Liquid and Dry Measure Equivalents

g = grams (dry measure) kg = kilograms dL = deciliters

The metric amounts represented here are the nearest equivalents.
See page 762 for formulas to convert precisely.

a pinch = slightly less than ¼ teaspoon
a dash = a few drops
3 teaspoons = 1 tablespoon
2 tablespoons = 1 ounce = ¼ dL (liquid), 30 g (dry)
1 jigger = 3 tablespoons = 1½ ounces
8 tablespoons = ½ cup = 4 ounces = 1 dL
2 cups = 1 pint = ½ quart = 1 pound* = ½ L (liquid), 450g (dry)*
4 cups = 32 ounces = 2 pints = 1 quart = 1 L
4 quarts = 1 gallon = 3¾ L
8 quarts(dry) = 1 peck = 7¼ kg
4 pecks(dry) = 1 bushel

*Dry ingredients measured in cups will vary in weight—see back inside cover for
specifics on flour, sugar, etc.*

When substituting cornstarch or arrowroot for flour as a thickener, use only half as much.

To correct a curdled or "broken" hollandaise or mayonnaise sauce, whisk in a teaspoon or two of boiling water, a drop at a time. If that doesn't work, put an egg yolk in a bowl and add the "broken" sauce slowly, beating with a whisk, and in time you'll have a smooth sauce.

An egg that is really stale will float or tip upward in a bowl of water. When cracked open, if the white and yolk cling together, the egg is very fresh. The older it gets, the flatter the yolk becomes and the runnier the white.

Basic Pastry Formula

For an 8-inch shell	1 cup (140 g) plus 2 tablespoons flour ¼ teaspoon salt	⅓ cup (¾ dL) shortening 2-3 tablespoons cold water
For an 8-inch two-crust pie	2 cups (280 g) flour ½ teaspoon salt	⅔ cup (1½ dL) shortening ⅓ cup (¾ dL) cold water
For a 9-inch pie shell	1½ cups (215 g) flour ¼ teaspoon salt	½ cup (1 dL) shortening 3-4 tablespoons cold water
For a 9-inch two-crust pie	2½ cups (350 g) flour ½ teaspoon salt	¾ cup (1¾ dL) shortening 6-7 tablespoons cold water

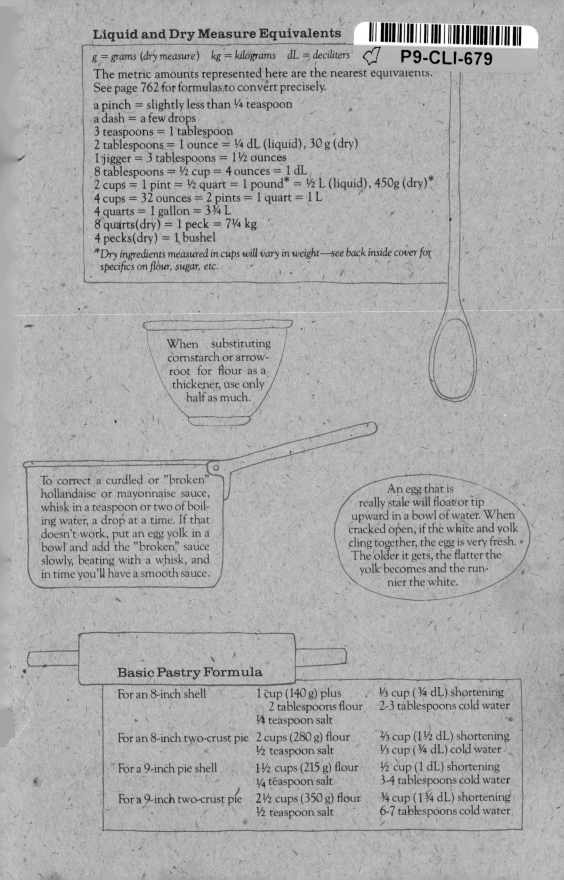

THE
FANNIE FARMER
COOKBOOK

THE
FANNIE FARMER
COOKBOOK

Twelfth Edition

Revised by Marion Cunningham
with Jeri Laber

Illustrated by Lauren Jarrett

ALFRED A. KNOPF
NEW YORK

THIS IS A BORZOI BOOK PUBLISHED BY ALFRED A. KNOPF, INC.

FANNIE FARMER IS A REGISTERED TRADEMARK
OWNED BY FANNY FARMER CANDY SHOPS, INC., AND
USED BY ALFRED A. KNOPF INC., UNDER LICENSE
FROM FANNY FARMER CANDY SHOPS, INC.

PUBLISHED ORIGINALLY IN 1896 UNDER THE TITLE
THE BOSTON COOKING-SCHOOL COOK BOOK BY FANNIE MERRITT FARMER.

LIBRARY OF CONGRESS CATALOGING IN PUBLICATION DATA
FARMER, FANNIE MERRITT   1857-1915.
THE FANNIE FARMER COOKBOOK.
INCLUDES INDEX.
1. COOKERY, AMERICAN. I. TITLE.
TX715.F234 1979 641.5 79-2097
ISBN 0-394-40650-8

MANUFACTURED IN THE UNITED STATES OF AMERICA

CONTENTS

INTRODUCTION
by James Beard

My first memory of Fannie Farmer and her *Boston Cooking-School Cook Book* came very early in my life, long before I ever thought of cooking myself. I can remember my mother talking at tea or luncheon with her friends and discussing recipes as people are wont to do, and there was always talk of where a recipe had been discovered. And if it wasn't from Miss Farmer's book it was apt to be out of one of the many charity cookbooks where a good many of the recipes were attributed to Fannie Farmer anyway.

So the name of Fannie Farmer was a household word. It was linked very closely to another woman, Mrs. Sara Tyson Rorer, who had also written a cookbook, a very large and complete one. And then there was the impressive *White House Cookbook,* which was almost *de rigueur* for every kitchen of that period.

But why did Fannie Farmer survive and not the others? There was something about the book, about her personality, that came right off the page. The book was not just *The Boston Cooking School Cook Book,* it was Fannie, and she was the voice of authority at all times, the final reference. Her book was so prized that it was something one could put confidently into the hands of a bride. The early editions reflect her love of all the good family foods of the time and she had pictures of them. Who else had sweetbreads under glass, for instance? She belonged to an era. And she never went in for vulgarities or common fads, such as "candlelight salad," a hideous concoction of a lettuce leaf with an upright piece of banana sitting on it (the candle), topped with a dribble of mayonnaise (melting wax), a shred of coconut (the wick), and a dot of red pimiento (to simulate the flame), that swept through the fashionable world at one time. Here and there in her books one would find delightful little quips about food that always gave you the feeling that this woman really appreciated what she ate. She must have had a delicate and beautiful palate. I remember her nephew, Dexter Perkins, once telling me that very often when she was on a trip to New York or Washington she would take part of a dish home in a little lace handkerchief to analyze and try out. She had great curiosity and undoubtedly the confidence that she could recreate and improve on many of the dishes she tested in this way. She never traveled a great deal, I think never went to Europe, but she was aware of the gradually increasing number of ethnic groups that were settling throughout our country, from the Atlantic to the Pacific, and of the good influences they had on home cookery; what the Polish people brought to the Middle West and the Czechs into Nebraska and Colorado, and the influence of the Scandinavians as people trekked farther west and settled along the Pacific, where I grew up.

Miss Farmer was apt to keep abreast of the times, and ethnic cookery was part of that. She also had the foresight to bring forth an edition in two languages so that the mistress of the household could work with a cook or hired girl who did not know English.

The decades following Miss Farmer's death in 1915 were not a particularly distinguished period in American cooking. Perhaps it was because the average American woman suddenly found herself with no help at all and, instead of wanting to learn cooking, she was interested in liberating herself from the kitchen. Perhaps Prohibition had its depressing influence. Whatever the reason, for a long time the emphasis was on oversimplification, shortcut methods, bastardization of traditional recipes and, as more convenience foods came on the market, there was more and more reliance on them. The magazines were full of casseroles covered with a condensed soup or packaged sauce, and ersatz products like flavored salts dulled the palate. It seemed that the spirit and influence of that great woman was drowned in a sea of jellied salad.

But after World War II things began to change for the better. G.I.'s had brought back some of the new tastes they had discovered abroad, more and more Americans began to travel, to eat out in ethnic restaurants and to appreciate the great foods of other lands. Gradually, Americans found new respect for good cooking and for the art of the kitchen and, in response to increasing demand, better and more interesting produce began appearing in our markets. Cooking schools sprung up like mad and cooking books of every description started flooding the bookstores. Today more than ever one is proud to be a good cook, and the time was ripe for the true spirit of Fannie Farmer to re-emerge, teaching young people the right way to deal with simple, fresh foods and offering them basic dependable American recipes that would provide a grounding in good cooking and offer opportunity for embellishment in creative ways.

When the publishing house of Alfred A. Knopf agreed to rise to this challenge, and the editor there, Judith Jones, was searching for someone who could recreate the book in Fannie's image, I recommended to her that Marion Cunningham be the one to take over and rebuild the great culinary edifice that Fannie Farmer had spent many years erecting. Mrs. Cunningham hails from California and has spent most of her life there, but we became great friends when she stepped across the border into Oregon to come to one of my cooking classes. Since then we have worked together, and she has conducted cooking classes on her own, given private lessons, traveled about, and judged cooking contests. Whenever she has done demonstrations and classes with me, I have been delighted with her never-ceasing enthusiasm for food and people. Her background knowledge of good cooking, her boundless curiosity, her sense for the roots of this country's culinary traditions, and her extraordinarily fine palate seemed to me to make her eminently qualified to take on this demanding assignment. And her determination to test out any kind of recipe just to satisfy herself, plus a kind, down-to-earth freshness and homeyness have served her singularly well in preparing Fannie Farmer's resurrection. Mrs. Cunningham was joined in this project by Jeri Laber, who worked out its structure and collaborated in its writing. Mrs. Laber is the editor of a number of the *Woman's Day* cookbooks, the coauthor of a book about weekend cooking, and has been a restaurant reviewer for the Connecticut edition of *The New York Times*. She loves gardening and her experience with growing and preserving vegetables was helpful. Also, being from the East Coast, she served as a balance for Mrs. Cunningham, so it proved an efficient working combination, which had its disagreements as well as agreements, and has brought forth something really special. And, of course, the overall surveillance and counsel from Judith Jones, whose appreciation and understanding and knowledge are almost earthshaking, have helped to form this book into something that is a model for the young cook to learn from and for the fine cook, as well as the professional, to consult as an authority on the basics of great American cooking. I spent a weekend not long since going through every page, one by one, reading and digesting, and I was filled with admiration for what has been done.

I know we are going to hear cries from many people that the book has changed, that a new philosophy has been developed and it is not the same old Fannie Farmer. But this is not the case at all. Rather, the new edition represents a rebirth of the principles of good cooking that Miss Farmer established at the turn of the century. And now it stands still blessed by generations of appreciation— a book that respects the past and yet embraces progress and all the good new methods in the field of cookery. So it is not only a new Fannie Farmer, it is a monument to the great past as well.

PREFACE

Our general approach to cooking has been set forth in the opening pages called About the Kitchen. These principles reflect, we feel, just what Fannie Farmer herself would be saying today about what good cooking is and how to develop good cooking habits. Were she alive now, she would be thrilled at how all kinds of Americans—young people, men, career women, as well as housewives—are rediscovering the joys of real cooking, making their favorite dishes from scratch, working with fresh ingredients, filling the kitchen with tempting cooking aromas, and setting tables of which they can be proud. There is an awakening interest in our own country's varied culinary heritage and in the natural, wholesome kind of produce that she championed.

Our efforts here to explain techniques, to define terms, and encourage using good fresh materials are in direct response to this genuine new interest in good cooking. In order to avoid offering too many alternatives, we have sought to concentrate on the very best way of making something. Throughout, we have recommended the use of timesaving appliances when they do the job well, but we've avoided the kind of shortcut method that calls for a can of mushroom soup, for instance, to masquerade as a sauce. We are more interested in showing how easy and satisfying—and so much more economical—it is to produce the real thing once you know how. We've tried to demonstrate that with intelligent planning you can have on hand your own preparations that will save you time and money in the long run.

We have tested every recipe that appears in this new edition, as well as many more we decided to exclude. We have been deliberately selective, rather than encyclopedic, focusing on dishes that Americans seem to eat and really enjoy, and adding a few introductory words about the taste of a dish when it has seemed useful. This is the book to which we hope you'll turn for such classics as a good New England boiled dinner; the best possible apple pie; a nostalgic, slow-cooking rice pudding; old-fashioned baked beans; anadama bread. We have adapted and restored from early editions of Fannie Farmer some wonderful, earthy recipes that disappeared during the years when things like breadbaking were not in vogue. And, even more, we have revised, expanded, and added other chapters, particularly hors d'oeuvre and appetizers, fish, vegetables, grains, fruits, and filled things (from sandwiches to pizzas and quiches), in keeping with the new tastes and styles of eating and entertaining.

We decided that this twelfth edition should be the first to take the plunge and introduce metrics in a basic cookbook. The metrics measurements that appear in parentheses alongside the standard American measurements have been simplified to the nearest equivalent, rather than made complicatedly precise. Our purpose is to familiarize you with the system that Europeans have been using for years, because eventually metrics are bound to become an integral part of our kitchen language.

All this has been a huge undertaking, one that has taken considerably longer than we originally anticipated, but every moment has been challenging and fun. We are grateful to Irene Sax, who joined us during the last six months of work and with cheerful enthusiasm helped us put the remaining chapters together. We are also indebted to Suzanne Hamlin for her expert assistance with the candy chapter. Our editor Judith Jones, continually setting the highest of standards, has put an inordinate amount of her own wisdom and work into every detail of this book. We feel lucky to have had this chance to work in the glow of the fine, radiant light that she brings to her profession.

All of us who have had a part in this edition feel certain that Fannie Farmer would have approved. And now the book is in your hands to use and enjoy.

Marion Cunningham
Jeri Laber

THE
FANNIE FARMER
COOKBOOK

ABOUT THE KITCHEN

What Is Good Everyday Cooking?

Cooking and eating together are among the great pleasures of family life and friendship. It's more than sustenance that brings people to the table at appointed times; a well-planned, satisfying, interesting meal is soothing to the spirit and provides an occasion when families can relax together, talk together, and share common interests.

Every meal should be a small celebration. If you acknowledge so joyous a fact of life, the pride you take in your efforts in the kitchen won't be confined to company occasions. You'll find it rewarding every day to see that the table is nicely set so that you won't have to jump up all the time to fetch things and disrupt the conversation. Butter should be in a butter dish with its own knife, milk in a pitcher, bottled sauces and condiments, unless the jar is particularly pretty, should be removed from their commercial containers and placed in small bowls with spoons. If your table looks like a hash-house counter, you encourage people to eat accordingly.

The prime attraction, of course, of any meal will always be what you serve, and no amount of table dressing will make up for food that is tasteless and monotonous. But don't let that intimidate you if you are new to cooking. Fortunately, experience is the greatest teacher. The more you cook, the more facile you become—and the more you enjoy it.

There is a tendency nowadays to make a separation between an everyday cook and a so-called gourmet cook. And the simpler cooks seem to stand in awe. Unfortunately *gourmet* has become synonymous with *fancy* and it conjures up the kind of cook who gussies up dishes with rich sauces and goes in for spectacular flambés. We'd all be better off today if we admitted that there is really no such thing as gourmet cooking—there is simply good cooking. It takes more sophistication to know when to serve something simply in its own good juices and more cooking sense—born out of experience—to get perfect results. You get there by trial and error. Experiment when you have the time and inclination but evaluate your own performance critically. Do only what you have the time for, but do it

3

well. And always shop carefully and respect the materials you work with. In other words, care. That is the path to good cooking and we should forget about "gourmet." Above all, don't get discouraged if something doesn't turn out perfectly the first time; too many fledgling cooks give up too easily, failing to realize that there are so many small unpredictable elements that confound even the most experienced cook: such as a staple loaf of bread that doesn't rise properly on one occasion just because the weather turned damp and heavy. So try to be resilient in the face of the unpredictable. Think of cooking as more of an art than a science. You'll have much more fun that way and you'll develop far more confidence than if you just rely on formulas.

Developing Good Cooking Habits

As a first good cooking habit, learn to read recipes through. Think about what you're supposed to be doing and why. Consider the time it will take and give yourself leeway so you don't get flustered. When you're making a complete meal, see if there is anything you can do ahead, like preparing your dessert just after breakfast. Then figure out what parts of the dinner are going to take longest and decide when you should start their preparation. If there are unfamiliar techniques involved in a recipe that is new to you, immerse yourself in all the general introductory material first so that you'll understand the principles underlying what you're about to attempt.

A second and almost equally important habit—one that develops with experience—is to start thinking in the market, especially when you're planning dishes that depend on specific fresh produce, like a particular cut of meat, or a kind of fish, certain vegetables and fruits. You will not only cook more economically if you look for what's "on special" or what's in season, but the end result will taste much better when you use ingredients that are at their peak of flavor. Try not to have your heart set on certain items and then pay an exorbitant price for hothouse versions that lack the quality of the real thing. Be flexible in choosing recipes, and be open to alternatives.

It's intelligent and creative to think ahead, both when you're in the market and in your own kitchen. Shop for several interrelated meals at a time and do the more time-consuming preparation when you know you're going to be around the house. For working people, as well as other cooks, it may be easiest to cook a big roast and a large stew on the weekend and then use the cooked meat in various ways on week nights when time is more limited. If you know you are having people for the weekend, pick a few hours earlier in the week to do a lot of the initial cooking so you'll be freer when your guests are around.

Don't let your family be scornful of the word "leftover"—a cook who plans two or three meals at a time deserves an "Oscar" for efficiency, economy, and imagination. By deliberately planning for leftovers, you'll find that you spend less time and money than if you always shop at the last minute for fresh hamburger, steak, chops. You will also have far more variety in your menus. For instance, even if your family is small, buy a pot roast at least twice the size you think you need for one meal. And, if you can, get the bones; you can make a good soup with them, some of the leftover gravy, and vegetables. The next day, using some of the pot roast ground up, you could have a main course of stuffed vegetables such as Green Peppers or Eggplant or Cabbage Leaves, depending on what's in season. And there would undoubtedly be enough left for a Beef-Noodle Casserole at another meal. Scraps are always good in someone's sandwich, particularly if there's a little gravy to drizzle over a crusty roll, or they could go into a taco filling, where a little goes far. Again, if you're planning to roast chicken for Sunday dinner or to sauté some cut-up chicken, get twice what you need. The carcasses and gizzards and necks will go into the soup pot. Later in the week you can have chicken hash, chicken salad, stuffed crêpes with mushrooms, a chicken gumbo, or chicken tetrazzini—any number of imaginative dishes.

By the same token, store away in small containers all the extra bits of vegetables, cooked rice, a little sauce, even pan scrapings. You'll be surprised how useful they can be. Soups, omelets, salads, baked dishes are an endless source of inspiration for such goodies. Think ahead when you're making those crêpes, or a pie dough, or bread, and make a double batch so that you have some ready in the freezer for an impromptu meal.

If you have a well-stocked freezer there is no need to buy a lot of "convenience" foods, which are expensive and usually not very satisfying. What you're doing is furnishing your own kinds of convenience supplies. If, in addition, you keep a well-stocked pantry and freezer (see pp. 725–734), you'll feel a great sense of well-being with everything at your fingertips.

Menu Planning for Family and Friends

Eating is much more a matter of individual taste today, and menus are more flexible. We are less rigidly a meat-and-potatoes society, although there are still plenty of Americans who feel they haven't eaten if that isn't the mainstay of the meal. But whether because of travel, economic necessity, ecological awareness, or vegetarian persuasion, more and more Americans are kicking over old traditions, borrowing from the European pattern of dividing the meal into more than one main course, putting less stress on the size of the meat portion and making it go further in all sorts of inventive ways. Sometimes you'll find a hearty soup as the centerpiece of a dinner. Or a platter of vegetables when they're at their summer best, accompanied by good whole-grain bread. Pasta dishes can be either a first or a main course; the same goes for salads, crêpes, fish and seafood, eggs. Cheese is appearing more often after the main course to be relished by itself with a crusty long loaf or with fresh fruit.

A well-planned meal should maintain a pleasing balance between contrasting textures, colors, and tastes. But don't make a fetish of it; just use common sense. If, for example, Chicken Divan with its Mornay sauce is to be your *pièce de résistance*, you won't want to precede it with a cream soup or an appetizer bathed in a cream sauce; nor would you want a creamy dessert. A white piece of fish with mashed potatoes and white onions, turnips, celery, or cauliflower would be depressingly colorless on the plate and cries out for an accent of fresh green beans or blanched broccoli, or at least some parsley and a few cherry tomatoes to relieve the monotony. If your main course is a stew full of sauce, soup is not your best bet as a starter; choose something with a contrasting texture—a cold vegetable or salad, or a small slice of quiche (in which case no pies for dessert, please).

A very spicy dish, in general, is best with something soothing; that is why hot curries are traditionally served with small side dishes of cooling cucumbers or bananas, and Mexican tacos, stuffed with peppery meat and sauce, have crisp lettuce, bland avocado, and chill sour cream to quench the fire. Dominant tastes like garlic, tomato sauces, and cabbagy flavors shouldn't be repeated. And watch out for heaviness—again, the tendency today is to want to leave the table pleasingly full but not glutted. Don't try to cap a triumphant rich dinner with an even richer dessert; if that torte or cake is to have star billing, plan accordingly so that it can be genuinely appreciated.

If you serve a vegetable as a first course—sliced tomatoes, for example, or an artichoke, or cold beans vinaigrette—you may not necessarily need a vegetable with your main dish. If you have a lot of gravy with your meat, you'll want something to sop it all up. That something doesn't always have to be potatoes, however; try rice, noodles, pasta, a grain like barley or cracked wheat, or a good homemade bread. If you follow the principle of good texture-color-and-taste contrast, you are very likely to end up with a good nutritional balance, too.

Lunches are generally lighter, of course, as are suppers when you have had dinner in the middle of the day—see Menu Suggestions at the back of the book. Lunch is always a pleasant, relaxed time to entertain, to set the table prettily, and to make a dish that is a little different. And brunch, that flexible meal that combines breakfast and lunch, is a grand time to indulge with family and friends in all those good old-fashioned breakfast delights like pancakes and sausages, kippered herring, corned beef hash with poached eggs, popovers, kidneys and bacon—things we so seldom have time for in the morning during the week.

ENTERTAINING

If you try to please your guests as you would your family, you'll realize that it is not necessary to do something extravagant to impress. Simplicity, using good ingredients well, is usually more impressive than a lot of fancy cooking that is sometimes too much to handle when you are doing everything yourself. Serve dishes that you know you can manage, and plan ahead so that you can enjoy your own company.

Dinner Parties

In planning what to have for a sit-down dinner, much depends on the guests. If you don't know them very well and suspect they may be fairly conservative in their eating habits, stick to a traditional menu: a first course of soup or an appetizer, a meat course (probably a roast) with vegetables and potatoes, and a dessert. If you know your guests love good food, be more experimental. Try special treats on those you know will appreciate them—a dish made with sweetbreads or crab or maybe game. Celebrate the seasons with their special bounty. Think seasonally, too—what tastes particularly good in certain kinds of weather, on a stormy winter night or a humid summer evening. If the dinner includes many young people, they may have vegetarian leanings and will appreciate less accent on the meat.

It is a good idea to plan dishes that don't require too much last-minute attention that will keep you in the kitchen away from your guests. Get as much cooking as possible done before the guests arrive. Decide when you will eat and figure out exactly when each dish should be put in the oven or heated on the stove.

"Complicated" dishes will seem easy if some of the component parts of a recipe are cooked well ahead, such as the making of a sauce, browning the meats, making stuffings. For instance, if you were making Cannelloni, a splendid party dish, you could do the crêpes well ahead (have them with your family the night you make them, stuffed a different way, and freeze an extra batch of crêpes). Have something that requires Tomato Sauce another night—a big bowl of spaghetti and meatballs, perhaps—and make lots of sauce, setting aside the 1½ cups required for the cannelloni (it freezes beautifully). You might even do a double batch of spinach for supper the night before, so that that would be ready, too, or something that requires cream sauce. What you'll have left to do the day of your party then is primarily an assembly job.

Always count on making a little more for guests than you would ordinarily. Offering seconds is a part of hospitality, and a dinner party is an occasion when people may want to indulge more than usual, particularly if your food is good—and it will be. If there are leftovers to be frozen, you'll welcome them eaten some evening when you'd rather not cook.

If you are serving more than nibbles with predinner drinks, choose your appetizers in relation to the rest of the meal; they should fit in with it appropriately and not be so overwhelming that they sate the appetite. Sometimes it's pleasant at a dinner party to serve a real first course in the living room with drinks—a portion of pâté on a plate, for instance, or a small hot tart, or a cup of soup; if your main dish does demand some finishing, having hors d'oeuvre in this way provides a natural break for you (moreover, you won't have to clear off a course and be away from the table).

While too many different courses may lead to a lot of scurrying and plate clearing, it is nice to stretch out a company meal with a pause for a separate salad and/or cheese course. There is nothing like lingering at the table when the conversation is good and everyone is enjoying the food and the slow rhythm of eating.

Cocktail Parties and Receptions
See also Appetizers and Hors d'Oeuvre (pp. 50–73).

Serve food that you can eat with your fingers at cocktail parties and receptions, so you don't have to bother with plates. The food should be substantial enough to fortify the stomach, especially when cocktails are being served. See suggested foods for cocktail parties and receptions (p. 50).

Since there are usually a few guests who stay on after a cocktail party is over, it's nice to plan for them by having one hot buffet dish, like a Chicken Pie (p. 254) or Scalloped Ham (p. 209) or Lasagne (p. 333), that you can pop into the oven and bring out for the late stayers-on.

Buffet Dinners
A buffet dinner is the simplest way to entertain a large group of people. Everything *must* be ready ahead of time, whether it is set out hot in a chafing dish or on a hot tray or is served cold or at room temperature.

Buffets present the interesting challenge of combining a number of dishes in a creative way. It is important that they look inviting on the table and that the dishes complement each other. (See suggestions for buffet dinners, p. 51.) Choose foods that can be cut with a fork; it's a lot easier than trying to handle a knife while you're balancing a plate on your lap. Don't serve dishes that are too soupy or everything will slop together on the plate.

Plan to serve at least one hot thing; there are always a few people who don't think they've had a real meal unless it includes something hot.

If you have a very large crowd, you can avoid long lines by setting the table up so guests may help themselves from either end.

Picnics and Barbecues
A picnic, or just eating out of doors, is a holiday from our daily table. Whether we are sitting in a meadow, on a mountaintop, by the shore, or in our own garden, nature creates a casual mood and whets our appetite. Prepare food that is easy to serve and easy to eat, tucking in extra just in case. If you are barbecuing, get your fire started well ahead.

An outdoor barbecue offers such a tempting way to get out of the kitchen on a warm evening that it is no wonder it has become a fixture in American life. It's also a means of getting the men in the family into the act of cooking, if they aren't already, and provides a simple answer to feeding a number of people, yet making a party of it as good cooking smells waft across the backyard. One is apt to get into a rut, however, and fall back too often on hamburgers or steaks as the standard barbecue fare. Don't let that happen. There are so many things that can be barbecued deliciously. Consult the fish chapter, for instance; any fish or seafood that broils successfully can be done as well on an open fire. The same goes for meats—Butterflied Lamb, for instance, or skewered chicken livers, or Shish Kebab—and chicken. If you have a spit, then try doing roast meats that way— duck is particularly delicious. Vegetables and potatoes can be wrapped in foil and tucked in among the coals, once your fire is going well (see p. 43), or some, like eggplant, can be grilled at the last minute after the meat is done.

A picnic basket could contain the welcome sight of something like cold vegetables, fresh scallions, small tomatoes, hearts of celery, avocado, slices of cold meat loaf, fried chicken, perhaps, ham on buttered homemade bread, cooked shrimp—the possibilities are endless. Think ahead so that you will have the cooked foods ready; fill small containers with pickles or preserves and olives; and don't forget the mustard. If something hot is deemed necessary, fill a thermos with soup. Wine, coffee, or lemonade can tend to the thirst. Cheese is simple to pack, and it's nice to have a variety. Cookies or a coarse, moist carrot cake would make the meal complete, with fresh fruit as the snack before starting home. As well as the necessary plates and cups and cutlery, the basket must have lots of paper napkins so crumbs and grease on fingers can be wiped away.

Communal Dinners
Like old-fashioned church suppers, communal dinners are coming into their own again. Whether they are planned as a family undertaking or a cooperative venture with friends, they are usually fun and full of surprises, everyone putting his or her best foot forward. It's a good way for working people, who might not otherwise have the time, to put together a festive dinner. And if everyone chips in, the financial burden is shared.

Sometimes friends like to cook all together, particularly if they love cooking and like to experiment with new dishes. If it's your first attempt at puff pastry, for instance, it is reassuring to make it with someone who has done it before; we learn a lot from each other in the kitchen. But more often for a communal dinner each member of the party prepares something at home and brings it. It is always wise to have someone coordinate the meal so that everything goes together well.

WINES
Learning About Wines
Americans are drinking more and more wine, before dinner as a light apéritif, throughout the meal, and at evening parties when cheese and other foods are apt to be served. In the last decade the per capita consumption of wine in the United States has more than doubled. This trend seems to reflect a growing respect for good cooking, for strong alcohol deadens the palate whereas wine awakens it and enhances the flavor of the foods with which it is served. As a matter of fact, except for the nondrinker, it seems right and natural today to offer wine with an appetizing lunch or dinner—even on a picnic.

You don't have to serve an elaborate wine. Fortunately, the more reasonably priced American jug wines are very drinkable, far better than the *vin ordinaire* you get from France. There is no reason to be ashamed of serving a jug wine. What with the rising cost of everything, more and more such blends are available at competitive prices, and when poured from a decanter they can be as festive and as much appreciated as a more ostentatious vintage wine from France or Germany. There are also increasing numbers of good table wines from Spain, Italy, Portugal, Greece, and South America, and they are available at more easily accepted prices.

Most quality American wines are sold under varietal labels (varietal refers to the dominant grape used). Reds include Cabernet Sauvignon, Pinot Noir, Gamay, Gamay Beaujolais, Barberra, Petite Sirah; whites include Chardonnay, Riesling, Gewürztraminer, Sauvignon Blanc, Chenin Blanc, Pinot Blanc, Semillon.

California wines labeled Burgundy and Chablis are usually generic in nature, not to be compared with wines of the same names produced in France. "Chablis," in fact, has become the vernacular term for white wines served in restaurant carafes. Be careful in buying a Sauternes; unless it is described as dry, it is apt to be sweet. California also uses the term Rhine Wine to refer to a sweet blend.

Also, in recent years more and more vineyards in different parts of the country have been developing good wines—Washington, Oregon, Illinois, Michigan, Ohio, Maryland, New York, Missouri, Arkansas, Virginia. There is something delightful about being able to serve the wines of one's own region, particularly as they are becoming more and more distinguished and can be drunk with pride, and it is so satisfying to taste the wine of a particular part of the country you may be visiting. Although most of these bottles carry varietal labels, in some areas where the climate is harsh, wine growers are experimenting with French hybrid grapes, and many of these less familiar wines have a lovely distinctive taste all their own.

Few American wines carry vintage dates as French wines do. Our wines are less apt to be affected by annual changes of climate, and our way of growing and producing wine makes the vintage year less important.

You can learn about wine only by experimenting, trying new wines, sampling and comparing. Try to find a wine merchant who is learning himself (and any good wine man is always learning)—someone who is willing to share his knowledge with his customers. Shopping for wines is not like buying canned goods. The more you establish a rapport with your source, the more you can enjoy developing your palate. Exciting things are happening in the world of wine and you should keep abreast; most local daily newspapers now have wine columns that are helpful. You don't have to be a connoisseur, but the more you know the more pleasure you will get—and the better buys you will make.

As for French wines, if you are just learning about them, you'll need more than ever the help of a reliable wine merchant. As a good red table wine, Beaujolais is probably the most popular in the world today. Although it should always be drunk young, it is hard to make generalities about quality because the vintage varies from year to year. The best Beaujolais are Fleurie, Moulin-à-Vent, Villages, Brouilly, and Morgon, and unless you have a dealer who knows his Beaujolais, it would be wise to look for one of those names on the label.

It is even harder to make generalities about fine French vintage wines, and there are a great many things to be learned, if you are serious, about reading French wine labels, including information about regions, growths (known in France as *crus*), the place of bottling, the importer, in addition to the vintage. But for a start you should at least be aware of the difference between Burgundy, always in the sloping-shouldered bottle, and Bordeaux in the high-shouldered bottle. One is inclined to think of Burgundy as primarily a full-bodied red wine, and the roster runs from the great labels like Aloxe-Corton and Romanée-Conti to the more accessible Chambertin, Côte de Beaune, Nuits-St.-Georges. But there are also excellent white Burgundies like Pouilly-Fuissé, Meursault, Montrachet, Chablis with which you will want to experiment when the opportunity arises. Bordeaux's greatest fame is for producing some of the most distinguished red wines (also known as clarets), such as Château Lascomes, Château Latour, Château Haut-Brion, Château Margaux, to name a few. All fine Bordeaux are characterized by the term "château," and there are many good bottles available for special occasions that aren't prohibitively expensive. Some of the more familiar white Bordeaux are Graves and Entre-Deux-Mers, named for local districts but varying considerably in quality. A true Sauternes—also from a Bordeaux district—is a rich, sweetish wine, something to serve with dessert or fruits.

Serving Wines with Meals

The general rule of thumb is that white wines—that is dry white wines—go with fish and poultry, and red wines with meats and usually cheese. Rosés are generally served with cold summer dishes, and are fine with poultry or ham. Sweet white wines are reserved for dessert, while champagne, which is particularly delightful with some sweet dishes, can be served also throughout a meal. Rules should never be inflexible, however. Some say wine shouldn't be served with salad, but others feel perfectly comfortable with that combination. Certainly if you are opening your dinner with some sort of salad as a starter, it can be refreshing to accompany it with a light white wine, then move on to a red with your meat course. It is pleasant to have red wine with a cheese course, if you are including one, but if you have served a white wine throughout the rest of the meal, there is no absolute reason why you must switch at this point.

White and rosé wines should be served chilled. An hour or so in the refrigerator is sufficient; you don't want them numbingly cold so you kill their flavor. Red wines should be served at room temperature. And champagne should be chilled; it really calls for an ice bucket.

Wines are always much more pleasant if they are served in stem glasses—clear, not colored. Don't settle for those that hold only tiny amounts. A wineglass should be ample enough so that you can swirl the wine around to appreciate its bouquet—seven ounces is right for an all-purpose glass—and it should be filled only about one-third to one-half full. Count on a minimum of half a bottle to a person when serving a full-course dinner.

Storing Wines

Wines should be kept in a relatively cool dry place. Bottles should be stored on their sides so the corks won't dry out. With fortified wines, like sherry, Madeira, and Port, and apéritifs, this is not important. Move bottles carefully so as not to disturb their sediment, and if you notice foreign matter in the bottom of a bottle, the wine should be decanted before serving—that is, carefully poured into a decanter, leaving behind the sediment.

If you have some wine left over in an open bottle, store it in the refrigerator and use it for cooking. Thus kept cool, it will last about a week and contribute flavor to many dishes; after that it turns vinegary.

STAPLES

Baking Powder. See also Leavening Agents (p. 16).

Baking powder, which comes in small, sturdy, airtight containers, is an early-nineteenth-century invention that changed the course of American cooking, making the art of baking much more predictable. It is used in making cakes, quick breads, muffins, cookies, and the like—the mysterious leavening agent that makes them rise. Recipes in this book call for *double-acting baking powder*, which is the most readily available everywhere today. Old-fashioned single-acting baking powder, technically *tartrate* or *phosphate baking powder*, goes to work as soon as it is mixed with liquid, thus demanding that the batter be baked immediately. Double-acting baking powder, on the other hand, acts twice—both when it is first mixed and again when the heat of the oven releases the full force of the leavening gases, so there is less urgency about baking your mixture. Both are equally effective in the long run, but it is important to note if you're using single-acting that you must double the amount called for in recipes because it is that much less potent.

There are those who prefer the old-fashioned baking powder, claiming that they can detect a chemical taste in double-acting. If you wish to make your own baking powder, combine ¼ teaspoon of baking soda with ½ teaspoon of cream of tartar and you will have the equivalent of 1 teaspoon of tartrate or phosphate baking powder. Do not store homemade baking powder; it will not keep well.

Store commercial baking powder in its own airtight container. If you have kept a tin around for months and months, you'd better test it for potency. Simply dissolve 1 teaspoonful in ¼ cup of hot water; if it doesn't foam and bubble within a few seconds, replace it.

Baking Soda. See also Leavening Agents (p. 16).

Baking soda is also a form of leavening, but it must be mixed with something acid like sour milk, sour cream, buttermilk, yogurt, molasses, or citrus juice to produce the gases that make a batter rise. About 1 teaspoon of soda is used for every cup of liquid, but the soda should be combined first with the dry ingredients. As soon as the batter is mixed it should be set to bake.

Many recipes using baking soda call for sour milk as the acid activator. This is fine if your milk is farm-fresh, but the pasteurized milk we usually buy will spoil without ever turning sour. *To "sour" pasteurized milk*, add 1 tablespoon of white vinegar or lemon juice to 1 cup of milk and let it stand at room temperature for 10 to 15 minutes. Or use buttermilk, a good substitute for sour milk in any bread or cake recipe.

Baking soda is also used *to destroy odors*. A large box left open in the refrigerator is surprisingly effective in absorbing odors and a tablespoon in a couple of cups of warm water is a refreshing cleanser.

Beans. For variety, preparation, cooking, and recipes, see Beans (p. 322).

Dried beans keep well in covered containers. Don't hold them for more than a year, though; eventually they will become stale.

Bouillon Cubes and Meat Concentrates. You'll get a better flavor from pure canned bouillon (not consommé), but cubes are all right in a pinch providing you adjust the seasoning accordingly; they are apt to be salty (unless, of course, you buy the unsalted kind).

Bouquet Garni. *Bouquet garni* means a bouquet for garnish—parsley, thyme, and bay leaf being the traditional ingredients; sometimes celery and other aromatic seasonings are added. Make a bundle of the herbs and tie with a piece of string or put the herbs in a cheesecloth bag so that it can be easily removed from the casserole or stewpot.

Bread Crumbs. It's easy—and economical—to make bread crumbs at home, and it's a good way to use up bits and ends of bread. Both *fresh and dry bread crumbs* are most easily made by pulverizing bread in a blender or food processor or by tearing up by hand; dry crumbs can also be made with a rolling pin. Use unsweetened white bread without crusts for fresh crumbs (sweetened bread crumbs are all right in a dessert). For dry crumbs dry out the bread first in a 250°F oven, and use some of the crust, if you wish. Whole-wheat or rye-bread crumbs add a robust touch to less delicate dishes. Do not use bread that is stale or the crumbs will have a stale taste.

If you store bread crumbs in the refrigerator for more than a short period of time, they may become moldy. It's best to put them in the freezer, wrapped tightly in a plastic bag, where they will keep and taste fresh for several weeks.

If you buy packaged bread crumbs, avoid the seasoned variety.

To make cracker crumbs, use unsweetened, unsalted soda crackers or common crackers. Never pulverize cracker crumbs completely: it's best to crush them with a rolling pin or whirl them quickly in a food processor.

Butter. See also Fats (p. 14); Oils (p. 17); Herb Butters (p. 20).

Butter has its own lovely flavor; there's nothing like it on vegetables, in sauces, and for certain kinds of cooking and baking. All the recipes will indicate when butter is preferred—no substitute will taste the same.

Whether you use *sweet (unsalted) butter* or *"lightly salted" butter* is a matter of personal preference. Sweet buttter is preferred by many, especially in pastrymaking, but we don't feel it's crucial.

To store butter, when refrigerating, make sure it's covered or well wrapped so that it doesn't absorb food flavors. Butter can be left out for a limited period if the kitchen is cool. Sweet butter will keep refrigerated for about a week; salted butter for about ten days. Butter freezes very well; it will hold for many months and can be defrosted and refrozen.

Measuring butter is easy when you buy it in ¼-pound sticks; there are 8 tablespoons or ½ cup to a stick. If you buy your butter in bulk, there's a cold-water trick for measuring it: to measure ½ cup of bulk butter, for example, fill a 1-cup measure with ½ cup of cold water, then add enough butter to bring the water level to 1 cup.

Creaming butter requires butter that is at room temperature. Do not try to force cold butter by heating; break it into bits instead and let it stand a while or massage it with your fingers.

Butter will burn at a lower temperature than other fats, and for this reason it is often mixed with oil or shortening for frying. If you clarify butter, however, by removing the milk solids, it will not burn and will keep almost indefinitely in a covered container in the refrigerator. *To clarify butter,* put it in a large glass measuring cup in a warm (225°F) oven and let it stand until it melts and the milky substance settles at the bottom. You can strain the clear liquid at the top into a container through damp cheesecloth or just put the melted butter in the refrigerator to harden and then scrape off the milky residue.

When *serving butter,* it's nice sometimes to use a butter mold to make a pretty pattern. You can also use a butter curler or two chilled wooden paddles to make butter balls, but that may take a bit of practice.

Cereals. Cereals keep well and are always good to have on hand (if you eat cereal). For varieties, cooking instructions, and recipes, see Cereals (p. 309).

Chestnuts. Chestnuts are most generally available around the Christmas holidays.

Buy them fresh (they should feel absolutely firm when you press them, with no shrinkage of the meat from the shell) and freeze them for long-term storage. Actually, chestnuts will peel a little more easily when they have been frozen. *To shell chestnuts,* see p. 87.

Chocolate. Chocolate for baking is available *unsweetened, semisweet, and sweet,* and comes divided into squares, usually weighing 1 ounce each. You may substitute chocolate bits or chips for semisweet chocolate, using the same number of ounces.

Storing chocolate is no problem; it keeps well, wrapped and in a cool place, not the refrigerator. When chocolate is exposed to air over a long period of time, it sometimes takes on a harmless white discoloration and becomes crumbly; this does not mean that it is stale, and it is perfectly usable.

To melt chocolate, put it in a pan over barely simmering water until the chocolate has melted. Chocolate when melting sometimes "tightens"; if that happens, add 1 teaspoon of solid vegetable shortening per ounce of chocolate and it will smooth out again.

Cocoa. *To substitute cocoa for chocolate,* use 3 tablespoons of unsweetened cocoa for each ounce of unsweetened chocolate and add 1 tablespoon of shortening.

Coconut. *Commercial flaked coconut* comes in cans or packages and is usually sweetened, unless you buy it in a natural-foods store. It's marvelous for cakes and fine in other sweet baked products. *Fresh unsweetened coconut* is best for nonsweet main-course dishes like salads, curries, and soups.

To open a fresh coconut, pierce the "eyes" of the coconut with a screwdriver and drain off the liquid. Put the coconut in a 400°F oven for 20 minutes. Tap it all over with a hammer to loosen the shell, then split it with a heavy knife or with a mallet or hammer. Pry out the white meat with a sharp knife, then pare off the dark skin.

To grate fresh coconut, put the white meat in a rotary grater, a blender, or a food processor. A medium-size coconut will produce 3 to 4 cups of grated coconut.

Coconut liquid has few uses and is usually discarded; despite a common misconception, it is not "coconut milk." *To make coconut milk,* steep the freshly grated coconut in boiling water to cover for 30 minutes. Then strain out the coconut, extracting all the flavorful juices by squeezing them through a towel back into the steeping liquid.

To toast fresh, grated coconut, spread it in a shallow pan in a 350°F oven for about 20 minutes, stirring frequently and watching carefully, until delicately brown.

Store fresh, grated coconut in the refrigerator for no more than four or five days or it will turn moldy. To keep longer, toast it and put it in a sealed jar; don't refrigerate.

Cream. For whipped cream recipes, see Dessert Sauces (p. 637); for freezing cream, see Frozen Foods (p. 729).

Half-and-half is more like milk than cream, but can be used instead of light cream; it will not whip, unless specially treated (see p. 644).

Light cream, also called "coffee cream," has a relatively low butterfat content and will not whip (see above). Use when you want a very light cream.

Heavy cream, also called "whipping cream," is the best for making whipped cream and is the richest cream you get commercially today. Depending on how fresh it is when purchased, it will last refrigerated anywhere from a few days to a week. The only test for sourness is to taste it.

To whip cream, use a whisk or an electric beater. Be careful to whip just until soft peaks form: cream that is beaten too long will begin to turn to butter, often quite suddenly, especially when electric beaters are used. It really doesn't matter when sugar or other flavorings are added.

Commercial whipped cream substitutes bear little resemblance in taste or texture to freshly whipped cream.

Ultrapasteurized (or sterilized) heavy cream has been sterilized at high temperatures so that it will keep for several weeks in the refrigerator. It is as thick as old-fashioned heavy cream and whips well, though its flavor is not quite as pure. It's good for desserts that must be held for a long time; sweetening will mask its slightly "boiled" taste.

Sour cream is thick with a slightly sour flavor. It is often used as a garnish, to flavor, and sometimes to thicken. *To avoid curdling* when adding sour cream to a hot sauce, have it at room temperature and stir it well before adding; do not let it boil.

Crème fraîche is what the French call their own fresh cream, which is thicker than ours and has a fine, tart edge. *For a homemade version,* add 1 teaspoon of buttermilk or 2 teaspoons of sour cream to 1 cup of heavy cream, put the mixture in a jar, shake it, and let it stand at room temperature, uncovered, for one or more days until it is thick, then cover. Refrigerate; it will keep for several weeks. Ultrapasteurized (sterilized) cream takes longer to thicken than regular, old-fashioned cream.

To reduce cream, boil it until it becomes thick and almost pale gold in color.

Cream of Tartar. See Baking Powder (p. 11).

Croutons. Croutons are small cubes of bread that have been dried out in the oven or fried, then seasoned. They are used as a garnish. When made at home (p. 492), they have a fresh flavor, far preferable to the packaged variety.

Eggs. Unless otherwise indicated, all eggs used in these recipes should be "large" in size.

For buying, storing, measuring and separating eggs, for beating and *folding egg whites,* for *tempering egg yolks* and for *cooking eggs,* see Eggs (p. 335). For *freezing leftover egg whites and egg yolks,* see Frozen Foods (p. 730).

If you have an excessive number of *leftover egg whites,* you might think of making meringues, an angel cake, or a dessert soufflé (check through the recipes). And don't forget that egg whites are essential for clarifying stocks and for certain bread glazes. If you have a lot of *leftover egg yolks,* maybe it's time for a hollandaise sauce, a custard, some mayonnaise. And remember how often you'll use yolks as a thickener in a sauce.

Fats. See Butter (p. 12); see Oils (p. 17).

Margarine. Margarine is a vegetable fat which is used as a substitute for butter. It does not have as fine a taste and texture as butter and does not hold up in cooking. Since margarine is no longer especially economical in comparison with butter, butter is always preferable, unless you have been told to avoid animal fats.

Solid vegetable shortening comes in cans and keeps indefinitely. It is usually white and has no taste. While its appearance is not exactly enticing, this vegetable fat has many uses; it tolerates high heat in frying, and it provides moisture and tenderness in baking, making a particularly flaky piecrust.

Lard is rendered pork fat. In its pure form, it's considered the best of all cooking fats. Commercial lards, however, are not always as dependable. Pick your brand carefully because some taste of preservatives; lard should have no taste. Refrigerate, well wrapped, and don't keep it too long.

Bacon fat has its own character and flavor. It's good for frying things like corn cakes and potatoes when you want a little of that flavor, and in the South it is often used in cooking field greens. After frying bacon, pour off the fat into a crock or coffee can and keep in a cool place.

Salt pork is cured pork fat. The crisp fried bits of salt pork that remain after the fat has been rendered are delicious in chowders, with greens, and mixed into biscuits. The fat itself is very salty, so salt judiciously.

Rendered chicken and goose fat have distinctive flavors and are marvelous for frying potatoes, onions, and root vegetables. Properly rendered fat will keep indefinitely. For rendering instructions, see p. 252.

Suet is beef fat; the best suet is the fat from around the kidney. It imparts a wonderful flavor—try it sometime for fried potatoes. It is particularly valued for steamed puddings and mincemeat, adding moisture as it melts in the cooking.

Flour. See also Thickening Agents (p. 19).

When recipes call for flour, unless otherwise noted, all-purpose white flour is to be used (unbleached or not, as you prefer).

For information about bread flour and meals, see Yeast Breads (p. 458).

For information about cake flours and about sifting and measuring flour, see Cakes (p. 502).

Garlic. Buy garlic that is firm and heavy to the touch, with no soft spots. Store it in an airy place, not in the refrigerator. A clove of garlic is one section of the bulb.

Always peel garlic unless otherwise directed. If you smash the unpeeled garlic clove lightly with the flat blade of a knife, you'll find it easy to peel.

Garlic is not always the highly aggressive seasoner that many people think it is. To understand the full range of its seductive power, you must sample it in its different stages.

Raw garlic is particularly assertive and its taste lingers long. Don't inflict chunks of it on a salad or in a sandwich, for instance. Use it sparingly—unless you deliberately want that dominant flavor—and always very finely minced. For a salad, if you don't know the tastes of your fellow diners, better just rub the bowl with a cut clove.

Chopped garlic cooked in hot fat will give a very pronounced garlicky flavor to a dish. Be careful not to let it brown or the flavor becomes bitter. If you add chopped raw garlic to something you are baking or broiling, it will have a dominant taste, too.

Garlic cloves, whole or crushed, cooked moist for a long time in a soup or stew or braised dish, for instance, impart a richness and an ineffable flavor to the sauce that never overwhelms.

Whole cloves of garlic, uncrushed, cooked slowly, either a whole head baked or the bulbs just separated and scattered around meat or poultry in a tightly covered baked dish, will surprise you the most with their mildness. When you crush the cooked cloves, the inside will be delicate and buttery, delicious to mop up with crusty bread.

A garlic *press* releases garlic oils in the most volatile way, leaving you with little but the juice. *Mincing* and/or *chopping* gives you more pulp with the juice and is more satisfactory, particularly if you sauté the pieces. When you *smash* or *crush* a whole clove of garlic, it releases its flavor but remains whole and can be removed from the cooking pot if desired.

Gelatin. For recipes using gelatin, see Molded Salads (p. 442); Gelatin Desserts (p. 620). For molding and unmolding, see Desserts (p. 605).

True gelatin is pure and unsweetened and will solidify any liquid. Don't use too much, however, or you will get a solid, rubbery block: 1 tablespoon of gelatin is enough to gel 2 cups of liquid mixed with 1 to 2 cups of solid ingredients (depending on water content of solids—see p. 442).

Gelatin *must* be softened for about 5 minutes in a cold liquid before it is dissolved in something hot. If the broth or juice that you wish to gel is cold, you can sprinkle the gelatin right onto it and then, when it is soft, heat the liquid until the gelatin dissolves. If the liquid is already hot—a freshly made chicken stock, for example—soften the gelatin in ¼ cup of cold water and then dissolve it in the hot stock.

Do not let gelatin mixtures boil; the gelatin will lose its vigor. Allow at least a few hours for a gelatin mixture to solidify, overnight if the mold is very large.

Leavening Agents. See also Yeast (p. 20); Baking Powder (p. 11); Baking Soda (p. 11).

Leavening agents are used to lighten a batter or dough by creating carbon dioxide gas, air, or steam that will make it rise.

Beaten eggs or *egg whites* (p. 336) are often used to leaven; they enclose air which is forced to expand in a hot oven.

Marrow. The soft interior of bones. It has a delicate taste and an almost gelatinous texture when poached, and it is highly prized for use in soups, sauces, as a garnish, and on toast.

Milk. To "*sour*" milk, see Baking Soda (p. 11).

To *scald milk*, heat it slowly in a small pan until tiny bubbles appear around the edges, but before the milk boils up.

Homogenized milk is whole milk that has been mechanically treated so that the globules of cream will not separate from the rest of the milk.

Skim milk is milk from which the cream has been removed.

Low-fat milk is skim milk which still retains a little of the cream. It tastes more like whole milk and looks less anemic than skim milk, although it's not rich.

Buttermilk is the product that remains after sweet or sour milk has been churned and the fat removed. *Cultured buttermilk* is the soured product after pasteurized skimmed milk is treated with a suitable lactic acid bacteria culture.

Evaporated milk is the whole cow's milk from which 60 percent of the water has been removed. It is homogenized and sealed in cans.

Sweetened condensed milk is made by evaporating half the water from whole milk and adding enough cane or corn sugar to preserve it. It is then heated, cooled, and canned.

Dry whole milk solids are what remain after all the water has been removed from whole milk. They can be reconstituted with water or another liquid.

Yogurt is fermented milk—delicious on its own, plain or mixed with fresh fruit. It can be used in salad dressings and is a good lower-calorie substitute for sour cream. It's simple and economical to make yogurt and you don't need a special yogurt maker, if you follow the simple method below.

To make yogurt

Heat 1 quart of milk to the boiling point for just 1 minute. Cool to 115°F. Gently mix in 2 tablespoons of fresh plain yogurt (the starter), pour into a crockery bowl or several small bowls, even custard cups, if that is more convenient. Cover tight with plastic wrap and set in a warm place, preferably an oven with just a pilot light burning, or place in a warm kitchen corner and drape a blanket over the bowls to prevent drafts. An ideal temperature of about 110°F will hasten the incubation. The yogurt should be ready in about five to eight hours: tilt the bowl to see if it holds together. It should then be chilled for at least three hours and it will firm up even more. If the yogurt sets for too long a time or if you use too much starter, it will be watery; the longer you incubate the more sour it will be.

Nuts. Almonds, walnuts, peanuts, pecans, hazelnuts (or filberts), and pistachios are the nuts most frequently used in cooking. Shelled and unshelled nuts keep well in the freezer.

To blanch (i.e., remove the inner skins of) almonds or pistachios, put them in a bowl, pour boiling water over them, and let them sit for just a minute. Drain, and then rub off the skins.

To blanch filberts, drop in boiling water for a minute, drain, then rub while still warm between Turkish towels to remove the skin. If any don't skin easily, return them to the boiling water for another minute. Don't try to remove every little bit—it's impossible; actually, peeling filberts is a refinement and for most cakes and cookies, you don't need to bother.

To roast nuts, spread them in a single layer on a cookie sheet and toast them for about 5 minutes in a 375°F oven. Shake the pan once or twice and watch them—they can burn suddenly. Blanched nuts should be roasted to restore their crispness in a 325°F oven for 10–15 minutes, watching carefully.

To grind nuts, a hand grinder is preferable to a food processor or a blender. Electric machines bring out the oils in nuts; if you use one, grind the nuts quickly, turning the machine on and off, and do only ½ cup at a time. Don't pack them down when measuring.

To shell chestnuts, see p. 87.

Oils. Don't refrigerate oils. If they are pure, they will keep indefinitely.

Olive oil should be a good-quality virgin olive oil. It's expensive: use it in salad dressings and in other dishes where the taste is noticeable—or as called for in recipes.

Vegetable oil is a good, all-purpose cooking oil. Corn oil and peanut oil are heavier than vegetable oil, excellent for frying and sautéing because they can be brought to a high temperature without burning.

Walnut oil, an expensive delicacy, makes an unusual salad dressing. Buy it in small quantities; it is perishable.

Onions. Onions should be peeled except when you deliberately leave the skin on to deepen the color of a stock. With a largish onion just strip off the skin and outer layer. (Incidentally, if you are prone to tears when peeling and cutting onions, chill them in the refrigerator first; the coldness will retard the volatile juices.) To peel small onions, drop them first in boiling water for a minute; the skins will then slip off easily. To keep them intact, don't trim the root end; but you can pierce the root for even cooking.

Pasta. Dried pasta—i.e., spaghetti, macaroni, noodles, etc.—keep well and are a staple one should always have on hand. For information and recipes, see Pasta (p. 327).

Preserves. For information about preserves of all kinds—Jams, Jellies, etc.—see p. 694.

Rice. Basic food for a large part of the world, rice belongs in every larder. For information and recipes, see Rice (p. 316).

Sour Cream. See Cream (p. 13).

Soybean Curd. As the name indicates, a bland cheeselike curd made from soybeans. Also known as tofu, it comes in white, square cakes and should be kept in cold water in the refrigerator; if the water is changed daily, it will keep up to a week. It is especially high in protein and is used a lot in Oriental cooking.

Sprouts. Alfalfa and mung bean sprouts, crunchy and healthful, have become staples these days in many supermarkets. Americans use them primarily in salads and sandwiches, sometimes in an omelet.

Stocks. A stock is a result of mingling the bones and flesh of meat, poultry, or fish, as the case may be, with vegetable aromatics and herbs, cooking slowly until the essence of flavor is extracted. For cooking, cooling, reducing, storing, freezing, and clarifying the different stocks and for substitutes, see About Stocks and Stockmaking (p. 76).

Sugar. *Granulated sugar* is the sugar most commonly used. It's what is called for in these recipes, unless otherwise indicated.

Superfine sugar is finely pulverized granulated sugar. You can buy it that way or pulverize it yourself in a blender. It's good to use in meringues and other delicate desserts and for sprinkling over fruit.

Confectioners' sugar is powdered sugar, often used in baking and in uncooked frostings.

Raw sugar is less refined than regular sugars and has a coarse texture. It's nice in beverages and for sprinkling when a coarse, less dissolvable texture is desired.

Brown sugar comes in a light and a dark form. They are not really interchangeable: the dark has a deeper, more intense flavor, light-brown sugar is more commonly used in baking. Recipes will specify which to use when it makes a difference; otherwise feel free to use either light or dark.

Brown sugar should be stored in an airtight container in a cool spot or in the refrigerator. Add to the container a small slice of apple in an open plastic bag; it will keep the sugar soft. If your brown sugar becomes hard, soften it by putting it in a covered bowl with a few drops of water in a warm (200°F) oven for about 20 minutes. Don't put hard brown sugar in the blender or food processor; it may damage the blades. Pack brown sugar firmly when you are measuring it.

Granulated brown sugar doesn't cake because much of its moisture has been removed. It's useful to have around if you like brown sugar on cereals and fruits and pancakes. But don't substitute it in baking for regular brown sugar—you won't get the same results.

Maple sugar has a wonderful, rich flavor and is very expensive. Don't waste it in cooking. Use it as a delicious topping for desserts and cakes.

Caramelized sugar is sugar that has been cooked long enough to turn a caramel color, and in the process it takes on a new flavor. To prepare for use in desserts, see p. 609. Caramel is also used to flavor and color gravy and sauces. To make it for this purpose and to store in liquid form, melt 1 cup of sugar over medium heat in a heavy-bottomed pan, stirring often until the sugar is a rich, golden color, about 5 or 6 minutes. Take care that the sugar doesn't burn. Remove from the heat and be sure to let it cool a little. Add 1 cup of hot water, stirring briskly; if it is partly thick and tacky at this stage, don't worry—it will always melt. Put the mixture back over medium heat until blended. Cool, pour into a container, cover, and store; it will keep indefinitely. (To clean the pot, soak it in hot water, or fill it with water and return to the heat to dissolve the bits of hard sugar syrup that cling to the pan.)

Syrups. *Molasses* is what remains after the granulated sugar has been removed from sugar cane. It comes in a light and in a dark form and should be stored in a tightly closed jar in a cool place. Unsulfured molasses is preserved, but is a purer, unrefined molasses. Blackstrap is also unrefined but to some it has an unpleasant bitter taste.

Corn syrup is available light and dark, and the difference is an intensity in flavor. Used exclusively in desserts—the recipes will indicate which kind is called for.

Honey has different flavors, depending on the kinds of flowers the bees have frequented. It comes in three forms: strained and clear; unstrained and thick; and in the edible comb. Thick honey is grand to spread on toast.

Maple syrup is boiled-down maple sap. Keep it in the refrigerator. It will turn dark after a while, but this will not affect its flavor. Pure maple syrup is expensive. If you read the labels carefully of less expensive syrups, you'll see that they are usually a mixture of syrups with some maple added in.

Thickening Agents. See also Eggs (p. 14); Cream (p. 13).
Flour, to be properly used as a thickener, is blended into melted butter or other fat over low heat, stirred constantly, and cooked for 2–3 minutes. This is called making a *roux*. When liquid is stirred into the roux and cooked to the boiling point, the roux will thicken the liquid. Incidentally, if the liquid is hot when you add it your sauce will not lump on you.
Beurre manié is French for "handled butter." To thicken a soup or sauce that is already cooked, make a beurre manié by blending equal amounts of flour and soft butter, working them together quickly with your fingers. Add the mixture, bit by bit, to a hot sauce, stirring after each addition, until it is absorbed and you have the thickness you want.
Instant-blending flour is expensive. It dissolves in hot liquid without lumping and may be added directly to a gravy or pan drippings, or to a sauce. Do not use it in bread, cakes, or cookies.
Cornstarch must be dissolved in cold water before it is added to a hot mixture or it will lump. It's used frequently in Oriental cooking and produces the glazy, translucent sheen so often associated with Chinese food.
Arrowroot is very expensive and not always easy to find. It must be dissolved in water first. It is clear and almost tasteless and gives a nice gleam to food.
Potato flour cooks quickly and smoothly in liquid, is transparent, and leaves no raw taste. It's nice in fruit and egg sauces, but it cannot be heated to more than 176°F without thinning out.

Vinegar. Vinegar is the result of the acetic fermentation of an alcoholic liquid and has an acid taste. There are four basic, common vinegars: white, all-purpose vinegar, which is very sharp; cider vinegar, which is strong and often used in pickling; gentler red and white wine vinegars, particularly nice in salads; and herb vinegars, available commercially but also easy to make yourself. Japanese rice vinegar, now generally available, is lovely and mild on fruit salad and tender-tasting vegetables. In addition to being essential in the kitchen as a seasoning, vinegar acts as a preservative and is also useful in marinades to break down tough tissues.

To make wine vinegar, put red or white wine in a large-mouthed bottle and let it stand, uncovered, in a warm, dark place for several months. Don't use a wine that has turned sour: it takes good wine to produce a good wine vinegar. If you add a "mother"—the thick glob of skin that forms in the bottom of a vinegar bottle—the wine vinegar will be ready much sooner, a matter of weeks.

Wines and Liquors. The reason for cooking with wines and liquors is that they impart an incomparable flavor and bouquet. Use the same quality wines and liquors in cooking that you would want to drink. Sweet wine should be used primarily with desserts, but sometimes the sweet cooked wines are used to flavor a savory sauce.

Alcohol evaporates during cooking: when you cook with wine, the finished dish will not be "alcoholic." The longer it cooks, the deeper and richer a wine sauce will be. Avoid special "cooking wines"; they are not the real thing and often give a harsh flavor. See Wines, p. 8.

Yeast. Yeast is a form of leavening that comes in dry, granular form, which can be stored simply in the cupboard, or in compressed cakes, which are more perishable and should be kept in the refrigerator or freezer. Both are equally satisfactory. For information about using yeast, see p. 457.

Yogurt. See Milk, p. 16.

HERBS, SPICES, AND SEASONINGS

Herbs should never overwhelm a dish. The purpose of any seasoning is to provide an accent that enhances natural flavors, and it is important in using *dried herbs* that they be as fresh-tasting and fragrant as possible. Colors should be bright, not faded, and a good sniff will tell you about pungency. Store dried herbs in a cool place away from strong light—the refrigerator is excellent, if you have room there. You'll be wise to buy in small quantities, because most herbs do turn stale quickly—some more than others. And even though it may hurt, throw out stale jars.

Fresh herbs are a great treat, and if you are fortunate enough to come by them, by all means use them in place of dried. The flavor is invariably more seductive and their fresh-cut look is so appealing in any dish, particularly as a final garnish. Increasingly farmers' markets and even supermarkets are carrying more common herbs like dill, basil, chives, and, of course, fresh parsley is now a standard fixture. If you have a kitchen garden, plant a small bed of your favorite herbs. Some herb-lovers manage to grow plants of basil, chives, rosemary, tarragon, and thyme on a sunny window sill or under plant lights, but indoor herb gardening under lights can be tricky so consult a good guide.

In *cooking with fresh herbs*, you will always need to use at least twice the quantity of dried herbs. In many cases it will be even more than that and your only gauge is to taste and make your own adjustments.

Should you have an overabundance of fresh herbs, try storing them by making *herb butters* which can be frozen and used during winter months on homemade bread, with vegetables, or swirled into a simple sauce to provide a lovely burst of summer flavor. To make herb butters, chop a cup or more of fresh herbs with a stick of butter and blend until smooth, adding a few drops of lemon juice (this can be done in a blender or food processor if you have one).

Spices are usually dried, either whole or ground. If you don't use a spice very often, it's a good idea to buy it whole and grind or grate it according to need.

In addition to the *seasonings* listed below, sauces, marinades, barbecue sauces, relishes, and stuffings are also used to enhance the flavor of foods. For recipes see Sauces, Marinades, Stuffings, and Quick Relishes (p. 264).

Allspice. Allspice comes whole or ground and it is a separate spice, not a collection of spices as the name might lead one to believe. Use it in baking and in pâtés and terrines.

Anise. Anise is a spice, usually bought ground. It has a strong licorice flavor and is good in cookies.

Aromatics. Aromatics are vegetables like onions, shallots, leeks, garlic, carrots, and celery used primarily to give off their flavor and aroma to foods they are cooked with. Sometimes they are simply dropped into the cooking pot or sometimes a combination of chopped aromatics will provide a bed on which meats, fish, and poultry are braised. A good kitchen is never without at least onions, carrots, garlic, and celery.

Basil. Basil has a robust flavor and lovely pungent smell. It's particularly good in tomatoey dishes and delicious fresh with salads and sliced tomatoes.

Bay Leaf. Bay leaf is very pungent and keeps its flavor well. The imported variety is far preferable, but if you have California bay use with great care: it's very strong. Bay leaf is essential in a bouquet garni, and something seems missing if a pot roast or pâté isn't cooked with a bay leaf.

Capers. Capers are the small buds of a shrub grown in the Mediterranean. They are pickled in vinegar or dried and salted. The salted should be washed before they are used. Capers are particularly good with seafood, in sauces and salads, and as a garnish.

Caraway Seed. A spiky seed, caraway is a flavor commonly associated with rye bread, but it also has other interesting uses—tossed with noodles, for instance, or embedded in sauerkraut and cole slaw.

Cardamom. Cardamom is a spice that is bought whole or ground and is used in baking.

Celery Leaves. Chopped, fresh celery leaves are apt to be on hand if you keep a fresh bunch of celery in the refrigerator (as you should). Finely chopped, the leaves are good added to soups, to a vegetable salad, and sometimes to the juices around a roast, rounding out the balance of flavors. Dried leaves are strong, so use only in soups, sparingly.

Celery Seed. Celery seed is not called for often but it is used sometimes in a potato salad and in aromatic vegetables. It is strong and should be used judiciously.

Chervil. Chervil, fresh or dried, has a delicate flavor, and the fresh leaves look a bit like parsley. It's lovely when subtle seasoning is desired—with fish, eggs, and delicate cream sauces.

Chili Powder. Made from chilies that have been dried, commercial chili powder is only mildly hot. *Ground chili* is usually labeled hot; use with more caution.

Chives. Chives belong to the onion family. Fresh are preferable when available; when they're not, use freeze-dried chives, rather than frozen, and be sure that they are very green. Chives have many uses—in soups, eggs, salads, with sour cream and cream cheese, and in simple sauces.

Cinnamon. Ground cinnamon is used in desserts and occasionally in main dishes and drinks. Mixed with sugar, it's wonderful on French toast or pancakes or sprinkled on a crisp slice of apple. Stick cinnamon is used primarily in mulled winter drinks and in sugar syrups for preserving.

Cloves. Ground cloves are used in baking while a few whole cloves, stuck into an onion or tied in a cheesecloth bag, often lend flavor to soups or stews; press them into a scored ham to bake, the more the merrier.

Coriander or Cilantro (Chinese Parsley). There are the seeds and there are the leaves, used quite differently. The ground coriander seeds are sometimes used in baking; the whole seeds are essential in pickling and making aromatic vegetables. The leaf, also known as Chinese parsley and cilantro, has a surprising, unfamiliar taste, one which must be acquired. But it is much appreciated by connoisseurs and used frequently in Mexican, Indian, and Chinese cooking.

Curry. Curry is not a single spice but a blend including turmeric, cumin, coriander, fenugreek, red peppers, and other strong spices. It's derived from the cooking of India and used in what we call curry dishes or to give a slight accent to a sauce or eggs. Since it varies in composition, buy a good, reliable blend of excellent quality.

Dill. Fresh dill is increasingly easy to find in the market in the right season and is better than the dried, which is sometimes called dillweed. Dill seed is often used in pickling. Dill is good with fish and with cucumbers and is basic to Scandinavian and Russian cooking. Although its flavor is lovely and mild, it should not be used with a heavy hand.

Duxelles. Minced mushrooms that have been sautéed in butter (p. 389) until all their liquid has evaporated, thus preserving them and condensing their flavor. They may be refrigerated or frozen in a tightly closed container and used, as needed, for seasoning.

Fennel. Fennel seed has a licoricelike flavor; use it judiciously or it can taste bitter. It is essential in aromatic vegetables. The fennel bulb like celery is used both as a vegetable and chopped raw in salads.

Ginger. Ground ginger is used primarily in baking. Candied ginger is used in desserts. Fresh ginger root, used especially in Chinese cooking, has become a staple in many markets recently. It will keep in the refrigerator for a week or so, but if you want to store longer, freeze and then just hack off a piece as you need it.

Horseradish. Horseradish is usually bought in a jar—the white or red variety being equally good—and it should be stored in the refrigerator. If you have a chance to buy fresh horseradish, grate it and use just as is—it's delicious. To keep, put it in a bottle with white vinegar to cover and add a little salt.

Juniper Berries. The berries are from a wild European shrub. Their aromatic flavor gives gin its characteristic taste, and they are used sometimes in meat marinades and sauces, providing a particularly good foil for game.

Lemon Juice. A few drops of lemon juice is often what's needed to properly sharpen the flavor of a great variety of dishes. Use fresh-squeezed lemon juice whenever possible. While frozen juice may do in a pinch, bottled lemon juice with its strong, medicinal taste is a poor substitute.

1. basil; 2. bay; 3. chervil; 4. chives; 5. dill; 6. mint; 7. coriander, also known as cilantro and Chinese parsley; 8. marjoram; 9. curly parsley; 10. oregano; 11. Italian parsley; 12. rosemary; 13. summer savory; 14. tarragon; 15. sage; 16. thyme.

It's hard to say how much juice one lemon gives; some lemons are juicier than others; some have thicker skins. The best way to be accurate is to measure the juice.

Ground Lemon Rind and Lemon Zest. The rind of the lemon skin should be pared away, leaving behind the bitter white. You can grate it, or strip it off with a vegetable parer or a special "zester." Lemon peels give a concentrated but beautifully refreshing lemony flavor to both desserts and main-course dishes.

Mace. Mace comes dried and ground. It is the outer covering of nutmeg, but has a lighter, milder flavor than the nutmeg it conceals. Classic with pound cake, it is used mainly in baking and in desserts.

Marinades. Marinades are used both to tenderize and to add flavor. They usually contain an acid liquid like lemon juice, vinegar, or wine, which helps to break down tough tissues, and they always have a variety of seasonings, sometimes with a liaison of oil. For recipes, see Marinades (p. 276).

Marjoram. Marjoram is a very pungent herb—even more so, surprisingly, when it is fresh. It requires discretion and is particularly good with grilled fish and with egg dishes. Dried, it loses its flavor quite quickly.

Mint. Dried mint is good; fresh mint is better. Iced tea is not its only use—it's good especially with fruit, in mint sauce for lamb, in peas, and in certain cold soups.

Monosodium Glutamate. Known also as MSG and produced under several brand names, this chemical product has been used and overused to bring out the flavors in food. If food is well seasoned, there's no need for it, especially since many people have a bad physical reaction to it and it is now considered unhealthful.

Mustard. Dry ground mustard is made of finely ground mustard seeds; it's very strong, so use in small quantities as directed. There are many kinds of prepared mustards, from ballpark to the imported French Dijon, and when a particular kind is called for, the recipe will specify.

Nutmeg. Ground nutmeg loses its flavor quickly when it sits around in a tin. Buy whole nutmeg instead and grate it fresh, using the small holes of your regular grater (or there are special small graters just for nutmeg). A few gratings give a wonderfully fragrant taste to certain vegetables and sauces, but nutmeg is used mostly in desserts.

Oregano. Dried oregano is much more pungent than fresh oregano. Don't keep it too long: it changes color and character as it gets stale.

Paprika. It pays to buy a good variety of Hungarian paprika; too many ordinary paprikas are more color than flavor. Recipes in this book call for sweet, not hot, paprika, so be sure to ask for the sweet if you are buying it imported. In making a stew or a sauce, if you cook paprika first in the fat, it helps to blossom the flavor.

Parsley. There is no excuse for using anything other than fresh parsley, particularly since it is so readily available today. The dried flakes are tasteless. Fresh parsley does much more than decorate a dish, although it is always a welcome garnish; like a drop of lemon, parsley is a seasoning that brings out other flavors in a dish. Curly parsley is tasty and decorative; Italian parsley has a flat leaf and a more pronounced flavor. When fresh chopped parsley is rubbed with dried herbs it is surprising how the herbs seem to come to life.

Pepper. For the brightest, most vivacious taste, buy *whole black peppercorns* and use them freshly ground: it really does make a difference. Experiment with different kinds of peppercorns. When whole peppercorns are called for be sure to crush them slightly first or they won't release any flavor.

White pepper has less flavor than black pepper. It's used in light-colored sauces because it doesn't show, but do a few black specks really matter very much?

Cayenne pepper is hot red pepper, dried and ground. It adds a lot of fire to a dish, so use it sparingly, respecting the palates of family and guests. Be sure it's fresh: it dies quickly.

Green peppercorns are the berries of a special species found primarily in Madagascar. They are preserved fresh in water or vinegar, water being preferable, even though the peppercorns won't last as long. Not as sharp as dried pepper, this relatively new seasoning is an exciting one, and adds zest to meats and poultry. Available in specialty stores.

Hot dried red pepper flakes are very hot and add verve to things like pasta and eggs. Again, use sparingly.

Tiny dried hot peppers, both red and green, should be seeded and chopped and used very sparingly in cooking. Be careful to wash your hands and not to rub your eyes when handling hot peppers.

Hot red pepper sauce is a liquid which mixes hot red pepper with vinegar, salt, and seasonings. It has its place, and not only in barbecue sauces or chili; a few drops added at the end to certain dishes bring out their flavors.

Pimientos are sweet red peppers that have been preserved in oil. Use them whole or chopped in salads, but always buy them whole, for the chopped pieces absorb too much water.

For information about pimientos and red and green peppers, both hot and sweet, see p. 395.

Pickling Spice. This mixture of whole spices—such as coriander, mustard seed, cinnamon, bay leaves, allspice, dill seed, ginger, cloves, and peppers—is used primarily for pickling.

Poppy Seeds. Used on rolls and in other baked products, poppy seeds are also good tossed with noodles and in an American favorite, poppy-seed salad dressing.

Rosemary. Rosemary has a strong, pungent flavor in both its fresh and its dried forms. It's good with pork, lamb, and beans and in stuffings.

Rosewater. Made of roses distilled with water, rosewater is a distinctive, delicate flavoring, often used in Middle Eastern cooking.

Saffron. Saffron is the stamen from the crocus. It gives a beautiful yellow color and lovely flavor to rice and other dishes; but never use more than is called for. Although good saffron is very expensive, don't settle for the cheaper varieties. Buy it in threads, rather than ground, for fresher flavor. Before using it, saffron *must* be steeped in hot liquid to bring out its flavor.

Sage. Sage is very pungent—even fresh (if using fresh try the pineapple sage for a fruity aromatic flavor). In the American kitchen it is used primarily in stuffings, in sausages, and with pork.

Salt. There's no substitute for salt. It adds its own flavor and also helps bring out the other flavors in food.

The effect of salt is quite variable, depending on whether it is added during cooking or after a dish is done. Because *the amount of salt* is very much a matter of personal taste, we have tried to avoid prescribing an exact amount when your own palate should be the guide: a good cook always tastes a dish as he goes along and adjusts the salt and other seasonings again at the end, if necessary. However, one must be precise when salt is mixed into raw ingredients before cooking, such as when baking, and in these instances the recipes will call for a precise amount. But whenever possible in these recipes we are asking you to use your own critical palate. Inexperienced cooks are often too timid using salt; there must be enough to develop the natural flavors of foods, so keep adding and sampling until the taste blossoms and pleases. There are times, however, when you must consider that those you are serving cannot tolerate much salt, and in that case try to use lots of fresh herbs instead.

Table salt is the fine-textured salt commonly used and therefore what is generally called for in these recipes; it has been dissolved, purified, and then recrystallized and is either iodized or uniodized. A little rice in your salt shaker helps to keep salt from getting too damp in humid weather.

Kosher salt is used by many good cooks and particularly by those who observe Jewish dietary laws. It has an even, coarse texture and measure for measure is not as strong as table salt.

Sea salt has a coarse texture and fresh flavor. It's often ground in a salt grinder when adding salt to cooked dishes. *Rock salt* is also used freshly ground.

Seasoned salt tends to taste dehydrated and is undesirable in cooking.

Savory. *Winter savory* is a perennial, strong in flavor with limited uses. *Summer savory* is a very versatile, all-purpose herb, used frequently in early American recipes.

Sesame Oil. Sesame oil is used to give a distinctive nutty flavor to foods and should be added in small quantities at the end of cooking. It's a very familiar taste in Chinese cooking.

Sesame Seed (Benne Seed). This seed, brought over from Africa by the slaves, has an especially good flavor. The flavor intensifies when the seeds are dry-roasted in a skillet.

Sorrel. Sorrel is sour grass, an easy-to-grow perennial that also grows wild in many parts of the United States. It's a wonderful, slightly sour addition to soups and sauces; cut in strips, it adds a tart taste to salads.

Soy Sauce. Soy sauce is made from soybeans, salt, yeast, wheat, and sugar. Used primarily as a seasoning in Oriental cooking, soy sauce has been adopted by Western cooks increasingly in the last few decades. It is particularly good for marinating meats, since it tenderizes them, and it adds flavor and color to sauces. It is apt to be salty so be careful about adding salt when using it.

Tabasco. Tabasco is a liquid pepper seasoning. It is hot, so use judiciously; a few drops go a long way.

Tarragon. Tarragon is a beautiful herb with a delicate, subtle, lemon-and-licorice flavor. It's especially good in dishes where flavors do not compete, like eggs, chicken, fish, veal, and certain sauces.

Thyme. Thyme is very strong and good, essential to a bouquet garni and to many soups and stews.

Tomato. Tomatoes in various forms are used frequently as a seasoning.

Tomato paste is made of puréed tomatoes that have been reduced at least by half. Because it is so concentrated, a spoonful of tomato paste is sometimes called for where a hint of tomato flavor is desired, but use judiciously to intensify a tomato sauce or perhaps to flavor a stew. You can freeze leftover tomato paste, either in its own small can or spooned into a plastic bag. It will be soft enough to spoon out in small quantities as you need it, and you can leave the remainder in the freezer for future use.

Tomato purée is unseasoned tomato pulp with some tomato juice. It is quite bland in taste.

Tomato sauce is made from tomatoes, salt, peppers, and spices. Make your own or choose from a variety of different brands, basically the same but seasoned differently. Taste and remember that you can add flavors to your own liking. Prepared sauces can be useful at certain times.

Solid-packed tomatoes are peeled whole unseasoned tomatoes in their own juice. They are the best substitute for fresh tomatoes, sometimes better to use when fresh tomatoes have little flavor.

Turmeric. Turmeric is an Indian spice made from a ground root that gives a yellow color and an exotic flavor to foods.

Worcestershire Sauce. This spicy sauce, based on a recipe from India, was first manufactured in Worcestershire, England—hence the name. It is good with meats and in some sauces, but use it sparingly so that it doesn't overwhelm natural flavors.

EQUIPMENT

For Food Preparation

Measuring Cups. It is important to have one set for dry measure and one for wet measure. For *dry measure* a graduated set of four cups: ¼ cup (½ dL), ⅓ cup (¾ dL), ½ cup (1 dL), and 1 cup (¼ L), which can be filled to the brim and then leveled off at the top with the flat edge of a knife, are the only kind that provide an accurate measure of flour and other dry ingredients. For *wet measure* use cups with a spout and made of see-through material so that the measure can be read at eye level. There is a little leeway at the top which is necessary as liquids are bound to spill over when carried. One-cup (¼-L) and 2-cup (½-L) sizes are essential; a 4-cup (1-L) measure is also very useful.

Measuring Spoons. A set of measuring spoons, shaped so that thez can easily be leveled off with a knife, is a must; ¼ teaspoon, ½ teaspoon, 1 teaspoon, and 1 tablespoon are the standard sizes.

Ruler. A ruler is necessary for taking the size of pastry shapes, for measuring pans, and for other kitchen needs.

Thermometers. The most common and least expensive *meat thermometer* is one that you insert in meat or poultry at the start and leave in throughout the cooking process. Far more accurate and convenient, however, are the smaller *instant thermometers*. These are not left in the oven: take the temperature at intervals by inserting the thermometer into whatever part of the flesh you want to test—such as the breast meat and the thigh meat of a chicken or a turkey. Furthermore, they can be slipped into the side of a steak, chops, or hamburgers to test for doneness. They are more expensive, but well worth the investment.

A *candy/frying thermometer* is important for measuring how hot the syrup or fat may be. For checking the accuracy of a candy thermometer, see p. 677.

A *freezer thermometer* is good if you wish to be sure that your freezer is cold enough for proper storage. See p. 726.

Timer. A timer is absolutely necessary in the kitchen. If your stove doesn't have one built into it, get a freestanding one.

Bowls. You will need mixing bowls in at least three different sizes. Stainless steel, glass, plastic, and earthenware are all fine; it's a matter of personal preference. A very large bowl is handy if you cook in large quantities or do a lot of entertaining.

Chopping Board. Your chopping board should be thick, solid, and large. Wood is the best material. A built-in chopping board is a wonderful convenience. Clean the chopping board from time to time with a baking soda solution or with lemon juice, especially after cutting up meat.

Knives. Whether you use stainless steel or carbon steel is a matter of personal preference. Stainless knives will not rust and are easy to keep shiny; many of the newer ones seem to hold an edge as fine as carbon steel knives. But there are still many traditional cooks who prefer good-quality carbon steel knives, which can be sharpened so easily after each use. You will need an 8- or 9-inch (20- or 23-cm) chef's knife, a paring knife or two, a bread knife with a serrated edge, and a carving knife. Knives should never be kept in a drawer unless the blades are protected by sheaths. It is really better to keep them on magnets attached to the wall or to slip them into slots, if you have that kind of knife holder.

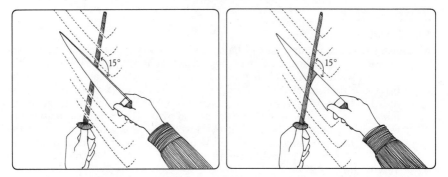

Knife Sharpener. Of the numerous knife sharpeners available, an ordinary whetting or sharpening stone does a good job. To sharpen, draw the blade across the stone at an angle of no more than 15 degrees, repeating until you get a good edge.

Kitchen Shears. You'll need a large pair of scissors in the kitchen for a number of jobs.

Vegetable Parer. Essential for peeling fruits and vegetables.

Openers. You will need a bottle opener, corkscrew, and beer opener. A jar opener that works for different sizes is also very handy. A substantial, heavy-duty *can opener* will make life easy. Electric ones are good, but keep a hand model around for when the power fails, and be sure to wipe off the blade occasionally, which can build up a residue.

Pepper Grinder. Essential for grinding fresh pepper. See Pepper (p. 25).

Rotary Egg Beater. Important if you don't have an electric hand beater (p. 30) and, again, for emergencies or just to save power.

Nutcracker. Get the sturdy, old-fashioned kind (see illustration, p. 30).

Funnel. Both a small and a large one are useful.

Grater. Use a four-sided, standing grater and a rotary hand grater for nuts and cheese. Even if you have a food processor, which grates most things successfully, a hand grater is less violent and will be wanted occasionally.

Colander. Good for draining many things, including pasta. Get a big, substantial one made of metal.

Strainer. You'll need a small one and a large one.

Juicer. A small hand juicer is necessary for squeezing lemons and other fruit for cooking. If you squeeze juice regularly for your family's breakfast, it's wonderful to have an electric juicer (p. 39).

Salad Spinner. A wire basket for drying greens is attractive and useful. The newer plastic salad spinners that will catch the water and whirl with great force are exceptionally efficient, particularly if you are an apartment dweller and don't have a backyard in which to swing a wet basket.

USEFUL BUT NOT ESSENTIAL

Grapefruit Knife. To loosen segments from a halved grapefruit.

Melon Baller. To scoop out perfect balls of melon and other fruit. It can also be used for potatoes.

Zester. To extract in thin strips the yellow rind of a lemon.

Egg Slicer. To cut perfect slices of hard-boiled eggs.

Chopping Bowl and Chopper. Particularly useful for chopping items that are going to jump around on a board.

Poultry Shears. To cut up poultry.

Apple Corer. To extract the core from an apple neatly.

Scales. Working with metrics does not mean that you have to start measuring with scales. However, it is useful to have kitchen scales that register both measures for easy translation and in order to familiarize yourself more readily with the metric system. And as you begin to use scales, you may find out how convenient it is to weigh rather than measure by cups.

Meat Grinder. A meat grinder is not absolutely necessary if you have a food processor (p. 39), although for tough meats it still does a better job, particularly if your food processor does not have a very strong motor.

Mortar and Pestle. For crushing and pulverizing and sometimes for mashing.

Trussing Needle. For sewing up meat, fish, and poultry.

Meat Pounder. To help tenderize and thin out pieces of meat and poultry.

For Cooking

Pots, Skillets, and Pans. Use good-quality *saucepans* of various sizes. They will last longer than pans of flimsy material, which burn easily and don't distribute the heat evenly. Some useful basic sizes are 1–2 cups (¼–½ L), 1 quart (1 L), 2 quarts (2 L), and 8 quarts (7½ or 8 L).

You'll need 7-inch (18-cm) and 12-inch (30-cm) *skillets* or *frying pans* (they mean the same thing); a 10-inch (25-cm) is also very handy. Skillets should have covers, or get a flat, "pigtail" lid which works for many sizes.

1. glass measuring cups for liquids; 2. measuring spoons; 3. measuring cups for dry ingredients (fill to top and level off with a knife); 4. scale; 5. can/bottle opener; 6. and 7. corkscrews; 8. manual can opener; 9. jar opener; 10. kitchen scissors; 11. ruler; 12. wall can opener; 13. garlic press; 14. juicer; 15. funnels; 16. nutcracker; 17. nut grinder; 18. and 19. pepper grinders; 20. nutmeg grater; 21. grater (with different size holes on its four sides); 22. cheese grater; 23. food mill; 24. rotary beater; 25. ricer.

1. colander; 2. strainers; 3. bowls; 4. salad spinner; 5. cutting board with (from top to bottom): boning knife, bread knife, knife sharpener, chef's knife, medium-size knife, paring knife; 6. salad basket; 7. grapefruit knife; 8. melon baller; 9. vegetable parer; 10. zester (for narrow strips of orange and lemon peel); 11. stripper (for wider strips); 12. apple corer; 13. egg piercer; 14. egg slicer; 15. poultry shears; 16. pitter; 17. wooden bowl and chopper; 18. carving knife and fork.

Nonstick surfaces, the kind that are bonded to the metal, are excellent for skillets, but not necessary for saucepans; it's helpful to have a 7-inch (18-cm) nonstick pan to make crêpes and omelets. Heavy enamel-coated frying pans are good for long, slow cooking, but they don't give a brown crust; the old-fashioned black cast-iron skillet is the best for that.

It is very useful to have a *flameproof casserole* or *Dutch oven* of heavy porcelain-coated iron or attractive stainless steel or lined copper which can be used on top of the stove, then go into the oven, and be presentable at the table. Three quart (2¾ L) is a basic size; 4–6 quart (3¾ L–5½ or 6 L) is good for a party or a large family.

There are many kinds of *casseroles and baking dishes*—glass, porcelain, earthenware—and you may want a variety, but most of them cannot be used on top of the stove, only for baking.

A shallow *roasting pan* for the oven, fitted with a V-shaped rack, is essential for roasts and can double as a baking dish or basin to hold smaller baking dishes that must be surrounded with boiling water.

A *double boiler* is not a necessity because you can always improvise by placing a heatproof mixing bowl over a larger pot filled with water. A glass *double boiler*, however, is useful because you can see the water level in the bottom and keep a check on it.

A *steamer* with a perforated top that sits above the water is very handy. An inexpensive, collapsible trivet made for steaming is equally satisfactory. A steamer can also be improvised by resting a heatproof plate on an empty tuna can in a large pot with a cover.

Kettle. Use a water kettle with a whistle so you'll be warned when the water has come to a boil.

Coffee Pot. The type of coffee pot you use is a matter of personal preference; but a metal pot is apt to retain a stale coffee taste and it must always be carefully cleaned.

Metal Ring Mold. It would be good to have these in 1- and 2-quart (1- and 2-L) sizes. Useful for gelatin salads and desserts, they are also used for cakes and molded rice dishes.

Wooden Spoons. There's a quiet, nice feeling about wooden cooking utensils: they don't conduct heat and/or scrape against the sides of the pan. Have several, one of them with a flat bottom that will scrape the bottom of the pan and get into the inside edges.

Rubber Spatula. Almost better than the human hand, a rubber spatula scrapes absolutely clean so there's no waste. One or two are a must in any kitchen.

Metal Utensils. Metal utensils should have plastic handles that won't heat up. Every kitchen needs a *metal spatula*, a *pancake turner*, a *slotted spoon*, a *cooking fork*, a *ladle*, and a *potato masher*. The best kind of potato masher is one with a spiral bottom.

Tongs. Tongs are particularly useful for turning something you don't want to risk piercing with a fork or in extracting something from a pot of boiling water.

Whisk. The whisk is designed so that its many strands of looped wire make it particularly effective for beating. A medium-size balloon whisk is a good size to start with.

Skewers. You will need both large and small depending on what you are skewering: the small ones are particularly useful for keeping stuffing from spilling out.

Bulb Baster. A marvelous kitchen invention for sucking up the juices from the pan in order to baste. It also works quite well for drawing off fat. The glass basters are apt to break; plastic melts if left carelessly near a heated surface; so metal is probably your best bet.

Brush. Good for basting and glazing.

USEFUL BUT NOT ESSENTIAL

Griddle. A flat metal surface for dry top-of-the-stove baking.

Old-Fashioned Bean Pot. The old-fashioned bean pot is a high-sided pot with a narrow neck usually made of earthenware with a tight-fitting top.

Wok. This round-bottomed Oriental cooking pot set on a collar is particularly good for stir-frying. Woks work only on a gas stove, however. There is an electric plug-in model available, but it doesn't respond very well to rapid temperature changes.

Skimmer. A flat, very fine mesh strainer, excellent for removing scum and particles from the surface of liquids.

Food Mill. A hand-operated food mill is especially useful if you don't have a food processor. It also does certain things a food processor can't do, like straining out the skins and seeds as you mash certain fruits and vegetables.

Ricer. Excellent for making mashed potatoes without any lumps.

Deep-Fat Fryer with a Basket. See Fry (p. 46).

Pudding Mold with a Lid That Seals. Necessary for steamed puddings (p. 39).

Espresso Pot. The only way to make strong Italian espresso coffee.

Scallop Shells. Nice for baking and serving seafood and other fishy appetizers.

Fish Poacher. A great convenience if you are apt to poach a whole fish quite often.

Stock Pot. Tall, narrow, and straight-sided, designed for the slow cooking-down of a stock, a stock pot is useful but not essential; any large pot will do.

Gratin Pan. An attractive, party-size gratin pan is useful to have; you can run it under the broiler, then bring it directly to the table. As an alternative, wrap a napkin or two around whatever baking pan you've used to present it at the table.

Pressure Cooker. A specially manufactured heavy pot with a lid that seals tightly, in which foods can be cooked rapidly under pressure. Useful when time is short, and many cooks swear by them. Check your instruction book for what pressure-cooks successfully. You must time very accurately (see pressure-cooking charts pp. 753–755).

Clay Cooker. Cooking in a covered clay pot, which seals in the juices so beautifully, is particularly satisfactory for lean, slightly tough meats and birds. The pots must always be soaked in water well before using and no cooking fat is necessary. If you turn the oven temperature up high at the end, the food inside will brown nicely, still covered.

Chafing Dish. The sauté pan usually sits over another pan of hot water warmed by canned heat, so the average chafing dish permits only relatively slow

1. meat grinder; 2. mortar and pestle; 3. trussing needle; 4. meat pounders; 5. instant
thermometer; 6. candy/frying thermometer; 7. oven thermometer; 8. timer;
9. wooden spoons; 10. spatula for cake frosting; 11. rubber spatulas; 12. cooking
spatulas; 13. kitchen fork; 14. slotted spoon; 15. ladle; 16. potato mashers;
17. tongs; 18. wire whisks; 19. bulb baster; 20. skewers; 21. pastry brushes;
22. skimmer.

1. *saucepans*; 2. *skillets, with pigtail lid*; 3. *steamer basket*; 4. *Dutch oven*; 5. *wok*;
6. *double boiler*; 7. *frying basket*; 8. *pressure cooker*; 9. *kettle*; 10. *large cooking pot*;
11. *fish steamer*; 12. *stock pot*; 13. *roasting pan and rack*.

cooking. But it is fine for dishes that require just that, and, of course, it can all be done at the table. It is also useful for keeping foods warm on a buffet table.

For Baking

Pastry Blender. The several wire strands cut shortening or butter into flour quickly and efficiently—sometimes better than you can do with your fingers.

Rolling Pin. Don't get a dinky rolling pin. A large heavy one is essential for rolling out dough successfully. For a *surface* you can use anything from a Formica counter top, a board at least 24 × 18 inches, (60 × 45 cm), or a marble slab. A lot of beginning cooks find a *pastry cloth* helpful.

Sifter. For sifting flour and sugar. The spring action kind that you squeeze with one hand is simplest to use and most readily available. Don't wash it every time you use it: just knock it and shake out any residue.

Cake Pans. If you do a fair amount of baking, you'll need two sizes of cake pans—a pair of 8-inch (20-cm) and a pair of 9-inch (23-cm) 1½ inches (4 cm) deep. Removable bottoms are not necessary. You'll also need an 8- or 9-inch (20- or 23-cm) *square cake pan* and a *9 × 12-inch (23 × 30–cm) rectangular pan*. Nonstick surfaces are a welcome feature, although we still recommend buttering them. A 10-inch (25-cm) *tube pan* (p. 38) is also useful, as are other specialized sizes.

Loaf Pans. For breads, quick breads, and loaf cakes. These come in two standard sizes: 9 × 5 × 3 inches (23 × 13 × 8 cm) and 8½ × 4½ × 2½ inches (21½ × 11½ × 6½ cm). The smaller size is preferable for the bread recipes in this book.

Cookie Sheets. You need at least two cookie sheets, as cookies take up a lot of space and must usually be baked in batches; the nonstick surfaces are good. You'll find you will use cookie sheets for other purposes as well, like toasting nuts and crackers and catching drippings.

Jelly-Roll Pan. Jelly-roll pans have a little edge around them; the standard size is 10½ × 15½ × 1 inch (26½ × 38½ × 2½ cm). They're used for classic jelly rolls, of course, and can also be used for cookies and other baked goods; they are particularly useful in making candy in case of too much spreading.

Muffin Tins. Muffin tins come in several sizes. The standard-size cups hold about ½ cup when full.

Pie Pans. Some recipes call for an 8-inch (20-cm) pan, others for 9-inch (23-cm), so get both of these standard sizes. A 10-inch (25-cm) pan is wonderful to have for entertaining. Glass is nice because you can see the color of the crust, but it cooks faster so you must lower your oven temperature by 25 degrees.

Tart Pan. A 10-inch (25-cm) tart pan with a removable rim is the right thing for tarts and quiches.

Soufflé Dish. A 2-quart (2-L) soufflé dish with straight sides will fill most needs, though for a small family a 1-quart (1-L) or 1½-quart (1½-L) is convenient. Porcelain and glass are both fine.

Custard Cups. Either glass or earthenware will do. Use them for custard, small soufflés, baked desserts, and popovers.

Cake Rack. Designed so that there is air space below, racks are necessary for cooling cakes, breads, and cookies.

USEFUL BUT NOT ESSENTIAL

Pastry Scraper. A flat-edged device for scraping dough from counter tops and boards. Good for cleanup, too.

Pastry-Pizza Cutter. For cutting various pastry shapes.

Biscuit Cutters. The rim of a glass will also do.

Doughnut Cutters. Necessary if you make doughnuts.

Cookie Cutters. They come in three standard sizes and in many fanciful shapes.

Springform Pans. A round tin with a removable rim, used particularly for cheesecakes.

Small Tart Tins. Good for making appetizers and desserts. Fit leftover pieces of pie dough into them and freeze (see Savory Tarts, p. 68).

Pastry Bag. The best kind is made of lightweight material that is washable with a set of standard-size nozzles. To make your own, see p. 534.

Cookie Press. For pressed cookies, see p. 548.

Appliances

In buying *large appliances,* ask a lot of questions, compare models, and consider not only what something costs but how much energy it is going to use.

For small electric appliances start out with only those that you need the most. Exciting as the food processor is, for instance, if you can learn to chop and slice and mix and knead with your hands first, you will understand food better and appreciate what any machine can and cannot do.

Space is also a consideration. If you haven't enough room for an appliance and have to store it somewhere, you tend not to use it. So consider your space before buying.

Refrigerator and Freezer. For owning and maintaining a freezer, see Frozen Foods, p. 725.

Select a refrigerator according to the way you live and how much cooking you do. Models with refrigerator and freezer side by side use more energy and provide a poor distribution of space. A freezer compartment on top is very much better: even if you have fewer cubic feet, it seems to hold more and you can get at things more easily.

Self-defrosting refrigerators and freezers use more energy but are a wonderful convenience. Since there is a constant evaporation in a frost-free refrigerator, foods dry out more rapidly and should always be tightly covered.

If you do a lot of freezing, you will probably need a separate freestanding freezer.

1. sifter; 2. pie dough/pastry blender; 3. pizza cutter; 4. rolling pin; 5. biscuit cutter; 6. doughnut cutter; 7. cookie cutters; 8. pastry bag and tips; 9. cookie press; 10. pastry scraper; 11. pie pan; 12. quiche pan; 13. cake pans; 14. square cake pan; 15. small tart tins; 16. ring mold; 17. springform pan; 18. tube pan; 19. bread pans; 20. cake rack; 21. muffin tin; 22. cookie sheet; 23. jelly roll pan.

1. clay cooker; 2. bean pot; 3. chafing dish; 4. gratin dish; 5. soufflé dish;
6. casserole; 7. pudding mold; 8. custard cups; 9. scallop shells; 10. hand electric
mixer; 11. electric juicer; 12. food processor; 13. standing electric mixer;
14. blender.

Ranges. If you have the opportunity to choose between a gas stove and an electric range, consider the advantages and drawbacks of each. Gas ranges respond more immediately when you turn up or lower the heat, which can be very important in certain kinds of cooking—making omelets, for instance, or quick browning followed by a slow braise. Electric ovens, however, are apt to be more dependable than gas. And the electric broiler goes on with the turn of a switch while all too often the pilot light on a gas broiler is knocked out by the heat of the oven and can be very difficult to relight. Many custom-designed kitchens feature gas burners and wall-hung electric ovens.

Both gas and electric ovens come with an optional self-cleaning feature. It's expensive and energy-consuming, but a great boon.

Microwave Ovens. Microwave ovens are good for thawing and defrosting frozen foods and for cooking certain things like vegetables and fish. There are now microwave ovens with a browning device, which is an important feature. Microwave cooking is an entirely new kind of cooking requiring special recipes; don't try to use the recipes in this book. It's as yet an unperfected appliance, so examine all the pros and cons before deciding to buy one.

Standing Electric Mixer. One of the most useful kitchen appliances, especially if you do a lot of baking. Select a heavy-duty model with a rounded bowl for even beating, and a dough hook for making bread.

Hand Electric Mixer. A relatively inexpensive appliance, an electric hand mixer is useful, whether or not you have a freestanding mixer. You can use it on the stove, to beat up sauces and frostings while they are heating.

Food Processor. The food processor is certainly the most exciting new appliance to appear on the market in many years. But although it has revolutionized many people's cooking habits, it does *not* do everything. It's particularly good for chopping, slicing, grating, grinding, and puréeing (without overblending) and for the tedious shredding of things like carrots and cabbage, and it is excellent for chopping meat.

There are some tricks for using a food processor properly. Feed it a little at a time, rather than filling up the entire bowl. Learn to turn the machine on and off again quickly and in rapid succession: this will chop foods more evenly rather than puréeing some of the pieces while leaving others in larger hunks.

The food processor is all right for making tart pastry but not for basic pastry (see p. 575). It can knead dough but only enough for one loaf at a time. Don't try to whip potatoes in it: they will turn gluey. Liquids that need to be aerated as they are beaten, such as egg whites and whipped cream, cannot be done in a food processor.

The food processor tends to extract liquid from raw vegetables such as onions and peppers while it is chopping them. Turning the machine on and off helps somewhat, but does not eliminate juiciness entirely. This is a problem, since you can't possibly brown a chopped vegetable that has been somewhat liquidized—it will simply steam in its own juice. The best solution is to pour off any liquid that has accumulated before attempting to brown (the juice can always be added later or used in a soup).

Blender. A blender does not chop, although it will pulverize a few absolutely dry ingredients like nuts and coffee beans—more satisfactorily than a food processor, incidentally. It's also better than a food processor if you want a very fine purée. But most owners of food processors find they can do without a separate blender.

Toaster. An "old-fashioned" toaster is still the best way of toasting bread, but it does not offer the other features of the dual-purpose toaster oven (see below).

Toaster Oven. For quick-grilled cheese sandwiches, baked potatoes, and small casseroles, it is more efficient and energy-saving to use a toaster oven rather than a large oven. It's not good for meat, however, which spatters—and the fat can not only catch fire but it makes it difficult to clean.

Waffle Iron and Griddle. Great for waffle lovers; the griddle will also make good grilled cheese sandwiches.

Electric Steamer. A useful piece of equipment if you do a lot of steaming. It is also convenient for heating up foods—and you won't burn the bottom of the pot since it turns off automatically when the water has boiled away.

Electric Skillet. An electric skillet is an auxiliary appliance that is helpful if your range has a limited number of burners. It is useful for outdoor patio cooking, too. You can also use it covered as an oven to heat small baked dishes.

Electric Rotisserie. Miraculously there is no spattering or smoking with the new electric rotisseries, so they can be used indoors. For spit-roasting meats and poultry they are great—the exterior becomes beautifully browned and the inside remains juicy and the house is filled with a wonderful fragrance as the spit turns. Many ovens are furnished with a rotisserie attachment which does almost as good a job and, of course, takes up less room.

Electric Deep-Fat Fryer. This appliance holds oil at an even temperature for deep frying. It is not always easy to pour off the oil from an electric fryer after using, and they are awkward to clean. A heavy pot with a strainer used on top of the stove with a thermometer to check the oil does just as well.

Electric Juicer. A great convenience if you make fresh juice regularly.

Electric Ice Cream Maker. The old-fashioned type of ice cream maker and its modern counterpart, both of which must be packed with ice and salt, still make the best ice cream, whether turned by hand or by electricity. The little ice-cream makers that can be put in the freezer compartment of the refrigerator, then plugged into the nearest outlet to churn, give satisfactory results, but the ice cream will not be as smooth and creamy and yields are small. For ice creams, sherbets, and ices, see Desserts and Dessert Sauces (p. 603).

Crock-Pot. These slow cookers are very popular, especially with working families. They require special recipes adapted to the Crock-Pot. A crock pot can also be improvised: an earthenware pot set over a hot tray or in a very slow oven will accomplish practically the same thing.

Electric Coffee Grinder. More and more people are grinding their own coffee; you can blend your own beans and the coffee tastes so good. Beans kept in the freezer stay freshest and you grind only the amount you need, still frozen. The simplest types of electric coffee grinders are the best. You can also use a blender.

Electric Coffee Pot. Electric coffee pots are available in drip and percolator models in a variety of makes and sizes. Be sure to clean the interior and the parts carefully because they retain a stale coffee flavor. A very large electric percolator is good if you do a lot of entertaining; the big pots taking up to a full pound of coffee usually make a surprisingly good cup.

Other Things

Canisters. Canisters, containers for keeping flour, sugar, rice, tea, and other dry things, should be easy to wash and have wide tops so that you can get into them with a scoop. Square canisters are better for storage, since they use space more efficiently. But it is also nice to have glass jars so that you can see at a glance what you have on hand; be sure that they have ground-glass tops.

Plastic Containers. See also Frozen Foods (p. 727). Plastic containers for refrigerator and freezer storage should vary in size. There's no reason why you can't use supermarket containers that you've saved, although they won't hold up as well as the sturdier kind you buy specifically for the refrigerator and freezer.

Aluminum Foil. Foil is a blessing in the kitchen. It can serve as a broiler lining, a drip catcher, a lid fitted snugly over an oven dish, and like old-fashioned parchment can be wrapped around foods which are to be baked. In addition it's an excellent, durable wrap, molding naturally to odd-shaped items, and it seals itself.

Plastic Wrap. Transparent plastic wrap tends to hold moisture and is excellent for wrapping because it clings tightly. It also makes a good covering for bowls. It's less good in the freezer, where it often doesn't stick well and should be used with ties or bindings of some kind.

Plastic Bags. Plastic bags with ties are excellent for freezing and refrigerator storage.

Wax Paper. Wax paper for spreading out on your working surface when measuring dry ingredients is very useful. It is also good for covering a sauce so that it won't form a skin and for wrapping things when you don't want the moisture that plastic wrap gives.

Parchment. Parchment paper is very handy in baking.

Paper Towels. Paper towels are essential in the kitchen these days for drying everything from hands to greens, from draining fried foods to sopping up fats from the surface of a broth.

Cheesecloth. It is always necessary to use fine-mesh cheesecloth when you want to strain out the residue to get a clear broth. It is also useful for binding something, for poaching, and for making a bouquet garni or herb bags.

String. You'll find you can't do without a ball of good strong kitchen twine.

COOKING TERMS AND PROCEDURES

Au Jus. A French expression meaning "with the juice" (pronounced "oh zhu"), it is a term applied to meat, usually roast beef, which is served in its own juices.

Bake. To cook by dry heat. Do not crowd things in the oven; the free circulation of air is important. Always preheat the oven 10–15 minutes, unless otherwise indicated, and use an oven thermometer to check the temperature.

Oven Temperatures

250°F (120°C)	Very slow
300°F (150°C)	Slow
325°F (165°C)	Moderately slow
350°F (180°C)	Moderate
375°F (190°C)	Moderately hot
400°F (205°C)	Hot
450–500°F (230°C–260°C)	Very hot

Barbecue. As commonly used, to cook on a grill over intense heat, usually a live fire made with charcoal or wood, sometimes called "charcoal broiling." True barbecuing requires basting with a sauce as the meat cooks (see p. 153). *To build an outdoor fire:* Calculate roughly to use a few more briquets than are needed to spread amply under the surface of the meat. Stack the charcoal briquets into a pyramid and ignite with charcoal lighter fluid or wood kindling. Start the fire 30–45 minutes before using. When the briquets are glowing and a little white ash is showing, the fire is ready. You can also determine how hot the fire is by putting your hand several inches above the briquets. Whenever it is possible to use natural wood chips and wood for kindling in place of charcoal and charcoal lighter fluid, do so—the smell and flavor of the meat is delicious.

Bard. To cover meats with a thin layer of fat before roasting them, usually done with very lean meats to keep them from drying out.

Baste. To moisten while cooking in order to add flavor and keep things from drying out. Use a bulb baster, a spoon, or a brush.

Batter. A mixture containing flour and liquid, thin enough to pour.

Beat. To mix rapidly in order to make a mixture smooth and light by incorporating as much air as possible. If you're beating by hand, use a whisk, a fork, or a wooden spoon in a rhythmic, circular motion, lifting and plopping; beat from the wrist without using your whole arm and you won't get tired. Rotary egg beaters and electric beaters are a great convenience. If you use an electric mixer it is better to have one with a rounded bowl for proper beating. For *beating egg whites*, see Eggs (p. 336); for *whipping cream*, see Cream (p. 14).

Beurre Manié. A mixture of butter and flour added at the last to thicken a hot sauce or soup. *To make a beurre manié*, mix equal amounts of flour and soft butter, working them together quickly with your fingers. Add small bits to a hot liquid, stirring and cooking after each addition until they are absorbed and you can determine the desired thickness. Use only as much as is needed.

Blanch. To boil rapidly in lots of water briefly, sometimes for just an instant. Blanching is done for various purposes: as a preliminary cooking process; as a way of setting color, sealing in juices, or sometimes removing strong flavors; as an aid in removing peels or shells; and as a way of destroying harmful enzymes when canning or freezing.

Blend. To incorporate two or more ingredients thoroughly. When the term is used in a recipe, it means to blend by hand or with an electric beater.

Boil. To heat a liquid until bubbles break continually on the surface. Boiling temperature at sea level is 212°F. At a high altitude it is much higher.

Braise. To cook slowly, usually covered, in a little liquid or fat, often on a bed of aromatics.

Broil. To cook on a grill under strong, direct heat. The term "broiling" is sometimes used loosely; "charcoal broiling" is really barbecuing or grilling, and "pan broiling" is closer to frying, although usually done with little or no fat.

Brown. Browning may be done under a broiler, in fat in a skillet, or in the oven. The purpose is to sear, to seal in juices, and to give good color. When browning meat for a stew, make sure it is absolutely dry, turn so all sides are seared, and when doing cut-up pieces, do not crowd the pan or they will steam rather than brown.

Bruise. To crush partially in order to release flavor, as with peppercorns and garlic cloves.

Caramelize. To heat sugar in order to turn it brown and give it a special taste.

Chop. To cut solids into pieces with a sharp knife or other chopping device. It is worth learning the right chopping techniques for different ingredients, because once you are proficient, you'll save yourself a lot of time—to say nothing of deriving satisfaction from your skill. To chop: Holding the blade at both ends, bring a large knife up and down firmly all over the material to be chopped.

Clarify. To separate and remove solids from a liquid, thus making it clear. *To clarify butter,* see p. 12; *to clarify stock,* see p. 78.

Coddle. To poach gently in barely simmering water.

Cream. To work one or more foods together until soft and blended. *To cream butter,* see Butter (p. 12).

Crimp. To seal together by pinching at intervals the edges of a two-crust pie, making a decorative edge (see illustration p. 572).

Curdle. Certain foods curdle—or separate—when too much heat is applied too quickly. Sometimes you can correct this; other times you have to start all over again, but you can incorporate the curdled mixture into the new one. Cream and custard sauces with a little flour in them will not curdle, even over high heat. See also Eggs (p. 337); Sour Cream (p. 14).

Cure. To preserve meats by drying and salting and/or smoking.

Cut in Shortening. To incorporate shortening into flour until it resembles coarse crumbs, uneven in size and texture. Use your fingers, two knives, or a pastry blender. It is better if the shortening is chilled.

Deglaze. To remove and preserve the natural glaze that accumulates in a cooking pan by adding liquid to the pan in which meat (or fish or poultry) has been cooked, scraping up any remaining bits. Sometimes the liquid is boiled down to a more concentrated form and sometimes additional butter is swirled in. Deglazing makes a small amount of natural sauce that can be poured over the meat or used as an enrichment for a more elaborate sauce.

Degrease. To remove grease from a soup, stock, gravy, or sauce. Skim the fat off the top with a spoon or skimmer, blotting out what remains with paper towels. It is difficult to degrease thoroughly when something is hot; the simplest way, whenever time permits, is to chill until the fat solidifies at the top and can be easily lifted off.

Dice. To dice: Remove, if necessary, a small slice from the bottom of the onion, or whatever you want to chop, so that it lies flat on the board.

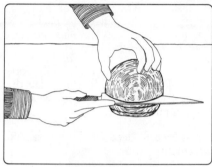 

a) Using one hand to hold it steady, first make horizontal cuts at even intervals, slicing not quite through to the root end (at the back).

b) Repeat with evenly spaced vertical cuts.

c) Slice straight down, making sure that the fingers at the edge are tucked under, and move them back with each slice. The chopped pieces will fall in uniform dice.

Dough. A mixture of flour, liquid, and other ingredients, stiff enough to shape and knead with your hands.

Dredge. To cover a solid food with sugar, flour, or other dry ingredients. Dredging can be done by dragging the solid food through the powdery substance, by shaking the two together in a bag, or by using a strainer or sifter.

Drippings. The juices, fats, and browned bits that collect in the pan after meat or poultry has been roasted. Unless burned or very greasy (and excess fat can be removed), the drippings are valuable for a little sauce (see Deglaze, opposite) and for gravy.

Drizzle. To sprinkle drops of liquid lightly over food in a casual manner.

Dust. To sprinkle food with dry ingredients. Use a strainer or a jar with a perforated cover, or try the good, old-fashioned way of shaking things together in a paper bag.

Eviscerate. To remove the entrails of a fish, fowl, or animal in preparation for cooking.

Fillet. As a verb, to remove the bones from meat or fish. A fillet (or filet) is the piece of flesh after it has been boned.

Flambé. To flame foods by dousing in some form of potable alcohol and setting alight. It's fun to do at the table, and if the alcohol is warmed beforehand, it will be sure to catch fire. Flambéing is enjoyed for the taste as much as for the spectacle.

Flute. To make a decorative scalloped or undulating edge on a piecrust or other pastry (see illustration p. 572).

Fold. To incorporate an aerated substance like whipped cream or beaten egg whites with what is usually a heavier substance. The purpose of folding is to retain volume and lightness by taking care not to deflate the pockets of air. Use your hands or a rubber spatula for folding. Cut through and turn over, rotating the bowl. For folding egg whites, see p. 336.

Fricassee. To stew gently in liquid and aromatic vegetables. It is usually done with poultry; a white sauce is then made from the broth. But today the term is used more loosely and a fricassee of vegetables or seafood could be made by stewing in butter and oil and natural juices.

Fritter. A food that is coated in a batter, then fried in deep fat. Fritters should be crispy on the outside, moist and succulent within.

Fry. Frying is cooking in a skillet with fat. *Pan frying* is done in a skillet. It can be a light sauté in a very small amount of butter, a quick browning in a layer of hot fat, or "pan broiling" over high heat of meats just in their own fat. *Deep-fat frying* requires a deep heavy pan with 3 or 4 cups of hot fat into which the food is lowered. Anything to be deep-fried should be thoroughly dried first or the fat will splatter. Sometimes foods are batter-coated first, sometimes just floured, according to the recipe. The frying temperature varies slightly according to the food (recipes will indicate). If you have no deep-fat thermometer, drop a 1-inch bread cube into the hot fat and count slowly to sixty; if the bread browns in just one minute, the fat should be around 365°F—the average deep-frying temperature. It is important that the fat be hot enough so that foods you are cooking will not absorb it and become greasy. Fry in batches, if necessary, so the pan is never crowded, and don't have the food ice-cold when it goes in. Do not let the fat smoke or you'll frizzle things too quickly on the outside, leaving an uncooked interior.

Vegetable or peanut oil or solid shortening is recommended for deep-fat frying. Do not use butter or olive oil. A deep-fat fryer is not essential, but a wire basket in which food can be lowered into the hot fat is a great convenience.

If you plan to reuse the oil, clarify it by adding a few slices of peeled potatoes to the hot oil to absorb flavors. Remove the potato, let the oil cool a bit, then strain it through cheesecloth. Store it in the refrigerator and taste it before reusing it to be sure it's still good. It will darken with each use.

Garnish. To decorate a dish both to enhance its appearance and to provide a flavorful foil. Parsley, lemon slices, raw vegetables, chopped chives, and other herbs are all forms of garnishes. See also Quick Relishes (p. 281).

Glaze. To apply a thickish liquid over the surface to give a final sheen. One refers also to meat glaze, which is reduced, highly concentrated stock, as well as the glaze left in the pan after cooking meat.

Grate. To break up a solid into small particles, usually by rubbing against a metal object or disk with sharp-edged holes.

Gratin. A shallow baking dish, usually round or oval, that can be slipped under the broiler. In common parlance the food baked and/or broiled in this kind of dish is called a gratin. Gratinéing is the browning process of the topping of crumbs or cheese.

Grill. To cook on a grill over intense heat.

Grind. To process solids by hand or mechanically to reduce them to tiny particles.

Julienne. To cut into thin strips. A julienne of vegetables would be a mixture of vegetables that have been so cut. To julienne: Make a stack of ⅛-inch slices (p. 49) and then cut downward at ⅛-inch intervals to make matchstick pieces.

Knead. To manipulate dough, with one's hands or mechanically, to develop the gluten in the flour.

Lard. To insert into a piece of meat strips of fat or sometimes other meat in order to tenderize, to give texture, and to add flavor.

Lukewarm. Neither cool nor warm, lukewarm means approximately body temperature.

Macerate. To toss fruits in sugar and lemon, wine, or a liqueur, and let them stand to absorb the flavors.

Marinate. To cover foods in seasoned liquid, always containing some acid, such as lemon, vinegar, or wine, to tenderize and to infuse flavor.

Mask. To improve the appearance or flavor of a food with a sauce or a seasoning.

Measure. When measuring, use accurate measuring cups and spoons (see p. 27) filled level. Do not pack ingredients except for brown sugar.

Mince. To chop very fine. To mince: After chopping roughly, with one hand on the tip of the blade and the other on the handle, rock the blade back and forth, marching from one end of the pile to the other; then repeat crosswise.

Mix. To combine two or more ingredients.

Mold. To form into an attractive shape by filling a decorative container (termed a mold) and steaming or baking or chilling, as the case may be.

Pan Broil. See Fry (p. 46). Sometimes the skillet is salted first; sometimes a piece of fat from the meat you are pan broiling is rubbed over the warm skillet.

Parboil. To precook in boiling water; see also Blanch (p. 43).

Pare. To finely shave away the skins of fruits.

Pâté. A baked, well-seasoned loaf of various meats, most of which are ground, sometimes studded with strips of other meats, well lubricated with fat. To be served cold.

Peel. To remove the peels from vegetables or fruits. The swivel-bladed vegetable peeler is a great tool.

Pickle. To preserve meats, vegetables, and fruits in brine.

Pinch. A pinch is the trifling amount you can hold between your thumb and forefinger.

Pipe. To squeeze a soft (but not runny) smooth food through a pastry tube in order to make decorative shapes or a border.

Planked. Cooked on a thick hardwood plank.

Plump. To soak dried fruits in liquid until they swell.

Poach. To simmer very gently.

Proof. To test yeast for potency.

Purée. To mash to a smooth blend. The result—the mashed substance—is also referred to as a purée.

Reduce. To boil down to reduce the volume.

Refresh. To run cold water over something that has been boiled.

Render. To make solid fat into liquid by melting it slowly.

Roast. To cook by dry heat in an oven. See also Bake (p. 42).

Roux. A mixture of melted fat and flour (see p. 264).

Sauté. A gentle cooking on top of the stove, less violent and requiring less fat than frying. Often one browns the food first, tossing to seal all sides, and then continues with a gentle sauté, covered or uncovered; at other times one does just a quick sauté.

Scald. To scald milk is to bring it just to the boil. To scald a solid food means to drop it in boiling water for a second.

Scallop. A word that has several meanings. The verb means to bake with a sauce or cream, or to make a decorative piecrust edge. The noun *scallop* can mean either a small, thin slice of meat or the bivalve scallops (see Fish and Shellfish chapter).

Score. To make shallow cuts in meat or fish both to tenderize and to help keep the shape.

Sear. To subject meat to very high heat in order to seal in the juices.

Shred. To cut or grate into shreds. To shred cabbage or lettuce: First cut the head in quarters. Place one flat side down on the board and cut against the perpendicular side, shaving as close to the edge as possible.

Sift. To remove possible lumps and to lighten the dry ingredients of a batter by putting them through a strainer or a sifter.

Simmer. To boil so gently that the liquid barely bubbles.

Slice. To slice: Holding the potato, or whatever, with fingers tucked under, bring the knife down firmly to make slices (⅛-inch thick if you are going to julienne).

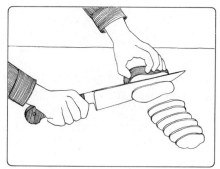

Spin a Thread. To cook a syrup to 238°F, at which point a thin brittle thread forms when a spoon is removed from the boiling liquid.

Steam. To cook or heat a food over boiling water without touching the water and allowing the steam to circulate (see illustration of steamer basket, p. 35). Sometimes foods are put into an airtight mold, as in steamed puddings, in which case they are simply lowered into gently boiling water to cook. Also when a food is enfolded in foil, sealed tightly, and then baked, the result is very much the same as steaming.

Steep. To pour boiling water over something and let it sit.

Stew. Long slow cooking in liquid.

Stir. To rotate ingredients in a bowl or in a pan, using a spoon or whisk, in order to mix, or to ensure even cooking and prevent sticking.

Temper. To prepare eggs for a hot liquid (see p. 337).

Toast. To broil or grill to crisp on the outside.

Truss. To bind a bird so that it will keep its shape during cooking (see p. 232).

Unmold. To turn out of a mold so that the interior keeps its shape.

Whip. To lighten and increase the volume by beating.

Whisk. To beat with a whisk or whip until well mixed.

APPETIZERS &
HORS D'OEUVRE

ABOUT FOOD TO SERVE WITH DRINKS
AND TO START OFF A MEAL

An appetizer should make an immediate appeal to the eye and the palate, stimulating without satisfying the appetite. The French word *hors d'oeuvre*, a term that has become a part of international cuisine, literally means "outside of the principal work or main course." You want such foods to demand attention with their bright colors and appealing arrangement; the hot dishes are served bubbling hot, and cold dishes well chilled. When served with drinks, salty or piquant tastes will encourage thirst while at the same time tempering the effects of alcohol; as an opener at dinner, their purpose is to awaken and stimulate the appetite. Portions are small: when passed with drinks, they are bite-size; when served on a plate either in the living room before dinner or at the table, a small plateful attractively arranged will suffice.

You are likely to serve different kinds of appetizers in different circumstances, so let's look at several typical occasions and consider which foods seem appropriate.

For a Large Cocktail Party or Reception

At this kind of affair you will want to concentrate on foods which can be eaten with the fingers—a combination of cold hors d'oeuvre and some hot ones. Most of these should be passed on trays; with a big crowd people cannot always make their way easily to a buffet table. It's nice to have placed strategically around the room some bowls of things to nibble, like nut mixtures, olives, freshly roasted popcorn, or potato chips, as well as some dips that can be scooped up with raw vegetables or crackers. Lots of small napkins for sticky fingers are a must; as for the appetizers passed on trays, avoid messy foods that are apt to drip before they can be popped into the mouth. Near the drinks, a buffet table might hold a pâté or something hot in a chafing dish, but this is the kind of cocktail party or reception where guests are expected to go on to their own dinners, so you need give them only enough for the road and to take away with them a lingering taste of your delicious tidbits. Count on about four appetizers per person, with the buffet offering and the snacks and dips as extra.

For a Stay-on Cocktail Party

This, too, could be a large party that dwindles down to a manageable number of more intimate friends you've asked to stay on. Or it could be a smaller gathering at which you really want your guests to hang around and talk, so you plan to feed them handsomely enough to sustain them for the whole evening. In either case have some nibbles and dips and a few simple appetizers available at the beginning of the party; at a smaller gathering it is easier for people to spread their own crackers. Then offer a satisfying spread of hot and cold dishes with small plates, forks, and napkins so that guests will help themselves as they feel the proddings of hunger (see ideas for the hot and cold buffet on the next page and also Buffet Dinners in Menu Suggestions at the back of the book). Everyone serves himself and eats perched on the edge of a chair or leaning against the dining-room wall. Eventually, the coffee urn and maybe even little cakes or cookies will be welcome.

Hors d'Oeuvre as a First Course at Dinner

Here your appetizers are usually more selective, very often just one delicious, tempting creation on a plate that fits in with the meal to come (see Menu Planning, p. 5) and can be served either in the living room or at table. There are such a lot of possibilities. For guidance in selection to determine what goes well with what, consult the sample menus in Menu Suggestions at the back of the book; a first course could be anything from hot stuffed clams to oysters Rockefeller, for particularly elegant occasions, or stuffed avocados, individual molds of a chilled mousse, a slice of quiche, and so on. If it's to be a salad, somehow that's more fitting when you're sitting down at the table. It is also splendid sometimes to have a large, colorful platter of mixed hors d'oeuvre, like an Italian antipasto, which can be passed around the table so everyone takes what he wants; make it a gorgeous arrangement with portions of homemade pâté, piles of aromatic vegetables, some shrimp or crabmeat with mustardy mayonnaise, thin slices of country ham or dry sausage, celery, olives, and sliced tomatoes.

Types of Appetizers and Hors d'Oeuvre

Dips and Spreads: These are more or less interchangeable: the same mixture that can be scooped up on the end of a carrot stick can be spread on a round of Melba toast. They are easy to prepare ahead of time, and have the advantage of allowing everyone to help himself. Surround the dip or the crock of spread with interesting crackers, potato chips, corn chips, fried tortillas, or toasted pita; set out some cold shrimp, scallops, cocktail sausages, or spears of ham; or present a colorful arrangement of raw vegetables.

Cold Appetizers: These can be made by piping different spreads onto crackers or thin slices of good bread cut into decorative shapes or into cornucopias of ham and salami. Such canapés can be made in the morning and refrigerated, covered with foil, plastic wrap, or a damp towel. For *stuffed vegetables* use the same spreads and savory butters to fill mushroom caps, hollowed-out cherry tomatoes, cucumber boats, or celery ribs. If it's a very warm evening, keep cold dishes chilled by presenting them on beds of chipped ice.

Hot Appetizers: All those piping hot, tempting morsels like cheese and crab puffs, cocktail sausages in pastry, tiny filled savory tarts, skewers of chicken livers and bacon, hot biscuits, fritters, and so on are included here. One can never get enough of them, but remember that if you are both host and cook, you'll have to keep your eye on the stove and replenish the platters, so don't attempt more than you can manage comfortably.

Hot and Cold Buffet: The buffet table might include a handsome pâté on a platter surrounded by tiny pickles or in a crock, accompanied by Melba toast, thin slices of French bread or of dark rye; a decorative ball of cheese or a mound of paprika-dusted Liptauer; aromatic vegetables; stuffed eggs; meatballs in a chafing dish, or a cheese fondue. Even though guests use their fingers, these things are easier to manage if they are laid out on a buffet table than from a passing tray. The food can be prepared well ahead, and it's the kind that always looks enticing on the table.

Nibbles: These are the seductive snacks that dare you to eat only one—popcorn, pretzels, salted nuts, and nut mixtures with dried fruit, pickled vegetables, olives. Most snacks are ready to serve when purchased and need only to be set out.

DIPS AND SPREADS

Crudités

A welcome offering with drinks is a plate of icy-crisp raw vegetables. They spoil neither the appetite nor the waistline, and are usually presented with a variety of sauces and dips. Look in other chapters for more ideas for dips to serve with raw vegetables: you might try Aïoli (p. 272) for garlic lovers, flavored Mayonnaises (p. 453), and Yogurt Green Sauce (p. 275) to start.

The culinary name *crudités* means raw, and the vegetables must be garden-fresh, crisp, and well washed. Sometimes it helps to scrub and scrape early in the day; keep certain vegetables (not tomatoes or mushrooms) in bowls of ice water in the refrigerator to crisp them. Choose one or many for your arrangement: cherry tomatoes, orange carrot sticks, snow-white cauliflower flowerets, jade-green broccoli, zucchini rounds or spears, peppery rounds of radish, sticks of turnip or kohlrabi, bland cucumber slices, green and red pepper chunks, and whole mushrooms. On the West Coast they serve jicama, a plain brown root vegetable that is sweet and crisp when it is peeled and sliced. The ultimate alternative to potato chips for dips is a trayful of chilled cooked artichoke leaves.

Guacamole

Don't purée the avocados; an authentic guacamole contains small chunks of avocado. Serve with tortilla chips.

(2 CUPS)

2 large ripe avocados
5 tablespoons minced onion
4 canned, peeled green chili peppers, chopped fine
1 clove garlic, minced
3 tablespoons lemon juice or vinegar
¼ teaspoon freshly ground pepper
Salt to taste

Peel and seed the avocados. Mash one avocado in a bowl, and finely chop the other. Mix the two with remaining ingredients. Cover and refrigerate for several hours before serving.

Eggplant Caviar

Serve with crackers or corn crisps.

(2 CUPS)

1 medium eggplant
2 scallions, minced
2 tablespoons minced parsley
½ teaspoon freshly ground
  pepper

3 tablespoons vinegar
4 tablespoons olive oil
Salt

Preheat the oven to 350°F (180°C). Bake the eggplant for 1 hour. When it is cool enough to handle, peel and chop coarsely. Blend the scallions, parsley, pepper, vinegar, and olive oil in the blender or food processor. Put the mixture in a bowl and add thecoarsely chopped eggplant and salt to taste. Serve chilled or at room temperature.

Yogurt Dip

(2 CUPS)

2 cups (½ L) plain yogurt
1 clove garlic, minced
½ cucumber, seeded and
  chopped fine

½ teaspoon dried mint,
  crumbled, or 1 teaspoon
  fresh, chopped

Mix all the ingredients and chill thoroughly to let the flavors develop.

Olive-Yogurt Dip

(1¾ CUPS)

1 cup (¼ L) plain yogurt
½ cup (1 dL) mayonnaise
¼ cup (½ dL) chopped green
  olives

1 clove garlic, minced

Mix all the ingredients, and chill.

Green Dip

(2½ CUPS)

1 cup (¼ L) parsley
5 scallions, chopped
1¼ cups (3 dL) mayonnaise
1 cup (¼ L) sour cream
1 tablespoon chopped fresh
  dill, or 1¼ teaspoons dried,
  crumbled

¼ teaspoon Tabasco
1 teaspoon curry powder
Salt

Liquefy the parsley, scallions, and ½ cup of the mayonnaise in a blender or food processor. Add the remaining ¾ cup mayonnaise, the sour cream, dill, Tabasco, curry powder, and salt to taste, and chill.

Sour-Cream Dip

Garden-fresh with raw vegetables in summer.

(2½ CUPS)

2 cups (½ L) sour cream
¼ cup (½ dL) mayonnaise
2 tablespoons chopped fresh
  dill, or 1 tablespoon dried,
  crumbled

1 tablespoon grated onion
1 tablespoon chopped chives
1 tablespoon chopped parsley
Salt
Freshly ground pepper

Mix the sour cream, mayonnaise, dill, onion, chives, and parsley. Season to taste with salt and pepper, and chill.

Health Dip

For the proper creamy texture you must use a blender or food processor.

(2 CUPS)

2 cups (½ L) cottage cheese
2 tablespoons vinegar
¼ cup (½ dL) chopped
  scallions
2 tablespoons chopped parsley

6–8 fresh basil leaves, or 1
  teaspoon dried, crumbled
Salt to taste
Freshly ground pepper to taste

Purée all the ingredients in a blender or food processor, and chill.

Red Caviar Dip

(2½ CUPS)

8 ounces (225 g) cream cheese,
  softened
1 cup (¼ L) sour cream

4-ounce (115-g) jar red caviar
2 teaspoons Worcestershire
  sauce

Mix all the ingredients, and chill.

Red Caviar Spread. Use only 2 tablespoons of sour cream and substitute *1 tablespoon grated onion* for the Worcestershire sauce, seasoning to taste with *salt* and *freshly ground pepper*. Spread on crackers or dark bread squares.

Clam Dip

(2½ CUPS)

8 ounces (225 g) cream cheese,
  softened
½ cup (1 dL) sour cream
6½-ounce (180-g) can minced
  clams

1 tablespoon Worcestershire
  sauce
1 teaspoon grated onion

Mix all the ingredients, and chill.

Hot Clam Dip

Surprisingly good with cold shrimp or scallops.

(2½ CUPS)

Two 6½-ounce (180-g) cans
  minced clams
¼ pound (115 g) butter
1½ cups (3½ dL) cracker
  crumbs

1 medium onion, chopped fine
½ teaspoon lemon juice

Preheat the oven to 350°F (180°C). Drain the juice from one can of clams (use it for another purpose). Melt the butter and add the drained clams, the other can of clams with juice, the crumbs, onion, and lemon juice. Pour into a shallow baking dish, bake for 30 minutes, and serve immediately.

Roquefort Dip

(1 CUP)

4 ounces (115 g) Roquefort
  cheese
3 ounces (85 g) cream cheese,
  softened

⅓ cup (¾ dL) light cream
Dash of cayenne pepper

Mix the Roquefort, cream cheese, and cream. Season to taste with cayenne, and chill.

Roquefort Spread. Omit the cream. Serve with crackers or toasted rounds of French bread.

Deviled Ham Spread

(1½ CUPS)

Two 4½-ounce (125-g) cans
  deviled ham
½ cup (1 dL) minced celery

1 tablespoon minced pimiento
1 tablespoon minced onion
⅓ cup (¾ dL) mayonnaise

Mix all ingredients, put into a crock, and chill.

Ham Spread

A good way to use up leftover bits from a baked ham.

(1 CUP)

1 cup (¼ L) chopped cooked
  ham
1 tablespoon grated onion

2 teaspoons prepared mustard
1 tablespoon chutney
2 tablespoons mayonnaise

Cut the ham into small pieces and purée in a blender or food processor. Add the rest of the ingredients, put into a crock, and chill.

Corned Beef Spread. Substitute *1 cup chopped cooked corned beef* for the ham.

Tuna Spread

(1¼ CUPS)

7-ounce (200-g) can tuna
1½ tablespoons mayonnaise
¼ teaspoon green peppercorns

Purée all the ingredients in a blender or food processor. Put into a crock and chill.

Salmon Spread

(2 CUPS)

7¾-ounce (225-g) can salmon
¾ cup (1¾ dL) sweet butter
1 tablespoon anchovy paste

2 teaspoons lemon juice
1 teaspoon Worcestershire
  sauce

Mix all ingredients, put into a crock, and chill.

Sardine-Parsley Spread

(2 CUPS)

Two 4⅜-ounce (125-g) cans
  sardines, mashed
8 ounces (225 g) cream cheese,
  softened

2 tablespoons chopped parsley
½ teaspoon paprika
1 tablespoon lemon juice

Mix all ingredients, put into a crock, and chill.

Sardine-Olive Spread. Omit the parsley and add *2 tablespoons chopped green olives* and *1 teaspoon grated onion.*

Flavored Butters

These butters are always good to have on hand and keep well frozen if tightly sealed. Make them when you have some of the following flavoring ingredients on hand and then they'll be ready to take out and use as spreads at a moment's notice. Or you can scoop out just a little bit to toss with fresh cooked vegetables or to use to round out the flavor of vegetables, meats, poultry, and fish.

(BETWEEN ¾ AND 2 CUPS)

To ¼ **pound butter** add any of the following ingredients, blending in a bowl or food processor until smooth. Put in a crock and chill (or freeze for later use).

For **Chive Butter:** *2 tablespoons minced chives and 2 tablespoons minced parsley.*

For **Shrimp Butter:** *½ cup finely chopped shrimp and 1 tablespoon lemon juice.*

For **Herb Butter:** *3–4 tablespoons finely chopped fresh herbs.*

For **Anchovy Butter:** *1 tablespoon anchovy paste.*

For **Horseradish Butter:** *1 tablespoon freshly grated or prepared horseradish.*

For **Watercress Butter:** *2 tablespoons chopped watercress.*

For **Blue Cheese Butter:** *1⅓ cups blue cheese and, if desired, ⅛ teaspoon finely chopped garlic.*

OTHER COLD APPETIZERS

Dried or Chipped Beef or Salami Rolls

(12 ROLLS)

3 ounces (85 g) cream cheese,
  softened
½ teaspoon dry mustard
3 drops Tabasco
1 tablespoon chopped chives

2 tablespoons minced parsley
3 tablespoons mayonnaise
Salt
12 slices dried beef or salami

Beat the cheese, mustard, Tabasco, chives, parsley, and mayonnaise until smooth and well blended. Add salt to taste. Spread some of the mixture on each beef or salami slice. Roll into cigarlike shapes, cover, and refrigerate.

Belgian Endive Appetizer

Tidy to eat and very elegant.

(6 PIECES)

¼ cup (½ dL) cooked crabmeat
  or 6 crab legs, smoked oysters,
  or mussels

6 Belgian endive leaves
1 tablespoon mayonnaise

Put a piece of crabmeat or a crab leg, oyster, or mussel and ½ teaspoon mayonnaise on the wide white end of each endive leaf.

Smoked Salmon Rolls

Serve whole or cut in bite-size pieces.

(8 ROLLS)

3 ounces (85 g) cream cheese,
  softened
2 tablespoons lemon juice
1 tablespoon capers, drained

2 teaspoons minced onion
1 teaspoon minced parsley
2 tablespoons mayonnaise
8 slices smoked salmon

Beat the cream cheese, lemon juice, capers, onion, parsley, and mayonnaise until smooth and well blended. Spread some of the mixture on each slice of smoked salmon. Roll up, cover, and refrigerate.

Cucumber Sandwiches

These used to be called tea sandwiches, but there's no reason why they shouldn't appear with cocktails as well.

(8 SMALL SANDWICHES)

4 thin slices fresh white bread
4 tablespoons butter, softened
1 large cucumber
Salt

2 tablespoons mayonnaise
¼ teaspoon dried tarragon, crumbled
Freshly ground pepper

Cut the crusts from the bread and spread slices with butter. Peel and seed the cucumber, chop coarsely, and sprinkle with salt. Let stand in a colander for 10 minutes. Pat dry, mix with the mayonnaise and tarragon, season to taste, and spread on the bread. Cover with the second slices, cut into quarters, and arrange on a plate.

Watercress Sandwiches. Substitute ⅓ *cup chopped watercress* for the cucumber, and omit the salting and draining.

Radish Bites

(16 PIECES)

4 slices thin black bread
¼ pound (125 g) sweet butter or ripe Camembert or Brie cheese

6–8 large radishes

Spread each slice of bread thickly with butter, or cheese, and cut each into four square pieces. Thinly slice the radishes and press into the butter or cheese.

Caviar Mound

(1 CUP)

8 ounces (225 g) cream cheese, softened
2 tablespoons mayonnaise
1 tablespoon grated onion
2 teaspoons Worcestershire sauce

Salt to taste
4-ounce (115-g) jar red or black caviar

Mix the cheese, mayonnaise, onion, Worcestershire sauce, and salt. Press into a small bowl and refrigerate. Just before serving, turn out onto a platter and cover with caviar.

Salmon Ball

(1½ CUPS)

7¾-ounce (225-g) can salmon, drained
3 ounces (85 g) cream cheese, softened
1 tablespoon lemon juice
½ teaspoon prepared horseradish

1 teaspoon grated onion
Salt to taste
¼ cup (½ dL) minced parsley
¼ cup (½ dL) finely chopped pecans

Mix the salmon, cream cheese, lemon juice, horseradish, onion, and salt. Refrigerate until firm enough to handle. Form into a ball, and roll in a mixture of parsley and pecans.

Liptauer Cheese

Very popular on the American cocktail scene, Liptauer is really an adaptation of a Hungarian recipe. The original uses a native, soft sheep's cheese called Liptó. Pile in a mound and serve surrounded with crackers.

(2 CUPS)

8 ounces (225 g) cream cheese, softened	2 teaspoons minced anchovies
4 tablespoons sour cream	2 shallots or scallions, minced
4 tablespoons butter, softened	1 tablespoon paprika
2 teaspoons drained capers	1 teaspoon caraway seed
	Salt to taste

Blend all the ingredients in a food processor, blender, or bowl. Press into a small bowl and chill.

Aromatic Vegetables

Vegetables cut in bite sizes and cooked in a broth of olive oil and Middle Eastern seasonings are unusual and delightfully refreshing with drinks. The vegetables should be firm enough so they can be speared with toothpicks. Each must be cooked separately, but sometimes it is nice to serve several kinds arranged colorfully on a platter.

(ABOUT 4 CUPS)

1 pound (450 g) mushrooms, small onions, or zucchini, in 1-inch pieces, or cauliflower in small flowerets, or 1 package frozen artichoke hearts	Pinch of celery seed
	2–6 scallions, in ½-inch pieces, using some green, or 5–6 shallots, peeled and sliced
⅓ cup (¾ dL) olive oil	Salt
2 tablespoons lemon juice	8–10 peppercorns, lightly crushed
¼ teaspoon coriander seed	2 tablespoons chopped parsley
¼ teaspoon fennel seed	

Place the mushrooms (quartered if large; halved if medium; left whole if small), or onions, or zucchini, or cauliflower flowerets, or artichoke hearts (thawed), in a heavy saucepan and cover with the remaining ingredients, except the parsley. Add indicated amount of water, salt liberally, and boil for the number of minutes recommended:

Mushrooms: ¼ cup water. Boil 5 minutes, uncovered, over medium-high heat, shaking pan frequently.

Onions: ¾ cup water and 2 tablespoons red wine vinegar (instead of lemon juice). Cook, covered, over medium-high heat 10 minutes, then remove cover and cook down 2 minutes, letting onions darken slightly.

Zucchini: ⅓ cup water. Cook, covered, 4 minutes, shaking the pan once or twice.

Cauliflower: ½ cup water. Cook, covered, 5 minutes, shaking pan once or twice.

Artichoke Hearts: ½ cup water. Boil rapidly, covered, 6 minutes, shaking once or twice.

Toss each vegetable with parsley, taste and correct seasoning. Chill several hours in its sauce. Bring to room temperature before serving so the oil is not congealed.

Cheese Ball

(2 CUPS)

8 ounces (225 g) cream cheese,
 softened
1 ounce (30 g) blue cheese,
 softened
¼ pound (125 g) sharp
 Cheddar cheese, grated

1 clove garlic, minced
Dash of Tabasco
¼ cup (½ dL) finely chopped
 almonds, toasted
¼ cup (½ dL) finely chopped
 parsley

Combine the cream cheese, blue cheese, and Cheddar cheese in a bowl. Add the garlic and Tabasco and blend until well mixed. Chill 2–3 hours. Form into a ball. Roll the ball in the almonds and then in the parsley, patting the coating in firmly. Chill; remove from the refrigerator 30 minutes before serving.

Chicken and Pork Pâté

A pâté is not unlike a meat loaf—and really not that much more difficult to prepare. But because pâtés are served cold as a tasty appetizer (and one slice goes a long way), they must be full of flavor, rich, and moist. Almost one-third of the mixture should consist of good pork fat because it is the fat that keeps the meat moist during the cooking. After the pâté has been baked, it should be weighted so that some of the fat runs out and the loaf is compressed, thus giving you dense slices that hold together when cut. This particular pâté uses a ground meat base of chicken, pork, and pork fat interlarded with strips of marinated chicken breast, which gives the finished slice a lovely marbled look. The most economical approach would be to buy a whole chicken, 3½–4 pounds, and bone it yourself using the dark meat in the ground mixture known as the forcemeat (and reserving all the meaty bones and carcass for a soup); but for those who don't have the time, buy instead the easily available chicken parts as recommended below. Pâtés are good served with thinly sliced sour pickles, mustard, and French or dark rye bread.

(ONE 2-QUART CASSEROLE)

1 whole chicken breast,
 skinned and boned
¼ cup (½ dL) brandy
1¾–2 pounds (800–900 g)
 chicken thighs
1¾ pounds (800 g) pork, with
 some fat on
1 pound (450 g) solid pork fat
3 eggs

½ cup (1 dL) Madeira
2 teaspoons salt
½ cup (1 dL) minced shallots
½ teaspoon ground allspice
¼ teaspoon ground cloves
Freshly ground pepper
¼ teaspoon ground thyme
¾ pound (340 g) bacon

Cut the chicken breast lengthwise into ½-inch strips. Toss them with the brandy and let marinate while preparing the other ingredients. Remove the skin and cut away the meat from the chicken thighs (if using a whole chicken, use all the meat you can cut off the bones, after you have put the breast meat to marinate); you should have about 1 pound dark chicken. Grind this along with the pork and the pork fat either by running through the food processor or putting through a meat grinder twice. Add the eggs, Madeira, salt, shallots, allspice, cloves, a generous amount of pepper, and thyme. Beat the mixture until smooth and well blended. If you want to taste to check the seasonings, fry a small amount of this forcemeat and taste when cooked through; it should be highly seasoned, so adjust seasonings if necessary, remembering that flavors are dulled when chilled. Preheat the oven to 325°F (165°C). Bring a large pot of water to a boil and drop the strips of bacon in; let them cook 2–3 minutes, just enough to reduce their saltiness, then drain, rinse, and pat dry. Line a 2-quart casserole with the bacon, as illustrated, leaving overhanging pieces to cover the top. Pat in a layer of

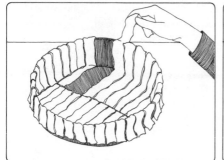

the forcemeat, then lay strips of chicken breast over in a neat line, about ½ inch apart. Add another layer of forcemeat, then chicken strips, ending with a final layer of forcemeat. Pull the bacon strips over to cover the top of the meat, trimming off excess to avoid a double layer anywhere. Cover with foil and with a snug-fitting lid. Place the casserole in a pan of hot water that comes halfway up the sides. Bake for 1–1¼ hours, or until the fat runs clear. Remove from the oven,

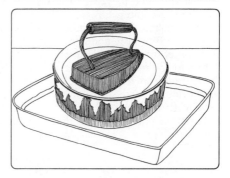

uncover, and weight down with a plate that just fits inside the casserole, on which you place heavy cans, or any solid object like an old iron. Let cool completely. Refrigerate, preferably 24 hours, then serve cool, but not ice cold.

Chicken Liver Pâté

(3 CUPS)

¼ pound (125 g) butter
1 onion, minced
1 pound (450 g) chicken livers
4 tablespoons brandy
1 teaspoon dry mustard
¼ teaspoon mace

¼ teaspoon powdered cloves
½ teaspoon freshly ground
  pepper
Pinch of cayenne pepper
Salt to taste

Melt the butter in a skillet. Add the onions and sauté until soft. Stir in the livers and cook 2–3 minutes over medium-high heat, stirring, until they are just cooked but still rosy inside. Purée the onions and livers in a food processor or blender, or put through a food mill. Over medium heat, pour the brandy into the skillet and scrape up the bits from the bottom of the pan. Add to the liver mixture along with remaining ingredients, and blend until smooth. Pack into a mold and refrigerate until chilled and set. Serve unmolded with thin toast or crackers.

Country Terrine

A terrine is the dish in which a meat loaf or pâté is baked. One usually serves the pâté in its terrine so it should be attractive enough to come to the table.

(ABOUT 10 CUPS)

1½ pounds (675 g) ground pork, approximately ⅓ fat
1 pound (450 g) ground veal
1 pound (450 g) fresh spinach, blanched, drained, and chopped
1 large onion, chopped fine
2 cloves garlic, minced
2 eggs, beaten
1 teaspoon thyme, crumbled

1 teaspoon dried basil, crumbled
¼ teaspoon nutmeg
¼ teaspoon mace
¼ teaspoon allspice
1½ teaspoons salt
1 teaspoon freshly ground pepper
10 slices bacon

Preheat the oven to 325°F (165°C). Put a shallow baking dish in the oven with 1 inch of hot water. Grease a 2½-quart terrine. Combine all ingredients except bacon. Use your hands to mix and blend well. Fry a spoonful of the mixture until no longer pink; taste and correct the seasoning. Lay 6 or 7 bacon strips crosswise over the bottom and sides of the terrine. Pack the meat mixture into the lined dish; fold the loose ends of bacon over the top and cover any blank spaces with the extra bacon strips. Cover the dish with foil, place in the pan of water, and bake 1 hour. The meat is done when the juices are clear. Remove from the oven, cover with a plate, and weight down with a heavy can to remove the fat and press out air pockets. Cool, drain off the fat, and refrigerate.

Meatballs Rémoulade

These are meatballs that can be made ahead and don't have to be reheated; they are served at room temperature.

(50 MEATBALLS)

1 pound (450 g) ground beef
Salt
½ teaspoon freshly ground pepper
4 tablespoons minced onion
3 tablespoons shortening
4 tablespoons prepared horseradish

½ cup (1 dL) tarragon vinegar
2 tablespoons catsup
¼ teaspoon cayenne pepper
1 cup (¼ L) vegetable oil
½ cup (1 dL) finely chopped scallions
½ cup (1 dL) minced celery
2 tablespoons minced parsley

Using your hands, mix the beef, about ½ teaspoon salt, pepper, and onion. Shape into 50 small meatballs about the size of marbles. Melt the shortening in a large skillet and fry the meatballs over medium heat, browning them on all sides. Put them in a shallow dish. Whisk together the horseradish, vinegar, catsup, cayenne, oil, scallions, celery, and parsley until well blended. Add salt to taste. Pour the sauce over the meatballs and let stand at room temperature for at least 1 hour before serving.

Parslied Liverwurst Pâté

With its border of cream cheese rolled in a carpet of green parsley, this liverwurst roll looks spectacular and tastes heavenly. Buy a good-quality liverwurst.

(7–8-INCH LOG, ABOUT 20 SLICES)

8-ounce (225-g) roll of liverwurst, approximately 5 inches long
8 ounces (225 g) cream cheese, softened

¾ cup (1¾ dL) finely chopped parsley

Peel the covering off the liverwurst. Spread the cream cheese out evenly on a lightly oiled piece of wax paper to the dimensions of 6 × 7 inches. Place the liverwurst in the center, then roll the wax paper around it, tucking up the ends. Chill until firm. Then peel off the wax paper and roll the cheese-covered liverwurst in the chopped parsley, covering completely and elongating the log to 7 or 8 inches. Serve cold, and when presenting slice off the end piece to display the interior design.

Beef Tartare

Serve with thin slices of dark bread spread with sweet butter. Only the best beef will do for this dish.

(SERVES SIX)

1 pound (450 g) lean ground beef: sirloin or filet
⅓ cup (¾ dL) minced onion
1 tablespoon capers, drained
4 anchovy fillets, chopped fine

4–5 drops Tabasco
1 egg yolk
Salt to taste
1 tablespoon minced parsley

With your hands, mix the beef, onion, capers, anchovy, Tabasco, and egg yolk. Add salt and put through the meat grinder or food processor once; the texture should be of ground, not puréed, meat. Pack into a small bowl to shape. Turn it out onto a platter and sprinkle with the parsley.

❁ Other Suggestions for Cold Hors d'Oeuvre

Consult the chapter on Filled Things for ideas for sandwiches that could be made on thin slices of bread with crusts removed and cut into triangles or finger shapes; see also Stuffed Eggs. In the Fish and Shellfish chapter you'll find Cold Mussels and also shrimp and lobster that can be skewered with a toothpick. For a buffet table try some of the mousses and aspics.

HOT APPETIZERS

Skewered Chicken Livers, Bacon, and Water Chestnuts

Before you begin, soak thirty small wooden skewers in water. This
will prevent their catching fire later.

(30 SKEWERS)

1 pound (450 g) chicken livers
1 can water chestnuts, drained
10–15 slices bacon

Preheat the broiler. Cut each liver in three or four pieces. Drain the water
chestnuts and cut in half. Cut each bacon slice in four pieces, and wrap a piece
around each water chestnut half. On each skewer, thread a piece of liver and a
piece of bacon-wrapped water chestnut. Repeat so that each skewer has at least
two pieces of liver. Place the threaded skewers on a broiler rack 4 inches below
the broiler element and cook 3 minutes each side or until the bacon is lightly
browned.

Crab Puffs

Miniature crab soufflés: luscious, hot, and puffy.

(48 PUFFS)

¾ cup (1¾ dL) mayonnaise
1 cup (¼ L) flaked cooked
   crabmeat
1 tablespoon finely chopped
   scallions
⅛ teaspoon cayenne pepper

2½ tablespoons lemon juice
Salt
2 egg whites
48 1½-inch (4-cm) rounds of
   bread

Preheat the broiler. Combine the mayonnaise, crabmeat, scallions, cayenne,
lemon juice, and salt to taste. Beat the egg whites until stiff and gently fold in
the crab mixture. Spoon a mound of mixture on each of the bread rounds. Place
on cookie sheets and put under the broiler until lightly browned. Serve
immediately.

Shrimp Puffs. Substitute *1 cup finely chopped cooked shrimp* for the crabmeat.

Hot Seafood with Mayonnaise

Serve these hot from the oven. Crabmeat, tiny shrimp, chopped
steamed mussels, tuna, or leftover cooked fish can be used, or
combinations thereof.

(2 CUPS OR 24 PIECES)

1½ cups (3½ dL) shellfish or
   boned and flaked cooked fish
¾ cup (1¾ dL) mayonnaise
3–4 tablespoons lemon juice
1 teaspoon minced onion

2 teaspoons minced parsley
Freshly ground pepper
Salt to taste
24 small bread rounds

Preheat the oven to 400°F (205°C). Combine the seafood and/or fish and the seasonings, and add salt and pepper to taste. Spread on bread rounds and bake 7–8 minutes.

Cold Seafood with Mayonnaise. Instead of baking the fish mixture, mound it in a bowl and serve cold, surrounded with crackers.

Clam Fritters

Spear with toothpicks to serve.

(30 FRITTERS)

Two 6½-ounce (190-g) cans
  minced clams, or 1 cup
  chopped clams
1 egg, beaten
⅔ cup (100 g) flour

1 teaspoon baking powder
½ teaspoon salt
⅛ teaspoon freshly ground
  pepper
Vegetable oil for frying

Preheat the oven to 250°F (120°C) and put in an ovenproof platter. Drain the clams and reserve the liquid; if necessary, add milk or bottled clam juice to make ⅓ cup of liquid. Combine the liquid, egg, flour, baking powder, salt, and pepper, and beat until well blended. Stir in the clams. Heat 1 inch of oil in a skillet. When it is very hot, drop in the clam batter by teaspoonfuls. Fry until brown on each side. Don't crowd the skillet; do a few at a time until all are fried. Remove with a slotted spoon, drain on paper towels, and transfer to the warm platter.

Cheese Straws

(36 STRAWS)

¼ pound (115 g) butter
2 cups (285 g) flour
¼ teaspoon cayenne pepper

1 pound (450 g) sharp Cheddar
  cheese, grated
Salt to taste

Preheat the oven to 400°F (205°C). Cream the butter until light; add the flour, cayenne, cheese, and salt. Roll out on a floured board or pastry cloth. Cut into strips 5 inches long and ⅜ inch wide. Place on a greased cookie sheet and bake 6 minutes, until golden.

Cheese Puffs

To freeze these unbaked, allow an extra 3–5 minutes of baking time.

(48 PUFFS)

2 cups (½ L) grated sharp
  cheese
¼ pound (115 g) butter

1 cup (140 g) flour
Salt to taste
48 pimiento-stuffed green olives

Preheat oven to 400°F (205°C). Put the cheese and butter in a mixing bowl or food processor, and blend until smooth. Add the flour and salt and mix well. Roll out to ¼-inch thickness. Cut the dough into 2-inch squares and wrap a square around each olive, sealing the seams. Place on a cookie sheet and bake 15 minutes. Check after the first 10 minutes to see puffs don't burn.

Cheese Wafers

Good to have at hand in the freezer: just cut slices from the frozen tube of dough.

(ABOUT FIVE DOZEN)

¼ pound (115 g) butter, softened
1 cup (140 g) flour
¼ teaspoon cayenne pepper

1 cup (¼ L) chopped pecans
2 cups (½ L) grated cheese
Salt to taste

Combine all ingredients. Make two rolls about 1½ inches in diameter. Wrap in foil and refrigerate at least 8 hours. Preheat the oven to 375°F (190°C). Slice the dough into thin wafers and bake 6–10 minutes, depending on the thickness of the wafers. Watch closely to see that they don't burn.

Easy Onion Bites

(16 PIECES)

¼ cup (½ dL) mayonnaise
¼ cup (½ dL) grated Parmesan cheese
4 slices good-quality white bread

1 medium onion, very thinly sliced

Preheat the broiler. Mix the mayonnaise and Parmesan. Remove the bread crusts and spread the bread with the cheese mixture. Cut each slice into four pieces. Top with an onion slice and cook 3–5 minutes, until brown and bubbling.

Hot Cream Cheese Canapés

Light and puffy, always popular.

(30 CANAPÉS)

8 ounces (225 g) cream cheese, softened
1 egg, lightly beaten
½ onion, minced

Freshly ground pepper
Salt
30 small bread squares, toasted

Preheat the broiler. Mix the cream cheese, egg, onion, and pepper together, mashing them well with a fork. Add salt to taste. Spread generously on toasted bread and run under the broiler until puffed and lightly browned. Serve at once.

Nachos

5-ounce (140-g) bag tortilla chips
1 pound (450 g) Monterey Jack or Cheddar cheese, grated

⅓ cup (¾ dL) chopped canned peeled green chilies
½ cup (1 dL) chopped onion

Preheat the oven to 400°F (205°C). Lay the tortilla chips on a cookie sheet. Toss together the cheese, chilies, and onion, and sprinkle over the tortilla chips. Bake for about 5 minutes, until the cheese has melted. Serve hot.

Montpelier Biscuits and Cheese

Long known among New Englanders by the town of their origin, Montpelier, these biscuits are old-fashioned water biscuits—the kind of hard cracker sold in country stores in barrels—and they are wonderful hot with melting cheese.

(2–3 PER PERSON)

Montpelier or other hard biscuits	Sharp Cheddar cheese
Butter, softened	Cayenne pepper (optional)

Preheat the oven to 425°F (220°C). Split the biscuits and spread with soft butter. Cover with a ¼-inch slice of Cheddar and bake for 8–10 minutes, until the cheese is bubbly. Add a dash of cayenne on top, if desired.

Benne Pastries

(MAKES 30)

½ cup (1 dL) sesame seeds	2½ tablespoons shortening
1 cup (140 g) flour	2½ tablespoons butter
½ teaspoon salt	

Put the sesame seeds in a skillet and toast over medium heat, shaking the pan often, until golden brown. Set aside. Place the flour and salt in a bowl and cut in the shortening and butter, using a pastry cutter or two knives, until it resembles coarse meal. Add the toasted sesame seeds. Beginning with 1 tablespoon, sprinkle on not more than 2½ tablespoons of ice water. Stir with a fork, using only enough water to allow the dough to stick together. Pat into a ball, cover, and chill. Preheat the oven to 400°F (205°C). Roll out the dough ¼ inch thick and cut into rounds or diamonds. Place on a cookie sheet and bake 7–8 minutes.

Savory Cream Puffs

Look to the section on spreads for filling suggestions; but don't forget Creamed or Curried Chicken, Mushroom Duxelles, Seafood Mayonnaise, or Creamed Chipped Beef.

(ABOUT 30 PUFFS)

1 recipe Cream Puffs (p. 596)
1 cup (¼ L) filling (see above)

Preheat the oven to 375°F (190°C). Make the cream puff dough and drop by rounded teaspoonfuls onto an ungreased cookie sheet. Bake 1½ inches apart for 25 minutes. Remove to racks, cut nearly in half, and let cool. Using a small spoon, push through the slice just enough filling to fill the puffs. Heat for a few minutes more before serving. The puffs can be made ahead of time, and even frozen, but they should be filled just before the final reheating or they will become soggy.

Small Biscuits and Ham

(25–30 BISCUITS)

1 recipe Baking Powder
  Biscuits (p. 490)
¼ pound (115 g) sweet butter,
  softened

½ pound (225 g) cooked ham,
  sliced thin
3 tablespoons prepared mustard

Preheat the oven to 450°F (230°C). Roll out the biscuit dough a little thinner than usual, and cut into rounds the size of a half-dollar. Place 1 inch apart on buttered cookie sheets and bake 8–10 minutes until golden. While still warm, split and generously butter the insides of the biscuits. Cut the ham to size and place two slices, with a dab of mustard, between the halves. Close the sandwiches and serve warm.

Cocktail Frankfurters in Pastry

(24 PIECES)

1 recipe Basic Pastry (p. 575),
  using 2 cups (285 g) flour
¾ pound (340 g) small cocktail
  frankfurters

1–2 tablespoons prepared
  mustard
1 egg, beaten with 1
  tablespoon water

Preheat the oven to 425°F (220°C). Divide the dough in half and roll out thin. Distribute the franks on the dough, leaving enough room between them so that the pastry can be wrapped around each one. Paint each frank generously with mustard. Cut the dough apart with a sharp knife or pizza cutter, and make a package of each frank, pinching the seams together. Place 1 inch apart on a lightly greased cookie sheet. Paint the tops and sides with the egg and water glaze and bake 12–15 minutes until crisp and golden.

Sardines in Pastry. Use *sardines* instead of frankfurters, brushing each with mustard and a *few drops of lemon juice,* and tucking a *sprig of dill* inside each package.

Savory Tarts

Make tart shells on the back of 1¾-inch muffin tins or in special small tartlet tins. A good way to use up extra dough: whenever you bake a pie, make and freeze tart shells from the leftovers until you have accumulated enough for a party.

(12 MUFFIN-SIZE SHELLS, OR 24 SMALLER SHELLS)

1 recipe Tart Pastry (p. 576),
  using 2 cups (285 g) flour

About 1½ cups (3½ dL) filling
  (see following recipes)

Preheat the oven to 425°F (220°C). Roll out the dough. For muffin tins, cut circles 3 inches in diameter and drape the dough circle on the greased outside of each muffin tin, pleating and pinching the edges and pressing tightly onto the tin. For tartlet tins, cut circles of dough just larger than the diameter and press them into the tins, trimming off the excess to make a neat edge. For partially baked shells, bake 8 minutes. For fully baked shells, bake 15 minutes for small tarts, 18–20 minutes for the muffin-size tarts.

Fillings for Partially Baked Tart Shells

These fillings are the right amount to fill one recipe of tart shells (see preceding). Preheat the oven to 375°F (190°C).

Ham and Cheese

2 teaspoons sharp prepared
   mustard
2 ounces (60 g) cooked ham,
   minced
¾ cup (1¾ dL) grated Swiss
   cheese

2 eggs, lightly beaten
½ cup (1 dL) cream
Salt to taste
Freshly ground pepper to taste

Paint the bottom of the shells with mustard and distribute the ham evenly over them. Mix the rest of the ingredients, pour into the shells, and bake 20 minutes.

Blue Cheese

½ pound (225 g) blue cheese,
   crumbled
½ cup (1 dL) heavy cream

2 eggs, lightly beaten
⅛ teaspoon cayenne pepper

Mix the ingredients, pour into the shells, and bake 20 minutes.

Spinach and Ricotta

1 cup (¼ L) chopped spinach,
   cooked and drained
½ cup (1 dL) ricotta cheese
2 eggs plus one egg yolk,
   lightly beaten

Salt to taste
Freshly ground pepper to taste
⅛ teaspoon nutmeg

Mix all the ingredients, pour into the shells, and bake 20 minutes.

Cheddar, Onion, and Bacon

6 strips bacon, cooked,
   drained, and crumbled
½ cup (1 dL) finely chopped
   onion

1 tablespoon butter
½ cup (1 dL) light cream
1¼ cups (3 dL) grated sharp
   Cheddar cheese

Distribute the crumbled bacon over the shells. Sauté the onions in the butter for 5 minutes. Remove from the heat, add the rest of the ingredients, pour into the shells, and bake 20 minutes.

Fillings for Fully Baked Shells

Preheat the oven to 450°F (230°C) and fill the baked shells straight from the freezer, if you like. These fillings are enough for one recipe of tart shells (p. 576).

Tomato and Mozzarella

1½ cups (3½ dL) seeded,
   peeled, chopped tomatoes
1 tablespoon olive oil
2 anchovies
1 clove garlic, minced
½ teaspoon dried basil,
   crumbled

Freshly ground pepper
¾ cup (1¾ dL) coarsely grated
   mozzarella cheese
6 black olives, pitted and
   halved
2 tablespoons grated Parmesan
   cheese

Cook the tomatoes in the oil until they are just soft and the liquid has evaporated. Mash the anchovies with the garlic and add to the tomatoes. Add basil and pepper to taste. Mix with the mozzarella and pour into fully baked tart shells. Top each with one half of a black olive and a sprinkle of Parmesan and bake 5 minutes, until bubbly.

Mushroom and Cream Cheese

1 cup (¼ L) Mushroom
    Duxelles (p. 389)
6 ounces (180 g) cream cheese
About ¼ cup (½ dL) heavy
    cream

1 tablespoon grated Parmesan
    cheese

Mix the mushrooms, cream cheese, and enough of the cream so that it spreads easily. Pour into fully baked tart shells, dust the top with Parmesan, and bake 5 minutes.

Rissolettes

(8 PASTRIES)

1 recipe 8-inch Basic Two-
    Crust Pastry (p. 575), or 1
    recipe Basic Puff Pastry
    (p. 598)

½ cup (1 dL) : Mushroom
    Duxelles (p. 389)

Preheat the oven to 450°F (230°C). Roll out the pastry ¼ thick and cut into 3-inch rounds. Place 1 teaspoon of filling in the center of half the pieces. Wet the edges, cover with the remaining pieces, and crimp the edges together with the tines of a fork. Set on a cookie sheet, prick the tops, and bake about 6 minutes, until pale brown.

Alternate Fillings: Chopped hard-boiled egg, red caviar, chopped cooked ham, or cooked sausage meat.

Stuffed Clams

You will need 24 clam shells, washed and dried, to make this savory appetizer.

(24 SHELLS)

1½ cups (3½ dL) chopped
    clams, or six 6½-ounce
    (195-g) cans minced clams
1 cup (¼ L) freshly made bread
    crumbs
⅓ cup (¾ dL) minced parsley
½ teaspoon dried oregano,
    crumbled

2 cloves garlic, minced
2 tablespoons olive oil
½ cup (1 dL) freshly grated
    Parmesan cheese
Salt to taste

Preheat the oven to 400°F (205°C). Put a 1-inch layer of rock salt in a shallow pan large enough to hold the clam shells and set it in the oven to warm. If you use canned clams, drain them and reserve the juice. Combine the clams and 2 tablespoons of the clam juice, ¾ cup of the bread crumbs, 3 tablespoons of the parsley, the oregano, garlic, olive oil, 5 tablespoons of the cheese, and salt. Toss lightly and spoon a small mound of the mixture in each shell. Mix the remaining 2 tablespoons of parsley, 3 tablespoons of cheese, and remaining bread crumbs, and sprinkle a little on each stuffed shell. Set the shells on the bed of rock salt or crumpled foil and bake for 6–7 minutes until the crumbs are lightly browned.

Barbecued Chicken Wings

(24 PIECES)

12 chicken wings
½ cup (1 dL) honey
2 tablespoons Worcestershire
  sauce

⅓ cup (¾ dL) soy sauce
Juice of 2 lemons
1 clove garlic, minced

Preheat the oven to 325°F (165°C). Remove the wing tips and break each wing into two pieces. Place in a shallow baking dish. Mix the remaining ingredients and pour over the wings. Bake for 1 hour and serve in the baking dish.

Oysters in Bacon

Oysters and bacon are a traditional pair.

(24 PIECES)

24 oysters, shucked and patted dry
12 strips of bacon, cut in half

Preheat the oven to 425°F (220°C). Wrap each oyster in a piece of bacon. Arrange the wrapped oysters, with bacon ends down, on a rack in a shallow pan. Bake only until the bacon is slightly browned. Drain on paper towels.

❂ Other Suggestions for Hot Hors d'Oeuvre

In the Fish and Shellfish chapter, there are Baked or Broiled Clams, which, if done in small shells, can be passed and eaten with the fingers; fried clams and oysters, tiny lobster croquettes, and small codfish cakes or balls also make good hot appetizers. In the Meat chapter, you'll find other kinds of meatballs that could be made into smaller balls and served from a chafing dish with toothpicks alongside. The Chicken chapter will give you ideas for Deviled Chicken-on-the-Bone, or try Delmonico's Deviled Chicken, using just wings; bite-size chicken croquettes are delicious, as would be small skewers of chicken livers. In Eggs & Cheese, try Cheese Toast cut into bite-size pieces, or Fried Cheese Balls. And in Filled Things, consult the quiche section; these can always be made in small tart tins or served in a big one and cut into bite-size pieces; you can do the same with pizza.

NIBBLES

Curried Peanuts

(2 CUPS)

2 cups (½ L) salted peanuts
2 teaspoons curry powder

Preheat the oven to 300°F (150°C). Combine the peanuts and curry powder in a
paper bag and shake well. Spread the coated peanuts in a single layer on a cookie
sheet and bake 20 minutes, shaking once or twice during that time.

Raisin-Nut Mix

Begin this recipe a week ahead by drying the orange rind. The mixed
seeds are the kind one buys in a health food store.

(ABOUT 3 CUPS)

2 oranges   ½ cup (1 dL) raisins
1 pound (450 g) salted mixed   ½ cup (1 dL) mixed seeds
    nuts

A week before you plan to serve the mix, remove thin strips of orange peel,
taking only the colored part, the "zest." Cut it into julienne strips and air-dry
on a pie plate or a sheet of wax paper. When thoroughly dried, toss with the
nuts, raisins, and seeds and store in an airtight container until ready to serve.

Trail Mix or Gorp

Created to provide energy for hikers, trail mix or "gorp" has become
an all-purpose snack.

(3½ CUPS)

2 cups (½ L) raisins   ¼ cup (½ dL) cashew pieces
¾ cup (1¾ dL) chocolate chips   ½ cup (1 dL) dried or grated
½ cup (1 dL) walnut pieces   coconut shavings

Toss all the ingredients together. Store in an airtight jar.

Sugared Nuts

Traditionally served with dessert, but irresistible as an appetizer.

(ABOUT 2 CUPS)

1 pound (450 g) pecan or   ½ cup (1 dL) sugar
    walnut halves   ½ teaspoon salt
1 egg white   ½ teaspoon cinnamon

Preheat the oven to 225°F (110°C). Beat the egg white with 1 tablespoon water,
and dip the nuts into it. Roll them in the mixed sugar, salt, and cinnamon,
spread on a cookie sheet, and bake 1 hour, stirring every 15 minutes. Let cool;
store in the refrigerator.

Popcorn

Popcorn kernels should be plump and fresh to pop up well. They keep well in a screwtop jar, even better in the freezer. For long storage, keep them in the refrigerator. If the kernels start to dry out, add a tablespoon or two of water for each two cups of kernels and shake together in the jar.

(3 QUARTS)

3 tablespoons vegetable oil
½ cup (1 dL) popcorn
    kernels

3–4 tablespoons melted butter
    (optional)
Salt

Put the oil (butter would burn) in a 4-quart heavy pot and let it heat over medium heat for 30 seconds. Stir in the kernels, turning with a spoon so that they are evenly covered with oil, then spread them in one layer on the bottom of the pot. Put on the cover, leaving a small air space at the edge for escaping steam. As soon as the first kernel pops, move the pot gently and continuously back and forth over medium-high heat until the popping stops. Turn into a warm bowl. If you like, toss with melted butter and salt to taste.

Corn Crisps

Crisp, coarse, and salty.

(ABOUT 30 CORN CRISPS)

2 tablespoons butter
½ cup (1 dL) yellow cornmeal
¼–½ teaspoon salt

Preheat the oven to 425°F (220°C). Butter a cookie sheet. Bring ¾ cup water and the butter to a boil in a small pan. Quickly stir in the cornmeal and salt and mix well. Drop by teaspoonfuls onto the cookie sheet and bake for 10–15 minutes.

SOUPS

ABOUT SOUP

Soup may be thick or thin, hot or cold, subtle or spicy, jellied, puréed, or creamed. It may be as clear as glass or full of chunky bits of vegetables and meats. Some soups derive their essential flavor from a rich stock; others depend upon water or milk to capture the pure taste of the ingredients. Certain soups can be cooked in thirty minutes (some do not even take cooking), but others require hours of slow simmering and taste even better when they've been left to mellow in the refrigerator for several days.

When to Serve Soup

There used to be an obligatory "soup course" in every formal meal. Today we use soup less conventionally: soup and a sandwich often constitute lunch; a really hearty soup can be the whole supper; a good soup can be the centerpiece of a meal with deliberately light dishes surrounding it—a salad, cheese, and dessert. When soup does preside as the first course, it is usually a clear, delicate soup to stimulate the appetite, unless the courses to follow are light and demand a rich or heavy soup at the outset.

Because the size of the portion you serve will vary considerably, depending upon the kind of soup and when you're having it, we have used the 8-ounce cup as the basic measure of yield per recipe, instead of the number of servings. Allow up to 1 cup of soup per person if the soup is a first course and as much as 2 cups if it is the main course. The quantity of soup that a recipe produces may vary a bit each time you make it, depending upon the proportion of liquid in the ingredients and how long and briskly it has been cooked.

Using Leftovers in Soup

Fortunately, soup recipes do not have to be precise: a little more or less of the ingredients prescribed, or the addition of something new, can often be an improvement. This flexibility presents the cook with a thrifty way to use leftovers:

the contents of the refrigerator shelves may even dictate what kind of soup to make. But a potpourri of tired, tasteless food that would otherwise be thrown away will not be transformed, nor will it improve the soup. Moreover, any leftovers you use must seem agreeable with the distinctive flavors of the soup. An equal amount of experience and good judgment is required to decide both what *should* and what *should not* go into the soup or stockpot.

Seasoning Soup
Most soups should be cooked in a covered pot to retain flavor and nutrients, although you may want to cover the pot only partially to reduce the soup a bit and to intensify its taste.

It is better to season a soup when it is nearly done because, as it simmers, it cooks down, so any salt you may have put in is intensified. Also, if it is a stock-based soup you are making, the salt content of the stock, particularly if it is a canned or dehydrated variety, is apt to vary greatly. For these reasons we have not given precise amounts of either salt or pepper in the recipes that follow. It is so much better to taste a soup toward the end of its cooking and let your palate be your guide. But don't be timid about seasoning; it may surprise you to discover how much salt is needed to bring out the good flavor of a soup. Nothing is less appealing than a bland soup.

Cold Soups
Many soups are equally good hot or cold. You can sometimes make one soup serve as two by offering it hot one day and cold the next. Soups thicken as they cool, and chilled soup may need to be thinned with extra broth or cream. If the stock base is rich and meaty, it may gel when refrigerated, in which case beat well with a wire whisk. Cold soups, like all cold foods, require more seasoning than hot.

Storing and Freezing Soup
Almost all soups can be made in advance. Many, in fact, are better on the second or third day, after the flavors have mingled. To keep refrigerated soups from spoiling, reheat them to the boiling point every third day.

Soup freezes very well, so it's good to make a lot and freeze what you do not use. Be sure to divide the soup into quantities that will be useful later: a portion which is enough to serve your family, for example, or another which may be added as a supplement for a few unexpected guests. Soups that have been held in the refrigerator for a while or frozen may need diluting and may also need reseasoning before they are served.

Binding and Thickening Soup
Flour is used with certain soups to add body and as a binder to inhibit separation and curdling. One tablespoon of butter to 1 of flour is the right proportion for every 2 cups of soup. Stir the flour into the melted butter and cook it for about 3 minutes over low heat; then stir in a little of the hot soup, whisk well, cook until thick, then add to the remaining soup; heat and stir until smooth.

Some soups are thickened with egg yolks: 1 egg yolk beaten with 1 teaspoon of milk or cream to each cup of soup shortly before serving. To prevent curdling, drizzle a little hot soup slowly into the egg yolks, whisking briskly, then pour into the pot of soup, reheating slowly and stirring until it thickens. Do not boil, or the eggs will curdle.

Canned Soups

Canned soups are unquestionably a convenience, and they can often be improved by the addition of fresh ingredients (see p. 442 for refreshing canned stocks, for instance). Sometimes several compatible kinds of canned soups are mixed together successfully, but there are no particular formulas so we are not including them here; follow your own instincts. It is really so very easy and economical to make wholesome, full-bodied soups from scratch, which have their own individual flavors, that you are urged to try some of the recipes that follow and discover for yourself the difference.

Soup Garnishes

The trend today is toward simple garnishes rather than the more elaborate garnishes that accompanied soups in our grandmothers' day. Small touches are all you need to enhance the appearance and flavor of a soup—a sprinkling of chopped parsley, chives, dill, or other fresh herbs, for instance, or a bundle of quickly blanched vegetables such as carrots, turnips, broccoli stems, or a scattering of raw ones like scallions and mushrooms; a dusting of freshly grated Parmesan cheese, chopped eggs, or nuts; a little rice or pasta for body; a hint of sherry or wine for accent; a dollop of sour cream, a slice of lemon, some chopped, cooked chicken, or a few crisp pork scraps added to each bowl at the last minute—these are all fine finishing touches and are suggested in specific recipes when they seem appropriate.

There are recipes for croutons, bread sticks, rolls and biscuits, garlic bread, cream bread fingers, and corn crisps, all of which are especially good with soup, as is almost any homemade bread, particularly when the soup is to be a full meal (see chapters on Yeast Breads and Quick Breads for ideas).

ABOUT STOCKS AND STOCKMAKING

Stock is water enriched by the good things that have been cooked in it: various combinations of meat, poultry, fish, vegetables, bones, and scraps. Full of flavor and nutritional value, it is the essential ingredient in many classic soups and sauces. Although commercially produced substitutes are often used, sometimes quite acceptably, there is no *true* replacement for the full-bodied flavor of good homemade stock.

Any strained stock can be served as a broth. Chicken soup is nothing more than chicken stock, seasoned to taste; beef bouillon is beef stock, clam broth and mushroom broth are also stocks. Since stock is almost always made in quantity, you can serve some as soup for dinner and freeze the rest for use later in soups and sauces.

Don't be intimidated by the common notion that stock is difficult to make. Although many stocks may take a long time to cook, they don't entail much work. The ingredients can be assembled quickly in the stockpot and left to simmer very slowly, requiring no attention other than a check from time to time to see that they are not cooking too briskly.

Keeping your own stock on hand can easily become a simple kitchen routine. And it makes you feel so provident to use up all those scraps and juices and carcasses that would otherwise go in the garbage. Once it becomes a habit, you'll find you may plan a boiled dinner or a stewed chicken just to replenish your stock when you see it running low. Blessed as we are with freezers today, it is always possible to have an adequate supply at the ready for an impromptu meal for your family on a stormy night or for unexpected guests.

Ingredients for Stock

The ingredients for stock should always be fresh and flavorful: don't use the stockpot for foods that have been refrigerated too long and have lost their flavor.

Most stock ingredients are readily found in a well-tended kitchen. In addition to staples like onions, celery, bay leaves, peppercorns, and cloves, most scraps and leftovers should be saved to use in stocks. Scallion, leek, and celery tops; stems from mushrooms, parsley, and dill; cooked vegetables; bits of leftover meats and stuffings; cooked carcasses; meat bones; chicken bones, skin, necks, and giblets; leftover gravies, sauces, and meat and vegetable juices—all of these add value to the stockpot and can be refrigerated or frozen until their moment arrives. There's no need to buy bones especially for stock, if you remember to ask the butcher to save them for you when he is boning your meat. Fish heads and skeletons can be had for the asking at many fish markets.

Smoked and corned meats, strongly flavored vegetables like cabbage and turnips, and dark, oily fish like mackerel may make the stock salty, bitter, or too overpowering and should be avoided.

Cooking Stock

Brown stocks are made by browning the ingredients in fat or roasting them in a very hot oven or under the broiler before they are put in the stockpot. Cold water is added so that the juices of the meat are drawn out into the soup as it is brought to a boil.

Stock should then be simmered—just a bubble or two breaking the surface is ideal. During the first half-hour of cooking, skim off any scum that rises to the surface. When the scum changes from a yellowish brown foam to a white froth, you may stop skimming; the foam that remains will disappear by itself.

If you keep the stockpot partially covered, the stock will be more easily maintained at a slight simmer and the liquid will be reduced a bit without any loss of flavor or vitamins.

If fish or vegetable stocks are allowed to cook for more than about 30 minutes, they may become bitter. Meat and poultry stocks, on the other hand, should be simmered as long as possible—all day when convenient.

If you want to cook some meat or poultry in the stock as it is simmering, both the stock and the meat will benefit from this exchange of flavors. Add the meat or chicken when the broth has begun to develop body, let it cook until it is tender enough to eat, then remove it and serve. Return to the stockpot any bones, skin, or leftover juices to cook longer and deepen the flavor of the soup.

Seasoning Stock

Always taste any juices or cooking liquids that you add to the stockpot. Season toward the end of the cooking and take into account any salty ingredients that you may be adding as a garnish or when the stock serves as a base for a soup. It is really better to hold back on the salting of a stock if you are storing it for later use because at that point you do not know how you will be using it; you may want to reduce it further, for instance, to add intense flavor to a sauce, but if you have already salted it, it will not stand the further reduction.

Cooling Stock

When the stock has finished cooking, strain it through a colander and let it cool, uncovered, as quickly as possible, in a cold place or the refrigerator. If stock is covered tightly while cooling, it may turn sour. Stock made with bones will gel when it is cold.

Removing Fat

The easiest way to remove fat from a stock is by chilling in the refrigerator until the fat congeals on the surface; it can then be lifted or spooned off.

If you do not have time to chill the stock, patiently spoon off the clear fat that will rise to the top. Run a paper towel over the surface to absorb the residue that you have not been able to trap in a spoon.

If you need to remove fat from just a small amount of stock—a cup or two for a sauce perhaps—pour it into a small metal bowl and put it in the freezer until the fat congeals.

Do not remove the fat until you are ready to use the stock. A layer of fat will serve as a seal which helps preserve the stock.

Reducing Stock

Strained stock, free of fat, can be evaporated to about half its volume by cooking it slowly, uncovered. The flavor will intensify as the stock becomes more concentrated, and the reduced stock will take less space in your freezer. You can later expand it with water if you need a larger quantity or if the flavor is too strong. This is another reason not to finish salting until serving: should you wish to reduce, any salt flavor will become greatly intensified.

A heavily reduced stock will ultimately become syrupy. When cool you will have the thick, jellylike substance that the French call *glace de viande*, meat glaze.

Storing and Freezing Stock

To keep stock from spoiling when it is being stored in the refrigerator for some time, reheat every three days and let it boil for about 2 minutes. The refrigerated stock should also be boiled whenever you add gravy or juice to it.

Stock freezes well. Freeze it in quantities calculated for use in soups and sauces. If you freeze the stock in clean tins or in heavy-duty plastic containers, you can take the container directly from the freezer and heat it in a pan of simmering water when you want to defrost the contents in a hurry. It's also convenient to freeze stock in ice-cube trays, then store the cubes in the freezer in plastic bags from which you can remove a few when you need a small quantity for a sauce.

Clarifying Stock

If you plan to use stock as a clear broth or in an aspic, you'll want it sparkling and crystal-clear. Start with a stock that is seasoned and fat-free and follow this procedure carefully.

To Clarify Stock
8 cups cold stock, strained
through a coffee filter
3 egg whites

Combine 2 cups of the stock in a large bowl with the egg whites, and beat well. Bring the remaining 6 cups of stock to a boil and slowly pour over the egg-white

mixture, whisking constantly. Return everything to the pan and heat over medium-low heat, whisking slowly, but continually, until a simmer is reached. Then stop whisking and turn the heat as low as possible, just so there is a bubble or two on the surface, barely quivering; keep the stock on this very low heat for 15 minutes, then turn off the heat and let rest 10 minutes. Carefully ladle or pour the liquid slowly through a colander lined with a clean napkin or dishcloth. (Don't use the commercial cheesecloth generally available today; it is coarse and made of harsh threads so that it does not do a good job of filtering.)

Stock Substitutes

You can substitute beef stock for chicken stock in many of these recipes—or chicken for beef, if you wish. Veal and chicken stock are completely interchangeable; the use of veal stock in a chicken dish will add a special, subtle touch. Vegetable stocks can be used instead of water in making beef stock, or instead of beef stock in making soups. Fish stock should be saved for fish soups and chowders or for sauces to be used with seafood.

Commercial products may be used, of course, as substitutes for stock (see p. 442 for suggestions on enriching their flavor). When the soup is very simple, that is when a high-quality stock makes the difference.

Canned beef and chicken broths are the most common commercial substitutes for beef or chicken stock. Some brands are better than others for this purpose. Try to find a canned broth that is not condensed and has good, but not overpowering, flavor. Do not use canned consommé as a stock substitute; it is too sweet. Bouillon cubes or powdered mixes, dissolved in water, may also be substituted if necessary, but they do not have as much body and are apt to be very salty, so watch your seasoning accordingly.

STOCKS, BROTHS, AND CLEAR SOUPS

Beef Stock

Beef stock made from bones alone will be rich in gelatin but will lack flavor unless some lean meat is included. One of the best cuts to use for stock is beef shank because it provides the shin bone with its marrow plus a solid piece of shank meat surrounding it. Have the shank cut up into 2-inch pieces. If you can't get that cut, use whatever bones are available (have them cracked if they are solid pieces like knuckle) and add an equal amount of lean stewing beef. Browning the meat, bones, and vegetables at the beginning will add color and flavor to the finished stock. If you want to be more provident and use the meat for a meal of sliced boiled beef, or in hash or a filling, remove it from the stockpot after 2½ hours, returning the bones to finish cooking.

(ABOUT 12 CUPS)

2 tablespoons shortening, cooking oil, or marrow
4–5 pounds (1¾–2¼ kg) beef shank or 2½ lbs (1¼ kg) beef bones and 2½ lbs (1¼ kg) stew meat
3 carrots, sliced

3 onions, sliced
3 stalks celery, sliced
1 teaspoon dried thyme
1 bay leaf
2 sprigs parsley
6 crushed peppercorns
Salt

Preheat oven to 450°F (230°C). Heat the shortening, oil, or marrow in a large roasting pan, add the pieces of shank (or the bones and stewing beef, cut into chunks) and brown them in the oven, stirring, turning, moving them about frequently. After about 10 minutes, add the carrots, onions, and celery to the roasting pan and let them brown, taking care that they do not scorch. When everything has browned, transfer it all to a stockpot or large cooking pot. Pour off the fat in the roasting pan, add a cup or so of boiling water, and scrape up all the browned bits in the pan, then pour into the stockpot. Add the thyme, bay leaf, parsley, and peppercorns, and cover with 4 quarts cold water. Bring the water slowly to a boil, then reduce the heat and simmer very gently, partially covered, for at least 4 or 5 hours, skimming off any scum that rises to the surface during the first 30 minutes or so. Strain and cool, uncovered. (See About Stock and Stockmaking, p. 76, for general information about seasoning, cooling, removing fat, reducing, storing, and clarifying stocks and about substitutes for beef stock.)

Beef Bouillon. Beef bouillon is a strong Beef Stock, reduced slightly if necessary to intensify the flavor, and seasoned to taste with *salt* and *freshly ground pepper*. It may be clarified and served as a consommé (see p. 82). Sprinkle each serving of bouillon with *finely chopped parsley, chives, or celery*.

Beef Bouillon with Noodles. Add ¼–½ *cup cooked egg noodles* or *broken-up vermicelli* for each 2 cups Beef Bouillon.

Beef Bouillon with Marrow Balls (16 marrow balls). Using a wooden spoon, a blender, or a food processor, blend to a smooth paste 2 *tablespoons marrow* (from marrow bones), 4 *tablespoons fine cracker crumbs, 1 egg, 1 teaspoon finely chopped parsley,* ¼ *teaspoon salt,* ⅛ *teaspoon freshly ground pepper,* and ⅛ *teaspoon nutmeg.* Shape into ½-inch balls and chill in the refrigerator until ready to use. Drop into simmering 1 quart Beef Bouillon and cook for 5 minutes, then turn each ball with a spoon and cook for another 5 minutes. Taste one to see if it is cooked through.

Chicken Stock

Simmering 4 to 5 hours enriches a stock, but longer than that isn't necessary. A very rich stock is good as a broth or in sauces, less necessary when used as the base for vegetable soups with many ingredients or for light soups with delicately flavored ingredients that should not be overwhelmed by the taste of the stock.

(ABOUT 7 CUPS, 1¾ L)

2 pounds (900 g) chicken backs, wings, necks, bones
1 onion, cut in half
2 carrots, cut in thirds
3 stalks celery with leaves, cut in half

1 bay leaf
6 crushed peppercorns
1 teaspoon dried thyme
Salt

Wash the chicken parts and put them in a large soup pot. Add 8 cups cold water and remaining ingredients, except salt. Bring to a boil, reduce heat, and simmer, skimming off the scum during the first 30 minutes. Simmer, partially covered, for 4 or 5 hours, longer if possible. Salt carefully to taste. Strain and cool quickly, uncovered. (See About Stocks and Stockmaking, p. 76, for general information about seasoning, cooling, removing fat, reducing, storing, and clarifying stocks and about substitutes for chicken stock.)

Chicken Stock Made by Cooking a Chicken (7–8 cups). Chicken stock can be made from the water in which a chicken is cooked, and you will have both stock and cooked chicken as the end result. To keep the chicken from being tough, stop cooking it when it is tender and use just the bones and skin to complete the stock.

Instead of the backs, wings, and necks used for regular Chicken Stock, substitute a *4-pound fowl or 4 pounds chicken parts.* Use the same amount of water, vegetables, and seasonings as in Chicken Stock, but set aside any white meat (if you are using chicken parts), adding it after everything else has simmered for about 20 minutes. Cook, covered, until the white meat is tender. Turn off the heat and remove all the chicken from the pot. When the chicken is cool enough to handle, separate the meat from the skin and bones and return the skin and bones to the pot. Continue to simmer, 4 or 5 hours in all. Strain and cool the stock, uncovered. Use the cooked chicken in soups, salads, sandwiches, crêpe fillings, or other dishes calling for cooked chicken.

Chicken Soup. Chicken soup is homemade Chicken Stock (above), seasoned to taste with *salt, pepper,* and a sprig or two of fresh *parsley* or *dill.*

Chicken Rice Soup. Add ¼ cup *cooked rice* for each 2 cups of well-seasoned Chicken Soup. Or add 1½ tablespoons *uncooked rice* for each 2 cups and cook in the soup until done.

Chicken Noodle Soup. Add ¼–½ cup *cooked egg noodles* or *broken-up vermicelli* for each 2 cups of Chicken Soup.

Cream of Chicken Soup. Slowly add ½ *cup warmed cream* for each 2 cups of Chicken Soup. Sprinkle with some *chopped parsley* and some *diced, cooked chicken.*

Veal Stock

Veal stock is a white stock with particularly good flavor. It may be used in any recipe calling for chicken stock and is especially distinctive in fine sauces.

(ABOUT 9 CUPS)

4-pound (1¾-kg) veal knuckle bone, cut in pieces	2 carrots, sliced
	1 bay leaf
1–2 pounds (450–900 g) lean veal	Pinch of dried thyme
	2 cloves
1 onion, sliced	6 crushed peppercorns
3 stalks celery, sliced	Salt

Put all the ingredients except salt in a stockpot with 3 quarts cold water and let them soak for up to an hour. Bring them slowly to a boil, reduce the heat, and simmer gently, partially covered, for 4 or 5 hours, skimming any scum from the surface during the first 30 minutes or so of cooking. Salt carefully to taste at the end of the cooking. Strain and cool, uncovered. (See About Stock and Stockmaking, p. 76, for general information about seasoning, cooling, removing fat, reducing, storing, and clarifying stocks and about substitutes for veal stock.)

Consommé

"Consommé" is generally used these days to describe any clear soup. In the earliest editions of *Fannie Farmer*, the definition was more specific: consommé then was described as a highly seasoned, clarified soup made from a combination of two or three different kinds of meat, usually beef, veal, and fowl.

You can make an excellent, old-fashioned consommé by substituting Veal Stock (above) and/or Chicken Stock (p. 81) for water in the recipe for Beef Stock (p. 79) or by adding 1–2 pounds chicken backs and necks and some veal bones to the beef stock ingredients. The finished stock should be cooled, degreased, seasoned well with salt and pepper, and then clarified (p. 78).

Serve consommé hot with a spoonful or two of mixed vegetables in each bowl: finely diced carrots, celery, green pepper, and scallions, which have been sautéed together in a little butter. Or serve consommé jellied, and flavored with a little lemon juice or sherry.

Turkey Soup

Serve turkey soup as a clear broth, or add some cooked noodles, rice, or barley. It can also be used as a base in many vegetable soups.

(7–8 CUPS)

1 turkey carcass	2 stalks celery, cut up
1 onion, sliced	6 crushed peppercorns
1 carrot, sliced	Salt

Break the turkey carcass into pieces and put them in a soup pot with any small pieces of turkey meat that you can spare. Add 8 cups water, onion, carrot, celery, and peppercorns. Bring to a boil, lower the heat, cover partially, and simmer for

3 or 4 hours. Strain the broth and cool it quickly, uncovered. Chill it and remove the fat when it solidifies, or scoop any fat off the surface with a spoon. Add salt to taste before serving.

Vegetable Stock

Vegetable stock is the liquid in which vegetables have been cooked. It contains many valuable vitamins and minerals. Use stocks from highly flavored vegetables like cabbage, turnips, and carrots sparingly and with discretion, and do not cook vegetable stocks for more than about 30 minutes or they may become bitter. You may use vegetable stock instead of water in making Beef Stock (p. 79) or instead of water or meat stock in many soups.

Mushroom Broth

Especially good when you're feeling frail.

(4 CUPS)

½ pound (225 g) mushrooms, chopped
½ teaspoon grated onion
Salt

Put the mushrooms, onion, and 4 cups cold water in a saucepan and simmer, partially covered, for about 1 hour. Remove from heat and let stand for at least 4 hours, overnight if possible. Strain and reheat, adding salt to taste. Mushroom broth can also be used as stock in vegetable soups or in place of water in making meat stocks.

Fish Stock or Court Bouillon

Use only white fish to make fish stock. If you use dark, oily fish like mackerel or if you cook a fish stock more than about 30 minutes, the stock will be too strong. Always save liquid in which fish has been cooked (it may be frozen) and add it to the fish stock. Clam Broth diluted half in half with water may be used instead of fish stock in many recipes.

(ABOUT 7 CUPS)

1½–2 pounds (675–900 g) fish skeleton, with heads if available
1 carrot, sliced
1 onion, sliced
2 stalks celery, sliced

2 cloves
½ bay leaf
6 crushed peppercorns
2 cups (½ L) dry white wine (optional)
Salt

Wash the fish trimmings. Combine them with the other ingredients except salt and 8 cups cold water (or 6 cups water and the wine) in a soup pot and simmer, uncovered, for about 30 minutes, skimming any scum from the surface. Season carefully to taste with salt. Strain and cool, uncovered. (See About Stocks and Stockmaking, p. 76, for general information about seasoning, cooling, removing fat, reducing, storing, and clarifying stocks and about substitutes for fish stock.)

Clam Broth

Do not overcook clams or they will be tough. If you are cooking soft-shelled "steamers," eat them as soon as the shells open, dipping each clam first in melted butter. If you are using hard-shelled clams, chop, mince, or freeze the clams to use in chowders, spreads, or other seafood dishes. The strained broth, seasoned to taste with salt and pepper, makes a fine soup, or it can be used instead of fish stock in chowders, soups, and sauces.

(ABOUT 2 CUPS)

1 quart (1 L) clams in shell   Salt
1 stalk celery, cut up   Freshly ground pepper
Small piece of bay leaf

Wash the clams in the shell, scrubbing them with a brush and changing the water several times. Put them in a kettle with the celery, bay leaf, and ½ cup water. Cover and steam until the shells open wide, 10–30 minutes, depending on the clams. Remove the clams from the broth. Let the broth stand for 15 minutes before straining so that the sediment will settle, or strain it through several layers of wet cheesecloth. Season to taste with salt (judiciously—clams can be very salty) and pepper before serving.

SOUPS WITH STOCK

Cream of Asparagus Soup

An appealing-looking soup with a pleasing asparagus taste.

(4 CUPS)

1 pound (450 g) fresh   2 tablespoons chopped onion
  asparagus, or 1 package   1 cup (¼ L) milk or cream
  frozen   Salt
1½ cups (3½ dL) Chicken   Freshly ground pepper
  Stock (p. 81) or canned
  broth

If using fresh asparagus, wash stalks and cut off the coarse ends. Cook the asparagus in 2 cups boiling water until tender. Drain, reserving 1 cup of the water. Cut off the asparagus tips, chop them, and reserve. Put the chicken stock, onion, and reserved water in a pan and bring to a boil. Add the asparagus and simmer for 5 minutes. Put through a strainer or vegetable mill or purée in a food processor or an electric blender. Return to the pot and add the milk or cream and salt and pepper to taste. Reheat and adjust the seasonings. Before serving, sprinkle with chopped asparagus tips.

Thick Cream of Asparagus Soup. Before adding the milk, melt 2 *tablespoons butter* in a large pot, stir in 2 *tablespoons flour*, and cook for a few minutes until smooth. Slowly add the milk or cream and salt and pepper. Then add the asparagus purée and reheat until thickened.

Cabbage and Beet Soup

A coarse, peasant soup that stirs up memories of farms and fields.

(8 CUPS)

1 quart (1 L) Beef Stock
   (p. 79) or beef bouillon
2 cups (½ L) peeled and diced
   raw beets
1 onion, chopped
2 cups (½ L) coarsely chopped
   cabbage

Freshly ground pepper
2 tablespoons cider vinegar
½ cup (1 dL) sour cream
Salt

Put the stock or bouillon, beets, onion, and cabbage in a soup pot. Bring to a boil, lower heat, and simmer, partially covered, replacing any liquid that evaporates with additional stock or water. Simmer for about 30 minutes or until the beets are tender. Season with pepper and vinegar, adding salt to taste. Serve hot or cold with a tablespoon of sour cream floated on top of each bowl.

Cheese Soup

This is a very nice change from meat and vegetable soups. The paprika adds good color.

(4 CUPS)

1 tablespoon butter
1 tablespoon finely chopped
   onion
1 tablespoon flour
1 cup (¼ L) well-seasoned Beef
   Stock (p. 79) or bouillon

2 cups (½ L) milk
¾ cup (1¾ dL) grated Cheddar
   cheese
2 teaspoons paprika

Melt the butter in a pot, add the onion, and cook slowly until limp. Stir in the flour and continue to cook for 3 minutes, stirring. Slowly add the seasoned stock and milk, and heat to the boiling point, stirring frequently. Stir in the cheese and paprika and whisk until the cheese has melted and the soup is very hot.

Pumpkin Soup

(7 CUPS)

2 medium onions, chopped
2 tablespoons butter
1 tablespoon flour
3 cups (¾ L) chicken broth
3 cups (¾ L) pumpkin purée
   (see p. 407)

Salt to taste
Freshly ground pepper
½ cup (1 dL) cream, whipped
Dusting nutmeg
3 tablespoons toasted pumpkin
   seed (optional)

Sauté the onions with the butter in the bottom of a heavy, large saucepan over low heat until soft. Sprinkle in the flour; stir and cook 2 or 3 minutes. Gradually add the chicken broth, whisking thoroughly, then the pumpkin purée, and cook gently about 15 minutes. Salt and pepper to taste. Pour into warm bowls and top with a dollop of whipped cream, a dusting of nutmeg, and, if you like, a scattering of toasted pumpkin seeds.

Creole Soup

A sharp and lively soup.

(4 CUPS)

2 tablespoons bacon fat
2 tablespoons finely chopped
  green pepper
2 tablespoons finely chopped
  onion
2 tablespoons flour
1 cup (¼ L) chopped tomatoes
3 cups (¾ L) Beef Stock
  (p. 79) or bouillon

⅛ teaspoon freshly ground
  pepper
1 tablespoon prepared
  horseradish
½ teaspoon vinegar
Salt to taste

Heat the bacon fat in a pot, add the green pepper and onion, and cook slowly for 5 minutes. Stir in the flour and cook for 2 or 3 minutes, then stir in the tomatoes and stock or bouillon. Simmer for 15 minutes. Strain and add remaining ingredients. Serve hot.

Cream of Almond Soup

A delicate soup to serve hot or cold. Use a mild chicken broth so that the almond flavor is not overwhelmed.

(4 CUPS)

½ cup (1 dL) blanched
  almonds, ground (p. 17)
2 cups (½ L) Chicken Stock
  (p. 81) or canned broth

¼ teaspoon almond extract
2 cups (½ L) cream
Salt to taste

Put the almonds and chicken broth in a soup pot, bring to a boil, then simmer, partially covered, for 20 minutes. Mix the almond extract with 2 tablespoons cold water, add it to the pot, and simmer 10 minutes more. Slowly stir in the cream, add salt if necessary, and heat without allowing to boil. Serve hot or cold.

Cream of Carrot Soup

(7 CUPS)

4 tablespoons butter
1 onion, chopped
4 carrots, sliced
1 stalk celery with leaves,
  chopped
2 medium potatoes, peeled and
  diced

2 sprigs parsley
5 cups (1¼ L) Chicken Stock
  (p. 81) or canned broth
1 cup (¼ L) heavy cream
Salt
Freshly ground pepper

Melt the butter in a large pot, add the onion, carrots, and celery, and cook for 10–15 minutes, stirring from time to time. Add the potatoes and parsley and stir until coated. Stir in the stock and cook, partially covered, until the potatoes are tender, about 20 minutes. Put through a strainer or vegetable mill or purée in a blender or food processor. Return to the pot, stir in the cream, add salt and pepper to taste, and reheat without boiling. Serve hot or cold.

Cream of Chestnut Soup

This soup has a good winter taste. It's worth the bother of shelling the chestnuts, a job for which there is no shortcut. To shell chestnuts, cut a slit on the flat side of each nut and drop several at a time into a pan of boiling water. Boil for a couple of minutes, remove from pot, and cut away the shell with a small knife. Peel off the dark skin. If the skin is stubborn, drop the chestnut back into boiling water for another minute or two; the heat will usually loosen the skin. Discard any chestnuts that are very hard and shriveled, and cut away any possible moldy spots.

(6 CUPS)

1 quart (1 L) Chicken Stock (p. 81) or canned broth
1 cup (¼ L) chestnuts, shelled (see above)
1 cup (¼ L) cream or milk
Salt to taste
1 teaspoon paprika

Put the stock and chestnuts in a large pot, heat to the boiling point, and simmer until the chestnuts are soft. Put through a strainer or vegetable mill or purée in a food processor or an electric blender. Return to the pot, stir in the cream or milk, and season with the salt and paprika. Reheat before serving.

Cream of Watercress Soup

Cream of Watercress soup is also good cold, as are the Spinach and Sorrel variations. Simply chill thoroughly, add ½ cup more cream, and adjust the salt. Wash the watercress, if necessary (you can always tell if it is gritty by tasting it), by submerging it in several changes of cold water. Pat it barely dry, wrap it in dampened paper towels, and keep in the refrigerator crisper until ready to use.

(6 CUPS)

2 bunches watercress, coarsely chopped
4 cups (1 L) Chicken Stock (p. 81) or canned broth
4 tablespoons butter
2 tablespoons flour
1 tablespoon lemon juice
1 cup (¼ L) cream
Salt
Freshly ground pepper

Put the watercress and the chicken stock in a pot and simmer for 10 minutes. Purée in a blender or food processor. Melt the butter in a large pot, stir in the flour, and cook slowly, stirring, for several minutes. Stir in a little of the purée and then add the rest. Bring the soup to the boiling point, stirring constantly. Stir in the lemon juice, cream, and salt and pepper to taste.

Cream of Spinach Soup (6 cups, 1½ L). Substitute ¾ *pound spinach* for the watercress.

Cream of Sorrel Soup (6 cups). Substitute ¾ *pound sorrel* for the watercress and omit the lemon juice.

Cream of Celery Soup

Don't use the dark-green outer stalks of the celery; the tender, inner stalks have a better consistency and flavor for this soup.

(4 CUPS)

6 stalks celery, chopped
½ onion, sliced
2 cups (½ L) Chicken Stock
   (p. 81) or canned broth

1½ cups (3½ dL) light cream
Salt to taste

Put the celery, onion, and chicken stock in a soup pot, bring to a boil, reduce heat, and simmer, partially covered, for 30 minutes or until the celery is tender. Put through a strainer or vegetable mill or purée in a blender or food processor. Return to pot. Add the cream and salt and reheat slowly.

Cream of Cucumber Soup

A pale cool-looking green soup with a light taste of cucumber.

(6 CUPS)

2 tablespoons butter
3 large cucumbers, peeled,
   seeded, and sliced
3 tablespoons chopped onion
3 tablespoons flour
3 cups (¾ L) Chicken Stock
   (p. 81) or canned broth

1 cup (¼ L) milk
½ cup (1 dL) cream
2 egg yolks, slightly beaten
Salt to taste

Melt the butter in a pot, add the cucumbers and onion, and cook over low heat for 10 minutes, stirring often. Stir in the flour and cook for 3 minutes. Slowly add the stock and milk and bring to the boiling point. Remove from heat and put through a strainer or vegetable mill or purée in a food processor or blender. Return to the pot, add the cream, egg yolks, and salt, and reheat, stirring, taking care not to boil.

Cream of Mushroom Soup

(3 CUPS)

4 tablespoons butter
¼ cup (½ dL) finely chopped
   onion
½ pound (225 g) mushrooms,
   finely chopped
1 tablespoon flour

2 cups (½ L) Chicken Stock
   (p. 81) or canned broth
½ cup (1 dL) cream
Salt
Freshly ground pepper

Melt the butter in a pot and add the onion and mushrooms. Cook over low heat for 15 minutes, stirring occasionally. Sprinkle with the flour and cook for a few minutes more. Slowly add the stock, and heat, stirring, until it reaches the boiling point. Reduce heat and simmer for 20 minutes. Stir in the cream, add salt and pepper to taste, and reheat before serving.

Cold Mushroom Soup. Use an additional ¼ cup cream and chill. Adjust salt. Serve in cold soupbowls with *chives* sprinkled on top.

Chicken Gumbo Soup

Diced cooked chicken, if you happen to have some, is a pleasant
addition to this and other chicken-based soups.

(6 CUPS)

2 tablespoons butter
1 onion, finely chopped
4 cups (1 L) Chicken Stock
  (p. 81) or canned broth
½ green pepper, chopped fine
1 cup (¼ L) sliced okra, fresh
  or frozen

1½ cups (3½ dL) canned
  tomatoes, undrained
¾ cup (1¾ dL) cooked rice
Salt
Freshly ground pepper

Melt the butter in a large pot, add the onion, and cook, stirring, for about 5
minutes or until golden. Stir in the stock, green pepper, okra, and tomatoes.
Bring to a boil, then simmer for about 30 minutes. Add the rice, season with salt
and pepper to taste, and reheat before serving.

Vegetable Gumbo Soup

(7 CUPS)

4 tablespoons butter
1 onion, finely chopped
4 cups (1 L) Chicken Stock
  (p. 81) or canned broth
1 green pepper, finely chopped
1 cup (¼ L) sliced okra, fresh
  or frozen

Pinch of cayenne
2 cups (½ L) canned tomatoes,
  chopped
Salt
Freshly ground pepper

Melt the butter in a pot, add the onion, and cook, stirring frequently, until limp.
Add the chicken stock, green pepper, okra, cayenne, and tomatoes. Simmer,
partially covered, for 1 hour. Add salt and pepper to taste before serving.

Philadelphia Pepper Pot

(8 CUPS)

3 tablespoons butter
1 small onion, chopped
1 stalk celery, chopped
1 green pepper, chopped
1 large potato, peeled and
  diced
3 tablespoons flour
5 cups (1¼ L) Veal Stock (p.
  82) or Chicken Stock (p.
  81) or canned broth

½ pound (225 g) honeycomb
  tripe, cooked (p. 222) and
  diced
Pinch of cayenne pepper
½ cup (1 dL) heavy cream
Salt
Freshly ground pepper

Melt the butter in a large pot, add the onion, celery, and green pepper, and cook
slowly for about 15 minutes. Stir in the potato and flour, and cook, stirring, for
about 5 minutes. Add the stock, tripe, and cayenne, simmer, partially covered,
until the potato is just tender, about 20 minutes. Before serving, stir in the
cream, add salt and pepper to taste, and reheat slowly.

Vegetable Soup

Other vegetables—tomatoes, shredded cabbage, green beans, corn—may be added to this soup, if you wish.

(6 CUPS)

4 tablespoons butter
2 carrots, diced
2 stalks celery with leaves, diced
½ onion, chopped
1 small turnip, peeled and diced
1 medium potato, peeled and diced

2 cups (½ L) Beef Stock (p. 79) or bouillon
1 tablespoon butter
1 tablespoon finely chopped parsley
Salt
Freshly ground pepper

Melt the butter in a soup pot, then add the carrots, celery, onion, turnip, and potato. Cook over low heat, stirring, for about 10 minutes. Add the stock and 2 cups water, partially cover, and simmer for about 30 minutes or until the vegetables are tender. Before serving, add butter, parsley, and salt and pepper to taste.

Cold Cucumber or Avocado Soup

These soups are very refreshing on a summer evening. They'll have a more interesting texture if you don't overblend them, and hold back enough cucumber to add a slice or two to each soup bowl or enough avocado to dice so you can add about two tablespoonsful to each serving.

(4 CUPS)

2 peeled and seeded cucumbers or avocados
2 tablespoons lemon juice
1 cup (¼ L) chicken broth

1 cup (¼ L) heavy cream
Salt to taste
4 tablespoons minced chives or scallion greens

If you have a blender or food processor, simply chop the cucumbers or avocados in rough pieces, leaving out enough for the garnish as suggested on p. 98, and whirl with all the other ingredients in the machine until just blended. Otherwise, grate the cucumbers or avocados and blend with the other ingredients by hand. Add salt and chill. Serve in bowls with their garnish, and chives and/or herbs scattered on top.

Queen Victoria Soup

Adapted from an old English recipe.

(6 CUPS)

2 tablespoons butter
1 small onion, chopped fine
½ cup (1 dL) chopped mushrooms

3 stalks celery, diced
Pinch of nutmeg
4 cups (1 L) Chicken Stock (p. 81) or canned broth

1 tablespoon quick tapioca
½ cup (1 dL) diced cooked
  chicken
½ cup (1 dL) diced cooked
  ham

2 hard-boiled eggs, finely
  chopped
1 cup (¼ L) cream
Salt
Freshly ground pepper

Melt the butter in a large saucepan, add the onion, and cook slowly until golden. Add the mushrooms, celery, and nutmeg, and cook for 10 minutes. Stir in the stock, tapioca, chicken, and ham and simmer for 20 minutes. Before serving, add the eggs and cream, season to taste, and reheat slowly, without boiling.

Vichyssoise

This splendid chilled soup was devised on American soil by a French chef, Louis Diat. It is also good served hot.

(6 CUPS)

4 tablespoons butter
1 onion, chopped
4 leeks, white part only, finely
  sliced
2 stalks celery, chopped
2 medium potatoes, peeled and
  sliced
2 sprigs parsley

4 cups (1 L) Chicken Stock
  (p. 81) or canned broth
1 cup (¼ L) heavy cream
1 tablespoon finely chopped
  chives
Salt
Freshly ground pepper

Melt the butter in a large pot, add the onion, leeks, and celery, and cook over low heat, stirring often, for 10–15 minutes or until limp but not brown. Stir in the potatoes, parsley, and stock. Cook, partially covered, until the potatoes are tender, about 20 minutes. Put through a strainer or vegetable mill or purée in a blender or food processor. Pour into a bowl, stir in the cream and chives, and chill in the refrigerator. Add more salt and pepper to taste before serving.

Oxtail Soup

(9 CUPS)

1½ pounds (675 g) oxtail, in
  2-inch pieces
2 tablespoons flour
2 tablespoons cooking oil
4 cups (1 L) Beef Stock
  (p. 79) or bouillon
2 carrots, diced
2 stalks celery, diced

½ cup (1 dL) diced turnip
1 medium onion, diced
1 tablespoon lemon juice
2 teaspoons Worcestershire
  sauce
Salt
Freshly ground pepper

Dust the oxtail pieces with flour. Heat the oil in a soup pot, add the oxtail, and brown slowly on all sides. Drain the oil from the pot, remove the meat, and slowly add the stock and 4 cups water, scraping the bottom of the pot to deglaze it. Return the meat to the pot, partially cover, and simmer for 2½ hours or until the meat is tender, adding more water to replace any that evaporates. Strain the soup and allow the meat and bones to cool enough to be handled. Remove the meat from the bones and return it to the soup. Add the carrots, celery, turnip, and onion to the soup and simmer for another 30 minutes or until tender. Stir in the lemon juice, Worcestershire, and salt and pepper to taste; serve very hot.

Mulligatawny Soup

This soup from India found its way into American cookery long before the Civil War. A recipe for it appeared in the original *Fannie Farmer Cook Book* of 1896.

(8 CUPS)

4 tablespoons butter
1 small onion, diced
1 carrot, diced
1 stalk celery with leaves,
  diced
1 green pepper, diced
1 apple, peeled and diced
1 cup (¼ L) diced raw chicken
  (about 1 pound)
⅓ cup (50 g) flour
1–2 teaspoons curry powder

¼ teaspoon nutmeg
5 cups (1¼ L) Chicken Stock
  (p. 81) or canned broth
2 cloves, crushed
2 sprigs parsley, chopped
1 cup (¼ L) canned or
  chopped tomatoes
2 cups (½ L) hot cooked rice
Salt
Freshly ground pepper

Melt the butter in a large soup pot. Add the onion, carrot, celery, green pepper, apple, and chicken, and cook slowly, stirring frequently, for about 15 minutes. Mix the flour with 1 teaspoon curry powder and the nutmeg, add it to the pot, and cook over low heat for about 5 minutes, stirring from time to time. Stir in the stock, then add the cloves, parsley, and tomatoes. Partially cover and simmer for about 1 hour. Add salt and pepper to taste and more curry powder if you wish. Pass the rice separately or spoon some into each bowl as you serve the soup.

SOUPS WITHOUT STOCK

Baked Bean Soup

It is worth making extra Baked Beans in order to have some leftovers to make this delicious soup.

(8 CUPS)

3 cups (¾ L) Baked Beans
  (p. 324)
1 onion, chopped
2 stalks celery, chopped
1½ cups (3½ dL) canned
  tomatoes

1½ teaspoons chili powder
Salt
Freshly ground pepper

Put the baked beans, onion, celery, tomatoes, and chili powder in a large pot with 6 cups water. Bring to a boil, reduce heat, and simmer, partially covered, for 30 minutes. Mash and beat until smooth or purée in a blender or food processor. Reheat, adding salt and pepper to taste.

Black Bean Soup

Black bean soup has a distinct personality. Robust and nourishing, it can be a complete meal in itself.

(8–10 CUPS)

2 cups (½ L) dried black beans
1 onion, sliced
2 stalks celery, chopped
1 ham bone
1½ cups (3½ dL) cooked ham
    chunks

1½ teaspoons dry mustard
2 tablespoons lemon juice
Salt to taste
Freshly ground pepper

Soak the beans, if necessary, overnight in water to cover (or see p. 323). Drain the beans and add enough cold water to the soaking liquid to make 2 quarts. Put the beans and water in a soup pot and add the onion, celery, and ham bone. Bring to a boil, then lower the heat and simmer, partially covered, for 3–4 hours or until the beans are soft, adding more water to replace any that evaporates. Remove the ham bone. Purée in a blender or food processor, or beat by hand. Add the cooked ham and reheat, seasoning with mustard, lemon juice, salt, and a generous amount of pepper.

Black Bean Soup with Sherry. Omit the lemon juice and add *sherry to taste* during the final seasoning.

Black Bean Soup with Rice. Top each serving with a tablespoonful of *hot cooked rice* and a sprinkling of *chopped onion*.

Black Bean Soup with Lemon and Egg. Top with a thin slice of *lemon* and a slice or two of *hard-cooked egg*.

Cream of Jerusalem Artichoke Soup

This soup has the delicate, unusual flavor of the Jerusalem artichoke, a root vegetable, sometimes called sunchoke, that was once very common in this country (see p. 359).

(4–5 CUPS)

1 pound (450 g) Jerusalem
    artichokes (about 4 large)
2 tablespoons butter
2 tablespoons flour
Dash of cayenne pepper

Dash of nutmeg
1 cup (¼ L) cream
½ cup (1 dL) milk
Salt to taste

Peel the Jerusalem artichokes with a potato peeler and drop them into cold acidulated water—a few drops of lemon juice will suffice. Save ⅓ of a large raw artichoke to dice fine just before serving and use as a garnish. Bring 4 cups water to a boil and add the remaining artichokes, cut in half. Cook them briskly, in a partially covered pot, for about 30 minutes or until they are just soft. Put the artichokes and the cooking liquid through a strainer or food mill or purée them in an electric blender or food processor. Melt the butter in a large pot, stir in the flour, cayenne, and nutmeg, and cook, stirring, for 3 or 4 minutes. Gradually stir in the puréed artichoke mixture and bring to a boil, stirring until smooth and thick. Just before serving, add cream, milk, and salt and reheat. Put a little of the reserved diced artichoke in each bowl of soup.

Bean and Vegetable Soup

Great Northern beans or pea beans are good choices for this soup.

(9 CUPS)

1 cup (¼ L) dried white beans
2-inch cube salt pork, diced small
2 cloves garlic, minced
1 onion, chopped
1 leek, sliced thin
2 carrots, sliced thin
1 cup (¼ L) diced zucchini or summer squash
4 fresh tomatoes, peeled and chopped, or 2 cups (½ L) canned tomatoes
1½ cups (3½ dL) coarsely chopped cabbage
Salt
Freshly ground pepper
Freshly grated Parmesan cheese

Soak the beans overnight in water to cover or use quick method, p. 323. Add enough water to the soaking liquid to make 6 cups. Set aside. Cook the salt pork in a small skillet over very low heat until it gives up its fat. Strain the fat and put 2 tablespoonfuls in a large soup pot; set aside the crisp scraps. Heat the fat and add the garlic, onion, leek, carrots, and squash. Cook over low heat, adding a little more fat or vegetable oil if necessary, for about 15 minutes. Stir in the tomatoes and the soaked beans and reserved liquid. Partially cover and simmer for about 1 hour, until the beans and the vegetables are tender. Add the cabbage and cook 15 minutes more. Add the pork scraps and salt and pepper to taste, and reheat before serving. Pass the Parmesan cheese separately.

Cream of Pea Soup

A fresh pea flavor with just a hint of sweetness.

(4 CUPS)

2 tablespoons butter
1 tablespoon chopped onion
2 cups (½ L) fresh or frozen peas
½ teaspoon sugar
1 cup (¼ L) milk or cream
Salt to taste

Melt the butter in a pot, add the onion, and cook, stirring, until transparent. Add the peas, sugar, and 2 cups water, cover, and cook until the peas are tender. Put through a strainer or vegetable mill or purée in a food processor or electric blender. Return to the pot, add the milk or cream and salt, and reheat before serving.

Clear Tomato Soup

A fresh, spicy flavor; fine hot or cold.

(4 CUPS)

2½ pounds (1¼ kg) fresh tomatoes, or 1 quart (1 L) canned
2 stalks celery, chopped
1 carrot, sliced
1 onion, chopped
1 small green pepper, chopped
3 whole cloves
2 tablespoons lemon juice
Salt
Freshly ground pepper

Cut up the tomatoes and put them and 1 cup water in a soup pot. Add the celery, carrot, onion, green pepper, and cloves. Bring to the boiling point, reduce heat, and simmer for 15 minutes. Strain and season with lemon juice and salt and pepper to taste.

Cream of Tomato Soup

Some consider it old-fashioned to add baking soda to cream of tomato soup, but it does seem to improve the taste.

(6 CUPS)

4 cups (1 L) milk or light
   cream
½ cup (1 dL) dry bread crumbs
½ onion, stuck with 6 cloves
Parsley sprig
½ bay leaf
2 teaspoons sugar

2 cups (½ L) chopped fresh or
   canned tomatoes
¼ teaspoon baking soda
4 tablespoons butter
Salt
Freshly ground pepper

Put the milk or cream in a pot and add the bread crumbs, onion with cloves, parsley, bay leaf, and sugar. Simmer gently over medium heat for about 5 minutes. Remove from heat and discard the onion with cloves and the bay leaf. Add the tomatoes and baking soda and simmer gently for about 15 minutes. Put through a strainer or vegetable mill or purée in a food processor or blender. Return to pot, add the butter and salt and pepper to taste, and reheat, stirring until the butter melts and the soup is very hot.

Leek and Potato Soup

Leeks tend to be gritty and need careful cleaning: cut off the roots and the coarse green tops, cut lengthwise through the remaining green tops starting within an inch of the white bottom, gently separate the stiff leaves, and rinse well under cold, running water.

(8 CUPS)

3 tablespoons butter
4 leeks, sliced very thin
3 stalks celery, sliced very thin
2 medium potatoes, peeled and
   diced

3 cups (¾ L) milk
Salt
Freshly ground pepper

Melt the butter in a large pot and add the leeks and celery. Cook for about 10 minutes over moderate heat, stirring often. Stir in 1 cup water, cover, and cook 10 minutes more. Add the potatoes and 2 more cups water, cover, and cook 10 minutes. Stir in the milk, cover, and cook until the potatoes are just tender, about 10 minutes more. Add salt and pepper to taste.

Cream of Vegetable Soup

Light in flavor and consistency, a good way to use leftover cooked vegetables.

(4 CUPS)

1 cup (¼ L) cooked vegetables	Salt
3 cups (¾ L) milk	Freshly ground pepper
2 slices onion	

Put the vegetables, milk, and onion in a saucepan and simmer, partially covered, for 20 minutes. Remove from heat; put through a strainer or vegetable mill or purée in a blender or food processor. Reheat, adding salt and pepper to taste.

Corn Chowder

You can use commercially frozen corn in this soup, but fresh summer corn is better. Cut the kernels from leftover ears of corn, cooked or uncooked. You can freeze them, if necessary, until you're ready to make this chowder.

(10 CUPS)

2-inch cube salt pork, diced small	2 cups (½ L) corn kernels
	3 cups (¾ L) milk
1 onion, finely chopped	3 tablespoons butter
4 medium potatoes, peeled and diced	Salt
	Freshly ground pepper

Cook the salt pork slowly in a deep pan until the fat has melted and the pieces are brown. Pour off all but 2 tablespoons of the fat, add the onion, and cook for 5 minutes. Add the potatoes and 3 cups water, cover, and cook until the potatoes are just tender. Add the corn and milk and cook 5 minutes more. Before serving, add the butter and salt and pepper to taste, and reheat.

Parsnip Stew

Parsnips are of the carrot family and have a faint sweetness. This soup has a nice, old-fashioned character.

(5 CUPS)

1½-inch cube salt pork, diced small	2 cups (½ L) milk
	1 tablespoon butter
2 medium parsnips, scraped and diced	1 tablespoon flour
	Salt
2 medium potatoes, peeled and diced	Freshly ground pepper

Cook the salt pork slowly in a pot until the fat has melted and the pieces are crisp. Pour off all but 1 tablespoon of fat, add the parsnips and potatoes, and cook for 5 minutes. Add 1½ cups water, cover, and cook about 15 minutes, until the vegetables are tender. Stir in the milk and keep over low heat. Melt the butter in a small pan and stir in the flour. Cook slowly, stirring, for 2 or 3 minutes. Add a little of the hot stew liquid and blend. Pour into the stew and cook for about 10 minutes until thick and hot. Add salt and pepper to taste.

Onion Soup

Allow about 45 minutes to cook the onions. Very slow cooking will give them a deep golden color and release their full flavor.

(4 CUPS)

3 tablespoons butter
4 cups (1 L) thinly sliced
   onions
½ teaspoon sugar
1 tablespoon flour
Salt

Freshly ground pepper
4 slices dried or toasted French
   bread
½ cup (1 dL) freshly grated
   Parmesan cheese

Melt the butter in a large pot, add the onions, and cook them very slowly over low heat, stirring often. Stir in the sugar and flour and cook for 3 minutes. Add 4 cups water and simmer, partially covered, for 30 minutes. Add salt and pepper to taste. Serve with a slice of French bread in each bowl. Pass the Parmesan cheese separately.

Onion Soup with Melted Parmesan Cheese. Before serving, sprinkle each filled bowl generously with grated Parmesan cheese and set the bowls in a 400°F (205° C) oven until the cheese is melted and brown.

Winter Squash Soup

Puréed pumpkin (p. 407) may be used instead of squash.

(5 CUPS)

1 cup (¼ L) mashed cooked
   winter squash
1 quart (1 L) milk
2 tablespoons grated onion

½ teaspoon powdered ginger
2 tablespoons butter
3 tablespoons flour
Salt

Mix the squash, milk, onion, and ginger in a pot and cook over moderate heat about ten minutes. Melt the butter in a small pan, stir in the flour, and cook several minutes until smooth and thick. Pour a little of the soup into the butter-flour mixture, stirring until blended, then slowly pour into the soup. Add salt to taste. Continue to cook, stirring frequently, until very hot.

Scotch Broth

Inexpensive cuts of lamb will give this soup the best flavor. Be patient and try to trim off as much of the fat as possible.

(8 CUPS)

3 pounds (1⅓ kg) lamb breast
   or neck
½ cup (1 dL) barley
2 tablespoons butter
2 carrots, finely diced
2 stalks celery, finely diced

1 small white turnip, peeled
   and diced
1 medium onion, finely diced
Salt
Freshly ground pepper

Remove most of the fat from the meat and cut meat into small pieces. Put it in a pot with 8 cups cold water. Bring to a boil and stir in the barley. Simmer, partially covered, for 1½ hours or until the meat and barley are tender, adding more water if any evaporates. Remove the meat from the bones. Cool the soup and skim off the fat. Melt the butter in a skillet and add the carrots, celery, turnip, and onion. Cook over low heat, stirring often, for 10 minutes. Add to the soup. Season with salt and pepper to taste, and cook for another 10 minutes or until the vegetables are tender. Serve piping hot.

Split Pea Soup

Whoever owned the 1912 edition of the *Fannie Farmer Cook Book* in which we found this recipe had written neatly alongside it: "Good." And she was right.

(10–12 CUPS)

1½ cups (3½ dL) dried split
    peas
Ham bone (optional)
2-inch cube salt pork
1 onion, chopped

3 tablespoons butter
2 tablespoons flour
2 cups (½ L) milk
Salt
Freshly ground pepper

Soak the peas overnight in water to cover or use quick method (see p. 323). Add enough water to the soaking liquid to make 2½ quarts. Put the peas and liquid in a large soup pot and the ham bone, if you are using it, and the salt pork and onion. Bring to a boil, reduce heat, and simmer, partially covered, for 1½–2 hours or until the peas are soft. Discard the salt pork. Put through a strainer or vegetable mill or purée the soup in a blender or food processor. Melt the butter in a small saucepan, stir in the flour, and cook over low heat for a few minutes. Add the milk, stirring constantly, and cook until smooth and thickened. Stir this sauce into the soup and add salt and pepper to taste.

Yogurt Soups

These are much lighter than the usual cold soups with a cream base and the yogurt gives a pleasant tangy taste. They're easy to make in a blender or food processor.

(4 CUPS)

2 peeled and seeded cucumbers
    or avocados or 2 cups (½ L)
    cooked beets
3 cups (¾ L) yogurt

2 scallions or 1 tablespoon
    chopped onion
Salt

Garnish

8 thin slices cucumber and 1
    tablespoon dill (for the
    cucumber)
4 slices lime (for the avocado)

4 tablespoons shredded beets,
    raw or cooked
Additional dollop yogurt or
    sour cream (optional)

Spin the cucumbers, avocados, or beets in a blender or food processor with the yogurt and scallions or onion until just smooth. Salt to taste and chill. Serve in chilled bowls with the suggested garnishes.

FISH SOUPS

Old-fashioned Fish Chowder

Use the head and bones from the filleted fish to make a rich fish stock for this chowder. If you can, let the chowder mellow in the refrigerator for a day before you eat it. Serve it with common crackers.

(10 CUPS)

2-inch cube salt pork, diced small
2 onions, thinly sliced
3 medium potatoes, peeled and diced
4 cups (1 L) Fish Stock (p. 83) or Clam Broth (p. 84) or juice

2 pounds (900 g) fillet of cod, haddock, or any firm white fish
2 cups (½ L) cream or milk
2 tablespoons butter
Salt
Freshly ground pepper

Cook the salt pork very slowly in a small skillet until the fat has melted and the scraps are brown. Strain, setting aside the crisp scraps, and put 2 tablespoons of the fat in a soup pot. Heat the fat, add the onions, and cook over low heat until golden. Stir in the potatoes and toss until well coated. Add the fish stock or clam liquid. Cut the fish in chunks, add it to the pot, and simmer, partially covered, for about 15 minutes, or until the fish is cooked through and the potatoes are tender. Stir in the cream or milk and heat slowly, without boiling. Add the pork scraps. Just before serving, stir in the butter, add salt and pepper to taste, and heat until butter melts.

Connecticut Fish Chowder (11 cups, 2¾ L). Omit the cream and substitute 4 *cups canned tomatoes, undrained.* If you wish, you may add ½ *teaspoon dried marjoram or thyme* along with the tomatoes.

Crab Bisque

A creamy texture and delicate taste. The faint flavor of onion and chicken broth does not overpower the crab.

(5 CUPS)

2 tablespoons butter
1 teaspoon finely chopped onion
1 tablespoon finely chopped parsley
1½ cups (3½ dL) chopped crabmeat, fresh-cooked, canned, or frozen

2 tablespoons flour
2 cups (½ L) Chicken Stock (p. 81) or canned broth
2 cups (½ L) light cream
Pinch of cayenne pepper
Salt

Melt the butter in a saucepan, add the onion, and cook slowly until golden. Add the parsley and crabmeat and cook over low heat, stirring often, for 5 minutes. Add the flour, stir to blend, and cook 3 minutes. Stir in the chicken broth and simmer, partially covered, for 20 minutes. Add the cream and cayenne pepper. Heat and add salt to taste before serving.

Lobster Bisque

A splendid soup with an excellent bouquet of flavors. Have the lobster killed and split at the market, if you can then cook it promptly. Or follow the directions on p. 133.

(8 CUPS)

2 cups (½ L) Beef Stock
   (p. 79) or bouillon
¼ cup (½ dL) rice
3 tablespoons butter
1 carrot, sliced
1 onion, chopped
¼ bay leaf
½ teaspoon dried thyme
1½ pounds (675 g) lobster,
   killed and split

1 cup (¼ L) dry white wine
4 cups (1 L) Chicken Stock
   (p. 81) or canned broth
1 tablespoon tomato paste
Lobster liver, if any
Lobster coral, if any
1 cup (¼ L) cream
Salt
Freshly ground pepper

Put the beef stock and rice in a saucepan, cover, and cook over moderate heat until the rice is done, about 15 minutes. Set aside. Melt 2 tablespoons of the butter in a large pot, add the carrot and onion, and cook slowly for 5 minutes. Add the bay leaf, thyme, and lobster, cover, and cook until the lobster shells are red, about 10 minutes. Add the wine and chicken stock, and simmer, partially covered, for another 15 minutes. Remove the lobster and strain the broth. Add the undrained cooked rice to the broth. Remove the lobster meat from the shell and cut it into bite-size pieces. Add it to the broth. Melt the remaining tablespoon of butter in a small pan and stir in the tomato paste and any lobster liver or coral. Cook until smooth, then add to the soup. Stir in the cream, add salt and pepper to taste, and heat to serving temperature without allowing the soup to boil.

Shrimp Bisque

Shrimp vary in size: small or medium-size ones are best in this soup.

(4 CUPS)

1¼ pounds (565 g) fresh
   shrimp, or 1 cup (¼ L)
   shelled or cooked
3 tablespoons butter
2 tablespoons finely chopped
   celery
¼ cup (½ dL) finely chopped
   mushrooms
¼ onion, finely chopped

¼ carrot, finely chopped
¼ bay leaf
Pinch of marjoram
Pinch of nutmeg
1 tablespoon lemon juice
2 cups (½ L) Chicken Stock
   (p. 81) or canned broth
1 cup (¼ L) cream or milk
Salt

Wash the shrimp, remove the shells, and devein them. If they are large, cut them in small pieces. Set aside. Melt the butter in a pot and add the celery, mushrooms, onion, carrot, bay leaf, marjoram, and nutmeg. Cook slowly, stirring occasionally, for 10 minutes. Add the lemon juice and chicken stock, cover partially, and simmer for 15 minutes. Add the shrimp and simmer for about 5 minutes, until they are cooked and pink. Add the cream or milk and heat, but do not allow to boil. Add salt to taste.

Clam and Tomato Bisque

(3 CUPS)

1 cup (¼ L) Clam Broth
  (p. 84)
1 cup (¼ L) peeled and stewed
  tomatoes or chopped canned
  tomatoes
1 cup (¼ L) milk or cream
Pinch of nutmeg

1 stalk celery, coarsely chopped
Parsley sprig
Small piece of bay leaf
3 tablespoons finely chopped
  onion
Salt

Simmer the clam broth and tomatoes together for 10–15 minutes. Stir in the milk or cream, nutmeg, celery, parsley, bay leaf, and onion. Heat slowly, without boiling. Strain and reheat, adding salt to taste before serving.

Oyster Soup

(6 CUPS)

4 cups (1 L) milk
1 thick slice onion
2 stalks celery with leaves
¼ teaspoon nutmeg
2 parsley sprigs
Small piece of bay leaf
2 cups (½ L) shucked or
  canned oysters and their
  juice

3 tablespoons butter
3 tablespoons flour
Salt
Pinch of cayenne pepper

Put the milk, onion, celery, nutmeg, parsley, and bay leaf in a pot, together with any oyster juice. Simmer for 15 minutes, then strain. Add the oysters and simmer for 10 minutes more. Melt the butter in a small pan, stir in the flour, and cook, stirring, for 3 minutes. Slowly add about 1 cup of the oyster mixture, stirring constantly, and cook until smooth and thick. Stir the thickened mixture into the remaining milk and oyster soup. Add salt to taste and the cayenne pepper and stir until smooth. Serve hot.

Mildred's Oyster Stew

Very fresh butter, milk, and cream will give this stew a pure, wonderful flavor.

(6 CUPS)

2 cups (½ L) milk
2 cups (½ L) light cream
2 cups (½ L) shucked or
  canned oysters and their
  juice

Salt
3 tablespoons butter

Heat the milk and cream in a pot; do not boil. Add the oysters and any oyster juice and simmer for 5 minutes. Season to taste with salt. Add the butter, heat until it melts, and serve very hot.

New England Clam Chowder

Raw, shucked clams and their undiluted juices are best for chowder; brief cooking in the chowder will keep the juice full of flavor and the clams very tender. Since it takes some skill and practice to shuck them easily, see if you can have this done for you at the fish store. Or steam the clams in a little water (see p. 84) until they open, and use them and the broth for the chowder. Clams are also available in cans and clam juice in bottles; these products will produce an acceptable chowder.

(9 CUPS)

3–4 cups (¾–1 L) shucked or steamed chowder clams, with their juice or broth
1½-inch cube salt pork, diced small
1 onion, finely chopped
2 tablespoons flour

3 medium potatoes, peeled and diced
3 cups (¾ L) milk
3 tablespoons butter
Salt
Freshly ground pepper

Measure the clam juice or broth from the shucked or steamed clams and add water, if necessary, to make 2½ cups. Cut the clams in small pieces and set aside. Cook the salt pork slowly in a small skillet until the fat has melted and the scraps are brown. Strain, set aside the scraps, and put 2 tablespoons of the fat in a large pot. Heat the fat, add the onion, and cook slowly until golden. Sprinkle the flour over the onion and cook, stirring, for 3 minutes. Add the potatoes and clam juice or broth. Cover and simmer 10 minutes. Add the clams and simmer 10 minutes more, or until the clams are cooked and the potatoes are tender. Add the milk, butter, and salt and pepper to taste, and heat until the butter has melted. Serve with a few crisp pork bits in each bowl.

Manhattan Clam Chowder

To prepare clams for chowder, see preceding recipe for New England Clam Chowder.

(6 CUPS)

2 cups (½ L) shucked or steamed chowder clams, with their juice or broth
1½-inch cube salt pork, diced small
1 onion, finely chopped
1 medium potato, peeled and diced

2 cups (½ L) stewed peeled tomatoes or chopped canned tomatoes
¼ teaspoon thyme
Salt
Freshly ground pepper

Measure the clam juice or broth from the shucked or steamed clams and add water, if necessary, to make 2½ cups. Cut the clams in small pieces and set aside. Cook the salt pork slowly in a small skillet until the fat melts and the scraps are brown. Strain, set aside the scraps, and put 2 tablespoons of the fat in a large pot. Heat the fat, add the onion, and cook until limp. Stir in the potatoes and clam juice. Cover and simmer 10 minutes. Add the tomatoes and simmer 10 minutes more. Stir in the clams and thyme, and cook for another 5–10 minutes, until the clams and the potatoes are done. Add salt and pepper to taste. Serve with a few crisp pork bits in each bowl.

Cream of Scallop Soup

(6 CUPS)

4 cups milk	4 cups (1 L) scallops, cut up
½ onion stuck with 2 cloves	3 tablespoons flour
½ bay leaf	Salt
5 tablespoons butter	Freshly ground pepper

Put the milk, onion with cloves, bay leaf, and 2 tablespoons of the butter in a large pot. Simmer, partially covered, for 15 minutes. Remove the onion with cloves and the bay leaf. Add the scallops and continue to simmer for 10 minutes. Melt the remaining 3 tablespoons of butter in a small pan and stir in the flour. Cook, stirring, for 5 minutes, then slowly add 1 cup of the soup, stirring until thick and smooth. Add this thickened mixture to the scallop soup, season to taste with salt and pepper, and stir until well blended and hot.

Cioppino

From Fisherman's Wharf, San Francisco: half Italian, all-American. This is really more of a stew than a soup and is usually served as a main course.

(SERVES SIX)

2 large onions, chopped	3 pounds (1⅓ kg) clams in
3 carrots, chopped	shell, scrubbed
3 cloves garlic, mashed	2 pounds (900 g) white fish
½ cup (1 dL) olive oil	fillets
1 cup (¼ L) chopped parsley	2 crabs, cooked and cracked
4 cups tomato sauce	¼ cup (½ dL) dry white wine
1½ teaspoons thyme, crumbled	Pinch of cayenne pepper
1 tablespoon basil, crumbled	Salt

In a large kettle, sauté the onions, carrots, and garlic in olive oil until the onions are soft. Add the parsley, tomato sauce, 2 cups water, thyme, and basil. Partially cover and simmer 45 minutes. If the soup gets too thick, add a little water. Add the clams and simmer 10 minutes. Add the white fish and crab, and simmer 5 minutes. Stir in the wine, cayenne pepper, and salt to taste, and simmer 10 minutes more. Ladle some of each variety of fish and shellfish into each bowl with a generous helping of broth.

FISH & SHELLFISH

ABOUT FISH AND SHELLFISH

America's coastal waters are rich with bounty—cod, swordfish, bass, various kinds of sole, bluefish, red snapper, pompano, mackerel, and others—and the fish lover has a wide variety to choose from. Inland the catch is more limited—trout, bass, perch, pickerel, catfish, and the like—and they are more often caught by sportsmen so are not readily available in supermarkets. But a good deal of coastal fish is shipped now all around the country and it is worth finding a market that handles it so that you can enjoy the delicious flavor of fresh fish at least once in a while.

Too many people have been put off by fish either because they *had to* eat it or because they have been subjected to it when it has been poorly prepared. The greatest enemy of fish is overcooking; next to that is frying it in deep fat—often not very fresh fat. Respect fish by giving it only the briefest cooking in a minimum of fat and by flavoring it delicately—as in the recipes that follow—and you will have the finest example of a perfect food. Fish has been recognized for its high-protein, low-calorie nutritional value, and thus it is not only a joy to the palate but eminently good for you. Try to make it a regular part of your diet.

Americans seem to have a more instinctive love of shellfish. A lobster or a shore dinner is considered a great treat. And look at how much shrimp we consume. Perhaps this is because shellfish are now considered a luxury, though that was certainly not the case in the nineteenth century when oysters, lobsters, and crab were so abundant that they were used almost profligately in American cooking. Many an old recipe, for instance, calls for oysters in a stuffing or to fill out a pie—a luxury today (but one that's still fun to indulge in for the superb taste they give).

Unlike fish, which have scales and fins and an interior skeleton, shellfish are either mollusks or crustaceans. Mollusks are shellfish without legs, such as oysters

104

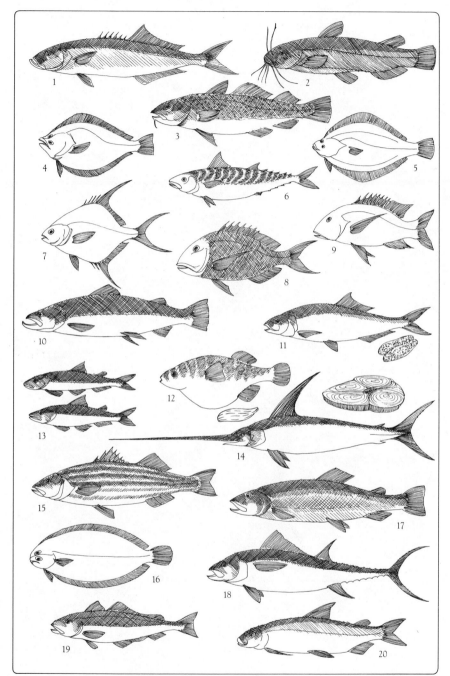

1. *bluefish;* 2. *catfish;* 3. *cod;* 4. *halibut;* 5. *flounder;* 6. *mackerel;* 7. *pompano;*
8. *porgy;* 9. *red snapper;* 10. *salmon;* 11. *shad and roe;* 12. *blowfish and meat* (*sea squab*); 13. *smelts;* 14. *swordfish and steak;* 15. *striped bass;* 16. *sole;* 17. *trout;*
18. *tuna;* 19. *whiting;* 20. *whitefish.*   Note: *fish are not drawn to scale.*

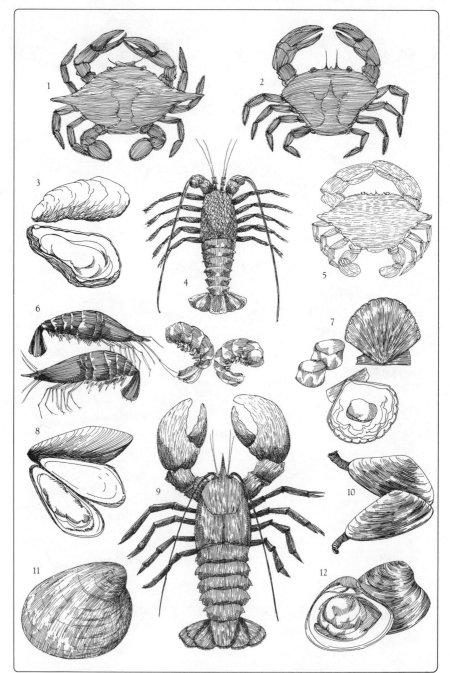

1. *blue crab*; 2. *rock crab*; 3. *oyster*; 4. *crayfish*; 5. *soft-shell crab*; 6. *shrimp (whole and shelled)*; 7. *scallops*; 8. *mussels*; 9. *lobster*; 10. *soft-shell clam*; 11. *abalone*; 12. *hard-shell clam*.

and scallops; some have one shell, while others have two. Crustaceans are shellfish that move about by means of claws and a tail.

Buying Fresh Fish and Shellfish

Buy the freshest fish you can get. Fresh fish has the clean scent of the sea; fresh-water fish should have barely any smell at all. Never buy fish that has a strong fishy odor. The eyes and skin should be shiny and bright, the scales tight to the skin, and the gills clear red; you may have to pull back the covering flap to check on this. The flesh should be firm to the touch, springing back when it is pressed. If fish looks dull, if its eyes are sunken, if it is soft to the touch or has a strong fishy odor, don't buy it. You won't be able to fix it up or to disguise the off-taste.

Allow ¾ pound of fish with bone per serving, and ⅓ to ½ pound of boneless steaks or fillets. Fish is sold whole; drawn (that is, gutted); dressed (drawn, with scales and fins removed); split (dressed and cut in half, with the backbone removed); and cut up into steaks, chunks, fillets, or sticks.

Boned fish is easier to eat than unboned, but is less flavorful. If you are going to cook a whole fish, leave on the head and tail. If you can't stand having the head looking up at you, at least don't let the fishmonger throw it away; save it for making fish stock and enriching a sauce.

Like fish, shellfish should always be bought impeccably fresh. As a matter of fact, much seafood is alive when purchased—lobsters, clams, oysters, mussels, soft-shell crabs. Shrimp today has usually traveled from its source frozen, unfortunately, so what you're buying has probably been thawed. It deteriorates quickly, so smell it for freshness and feel whether it has gone soft; this is difficult with a plastic, sealed wrap, so try to avoid buying shrimp that way.

Buying Frozen Fish and Shellfish

Fresh fish is always preferable to frozen or canned. However, for many people in inland areas of the country, frozen fish is what is primarily available, and if you shop carefully, you will get quite a variety now that has been flash-frozen (rapidly at a very low temperature) successfully. If it is handled well by the various purveyors, there is no reason why it shouldn't be fine. Select only solidly frozen packages; if there is ice on the outside of the box, it may have been thawed and then refrozen, and this can ruin fish. If there is any odor at all, don't buy it. Take frozen fish home and put it in your freezer immediately. Defrost it slowly, preferably in the refrigerator. It is best prepared with a sauce or lively seasoning, since it does not have quite the lovely pure taste of fresh fish.

Storing Fish and Shellfish

Do not keep any fish longer than two days without freezing it. When you bring it home, rinse it thoroughly under cold running water and pat it dry with paper towels. Cover loosely with wax paper so that the air can circulate around it, and store in the coldest part of the refrigerator, preferably on a bed of ice.

Shellfish is very perishable and should be used as quickly as possible. Fresh crab and shrimp can be frozen, but they will lose something in taste and texture. Hard-shell seafood, like oysters, clams, and mussels, can't be frozen, but they will keep several days, if you store them on ice in the refrigerator, pouring off water as it accumulates.

Scaling Fish and Removing Fins

Cover a table or counter top with newspaper. Take hold of the fish tail with a clean cloth, and scrape off the scales, using a fish scaler or a straight sharp knife. Scrape from the tail toward the head, slanting the knife slightly to keep the scales from flying. Turn the fish over and repeat on the other side.

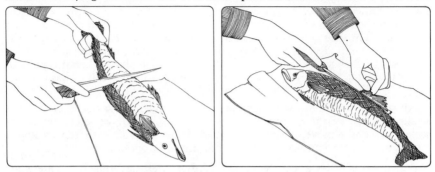

To remove the fins, insert the tip of the knife at one end of the fin. Run the blade up one side of the fin and then down the other, tilting the blade so that the cuts meet. Lift out the fin with a tug.

Cleaning Fish

Lay newspapers on a table or counter top. Cut a gash in the underside of the fish with scissors or a sharp knife, slitting from the anal opening to the head. Cut at the throat where attached and remove the entrails; rinse under running water to get rid of any clotted blood clinging to the backbone. Wipe inside and out with a paper towel or a damp cloth.

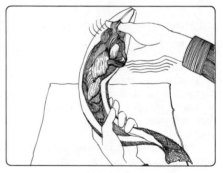

Skinning Fish

Cut off a narrow strip of skin along the entire length of the backbone. Loosen the skin on one side from the bony part of the gills. If the flesh is very firm, the skin will peel off easily. If it is soft, you will have to work slowly and carefully, pushing the flesh away from the skin with the back of the knife. Turn over and skin the other side.

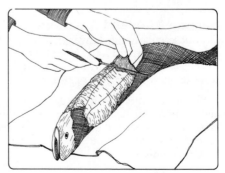

Boning Fish

Lay the fish on newspapers on a table or counter top. Beginning at the tail, run a long sharp knife under the flesh close to the backbone. Follow the bone for its entire length, making as clean a cut as possible. Cut away the flesh, laying the knife flat, and lift it off in one piece. Turn over and repeat, cutting off the flesh from the other side. Pick out any small bones that remain.

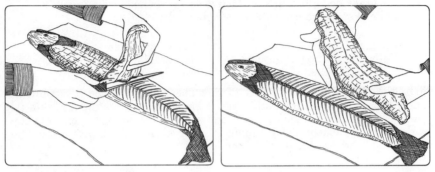

Cooking Fish

Fish should be moist when it is served, but it is commonly so overcooked that it is dry and tasteless. Many books recommend that it be cooked until it is flaky, a measurement that results in overdone fish. If the fish is cooked whole, probe with a fork to look at the flesh around the bone. When this is opaque (usually white, or pink in the case of salmon) and no longer raw-looking, and when it pulls away easily from the bone, the fish is done. Fillets are done when the flesh has turned opaque at the thickest part.

Using Leftover Fish and Shellfish

Leftover fish and shellfish will last two or three days if it is well chilled and covered. Too often, little bits are thrown away that could be used to good advantage in a salad, a crêpe, or an omelet. Larger pieces can be stretched by garnishing with quartered hard-boiled eggs, tomato wedges, and black olives, and serving with homemade mayonnaise with herbs or a yogurt dressing. Save fish heads and skeletons to use in a court bouillon or a fish soup, lobster shells and shrimp peelings for seafood bisques.

Using Canned Fish

The familiar small flat can of tuna delivers honest value and has aided many a fledgling cook in preparing a tasty dish for little money. Canned salmon is also a provider of good and thrifty meals. Canned shrimp, clams, and mackerel have their uses, too. There is a difference among brands; experiment until you discover the brand that pleases you. Use canned and leftover cooked fish interchangeably in recipes.

FISH

Broiled Bluefish

A dark-fleshed fish with a distinctive flavor, young bluefish is delicate and makes superb eating when simply broiled.

(SERVES TWO)

1 lemon	2 teaspoons butter
1½-pound (675-g) bluefish, split and boned	Salt
	Sprinkling of fresh herbs

Preheat the broiler. Squeeze half the lemon over the fish and let it sit while the broiler heats. Smear a little butter on the broiler rack. Place the fish, skin side down, on the rack, sprinkle with salt, and dot with remaining butter. Broil close to the broiling element about 6 minutes. Do not turn. Serve with a sprinkling of herbs and the remaining half of the lemon, cut in wedges.

Bluefish Baked with Aromatic Vegetables

A particularly good way to cook larger bluefish fillets. They are also tasty when baked like mackerel over potatoes with bacon, tomatoes, and peppers (p. 114).

(SERVES FOUR)

4 tablespoons butter	2 tablespoons chopped parsley
1 onion, chopped	¼ cup (½ dL) dry white wine
1 carrot, chopped	3–4-pound (1⅓–1¾-kg)
1 stalk celery, chopped	bluefish, split and boned
¼ pound (115 g) mushrooms, chopped	Salt
	⅛ teaspoon paprika

Preheat the oven to 425°F (220°C). Heat the butter in a flameproof baking dish large enough to accommodate the fish. Add the onion, carrot, celery, mushrooms, and parsley, and cook, stirring often, for about 5 minutes. Add the wine and cook 3–4 minutes more. Remove half the vegetables, lay the fish on top. Cover with the remaining vegetables, and sprinkle with salt and paprika. Cover loosely with foil, and bake 20 minutes.

Stuffed Baked Buffalofish

Buffalofish is bony with firm white flesh.

(SERVES THREE OR FOUR)

1 whole buffalofish, about 4 pounds (1⅘ kg), dressed	5 tablespoons butter
½ recipe Celery Stuffing (p. 280)	Salt
	Lemon wedges

Preheat the oven to 450°F (230°C). Cover the bottom of a baking dish with heavy-duty foil and butter the foil. Rinse the fish inside and out under cold running water; pat dry with paper towels. Fill with the stuffing and close with skewers. Rub the outside of the fish with 2 tablespoons butter and sprinkle with salt. Melt the remaining butter with 3 tablespoons water. Place the fish on the foil and bake 30–40 minutes, basting every 10 minutes with the melted butter. The fish is done when the flesh around the bone is opaque. To serve, make a deep cut along the backbone, then cut into pieces at right angles to the backbone. Serve with lemon wedges.

Broiled Marinated Carp

Carp has lean, firm, rather tasteless flesh, and is particularly good when it is marinated and then broiled.

(SERVES FOUR)

3–4-pound (1⅓–1¾-kg) carp,
   dressed and split
⅓ cup (¾ dL) oil
½ cup (1 dL) thin onion rings
2 tablespoons lemon juice

1½ teaspoons salt
½ teaspoon freshly ground
   pepper
1½ teaspoons basil, crumbled

Rinse the carp with cold water and pat dry with paper towels. Combine the oil, onions, lemon juice, salt, pepper, basil, and 3 tablespoons water in a jar. Cover tightly and shake until well blended. Put the fish in a shallow baking dish, cover with the marinade, and let stand at room temperature for 1 hour. Preheat the broiler. Place the fish skin side down on a heavily buttered piece of foil in the broiler pan. Spoon on the marinade. Place the pan 4 inches beneath the broiler element and cook 10 minutes, until the meat is opaque throughout.

Pan-fried Catfish

A firm-flesh fish popular all over the southern United States, catfish is sold whole or in fillets. It can be fried, baked, or broiled. Pan fry whole catfish according to the recipe for Pan-fried Porgy (p. 116).

(SERVES THREE)

1½ pounds (675 g) catfish
   fillets
⅓ cup (¾ dL) flour
1½ teaspoons salt
½ teaspoon freshly ground
   pepper

2 eggs, slightly beaten
1 cup (¼ L) cornmeal
Oil for frying
Lemon wedges

Rinse the fish under cold water and pat dry with paper towels. Mix the flour with salt and pepper, and spread it on a piece of wax paper. Put the eggs in a shallow bowl and the cornmeal on another piece of wax paper. Lightly dust each fillet in the seasoned flour and shake off the excess. Dip the fillet into the egg. Hold over the bowl to let excess egg drip off. Dip into the cornmeal. Warm a platter in a 250°F (120°C) oven. In a large skillet, heat ¼ inch of oil. Put your hand over the oil in the skillet, and when you can feel a good amount of heat rising, put in the fish and brown on each side. This should take 1½–2 minutes on each side. Don't crowd the skillet; do only a few at a time. Remove to a paper towel to drain, transfer to the warmed platter, and continue frying the fillets. Serve with lemon wedges.

Foil-steamed Cod Steaks

Heavy foil, securely sealed around a piece of fish, serves much the same purpose as steaming: it locks in the juices so that the flavors are beautifully preserved. This process works on an outdoor grill as well, and is a clean and easy method of cooking. The package is brought right to the table, and the taste of a bland fish like cod, tilefish, halibut, or flounder is greatly enhanced.

(SERVES FOUR)

6 tablespoons butter
Four ½-pound (225-g) cod
  steaks
Salt
Freshly ground pepper
Juice of 1 lemon

2 tablespoons chopped parsley,
  chives and fresh basil,
  tarragon, chervil, or dill (or
  1 teaspoon dried)
Lemon wedges

Preheat the oven to 425°F (220°C). Liberally butter four pieces of aluminum foil large enough to enclose the fish steaks generously. Sprinkle the fish with salt, pepper, lemon juice, and herbs. Dot with remaining butter and wrap the foil around the fish, folding the edges to seal well. Place on a baking sheet and bake 15 minutes for fillets, 20 minutes for steaks 1 inch thick or more. Serve with lemon wedges.

Foil-steamed Cod with Mushrooms. Instead of using lemon juice, sprinkle a *few drops of white wine* over each piece of fish and spread with *1 tablespoon Mushroom Duxelles* (p. 389).

Foil-steamed Cod with Aromatic Vegetables. Sauté *1 carrot, chopped, 1 stalk celery, chopped,* and *1 onion, chopped,* in *2 tablespoons butter* for 5 minutes, then spread over the pieces of fish along with the lemon juice and herbs.

Halibut with Cheese Sauce

Halibut is a member of the flounder family. It has fine firm white meat and a delicate flavor. Steaks may be broiled like swordfish (p. 124) or baked like mackerel (p. 114).

(SERVES FOUR)

1½ pounds (675 g) halibut
  steak
1 onion, sliced
2 bay leaves, broken in pieces
4 tablespoons butter
4 tablespoons flour
2 cups (½ L) milk

1½ cups (3½ dL) grated
  Cheddar cheese
Freshly ground pepper
Salt
1 cup freshly made buttered
  bread crumbs

Preheat the oven to 350°F (180°C). Put the halibut steaks in a steamer and cover with the onion slices and bay leaves. Cover and steam 5 minutes. Meanwhile, melt the butter in a saucepan. Add the flour and blend until smooth. Slowly add the milk and stir over medium heat until smooth and thickened. Add the cheese and cook until melted. Add pepper and salt to taste. Cut the halibut into bite-size pieces, remove any bones, and place fish in a shallow, buttered casserole. Spoon the cheese sauce evenly over the halibut. Sprinkle with the bread crumbs and bake for 25 minutes.

Halibut Creole

In this recipe, as in many others, cod and halibut may be used interchangeably.

(SERVES FOUR)

1¾–2 pounds (800–900 g) halibut steaks
Salt
Freshly ground pepper
3 large tomatoes, peeled, seeded, and chopped
½ cup (1 dL) finely chopped green pepper

½ cup (1 dL) finely chopped onion
6 tablespoons butter
3 tablespoons lemon juice
⅛ teaspoon Tabasco

Preheat the oven to 400°F (205°C). Butter a shallow baking dish large enough to hold the fish in one layer, and place the fish in it. Season with salt and pepper to taste and spread the tomatoes, green pepper, and onion over the top. Melt the butter with the lemon juice and Tabasco and drizzle it over the fish and vegetables. Bake about 25 minutes, basting with pan juices every 10 minutes.

Hollendon Halibut

The salt pork melts into the fish, making it moist and delicious.

(SERVES FOUR)

⅛ pound (60 g) salt pork, sliced thin
1 onion, sliced thin
2 bay leaves
Two 1-pound (450-g) halibut steaks
Salt
Freshly ground pepper

4 tablespoons butter, softened
3 tablespoons flour
½ cup (1 dL) fresh bread crumbs
¼ teaspoon paprika
Chopped parsley
Lemon slices

Preheat the oven to 350°F (180°C). Place all but three or four slices of salt pork in the bottom of a shallow baking dish. Cover with onion and bay leaves and place halibut steaks on top. Season with salt lightly, pepper liberally. Cream together 3 tablespoons of the butter and the flour, and smear it over the fish. Cover with remaining salt pork slices, top with the bread crumbs, and dot with the remaining 1 tablespoon butter. Cover with foil and bake 40 minutes; remove foil and bake another 10 minutes to brown. Serve sprinkled with paprika and parsley and surrounded with lemon slices.

Steamed Ling Cod with Soy and Ginger

In spite of its name, ling cod is not a member of the cod family. It is sold whole or in fillets, fresh or frozen. It is excellent roasted, like pompano (p. 115), broiled, like shad (p. 119), or steamed Chinese-style with delicate seasonings.

Steamed Ling Cod with Soy and Ginger (continued)

(SERVES FOUR)

3-pound (1⅓-kg) ling cod,   4 tablespoons vegetable oil
  dressed   ½ teaspoon sesame seed oil
6 scallions, in 1-inch pieces   1 teaspoon soy sauce
4 slices fresh ginger root, in ½- 3 tablespoons dry sherry
  inch slices

Rinse the fish under cold water and pat dry. Make four or five 1½-inch incisions to the bone on each side of the fish. Put the scallions and ginger inside the cavity. If you don't have a steamer, use a roasting pan with a heatproof platter or rack to support the fish above the boiling water (p. 32). Place the fish on the steamer, cover, and cook 20–25 minutes, until the meat is opaque. In a small saucepan, whisk together the vegetable oil, sesame seed oil, soy sauce, and sherry. Heat and spoon over each portion of fish.

Mackerel Broiled in Milk

Small mackerel are good filleted and simply broiled with lemon, like bluefish (p. 110). Oily fish, they also take well to being grilled with milk. Whole fillets from a larger mackerel are delicious baked on a bed of potatoes with pungent flavorings to balance the richness of the fish as in the recipe that follows this one.

(SERVES FOUR)

1¾–2 pounds (800–900 g)   2 tablespoons chopped parsley
  mackerel fillets   1 tablespoon chopped fresh
¾ cup (1¾ dL) milk   dill, or 1 teaspoon dried,
Salt   crumbled
Freshly ground pepper

Preheat the broiler. Pour the milk in a baking dish large enough to hold the mackerel in one layer. Season the fillets with salt and pepper. Lay them in the dish and broil about 6 inches below the heat for 10 minutes, basting twice. Sprinkle with herbs and broil 5 minutes more.

Baked Mackerel Hungarian

(SERVES SIX)

6 medium potatoes   ¼ pound (115 g) bacon, in
2½ pounds (1¼ kg) large   1-inch slices
  mackerel fillets   1 teaspoon paprika
1 green pepper, sliced   1 cup (¼ L) sour cream, at
2 tomatoes, sliced   room temperature

Preheat the oven to 400°F (205°C). Peel and cut the potatoes into ¼-inch slices. Boil them in salted water for 5 minutes; drain and scatter over the bottom of a large buttered baking dish. Make slashes in the mackerel about ¾ inch apart and insert in each one a slice of green pepper, tomato, and bacon. Place the fish over the potatoes, sprinkle with paprika, and bake for 20 minutes. Spread with sour cream and bake 5 minutes more.

Ocean Perch Fillets, Filled and Baked

Ocean perch is the most common of the frozen fish fillets in our supermarkets. This easy cooking method lends tastiness to the rather bland, lean fish cut from a variety of large ocean fish: to be distinguished, incidentally, from small fresh lake perch, which should be cooked the way you would trout (p. 125). For this recipe you may substitute any other fillet, such as halibut, flounder, or sole.

(SERVES FOUR)

1¾–2 pounds (800–900 g) ocean perch or other fillets
Salt
Freshly ground pepper

2 tablespoons butter, melted
2 tablespoons lemon juice or dry vermouth
2 tablespoons heavy cream

Fillings

½ cup (1 dL) Bread Stuffing (p. 278), or
⅓ cup (¾ dL) Mushroom Duxelles (p. 389), or

½ cup (1 dL) finely chopped cooked seafood

Preheat the oven to 425°F (220°C). Butter a shallow casserole large enough to hold half the fillets in one layer. Lay down half the fish, and sprinkle with salt and pepper. Brush with half the butter and sprinkle with the lemon juice or vermouth. Spread with one of the fillings, and cover with the remaining fillets. Season again with salt, pepper, and remaining butter, and pour on the cream. Cover loosely with foil and bake 20–30 minutes, depending on the thickness of the fillets.

Whole Roasted Pompano

Serve these superb silvery fish from the Gulf of Mexico by roasting them simply, one to a person.

(SERVES TWO)

2 whole pompano, about ¾ pound (340 g) each
1 tablespoon oil

Salt
Freshly ground pepper
Lemon wedges

Preheat the oven to 400°F (205°C). Rub the fish with oil. Season lightly inside and out with salt and pepper. Bake in a shallow pan 25–30 minutes or until you see the skin bubbling slightly and swelling from the flesh—the sign that it is done. Serve with lemon wedges.

Pompano en Papillotte

A spectacular dish created at Antoine's restaurant in New Orleans. The fish is baked in "papillottes," heart-shaped pieces of parchment, 8 × 10 inches, which you oil lightly on the inside, fill with fish, and then seal with a tight, firm roll. When papillottes are pierced, the aromatic steam is released, whetting appetites. Aluminum foil can be substituted for parchment, but the presentation will not be the same.

Pompano en Papillotte (continued)

Three 1½-pound (675-g)
   pompano, filleted, with
   skeletons and heads reserved
1 carrot, chopped
1 onion, chopped
1 stalk celery, chopped
1½ cups dry white wine
Salt
⅛ teaspoon cayenne pepper

3 scallions, white part only,
   chopped
1 garlic clove, minced
5 tablespoons butter
2 cups small cooked shrimp
2 cups crabmeat
⅛ teaspoon thyme
1 bay leaf
2 tablespoons flour

Preheat the oven to 450°F (230°C). Make a stock with the fish skeletons and heads, the carrot, onion, celery, wine, and 2 cups water. Simmer for 40 minutes, then strain. Season the fillets with salt and cayenne pepper, put in a flameproof dish, and cover with the stock. Cover and simmer gently 5–6 minutes. Remove from heat and let rest in the liquid. In a skillet, sauté the scallions and garlic in 3 tablespoons of the butter. Add the shrimp, crabmeat, thyme, and bay leaf, and warm through. In a saucepan, melt the remaining butter. Add the flour and cook 2 minutes, until blended. Slowly add 1¼ cups of the stock and stir until thick. Stir in the shrimp and crabmeat mixture. Remove the bay leaf, and correct the seasoning. Now drain the fish, reserving the stock for another use. Place one fillet on one half of an oiled parchment heart or foil. Cover with one-sixth of the shrimp-crabmeat sauce, fold the paper over, and seal the edges. Repeat with the other parchments. Place on a large baking sheet and cook 15 minutes. Serve, still sealed, one to a person.

Pan-fried Porgy

A popular game fish in Atlantic waters, porgy is usually sold whole.

4 porgies, ½–¾ pound
   (225–340 g) each
½ cup (1 dL) cornmeal
½ teaspoon salt
Freshly ground pepper
4 tablespoons oil

1 clove garlic, minced
   (optional)
½ teaspoon marjoram or basil
1 lemon
1 tablespoon butter

Wash the porgies and pat dry. Season the cornmeal with salt and pepper, and dredge the fish. Heat the oil in a large skillet, and brown the fish quickly on both sides. Turn the heat to medium, add the garlic (if desired) and herbs, and cook 10–15 minutes. Remove to a warm platter. Squeeze half a lemon into the pan with the butter, scrape up the browned bits, and pour the juices over the fish. Cut the other half of the lemon into slices and garnish the fish with them.

Red Snapper, Stuffed and Baked

One of our finest fish from the Gulf Coast, so handsome on the platter when served whole with its glistening silver and pinkish red skin.

6 tablespoons butter
¼ pound (115 g) mushrooms,
  finely chopped
4 scallions, chopped
1 stalk celery, chopped
½ cup (1 dL) bread crumbs

½ teaspoon rosemary
½ teaspoon salt
Freshly ground pepper
1 whole red snapper, about 2½
  pounds (1¼ kg)
2–3 tablespoons dry white wine

Preheat the oven to 400°F (205°C). Melt 5 tablespoons of the butter, add the mushrooms, scallions, and celery, and sauté about 10 minutes. Mix in the bread crumbs, rosemary, salt, and pepper to taste. Fill the cavity of the fish with the stuffing and skewer or sew up the opening. Brush the fish with some of the remaining butter and bake for 30 minutes, basting with what's left of the butter and a little wine twice during the cooking.

Red Snapper Fillets, Florida Style

1½ pounds (675 g) red snapper
  fillets
Salt
Freshly ground pepper
A few gratings of nutmeg
1½ teaspoons grated orange
  rind

1 teaspoon grated grapefruit
  rind, or a combination of
  lemon and lime

Preheat the oven to 400°F (205°C). Put the fillets in a lightly buttered baking dish. Sprinkle them lightly with salt and pepper and nutmeg and distribute the grated rinds on top. Cover with foil and bake 15 minutes.

Broiled Rockbass with Fennel Seed

Rockbass is from the bass family, a lean fish found in the Midwest and South. Sold whole or in fillets, it benefits from added seasonings and sauces.

3-pound (1⅓-kg) rockbass,
  split, with backbone
  removed
4 tablespoons butter
¾ cup (1¾ dL) dry white wine
2 teaspoons fennel seed

Salt
Freshly ground pepper
1 large tomato, peeled, seeded,
  and chopped
1 tablespoon finely chopped
  parsley

Rinse the fish and pat dry. Place it, skin side down, on a well-oiled broiler pan. Melt the butter with the wine and fennel. Let simmer 2 minutes, remove from the heat, and let steep 15 minutes. Preheat the broiler. Sprinkle the fish with salt and pepper, and pour on the butter mixture. Place 4 inches beneath the broiler element and cook 6–8 minutes, depending on the thickness of the fish. Remove to a warm platter. Mix the tomato with parsley and spoon it on the fish.

Poached Salmon

Salmon is one of the most flavorful fish. It weighs between 5 and 10 pounds when whole; larger salmon are generally cut into steaks or sections. The meat is pink, tender, and firm, the flavor mild and delicious. It lends itself to poaching whole, baking split, or broiling (planked or not, as you wish). It is equally delicious cold, and makes a splendid buffet dish.

(SERVES EIGHT TO TEN)

6-pound (2¾-kg) whole dressed salmon
2 cups (½ L) dry white wine
1½ tablespoons salt
4 carrots, sliced
3 onions, sliced thin

4 bay leaves, in pieces
12 sprigs parsley
1 teaspoon freshly ground pepper
1 recipe Hollandaise Sauce (p. 272)

Rinse the salmon under cold running water. In a fish poacher or a large roasting pan with a lid and rack to hold the fish, combine 4 quarts water with the wine, salt, carrots, onions, bay leaves, parsley, and pepper. Bring to a boil and simmer 15 minutes. If you want to make sure that the salmon remains in one piece, wrap it in a cheesecloth sling before placing it in the broth; it will be easy to lift out later. Lay the fish on the rack; if there is not enough broth to cover it, add some more water. Put on the lid and simmer 25–30 minutes or until meat loses its deep pink color around the backbone. A thermometer will register 140°F (60°C) when the fish is done. Remove the pan from the heat and let the fish remain in the broth until you are ready to serve it, up to 45 minutes. Serve with hollandaise.

Cold Poached Salmon. Follow the recipe for Poached Salmon, but remove the fish from the broth and refrigerate until it is cool. Place on a platter and decorate with tomato wedges, cucumber slices, black olives, and watercress. Serve with Mayonnaise (p. 452), Green Mayonnaise (p. 453), or Cucumber Sauce (p. 274).

Broiled Salmon

(SERVES FOUR)

6 tablespoons butter, melted
4 salmon steaks, about ¾ inch (2 cm) thick
Salt to taste
Freshly ground pepper to taste

1 tablespoon mixed chopped parsley, chives, and dill
Juice of 1 lemon
Lemon wedges

Preheat the broiler. Brush 2 tablespoons of the butter over the salmon steaks. Mix remaining butter with salt, pepper, herbs, and lemon juice. Place salmon steaks on the broiler pan and put it on the highest level under the broiling element. Cook 5 minutes each side. For the last minutes of cooking, pour on the remaining butter mixture. Serve with accumulated pan juices and surround with lemon wedges.

Broiled Scrod

Scrod is young cod. It is most delicious when very fresh, split down the back and broiled quickly with a crusty topping to contrast with the tender flesh.

(SERVES FOUR)

Four ½-pound (225-g) pieces
   split scrod
6 tablespoons butter, melted
Salt
Freshly ground pepper

½ cup (1 dL) fresh bread
   crumbs
¼ cup (½ dL) grated Swiss
   cheese
Lemon wedges

Preheat the broiler. Oil the broiler pan, and place the scrod on it. Sprinkle with half the melted butter, salt, and pepper, and place beneath the broiling element. Cook 6 minutes on one side. Turn, cook 4 minutes, and then sprinkle on the bread crumbs mixed with cheese. Top with the remaining butter and broil another minute or two until nicely browned. Garnish with lemon wedges.

Sautéed Sea Squab

The sea squab, a small portion extracted from the blowfish, is an oval lump of flesh covering a slender backbone. It is a rare delicacy with an exquisite flavor and a firm, succulent texture. Blowfish are increasingly hard to find, but a treasure to be savored when you come across them. They may be pan-fried in butter, added to a fish stew, or sautéed with aromatic vegetables as in this recipe.

(SERVES FOUR)

⅓ cup (50 g) flour
½ teaspoon salt
Freshly ground pepper
1½ pounds (675 g) sea squab,
   about 3 per person
2 tablespoons olive oil
2 tablespoons butter

2 tomatoes, peeled, seeded
   and chopped
4 scallions, chopped
6 mushrooms, chopped
¼ cup dry white wine, or 2
   tablespoons lemon juice

Season the flour with salt and pepper, and dust the fish, shaking off the excess. Heat the oil and butter in a large skillet and toss in the squab with the chopped tomatoes, scallions, and mushrooms. Cook 5 minutes on each side. Remove to a platter. Add the wine or lemon juice to the pan and stir, scraping up all the vegetables. Pour over the sea squab.

Broiled Shad

Like asparagus, fresh broiled shad is one of the pleasures of spring— that is, for those lucky enough to live in parts of America where the shad run. It used to be an onerous task to pull out all the small bones, but now one can buy fillets impeccably boned. If you should be confronted with an unboned shad, try the next recipe, in which the fish is cooked so long that the bones melt away.

(SERVES FOUR)

2 tablespoons butter
2 sides of shad, boned, about 2
   pounds (900 g)

Salt
Freshly ground pepper
Lemon wedges

Preheat the broiler. Rub a little butter on the rack and place the shad on it, skin side down. Season with salt and pepper and dot with remaining butter. Broil at highest level for 8 minutes, without turning. Serve garnished with lemon wedges.

Old-fashioned Whole "Boneless" Shad

This method of cooking will melt away the tiny bones should you
have a whole unboned shad. Despite the long cooking, the flesh stays
moist and has a fine flavor. If your shad is female, and there is roe,
remove it and cook it separately.

(SERVES EIGHT)

1 whole shad, 4–5 pounds   1 tablespoon olive oil
  (2–2¼ kg)   4 strips bacon
½ recipe Savory Bread Stuffing
  (p. 278)

Preheat the oven to 225°F (110°C). Fill the shad cavity with the stuffing and
skewer the opening together. Rub the outside with olive oil and place the fish
on a piece of heavy foil large enough to fold comfortably around it. Lay strips of
bacon over the top, and then tuck the foil over the fish, folding the edges
together securely. Place on a baking sheet and cook for 6 hours.

Shad Roe in a Chafing Dish

The roe of the shad, sold in pairs, is one of our finest culinary
treasures. It is often broiled with bacon, which tends to dry and
toughen it. It is much more delicate and tender cooked this way,
either done at the table or in a kitchen skillet.

(SERVES TWO)

2 pairs shad roe   1 lemon
6 tablespoons butter   2 tablespoons chopped parsley
Salt   4 slices bacon, fried
Freshly ground pepper

Sauté the shad roe in the butter in a chafing dish or skillet. Using moderate heat,
cover and cook for 15 minutes, turning several times. Season with salt and
pepper and squeeze on the juice of half the lemon, slicing the other half to use
as garnish. Sprinkle with parsley and serve with crisp bacon.

Shad Stuffed with Roe

(SERVES SIX)

2 pairs shad roe   2 sides of large shad, boned,
2 tablespoons butter   about 3 pounds (1⅓ kg)
2 tablespoons minced scallions   1 teaspoon cornstarch
½ cup (1 dL) dry vermouth   1 cup (¼ L) heavy cream
Salt   1 teaspoon tarragon, crumbled
Freshly ground pepper

Preheat the oven to 350°F (180°C). Sauté the roe in the butter with the scallions
for 1–2 minutes. Add the vermouth and ¼ cup water and simmer 10 minutes.
Remove the roe, mash and season with salt and pepper, and stuff into the two
sides of the shad. There are natural flaps to tuck the roe under. Put the stuffed
fish in a pan, cover with foil, and bake 30 minutes. Meanwhile, boil down the
roe poaching liquid to about ¼ cup. Dissolve the cornstarch in a little of the

cream, then add to the roe liquid along with the remaining cream. Blend well, cook until thickened, add the tarragon, and adjust the seasoning. Pour this sauce over the baked fish.

Planked Shad with Creamed Roe

In the old days, shad was baked on a hardwood plank. You can do the same by soaking the plank in cold water and then rubbing it all over with butter or oil. It makes a handsome presentation of an early New England recipe, but of course a flameproof baking dish will do just as well.

(SERVES SIX)

2 sides of shad	1½ tablespoons flour
1 pair shad roe	¾ cup (1¾ dL) heavy cream
1 tablespoon plus ½ teaspoon lemon juice	Salt
	Freshly ground pepper
1 teaspoon finely chopped shallots or scallions	¾ cup (1¾ dL) fresh buttered bread crumbs
3 tablespoons butter	

Soak a plank in cold water for 1 hour. Pat it dry, and oil or butter it. Preheat the oven to 425°F (220°C), or preheat the broiler. Place the shad on the plank and bake for 20 minutes (or broil for 12 minutes about 6 inches from the heat). Meanwhile, simmer the roe in water to which you have added 1 tablespoon lemon juice. Cook for 5 minutes, until the roe whitens. Drain and mash the roe. Sauté the shallots or scallions in the butter 4–5 minutes. Stir in the flour and cook until blended. Slowly add the cream and cook until thick and smooth. Then add the mashed roe, and season with salt and pepper and a few drops of lemon juice. Spread the creamed roe over the cooked shad, cover with the buttered crumbs, and run it quickly under the broiler to brown. Serve on the plank or in a baking dish.

Pan-fried Smelts with Spinach

Small bony fish that are wonderful fried crisp and eaten with the fingers. Nibble the flesh off the larger bones; the smaller ones are tender enough to eat.

(SERVES FOUR)

2 pounds (900 g) smelts	¼ pound (115 g) butter
⅓ cup (50 g) flour	2 tablespoons oil
1½ teaspoons salt	1 pound (450 g) fresh spinach, washed and stemmed
¼ teaspoon freshly ground pepper	3 tablespoons lemon juice

Preheat the oven to 225°F (110°C) and put in an ovenproof platter. Rinse the smelts under cold water and pat dry. Mix the flour with 1 teaspoon of salt and the pepper, put it on a piece of wax paper, and drag each smelt through it so each side is coated. Melt the butter and oil in a large skillet. When it is hot, put in as many smelts as you can without crowding the skillet. Fry 1–1½ minutes on each side over high heat. Transfer to a warm platter and continue until all are fried. Put the spinach in the skillet, sprinkle with the remaining ½ teaspoon salt, and stir in the lemon juice. Cover and cook 3 minutes, until just wilted. Serve covered with the smelts.

Smelts with Brown Butter. Omit the spinach. Remove the fried fish to a platter. Add another *4 tablespoons butter* to the pan and heat until it turns brown. Mix in *2 tablespoons capers* with a little of their juice. Pour over the smelts and sprinkle with *chopped parsley.*

Smelts with Anchovy Butter. Omit the spinach. Remove the fried fish to a platter. Stir *1 tablespoon anchovy paste* into the pan juices with *several squirts of lemon.* Pour over the smelts and sprinkle with *chopped parsley.* Serve with *lemon wedges.*

Sole with Butter, Lemon, and Parsley

All species of sole are members of the flounder family: the most common are Dover, grey, lemon, rex, and petrale. Sole is a lean fish, usually sold in fillets, whose white delicate meat lends itself to all kinds of adornment.

(SERVES FOUR)

⅓ cup (50 g) flour
1¼ teaspoons salt
¼ teaspoon freshly ground
    pepper
1½ pounds (675 g) sole fillets

6 tablespoons butter
1 tablespoon oil
2 tablespoons lemon juice
1½ tablespoons minced parsley

Preheat the oven to 225°F (110°C). Put in an ovenproof platter. Combine the flour, salt, and pepper, spread it on wax paper, and drag each of the fillets through it so they are well coated. Shake off excess flour. In a large skillet, heat 3 tablespoons of the butter with the oil. Without crowding, put some of the fillets in the skillet and pan fry over medium heat until golden. Unless they are unusually thick, this should take 1–2 minutes on each side. Transfer to the warm platter and cook the rest of the fillets, adding the remaining butter as needed. When all the fish is cooked, turn the heat to high, stir in the lemon juice, and cook for a few seconds. Add the parsley, stir, and drizzle over the fillets.

Sole with Almonds. Omit the parsley and, after the fillets are done, sauté *½ cup sliced almonds* in *2 tablespoons butter* until they are golden. Distribute over the fish before serving.

Sole Baked in Herbed Cream

(SERVES FOUR)

5 tablespoons flour
1½ teaspoons salt
¼ teaspoon freshly ground
    pepper
1½ pounds (675 g) sole fillets
½ teaspoon tarragon, crumbled

2 tablespoons finely chopped
    chives
2 tablespoons minced parsley
3 tablespoons lemon juice
1½ cups (3½ dL) heavy cream

Preheat the oven to 450°F (230°C). Butter a shallow baking dish large enough to hold the fillets in a single layer, slightly overlapping. Mix the flour, salt, and pepper, spread it on wax paper, and drag the fillets through it to coat each side, shaking off any excess flour. Lay the fillets in the baking dish and sprinkle with the tarragon, chives, parsley, and lemon juice. Pour on the cream and bake about 15 minutes.

Sole Baked with Wine, Grapes, and Cream. Omit the tarragon, chives, parsley, and lemon juice. Add *1½ cups seedless green grapes* to the baking dish, and pour *½ cup dry white wine* over the fillets and grapes before baking for 12–15 minutes. Heat *1 cup heavy cream* in a saucepan. When the fillets are done, spoon 6 tablespoons of the baking liquid into the hot cream and whisk for a few seconds until blended. Transfer the fish to a warm platter and pour on the cream sauce; when serving, give everyone a few grapes.

Sole Baked with Cream and Mushrooms. Sauté *3 cups sliced mushrooms* in *5 tablespoons butter,* just before serving, pour over the fish.

Seviche

An unusual cool and refreshing dish from South of the Border which has become popular in the States in recent years. Don't be put off by the fact that the fish is raw: it really "cooks" in its marinade of lime and lemon juices, becoming firm and white. Delicious as a first course, seviche also makes a nice summer lunch, served in small chilled bowls or plates garnished with avocado slices and watercress.

(SERVES FOUR)

1 pound (450 g) fillets of sole, halibut, or other lean white fish	½ teaspoon salt
	Freshly ground pepper
	1 clove garlic, minced
½ cup (1 dL) freshly squeezed lime juice	½ large red onion, sliced thin
	1 tablespoon minced seeded
¼ cup (½ dL) freshly squeezed lemon juice	canned green chili pepper, or ¼ teaspoon pepper flakes
1 teaspoon finely chopped ginger root	3 tablespoons chopped Chinese parsley

Slice fillets in half lengthwise and cut into ½-inch pieces. Spread in one layer in a dish. Combine the remaining ingredients, reserving 1 tablespoon of Chinese parsley. Pour over the fish, cover with plastic wrap, and refrigerate for at least 6 hours, turning once. Sprinkle with reserved Chinese parsley before serving.

Whole Striped Bass, Steamed

Striped bass is one of the most highly prized of Atlantic fish. The flesh is so delicate and succulent that it is good hot or cold, poached, steamed, or baked. Served whole with the head and tail on, the large black-striped silvery-skinned bass makes a handsome dish.

(SERVES SIX)

4½-pound (2-kg) striped bass, or 2 bass, 2¼ pounds (1 kg) each	Salt
	Freshly ground pepper

Season the fish inside and out with salt and pepper. If you haven't a steamer, see p. 32 for suggestions on improvising one. Lightly oil the steaming rack. Wrap the fish in cheesecloth and place on the rack. Pour in enough boiling water to cover the bottom of the pot without touching the rack. Put on the cover and steam 25–30 minutes for the larger fish (you may have to replenish the water) and 15 minutes for the smaller. Remove carefully, pouring juices that accumulate on the platter back into the water remaining in the steamer. Reduce this, if necessary, to about 2 tablespoons and use it in making Hollandaise Sauce (p. 272) if you are serving the fish warm. If you are serving it cold, chill for several hours and serve with Green Mayonnaise (p. 453), or Yogurt Green Sauce (p. 275), or Cucumber Sauce (p. 274).

Poached Striped Bass. Follow the recipe for Poached Salmon (p. 118), cooking 25 minutes for a 4½-pound bass, 15 minutes for a 2-pounder.

Baked Stuffed Striped Bass. Follow the recipe for Red Snapper, Stuffed and Baked (p. 116), baking a 4½-pound bass 45 minutes, and a 2-pound bass 25 minutes.

Striped Bass Baked with Vegetables

When a bass is very large, its steaks are cut about ⅓ to ½ pound apiece. Cod, halibut, tilefish, and kingfish steaks are also cooked this way.

(SERVES FOUR)

2 tablespoons oil	Cayenne pepper to taste
1 large onion, chopped	¼ teaspoon oregano
1 clove garlic, chopped	½ teaspoon salt
2 large tomatoes, peeled, seeded, and chopped, or ¾ cup (1¾ dL) canned tomatoes, drained and chopped	Freshly ground pepper to taste 4 striped bass steaks 2 tablespoons lemon juice ¼ cup (½ dL) fresh bread crumbs
1 green pepper, chopped	2 tablespoons butter

Preheat the oven to 375°F (190°C). In a skillet, heat the oil and sauté the onion, garlic, tomatoes, and green pepper over low heat for 10 minutes. Add the cayenne and oregano and spread half the mixture in a shallow baking dish large enough to hold the fish in one layer. Season the fish steaks with salt and pepper, place them on the vegetables, and cover with the remaining vegetable mixture. Sprinkle with lemon juice and bread crumbs and dot with butter. Bake for 25 minutes.

Broiled Swordfish

Even people who don't like fish like swordfish, because its firm, oily flesh so resembles meat. Swordfish steaks should be cut about 1 inch thick for broiling. Thicker than that, the outside is apt to get too dry while the inside is undercooked; thinner than that, the steaks dry out completely and are better pan-fried. Swordfish is also very good cooked on an outdoor grill.

(SERVES FOUR)

2-pound (900-g) swordfish steak	Freshly ground pepper ½ teaspoon anchovy paste (optional)
4 tablespoons butter, melted Salt	Lemon wedges

Preheat the broiler. Brush both sides of the swordfish with some of the melted butter, and season with salt and pepper. Broil on the highest level for 5 minutes; then turn, pour on a tablespoon of butter, and broil another 4–5 minutes. Mix the remaining butter with the anchovy paste, if you like a sharper accent, and pour it over the fish. Surround with lemon wedges.

Tilefish with Tomatoes and Ripe Olives

A large, moist, fairly bland fish that has recently returned to Atlantic waters, tile is best cut into thick steaks and cooked bathed in a tasty sauce. Steaks from a large striped bass or cod could be done the same way.

(SERVES FOUR)

3 tablespoons oil	Freshly ground pepper
2 cloves garlic	1-pound 12-ounce (800-g) can
1 medium onion, sliced	whole tomatoes
4 tilefish steaks, ⅓–½ pound	8–10 large pitted ripe olives,
(150–225 g) each	sliced
Salt	2 tablespoons chopped parsley

Heat the oil in a large skillet. Sauté the garlic cloves until they begin to turn color. Remove, and cook the onion in the oil about 3 minutes. Push to the side and add the fish, browning lightly on one side for 1 minute before turning. Season with salt and pepper. Drain the tomatoes, chop the pulp roughly, and add to the skillet with 2–3 tablespoons of the juice. Cover and cook over medium heat 12–15 minutes. Remove the fish to a warm platter. Boil down the tomatoes if too liquid, add the olives until warm through, spoon over the fish, and sprinkle with parsley.

Pan-fried Brook Trout

Fresh-water trout is unequaled when cooked straight from the stream, but it is beautiful eating any time.

(SERVES FOUR)

4 brook trout, cleaned, with	7 tablespoons butter
head and tail left on	3 tablespoons oil
2 tablespoons flour	2 tablespoons lemon juice
Salt	2 tablespoons minced chives

Rinse the fish under cold running water and pat dry with paper towels. Dust lightly with flour, and sprinkle with salt. In a large skillet, melt 3 tablespoons of the butter and the oil. When it is hot, put in the trout and fry over medium-high heat. When browned, turn and brown the other side: each side will take about 3 minutes. Melt the remaining 4 tablespoons butter with lemon juice and chives in a small saucepan. When the trout is done, transfer to a warm platter and pour on the sauce.

Broiled Rainbow (or Speckled or Brown) Trout

(SERVES FOUR)

4 rainbow trout, cleaned, with	Freshly ground pepper
head and tail left on	Oil
Salt	Lemon wedges

Preheat the broiler. Sprinkle the cavity of the fish with salt and pepper. Rub the outside with oil. Place on an oiled rack 5 inches beneath the broiler (at the second level) and broil for 5 minutes on each side. The skin will just be spottily charred and the flesh moist and tender. Serve with lemon wedges.

Broiled Trout with Rosemary. Place a *sprig of fresh rosemary* in the cavity of each trout before cooking.

Broiled Trout with Cream. Use a shallow pan instead of the broiler rack. After broiling 2–3 minutes on the second side, pour *¾ cup heavy cream* over the trout and broil another 5 minutes, basting a couple of times. Omit lemon wedges and sprinkle with *1 tablespoon chopped parsley* and *1 tablespoon chopped fresh tarragon, or 1 teaspoon dried, crumbled.*

Baked Fresh Tuna

Once in a while, fish markets will advertise fresh tuna, and it is well worth experimenting with the red-fleshed steaks and tasting the difference between them and the canned version. Swordfish and kingfish are both good prepared this way.

(SERVES FOUR)

1¾ pounds (800 g) fresh tuna steaks	1 large red onion, sliced thin
2 tablespoons olive oil	4 medium tomatoes, peeled, seeded, and chopped
Salt	½ cup (1 dL) dry vermouth
Freshly ground pepper	1 teaspoon basil, crumbled

Preheat the oven to 425°F (220°C). Rub the tuna steaks with 1 tablespoon olive oil and season lightly with salt and pepper. In a skillet, sauté the onion in the remaining oil until it is limp. Add the tomatoes and vermouth and cook briefly. Place the steaks in a shallow baking dish, pour on the onion-tomato mixture, and bake 12–15 minutes, depending on their thickness. Sprinkle with basil.

Whitefish Broiled with Sesame Seeds

This tasty fish from the Great Lakes and other northern inland waters can also be pan-sautéed, particularly if you have fillets, but do run the pan under the broiler if you sprinkle the fish with sesame seeds— just long enough to toast them as here.

(SERVES FOUR)

1 whole whitefish, about 2½ pounds (1¼ kg)	3 tablespoons sesame seeds
Salt	Lemon wedges
2 tablespoons melted butter with ½ teaspoon lemon juice	

Preheat the broiler. Rub the fish inside and out with a little salt and melted butter with lemon juice. Broil 5 inches from the heat 5 minutes, basting once or twice, then turn and broil 4 minutes, brush well with butter, and coat with sesame seeds. Broil another minute or so until seeds are golden brown. Serve with lemon wedges.

Pan-sautéed Whiting

Whiting is an Atlantic fish with a mild flavor. People who think they object to fishy flavors, often favor a whiting. It is usually served whole, one to a person.

(SERVES FOUR)

4 whole whitings, about ¾
    pound (340 g) each
Salt
Freshly ground pepper
½ cup (70 g) flour

¼ teaspoon paprika
3 tablespoons butter
2 tablespoons oil
1 lemon
1 tablespoon chopped parsley

Rinse the whitings inside and out, pat dry, and sprinkle with salt and pepper. Mix the flour and paprika, dust the fish with it, and shake off excess. In a large skillet heat 2 tablespoons of butter and the oil until the foam subsides. Add the fish and brown on both sides. Lower the heat and cover, cooking about 12 minutes or until the flesh is opaque around the rib cage. Remove to a warm platter. Squeeze half the lemon into the pan, add the remaining butter, and cook 1 minute more, scraping up the bits from the pan. Pour over the fish and garnish with parsley and the remaining lemon cut in wedges.

SHELLFISH

Pan-fried Abalone

Abalone is a large single-shelled mollusk that is found along the California coast. It is in short supply, and cannot be canned or shipped fresh or frozen out of California. Preserved abalone from Japan is sometimes available. Should you be so lucky as to obtain abalone steaks, tenderize them by pounding with a wooden mallet. Use persistent, firm strokes, and flatten them to quarter-inch thickness. Do not overcook, or the abalone will be tough and rubbery. Thirty seconds to a side is enough; less is better.

(SERVES TWO)

2 abalone steaks, tenderized
3 tablespoons butter
1 tablespoon oil
Salt

Freshly ground pepper
1 tablespoon lemon juice
2 parsley sprigs

Pat the abalone dry with paper towels. Melt the butter with the oil in a large skillet. When the butter foams and is very hot, add the steaks. Season with salt and pepper and fry 30 seconds on each side. Transfer to a warm platter, drizzle with lemon juice, and garnish with parsley.

Steamed Clams

Clams are a bivalve, or two-shelled, mollusk. There are three principal
varieties, soft-shelled, hard-shelled, and razor clams from the Pacific.
The so-called soft-shelled are oval and come from northern New
England. The hard-shelled are round and come in small littlenecks,
medium cherrystones, and large quahogs or chowder clams. Small
clams are eaten raw, steamed, or on the half-shell; quahogs are good
minced and in soups. When buying clams, be sure the shells are
clamped tightly together; this indicates that the clam is alive. Discard
broken or cracked shells. To get rid of all the sand, scrub under
running water and then soak in a salt-water brine for about ½ hour.

(1 QUART PER SERVING)

1 quart (1 L) clams per serving   Lemon juice or vinegar
¼ cup (½ dL) butter, melted,
   per serving

Scrub the shells with a brush, changing the water until there is no trace of sand.
Put the clams in a deep kettle with 2 tablespoons water for each quart of clams.
Cover tightly and cook over low heat until the shells open, about 15 minutes.
Don't overcook. Using a slotted spoon, remove the clams to large soup plates.
Strain the broth into small glasses and serve with the clams. Set out individual
dishes of melted butter, to which you may add a little lemon juice or vinegar, and
a small amount of boiling water which will make the butter float to the top and
stay hot. To eat, lift the clam from the shell by the black neck. Dip in the clam
broth, then in the butter, and eat; some like the neck, some don't.

Baked or Broiled Clams

To open clams for serving on the half-shell, insert a knife between
the shells near the muscle. Cut through the muscle and twist the
knife a little to pry the shells apart. Drain the juice into a bowl.

(SERVES FOUR)

24 medium-size clams
¼ pound (115 g) butter, melted
1 lemon, quartered

Preheat the oven to 400°F (205°C) or preheat the broiler. Remove the top shell
from hard-shelled clams. Spoon a teaspoon of melted butter on each clam and
bake for 6 minutes or broil 3–4 minutes. Serve hot with lemon quarters.

Seashore Clambake

1 quart (1 L) clams per person
1 small lobster per person
1–2 ears corn per person

Dig a pit in the sand about 1 foot deep. Put down a layer of stones and build a
wood fire on the stones. Burn until the fire dies down and the stones are white-
hot, about 1 hour. Meanwhile, scrub the clams in sea water, kill the lobsters

(p. 133), and dip the corn in sea water. Rake off the ashes and spread a thin layer of seaweed on the stones. Put a piece of chicken wire over the seaweed and pile on the clams, lobsters, and corn. Cover with more seaweed and a piece of canvas to keep in the steam, working quickly so that the rocks do not cool. Steam about 1 hour.

Fricassee of Clams

(SERVES FOUR AS FIRST COURSE)

2 tablespoons butter
2 tablespoons flour
¾ cup (1¾ dL) heavy cream
Salt

Pinch of cayenne pepper
2 tablespoons dry sherry
1 pint (½ L) chopped clams

Melt the butter in a saucepan. Stir in the flour and cook over medium heat until smooth and blended. Slowly add the cream, stirring constantly, until the sauce is smooth. Stir in the salt, cayenne pepper, sherry, and clams, and cook over low heat for 3 minutes, stirring constantly. Serve on toast.

Stuffed Clams Union League

(SERVES FOUR)

¼ pound (115 g) butter
1 tablespoon finely chopped
  shallot or onion
36 small clams in the shell
1 cup (¼ L) dry white wine
3 tablespoons flour
½ cup (1 dL) heavy cream

5–6 drops Tabasco
2 teaspoons finely chopped
  parsley
1 cup (¼ L) freshly made bread
  crumbs
½ cup (1 dL) freshly grated
  Parmesan cheese

Melt 5 tablespoons of the butter in a large saucepan. Add the shallot or onion and stir over low heat for 5 minutes. Add the clams and wine, cover, and cook until the shells open, 12–15 minutes. Remove the clams from the shells and chop them. Save the shells. Preheat the oven to 400°F (205°C). Melt the remaining 3 tablespoons butter in a saucepan. Blend in the flour and cook 1 minute. Slowly add ½ cup of the clam liquid and the cream, and stir until the sauce is smooth. Add the clams and Tabasco and stir constantly until the sauce is thickened. Remove from the heat, add the parsley, and spoon the clams and sauce back into the shells. Mix the bread crumbs and cheese and sprinkle on each clam. Bake for 15 minutes or until the crumbs are lightly browned.

Boiled Crabs

There are three types of crab on the market: blue crabs from the Atlantic and Gulf coasts, Dungeness crabs from the Pacific, and king crab from North Pacific waters. Crab is sold alive, frozen, or cleaned and packed in refrigerated tins. Canned crab is good, but lacks the delicate flavor of fresh. The best way to learn to eat a hard-shelled crab is to go to a Baltimore crab house and ask a waiter to show you. Failing that, we offer instructions below. Choose lively crabs.

Boiled Crabs (continued)

(SERVES FOUR)

Salt
6 live blue crabs

Bring a large kettle of salted water to the boil. Drop in the crabs and boil 15 minutes; they will turn pink. Drain and run them under cold water to make them cool enough to handle. Twist off the large legs and crack with a nutcracker or pliers. Pull and break off the apron. Remove the gills, intestine, and the rest of the innards. Reserve the roe, which is orange, and the tomalley, which is pale green—both are delicious. Dig out the small amount of precious meat, to be found beneath the gills. If the shell is to be stuffed, remove the stomach sac, rinse the shell well, and dry.

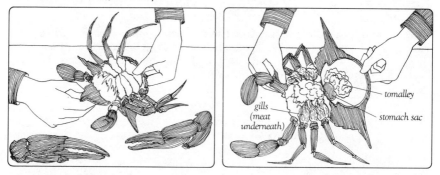

Steamed Crabs. Set the crabs on a steamer over boiling water. Sprinkle them with *Tabasco* and *vinegar,* cover the pot, and steam about 10 minutes.

Soft-shelled Crabs, Sautéed

Soft-shelled crabs are a seasonal delicacy. All crabs have hard shells, which they shed as they outgrow them. It is at the time of molting, in late spring and summer, that they are caught and sold as soft-shelled crabs. Buy them alive, whole, and have them killed and cleaned just before you bring them home.

(SERVES THREE)

¼ cup (35 g) flour
Salt
Freshly ground pepper
6 soft-shelled crabs

6 tablespoons butter
1 tablespoon oil
Juice of 1 lemon

Season the flour with salt and pepper, dust the crabs with it, and shake off excess. In a large skillet, heat the butter and oil. Toss in the crabs and cook over moderately high heat about 3 minutes each side. Remove to a warm platter. Squeeze in the lemon juice and stir, scraping up all the brown bits. Pour over the crabs.

Soft-shelled Crabs Amandine. Before adding the lemon juice, sauté ⅓ *cup slivered almonds* in the pan, adding additional *butter* if necessary. When the nuts are golden, scatter them over the crabs, and finish with the lemon juice.

Ipswich Deviled Crab

Baked in a creamy, sharp sauce to set off the crab.

(SERVES SIX)

½ teaspoon dry mustard
⅛ teaspoon cayenne pepper
1½ cups (3½ dL) freshly made
  bread crumbs

2 tablespoons butter
2 tablespoons heavy cream
2 cups (½ L) crabmeat
Salt

Preheat the oven to 350°F (180°C). Butter a gratin pan or 6 ramekins. Combine the mustard, cayenne, 1 cup of the bread crumbs, butter, cream, and 1 cup hot water in a saucepan. Bring to a boil, reduce heat, and simmer 5 minutes. Add the crabmeat and salt to taste, and cook 1 minute more. Fill the baking dish or ramekins, and sprinkle with the remaining ½ cup bread crumbs. Bake 20 minutes, until the crumbs are lightly browned and the sauce is bubbling.

Creamed Crab

Serve on toast or over rice.

(SERVES FOUR)

3 tablespoons butter
3 tablespoons flour
1½ cups (3½ dL) light cream
Dash of Tabasco

3–4 tablespoons dry sherry
1½ cups (3½ dL) crabmeat
Salt

Melt the butter in a saucepan. Stir in the flour and blend until smooth. Slowly add the cream, stirring constantly, until smooth and thickened. Add Tabasco and sherry and cook over very low heat for 3 minutes. Add the crab and salt to taste, and cook only until heated through.

Creamed Crab with Mushrooms. Add *1 cup sliced mushrooms* sautéed in *2 tablespoons butter* to the cream sauce.

Crabmeat Terrapin Style

Serve over rice or in patty shells.

(SERVES FOUR)

3 tablespoons butter
¼ cup (½ dL) finely chopped
  onion
1½ cups (3½ dL) crabmeat
3 tablespoons dry sherry

½ cup (1 dL) heavy cream
3 egg yolks
Salt
Dash of cayenne pepper

Melt the butter in a saucepan. Stir in the onion and cook over low heat until soft and yellow. Remove the onion and set aside. Stir in the crabmeat, add the sherry, and cook over low heat, stirring constantly, for 3 minutes. Beat the cream and egg yolks together. Slowly add to the saucepan, stirring briskly. Add the onion and cook for 2 minutes until the sauce is smooth and thickened. Remove from the heat and season to taste with salt and cayenne.

Crabmeat Indienne

This is good on rice.

(SERVES FOUR)

3 tablespoons butter
1 tablespoon finely chopped
  onion
4 tablespoons flour

2 teaspoons curry powder
2 cups (½ L) chicken broth
1½ cups (3½ dL) crabmeat

Melt the butter in a saucepan. Add the onion and cook over low heat for 3 minutes, stirring often. Stir the flour and curry powder into the skillet and cook 2 minutes more. Add the chicken broth slowly and cook and stir for 5 minutes. Add the crabmeat and cook only until heated through.

Crabmeat Casserole

(SERVES EIGHT)

1 cup (¼ L) heavy cream
1 cup (¼ L) mayonnaise
1 tablespoon minced parsley
1 tablespoon minced onion
Salt

Freshly ground pepper
3½ cups (⅘ L) crabmeat
6 hard-cooked eggs, chopped
1 cup (¼ L) buttered bread
  crumbs

Preheat the oven to 350°F (180°C) and butter a shallow baking dish. Combine the cream, mayonnaise, parsley, onion, salt and pepper to taste, crabmeat, and chopped egg. Toss lightly, put into a baking dish, and sprinkle with the bread crumbs. Bake for 30 minutes.

Boiled Live Lobster

Lobsters are found in waters all over the world. They range from one to thirty pounds. The commercial grading is: "chicken," 1 pound; "quarters," under 1½ pounds; "large," 1½–2½ pounds; and "jumbo," over 2½ pounds. When buying a live lobster, look for one that is active and lively and heavy for its size. Killed lobsters should be cooked as soon as possible after purchase. The meat of the claws, body, and tail are wonderful to eat. The green liver or tomalley is a choice morsel, as is the roe or "coral" of the female lobster.

Salt
Lobsters

Fill a kettle with plenty of water to cover the lobsters. Add 2 teaspoons salt for each quart of water used. Bring to a rolling boil and put the lobsters in the pot. Allow 10 minutes cooking time for small lobsters, 15 minutes for medium, and as much as 25 minutes for large. Using tongs, lift from the water and cool just enough to handle. To prepare a boiled lobster to be eaten, first twist off the claws. Break the claws with a hammer or nutcracker so the meat is easily removed. Gently pull apart the tail from the body. Holding the tail with the hard shell down, cut the length of the cartilaginous tail with scissors. Bend it apart so the meat comes loose. Insert a small knife down the center and remove the dark line of intestine. Take the body and carefully remove the meat, discarding the lungs and stomach. Pick carefully for any small shell-like particles.

Coral Butter. Put the lobster coral into a blender or food processor and slowly add 4 *tablespoons butter, softened.* Spread on toast or use in a sauce.

Broiled Lobster

Lobster
Melted butter

Preheat the broiler. Kill the lobster by inserting a sharp knife where the head meets the shell. Turn on its back and make a deep cut through the length of the body with a heavy sharp-pointed knife. Spread the halves apart and remove the black line and the stomach. Leave the tomalley (the green-black soft matter) and the orange roe—both are delicious. Crack the claw shells with a hammer. Drizzle melted butter over the body. Place on rack in the broiler, meat side up, and broil for about 15 minutes without turning. Serve with more melted butter.

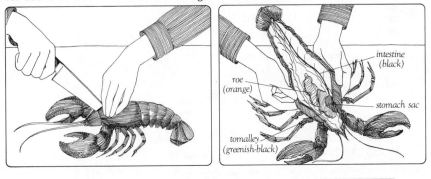

Rock Lobster Tails, Boiled

Rock lobster tails are imported frozen from South Africa, New Zealand, and Australia. They vary in size from 4 ounces to 1½ pounds.

(½ POUND PER SERVING)

Salt
Rock lobster tails
Melted butter

Bring a large pot of salted water to a boil. Drop in the frozen lobster tails and boil 3 minutes for small and 5 minutes for large tails. Drain until just cool enough to handle. With a knife, remove the shell-like covering on the underside of the tail. Cut down the center of the flesh deeply enough to remove the dark vein. Serve with melted butter.

Rock Lobster Tails Broiled. Drizzle lobster tails with melted butter and put them on a baking sheet, shell side down. Broil in a preheated oven 3–4 minutes.

Lobster à l'Américaine

(SERVES FOUR)

2 large lobsters, about 1½
  pounds (675 g) each
4 tablespoons oil
6 tablespoons butter
1 bay leaf, crumbled
1 teaspoon thyme, crumbled

4 tablespoons finely chopped
  shallots
⅛ teaspoon cayenne pepper
2 tablespoons tomato paste
⅓ cup (¾ dL) dry white wine

Kill and split the live lobsters (p. 133). Cut in 8 pieces, remove any liver and coral, and set aside. In a large skillet, heat the oil and butter. When they are hot, add the lobster pieces, bay leaf, thyme, and shallots. Lower the heat, cover, and simmer 5 minutes. Mix the cayenne pepper, tomato paste, and wine in a small bowl. Add to the lobster, stirring with the juices in the skillet. Cover and simmer another 10–15 minutes, until the shells are red. Take out the lobster and remove the meat. Strain the liquid and return it to the pan with the liver and coral. Blend, add the lobster meat, and heat through.

Lobster Thermidor

Serve this with steamed rice.

(SERVES EIGHT)

8 tablespoons butter
½ pound (225 g) mushrooms,
  sliced
3 tablespoons flour
2 cups (½ L) heavy cream
¼ cup (½ dL) dry sherry

4 cups (1 L) cooked lobster
  meat
Salt
⅓ cup (¾ dL) freshly grated
  Parmesan cheese

Preheat the oven to 450°F (230°C). Butter a shallow baking dish. Melt 5 tablespoons of the butter in a saucepan. Add the mushrooms and cook until they are softened. Remove and set aside. Melt the remaining 3 tablespoons of butter, stir in the flour, and cook until smooth and blended. Slowly stir in the cream and cook over low heat, stirring until the sauce is smooth and thickened. Add the sherry and cook 1 minute more. Remove from the heat and add the lobster and salt to taste. Spoon into the baking dish, sprinkle with cheese, and bake about 10 minutes, until the cheese is melted and lightly browned.

Creamed Lobster

(SERVES FOUR)

5 tablespoons butter
5 tablespoons flour
2 cups (½ L) light cream
½ teaspoon nutmeg
Pinch of cayenne pepper
3 tablespoons lemon juice

2 cups (½ L) cooked lobster
  meat
Toast or patty shells
1 tablespoon finely chopped
  parsley

Melt the butter in a saucepan. Stir in the flour and cook over low heat until smooth and blended. Slowly add the cream, stirring constantly, and the nutmeg, cayenne pepper, and lemon juice. Cook, stirring, until the sauce is smooth and thickened. Add the lobster meat and heat through. Spoon over toast or patty shells and sprinkle with parsley.

Lobster Timbales

A first course or elegant lunch dish with a Lobster Velouté Sauce (p. 266).

(SERVES SIX)

1 tablespoon butter	1 cup (¼ L) chopped cooked
1 tablespoon flour	lobster meat
⅓ cup (¾ dL) milk	⅓ cup (¾ dL) heavy cream,
¾ teaspoon salt	beaten stiff
2 egg yolks	1 egg white, beaten stiff

Preheat the oven to 350°F (180°C). Butter six 1-cup custard cups. Select a shallow pan large enough to hold the custard cups without touching: fill it with 1½ inches of hot water and place in the oven. Melt the butter in a saucepan. Stir in the flour, blend until smooth, and slowly stir in the milk and salt. Cook over low heat, stirring constantly, until the sauce is smooth and thickened. Beat a spoonful of sauce into the yolks, and then return the yolk-sauce mixture to the saucepan. Cook, stirring, for 1 minute; remove from the heat and mix in the lobster. Pour the lobster mixture into a bowl and gently fold in the whipped cream and beaten egg white. Spoon mixture into the custard cups, place in the pan of hot water in the oven, and bake for 35 minutes. Remove from the oven and unmold.

Lobster Croquettes

Golden, crisp, and delightful.

(12 CROQUETTES)

2 cups (½ L) chopped cooked	1 cup (¼ L) Thick Cream
lobster meat	Sauce (p. 265)
½ teaspoon salt	1½ cups (3½ dL) freshly made
½ teaspoon dry mustard	bread crumbs
Pinch of cayenne pepper	Oil for frying
1½ tablespoons lemon juice	

Warm a platter in a 250°F (120°C) oven. Combine the lobster, salt, mustard, cayenne pepper, lemon juice, and sauce. Refrigerate at least 1 hour, until the mixture is well chilled. Make small conelike shapes and roll in the bread crumbs. Heat 1 inch of oil in a heavy-bottomed pan to 360°F (182°C). Without crowding, fry a few croquettes at a time until they are golden. Don't fry too quickly, or the insides will be cold. Drain on paper towels and keep warm in the oven until all are done.

Steamed Mussels in White Wine

Another bivalve mollusk like the clam, the mussel in its blue-black oval shell is a great delicacy as well as one of the most abundant of seafoods. Mussels must be very well scrubbed, have their beards scraped away, and any open raw mussels should be discarded. Also, try to move the halves of the shell. If they slide, discard the mussel, for it may be full of mud.

(SERVES FIVE)

2 cups (½ L) dry white wine, or 1½ cups (3½ dL) dry vermouth mixed with ½ cup (1 dL) water
¼ cup (½ dL) finely chopped shallots or scallions

Pinch of thyme
1 bay leaf
4 pounds (1800 g) mussels, scrubbed and scraped
⅓ cup (¾ dL) chopped parsley

Put the wine, shallots or scallions, thyme, and bay leaf in a large pot and boil briskly for 10 minutes. Add the mussels, cover tightly, and boil 3–5 minutes, giving the pot a shake once or twice. If the mussels have opened, they are done; if not, cover and cook 1–2 minutes longer until all are opened. Spoon into large soup plates with a portion of broth. Sprinkle with parsley and serve with crusty bread.

Cold Mussels on the Half-Shell

(SERVES FOUR)

2½ dozen steamed mussels (see preceding recipe)
Juice of 1 lemon
½ cup (1 dL) Mustard Sauce (p. 273) or Green Mayonnaise (p. 453)

3 tablespoons mixed chopped parsley and chives
Lemon slices

Loosen each cooked mussel from its shell, break the shells apart. Then place a mussel on each half. Squeeze a drop or two of lemon juice on each, cover with the sauce or mayonnaise, and sprinkle generously with parsley and chives. Chill, then serve with lemon slices.

Oysters on the Half-Shell

Oysters have a long history on this continent; ancient Indian settlements have been located because their inhabitants left heaps of empty oyster shells. Oysters are two-shelled mollusks, having one half of the shell flatter than the other. When they are served "on the half-shell," the deep half is always used. They vary in size from the tiny western Olympias to the huge Japanese variety. On the East Coast, Maryland's Chincoteagues are famous. Buy oysters with shells tightly clamped together, indicating they are still alive. The pure and perfect way to eat an oyster is to have it fresh, raw, and alive with, at most, a few drops of lemon juice. Clean, briny, and tender, they are the perfect first course, preparing the palate for the meal to follow.

(SERVES FOUR)

24 oysters in the shell
Lemon wedges

Use a blunt-ended oyster knife to shuck the oysters. Insert the end of the knife between the shells near the hinge; work it until you cut through the muscle that holds the shells together. Catch the oyster liquor in a bowl. When the oysters are all shucked, strain the liquor through muslin before setting aside to use in sauces. Place an oyster in the deep half of each shell; serve with lemon wedges.

Oysters Casino

Clams are delicious prepared this way, too.

(SERVES FOUR)

24 oysters on the half-shell (see preceding recipe)
2 tablespoons lemon juice
3 tablespoons minced green pepper

2 tablespoons minced parsley
Salt
Freshly ground pepper
6 strips bacon

Preheat the broiler. Spread 1 inch of rock salt in a shallow baking dish large enough to hold the oyster shells, or use crumpled foil—anything to hold the oysters steady. Arrange the oysters on the salt. Sprinkle each with a few drops of lemon juice. Mix the green pepper, parsley, and salt and pepper to taste, and sprinkle over each oyster. Cut the bacon into 1½-inch lengths and put one piece on each oyster. Broil until the bacon is slightly brown.

Oysters Rockefeller

(SERVES FOUR)

3 scallions, including 1 inch of green tops
¼ cup (½ dL) chopped celery
2 tablespoons chopped parsley
½ cup (1 dL) chopped spinach
2 tablespoons freshly made bread crumbs
Dash of Tabasco

¼ teaspoon Worcestershire sauce
½ pound (225 g) butter, softened
Salt
24 large oysters on the half-shell (above)

Preheat the oven to 450°F (230°C). Combine the scallions, celery, parsley, and spinach and mince them with a knife or chop in a blender or food processor. Put the mixture into a bowl with the bread crumbs, Tabasco, and Worcestershire sauce. Add the butter and salt to taste, and cream all together into a smooth paste. Spread 1 inch of rock salt over a pan or baking dish large enough to hold the oyster shells or use crumpled foil. Arrange the oysters on top. Put 1 tablespoon of butter mixture on each oyster and bake 10 minutes or until the mixture has melted.

Panned Oysters

6 slices bread
¼ pound (115 g) butter,
   softened
2 tablespoons lemon juice

24 medium oysters, shucked
Salt
Freshly ground pepper

Preheat the oven to 400°F (205°C). Toast the bread. Cream the butter with lemon juice and spread it on the toast. Cut each slice of toast into four squares. Place an oyster on each square and sprinkle lightly with salt and pepper. Place the squares on a flat baking sheet and bake 5–6 minutes: only long enough to plump up oysters. The bread soaks up the lovely oyster liquor.

Oyster Fricassee

Spoon over toast or patty shells.

2 tablespoons butter
2 tablespoons flour
1 pint (½ L) shucked oysters,
   with their liquor
Milk

1½ tablespoons dry white wine
2 teaspoons minced parsley
Salt
Freshly ground pepper

Melt the butter in a saucepan. Stir in the flour and blend until smooth. Measure oyster liquor, add enough milk to make 1 cup, and slowly stir mixture into saucepan. Cook, stirring constantly, until the sauce is smooth and thickened. Stir in the wine and oysters and cook 1 minute. Add parsley and salt and pepper to taste, and simmer 2 minutes more.

Deviled Oysters

Try making clams this way, too.

1 pint (½ L) shucked oysters
2 tablespoons butter
3 shallots, chopped fine
2 tablespoons flour
1 cup (¼ L) light cream
⅛ teaspoon nutmeg
Pinch of cayenne pepper

1 teaspoon dry mustard
2 teaspoons Worcestershire
   sauce
2 tablespoons minced parsley
1 cup (¼ L) freshly made bread
   crumbs, buttered

Preheat the oven to 400°F (205°C). Have on hand 6–8 deep halves of oyster shells or 4–6 scallop shells. Chop the oysters coarsely and set aside. Melt the butter in a saucepan and add the shallots, cooking until soft. Stir in the flour, cook for 2 minutes, and slowly add the cream, nutmeg, cayenne, mustard, and Worcestershire sauce. Cook over medium-low heat, stirring constantly, for 4–5 minutes, until the sauce is smooth and thickened. Stir in the oysters and 1 tablespoon of the parsley. Remove from the heat and spoon into the shells. Place the shells on a baking sheet. Mix the remaining parsley and bread crumbs and sprinkle evenly over the oyster mixture. Bake 15–20 minutes.

Scalloped Oysters

(SERVES FOUR)

¼ pound (115 g) butter
½ cup (1 dL) freshly made
 bread crumbs
1 cup (¼ L) freshly made
 cracker crumbs

1 pint (½ L) shucked oysters,
 with their liquor
Salt
Dash of Tabasco
1 tablespoon cream

Preheat the oven to 425°F (220°C). Melt the butter in a skillet and toss in the bread and cracker crumbs, coating with the butter. Spread half the crumbs over the bottom of a shallow baking dish. Drain the oysters, reserving liquor, and arrange them in a single layer over the crumbs, and sprinkle with salt. Mix a healthy dash of Tabasco with the cream and 2 tablespoons oyster liquor, and dribble over oysters. Cover with remaining crumbs and bake 25 minutes.

Fried Oysters

(SERVES FOUR)

1 quart (1 L) shucked oysters
3 eggs
Salt
Freshly ground pepper

1½ cups (3½ dL) freshly made
 fine cracker crumbs
Oil for frying

Preheat the oven to 225°F (110°C) and warm an ovenproof platter. Pat the oysters dry on paper towels. Beat the eggs with a sprinkle of salt and pepper. Dip each oyster in egg, letting the excess drip back into the bowl, then dip in the cracker crumbs. Shake so that the excess falls off. Each oyster should be well covered with crumbs. In a heavy skillet, heat 1 inch of oil. When the oil is hot enough to brown a cube of bread in 30 seconds or registers 360°F on a fat thermometer, add the oysters. Don't crowd the skillet: do a few at a time. Drain on paper towels and keep warm in the oven.

Sautéed Scallops

Scallops, like oysters and clams, are bivalve mollusks. The part of the scallop we eat is the muscle that opens and closes the shell. Buy tiny bay scallops or larger sea scallops; they should have a shiny moist look and a faint fresh scent of the sea. Scallops, even more than other seafood, tend to toughen and lose their fine character when they are overcooked. Clean by rinsing under cold water; pat dry with paper towels, and then cook them briefly, just until they lose their translucency and become creamy-white.

(SERVES FOUR)

1½ pounds (675 g) scallops
¼ pound (115 g) butter
1½ tablespoons lemon juice

1 tablespoon minced parsley
Salt

Rinse the scallops and pat dry with paper towels. Melt the butter in a skillet and, when it foams, add the scallops. Cook over high heat about 1 minute each side. Remove to a warm platter and sprinkle with lemon juice, parsley, and salt.

Fried Scallops

1½ pounds (675 g) scallops
1¼ (3 dL) cups freshly made
   dry bread crumbs
2 eggs, well beaten

Oil for frying
Salt
Lemon wedges
Watercress sprigs

Preheat the oven to 225°F (110°C) and warm an ovenproof platter. Rinse the scallops, shake off excess water, and roll in the bread crumbs. Dip into the beaten eggs and again in the crumbs. Heat ½ inch of oil in a heavy skillet. When it is very hot, put in the scallops without crowding the pan. Do only a few at a time, and fry until the crumbs are nicely browned. Turn and brown the other side. Drain on paper towels and place on the warm platter. Season with salt and garnish with lemon wedges and watercress.

Deviled Scallops

1 pint (½ L) scallops
4 tablespoons butter, softened
½ teaspoon dry mustard

Dash of cayenne pepper
1 cup (¼ L) freshly made
   buttered bread crumbs

Preheat the oven to 375°F (190°C). Butter a small baking dish or three scallop shells. Rinse the scallops and pat dry with paper towels. Cream the butter, mustard, and cayenne in a small bowl. Put the scallops in the baking dish or shells, dot with the creamed butter, and cover with buttered crumbs. Bake for 20 minutes.

Coquilles Saint-Jacques

1½ pounds (675 g) scallops
6 tablespoons butter
¼ cup (½ dL) finely chopped
   scallions
2 tablespoons minced parsley
¼ pound (115 g) mushrooms,
   chopped
1 cup (¼ L) dry white wine

Pinch of cayenne pepper
2 tablespoons flour
1 cup (¼ L) heavy cream
2 egg yolks, lightly beaten
Salt
½ cup (1 dL) freshly grated
   Parmesan cheese

Butter 6–8 scallop shells or a shallow baking dish. Rinse the scallops and pat dry with paper towels. Cut them in half. Melt 4 tablespoons of the butter in a skillet and add the scallions, parsley, and mushrooms. Stir over medium heat for 3–4 minutes, until the mushrooms have darkened and are soft. Add the scallops, wine, and cayenne, and simmer covered for 3 minutes. Drain and set aside, reserving the liquid. Melt the remaining 2 tablespoons butter in the skillet. Stir in the flour and cook until smooth and blended. Slowly add the reserved liquid and the cream and cook until the sauce is thick. Beat 2 spoonfuls of the sauce into the yolks, then stir the yolk-sauce mixture back into the sauce. Stir and cook until smooth and thickened. Add salt to taste. Spoon into the buttered scallop shells or baking dish, sprinkle with Parmesan cheese, and put under the broiler just long enough to brown the cheese.

Scallops Newburg

Scallops in a fresh creamy sauce, good with pasta, rice, or in patty shells.

(SERVES THREE)

1 pint (½ L) scallops
4 tablespoons butter
1 tablespoon lemon juice
2 teaspoons flour

¾ cup (1¾ dL) heavy cream
2 egg yolks, slightly beaten
2 tablespoons dry sherry
Salt

Rinse the scallops and pat dry with paper towels. Cut them in half. Melt 3 tablespoons of the butter in a skillet and add the scallops and lemon juice. Cook for 1 minute, remove, and set aside. Melt the remaining tablespoon of butter in the skillet, stir in the flour, and cook until smooth and blended. Slowly add the cream, stirring constantly. Stir over low heat until thickened and smooth. Beat 2 spoonfuls of sauce into the yolks, and then stir the yolk-sauce mixture back into the sauce. Add the sherry and cook for 1 minute. Add the scallops and cook 2–3 minutes more. Add salt to taste.

Savoy Scallops

(SERVES FOUR)

1 quart (1 L) scallops
3 tablespoons butter
3 tablespoons flour

¼ teaspoon thyme, crumbled
½ cup (1 dL) mayonnaise
Salt

Rinse the scallops and pat dry with paper towels. Cut in half. Put them in a saucepan, add about 1 quart water, and simmer 5 minutes. Drain and set aside, reserving the liquid. Melt the butter in a saucepan. Stir in the flour and cook until blended and smooth. Slowly add 1½ cups of reserved liquid and the thyme. Stir over low heat until smooth and thickened; stir in the mayonnaise and salt to taste. Add the scallops and cook only until heated through.

Boiled Shrimp

Shrimp are bright in texture and flavor, full of protein and low in calories. Americans buy more shrimp than any other shellfish: fresh, canned, and frozen, raw and cooked, shelled and unshelled. Two pounds of shrimp yield slightly more than a pound after shelling; depending on the recipe and appetites, that pound serves two people or six. If you shell shrimp before cooking, add the shells to the cooking liquid to give extra flavor. Shrimp should be cooked only until they turn pink: 3 to 5 minutes at most. If they are going into a sauce or casserole they should not be cooked first or they will become rubbery.

(SERVES TWO TO SIX)

Salt
2 pounds (900 g) raw unshelled shrimp

Bring 4 quarts of salted water to the boil and add the shrimp. Turn the heat down so the water is boiling gently, and cook the shrimp until they turn pink, 3–5 minutes. Drain. When cool enough to handle, shell and devein the shrimp: gently pull the shells apart, and with the tip of a knife, remove the black vein that runs down the center of the back. Don't be too fussy about this: some people mangle the shrimp getting out the last unappetizing but harmless speck.

Shrimp in Court Bouillon

Shrimp is sometimes cooked in a flavored broth, called a court bouillon, that provides additional taste.

(SERVES TWO TO SIX)

4 tablespoons butter
⅓ cup (¾ dL) chopped carrot
⅓ cup (¾ dL) chopped celery
⅓ cup (¾ dL) chopped onion
4 sprigs parsley
6 peppercorns, crushed

2 cloves
½ bay leaf
2 tablespoons vinegar
1 tablespoon salt
2 pounds (900 g) raw unshelled
  shrimp

Melt the butter in a large saucepan. Add the carrot, celery, and onion, and cook for 3 minutes. Add the parsley, peppercorns, cloves, bay leaf, vinegar, salt, and 2 quarts water. Bring to a boil, add the shrimp, and cook only until they turn pink, 3–5 minutes. Drain, cool, and shell. If you are making a sauce, reduce the court bouillon to 2 cups, strain, and use the reduced liquid in the sauce.

Shrimp Wiggle

Serve on buttered toast for lunch or supper.

(SERVES SIX)

4 tablespoons butter
4 tablespoons flour
1 cup (¼ L) milk
1 cup (¼ L) light cream

2 cups (½ L) small cooked
  shrimp, shelled (p. 141)
1 cup (¼ L) cooked peas
Salt to taste

Melt the butter in a saucepan and stir in the flour. Stir constantly over low heat until smooth and blended. Slowly add the milk and cream, and cook over medium-low heat for 5 minutes, until smooth and thickened. Add the shrimp, peas, and salt, and cook only long enough to heat through.

Shrimp Jambalaya

One version of a fine Cajun dish of Spanish origin.

(SERVES SIX)

3 slices bacon, diced
½ cup (1 dL) chopped celery
½ cup (1 dL) chopped onion
½ cup (1 dL) chopped green
  pepper
1 tablespoon minced garlic
4 cups (1 L) canned tomatoes
  with liquid
⅛ teaspoon cayenne pepper

1 teaspoon chili powder
¼ teaspoon thyme, crumbled
2 pounds (900 g) shrimp,
  cooked, shelled, and
  deveined (p. 141)
¼ cup (½ dL) finely chopped
  parsley
Salt to taste
4 cups (1 L) hot cooked rice

Fry the bacon in a skillet and, when it is crisp, drain on paper towels. If the skillet is very hot, let it cool down a bit. Put it over medium heat and cook the celery, onion, and green pepper in the bacon fat until the onion is soft. Add the garlic, tomatoes, cayenne pepper, chili powder, and thyme. Lower the heat and simmer 20 minutes. Add the shrimp, parsley, and salt to the tomato sauce and cook for a few minutes until the shrimp is hot. Mound the rice on a platter, spoon the shrimp and tomato sauce over it, and garnish with bits of crisp bacon.

Shrimp Newburg

Elegant prepared in a chafing dish, or spooned over toast or into patty shells.

(SERVES FOUR)

3 tablespoons butter	½ cup (1 dL) cream
2 cups (½ L) raw small shrimp, shelled (p. 141)	2 egg yolks, slightly beaten
	1 tablespoon dry sherry
1 teaspoon lemon juice	1 tablespoon brandy
1 teaspoon flour	

Melt 2 tablespoons of the butter in a skillet or chafing dish. Add the shrimp and cook over low heat for 3 minutes. Stir in the lemon juice, and set pan aside. Melt the remaining tablespoon of butter, add the flour, and cook 1 minute, stirring. Slowly add the cream and cook and stir until the sauce is slightly thickened. Beat 2 spoonfuls of the sauce into the egg yolks. Return the egg-sauce mixture to the sauce and add the sherry and brandy. Over low heat, stir in the shrimp and cook only until heated through.

Sautéed Shrimp

(SERVES FOUR)

2 pounds (900 g) raw shrimp	2 teaspoons minced parsley
4 tablespoons butter	Lemon wedges

Shell and devein the shrimp (p. 141), leaving the tails on. Melt the butter in a skillet and, when it foams, add the shrimp. Cook over high heat, shaking the pan and turning the shrimp once or twice, until they turn pink. This should take about 5 minutes, depending on size. Remove from the heat, sprinkle with parsley, and serve with lemon wedges.

Fried Shrimp

Serve with Chili Sauce (p. 284) or Tartar Sauce (p. 274).

(SERVES SIX)

1 cup (140 g) flour	2 tablespoons oil
½ teaspoon salt	2½ pounds (1¼ kg) raw shrimp
½ teaspoon sugar	Oil for frying
1 egg	

Preheat the oven to 225°F (110°C) and warm an ovenproof platter. Beat the flour, salt, sugar, egg, 2 tablespoons oil, and 1 cup ice water in a bowl and refrigerate. Shell and devein the shrimp (p. 141). Pat the shrimp dry with paper towels. Heat 3 inches of oil to 365°F (185°C) in a heavy pot or skillet. Dip each shrimp into the batter and drop into the hot oil. Don't crowd the pot. Do a few at a time, frying for about 1 minute or until golden. Proceed until all the shrimp are fried, draining each batch and keeping warm on the platter in the oven.

Broiled Shrimp

If you can find large shrimp, broil them this Italian way. And serve lots of crusty Italian bread to mop up the sauce.

(SERVES FOUR)

1½ pounds (675 g) large shrimp	Freshly ground pepper to taste
½ cup (1 dL) olive oil	1 teaspoon minced garlic
1 tablespoon lemon juice	1 teaspoon oregano, crushed
½ teaspoon salt	1 tablespoon finely chopped parsley

Remove the shell from the shrimp, except around the tail; leave that intact. If there is a dark vein running just under the surface on the outside, scrape it out. Mix all the rest of the ingredients in a large bowl and add the shrimp to marinate for at least 1 hour, turning once or twice. Preheat the broiler. Place the shrimp in a large shallow pan with their marinade and broil as close to the heat as possible, about 3–4 minutes each side.

COOKED AND CANNED FISH

Creamed Fish

Many recipes for cooked fish can be made with canned fish as well. Serve this over toast or rice, or use it in an omelet or crêpe.

(SERVES FOUR)

3 tablespoons butter	Salt
3 tablespoons flour	Freshly ground pepper
2 cups (½ L) milk	1 tablespoon minced parsley
1 tablespoon lemon juice	
1–1½ cups (2–3½ dL) cooked or canned fish	

Heat the butter in a heavy-bottomed saucepan. Stir in the flour and cook until smooth, about 2 minutes. Slowly add the milk, continuing to stir. Simmer for 2 minutes. Mix the lemon juice into the fish and add to the cream sauce. Add salt and pepper to taste. Heat thoroughly, remove from the heat, and sprinkle with parsley.

Creamed Fish with Mushrooms. Add ½ cup mushrooms, sautéed in 2 tablespoons butter, to the sauce.

Creamed Fish with Tarragon. Add ¼ teaspoon dried tarragon, crumbled, with the milk.

Creamed Fish Florentine. Cook 1½ pounds of spinach in boiling salted water. Drain well and spoon the creamed fish over the spinach.

Kedgeree

A popular breakfast dish in England.

(SERVES SIX)

4 tablespoons butter
2 cups (½ L) cooked rice
2 cups (½ L) cooked fish
3 tablespoons raisins
¾ cup (1¾ dL) heavy cream

1 teaspoon curry powder
Salt to taste
4 hard-cooked eggs, chopped
3 tablespoons finely chopped
   parsley

Melt the butter in a heavy-bottomed pan. Stir in the rice, fish, raisins, cream, curry powder, and salt. Mix well and cook only until heated through. Arrange on a warm platter and garnish with chopped egg and parsley.

Seafood Chesapeake

A tangy luncheon dish.

(SERVES SIX)

4 cups (1 L) cooked fish,
   including crabmeat, if
   possible
1 cup (¼ L) mayonnaise
1 tablespoon dry mustard
1 tablespoon Worcestershire
   sauce
¼ cup (½ dL) slivered
   blanched almonds

½ cup (1 dL) minced celery
Salt to taste
Freshly ground pepper to taste
¼ cup (½ dL) freshly grated
   Parmesan cheese

Preheat the oven to 375°F (190°C) and butter a shallow baking dish or six scallop shells. Mix all ingredients except the cheese, tossing lightly. Place in the baking dish or the shells, sprinkle with cheese, and bake 25 minutes.

Fish Hash

Serve with thick slices of fresh tomatoes.

(SERVES FOUR)

¼ pound (115 g) salt pork,
   diced small
1 onion, chopped
1½ cups (3½ dL) diced boiled
   potatoes

1½ cups (3½ dL) cooked fish
Salt
Freshly ground pepper

In a hot skillet, cook the salt pork until the fat is rendered and the bits of pork are brown and crisp. Remove, drain on paper towels, and set aside. Toss together the onion, potatoes, fish, and salt and pepper to taste—take care not to oversalt: the salt pork may supply enough. Stir into the fat in the skillet and cook over medium heat. Press down with a spatula and cook about 5 minutes, until the bottom is brown. Turn the hash over and cook until the underside is nicely browned. Tip out onto a warm platter and sprinkle with the crisp bits of salt pork.

Scalloped Fish

(SERVES FOUR)

5 tablespoons butter
2 tablespoons finely chopped
   shallots or scallions
1 cup (¼ L) toasted bread
   crumbs
2 tablespoons flour

1½ cups (3½ dL) light cream
1 cup (¼ L) cooked fish
2 tablespoons dry sherry
Salt
Freshly ground pepper

Preheat the oven to 425°F (220°C). Butter a shallow baking dish. Melt 3 tablespoons of the butter in a saucepan and sauté the shallots or scallions until soft. Stir in the bread crumbs and toss. Remove and set aside. Melt the remaining 2 tablespoons of butter in the skillet. Stir in the flour and cook for 2 minutes, until smooth. Slowly add the cream, and cook, stirring constantly, until thickened, about 3 minutes. Add the fish, sherry, and salt and pepper to taste. Spread half the fish mixture in the baking dish and cover with half the bread crumbs; repeat the two layers. Bake 20 minutes, until the sauce bubbles.

Fish Mousse

Try making this with leftover or canned salmon.

(SERVES FOUR)

2 cups (½ L) cooked fish
Dash of cayenne pepper
1 tablespoon lemon juice
Salt
3 egg whites

⅓ cup (¾ dL) heavy cream,
   whipped
1 recipe Hollandaise Sauce
   (p. 272)

Preheat the oven to 350°F (180°C). Butter a 1½-quart mold or baking dish. Put 1 inch of hot water in a pan larger than the mold, and place it in the oven. Combine the fish, cayenne pepper, lemon juice, and salt to taste. Add ¼ teaspoon of salt to the egg whites, and beat until stiff. Fold the whipped cream and the whites gently into the fish mixture. Spoon into the buttered mold, place in the oven in the pan of water, and bake about 20 minutes, until firm. Remove, unmold on a warm platter, and serve with hollandaise.

Fish Soufflé

(SERVES FOUR)

2 cups (½ L) well-drained
   cooked or canned fish
Pinch of cayenne pepper
1 tablespoon lemon juice
½ cup (1 dL) freshly made
   bread crumbs

½ cup (1 dL) milk
3 egg yolks, beaten
3 egg whites, beaten stiff but
   not dry
Salt
1 recipe Lemon Sauce (p. 266)

Preheat the oven to 350°F (180°C). Butter a 1½-quart mold or baking dish. Put 1 inch of hot water in a pan larger than the mold, and place it in the oven. Toss together the fish, cayenne pepper, and lemon juice. In a saucepan, heat the bread crumbs and milk and stir in the fish mixture. Beat a little of the hot mixture into the egg yolks and return the yolk-crumb mixture to the fish blend. Add salt to taste. Cook over low heat, stirring, for 1 minute. Remove from the heat and gently fold in the egg whites. Spoon into the buttered dish and bake until firm, about 25 minutes. Serve with the sauce.

Salmon or Tuna Loaf

(SERVES SIX)

2 cups (½ L) well-drained cooked or canned salmon or tuna
½ cup (1 dL) freshly made bread crumbs
4 tablespoons butter, melted
2 eggs, well beaten
1½ tablespoons minced onion
2 teaspoons minced parsley

1 tablespoon minced green pepper
¼ teaspoon Worcestershire sauce
Dash of Tabasco
Salt to taste
1 recipe Mustard Sauce (p. 273)

Preheat the oven to 350°F (180°C). Butter a 1-quart loaf pan. Combine the fish, bread crumbs, butter, eggs, onion, parsley, green pepper, Worcestershire, Tabasco, and salt. Mix well, press into the loaf pan, and bake about 35 minutes. Serve with the sauce.

Tuna-Noodle Casserole

(SERVES FOUR)

7-ounce (200-g) can tuna, well drained
2 cups (½ L) cooked narrow noodles
3 hard-cooked eggs
2 cups (½ L) White Sauce (p. 265)

1 cup (¼ L) sliced mushrooms, sautéed
1 tablespoon minced onion
4 tablespoons butter
1 cup (¼ L) freshly made bread crumbs

Preheat the oven to 350°F (180°C). Butter a 1½-quart baking dish. Combine the tuna, noodles, eggs, sauce, mushrooms, and onion, mix carefully, and put into the baking dish. Melt the butter in a skillet and toss the bread crumbs until they are coated and lightly browned. Sprinkle evenly over the tuna mixture and bake 20 minutes, until very hot.

Tuna Pie

(SERVES SIX)

1 recipe Basic Pastry for 9-inch shell (p. 575)
Two 7-ounce (200 g) cans tuna, well drained
2 cups (½ L) White Sauce (p. 265)

1½ teaspoons Worcestershire sauce
1½ tablespoons lemon juice
1 tablespoon minced parsley

Preheat the oven to 425°F (220°C). Line a 9-inch pie plate with the pastry. Combine the tuna, sauce, Worcestershire, and lemon juice. Spoon into the pie shell and bake 25 minutes. Sprinkle with parsley.

Tuna and Rice

(SERVES FOUR)

3 tablespoons butter
¼ cup (½ dL) finely chopped
    onion
¼ cup (½ dL) finely chopped
    celery
7-ounce (200-g) can tuna,
    drained and flaked

2 cups (½ L) cooked rice
¼ cup (½ dL) minced parsley
Salt to taste
½ cup (1 dL) chopped cashews

Melt the butter in a saucepan. Add the onion and celery and cook over medium heat, stirring often, until the onion is soft. Stir in the tuna, rice, parsley, and salt and heat through. Sprinkle with cashews and serve hot.

Creamed Sardines

An unusual dish; serve it on toast.

(SERVES TWO)

4 tablespoons butter
4 tablespoons freshly made
    bread crumbs
1 cup (¼ L) heavy cream

1 small can sardines, drained
2 hard-boiled eggs, chopped
    fine
Salt to taste

Melt the butter and add remaining ingredients. Heat thoroughly, stirring to blend.

Kippered Herring in Cream

The word "kippered" has become a general term for various hot-smoked products. Kippered herring is put briefly into a salt solution, then air-dried and cold-smoked. It is available fresh, frozen, or canned.

(SERVES FOUR)

1 pound (450 g) kippered
    herring
2 tablespoons butter
½ cup (1 dL) finely chopped
    onions

¾ cup (1¾ dL) heavy cream
Lemon wedges

Cover the herring with boiling water and soak for 20 minutes. Drain and dry. If you are using canned herring, simply rinse off the brine. Melt the butter in a skillet and cook the onions until they are soft. Add the herring and cook 30 seconds on each side. Stir in the cream and heat thoroughly without boiling. Serve with lemon wedges.

Codfish Cakes

Salt-cured codfish is available in a few markets and Italian delicatessens. It is generally packaged in small wooden 1-pound boxes or 1-pound packages in the refrigerated section. It must be freshened before use to get rid of excess saltiness; this is done by soaking overnight or at least 6 hours in several changes of cold water.

(15 CAKES)

1 pound (450 g) salt cod,
  freshened
3 cups (¾ L) mashed potatoes
⅓ cup (¾ dL) light cream
4 tablespoons butter, softened

½ teaspoon freshly ground
  pepper
5 tablespoons shortening
2 tablespoons minced parsley

When you have freshened the salt cod as directed above, simmer it for 10 minutes in a pan with water to cover. Drain, and flake the fish or chop it in a food processor. Add the potatoes, cream, butter, and pepper and blend well. Pat into cakes about 2½ inches in diameter. Melt half the shortening in a large skillet over medium-high heat. When it is hot, put in as many cakes as possible without having them touch. Fry quickly on each side until golden-brown, then remove. Add remaining shortening and fry rest of cakes. Sprinkle cakes with parsley and serve immediately on a warm platter.

Creamed Codfish

Serve on toast or mashed potatoes for a wholesome family supper.

(SERVES FOUR)

1 pound (450 g) salt cod
4 tablespoons butter
2 tablespoons flour
2 cups (½ L) milk

Dash of Tabasco
1 tablespoon minced parsley
2 teaspoons chopped chives
2 hard-boiled eggs, chopped

Freshen the salt cod as directed above, then simmer it for 10 minutes in a pan with water to cover. Drain, and shred or chop in a food processor. Melt the butter in a heavy-bottomed pan. Stir in the flour and cook until smooth. Slowly add the milk and cook, stirring constantly, until smooth and thickened. Add the Tabasco, parsley, chives, and cod, and cook, stirring, until heated through. Add the eggs and cook 1 minute more.

Salt Codfish Hash with Tomatoes and Garlic

(SERVES FOUR)

1 pound (450 g) salt cod
5 tablespoons oil
1 cup (¼ L) finely chopped
  onion
2 cloves garlic, chopped fine
3 tomatoes, peeled, seeded,
  and chopped

3 cups (¾ L) cooked potatoes
  in small dice or mashed
¾ teaspoon freshly ground
  pepper

Freshen the salt cod as directed above, then simmer it for 10 minutes in a pan with water to cover. Drain, and flake or chop in a food processor. Heat 2 tablespoons of the oil in a large skillet. Add the onion and garlic and sauté over medium heat until the onion is soft. Toss together the onion, garlic, tomatoes, potatoes, cod, and pepper in a bowl. Heat the remaining 3 tablespoons oil in the skillet, and when it is hot, spread the hash over the bottom. Fry over medium-high heat until it is brown on the bottom. Turn over and brown the other side.

Finnan Haddie Baked in Milk

Finnan haddie is smoked haddock. It is usually sold in fillets, but occasionally sold whole.

(SERVES FOUR)

1½–2 pounds (675–900 g)
   smoked haddock
4 tablespoons butter
1 medium onion, sliced fine
½ teaspoon freshly ground
   pepper

1 cup (¼ L) milk
1 bay leaf
⅛ teaspoon nutmeg
Dash of cayenne pepper

Soak the haddock in warm water for 1 hour. Butter a shallow baking dish. Drain and place the haddock in the baking dish. Preheat the oven to 375°F (190°C). Melt the butter in a skillet and cook the onion over medium heat until soft. Stir in remaining ingredients, and pour mixture over the haddock. Bake for 45 minutes.

Finnan Haddie Delmonico

This works well in a chafing dish for a late Sunday breakfast.

(SERVES FOUR)

1 pound (450 g) smoked
   haddock
1 cup (¼ L) heavy cream
4 hard-boiled eggs, sliced thin

1 tablespoon butter
Dash of Tabasco
1 tablespoon minced parsley

Cut the haddock into strips. Put in a pan, cover with water, bring to a boil, and simmer 20 minutes. Drain and rinse thoroughly with cold water. Press dry and separate into flakes. Combine with remaining ingredients in a skillet or chafing dish and heat through before serving.

❁ Other Suggestions for Using Leftover Cooked Fish and Seafood

Cooked fish, boned and flaked, as well as seafood of all kinds, can be used effectively in appetizers; try the Hot Seafood with Mayonnaise, improvise with the recipe for Salmon Spread, or make fillings for Savory Cream Puffs, tarts, and risolettes. For an entree, substitute cooked fish or seafood, or a combination thereof, for chicken in Chicken Soufflé, Chicken Divan, and Chicken Croquettes; try also Fish Timbales. See also Filled Things for ideas on using leftover fish and seafood as fillings for crêpes or for a vegetable like cucumbers, and the Egg chapter for omelets and frittatas. There are a number of seafood recipes in the Salad chapter and a lovely Seafood Aspic using both cooked fish and shellfish.

MEAT

ABOUT MEAT

Americans have long been big meat-eaters. What with our rich farms and vast grazing lands, the supply of good meat has seemed inexhaustible and the American table has been notoriously generous with its home-cured hams and thick slabs of beef (often served for breakfast, too). Even today, when many of us are eating less meat, Americans manage to consume more meat per capita than any other country in the world. Our meals are usually planned around meat, and meat consumes more of our food dollar than anything else we eat.

Buying Meat

The United States Department of Agriculture inspects all the beef, veal, and lamb sold in interstate commerce, marking it with a purple vegetable dye according to grade. "Prime," the highest grade, is generally sold only to fancy butchers and restaurants. Supermarkets carry both "choice" and "good": while "choice" is more tender and juicy, "good" is quite adequate for cuts of meat that require long, slow cooking. Few of the many lower grades of meat are offered for retail sale.

Each section of this chapter—beef, veal, lamb, and pork—is introduced by an illustration pointing out the tender cuts that can be broiled, pan-fried, or roasted, and the tougher cuts that need long, slow braising or stewing. Notice on the beef one, p. 155, for instance: the most heavily exercised parts of the animal produce meat with the toughest muscle fibers, while the least-used parts are the most tender. If you compare this chart with the others, you will see that the rear portion of the steer that produces tender sirloin and rump is the same as the part of the lamb that produces leg of lamb; also, from the rear portion of a calf we get the leg and scallops, and from the pig we get the ham. In a similar way, there is a relationship between beef rib steaks, lamb and veal rib chops, and the tender meat on pork spareribs. And the shoulder of all these animals produces a tough but flavorful cut, delicious when cooked gently.

To determine how much meat to buy, take into account the amount of fat and bone in a particular cut, as well as individual appetites. A quarter-pound of meat with no bone and little fat—lean hamburger, for instance—may make an adequate serving for a nonravenous eater, but meat with even a little bone, such as a chop or steak, will provide only two servings per pound. With short ribs and breast veal, which have an even greater proportion of bone, you allow a pound per person.

Storing Meat

As soon as you bring meat home, either open the wrappings or rewrap the meat loosely. This allows air to circulate freely, drying the surface of the meat and retarding the growth of moisture-loving bacteria. Store in the coldest part of the refrigerator. Variety meats will keep for a day, chopped meat for two, and roasts for as much as four or five days. Beef usually keeps longer than other meats, larger cuts better than small pieces. Smoked and cured meats are good for at least several weeks, sometimes much longer depending on how they have been cured. Tenderized hams are all right for about ten days, but bacon, once the package has been opened, tastes fresher if used within a week.

To store a cooked roast, let it cool thoroughly before putting it in the refrigerator; if you don't, when the hot meat encounters the cool refrigerator air a steamy cloud will form that will encourage the growth of bacteria. Cover cooked meats loosely to permit air circulation.

For freezing meat, see p. 730.

Cooking Meat

Salting. The question of whether to salt or not before or after cooking depends on the cut of the meat and the way it is cooked. In general, don't salt roasts, steaks, and chops before cooking because it tends to draw out the juices. With stews and braised dishes, it is better to salt after browning the meat, unless you are browning in flour, which acts as a seal. All chopped meats should always have salt and other seasonings mixed in before cooking.

Roasting. Always preheat the oven. Some cooks prefer to start roasting at 500°F, then to reduce the heat to 325° F after the meat is seared and has browned. We prefer a consistent temperature of 325°F (or 350 for pork), having found that this steady temperature seems to reduce shrinkage. Either way, place your roast on a rack in a shallow pan, with the fat top side up, so that it seeps down and bastes the meat as it cooks.

Take the meat out when the thermometer registers 5 degrees less than is called for. Set it on a warm platter or a carving board and cover loosely with a tent of foil. The meat will continue to cook for the next 15 minutes while the juices settle; it will also be easier to carve after resting for a while.

Testing for Doneness. Recipe directions and charts for roasting meat can give only approximations about doneness of meat. Cooking times will vary not only according to weight but also shape (a long-and-thin roast cooks more quickly than a short, fat roast), the amount of marbling fat, and whether or not it has been boned. Always have meat at room temperature before cooking, and preheat the oven or broiler.

When the recommended time is almost up, start testing with an instant meat thermometer—by far the most accurate kind (see p. 27). Stick it into the center of the meat, avoiding any bone, and you'll get an immediate reading. For rare meat you want 130°F, 160 for medium, and 180 for well done. Pork should always be cooked to 160°F; any longer will make it dry. Don't follow the recommended temperatures on old-style meat thermometers; they are almost invariably too high.

Here are some good old-fashioned methods for testing meat. (1) Prod it with your finger. If the meat feels soft, it is rare; if it is hard, it is well done. Medium falls somewhere in between. (2) A more persistent nudge will make juices flow: if they are red, the meat is still bloody-rare; if they are pink, it is medium; if they run clear, it is well done. Pork juices, of course, should always run clear—and to be safe, test with a meat thermometer.

Broiling. Remove the broiler rack and preheat the broiler. If the meat is very lean, grease the rack with some fat cut from the meat or with vegetable oil.

Score the edges of the meat by making shallow cuts in the outside every 2 inches to prevent curling while it cooks. In general, set the rack 3 inches below the broiler element (usually the highest rung); very thick cuts of steak should be placed lower down.

Cook on one side until nicely brown—the cooking time will depend on the thickness of the meat—then turn and cook on the other side. Test with a meat thermometer or your forefinger. When the meat is nearly done, remove it from the rack, season with salt and pepper, and place, loosely covered with foil, on a carving board. It will finish cooking in its own heat.

Charcoal Grilling. Any meat that can be broiled can also be grilled over charcoal. Ignite the coals and let them become white-hot. This will take at least 1 hour. Then place the meat on a rack over the coals. Small pieces, like patties, sausages, and kidneys, are easier to turn if placed in folding grills or threaded onto skewers. Spray water on the coals to control the flames that flare up when fat drips on them. Cook the meat on one side; turn to cook the other side. Season when done.

Pan Broiling. Use a heavy skillet that heats evenly and will not scorch. If the meat is lean, brush the surface of the pan with oil. Heat, and when the surface looks wavy, add the meat. Brown it quickly until the blood rises to the top surface, then turn and sear the other side. Pour off any fat that accumulates.

Remove to a hot platter as soon as the meat is done: it will toughen if it overcooks. You can add broth, cream, or wine to deglaze the pan (p. 44), and pour over the pan-broiled meat.

Sautéing and Frying. Sautéed and fried meats are cooked in hot fat, such as butter, lard, or vegetable oil or a combination. Butter, which gives the most delicate flavor, burns easily; it helps to add a tablespoon of oil for every 2 or 3 tablespoons of butter.

In a skillet, heat the amount of fat called for in the recipe, then add the meat, a few pieces at a time. Do not crowd the pan, or the temperature of the fat will be lowered and the frying process will stop. Cook the meat in shifts, removing the cooked pieces to a warm platter as they are done.

For deep-fat frying, see p. 46.

Stewing and Braising. Some of the world's great dishes are made by stewing or braising tougher cuts of meat slowly and gently in aromatic liquid until they are tender, thus making a virtue of necessity. Usually the meat is first browned in fat to produce good color, then a well-seasoned liquid, such as wine, broth, the juice of tomatoes, water, or a combination thereof, is added, and the pot, tightly covered, is set in a slow oven or over a gentle burner for several hours. The trick is to keep the liquid just at a simmer—not over 185°F—for the entire cooking time; any more strenuous boiling toughens the meat fibers.

The resulting gravy is apt to have a considerable amount of fat, which you should skim off with a spoon; let it rest a moment and the fat will rise to the top. If you wish to remove every last bit of fat (and if you allow enough time) it will be simpler to remove if you let it chill and solidify; just put the pot in the refrigerator, or pour the juices into a separate, metal bowl, then refrigerate or set in the freezer or cool quickly over ice.

Tenderizing. In addition to stewing and braising, there are other ways to deal with tough cuts of meat. Grinding is one way; most of our hamburger meat comes from less tender cuts of meat. Tough fibers are also broken down and tenderized by pounding with a meat mallet or with the edge of a saucer. Some steaks, such as flank or round, can be scored in a diamond pattern, the cuts running through some of the tough fibers.

Tough roasts and steaks may be tenderized by soaking them in flavorful marinades that contain an acid liquid such as wine or vinegar. There are also chemical meat tenderizers, usually papaya derivatives. When too heavily applied, they produce an unpleasant, pulpy piece of meat, but, used judiciously, they will help make a piece of braising steak more tender.

BEEF

About Beef

The quality of beef depends on the feeding of the animal, the age at which it is slaughtered, and the handling of the meat. Although the very best beef goes to restaurants and fancy butchers, it is possible to choose intelligently in a supermarket. In *color,* look for bright pink-red flesh, light-colored bones, and creamy-white fat. In *texture,* look for fine flesh, soft-looking bones, and crumbly suet or exterior fat. The best beef—the sort that is served at top-notch steak houses—has a delicate network of fat running through the flesh. This is the "marbling," which dissolves during cooking, providing automatic internal basting.

Since tender and less tender cuts have practically the same food values, it is good to be able to recognize and use a variety of beef cuts. Then you can experiment with unfamiliar recipes and take advantage of sales and specials. Tender beef, like the tenderloin roast and steak, is cooked dry for short periods of time, while tougher cuts, like the chuck, round, and brisket, need slow moist cooking, as in Pot Roast (p. 159). Stew beef is cut from small pieces and ends of the less tender roasts. The best stew beef has some bone in it to add sweetness and moisture. For some reason, it is seldom packaged this way; ask the butcher to give you 1 pound of short rib or shank to every 2 pounds of chuck, or simply combine two packages of supermarket "stewing beef" with one package of soup bones, and you will make an Old-fashioned Beef Stew (p. 163) of surprising quality.

As for the great American hamburger, it is in fact made from almost any part of the steer. Our grandmothers used to buy their steaks whole and watch suspiciously while the butcher ground them to order. It is good to find a market you can trust, or, if you shop in a supermarket, get to know the butcher out back who cuts the meat. If you have a food processor, it is simple to buy labeled cuts such as chuck or skirt and grind your own; that way you know exactly what your hamburger consists of. Except for people on special diets, some fat is needed in the meat to give it flavor and hold it together: 20 percent of the hamburger should be fat. Too much fat, on the other hand, simply melts away in the broiler, wasting flavor and money.

Standing Rib Roast

Cooking time varies widely, depending on the shape of the roast and internal temperature. You'll need a meat thermometer. For Yorkshire Pudding, traditionally served with Roast Beef, see p. 492.

(ALLOW ½–1 POUND PER SERVING)

1 standing rib roast, at least 4 pounds (1¾ kg)	Salt
	Freshly ground pepper
¼ cup (½ dL) beef broth, red wine, or sherry	

Preheat the oven to 325°F (165°C). Place the meat, fat side up, in a shallow open pan and allow it to come to room temperature. Roast for approximately 20

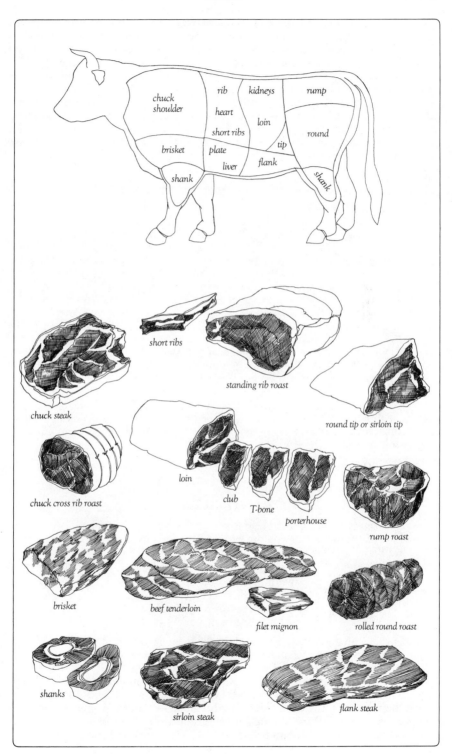

chuck steak

short ribs

standing rib roast

round tip or sirloin tip

chuck cross rib roast

loin

club

T-bone

porterhouse

rump roast

brisket

beef tenderloin

filet mignon

rolled round roast

shanks

sirloin steak

flank steak

minutes to the pound. Insert a meat thermometer toward the end of the estimated cooking time: the meat is rare at 130°F, medium at 140°F, and well done at 160°F. Remove from the oven when the thermometer registers 5 degrees lower than the desired temperature, and let the roast sit on a carving board while the Yorkshire pudding bakes, if you are making it, and while you make a simple gravy: the roast will continue to cook and become easier to carve. Drain off most of the fat and place the roasting pan over a burner. Add the broth, wine, sherry, or simply ¼ cup water, and stir and scrape with a large kitchen spoon, loosening the brown glaze on the bottom of the pan. Add more liquid if you wish and salt and pepper to taste, and cook over low heat until well blended, about 2 minutes. Spoon over slices of carved beef.

To carve a rib roast: 1. *The old-fashioned way has always been to stand the roast on its ribs and carve downward in slices as thin as you wish.*

2. *The more professional method, particularly for a many-ribbed roast and thicker slices, is to lay the roast on its side. First cut along the rib to loosen the meat from the bone, then make horizontal slices.*

Rolled Rib Roast. Place meat in a V-shaped rack and increase cooking time to approximately 30 minutes to the pound. Allow ⅓ pound per serving. Carve as you would Pot Roast, p. 159.

Tenderloin Roast

The tenderloin or fillet of beef is very costly because it is the tenderest part of the steer, but you are buying 4–6 pounds of pure meat with no bones and fat to discard.

(ALLOW ⅓ POUND PER SERVING)

> 1 whole tenderloin
> ¼ cup (½ dL) vegetable oil or
>   butter; or thin strips beef fat
>   or blanched salt pork

Preheat the oven to 450°F (230°C). Have the meat at room temperature and place it on a rack in an open shallow pan, tucking the thin end under to make it as thick as the rest of the roast. Brush the meat with vegetable oil, dot with butter, or lay strips of fat over the top. Roast for about 30–35 minutes. A meat thermometer will show 130°F for rare, 140° for medium, and 160° for well done. Take the roast from the oven when the thermometer reads 5 degrees short of the desired temperature. Place the meat on a warm platter, cover loosely with a towel or foil, and let sit for 15 minutes. It will be fork-tender and easy to slice.

Broiled Steak

For broiling, select a steak that is at least 1 inch thick. Trim its
excess fat and slash the steak every 2 inches to prevent curling.

(ALLOW ½ POUND PER SERVING)

1 steak, such as sirloin, porterhouse, club, rib	Salt
	Freshly ground pepper
1 tablespoon oil	

Allow the meat to come to room temperature. Preheat the broiler. Rub oil on
a broiler rack set in a drip pan, and place the meat on the rack. Cook it 2 inches
beneath the broiler if it is thin or as much as 4 inches beneath the broiler if it
is thick. Broil for at least 4 minutes per side for rare, depending on the thickness
and temperature of the meat and the heat of the oven. Cut into the steak to see
if it is done; eventually you will be able to test this by pressing the surface of the
meat with a forefinger protected by a paper towel: rare steak feels soft, well done
feels hard, and medium is somewhere in between. Remove from the broiler when
slightly underdone, sprinkle liberally with salt and pepper, slice, and serve.

Carpetbag Steak

Oyster and steak was a familiar combination in the improvident days
of the nineteenth century, but it is a rare and delicious treat today.
Multiply the ingredients to serve as many as you like.

(ONE STEAK PER SERVING)

Tenderloin steaks, cut 2 inches thick	4–5 oysters per steak
	Salt
3 tablespoons butter per steak	Freshly ground pepper

Allow ½–¾ pound of meat for each person. With a sharp knife, cut a slit on the
side of each steak and make a deep pocket nearly all the way through. Preheat
the broiler. For each serving, melt 2 tablespoons of the butter in a skillet, and
sauté the oysters for 2–3 minutes. Drain the oysters and stuff 4–5 into the pocket
of each steak. Skewer or sew up the opening. Rub the steaks with the remaining
butter and broil them on a rack placed 3 inches beneath the broiling element.
Cook 5–7 minutes on each side for rare and season with salt and pepper before
serving.

London Broil

A chewy, flavorful cut of meat that becomes tender when it is carved
diagonally across the grain into thin slices. A hearty marinade aids
the tenderizing process.

(SERVES FOUR)

1 clove garlic, peeled (optional)	1½ tablespoons vegetable oil
	Salt
1½ pounds (675 g) flank steak	Freshly ground pepper

Preheat the broiler. If you want a garlic flavor, rub the clove of garlic vigorously
on both sides of the steak. Rub with oil and place the meat on a rack over a drip

pan. Broil 1½ inches beneath the broiling element 4–5 minutes each side for medium, 3–4 for medium-rare. Remove, sprinkle with salt and pepper, and slice as directed above.

Marinated London Broil. Early in the day, mix ¾ *cup red wine,* ¼ *cup oil, 1 small onion, chopped, 1 tablespoon oregano, crumbled,* and *1 teaspoon salt.* Marinate the steak in this mixture until ready to cook. Remove, pat dry with paper towels, and follow the recipe, eliminating the salt, pepper, and garlic.

Pan-broiled Steak

The term "broiling" is used because here thin slices of tender steak are done in a pan with almost no fat, so the effect is much the same. A heavy frypan, such as one made of cast iron, is necessary for this method.

(ALLOW ⅓–½ POUND PER SERVING)

1 thin steak, such as tenderloin or minute steak	Freshly ground pepper
1 tablespoon oil	¼ cup (½ dL) beef broth, red wine, or sherry (optional)
Salt	

Allow the meat to come to room temperature. Heat the oven to 225°F (110°C) and warm an ovenproof serving platter. Rub the pan with fat cut from the meat or with a paper towel lightly dipped in oil: just slick the surface. When the pan is searing hot and the fat looks wavy, add the steak. Cook on·one side until brown, then turn and brown the other side. If necessary, turn the heat down and cook longer, but pour off any accumulated liquid, so that the meat will cook by dry heat. Cook as little as 2–3 minutes on each side and remove to the warm platter. Season and serve as is, or return any cooking juices to the pan along with the broth, red wine, or sherry. Cook down, scraping the bottom of the pan, adjust the seasoning, and pour the sauce over the steaks.

Pepper Steak

A lively way to serve tender steaks, and an exception to the rule against seasoning before cooking.

(SERVES FOUR)

4 shell or fillet steaks, about ½ pound (225 g) each	3 tablespoons butter
1 teaspoon salt	1 tablespoon oil
3 tablespoons peppercorns, coarsely crushed	4 tablespoons bourbon

Heat the oven to 225°F (110°C) and warm an ovenproof platter. Rub the steaks with salt. Sprinkle with the peppercorns and use a meat pounder or the bottom of a pot to pound the pepper into the steak. Turn the meat over, and repeat the seasoning on the other side. Heat the butter and oil in a heavy skillet and sauté the steaks about 4 minutes on each side. Transfer to the warm platter. Add the bourbon and 2 tablespoons water to the skillet and cook rapidly, stirring and scraping, to incorporate the bits of meat and fat in the pan. Boil down for 1 minute and spoon the sauce over the steaks.

Pot Roast

The secret of tender pot roasts lies in keeping the heat below the boil. Violent boiling toughens meat fibers. Cooking ahead allows you to chill the meat and remove the fat on the surface; chilled meat is also easy to slice.

(SERVES EIGHT TO TEN)

2 tablespoons flour
1½ teaspoons salt
½ teaspoon freshly ground
    pepper
4–5 pounds (2–2¼ kg)
    boneless chuck or rump roast

3 tablespoons shortening
1 onion, sliced
2 teaspoons thyme, crumbled
1 cup (¼ L) tomato juice
¼–½ teaspoon Tabasco

Combine the flour, salt, and pepper. Rub it all over the roast. Melt the shortening in a heavy casserole with a lid or a Dutch oven. When the shortening is hot, add the roast and brown it to a deep rich color on all sides. Lower the heat and add the onion, thyme, tomato juice, and Tabasco. Cover and simmer for 3–3½ hours, turning once or twice during the cooking. When fork-tender, cool. Remove the fat, slice the meat, and reheat in the degreased sauce, or skim off the fat, reheat, and bring to the table to carve.

Beef à la Mode

Call it pot roast, braised beef, or beef à la mode, but the process is the same: long, slow cooking in liquid tenderizes and flavors a tough cut of meat. The savory sauce is the bonus.

(SERVES TEN)

⅛ pound (60 g) salt pork, cut
    in small dice
2 tablespoons flour
4 pounds (1¾ kg) boneless
    round or chuck roast
⅓ cup (¾ dL) diced carrot

⅓ cup (¾ dL) diced turnip
⅓ cup (¾ dL) diced celery
Salt
Freshly ground pepper
3 sprigs parsley
1 bay leaf

Place a Dutch oven or heavy pot with a lid over medium-high heat. Add the salt pork and cook, stirring often, until the bits are crisp and golden. Remove and drain on paper towels, leaving fat from the pork on the bottom of the pot. Flour the beef on all sides and brown in the melted pork fat. Remove and set aside. Spread the diced vegetables on the bottom of the pot. Place the beef on top and sprinkle with salt and pepper. Add the parsley, bay leaf, and 2 cups of water. Cover closely and simmer for 3 hours. Remove the meat. Slice it and sprinkle with bits of salt pork. Strain the juices, spoon some over the meat, and serve the rest as a sauce.

New England Boiled Dinner

Serve this American classic with Mustard Sauce (p. 273), Horseradish Cream (p. 273), corn muffins, and sweet butter. Plan for some leftovers for corned beef hash.

(SERVES SIX TO EIGHT)

4–5 pounds (2–2¼ kg) corned beef brisket
4 medium onions, outer skins removed
6 medium potatoes, peeled

8 small young beets
6 carrots, scrubbed and scraped
6 small turnips, scrubbed
1 medium head green cabbage, quartered and cored

Rinse the corned beef under cold running water to remove the brine. Place in a large pot, cover with cold water, and bring to a boil, skimming off the scum that rises to the surface during the first 10 minutes. Cover and simmer for 2 hours. Then add the onions and potatoes, and continue to simmer. Meanwhile, bring a quantity of water to boil in another saucepan and add the beets. Boil them for 30–40 minutes, or until they are barely tender when pierced with a knife. Drain and put them in a 250°F (120°C) oven to keep warm. When the onions and potatoes have cooked for 15 minutes, add the carrots and turnips to the pot and simmer for 30 minutes more. Remove and slice the meat and arrange, surrounded by vegetables, on an ovenproof platter. Place in the warm oven, along with the dish of beets. Turn up the heat under the broth and, when it boils, add the cabbage. Boil for 3 minutes, drain, and place in a separate serving bowl. Serve the beef surrounded by carrots, turnips, onions, and potatoes, with the beets and cabbage in separate bowls.

Beef Stroganoff

Tender beef in a lightly tangy sauce with the flavor of mushrooms: good over brown rice. If your pocketbook can't manage tenderloin, try making it with thin slices of flank steak, cut diagonally across the grain, or very rare leftover roast beef or steak. Incidentally, if you freeze the meat for an hour or so—just enough for it to firm up—it will be easier to slice thin.

(SERVES SIX)

6 tablespoons butter
2 tablespoons minced onion
2 pounds (900 g) beef tenderloin, cut thin in 1 × 2½-inch strips
½ pound (225 g) mushrooms, sliced

Salt to taste
Freshly ground pepper to taste
⅛ teaspoon nutmeg
1 cup (¼ L) sour cream, at room temperature

Melt 3 tablespoons of the butter in a heavy skillet. Add the onion and cook slowly until transparent. Remove and set aside. Turn the heat to medium-high, add the beef, and cook briefly, turning to brown on all sides. Remove the beef and set aside with the onions. Add the remaining 3 tablespoons butter to the skillet. Stir in the mushrooms, cover, and cook 3 minutes. Season with salt, pepper, and nutmeg. Whisk the sour cream and add to the pan, but do not allow it to boil. Return the beef and onions to the pan and just heat through.

Corned Beef Hash

The chopped corned beef is mixed with potato and onion, doused with rich cream, and fried to form a crust top and bottom. Thick slices of fresh tomatoes, warm bread, and butter go well with it. So does a poached egg on each serving.

(SERVES FOUR)

2 cups (½ L) chopped cooked corned beef	Freshly ground pepper Salt
2 cups (½ L) chopped boiled potatoes	4 tablespoons butter 5 tablespoons heavy cream
1 small onion, chopped fine	

Mix the beef, potatoes, onion, and pepper and salt to taste (be careful: the beef is salty!). Melt the butter in a 10-inch skillet: iron is best, if you have one. Spread the beef mixture over the bottom and press down with a spatula. Fry over medium-low heat for 15–20 minutes. Use the spatula and take a peek at the underside. If it is nicely browned, turn the hash over. Slide it out onto a dinner plate, and invert the plate over the skillet. Pour the cream evenly over the meat and cook another 15–20 minutes, until the second side is nicely brown.

Red Flannel Hash. Mix *1 cup finely diced cooked beets* with the hash and fry.

Sauerbraten

Long a standby in German-American households, sauerbraten displays the thrift and foresight of the cook. A less than tender cut of meat is placed in a marinade for two days. It is slow-cooked, then sliced, and its piquant sweet-and-sour sauce is complemented by bland potatoes, thin slices of dark bread, and butter.

(SERVES TEN)

4-pound (1¾-kg) top or bottom round roast	2 bay leaves 2 tablespoons pickling spices
1 cup (¼ L) dry red wine	3 tablespoons shortening
1½ teaspoons salt	½ cup (1 dL) gingersnaps, crushed fine
10 peppercorns, crushed	½ cup (1 dL) sour cream
1 onion, sliced thin	

Two days before you plan to use it, put the beef in a deep glass or pottery bowl. In a saucepan, mix the wine, salt, peppercorns, onion slices, bay leaves, and pickling spices with 2 cups water and bring to a boil. Remove from the heat. When it is cool, pour over the beef. Cover the bowl tightly with foil and refrigerate for at least two days, turning the meat in the marinade twice a day. Preheat the oven to 350°F (180°C). Melt the shortening in a covered roasting pan or casserole. Remove the meat from the marinade, pat it dry with paper towels, and brown it well on all sides in the hot shortening. Drain off the fat, strain the marinade, and pour it over the meat. Cover and cook in the oven for 2–2½ hours, or until tender. Remove the meat and keep warm on a platter. Put the roasting pan on a burner and add the gingersnap crumbs, stirring until the gravy is smooth and thickened. Stir in the sour cream, letting it get hot but not allowing it to boil, lest it curdle. Slice the meat, pour the gravy into a sauce bowl, and serve with the sauerbraten.

Swiss Steak

Midway between pot roast and stew, this is a fine way to use a less than tender steak. Lots of gravy to go over mashed potatoes or noodles.

(SERVES FOUR)

1½ pounds (675 g) rump,
    round, or chuck steak
2 tablespoons flour
¾ teaspoon salt
½ teaspoon freshly ground
    pepper

3 tablespoons shortening
1½ cups (3½ dL) canned
    stewed tomatoes
1 onion, sliced

Preheat the oven to 325°F (165°C). Trim excess fat from the steak. Combine the flour, salt, and pepper. Sprinkle half the flour mixture on one side of the meat and pound it in with a meat-tenderizing mallet or the rim of a saucer. Turn the meat over and repeat the flouring and pounding. Melt the shortening in a covered pan or Dutch oven. When it is hot, add the meat and brown over medium heat until both sides are well colored. Add the tomatoes and onion, cover, and place in the oven for about 2 hours or until tender.

Hungarian Goulash

Goulash can resemble stew or soup: this one must be eaten in bowls with a spoon to manage its abundant paprika and onion sauce.

(SERVES FOUR)

3 tablespoons butter
1 onion, chopped
2 tablespoons sweet Hungarian
    paprika
2 pounds (900 g) beef round,
    in 1½-inch cubes
2 tablespoons flour

Salt
¾ teaspoon marjoram,
    crumbled
4 cups (1 L) beef broth
1½ cups (3½ dL) potato cubes
1½ tablespoons lemon juice

Melt the butter in a covered casserole. Add the onion, stir, and cook until soft. Stir in the paprika and cook slowly 1–2 minutes. Roll the meat in flour and add to the onion, cooking only long enough to brown lightly. Sprinkle with a little salt, and add marjoram. Pour in broth and bring to a boil. Cover and simmer for about 1 hour, or until tender. Add the potato cubes and cook 15–20 minutes, until done. Remove from heat, stir in the lemon juice, and add more salt if necessary.

Goulash Stew

A drier goulash than the previous one, this is good served over broad noodles.

(SERVES FOUR)

3 tablespoons butter
2 large onions, sliced thin
2 tablespoons paprika

½ teaspoon salt
1 clove garlic, minced
2 pounds (900 g) beef round

2 cups (½ L) canned tomatoes   ¼ cup (½ dL) sour cream, at
  without juice   room temperature

Melt the butter in a casserole with cover. Add the onion slices and cook gently for 10 minutes. Stir in the paprika, salt, and garlic, and cook 2 minutes more. Remove the onions with a slotted spoon and set aside. Turn up the heat and brown the beef, a few pieces at a time, in the pan oils. Return the onions to the pot with all the meat and the tomatoes. Cover and simmer for 2½ hours. When it is done, remove the pot from the burner and briskly stir in the sour cream.

Old-fashioned Beef Stew

A stew you will serve in soupbowls: dark-brown beef and vegetables in lots of rich gravy.

(SERVES FOUR)

⅓ cup (50 g) flour   1 large onion, sliced
1 teaspoon salt   2 bay leaves
¼ teaspoon freshly ground   ¼ teaspoon allspice
  pepper   12 small carrots, trimmed and
2 pounds (900 g) stewing beef   scraped
  plus bones (see p. 154)   12 small white onions,
4 tablespoons shortening   trimmed
1 tablespoon lemon juice   8 small new potatoes, peeled
1 tablespoon Worcestershire
  sauce

Mix the flour, salt, and pepper and roll the beef cubes in the mixture. Shake off excess. Melt the shortening over high heat in a Dutch oven or heavy-bottomed pot with a cover. When the fat is very hot add the beef, about 5 or 6 pieces at a time so as not to crowd them, brown on all sides, and remove. When the last batch of meat is a richly dark color, return all to the pot and pour on 4 cups boiling water. Stand back when you do it, because it will spit and sputter. Stir and add the lemon juice, Worcestershire sauce, onion, bay leaves, and allspice. Lower the heat, cover, and simmer for 1½–2 hours, or until the meat is tender. Add the carrots, onions, and potatoes and cook another 20–25 minutes or until they can be pierced easily with a fork.

Creamed Dried Beef

A "shelf supper," old-fashioned and simple to fix. Dried or chipped beef, once a kitchen staple, is paper-thin dried beef that comes packed in jars or plastic bags. The salty taste is soothed by a rich cream sauce and the small amount of beef goes far; serve on a base of buttered toast or mealy baked potatoes, split open.

(SERVES FOUR)

¼ pound (115 g) dried beef   1 cup (¼ L) light cream
4 tablespoons butter   ¼ teaspoon freshly ground
3 tablespoons flour   pepper
1 cup (¼ L) hot milk

Separate the slices of beef and set aside. In a saucepan, melt the butter, and when it foams, sprinkle on the flour and stir until well blended. Add the milk and cook over low heat, stirring. Add the cream slowly, continuing to stir constantly until the cream sauce is thickened. Add the pepper and the dried beef and mix well until heated through.

Burgundy Beef

Beef and red wine just seem to go together. Steamed potatoes, salad, and crusty bread finish off the meal.

(SERVES FOUR)

⅛ pound (60 g) salt pork, diced fine
1 large onion, chopped
3 tablespoons flour
½ teaspoon salt
¼ teaspoon freshly ground pepper
2 pounds (900 g) stewing beef plus bones (see p. 154)
½ teaspoon marjoram, crumbled
1 teaspoon thyme, crumbled
1 cup (¼ L) Burgundy or other red wine
1 cup (¼ L) beef broth
12 small white onions, trimmed and peeled
½ pound (225 g) mushrooms

Melt the salt pork over medium heat in a heavy Dutch oven or covered casserole. When crisp and golden, remove and drain on paper towels. Add the chopped onions to the melted fat in the pan, slowly cook them to a light golden brown, remove, and set aside. Mix the flour, salt, and pepper on a dinner plate and roll the meat in the mixture. Brown the beef, a few pieces at a time, and add the marjoram, thyme, wine, and beef broth. Return the pork and onions to the pot, cover, and simmer for 1½ hours. Add the small onions and cook 20 minutes, then add the mushrooms and cook 10 minutes more. Correct seasoning. When the onions are fork-tender, the stew is done.

Braised Oxtail

When your supermarket features oxtail, don't pass it up. Try this simple recipe for hearty beef in dark-brown sauce, but plan to cook ahead so that you can cool it and remove the fat easily.

(SERVES FOUR)

3 tablespoons shortening
3 tablespoons flour
½ teaspoon salt
Freshly ground pepper
3–4 pounds (1⅓–1¾-g) oxtail, in 2-inch pieces
2 onions, sliced thin
1½ cups (3½ dL) beef broth
1½ cups (3½ dL) canned tomatoes
2 bay leaves

Preheat the oven to 300°F (150°C). Melt the shortening in a heavy skillet. Mix the flour, salt, and pepper, and roll the oxtail pieces in it. Brown the meat in the shortening, turning so that all sides are colored. Transfer to a covered casserole and cook the onions in the fat remaining in the skillet. When they are lightly brown, add them to the meat in the casserole. Pour on the beef broth, tomatoes, and 1 cup water. Stir, add the bay leaves, cover, and bake for 3 hours. Remove the bay leaves, cool the whole dish, and remove the fat. Reheat and serve.

Beefsteak and Kidney Pie

The essence of winter goodness, this traditional favorite mingles tender steak and pieces of kidney under a flaky crust or baking-powder biscuits. Because kidneys are not always readily available, buy them when you can, and freeze the extras. They will keep well in your freezer for two months.

(SERVES EIGHT)

1 beef kidney
4 tablespoons shortening
2 onions, chopped
2 pounds (900 g) round steak, in 1-inch cubes
1½ tablespoons Worcestershire sauce
½ teaspoon salt
½ teaspoon freshly ground pepper

2 tablespoons butter, softened
2 tablespoons flour
2 tablespoons minced parsley
1 recipe Basic Pastry for 9-inch shell (p. 575), or 1 recipe Baking Powder Biscuits (p. 490)

Wash the kidney, remove membranes and fat, and cut kidney in 1-inch cubes. Melt the shortening in a heavy pot. Add the onions and cook, stirring often, until well browned. Add the steak and kidneys. When the meat is browned on all sides, pour on 2 cups boiling water, Worcestershire, salt, and pepper. Cover and cook over very low heat for 1½ hours, or until the steak is tender. Preheat the oven to 400°F (205°C). Blend the butter with the flour to make a beurre manié. Drop small pellets of this paste into the sauce and stir to thicken it. Put meat and sauce into a deep pie plate and sprinkle with parsley. If you wish to use a pastry topping, roll out the dough and cover the pie plate. Slash the top, crimp the edges, and bake about 30 minutes, or until well browned. Or form enough baking powder biscuits to cover the meat and bake 20–25 minutes until done.

Braised Short Ribs

Meat with lots of bone makes an especially tasty and juicy stew, and you have the fun of nibbling at the bones! Serve with big napkins.

(SERVES FOUR)

3 tablespoons flour
1½ teaspoons salt
½ teaspoon freshly ground pepper
4 pounds (1¾ kg) beef short ribs
4 tablespoons shortening
8 small carrots, scraped

2 large onions, peeled and quartered
1 cup (¼ L) sliced celery
4 parsley sprigs
2 bay leaves
1 teaspoon marjoram, crumbled
1 cup (¼ L) red wine

Preheat the oven to 350°F (180°C). Combine the flour, salt, and pepper in a brown paper bag. Shake the short ribs in the bag with the flour, coating it on all sides. Melt the shortening in a heavy casserole or Dutch oven. When it is hot, add the meat and brown to a rich dark color. Pour off the fat in the pan, reduce the heat, and add 1 cup water and remaining ingredients. Cover and cook in the oven for 1½–2 hours. Since this is very fatty meat, it is good to chill it and remove the fat if there is time. Then reheat to serve.

Meat Loaf

A hearty family meal, susceptible to many variations. The second day, slice it thin and make sandwiches on rye bread with sweet pickles.

Meat Loaf (continued)

2 cups (½ L) freshly made
   bread crumbs
1 onion, chopped fine
2 eggs, slightly beaten
2 pounds (900 g) ground beef
2 tablespoons Worcestershire
   sauce

1½ teaspoons dry mustard
1½ teaspoons salt
½ teaspoon freshly ground
   pepper
¾ cup (1¾ dL) milk

Preheat the oven to 350°F (180°C). Butter a loaf pan. Combine all the ingredients in a large bowl; your freshly washed hands are the best tools for the job. Pat into the loaf pan and bake for 45 minutes.

Meat Loaf with Parsley and Tomato. Omit the Worcestershire sauce and mustard; in place of the milk, use *¾ cup of juice from a can of tomatoes* and add *¼ cup minced parsley* plus *½ teaspoon basil, crumbled.* Pat into pan and cover with *¾ cup of the tomatoes* from the can, roughly chopped, or *¾ cup tomato sauce.*

Meat Loaf with Cheese. Omit the Worcestershire sauce and add *½ cup grated cheese.*

Meat Loaf with Bacon. After patting the loaf into the pan, cover with *4 strips uncooked bacon.*

Meat Loaf with Three Meats. Instead of 2 pounds ground beef, use *1 pound ground beef* mixed with *⅔ pound ground veal* and *⅓ pound ground pork. Red wine* may be used instead of milk if desired. Bake 1 hour.

Individual Muffin-Size Meat Loaves. Instead of using a loaf pan, pack the meat into muffin tins or Pyrex baking cups, top each with a square of *bacon,* and bake for only 25 minutes at 400°F (205°C). Turn out and serve with *tomato sauce.*

Hamburgers

The secret of first-rate hamburgers is to use medium-lean meat. Chuck is about the best, or grind your own from the skirt, particularly if you have a food processor, which does a good job. The more you handle or grind hamburger the more compact and dry it becomes. Divide and shape the patties as lightly as possible and don't press down on them when cooking or you'll squeeze all the juice out. For hamburger patties in buns with various trimmings, see p. 289.

Salt
Freshly ground pepper
1½ pounds (675 g) medium-
   lean ground beef

1 tablespoon butter
1 tablespoon cooking oil

Salt and pepper the meat and mix with a light hand. Shape into four patties about ¾ inch thick. Melt the butter and oil in a skillet until bubbling, then add the hamburgers. Fry 2–3 minutes on each side for rare; 4–5 minutes each side for medium; 6 minutes each side for well done. Pour pan drippings over and serve.

Broiled Hamburgers. Put the patties on a lightly oiled broiler rack and place 4 inches below a preheated broiler. Broil 4–5 minutes on each side for medium-rare; 5–6 for well done.

Hamburgers with Red Wine Sauce. After removing the hamburgers from the pan sauté *2 tablespoons minced shallots* or *scallions* for 1 minute, then add *⅓ cup red wine.* Cook down rapidly to half, swirl in *2 tablespoons butter,* and pour over the hamburgers.

Hamburger Stroganoff. Keep the cooked hamburgers warm while you prepare the stroganoff sauce: melt *2 tablespoons butter* in the same skillet, add *1 onion, finely chopped,* and sauté until translucent. Add *¼ pound sliced mushrooms* and cook 5 minutes, then stir in *¾ cup sour cream.* When warm through, return the hamburgers to the skillet and spoon sauce over them to heat. Serve dusted with *paprika.*

Salisbury Steak

(SERVES FOUR)

2 slices white bread	1 teaspoon Worcestershire
¼ cup (½ dL) milk	sauce
1¾ pounds (800 g) medium	4 strips bacon, cooked and
lean ground beef	crumbled
1 teaspoon salt	⅓ cup (¾ dL) bread crumbs
Freshly ground pepper	

Remove the crusts from the bread and soak bread in the milk until soft. Squeeze out excess milk, then lightly mix the moist bread with the ground beef until thoroughly absorbed. Add the seasonings and shape into a large round about 1 inch thick. Preheat the broiler. Place meat on an oiled broiler rack and cook 4 inches from heat on one side for 5 minutes, then turn and sprinkle the bacon and the bread crumbs over the top and broil another 4–5 minutes for medium-rare; add another minute each side for better done.

Texas Hash

(SERVES SIX)

1 onion, chopped	1 teaspoon chili powder
4 stalks celery, chopped	16-ounce (450-g) can tomatoes
1 small green pepper, chopped	1½ cups (3½ dL) cooked rice
2 tablespoons vegetable oil	Salt to taste
1½ pounds (675 g) medium-	¾ cup (1¾ dL) grated sharp
lean ground beef	Cheddar cheese

Sauté the onion, celery, and green pepper in the oil until just tender. Add the meat and cook until it loses its color. Add the chili powder and tomatoes. Cook 10 minutes over medium heat. Stir in the rice and salt, and warm through. Then turn out into a shallow baking dish, scatter the cheese over the top, and run under the broiler until bubbling.

Chili con Carne

In Texas, where this dish originated, strong men have been known to do battle over the proper way to cook chili con carne. This recipe can be made with ground beef, but cubed beef has more character. Serve in the traditional manner, with red pinto beans and fluffy rice.

Chile con Carne (continued)

(SERVES SIX)

2 pounds (900 g) beef chuck,
  in 1-inch cubes
2 tablespoons flour
4 tablespoons shortening

2 cloves garlic, minced
2 tablespoons chili powder
Salt

Roll the beef cubes in the flour. Heat the shortening in a heavy pot or covered skillet and brown the meat, turning to color it on all sides. Lower the heat, add the garlic, and cook for 1 minute, stirring so that it doesn't burn. Add 1 cup water and the chili powder, stirring to blend. Cover and simmer for 2 hours. Add salt to taste.

Revoltillos

An unusual dish with a strong flavor of bay and the contrasting tastes of sweet raisins and salty olives.

(SERVES EIGHT)

¼ cup (½ dL) oil
3 green peppers, chopped
3 onions, chopped
2 cloves garlic, minced
2 pounds (900 g) chopped beef

¾ cup (1¾ dL) raisins
¾ cup (1¾ dL) ripe olives
5 bay leaves
2 cups (½ L) beef broth
1 cup (¼ L) rice

Heat the oil in a large skillet with a lid. Stir in the peppers, onions, and garlic. Cook, stirring, until they are soft. Add the beef and break it up with a fork, cooking until it loses its pink color. Add the raisins, olives, and bay leaves, cover, and simmer for 30 minutes. Remove the bay leaves. Meanwhile, bring the beef broth to a boil in a saucepan and slowly add the rice. Shake the pan so the rice will level and cook evenly. Cover and cook 20 minutes. When the liquid is absorbed, toss the rice with a fork, add to the meat mixture, and serve.

Meatballs in Onions and Sour Cream

Light and creamy, these meatballs with lots of sauce are good with rice or noodles.

(SERVES FOUR)

4 slices white bread, crusts
  removed
¾ cup (1¾ dL) milk
4 medium onions, sliced
3 tablespoons butter
1 pound (450 g) lean ground
  beef

1 teaspoon salt
Freshly ground pepper to taste
1 tablespoon minced parsley
1 teaspoon Dijon mustard, or
  ¼ teaspoon dried
1¼ cups (3 dL) sour cream
Paprika

Soak the bread in the milk for 20 minutes. Meanwhile sauté the onions in the butter very slowly, covered so they do not brown, until they are translucent. When the bread is swollen with milk, break it up with a fork, and pour off any extra liquid. Mix the bread lightly with the ground beef, adding salt, pepper, parsley, and mustard. With a light hand form the meat mixture into balls just a little smaller than golf balls. Put the meatballs in with the onions, cover, and cook gently, turning each one carefully after about 10 minutes. Cook on the other side another 5 minutes. They should be soft, not browned, and just cooked through. Add the sour cream and heat, stirring it in gently around the meatballs. Dust with paprika and serve.

Corn Pone Pie

(SERVES SIX)

3 tablespoons bacon fat
1 onion, chopped
1 pound (450 g) lean ground
  beef
1 clove garlic, chopped
1½ cups (3½ dL) chili beans

2 cups (½ L) stewed or canned
  tomatoes
1 tablespoon chili powder
Salt
1 recipe Corn Bread batter
  (p. 493)

Melt the bacon fat in a large skillet, add the onion, and cook over medium heat until it is soft. Add the beef, breaking it up into small bits. Stir and mix with the onion, and cook until the beef loses its redness. Stir in the garlic, chili beans, tomatoes, and chili powder. Mix well and add salt to taste. Simmer for 45 minutes, stirring often. Preheat the oven to 400°F (205°C). Spread the chili mixture into a shallow 2- or 2½-quart baking dish. Spread the corn bread batter over the top and bake about 20 minutes.

Little Joe's

This is a version of a very popular San Francisco dish.

(SERVES SIX)

3 tablespoons oil
1 onion, chopped
1 pound (450 g) lean ground
  beef
1 pound (450 g) spinach,
  blanched, well drained,
  chopped

Salt
Tabasco
4 eggs, slightly beaten
4 tablespoons freshly grated
  Parmesan cheese

Heat the oil in a large skillet, add the onion, and cook over medium heat until soft. Add the beef, mixing with the onion and breaking it up into small bits with a fork; cook until the redness is gone. Add the spinach and mix well. Stir and cook for 3–4 minutes, then salt to taste. Mix a dash or so of Tabasco with the eggs, then pour them over the beef mixture and stir until the eggs are set. Remove from heat and put on a warm platter. Sprinkle the Parmesan cheese over.

Beef and Corn Casserole

(SERVES SIX)

2 tablespoons oil
1 green pepper, chopped
1 onion, chopped
1 pound (450 g) lean ground
  beef
1-pound 1-ounce (480-g) can
  cream-style corn

Salt
2 firm ripe tomatoes, peeled,
  sliced
1 cup (¼ L) buttered bread
  crumbs

Preheat oven to 350°F (180°C). Heat the oil in a skillet, add the pepper and onion, and cook, stirring often, until the onion is soft. Add the ground beef, breaking it up into small bits, and cook until it loses its redness. Stir in the corn and salt to taste. Mix well. Place in a baking dish, cover with tomato slices, and sprinkle the crumbs over the top. Bake 25 minutes, or until the crumbs are brown.

Cannelon of Beef

This moist loaf will be dense, smooth-textured, and easy to slice.

(SERVES SIX)

2 pounds (900 g) lean ground
  beef
Grated rind of ½ lemon
2 tablespoons minced parsley
1 egg
2 tablespoons minced onion
2 tablespoons butter, melted

1 teaspoon nutmeg
½ teaspoon salt
¼ teaspoon freshly ground
  pepper
4 slices salt pork
1 recipe Mushroom Sauce
  (p. 270)

Preheat the oven to 400°F (205°C). Combine the beef, lemon rind, parsley, egg, onion, melted butter, nutmeg, salt, and pepper (you can do it all in a food processor). Mix until very well blended. Chill, then shape into a roll 6 inches long. Place on a rack in a roasting pan, arrange the slices of salt pork over the top, and bake for 30 minutes. Remove to a warm platter. Serve with the mushroom sauce, garnished with the salt pork cut into small dice.

Beef à la Lindstrom

A spicy mix of beef, potatoes, beets, and capers. Fry it in patties, bake in a loaf, or fashion a crisp hashlike pancake.

(SERVES SIX)

2 potatoes, boiled and mashed,
  or about 1¼ cups (3 dL)
  mashed potatoes
1½ pounds (675 g) ground beef
2 egg yolks, lightly beaten
½ cup (1 dL) heavy cream
2 pickled beets, diced fine

2 tablespoons minced onion
3 tablespoons capers
¾ teaspoon salt
½ teaspoon freshly ground
  pepper
2 tablespoons butter (optional)
1 tablespoon oil (optional)

If you are going to make a meat loaf, preheat the oven to 350°F (180°C). Mix the mashed potatoes, beef, egg yolks, cream, beets, onion, capers, salt, and pepper. Shape to fit a loaf pan, and bake 45 minutes. Or, shape the mixture into six patties. Melt the butter and oil in a skillet and fry the patties over medium heat, turning as they brown. Or, preheat the broiler. Melt the butter and oil in a skillet and press the mixture flat with a spatula. When it has formed a crust on the bottom, place under the broiler to brown the top. Serve in pie-shaped wedges.

Swedish Meatballs

These small meatballs, faintly flavored with allspice and nutmeg in a creamy sauce, would be good at a cocktail buffet speared with toothpicks. They are equally good served six to a person over noodles for dinner.

(30 MEATBALLS)

1 pound (450 g) lean beef
¼ pound (115 g) salt pork
5 slices whole-wheat bread

1 egg, lightly beaten
1 teaspoon sugar
¾ teaspoon allspice

¾ teaspoon nutmeg
½ teaspoon salt
¼ teaspoon freshly ground
  pepper

2 tablespoons shortening
1½ cups (3½ dL) beef broth
½ cup (1 dL) heavy cream

Preheat the oven to 325°F (165°C). Grind the beef, salt pork, and bread together twice, using a meat grinder or food processor. Combine with the egg, sugar, allspice, nutmeg, salt, and pepper. Shape into 1-inch balls. Melt the shortening in a skillet and brown the meatballs. Transfer to a shallow casserole, pour on the beef broth, cover with foil, and bake for 45 minutes. Add the cream and cook without a cover for 15 minutes more.

Meatballs in Sauce for Spaghetti

This family favorite is particularly good made from scratch with your own homemade tomato sauce, prepared only yesterday or frozen months earlier when tomatoes were ripe and plentiful.

(SERVES FOUR TO SIX)

1 pound (450 g) ground beef
½ cup (1 dL) dried bread
  crumbs
1 clove garlic, minced
2 tablespoons minced parsley
1 tablespoon basil, crumbled
1 egg, lightly beaten
½ teaspoon salt

¼ teaspoon freshly ground
  pepper
2 tablespoons oil
4 cups (1 L) Tomato Sauce
  (p. 271)
½ pound (225 g) grated
  Parmesan cheese

Combine the beef, bread crumbs, garlic, parsley, basil, egg, salt, and pepper. Mix thoroughly and shape into balls 1½ inches in diameter. Melt the oil in a saucepan. Brown the meatballs lightly on all sides; drain off the fat. Add the tomato sauce, cover, and simmer 40 minutes. Serve over spaghetti, and pass the grated cheese.

DISHES USING LEFTOVER BEEF

Roast Beef Hash

The secret to good roast beef hash is the gravy. If you have not saved enough from your leftover roast you will have to improvise (see p. 268). Be sure to include any beef juice or drippings to add flavor.

(SERVES FOUR)

4 tablespoons shortening
3 cups (¾ L) finely chopped
  cooked roast beef
3 medium potatoes, cooked,
  peeled, and chopped

1 onion, chopped
1 cup (¼ L) gravy, leftover or
  improvised (p. 268)
Salt
Freshly ground pepper

Heat the shortening in a sauté pan and when it is hot add the beef, potatoes, onion, and gravy. Cook over high heat, stirring and turning often, until brown underneath. Add salt and pepper to taste. Turn over and cook on the other side—about 10–15 minutes in all.

Gratin of Beef

(SERVES SIX)

2 onions, finely chopped
1 large green pepper, finely
  chopped
2 tablespoons oil
2 large tomatoes, peeled and
  chopped, or 1 cup canned
2 cloves garlic, minced
1 bay leaf
¾ teaspoon dried rosemary, or
  1 teaspoon fresh

Salt to taste
Freshly ground pepper to taste
½ cup (1dL) chopped parsley
1 tablespoon capers
3 tablespoons beef juice, gravy,
  or bouillon
About 6 slices cooked beef
¾ cup (1¾ dL) bread crumbs
2 tablespoons melted butter

Sauté the onions and green pepper in the oil until slightly done, about 5 minutes.
Add the tomatoes and garlic and cook another 10 minutes or more until liquid
has evaporated and you have a soft purée. Add all the seasonings and capers, and
the beef liquid; mix well and spread over the bottom of a large shallow baking
dish. Place the beef slices on top; you should have enough to cover—use scraps
or whatever size pieces you have left over. Sprinkle the bread crumbs on top and
drizzle butter over. Bake in a pre-heated 400°F (205°C) oven 15 minutes.

Beef, Peas, Onions

Serve with buttered noodles.

(SERVES FOUR)

¼ pound (115 g) salt pork, cut
  in small dice
1 onion, coarsely chopped
½ pound (225 g) mushrooms,
  wiped clean, cut in half
2 cups (½ L) peas, cooked

1½ cups (3½ dL) cooked beef,
  cut into bite-size pieces
1 cup (¼ L) gravy from stew or
  roast (or see p. 268)
¼ cup (½ dL) dry red wine
Salt

Fry the salt pork over medium-high heat until most of the fat has melted and
small pieces are crisp and golden. Remove with a slotted spatula or spoon and
pat dry on paper towels. Set aside. Add the onion and mushrooms to the fat and
stir constantly, cooking until the onion is soft. Add the peas, beef, gravy, and
wine, stir to mix, and lower the heat to simmer. Cook for 10 minutes, then salt
to taste. Sprinkle the pork bits over the top.

Beef, Brown Rice, and Feta Casserole

(SERVES FOUR)

6 large dried mushrooms, or ¼
  cup (½ dL) pieces
1 onion, chopped
1 tablespoon oil
1½ cups (3½ dL) canned
  tomatoes
1 clove garlic, minced
Salt
Freshly ground pepper

2 cups (½ L) cooked brown
  rice
1½ cups (3½ dL) cooked beef
  in medium chunks
3 ounces (90 g) feta cheese,
  crumbled
6 black olives, pitted and sliced
2 tablespoons grated Parmesan
  cheese

Put the dried mushrooms in ½ cup hot water and let stand 20 minutes. Sauté the onion in the oil slowly for 5 minutes, then add the tomatoes and garlic, and let cook gently uncovered about 10 minutes. Salt and pepper to taste, then add the dried mushrooms, cut in quarters if large, with any tough stems removed, and the mushroom soaking liquid. Cook another 5 minutes. Preheat oven to 400°F (205°C). Line the bottom of 1½-quart casserole with 1 cup of the rice, add the cooked beef, and strew over the top the feta cheese, the olives, and half the sauce. Add the remaining rice and the rest of the sauce, and sprinkle with Parmesan. Bake 20 minutes.

Beef Pot Pie

Serve with rice, brown rice, or bulgur wheat.

(SERVES FOUR)

4 slices bacon
1 onion, chopped
1 pound (450 g) cooked beef, in bite-size pieces
1½ cups (3½ dL) gravy, leftover or improvised (p. 268)
4 carrots, cooked, sliced

3 potatoes, cooked, peeled, diced
¼ teaspoon cinnamon
Salt
Freshly ground pepper
1 recipe Basic Pastry for 9-inch shell (p. 575)

Fry the bacon until soft but cooked and drain on paper towels. Discard all but 3 tablespoons of the bacon fat in the skillet, add the onion, and cook until soft. Add the beef, gravy, carrots, potatoes, and cinnamon, stirring constantly until bubbling. Salt and pepper to taste. Put beef mixture into a deep pie dish or shallow casserole. Preheat the oven to 425°F (220°C). Roll out the pastry and place on top; crimp the edges and cut a small vent on top. Bake about 20 minutes, or until bubbling and top is golden.

Beef and Scallions, Mushroom Sauce

(SERVES SIX)

¼ pound (115 g) butter
1 pound (450 g) mushrooms, wiped clean, cut in half
1 cup (¼ L) chopped scallions
2 teaspoons minced garlic
2 tablespoons tomato paste
½ teaspoon thyme, crumbled
2 bay leaves
1½ cups (3½ dL) beef broth

¼ cup (½ dL) Burgundy wine
1 cup (¼ L) tomato purée
Salt to taste
½ teaspoon freshly ground pepper
1½–2 pounds (675–900 g) cooked beef, in bite-size pieces

Melt the butter in a large sauté pan, add the mushrooms, and cook, stirring often, until they are soft. Add the scallions, garlic, tomato paste, thyme, bay leaves, broth, wine, tomato purée, salt, and pepper. Mix well, turn the heat to low, and simmer for 1 hour. Stir in the beef and cook until just hot through.

◉ Other Suggestions for Using Leftover Beef

For an appetizer, try using a mixture of cooked beef and mushroom duxelles in savory tarts or rissolettes. And any scraps are always good in the soup pot. Cooked beef can be substituted for raw in many of the recipes in this chapter—Texas Hash, Beef and Corn Casserole, Beef à la Lindstrom, Beefsteak and Kidney Pie, and Beef Stroganoff, provided you have some rare leftover pieces; also, beef can be used in place of lamb in a Shepherd's Pie. Ground-up leftover beef makes good stuffings; check the pastas, enchiladas, and stuffed vegetables in Filled Things. Leftover beef is good in sandwiches and salads. There is also a fine Aspic of Cold Beef and Vegetables in the Salad chapter.

VEAL

About Veal

The finest and most expensive veal comes from calves that were slaughtered when they were less than six months old, so young that the animal was not yet weaned. This "milk-fed" or "dairy" veal is white and tender, but, although widely enjoyed in Europe, it is hardly ever found in American markets. Recently many states have been sponsoring the careful raising and milk-feeding of calves up to about twelve weeks, which produces much more tender veal than has been available in the past in this country. Usually here the animals have been allowed to graze, and the iron in the grass gives the flesh a pinkish red color, more like the color of young beef.

Veal has little fat and no visible marbling. It should, therefore, be cooked slowly and gently, preferably by moist heat (except when you are quickly sautéing thin slices). A very good leg or loin of veal can be oven-roasted, but care must be taken to add fat to the meat and to baste it frequently while it is cooking. Veal roasts from the breast or shoulder are gently braised in a flavorful liquid.

Veal cutlets are steaks cut from the leg of the calf. Trimmed and pounded thin, they become scallops, the most tender, delicate morsels imaginable. Because veal is scarce and costly, many of the recipes that specify veal scallops can be made instead with pounded slices of boned chicken or turkey breast. These are a reasonable alternative to the more expensive meat, although they lack the succulence and special flavor of veal scallops.

Since its delicate taste and texture are perfect foils for cooking embellishments, veal is usually presented with a little sauce.

Oven-roasted Veal

If you have your butcher remove the bone, you can fill the cavity with any desired stuffing, such as Savory Bread Stuffing (p. 278). A 6-pound roast will then serve eight or ten hungry people.

(SERVES SIX TO EIGHT)

Pork fat for barding, or 6 tablespoons oil	1 recipe Onion Sauce (p. 267)
4–6-pound (1¾–2¾-kg) veal roast, leg or loin	

Preheat the oven to 325°F (165°C). Tie strips of fat over the roast or rub it with oil. Place meat on a rack in a shallow pan in the oven. Roast 30 minutes per pound, basting frequently with drippings, until the veal registers 160°F on a meat thermometer. Serve with the sauce.

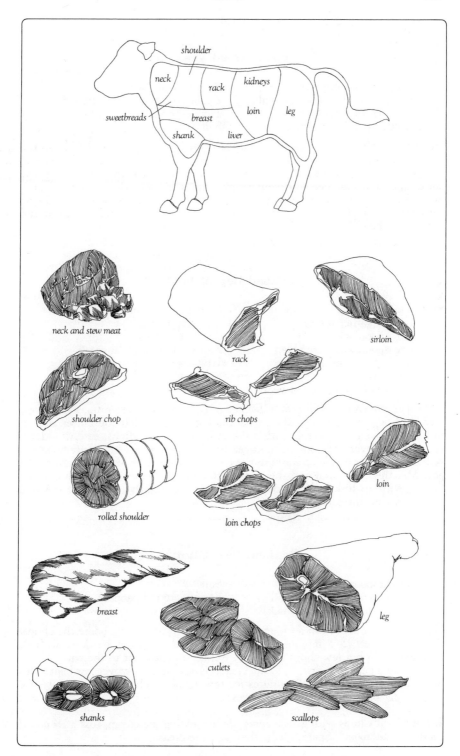

shoulder

neck rack kidneys

sweetbreads breast loin leg

shank liver

neck and stew meat

rack

sirloin

shoulder chop

rib chops

loin

rolled shoulder

loin chops

breast

leg

cutlets

shanks

scallops

Pot-roasted Veal

(SERVES SIX TO EIGHT)

4 tablespoons oil
4–6-pound (1¾–2¾-kg) veal
  roast, shoulder or breast
½ cup (1 dL) chicken broth

½ cup (1 dL) white wine
2 tablespoons butter, softened
2 tablespoons flour
Salt

Preheat the oven to 325°F (165°C). Heat the oil in a Dutch oven and brown the roast on all sides. Pour the chicken broth and wine over the meat. Cover and cook until tender, about 2 hours. Remove the meat and keep warm. Work the butter and flour together with your fingers into a smooth paste. Set the Dutch oven over a medium flame and drop pellets of this paste into the broth, stirring constantly, until thickened to your liking. Add salt to taste. Slice the meat and serve with the sauce.

Braised Leg of Veal

(SERVES SIX)

2 tablespoons shortening
1 clove garlic, minced
1 teaspoon salt
1 teaspoon sage, crumbled
½ teaspoon freshly ground
  pepper
5-pound (2¼-kg) leg of veal

6 tablespoons butter
2 tablespoons oil
2 onions, sliced
2 ribs celery, with leaves
1 tablespoon cornstarch
¼ cup (½ dL) dry sherry

Preheat the oven to 350°F (180°C). Cream together the shortening, garlic, salt, sage, and pepper. Spread mixture over the leg of veal. Melt the butter and oil in a Dutch oven or casserole with a lid. Add the meat, onions, celery, and 1½ cups water. Cover and cook in the oven until tender, 1½–2 hours. Remove the veal from the pot and keep warm in the oven. Strain the broth and return to the pot. Mix the cornstarch and sherry and stir into the broth over medium heat, beating with a whisk until smooth, thickened, and slightly clear. Slice the veal and serve with the sauce.

Braised Veal Chops

(SERVES SIX)

2 tablespoons butter
2 tablespoons vegetable oil
6 veal chops (¾ inch thick)

Salt
Freshly ground pepper
¾ cup (1¾ dL) cream

Heat the butter and oil in a frying pan large enough to accommodate the chops. Brown the meat 2–3 minutes on each side; if this cannot be done without crowding, brown a few chops at a time. Return all the meat to the pan. Season with salt and pepper to taste, add the cream, cover, and cook over low heat. This will take anywhere from 20 minutes for tender young chops to 40 minutes for tough older ones. Serve with pan juices.

Braised Veal Chops with Mushrooms. Before adding the cream, toss in ¾ *pound quartered mushrooms.* Sauté briefly, then add the cream.

Braised Veal Chops with Vegetables. Parboil *16 small white onions*. When the chops are brown, remove and set aside. Pat the onions dry and brown lightly in the pan. Return the chops, omitting the cream and adding instead *½ cup chicken broth*. Cover and cook until tender, adding up to *¼ cup chicken broth* if needed. Serve, sprinkled with *1 tablespoon grated lemon peel*. Or, instead of the onions, cut *1 fennel bulb* into julienne strips (these will not require parboiling). Toss into the pan and cook gently.

Braised Veal Chops with Artichoke Hearts. Parboil *1 package frozen artichoke hearts*, drain, and pat dry. Add to the pan along with *¾ cup diced carrots* and *½ cup chopped scallions* and cook for 1 minute. Omit the cream and add *½ cup chicken broth* and *2 tablespoons butter*. Cover and cook until tender, adding up to *¼ cup chicken broth* if needed. Serve, sprinkled with *¼ cup chopped parsley*.

Breaded Veal Cutlets

(SERVES FOUR)

3 tablespoons flour	1½ tablespoons butter
2 eggs, lightly beaten	1½ tablespoons oil
1½ cups (3½ dL) bread crumbs	1 tablespoon finely chopped
1 teaspoon salt	parsley
½ teaspoon freshly ground	1 lemon, in 4 wedges
pepper	
1 pound (450 g) veal cutlets,	
about ¼–⅓ inch thick,	
pounded	

Put the flour, eggs, and crumbs in three separate shallow dishes. Mix the salt and pepper into the crumbs. Dip the cutlets one at a time into the flour, shaking off any excess, then into the beaten eggs, letting any excess drip off. Then drag the cutlet lightly through the seasoned crumbs. Set aside for 15 minutes so that the coating can dry. Heat the butter and oil in a skillet, and fry the cutlets over medium heat, 3–5 minutes on each side, or until brown and cooked through. Sprinkle with parsley and serve with lemon wedges.

Sautéed Veal Cutlets

A cutlet is a ½-inch cut from the leg. When it is neatly trimmed of bone, gristle, and fat and pounded very thin, it is also called a scallop.

(SERVES THREE)

1 pound (450 g) veal cutlets,	2 tablespoons oil
trimmed and pounded thin	¼ cup (½ dL) dry white wine
Salt	1 teaspoon finely chopped
Freshly ground pepper	parsley
2 tablespoons butter	

Sprinkle the cutlets with salt and pepper. Heat the butter and oil in a skillet, add the cutlets, and cook over medium heat for 1–2 minutes on each side. Remove the veal to a warm platter. Pour in the wine and turn the heat up high, letting the wine and pan juices bubble for another 1–2 minutes. Pour over the veal, sprinkle with the parsley, and serve.

Veal Cutlets with Mushrooms. Sauté ½ *pound sliced mushrooms* in 4 *tablespoons butter* for 3–4 minutes. Sprinkle with *salt* and set aside. Follow the recipe for Sautéed Veal Cutlets, omitting the wine, and serve the veal with the mushrooms.

Veal Cutlets aux Fines Herbs. Omit the wine and sprinkle 3 *tablespoons minced parsley,* 1 *tablespoon minced chives,* and the *juice of 1 lemon* over the veal just before serving.

Veal Cutlets in Wine

(SERVES THREE)

1 pound (450 g) veal cutlets	1 tablespoon chopped parsley
1 tablespoon butter	2 tablespoons finely chopped
1 tablespoon oil	ham
2 tablespoons finely chopped	1 clove garlic, split
onion	¼ cup (½ dL) dry red wine

Pound the veal cutlets with a meat mallet or the edge of a saucer until they are ¼ inch thick. Melt the butter and oil in a skillet. Add the cutlets and brown lightly on both sides. Add the onion, parsley, ham, and garlic. Cover and simmer for 20 minutes. Add the wine and ¼ cup water, cover, and cook 10 minutes more. Remove the veal and keep warm in the oven. Boil down the pan juices to reduce by a third, and pour over the meat before serving.

Veal Paprika

A good-quality Hungarian paprika makes all the difference in this dish.

(SERVES SIX)

2 pounds (900 g) veal cutlets,	1½ tablespoons paprika
trimmed and pounded thin	1½ cups (3½ dL) chicken
2 tablespoons butter	broth
1 tablespoon oil	1 cup (¼ L) sour cream
2 onions, sliced thin	Salt

Cut the veal into 2-inch squares. Melt the butter and oil in a skillet, add the onions, and cook, stirring, until golden brown. Push the onions to the side of the pan, add the veal, and brown lightly. Stir in the paprika and then the chicken broth. Simmer, uncovered, until most of the liquid has evaporated. Before serving, turn down the heat, whisk in the sour cream, add salt to taste, and heat through without boiling.

Scaloppine of Veal Marsala

(SERVES THREE)

1 pound (450 g) veal cutlets,	1 tablespoon oil
trimmed and pounded thin	1 clove garlic, peeled
⅓ cup (¾ dL) freshly grated	¼ cup (½ dL) beef broth
Parmesan cheese	¼ cup (½ dL) Marsala wine
3 tablespoons butter	

Cut the veal into 2-inch pieces. Dip in Parmesan cheese to coat both sides. Melt the butter and oil in a skillet, add the garlic and the veal, and cook until lightly browned on both sides. Discard the garlic. Remove the veal to a warm platter. Turn the heat up and add the beef broth, stirring and scraping the bits of meat clinging to the bottom of the skillet. Cook 1 minute over high heat, then add the wine and cook 1 minute more. Pour over the veal and serve.

Veal Birds

Thin slices of boneless veal wrapped around succulent stuffing. Nice with hot tart applesauce.

(SERVES FOUR)

1½ pounds (675 g) veal cutlets, trimmed	Salt
	Freshly ground pepper
1½ cups (3½ dL) Celery Stuffing (p. 280)	1½ cups (3½ dL) chicken broth
2 tablespoons butter	½ cup (1 dL) heavy cream
1 tablespoon oil	

Preheat the oven to 350°F (180°C). Pound the veal with a meat mallet or the edge of a saucer until ¼ inch thick. Cut into 4 × 6-inch pieces. Spread some stuffing down the middle of each piece and roll lengthwise. Tie securely with string. Melt the butter and oil in a pan and brown the veal birds on all sides, a few at a time. Transfer to a casserole, sprinkle with salt and pepper, and pour the chicken broth over them. Cover and cook in the oven 45 minutes. Stir in the cream and cook, uncovered, for 20–30 minutes more.

Blanquette of Veal

Serve gently sautéed spring vegetables and fried bread triangles or rice with this creamy veal stew.

(SERVES SIX)

2 pounds (900 g) stewing veal in 2-inch pieces	3 tablespoons butter
6 small white onions	3 tablespoons flour
1 medium onion, stuck with 2 cloves	3 egg yolks
	Juice of 1 lemon
2 carrots, in thick slices	¼ teaspoon nutmeg
1 bay leaf	Salt
2 teaspoons thyme, crumbled	Freshly ground pepper

Put the veal into a pot and cover with cold water. Add the small onions, onion with cloves, carrots, bay leaf, and thyme. Bring to a boil, then simmer, covered, for 1½ hours or until tender. Skim off the scum as it rises. Remove the meat and keep warm. Strain the broth. Melt the butter in a saucepan. Stir in the flour and cook over medium heat for a few minutes, then slowly add 3 cups of the veal broth. Stir constantly over medium heat until well blended, smooth, and thick. In a separate bowl, beat the egg yolks with the lemon juice. Pour a spoonful or two of the hot sauce into the egg mixture, then remove the sauce from the heat and briskly stir the egg mixture into the remaining sauce. Add nutmeg, salt and pepper to taste, put the meat in a serving dish, and pour the sauce over it.

English Veal Pie

(SERVES EIGHT)

2 pounds (900 g) or more veal bones
3 pounds (1⅓ kg) shoulder of veal, in chunks
½ onion, sliced
2 carrots, in 1-inch pieces
1 bay leaf
3 parsley sprigs
12 peppercorns, crushed

½ teaspoon mace
½ pound (225 g) lean ham, in chunks
4 tablespoons butter
4 tablespoons flour
Salt
1 recipe Basic Pastry for 9-inch shell (p. 575)

Put the bones in a soup pot and cover with cold water. Add the veal chunks, onion, carrots, bay leaf, parsley, peppercorns, mace, and simmer for 20 minutes, removing the scum that rises to the top. Partially cover and simmer for 1 hour or until the meat is very tender. Remove the meat and set aside. Boil down the broth to 2 cups. Strain. Melt the butter in a skillet and let it brown lightly. Blend in the flour and cook for a few minutes. Slowly add the broth, stirring constantly, and cook until thickened. Add the veal and ham, and simmer for 5 minutes. Add salt to taste. Meanwhile, prepare the Basic Pastry and preheat the oven to 425°F (220°C). Put the meat mixture into a 2-quart casserole and cover with the pastry. Cut several vents in the crust and bake until it is brown, about 20 minutes.

Vienna Steaks

The sour cream makes a natural sauce for these ground meat patties.

(SERVES TWO TO THREE)

½ pound (225 g) ground veal
½ pound (225 g) ground beef
1 teaspoon salt
½ teaspoon freshly ground pepper

¼ teaspoon nutmeg
1 tablespoon lemon juice
1 egg, well beaten
2 tablespoons shortening
1 cup (¼ L) sour cream

Combine the veal, beef, salt, pepper, nutmeg, lemon juice, and egg. Mix lightly and form into six ½-inch-thick patties. Heat the shortening in a skillet and sauté the patties until brown on each side and cooked through. Remove and keep warm. Remove all but 2 tablespoons of drippings from the skillet. Whisk the sour cream, then stir it into the pan with the heat turned off. Heat it through without boiling, to prevent curdling. Serve over patties.

Veal Loaf

Expensive milk-fed veal is not necessary for this dish.

(SERVES SIX)

2 pounds (900 g) ground veal
½ pound (225 g) ground pork
½ green pepper, chopped fine
1 onion, chopped fine
1 tablespoon lemon juice
1 teaspoon salt

½ cup (1 dL) cracker crumbs
1 egg
½ cup (1 dL) milk
2 teaspoons Worcestershire sauce

Preheat the oven to 325°F (165°C). Combine all ingredients and mix until well blended, using a large spoon or your hands. Press into a loaf pan. Cover with foil and bake for 40 minutes. Uncover and bake 20 minutes more to brown the top.

Pressed Veal

A jellied veal loaf with the subtle flavor of tarragon. Serve it cold, sliced thin, with Horseradish Cream (p. 273).

(SERVES SIX)

1½ pounds (675 g) veal, in cubes
1 rib celery with leaves, chopped
1 small onion, stuck with 1 clove
Salt

Freshly ground pepper
½ teaspoon tarragon, crumbled
1 package gelatin
3 tablespoons cider vinegar
1 tablespoon finely chopped parsley

Put the veal, celery, onion with clove, salt, and pepper in a pot. Cover with 3 cups water, bring to a boil, and simmer for 1 hour or until very tender. Strain and reserve the broth. Put the veal and tarragon through a meat grinder or food processor. Soften the gelatin in ¼ cup cold water. Boil down the broth to about 2 cups. Stir the gelatin into the hot liquid until dissolved and clear, then add the vinegar and parsley. Blend in the veal and tarragon. Add salt and pepper to taste, remembering that when the loaf is chilled the flavors will be less intense. Pour into a mold and chill until firm, at least 6 hours. Unmold before serving.

Vitello Tonnato

This Italian favorite (it means veal tuna) makes a marvelous summer dish, lovely with an accompanying platter of freshly sliced tomatoes, cucumbers, blanched green beans. You can also substitute an equal amount of skinned turkey breast for the veal.

(SERVES SIX)

12-ounce (340-g) can oil-packed tuna
3 pounds (1⅓ kg) boned veal roast
1 onion, chopped
2 carrots, chopped
2 ribs celery, chopped
2 bay leaves
½ teaspoon thyme, crumbled

2 tablespoons anchovy fillets, drained and mashed
1½ cups (3½ dL) chicken broth
3 tablespoons lemon juice
1 cup (¼ L) homemade Mayonnaise (p. 452)
3 tablespoons capers, drained
Salt

Heat a heavy casserole and add the oil drained from the can of tuna, then sear the meat, browning on all sides. Remove and set aside. Add a little vegetable oil to the pan if less than 3 tablespoons remain, and cook the onion, carrots, and celery in it, stirring often, until soft. Add the bay leaves, thyme, mashed anchovy fillets, chicken broth, and lemon juice, and mix well. Add the meat, cover, and lower heat to simmer; cook for about 1 hour, or until tender. Remove the meat, cover, and refrigerate until needed. Meanwhile turn the heat up to reduce the juices in the casserole until quite thick. Remove from the heat and cool. Put the reduced juices and vegetables through a food mill or processor to purée along with the mayonnaise, tuna, capers, and salt to taste. Refrigerate until ready to serve. Slice the meat rather thin and spoon some of the sauce over. Pass remaining sauce in a bowl.

DISHES USING LEFTOVER VEAL

Minced Veal in Cream with Mushrooms

Serve on toast or nestled in rice.

(SERVES FOUR)

2 tablespoons butter
1 cup (¼ L) minced
  mushrooms
1 tablespoon minced scallions
  or shallots
2 cups (½ L) minced cooked
  veal

1 cup (¼ L) heavy cream
Salt
Freshly ground pepper
½ teaspoon tarragon

Melt the butter in a skillet and add the mushrooms and scallions or shallots. Cook slowly for 5 minutes. Add the veal, cream, salt and pepper to taste, and tarragon, and cook over medium heat, stirring often, for about 5 minutes, until the cream has reduced and thickened somewhat.

Baked Veal with Green Peppers

(SERVES FOUR)

2 tablespoons butter
1 small onion, chopped
¼ cup (½ dL) chopped green
  pepper
2 cups (½ L) cubed cooked
  veal
1 tablespoon flour

¾ cup (1¾ dL) milk
¼ cup (½ dL) dry white wine
Salt
Freshly ground pepper
1 5-ounce (150-g) can fried
  chow mein noodles

Preheat oven to 350°F (180°C). Melt the butter in a flameproof 1-quart casserole and cook the onion and green pepper slowly for 5 minutes. Add the veal and sprinkle on the flour, cooking a minute and turning to coat all sides. Pour in the milk and wine and bring to a boil, stirring to blend. Salt and pepper to taste. Bake covered for 25 minutes, then uncover and scatter the crisp chow mein noodles on top. Return to the oven a few minutes to heat through.

Quick Vitello Tonnato

(SERVES FOUR)

⅔ cup (1½ dL) mayonnaise
½ cup (1 dL) drained tuna
2 anchovy fillets
2 teaspoons capers

Salt to taste
Freshly ground pepper
8–10 slices cooked veal

Spin the mayonnaise, tuna, anchovies, and all but 8 capers in the blender or food processor or beat well together until blended. Salt and pepper to taste. Spread over the veal and chill for several hours. Dot the remaining capers on top.

⚙   **Other Suggestions for Using Leftover Veal**

Cooked veal could be used perfectly well to make the Blanquette in this chapter, provided you simmer the stew for only about one-half hour and substitute chicken broth if you don't have any veal stock, and for the English Veal Pie, again substituting chicken broth. Try leftover veal instead of lamb in Shepherd's Pie, Lamb à la Breck, Curry, and the Casserole of Rice and Lamb. In recipes in the Poultry chapter, veal could be used in place of chicken in Creamed Chicken in patty shells, or any of the variations, like Creamed Chicken and Mushrooms or Chicken à la King, as well as in Tetrazzini, Chicken Divan, and Croquettes. Cold veal is good sliced in a sandwich and also in Filled Things look for stuffed vegetables and crêpes for ways of using ground veal as a filling.

LAMB

About Lamb

Lamb is the meat from sheep that were less than a year old when they were slaughtered. Older sheep give us mutton, long popular in England, but rarely seen in American markets.

The choicest, most tender lamb, called "spring lamb," was once available only between March and September, making it a traditional Easter dish. Its mild flavor came from the kind of feed available in the spring. Now that sheep are imported from all over the world, we can get Australian or New Zealand "spring lamb" even in January. A spring leg of lamb will weigh between 4 and 7 pounds, while a winter leg may weigh as much as 9 pounds and is generally considered less desirable since it is older. When choosing lamb, look for bright pink flesh, pink bones, and white fat. Older lamb has dark-red meat and bones.

A leg of lamb makes a meaty, tender roast. You can buy half the leg for a small family, but it is most economical to buy the whole joint, and there are many good ways to use leftover lamb. Choicer, but far less economical, is the rack, consisting of a series of rib chops, and the crown roast, made by tying two racks back to back in a circle. Other cuts, such as the shank, breast, and flank, are flavorful but not so tender and require gentle, moist braising. Chops cut from the rib or loin are broiled or pan-fried.

Europeans eat only very pink lamb and think it a desecration to cook it beyond an internal temperature of 140°F. Pink lamb is very tender and gives off delicious juices. As with roast beef, the degree to which it is cooked is ultimately a matter of personal preference. Lamb will be medium-rare when the meat thermometer registers 145°F, and will be well done at 165°. Allow the meat to set, lightly covered with a towel or foil, for 15 minutes before you carve and serve it.

Roast Leg of Lamb

Allow about a pound per person when cooking a leg of lamb with the bone in; if it has no bone, a 4-pound roast will serve twice as many people.

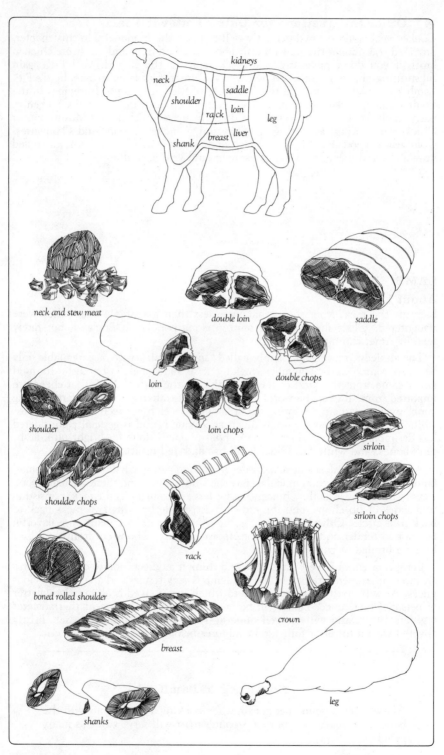

neck and stew meat

double loin

saddle

loin

double chops

shoulder

loin chops

sirloin

shoulder chops

sirloin chops

boned rolled shoulder

rack

crown

breast

shanks

leg

Roast Leg of Lamb (*continued*)

5–6-pound (2¼–2¾-kg) leg
  of lamb
Oil
Salt

Freshly ground pepper
½ teaspoon rosemary, crumbled
2 cloves garlic, in slivers
  (optional)

Preheat the oven to 350°F (180°C). Have the meat at room temperature. Place the lamb, fat side up, in a shallow open roasting pan. Rub with oil, salt, pepper, and the rosemary. If using garlic (and it's delicious with lamb) make 8–10 slits in the meat with the point of a paring knife, and tuck a sliver of garlic into each slit. Roast for about 1½ hours, or until a meat thermometer registers 145°F for medium-rare, 165°F for well done. Let the roast rest for 5–10 minutes, then carve at the table as illustrated.

Crown Roast of Lamb

A crown roast of lamb is an expensive delicacy: two racks of lamb set upright and tied back to back to form a circle. Have the butcher prepare it and ask him to crack the chine bone between each rib so it will be easy to carve. Because there are only small morsels of meat on each rib, it's a good idea to stuff the inside of the crown. If you want to be very elegant, serve with paper frills, but add only at the last; when cooking, protect the ends of the rib bones by wrapping them in foil.

1 crown roast of lamb,
  approximately 12 ribs
Oil
½ teaspoon rosemary, crumbled
2 cloves garlic, in slivers
  (optional)

1 recipe Bread Stuffing
  (p. 278)
¼ pound (115 g) mushrooms,
  chopped, or ¼ pound
  (115 g) lightly browned
  sausage meat

Preheat the oven to 350°F (180°C). Have the roast at room temperature. Place it in a shallow open roasting pan. Rub all over with oil and then with the rosemary. If using garlic, make 8–10 slits in the meat with the point of a paring knife, and tuck a sliver of garlic into each slit. Prepare the stuffing, adding the mushrooms or sausage meat. Fill the cavity of the roast with stuffing. Roast for 1¼ hours, or until a meat thermometer registers 145°F for medium-rare, 165° for well done.

Broiled Lamb Chops

A loin or rib chop cut 1½ inches thick makes an ample serving for one moderate eater.

Broiled Lamb Chops (continued)

> 6 loin or rib lamb chops
> Salt
> Freshly ground pepper

Trim excess fat from the chops. Preheat the broiler and place the meat 3 inches below the heat. Broil 1-inch chops 3–4 minutes on each side for medium-rare; broil 1½-inch chops 5–6 minutes each side. Salt and pepper to taste.

Broiled Chops with Bacon. Follow the recipe for Broiled Lamb Chops, but have the butcher bone the chops and wrap each one in *1 strip bacon.*

Pan-broiled Chops

Pan broiling works best on chops that are less than 1 inch thick. Serve two to each hungry eater.

> 8 thin loin or rib lamb chops
> Salt
> Freshly ground pepper

Trim excess fat from the chops, and rub a hissing-hot heavy skillet with a piece of the fat. Brown the chops quickly on each side, reduce the heat, and finish cooking, allowing 3 minutes on each side for 1-inch chops. Pour off any excess fat during the cooking. Salt and pepper to taste.

Mixed Grill

Potatoes fried with lots of onion and parsley go well with this dish.

3 tablespoons vegetable oil	Salt
4 lamb kidneys, cut in half lengthwise, cleaned and trimmed (see p. 216)	Freshly ground pepper 4 lamb chops, about 1 inch thick
4 tomatoes, cut in half	8 breakfast sausages, parboiled 3 minutes
8 large mushrooms, stems removed	

Preheat the broiler. Rub oil over the kidneys, tomatoes, and mushrooms. Sprinkle salt and pepper over the chops, kidneys, tomatoes, and mushrooms. Place the chops and kidneys on a rack 3 inches beneath the broiler, cook for 3 minutes, then turn them over. Add the sausages, tomatoes (cut side up), and mushrooms (top side up) to the rack. Broil 3–4 minutes more, or until the chops are browned. The tomatoes and mushrooms should just be heated through.

Shish Kebab

Start your marinade early in the day or the night before. Shish kebab is at its best if it can be cooked over coals, but if that isn't possible, broiling works very well. You cannot, incidentally, use cheaper cuts because they'll be too tough cooked this way. Be sure to push the cubes of meat together on the skewer, so they do not dry out while they cook. Try separate skewers of vegetables—the cooking time will be different from the lamb. Serve with rice.

(SERVES EIGHT)

1 leg of lamb, boned, in 1½-
   inch cubes
2 medium onions, sliced
2 teaspoons salt
½ teaspoon freshly ground
   pepper

½ cup (1 dL) dry sherry
1 tablespoon vegetable oil
⅛ teaspoon oregano, crumbled

Trim most of the fat from the meat. Mix remaining ingredients in a small bowl and blend well. Spread the meat in a shallow dish and cover with the marinade, tossing so meat is well coated. Cover the dish with foil and refrigerate several hours or overnight. When you are ready to cook, place the lamb on skewers, pushing the pieces snugly together. Cook over charcoal or place on a rack 3 inches under the broiler and broil 4–5 minutes on each side. Serve either on the skewers or pushed off on a plate.

Shish Kebab with Vegetables. On two separate skewers, place *4 small onions, parboiled 5 minutes, 4 large mushrooms, 4 cherry tomatoes* or *tomato quarters, 4 squares green pepper,* and *4 chunks canned pineapple* or other vegetables. Brush with *1 tablespoon oil* and cook for 2 minutes on each side. Serve with the skewers of lamb.

Fillets of Lamb

Mix your marinade early in the day or the night before you make these tender lamb fillets.

(SERVES SIX)

2 pounds (900 g) lamb steak
   cut from the leg, in strips ¾
   inch thick and about 2½
   inches long
4 tablespoons olive oil
3 tablespoons vinegar

½ teaspoon salt
½ onion, finely chopped
1 tablespoon finely chopped
   parsley
2 tablespoons butter

Pound the strips of lamb with the edge of a saucer to break down the fibers. Mix 3 tablespoons of the olive oil, vinegar, salt, onion, and parsley together and pour over the lamb strips in a shallow dish. Cover with aluminum foil and refrigerate at least 6 hours, turning the meat once or twice in the marinade. When you are ready to cook, remove the lamb from the marinade and pat dry with paper towels. Heat the butter and remaining tablespoon of oil in a skillet. When the foam begins to subside, add the lamb and cook quickly over high heat, about 2 minutes on each side.

Braised Breast of Lamb

A thrifty family dish, good with fresh green beans and corn bread. There is excess fat on lamb breast, so trim away all you can before you cook it, and remove the fat when the dish is finished.

Braised Breast of Lamb (continued)

(SERVES FOUR)

1 tablespoon shortening
3 pounds (1⅓ kg) lamb breast
1 tablespoon thyme, crumbled
1 carrot, chopped
½ onion, stuck with 3 cloves

½ cup (1 dL) cubed turnip
½ teaspoon freshly ground
   pepper
Salt

Melt the shortening in a heavy pot with a cover or a Dutch oven. Add the lamb breast and brown lightly on both sides. Sprinkle with thyme and pour 2 cups of boiling water over it. Add carrot, onion stuck with cloves, turnip, and pepper. Lower the heat, cover, and simmer for 1½ hours. Salt to taste. Remove as much fat as possible with a spoon. Cut the ribs apart before serving.

Grilled Butterflied Leg of Lamb

A tender lamb steak that may be cooked over coals or in the broiler, offering both a crisp well-done exterior and succulent rare insides. Start to marinate in the afternoon.

(SERVES SIX)

4 tablespoons olive oil
2 cloves garlic, minced
1 teaspoon rosemary, crumbled
1 teaspoon salt

1 teaspoon freshly ground
   pepper
5-pound (2¼-kg) leg of lamb,
   split open and bone removed

Put the olive oil in a small bowl and add the garlic, rosemary, salt, and pepper. Mix well, and rub mixture all over the lamb. Put the meat on a broiler rack and cover it lightly with wax paper. Let stand for 2–3 hours before broiling. Preheat the broiler. Remove the wax paper and place the lamb on the rack 4 inches below the broiler. Cook 15 minutes on each side. Test by cutting a small slit in the thickest part. It should be slightly pink inside and nicely browned on top. Slice across the grain on the diagonal, and serve with natural juices.

Fricassee of Lamb

A succulent dish to serve with parslied boiled potatoes.

(SERVES SIX)

2 pounds (900 g) boneless
   shoulder of lamb, in 1½-
   inch cubes
2 tablespoons flour
2 tablespoons vegetable
   shortening
2 cups (½ L) boiling tomato
   juice

1 medium onion, chopped
2 carrots, chopped
4 parsley sprigs, chopped
1 bay leaf
4 cloves
Salt
Freshly ground pepper

Trim off most of the lamb fat. Dust the lamb cubes with the flour. Melt the shortening in a heavy pot with a cover or a Dutch oven. Brown the lamb pieces on all sides. Pour the boiling tomato juice over the meat, then add the onion, carrots, parsley, bay leaf, and cloves. Lower the heat, cover, and simmer for 1½–2 hours, or until lamb is very tender. Salt and pepper to taste. Remove the bay leaf and serve.

Irish Stew

The simple goodness of lamb and roast vegetables tasting of themselves. Try that fine old-fashioned twosome—Irish Stew and Dumplings (p. 245).

(SERVES SIX)

2 pounds (900 g) boneless shoulder of lamb, in 1½-inch cubes
2 tablespoons shortening
1 cup (¼ L) ½-inch carrot slices

1 cup (¼ L) cubed white turnip
1 potato, peeled and cubed
1 onion, sliced
Salt to taste
Freshly ground pepper

Take care to trim off most of the lamb fat. Melt the shortening in a heavy pot, add the lamb cubes, and brown them well on all sides. Stand back while you pour 2 cups of boiling water over the lamb—it will sizzle and sputter. Cover and simmer for 1 hour. Add the carrot, turnip, potatoes, onion, salt and pepper, cover, and simmer 30 minutes more. Taste, correct for seasoning, and serve.

Savory Lamb Patties

(SERVES FOUR)

1 pound (450 g) lean ground lamb
1 cup (¼ L) freshly made dry bread crumbs
¾ teaspoon salt
¼ teaspoon freshly ground pepper
½ cup (1 dL) finely chopped celery

2 teaspoons Worcestershire sauce
½ teaspoon rosemary, crumbled
2 tomatoes, peeled, seeded, chopped fine
1 egg, slightly beaten
2 tablespoons shortening

Combine the lamb, bread crumbs, salt, pepper, celery, Worcestershire sauce, rosemary, tomatoes, and egg in a large bowl. Mix together and shape into six patties. Melt the shortening in a skillet and fry the patties over medium heat for 5 minutes on each side or until brown and cooked as desired.

Braised Lamb Shanks

The meat on lamb shanks is particularly succulent from lying close to the bone. You will need one per person because there is not actually much meat on them.

(SERVES FOUR)

4 lamb shanks
2 fat cloves garlic, each in 8 slivers
2 tablespoons flour
3 tablespoons shortening
1 bay leaf

1 tablespoon grated lemon rind
⅓ cup (¾ dL) lemon juice
Salt
Freshly ground pepper
4 carrots, in ½-inch pieces
8 small onions, peeled

Cut four slits in the flesh of each lamb shank; insert a sliver of garlic in each slit. Lightly dust the shanks with flour. Heat the shortening in a Dutch oven or a heavy pot with a lid. Put the shanks in and brown on all sides. Remove all but 1 tablespoon fat. Add the bay leaf, lemon rind, lemon juice, and ¼ cup water, and sprinkle salt and pepper over all. Lower the heat, cover, and simmer for 1½–2 hours, depending on the tenderness of the shanks. Add the carrots and onions for the last 40 minutes of cooking. Remove shanks and vegetables to a platter and keep warm. Serve with the pot juices or make a gravy following the recipe for Brown Gravy (p. 269).

Lamb Curry

A mild curry: add more curry powder if a spicy dish is desired. If you use leftover lamb, substitute beef broth for the lamb broth. Serve with rice and chutney.

(SERVES SIX)

2 pounds (900 g) boned lean
   lamb, in 1½-inch cubes
3 onions, sliced
1 teaspoon thyme, crumbled
2 parsley sprigs

3 tablespoons butter
3 tablespoons flour
2 teaspoons curry powder
Salt
Freshly ground pepper

Put the meat in a heavy pot with a lid or a Dutch oven and cover with 1 quart of boiling water. Add the onions, thyme, and parsley. Simmer for 1 hour, skimming the scum that rises to the top during the first 15 minutes. Remove the meat, strain the liquid, and set aside. In a skillet, melt the butter and gradually stir in the flour and curry powder. Cook over low heat, stirring constantly, for 3 minutes. Slowly add the lamb broth and stir. Add salt and pepper to taste, and cook, stirring, for several minutes, until the sauce thickens.

DISHES USING LEFTOVER LAMB

Moussaka I

Pronounced "*moo*-sah-kah," this is a traditional Greek dish. Make it with either uncooked or leftover lamb. For best results when frying eggplant, see p. 383.

(SERVES SIX TO EIGHT)

6 tablespoons vegetable oil
¼ cup (½ dL) chopped onion
1 pound (450 g) fresh or
   cooked ground lamb
½ teaspoon allspice
½ teaspoon salt
½ teaspoon freshly ground
   pepper

1 cup (¼ L) tomato sauce
3 eggplants
3 eggs, lightly beaten
2 cups (½ L) light cream
2 tablespoons minced parsley
1 cup (¼ L) freshly made dry
   bread crumbs
4 tablespoons butter, melted

Preheat the oven to 350°F (180°C). Grease a 2½-quart baking dish. Heat 2 tablespoons of the oil in a skillet, add the onion, and cook, stirring, until soft.

If using fresh lamb, add to the onion and cook, stirring, until most of the pinkness disappears. Add the allspice, salt, pepper, and tomato sauce to the skillet, along with the cooked lamb if you are using it. Cover and simmer for 30 minutes. Heat the remaining 4 tablespoons of oil in a skillet. Cut the eggplants into ¼-inch slices. Have the oil very hot, and quickly brown each side of the eggplant slices, then pat them dry of excess oil. Mix the eggs, cream, parsley, and ½ cup of the bread crumbs. Put a layer of eggplant on the bottom of the casserole and spread a layer of the lamb mixture over it. Continue layering, ending with eggplant on top. Pour the egg mixture over all, sprinkle the remaining ½ cup of crumbs on top, and drizzle the butter over. Bake 40 minutes or until the egg custard is set.

Moussaka II

Another version of the Greek classic, in which the ground lamb is wrapped in shiny eggplant skins. It takes a little care to make but is a beautiful dish.

(SERVES SIX)

4 medium eggplants
2 tablespoons olive oil
1 cup (¼ L) finely chopped onion
½ pound (225 g) mushrooms, chopped fine
2 cups (½ L) ground cooked lamb
3 cloves peeled garlic, chopped fine

1 teaspoon thyme, crumbled
1 teaspoon rosemary, crumbled
1 teaspoon salt
½ teaspoon freshly ground pepper
2½ cups (6 dL) Tomato Sauce (p. 271)

Preheat the oven to 375°F (190°C). Oil a 2-quart mold that is about 7 inches in diameter and 4 inches deep, such as a charlotte mold or a deep cake pan. Rinse a cookie sheet with cold water and shake off the excess. Slice the eggplants in half and make several deep gashes in their flesh, taking care not to cut down through the skin. Rub the cut surfaces with olive oil and place, skin side down, on the cookie sheet. Bake for 30 minutes, or until the flesh is tender. Set aside to cool. In a large bowl, mix the onion, mushrooms, lamb, garlic, thyme, rosemary, salt, and pepper. Carefully scoop out the eggplant flesh, chop it, and mix well with the lamb mixture. Use the skins to line the mold, placing the purple outer sides against the mold. If necessary, patch so that none of the mold is exposed. Let 3–4 inches of the skins hang down outside the mold. Pack the lamb mixture into the skin-lined mold, and enclose it by folding the ends of the skins over the top. Place in a pan of boiling water and bake for 1½ hours. Remove from the oven and let stand for 10 minutes while you heat the tomato sauce. Turn the moussaka out onto a warm platter and spoon a little sauce over the top. Pass the rest of the sauce at the table.

Shepherd's Pie

Not really a pie, but a fragrant dish of lamb, onion, rosemary, and garlic, under a "crust" of browned mashed potatoes. Use any kind of cooked lamb.

Shepherd's Pie (continued)

(SERVES SIX)

3 cups (¾ L) chopped cooked
   lamb
1 large clove garlic, peeled
1 small onion
1 teaspoon rosemary, crumbled
4 tablespoons butter
2 tablespoons flour

¾ cup (1¾ dL) beef or lamb
   broth
Salt
Freshly ground pepper
4 medium potatoes, cooked
   and mashed, about 3 cups
   (¾ L)

Preheat the oven to 375°F (190°C). Combine the lamb, garlic, onion, and rosemary. Put through a meat grinder twice, or chop until fine in a food processor. Melt the butter in a skillet and stir in the flour. Cook for a few minutes until smooth and blended. Slowly add the beef or lamb broth. Stir and cook until the gravy is thickened, cooking at least 5 minutes to get rid of the raw flour taste. Add the lamb mixture, stir to blend, and add salt and pepper to taste. Spoon into a 1½-quart casserole or deep pie dish. Spread the mashed potatoes on top and cover evenly to the edge of the casserole. Make a crisscross design with a fork. Bake for 35–40 minutes or until the meat is bubbling hot and the potatoes are browned.

Lamb à la Breck

A pleasing, rather mild custard made with leftover lamb. Nice for Sunday supper.

(SERVES SIX)

2 cups (½ L) finely chopped
   cooked lamb
Salt to taste
Freshly ground pepper to taste
2 tablespoons minced onion

2 tablespoons minced celery
   with leaves
2 cups (½ L) cooked macaroni
3 eggs, slightly beaten
2 cups (½ L) milk

Preheat the oven to 350°F (180°C). Butter a 1½-quart baking dish. Combine the lamb, salt, pepper, onion, and celery in a bowl and mix well. Spread the cooked macaroni on the bottom of the baking dish and put the lamb mixture over it. Mix the eggs and milk together and pour on top. Bake for 30–40 minutes or until the custard is firm. Serve very hot.

Lamb in Barbecue Sauce

Serve cooked lamb in a plum-colored sweet-and-sour sauce. A trifle fiery and very good.

(SERVES SIX)

4 tablespoons butter
2 tablespoons vinegar
½ cup (1 dL) currant jelly
½ teaspoon dry mustard

⅛ teaspoon cayenne pepper
Salt to taste
6 slices cooked lamb

Melt the butter in a skillet. Stir in the vinegar, jelly, mustard, cayenne, and salt. Stir and cook over medium heat until the sauce is smooth and hot. Add the lamb to the skillet. Turn it over in the sauce, coating the slices and heating them thoroughly.

Casserole of Rice and Lamb

Cooked lamb and cooked rice are combined in this moist and mild hash with rather a tang.

(SERVES FOUR)

2 cups (½ L) finely chopped
  cooked lamb
2 cups (½ L) cooked rice
2 tablespoons minced onion
Pinch of cayenne pepper
¾ cup (1¾ dL) lamb gravy or
  juices or chicken broth

3 tablespoons lemon juice
Salt
Freshly ground pepper
3 tablespoons butter, melted
½ cup (1 dL) fresh cracker
  crumbs

Preheat the oven to 350°F (180°C). Butter a 1½-quart baking dish. Combine the lamb, rice, onion, cayenne, gravy or broth, and lemon juice in a large bowl. Mix well, add salt and pepper to taste, and put into the baking dish. Toss the melted butter and crumbs together and sprinkle over the top. Cover the dish with a piece of buttered wax paper and bake for 20 minutes. Remove the paper and bake 15 more minutes, until the crumbs are brown.

Quick Lamb Curry

(SERVES FOUR)

2 onions, roughly chopped
2 tablespoons butter
2 cups (½ L) cooked lamb in
  medium pieces
2 tablespoons flour
1¼ cups (3 dL) hot beef or
  chicken broth

2 teaspoons curry powder
2 tart apples, peeled and cut in
  wedges
1 tablespoon raisins
Salt to taste
Freshly ground pepper

Sauté the onions in the butter slowly in a large heavy skillet, until they are translucent. Add the lamb and when warm through sprinkle on the flour. Stir to blend into the meat and onions thoroughly, then add the hot broth, stirring constantly until thick. Add the curry, apples, raisins, salt and pepper to taste and simmer, covered, for 5 to 10 minutes until the apples are just cooked but still hold their shape. Serve with rice.

❀ Other Suggestions for Using Leftover Lamb

Cooked lamb could be used in the Fricassee of Lamb in this chapter, but cook the stew only one-half hour, and also in the Savory Lamb Patties. Lamb croquettes are particularly delicious—just follow the recipe for Chicken Croquettes and add a touch of dill. Use lamb instead of veal in Blanquette of Veal and instead of pork in Pork Turnovers. Leftover lamb makes a good sandwich, particularly nice when stuffed into pita bread—see the recipe in Filled Things; see also stuffed vegetables there, especially the eggplant which is so good with lamb. And try Lentils and Lamb, a fine main-course bean dish.

PORK
About Pork
Fresh pork is flavorful, high in protein and in vitamin B_1. Unfortunately, it is too often served tasteless and dry, overcooked in an effort to make it safe to eat. It is true that pork should be cooked enough to destroy any trichinae, but an internal temperature of 140°F is considered safe, and you can be absolutely sure when a thermometer registers 160°F, well before the pork loses its wonderful succulence.

Nearly every part of the pig is edible and delicious, from the costly tenderloin to the lowly pig's feet. In general, allow ⅓ pound of meat for a serving. Look for light pink to white meat, pink bones, and white fat. The graining in pork is not fat, but muscle, which is why it is sometimes dry. Contrary to our preconceptions, some cuts of pork, such as the tenderloin, are so lacking in fat that they need some added fat in cooking.

For roasting, choose the loin, shoulder, or leg, or, for a very special occasion, a whole suckling pig. Chops, too, are cut from the loin, rib, and shoulder; although they are tender, they dry out quickly when they are broiled, and are usually baked or braised instead. Wonderful meals can be made from the spareribs, the feet, or salt pork. Cured in salt or in brine, salt pork, which is used to add flavor to many complicated stews, also stands on its own in the traditional Fried Salt Pork, Country Style (p. 200).

Roast Pork

Ask the butcher to cut through the chine bone, and the roast will be easy to carve. If you want to do a 5- to 7-pound roast, it will need three or more hours of cooking time. Serve with hot applesauce and horseradish.

(SERVES FOUR)

4-pound (1¾-kg) loin of pork	Freshly ground pepper
Salt	½ teaspoon thyme, crumbled

Preheat the oven to 350°F (180°C). Put the roast, fat side up, on a rack in a shallow open pan. Rub lightly with salt, pepper, and thyme. Roast 1¾–2 hours, or until the internal temperature is 160°F. Remove from the oven and let rest for 15 minutes for easy carving.

Broiled Pork Tenderloin

The leanness of the meat requires a strip or two of fat to be placed over it before it is broiled.

(SERVES SIX)

2 pork tenderloins, about
¾ pound (340 g) each
4 strips bacon

Preheat the broiler. Tie the bacon in place on top of the tenderloin. Place the meat on a rack over a shallow pan, 4 inches beneath the broiler element. Cook about 12 minutes in all. Slice and serve.

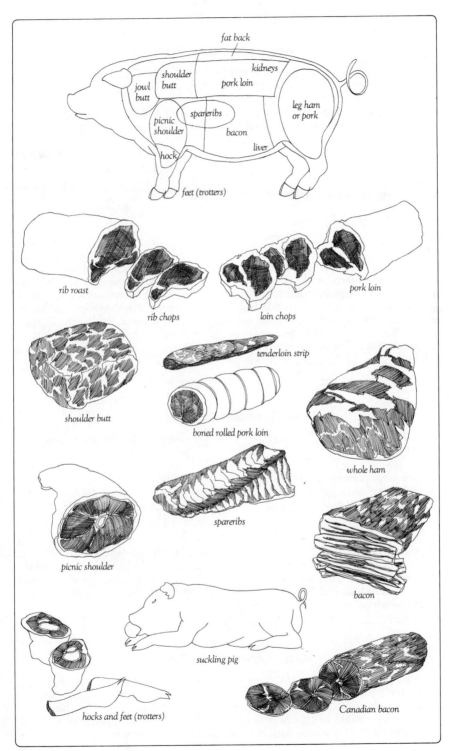

fat back

kidneys

shoulder butt

pork loin

jowl butt

leg ham or pork

picnic shoulder

spareribs

bacon

hock

liver

feet (trotters)

rib roast

rib chops

loin chops

pork loin

shoulder butt

tenderloin strip

boned rolled pork loin

whole ham

picnic shoulder

spareribs

bacon

suckling pig

hocks and feet (trotters)

Canadian bacon

Roast Suckling Pig

The butcher will prepare the pig for you, cleaning it, propping the mouth open with a small piece of wood, and slashing the skin on either side of the backbone so that it doesn't swell and burst. Garnish this splendid pig with parsley or watercress, or put a wreath of laurel or holly around its neck. Remove the wood and put a rosy apple in its mouth.

(SERVES TEN)

10–15-pound (4½–6¾-kg) suckling pig
½ cup (1 dL) vegetable oil
Salt
Freshly ground pepper

Two recipes Bread Stuffing (p. 278), plus 2 teaspoons sage, crumbled
¼ pound (115 g) butter, melted

Preheat the oven to 350°F (180°C). Rub the pig with the oil and sprinkle with salt and pepper. Stuff lightly with the stuffing and sew the cavity shut. Put the pig on its side on a rack in a shallow roasting pan or, if your oven is large enough, lay it on its stomach, with its front knees bent and tied to the rack and its hind legs stretched backward, tied together. Cover the ears and tail with foil so they don't burn. Place in the oven and baste every 20 minutes with the melted butter until there are enough pan juices for basting. Roast about 2½ hours, basting often, then remove foil. Roast about 30 minutes more, until the internal temperature is 165°F. Remove and let rest at room temperature for 10–15 minutes before carving. Make gravy from the pan juices (p. 268).

Pork Tenderloin Teriyaki

Add flavor to pork tenderloin with this Oriental marinade, mixed early in the day.

(SERVES SIX)

4 tablespoons soy sauce
1 clove garlic, minced
½ teaspoon freshly ground pepper
2 teaspoons light-brown sugar

2 tablespoons olive oil
1 teaspoon ground ginger
2 pork tenderloins, about ¾ pound (340 g) each

Combine the soy sauce, garlic, pepper, brown sugar, oil, and ginger in a jar. Cover tightly and shake until all the ingredients are well blended. Pour over the tenderloins and let them marinate for several hours. Drain and place on a rack over a shallow pan 4 inches beneath the broiler element. Broil for 12–15 minutes. Slice and serve.

Skillet-fried Pork Chops

Fried pork chops retain their tenderness and moisture when they aren't cooked to death. Cook ½-inch chops 5 minutes each side; ¾-inch chops only 8 minutes; 1-inch chops 10 minutes a side. Anything thicker should be lightly browned and then braised in liquid. All are especially nice served with a snowdrift of mashed potatoes.

6 pork chops, cut ½–¾ inch
   thick
2 tablespoons flour
Salt

Freshly ground pepper
3 tablespoons shortening
½ cup (1 dL) cider or chicken
   broth

Lightly dust the pork chops with flour, shaking off the excess. Sprinkle with salt and pepper. Heat the shortening in the skillet and brown the chops over medium heat for 5–8 minutes, as directed above. Remove to a warm platter. Pour off all but 2 tablespoons of fat. Splash in the cider or broth, cook down 1 minute, and spoon over the chops.

Braised Pork Chops with Sweet Potatoes

4 sweet potatoes
6 pork chops, cut 1½ inches
   thick
2 tablespoons flour

Salt
Freshly ground pepper
3 tablespoons shortening

Parboil the sweet potatoes for 20 minutes in boiling water. Peel, cut into ½-inch slices, and set aside. Lightly dust the chops with flour, shaking off the excess. Sprinkle with salt and pepper. Melt the shortening in the skillet and brown the chops over medium-high heat for 1 minute on each side. Add the sweet potatoes to the pan, cover, and cook over medium heat for 30 minutes.

Braised Pork Chops with Apples. Omit the sweet potatoes and add 4 *apples, peeled, cored, and sliced,* to the chops in the skillet.

Braised Pork Chops with Cabbage. Omit the sweet potatoes and add 4 *cups finely shredded cabbage* and ½ *teaspoon caraway seeds* to the chops in the skillet.

Braised Pork Chops with Sauerkraut. Omit the sweet potatoes and add 2 *cups sauerkraut* and 6 *juniper berries* to the chops in the skillet.

Casserole of Pork Chops, Sweet Potatoes, and Apples

4 large sweet potatoes
3 tablespoons shortening
Six 1½-inch-thick pork chops,
   trimmed
Salt

Freshly ground pepper
½ recipe Onion Stuffing
   (p. 279)
3 large tart apples
½ cup (1 dL) raisins

Preheat the oven to 400°F (205°C). Peel the sweet potatoes and cut into thirds. Put the pieces into a pan, cover with water, bring to a boil, and cook about 10 minutes or until barely tender when pierced with a fork; drain and set aside. Melt the shortening in a large skillet. Add the chops and brown quickly on both sides. Sprinkle with salt and pepper, remove, and set aside to cool. Cut a slit in the side of each chop, deep enough to make a pocket. Fill each pocket with stuffing. Arrange the chops in a shallow baking dish and place the sweet potatoes around them. Peel, halve, and core the apples. Fill the cores with most of the raisins, and place the apples around the chops. Sprinkle remaining raisins on top. Cover snugly with foil, and bake for 45–60 minutes, or until the chops and apples are tender.

Rib Chops with Celery Stuffing and Apples

Apples and meat juices add flavor to the stuffing.

(SERVES SIX)

2 tablespoons shortening
6 thick rib pork chops,
    trimmed
Salt
Freshly ground pepper

1 recipe Celery Stuffing
    (p. 280)
3 firm red apples, cored and
    halved

Preheat the oven to 350°F (180°C). Grease a 1½-quart covered casserole. Melt the shortening in a skillet and brown the chops on each side. Sprinkle with salt and pepper. Spread the stuffing on the bottom of the casserole and place the browned pork chops over it. Put one half-apple, cut side down, on top of each pork chop. Cover snugly and bake about 45 minutes.

Braised Mexican Pork Chops

(SERVES SIX)

2½ cups (6 dL) tomato juice
1 tablespoon chili powder
1 teaspoon salt
½ teaspoon freshly ground
    pepper
1 cup (¼ L) rice

2 tablespoons shortening
1 green pepper, chopped
1 onion, chopped
Six 1-inch pork chops,
    trimmed

Preheat the oven to 350°F (180°C). Grease a 1½-quart covered casserole. Combine the tomato juice, chili powder, salt, and pepper in a saucepan. Bring to a boil and add the rice. Shake the pan to level the rice, cover, and simmer for 20 minutes. Remove from heat and set aside. Meanwhile, melt the shortening in a skillet and add the green pepper and onion. Stir over medium heat until transparent. Add the pepper and onion to the rice and toss with a fork. There should be a film of shortening left in the skillet. If not, add a little shortening before you heat the skillet and add the pork chops. Salt lightly and brown well on both sides. Spread the rice over the bottom of the casserole and place the pork chops on it. Cover and bake 1 hour.

Spareribs with Vegetables

(SERVES FOUR)

2 tablespoons shortening
3 pounds (1⅓ kg) spareribs
1 bay leaf
1½ teaspoons salt
1 teaspoon peppercorns,
    crushed

4 potatoes, peeled and
    quartered
1 small head cabbage,
    quartered

Melt the shortening in a Dutch oven. Brown the spareribs on each side; drain the fat from the pan. Add 4 cups water and bring to a boil. Add the bay leaf, salt, and peppercorns, and simmer for 45 minutes. Add the potatoes and simmer for 10 minutes, then add the cabbage and simmer 10 minutes more. Drain and arrange on a warm serving platter.

Barbecued Spareribs

Marinate these ribs for several hours before cooking.

(SERVES SIX)

1¼ cups (3 dL) tomato juice	2 tablespoons finely grated
2 tablespoons soy sauce	onion
¾ cup (1¾ dL) vinegar	1 cup (¼ L) vegetable oil
1 teaspoon dry mustard	¾ cup (145 g) sugar
1 tablespoon Worcestershire	6 pounds (2¾ kg) spareribs in
sauce	1 or 2 pieces or racks

Combine all ingredients except spareribs in a blender or large lidded jar, and blend or shake until the mixture is thoroughly combined. Place the spareribs in a large shallow baking pan and cover them with the sauce. Cover with aluminum foil and marinate at room temperature for several hours. Preheat the oven to 350°F (180°C). Leave the foil in place and bake for 45 minutes; uncover and bake another 30–40 minutes. Serve, cut in portions of 2–3 ribs.

Stuffed Spareribs

(SERVES SIX)

5 pounds (2¼ kg) spareribs
in racks
2 recipes Celery Stuffing (p. 280)

Preheat the oven to 350°F (180°C). Place half the spareribs on the bottom of a shallow baking pan. Spread the stuffing over them, and cover with the remaining spareribs. Bake for 1½ hours. Divide the ribs and serve with the stuffing.

Spareribs and Sauerkraut

(SERVES FOUR)

4 cups (1 L) sauerkraut,	1 teaspoon salt
drained	½ teaspoon freshly ground
3 tart apples, peeled, cored,	pepper
and sliced thin	1 cup (¼ L) dry white wine
1 onion, cut in thin rings	4 pounds (1¾ kg) spareribs,
2 bay leaves	trimmed

Preheat the oven to 350°F (180°C). Spread the sauerkraut over the bottom of a shallow baking dish. Cover with the apples, onion rings, bay leaves, salt, and pepper. Drizzle the wine over and lay the spareribs on top. Cover snugly with foil and bake for 1 hour. Uncover, and bake another 20 minutes. Cut the ribs into 3-rib portions and serve each over a spoonful of apples, onions, and sauerkraut.

City Chicken

A favorite recipe from Depression days when chicken was more expensive than pork.

City Chicken (continued)

1 pound (450 g) pork, trimmed, in 1-inch cubes	Salt
	Freshly ground pepper
1 pound (450 g) lean veal or skinned, boned chicken in 1-inch cubes	4 tablespoons butter
	2 tablespoons oil
	1 cup (¼ L) chicken broth
1 egg, slightly beaten	1 tablespoon cornstarch
1½ cups (3½ dL) freshly made bread crumbs	

Place alternating cubes of pork and veal or chicken on eight wooden skewers. Push the meat cubes together snugly. Mix the egg with 1 tablespoon water and dip the skewered meat in it. Roll meat in the crumbs and sprinkle with salt and pepper. Heat the butter and oil in a large skillet and brown the meat lightly. Add ½ cup of the chicken broth, cover, and simmer for 20–30 minutes. Dissolve the cornstarch in the remaining ½ cup of chicken broth and add it to the pan juices, cooking and stirring until clear and thickened. Serve the skewers with sauce poured over them.

Fried Salt Pork, Country Style

Creamed potatoes and crisp salt pork covered with creamy milk gravy. A country meal, served with fresh peas and baked apples.

½ pound (225 g) salt pork	¼ teaspoon freshly ground pepper
3 tablespoons yellow cornmeal	
5 tablespoons flour	1½ cups (3½ dL) cooked potatoes, peeled and cubed
1 tablespoon butter	
1¼ cups (3 dL) milk	

Blanch the salt pork to get rid of the excess salt: place it in a pan of cold water, bring to a boil uncovered, and simmer for 5 minutes. Then drain and rinse in cold water and pat dry with paper towels. Mix the cornmeal and 3 tablespoons of the flour. Slice the salt pork into pieces about 3 inches long and ½ inch wide. Dip into the cornmeal-flour mixture. Heat the butter in a skillet and cook the pork until crisp and well browned, turning it several times. In about 5 minutes, remove and drain on paper towels. Keep warm. Remove all but 2 tablespoons fat from the skillet. Over medium heat, stir in the remaining 2 tablespoons of flour. Stir for several minutes until smooth and well blended. Slowly stir in the milk, and add the pepper. Cook over low heat for 4–5 minutes, stirring until thickened and smooth. Add the cooked potato cubes and cook only until heated through. Spoon the creamed potatoes in the center of a warm serving platter and surround with the crisp pork.

Pig's Feet (Hocks)

Allow one or two hocks per person. Serve with a pot of Great Northern white beans.

8 pig's feet or hocks	1 teaspoon peppercorns, crushed
1 onion, sliced	
1 carrot, sliced	2 bay leaves
3 parsley sprigs	1½ teaspoons salt

Wash the pig's feet and tie individually in cheesecloth so they will hold their shape. Put into a deep pot and cover with cold water. Add the remaining ingredients. Bring to a boil, skim the scum from the top, reduce the heat to simmer, cover, and cook gently for about 1½ hours, or until the meat is tender. Remove from the liquid, discard the cheesecloth, and serve.

Broiled Pig's Feet. Remove the cheesecloth when the pig's feet are cooked. Rub *1 tablespoon butter* all over each foot and roll in about *2 cups freshly made bread crumbs* mixed with *2 tablespoons minced parsley, 1 teaspoon salt,* and *½ teaspoon freshly ground pepper*. Place the hocks 6 inches below the broiling element and cook until golden, turning once. Serve with mustard.

Pickled Pig's Feet. Add *1 cup cider vinegar* for each 3 cups of water in the pot.

Jellied Pig's Feet. Strain the broth and remove the meat, discarding the skin and bones. Adjust the seasonings in the broth and replace the meat. Pour into a mold and chill until firm.

Scrapple

A fine old Philadelphia tradition, served at breakfast or Sunday supper. Homemade takes some time, but it is much better than the canned product.

(SERVES SIX)

1 pound (450 g) pork, with bones	⅔ cup (1½ dL) cornmeal
2 pig's feet	2 tablespoons chopped onion
Salt	Freshly ground pepper

Place the pork, pig's feet, and a sprinkle of salt in a large pot and cover with 1 quart of water. Bring to a boil, cover, and simmer until the meat falls from the bones, at least 1½ hours. Remove the meat and reserve the broth. Discard the bones and grind the meat in a meat grinder or food processor. Add cornmeal to the broth, and cook, stirring, for 5 minutes. Add the ground meat and onion. Place in the top of a double boiler, and cook over simmering water for an hour. Add salt and pepper to taste. Pack into a small loaf pan that has been rinsed with cold water and chill until set. To serve, cut into ½-inch slices and pan-fry until crisp and brown.

DISHES USING LEFTOVER PORK

Pork Baked with Cabbage and Cream

You could use any kind of leftover cooked pork to make this delicious dish—slices or chops from a roast—or even cook up extra chops when next you are frying some so you'll have them handy.

Pork Baked with Cabbage and Cream (continued)

1 small cabbage or ½ large
   (about 1½ pounds, 675 g)
½ cup (1 dL) heavy cream
Salt
Freshly ground pepper
1 teaspoon caraway seeds

½ teaspoon paprika
4 thick slices cooked pork or
   leftover chops
½ cup (1 dL) grated Swiss
   cheese

Preheat oven to 350°F (180°C). Shred the cabbage, discarding the core. Boil in several quarts of salted water for 5 minutes. Drain. Bring the cream to a boil, then add the well-drained cabbage, salt and pepper to taste, caraway, and paprika, and cook briskly, stirring occasionally, for 5 minutes. Distribute half the cabbage and cream over the bottom of a baking dish, place the pork on top, seasoning it well to taste and adding any drippings that may be left over from cooking; add the rest of the cabbage, and top with the cheese. Bake for 40 minutes.

Pork–Lima Bean Casserole

2 cups (½ L) large dried lima
   beans, soaked overnight in
   water
½ pound (225 g) salt pork, cut
   at ¼-inch intervals almost to
   rind
2 tablespoons vegetable oil
1 large onion, chopped
1 clove garlic, minced
1½ tablespoons chili powder

1 can tomato soup
2 teaspoons Worcestershire
   sauce
2 teaspoons prepared mustard
½ cup (100 g) dark-brown
   sugar
¼ cup (½ dL) vinegar
Salt to taste
1½ pounds (675 g) cooked
   pork, trimmed of fat

Preheat the oven to 350°F (180°C). Bring the water to boil in a large pot. Add the lima beans and keep the water boiling, reduce the heat, and add the salt pork. Simmer for 1½ hours, or until the lima beans are tender. Drain and reserve the liquid and salt pork. Heat the oil in a sauté pan and add the onion; cook, stirring often until soft, then add the garlic, and sauté another minute. Stir in the chili powder, tomato soup, 1 cup of liquid from lima beans, Worcestershire sauce, mustard, sugar, vinegar, and salt. Heat sauce until it bubbles. Cut the pork into large pieces, add to the sauce, and cook a minute. Remove from heat. Fill a casserole with a layer of lima beans, sauce, another layer of lima beans, sauce, and place the salt pork on top. Bake covered for 45 minutes. Uncover and bake 30 minutes more.

Pork Turnovers

4 tablespoons butter
½ large onion, finely chopped
3 tablespoons flour
1 cup (¼ L) heavy cream
1½ cups (3½ dL) finely
   chopped cooked pork
1 tart apple, peeled, cored,
   chopped

Grated rind of 1 lemon
1 tablespoon lemon juice
½ teaspoon rosemary, crumbled
Salt
1 recipe Basic Pastry for two-
   crust pie (p. 575)

Preheat the oven to 425°F (220°C). Grease a cookie sheet. Melt the butter in a sauté pan and add the onion; cook, stirring often, until the onion is soft. Sprinkle in the flour and stir to blend, cooking over medium-low heat for 1–2 minutes or until smooth and bubbling. Slowly add the cream, stirring constantly; cook, continuing to stir, until the sauce is thick and smooth. Add the pork, apple, lemon rind, lemon juice, and rosemary. Stir to blend and heat thoroughly. Salt to taste. Prepare the pastry and roll out a little less than ¼ inch thick on a floured surface. Cut in 3½-inch circles. Fill one-half of the circle, leaving an edge so the turnover can be crimped together. Dampen the edges with a few drops of water, then fold in half; press or crimp the edges together with the tines of a fork or your fingers. Place turnovers on cookie sheet and pierce a few holes on top of each to allow steam to escape during baking. Bake for 20–25 minutes, or until the turnovers are golden brown. Serve hot or cold.

Pork Sweet and Sour

(SERVES SIX)

1½ pounds (675 g) cooked pork
¾ cup (1¾ dL) soy sauce
3 tablespoons oil
3 green peppers, cut in narrow strips

1 onion, cut in narrow strips
1-pound 4-ounce (560-g) can pineapple tidbits

The Sauce

3 tablespoons cornstarch
1 tablespoon soy sauce

3 tablespoons vinegar
⅓ cup (65 g) sugar

Trim the pork of excess fat and slice. Put the pork in a shallow dish and cover with the ¾ cup soy sauce. Let stand for 1 hour, turning the meat often so it thoroughly marinates. Heat the oil in a sauté pan, add the peppers and onion, and cook over high heat for just a minute, stirring constantly. Remove from the pan and set aside. Drain the pork, add to the skillet along with the juice from the pineapple tidbits, and bring to a boil. Lower the heat and simmer for 5 minutes. Add the pineapple, peppers, and onion, stir to mix and simmer a minute. Combine thoroughly the sauce ingredients with ⅓ cup water and add to the pork mixture, stirring constantly. Cook until sauce thickens.

❁ Other Suggestions for Using Leftover Pork

Use pork instead of beef in Beef and Corn Casserole; Beef and Scallions, Mushroom Sauce; Beef, Peas, Onions; and Beef Pot Pie and instead of lamb in Lentils and Lamb, Lamb in Barbecue Sauce, Shepherd's Pie, Casserole of Rice and Lamb, Fricasee of Lamb, Moussaka, and Curry. Pork is good instead of ham in Ham and Noodle Casserole. Chopped cooked pork can be used to make Fried Rice and ground up it can serve you well for fillings for savory tarts, stuffed pasta, and vegetables.

HAM

About Ham

A ham is, correctly, a leg of pork, but that meaning has faded, and the word "ham" (unless labeled "fresh ham") is now used to describe any cut of pork that has been through a preserving process. Although refrigeration has made it unnecessary to preserve pork this way, our palates have learned to enjoy the salty, smoked flavor of ham.

Salt curing destroys the organisms that cause meat to spoil. There are two methods of salt curing: salt brining and dry curing. Brined pork is soaked in or, more often, injected with a brine solution. Dry-cured pork is rubbed all over with salt and then aged in a cool place. The most famous hams are dry-cured, such as our own Smithfield and Virginia hams and imported Parma ham or prosciutto. Different packers have their own recipes, which often include sugar, spices, and pepper. These recipes are closely kept secrets.

Smoking is the next step in curing, although not all ham is smoked. Smoked ham has a robust, country character, and many people prefer the milder flavor of salt curing. Smoking is done over wood in airtight containers or rooms, where a low fire of beechwood or hickory provides a constant cloud of aromatic smoke.

Country-style hams, usually ordered by mail or bought in specialty shops, have been dry-salted and rubbed with black pepper, then smoked and aged for about a year. Most of them arrive with detailed directions for their preparation, which involves soaking, blanching, boiling, scrubbing, peeling, glazing, and baking.

Among the many cuts of ham that are available in supermarkets, the best are those that have the bone left in. Water is sometimes injected into these hams, but it must be noted on the label and cannot exceed 10 percent of the fresh meat weight. A whole ham is usually 10–14 pounds in weight, but you can also buy the meaty butt end or the flavorful shank end of the ham. The loin of pork—not, strictly speaking, ham—has an excellent flavor. Picnic ham is the smoked pork shoulder, which has very good flavor but a great deal of waste, and the smoked or Boston butt is also good but extremely fatty. Boned hams are less flavorful, but have little waste and are easy to carve.

Most of these hams are available either partially or fully cooked. If they are fully cooked, they have been kept at an internal temperature of 160°F for at least half an hour, destroying any possibility of trichinosis. But almost all hams on the market today have been held at 137°F for half an hour, and need only heating through to be safe. Canned hams tend to be bland and dull and coated with gelatin.

Baked Ham

Be sure to read the label on the ham: some are precooked, some partially cooked. If the ham has not been precooked at all, allow 20 minutes per pound in a 350°F oven, then use a meat thermometer to be sure that the internal temperature is 160°F. If the ham is precooked, you must still allow 10 minutes per pound to warm the meat and melt the glaze.

(ALLOW ½ POUND PER SERVING)

1 ham	2 teaspoons dry mustard
1 cup (200 g) brown sugar	15 or more cloves
¼ cup (½ dL) honey, maple syrup, or cider vinegar	1 can pineapple rings (optional)

Basting Sauce (optional)
1 cup (200 g) brown sugar
1 teaspoon dry mustard
1 cup (¼ L) orange juice

Preheat the oven to 350°F (180°C). Place the ham on a rack in a shallow roasting pan, fat side up. Bake the ham unglazed until the thermometer reads 130°F (54°C), or until 1 hour before the ham is done. Prepare for glazing by scoring the outside fat in a diamond pattern, cutting ¼ inch deep with a sharp knife. Combine the brown sugar with the honey, syrup, or vinegar and the mustard. Mix well and spread over the outside of the ham. Stud with whole cloves set decoratively in the center of each diamond. Or if you like pineapple rings, set them in place with toothpicks, putting the cloves in the holes. Return to the oven for 1 hour to finish baking, 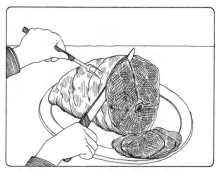 brushing, if you wish, every 15 minutes with basting sauce. Let it rest and carve at the table as illustrated.

Picnic Ham

A picnic ham is a pork shoulder that has been cured and smoked. Its waste in bone and fat (thus you need more per person) is made up for by its flavor.

(ALLOW 1 POUND PER SERVING)

5–8-pound (2¼–3½-kg) picnic ham

Put the ham into a large pot and cover it with cold water. Bring to a boil and reduce the heat. Simmer for 1½–2 hours, depending on the size. A 5-pound ham cooks in 1½ hours, an 8-pound ham in 2 hours. Add more water as it cooks away. When it is done, drain and remove the rind. Preheat the oven to 325°F (165°C). Place the ham on a rack in a shallow pan and bake for 2 hours.

Boiled Country Ham

Begin preparing home-cured ham the day before you serve it. Long soaking and cooking make country ham a special treat.

(ALLOW ½ POUND PER SERVING)

1 home-cured Smithfield or   1 cup (200 g) dark-brown sugar
    Virginia ham   8 cloves

Soak the ham overnight in cold water to cover. Drain, scrub with a stiff brush, and place in a large pot. Cover with water, heat, and simmer for 25 minutes per pound, or until an instant meat thermometer shows an internal temperature of 150°F. Add more water as it cooks away. Allow the ham to cool in the water in which it cooked, then remove it and peel or cut off the tough outer skin and most of the fat. The ham is now ready to eat, but a brief glazing and baking will make it even better. Preheat the oven to 350°F (180°C). Place the ham on a rack in a shallow roasting pan, and rub it all over with the brown sugar. Stud with cloves and bake for 10 minutes per pound, until the meat is heated through and the glaze is melted and shining.

Slice of Ham Baked in Milk

(SERVES FOUR)

2 pounds (900 g) ham, cut in   1 tablespoon brown sugar
  1½-inch slice   2 cups (½ L) milk
1 tablespoon prepared mustard

Preheat oven to 300°F (150°C). Put the ham in a shallow baking dish. Paint the top with the mustard and sprinkle the brown sugar over. Pour the milk around the ham and bake for 2 to 2½ hours. Serve with a little of the clotted milk spooned over the top.

Thin Slices of Ham in Milk. A good way to use leftover baked ham, particularly when it is salty. Cut serving slices of ham, paint lightly with mustard, and sprinkle with brown sugar. Arrange in a baking dish and cover with milk. Bake about ½ hour.

Ham with Red-eye Gravy

In this regional southern dish, the fried ham lends a slightly reddish tint to pan gravy. Often a few drops of coffee are added for a richer color. Serve with grits or hot biscuits.

(ALLOW ⅓ POUND PER SERVING)

⅓-pound (150 g) slice of ham   Salt
1 tablespoon flour   1½ tablespoons coffee

Cut a piece of fat from the ham and melt it in a skillet. Add the ham and fry over medium heat until the edges are slightly brown. Remove and keep warm. Turn the heat to high and stir in the flour. Cook flour slowly until golden, then add 1 cup water, stirring constantly. Sprinkle in salt and the coffee. Turn the heat to medium-low and cook 5–7 minutes, stirring often to keep the gravy smooth. Return meat to the gravy to heat through.

Ham Casserole Country Style

(SERVES FOUR)

2 cups (½ L) potatoes, sliced   2 teaspoons thyme, crumbled
  thin   1 thick slice ham, trimmed
Salt   (1½–2 pounds, 675–900 g)
Freshly ground pepper   2 cups (½ L) milk
1 large onion, sliced thin

Preheat the oven to 350°F (180°C). Butter a 1½-quart covered casserole. Cover the bottom of the casserole with the potatoes and sprinkle with salt and pepper. Spread the onions on top and scatter with thyme. Lay the ham slice over the onions, pour on the milk, cover, and bake for about 1 hour, or until the potatoes are tender.

Tomato-Ham Casserole Country Style. Omit the milk and substitute *2 cups chopped tomatoes and juice.*

Ham Roll

(SERVES FOUR)

3 cups (¾ L) freshly made
  bread crumbs
6 tablespoons butter, melted
¼ teaspoon freshly ground
  pepper
½ cup (1 dL) raisins

½ cup (1 dL) walnuts, chopped
2 trimmed ½-inch-thick ham
  slices
¾ cup (1¾ dL) unsweetened
  pineapple juice

Preheat the oven to 350°F (180°C). Mix the crumbs, melted butter, pepper, raisins, and walnuts. Spread this stuffing evenly over each ham slice, roll it up, and tie loosely (because the stuffing will expand) in two places with string. Place the rolls in a baking pan. Mix the pineapple juice with ¾ cup water and pour over the rolls. Cover with a lid or foil and bake 45 minutes. Remove the strings, slice the rolls in half, and serve.

German Loaf

You need a large piece of cheesecloth and a low rack or trivet to make this fine-textured loaf.

(SERVES SIX)

1 pound (450 g) ham, trimmed
  of fat
1 pound (450 g) fresh pork
2 cloves garlic
1 onion
1 teaspoon freshly ground
  pepper

2 teaspoons curry powder
1 tablespoon sage, crumbled
2½ teaspoons salt
1 egg white
½ cup (1 dL) cream
¼ cup (½ dL) vinegar

Grind the ham, fresh pork, garlic, and onion together in a meat grinder or food processor. Add the pepper, curry powder, sage, and 1½ teaspoons salt, and mix very well. Add the egg white and cream and blend thoroughly. Put 3 quarts of water, vinegar, and 1 teaspoon salt in a large pot and bring to a boil. Spread a large square of cheesecloth on the counter, put the meat mixture in the center, and pat into a loaf shape. Fold the cheesecloth around the meat, tie it snugly in shape, and place it on a rack or trivet in the boiling water. Cover, reduce heat, and simmer for 1½ hours. Remove and drain the meat. Cover it with a weight (see p. 61), and cool before cutting in thin slices. Serve cool or reheated in a moderate oven.

DISHES USING LEFTOVER HAM

Nancy's Ham Loaf

Buy ground meat, or do it yourself in a meat grinder or food processor. Use a brave hand with the Tabasco.

Nancy's Ham Loaf (continued)

1 pound (450 g) ground ham
½ pound (225 g) ground beef
½ pound (225 g) ground pork
1 cup (¼ L) freshly made bread
    crumbs
¼ teaspoon Tabasco

¾ cup (1¾ dL) instant dry
    milk
1 onion, chopped fine
1 egg, lightly beaten
1 cup (¼ L) tomato juice

Preheat the oven to 325°F (165°C). Butter a 1½-quart casserole. Lightly mix all the ingredients in a large bowl. Pack into the buttered casserole and bake for 50–60 minutes.

Ham and Spinach Soufflé

A soufflé must go right from the oven to the table, or it will fall. The extra egg whites make this soufflé extra light!

3 tablespoons butter
3 tablespoons minced onion
3 tablespoons flour
¾ cup (1¾ dL) milk
½ teaspoon salt
¼ teaspoon freshly ground
    pepper
2 teaspoons dry mustard

3 egg yolks, lightly beaten
1 cup (¼ L) cooked or
    defrosted spinach, squeezed
    dry
¾ cup (1¾ dL) diced cooked
    ham
6 egg whites

Preheat the oven to 350°F (180°C). Grease the bottom and sides of a 2-quart soufflé mold. Melt the butter in a saucepan, add the onion, and cook over low heat until the onion is limp. Stir in the flour and cook for 2 minutes. Slowly pour in the milk, stir, and cook for 1 minute. Add the salt, pepper, and dry mustard and cook for 3–4 minutes, stirring, while the sauce boils. Remove from the heat and vigorously stir in the egg yolks. Put back on the heat and cook, stirring constantly, for another minute, no more. Remove from the heat and add the spinach and ham. Mix thoroughly and set aside to cool to lukewarm. Beat the egg whites until they are stiff but moist, then stir a large spoonful into the ham mixture. Fold the mixture gently into the remaining egg whites. Gently spoon into buttered soufflé mold. Bake for 30–40 minutes, or until just set, and serve immediately.

Ham Mousse Alexandria

½ pound (225 g) cooked ham,
    ground fine
4 egg whites
¼ teaspoon nutmeg

⅛ teaspoon freshly ground
    pepper
½ cup (1 dL) heavy cream
1 recipe Russian Sauce (p. 266)

Preheat the oven to 350°F (180°C). Butter four custard cups or molds with a ¾-cup capacity. Blend the ham and egg whites until smoothly puréed by whirring them through a blender or food processor or rubbing them through a sieve. Add the nutmeg and pepper, stir in the cream very slowly until blended, and spoon into the cups or molds. Set them in a shallow pan containing 1 inch of hot water and bake until firm, 25–35 minutes. A knife stuck in the center should come out clean. Turn out onto a platter or individual plates and serve hot with the sauce.

Scalloped Ham

(SERVES SIX)

1½ cups (3½ dL) freshly made
  bread crumbs
1½ cups (3½ dL) cooked
  spinach, drained and
  chopped
4 hard-cooked eggs, chopped
2 cups (½ L) chopped cooked
  ham

½ teaspoon nutmeg
½ teaspoon freshly ground
  pepper
3 cups (¾ L) White Sauce
  (p. 265)

Preheat the oven to 350°F (180°C). Butter a 1½-quart casserole and sprinkle ½ cup of the crumbs over the bottom. Spread ¾ cup of the spinach over the crumbs, then half the chopped eggs and 1 cup of the ham. Stir the nutmeg and pepper into the sauce and spoon half the sauce over the ham. Repeat the layers, finishing with the remaining cup of bread crumbs. Bake for 45 minutes, until bubbling and brown.

Ham Patties

Ham sharpened with dry mustard. A salad of chilled cucumbers in a sugar and vinegar dressing makes a good accompaniment.

(SERVES FOUR)

2 cups (½ L) ground cooked
  ham
1 egg, slightly beaten
½ cup (1 dL) freshly made
  bread crumbs

1 tablespoon dry mustard
3 tablespoons heavy cream
2 tablespoons bacon fat or
  shortening

Mix the ham, egg, crumbs, mustard, and cream until thoroughly combined. Shape the mixture into four equal patties. Melt the bacon fat or shortening in a large skillet, and sauté the patties until well browned on each side.

Ham Croquettes

(ABOUT 15 CROQUETTES)

3½ cups (8 dL) ground cooked
  ham
2 cups (½ L) Thick White
  Sauce (p. 265)
1 tablespoon minced parsley
1 tablespoon Dijon mustard
3 tablespoons minced onion

¼ teaspoon freshly ground
  pepper
1½ cups (3½ dL) freshly made
  bread crumbs
1 egg
Vegetable oil

Combine the ham, sauce, parsley, mustard, onion, and pepper, in a bowl and blend well. If mixture is slightly warm, chill in the refrigerator until firm. Put the bread crumbs in a shallow dish, and in another dish beat the egg with 1 tablespoon water. Shape the meat into 1½-inch balls or cylinders. Roll them in the crumbs, then dip into the egg, and again roll in the crumbs. Let the croquettes dry in the refrigerator for at least 30 minutes to set the coating. Fill a skillet halfway with vegetable oil and heat to about 360°F (181°C). Fry a few croquettes at a time to golden brown, turning to brown on all sides. Remove with a slotted spoon and dry on paper towels.

❀ Other Suggestions for Using Leftover Ham

It seems almost superfluous to make suggestions for using leftover ham, it has so many uses. In fact, ham is something you never want to be without. As a Virginia-born friend, Edna Lewis, said of her childhood: "Ham held the same rating as the basic black dress. If you had a ham in the meat house any situation could be faced. On short notice it would be sliced and fried with special red gravy. . . . The smoked shoulder was indispensable as a seasoning for other meat dishes; a slice would be added in to fried chicken, guinea fowl, rabbit, squirrel, or quail. It was used also in boiled pots of cabbage, beans, watercress, and green black-eyed peas." Today, ham is as indispensable as ever. In Appetizers you'll find ham used as spreads, in pâtés, on small hot biscuits, in savory tarts and risolettes; thin slices of smoked country ham are good with slices of melon as a starter. It is the leftover ham bone that makes Split-Pea Soup special and gives that authentic taste to Mixed-Greens Southern Style. You can always whip up an omelet or a frittata or a quiche if you have some scraps of ham on hand, to say nothing of fried or shirred eggs and ham. Soufflés, croquettes, timbales, bean dishes, pumpkin, and macaroni casseroles all make hearty main-course dishes when you have some ham. And what would we do without ham for ham and cheese sandwiches and chef's salad?

SAUSAGE AND FRANKFURTERS

About Sausage and Frankfurters

Sausage meat is nothing more than ground pork and fat with seasonings. The simplest "fresh" or "country" sausages are made by combining newly ground pork with such seasonings as thyme, basil, salt, and pepper. You can make sausages yourself; season the meat lightly, fry a tablespoonful to kill any trichinae, and then taste. Add more seasoning to the raw mixture if it is needed. You will find the results quite an improvement on commercial sausage meat. Commercial brands of sausage meat are bought either loose or in casings, and many brands are advertised as precooked: that is, they have been kept at 160°F for half an hour and need only to be heated through for palatability.

Smoking, another form of precooking, is the method that produces the familiar taste in hot dogs. Frankfurters can be all-beef, all-meat, or a blend of meat with soy and milk fillers. Although they, too, are perfectly safe to eat raw, we'd as soon eat them uncooked as without mustard and relish!

Finally there are dry sausages, the group that includes salami, bologna, peperoni. Like dried hams, they are highly seasoned, unparalleled in flavor and keeping power, and delicious to eat without further cooking. Leftover sausages are best used in stuffings or omelets or to top the filling of a quiche or pizza.

Sausage Meat

Many people are going back to making their own sausage meat: it's easy, fresh, and preservative-free. You need to use proportions of 2 parts lean meat to 1 part fat in order to have a moist sausage (much of the fat will cook out). Remember to fry a tablespoonful of the mixture before you taste it to adjust the seasonings.

(ABOUT 3 CUPS; SERVES FOUR)

1 pound (450 g) pork, ground	½ teaspoon freshly ground
½ pound (225 g) fresh pork	pepper
fat, ground	½ teaspoon sage, crumbled
1 teaspoon salt	

Mix all the ingredients. Use in recipes requiring sausage meat, or shape into patties and cook in a skillet about 8 minutes a side, pouring off the fat as it accumulates.

Herbed and Spiced Sausage Meat. Instead of the sage, use ¾ *teaspoon ground* herbs and spices combined: *allspice, paprika, bay leaf, and thyme.*

Bubble-and-Squeak

An old-fashioned English dish.

(SERVES FOUR)

1 pound (450 g) sausage meat	Salt to taste
½ onion, chopped	2 cups (½ L) White Sauce
2 cups (½ L) cooked chopped	(p. 265)
cabbage	

Preheat the oven to 350°F (180°C). Butter a 1½-quart casserole. Cook the sausage meat in a skillet, breaking it up with a fork as it cooks. When no pink shows, transfer it to a bowl. Add the chopped onion to the sausage drippings in the skillet and cook until limp. Add to the meat and mix well. Spread the meat in the bottom of the casserole. Cover with the cabbage, add salt to taste, then cover with the sauce, and bake 30–40 minutes, or until bubbling hot.

Sausage-stuffed Prunes

Good for breakfast with scrambled eggs and wheat toast.

(SERVES FOUR)

½ pound (225 g) large prunes	1 tablespoon butter
½ pound (225 g) sausage meat	1 tablespoon flour
½ cup (1 dL) freshly made	1 cup (¼ L) prune juice
bread crumbs	1 tablespoon lemon juice
Salt	1 teaspoon grated lemon rind
¼ teaspoon freshly ground	
pepper	

Preheat the oven to 400°F (205°C). Butter a shallow baking pan. Put the prunes in a saucepan and cover with water. Cook until tender, drain, and pit. Mix the sausage, crumbs, about ½ teaspoon salt, and pepper together. Stuff the prunes generously with the mixture. Place in the pan and bake 20–25 minutes. While the prunes are cooking, melt the butter in a saucepan and stir in the flour. Cook, stirring, for 2 minutes. Add prune juice, lemon juice, lemon rind, and salt to taste. Cook, stirring constantly, for several more minutes, or until the sauce is thickened. Arrange the prunes on a plate and spoon the sauce over the top.

Sausage-stuffed Apples

Serve these hot, with a little maple syrup over the top, for breakfast or brunch.

(SERVES FOUR)

1 pound (450 g) sausage meat	½ cup (1 dL) dark-brown sugar
4 tablespoons minced onion	Maple syrup
4 large cooking apples	

Preheat the oven to 350°F (180°C). Butter a shallow pan. Sauté the sausage and onions in a skillet over medium heat, breaking the meat with a fork, until the rawness disappears. Core the apples, making a hole about 1¼ inches in diameter, and cut them in half horizontally. Place them in the pan and stuff firmly with the sausage. Sprinkle on the brown sugar and bake for about 40 minutes, or until the apples are tender. Serve with maple syrup.

Cooked Frankfurters, Kielbasa, Bratwurst, Knockwurst

The simplest and most effective way to cook all of these sausages is to simmer in water to cover until heated through (see page 290 for Frankfurters or Hot Dogs). Kielbasa, Bratwurst, and Knockwurst should be pricked in several places and will take 10–15 minutes to cook. Count on 1 pound of sausage serving 2–3 people.

Another method is to partially cover with simmering water, turn often as they are cooking, then turn up the heat the last few minutes to boil off the water. Let the sausages brown finally in a little of their own fat. Serve with mustard and pickles and hash brown potatoes.

Pan-fried Frankfurters

Cooked this way, frankfurters taste like the ones we get at ball games. Serve with mustard and, if you like, sauerkraut.

(SERVES FOUR)

8 frankfurters

Heat a skillet with barely enough oil to film the bottom of the pan. Slice the frankfurters in half lengthwise; don't cut through entirely, but leave a "hinge" of skin. Put them, cut side down, in the hot skillet and fry until nicely browned around the edges. Turn and cook until lightly browned on both sides.

Charcoal-grilled Frankfurters

(SERVES FOUR)

8 frankfurters

Ignite coals in a barbecue. When they are white-hot, place the frankfurters on the grill. Turn and cook until frankfurters are shiny and brown.

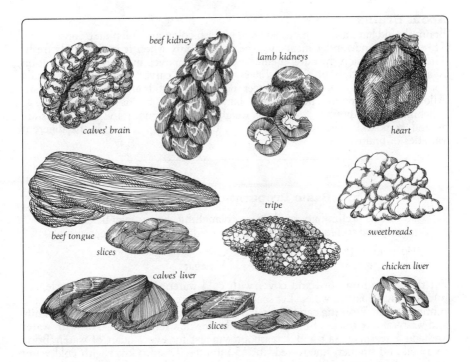

beef kidney

lamb kidneys

calves' brain

heart

beef tongue

tripe

slices

sweetbreads

calves' liver

chicken liver

slices

VARIETY MEATS

About Variety Meats

In America, we call them variety meats, innards, organs, or glands. In England, they call them "offal," which many Americans think is a pun for "awful." Whatever we call them, we mean certain organ and muscle meats such as tongue, heart, kidney, liver, tripe, sweetbreads, and brains.

Colonial Americans enjoyed variety meats: old cookbooks are studded with instructions for preparing sweetbreads and brains. But today, some of us feel a certain distaste for innards, reflecting a cultural attitude that makes no sense. On the other hand, many fine cooks consider them a treat and a delicacy. Aside from the fact that variety meats are high in protein, minerals, and iron, we also have an obligation to make good use of all our resources.

Variety meats are very perishable and require careful purchasing and storage. They should be stored, loosely wrapped, in the refrigerator, and cooked within 24 hours. Loose wrapping will allow air to circulate around the meat, drying its surface and retarding the growth of bacteria. Most variety meats freeze very well. Often you will find them frozen in the meat counter, and most are perfectly satisfactory bought that way.

Pay careful attention to the directions here for cleaning and precooking. It can make all the difference between a clumsy dish and one that is done with finesse.

About Brains

Brains should have a shiny moist surface, pinkish color, and full plump consistency. This delicate and tender meat must be bought only when it is absolutely fresh. The ease with which the outer membrane can be removed in the basic preparation is a good indication of the freshness. Although calves' brains are generally considered to be the most choice, beef, pork, and lamb brains are also excellent. Allow about ¼ pound per serving: lamb and pork brains are the smallest, weighing only ¼ pound; veal brains weigh about ½ pound; and beef brains are around ¾ pound. The recipes can be used interchangeably with the different varieties of brains.

Basic Preparation of Brains

After this preliminary soaking and blanching, brains may be covered loosely and stored in the refrigerator for a day before final preparation.

1½ pounds (675 g) brains	Salt
Lemon juice	Vinegar

Put the brains in a bowl and cover with cold water. Add 2 tablespoons lemon juice for each quart of water. Let soak for 30 minutes. Drain and rinse under cold running water. Working carefully, remove the outer membrane with a sharp knife and wash off any traces of blood. Put the brains in a saucepan. Cover with water and add 1 teaspoon salt and 1 teaspoon vinegar for every quart of water. Bring to a boil and simmer, uncovered, for 15 minutes. Drain. Cover with cold water again and let stand 15 minutes more to keep the brains firm, or, better yet, refrigerate a few hours with a plate on top.

Brains with Brown Butter

Serve with triangles of warm dry toast.

(SERVES FOUR)

1½ pounds (675 g) brains	2 tablespoons vinegar
¼ pound (115 g) butter	1 tablespoon minced parsley
2 tablespoons lemon juice	1 tablespoon capers

Prepare the brains as directed (above). Cut them into thick slices. Melt 4 tablespoons of the butter in a skillet. Sauté the brains quickly and place them on a warm plate. Add the remaining 4 tablespoons of butter to the skillet, turn the heat to high, and heat until butter turns brown. Stir in the lemon juice and vinegar, and let them bubble together for about 30 seconds. Remove from heat, then add parsley and capers and pour over the brains.

Brains Sautéed with Bacon

(SERVES FOUR)

1½ pounds (675 g) brains	Freshly ground pepper
8 slices bacon	1 bunch watercress

Prepare the brains as directed (above). Fry the bacon until crisp; drain on paper towels and keep warm in the oven. Remove all but 4 tablespoons of bacon fat from the skillet. Keep the skillet medium hot. Cut the brains into thick slices and brown them lightly on each side in the bacon fat. Sprinkle with pepper and arrange on a platter, surrounded by bacon and garnished with watercress.

Scrambled Eggs and Brains

(SERVES FOUR)

½ pound (225 g) brains
6 eggs, lightly beaten
¼ teaspoon Tabasco

2 tablespoons minced scallions
1 teaspoon salt
5 tablespoons butter

Prepare the brains as directed (opposite). Cut them into ½-inch cubes and add to the eggs. Stir in the Tabasco, scallions, and salt. Melt the butter over medium heat. When it foams, pour in the egg and brain mixture. Cook over low heat, stirring and scraping the bottom of the pan so the eggs don't dry out and stick to the bottom; don't overcook. Remove when partially set, but still very moist.

Calves' Brains in Mushroom-Cream Sauce

Serve in patty shells or with triangles of sautéed toast.

(SERVES FOUR)

1 pound (450 g) calves' brains
½ cup (1 dL) sherry
4 tablespoons butter
¼ pound (115 g) mushroom
  caps, sliced

1½ cups (3½ dL) White Sauce
(p. 265)

Prepare the brains as directed (opposite). Cut them into ½-inch pieces, cover with the sherry, and let stand for 1 hour. Melt the butter in a skillet, add the mushrooms, and sauté until slightly soft. Add the sauce, the brains, and 4 tablespoons of the sherry. Stir until blended and heat to serving temperature.

About Heart

Heart has a mild flavor, similar to that of liver, although not as pronounced in taste. The texture is firm and dense. Like all variety meats, it is perishable and should be used within a day or two of purchase. Parboiling helps to prevent rapid spoilage, but is not necessary if the heart will be used soon or undergo long cooking, as in the recipe for Stuffed Hearts with Vegetables (p. 216). A lamb heart weighs ¼ pound, a pork heart about ½ pound, a veal heart about 1 pound, and a beef heart 3–4 pounds. Allow ⅓ pound for each serving.

Basic Preparation of Heart

Wash the heart thoroughly under cold water, cutting away any arteries, fat, or connective tissue. Heart is tender, and so it must be either sautéed quickly, in which case it should be served slightly pink in the center, or braised slowly as in Stuffed Hearts with Vegetables.

Sautéed Heart

(SERVES FOUR)

1 pound (450 g) veal heart	Salt
3 tablespoons butter	Freshly ground pepper
1 tablespoon oil	1 cup (¼ L) freshly made bread
½ teaspoon rosemary, crumbled	crumbs

Prepare the hearts as directed above. Slice them in half lengthwise and then into ½-inch slices crosswise. Heat the butter and oil in a skillet, add the heart slices, and sprinkle with rosemary, salt, and pepper. Cook slowly, turning and stirring until the heart slices are done—about 5 minutes. Meanwhile, brown the bread crumbs on a cookie sheet in a 350°F (180°C) oven for about 5 minutes. Put the heart slices on a serving dish and sprinkle with crisply brown bread crumbs.

Stuffed Hearts with Vegetables

(SERVES SIX)

2 calves' hearts or 1 beef heart	2 tablespoons flour
1½ cups (3½ dL) Bread	3 tablespoons shortening
Stuffing (p. 278), seasoned	1 rib celery with leaves, sliced
with 3 tablespoons minced	4 parsley sprigs, chopped
onion and 1 teaspoon	1 carrot, sliced
thyme, crumbled	1 bay leaf
½ teaspoon salt	¼ teaspoon ground cloves
¼ teaspoon freshly ground	¾ cup (1¾ dL) red wine
pepper	

Prepare the hearts as directed (above), enlarging the openings if necessary for stuffing. Fill with seasoned stuffing and sew or skewer close. Mix the salt and pepper with the flour and lightly coat the hearts. Melt the shortening in a Dutch oven and add the hearts with the celery, parsley, carrot, and bay leaf, turning and stirring until the meat is lightly browned. Add the cloves, wine, and ¼ cup water. Cover and cook over very low heat for about 1¼ hours or ½ hour longer for beef. Remove hearts to a warm platter, strain the liquid, and serve as a sauce.

About Kidneys

Kidneys taste something like liver and, like liver, tend to toughen quickly when overcooked. Choose kidneys that have a bright, shiny appearance. Like the other variety meats, they are very perishable and should be cooked within a day of purchase or defrosting. Veal kidneys are especially highly prized; pork kidneys are scarce because they are used for commercial preparations and pâtés.

A beef kidney serves four; a veal kidney, three; and pork kidney, one. Two or three lamb kidneys are required for one serving.

Basic Preparation of Kidneys

Remove the outside membrane from the kidneys. If you are preparing large beef or pork kidneys, cut them in half lengthwise and remove the white core and fat from the center. The fat around the outside of a pork kidney is called "leaf lard" and is considered the purest fat for cooking and baking.

Don't soak veal or lamb kidneys; they need only to be rinsed and dried off. Beef and pork kidneys, however, must be soaked for 1 hour in acidulated water. Use 2 tablespoons vinegar or lemon juice for every quart of water. Soak, rinse, and pat dry. Then plunge the kidneys into boiling water for a minute to refresh. Drain, rinse quickly under cold running water, and pat dry. If any unpleasant odor lingers, rub the kidneys with a little baking soda and rinse again.

Broiled Kidneys

(SERVES FOUR)

1 pound (450 g) veal or lamb
   kidneys
⅓ cup (¾ dL) olive oil
3 tablespoons red wine
¼ teaspoon oregano, crumbled

½ teaspoon thyme, crumbled
½ teaspoon salt
¼ teaspoon freshly ground
   pepper

Prepare the kidneys as directed (opposite). Mix remaining ingredients in a jar, cover closely, and shake. Slice the kidneys crosswise in 3 slices for lamb kidneys, about 5 for veal. Place them in a shallow dish, pour on the marinade, and marinate for 1 hour. Preheat the broiler. Thread the kidneys on skewers and place 3 inches beneath the broiler element. Cook 1–2 minutes on each side or until lightly browned.

Sautéed Kidneys

(SERVES FOUR)

1 pound (450 g) veal or lamb
   kidneys
3 tablespoons butter
1 tablespoon oil
4 tablespoons finely chopped
   onion

1 cup (¼ L) sliced mushrooms
¼ cup (½ dL) red wine
Salt
Toast

Prepare the kidneys as directed (opposite). Melt the butter and oil in a skillet. Quickly brown the kidneys, cooking for just a minute before removing to a warm plate. Add the onion and mushrooms to the pan and cook, stirring, until the onion is soft. Pour in the wine and cook a minute; then return the kidneys to the pan, add salt to taste, and heat through. Serve on toast.

Kidney Stew

(SERVES SIX)

1½ pounds (675 g) beef
   kidneys
4 tablespoons flour
2 tablespoons shortening
½ cup (1 dL) finely chopped
   onion

2 cloves garlic, minced
Freshly ground pepper
Salt
1 cup (¼ L) beef broth
¼ cup (½ dL) red wine

Prepare the kidneys as directed (opposite). Cut them in ½-inch slices. Roll them in flour and shake off the excess. Melt the shortening in a skillet with a lid. Cook the onion and garlic until soft. Add the kidneys and cook until lightly browned. Sprinkle with pepper and salt, and add the broth and wine. Cover and simmer for 30 minutes, or until the kidney slices are tender.

About Sweetbreads

Sweetbreads, with brains, are the most delicate of all variety meats, the lightest in taste, and the most expensive. They are also among the most perishable, and should be used on the day they are purchased. If this is not possible, they can be frozen with good results.

A sweetbread is the thymus gland of an animal. This gland has two lobes. One lobe, called the "throat," is uneven and veiny, and disappears almost completely as the animal matures. The other, the "heart" or "belly" lobe of the thymus, grows larger in the maturing animal. It is smooth and round and, when it comes from a calf, is considered the choicest piece of sweetbread available.

When shopping for sweetbreads, look for moisture and freshness. They should be rosy-colored if they come from steer and whitish if they come from calves or lamb. A pound of sweetbreads serves four people.

Basic Preparation of Sweetbreads

After this preliminary soaking and blanching, the sweetbreads may be covered loosely and stored in the refrigerator for a day before final preparation.

Sweetbreads
Lemon juice or vinegar
Salt

Soak the sweetbreads in cold water for 1 hour. Bring to a boil a pot full of acidulated water: for every quart of water, add 2 tablespoons lemon juice or vinegar and ½ teaspoon salt. Add the sweetbreads and boil gently for 15 minutes. Drain, then plunge immediately into cold water. Allow the cold water to run over the sweetbreads to cool them rapidly. Working gently with a sharp knife, trim away the membranes and connecting tubes. Pat dry.

Broiled Sweetbreads

Serve on toast triangles.

(SERVES FOUR)

1 pound (450 g) veal   Juice of 1 lemon
  sweetbreads   4 tablespoons butter, melted
Salt

Prepare the sweetbreads as directed (above). Preheat the broiler. Split the sweetbreads crosswise, sprinkle with salt, place 3 inches under the broiler element, and cook 2–3 minutes on each side. Put on a platter and pour lemon juice and butter on top.

Sautéed Sweetbreads

(SERVES FOUR)

1 pound (450 g) sweetbreads   Salt
3 tablespoons butter   ½ cup (1 dL) dry sherry
1 tablespoon oil   1 tablespoon minced parsley

Prepare the sweetbreads as directed (above). Slice them. Melt the butter and oil in a skillet, and brown the sweetbreads quickly over high heat. Sprinkle with salt and transfer to a warm plate. With heat kept high, pour the sherry into the skillet and let it boil for 1 minute. Pour over sweetbreads and sprinkle with parsley.

Creamed Sweetbreads

Serve on toast or in patty shells.

(SERVES FOUR)

1 pound (450 g) sweetbreads
4 tablespoons butter
4 tablespoons flour
1 cup (¼ L) chicken broth

1 cup (¼ L) light cream
Salt to taste
¼ teaspoon grated nutmeg

Prepare the sweetbreads as directed (opposite). Cut them into small cubes. In a saucepan, heat the butter until it foams. Stir in the flour and cook over low heat, stirring constantly for several minutes, so that the flour loses its raw taste. Slowly add the chicken broth and cream. Simmer for 5 minutes, stirring often. Add salt, nutmeg, and sweetbreads, and heat through.

Sweetbreads à la Napoli

(SERVES FOUR)

1½ cups (3½ dL) heavy cream
1 pound (450 g) sweetbreads
6 tablespoons butter
2 tablespoons beef broth
Salt

1 cup (¼ L) grated Parmesan
  cheese
8 pieces of toast, in 3½-inch
  rounds
8 mushroom caps

Preheat the oven to 350°F (180°C). Prepare four individual baking dishes by putting 2 tablespoons of cream in each. Prepare the sweetbreads as directed (opposite). Cut them into eight pieces. Melt 2 tablespoons of the butter in a skillet and sauté the sweetbreads quickly. When they are lightly brown, add the beef broth, stirring to blend, until glazed; salt lightly, remove and set aside. Mix the remaining cream with the cheese. Spread it on the toast rounds. Melt the remaining 4 tablespoons butter in the skillet. Sauté the mushroom caps until they darken slightly but are still firm; set aside. Put two toast rounds in each dish. On each piece of toast, place a slice of sweetbread and then a mushroom cap. Bake, covered with foil, for 8 minutes.

About Tongue

Tongue is available pickled, smoked, and fresh. Fresh tongue has the most delicate flavor, but the others are equally good; and canned tongue is convenient to have in the pantry. Although pickled and smoked tongues have been partially preserved, they need the same scrubbing and long simmering as fresh tongue, and may be used interchangeably in the recipes.

We are most familiar with the 4–6-pound beef tongue and the 1½-pound calves' tongue. Lamb and pork tongues are scarce, tiny, and delicious. For fine texture, choose a tongue that is 3 pounds or less in weight. With little waste, it will easily provide three servings per pound. Remember to allow for leftovers, since this is one meat that is just as good cold as hot.

Basic Preparation of Tongue

After it is cooked and trimmed, this is ready to serve with Mustard Sauce (p. 273) or to be used in one of the preparations that follows.

1 tongue, fresh, pickled, or
  smoked
½ lemon, sliced
1 onion, sliced

2 bay leaves
2 teaspoons salt
8 peppercorns, crushed
6 cloves

Scrub the tongue with a vegetable brush in warm running water. Soak for 1 hour in cold water. Put into a pot of boiling water along with remaining ingredients. Partially cover and simmer gently until tender: a beef tongue takes 3–4 hours, veal 1½–2 hours, pork 1–1½ hours, and lamb about 1 hour. Let the tongue cool in the broth. Split the skin and peel it off. Trim away all the small bones and gristle at the root end. To serve, slice thin on a slight angle.

Braised Tongue

Serve with Horseradish Cream (p. 273).

(SERVES FOUR, WITH LEFTOVERS)

1½ pounds (675 g) fresh
  tongue
1 cup (¼ L) sliced carrots
1 cup (¼ L) sliced celery with
  leaves
1 onion, sliced

3 parsley sprigs
2 tablespoons butter
2 tablespoons flour
1 teaspoon salt
½ teaspoon coarsely ground
  pepper

Prepare the tongue as directed (above), reserving 2 cups of the broth. Preheat the oven to 325°F (165°C). Put the carrots, celery, onion, and parsley in a heavy casserole with a lid and set aside. Melt the butter in a saucepan and stir in the flour. Stirring constantly, let the flour cook over low heat 2–3 minutes. Slowly pour in the reserved broth and continue to cook, stirring, for 5 minutes. Add salt and pepper. Slice the tongue on a slight angle and lay the slices over the bed of vegetables in the casserole. Pour the sauce on top; if it is too thick to flow easily from a spoon, thin it with a little water. Cover and bake for 1 hour.

Sweet-and-Sour Tongue

(SERVES SIX)

1½ pounds (675 g) tongue
1 lemon, sliced paper-thin
1 cup (¼ L) mild vinegar
1 cup (200 g) dark-brown sugar
12 gingersnaps, crumbed
1 bay leaf

⅓ cup (¾ dL) raisins
1 cinnamon stick
8 cloves
1 small onion, sliced paper-
  thin

Prepare the tongue as directed (above) or use canned tongue. Slice it thin. Combine the remaining ingredients in a large pan. Cook over medium-low heat, stirring to dissolve the sugar and gingersnap crumbs. Bring to a boil, lower the heat, and simmer for 10 minutes. Add the sliced tongue and cook until heated through. Remove the meat, place it on a platter, and strain the sauce over it.

Fresh Tongue with Vegetables

If the onions are larger than ½ inch in diameter, cut them in half before using.

(SERVES EIGHT, WITH LEFTOVERS)

4–6-pound (1¾–2¾-kg) fresh beef tongue
4 carrots, in ¼-inch slices
2 turnips, in small dice
4 ribs celery, in ¼-inch slices
1 pound green beans, in ½-inch lengths

3 potatoes, peeled and diced
1 pound (450 g) onions, peeled
3 tablespoons butter, softened
3 tablespoons flour
Salt
Freshly ground pepper

Prepare the tongue as directed (opposite). Drain and reserve the liquid. Preheat the oven to 300°F (150°C). Spread the carrots, turnips, celery, green beans, potatoes, and onions over the bottom of a roasting pan. Place the tongue on the vegetables. Add 3 cups of the reserved liquid, cover snugly with foil, and bake for 2 hours. Remove the meat and vegetables and keep warm. Blend the soft butter and flour into a smooth paste. Drop pellets of this paste into the simmering pan liquid, whisking it briskly until it is properly thickened. Add salt and pepper to taste, and cook, stirring, for 5 minutes. Cut the tongue into thin, slanted slices, and serve on a platter surrounded by the vegetables. Pass the gravy separately.

Tongue in White Wine

Serve with whipped cream to which you have added freshly grated horseradish.

(SERVES EIGHT, WITH LEFTOVERS)

4–6-pound (1¾–2¾-kg) beef tongue
3 tablespoons butter
1 tablespoon oil

¾ cup (1¾ dL) dry white wine
½ teaspoon salt
½ teaspoon freshly ground pepper

Prepare the tongue as directed (opposite) and pat it dry. Melt the butter and oil in a deep pot. Add the tongue and brown it lightly. Lower the heat and add the wine, salt, pepper, and barely enough water to cover. Simmer for 2½ hours or until tender. Remove the tongue and slice it thin, on the diagonal.

About Tripe

Tripe is the gastronomic name for part of the stomach of an animal that chews its cud. In this country, only beef tripe is generally available, and of the four kinds of beef tripe, we can usually find only two: smooth and honeycomb. The honeycomb is considered the more desirable.

Before it is offered for sale, tripe is processed by soaking in lime, brining, and boiling. The preparation of tripe used to be long and arduous before this process became common: some old recipes call for more than 24 hours of cooking time.

Basic Preparation of Tripe

Tripe is tough, with a texture like that of gristle, and if it has not been precooked, it requires long cooking to be edible. The only way to tell is to taste—it is cooked when the meat still has some resistance; a slight chewiness, before it has become completely soft.

Tripe
Salt
1 onion, stuck with 3 cloves
1 bay leaf

½ cup (1 dL) chopped celery
with leaves
6 peppercorns, crushed

Scrub the tripe with a vegetable brush. Blanch it by covering with cold water and bringing to a boil. Drain, and plunge it into a bowl of cold water. Fill the saucepan with water again, adding 2 teaspoons salt for every quart of water. Add the tripe and simmer until it is tender: anywhere from 30 minutes to 2 hours, depending on how much previous tenderizing was done. After it has simmered for 20 minutes, add the onion, bay leaf, celery, and peppercorns. This will produce a good flavorful broth to use in further preparations.

Broiled Tripe

(SERVES FOUR)

1 pound (450 g) honeycomb
tripe
1¼ cup (3 dL) cracker crumbs
½ pound (225 g) butter,
melted

Salt
Lemon wedges

Prepare the tripe as directed (above). Preheat the broiler. Cut the tripe into serving pieces and dip first into cracker crumbs, then into the melted butter. Sprinkle with salt and place, smooth side up, 3 inches beneath the broiler element. Cook 2–3 minutes on each side or until lightly browned. Serve garnished with lemon wedges.

Tripe in Batter

Serve with Chili Sauce (p. 284).

(SERVES FOUR)

1 pound (450 g) tripe
1 cup (140 g) flour
½ teaspoon salt
1 teaspoon baking powder

1 egg, beaten
⅓ cup (¾ L) milk
1 cup (¼ L) plus 1 teaspoon
vegetable oil

Prepare the tripe as directed (above) and cut into serving-size pieces. Make a batter by combining the flour, salt, baking powder, egg, milk, and 1 teaspoon oil in a bowl. Beat until well blended. Dip pieces of tripe in the batter. Heat the remaining cup of oil in a large skillet. When it is very hot, fry the battered tripe until brown on both sides. Don't crowd the pan: do a few pieces at a time and keep those that are done warm in the oven.

Tripe Lyonnaise

1 pound (450 g) tripe	Salt
2 tablespoons butter	Freshly ground pepper
2 tablespoons finely chopped	3 tablespoons lemon juice
onion	1 tablespoon minced parsley

Prepare the tripe as directed (opposite) and cut it into ½ × 2-inch pieces. Melt the butter in a skillet and add the onion. Cook over moderate heat, stirring often, until onion is soft. Add the pieces of tripe and cook 4 minutes. Sprinkle with salt, pepper, and lemon juice; arrange on a platter and garnish with parsley.

About Liver

Liver is unquestionably the most generally used variety meat in America. With no waste, it provides four highly nutritious servings a pound. Look for a bright, shiny surface when you buy it; avoid liver that is dull-colored. The butcher will probably not have removed the outer membrane for you. Scrape and peel it off, then wipe the liver clean with a paper towel. Keep it loosely wrapped in the refrigerator, and plan to use it within 24 hours. If that is not possible, freeze it; like all variety meats, liver freezes well.

The best quality, flavor, and tenderness are found in calves' liver. Beef liver is tougher and stronger in flavor, though still very good, while pork liver has a stronger odor and flavor but is very nutritious. Pork and goose livers are both widely used for making pâtés. Chicken, duck, turkey, and goose livers are all tender, flavorful, and highly perishable.

Even the most tender piece of calves' liver, if overcooked, will tighten and toughen. Never overcook it: either sauté it quickly over high heat, a minute on each side, or cook it gently over medium heat only to the point of tenderness.

Liver Sautéed in Butter

1 pound (450 g) liver, in	1 tablespoon oil
⅛–¼-inch slices	Salt
3 tablespoons flour	Freshly ground pepper
3 tablespoons butter	

Dip the liver in flour and shake off any excess. Heat the butter and oil in a skillet until foaming, then add the liver. Cook about 1 minute—or less for very thin pieces—on each side or until the red color is gone. Sprinkle with salt and pepper.

Liver and Bacon. Fry 8 slices of bacon, drain on paper towels, and keep warm. Remove all but 3 tablespoons bacon fat from the skillet, and use this instead of butter and oil to sauté the liver. Serve with the cooked bacon.

Liver and Onions. Slice 2 large onions thin, and separate the rings. Melt 2 tablespoons butter in a skillet over medium heat, and cook the onions until light golden. Remove and keep warm. In sautéing the liver, omit the oil. Serve covered with onions.

Liver Venetian Style

(SERVES FOUR)

1 pound (450 g) liver, in ⅛-
inch slices
4 tablespoons vegetable oil

4 onions, sliced thin
Salt
Freshly ground pepper

Cut the liver into matchlike pieces, using scissors or a sharp knife. Heat the oil
in a large skillet. Add the onions and cook, stirring often, over medium heat
until soft and lightly browned. Push the onions to the side of the pan, turn the
heat up, and sauté the liver for about 1 minute, until it turns from red to brown.
Sprinkle with salt and pepper.

Broiled Liver

Liver for broiling should be cut at least ½ inch thick; otherwise, the
intense heat toughens it to a leathery consistency.

(SERVES FOUR)

3 tablespoons butter, softened
½ teaspoon salt
¼ teaspoon freshly ground pepper

¾ teaspoon tarragon or savory,
crushed
1 pound (450 g) liver

Preheat the broiler. Blend the butter with salt, pepper, and tarragon or savory.
Place the liver on a rack 3 inches below the broiling element and cook about 2
minutes on each side, depending on the thickness of the slices. Don't overcook
it! Remove, and top each serving with a lump of seasoned butter.

Liver Loaf

Serve hot or cold; nice on sandwiches, too.

(SERVES SIX)

1 pound (450 g) liver
½ pound (225 g) pork,
chopped fine
1 onion, chopped fine
1 cup (¼ L) freshly made bread
crumbs
1 egg, well beaten

1 teaspoon salt
¼ teaspoon freshly ground
pepper
4 tablespoons catsup
Juice of 1 lemon
8 slices bacon
1 bay leaf

Preheat the oven to 350°F (180°C). Cover the liver with water in a skillet and
simmer for 5 minutes. Drain and chop fine with a knife or in a food processor.
Mix the liver, pork, onion, crumbs, egg, salt, pepper, catsup, and lemon juice.
Your freshly washed hands will do the most efficient job. Line a loaf pan with six
slices of the bacon. Pack the liver mixture into the pan, patting the top to make
it even. Lay the remaining bacon slices over the top, forming a cross. Put the
bay leaf on top and bake for 45–50 minutes or until done.

RABBIT

About Rabbit

The rabbit we get in this country has been raised domestically, so we cannot consider rabbit as game. The meat tastes very much like chicken, a little more dense and dry, and it would be worthwhile experimenting by substituting rabbit in some of the chicken recipes. Rabbit usually comes packaged, cut up in pieces, more often than not frozen. Defrost slowly in the refrigerator.

Fried Rabbit

Like fried chicken, this tastes good served hot or cold.

(SERVES FOUR TO FIVE)

4-pound (1¾-kg) domestic rabbit, in serving pieces	Salt
4 tablespoons flour	Freshly ground pepper
	3 tablespoons shortening

Wipe the rabbit pieces with a damp towel and pat dry. Lightly dust each piece with flour and sprinkle with salt and pepper. Heat the shortening in a large skillet, then add the rabbit and brown. Lower the heat and fry, turning often, for 25 minutes or until the juices run clear when a small slit is made in the thick part of the thigh.

Rabbit Sautéed with Cream

A lovely, tender dish. Serve with applesauce.

(SERVES FOUR TO FIVE)

4-pound (1¾-kg) domestic rabbit, in serving pieces	Freshly ground pepper
6 tablespoons flour	2 tablespoons butter
Salt	2 tablespoons oil
	1½ cups (3½ dL) light cream

Wipe the rabbit pieces with a damp towel and pat dry. Dust with 4 tablespoons of the flour, and sprinkle with salt and pepper. Heat the butter and oil in a large skillet, brown the pieces on each side, cover, and cook for 25 minutes, or until the juices run clear. Transfer the rabbit to a warm platter. Add the remaining 2 tablespoons of flour to the pan drippings, stirring and scraping the bits from the bottom of the pan. Slowly stir in the cream and cook, stirring, over medium heat until the sauce is thickened, at least 5–6 minutes. Spoon some of the sauce over the rabbit and serve the remaining sauce in a bowl.

VENISON

About Venison

Venison is seldom available in our markets, so you have to know a hunter to enjoy this treat. Also, only he will know the approximate age of the deer when killed, which is important because that is your guide to how to cook the meat. Tender young venison will need no marinating and can be cooked very briefly, as in Broiled Venison Steak, or you may use some of the recipes for lamb—chops or roasts. Older venison should always be marinated before cooking.

Venison Steak and Chestnut Sauce

(SERVES FOUR)

3 tablespoons butter
½ onion, chopped
½ carrot, chopped
3 tablespoons flour
1½ cups (3½ dL) beef broth
½ bay leaf, crumbled
1 teaspoon coarsely ground
  pepper

1 teaspoon salt
4 tablespoons Madeira
1 cup (¼ L) cooked chopped
  chestnuts
1 or 2 venison steaks, 1¼
  inches thick

Melt the butter in a skillet. Add the onion and carrot and cook until lightly browned, about 5 minutes. Stir in the flour and cook until brown. Add the beef broth, bay leaf, pepper, and salt, and simmer for 10–15 minutes. Strain, then add the Madeira and chestnuts and set aside. Preheat the broiler. Place the venison steaks on a rack 5 inches beneath the broiler element. Cook 5 minutes on each side. Remove to a hot platter and cover with the hot chestnut sauce.

Broiled Venison Steak

(SERVES TWO)

1 venison steak, ¾–1 inch
  thick
4 tablespoons butter, softened
Salt

Freshly ground pepper
1 cup (¼ L) dry red wine
¼ teaspoon allspice
½ cup (1 dL) currant jelly

Preheat the broiler. Rub the venison steak with butter and sprinkle liberally with salt and pepper. Place the steak 4 inches beneath the broiling element on a rack in a shallow pan. Broil 4 minutes each side. Remove the steak to a warm platter and set the pan over a burner. Add the wine, allspice, and jelly to the pan drippings. Bring to a boil and stir until smooth and blended. Spoon a little sauce over the steak and pass the rest in a bowl.

Marinated Leg of Venison

Start to marinate the meat two days before you plan to cook it.

(SERVES EIGHT TO TEN)

5-pound (2¼-kg) leg of
  venison
2 cups (½ L) dry red wine
½ cup (1 dL) olive oil
2 bay leaves
4 cloves garlic, chopped
2 teaspoons dry mustard

1 teaspoon rosemary, crumbled
1 teaspoon salt
1 teaspoon coarsely ground
  pepper
4 slices bacon
3 tablespoons flour
½ cup (1 dL) red currant jelly

Place the leg of venison in a deep bowl. Combine the wine, oil, bay leaves, garlic, mustard, rosemary, salt, and pepper, and pour over the venison. Cover with foil and refrigerate two days, turning the meat several times. Preheat the oven to 450°F (230°C). Drain the venison and reserve the marinade. Place the meat on a rack in a shallow pan and cover with the bacon strips. Roast for 30 minutes, basting several times with the marinade, then reduce the heat to 350°F (180°C) and continue to roast another 40–60 minutes (to an interior temperature of 130° for rare; 140° for medium). Put the venison on a platter and keep warm. Set the roasting pan over a burner, add the flour to the pan drippings, and cook until it is browned. Strain the reserved marinade and stir into the pan, cooking until smooth and thickened. Add the currant jelly; cook only until the jelly is melted and blended with the sauce. Carve at the table the way you would a roast of lamb, with the gravy in a sauceboat.

POULTRY &
GAME BIRDS

ABOUT POULTRY

The dream of the good life in America is embodied in the promise of "a chicken in every pot." Domestic and wild fowl have always been abundant and popular, and each wave of immigrants has brought along favorite dishes—such as paella and chicken cacciatore—which have soon become naturalized citizens.

Thanks to modern scientific techniques, the birds we buy today are rich in nutrition, low in fat, and reasonable in price. Whereas once we had to wait for spring broilers, summer fryers, fall roasters, and the stewing hens of deep winter, we now have an endless supply of tender wholesome poultry all year round.

Types of Poultry

By "poultry" we mean all the domestic birds that are raised for food: chicken, turkey, duck, goose, Cornish game hen, and squab or pigeon.

Chicken. Chicken is classified by its age and weight and sold with names that are suggestions rather than prescriptions for cooking. Fryers, for example, are good roasted or poached as well as fried. They weigh from 2 to 3½ pounds, somewhat larger than 2-pound broilers. The distinction between broilers and fryers is disappearing, however, and these days you are more likely to find broiler-fryers weighing 2 to 3½ pounds. Roasters are larger, 3 to 5 pounds, and capons—desexed male chickens—provide especially tender meat at the same weight. An old hen may weigh as little as a fryer, but most are considerably larger; they have stringy meat and a lot of body fat, but slow simmering makes them tender and brings out their deep flavor.

Turkey. Turkey also comes in various weights. There are fryer-roasters at 4 to 8 pounds and young hens weighing 7 to 15 pounds. Fully mature hens or tom turkeys—both have their enthusiasts—weigh up to 30 pounds and are splendid for holiday feasts. Their appearance is generous, and they are more economical than smaller birds, costing less per pound and having a higher ratio of meat to bone than less imposing fowl.

Other Poultry. The smallest bird raised for food is the Rock Cornish game hen, produced by cross-breeding a Plymouth Rock chicken and a Cornish gamecock. These tiny fowl, served one to a person, have delicate, nongamy meat. Domestic ducklings, only 3 to 4 pounds in weight, are tender and delicate when fried or broiled; mature ducks at 5 to 6 pounds should be roasted or braised. Goose is still larger, ranging from 8 to 16 pounds.

Buying Poultry

All the poultry offered for sale in this country has been inspected by the United States Department of Agriculture, and the clip, tag, or stamp on each bird certifies its freshness. A flexible breastbone is a good sign of youth; if it is stiff and unyielding, try some long slow cooking.

The color of the chicken does not indicate its quality: in the midwestern states white-skinned chicken is preferred, while corn-feeding produces yellow skin in chickens, considered desirable in California.

About 1 pound of chicken or turkey with bones makes a serving, but allow at least 1½ pounds of raw duck or goose for each person, for they have a large amount of body fat that melts away during cooking, making their raw weight misleading. Buy more rather than less: using up leftover poultry is no problem.

If your family strongly prefers white or dark meat, you may decide to buy cut-up poultry in packages containing only the parts that you want. Resist the temptation to buy either prebasted or frozen stuffed turkeys; you will be paying someone else to do jobs that are simple and so much better done at home.

Storing Poultry

Poultry is among the most perishable of meats. Take it straight home from the market and remove it from its wrappings. Rewrap it loosely and refrigerate it immediately, keeping it no more than a day or two. Chicken parts are even more perishable than whole chickens. For freezing poultry, see p. 730.

Preparing Poultry for Cooking

Today's poultry is usually ready to cook; all you need do is to wipe it with a damp paper towel or rinse it quickly under cold running water, patting it dry so that it will brown nicely. Remove any lumps of fat around the cavities, particularly the tail. Save chicken and goose fat and render it so that it can be used in cooking.

To Render Chicken Fat. Pick the yellow fat off each chicken you cook; you'll find most of it around the tail. Collect raw chicken fat in the freezer until you have enough to render, about ½ to 1 cup. One pound of raw chicken fat will produce about 2 cups of rendered fat.

    Cut the fat into very small pieces and put them in a large skillet over very low heat until the fat has melted and the small pieces are crisp and brown. Remove them from the pan and drain on paper towels. If you wish, flavor the rendered fat in the pan by browning a diced onion or two in it. Strain the fat into a jar or container, cover tight, and refrigerate. It will keep almost indefinitely.

    The browned bits of fat and onions are traditionally mixed into chopped liver or mashed potatoes or sprinkled with salt and served as a snack.

To Melt Chicken Fat. This is a simple way to render chicken fat. The fat will be pure and unflavored and will keep indefinitely.

    Pick fat off the chicken. Preheat the oven to 275°F (135°C). Put the chicken fat in a heatproof cup or bowl and fill two-thirds full with water. Place in the oven and let the fat melt slowly; this will take an hour or more, depending on the amount of fat. Remove and cool. The fat will rise to the top and should then be carefully spooned into a container, covered, and stored in the refrigerator.

Cutting Up a Whole Chicken

You not only save money by cutting up your own chicken but, when you do it yourself, it is neater, with none of the little splintered bones that the electric saw sometimes produces.

1) Place the chicken breast side down. Using a very sharp knife, cut through the backbone along the spinal column.

2) Turn the chicken over and break both sides of the breastbone by pushing down on it with the heel of your hand. Firmly flatten the chicken as much as possible.

3) Wiggle the wing joint at the shoulder, poking around with the tip of your knife until you feel the connecting tissue.

4) Cut through to remove the wing. Repeat with the other wing.

5) Wiggle the leg back and forth to see where it connects to the body. Pull it down to help detect the connecting joint; when you find the socket, cut through it and remove both legs.

6) Cut the thigh from the drumstick at the joint.

7) Cut away the side of the breast, still attached to the back, severing the tiny bones. (Use the back bone for making stock.)

8) Cut the breast in half, starting just above the cartilage and probing with your knife to feel where the tissue gives way. Make the cut a little off-center, where the bones are thin.

The chicken is now in eight pieces, ready to be fried or broiled. Collect and freeze the backbones, necks, gizzards, and hearts until you have enough to make a rich chicken stock or soup. Freeze the liver separately to use in liver dishes.

Boning Chicken Breasts. Chicken breasts, skinned, boned, and pounded thin, are the basis for many interesting, delicate dishes and, like turkey, make a delicious and thrifty substitute in recipes calling for veal cutlets. Save

money by boning them yourself, using a sharp knife: following the breastbone cut the meat in half lengthwise, then scrape it away from the breastbone as you gently tug it. The bones should go into the stockpot. Three pounds of chicken breasts will weigh about 2¼ pounds after boning.

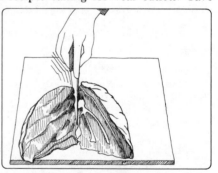

A boned breast will be about ½ inch thick. To make a cutlet, place it between two sheets of wax paper and pound it with a mallet or rolling pin until it is only ¼ inch thick. Cooked for 10 minutes or less, it should be tender, moist, and delicately flavored.

Stuffing Poultry

For stuffings, see p. 277.

To stuff a bird, wash it briefly and pat it dry with paper towels. Season it inside and out. You can prepare the stuffing ahead of time, but don't put it into the bird more than a few hours before you cook it and be sure to refrigerate. Even after it has been cooked, stuffing should not sit around too long in the bird. It's a good

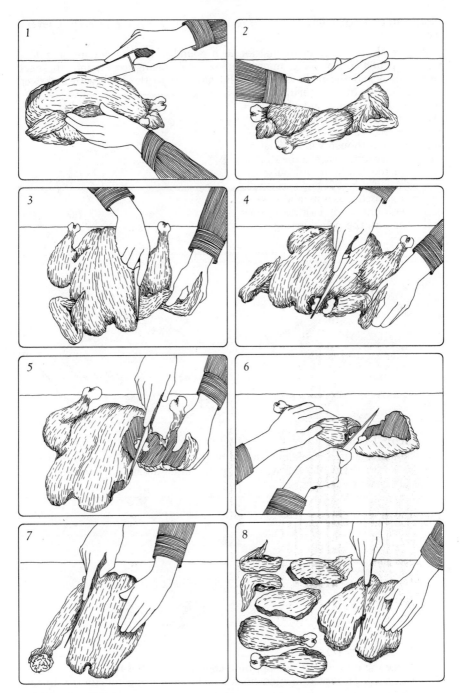

idea to store it separately in the refrigerator if you are going to keep it several days.

Prepare about ¾ cup of stuffing for each pound of poultry; 9 cups of stuffing for a 12-pound turkey, for example. Pack a little stuffing loosely into the neck cavity, then pull the neck skin over and fasten it to the back with a skewer.

Spoon the rest of the stuffing lightly into the body cavity and either sew the opening shut or stick it through with skewers, wrapping string around the skewers as though you were lacing a boot. Leave some space: if the stuffing is packed too firmly, it will burst the skin as it expands. Put any extra stuffing in a greased casserole and bake it along with the bird, basting it now and then with the pan drippings.

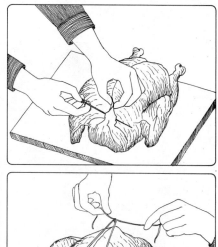

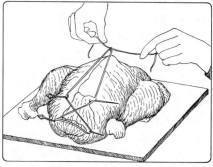

Trussing Poultry

Stuffed or unstuffed, a whole bird should be trussed before it is roasted or braised to keep it from drying out during cooking, to ensure an attractive presentation, and to add ease to carving.

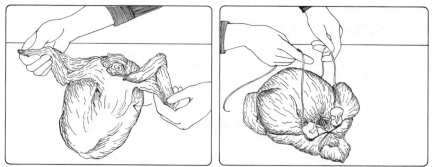

1) Place the bird, breast side up, on a counter top. Bend the second joints of the wings back. 2) Place the middle of a long piece of string underneath the tail, bring the ends over the tail, and cross them over the body, looping around the ends of the drumsticks. 3) Run the string snugly across the sides of the body,

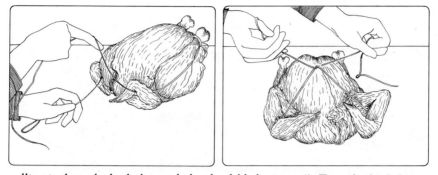

pulling it through the holes made by the folded wings. 4) Turn the bird, breast side down, and tie the string in a knot in the back. One snip before carving will remove the string, while the bird stays neatly in shape.

Cooking Poultry

Poultry may be roasted, broiled, fried, stewed, braised, or poached. Steaming is used primarily in Chinese cooking and for special fat-free diets.

When you are roasting or broiling, basting helps to keep the skin from drying out. Birds can be roasted stuffed or unstuffed; stuffed poultry requires extra cooking time. If you don't want to bother with a stuffing, season the cavity with salt and pepper and put in a whole onion, a handful of fresh herbs, or perhaps a half a lemon, for flavor. Roasting times vary considerably: tiny game hens take less than an hour, but a stuffed goose weighing 12 or more pounds will take nearly 4 hours to become succulent and brown.

When you fry small, tender chickens, they will become crisp and brown in a very short time. Less tender birds should be browned in butter and then gently simmered in liquid, as in Coq au Vin and Chicken Fricassee. Older chickens when gently cooked in lots of liquid will produce a rich broth, as in chicken and dumplings.

Testing for Doneness

The poultry we get today has been fed scientifically; it's tender and moist, and the cooking time is shorter than it was some years ago. Test to see if poultry is done by cutting a deep slit in the flesh between leg and body: if the juices run clear the bird is done; pink blood indicates that more cooking is required. The old test of "shaking hands with the bird" is unreliable, for if the leg moves easily in its socket, the dark meat is probably overdone. With experience you will be able to feel when the meat is done by pressing the thigh and breast with your finger.

An instant meat thermometer provides real assurance, of course. When the approximate cooking time is coming to an end, insert the tip of the thermometer into the breast meat or the thickest part of the thigh, being careful not to touch the tip of the thermometer to a bone. The bird is done when the temperature of the breast meat reads 170°F and that of the thigh meat is at 185°F. This slight disparity in required cooking time makes it advisable, if you are cooking poultry cut up into parts, to start dark meat cooking a few minutes before white meat when possible; it also explains why roast turkeys sometimes have dried-out white meat while their dark meat is still succulent and flavorful.

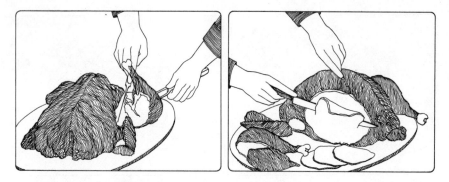

Carving Cooked Poultry

Carving will be easier if you let the bird rest at room temperature for 15 minutes after it is cooked. Use a freshly sharpened carving knife. Place the cooked chicken or turkey on a platter breast side up, with the legs to your right. (Reverse this position, of course, if you are left-handed.) Holding a large fork in your fist, stick it firmly into the fleshy part of the drumstick near you. Cut through the skin that joins the leg to the body. Pull the leg away from the body, finding the connecting joint with the tip of your knife so you can sever it. Once removed, detach the drumstick from the second joint. Next, cut off the wing, again probing with the tip of your knife to find the socket before you cut. Then carve the breast meat into thin slices, sticking the fork into the meat above. Repeat on the other side as more meat is needed.

Using Leftovers

For specific dishes using leftover chicken, turkey, and other poultry, see p. 253.

Poultry Livers

Liver, with its pronounced flavor, should never go into a stock. Save the livers for another use; even if there's just one liver, save it and freeze it until you have enough to make a dish. Or if you are roasting the poultry, add the liver to the pan during the last 5 minutes (10 minutes for a large turkey liver). The liver will absorb a little of the pan drippings and turn brown while retaining its rosy center, and is delicious chopped and added to your gravy (or just eaten whole).

Chicken, turkey, duck, and goose livers should be cooked only long enough to brown them, leaving them lightly pink inside. Overcooking makes them tough and rubbery and destroys the good, creamy texture.

TURKEY

Roast Stuffed Turkey

Before you place the turkey on its V-shaped rack, cover the rack with heavily greased parchment, foil, or brown paper to keep the skin from tearing when you turn the turkey. Check p. 230 to determine the amount of stuffing per pound of turkey you will need.

1 turkey	Salt
Stuffing (pp. 277–281)	Freshly ground pepper
¼–½ pound (115–225 g) butter, depending on size of turkey	

Preheat the oven to 325°F (165°C). Rinse the turkey and pat it dry. Stuff the body and neck cavities before trussing (p. 232). Soften ⅛–¼ pound butter and rub all over the turkey, depending on its size—it should be thoroughly buttered. Sprinkle with salt and pepper and place, breast down, on the paper-covered rack in a roasting pan. Put in the oven. Melt the remaining butter (about ¼ pound) with ¼ cup water and baste the turkey every 20 minutes with this mixture until enough pan drippings for basting have accumulated in the bottom of the roasting pan. Cook 15 minutes per pound if the turkey weighs less than 16 pounds; 12 minutes per pound if it is heavier. Turn breast up after 1 hour if the turkey weighs less than 12 pounds; after 1½ hours if it weighs more. When a meat thermometer registers 170°F in the breast meat and 185°F in the thigh meat, remove the turkey to a warm platter and cover loosely with a towel or foil. Let rest 15 minutes before carving.

Unstuffed Roast Turkey. Omit the stuffing. Sprinkle the body cavity with *1 teaspoon salt* and *½ teaspoon poultry seasoning,* then place in the cavity *5 sprigs parsley, 4 stalks celery,* and *3 onions, peeled and quartered.*

Basic Chicken or Turkey Gravy

Two factors help make a lovely deep-brown gravy: the drippings on the bottom of the roasting pan and the slow browning of the flour in the fat.

(2 CUPS)

4 tablespoons fat from poultry pan drippings	Freshly ground pepper
3 tablespoons flour	2 cups (½ L) liquid: stock, giblet broth, water, or milk
Salt	

When the bird has been removed from the roasting pan, skim off all but 4 tablespoons of fat in the pan. If there is not enough fat in the drippings, add butter. Place the pan over a burner and heat it, scraping the bottom of the pan to loosen all the browned bits. (If the roasting pan is clumsy to handle, scrape and pour the drippings into a saucepan.) Stir in the flour and blend well over medium heat for 3 minutes or more, until lightly browned. Add salt and pepper to taste, and slowly pour in the liquid, stirring constantly, until smooth. Simmer for 10 minutes to develop the flavor.

Giblet Broth

In general "giblets" refers to all the loose parts—the neck, heart, liver, and gizzard of poultry. A broth made of giblets and vegetables will add richness to gravy, as will the chopped giblets themselves. Because of its strong flavor, the liver should not be cooked in the broth, but separately.

Giblets	Salt
1 teaspoon thyme, crumbled	Freshly ground pepper
1 thick slice onion	Butter (optional)
1 rib celery with leaves, sliced	

Rinse the gizzard, heart, and neck, and trim all fat, membranes, and blood. Put the giblets in a saucepan, cover with cold water, and add the thyme, onion, celery, and a sprinkle of salt and pepper. Bring to a boil and simmer 45 minutes, or until the gizzard is tender. Meanwhile, cook the liver under the roasting bird 5–10 minutes or sauté lightly in some butter. Strain the giblets, reserve the broth, and finely dice the gizzard, liver, and heart. Using this broth, make the gravy following Basic Chicken or Turkey Gravy (preceding recipe) and add the giblets at the end.

Roast Turkey Breast

To bone a turkey breast, slip a knife between the bone and the meat and separate the two, using a sawing motion. Tie the two halves together to make a cylindrical roll.

(1 POUND SERVES THREE)

1 whole boned turkey breast	Salt
4 tablespoons butter	Freshly ground pepper

Preheat the oven to 325°F (165°C). Rub the turkey breast liberally with butter and sprinkle with salt and pepper. Place in a shallow pan and roast for 25 minutes per pound or until the meat thermometer registers 170°F.

Turkey Breast with Red Currant Sauce. Mix ½ cup red currant jelly, 4 tablespoons port wine, 3 tablespoons butter, and 1½ teaspoons Worcestershire sauce in a small saucepan. Stir over low heat until melted and simmering, then brush on the roasting turkey breast every 15 minutes. Spoon some of the sauce over the sliced meat.

CHICKEN

Roast Chicken

Although a 3–5-pound chicken is called a roaster, small broiler-fryers can also be cooked this way. Use a roasting pan that accommodates the bird comfortably; if the pan is too big, the good pan drippings will spread out and cook away.

(1 POUND PER SERVING)

2½–5-pound (1¼–2¼-kg) chicken	¼–⅓ pound (85–115 g) butter
	Salt
Stuffing (p. 277; optional)	Freshly ground pepper

Preheat the oven to 325°F (165°C). Rinse the chicken and pat it dry. Stuff the body and neck cavities, if desired, before trussing (p. 232). Soften 3–4 tablespoons of the butter and rub it all over the chicken. Sprinkle with salt and pepper and place the chicken in the oven, breast up, on a V-shaped rack in a roasting pan. Melt the remaining butter in a saucepan. Baste every 15 minutes with the melted butter until enough pan drippings for basting have accumulated in the bottom of the roasting pan. Cook about 25 minutes a pound, or until a meat thermometer registers 170°F in the breast meat and 185°F in the thigh meat. Remove the chicken to a warm platter and cover loosely with a towel or foil. Let rest 10 minutes to distribute the juices and settle the meat for carving.

Thyme-roasted Chicken. Omit the stuffing and rub ½ *teaspoon salt* in the body cavity before inserting 1 *carrot, sliced,* and 1 *rib celery with leaves, sliced.* Add 1 *teaspoon thyme, crumbled,* to the butter rubbed on the chicken. Make basic gravy (p. 268), using 1 *cup chicken broth* and 1 *cup water* and adding the *juice of 1 lemon* before serving.

Oven-broiled Chicken

Unlike real broiled chicken, fowl cooked by this simple method does not require careful watching. It is good when hot, and unequaled later in salads or sandwiches.

(SERVES FOUR)

2½–3-pound (1¼–1½-kg) chicken, in halves or quarters	3 tablespoons oil Salt Freshly ground pepper

Preheat the oven to 400°F (205°C). Lightly oil a shallow pan. Coat the chicken with oil and season with salt and pepper. Place skin side up in the pan. Bake for 35–45 minutes, or until a meat thermometer reads 170°F in the breast meat, 185°F in the dark meat.

Broiled Chicken

Quick and juicy, but requiring careful watching.

(SERVES FOUR)

2½–3-pound (1¼–1½-kg) chicken, in halves or quarters	Salt Freshly ground pepper 4 tablespoons butter, melted

Preheat the broiler. Sprinkle salt and pepper on the chicken and place it on the broiler pan, skin side down. Brush with the melted butter. Place the pan 5 inches beneath the broiling element and cook 10 minutes. Turn the chicken, brush with melted butter, and broil 10 minutes more. Turn and brush with melted butter again. Check with a meat thermometer (see p. 27) or cut a slit in the thickest part of the thigh and see if the juices run clear. Turn and cook longer if necessary.

Orange-broiled Chicken. Baste with a mixture of ½ *cup orange juice,* ¼ *cup oil,* 2 *tablespoons grated orange rind,* ½ *teaspoon dry mustard,* ¼ *teaspoon salt,* and a *dash of Tabasco* instead of the melted butter.

Barbecue-roasted Chicken

This may be done on an indoor rotisserie as well as over hot coals.

(SERVES FOUR)

2½–3-pound (1¼–1½-kg) chicken ¼ cup oil Salt	Freshly ground pepper 1 recipe Light Barbecue Sauce (p. 277)

Light the coals. Truss the chicken (p. 232), rub it with oil, and sprinkle it with salt and pepper. Arrange on a spit. When the fire is ready, place the spitted chicken on the rotisserie and cook for 1–1½ hours or until a meat thermometer registers 170°F in the breast meat and 185°F in the thigh meat, basting every 15 minutes with the sauce.

Barbecue-broiled Chicken. Cut the chicken into halves or quarters. (Smaller pieces tend to dry out and overdarken.) Place on the grill, bone side down, and cook 10 minutes. Turn and baste every 10 minutes until done, about 40 minutes in all.

Pan-fried Chicken

Remember all the nice things that go with this: biscuits with butter and maybe honey, cream gravy—and mustard greens cooked with salt pork for a real southern dinner.

(SERVES FOUR)

2½–3-pound (1¼–1½-kg) chicken, in 8 pieces
Milk
¾ cup (1¾ dL) flour
1 teaspoon salt

½ teaspoon freshly ground pepper
Oil for frying
Cream Gravy (following recipe)

Wash and dry the chicken pieces. Place them snugly together in one layer in a shallow dish. Pour on milk to cover, and steep 1 hour, turning once. Mix the flour, salt, and pepper on a piece of wax paper or in a paper bag. Remove chicken from the milk and roll it in the seasoned flour or shake vigorously in the paper bag. Pour oil into a large skillet to a depth of ½ inch. Heat until a small cube of bread browns in 60 seconds or a frying thermometer registers 375°F. Put the dark meat into the pan first, adding the white meat 5 minutes later. Do not crowd the chicken; if necessary, cook in two batches. Fry about 20–30 minutes, turning often with a pair of tongs. Remove, drain on paper towels, and keep warm while you make the gravy. Serve hot with the gravy.

Cream Gravy

A must with all types of fried chicken!

(1¾ CUPS)

3 tablespoons pan drippings and butter
3 tablespoons flour
1½ cups (3½ dL) cream

Salt
¼ teaspoon freshly ground pepper

Heat the pan drippings in the skillet, adding butter, if necessary, and scraping up any brown bits in the pan. Stir in the flour and blend, cooking over low heat until lightly browned. Slowly add the cream, stirring constantly until smooth. Season with salt to taste and pepper, and cook for about 7 minutes.

Batter-fried Chicken

The batter coating makes a crunchy crust. An electric deep-fat fryer with automatic temperature controls is good for this, but you can use an ordinary heavy-bottomed pan.

2½–3-pound (1¼–1½-kg)   1 recipe Beer Fritter Batter (p. 358)
   chicken, in 8 pieces   Oil for deep frying

Wash and dry the pieces of chicken. Prepare the fritter batter. Heat at least 3 inches of oil until a small cube of bread browns in 60 seconds or a frying thermometer registers 365°F. Dip the chicken pieces into the batter and submerge them carefully in the oil. Use tongs to move the pieces about so they don't stick together. Fry 15 minutes or until done, and drain on paper towels.

Maryland Fried Chicken

In Maryland, it seems, they dip their chicken in flour, egg, and soft bread crumbs before frying it.

½ cup (70 g) flour   1 egg
1 teaspoon salt   2½–3-pound (1¼–1½-kg)
½ teaspoon freshly ground   chicken, in 8 pieces
   pepper   Oil for frying
2 cups (½ L) freshly made   Cream Gravy (opposite)
   bread crumbs

Mix the flour with the salt and pepper on wax paper. Spread the bread crumbs on another piece of wax paper. Lightly beat the egg in a shallow bowl with 2 tablespoons of water. Wash and dry the chicken pieces. Coat them with flour, dip in the egg, then roll them in the bread crumbs. Heat ½ inch of oil until a small cube of bread browns in 60 seconds or a frying thermometer registers 365°F. Using tongs, put the chicken in the hot oil and fry for about 20 minutes, turning often, until brown and done. Drain on paper towels and keep warm while you make the gravy.

Coq au Vin

A wonderfully robust dish, full of friendly flavors in a rich dark sauce—and a good way to use a middle-aged hen.

6 tablespoons butter   2 bay leaves
2 tablespoons oil   10 whole mushrooms
5-pound (2¼-kg) chicken, in 8   1 teaspoon salt
   pieces   ½ teaspoon freshly ground
½ cup (1 dL) chopped ham   pepper
10 small white onions   4 tablespoons Cognac or other
2 cloves garlic, crushed   brandy
1 teaspoon thyme, crumbled   1 cup (¼ L) dry red wine
3 parsley sprigs

Preheat the oven to 275°F (135°C). Melt the butter and oil in a large pot. Brown the chicken pieces on all sides. Remove and place in a casserole with the drippings. Add the ham, onions, garlic, thyme, parsley, bay leaves, mushrooms, salt, and pepper. Warm the brandy slightly in a small saucepan. Ignite it with a match and pour it, flaming, over the chicken. When the flames die, pour on the red wine. Cover and bake 1½–2 hours.

Delmonico's Deviled Chicken

"Deviled" here means that the chicken is split, seasoned, and then sprinkled with crumbs.

(SERVES FOUR)

2½–3-pound (1¼–1½-kg)
   chicken, in quarters
4 tablespoons butter, softened
1 tablespoon prepared mustard
1 tablespoon vinegar

½ teaspoon salt
½ teaspoon paprika
1 cup (¼ L) freshly made bread
   crumbs

Preheat the oven to 375°F (190°C). Wipe the chicken with a paper towel. Mix the butter, mustard, vinegar, salt, and paprika, and rub the mixture all over the skin side of the chicken. Place the quarters, skin side up, in a shallow roasting pan. Sprinkle evenly with the crumbs and bake for about 40 minutes or until a meat thermometer registers 170°F in the breast meat, 185°F in the dark meat.

Savory Casserole of Chicken

(SERVES FOUR)

2½–3-pound (1¼–1½-kg)
   chicken, in 8 pieces
4 tablespoons flour
4 tablespoons oil
¼ cup (½ dL) finely chopped
   onion
¼ cup (½ dL) finely chopped
   celery

1 tablespoon finely chopped
   green pepper
1½ cups (3½ dL) chopped
   canned or fresh tomatoes
¾ teaspoon oregano, crumbled
1¼ teaspoons salt
½ teaspoon freshly ground
   pepper

Preheat the oven to 325°F (165°C). Wash and dry the chicken pieces and lightly dust with flour. Heat the oil in a skillet and quickly brown the chicken pieces. Put the chicken into a casserole with a lid. Add the remaining ingredients, cover, and bake 1 hour.

Chicken Cacciatore

An Italian dish—*cacciatore* meaning "hunter's"—which has a good earthy taste. The final garnish adds wonderful zest to the finished dish—and those shy of garlic *can* always leave the garlic out.

(SERVES FOUR)

1 ounce (30 g) dried
   mushrooms
4 tablespoons olive oil
1 medium chicken, cut in 8
   pieces
1 large onion, chopped
½ cup (1 dL) dry white wine
1 clove garlic, minced
1 tablespoon tomato paste

2 cups (½ L) fresh tomatoes,
   peeled, seeded, and chopped
   or canned drained
½ teaspoon allspice
Freshly ground pepper
2 bay leaves
½ teaspoon thyme, crumbled
Salt to taste

Garnish

Grated rind of 1 lemon   3 tablespoons minced parsley
½ clove garlic, minced

Put the mushrooms to soak for ½ hour in a cup with just enough warm water to cover. Heat the oil in a large skillet and cook the chicken until lightly browned on all sides. Add the onion and sauté a minute or two, then splash in the wine and let it boil up. Lower the heat and add the garlic, paste, and tomatoes, the soaked mushrooms and their liquid, carefully strained, and the seasonings. Cover and cook slowly for about 40 minutes, or until done. Remove bay leaves, taste and correct the salt. Mix together the lemon rind, minced garlic, and parsley and scatter over the top.

Chicken Contadine

(SERVES FOUR TO SIX)

6 tablespoons butter   ½ cup (1 dL) dry vermouth
2 tablespoons oil   1 teaspoon tomato paste
2 onions, chopped fine   ⅛ teaspoon cinnamon
2 small chickens, in quarters   Salt

Melt the butter and oil in a large skillet. Add the onions and cook slowly until soft. Add the chicken pieces and cook until lightly browned on all sides. Remove the chicken from the pan, stir in the vermouth, and bring to a boil. Lower the heat and stir in the tomato paste, cinnamon, and salt to taste. Return the chicken to the pan, cover, and cook over low heat for about 30 minutes.

Chicken Jambalaya

From the South: chicken, ham, and vegetables in tomato-flavored rice.

(SERVES SIX)

4–5-pound (2–2¼-kg) chicken,   ½ cup (1 dL) chopped celery
   in quarters   1 large onion, chopped
2 tablespoons oil   2 cloves garlic, minced
2 tablespoons bacon fat   5 cups (1¼ L) chicken broth
Salt   ¼ cup (½ dL) minced parsley
Freshly ground pepper   1 bay leaf
⅛ teaspoon cayenne pepper   1½ teaspoons thyme, crumbled
1 cup (¼ L) diced ham   1 cup (¼ L) chopped canned
½ cup (1 dL) chopped green   or fresh tomatoes
   pepper   2 cups (½ L) rice

Preheat the oven to 325°F (165°C). Rinse the chicken pieces and wipe dry. Heat the oil and bacon fat in a large skillet. Brown the chicken pieces and sprinkle them with salt, pepper, and cayenne pepper. Remove from the pan and set aside. Add the ham, green pepper, celery, onion, and garlic to the pan and cook until the vegetables are soft. Add the chicken broth, parsley, bay leaf, and thyme; bring to a boil and cook uncovered until the broth is reduced to 4 cups. Remove the chicken meat from the bones in large pieces. Put the chicken meat, the unstrained broth, the tomatoes, and rice in a casserole. Stir, cover, and bake for 1 hour, checking every 20 minutes and adding more hot broth or water if it dries out. Remove the bay leaf before serving.

Chicken Marengo

(SERVES FOUR)

4–5-pound (2–2¼-kg) chicken,
  in 8 pieces
⅓ cup (¾ dL) olive oil
Salt
Freshly ground pepper
1 onion, chopped

2 cloves garlic, crushed
½ cup (1 dL) dry white wine
1 cup (¼ L) chopped canned
  or fresh tomatoes
½ pound (225 g) mushrooms,
  sliced

Rinse the chicken and wipe dry. Heat the oil in a skillet. Add the chicken, brown lightly on all sides, and sprinkle with salt and pepper. Remove the chicken and set aside. Cook the onion and garlic until soft. Return the chicken to the pan with the wine, tomatoes, and mushrooms. Cover and simmer 30–40 minutes.

Mexican Chicken

(SERVES SIX)

2 small chickens, each in 8
  pieces
4 tablespoons oil
Salt
Freshly ground pepper
1½ cups (3½ dL) chopped
  onion
2 cloves garlic, minced
1 green pepper, chopped

¼ teaspoon ground cloves
2 teaspoons chili powder
1½ cups (3½ dL) chopped
  canned or fresh tomatoes
⅓ cup (¾ dL) raisins
4 tablespoons dry sherry
⅓ cup (¾ dL) stuffed green
  olives, sliced

Rinse the chicken and pat dry. Heat the oil in a heavy pan with a lid. Sprinkle the chicken with salt and pepper and brown in the hot oil. Remove the chicken and set aside. Add the onion, garlic, and green pepper to the pan and cook until soft. Stir in the cloves, chili powder, tomatoes, raisins, and browned chicken. Pour on the sherry, cover the pan, and simmer 30–40 minutes. Add the sliced olives just before serving.

Chicken Paprika

A Hungarian dish that is good served with wide noodles.

(SERVES FOUR)

3-pound (1⅓-kg) chicken, in
  quarters
4 tablespoons butter
½ cup (1 dL) chopped onion
Salt
2 tablespoons sweet Hungarian
  paprika

1 tomato, peeled and chopped
½–1 cup (⅛–¼ L) chicken
  broth
3 tablespoons flour
¼ cup (½ dL) heavy cream
½ cup (1 dL) sour cream, at
  room temperature

Rinse the chicken and pat it dry. Melt the butter in a heavy pan. Cook the onion until lightly browned, then add the chicken and sprinkle with salt. When the chicken pieces are browned, remove them from the pan and set aside. Mix in the paprika and cook for 1 minute; add the tomato and ½ cup chicken broth, lower the heat, and simmer for 7 minutes. Return the chicken to the pan, cover, and cook 30–40 minutes. Remove the chicken to a warm platter. Sprinkle the flour over the pan drippings, stirring briskly to smooth and blend, and cook for 3 minutes. Gradually add enough chicken broth to make 1 cup of liquid, then stir in the heavy cream. When it is heated through, turn off the heat, whisk the sour cream in a small bowl, and add it to the sauce, blending it quickly without letting it boil. Spoon over the chicken pieces to serve.

Chicken Fricassee

A great old-fashioned dish, the essence of chicken in a creamy sauce.

(SERVES SIX)

5-pound (2¼-kg) chicken, cut in large pieces	1 carrot, sliced
¼ pound (115 g) butter	1 bay leaf
2 tablespoons oil	4 tablespoons flour
1 small onion, sliced	1 cup (¼ L) heavy cream
2 ribs celery with leaves, cut in pieces	2 tablespoons lemon juice
	Salt
	Freshly ground pepper

Rinse the chicken and pat it dry. Heat 4 tablespoons of the butter with the oil in a Dutch oven, and brown the chicken on all sides. Lower the heat, pour on boiling water to cover the chicken, and add the onion, celery, carrot, and bay leaf. Cover and simmer 40–45 minutes. Remove the chicken to a platter and keep warm. Strain the broth and remove any surface fat. Bring the broth to a boil and reduce to 1½ cups. Melt the remaining 4 tablespoons of butter in a saucepan. Stir in the flour and cook for 2–3 minutes. Slowly add the cream and broth, continuing to stir and simmer for 4–5 minutes until thickened and smooth. Add the lemon juice and salt and pepper to taste, spoon over the chicken, and serve.

Chicken Fricassee with Mushrooms. Add *1 cup mushrooms* sautéed in *2 tablespoons butter* to the sauce just before adding the lemon juice.

Chicken Gumbo

Use fresh okra if you can get it, frozen okra if you can't.

(SERVES FOUR)

3-pound (1⅓-kg) chicken, in 8 pieces	½ cup (1 dL) chopped sweet red pepper
Salt	1½ cups (3½ dL) chopped fresh or canned tomatoes
Freshly ground pepper	2 teaspoons basil, crumbled
3 tablespoons bacon fat	1 cup (¼ L) cooked rice
½ onion, chopped	
4 cups (1 L) sliced okra	

Rinse the chicken, pat it dry, and sprinkle with salt and pepper. Melt the bacon fat in a large skillet and brown the chicken on all sides. Remove from the pan and set aside. Add the onion, okra, and pepper and cook over medium heat, stirring constantly, for 5 minutes. Stir in the tomatoes, basil, and 3 cups of boiling water. Mix in the chicken and about a teaspoon of salt. Cover and simmer 30–40 minutes. Add the cooked rice, mix well, and cook 5 minutes more to heat through. There will be lots of spicy liquid to serve in soupbowls.

Paella

A saffron-colored dish from Spain, allowing for much improvisation
in the ingredients.

(SERVES EIGHT)

Pinch of saffron
4 cups (1 L) chicken broth
4–5-pound (2–2¼-kg) chicken,
    in 8 pieces
Salt
Freshly ground pepper
4 tablespoons olive oil
1 teaspoon oregano, crumbled
12 thin slices spicy Italian or
    Spanish sausage

1 cup (¼ L) chopped onion
2 cloves garlic, sliced
4 tablespoons butter
2 cups (½ L) rice
1 pound (450 g) shrimp,
    cooked and shelled
1½ dozen clams in the shell
1 package frozen tiny peas, or
    1½ cups (3½ dL) fresh

Preheat the oven to 350°F (180°C). Put the saffron to soak in 2 tablespoons of
the chicken broth. Rinse the chicken, pat it dry, and sprinkle liberally with salt
and pepper. Heat the olive oil in a large skillet, add the chicken, and brown well
on all sides. Add 4 tablespoons water and the oregano. Cover and cook over low
heat for 20 minutes or until the chicken is done. Remove the chicken and set
aside. Lightly brown the sausage slices; remove and set aside. Add the onion and
garlic to the pan and cook, stirring, for 5 minutes. Melt the butter in the pan
and stir in the rice, saffron, and about a teaspoon of salt, cooking for 5 minutes.
Add the remaining chicken broth, bring to a boil, cover, and simmer 20 minutes.
In a shallow 4-quart casserole, arrange the rice, chicken, shrimp, sausage, and
clams so that some of each shows on the top. Heat in the oven until the clams
open, about 15–20 minutes. Meanwhile either pour boiling water over frozen
peas or blanch fresh peas 2 minutes. Scatter over the casserole and serve.

Paella improvisations

2 cups (½ L) green and red peppers, cut in strips and
    added when clams are

1 cup (¼ L) black olives, pitted, scattered over the top for the
    last 5 minutes in the oven

1 package artichoke hearts, cooked, and added at the last

1 cup (¼ L) ham in strips, added during the last 5 minutes of cooking

Poached Chicken

Chicken prepared this way stays juicy and moist for salads and
sandwiches. The broth may be saved and used for stock, for boiling
noodles or rice, or for poaching another chicken.

(SERVES FOUR)

3-pound (1⅓-kg) chicken, whole
Salt

Wash the chicken with cold water. Truss (p. 232) and place in a large saucepan.
Add water halfway up the chicken, with ½ teaspoon salt for every quart of water
used. Cover and simmer over medium-low heat for 1 hour, turning the chicken

over once or twice during the cooking. Cool the chicken in the broth and refrigerate until needed.

Chicken à la Providence

(SERVES FOUR)

3-pound (1⅓-kg) chicken, whole	3 parsley sprigs
1 rib celery with leaves, in 4 pieces	1 bay leaf
	1 carrot, sliced
½ onion, sliced	3 tablespoons butter
1 teaspoon thyme, crumbled	3 tablespoons flour
½ teaspoon freshly ground pepper	2 egg yolks, lightly beaten
	2 tablespoons lemon juice
	Salt

Wash and truss the chicken (p. 232). Place it in a large saucepan and add water halfway up the chicken. Add the celery, onion, thyme, pepper, parsley, bay leaf, and carrot. Partially cover and simmer for 1 hour. Remove the chicken and keep it warm in the oven. Strain the broth, return it to the pan, and boil until reduced to 2 cups. Melt the butter in a second saucepan. Stir in the flour and cook, stirring, 2–3 minutes until smooth. Slowly add the reduced broth, stirring over low heat for 3–4 minutes more. Little by little, add ½ cup of simmering sauce to the egg yolks, beating constantly. Return the sauce-egg mixture to the sauce remaining in the pan, and cook 1 minute more. Remove from the heat, stir in the lemon juice, then add salt to taste. Serve the sauce alongside the chicken.

Chicken with Dumplings

Serve in soupbowls: pieces of chicken in broth with a dumpling floating on top.

(SERVES SIX)

4–5-pound (2–2¼-kg) chicken, in 8 pieces	1½ teaspoons thyme, crumbled
	½ teaspoon rosemary, crumbled
2 carrots, sliced thin	2 teaspoons salt
2 ribs celery with leaves, sliced fine	½ teaspoon freshly ground pepper
1 large onion, chopped	

Dumplings

2 cups (285 g) flour	2 tablespoons minced parsley
3 teaspoons baking powder	4 tablespoons shortening
1 teaspoon salt	¾–1 cup (1¾ dL–¼ L) milk

Rinse the chicken pieces, put them in a large pot, and cover with water. Add the carrots, celery, onion, thyme, rosemary, 2 teaspoons salt, and pepper. Bring to a boil and reduce to a simmer. Combine the flour, baking powder, 1 teaspoon salt, and parsley in a bowl. Cut in the shortening until the mixture resembles coarse meal. Add ¾ cup milk and stir briefly with a fork. Add only enough of the remaining ¼ cup milk to make the dough hold together. When the chicken has simmered for 20 minutes, drop spoonfuls of dough on top of the bubbling broth. Cover and steam for 20 minutes without lifting the cover.

Chicken and Onion Stew

(SERVES FOUR)

4–5-pound (2–2¼-kg) chicken,   ½ cup (1 dL) heavy cream
   in quarters   1 egg yolk, slightly beaten
12 small onions, peeled   2 tablespoons lemon juice
2 tablespoons butter   Salt
3 tablespoons flour   Freshly ground pepper

Rinse the chicken and place in a large pot with the onions and enough water to cover. Bring to a boil and simmer for 40 minutes. Remove the chicken and onions and keep them warm in a barely heated oven. Briskly boil the broth from the chicken until it is reduced to 1¼ cups. Melt the butter in another saucepan and stir in the flour. Cook, stirring to blend, for 2 minutes. Slowly add the chicken broth and cream, stirring constantly 4–5 minutes, until smooth and thickened. Remove from the heat. Little by little, add ¼ cup of the hot sauce to the egg yolk, beating constantly. Return the sauce-yolk mixture to the sauce remaining in the pan and briskly stir in the lemon juice and salt and pepper to taste. Heat without boiling for 1 minute. Spoon over the chicken pieces to serve.

Brunswick Stew

A southern stew that is traditionally long-cooked so that the vegetables become soft and the potatoes are cooked to a thickening paste.

(SERVES SIX)

4–5-pound (2–2¼-kg) chicken,   1 cup (¼ L) green lima beans
   in quarters   3 potatoes, peeled and diced
Salt   1 cup (¼ L) whole-kernel corn
1 cup (¼ L) chopped canned   1 teaspoon sugar
   or fresh tomatoes   ⅛–¼ teaspoon cayenne pepper
2 onions, sliced thin

Rinse the pieces of chicken and put them into a large pot with 2 teaspoons salt and water to cover. Bring to a boil and simmer for 40 minutes. Remove the chicken from the broth, take the meat off the bones, and set aside. Put the tomatoes, onions, lima beans, potatoes, corn, sugar, and cayenne pepper into the broth and boil gently for 30 minutes covered. Add the pieces of chicken and simmer for 10 minutes more uncovered. Taste and add cayenne pepper and more salt if needed.

Sautéed Chicken Breasts

Buy 3 pounds of unboned chicken breasts if you are boning them yourself. This is equally good made with thin slices of turkey breast.

(SERVES FOUR)

⅓ cup (¾ dL) flour   2 tablespoons oil
1½ pounds (675 g) skinned   Juice of 1 lemon
   and boned chicken breasts   Salt
   (p. 230)   Freshly ground pepper
4 tablespoons butter   1 tablespoon minced parsley

Spread the flour on a piece of wax paper and dredge each chicken breast. Melt the butter and oil in a skillet. When it foams, add the chicken, and cook over medium-high heat for about 3 minutes on each side. Remove to a warm platter. Pour off all but 2 tablespoons of fat from the pan, and stir in the lemon juice and salt and pepper to taste. When it is very hot, spoon this sauce over the chicken and sprinkle with parsley.

Baked Chicken Breasts. Omit the flour. Season each breast with salt and pepper, place in a shallow pan, and dot with 4 *tablespoons butter*. Cover with foil and bake in a preheated 375°F (190°C) oven for 20 minutes or until done. Remove the foil, drizzle on the lemon juice, and sprinkle with the parsley.

Chicken Lake Como

Also good made with thin slices of turkey breast.

(SERVES FOUR)

1 egg, lightly beaten	Freshly ground pepper
1 cup (¼ L) freshly made bread crumbs	2 tablespoons lemon juice
	¼ teaspoon nutmeg
½ cup (1 dL) freshly grated Parmesan cheese	1½ cups (3½ dL) chopped cooked spinach, or 1 package frozen chopped spinach, cooked
1½ pounds (675 g) skinned and boned chicken breasts (p. 230)	
	4 tablespoons butter
⅓ cup (50 g) flour	2 tablespoons oil
Salt	1 cup (¼ L) heavy cream

Mix the egg with 2 tablespoons water in a shallow bowl. Combine the bread crumbs and cheese on a piece of wax paper. Coat the chicken breasts with flour, and sprinkle with salt and pepper. Dip them into the egg and then into the bread crumb–cheese mixture; set aside. Add the lemon juice and nutmeg to the spinach and stir over low heat until it is warm. Melt the butter and oil in a large skillet. When it foams, add the chicken and sauté over medium-high heat for 2–3 minutes on each side, or until just done. Spread the spinach on a warm platter, place the chicken on top, and keep warm. Remove all but 3 tablespoons of butter from the skillet. Place it over high heat and add the cream. Stir, scraping the bottom of the pan, until the cream comes to a boil. Spoon a little of this sauce over the chicken and spinach, and pour the rest into a serving bowl.

Mushroom-stuffed Chicken Breasts

(SERVES FOUR TO SIX)

¼ pound (115 g) plus 4 tablespoons butter	1½ cups (3½ dL) freshly made bread crumbs
½ pound (225 g) mushrooms, chopped fine	¼ teaspoon nutmeg
	4 chicken breasts, skinned, boned, and halved (p. 230)
½ teaspoon salt	1 cup (¼ L) heavy cream
¼ teaspoon freshly ground pepper	

Preheat the oven to 350°F (180°C). Melt ¼ pound of the butter in a skillet. Add the mushrooms, salt, and pepper, and cook, stirring often, until the mushrooms turn very dark and absorb all the butter. Remove from the heat and stir in ¾ cup of the bread crumbs and the nutmeg. Divide the mushroom stuffing into 8 portions and place a portion in the center of each piece of chicken. Fold the chicken around the stuffing, and place, seam side down, in a shallow casserole. Melt the remaining 4 tablespoons butter and brush over the chicken. Sprinkle with the remaining ¾ cup of bread crumbs. Pour on the cream and bake for 30 minutes until lightly brown.

Chicken Kiev

Boned chicken breasts, wrapped around nuggets of flavored butter, then breaded and deep-fried. When the chicken breasts are cut open, hot butter spurts out onto a bed of kasha or brown rice.

(SERVES FOUR)

4 chicken breasts, skinned, boned, and halved (p. 230)
Salt
¼ pound (115 g) butter, softened
1 tablespoon lemon juice
2 teaspoons minced parsley

1 clove garlic, minced (optional)
⅓ cup (50 g) flour
1½ cups (3½ dL) freshly made bread crumbs
2 eggs, lightly beaten
Oil for frying

Sprinkle the halves of chicken breasts with salt, cover with wax paper, and refrigerate. Cream the butter, lemon juice, parsley, and garlic (if desired), and refrigerate for 20 minutes or until firm enough to shape into 8 pieces the size of a little finger. Roll each halved breast around a butter finger, tucking in the ends. Place the flour and bread crumbs on separate sheets of wax paper, and beat the eggs in a shallow bowl. Dust the breasts with flour, dip in the eggs, then roll in the bread crumbs. Place the cutlets on a plate and refrigerate at least 2 hours to set the crust. Heat about 1½ inches of oil in a skillet to 365°F (185°C) or until a small cube of bread browns in 60 seconds. Fry the chicken until the rolls are golden, drain on paper towels, and serve immediately with Kasha (p. 315) or brown rice.

CHICKEN LIVERS

Sautéed Chicken Livers with Madeira

Serve the livers and sauce spooned over toast with broiled tomato halves.

(SERVES FOUR)

2 tablespoons butter
2 tablespoons oil
1 pound (450 g) chicken livers

4 tablespoons Madeira
Salt
Freshly ground pepper

Heat the butter and oil in a skillet, toss in the chicken livers, and cook very quickly, shoving them about in the pan, until dark brown; remove to a warm platter. Turn the heat up very high and add the Madeira. Let it come to a boil as you scrape up the pan juices. Add salt and pepper to taste.

Chicken Livers with Mushrooms

(SERVES FOUR)

1 pound (450 g) chicken livers
5 tablespoons butter
2 cups (½ L) sliced mushrooms
3 shallots or scallions, minced
  fine

1½ tablespoons lemon juice
¾ cup (1¾ dL) beef broth
Freshly ground pepper
1 tablespoon minced parsley

Trim the chicken livers of any discolored membranes or tough connective tissue, and wipe with a paper towel. Melt the butter in a skillet. Add the mushrooms and cook, stirring, over medium heat for 1½ minutes. Add the livers, shallots or scallions, lemon juice, broth, and salt and pepper to taste. Turn the heat to high and cook, stirring, for another 1½ minutes. Serve, sprinkled with the parsley.

Chicken Livers en Brochette

(SERVES FOUR)

1 pound (450 g) chicken livers
¼ pound (115 g) bacon slices,
  cut in 1-inch pieces

20 whole mushrooms
12 whole cherry tomatoes

Preheat the broiler. Thread chicken livers, bacon, mushrooms, and cherry tomatoes on skewers. Place them on a broiler rack 3 inches beneath the broiler element. Broil 3–5 minutes on each side.

Curried Chicken Livers

(SERVES FOUR)

4 tablespoons butter
½ cup (1 dL) finely chopped
  onion
1 pound (450 g) chicken livers
2 teaspoons curry powder

1 cup (¼ L) chicken broth
Salt to taste
4 cups (1 L) hot cooked rice
1 cup (¼ L) peanuts, chopped
  (optional)

Melt the butter in a skillet. Stir in the onion and cook for 5 minutes over low heat. Turn the heat to medium, add the chicken livers, and cook until brown, about 2 minutes on each side. Remove livers to a warm plate. Add the curry powder to the skillet and stir to blend with the onion and pan juices. Add the chicken broth, bring to a boil and reduce to about ¾ cup, taste, and add salt. Put the hot rice on a platter with the chicken livers on top, and pour the curried sauce over it. Sprinkle with the peanuts, if you wish.

OTHER POULTRY

Roast Duck

For a crisp brown duck, try this recipe: the secret is basting it with water.

(SERVES FOUR)

5-pound (2¼-kg) duck
Salt
Freshly ground pepper

Preheat the oven to 450°F (230°C). Rub the inside of the duck with salt and pepper. Prick the skin all over, especially along the sides under the breast, to allow the fat to run out while the duck roasts. Place the duck breast up on a rack in a shallow roasting pan. Baste every 15 minutes, pouring off the fat from the pan as it accumulates. Turn the duck breast down after the first 45 minutes of roasting. Turn it breast up again after the second 45 minutes. Roast the duck for 1¼ hours, then baste it with 3–4 tablespoons of ice water and roast another 15 minutes—1½ hours altogether or until a meat thermometer reads 180°F in the thigh. If you like your duck very well done, roast it another 20–30 minutes, but be forewarned, the meat is going to be dry. Remove from the oven and let rest for 15 minutes before carving.

Duck à l'Orange

(SERVES FOUR)

5-pound (2¼-kg) duck
Salt
Freshly ground pepper
5 oranges
2 lemons
3 tablespoons sugar

3 tablespoons wine vinegar
2 cups (½ L) beef broth
1 tablespoon cornstarch
2 tablespoons red currant jelly
4 tablespoons dry white wine

Preheat the oven to 350°F (180°C). Prick the duck skin all over and rub the cavity with salt and pepper. Roast for 1¾ hours (or until interior temperature is 180°F in the thigh) on a rack in a shallow roasting pan, pouring off the fat every 20 minutes. Using a vegetable peeler, remove the colored part, or "zest," of the skins of 2 of the oranges and 1 of the lemons. Cut the zest into thin strips. Squeeze the juice from the peeled fruit and set aside. Bring a pan of water to a boil and add the strips. Steep them 5 minutes, drain, and set aside. Cut the pieces of fruit free from the membranes of the remaining 3 oranges and 1 lemon. Put the sections in a bowl and set aside. In a small heavy-bottomed pan, cook the sugar over medium-high heat. Caramelize it by moving the pan over the heat so that the sugar turns golden, taking care that it does not burn. Add the vinegar, orange juice, and lemon juice, and boil rapidly until the liquid is reduced by half. Stir in the broth and simmer for 5 minutes more. In a small bowl, dissolve the cornstarch in 2 tablespoons water. Add it to the caramelized sauce with the currant jelly, stirring until the sauce is clear and thickened. When the duck is roasted, put it on a warm platter. Pour off the fat from the roasting pan and place it over a burner. Add the wine, scrape up the bits from the bottom of the pan, and boil rapidly for 1 minute. Strain into the sauce. Sprinkle the duck with the fruit rind strips, surround with fruit sections, and pour enough of the rich brown sauce over to glaze the duck, serving the rest in a sauceboat.

Braised Duck with Olives

(SERVES FOUR)

2 tablespoons butter
5-pound (2¼-kg) duck
½ cup (1 dL) Port wine
1½ cups (3½ dL) chicken
  broth
1 bay leaf
4 parsley sprigs

1 rib celery with leaves,
  chopped
2 teaspoons thyme, crumbled
12 green olives
Salt
Freshly ground pepper

Melt the butter in a heavy pot. Prick the duck all over and brown it on all sides. Drain the fat from the pot and stir in the wine, chicken broth, bay leaf, parsley, celery, and thyme. Cover and simmer 1 hour. In another pan, simmer the olives for 5 minutes, drain, and set aside. Remove the duck to a warm platter and skim off all the fat from the liquid. Strain the liquid, return it to the pan, and boil rapidly until reduced by one-third. Add salt and pepper to taste. Carve the duck, garnish with the olives, and spoon the concentrated broth over both.

Salmi of Duck

A salmi is a dish made from cooked game. If you should have some leftover duck, you could use it this way, adjusting the proportions of the other ingredients according to the amount of duck you have.

(SERVES FOUR)

5-pound (2¼-kg) duck, roasted
  (opposite)
4 tablespoons butter
1 tablespoon finely chopped
  onion
1 rib celery, chopped fine
1 small carrot, chopped fine
3 tablespoons finely chopped
  ham

4 tablespoons flour
2 cups (½ L) beef broth
½ bay leaf
2 parsley sprigs
¼ teaspoon mace
Pinch of powdered cloves
3 tablespoons dry sherry
12 black olives, pitted
Salt to taste

Carve the duck into serving pieces. Melt the butter in a saucepan and add the onion, celery, carrot, and ham. Cook, stirring often, until the vegetables are browned. Stir in the flour; when it is nicely browned, slowly add the broth, bay leaf, parsley, mace, and cloves. Cook, stirring constantly, for 5 minutes. Strain the sauce and return to the saucepan. Add the duck, sherry, olives, and salt, and heat through. Arrange the duck on a warm platter surrounded with the olives and covered with a glaze of sauce.

Roast Goose with Apples and Prunes

(SERVES SIX)

2 dozen prunes, pitted
1 cup (¼ L) red wine
5 tart green apples
8–10-pound (3½–4½-kg)
  goose

Salt
Freshly ground pepper
2 tablespoons flour
1½ cups (3½ dL) chicken or
  goose* broth

Roast Goose with Apples and Prunes (continued)

Soak the prunes in wine for 30 minutes. Peel, core, and quarter the apples. Preheat the oven to 325°F (165°C). Rub the goose inside and out with salt and pepper. Drain the prunes, toss with the apple sections, and stuff into the goose cavity. Sew up or skewer the opening. Place the goose on a rack in a shallow pan, pricking the skin all over to release the fat as the bird roasts. Cook 3–3½ hours, until the juices run clear when the skin is cut at the upper thigh or a meat thermometer registers 185°F. During the roasting, pour off the fat every 20 minutes, using a bulb baster or spoon. Save and process the fat (see below). Remove the goose to a platter and keep warm. Remove all but 1 tablespoon fat from the roasting pan. Set it over a burner, stir in the flour, and brown it lightly. Slowly add the chicken broth, stirring until thickened. Season the gravy with salt and pepper, strain it, and pass with the goose.

> *If the neck and gizzards come with the goose, simmer them with a small carrot and onion in about 4 cups water for 1½–2 hours, it will reduce to about 1½ cups.

Roast Goose with Potato Stuffing

(SERVES SIX)

4 medium potatoes	Freshly ground pepper
4 tablespoons butter	8–10-pound (3½–4½-kg)
2 onions, chopped	goose
½–¾ cup (1–1¾ dL) heavy	2 tablespoons flour
cream	1½ cups (3½ dL) chicken or
Salt	goose broth

Peel, quarter, and boil the potatoes until tender. Melt the butter in a skillet and cook the onions until soft. Mash the potatoes with enough cream to make a fluffy mixture. Add the onions and salt and pepper to taste, and stuff into the cavity of the goose. Sew up or skewer it closed. Rub the outside of the goose with more salt and pepper and prick the skin all over to release the fat as it melts during roasting. Preheat the oven to 325°F (165°C). Place the goose on a rack in a shallow roasting pan and roast 3–3½ hours. Pour off the fat every 20 minutes, saving it as directed below. Spoon 3–4 tablespoons ice water over the goose during the last 15 minutes of roasting in order to crisp the skin. Prepare gravy as in the preceding recipe.

Rendered Goose Fat

Goose fat is a kitchen treasure. Use it to fry golden-brown potatoes or to season a bowl of freshly cooked vegetables.

Fat from an 8–10-pound (3½–4½-kg)
goose, raw or melted

Cut raw goose fat into small dice. Place in a deep saucepan over very low heat, adding ¼ cup water for every pound of fat. When it is melted, pour the fat through a fine strainer or cheesecloth. If you are roasting the goose, remove the fat every 20 minutes with a bulb baster or spoon. Strain it through a fine strainer or cheesecloth and set aside. When it congeals, it will separate from the liquid. Remove it and preserve by placing it in a covered jar in the refrigerator. Goose fat must be free of liquid and clean of all residue or it will spoil; cleaned and chilled, it will keep for months—up to a year, in fact, if well refrigerated.

Rock Cornish Game Hens with Wild Rice Stuffing

Serve one hen to a person, garnished with watercress.

(SERVES SIX)

¼ pound (115 g) butter	½ teaspoon marjoram,
½ onion, chopped fine	crumbled
1 cup (¼ L) chopped	Salt
mushrooms	Freshly ground pepper
1½ cups (3½ dL) cooked wild	6 Rock Cornish game hens
rice	1 cup (¼ L) chicken broth
½ teaspoon thyme, crumbled	½ cup (1 dL) dry vermouth

Preheat the oven to 400°F (205°C). Melt 4 tablespoons of the butter in a saucepan. Add the onion and mushrooms and cook over medium heat until soft. Mix in the rice, thyme, and marjoram. Stuff loosely into the cavities of the hens. Rub them all over with the remaining butter and sprinkle with salt and pepper. Place the hens, not touching, in a shallow pan and roast, basting every 10–15 minutes with a mixture of chicken broth and vermouth. After 15 minutes, reduce the heat to 300°F (150°C) and cook another 30–40 minutes, or until the juices run clear when a small slit is made in the upper thigh. Serve with pan juices as a natural sauce.

Rock Cornish Game Hens with Rice-Raisin Stuffing

(SERVES SIX)

¼ pound (115 g) plus 4	½ cup (1 dL) raisins
tablespoons butter	3 cups (¾ L) chicken broth
½ onion, chopped fine	12 juniper berries
1½ cups (3½ dL) white rice	6 Rock Cornish game hens
Salt	1 cup (¼ L) red wine
Freshly ground pepper	

Preheat the oven to 325°F (165°C). Melt 4 tablespoons of the butter in a saucepan. Add the onion and cook over medium heat until soft. Add the rice, a sprinkle of salt and pepper, and the raisins. Slowly stir in the chicken broth. Cover and simmer for 20 minutes, until the rice is tender. Put 2 juniper berries in each hen's cavity, stuff with the rice, and skewer closed. Rub the hens with 4 tablespoons of the butter and sprinkle with salt and pepper. Place hens in a shallow pan, not touching, and brush with the remaining 4 tablespoons of butter, melted and mixed with the wine. Roast 50–60 minutes, basting with the wine-butter marinade every 10 minutes. Serve with pan juices as a natural sauce.

☼ Recipes for Cooked Chicken, Turkey, and/or Other Poultry

There are so many good ways of using cooked turkey and chicken. In recipes calling for one or the other, feel free to use them interchangeably, or to substitute any other leftover poultry meat for that matter; there may be a little difference in flavor, but that lends variety to any dish. Cool cooked poultry that you plan to use again, then scrape and save the bones, skins, bits of gristle—they will go into the soup pot, and the jellied juices that accumulate can go into whatever sauce you may be making for the poultry leftovers. If you are not going to use the meat within a few days, freeze it.

Chicken Pie

(SERVES SIX)

6 tablespoons butter
6 tablespoons flour
2 cups (½ L) chicken broth
1 cup (¼ L) heavy cream
½ teaspoon freshly ground
   pepper
Salt

4 cups (1 L) cooked chicken,
   cut in large chunks
12 small white onions, cooked
¾ cup (1¾ dL) peas, cooked
1 recipe Basic Pastry for 9-inch
   shell (p. 575)

Preheat the oven to 425°F (220°C). Melt the butter in a saucepan, stir in the flour, and cook, stirring, for 2 minutes. Slowly add the broth, cream, pepper, and salt to taste. Cook for 5 minutes, until thickened and smooth. Put the chicken pieces in a deep pie plate or casserole, cover with sauce, and stir in the small onions and peas. Place the prepared piecrust over the casserole, allowing enough overhang so that the edges can be crimped. Cut vents in the crust to allow the steam to escape. Bake for 25–30 minutes or until the crust is nicely browned.

Louisburg Chicken Pie. Add to the cooked onions and peas *1 cup sliced mushrooms, sautéed in butter,* and *½ pound sausage meat* that has been shaped into tiny balls and sautéed.

Chicken Pie, Country Style. Use *1 recipe Baking Powder Biscuits* (*p. 490*) instead of Basic Pastry. Roll out the biscuit dough ½ inch thick, cut into 2-inch rounds, and place them, edges touching, all over the top of the pie. Bake at 450°F (230°C) for 15–20 minutes until browned.

Deviled Chicken-on-the-Bone

"Deviled" here means a spicy sauce with mustard and cayenne.

(SERVES FOUR)

2 tablespoons butter
2 tablespoons chili sauce
2 tablespoons Worcestershire
   sauce
2 teaspoons prepared mustard
⅛ teaspoon cayenne pepper

8 pieces cooked chicken, on
   the bone
1 cup (¼ L) chicken broth
Salt
Freshly ground pepper

Heat the butter, chili sauce, Worcestershire sauce, mustard, and cayenne pepper in a saucepan. Add the chicken pieces, turning them in the sauce so they are coated, and cook, stirring often, for 4–5 minutes. Add the chicken broth and salt and pepper to taste, and simmer 3 minutes more.

Creamed Chicken

Serve this slightly lemony creamed chicken over toast or biscuits.

(SERVES TWO)

2 tablespoons butter
3 tablespoons flour
1 cup (¼ L) milk

⅓ cup (¾ dL) heavy cream
⅛ teaspoon freshly ground
   pepper

1½ cups (3½ dL) cubed
    cooked chicken

2½ tablespoons lemon juice
Salt

Melt the butter in a saucepan and stir in the flour. Cook for 2–3 minutes over medium heat, stirring constantly, until well blended. Gradually add the milk and cream and stir for 5 minutes until thickened and smooth. Add the pepper, chicken, lemon juice, and salt to taste. Simmer 5 minutes more.

Creamed Chicken with Vegetables. Add to the cream sauce *2 hard-cooked eggs, chopped, ¼ cup finely sliced cooked celery, ½ cup cooked peas,* and *½ cup sliced cooked mushrooms.*

Blanquette of Chicken. Stir ½ cup of the finished sauce into *1 egg yolk, lightly beaten.* Return to the creamed chicken in the pan, stirring constantly. Sprinkle with *2 tablespoons minced parsley.*

Chicken Curry. Stir in *2 teaspoons curry powder* and *¼ cup raisins* after adding the milk and cream.

Creamed Chicken and Mushrooms

(SERVES THREE)

4 tablespoons butter
12 mushrooms, sliced
2 cups (½ L) cubed cooked
    chicken
4 tablespoons flour

2 cups (½ L) chicken broth
Pinch of cayenne pepper
4 tablespoons sherry
Salt to taste

Melt the butter in a saucepan. Add the mushrooms and chicken and cook for 3 minutes. Stir in the flour and cook for 2 minutes; gradually add the chicken broth and simmer for 10 minutes more. Add the cayenne pepper, sherry, and salt, and heat through.

Chicken and Noodles

A golden sauce, sharp with the tang of cheese.

(SERVES FOUR)

¼ pound (115 g) broad egg
    noodles or green noodles
¾ cup (1¾ dL) freshly grated
    Parmesan cheese
2 tablespoons butter
2 tablespoons flour

1 cup (¼ L) heavy cream
1 cup (¼ L) chicken broth
2 cups (½ L) cubed cooked
    chicken
2 egg yolks, lightly beaten
Salt

Preheat the oven to 375°F (190°C). Butter a 2-quart baking dish. Cook the noodles until just done. Drain them, and, while they are still hot, stir in all but 2 tablespoons of the cheese. Melt the butter in a saucepan, add the flour, and cook for 2–3 minutes. Gradually stir in the cream and broth. Cook over low heat, stirring often, for 5 minutes. Add the chicken and cook another minute. Beat ¼ cup of the hot sauce into the egg yolks, then return the yolk-sauce mixture to the chicken mixture. Stir briskly for 1 minute, remove from the heat, and add salt to taste. Place the chicken mixture over the noodles. Sprinkle with the reserved 2 tablespoons of cheese, and bake 20–30 minutes, until golden.

Chicken à la King

Serve in flaky patty shells.

(SERVES TWO TO THREE)

½ cup (1 dL) sliced mushrooms
2 tablespoons butter
1½ cups (3½ dL) Velouté
   Sauce (p. 266)
1 cup (¼ L) cubed cooked
   chicken

4 tablespoons canned
   pimientos, in strips
1 egg yolk, lightly beaten
2 tablespoons dry sherry
Salt to taste

Sauté the mushrooms in butter. Mix them into the sauce together with the chicken and pimientos in a saucepan over low heat. When it is hot, add ¼ cup of this mixture to the egg yolk, beating constantly. Return the yolk-sauce mixture to the saucepan with the sherry and salt and blend well.

Chicken-Almond Supreme

(SERVES THREE TO FOUR)

2 cups (½ L) cooked chicken
   in large pieces
3 tablespoons butter
1½ cups (3½ dL) sliced
   mushrooms
1 cup (¼ L) canned water
   chestnuts, sliced thin

1 tablespoon soy sauce
1 recipe Supreme Sauce
   (p. 266)
⅓ cup (¾ dL) slivered almonds

Preheat the oven to 350°F (180°C). Spread the chicken pieces in a shallow baking dish. Melt the butter in a skillet, add the mushrooms, and cook until soft. Sprinkle the mushrooms and water chestnuts over the chicken. Add the soy sauce to the supreme sauce, and pour over the chicken mixture. Sprinkle with the almonds and bake 20–25 minutes or until heated through.

Chicken Tetrazzini

(SERVES FOUR)

4 cups (1 L) cooked spaghetti
   (about ½ pound)
¼ teaspoon nutmeg
3 tablespoons dry sherry
Salt to taste
1 recipe Velouté Sauce
   (p. 266)

2 tablespoons butter
1 cup (¼ L) sliced mushrooms
8 or more slices cooked
   chicken
½ cup (1 dL) freshly grated
   Romano or Parmesan cheese

Preheat the oven to 400°F (205°C). Butter a 2-quart shallow baking dish, and spread the cooked spaghetti in it. Stir the nutmeg, sherry, and salt into the warm velouté sauce and set aside. Melt the butter in a skillet, add the mushrooms, and cook, stirring, until soft. Spoon half the sauce over the spaghetti. Place the chicken slices and mushrooms on top, and spoon on the remaining sauce. Sprinkle with the grated cheese and bake for 30 minutes.

Chicken Divan

(SERVES FOUR)

3 cups (¾ L) cooked broccoli
8 or more slices cooked
  chicken
4 tablespoons dry sherry
2 cups (½ L) White Sauce (p. 265)

2 egg yolks, lightly beaten
Salt to taste
½ cup (1 dL) freshly grated
  Romano or Parmesan cheese

Preheat the oven to 375°F (190°C). Butter a shallow baking dish and lay the broccoli over the bottom. Put the chicken over the broccoli. Add sherry to the white sauce, heat, beat 2 tablespoonfuls of sauce into the egg yolks, then stir the yolk-sauce mixture back into the sauce. Add salt to taste. Spoon evenly over the chicken, sprinkle with cheese, and bake 15–20 minutes, until very hot.

Chicken-Asparagus Divan. Use *1 pound asparagus, cooked,* instead of broccoli.

Chicken Hollandaise

Wonderfully crunchy, with a touch of lemon. Serve on whole-wheat toast.

(SERVES THREE)

3 tablespoons butter
1 tablespoon minced onion
4 tablespoons cornstarch
2 cups (½ L) chicken broth
½ cup (1 dL) finely chopped
  celery

1 tablespoon lemon juice
2 cups (½ L) cubed cooked
  chicken
2 egg yolks, lightly beaten
Salt

Melt the butter in a saucepan and add the onion. Cook, stirring, until soft. Stir in the cornstarch and cook over medium-low heat until smooth and blended. Slowly add the chicken broth, celery, lemon juice, and chicken. Cook, stirring, for 3–4 minutes. Beat ¼ cup of the hot sauce into the yolks and then return the yolk-sauce mixture to the saucepan. Cook for 1 minute more, and add salt to taste.

Chicken Hash

(SERVES FOUR)

3 tablespoons butter
2 cups (½ L) cubed cooked
  chicken
2 cups (½ L) cubed cooked
  potatoes
1 cup (¼ L) chicken gravy or
  heavy cream or mixture of
  both

Salt
Freshly ground pepper
1 tablespoon finely chopped
  parsley

Heat the butter in a large skillet until foaming. Add the chicken and potatoes, stir well, and cook for 3–4 minutes, pressing down with a spatula to form a flat cake. Lower the heat to medium low and pour in the gravy and/or cream. Sprinkle with salt and pepper and cook for 5 minutes more. Turn out onto a serving platter and sprinkle with parsley.

Chicken Soufflé

Mild and light, good for a gentle lunch or supper.

(SERVES FOUR)

2 tablespoons butter
1 tablespoon finely chopped
  onion
2 tablespoons flour
1 cup (¼ L) chicken broth
1 cup (¼ L) heavy cream
½ cup (1 dL) soft bread crumbs
½ teaspoon salt

Pinch of cayenne pepper
2 teaspoons Worcestershire
  sauce
2 cups (½ L) finely chopped
  cooked chicken
3 eggs, separated
1 tablespoon chopped parsley

Preheat the oven to 325°F (165°C). Butter a 2-quart soufflé dish. Melt the butter in a saucepan and add the onion. Cook for 2 minutes and stir in the flour, cooking for another 2–3 minutes. Slowly add the chicken broth and cream, stirring until smooth and thickened. Add the crumbs, salt, cayenne, and Worcestershire sauce. Cook for another minute and add the chicken. Beat the egg yolks lightly, add ¼ cup of the hot sauce, mix well, then return the mixture to the saucepan. Add the parsley and remove from the heat. Let cool slightly. Beat the egg whites until stiff but not dry, stir a third of them into the chicken sauce, then gently fold in the remaining whites. Spoon into the soufflé dish and bake in the bottom half of the oven 30–35 minutes or until high and set.

Chicken Croquettes

A firm, creamy blend of chicken and crisp brown crumbs. Tradition dictates that they be shaped like small upside-down ice cream cones, but other shapes taste just as good.

(6–8 CROQUETTES)

2 cups (½ L) finely diced
  cooked chicken
½ teaspoon salt
2 teaspoons minced celery with
  leaves
Pinch of cayenne pepper
2 teaspoons lemon juice
2 teaspoons minced onion

1 teaspoon minced parsley
1 cup (¼ L) Thick Cream
  Sauce (p. 265)
2 eggs, lightly beaten
2 cups (½ L) freshly made
  bread crumbs
Oil for frying

Mix the chicken, salt, celery, cayenne pepper, lemon juice, onion, parsley, and cream sauce until well blended. Cover with foil, refrigerate until chilled, then form into small cones, 1½ inches at the base and about 2 inches high. Dip them into the beaten eggs, then roll them in the crumbs. Set them to dry on a piece of wax paper. Heat 3 inches of oil in a heavy pot, until medium hot—360°F. Add the croquettes, let them brown, turn, and brown on the other side. Don't crowd the pot; do in two batches, if necessary. Drain on paper towels. Place on a warm platter and serve with White Sauce.

Chicken and Almond Croquettes. Add *½ cup blanched, chopped almonds* to the mixture. Serve with *Brown Sauce* (p. 269).

Chicken and Mushroom Croquettes. Sauté *1 cup chopped mushrooms* in *2 tablespoons butter* and add to the chicken mixture. Serve with White Sauce.

Chicken Croquettes Macédoine

"Macédoine" means a mixture of vegetables and flavorful meat, such as the mixture in these croquettes.

(SERVES SIX)

3 tablespoons butter
1 tablespoon finely chopped
  shallot or onion
4 tablespoons flour
½ teaspoon salt
¼ teaspoon paprika
⅛ teaspoon nutmeg
1 cup (¼ L) chicken broth
3 egg yolks, lightly beaten
1 cup (¼ L) finely diced
  cooked chicken

½ cup (1 dL) finely diced
  cooked ham
¼ cup (½ dL) finely chopped
  mushrooms
1 large egg, lightly beaten
2 cups (½ L) freshly made
  bread crumbs
Oil for frying
White Sauce (p. 265)

Melt the butter in a saucepan and stir in the shallot or onion. Cook, stirring, over medium heat until soft. Stir in the flour, salt, paprika, and nutmeg, and cook 2–3 minutes more. Gradually add the chicken broth and bring to the boiling point. Stir ¼ cup of the sauce into the egg yolks, and then return the yolk-sauce mixture to the hot sauce. Add the chicken, ham, and mushrooms, and cook over low heat, stirring constantly, for 4–5 minutes. Pour into a shallow bowl and refrigerate until chilled. Shape into small cones, 1½ inches at the base and about 2 inches high. Dip into the beaten egg and roll gently in the bread crumbs. Set to dry on a rack or a piece of wax paper. Heat 3 inches of oil in a heavy pot, until medium hot—360°F. Add the croquettes, and let them brown, turning them, on all sides. Drain on paper towels and place on a warm platter and serve with the sauce.

Chicken and Oysters for a Chafing Dish

A chafing dish is an elegant way of cooking right at the table with family or friends.

(SERVES SIX)

6 tablespoons butter
½ pound (225 g) mushrooms,
  sliced
4 tablespoons flour
2 cups (½ L) cream
2 cups (½ L) diced cooked
  chicken

2 cups (½ L) oysters, drained
  and cut into ½-inch pieces
  (or use tiny Olympias)
3 tablespoons dry sherry
Salt to taste
Toast

Melt the butter in the chafing dish. Add the mushrooms and cook for 5 minutes, stirring often. Stir in the flour and cook 2–3 minutes. Slowly pour in the cream and cook until thick and smooth. Add the chicken, oysters, sherry, and salt, and spoon over toast.

Chicken-Corn Casserole

(SERVES FOUR)

4 tablespoons butter
6 tablespoons flour
1 cup (¼ L) light cream
1 cup (¼ L) chicken broth
Pinch of cayenne pepper
3 eggs, lightly beaten
1½ cups (3½ dL) diced cooked
  chicken

1 cup (¼ L) whole-kernel corn
3 tablespoons diced green
  pepper
3 tablespoons diced canned
  pimiento
Salt

Preheat the oven to 300°F (150°C). Butter a 2½-quart casserole. Melt the butter in a heavy-bottomed saucepan. Blend in the flour and cook, stirring, for 2–3 minutes. Slowly add the cream, broth, and cayenne pepper, and cook for 5 minutes, stirring constantly, until thickened and smooth. Remove from the heat and beat ¼ cup of the sauce into the eggs. Return the egg-sauce mixture to the pan with the chicken, corn, green pepper, and pimiento, and salt to taste. Pour into the casserole and bake for 25–35 minutes, or until a knife inserted in the center comes out clean.

Scalloped Turkey

(SERVES THREE)

2 cups (½ L) minced cooked
  turkey
About 1½ cups (3½ dL) turkey
  gravy
1½ cups (3½ dL) cracker
  crumbs

Salt
¼ teaspoon freshly ground
  pepper
4 tablespoons butter

Preheat the oven to 350°F (180°C). Butter a 1½-quart casserole. Combine the turkey, the gravy, and ¾ cup of the cracker crumbs. Mix well, and season with salt and pepper to taste. Melt the butter in a skillet and lightly brown the remaining ¾ cup cracker crumbs. Spoon the turkey mixture into the casserole, sprinkle the buttered crumbs on top, and bake for 25–35 minutes, or until bubbling hot.

❋ Other Suggestions for Using Leftover Chicken and Turkey

Use thin strips of cooked poultry to garnish a clear broth or a cold soup like Avocado. Chicken or turkey could be used in place of lamb to make a curry or Lamb à la Breck, and in place of veal to make a Veal Loaf. Cooked chicken is called for in Turkish Pilaf with Chicken, Chicken-Noodle Casserole, Chicken-stuffed Manicotti, Enchilladas with Chicken and Green Sauce, and it would be good in a Wild Rice Casserole. And there are always omelets, crêpes, stuffed vegetables, sandwiches, and all those delicious ways to use chicken and turkey in salads.

ABOUT GAME BIRDS

Wild birds, lacking the fat that comes from an easy domestic life, tend to be tough, especially as they grow older. Fat is often added by basting or by barding, that is, by placing thin sheets of pork fat over the fowl while it is cooking.

The flavor we call "gamy" develops when a bird is hung properly. Also, the flesh tends to be richer and tastier because the bird has fed on wild things. This special flavor, which gives game its character, is often complemented by tart currant jelly or sour applesauce, and as an accompaniment wild rice and a robust vegetable, preferably of the cabbage family.

Game birds such as wild duck, Canada goose, guinea hen, partridge, pheasant, quail, and grouse make festive eating. Very small birds can be prepared the same way quail is done on page 263; pheasant and partridge should be cooked the same as guinea hen; wild goose is similar to wild duck but takes longer. You'll need to buy these birds in a special market, unless you have a hunter in the family. Be fastidious about cleaning and cooking wild game birds: wash them thoroughly in cold water, inside and out; dry them well; and don't overcook them!

Roast Guinea Hen

Because guinea hen is naturally dry, it should be covered with sheets of barding fat during roasting.

(SERVES FOUR)

2 young guinea hens	¼ pound (115 g) salt pork, in
Salt	thin sheets
Freshly ground pepper	

Preheat the oven to 350°F (180°C). Rub the guinea hens liberally inside and out with salt and pepper. Place them on a rack in a shallow roasting pan and lay sheets of salt pork over the breasts. Roast for 45–60 minutes.

Guinea Hen Braised in Cream

(SERVES FOUR)

¼ pound (115 g) butter	12 small white onions
2 guinea hens, in quarters	1½ cups (3½ dL) heavy cream
Salt	3 tablespoons lemon juice
Freshly ground pepper	2 tablespoons cranberry jelly

Melt the butter in a large skillet over medium heat. Lightly brown the guinea hens in the butter, sprinkle them with salt and pepper, remove from the pan, and set aside. Brown the onions in the fat remaining in the pan. Return the guinea hens to the pan and pour the cream over them. Cover and simmer for 40 minutes, basting with the cream every 10 minutes. When done, remove the guinea hens to a warm platter. Add the lemon juice and cranberry jelly to the cream and pan drippings and simmer, stirring, for 2–3 minutes. Spoon over the guinea hens before serving.

Broiled Wild Duck

(ALLOW ONE-HALF DUCK PER SERVING UNLESS VERY SMALL)

2 wild ducks
4 tablespoons olive oil
Salt
Freshly ground pepper

¼ pound (115 g) butter
4 tablespoons lemon juice
2 tablespoons minced parsley

Preheat the broiler and place the rack 5 inches beneath it. Split the ducks down the back and flatten them by pressing the breastbone with the heel of your hand. Rub both sides with olive oil and sprinkle with salt and pepper. Place the ducks, skin side down, on the broiler rack and cook 5–7 minutes on each side for rare, 10–12 for medium. In a small saucepan melt the butter and add the lemon juice and parsley. Put the ducks on a warm platter and pour the butter sauce over them.

Roast Wild Duck

A hunter with thirty years of duck-shooting experience claims this is the best way to cook a wild duck. He serves it with an extravagant amount of wild rice and currant jelly, and a wedge or two of lemon alongside each serving. If anyone finds the duck too rare, a hearty squeeze of lemon juice will turn the rosy meat instantly brown.

(ALLOW ONE-HALF DUCK PER PERSON)

1 wild duck
Lemon wedges

Preheat the oven to 500°F (260°C). Rinse the duck inside and out with cold water and dry thoroughly. Place on a rack in a shallow pan and roast for 18 minutes for very rare, 25–30 minutes for pink duck.

Wild Duck with Peanut Stuffing

The peanuts add a congenial taste and a nice crunch to the meat.

(ONE-HALF DUCK PER SERVING UNLESS VERY SMALL)

¾ cup (1¾ dL) cracker crumbs
½ cup (1 dL) chopped dry-
    roasted peanuts
½ cup (1 dL) or more heavy
    cream
2 tablespoons butter, melted

2 teaspoons grated onion
Pinch of cayenne pepper
1 wild duck
Salt
Freshly ground pepper
2 slices salt pork

Combine the crumbs, peanuts, cream, butter, grated onion, and cayenne pepper. If the stuffing seems too dry, add a little more cream. Preheat the oven to 450°F (230°C). Rinse the duck inside and out with cold water; dry thoroughly. Stuff and skewer shut, then truss by winding string twice around one leg, then leaving an inch of slack and winding it around the other leg. Place the duck breast up on a rack in a shallow pan. Sprinkle with salt and pepper and cover the breast with the salt pork. Roast for 20–30 minutes, basting every 5 minutes with the melted fat.

Broiled Quail

Place a tiny bird on a piece of toast, with currant jelly, watercress, and thin slices of lemon on the side.

(SERVES ONE)

2 quail
4 tablespoons butter, melted

Preheat the broiler. Split each bird in two pieces down the center. Brush with melted butter and place, skin side down, on a rack in a shallow pan, about 5 inches below the broiler element. Baste frequently with melted butter. Turn the birds once, broiling about 5 minutes on each side until well done.

Roast Quail

(SERVES ONE TO TWO)

2 quail
¼ pound (115 g) butter, softened

Pork fat, in thin sheets
1 cup (¼ L) coarse bread crumbs

Preheat the oven to 450°F (230°C). Rinse the quail under cold water and pat dry. Rub all over with 4 tablespoons of the softened butter. Place on a rack in a shallow pan, covering the breasts with sheets of pork fat. Bake for 20–25 minutes, basting three times with the remaining 4 tablespoons of butter. Remove the birds and place on a warm platter. Toss the bread crumbs in the pan drippings over high heat until they are coated with fat and lightly browned. Split the quail in half and sprinkle with the browned crumbs.

SAUCES, MARINADES, STUFFINGS, & QUICK RELISHES

ABOUT SAUCES AND GRAVIES

Today there seems to be a movement toward serving foods more naturally, and thick gravies and rich cream and egg sauces are not as prevalent on the American table as they once were. Still, no cook should be without the basic skills of saucemaking. There are times when a well-made sauce or gravy is the very thing that is needed to complement a roast, to stretch leftovers, to elevate a modest dish, or simply to provide variety and please the palate. A scant spoonful of good hollandaise sauce makes it pleasurable for the dieter to fill up on great quantities of blanched broccoli.

The simplest gravies or sauces can be made from pan juices, adding perhaps a dollop of cream or a little broth and/or wine, boiling up and blending well to incorporate all the tasty browned bits in the pan. But you can produce only a little bit of sauce this way. When a gravy is wanted, you must add flour to the pan drippings and then liquid to increase the volume (see p. 268). The basic fat (whether it be drippings, butter, or other fat) and flour mixture is called a roux, and it is the beginning of many sauces. It is always important to cook the flour in the fat for several minutes to remove its raw pasty taste. Sometimes a roux is cooked longer until it turns a nut-brown color, which then gives a definite flavor to the finished dish, a taste that is very characteristic of New Orleans cooking. But for most delicate sauces, the roux is cooked so briefly that it does not take on color. Two tablespoons of flour will thicken a cup of liquid; one tablespoon makes a thin sauce; three tablespoons a thick sauce. If you have the liquid hot when you add it, and you stir well, you will never have trouble with lumping.

Egg yolks are the thickening agent in sauces like hollandaise and mayonnaise (to be found in the Salad chapter, p. 420), a pair that is intimidating to many cooks. The trick is to whisk rapidly, adding oil or butter to the egg yolks slowly, either by hand, or in the blender or food processor. And, if the sauce *should* curdle or separate, there are reliable techniques for rescuing it.

To correct a curdled or "broken" hollandaise or mayonnaise sauce, whisk in a teaspoon or two of boiling water, a drop at a time. If that doesn't work, put an egg yolk in a bowl and add the "broken" sauce very slowly, beating with a whisk. Be patient and take lots of time; eventually you will have a smooth sauce.

Thickening for sauces is also provided by crumbs, or by a cornstarch and water mixture, the latter giving the sauce a somewhat translucent look. A tablespoon of cornstarch will thicken lightly 2 cups of liquid. Rapid boiling down will also thicken a sauce and intensify its flavor.

In general, a sauce should be thick enough to flow from a spoon and should be smooth and well flavored. All of these recipes should be seasoned to taste at the end. The effort spent in learning to make sauces will be well repaid. After all, who wants to live on broiled meat and steamed vegetables alone?

White Sauce or Béchamel Sauce

This used to be one of the first lessons in any high school home economics class. White and pasty, this sauce formed the foundation for many bland dishes. When it is well made, however, it has a proper place in homey creamed dishes, often making leftovers stretch or giving cooked foods an entirely new life. And it is important as a base for soufflés. This medium-thick white sauce is sometimes called a *béchamel*. The foolproof way to attain a perfectly smooth sauce is to have your milk hot when you add it to the butter and flour. It uses an extra pot and as you become more proficient, this cautionary measure may not be necessary.

(1 CUP)

2 tablespoons butter	Salt
2 tablespoons flour	Freshly ground pepper
1 cup (¼ L) milk, heated	

Melt the butter in a heavy-bottomed saucepan. Stir in the flour and cook, stirring constantly, until the paste cooks and bubbles a bit, but don't let it brown—about 2 minutes. Add the hot milk, continuing to stir as the sauce thickens. Bring to a boil. Add salt and pepper to taste, lower the heat, and cook, stirring, for 2–3 minutes more. Remove from the heat. You may cool this sauce for later use; in that case, cover it with wax paper or pour a film of milk over it to prevent a skin from forming.

Thick Cream Sauce. Use *3 tablespoons flour* to *1 cup milk*. This is the consistency needed as a base for croquettes and for soufflés.

Curry Cream Sauce. Add *1 teaspoon curry powder* and *¼ teaspoon ground ginger* with the flour.

Mock Hollandaise. Just before serving, beat in *2 egg yolks*, *6 tablespoons butter* (1 tablespoon at a time), and *1 tablespoon lemon juice*.

Cheese Sauce. Stir in *½ cup grated Cheddar cheese* during the last 2 minutes of cooking, along with a *pinch of cayenne pepper*.

Mornay Sauce. Add *2 tablespoons grated Parmesan cheese* and *2 tablespoons grated Swiss cheese* during the last 2 minutes of cooking. Stir until blended. Just before removing from the heat, beat 2 tablespoons of the sauce into *1 lightly beaten egg yolk*. Stir the sauce-yolk mixture back into the sauce and add *2 tablespoons butter*. Cook, stirring, 1 minute more.

Velouté Sauce

Another basic sauce: creamy with a background taste of well-flavored broth.

(1½ CUPS)

2 tablespoons butter	⅓ cup (¾ dL) heavy cream
3 tablespoons flour	Salt to taste
1 cup (¼ L) hot chicken broth	

Melt the butter in a heavy-bottomed pan. Stir in the flour and blend over moderate heat until smooth. Continue to cook, stirring constantly, for 2 minutes. Add the chicken broth, continuing to stir as the sauce thickens. Bring to a boil, lower the heat, and cook 2 minutes more. Pour in the cream, add salt, and heat thoroughly.

Supreme Sauce. Just before serving, lightly beat *2 egg yolks* in a small bowl. Beat 2 tablespoons of the sauce into the yolks, then stir the sauce-yolk mixture back into the sauce with ¼ *teaspoon nutmeg* and the *juice of ½ lemon.*

Lobster Velouté Sauce. Cover the *shells of 1 (or more) lobster* with water and simmer for 1 hour. Strain the broth and return to the boil, reducing to 1 cup. Omit the chicken broth and use the lobster broth instead. If a richer sauce is desired, beat *2 egg yolks* in a small bowl. Beat 2 tablespoons of the sauce into the yolks, then stir the sauce-yolk mixture back into the sauce. Add *1 tablespoon lemon juice.* Stir to blend.

Russian Sauce. Before adding cream, add ½ *teaspoon finely chopped chives,* ½ *teaspoon prepared Dijon mustard, 1 teaspoon grated horseradish* (or *prepared horseradish*). Cook 2 minutes, then add the cream and *1 teaspoon lemon juice.*

Bercy Sauce

Creamy yellow, with the flavor of shallots. A good sauce for heating leftover chicken or veal; also good on fish.

(1 CUP)

3 tablespoons butter	1 cup (¼ L) hot chicken broth
1 tablespoon minced shallots	Salt
2 tablespoons flour	

Melt 1 tablespoon of the butter in a small pan. Add the shallots and cook, stirring, for 2–3 minutes. Add the flour, blend well, and cook, stirring for 2 minutes more. Slowly pour in the chicken broth, stir until smooth, and simmer for 15 minutes. Strain the sauce through cheesecloth or a fine sieve, and add the remaining 2 tablespoons of butter and salt to taste.

Lemon Sauce

Pale yellow, with a nice lemony bite. Good over cauliflower, spinach, or broccoli.

(1½ CUPS)

1 cup (¼ L) chicken broth
1 tablespoon butter
2 tablespoons cornstarch

2 egg yolks, lightly beaten
Juice and grated rind of 1
lemon

Heat the chicken broth and butter in a heavy-bottomed pan. In a small dish, blend the cornstarch with 4 tablespoons cold water until smooth; slowly stir the mixture into the chicken broth. Cook over low heat for 5 minutes, stirring constantly, until thickened and smooth. Beat 2 tablespoons of the thickened broth into the yolks, then stir the broth-yolk mixture back into the broth. Add the lemon juice and rind and cook 1 minute more. Do not boil. This sauce will keep for a couple of days if it is well covered in the refrigerator. It can be reheated by stirring over low heat.

Onion Sauce or Soubise

(2 CUPS)

3 medium onions, chopped
4 tablespoons butter
1½ recipes White Sauce
  (p. 265)

¼ teaspoon nutmeg
½ cup (1 dL) heavy cream
Salt to taste

Preheat the oven to 350°F (180°C). Bring a pan of water to a boil and plunge in the chopped onions. Cook for 1 minute, then remove and drain the onions on paper towels. Melt the butter in a saucepan and, when it bubbles, stir in the onions. Cover and cook over very low heat, shaking the pan often to keep the onions from sticking or scorching. Cook until tender. Put the onions in a shallow baking dish, add the white sauce and nutmeg, and stir to blend. Cover with foil and bake 30 minutes or until the onions are mushy. Remove and put through a food processor or press through a sieve. Stir in the cream and salt, and heat thoroughly without boiling.

Parsley Butter

Good on steaks, chops, broiled fish, as well as vegetables. For other variations on the flavored butter theme, see p. 56, and try to marry compatible flavors.

(½ CUP)

¼ pound (115 g) butter,
  softened
⅛ teaspoon freshly ground
  pepper

2 tablespoons finely chopped
  parsley
1 tablespoon lemon juice
Salt

Put the butter into a bowl with the pepper and parsley and blend with the back of a spoon. Or spin the ingredients in a food processor. Slowly add the lemon juice, a few drops at a time, then salt to taste. Form into a cylinder, wrap in wax paper or foil, and chill in the refrigerator. Once it is chilled, cut it into slices and place a slice or two to melt on each serving of meat or fish.

Herb Butter. Omit the parsley. Substitute a combination of herbs, making approximately *1 tablespoon fresh herbs or 1–1½ teaspoons dry herbs. For example, use 1½ teaspoons chopped chives, ½ teaspoon dried thyme or tarragon, and ½ teaspoon chopped parsley.*

Improvised Gravy

When you don't have enough natural pan juices and drippings to make a gravy or need a gravy to create a tasty dish out of leftover meat, here is a basic recipe that will serve well. You can add compatible seasonings like fresh herbs or a little duxelles. Use beef bouillon for red meat and chicken for poultry.

(ABOUT 1½ CUPS)

2 tablespoons minced shallots, scallions, or onion
3 tablespoons butter
3 tablespoons flour
¼ cup (½ dL) red wine or dry vermouth (optional)

1½ cups (3½ dL) beef or chicken broth
Leftover drippings or additional tablespoon butter
Salt
Freshly ground pepper

Sauté the minced shallots or other kind of onion in the butter until translucent. Stir in the flour and, cooking slowly, stir until it turns light brown. Remove the pan from the fire, add the wine, if you are using it, and an equal amount of broth. Stir until smooth, return to the fire, and slowly add the remaining broth, stirring constantly. Continue to cook, stirring often, for another 5 minutes. Swirl in leftover drippings or butter, salt and pepper to taste.

Brown Butter

A dark-brown sauce with a nutty, tart taste. Traditional with sweetbreads, brains, white fish.

(5 TABLESPOONS)

5 tablespoons butter
2 teaspoons vinegar

Melt the butter over low heat. Stir and cook until the butter turns dark brown. Add the vinegar and blend well.

Pan Gravy

The simplest, purest gravy imaginable.

(½ CUP)

2 tablespoons melted fat from cooked meat

Salt
Freshly ground pepper

Spoon off all but 2 tablespoons of fat from the roasting pan or from a skillet in which you have cooked chops, steaks, hamburger, or liver. Using a spatula or a wooden spoon, stir and scrape the bits from the bottom of the pan over low heat. Deglaze by pouring ½ cup boiling water or broth (beef or chicken depending on the meat) into the pan. Season with salt and pepper to taste, and cook for 1 minute.

Pan Gravy with Cream. Instead of using water or broth, add ½ *cup cream* and cook down rapidly for a minute or two.

Pan Gravy with Wine. Instead of using water or broth, add ½ *cup red or white dry wine* and cook down rapidly; you could also use a combination of broth and wine.

Brown Gravy

(2 CUPS)

2 tablespoons fat from a roast   Salt
2 tablespoons flour   Freshly ground pepper
1½ cups (3½ dL) liquid: pan
  juices, water, stock, wine, or
  a combination

Remove the meat from the roasting pan. Pour all the pan juices into a measuring cup. When the fat rises to the top, spoon off 2 tablespoons and return them to the pan. Discard the excess fat but save whatever juices are left in the cup. Put the pan over a burner and heat gently. Stir in the flour. Cook it thoroughly for several minutes, stirring to keep it smooth. Add enough additional liquid to the juices in the cup to make 1½ cups in all. Slowly stir the liquid into the roasting pan and cook for 5–6 minutes. If the gravy is too thick to flow easily from a spoon, add more liquid and cook for 1 minute. Season with salt and pepper to taste.

Clear or Transparent Gravy. Omit the flour. Dissolve *1 tablespoon cornstarch* in *½ cup cold stock, wine, or water.* Pour the pan juices into the pan. Heat gently, and stir in the cornstarch mixture until the gravy is clear and thickened.

Brown Sauce

(1 CUP)

2 tablespoons butter   2 tablespoons flour
1 slice onion   1 cup (¼ L) beef stock
⅛ teaspoon freshly ground   Salt to taste
  pepper

Melt the butter in a saucepan and add the onion. When the butter is barely brown, stir in the pepper and flour, and cook slowly until the flour is brown. Gradually add the stock, stirring, and boil gently for 1 minute. Remove the onion, add salt, turn the heat to simmer, and cook 15 minutes. Add more liquid if the sauce is too thick.

Onion-Brown Sauce. Omit the onion slice. Cook *4 tablespoons finely chopped onion* in the butter, and do not remove.

Bordelaise Sauce. Omit the onion slice. After adding the broth, stir in *2 green onions, minced, 1 tablespoon minced carrot, 1 sprig parsley, ½ bay leaf, 1 whole clove,* and *1½ teaspoons Worcestershire sauce.* After cooking 15 minutes, strain.

Brown Curry Sauce. Add *1 teaspoon curry powder* and *½ teaspoon dry mustard* to the flour-butter mixture.

Currant Jelly Sauce. Omit the onion slice. After adding the broth, stir in *3 tablespoons currant jelly* and *2 tablespoons cider vinegar.*

Sauce Piquante. Omit the onion slice. After adding the broth, stir in *1 tablespoon vinegar, 2 teaspoons minced green onions, 2 teaspoons capers, 1 tablespoon minced dill pickle,* and a *dash of cayenne pepper.*

Marchand de Vin Sauce

Meaning "wine merchant's sauce," this has a nice winy flavor, although the alcohol will cook out completely. Use with steak—wonderful, too, on hamburger.

(2 CUPS)

6 tablespoons butter
6 scallions, minced (use the
   white and a little of the
   green)
¾ cup (1¾ dL) red wine

1 cup (¼ L) Brown Gravy
   (p. 269) or Brown Sauce
   (p. 269)
2 tablespoons lemon juice

Melt 4 tablespoons of the butter in a saucepan and stir in the scallions. Cook, stirring, for 5 minutes. Add the wine, partially cover, and let simmer for 15 minutes. Add the gravy or sauce and the lemon juice, and simmer another 3–4 minutes. Just before serving, add the remaining butter bit by bit.

Mushroom Sauce

Unless mushrooms are very dirty, trim off the hard end of the stems and just wipe them clean with a damp cloth or paper towel.

(1½ CUPS)

5 tablespoons butter
½ pound (225 g) mushrooms,
   sliced
2 tablespoons flour

Juice of ½ lemon
1 cup (¼ L) heavy cream
Salt to taste

Melt the butter in a large skillet. Stir in the mushrooms and cook for 2–3 minutes, until they darken a little. Stir in the flour, blend to smooth, and cook 2 minutes. Slowly stir in the lemon juice, cream, and salt, and cook only until hot.

Sauce Robert

A lively, robust flavor—good with beef, liver, and leftover lamb.

(1 CUP)

1 tablespoon butter
2 tablespoons minced shallots
   or scallions
1 teaspoon flour
1 tablespoon vinegar

1 cup (¼ L) chicken broth
2 tablespoons minced dill
   pickle
1 teaspoon dry mustard
Salt to taste

Melt the butter in a saucepan. Add the shallots or scallions and the flour, and cook and stir for 3 minutes. Add remaining ingredients. Simmer, stirring often, for 5 minutes.

Fresh Tomato Sauce

(5 CUPS)

5 tablespoons olive oil
4 shallots, finely chopped
1½ teaspoons thyme, crumbled

5 fresh tomatoes, peeled and
   chopped
1 carrot, grated

½ teaspoon freshly ground
  pepper

½ cup (1 dL) chopped parsley
Salt to taste

Heat the oil in a sauté pan and add the shallots. Cook, stirring, for 1 minute. Add the thyme, tomatoes, carrot, and pepper. Simmer for 20 minutes. Add parsley and salt.

Tomato Sauce

This is a simple sauce with no onions or garlic; the grated carrot adds a little sweetness, but if you prefer, use a little sugar to counter the acidity of the tomatoes. For a more robust flavor, try one of the variations.

(4 CUPS SAUCE)

2 tablespoons olive oil
¾ cup (1¾ dL) tomato paste
2½ cups (6 dL) peeled and
  chopped fresh or canned
  tomatoes
1 carrot, grated, or 1 teaspoon
  sugar

½ teaspoon freshly ground
  pepper
1 tablespoon basil, crumbled
5 tablespoons butter
Salt to taste

Heat the oil in a heavy-bottomed saucepan. Stir in the tomato paste, tomatoes, carrot, pepper, and basil. Simmer for 30 minutes. If the sauce becomes too thick, add a little water. Cook 15 minutes more, then stir in the butter and salt. Serve with cooked pasta.

I. Italian Tomato Sauce with Ground Beef. Add *1 pound ground beef* to the heated oil. Cook, stirring and breaking the beef into tiny pieces, until the meat loses its pinkness. If the beef is fat, spoon off all but 3 tablespoons of fat and proceed as directed.

II. Italian Tomato Sauce with Garlic and Onions. Cook *1 onion, chopped,* and *2 cloves garlic, minced,* in the heated oil for 3 minutes before adding the remaining ingredients.

Mexican Tomato Sauce

Not really a sauce, but a wonderfully fresh-tasting combination of vegetables. Just right with fish.

(1 CUP)

2 tablespoons butter
1 onion, chopped fine
1 red pepper, chopped fine
1 green pepper, chopped fine
1 clove garlic, minced

2 tomatoes, peeled and
  chopped
2 teaspoons Worcestershire
  sauce
Salt to taste

Melt the butter in a saucepan. Add the onion and cook 3–4 minutes. Add the red pepper, green pepper, garlic, and tomatoes. Partially cover and simmer for 15 minutes. Stir in the Worcestershire sauce and salt. Remove and serve, or refrigerate in a tightly covered jar.

Hollandaise Sauce

There's no reason to fear this classic sauce, yellow with butter and egg and tart with lemon juice. Made the traditional way, or whirred in the blender (following recipe), it should cause no problems for the careful cook. And if it does, there are two sure-fire ways to fix it (p. 264).

(1 CUP)

3 egg yolks
1 tablespoon lemon juice
¼ pound (115 g) butter,
  melted

Dash of cayenne pepper
Salt to taste

Use a double boiler or a metal bowl placed over hot, but not simmering, water. Put the egg yolks in the boiler top, and beat with a wire whisk until smooth. Add the lemon juice and gradually whisk in the melted butter, pouring in a thin stream. Slowly stir in 2 tablespoons hot water, the cayenne, and salt. Continue to mix for 1 minute. The sauce should be thickened. Serve immediately, or hold over warm water for an hour or two, but don't try to keep it too long without refrigerating.

Béarnaise Sauce. Cook *1 tablespoon minced shallots* or *white ends of scallions* until reduced to 1 tablespoon; then strain. Use this in place of the lemon juice. Add *1 teaspoon minced parsley* and *½ teaspoon dried tarragon, crumbled,* or *1 teaspoon minced fresh tarragon* to the sauce when thickened.

Sauce Mousseline. Fold in *⅓ cup heavy cream, whipped,* just before serving. This is a good way to stretch the sauce.

Blender or Food Processor Hollandaise

Smooth, buttery, tart, and easy. Fish, broccoli, asparagus, and eggs all benefit from a cover of hollandaise. The same variations as in the preceding recipe can be made with this Hollandaise and the same rules about storage apply.

(1¼ CUPS)

2 egg yolks
½ pound (225 g) butter,
  melted

1 tablespoon lemon juice
Dash of cayenne pepper
Salt to taste

Put the egg yolks in the electric blender or food processor. If using the blender, turn to low speed. Slowly add 1½ tablespoons boiling water, and then add the butter very slowly in a thin stream. Add the lemon juice, cayenne, and salt. Taste and correct the seasonings.

Aïoli

Pronounce it "i-oh-lee." It is robust with garlic, adds zest to fish, especially cod, and boiled new potatoes, hard-cooked eggs, or green beans.

(1½ CUPS)

3 egg yolks
½ teaspoon salt
6 cloves garlic, peeled

1½ cups (3½ dL) olive oil
1 tablespoon lemon juice

Put the yolks in a bowl. Put the salt on a cutting board with the garlic on top.
Mince the garlic, incorporating the salt as you chop. At the end, use the flat
edge of the knife blade to mash and crush the garlic and salt into a paste. Add
this to the yolks. Blend in the oil, drop by drop, whisking or stirring briskly with
a fork. Be patient. When the sauce has thickened a little, increase the speed of
the oil to a thin slow stream. When all the oil is incorporated, add the lemon
juice, blend well, and correct the seasoning.

Horseradish Cream

A creamy, sharp accompaniment to roast beef.

(1 CUP)

¾ cup (1¾ dL) heavy cream
4 tablespoons prepared
  horseradish

2 tablespoons vinegar
Salt to taste

Beat the cream until stiff. Gently stir in the horseradish, vinegar, and salt.
Refrigerate until needed.

Mustard Sauce

Adds sharpness to beef, ham, spinach, and sausage.

(1½ CUPS)

2 tablespoons dry mustard
1 teaspoon flour
1 cup (¼ L) light cream
1 egg yolk

1 teaspoon sugar
½ cup (1 dL) vinegar, heated
Salt to taste

Blend the dry mustard, flour, and ¼ cup of the cream. Put the remaining ¾ cup
cream in a heavy-bottomed pan. Heat, then stir in the mustard mixture. Beat
the egg yolk in a small bowl. Beat in 2 tablespoons of the hot mustard mixture,
then stir the yolk-sauce mixture into the saucepan. Add the sugar, and cook,
stirring constantly, until thickened. Stir in the heated vinegar and salt.

Raisin Sauce

Very good with ham or tongue.

(2½ CUPS)

½ cup (1 dL) dark-brown sugar
1½ teaspoons dry mustard
1 tablespoon flour
2 tablespoons vinegar

2 tablespoons lemon juice
¼ teaspoon grated lemon rind
⅓ cup (¾ dL) raisins
Salt to taste

Combine the brown sugar, dry mustard, and flour in a heavy-bottomed pan off
the heat. Slowly stir in the vinegar, lemon juice, lemon rind, and 1½ cups water.
Place over medium heat and bring to a boil, stirring constantly. Lower the heat
and add the raisins and salt. Cook and stir until the sauce is thick.

Sweet-and-Sour Sauce

This sauce adds a spicy Christmas taste to tongue or ham.

(2 CUPS)

⅓ cup (¾ dL) vinegar
1 onion, sliced thin
¼ cup (½ dL) raisins
½ lemon, sliced paper-thin
¼ cup (½ dL) brown sugar
½ teaspoon allspice

1 bay leaf
Dash of cayenne pepper
½ cup (1 dL) finely crumbed
  gingersnaps
Salt to taste

Combine 2 cups of water with the vinegar, onion, raisins, lemon, brown sugar, allspice, bay leaf, and cayenne pepper in a saucepan. Bring to a boil and simmer until the onion and lemon are tender, about 15 minutes. Remove the bay leaf, add the gingersnap crumbs and salt, and stir over medium heat until thickened. Serve hot.

Tartar Sauce

Traditional with fish and seafood—and so much superior when you make it yourself.

(1 CUP)

¾ cup (1¾ dL) mayonnaise,
  preferably homemade
  (p. 452)
2 teaspoons minced scallion
1 teaspoon capers

1 teaspoon minced sweet pickle
1 teaspoon minced parsley
1 tablespoon vinegar

Combine all ingredients in a bowl. Stir until well blended.

Cucumber Cream

More a relish than a proper sauce, this is lovely and fresh-tasting with fish.

(1¼ CUPS)

1 cucumber
½ cup (1 dL) sour cream

2 tablespoons vinegar
Salt to taste

Pare and finely chop the cucumber. Pat dry of excess liquid, put in a bowl, and stir in the sour cream, vinegar, and salt.

Cucumber Sauce

Another fresh cucumber relish to serve with fish.

(ABOUT ¾ CUP)

1 medium cucumber
⅛ teaspoon freshly ground
  pepper

1 tablespoon white vinegar
Salt to taste

Pare the cucumber. Grate it by hand or in a food processor, and squeeze out most of the juice. Mix with the pepper, vinegar, and salt.

Yogurt Green Sauce

The tartness of the yogurt makes this a particularly good foil for cold fish or chicken. When you have some homemade green mayonnaise on hand in the refrigerator, try this interesting sauce. It is easy enough to increase or decrease the ingredients according to your needs.

(1 CUP)

½ cup (1 dL) Green
  Mayonnaise (p. 453)
½ cup (1 dL) yogurt
1 tablespoon capers, drained
Fresh lemon juice

Salt to taste
Freshly ground pepper
1 tablespoon fresh chopped
  herbs

Beat the mayonnaise and yogurt together. Add the capers and a few drops of lemon juice to taste, and salt and pepper. Sprinkle on fresh herbs.

Orange Sauce

Pleasing with lamb.

(1 CUP)

⅓ cup (¾ dL) currant jelly
3 tablespoons sugar
Grated rind of 2 oranges
2 tablespoons Port wine

2 tablespoons orange juice
2 tablespoons lemon juice
⅛ teaspoon cayenne pepper
Salt

In a saucepan, combine the jelly, sugar, and grated orange rind and beat until smoothly blended. Stir in the wine, orange juice, lemon juice, and cayenne pepper. Heat through to melt the jelly. Add salt to taste.

Oyster Sauce

A creamy sauce for fish.

(2 CUPS)

1½ cups (3½ dL) shucked
  oysters and their liquor
4 tablespoons butter
3 tablespoons flour

1¼ cups (3 dL) milk
Salt to taste
¼ teaspoon freshly ground
  pepper

If the oysters are very large, cut into pieces about the size of a grape. Put the oysters and oyster liquor in a pan and cook over low heat for about 3 minutes, or until the oysters look plump. Remove the oysters and pour the liquor into a cup. Melt the butter in a pan and, when it foams, stir in the flour. Cook and stir for 2 minutes. Slowly add the oyster liquor and milk, stirring constantly. Add the salt and pepper and cook another 5 minutes over low heat. The sauce should flow easily from a spoon; if it becomes too thick, add more milk. Stir in the oysters and cook only until they are heated through.

Mint Sauce

A slightly sweet sauce of fresh mint in tart vinegar: so much better than the bright-green commercial mint jelly.

Mint Sauce (continued)

(½ CUP)

> ½ cup (1 dL) white vinegar
> ¼ cup (½ dL) sugar
> ½ cup (1 dL) minced fresh mint leaves

Put the vinegar and sugar in a small pan. Heat until it boils and the sugar dissolves. Pour the hot sauce over the mint and let stand at least 1 hour.

ABOUT MARINADES AND BARBECUE SAUCES

Marinades and barbecue sauces are similar in composition but are used differently. Each usually contains oil, seasoning, and an acid liquid such as wine, vinegar, tomatoes, or lemon juice. Meat is soaked in a marinade so that the seasonings can add flavor while the acid in the liquid softens tough fibers. A plastic bag, sealed tightly, can be used instead of a bowl, thus making it easy to turn the meat. Then the meat is patted dry and cooked in one of several ways; often the marinade is used in the cooking. A barbecue sauce sometimes serves as a marinade as well, seasoning and softening meat put to soak in it, but ordinarily it is brushed over food as it is baked or grilled, imparting a surface flavor.

Wine Marinade

Red wine is good with beef and lamb. Let the meat marinate for at least 3 hours before cooking, turning it several times in the marinade.

(2 CUPS)

1 cup (¼ L) red wine	½ teaspoon rosemary, crumbled
1 cup (¼ L) olive oil	1 teaspoon thyme, crumbled
3 cloves garlic	4 tablespoons minced parsley
1 teaspoon salt	1 teaspoon coarsely ground
½ teaspoon marjoram,	pepper
crumbled	

Mix the wine and oil together in a jar with a tight-fitting lid. Crush and chop the garlic with the salt until almost a paste. Add to the wine and oil, along with remaining ingredients. Cover tight and shake until all ingredients are well blended.

Barbecue Sauce

A basic barbecue sauce, good on pork chops, spareribs, hamburgers.

(ABOUT 2 CUPS)

2 tablespoons butter	4 tablespoons vinegar
1 onion, grated	4 tablespoons Worcestershire
2 cloves garlic, minced	sauce
¼ teaspoon salt	1 cup (¼ L) catsup
1 tablespoon chili powder	1 teaspoon Tabasco
4 tablespoons brown sugar	

Melt the butter in a saucepan and cook the onion and garlic until soft. Add 2 cups of water and remaining ingredients. Stir until well mixed. Place over medium-low heat and simmer for 30 minutes.

Light Barbecue Sauce

A sauce that allows meat and poultry to keep their own character.

(1½ CUPS)

1 cup (¼ L) dry white wine
¼ cup (½ dL) olive oil
2 tablespoons butter
1 medium onion, chopped fine

1 clove garlic, crushed
1 teaspoon salt
1 teaspoon rosemary, crumbled

Combine all ingredients in a saucepan. Simmer for 30 minutes.

Chicken Barbecue Sauce

Brush on chicken parts as they cook over the coals. Also good with pork.

(1½ CUPS)

1 egg, well beaten
½ cup (1 dL) cooking oil
1 cup (¼ L) cider vinegar
1 tablespoon salt

1 teaspoon sage, crumbled
¼ teaspoon freshly ground
  pepper

Combine all ingredients in a jar. Shake well and let stand for several hours before using.

ABOUT STUFFINGS

Use day-old bread for stuffing or let fresh bread dry out slightly in the oven. Don't economize by using old, stale bread: its tired flavor will haunt the stuffing unless the seasoning is very strong. You don't always have to use breadcrumbs—try croutons, cracker crumbs, crumbled corn bread, wild rice, white rice, and barley, or kasha.

Always taste and correct the seasoning before you use the stuffing. Fry a tablespoonful in a small skillet before tasting it, and bear in mind that the stuffing will absorb additional flavor and moisture as it cooks from the juices of the meat, poultry, or vegetable in which it is encased.

The amount of liquid in stuffing is a matter of personal taste; some people prefer a steaming, porridgy stuffing, while others like the crunch of croutons or dry buttery crumbs. Stuffing expands as it cooks: handle it lightly, tossing rather than beating it, and pack it gently to allow plenty of room for expansion. (For stuffing poultry, see p. 230.)

To store leftovers, remove the stuffing from the cavity, put it in a casserole, and refrigerate. To reheat, place the casserole in a 325°F (165°C) oven for half an hour, or toss the stuffing in a skillet in a few tablespoons of melted butter.

Suggested Uses for Stuffings

These are only suggestions, not inflexible rules, in an area in which cooks should use their imaginations. Vegetables such as tomatoes, peppers, eggplants, onions, zucchini, and mushrooms are all delicious when baked with stuffings (see recipes in Filled Things), and there is no reason why a number of the stuffings below could not also be used to stuff such vegetables.

Bread Stuffing

Savory Bread Stuffing	Chicken, Turkey, Fish
Raisin-Nut Stuffing	Chicken, Turkey, Pork
Corn Bread Stuffing	Turkey, Pork, Ham
Corn Stuffing	Turkey, Ham
Giblet Stuffing	Chicken, Turkey
Herb Stuffing	Chicken, Turkey, Fish
Mushroom Stuffing	Chicken, Turkey, Cornish Game Hens, Fish
Onion Stuffing	Chicken, Veal, Ham
Oyster Stuffing	Chicken, Turkey, Fish
Apple Stuffing	Duck, Goose, Pork, Veal
Celery Stuffing	Chicken, Duck, Fish
Mint Stuffing	Lamb, Chicken, Cornish Game Hens
Orange Stuffing	Duck
Lemon Stuffing	Chicken, Fish, Veal
Prune and Apple Stuffing	Duck, Goose, Pork, Veal
Wild Rice and Mushroom Stuffing	Cornish Game Hens, Goose, Turkey, Chicken
Sausage Stuffing	Turkey
Sausage and Chestnut Stuffing	Turkey, Squabs, Chicken

Bread Stuffing

A pleasant basic stuffing.

(ABOUT 3 CUPS)

¼ pound (115 g) butter
4 tablespoons finely chopped onion
4 tablespoons finely chopped celery

4 cups (1 L) dry bread crumbs
¼ teaspoon freshly ground pepper
Salt to taste

Melt the butter in a skillet and stir in the onion and celery. Cook over low heat until the onion is soft. Add this mixture to the crumbs and toss lightly with plenty of pepper and salt.

Savory Bread Stuffing. Add *1 teaspoon sage, crumbled, or 1 teaspoon poultry seasoning.*

Raisin-Nut Stuffing. Add *½ cup raisins and ½ cup walnuts.*

Giblet Stuffing. Cover the *giblets* with 1 quart cold water in a saucepan. Bring to a boil and simmer. When the liver is tender, remove it. Continue to cook the gizzard until it is tender, about 45 minutes. Drain the giblets and chop into small bits, and add to the stuffing. Save the liquid for soup.

Herb Stuffing. Add *1 teaspoon thyme, crumbled, 1 teaspoon basil, crumbled,* and *½ teaspoon marjoram, crumbled.*

Mushroom Stuffing. Omit the celery and cook *2 cups chopped mushrooms* with the onions. Add *½ teaspoon nutmeg.*

Onion Stuffing. Add *6 onions,* boiled until barely tender, drained, and chopped.

Oyster Stuffing. Add *2 cups oysters,* in bite-size pieces, and use about ¼ *cup* of *oyster liquor* for moistening the crumbs.

Corn Bread Stuffing. Substitute *2 cups corn bread crumbs* for 2 cups of the bread crumbs. For *Corn Stuffing,* add *1 cup cooked whole-kernel corn.*

Apple Stuffing

The apples, which turn lightly brown and tender, are mixed with spices and crumbs to make a fine Christmas stuffing.

(2½ CUPS)

4 tablespoons bacon fat
2 cups (½ L) diced unpeeled
   tart apples
2 teaspoons sugar

½ cup (1 dL) dry bread crumbs
¼ teaspoon nutmeg
¼ teaspoon cinnamon

Melt the bacon fat in a skillet. Add the apples and sugar and cook over medium-low heat, stirring, for 5 minutes. Remove from the heat and toss in the crumbs, nutmeg, and cinnamon.

Prune and Apple Stuffing

(2 CUPS)

1 cup (¼ L) dried prunes,
   pitted
2 tablespoons raisins
2 tablespoons fine cracker
   crumbs

2 teaspoons sugar
1 large apple, peeled, cored,
   and diced small
Salt to taste

Put the prunes and raisins in a bowl and pour on 1½ cups boiling water. Let stand 5 minutes. Drain and cut the prunes into pieces. Add remaining ingredients, and toss to blend well.

Wild Rice and Mushroom Stuffing

(3 CUPS)

1 cup (¼ L) wild rice
4 tablespoons butter
2 cups (½ L) chopped
   mushrooms
1 small onion, chopped fine

¼ teaspoon freshly ground
   pepper
¼–½ teaspoon ground nutmeg
Salt to taste

Steam the rice (p. 321). Melt the butter in a saucepan, add the mushrooms and onion, and cook over low heat until soft. Toss in the rice with the pepper, nutmeg, and salt.

Celery Stuffing

This is a more moist stuffing.

(6 CUPS)

4 tablespoons butter
1 cup (¼ L) chopped celery
4 tablespoons finely chopped
  onion
4 tablespoons minced parsley

4 cups (1 L) dry bread crumbs
¼ teaspoon freshly ground
  pepper
¼ cup (½ dL) chicken broth
Salt to taste

Melt the butter in a skillet. Stir in the celery and onion and cook over low heat for 3–4 minutes. Remove from the heat and blend in the parsley, crumbs, pepper, chicken broth, and salt.

Mint Stuffing

Dry, crisp, with lots of fresh mint flavor; a natural kin to lamb.

(3½ CUPS)

6 tablespoons butter
2 tablespoons minced onion
3 tablespoons finely chopped
  celery
½ cup (1 dL) finely cut fresh
  mint leaves

3 cups (¾ L) fine dry bread
  crumbs
Salt to taste

Melt 3 tablespoons of the butter in a skillet. Add the onion and celery and cook for 3 minutes. Add the mint leaves and cook until most of the liquid has evaporated. Remove from the heat and toss with the remaining 3 tablespoons of butter, the crumbs, and salt.

Sausage Stuffing

(8 CUPS)

1 pound (450 g) sausage meat
4 tablespoons minced onion
8 cups (2 L) freshly made dry
  bread crumbs

1 teaspoon freshly ground
  pepper
2 tablespoons minced parsley
Salt to taste

Heat a skillet and add the sausage, crumbling it into small bits as it cooks. Brown lightly and remove to a bowl, leaving the drippings in the skillet. Add the onion and cook, stirring, for 2 minutes. Add the crumbs, pepper, and parsley, and cook 1 minute more, stirring to mix well. Toss with the sausage meat and salt.

Sausage and Chestnut Stuffing

(5 CUPS)

2 cups (½ L) braised chestnuts
  (p. 376)
4 tablespoons butter

1 small onion, chopped
1 pound (450 g) sausage meat
1 teaspoon thyme, crumbled

½ teaspoon freshly ground
  pepper
1 tablespoon minced parsley

2 cups (½ L) freshly made
  bread crumbs
Salt to taste

Cut the chestnuts into quarters. Melt the butter in a skillet, add the onion, and cook, stirring often, over medium heat until soft. Scrape into a bowl and mix with the chestnuts. Cook the sausage in the skillet, crumbling it into tiny bits until it is brown. Add the sausage, with some of its fat, to the chestnut mixture with the thyme, pepper, parsley, bread crumbs, and salt.

Orange Stuffing

(4 CUPS)

3 cups (¾ L) croutons
  (p. 492)
¼ cup (½ dL) orange juice
2 teaspoons grated orange rind
⅔ cup (1½ dL) orange sections,
  with membranes removed

2 cups (½ L) finely chopped
  celery
5 tablespoons butter, melted
Salt to taste

Put the croutons in a bowl and stir in the orange juice. Let stand 15 minutes. Mix in remaining ingredients.

Lemon Stuffing. Use *2 tablespoons lemon juice* and *2 teaspoons lemon rind* instead of the orange juice and rind. This is particularly nice with chicken, fish, and veal.

ABOUT FRUIT RELISHES AND QUICK RELISHES

A longstanding tradition of the American table is the assortment of relishes served before or with a meal. They look nice and provide both color and flavor, often perking up a bland dish. Fruit relishes go especially well with pork, veal, and poultry. Quick relishes resemble pickles but are not so long-keeping.

Spiced Crabapples

(SERVES EIGHT TO TEN)

1 cup (¼ L) sugar
24 whole cloves
6 allspice berries

2-inch stick of cinnamon
Salt to taste
1 pound (450 g) crabapples

Put all the ingredients in a pot with 2 cups boiling water and simmer gently until the apples are just tender. Spoon out the fruit and pour a little juice over it. Serve hot or cold.

Spiced Carrots. Substitute *1 pound tiny new scraped carrots* for the crabapples.

Spiced Apricots or Peaches. Cook the syrup (without the crabapples) for about 10 minutes, then pour it over *peach or apricot halves, cooked and pitted,* and let stand until cool.

Fried Apple Rings

Serve these instead of applesauce with ham, pork dishes, or duck.

(SERVES FOUR)

>   2 tart apples
>   4 tablespoons butter
>   2 tablespoons sugar

Core the apples. Peel them only if the skins are very tough. Cut them in ½-inch slices and sauté the slices in butter until just barely tender. Sprinkle with sugar, cover the pan, and cook a few minutes more, until they are glazed and golden.

Cranberry Sauce

(SERVES EIGHT–TEN)

>   1 pound, 450 g (4 cups, 1 L)
>   fresh cranberries
>   1½ cups (275 g) sugar

Wash the cranberries. Bring 2 cups of water to a boil, then add the cranberries and sugar. Cook for 10 minutes or until the skins pop. Skim off the white froth and cool. Refrigerate until ready to serve.

Cranberry Jelly

This is a tart, soft-textured jelly, very unlike its canned counterpart.

(2½ CUPS)

> 1 pound, 450 g (4 cups, 1 L)   2 cups (400 g) sugar
>   fresh cranberries   Salt

Wash the cranberries. Bring 2 cups of water to a boil, add the cranberries, and boil for 20 minutes, stirring occasionally to keep from burning, especially at the end. Put the berries through a strainer or food mill. Return them to the pot and cook over low heat for 3 minutes, stirring frequently. Add the sugar and a pinch of salt and cook 2 minutes more. Pour into a bowl and chill.

Spiced Cranberry Jelly. Add with the cranberries a *2-inch stick of cinnamon, 3 whole cloves,* and *3 allspice berries.*

Cranberry and Orange Relish

(SERVES SIX)

> ½ pound, 225 g (2 cups, ½ L)   1 small orange
>   cranberries   ¾ cup (1¾ dL) sugar

Wash the cranberries. Cut the orange in pieces and remove the seeds; do not peel. Chop the cranberries and orange with a food chopper or in a food processor. Add the sugar and stir well. Let stand at least 30 minutes before serving.

Fruit Kabobs

Good with barbecued chicken or spareribs.

Fresh pineapple, cubed
Spiced Apricots or Peaches
   (p. 281)

Prunes, pitted and cooked
Butter

Arrange the fruit on skewers, brush with butter, and broil, indoors or out, for 5 minutes.

Baked Oranges

These should be baked alongside a roasting turkey or duck.

(SERVES SIX)

6 seedless oranges
2 tablespoons sugar

Cover the oranges with cold water. Bring to the boiling point, simmer 30 minutes, and drain. Cut a slice off the top of each orange and place 1 teaspoon sugar in each. Bake in the roasting pan for about 1 hour.

Broiled Peaches or Apricots

This relish also makes a delicious and simple dessert.

(SERVES SIX)

6 fresh peaches or apricots
4 tablespoons butter
4 tablespoons brown sugar

Wash peaches or apricots. Cut them in half and remove the stones. Place them in a shallow pan, cut side up. Dot each half with 1 teaspoon butter and sprinkle with 1 teaspoon brown sugar. Broil until the sugar melts.

Broiled Peaches with Blueberries. Fill each cavity of the peaches or apricots with a spoonful of *blueberries* before dotting with butter and sugar.

Broiled Brandied Peaches. Add ½ *teaspoon brandy* to each cavity before dotting with butter and sugar.

Beet Relish

(1½ CUPS)

1½ cups (3½ dL) chopped
   cooked or canned beets
3 tablespoons prepared
   horseradish, well drained

2 tablespoons lemon juice
2 teaspoons sugar
Salt to taste

Toss together all ingredients. Refrigerate before serving.

Uncooked Tomato Relish

You can keep this uncooked mixture in a cool, dark place for about six months. It lacks the subtlety of cooked relishes, but has a fresh, piquant quality that is decidedly different.

(2 PINTS)

12 large ripe tomatoes, peeled and chopped
½ cup (1 dL) chopped celery
2 tablespoons chopped sweet red or green pepper
2 tablespoons chopped onion
1½ tablespoons salt

2 tablespoons sugar
1½ tablespoons mustard seed
¼ teaspoons nutmeg
¼ teaspoon cinnamon
Pinch of ground cloves
½ cup (1 dL) cider vinegar

Drain off the liquid from the tomato. Combine the pulp with the remaining ingredients. Put the mixture in a covered crock and let it stand for at least one week before using.

Celery Relish

(1½ CUPS)

1½ cups (3½ dL) chopped celery
1 tablespoon sugar
½ teaspoon mustard

¼ cup (½ dL) vinegar
Salt to taste

Combine all ingredients. Cover and refrigerate at least 1½ hours. Drain before serving.

Chili Sauce

(1½ CUPS)

2 cups (½ L) canned tomatoes
1 onion, chopped
Dash of cayenne pepper
⅛ teaspoon ground cloves
⅛ teaspoon cinnamon

1 tablespoon sugar
¼ cup (½ dL) vinegar
2 tablespoons chopped green pepper
About ½ teaspoon salt

In a heavy-bottomed saucepan, combine the tomatoes, onion, cayenne, cloves, cinnamon, sugar, and vinegar. Simmer, uncovered, for 1 hour. Add the green pepper and simmer 30 minutes more. Add salt to taste. Chill before serving.

Philadelphia Relish

(2½ CUPS)

2 cups (½ L) finely shredded cabbage
2 green peppers, diced fine
1 teaspoon celery seed

¼ teaspoon mustard seed
2 tablespoons brown sugar
¼ cup (½ dL) vinegar
Salt to taste

Toss together all ingredients. Chill before serving.

Mustard Relish

A food processor makes light work of preparing the chopped vegetables for this relish.

(3 CUPS)

2 cups (½ L) shredded cabbage
1 sweet red pepper, chopped fine
½ large green pepper, chopped fine
⅓ cup (¾ dL) chopped onion
1½ cups (3½ dL) vinegar

Salt
¼ cup (50 g) sugar
3 tablespoons flour
2 teaspoons dry mustard
¼ teaspoon turmeric
¼ teaspoon celery seed

Mix the cabbage, red pepper, green pepper, onion, 1 cup of the vinegar, 1 cup of water, and 2 tablespoons salt, and let stand for several hours. In a heavy-bottomed pan, whisk the sugar, flour, mustard, turmeric, and celery seed. Slowly add the remaining ½ cup of vinegar with ½ cup of cold water. Stir and cook over low heat until thick; cover and cook gently 10 minutes. Drain the vegetables. Add them to the dressing and simmer 5 minutes more. Taste, and add more salt if you wish. Chill before serving.

FILLED THINGS

ABOUT FILLED THINGS

Hamburgers, hot dogs, and sandwiches make up our great movable feast, the foods that can be eaten with the fingers and on the run: at the desk, in the lunchroom, at ball games, and at picnics. While there is no need to decry the fast-food vendors, it's far better to prepare these foods yourself from the highest-quality ingredients. Since portable foods constitute about one-third of the American diet, they should be prepared with great care, and attention should be paid to both their taste and their nutritional quality.

They include not only sandwiches, but also the many varieties of filled doughs that weren't in the American vocabulary before World War II but are now part of the national cuisine; foods such as crêpes, quiches, pizzas, and tortillas. There are also stuffed vegetables and eggs that can be served as a first course, at a picnic, or for a light lunch.

All these filled things offer thrifty ways to use up leftover cooked foods, stretch a quarter-pound of expensive crabmeat or fillet, or transform lesser cuts of meat so that no one would guess they were economical. They provide a sensible and delicious way of reducing meat intake and increasing the amount of grains and vegetables in the diet.

Sandwiches

What makes a good sandwich? Good bread, generous filling, contrasting textures, and the mysterious mating of the right filling with the right bread. There was a time when you couldn't get a sandwich in this country on anything but soft white bread: the choice was to have it plain or toasted. Now Americans have not only adopted French, Italian, and Portuguese breads, Greek pitas and Scandinavian flatbreads and ryes, but revived whole-grain breads to the great enrichment of the noonday meal.

What makes a bad sandwich? Dryness, a poor proportion of filling to bread, staleness, incompatible combinations, and wet greens that make everything soggy

286

or undrained tomatoes that sit too long on the bread. Firm, tastily ripe tomatoes are wonderful in sandwiches, adding moisture and goodness.

Unless you must, don't make sandwiches until just before they are to be eaten. When they have to be made in advance for picnics or lunchboxes, wrap each sandwich individually, making an airtight package with plastic wrap or foil. A good idea is to put the lettuce and sliced tomato in a separate plastic bag, to be tucked into the sandwich just before eating.

Crêpes, Filled Pasta, Quiches, and Pizza

Every nation has its own way of wrapping savory fillings in envelopes of dough. Crêpes are thin pancakes that are rolled around a filling (see basic recipe, p. 497). In spite of their elegant reputation, they are actually a great convenience food, reacting well to being prepared ahead of time, frozen, and then defrosted when they are needed. Many of the fillings recommended for crêpes also go well in omelets.

In Italy, pasta dough is rolled out and used to contain different fillings, such as small, square ravioli, fat, tubular manicotti, and cannelloni, which works much the way a crêpe does. This pasta dough can be homemade or purchased; lucky for you if you have a commercial source of fresh pasta nearby.

From France come quiches, unsweetened piecrust shells that are filled with mixtures of different foods and seasoned custard. They are a wonderful way of using up leftover meat and vegetables.

And finally, there is pizza, once Italian, now the quintessential American meal. Far more nutritious than our children imagine, pizza is a worthwhile combination of bread, cheese, and tomatoes. In addition to the familiar garnishes of sausage, anchovy, and mushrooms, pizza can serve as a delicious base for chopped leftover meat and vegetables. Even people who hate leftovers will eat them spread over a bed of yeasty dough and tomato sauce, covered with a blanket of bubbling mozzarella cheese.

Tortillas, Tacos, and Enchilladas

Tortillas, tacos, and enchilladas are common in the Southwest, new to most of the rest of the country. Tortillas are Mexican pancakes made of a flour ground of cooked corn grain, called *masa harina*. You can make them yourself if you have either a tortilla press or a lot of experience: they are tricky. Luckily, many markets now carry tortillas in the frozen food section and some markets even have them fresh, so it isn't necessary to create your own. Enchilladas are softened tortillas that are filled and rolled. The tortilla is put in hot oil to soften and then whisked through a warm sauce, filled, and rolled. Tacos are fried tortillas, usually made very crisp. They are folded in half while they are being fried and are then removed, filled, and served.

Stuffed Vegetables and Eggs

Stuffed vegetables are a centuries-old way of using cooked foods. They are both elegant and economical, and make a glorious antipasto or a summer lunch. Serve them hot, or let them cool and serve chilled and sprinkled with freshly chopped herbs. And what would a picnic be without stuffed eggs? To say nothing of their role as an hors d'oeuvre and a salad or cold platter garnish.

SANDWICHES

Sandwiches with Meat or Fish Fillings

(SERVES ONE)

Sliced Chicken or Turkey

Season at least 3 or 4 slices of the white meat with salt and pepper. Because they're apt to be dry, top the slices with a good tablespoon of mayonnaise, preferably homemade. Pile on buttered white or whole-wheat bread and add 2 or 3 generous sprigs of watercress or a crisp lettuce leaf.

Ham

Use 3 thin slices of ham, preferably good baked ham, on buttered rye bread with 1 tablespoon of mayonnaise on one side, and 1 teaspoon of mustard on the other—mild or Dijon according to preference.

Ham and Cheese: Eliminate the mayonnaise and add a slice or two of Swiss or other mild cheese.

Roast Beef

Use beef that is somewhat rare, or else it will be dry. Pile a generous 2 or 3 slices on buttered white or rye bread. Add salt and pepper, a teaspoon of mustard, and a crisp lettuce leaf. Serve with dill pickle.

Hot Roast Beef

Hot roast beef is particularly good on a hard roll, such as Kaiser, onion, or sesame seed, with the juices poured over. Salt and pepper to taste and pass the mustard.

Corned Beef or Tongue

Most aficionados like 4 or 5 generous slices with mustard only on buttered rye bread. Serve with dill pickle.

Hot Pastrami

This spicy cousin of corned beef must always be served warm, 4 or 5 slices on buttered pumpernickel or rye with a good teaspoon of mustard.

Cold Sliced Pork, Veal, or Lamb

These meats are apt to be a little dry when cold, so serve 3 or 4 slices with a generous tablespoon of mayonnaise, and watercress or crisp lettuce, on well-buttered bread. A relish such as chutney or bread-and-butter pickle can be good on the meat, especially the pork.

Bologna, Liverwurst, or Salami

Place 3 or 4 good slices of bologna, liverwurst, or salami on dark buttered rye or whole-wheat bread, with 1 teaspoon prepared horseradish or 2 teaspoons peppery mustard, or 2 teaspoons mayonnaise. Serve with dill pickle.

Sardine

Place a row of well-drained sardines on a thin slice of buttered rye bread. Squeeze 1 teaspoon of lemon juice on top, sprinkle with ½ teaspoon chopped dill, and cover with buttered slice of rye.

Sandwiches with Salad Fillings

(SERVES ONE)

Chicken or Turkey Salad

Mix ¼ cup chopped cooked chicken with 1 tablespoon finely chopped celery, ½ hard-cooked egg, chopped, 2 tablespoons mayonnaise, salt, and freshly ground pepper. Spread the chicken mixture between 2 slices of buttered fresh white bread, and add a crisp lettuce leaf or sprigs of watercress.

Curried Chicken or Turkey Salad

Follow the directions for Chicken Salad, but add ¼ teaspoon curry powder and 1 teaspoon chutney. Omit the lettuce or watercress and use whole-wheat bread instead of white.

Tuna or Salmon Salad

Mix ¼ cup drained flaked tuna with ½ hard-cooked egg, chopped, 1 teaspoon sweet relish (optional), 2 teaspoons chopped celery, 1½ tablespoons mayonnaise, and ½ teaspoon lemon juice. Spread between 2 slices buttered white or whole-wheat bread and cover with a crisp lettuce leaf.

Shrimp, Crab, or Lobster Salad

Mix ⅓ cup cooked shrimp, crab, or lobster with 2 tablespoons mayonnaise, 1 teaspoon lemon juice, 4 drops Tabasco, and salt to taste. Butter two slices of fresh French bread, preferably sourdough, sliced ⅜ inch thick. Spread the seafood salad over the bread, and cover with other slice.

Shrimp-Cucumber Salad

Follow the recipe for Shrimp Salad using ¼ cup, and add about 2 tablespoons chopped, seeded cucumber.

Lobster Roll

Follow the recipe for Lobster Salad, and serve on a toasted hot-dog roll.

Egg Salad

Mash 1 hard-cooked egg with 1 tablespoon mayonnaise. Scrape the cut side of an onion and add ½ teaspoon of the juicy purée to the egg. Spread between 2 buttered slices of fresh white bread or a whole-grain bread, adding a crisp lettuce leaf.

Ham, Tongue, or Corned Beef Salad

Coarsely chop cooked ham, tongue, or corned beef to make ¼ cup. Add 2 teaspoons mayonnaise, 1 teaspoon prepared horseradish, and 1 teaspoon prepared mustard. Spread between 2 slices of rye bread, either light or dark.

Hamburger

One pound of ground beef makes four ample patties. Use medium-lean beef, since a little fat is needed for moistness. The more you handle or grind hamburger the more compact and dry it becomes. Try to divide and shape each patty as lightly as possible, and don't press down on it when it is cooking, since that pushes out the juice. Have the hamburger roll hot or toast it lightly. Some like a hamburger plain; some prefer it dressed up in one or more of the following garnishes: *catsup, prepared mustard, sliced raw onion,* a mixture of *mayonnaise* and finely chopped *onion* or *scallions, sweet pickle relish,* slices of *dill pickle,* thin slices of *tomato,* a slice of *Cheddar, Monterey Jack,* or *Swiss cheese, chili sauce,* and either a crisp dry leaf or a small mound of shredded iceberg *lettuce.*

(ONE HAMBURGER)

¼ pound (115 g) medium-lean ground beef	Freshly ground pepper
Salt	1 teaspoon shortening

Salt and pepper the ground beef as liberally as you like it, then, lightly, handling as little as possible, shape it into a patty about 3½ inches in diameter, about the size of a hamburger bun. To fry, melt the shortening in a skillet. When it is hot, add the patty and fry a few minutes on each side, 2 for rare, 3 for medium, 4 or more for well done. To broil, place patty on a rack 2 inches beneath a preheated broiler, and broil a minute longer for each side than you would for frying. Serve garnished with any of the above suggestions according to your taste on buttered hot hamburger rolls, or on toasted English muffins, Kaiser rolls, or just toast, as you wish.

Hot Dogs

Hot dogs or frankfurters are ready-to-eat when bought, but their flavor and texture are improved with heating. Again, some like their frankfurters plain, some like them with all the trimmings, which can include one or more of the following: prepared *mustard, chopped onions,* some *chili beans, sweet pickle relish,* slices of *dill pickle, chopped tomato,* or *sauerkraut.* Have your hot-dog rolls warm or toasted. The different methods of cooking are:

Boiling. Bring a pan of water to boil, lower the heat so water is simmering, and add the hot dogs. Cook keeping at a simmer for 5 minutes; if the water boils too hard, the frankfurters will break out of their casings.

Frying. Heat a teaspoon of fat in skillet. Cut the hot dogs lengthwise down the middle, but not completely through; or cut diagonal slashes. Place cut side down in the hot fat and fry for 2 minutes over medium heat on each side.

Grilling. Place the hot dogs over glowing coals (or under a preheated broiler, as close to the heat as possible) and grill, turning until all sides are well browned.

Bacon, Lettuce, and Tomato Sandwich (BLT)

Don't be skimpy with the bacon: use at least three strips. The authentic bacon, lettuce, and tomato sandwich is on toasted white bread.

(ONE SANDWICH)

3 strips bacon	4 slices tomato
2 slices white bread	Salt
2 tablespoons mayonnaise	Leaf of crisp iceberg lettuce

Fry the bacon crisp and drain on a paper towel. Toast the bread, and spread mayonnaise on each slice. Pile the tomatoes on one slice, salt to taste and top with bacon, lettuce, and the second slice of bread. Cut in half.

Denver Sandwich

This is also known as a Western Omelet Sandwich. Part of the delight is having the egg soak into the soft bread.

(TWO SANDWICHES)

3 tablespoons butter	3 eggs, slightly beaten
⅓ cup (¾ dL) finely chopped onion	Salt to taste
	Cayenne pepper to taste
⅓ cup (¾ dL) finely chopped green pepper	4 slices buttered bread
	Prepared mustard
2 slices ham, chopped	

Melt the butter in a skillet. Add the onion, pepper, and ham, and cook until the onion is soft. Pour the beaten eggs over the ham and vegetables, and add salt and cayenne pepper. Cook over low heat until lightly golden. Turn over with a spatula and quickly brown only lightly the other side (the center should remain moist). Divide the omelet in half and place each half on a piece of buttered bread. Spread with mustard and close with the other slice of bread. Serve warm.

Reuben Sandwich

(ONE SANDWICH)

2 slices corned beef	4 tablespoons sauerkraut
1 slice Swiss cheese	1½ tablespoons Russian
2 slices dark rye or pumpernickel bread	Dressing (p. 453)
	3 tablespoons butter

Put 1 slice corned beef and 1 slice Swiss cheese on a piece of bread. Heap on sauerkraut and spread the dressing over it. Put on the second slice of corned beef and second slice of bread. Melt the butter in a skillet over medium-low heat. Put in the sandwich and grill on each side until the cheese melts, or grill in a sandwich toaster. Serve warm.

Club Sandwich

Quite a perfect sandwich, particularly made of newly baked bread freshly toasted with ample slices of breast of chicken and thin slices of tomatoes. (The faint of heart *can* use only two slices of bread—but then it hardly qualifies as a genuine lofty club sandwich.)

(ONE SANDWICH)

Butter	Freshly ground pepper
2 tablespoons mayonnaise	3 thin slices ripe, firm tomato
3 slices fresh bread, toasted crisp	3 slices bacon, fried crisp and drained
4 thin slices cooked chicken breast	Green olives
Salt	Sweet pickles

Spread butter and mayonnaise on one side of each slice of toast, cover with chicken, sprinkle with salt and pepper, and cover with a slice of toast. Place the tomatoes and bacon on it, and season with salt and pepper. Cover with the last slice of toast. Cut in quarters, diagonally, and serve with olives and pickles.

Barbecued Pork Sandwich

Serve with pickles and/or cole slaw.

(FOUR SANDWICHES)

4 French rolls, split and buttered 1½ cups (3½ dL) Barbecue
8 slices roast pork   Sauce (p. 276)

Put the rolls under the broiler and toast only on the buttered side. Put the pork slices in a skillet with the barbecue sauce, and heat gently. Put the pork on the toasted rolls and spoon sauce over the top.

Grilled Cheese Sandwich

A perennial favorite: soft melted cheese and pressed, buttery toast.

(ONE SANDWICH)

2 slices Cheddar, American, 2 slices white bread
   or Swiss cheese   2 tablespoons butter

Put the cheese between the slices of bread. Heat 1 tablespoon of the butter in a skillet or grill and when it is melted add the sandwich. Gently press down with a spatula once or twice during the grilling. When one side is golden, add the remaining tablespoon of butter, turn the sandwich over, and brown.

Grilled Cheese with Bacon. Fry 3 *slices bacon* until cooked but not crisp. Pat dry of excess fat, add on top of the cheese, and grill as directed.

Grilled Cheese with Ham. Put 2 *thin slices ham* on the cheese and grill as directed. Serve with sweet pickle.

Onion-Cheese Sandwich. Follow the recipe for Grilled Cheese Sandwich, but lightly coat 1 slice of bread with *Dijon mustard*. Sauté 3–4 *slices onion* in *butter* and put on top of the cheese. Cover and grill.

Tomato-Cheese Sandwich. Follow the recipe for Grilled Cheese Sandwich, but add 2 *thin slices tomato* to the sandwich before grilling.

Poor-Boy Sandwich

In New Orleans they make poor-boy sandwiches with fillings that start with fried potatoes and ascend to crabmeat. The classic is this hot sandwich made with leftover roast beef and gravy; if you don't have enough leftover gravy, use the improvised recipe, p. 268.

(SERVES TWO TO THREE)

12-inch loaf French bread   About ½ cup (1 dL) beef
½ cup (1 dL) mayonnaise   gravy, warmed
1 cup (¼ L) shredded lettuce   2 tomatoes, sliced thin
6 thin slices cooked beef

Split the bread lengthwise and warm it in the oven. Spread the bottom half with mayonnaise. Pile on shredded lettuce and top with overlapping slices of beef. Spoon warm gravy over the meat, top with tomato slices, and add the top half of the bread. Cut in 2–3 pieces and serve warm.

Hero Sandwich

Depending on where you live, you may call it a hero, hoagie, submarine, or grinder. Make it in individual 6-inch rolls as below, in loaves of French bread cut in 4-inch wedges, or, heroically, for a party in a special 2-foot-long loaf—increasing amounts of filling proportionately.

(ONE SANDWICH)

6-inch French roll	4 slices salami, bologna,
4 tablespoons butter	mortadella, ham, or other
¼ cup (½ dL) mayonnaise	cooked meat
2½ tablespoons prepared	Tomato slices
mustard	Onion rings
4 slices cheese: Cheddar, Swiss,	Pickle slices
Fontina, or others	Shredded lettuce

Split the roll lengthwise. Butter each half and spread with mayonnaise and mustard. Place the cheese and meat, overlapping, along the length. Add any of the remaining ingredients you like: the more, the better. If you want to serve it warm, omit the lettuce and tomato, wrap snugly in foil, and cook in a 350°F (180°C) oven for 30 minutes.

Mexican Hero Sandwich. Add *2½ tablespoons chopped, canned green chili to 6 ounces softened butter.* Omit the mustard and mayonnaise. Spread chili butter on the loaf, and use *salami* and *Monterey Jack cheese.* Wrap in foil and heat in a 350°F (180°C) oven for 30 minutes.

Italian Hero Sandwich. Omit the mustard. Use sliced *prosciutto ham* and *Genoa salami* and *Fontina, Romano,* or *Parmesan cheese.* Top with *onion* and *green pepper slices* and *olive relish.* Serve cold.

Meatball Hero

(SERVES FOUR)

Two 12-inch loaves French bread	1 cup (¼ L) grated Parmesan
1 recipe Meatballs in Sauce	cheese
(p. 171)	

Preheat the oven to 300°F (150°C). Split the bread lengthwise. Spoon some tomato sauce on the bottom half. Cut the meatballs in half and lay them along the length. Cover with more sauce and with a good sprinkling of Parmesan cheese. Cover with top half of bread, wrap in foil, and warm 20 minutes.

Lunchbasket Pita

Flatbreads, commonly known as pita, can be found in most super-markets today. The smaller size is often labeled pocket bread and makes a lovely sandwich when stuffed. Plain white pita is the most readily available but sometimes you can find whole wheat and the kind baked with sesame seeds (which can be improvised in this recipe; if sesame seed pita is available, skip the next to last step). Pita is also delicious cold with fillings of cheese and bean sprouts and other vegetables.

Lunchbasket Pita (*continued*)

(ONE SANDWICH)

1 small pita
Butter, softened
3 thin slices ham
2 slices mozzarella, fontina, or
    other melting cheese

Several thin slices sweet pickle
1 egg yolk beaten with 1
    teaspoon water (optional)
Sesame seeds (optional)

Slit open the side of the pita and spread the interior with soft butter. Stuff in slices of ham, alternating with cheese, and distribute the pickle inside evenly. Place under the broiler and toast one side until warm. Then turn and brush the top with a little egg glaze and sprinkle sesame seeds over. Toast until just light brown.

Lamb-filled Pita. A traditional filling. Be sure to save some lamb and a little juice from your next roast. Stuff pita with *3–4 slices of warm cooked lamb,* moistened with juices or gravy.

Corned Beef Pita. Use *3–5 slices cooked corned beef brushed with mustard.* Toast or not, as you wish. Particularly good with whole-wheat pita.

Open Sandwiches

Health Sandwich

Nutritionally this is just about everything you need in a sandwich: vary the ingredients with fresh things in season, such as tomatoes or other raw vegetables.

(ONE SANDWICH)

¼ cup (½ dL) shredded lettuce
¼ cup (½ dL) fresh bean
    sprouts
¼ cup (½ dL) grated Cheddar
    cheese
3 tablespoons grated carrot
2 tablespoons raisins

2 tablespoons chopped walnuts
1 slice good whole-grain bread
2 teaspoons honey
2 teaspoons lemon juice
4 tablespoons yogurt
2 tablespoons alfalfa sprouts

Toss the lettuce, bean sprouts, cheese, carrot, raisins, and walnuts together, and place on the bread. Combine the honey, lemon juice, and yogurt and blend until smooth. Spoon the dressing over the vegetables and sprinkle alfalfa sprouts on top.

Open-faced Swedish Sandwich

There are two requirements: dark bread and sweet butter. After that, the possibilities are endless.

(ONE SANDWICH)

1 slice thin dark bread
1–2 tablespoons sweet butter
1 slice smoked salmon

Capers
Dill sprigs

Spread the bread thickly with the butter. Arrange the salmon over it, and garnish with capers and dill.

Meatball Sandwich. Top the buttered bread instead with *sliced Swedish Meatballs* (p. 170), *pickled onions,* and *parsley.*

Tongue Sandwich. Lay over the buttered bread *2 slices tongue, 4 slices cucumber,* and a *dab of red currant jelly.*

Egg Sandwich. Lay over the buttered bread *1 hard-cooked egg, sliced,* and *2 anchovies.*

Silver Dollar

An extravaganza from the silver mine area of the Rockies, where sandwiches are big, open, and healthful. Vary it as you like, but keep in mind contrasts of texture and flavor.

(FOUR SANDWICHES)

8 broccoli spears
1 recipe Welsh Rabbit (p. 351)
4 large slices whole-grain
  bread, buttered
8 slices Canadian bacon, fried
  in butter

8 generous slices cooked turkey
  breast
2 tablespoons sesame seeds

Drop the broccoli spears into a large pot of salted boiling water and cook 5 minutes, then drain well. Meanwhile, make the rabbit. On each buttered bread slice, pile the bacon, turkey, and broccoli. Spoon on a generous portion of sauce and sprinkle with sesame seeds.

Golden Eagle. Use *8 slices cooked ham* instead of Canadian bacon, *8 asparagus spears* instead of broccoli, and top with *Cheese Sauce* (p. 265).

Crabmeat Special on English Muffins

(SERVES TWO)

2 English muffins
Butter
6 ounces (180 g) crabmeat,
  canned or fresh
3 tablespoons mayonnaise

Fresh lemon juice
Salt
Freshly ground pepper
1 large tomato, sliced thin
4 slices Swiss cheese

Split and toast the muffins and butter them while they are warm. Drain the crabmeat and toss with mayonnaise and a few drops of lemon juice, and salt and pepper to taste. Spread evenly over the muffin halves, cover with tomato slices, and top with cheese. Slip under the broiler until the cheese melts and is bubbly.

CRÊPES
About Crêpes
Crêpes are simply thin pancakes, also known as French pancakes, and the instructions for making them appear on page 497. They are a great boon to have on hand in your freezer so that you can whip up an impromptu but elegant meal with whatever bits and pieces you may have in your refrigerator, bound together

with a simple cream sauce. Use the proportions indicated in the recipes that follow and then create your own variations with whatever is at hand.

Chicken or Turkey Crêpes

(FILLING FOR 12 CRÊPES)

4 tablespoons butter
2 tablespoons finely chopped
  shallots or scallions
4 tablespoons flour
1¼ cups (3 dL) light cream
¾ cup (1¾ dL) chicken broth
¼ cup (½ dL) dry white wine

¼ teaspoon tarragon, crumbled
2 egg yolks, slightly beaten
2 cups (½ L) diced cooked
  chicken or turkey
Salt
1 recipe Crêpes or French
  Pancakes (p. 497)

Melt the butter in a saucepan, add the shallots or scallions, and cook, stirring, for 2 minutes. Add the flour, stir to blend, and slowly add 1 cup of the cream, stirring constantly. Add the broth, wine, and tarragon, and stir over medium-low heat until the sauce thickens. Cook for 5 minutes. Beat 3 tablespoons of hot sauce into the yolks, and then return the yolk-sauce mixture to the saucepan, stirring briskly. Cook 1 minute more, and remove from the heat. Mix half the sauce with the chicken or turkey and add salt to taste. Preheat the oven to 350°F (180°C). Fill each crêpe with 3 tablespoons of the filling. Roll and place seam side down in a baking dish approximately 13 × 9 × 2 inches. Thin the rest of the sauce with the remaining ¼ cup cream and spread it over the crêpes. Bake for 25 minutes, or until the sauce begins to bubble.

Chicken and Mushroom Filling. Omit the shallots or scallions and the tarragon. Sauté *2 cups sliced mushrooms* in the melted butter. Toast *1 cup slivered almonds* and add half of it to the sauce with the chicken. Sprinkle the rest over the crêpes just before serving.

Seafood Crêpes

Different varieties or combinations of seafood may be used: chopped shrimp, clams, mussels, scallops, or crabmeat, cooked lean fish, salmon, cod, or sole.

(SERVES SIX)

5 tablespoons butter
3 tablespoons minced shallots
  or scallions
4 tablespoons flour
1 cup (¼ L) hot chicken broth
  or fish stock
½ cup (1 dL) light cream
3 tablespoons dry sherry
2 cups (½ L) flaked cooked
  shellfish and/or fish

Tabasco to taste
Salt to taste
1 recipe Crêpes or French
  Pancakes (p. 497)
½ cup (1 dL) heavy cream
¼ teaspoon nutmeg
2 tablespoons minced parsley
Lemon slices

Preheat the oven to 350°F (180°C). Butter a baking dish approximately 13 × 9 × 2 inches. Sauté the shallots or scallions in the butter for 2 minutes. Sprinkle on the flour, stir, and cook for 2 minutes. Slowly add the hot broth or stock. Stir until thick and smooth, then add the cream and sherry. Cook for 5 minutes, stirring constantly, until sauce is smooth and thickened. Add the shellfish and/or fish, taste and season with Tabasco and salt. Stir a minute and remove from the heat. Fill each crêpe with 3 tablespoons of filling. Roll and place seam side down in the baking dish. Spoon any extra filling around the edges and between the crêpes. Lightly whip the heavy cream, add the nutmeg, and spread over the crêpes. Bake for 20–25 minutes or just until the sauce bubbles. Sprinkle the parsley on top and serve garnished with lemon slices.

Mushroom Crêpes

(SERVES SIX)

1¼ pounds (565 g) mushrooms
5 tablespoons butter
4 tablespoons minced shallots
  or scallions
5 tablespoons flour
1½ cups (3½ dL) hot chicken
  broth

1½ cups (3½ dL) heavy cream
Salt to taste
Freshly ground pepper
1 recipe Crêpes or French
  Pancakes(p. 497)

Preheat the oven to 350°F (180°C). Butter a shallow baking dish, approximately 13 × 9 × 2 inches. Slice the mushrooms, including the stems, and sauté them in the butter with the shallots or scallions, for about 4 minutes, until soft. Sprinkle on the flour and cook for 2 minutes. Slowly add the broth, stir until thick and smooth, then add the cream, and season with salt and pepper to taste. Continue cooking, stirring, for 5 minutes to reduce and thicken slightly. Spoon 3 tablespoons of filling in the center of each crêpe. Fold the ends over and place each crêpe end side down in the baking dish. Spoon the remaining mushroom filling over the top of the crêpes. Bake for 25 minutes or until sauce bubbles.

FILLED PASTA

Cannelloni

This cannelloni is made with crêpes, which gives the finished dish a delightful texture. It can also be made with the pasta that is sold as cannelloni, if you can find it; or make your own (p. 328). The same filling could go into manicotti and ravioli.

(SERVES EIGHT)

1 recipe Crêpes or French Pancakes (p. 497)

Filling

1 onion, chopped fine
3 tablespoons olive oil
1 clove garlic, minced
1 pound (450 g) lean ground
  beef
2 tablespoons cream
1 teaspoon oregano, crumbled
2 eggs

1½ pounds (675 g) fresh
  spinach, cooked, drained,
  and chopped; or one 10-
  ounce (285-g) package frozen
  spinach, thawed and drained
Salt to taste
Freshly ground pepper

Sauté the onion in the olive oil until just soft, then add the garlic and cook, stirring, a minute more. Remove to a bowl. Add the beef to the skillet, breaking it up, and cook until it loses its pinkness. Scrape into the onion and garlic, then add the cream, oregano, eggs, spinach, salt, and pepper. Mix vigorously with a wooden spoon or with your hands until the ingredients are well blended. Set aside.

Sauce I

6 tablespoons butter	¼ teaspoon nutmeg
6 tablespoons flour	Salt to taste
1 cup (¼ L) hot milk	Freshly ground pepper
1 cup (¼ L) heavy cream	

Melt the butter in a saucepan, add the flour, and cook, stirring constantly, over medium heat 3–4 minutes. Add the milk, stirring until the sauce is smooth and thick, then add the cream and continue to cook gently a few minutes. Sprinkle in the nutmeg, salt and pepper to taste. Set aside.

Sauce II
1½ cups (3½ dL) Tomato Sauce (p. 271)

To Assemble the Cannelloni: Preheat the oven to 375°F (190°C). Film the bottom of a shallow baking dish, about 13 × 9 × 2 inches, with tomato sauce. Fill each crêpe with 4 tablespoons of the filling. Roll up and place each crêpe seam side down in the baking dish. Proceed until the crêpes are filled and in a single layer. Spoon the white sauce, Sauce I, over the top and drizzle the remaining tomato sauce lengthwise in two rivulets over the white sauce. Bake for 40 minutes or until the sauce bubbles around the edges.

Cheese-stuffed Manicotti

Manicotti are large tubular pasta shapes, about 4 inches long and 1½ inches in diameter. Here are three fillings for manicotti: a mild cheese filling, a heartier meat filling (for which you could use cooked beef if you have some leftovers), and a subtle chicken or turkey filling. All are quite rich and the dish will serve eight as a first course or lunch dish, but for a main dinner dish, count on its serving only four with just a green salad.

(SERVES FOUR OR EIGHT)

8 manicotti, cooked, slightly
underdone, and drained

Stuffing

2 cups (½ L) ricotta or small-curd cottage cheese	1 teaspoon basil, crumbled
1 egg, slightly beaten	¼ teaspoon nutmeg
2 tablespoons minced parsley	½ teaspoon salt
4 tablespoons freshly grated Parmesan cheese	¼ teaspoon freshly ground pepper

Combine the ricotta or cottage cheese with remaining ingredients. Mix well and use it to stuff the manicotti.

Sauce

¼ pound (115 g) butter	2 cups (½ L) grated Monterey Jack cheese
7 tablespoons flour	
3 cups (¾ L) chicken broth	¼ teaspoon Tabasco
1 cup (¼ L) heavy cream	Salt to taste

Melt the butter in a saucepan. Stir in the flour and cook, stirring constantly, for 3 minutes. Slowly stir in the broth and cream and cook 3 minutes more, until sauce is smooth and thickened. Add the cheese, Tabasco, and salt and cook until the cheese melts.

To Assemble the Manicotti: Preheat the oven to 375°F (190°C). Film the bottom of an 11¾ × 7½ × 1¾-inch baking pan with the sauce. Make a single layer of the stuffed manicotti. Cover with the remaining sauce, cover with foil, and bake 1 hour.

Beef-Spinach Stuffed Manicotti

8 manicotti, cooked, slightly underdone, and drained
3 tablespoons olive oil
½ pound (225 g) lean ground beef
½ cup (1 dL) minced onion
1 cup (¼ L) freshly made bread crumbs
3 tablespoons freshly grated Parmesan cheese
3 eggs, slightly beaten

1½ pounds (675 g) fresh spinach, cooked, drained, and chopped, or 10-ounce (285-g) package frozen spinach, thawed, drained, and chopped
½ teaspoon salt
¼ teaspoon freshly ground pepper
2 cups Tomato Sauce (p. 271)

Preheat the oven to 375°F (190°C). Heat the olive oil in a skillet and add the beef and onion. Cook, breaking the meat into tiny bits with a fork, until it has lost its pinkness. Put the meat and onion in a bowl and mix with the bread crumbs, cheese, eggs, spinach, salt, and pepper. Stuff the cooked manicotti with the mixture and make a single layer in an 11¾ × 7½ × 1¾-inch baking dish, allowing space between the manicotti for expansion. Spoon the tomato sauce evenly over the top, cover with foil, and bake 45 minutes.

Chicken-stuffed Manicotti

Stuffing

8 manicotti cooked, slightly underdone, and drained
2 cups (½ L) finely chopped cooked chicken
4 tablespoons minced parsley
1 teaspoon thyme, crumbled

½ cup (1 dL) finely chopped celery
1 cup (¼ L) grated Monterey Jack cheese
3 tablespoons dry white wine
½ teaspoon salt

Combine the chicken with remaining ingredients. Divide the stuffing into 8 parts and stuff the manicotti.

Sauce

6 tablespoons butter
6 tablespoons flour
3 cups (¾ L) chicken broth
1 teaspoon tarragon, crumbled

1 cup (¼ L) grated Monterey Jack cheese
Salt to taste

Melt the butter in a saucepan and slowly stir in the flour, cooking 3 minutes. Slowly add the chicken broth, cooking 3 minutes more, until the sauce is smooth and thickened. Add the tarragon, cheese, and salt, and cook until the cheese is melted. Preheat the oven to 350°F (180°C). Spoon a light film of the sauce over the bottom of an 11¾ × 7½ × 1¾-inch baking dish. Make a single layer of manicotti, leaving room for expansion, and spread the remaining sauce over it. Cover with foil and bake 40 minutes.

Ravioli

1 recipe Homemade Italian
Noodles (p. 328)

Filling for Ravioli

½ cup (1 dL) finely chopped
cooked meat or chicken
½ cup (1 dL) finely chopped
cooked spinach
1 egg
2 tablespoons freshly grated
Parmesan cheese

¼ teaspoon salt
¼ teaspoon freshly ground
pepper
⅛ teaspoon nutmeg
¼ teaspoon oregano, crumbled

Combine all the filling ingredients in a bowl. Mix until well blended and set aside.

Cut the pasta dough into two even pieces and roll paper-thin into rectangular sheets. Put teaspoonfuls of filling on half the strips, dotting them 2 inches apart. Using a narrow brush, or your finger, moisten with water a rectangle around each mound of filling. Cover with the other sheet. Seal between the mounds of filling by pressing with your thumbs. Cut apart and let dry 2 hours before cooking.

Cooking Ravioli

Bring 6 quarts salted water to boil in a large pot. Drop in the ravioli and boil for 5–6 minutes. Stir gently with a wooden spoon to keep them from sticking to one another. Lift them out with a skimmer or strainer and place on a warmed platter.

Assembly of Ravioli

1 cup (¼ L) Tomato Sauce
(p. 271)

½ cup (1 dL) freshly grated
Parmesan cheese

Drizzle the sauce over the platter of ravioli and sprinkle with the cheese.

QUICHES AND PIZZAS

About Quiches

A quiche is a custard cooked in a tart shell. Learning to make quiches is a **very** useful addition to your cooking knowledge because you can use so many different things in the custard filling to vary it. Follow this first basic recipe and improvise with your fillings. Try 1½ cups of cooked vegetables, or different cheeses, or slices of sausage or ham. For other ideas see fillings of Savory Tarts on p. 68.

Cheese and Bacon Quiche

(SERVES SIX)

10 slices bacon, fried crisp and crumbled
1 partially baked Tart Pastry (p. 576), without sugar
4 eggs
2 cups (½ L) light cream
½ teaspoon salt
⅛ teaspoon nutmeg
Pinch of cayenne pepper
1¼ cups (3 dL) grated Swiss cheese

Preheat the oven to 425°F (220°C). Sprinkle the crumbled bacon over the bottom of the tart shell. Combine the eggs, cream, salt, nutmeg, and cayenne pepper in a bowl and beat to mix thoroughly. Sprinkle the cheese over the bacon and ladle the custard over all. Bake for 15 minutes at 425°F (220°C); then lower the heat to 350°F (180°C) and bake for 30 minutes more, or until a knife inserted in the center comes out clean. Serve in wedges, hot or cold.

Spinach Quiche. Omit the bacon and use only ½ cup grated Swiss cheese. Add *1 cup cooked, chopped spinach, well drained, and 2 tablespoons minced onions* sautéed in *1 tablespoon butter* to the custard mixture.

Onion Quiche. Omit the bacon and add to the custard mixture *2 onions, thinly sliced and sautéed in 3 tablespoons butter.*

Eggplant Quiche with Tomatoes and Olives

This is a particularly tasty filling for a quiche.

(SERVES SIX)

1 small eggplant
2 tomatoes, peeled, seeded, chopped, and drained
½ cup (1 dL) chopped onions
4 tablespoons olive oil
1 clove garlic, minced
¼ cup (½ dL) sliced black olives
Salt
¼ teaspoon freshly ground pepper
½ teaspoon oregano, crumbled
4 eggs
1½ cups (3½ dL) heavy cream
1 unbaked Tart Pastry (p. 576), without sugar
½ cup (1 dL) freshly grated Parmesan cheese

Preheat the oven to 350°F (180°C). Put the eggplant on an oiled pie plate and bake in the oven for 45 minutes to 1 hour or until tender when pierced with a fork. Turn up the oven to 425°F (220°C). When the eggplant is cool enough to handle, peel it and coarsely chop the pulp. Put in a colander with the tomatoes, press once gently to drain, and let stand for 15 minutes. Heat skillet and sauté the onions in the oil slowly until soft; add the garlic, eggplant and tomatoes, sauté 2 minutes, then add the olives, salt, pepper, and oregano. Cook 2 minutes more. Remove from the heat. Put the eggplant mixture in the colander and drain 2–3 minutes. Beat the eggs and cream in a bowl until mixed. Spread the eggplant mixture over the bottom of the tart shell. Pour the egg mixture over the eggplant and sprinkle with the cheese. Bake for 15 minutes, lower the heat to 300°F (150°C), and bake for 30 minutes more, or until a knife inserted in the center comes out clean. Serve in wedges, hot or cold.

About Pizzas

Homemade pizza is fun to make—the dough is no harder to put together than a bread dough and while the stretching may take a little practice you can always roll out the dough instead. And they taste so good fresh from the oven. Try other fillings, using the same proportions as those in the variations that follow this basic recipe.

Pizza

(TWO 12-INCH PIZZAS)

1 package dry yeast
4 cups (560 g) flour
Olive oil
2 teaspoons salt
2 cups (½ L) Tomato Sauce
   (p. 271)

2 cups (½ L) grated mozzarella
   cheese
2 teaspoons oregano, crumbled

Dissolve the yeast in ⅓ cup warm water. Add the flour, 2 tablespoons oil, 1 cup warm water, and the salt, and knead for 10 minutes. Put in an oiled bowl to rise, covered with plastic wrap. When the dough has doubled in bulk, about 2 hours, punch it down and divide in two. Let rest 5 minutes. Preheat the oven to 400°F (205°C). Roll the dough with a rolling pin or stretch it over your fists until you have two 12-inch circles. Place on pizza pans or cookie sheets and prick all over. On each circle, spoon 1 cup tomato sauce; sprinkle with 1 cup mozzarella and 1 teaspoon oregano. Drizzle with about 1 tablespoon olive oil. Let rest another 10 minutes and then bake for 25 minutes, until lightly brown. Cut into wedges and serve hot.

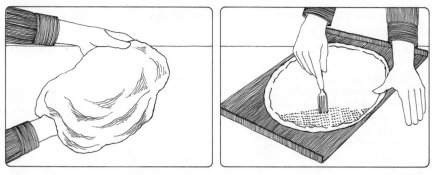

Pizza with Tomato-Mushroom Filling. Add to the filling *2 cups sliced mushrooms* sautéed 3 minutes in *2 tablespoons olive oil* and sprinkle *2 tablespoons capers* on top.

Pizza with Anchovy Filling. Arrange over the tomato filling *16 anchovy fillets* like the spokes of a wheel and decorate each pizza with *½ cup black olives.*

Pizza with Sausage. Distribute over the tomato filling *¾ pound peperoni* cut in thin slices, or *1 pound other cooked sausage* sliced.

TORTILLAS, TACOS, AND ENCHILLADAS

About Tortillas, Tacos, and Enchilladas

Remember, a tortilla is the plain flat pancake; the taco is a tortilla fried crisp with the sauce and filling tucked inside; and an enchillada is a filled soft tortilla that has sauce over it.

Enchilladas with Chicken and Green Sauce

(SERVES SIX)

½ cup (1 dL) peanut oil
12 flour tortillas
3 cups (¾ L) shredded cooked
  chicken
1 pound (450 g) grated
  Monterey Jack cheese
¼ cup (½ dL) heavy cream
½ cup (1 dL) finely chopped
  scallions
Salt

1½ cups (3½ dL) chopped
  Mexican green tomatoes or
  tomatillos verdes, fresh or
  canned (drain if canned)
1 cup (¼ L) chopped cilantro
4-ounce (115-g) can peeled
  green chilies, drained and
  chopped
1½ cups (3½ dL) sour cream

Heat the oil in a skillet. Put each tortilla into the hot oil for a few seconds, turning over so it softens. Stack the tortillas in a pan. Preheat the oven to 375°F (190°C). Oil a baking dish about 14 × 9 × 2 inches. Put some chicken, cheese, 1 teaspoon of the cream, a sprinkling of scallions, and salt to taste down the center of each tortilla. Roll them loosely and set side by side in the baking dish, with ends overlapping. Cover the dish snugly with foil and bake 30 minutes, until the cheese melts and bubbles a little. Meanwhile, prepare the sauce. Finely chop the tomatoes, cilantro, and green chilies. These can be run through the food processor very briefly so that the texture is in chunks instead of puréed. Stir in the sour cream until it is well blended. Remove the enchilladas from the oven, spoon a little of the green sauce over the top, and pass the rest of the sauce in a bowl.

Beef Filling for Tacos or Enchilladas

(FILLS TEN TO TWELVE TACOS OR ENCHILLADAS)

3 tablespoons vegetable oil
1 onion, finely chopped
2 cloves garlic, finely chopped
2 teaspoons chili powder

1 pound (450 g) lean ground
  beef, or 2 cups (½ L)
  chopped leftover beef
Salt to taste

Heat the oil in a large skillet, add the onion, and stir often until the onion is soft. Add the garlic and cook, stirring for 2 minutes; add the chili powder, beef, and salt. Mix and cook, stirring, breaking the meat into tiny bits, until the meat loses it pinkness. If using leftover beef, simply heat through. With a slotted spoon, leaving the fat behind in the skillet, remove the meat mixture to a bowl. Use about 2 tablespoons per taco or enchilada when filling.

Taco Filling

Crisp tacos may be filled with many different things, such as cold cooked meats or poultry or vegetables. This is a general outline of a typical taco filling. If the suggested taco sauce is too potent for those who shy away from raw onion and garlic, use sour cream instead. The

Taco Filling (continued)

sauce will keep for a few days, it is at its best if used as soon after making as possible, since the cilantro tends to fade quickly. If you can't find cilantro, try flat-leaved Italian parsley. Add more fresh cilantro if possible just before using.

(FILLING FOR 8 TACOS)

1 cup (¼ L) shredded or chopped cooked meat or poultry
8 fried tacos
1¼ cups (3 dL) shredded iceberg lettuce
½ cup (1 dL) finely chopped onion

1 cup (¼ L) chopped fresh tomato
Taco Sauce (following recipe) or approximately 2 cups (½ L) sour cream
1 cup (¼ L) grated Cheddar or Monterey Jack cheese

To Make Fried Tacos

In a skillet, heat ⅓ inch of oil, preferably peanut oil, to 360°F. Then slip a tortilla into the hot fat. After just one second, take a spatula and fold the tortilla in half. Insert the spatula between the folds and press down and fry for about 30 seconds to 1 minute until golden, then turn it over and repeat. Drain on paper towels, standing it curved side down like a rocking horse so the oil will drip off. Keep warm while you fry others.

Spread the meat or poultry across the bottom of the taco. Add the lettuce, and sprinkle with the onion and tomato. Spoon the sauce or sour cream on top, and evenly sprinkle with cheese. Serve.

Taco Sauce

(ABOUT 2 CUPS)

3 fresh tomatoes, chopped, or 1½ cups (3½ dL) canned tomatoes with juice, chopped
½ cup (1 dL) chopped onion
2 cloves garlic, chopped fine
¾ teaspoon salt

½ cup (1 dL) cilantro, washed, dried, and chopped
One half a 4-ounce (115-g) can peeled green chilies, drained and chopped
Pinch of sugar

Combine all ingredients with ¼ cup water in a bowl. Beat until well blended.

STUFFED VEGETABLES AND EGGS

Stuffed Zucchini

These are also good served cold.

(SERVES FOUR)

4 medium zucchini
4 tablespoons olive oil
½ cup (1 dL) finely chopped onion
1 clove garlic, minced
¼ pound (115 g) ground beef, or 1 cup (¼ L) leftover cooked beef or pork, ground

2 tomatoes, peeled, seeded, and chopped
½ cup (1 dL) freshly made dry bread crumbs
1 tablespoon minced parsley
Salt
Freshly ground pepper
¼ teaspoon basil, crumbled

Preheat the oven to 350°F (180°C). Oil a shallow baking dish large enough to hold the eight halves of zucchini in one layer. Trim the ends off the zucchini and cook in a large pot of boiling salted water for 3 minutes. Drain, cut in half lengthwise. Scoop out the pulp, leaving a sturdy shell; chop and reserve the pulp. Sauté the onion slowly in the oil for 5 minutes, then add the garlic and meat. Cook, stirring constantly, until the meat loses its color. Remove from the skillet and set aside. Pour off all but 2 tablespoons of oil from the skillet, heat again, and add the chopped zucchini pulp and tomatoes. Sauté for 1 minute and add to the meat mixture. Add the bread crumbs, parsley, salt, pepper, and basil. Toss together lightly until mixed. Fill the zucchini shells, without packing down, and place on baking dish. Bake for 30 minutes.

Stuffed Green Peppers

A good way to serve leftover meats in a fresh way.

(SERVES SIX)

3 large green peppers, halved and seeded
3 tablespoons olive oil
1 onion, finely chopped
1 pound (450 g) ground cooked or uncooked beef, pork, veal, or lamb
2 tomatoes, peeled and coarsely chopped

2 tablespoons minced parsley
1 tablespoon chopped fresh basil, or 1½ teaspoons dried, crumbled
Salt
¼ teaspoon freshly ground pepper
1 cup (¼ L) freshly made bread crumbs

Preheat the oven to 350°F (180°C). Oil a shallow baking dish. Cook the peppers in boiling water for 2 minutes; drain and set aside. Heat the oil in a skillet and add the chopped onion. Cook, stirring, until soft. If using uncooked meat, add it and cook lightly for 5–10 minutes. Otherwise, mix the onion and meat together, then add the tomatoes, parsley, basil, salt to taste, and pepper, combining thoroughly. Lightly fill each pepper half with some of the meat mixture. Sprinkle the tops with bread crumbs. Bake for 30–40 minutes.

Stuffed Cucumbers

Minced clams or bits of leftover fish or chicken mixed with buttered crumbs inside a hollowed-out cucumber—a nice first course, luncheon, or light supper, served hot or cold. The cucumber is tender but firm; its taste mingles with the filling.

(SERVES FOUR)

2 large cucumbers
1 cup (¼ L) canned, drained minced clams or chopped, cooked fish or chicken
1 cup (¼ L) freshly made bread crumbs
2 tablespoons butter, melted

1 teaspoon finely chopped chives
Salt to taste
Pinch of cayenne pepper
1 cup (¼ L) chicken broth

Cut the cucumbers in half lengthwise and carefully scoop out the seeds and centers with a teaspoon. If they have been waxed, peel off the skins. Mix the clams, fish, or chicken with the bread crumbs, butter, chives, salt, and cayenne;

toss well. Divide the filling evenly, and lightly fill each cucumber half; don't pack the filling down. Put the halves together and tie with string. Place the tied cucumbers in a pan, add the chicken broth, cover, and simmer for 20–25 minutes. Slice in the middle and serve one-half per person.

Stuffed Eggplant

Eggplant and lamb always seem to marry well. This is a good dish to make when you have some leftover roast lamb or stew with some juice; if the lamb is dry and no gravy or juice is left, use canned tomatoes to moisten the filling.

(SERVES FOUR)

1 medium or 2 small eggplants	¾ cup (1¾ dL) lamb gravy,
Salt	drippings, or stew liquid, or
4–5 tablespoons olive oil	1 cup (¼ L) canned
1 onion, chopped	tomatoes, chopped, with
1 garlic clove, minced	juice
(optional)	Freshly ground pepper
2 cups (½ L) minced or ground	1 dozen whole almonds,
cooked lamb	blanched
1½ cups (3½ dL) cooked rice	¼ cup (½ dL) chopped parsley

Cut the eggplant(s) in half lengthwise. Leaving the shell intact, about ¼ inch thick, carefully scoop out the flesh and chop into rough pieces. Place in colander, sprinkle liberally with salt, and drain for at least 30 minutes. Salt the empty shells and turn upside down to drain. Heat the oven to 350°F (180°C). Rinse off the eggplant pieces, pat dry, and sauté in hot olive oil in a large skillet until browned on all sides. Add the onion and a little more oil if necessary and cook until almost soft. Add the garlic (if you wish), the lamb, rice, and lamb sauce or tomatoes. Mix well, cook a few minutes, add pepper and salt to taste, then pile into the drained eggplant shells. Toss the almonds in a little hot oil to brown, and poke them into the eggplant mixture at intervals. Bake 50 minutes. Sprinkle parsley over the tops before serving.

Stuffed Cabbage Leaves

A wonderful way to transform cooked beef or pork, particularly if you save some sauce—meat juices, drippings, or leftover gravy—to add flavor and moisture to the filling. If you use ham or corned beef, add 1 teaspoon mustard in place of leftover gravy. The inner part of the cabbage, chopped and sautéed with a little butter and cream, makes a vegetable course for another meal.

(SERVES FOUR)

1 head cabbage	½ teaspoon rosemary, crumbled
2 onions, chopped	Salt
4 tablespoons butter	Freshly ground pepper
1 teaspoon sweet paprika	¾ cup (1¾ dL) meat sauce—
2 cups (½ L) minced cooked	gravy, juice, or strong
beef or pork	bouillon
2 cups (½ L) cooked rice	16-ounce (450-g) can tomatoes
¼ cup (½ dL) chopped parsley	

Preheat the oven to 350°F (180°C). Cut a circle around the core of the cabbage to loosen the leaves, then drop them into a large pot of boiling, salted water. Lift out after 3–4 minutes. Carefully select 8 of the large outer leaves. Lay them out flat, and cut out a small V from the root end to remove the hard spine. Sauté

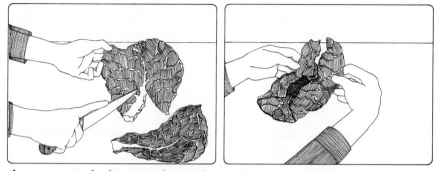

the onions in the butter with paprika until soft. Leaving 2 tablespoons of the onion in the pan, spoon the rest into a bowl and add the meat, rice, parsley, most of the rosemary, some salt and pepper, and ½ cup of the meat sauce or other liquid. Place one-eighth of the filling in the center of each leaf. Fold in the sides, then roll to make a neat sausage-shaped package. Place the rolls, seam side down, in a shallow baking dish that holds them snugly. Add the tomatoes and their juice to the onions remaining in the skillet, breaking them up roughly. Add the remaining ¼ cup meat sauce and boil hard for 5 minutes until the liquid is somewhat reduced. Season to taste with salt, pepper, and a pinch more rosemary, and pour

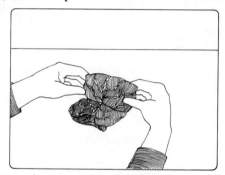

around the stuffed cabbage leaves. Cover loosely with foil and bake for 50 minutes.

Stuffed Onions

Large round Spanish onions that range in color from yellow to red are ideal for this dish. You could use tongue or corned beef instead of ham—any tasty cooked meat.

(SERVES FOUR)

4 large onions
6 tablespoons butter, melted
Salt
Freshly ground pepper
½ cup (1 dL) coarsely chopped cooked ham
⅓ cup (¾ dL) freshly made bread crumbs
1½ teaspoons finely chopped parsley
¼ teaspoon nutmeg
2 tablespoons dry sherry

Preheat the oven to 300°F (150°C). Butter a casserole or baking dish large enough to hold the onions. Put the onions in a pan of boiling water to cover, and parboil for 10 minutes. Drain and refresh under cold water. Scoop out the centers, but leave a sturdy shell. Brush the insides with a little of the melted butter, and sprinkle with salt and pepper. Set aside. Combine the ham, crumbs, parsley, and nutmeg in a small bowl, add salt and pepper to taste, and toss until mixed well. Divide the ham filling and stuff the four onions. Add the sherry to the remaining melted butter, and pour over each of the onions. Cover and bake for about 1 hour or until tender.

Stuffed Eggs

If you want the eggs to look elegant, use a pastry tube to pipe the creamy yolk mixture into the white. Imaginative garnishes such as a fat caper on top or a cross of slivers of green or red pepper, a slice of olive or pickle, a sprinkling of fresh herbs or watercress, can make stuffed eggs particularly lovely.

1 egg, hard-boiled (p. 338)	Freshly ground pepper
2 teaspoons mayonnaise	½ teaspoon minced parsley or
¼ teaspoon Dijon mustard	fresh herbs (optional)
Salt	

Shell the egg and slice it in half lengthwise. Remove the yolk and mash it with the mayonnaise, mustard, and salt and pepper to taste until it is smoothly blended and creamy. Stuff it into the hollow of the egg white. Sprinkle parsley or fresh herbs on top, if desired.

Anchovy-stuffed Eggs. Omit the mustard and add ¼–½ *teaspoon anchovy paste*, to taste.

Ham-stuffed Eggs. Add 1 *teaspoon finely chopped ham* to the filling.

Cheese-stuffed Eggs. Use 1½ *teaspoons freshly grated Parmesan cheese* instead of the mustard.

Curried-stuffed Eggs. Add ½ *teaspoon curry powder* to the filling.

CEREALS, RICE, BEANS, & PASTA

Cereals, rice, beans, and pasta: these are wholesome foods that fill the stomach and warm the heart, that provide energy for a snowy morning and restore courage at the end of a long day. Basic foods for the world's poorer nations, they often replace meat on the American table as well, for, in the right combinations, they provide a valuable source of low-fat protein.

ABOUT CEREALS

Grains are the dried seeds of grass plants; those that are used for food are called cereals. About one-quarter of our diet is made up of grains such as wheat, rice, corn, oats, barley, and rye.

All cereals contain a high percentage of carbohydrate, with varying amounts of protein, minerals, and vitamins. Although they don't provide complete protein by themselves, they become highly valuable foods when they are mixed with milk products, eggs, dried beans, or animal proteins. In many parts of the world where meat is scarce, people live largely on grains.

Breakfast Cereals

Be careful when you are buying cold cereals for your family that you get ones that supply real food value. Many whole-grain or enriched cold cereals are available now. Read the list of contents on cereal boxes carefully: sugar appears under many guises, and "refining" often means the removal of nutritional value. If you want real value and goodness, try making your own granola (p. 311).

Consider sometimes starting the day with an "old-fashioned" hot cereal! A steaming bowl of whole-grain cereal is a complete meal. "Real meal" cereals like Wheatena, hominy grits, cornmeal, and oatmeal will increase in bulk as they are cooked in liquid. Add more liquid for a thinner cereal; add more cooking time for a smoother cereal. Use skim milk instead of water for extra nutrition, and cover the pot at the end of the cooking time to prevent a crust from forming.

Stir in some applesauce, nuts, or chopped dried fruits and top with a big spoonful of yogurt, honey, brown sugar, or maple syrup—you will face the morning well fortified.

Lunch and Dinner Cereals

Cereals often take the place of potatoes at lunch or dinner. They are low in fat, high in vitamins, and, combined with a little cheese or served with meat, are a good source of protein. Cereals are also inexpensive and satisfying.

Turkey is well served by a casserole of buckwheat and onions; hominy grits are delicious with fried ham; bland cornmeal is a natural background for spicy sausages. A new dinner can be created when leftover meat and pan drippings are mixed into rice or barley. And, if calories are a concern, it's comforting to know that it takes 1½ cups of rice or 2⅔ cups of cooked cornmeal to equal the calories in one small, unadorned hamburger!

Kinds of Cereals

Barley. Barley was probably the first cereal cultivated by man. In Scotland it is exceedingly popular, used in soups as a thickener, as a porridge, in cake, and in the distillation of Scotch whisky. Pot barley has had the outer hull removed; pearled barley has been processed to remove both hull and germ, leaving small, cream-colored balls that look like pearls. Cooked barley has a mild flavor and chewy texture; it is very good steamed and buttered, particularly delicious served with lamb.

Wheat Berries. The health-food movement is responsible for the popularity of this delicious, chewy grain, made from whole-wheat kernels with only the outer layer removed. Without the strawlike chaff or husk, wheat berries have a nutlike taste and are bursting with nutrients. They are very good mixed with hot rice, or chilled and added to salads.

Bulgur Wheat. Bulgur is made by boiling, drying, and cooking whole-wheat grains. It resembles brown rice in its chewy texture, hearty flavor, and nutritional makeup. Because bulgur is dehydrated, it must be reconstituted by soaking in liquid for an hour if you are using it raw, as in a salad, but not when it is cooked. Use a ratio of one part bulgur to two parts water, broth, tomato juice, or other liquid, depending on the flavor you wish to add. Long popular in the Middle East, bulgur is increasingly familiar here, where it is used in soups, stuffings, breakfast cereals, salads, and as a side dish with meat and poultry.

Cornmeal. The only native American grain, corn was used by the Indians before Columbus and was introduced to Europe by the early explorers of this continent. Cornmeal is made of ground corn kernels. Water-ground meal retains the vitamin-rich germ, while commercially ground meal is made from only the starchy part of the kernel. As with all ground kernels, the texture of the meal can range from coarse to fine, depending on the dish being prepared. A coarse grind is ideal for Italian polenta, while finer grinds are usually used for American southern favorites such as spoon bread, muffins, and mush, although some prefer a coarser texture in these dishes as well. Cornmeal dishes are traditionally cooked in heavy iron pans to encourage the formation of a thick, dark crust. Both yellow and white cornmeal are available. The difference is really only in the color, but there are strong partisans of each kind in different regions of the country.

Hominy. Hominy is a staple in the American South: dried corn that has had its hull and germ removed with lye or soda. Hominy grits are ground hominy grains. They are white, about the size of toast crumbs. Cooked, their texture is thick and chewy and their flavor rather mild. You can stir in a keen-flavored cheese, spread the grits in a casserole with more cheese on top, and bake until the cheese melts. Serve grits with fish, ham, or sausage, or make them into a breakfast cereal with raisins, butter, and brown sugar. The unflavored porridge is delicious cooled, sliced, and fried in butter.

Buckwheat. Buckwheat has nothing to do with wheat: wheat is a grass, whereas buckwheat is a low, shrublike plant producing a seed that is often ground into flour. Buckwheat flour has a distinctive flavor that is popular in Asian and Russian cooking and in American pancakes. When the seed is parboiled, dried, and coarsely ground, it is called buckwheat groats or kasha. Groats make wonderfully hearty side dishes for turkey, duck, venison, and other game.

CEREALS

Granola

(10 CUPS)

¾ cup (1¾ dL) peanut oil
4 cups (1 L) rolled oats
½ cup (1 dL) sesame seeds
½ cup (1 dL) wheat germ
1 cup (¼ L) soy grits
1 cup (¼ L) shredded coconut
1 cup (¼ L) honey

1 teaspoon vanilla
¾ cup (1¾ dL) sunflower seeds
1 cup (¼ L) roasted unsalted
   peanuts
1 cup (¼ L) raisins
Salt

Preheat the oven to 350°F (180°C). Bring 1 cup water to a boil, and mix it with the oil. In a large heavy pot combine the oats, sesame seeds, wheat germ, soy grits, and coconut. Combine the honey with the oil and water and vanilla, stirring well, and mix into the dry ingredients a little at a time; when all the particles are covered with the honey mixture, put the pot in the oven and toast for 15 minutes. Stir well. Reduce the heat to 275°F (135°C) and repeat the process, stirring every 10 to 15 minutes for 1½–2 hours, until the granola is thoroughly toasted. Let the granola cool, then stir in the sunflower seeds, peanuts, raisins, and salt to taste. To store, refrigerate in a tightly closed jar.

Barley

(SERVES FOUR)

Salt
1½ cups (3½ dL) pearl barley

Bring 3 cups water to a boil with about 1 teaspoon salt. Stir in the barley, cover, and simmer for 25 minutes.

Barley in Broth. Substitute *3 cups chicken or beef broth* for the water.

Barley and Rice. Substitute *½ cup white rice* for ½ cup of the barley.

Barley and Walnuts. Add *½ cup chopped walnuts* just before serving.

Curried Barley. Add *1 teaspoon curry powder* and *¼ cup raisins* to the water before adding the barley.

Barley Casserole

Serve by itself or with cold sliced beef or chicken.

(SERVES FOUR)

3 tablespoons butter
1 cup (¼ L) barley
1 small onion, chopped
¼ cup (½ dL) finely chopped
  green pepper
½ cup (1 dL) cashews,
  chopped

3 cups (¾ L) chicken broth,
  boiling
Salt
Freshly ground pepper

Melt the butter in a saucepan. Add the barley and onion, and cook, stirring often, until the onion is slightly cooked and the grains of barley are coated. Add the green pepper and cook 2 minutes more. Add the cashews, boiling chicken broth, and salt and pepper to taste. Cover and simmer 25 minutes; or bake for 1 hour at 350°F (180°C) in a covered casserole.

Wheat Berries

(SERVES SIX)

1 cup (¼ L) wheat berries
4 tablespoons butter
Salt to taste

Combine the wheat berries with 4 cups water in a saucepan. Bring to a boil and cook gently for 2 minutes. Remove from the heat, cover, and soak for 1 hour. Return to the heat and simmer 1 hour more. Stir in the butter and salt.

Bulgur

One cup of dry bulgur becomes three when it is cooked. Vary by using different liquids in place of water, such as beef or chicken broth, tomato juice, orange juice, or milk.

(SERVES FOUR)

2 tablespoons butter
1 cup (¼ L) bulgur

Salt
Freshly ground pepper

Melt the butter in a saucepan. Stir in the bulgur and cook, stirring, for 2 minutes. Add salt and pepper, pour in 2 cups water, cover, and simmer 15 minutes.

Bulgur Pilaf. Cook ¼ teaspoon *turmeric* in the butter. Use *beef broth* instead of water, and add *½ cup frozen peas* and *1 small onion, chopped and sautéed.*

Bulgur Stuffing. Use *chicken broth* instead of water and add *½ cup chopped celery, ½ cup chopped onion,* and *½ teaspoon sage, crumbled.*

Cornmeal Mush

Good with fried chicken and cream gravy or with fried pork.

(SERVES SIX)

1 cup (¼ L) cornmeal
1½ teaspoons salt

Mix the cornmeal with 1 cup cold water. In a saucepan, bring 3 cups water and the salt to a boil. Add the cornmeal mixture to the boiling water and cook, stirring often, over medium heat for 7 minutes or until thick.

Fried Cornmeal Mush

Good both as an accompaniment to meats and for breakfast with butter, honey, or maple syrup.

(SERVES SIX)

1 cup (¼ L) cornmeal
6 tablespoons bacon fat, or
   4 tablespoons butter plus
   2 tablespoons oil

Follow the directions for Cornmeal Mush (preceding recipe). Spread the mush in a loaf pan and refrigerate. When it is thoroughly chilled, cut in ½-inch slices. Melt the fat or butter and oil in a skillet and fry the slices until golden on both sides.

Spoon Bread

A southern favorite with spareribs, poultry, ham, and pork.

(SERVES SIX)

1 cup (¼ L) yellow cornmeal   4 eggs, well beaten
1 teaspoon salt   1 cup (¼ L) milk or buttermilk
2 tablespoons butter

Preheat the oven to 400°F (205°C). Butter a 1½-quart casserole. Bring 2 cups water to a boil. Add the cornmeal and salt slowly in a steady stream and cook, stirring, for 1 minute. Beat in the butter, eggs, and milk, beating until smooth. Pour into the casserole and bake about 40 minutes, until a straw inserted in the center comes out clean.

Light Spoon Bread

(SERVES SIX)

1 cup (¼ L) white cornmeal   1 teaspoon salt
1 tablespoon butter, melted   1 teaspoon sugar
3 eggs, separated   1 teaspoon baking powder
1 cup (¼ L) buttermilk   ¼ teaspoon baking soda

Preheat the oven to 375°F (190°C). Butter a 2-quart casserole. Bring 1½ cups water to a boil, and pour it over the cornmeal in a bowl, briskly stirring so no lumps form. Add the butter, egg yolks, buttermilk, salt, sugar, baking powder, and baking soda. Stir until well blended. Beat the egg whites until stiff but not dry. Gently stir a fourth of the whites into the cornmeal mixture, then fold in the remaining whites. Spoon into the casserole. Bake about 45 minutes or until the center is dry when a straw is inserted.

Polenta

A more recent import from northern Italy, polenta is not unlike the old southern standby cornmeal mush. Buy coarsely ground cornmeal at an Italian delicatessen or health-food store. Serve the polenta with a sauce chunky with mushrooms, sausages, and cheese.

(SERVES SIX)

Salt
2 cups (½ L) coarsely ground
  cornmeal
6 tablespoons olive oil
1 large onion, chopped
2 Italian sausages, in ½-inch
  slices

½ pound (225 g) mushrooms,
  sliced
2 cups (½ L) Italian Tomato
  Sauce II (p. 271)
1 tablespoon basil, crumbled
½ pound (225 g) Cheddar or
  Monterey Jack cheese, cubed

Add 1 tablespoon salt to 7 cups boiling water and slowly stir in the cornmeal in a thin, steady stream. Cook, stirring occasionally, for 20 minutes, until the polenta is stiff and leaves the sides of the pan. Spread in a baking dish to a depth of 1½ to 2 inches. Cover, refrigerate, and use later, or keep warm in a 250°F (120°C) oven while making the sauce. For the sauce, heat 3 tablespoons of the oil in a saucepan, add the onion, and cook over medium heat until soft. Add the sausages and cook another 3–4 minutes; stir in the mushrooms and cook 2 minutes more. Add the tomato sauce, basil, and salt to taste. Cover and simmer for 30 minutes. If the sauce becomes too thick, add ½ cup water, stir, and continue to cook. Add the remaining 3 tablespoons oil and cook 10 minutes more. Remove the polenta from the oven and dot with cubes of cheese. Turn the oven up to 350°F (180°C) and bake the polenta and cheese until it is hot and the cheese is melted. Cut in squares and spoon the sauce over the top.

Hominy Grits

(SERVES FOUR)

1 cup (¼ L) hominy grits
1 teaspoon salt

Bring 4 cups of water to boil in a saucepan. Slowly stir in the grits and salt and cook 3–5 minutes (for quick-cooking grits, otherwise 15–20 minutes), stirring occasionally, until thick.

Fried Grits

Good as a meat accompaniment and with eggs, sausage, and maple syrup for breakfast.

(SERVES SIX)

1 cup (¼ L) hominy grits
6 tablespoons bacon fat, oil,
  butter, or combination

2 eggs, beaten
1½ cups (3½ dL) freshly made
  bread crumbs

Cook the grits as directed (preceding recipe). Spread in a loaf pan, refrigerate until thoroughly chilled, then cut into ½-inch slices. Melt the bacon fat or butter and oil in a large skillet. Dip the slices into the egg and then into the crumbs, coating both sides completely. Place in the skillet and cook for 3 minutes on each side or until hot and golden brown.

Hominy Grits Casserole

(SERVES SIX)

1 cup (¼ L) hominy grits
3 cups (¾ L) milk
1 teaspoon salt
2 eggs, lightly beaten
6 tablespoons butter

1 cup (¼ L) grated Cheddar or
   Monterey Jack cheese
½ cup (1 dL) canned green
   chilies, rinsed and chopped

Preheat the oven to 350°F (180°C). Stir the hominy grits into the milk in a saucepan, add the salt, and cook over medium heat, stirring often so the mixture doesn't scorch. When it is thick, remove from the heat and add the eggs and 1 cup water, stirring vigorously. Return to the burner and cook until thickened again. Stir in the butter, cheese, and chilies. Spread in a casserole and bake for 30 minutes.

Alace's Spoon Bread

The surprising texture of canned whole hominy mixed with hominy grits in a baked pudding.

(SERVES FOUR)

2 eggs, well beaten
1 cup (¼ L) milk
½ cup (1 dL) hominy grits
½ cup (1 dL) canned hominy,
   drained

1 teaspoon baking powder
3 tablespoons butter, softened
½ teaspoon salt

Preheat the oven to 375°F (190°C). Butter a 1½-quart casserole. Combine all ingredients, and beat until well blended. Pour into the casserole and bake 50–60 minutes, or until a straw inserted in the center comes out clean.

Buckwheat Groats or Kasha

(SERVES FOUR)

1 egg, slightly beaten
1 cup (¼ L) buckwheat groats

2 tablespoons butter
Salt to taste

Put the egg and groats in a bowl and mix well. Put the mixture in a dry skillet and cook over medium-high heat, stirring constantly, until each grain is separate and dry; set aside. Heat a saucepan, add the egg-groats mixture, and quickly pour in 2 cups boiling water. Cover and simmer for 15 minutes. Add the butter and salt; stir, cover, and cook 5 minutes more.

Kasha in Broth. Substitute *2 cups chicken or beef broth* for the water.

Kasha with Onion. Sauté *1 large onion, chopped,* in *2 tablespoons oil* and add to the saucepan with the boiling water.

Kasha with Mushrooms. Sauté *1 cup sliced mushrooms* in *2 tablespoons butter,* and add to the saucepan with the boiling water. Just before serving, stir in *½ cup yogurt.*

RICE

Rice is the staple food for most of the world's population. Although it comes in many forms, we know only a few in this country.

Kinds of Rice

White Rice. White rice has had its outer covering removed by a process called "polishing" that takes away many of the B vitamins as well; nonetheless, it remains more popular than unpolished rice. *Long-grain white rice,* when it is cooked, tends to separate nicely into individual fluffy grains. Kernels of *short-grain white rice* cook up tender and moist, clinging together; they are best used in croquettes, puddings, and rice rings.

Converted Rice. Converted rice is hulled under moist conditions, steamed, and dried so that all the nutrients are incorporated back into the grain and not lost. It always tastes a little pasty and doesn't have the same good texture as plain long-grain rice.

Brown Rice. Brown rice is superior to white rice in nutrients because it retains its outer coating. Although it takes longer to cook than white rice, its good, nutty flavor and high food value are making it ever more popular.

Dehydrated, Precooked Rice, usually known as Instant or Minute Rice. Dehydrated, precooked rice, the sort you rehydrate by covering with boiling water and soaking for five minutes, is the least desirable kind of rice. The exterior has an unnatural fluffiness when cooked and the center seems raw. It is at best a convenience food to be used when in a hurry.

Wild Rice. Wild rice, also known as Indian rice or water oats, is not a rice at all, but the seed from a grass that grows wild along the edges of lakes in Minnesota, Wisconsin, and southern Canada. There it is harvested in the old-time way by Indians who paddle along the water's edge, bending the grasses and beating the seeds into their boats. It is expensive, dark in color, strong, and intriguing in taste, well worth an occasional indulgence.

Boiled Rice

There is no reason to worry about failures if you cook rice like pasta in lots of boiling salted water and watch the timing.

(3 CUPS WHITE RICE OR 2 CUPS BROWN RICE)

1 teaspoon salt
1 cup (¼ L) rice

Bring about 3 quarts water and salt to a boil in a deep pot. Trickle the rice slowly into the water so that it doesn't stop boiling. Don't stir, but give the pan a shake so the rice levels. Keep the water boiling over medium-high heat. White rice will be done in 15–18 minutes; brown rice will be done in 35–40 minutes. Test at the minimum time by removing a few grains with a slotted spoon; bite into the kernel—it should be firm, not mushy and splayed out at the ends. If in doubt, it is better to undercook rice slightly and steam it longer at the end, particularly if you are planning to hold the rice 10 or 15 minutes before serving. Drain the rice in a colander. Keep warm by placing the colander over gently boiling water, covering the rice with a dish towel.

Steamed Rice

Steamed white rice will cook in 20 minutes; brown rice in 40 minutes.

(3 CUPS WHITE RICE OR 2 CUPS BROWN RICE)

¾ teaspoon salt
1 teaspoon butter (optional)
1 cup (¼ L) rice

Using a deep, heavy-bottomed pot, bring to a boil 2 cups water, the salt, and the butter, if desired. Add the rice slowly so that the boiling doesn't stop. Cover and simmer without stirring and don't remove the cover for 20 minutes. Then check: the rice should be just soft and the water absorbed. Fluff up with a fork before serving.

Rice with Peanuts. Add *1 cup finely chopped celery* and *½ cup chopped salted peanuts* to the rice before cooking.

Mushroom Rice. Just before serving add *¼ teaspoon nutmeg* and *1 cup chopped mushrooms,* sautéed in *2 tablespoons butter.*

Baked Rice

A nice way to serve rice when the meat is rather plain and the casserole, popped in the oven about a half an hour before serving, is all ready to come to the table.

(SERVES FOUR)

⅓ cup (¾ dL) chopped onion
2 tablespoons butter
1 cup (¼ L) rice

2 bouillon cubes, chicken or beef

Preheat the oven to 375°F (190°C). Sauté the onion in the butter about 3 minutes. Add the rice and stir, cooking just long enough to coat it, 2 or 3 minutes. Pour in 2 cups water, bring to the boil, stir in the bouillon cubes, dissolve, and mix well. Turn into a 1-quart casserole, cover, and bake for 30 minutes.

Baked Rice with Pepper and Ham. Add *½ cup chopped green* or *red pepper* along with the onion. After the rice has been coated, add up to *1 cup chopped ham.* Sprinkle the top with *2–3 tablespoons Swiss* or *Parmesan cheese* and remove the cover for the last 5 minutes of baking.

Saffron Rice with Raisins and Pine Nuts. Before turning the mixture into the casserole, remove ¼ cup of the hot liquid and pour over *⅛ teaspoon crumbled saffron;* let steep 5 minutes. Remove to the casserole and stir in *½ cup raisins* and *2 tablespoons pine nuts.*

Rice with Cheese

If you use brown rice and mix wheat germ with the cracker crumbs, you'll have a fine vegetarian dish.

Rice with Cheese (continued)

(SERVES FOUR)

4 cups (1 L) cooked rice,
  slightly underdone
1 cup (¼ L) grated Cheddar
  cheese
Pinch of cayenne pepper

Salt to taste
4 tablespoons butter
1 cup (¼ L) milk
1 cup (¼ L) buttered cracker
  crumbs

Preheat the oven to 350°F (180°C). Butter a 1½-quart baking dish. Spread half the rice on the bottom of the baking dish, sprinkle with half the cheese, cayenne pepper, and salt, and dot with 2 tablespoons of the butter. Repeat. Finish by pouring the milk evenly over all and sprinkling the top with buttered crumbs. Bake for 30 minutes.

Green Rice

A creamy, green-flecked dish to go with tuna, chicken, or chipped beef.

(SERVES FOUR)

1½ cups (3½ dL) cooked rice,
  slightly underdone
1 cup (¼ L) milk
4 tablespoons butter, melted
½ cup (1 dL) grated Swiss
  cheese

½ onion, chopped fine
½ cup (1 dL) finely chopped
  parsley, spinach, watercress,
  or dandelion greens
1 egg, well beaten
Salt to taste

Preheat the oven to 350°F (180°C). Butter a 1½-quart casserole or ring mold. Combine all ingredients. Pour into the casserole or mold and bake uncovered for 40 minutes or until set.

Turkish Pilaf I

Pilaf is a seasoned rice dish common to many Eastern countries. It can be a whole meal made with fish, poultry, or meat, or a simple side dish made with herbs, spices, nuts, or raisins.

(SERVES FOUR)

3 tablespoons olive oil
3 tablespoons finely chopped
  onion
1 cup (¼ L) long-grain rice

½ teaspoon salt
¼ teaspoon freshly ground
  pepper
2 cups (½ L) beef broth

Heat the oil in a saucepan. Add the onion and cook, stirring often, until soft. Add the rice and cook over low heat, stirring constantly, for 3 minutes. Add the salt, pepper, and beef broth. Cover and simmer 20 minutes or transfer to a covered casserole and bake in a 350°F (180°C) oven for 1 hour.

Mushroom Pilaf. Add the broth to *1 cup chopped mushrooms* that have been sautéed in *2 tablespoons butter.*

Chicken Pilaf. Substitute *2 cups chicken broth* for the beef broth, and with the broth add *1 cup diced cooked chicken* and *½ teaspoon tarragon, crumbled.*

Turkish Pilaf II

Fragrant with spices, this pilaf is good with poultry and curries.

(SERVES FOUR)

6 tablespoons butter
1 cup (¼ L) rice
1½ cups (3½ dL) finely
  chopped onion
½ teaspoon salt
1 bay leaf, crumbled

¼ teaspoon cinnamon
½ cup (1 dL) raisins
½ cup (1 dL) sliced, toasted
  almonds
2 cups (½ L) chicken broth

Preheat the oven to 375°F (190°C). Melt the butter in a skillet. Stir in the rice and cook over low heat until all the grains glisten. Add the onion and cook, stirring, until they are soft. Put the mixture into a 1½-quart casserole. Add the salt, bay leaf, cinnamon, raisins, and almonds. Heat the broth to a boil, mix with all the ingredients, cover, and bake for 45 minutes.

Spanish Rice

(SERVES FOUR)

4 tablespoons olive oil
1 onion, chopped
1 small green pepper, chopped
2 cloves garlic, minced
1 rib celery, diced
1 cup (¼ L) chopped
  mushrooms

2 large tomatoes, peeled and
  chopped
1 cup (¼ L) long-grain rice
½ teaspoon salt
¼ teaspoon freshly ground
  pepper
2 cups (½ L) chicken broth

Preheat the oven to 375°F (190°C). Lightly oil a 2-quart casserole. Heat the olive oil in a skillet and add the onion, green pepper, garlic, celery, and mushrooms. Cook over medium-low heat, stirring often, for 5 minutes. Transfer to a casserole and add the tomatoes, rice, salt, and pepper. Pour in the broth, stir, cover, and bake 30 minutes. Stir again and bake for another 30 minutes.

Sauternes Rice

An elegant side dish with game hens, chicken, or veal.

(SERVES EIGHT)

½ cup (1 dL) currants
5 tablespoons butter
2 cloves garlic, halved
2 cups (½ L) long-grain rice
1½ cups (3½ dL) dry white
  wine

1 tablespoon salt
¼ teaspoon freshly ground
  pepper
¼ teaspoon nutmeg
¼ teaspoon allspice
2 teaspoons sugar

Pour 1 cup boiling water over the currants. Soak for 10 minutes, drain, and set aside. Melt the butter in a skillet. Add the garlic and mash with the back of a fork. Cook for 1 minute to flavor the butter and then remove the garlic. Add the rice and cook, stirring, for 2 minutes. Bring 3 cups water to a boil with the wine in a deep pot. Add the buttered rice with remaining ingredients. Cover and simmer 25 minutes. Add the plumped currants, toss with a fork, and serve.

Rice Croquettes

Delicate golden patties, especially good with poached fish.

½ cup (1 dL) short-grained rice
½ teaspoon salt
1 cup (¼ L) milk
2 eggs

6 tablespoons butter
1½ cups (3½ dL) freshly made
  bread crumbs
2 tablespoons oil

Sprinkle the rice and salt into ½ cup boiling water. Cover and cook slowly until the water is absorbed, 7–10 minutes. Add the milk, stir, cover, and cook 10–12 minutes more, or until the rice is tender. Stir in 1 egg and 2 tablespoons of the butter. Spread the mixture on a shallow plate, cover with plastic wrap, and refrigerate. Beat the remaining egg in a shallow dish and put the crumbs on a piece of wax paper. Shape the chilled rice mixture into 6 conical or patty shapes. Dip each croquette into the egg and then cover with crumbs. Melt the remaining 4 tablespoons of butter in a skillet with the oil. When hot, fry the croquettes until golden brown; don't cook them too quickly or the insides will remain cold.

Fried Rice

Add cooked diced shrimp, pork, or chicken, if you wish, and serve as a supper dish.

4 tablespoons oil
4 cups (1 L) cooked rice
4 tablespoons chopped scallions
1½ tablespoons soy sauce

¼ teaspoon freshly ground
  pepper
2 eggs, slightly beaten

Heat the oil in a large skillet, and add the rice, scallions, soy sauce, and pepper. Cook over medium-high heat, stirring often, for 6 minutes. Add the eggs and stir briskly so they cook and break into small bits throughout the rice. As soon as the egg is set, remove and serve.

Rice and Pecan Loaf

An old southern tradition, utterly simple and delicious.

1½ cups (3½ dL) cooked
  brown rice
1½ cups (3½ dL) coarsely
  chopped pecans
1½ cups (3½ dL) cracker
  crumbs
1 egg, well beaten

1¼ cups (3 dL) milk
1 teaspoon salt
½ teaspoon freshly ground
  pepper
3 tablespoons butter, melted
1 recipe Onion Sauce (p. 267)

Preheat the oven to 350°F (180°C). Butter a 2-quart loaf pan or casserole. Mix rice, pecans, crumbs, egg, milk, salt, and pepper until well blended. Turn into the loaf pan or casserole and pour melted butter on top. Bake 50–60 minutes and serve with the sauce.

Curried Rice

(SERVES FOUR)

3 tablespoons oil
1 onion, chopped fine
1 cup (¼ L) long-grain rice
2 teaspoons curry powder

½ teaspoon salt
2 tablespoons butter
½ cup (1 dL) raisins
2 cups (½ L) chicken broth

Preheat the oven to 375°F (190°C). Butter a 1½-quart casserole. Heat the oil in a skillet, add the onion, and cook until it is soft. Stir in the rice and cook, stirring, for 3 minutes. Add the curry powder, salt, butter, and raisins, and cook 1 minute more. Transfer to a casserole, pour in the chicken broth, stir, cover, and bake for 1 hour.

Parched Rice with Tomato Sauce and Cheese

Dandy for a meal when you don't want to fuss—be sure to use freshly grated cheese.

(SERVES SIX)

6 tablespoons butter
6 cups (1½ L) cooked white
rice
2 cups (½ L) Tomato Sauce
(p. 271)

1¼ cup (3 dL) freshly grated
Parmesan cheese

Melt the butter in a skillet. Add the rice and cook, stirring, until heated through and lightly browned. Put into a warm serving bowl, heat the tomato sauce, and cover the rice; then sprinkle with the cheese. Lift and toss the rice with a fork so that every kernel is coated.

Wild Rice

Wild rice is expensive and special. Cook it simply to enjoy its distinctive flavor and texture.

(3 CUPS)

1 cup (¼ L) wild rice
1 tablespoon salt
4 tablespoons butter

Rinse the rice several times in cold water and remove any foreign particles. Boil 3 cups water with the salt and slowly add the rice. Simmer for 45–50 minutes or until the grain is tender and has absorbed all the water. Stir in the butter, toss with a fork, and serve.

Wild Rice Casserole

Wild rice needs little adornment; serve this casserole with duck or game. You could even tuck pieces of leftover duck or game into the casserole as it bakes and serve as a main course.

Wild Rice Casserole (continued)

¼ pound (115 g) butter
½ cup (1 dL) finely chopped
  onion
2 cups (½ L) sliced mushrooms
1 cup (¼ L) wild rice

3 cups (¾ L) chicken broth
1 teaspoon salt
½ teaspoon freshly ground
  pepper

Preheat the oven to 325°F (165°C). Butter a 1½-quart casserole. Melt the butter in a skillet, add the onion, and cook until soft. Add the mushrooms and cook, stirring, until they darken. Put the onion and mushrooms into the casserole with remaining ingredients. Cover and bake for 1 hour or until the broth is absorbed and the rice is tender.

DRIED BEANS

About Dried Beans

Dried beans are wholesome, filling, and inexpensive. When cooked with rice, as in the traditional black beans and rice combination, they provide a complete protein. They are splendid in casseroles, robust and satisfying in soups and salads, and, on a hike, a cold bean sandwich has no peers.

Kinds of Dried Beans

Of the many varieties of dried beans available in our markets, some are more familiar than others.

Kidney Beans and Red Beans. Kidney beans and red beans are used in chili, casseroles, and pork dishes. *Cannellini,* a white kidney bean, is a great favorite in Italian cooking and is available both dried and canned in Italian markets.

Black Beans. Black beans are a national winner in South America and the Caribbean. They make a wonderful soup, flavored with lemon, sherry, or rum, and are excellent boiled, mashed, and served with melting squares of cheese.

Chickpeas or Garbanzo Beans. A roundish, wrinkled bean used a great deal in Mexican cooking. They take a lot of cooking to soften; add ½ teaspoon of baking soda to the water when boiling. They are delicious puréed and particularly good in salads.

Pinto Beans and Pink Beans. These are the beans used in Mexican dishes such as refried beans. They provide a good base for intense spices.

Lima Beans and Baby Lima Beans. Limas are good in lamb, pork, or ham casseroles and as a side dish with barbecued meats.

Great Northern Beans and Navy Beans (Small White Beans). These are the beans used to make Boston baked beans and in minestrone-type soups. They also make a fine meal when simmered with a ham bone, celery leaves, and onions.

Lentils. Lentils, traditional with lamb at Easter time, are served year-round in hearty soups and robust sausage and vegetable casseroles.

Black-eyed Peas. Black-eyed peas are as common in the South as the navy bean is in the Northeast. Cook them with molasses or with chili; serve them in soups or with ham or rice.

Split Peas. Split peas and ham are a classic combination. Both green and yellow make satisfying winter soups.

Amount of Dried Beans to Cook

A cup of cooked beans will provide two servings, but different varieties of dried beans will produce different amounts of cooked beans, as the following chart shows. The time represents the amount of time for cooking *after* soaking.

Cook 1 cup:	In:	For:	Yield:
Baby Lima Beans	4 cups water	1 hour	3½ cups
Black Beans	8 cups water	1½ hours	4 cups
Black-eyed Peas	6 cups water	1 hour	4 cups
Chickpeas or Garbanzo Beans	8 cups water (plus ½ teaspoon baking soda)	2½–3 hours or more	4 cups
Great Northern Beans	7 cups water	1 hour	4 cups
Kidney Beans	6 cups water	¾–1 hour	4 cups
Lentils	6 cups water	35 minutes	4½ cups
Lima Beans	6 cups water	1½ hours	2½ cups
Pink Beans	6 cups water	1 hour	4 cups
Pinto Beans	6 cups water	1½ hours	4 cups
Red Beans	6 cups water	2 hours	4 cups
Small White Beans or Navy Beans	6 cups water	¾–1 hour	4 cups
Split Peas	6 cups water	45 minutes	4½ cups

Preparing Dried Beans for Cooking

Wash beans by covering them with cold water and picking out any pebbles or floating particles. Soak them overnight to reduce the cooking time, or, if you forget to do this or are short of time, use the following short method: put 2 cups of beans in a pot, cover with 6 cups water, bring to a boil, and cook for 2 minutes; remove from the heat, cover the pot, and let stand for 1 hour before cooking.

Lentils do not have to be soaked before cooking, nor do those beans with package directions that say "no soaking necessary."

Cooking Dried Beans

To preserve food values, don't drain off the soaking liquid before proceeding with the cooking: just add enough additional liquid to cover the beans. Add about ½ teaspoon of salt for every cup of dried beans, cover, and simmer until the beans are tender. The amount of liquid does not have to be exact; just keep the beans covered with water while they are cooking.

An old-fashioned bean pot is usually tall and made of clay. Heated in a slow oven, it's ideal for keeping beans and liquid at a slow simmer. If you don't have a bean pot, use a good, heavy casserole.

To use a pressure cooker for dried beans or peas see chart p. 755.

Boston Baked Beans

(SERVES EIGHT)

2 cups (½ L) navy beans, small white beans, or Great Northern beans	¼ pound (115 g) salt pork
	2 teaspoons dry mustard
	5 tablespoons dark-brown sugar
About 1 teaspoon salt	4 tablespoons molasses

Wash the beans. Soak overnight or use the short method (p. 323). Add salt, stir and drain, reserving the liquid. Preheat the oven to 300°F (150°C). Cut off a third of the salt pork and place the piece on the bottom of a bean pot. Add the beans to the pot. Blend the mustard, brown sugar, and molasses with the reserved bean liquid and pour over the beans. Cut several gashes in the remaining piece of salt pork and place on top of the beans. Cover and bake for about 6 hours, adding water as needed. Uncover for the final hour of cooking so the pork will become brown and crisp. Taste and correct seasoning.

Chili Beans

A touch of cayenne pepper heightens the taste of this old favorite.

(SERVES EIGHT)

2 cups (½ L) red, pink, or pinto beans	¾ teaspoon oregano, crumbled
¼ pound (115 g) salt pork, diced fine	½ teaspoon sage, crumbled
	½ teaspoon cumin
2 large onions, chopped	2 tablespoons chili powder
2 cloves garlic, chopped	¼ teaspoon cayenne pepper (optional)
2 tablespoons bacon fat, if needed	2 tablespoons cornmeal
1 teaspoon freshly ground pepper	1 cup (¼ L) peeled and chopped fresh or canned tomatoes
About 1 teaspoon salt	

Wash the beans. Soak overnight. Or use the short method (p. 323), in either case do not drain. Sauté the salt pork; after 5 minutes, add the onions and garlic and cook until the onions are golden. If the pork does not render enough fat, add 2 tablespoons bacon fat. Add black pepper, salt, oregano, sage, cumin, chili powder, cayenne pepper (if you wish), cornmeal, tomatoes, and 1 cup of the bean liquid. Cook, stirring constantly, for 5 minutes and add to the pot of beans and liquid. Stir to blend, and simmer for 2 hours, checking frequently to see if the liquid needs replenishing. Taste, and correct seasoning.

Chickpea Purée

Particularly delicious mingling with the meat juices from a roast of lamb or of pork. You can use canned chickpeas or garbanzo beans.

(SERVES SIX)

3 cups (¾ L) cooked chickpeas	Freshly ground pepper
1 clove garlic, minced	2 tablespoons butter
Salt	1 tablespoon chopped parsley

Purée the chickpeas in a food mill, a blender, or a food processor. Add the minced garlic and a little of the cooking liquid to make a smooth purée, and season to taste with salt and pepper. Heat and add the butter. Sprinkle parsley on top.

Beans Bretonne

(SERVES SIX)

1½ cups (3½ dL) navy beans, small white beans, or Great Northern beans
1 cup (¼ L) stewed tomatoes, drained
1 cup (¼ L) chicken broth
1 onion, chopped fine

4-ounce (115-g) can whole pimientos, puréed
2 cloves garlic, minced
4 tablespoons butter
About 1 teaspoon salt
Freshly ground pepper

Wash the beans. Soak overnight or use the short method (p. 323). Preheat the oven to 300°F (150°C). Drain the beans and place in a bean pot with remaining ingredients. Stir, cover, and bake until the liquid is nearly absorbed, about 2 hours. Correct seasoning.

Refried Beans with Cheese

A classic dish south-of-the-border. "Refried" means that they are first simmered and then fried.

(SERVES EIGHT)

2 cups (½ L) pink or pinto beans
About 1½ teaspoons salt
½ teaspoon freshly ground pepper

5 tablespoons bacon fat
1½ cups (3½ dL) cubed Cheddar or Monterey Jack cheese

Wash the beans. Soak overnight or use the short method (p. 323). Return to the heat and simmer about 1½ hours, or until tender. Add salt and pepper. Heat the bacon fat in a skillet. Drain 1 cup of beans and put in the skillet. Mash thoroughly, adding ½ cup of the reserved liquid. Stir and cook for 1–2 minutes. Add and mash more beans with more of the reserved liquid. Repeat until all the beans and liquid have been used and the mixture is creamy. Add the cheese, blend, and cook until the cheese is melted.

Lima Beans Fermière

(SERVES SIX)

2 cups (½ L) dried lima beans
1 teaspoon salt
¼ teaspoon freshly ground pepper
¼ pound (115 g) salt pork, diced

1 onion, chopped
1 cup (¼ L) finely diced carrot
2 tablespoons butter

Wash the lima beans. Soak overnight or use the short method (p. 323). Drain the beans and put in a casserole, reserving the liquid. Stir in the salt and pepper.

Preheat the oven to 300°F (150°C). Cook the salt pork in a skillet until it is golden brown. Add the onion and carrot, and cook, stirring, until the vegetables are golden. Mix the vegetables and butter into the casserole with the lima beans. Pour in 1 cup reserved bean liquid, cover, and bake for 2 hours, adding more bean liquid as needed.

Barbecued Lima Beans

Spicy and perfect with grilled beef at a summer barbecue.

(SERVES FOUR)

1 cup (¼ L) dried baby lima beans	1 tablespoon prepared mustard
⅛ pound (60 g) salt pork, diced	1 teaspoon Worcestershire sauce
½ onion, chopped	1 teaspoon chili powder
1 large clove garlic, chopped fine	¼ cup (½ dL) puréed tomatoes
	1 tablespoon cider vinegar
	2 teaspoons brown sugar

Wash the beans. Soak overnight or use the short method (p. 323). Add enough water to cover well, and boil the beans gently for 1 hour, or until they are tender. Drain, put into a bean pot or casserole, and reserve the liquid. Preheat the oven to 350°F (180°C). Cook the salt pork in a skillet until it is golden. Add the onion and garlic, and cook until the onion is soft. Stir in remaining ingredients and ½ cup reserved bean liquid. Simmer for 3 minutes and pour over the beans. Bake for 45 minutes.

Lentils and Lamb

This classic combination is a harbinger of spring.

(SERVES SIX)

1 cup (¼ L) dried lentils	1 teaspoon salt
1 onion, chopped	2 tomatoes, peeled, seeded, and chopped
2 tablespoons finely chopped parsley	2 cups (½ L) cooked lamb, in bite-size pieces
2 cloves garlic, minced	
½ cup (1 dL) chopped celery	
¼ teaspoon freshly ground pepper	

Wash the lentils. Add 5 cups water with the onion, parsley, garlic, celery, pepper, salt, and tomatoes. Bring to a boil and simmer 30 minutes, or until the lentils are tender. Drain, reserving the liquid, and put the lentils into a casserole. Preheat the oven to 350°F (180°C). Put 2½ cups of liquid into a saucepan and boil briskly until it is reduced by half, about 15 minutes. Pour over the lentils, stir in the lamb, cover, and bake 1 hour.

Lentils and Ham. Omit the lamb and salt and add *2 cups chopped cooked ham.*

Lentils and Sausage. Omit the lamb and add *1 pound sausage meat,* browned in a skillet. Cover the lentils with *3 strips of bacon* and uncover the pot for the last 30 minutes of cooking so the bacon will crisp.

PASTA

About Pasta

Pasta Shapes. Pasta is the general name for the many variously shaped flour-and-water-dough products that we sometimes incorrectly call "macaroni." *Macaroni* is only one member of the pasta family, which ranges from broad *lasagna* to tiny *pastini*, from simple *tagliatelle* to intricate *tortellini*—names that mean things like "angel hair," "badly cut," and "little hat." Pasta may be white, or egg-enriched yellow, or spinach-touched green.

The real difference between pastas, however, lies not in their shapes but in their origins—domestic, imported, or homemade.

Domestic Pasta. Unfortunately, because of the kind of flour used, American-made pastas tend to become gummy when cooked, and it is often hard to separate the strands. Adding a little oil to the cooking water, as is often recommended, does not really help much. It *does* help if you are careful not to overcook the pasta; if pasta sticks, pour boiling water over it after draining it and separate the strands with a fork.

Imported Pasta. If you have an Italian grocery nearby, you may be able to buy imported, factory-made dry pasta. More expensive than local brands, it is still well worth trying if you care about the texture. Italian pasta, made with flour ground from the heart of hard durum wheat, is firm and chewy without a trace of gumminess.

Homemade Pasta. If you live near an Italian neighborhood you can sometimes find a shop that sells its own fresh, homemade pasta; made with flour, eggs, and sometimes a little water, it is both tender and firm, with a roughish surface that catches the sauce, and it takes less than a minute to cook. To make your own takes some skill, but if you have a hand-cranked pasta machine, the task becomes really simple and it is fun to do, particularly when children join in to catch the strands as they roll out and to lay them across a broomstick. There is another recipe for an American-style egg noodle and these are simpler to do with a rolling pin, partially because you don't need to get them so thin.

Cooking Pasta

Bring a large amount of salted water to a boil, using at least 8 quarts for 1 pound of pasta. When the water is boiling violently, add the noodles gradually so as not to slow the boiling. Stir gently to separate the strands. Put your serving bowl or platter into a 250°F oven so that it will be warm and ready when the pasta is done. (If you are cooking fresh pasta, begin heating the bowl 5 minutes before the noodles go into the water, since they cook so quickly.)

Underdone pasta has a core of uncooked dough, while overcooked pasta is mushy and unappetizing. Italians cook spaghetti until it is *al dente*, that is, resistant to the bite. Since cooking times vary considerably, begin testing before you expect the noodles to be ready, and disregard the cooking times recommended on the box—they are almost always too long. Use a fork to remove a strand of pasta from the boiling water, run the pasta under cold water, and bite into it. It should be tender, but quite firm, with no hard core. Test every minute until the pasta is ready.

Serving Pasta

Pour the cooked pasta into a colander, letting the water run out. Transfer the noodles immediately to a heated bowl and stir in the sauce. A 1-pound box of pasta makes 8 cups of cooked noodles, enough to serve four as a main course, six as a first course.

Homemade Italian Noodles

This recipe calls for a hand-cranked Italian pasta machine. If you
don't have one, you can try rolling the dough out by hand, following
the instructions in the recipe that follows for American-style noodles,
but it won't be an easy job.

(MAKES ABOUT 1 POUND TO SERVE FOUR).

2 cups (½ L) flour
3 eggs

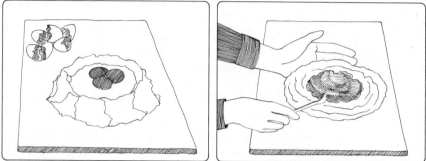

Put the flour in a heap on a clean counter or pastry board. Make a hole in the
center and crack the 3 eggs and drop them in. Add 2 tablespoons water and
break up gently with a fork, continuing to beat until frothy and gradually
incorporating a little of the flour around the sides. Continue beating and
incorporating the flour until it is all used up. If the dough gets too dry, add a little
bit more water until you have a manageable ball of dough with no dry pieces that
aren't absorbed. Scrape and clean the counter and then start kneading with the
palm of your hand as you would bread, until the dough holds together and
becomes flexible. If you have a food processor, it can do the kneading: add a little
more water and process until the dough forms a mass. Divide the dough in half
and start feeding one half into the machine rollers opened to their largest
opening, usually number 8. Using the hand crank, roll the dough through. Then

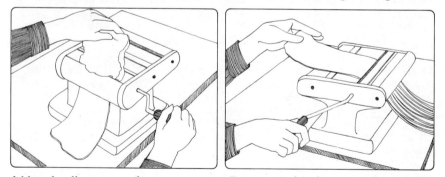

fold and roll again at the next setting. Repeat until it has gone through the
narrowest setting at which point it will look like a long, smooth stocking. Do
the same with the other half of the dough. For broad noodles, put the smooth
pieces of dough through the wider cutters, catching them as they come out and
spreading them over a broomstick or on large cookie sheets. For thinner noodles,

use the narrower cutters. They need to dry long enough to remove surface moisture. To cook, plunge into a large pot of boiling salted water and start tasting 30 seconds after it has returned to the boil; the noodles are usually done in less than a minute. Drain and toss with butter and lots of freshly grated Parmesan cheese.

Pasta for Ravioli. After you have rolled out each half of dough into a long, smooth piece, place one on a lightly floured surface and distribute filling over it as directed on p. 300, using the other half to cover.

Pasta for Cannelloni. After you have rolled out each half, cut squares roughly 4 × 4 inches and cook them in rapidly boiling salted water until just tender, a minute or two. Drain, separate, and pat off excess water before filling. Use instead of the crêpes to make Cannelloni, p. 297.

Homemade American-style Noodles

Noodles freeze very well placed uncooked in a plastic bag or container.

(1 POUND)

3 egg yolks	1 tablespoon salt
1 egg	2 cups (½ L) flour

Beat the yolks and egg until they are light. Beat in the salt and 3 tablespoons cold water. Using your hands, work the flour into this mixture to make a stiff dough. Cut into three equal parts. Cover with plastic wrap and let rest a few minutes. Dust a board or pastry cloth with flour and roll out one part of the dough as thin as possible. Cover with a dishcloth and let rest for 10 minutes.

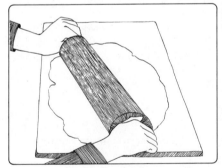

Repeat with the other two pieces. Sprinkle one sheet of dough very lightly with flour and roll up like a jelly roll. With a sharp knife, cut across the roll into ⅛-inch-wide strips for fine noodles and ½-inch-wide strips for broad noodles. Open out the strips and hang over a broomstick or chair back to dry. They will be ready to cook when they have lost their surface dampness. About ten minutes should be enough. Bring a large pot of boiling salted water 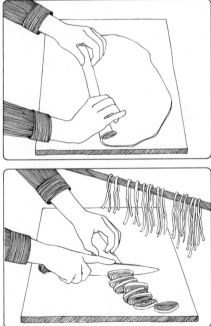 to a rolling boil and drop the noodles in. Boil vigorously until just tender—between 5 and 10 minutes, depending on how thin you have succeeded in rolling them; fork out one and taste to determine doneness.

Truman's Sauce for Pasta

(4 CUPS)

2 slices bacon, diced
1 cup (¼ L) chopped green
  pepper
1 onion, chopped
2 cloves garlic, cut in half
1 pound (450 g) lean ground
  beef
1½ cups (3½ dL) tomato paste
1½ cups (3½ dL) canned
  consommé, undiluted

1 tablespoon Worcestershire
  sauce
4 tablespoons freshly grated
  Parmesan cheese
Salt to taste
¼ teaspoon freshly ground
  pepper
1 teaspoon oregano, crumbled
1 pound (450 g) pasta

Fry the bacon in a saucepan until some of the fat is melted. Add the green pepper, onion, and garlic, and cook until soft. Add the beef and break it into tiny pieces with a fork until it loses its pinkness. Stir in the tomato paste, consommé, Worcestershire sauce, cheese, salt, pepper, and oregano. Simmer for 1½ hours, adding water if it becomes too thick. Serve with cooked pasta.

Alfredo's Noodles

You may know this creamy, delicate dish as Fettucine Alfredo. As a first course, which is the way Italians would serve it, this recipe makes enough for four.

(SERVES THREE TO FOUR)

½ pound (225 g) noodles,
  ¼ inch wide
¼ pound (115 g) sweet butter,
  melted
1 cup (¼ L) heavy cream,
  warmed

¾ cup (1¾ dL) freshly grated
  Parmesan cheese
Salt to taste
¼ teaspoon freshly ground
  pepper

Have a large bowl warmed and ready before you cook the noodles. Drain the cooked noodles and put them into the bowl. Quickly add remaining ingredients, tossing briskly to coat all the noodles, and serve at once.

Noodles with Poppy Seeds. Omit the Parmesan cheese and add *3 tablespoons poppy seeds.*

Sour-Cream Noodles

This recipe has infinite variations. Use the butter to sauté any one or more of the following, then add to the noodles: *¼ cup chopped onion, ¼ cup chopped green pepper, ½ cup chopped celery, 1 cup sliced mushrooms, 1 cup well-drained flaked tuna, or 1½–2 cups diced cooked poultry.*

(SERVES FOUR)

¼ pound (115 g) noodles, ¼
  inch wide or wider, cooked
1 cup (¼ L) cottage cheese

1 cup (¼ L) sour cream
1 egg, slightly beaten
½ teaspoon salt

⅛ teaspoon freshly ground   4 tablespoons butter, melted
  pepper

Preheat the oven to 375°F (190°C). Butter a 1½-quart casserole. Put the cooked noodles into a bowl and toss with the remaining ingredients. Put into the casserole and bake 50–60 minutes, or until bubbling and set.

Noodle Pudding. Add *1 cup finely chopped ham* and *½ cup raisins* to the mixture before baking.

Ham and Noodle Casserole

(SERVES SIX)

4 tablespoons butter   1½ cups (3½ dL) finely
1 small onion, chopped fine   chopped cooked ham
2 eggs, slightly beaten   Salt
1 cup (¼ L) sour cream   ½ pound (225 g) noodles, ¼
½ cup (1 dL) grated Gruyère   inch wide, cooked
  or Swiss cheese

Preheat the oven to 350°F (180°C). Butter a 2-quart casserole. Melt the butter in a skillet and cook the onion over medium heat until soft. In a small bowl, mix the eggs and sour cream, then add the onion, cheese, and ham. Add salt to taste. Put the noodles in the casserole, then add the sauce and toss gently. Bake for 45 minutes or until a straw inserted in the middle comes out clean.

Beef-Noodle Casserole. Substitute *1½ cups diced cooked beef.* If the beef is left over from a pot roast or stew and you have some gravy, add it to the casserole, adjusting the amount of sour cream accordingly.

Chicken-Noodle Casserole. Substitute *1½ cups finely chopped cooked chicken or turkey* for the ham.

Spaghetti with Clams

(SERVES FOUR)

¼ pound (115 g) butter   1 cup (¼ L) clam juice, fresh
⅓ cup (¾ dL) olive oil   or bottled
½ teaspoon freshly ground   Salt
  pepper   1 pound (450 g) spaghetti
1 teaspoon oregano, crumbled   ½ cup (1 dL) freshly grated
2 tablespoons basil, crumbled   Parmesan cheese
3 cloves garlic, minced   3 tablespoons minced parsley
1½ cups (3½ dL) minced
  clams, fresh or canned

Melt the butter in a skillet and add the olive oil, pepper, oregano, basil, garlic, clams, and clam juice. Simmer for 30 minutes. Add salt to taste. Warm a large bowl while you cook the spaghetti. Drain the spaghetti, put it into the bowl, and add the clam sauce. Toss with the cheese and parsley and serve immediately.

Spaghetti Carbonara

Eggs make the strands of pasta glisten; cheese adds sharpness; lots of coarse black pepper heightens the spiciness.

(SERVES SIX)

1 pound (450 g) bacon
1 pound (450 g) spaghetti
¾ cup (1¾ dL) freshly grated
Parmesan cheese

3 tablespoons butter
Freshly ground pepper
2 eggs, slightly beaten

Fry the bacon until it is just crisp, drain on paper towels, chop into bite-size pieces. Cook the spaghetti in a very large pot of boiling salted water, until just tender, about 8 to 10 minutes. Meanwhile warm a serving bowl. Drain the spaghetti well and toss in the bowl with the bacon, cheese, butter, and lots of freshly ground pepper—as much as a teaspoonful—for a few seconds, allowing to cool slightly. Add the eggs and stir vigorously to coat all the strands. Serve immediately.

Vermicelli in Fresh Tomato Sauce

(SERVES SIX)

6 vine-ripened tomatoes,
peeled and chopped
1 tablespoon lemon juice
2 teaspoons basil, crumbled
¼ teaspoon freshly ground
pepper
4 tablespoons finely chopped
parsley

½ cup (1 dL) olive oil
3 cloves garlic, minced
½ cup (1 dL) sliced scallions
Salt to taste
1 pound (450 g) vermicelli

Mix the tomatoes, lemon juice, basil, pepper, and parsley in a bowl. Heat the olive oil in a saucepan. Add the garlic and cook, stirring, for 2 minutes; add the scallions and continue to cook and stir for 1 minute more. Add the tomato mixture and salt, and simmer for 10 minutes as you cook the vermicelli. Drain the pasta, place in a large warm bowl, add the tomato mixture, and mix well.

Macaroni and Cheese

It is so easy and inexpensive to make this favorite dish from scratch.

(SERVES FOUR)

9 ounces (250 g) macaroni,
cooked
2 cups (½ L) Cheese Sauce
(p. 265)

½ cup (1 dL) grated sharp
Cheddar cheese
½ cup (1 dL) freshly made
buttered bread crumbs

Preheat the oven to 375°F (190°C). Butter a 1½-quart casserole. Put the cooked macaroni into the casserole, pour the cheese sauce over it, and mix gently with a fork. Sprinkle the grated cheese evenly over the top and spread the crumbs over the cheese. Bake uncovered, until the top is golden and the sauce is bubbling, about 30 minutes.

Macaroni and Cheese with Chipped Beef. Take ¼ *pound dried beef,* separate the slices, cover with boiling water, and let stand 5 minutes. Drain well, chop into coarse pieces, and mix in with the cheese sauce before adding it to the macaroni.

Macaroni Mousse

Cook in a ring mold, and fill the center with creamed chicken or fish.

(SERVES FOUR)

1 cup (¼ L) cooked elbow macaroni
1½ cups (3½ dL) milk
2 eggs, well beaten
1 tablespoon finely chopped pimiento
⅓ cup (¾ dL) finely chopped green pepper

1 tablespoon finely chopped onion
½ cup (1 dL) grated Swiss cheese
Salt to taste
½ cup (1 dL) soft bread crumbs

Preheat the oven to 350°F (180°C). Butter a 9 × 5-inch loaf pan or a ring mold, and put in the macaroni. In a bowl, mix the milk, eggs, pimiento, green pepper, onion, cheese, and salt. Pour over the macaroni, mix gently, and sprinkle with bread crumbs. Bake 50–60 minutes or until set.

Lasagne

(SERVES SIX)

3 tablespoons olive oil
½ cup (1 dL) chopped onions
⅓ cup (¾ dL) chopped carrots
3 cloves garlic, minced
1 pound (450 g) lean ground beef
3 cups (¾ L) canned Italian plum tomatoes
3 tablespoons butter, melted
1 teaspoon oregano, crumbled
1 tablespoon basil, crumbled

1 teaspoon salt
½ teaspoon freshly ground pepper
½ pound (225 g) lasagna noodles, cooked
½ pound (225 g) mozzarella cheese, grated
2 cups (½ L) ricotta cheese
¼ pound (115 g) freshly grated Parmesan cheese

Heat the oil in a skillet. Add the onions, carrots, and garlic, and cook, stirring, until they are lightly browned. Push to the side of the pan and add the beef. Break it up into bits, cooking until it loses its pink color. Purée the tomatoes in a blender or food processor, add to the meat, and simmer 15 minutes. Add the butter, oregano, basil, salt, and pepper, partially cover, and simmer 30 minutes. Preheat the oven to 375°F (190°C). Assemble the lasagne by drizzling some sauce over the bottom of a shallow rectangular baking dish. Put in a layer of noodles, sprinkle with some of the mozzarella, and spread on a layer of ricotta. Make another layer of noodles, sauce, mozzarella, and ricotta. Finish with noodles and sauce. Sprinkle Parmesan cheese evenly over the top and bake 20 minutes or until hot and bubbling.

Gnocchi alla Romana

The good graininess of gnocchi comes from semolina, coarsely ground durum wheat that is available in Italian markets and health-food stores.

(SERVES SIX)

3 cups (¾ L) milk
1 teaspoon salt
¼ teaspoon nutmeg
¼ teaspoon freshly ground
   pepper

1 cup (¼ L) semolina
3 eggs, lightly beaten
1 cup (¼ L) freshly grated
   Parmesan cheese
6 tablespoons butter, melted

Butter a jelly-roll pan (18 × 13 × 1 inch). Combine the milk, salt, nutmeg, and pepper in a heavy-bottomed pan, bring to a boil, and slowly drizzle in the semolina, stirring constantly with a wooden spoon. Cook for about 2 minutes or until thick enough so that the spoon will stand up in the mixture. Cool slightly, beat in the eggs vigorously, and add the cheese and butter. Beat until well blended. Spread the mixture in the buttered pan and chill for 2 hours or longer. Preheat the oven to 400°F (205°C). Cut the dough into 1½- or 2-inch squares, triangles, or circles. Arrange the pieces in a buttered baking dish, spoon the melted butter over the top, and bake for 20–25 minutes, or until piping hot and lightly golden.

✸ Other Suggestions for Pasta Dishes

All of the recipes for stuffed pastas—ravioli, cannelloni, manicotti—will be found in the chapter on Filled Things. For a fine dish of spaghetti and meatballs, see Meatballs in Sauce, p. 171. Leftover pasta is always good in soup, and cold unbuttered macaroni can be used in salad.

EGGS & CHEESE

EGGS

About Eggs

Eggs are simple, complete, and infinitely versatile. They begin our day—soft and golden, spooned from an eggcup, or fried with country ham. They can be the centerpiece of a meal—baked, shirred, in omelets, soufflés, and frittatas. Eggs serve as leavening for cakes and soufflés, thickening for sauces and custards, binding for batters. They help in clarifying broth and make a simple glaze for cakes and rolls.

Buying Eggs

It's heaven when you are in the country to enjoy the taste of a newly laid farm egg for breakfast. But supermarket eggs are reliable and certainly fresh enough for general purposes. Commercial eggs are grated A or B, depending on their quality and freshness. Grade A eggs are the best; grade B are adequate for baking and cooking but don't have the fresh flavor necessary for plain boiling and poaching.

An old-fashioned method for determining whether an egg is really stale is to see if it floats in a bowl of water; if it does, or tips noticeably upward, it means an air sac has formed as the interior has shrunk away from the shell and the egg is definitely old. However, it would take at least three weeks for eggs left at room temperature to reach this state so it is not likely to occur with modern methods of fast distribution and refrigeration.

If an egg is fresh, the white and yolk will cling together tightly when you crack it open. The older it gets, the flatter the yolk becomes and the runnier the white. You don't have to throw the eggs out at that stage, but where flavor counts, they certainly won't have a pleasant fresh taste; however, the eggs would still retain their rising power.

The color of an egg's shell has nothing to do with its quality or taste, despite local prejudices. Buy whichever is least expensive. Yolks also vary in color, from pale yellow to nearly orange. This comes from variations in the chicken's feed and makes little difference in taste. A speck of blood in a yolk is not harmful.

Storing Eggs

If you use several whites in a meringue or a cake, you can keep the uncooked yolks for two or three days in the refrigerator, using them to enrich scrambled eggs or to thicken a sauce. Cover them with a film of cold water and some plastic wrap to prevent a skin from forming. For freezing egg yolks, see p. 730.

If you are going to use leftover egg whites within a few days, store them in a covered container in the refrigerator. For freezing egg whites, see p. 730.

Measuring Eggs

Egg size is standardized by the government. The recipes in this book call for "large" eggs, weighing 2 ounces each or 24 ounces a dozen. A dozen "small" eggs weigh 18 ounces, "medium" weigh 21, and "extra large" weigh 27 ounces. To make 1 cup of eggs requires 7 "smalls," 6 "mediums," 5 "large," or 4 "extra large." It's easy enough to adapt egg sizes in recipes where it matters, like cakes, custards, and soufflés.

An egg is one-third yolk, two-thirds white. A cup of egg whites contains 10 "small," 8 "medium," 7 "large," or 6 "extra large" egg whites, while a cup of yolks uses 18 "small," 16 "medium," 14 "large," or 12 "extra large" yolks.

If, on doubling or halving a recipe, you wind up needing to use half an egg, just break it, beat it, and measure off half: about 1½ tablespoons.

Separating Eggs

To separate an egg, crack it with a knife or against the edge of a bowl and split the shell into two parts. Pass the yolk back and forth between the halves of the shell, letting the white fall into a cup underneath. Or pass the shelled egg from one hand to the other, letting the white fall through your fingers. Play safe: drop each white into a cup before adding it to the other egg whites in the bowl. In that way, if some yolk breaks into the white, it will not ruin the whole bowl.

Beating Egg Whites

When beating egg whites, aim for as much volume as possible. Start with whites that are at room temperature. Make sure that the bowl and beater are absolutely grease-free: you can remove unwanted bits of broken egg yolk by using the shell or the corner of a paper towel. Beat with a whisk or a mechanical beater. Some believe that an unlined copper bowl produces the greatest volume, but glass, earthenware, or stainless steel is also fine for beating egg whites. Aluminum and plastic are less than satisfactory. If you are using an electric beater, start out on slow speed until whites are foamy, then increase to medium; if it is a hand-held beater, circulate it around the bowl. Many recipes instruct you to beat egg whites until they are "stiff but not dry." This is a way of describing the point at which the beaten whites have achieved their greatest degree of elasticity. That point is reached when a whisk or beater removed from the mixture pulls with it stiff peaks of egg white that have a shiny, glossy surface.

 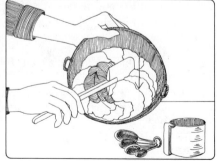

Folding Egg Whites

Properly beaten, egg whites will grow to as much as six times their original volume. Use beaten whites immediately, before they begin to shrink and separate, and always fold the light whites into the heavier mixture. Start by spooning the egg whites on top of the heavier batter, using a rubber spatula. Cut down into the batter and back up again in a circular motion, using the spatula or your hands and turning the bowl as you fold. Your aim is to incorporate the air captured in the beaten egg whites; if you overfold, the tiny air pockets will be flattened.

Tempering Egg Yolks

Egg yolks are frequently added to hot mixtures, often to sauces, so that as the heat works on the yolks, it will cause them to thicken the sauce. Yolks must be tempered first so that they do not cook too quickly and wind up floating, scrambled, in the sauce. To temper them, gently beat the yolks with a fork in a separate bowl, then add a bit of the hot sauce to them in a thin stream. When this mixture has become warm and thick, you can stir it into the whole potful of simmering liquid. Keep it below the boiling point unless the sauce is bound by flour, which prevents curdling.

Cooking Eggs

There are about ten basic ways to cook an egg, and a nearly infinite number of variations. *Soft-boiled eggs* are simmered in the shell for 3–4 minutes until the whites are opaque but still soft. *Medium-boiled eggs* are cooked in the shell for 4–5 minutes until the white is solid, but the yolk still liquid. They are also called *coddled eggs* or *eggs mollet* and, when peeled, they may be substituted for poached eggs. *Hard-boiled eggs* are simmered for 12 minutes, until both white and yolk are solid.

Poached eggs are turned out of their shells and cooked in simmering liquid until the whites become opaque. *Fried eggs* are broken into hot butter or oil and cooked in a skillet to the same point. *Scrambled eggs* are first mixed in a bowl with a tablespoonful of liquid, then dropped into a buttered pan and stirred lightly over the heat until curds form.

Shirred eggs are dropped into a flat dish and baked in the oven, while *eggs en cocotte* are placed in covered porcelain cups that are then immersed in simmering water. Finally, there are *omelets* and *soufflés*, perhaps the most elegant of ways to present eggs.

No matter what the technique, it is essential to use low, gentle heat when cooking eggs: egg protein begins to thicken at only 144°F, and toughens rapidly. The only exception is omelets; there the bottom is cooked quickly over medium-high heat, but the surface remains slightly runny, making for a soft interior when folded. Serve cooked eggs on warm, not sizzling hot, plates or they will continue to cook after they are removed from the pan.

Soft-boiled Eggs

Soft-boiled eggs have softly set whites and runny yolks.

Fill a saucepan with enough water to cover the egg, and heat to a gentle boil. Pierce the large end of the egg with an egg piercer (see illustration p. 31) or a needle; this will release the pressure that often cracks the shell.

When the water is gently simmering, lower the egg on a tablespoon. Set the timer; it will take 3–4 minutes for a "large" egg to be soft-boiled. If you are cooking many eggs at the same time, it is helpful to lower them into the water in a wire basket such as those used for deep frying.

Medium-boiled Eggs

Coddled or medium-boiled eggs have firm opaque whites and soft yolks. They can be shelled and used in place of poached eggs.

Fill a saucepan with enough water to cover the egg, and heat to a gentle boil. Pierce the large end of the egg with an egg piercer or with a needle; this releases the pressure that often cracks the shell.

When the water is gently boiling, lower the egg on a tablespoon. Cover the pan, remove from the heat, and let the egg stand for 4–5 minutes, depending on how firm you want it to be.

Hard-boiled Eggs

Hard-boiled eggs have firm whites and yolks.

Pierce the large end of the egg with an egg piercer or a needle; this will release the pressure that often cracks the shell. Put the egg in a pan and fill it with water. Bring it to a boil, and simmer for 12 minutes.

Remove from the heat and place the egg in cold water immediately. An overcooked egg develops a harmless dark ring that isn't as appetizing as the bright-yellow yolk.

Shirred Eggs

Shirred eggs are baked with butter in a shallow dish until they are barely set. A wonderful way for an inexperienced cook to fix eggs, particularly since you can add garnishes to make a delicious and satisfying dish.

(SERVES ONE)

1½ teaspoons butter   Salt
2 eggs   Freshly ground pepper

Preheat the oven to 400°F (205°C). Use baking dishes that accommodate no more than two eggs, such as gratin dishes. Put the butter in the dish and place it in the oven until the butter melts. Swirl it to coat the bottom and sides. Crack the eggs, put them in the dish, and cover snugly with foil. Bake for 7 minutes. Uncover, and season to taste.

Shirred Eggs with Crumbs. Sprinkle *2 tablespoons freshly made bread crumbs* over the buttered bottom of the baking dish. Add the eggs, and sprinkle with another *2 tablespoons bread crumbs.*

Shirred Eggs in Cream. For each egg add *1½ tablespoons heavy cream* to the bottom of the baking dish and spoon another *1½ tablespoons heavy cream* over the eggs.

Shirred Eggs with Sausage. For each 2 eggs cook *4 small sausages* until done. Drain and place the sausages around the eggs in the baking dish.

Shirred Eggs with Chicken Livers. For each 2 eggs add *2 or 3 chicken livers,* sautéed first in *1 tablespoon butter* for 2 or 3 minutes. Add *1 teaspoon sherry,* scrape up the livers and butter and browned bits from the sauté pan, and place around the eggs in the baking dish.

Shirred Eggs with Ham. For each 2 eggs add 2–3 *tablespoons diced cooked ham (or other tasty meat) such as corned beef, tongue, chipped beef* to the baking dish.

Shirred Eggs Mornay. Make a *Mornay Sauce* (p. 265); one recipe will be enough for 6 eggs. Divide the sauce in three parts and spoon each third over 2 eggs. Cover the dish and bake for 5 minutes; uncover and slip under the broiler for 1 minute more to brown lightly.

Shirred Eggs Florentine. Spread 1 *tablespoon chopped cooked spinach* for each egg on the bottom of the baking dish. Put the egg on top and sprinkle with 1 *tablespoon freshly grated Parmesan cheese.*

Poached Eggs

A poached egg is cooked out of its shell in simmering liquid until its white is opaque and firm and its yolk is still runny. Delicious on toast, on hash, or on English muffins.

(SERVES TWO TO FOUR)

4 eggs, at room temperature
1 teaspoon vinegar (optional)
½ teaspoon salt

Fill a nonstick 10–12-inch skillet two-thirds full of water. Add 1 teaspoon vinegar, if eggs are very fresh, to help coagulate the egg white. Bring the water to a simmer, break each egg, one by one, into a saucer, and slide it tenderly into the water. Slip each additional egg into a different place in the skillet. Add salt. Spoon the simmering water over the eggs for 2–3 minutes until they are set; or turn off the heat, cover the pan, and let the eggs stand in the water for 5–6 minutes. The eggs are done when the whites become opaque and the yolks lose their shine. Remove one by one with a slotted spoon. If you prepare the eggs ahead of time, place the poached eggs in a bowl of cold water and refrigerate until needed. Just before serving, place them in a bowl of very hot water for a few minutes to warm them or slide them into a skillet full of simmering water and cook for 1 minute.

For a single poached egg, simply use a smaller skillet. Until you get the knack of poaching eggs, you may find it easier to do one at a time.

Fried Eggs

Use a heavy skillet or nonstick pan, and don't cook the eggs over high heat or the whites will become tough and rubbery.

2 teaspoons butter, oil, or bacon fat
1 egg

Melt the fat in a skillet. Break the egg into a saucer. When the fat is hot, slide in the egg and reduce the heat. If the eggs are to be cooked "sunny side up"— that is, not turned over—spoon the hot fat over them until the white is set and the yolk loses its shine, or else cover the skillet and let the eggs cook for 2–3 minutes. If they are to be turned over, use a spatula to lift each egg gently. Turn and cook for 30 seconds more until white is set over yolk. Remove to a warm plate.

Scrambled Eggs

Some like their scrambled eggs moist and some like them rather dry. The longer they cook, the drier they become. Either way, use low heat so the texture remains soft and creamy.

(SERVES THREE)

4 tablespoons butter	⅛ teaspoon freshly ground
5 eggs	pepper
¼ teaspoon salt	

Melt the butter in a heavy skillet or nonstick pan. Combine the eggs, salt, pepper, and 2 tablespoons water in a bowl. Briskly whisk, pour into the skillet, and turn the heat very low. Gently stir the egg mixture, lifting it up and over from the bottom as it thickens. Continue to stir until the desired texture is achieved. They thicken and dry out very quickly toward the end, so if you like them soft and moist, remove them from the heat a little before they reach the desired texture; they will continue to cook after being removed from the pan.

Scrambled Eggs with Ham. Add ½ cup finely chopped cooked ham to the egg mixture.

Scrambled Eggs with Cream Cheese. Cut 4 ounces cream cheese into small cubes and add to the eggs after they begin to thicken in the skillet.

Scrambled Eggs with Chives. Add 1 tablespoon chopped chives and 1 tablespoon chopped parsley to the egg mixture, and substitute 2 tablespoons cream for the water.

Scrambled Eggs with Lox. Fry ½ onion, sliced, and 2 slices lox in the butter before adding the eggs, and eliminate the salt from the mixture.

Scrambled Eggs with Chicken Livers. Fry 2 chicken livers, diced, in the butter before adding the egg mixture.

French Omelet

Read this recipe from beginning to end before starting to cook. A perfectly made omelet is a mass of creamy scrambled eggs enclosed in an envelope of coagulated egg. The keys to making a good omelet are quickness and proper heat. Almost any leftover food makes a good filling, as long as it isn't too liquid. It is always better to make omelets one at a time. You cannot achieve the same result working with more than two or three eggs and a larger pan.

(SERVES ONE)

2 "large" eggs	3–4 tablespoons filling
Salt	(optional: see following)
Freshly ground pepper	1 tablespoon butter
Tabasco (optional)	

Beat the eggs in a bowl only until they are just blended. Add a pinch of salt and pepper or a dash of Tabasco. If a filling is to be used, have it prepared and warm, if necessary. Heat a 7- or 8-inch nonstick skillet until hot. Add butter. When

it foams and sizzles, quickly pour in the eggs. Shake the skillet with a short forward and backward motion. Using a fork, pull back a little of the edge of the egg that will have started to curl up and, by tipping the skillet, allow the liquid egg in the center of the pan to run over. Continue to shake and fork around the edges, but work quickly: it should take only 15 seconds from the time the eggs are poured into the skillet until the filling (if you are using one) is added. Spread the filling across the center of the omelet. Have a warm plate ready. Use a spatula or the fork and roll one-third of the omelet over onto itself, then out of the skillet onto the plate, encouraging it to make the second fold as it falls. Don't cook the omelet dry; the center of a finished omelet should be moist, which means that you start to roll it when the surface is still a little runny.

Herb Omelet. Add *1 teaspoon minced parsley, 1 tablespoon minced chives,* and *⅛ teaspoon tarragon, crumbled,* to the egg mixture.

Crouton Omelet. Lay *¼ cup freshly made buttered croutons* over the omelet just before folding.

Cheese Omelet. Sprinkle *¼ cup freshly grated Gruyère or Swiss cheese* over the omelet just before folding.

Mushroom Omelet. Spread *½ cup sliced mushrooms,* first sautéed in a little butter, over the center of the omelet just before folding.

Bacon Omelet. Fry *2 slices bacon.* Drain, break into small pieces, and sprinkle over the omelet just before folding.

Other excellent omelets can be made by using ¼–½ cup of any of the following fillings. Heat and spread over the omelet just before you fold it.

Chicken or turkey, cooked and creamed

Chicken livers, chopped and sautéed

Fish, cooked and flaked or creamed

Ham, cooked and chopped

Tomato, chopped with onions, peppers, or canned green chilies

Cooked vegetables, diced and heated in butter

Lobster, shrimp, tuna, or crabmeat, cooked and
    creamed or heated in butter

For a special dessert, follow the recipe for Sweet Omelet (p. 614).

Puffy Omelet

This is a light dish akin to a soufflé. Any of the fillings for the French
Omelet (preceding recipe) may be used for the Puffy Omelet. If you
use a filling, have it warm and spread it over the top when the omelet
is done.

(SERVES TWO)

2 teaspoons butter
4 eggs, separated
¼ teaspoon salt

⅛ teaspoon freshly ground
    pepper

Preheat the oven to 400°F (205°C). Spread the butter around the sides and bottom
of a 10-inch skillet. Beat the egg yolks, 4 tablespoons hot water, salt, and pepper
until thick and lemon-colored. In another bowl beat the egg whites until stiff but
not dry. Gently stir a fourth of the whites into the yolk mixture and then fold
the yolk mixture into the remaining whites. Heat the buttered skillet over low
heat. Spoon the omelet mixture into the pan and spread it evenly. Cook very
slowly over low heat. When the omelet is nicely puffed, transfer the skillet to
the oven and bake it 3–4 minutes, or until it is lightly browned. Or, if a moist
interior is desired, slip the pan under the broiler to brown the top instead of
cooking it longer in the oven.

Potato and Leek Frittata

A frittata is the flat omelet served in Mediterranean countries that
is often a background for spicy vegetables. It is easier to make (than
separate omelets) for four or more and a most satisfying way to use
up bits of cooked vegetables—see suggestions in this and the recipe
that follows.

(SERVES FOUR)

4 tablespoons butter
1 tablespoon oil
1 cup (¼ L) cooked peeled
    potatoes, in ½-inch cubes
½ cup (1 dL) cooked leeks
    sliced in thin rounds
1 tablespoon minced parsley

¼ cup (½ dL) freshly grated
    Parmesan cheese
5 eggs
½ cup (1 dL) heavy cream
¼ teaspoon salt
⅛ teaspoon freshly ground
    pepper

Heat 2 tablespoons of the butter and the oil in a skillet. Add the potatoes and
leeks and cook until the potatoes are lightly browned. Put into a bowl, toss in
the parsley and cheese, and set aside. Combine the eggs, cream, salt, and pepper,
and add to the potatoes and leeks. Melt the remaining 2 tablespoons of butter
in the skillet. Pour in the egg mixture and cook very slowly over low heat,

pricking the top with a fork and lifting the bottom gently. Continue to cook until the bottom is brown and set. Slide out onto a dinner plate and invert into the pan. Or else place the frittata under a preheated broiler until the top is brown.

Spinach-Cheese Frittata. Eliminate the potatoes and leeks. Sauté ½ *cup chopped spinach* and ½ *onion, chopped,* in the butter and add ¼ *cup freshly grated Parmesan cheese* to the egg mixture.

Frittata with Cheese and Vegetables

Makes a fine hot lunch or may be cut into wedges and served cold as a summer appetizer.

(SERVES FOUR)

3 tablespoons olive oil
2 cloves garlic
1 small onion, chopped
6 eggs
3 tablespoons finely chopped parsley
½ cup (1 dL) freshly grated Parmesan cheese
½ teaspoon thyme, crumbled

¾ cup (1¾ dL) cooked vegetables, drained and diced, a combination of 2 or more: zucchini, asparagus, spinach, green beans, eggplant, artichoke hearts, tomatoes
Salt to taste
¼ teaspoon freshly ground pepper

Preheat the broiler. Heat the oil in a heavy skillet. Cook the garlic until it is lightly brown, and add the onion and cook until soft. Discard the garlic and remove the skillet from the heat. In a bowl, combine remaining ingredients. Put the skillet back on very low heat. Pour in the egg mixture, stirring to incorporate the onions. Cover and cook 2–3 minutes, until the edges shrink a little. Slip under the broiler to brown lightly.

Sausage and Pepper Frittata. Instead of using the ¾ cup cooked vegetables, sauté with the onion and garlic ½ *green pepper, in ½-inch squares,* and 8 *thin slices peperoni sausage* in the oil before adding the eggs.

Mushrooms, Ham, and Red (or Green) Pepper Frittata. Instead of using ¾ cup cooked vegetables, sauté with the onion and garlic ¼ *pound small mushrooms (or large ones cut in quarters),* about ⅓ *cup diced ham,* and ½ *sweet red or green pepper, diced.*

Fluffy Egg Nest

One golden yolk nestles in a tender nest of egg white.

(SERVES FOUR)

4 eggs
½ teaspoon salt
4 slices toast

4 teaspoons butter
4 teaspoons heavy cream

Preheat the oven to 375°F (190°C). Separate the eggs and beat the whites with the salt until they are stiff but not dry. Put the toast on a cookie sheet. Mound a fourth of the whites on each piece of toast. Using the back of a teaspoon, make a dent or nest in the center of each mound. Put 1 teaspoon of butter and 1 egg yolk in each nest. Spoon 1 teaspoon of cream over each yolk. Bake for 10–12 minutes, or until the whites are golden and the yolk is slightly set.

Creamed Eggs

(SERVES FOUR)

8 hard-boiled eggs (p. 338)
3 cups (¾ L) Cream Sauce
  (p. 265)
8 slices toast

Dusting of paprika
2 tablespoons minced parsley
  and chives or other fresh
  herbs (optional)

Chop the eggs into small dice. Stir them into the warm sauce and cook until very hot. Spoon over the toast and dust with paprika and/or fresh parsley and herbs.

Curried Eggs. Add *1 tablespoon curry powder* and, if you like, *½ cup peanuts* to the egg sauce. Serve with *chutney or raisins.* Omit the paprika and parsley.

Goldenrod Eggs. Sieve and set aside the egg yolks. Chop and add only the whites to the sauce. To serve, spoon the sauce over toast and garnish with sieved yolks. Omit paprika and use parsley and herbs if you wish.

Eggs Chasseur

(SERVES FOUR)

2 tablespoons butter
2 shallots, chopped fine, or 2
  tablespoons finely chopped
  onion
6 mushrooms, chopped
½ cup (1 dL) chicken broth
2 tablespoons dry sherry

¼ teaspoon salt
Pinch of cayenne pepper
8 poached eggs (p. 339)
4 tablespoons heavy cream
2 tablespoons freshly grated
  Parmesan cheese

Preheat the oven to 400°F (205°C). Melt the butter in a saucepan. Add the shallots or onion and cook over low heat for 3 minutes. Add the mushrooms and cook until soft. Add the chicken broth, sherry, salt, and cayenne pepper, bring to the boiling point, and simmer for 10 minutes. Pour the sauce into a shallow baking dish that will accommodate 8 poached eggs. Put the eggs in the sauce and spoon cream over them. Sprinkle with cheese and bake until the cheese is melted, about 3–5 minutes.

Eggs Benedict

Multiply this recipe according to the number of persons being served, and encourage heartier appetites to have two.

(SERVES ONE)

⅓ cup (¾ dL) Hollandaise
  Sauce (p. 272)
1 slice cooked ham, ⅜ inch
  thick, the size of the muffin,
  or 1 slice Canadian bacon

½ English muffin
Butter
1 egg

Prepare the Hollandaise and keep it warm. Put the ham in a small skillet and heat thoroughly or fry the Canadian bacon. Spread the English muffin with butter, and toast under the broiler. Poach the egg (p. 339). To assemble, put the English muffin on a plate, place the ham or bacon on the muffin, carefully place the egg on the ham, and cover with hollandaise sauce.

Luncheon Custard

Serve with a tomato or mushroom sauce to add distinction to this mild custard.

(SERVES FOUR)

4 eggs, slightly beaten
1 cup (¼ L) milk
½ teaspoon salt
⅛ teaspoon freshly ground
 pepper
Pinch of cayenne pepper

1 tablespoon minced onion
1 cup (¼ L) Tomato Sauce
 (p. 271) or Mushroom Sauce
 (p. 270)

Preheat the oven to 350°F (180°C). Butter four 1-cup molds or ramekins and place them in the oven in a shallow pan with 1 inch of hot water. Combine the eggs, milk, salt, pepper, cayenne pepper, and onion. Divide the mixture among the molds and bake 25–30 minutes until set. Serve with a sauce.

Ham Timbales

A timbale is a cross between a custard and a soufflé, made in individual custard cups, or small molds, or even muffin tins; the timbales are then unmolded and served with a sauce. They may be made of almost any mixture of tasty cooked meat, poultry, fish and shellfish, or vegetables and cheese, so they provide a good way of transforming leftovers into a delicious luncheon dish.

(SERVES FOUR)

Softened butter
4 tablespoons butter
½ cup (1 dL) bread crumbs
1¼ cups (3 dL) milk
2 cups (½ L) minced ham

2 tablespoons minced parsley
4 eggs, lightly beaten
Salt to taste
Freshly ground pepper

Preheat the oven to 350°F (180°C). Lightly butter eight custard cups or muffin tins. Melt the 4 tablespoons of butter, add the bread crumbs and milk, and cook over medium-low heat 5 minutes, stirring constantly. Add the ham, parsley, and eggs. Season to taste with salt and pepper. Fill the cups—they should be about two-thirds full—and place them in a pan of hot water that comes about two-thirds of the way up the sides. Bake for 20 minutes. Remove and let stand 5 minutes, then unmold by slipping a knife around the inside of each cup and turning onto warm plates or a platter. Surround with *Mushroom Sauce* (p. 270) or *Curry Cream Sauce* (p. 265).

Chicken or Turkey Timbales. Use *2 cups minced cooked chicken* or *turkey* instead of ham and add *½ teaspoon dried* or *2 teaspoons fresh tarragon.* Serve with *Mushroom Sauce* (p. 270) or *Lemon Sauce* (p. 266).

Fish or Shellfish Timbales. Use *2 cups minced cooked fish* or *shellfish* instead of ham and add *¼ teaspoon dried dill* or *1 teaspoon fresh chopped dill* and a few drops of *lemon juice.* Surround with *Lobster Velouté Sauce* (p. 266) or *Sauce Mousseline* (p. 272).

Cheese Soufflé

This is a light fragile soufflé that must be brought to the table as soon as it is ready. Soufflés can be made of many kinds of leftovers—ground meat or poultry that has a good flavor, a bit of fish, finely chopped vegetables that have intense color and taste. Follow the proportions for the Spinach Soufflé variation.

(SERVES FOUR)

1 cup (¼ L) plus 2 tablespoons grated Cheddar cheese
4 tablespoons butter
4 tablespoons flour
1 cup (¼ L) hot milk

½ teaspoon salt
Pinch of cayenne pepper
4 egg yolks, slightly beaten
5 egg whites

Preheat the oven to 375°F (190°C). Butter a 1½-quart straight-sided soufflé dish and sprinkle 2 tablespoons of the cheese over the bottom and around the sides. Melt the butter in a saucepan, add the flour, and cook gently 2–3 minutes, stirring constantly. Add the milk and continue to cook over low heat 2–3 minutes, stirring, until thick and smooth. Add the salt, cayenne pepper, and the rest of the cheese, blending in the cheese thoroughly; the sauce should be very thick. Beat 3 tablespoons of the hot cheese mixture into the egg yolks and then return to the saucepan, stirring 1 minute over low heat. Remove and pour into a large bowl. Beat the egg whites until they are stiff but not dry. Stir a fourth of the whites into the cheese sauce, then fold in the remaining whites. Spoon into the soufflé dish. Bake on the middle rack of the oven for 35 minutes. Serve immediately.

Herb Soufflé. Omit the cheese and add *1½ tablespoons minced onion, 1 teaspoon basil, crumbled, 1 teaspoon tarragon, crumbled,* and *1 tablespoon minced parsley* to the cream sauce base.

Spinach Soufflé. Instead of the 1 cup Cheddar cheese, use *¾ cup well-drained, finely chopped cooked spinach* and *⅓ cup grated Swiss cheese.*

Sturdy Soufflé

This light but dense soufflé comes from the oven nicely rounded and shiny. Although it will fall in about 10 minutes, it will not really flatten, unlike the preceding cloudlike soufflé made of separated eggs. Serve hot or at room temperature, and try making it in a colorful ovenproof bowl or casserole instead of a classic soufflé dish.

(SERVES THREE TO FOUR)

4 tablespoons butter
¼ cup (½ dL) flour
1 cup (¼ L) hot milk
Pinch of salt

Pinch of cayenne pepper
½ cup (1 dL) grated Parmesan cheese
4 eggs, well beaten

Preheat the oven to 375°F (190°C). Butter a 3-cup or 1-quart ovenproof bowl or baking dish. Place it in the oven in a pan containing 1 inch of hot water. Melt the butter in a saucepan. Stir in the flour and blend until smooth. Cook over low heat for 2–3 minutes. Slowly add the milk and cook, stirring constantly, for 3 minutes, until smooth and thick. Add the salt, cayenne pepper, and cheese. Stir until the cheese is melted and blended into the sauce. Remove from the heat. Beat 3 tablespoons of sauce into the eggs, then return the egg-sauce mixture to the saucepan and beat until smooth. Pour into the baking dish and bake for about 20 minutes, until set.

Eggs à la Suisse

A simple dish to make if you keep the heat very low.

(SERVES TWO)

1 tablespoon butter	Pinch of cayenne pepper
½ cup (1 dL) heavy cream	2 tablespoons freshly grated
4 eggs	Gruyère or Swiss cheese
Salt	2 slices toast, buttered

Melt the butter in a skillet. Add the cream, gently break in the eggs one by one, and sprinkle with salt and cayenne pepper. Cook over very low heat, basting with the cream, until the whites are almost firm. Sprinkle the cheese evenly over the top. Place 2 eggs and a spoonful of cream on each piece of buttered toast.

Scrambled Eggs Creole

These flavorful eggs are particularly good with warm tortillas.

(SERVES FOUR)

2 tablespoons butter	½ teaspoon salt
4 tablespoons finely chopped onion	¼ teaspoon freshly ground pepper
1 cup (¼ L) tomatoes, peeled, seeded, and chopped fine	5 eggs, slightly beaten
1 teaspoon sugar	4 tablespoons freshly grated Parmesan cheese

Melt the butter in a skillet and cook the onion over medium heat until soft. Add the tomatoes, sugar, salt, and pepper and cook 5 minutes. Stir in the eggs. Cook over low heat, stirring as they set, until they are creamy. Sprinkle with the cheese.

Scrambled Eggs with Mushrooms

(SERVES FOUR)

4 tablespoons butter	5 eggs, slightly beaten
1½ cups (3½ dL) sliced mushrooms	½ teaspoon salt
1½ tablespoons flour	Pinch of cayenne pepper
4 tablespoons finely chopped onion	

Melt the butter in a skillet. Dust the mushrooms with flour and put in the skillet with the onion. Cook and stir 4–5 minutes, until the mushrooms darken and become soft. Lower the heat. Stir in the eggs, salt, and cayenne pepper and cook, following the recipe for Scrambled Eggs, p. 340, until the eggs are creamy and set.

Baked Eggs in Mornay Sauce

A good Sunday supper: eggs nestling in a cheese-flavored cream sauce.
Spoon each egg with some sauce over toast or English muffins.

(SERVES THREE TO FOUR)

2 recipes Mornay Sauce (p. 265)
6 eggs

Preheat the oven to 375°F (190°C). Butter a shallow gratin dish or baking dish
large enough to hold the eggs and the sauce. When the sauce is very hot, pour
it into the dish. Break the eggs, one by one, into a saucer, and drop each one
gently at evenly spaced intervals over the sauce. Butter a piece of wax paper,
cover the baking dish, and bake for 6–7 minutes, just long enough to set the
whites and slightly set the yolks. The yolks should remain runny.

CHEESE

About Cheese

There is no part of the Western world where cheese is not made, whether it be
a subtle, well-ripened Brie, the comfortable American cheese we use for toasted
cheese sandwiches, or the country Cheddar that makes such a natural partner to
autumn's first crisp McIntosh apples.

Cheese, like wine, varies from one season to another and from one location
to another. It is highly nutritious, and a good substitute for meat. It developed
as a method of preserving surplus milk, and thus is made where there are milk-
producing herds, in such places as Switzerland and the American Midwest among
others. The milk may be sweet or sour, whole, skim, or mixed with additional
cream; it may come from cows, goats, or ewes, or even, in the case of old-
fashioned mozzarella and provolone, from water buffaloes.

Kinds of Cheese

Natural Cheese. Natural cheese is made when milk is separated into a firm curd
and liquid whey by the action of gentle heat or lactic acid. The whey is
drained off, the curd cut into cubes, and cream is added. We call this
simplest natural cheese "fresh" or "unripened," by which we mean that it
is unfermented. To this category belong cottage, pot cheese, and farmer
cheese, whose names describe their rustic origins; every farmwife used to
make her own cottage cheese from milk that otherwise would have gone
bad. Some other fresh cheeses are ricotta, feta, fresh cream cheese, and
Neufchâtel. They are all quite perishable and, unlike other cheeses, should
be served straight from the refrigerator.

Ripened Cheese. Ripened natural cheese is made when the curds are fermented
through the action of rennet or various bacteria cultures. The amount of
liquid whey left with the curd determines whether the cheese is soft, like
Brie and Camembert, semifirm, like Muenster, Cheddar, and Gruyère, or
hard, like Parmesan and Romano. The blue cheeses—Roquefort, Stilton,
and Danish blue—are considered semifirm. It is not only the amount of
whey in the cheese that accounts for the differences in type, however, but
rather such mysterious factors as the quality of the milk, the length of the
aging process, the humidity and temperature of the place where the cheese
is ripened, and the differences in molds from one cave or cellar to another.

1. *Cheddar*; 2. *Swiss*; 3. *Jarlsberg*; 4. *Edam*; 5. *Stilton*; 6. *Roquefort*; 7. *Parmesan*;
8. *Romano*; 9. *Provolone*; 10. *Liederkranz*; 11. *Brick*; 12. *Fontina*; 13. *Port Salut*;
14. *Chèvres (goat cheese)*; 15. *Feta (in brine)*; 16. *Brie*; 17. *Camembert*;
18. *Boursin*.

Processed Cheese. American technology has tried to standardize the quality of cheese and improve its longevity. The result has been a variety of long-keeping processed cheeses and cheese foods available in American markets.

Processed cheese is natural cheese that has been ground up, pasteurized, reblended, and packaged. Cheese food is a blend of various ground cheeses with whey solids, whey albumins, seasonings, color, and water. Cheese spreads are made by adding gums, fat, and liquid to processed cheese. Processed cheese is lower in butterfat and, therefore, in calories, than natural cheese. It has less food value than natural cheese, however, and lacks its interesting texture and fine flavor.

Buying Cheese

Most supermarkets offer a good variety of cheeses, and local delicatessens often carry cheeses like Jarlsberg, Fontina, and Cheddar in bulk. Specialized cheese shops are great fun to explore, and most owners are happy to let you sample before you buy. The more you taste good cheeses, the more you will want to serve them and be confident about your selections.

Storing Cheese

The softer a cheese is, the more perishable it will be. Still, even soft cheese should always be removed from the refrigerator one-half to one hour (depending on the temperature of your kitchen) before serving to develop flavor and the proper consistency; then carefully wrap again in plastic right after using and refrigerate. Only cottage cheese should be served chilled. Semisoft and medium-firm cheeses should also be kept in the refrigerator, wrapped tightly in plastic wrap to seal out the air, and brought to room temperature before serving. Incidentally, if a cheese develops a little mold on the outside, that doesn't mean it is spoiled; just scrape the mold away. Very hard cheeses actually need no refrigeration at all—think of the waxy balls of provolone that hang from the ceilings of Italian delicatessens—but they should be well wrapped or kept under a bell in a relatively cool place. Hard and semihard cheeses freeze well; soft cheeses are apt to break down in texture.

Grating Cheese

Try always to grate your own cheese. It will taste so much better and is more economical. A standard four-sided grater or a small cylindrical one with a handle works best. You can also use a blender or food processor if your cheese is not too hard. Keep a piece of imported Parmesan and another of sharp Cheddar for just this purpose; well wrapped in the refrigerator they will keep a long time.

Cooking Cheese

Use natural cheeses for cooking and never overheat them, lest they become tough and stringy. Try substituting one cheese for another in recipes: although the taste of the finished dish will be altered, it may be improved.

Serving Cheese

Cheese may be served before dinner or during the evening with drinks, passed with the salad, or served after as a separate course with or without fruit. In arranging a cheese board, choose varieties that will contrast in flavor and texture with one another. Try buttery Camembert, rich blue-veined Stilton, and sharp Vermont Cheddar, or combine tangy chèvre (French goat cheese), stolid Edam, and pungent Limburger or Liedercranz. And don't forget about bringing the cheeses to room temperature. Pass a basket of plain crackers or some French bread with your cheese platter.

Cheese Toast

Like a serving of cheese soufflé on toast, these puffs are nice with a cup of soup; they must be eaten as soon as they are prepared.

(SERVES SIX)

2 tablespoons butter	Salt
1 tablespoon flour	2 egg yolks, slightly beaten
⅛ teaspoon cayenne pepper	2 egg whites, stiffly beaten but
1 cup (¼ L) hot milk	not-dry
¾ cup (1¾ dL) grated Cheddar cheese	6 slices toast

Melt the butter in a saucepan. Blend in the flour and cayenne pepper, and cook for 2–3 minutes, stirring. Slowly add the milk, stirring constantly until smooth and thickened. Stir in the cheese and cook until it is melted. Add salt to taste. Beat 2 tablespoonfuls of hot cheese mixture into the yolks. Return the yolk-cheese mixture to the saucepan and cook over medium heat, stirring constantly, for 1–2 minutes, until thickened. Remove from the heat, gently fold in the egg whites, and mound on toast.

Fried Cheese Balls

Serve hot or cold, with a salad or with pre-dinner drinks.

(15 SMALL BALLS)

1 cup (¼ L) grated mild cheese	2 egg whites, stiffly beaten
2 teaspoons flour	¾ cup (1¾ dL) fine cracker
¼ teaspoon salt	crumbs
⅛ teaspoon cayenne pepper	½ cup (1 dL) vegetable oil

Combine the cheese, flour, salt, and cayenne pepper. Using your hands, gently stir in the egg whites. Pat the mixture into small balls and roll them in cracker crumbs until thoroughly coated. Heat the oil in a skillet. When it is hot, put the balls in the pan without crowding them. Cook over medium-high heat, turning so all sides become golden brown. Drain on paper towels.

Welsh Rabbit

(SERVES FOUR)

½ pound (225 g) sharp Cheddar cheese, in small dice	Cayenne pepper to taste
	1 egg, slightly beaten
	Salt
1 tablespoon butter	½ cup (1 dL) beer
½ teaspoon dry mustard	4 slices toast

Combine the cheese, butter, mustard, and cayenne pepper in a heavy-bottomed pan, a chafing dish, or the top of a double boiler. Cook over low heat, stirring constantly, until the cheese has melted. Beat a little of the hot cheese mixture into the egg, and then return the egg-cheese mixture to the pan. Add salt to taste. Add the beer and cook 1–2 minutes more, until very hot but not boiling. Spoon over toast.

Mild Rabbit. Substitute ½ *cup milk* for the beer.

English Monkey

This pleasant sauce is only as tasty as the cheese you use. A good recipe for young cooks to try.

(SERVES FOUR)

1 cup (¼ L) dry bread crumbs
1 cup (¼ L) grated Cheddar
  cheese

1 cup (¼ L) milk
1 teaspoon prepared mustard
4 slices toast

Combine the crumbs, cheese, milk, and mustard in a heavy-bottomed pan and heat, stirring, over medium-low heat. Cook until the cheese has melted and all the ingredients are hot and blended. Spoon over toast.

Tomato Rarebit

(SERVES SIX)

2 tablespoons butter
2 tablespoons flour
1 cup (¼ L) light cream,
  heated
½ cup (1 dL) finely chopped
  canned or fresh tomatoes
⅛ teaspoon baking soda

2 cups (½ L) grated Cheddar
  cheese
2 eggs, slightly beaten
1 teaspoon dry mustard
Cayenne pepper to taste
Salt
6 slices toast

Melt the butter in a saucepan. Stir in the flour and cook for 2–3 minutes, stirring. Slowly pour in the cream, and cook and stir until the mixture thickens. Add the tomatoes mixed with baking soda, cheese, eggs, mustard, and cayenne pepper. Cook over gentle heat, stirring, until the cheese melts. Salt to taste. Do not boil. Spoon over toast.

Chilaly

(SERVES FOUR)

1 tablespoon butter
2 tablespoons finely chopped
  green pepper
2 tablespoons finely chopped
  onion
½ cup (1 dL) finely chopped
  tomato pulp
¼ teaspoon salt
⅛ teaspoon cayenne pepper

1½ cups (3½ dL) grated
  Monterey Jack or Cheddar
  cheese
2 tablespoons milk
1 egg, slightly beaten
4 pieces toast

Melt the butter in a skillet. Add the green pepper and onion and cook, stirring, until soft. Add the tomatoes and stir over low heat for 5 minutes. Add the salt, cayenne pepper, and cheese and cook, stirring constantly, until the cheese melts. Briskly stir in the milk mixed with the egg, cook 1 minute more, and spoon over toast.

Swiss Fondue

Make the fondue in a chafing dish, a special fondue dish, or in a heavy earthenware casserole placed over very low heat on an asbestos mat. Then sit around and dunk. If it thickens too much as it cools, thin it with a little more warm wine.

(SERVES FOUR)

1 clove garlic
1 cup (¼ L) dry white wine
1 pound (450 g), about 2½ cups (6 dL) Swiss cheese, grated or diced small
¼ teaspoon nutmeg

¼ teaspoon freshly ground pepper
3 tablespoons kirsch
Salt to taste
1 loaf French bread, in 1-inch cubes

Vigorously rub the inside of the casserole with the garlic clove. Pour the wine into the casserole and heat until it barely simmers. Over low heat, add the cheese a little at a time, stirring with a wooden spoon until it is melted. Stir in the nutmeg, pepper, kirsch, and salt. Give guests long-handled forks, and let them spear cubes of bread to dunk into the creamy fondue.

Fondue Celestine

For a special supper.

(SERVES SIX)

1 pound (450 g) cooked or canned lobster meat, chopped
1 cup (¼ L) finely chopped celery
2 tablespoons finely chopped onion
½ cup (1 dL) mayonnaise
1½ tablespoons prepared mustard

3 tablespoons lemon juice
16 thin slices white bread, crusts removed
2 cups (½ L) milk
1 cup (¼ L) grated Swiss cheese
1 egg, slightly beaten
Salt to taste
¼ teaspoon freshly ground pepper

Preheat the oven to 325°F (165°C). Combine the lobster, celery, onion, mayonnaise, mustard, and lemon juice in a bowl. Spread 8 slices of the bread with the lobster filling, and place the remaining slices of bread on top. Cut the sandwiches into quarters and lay them in one layer in a shallow baking dish. Scald the milk, cool slightly, and beat in the cheese, egg, salt, and pepper. Pour over the sandwiches. Let stand for 1 hour. Put the baking dish in a larger pan with 1 inch of hot water and bake until firm, 35–40 minutes.

Cheese-Bread Pudding

(SERVES FOUR)

5 slices bread, without crusts
1½ cups (3½ dL) milk
1 cup (¼ L) grated Cheddar cheese

3 eggs, slightly beaten
1 teaspoon Worcestershire sauce
Salt to taste

Preheat the oven to 300°F (150°C). Butter a 1-quart casserole. Cut the bread into

1-inch squares. Scald the milk, cool slightly, and beat in the cheese, eggs, Worcestershire sauce, and salt. Pour into the casserole, add the bread squares, and bake 40–50 minutes, or until firm.

Hot Cheese Savory

Two kinds of cheese make the rich flavor of this custard.

(SERVES FOUR)

2 eggs, slightly beaten
⅔ cup (1½ dL) heavy cream
½ cup (1 dL) finely diced Swiss
  cheese
½ cup (1 dL) freshly grated
  Parmesan cheese

¼ teaspoon freshly ground
  pepper
Pinch of cayenne pepper
¼ teaspoon nutmeg

Preheat the oven to 450°F (230°C). Combine all ingredients. Beat well and pour into a small casserole or four ramekins. Bake 15 minutes.

New England Cheddar Pie

(SERVES SIX)

1½ cups (3½ dL) grated sharp
  Cheddar cheese
1 recipe Basic Pastry for 9-inch
  pie shell (p. 575)
4 eggs
2 cups (½ L) heavy cream

2 hearty shakes of the Tabasco
  bottle
Salt to taste
½ cup (1 dL) coarsely chopped
  walnuts (optional)

Preheat the oven to 425°F (220°C). Sprinkle the cheese evenly over the bottom of the pie shell. In a bowl, beat the eggs and stir in the cream and Tabasco. Pour over the cheese in the pie shell. Taste and add salt as needed. Bake for 15 minutes, lower the heat to 300°F (150°C), and bake 25–30 minutes more or until a knife inserted in the center comes out clean. Remove from the oven, sprinkle with chopped walnuts, if desired, and let stand for 5 minutes to make it easier to cut and serve.

VEGETABLES

ABOUT VEGETABLES

Attitudes toward vegetable cooking have changed dramatically over the years. Today the emphasis in on preserving the natural goodness of vegetables, cooking them for the shortest time possible, until just barely tender with a slight suggestion of crispness or crunchiness.

Those of us who were brought up on soggy, overcooked vegetables and learned at an early age to dislike them thoroughly have since discovered that the same vegetables, properly cooked to retain color, flavor, shape, and texture, are not only nourishing but very delicious. And proper cooking is only part of the secret—it is also important to know *when* to buy fresh vegetables, *what* to look for, and *how* to serve them.

Buying Vegetables

Careful selection of green groceries is important: if vegetables are weary when purchased, you will not be able to perk them up by cooking them. It's worth going out of your way to find a special produce market or to drive to a country farm stand in order to get crisp, firm, fresh vegetables with bright, natural color. Or try growing them in your own backyard.

Whenever possible, try to get fresh rather than canned or frozen vegetables. Buy them when they are in season: they are less expensive and also at their best when they have been born and nurtured in rhythm with the earth's master plan. Somehow man's forced system for producing certain vegetables all year round results in vegetables that lack character, although they often look glamorously bright and large.

Storing Vegetables

Try to buy vegetables shortly before you plan to use them, and do not buy more than you need. Even vegetables like peas and corn, which do not change in appearance as they get older, will become starchy and lose their sweetness when they are held for any time.

Most vegetables should be kept in the refrigerator or in a cool place.

Cooking Vegetables

The taste and tenderness of a vegetable will vary, according to its age, size, and freshness. These recipes give general guidelines for cooking times and seasonings, but the best test of all is your own taste. If in doubt, it is always better to undercook vegetables than to let them get limp and lifeless.

A wonderful way to cook many vegetables—such as broccoli, green beans, spinach, cauliflower, Brussels sprouts, cabbage, and carrots—is to give them a brief baptism in boiling water. Fresh natural flavors and bright colors intensify when vegetables are cooked briskly in an uncovered pot. It's easy to tell when the vegetable is done: just pluck one out and taste it. Use lots of water so that it returns quickly to a boil after the vegetables are added to the pot. Cook the vegetables as briefly as possible, just until they are tender-crisp. Drain, add salt and butter, and serve, or drain and set aside until later, reheating them quickly, just before serving, in a little melted butter.

Some vegetables, like broccoli, cauliflower, and green beans, taste very good steamed, although green vegetables lose some of their color. Steam them in a covered steamer basket over briskly boiling water. Steaming will take longer than boiling. There are several kinds of steamer pots available, as well as a collapsible vegetable holder that will adjust to any pot. The new electric steamers are excellent, enabling you to steam more than one vegetable at a time.

Roasting vegetables around meat mingles lovely juices and turns the vegetables a rich brown. Potatoes, turnips, carrots, and onions blossom this way. Parboil potatoes and turnips before they join the roast by peeling them and dropping them into a large pot of boiling water. Let them boil merrily for 10 to 20 minutes until they are barely tender when pierced with a knife. Then place them around the roast about an hour before the meat is done. See White Turnips Roasted with Meat or Fowl (p. 419) for a master recipe.

Crisp, batter-coated, deep-fried vegetables, or fritters, make a light, yet crunchy accompaniment to roasts and broiled meats. Or a whole platter of various combinations when the garden abounds with tender young vegetables is such a treat that one might want little else for supper. Zucchini and eggplant cut in 1-inch pieces, cauliflower and broccoli flowerets, mushrooms and whole green beans take particularly well to the fritter treatment. See p. 358 for Beer Fritter Batter which has a tangy flavor, particularly well-suited to vegetables.

Vegetable custards are light suppers in themselves and are also good for lunch. Use Broccoli in Cheese Custard (p. 367) as a basic recipe and vary it with other vegetables.

The food processor, with a flick of the wrist, will purée cooked vegetables in a matter of seconds. Add butter, seasonings, and a bit of cream, perhaps, and try combining several vegetables in a purée. Turnips with potatoes, celeriac with potatoes, and pumpkin with yams are among many happy unions. Use the recipe for Mashed or Puréed Parsnips (p. 393) and try it with other vegetables as well. You can also use a blender to purée, but you're apt to have to add more liquid to get it going—more cream or a little of the vegetable cooking juice.

Vegetables can be cooked in many other interesting ways, as the recipes in this chapter indicate: sautéed or stir-fried in butter or oil, braised in broth or wine, baked with buttered crumbs, broiled, glazed or candied, or stuffed with tangy fillings.

You can also cook vegetables in a pressure cooker, which is time-saving with certain vegetables and a good way to preserve healthful vegetable juices. Pressure cooking has its disadvantages, however: since you cannot remove the cover to taste a sample bean or pea, you can't test for doneness and adjust the cooking time accordingly.

If you use a pressure cooker, be sure to follow the manufacturer's directions carefully (on p. 753 there is a general guide to timing pressure-cooked vegetables).

Serving Vegetables

Vegetables are used in soups, stews, and salads. They are also good combined with rice, beans, or pasta or served with a variety of sauces, both hot and cold. Make them the appetizer to a meal, use them as side dishes to a main meat course, or plan an all-vegetable meal or a country corn boil with vegetables as the main attraction.

You'll want to use the same vegetable frequently while it's in season. This can be made less repetitious with a few small innovations—a light blanket of cream, some buttered crumbs, perhaps a sprinkling of a friendly herb.

Use restraint, however, in adding sauces, garnishes, and herbs to vegetables. Think of the total meal and adorn the vegetable only when the other dishes are very plain. Many times a light salting and a dollop of butter over a spanking-fresh vegetable are just enough.

Think also of color, texture, and taste when you select a vegetable, so that it will balance and enhance the other dishes you are serving. It is dreadful to face a dinner plate on which everything is pale and white or of a uniformly soft consistency. It is even worse to eat a combination of highly seasoned dishes that compete with or cancel out one another's tastes.

Leftover Vegetables

Soups and stocks are good catch-alls for vegetable juices and for leftover vegetables, whether raw or cooked, in large quantities or just a few scraps. Use leftover vegetables in custards, in soufflés, or in omelets and frittatas. You can also purée leftover vegetables in a blender or food processor and heat them with a little butter, salt, and cream. Or add puréed vegetables to soups, soufflés, or custards.

Leftover cooked vegetables are seldom very good when simply reheated the next day. It's better to serve them cold in French Dressing or Basic Vinaigrette (p. 450) or to cut them up and add them to a tossed salad. If the vegetables have been buttered, you can wash off the congealed butter with a little hot water before adding them to a salad.

If you must reheat vegetables, do so in a double boiler and do not heat them any longer than necessary. Try serving them with White Sauce (p. 265) or Cheese Sauce (p. 265).

Frozen or Canned Vegetables

Frozen or canned vegetables, always second best to fresh, may be used in some of these recipes. Check under the individual vegetable listings to see if such substitutions are advisable.

Frozen vegetables are generally preferable to canned and usually work best when combined with sauces or other vegetables. When cooking frozen vegetables, it's often best to disregard the package directions, allowing the vegetable to defrost enough so that it can be broken up easily; then cook as quickly as possible in a very small amount of water.

For canning vegetables, see p. 694.

For freezing vegetables, see p. 733.

Beer Fritter Batter

This is good not only for vegetables but for seafood and chicken, as well as for fruit fritters, such as banana, pineapple, and apple.

(1½ CUPS)

1 cup flour	Salt
1 egg	½ cup (1 dL) beer
1 tablespoon butter, melted	

Combine the flour, egg, butter, salt, and beer in a blender, or processor, or a bowl. Beat until the batter is smooth. Let the batter stand, covered, for 4 hours before using. Have vegetables well drained and patted dry if they have been washed. Cut into 1-inch pieces or use whole flowerets; leave green beans and mushrooms whole. Dip in batter and fry in deep fat, 360°F, until golden. Remove quickly and drain on paper towels.

ABOUT GLOBE ARTICHOKES

Height of Season: April and May.
What to Look For: Green stems and firm, unblemished leaves. Size does not affect
   taste.
Uses: Cooked, as a first or separate course; bottoms or hearts in salads.
Amount: One per person.
Alternatives to Fresh: Both frozen and canned hearts and bottoms are available
   and good.

Globe artichokes, sometimes called French or Italian artichokes, resemble a flower bud with a fascinating, complex construction.

   If you've never eaten an artichoke, here's how you proceed. Start with the outer leaves and work toward the center, taking off each leaf with your fingers and dipping it in melted butter or a special sauce. Scrape off the edible bottom part of the leaf with your teeth and discard what remains. In the center of the artichoke is a light green cone of tiny leaves which can be removed in one piece. Under this cone is the prickly center, or "choke," which is inedible and should be scraped off. (See illustration of cross section, p. 363).

   The tender, delicious artichoke bottom, sometimes erroneously called the "heart," is just below the choke. It is slightly cuplike in shape and captures the intense, delicious flavor of the artichoke.

   The heart is actually the whole tender center of an artichoke, including the bottom and some of the most tender leaves; the bristly choke is removed. The hearts of tiny artichokes are sold frozen and in jars.

Basic Method for Cooking Artichokes

(ALLOW ONE PER PERSON)

Cooked artichoke stems are delicious. Do not detach them until after cooking, and use them in salads or as an hors d'oeuvre.

   To prepare for cooking, peel the coarse fibers from the artichoke stem. Remove the tough bottom leaves, then slice off about an inch from the leaves at the top. With scissors, snip off the prickly tops of the remaining side leaves. Plunge the

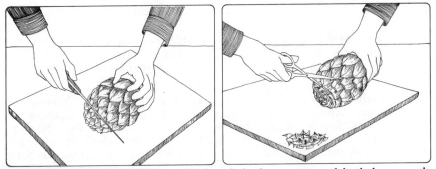

artichokes into a very large pot filled with boiling water and boil them gently until done. Allow 25–40 minutes: they are done when an outer leaf pulls off easily and the bottom is tender when pierced with a fork. Drain them upside down. Serve them hot or warm, with *melted butter* or *Hollandaise Sauce* (p. 272) on the side, or cold with *French Dressing* (p. 450) or *mayonnaise seasoned with lemon juice and a drop of prepared mustard.*

Sautéed Artichoke Hearts

(SERVES FOUR)

Two 8½-ounce (240-g)   6 tablespoons butter
    packages frozen artichoke   Salt to taste
    hearts, or two 9-ounce (250-g)   2 tablespoons minced parsley
    cans drained, rinsed hearts

If you are using frozen, thaw them enough to break apart. Then cook them in ¼ cup water, covered, for 5 minutes. Melt the butter in a skillet and add the drained artichoke hearts. Stir often so they are well coated with butter, sprinkle with salt and parsley, and serve when thoroughly hot.

ABOUT JERUSALEM ARTICHOKES

Height of Season: Winter months.
What to Look For: Firm, hard tubers.
Uses: Raw, peeled, then sliced or grated, as an hors d'oeuvre or in salads. *Cooked,* in soups (see p. 93). *As a vegetable accompaniment,* particularly good with red meat.
Amount: One pound serves four.

Jerusalem artichokes, often called sunchokes, are not related to globe artichokes. They are tubers and look something like ginger root, with a knobby, irregular shape, a mild sweetness in taste, and a crunchy, slightly watery consistency. They are very easy to grow in backyard gardens and will return and multiply year after year.

Basic Method for Cooking Jerusalem Artichokes

Peel Jerusalem artichokes with a vegetable peeler. If you remove the bumps, the artichokes will cook more evenly. Don't be a perfectionist—a little of the skin tastes fine.

Basic Method for Cooking Jerusalem Artichokes (continued)

(SERVES THREE TO FOUR)

1 pound (450 g) Jerusalem artichokes	3 tablespoons butter
2 tablespoons finely chopped parsley	Salt to taste
	Freshly ground pepper

Scrub the artichokes with a brush, peel, and drop into cold water with a teaspoon of lemon juice. Then boil in water to cover for 10–20 minutes, depending on their size. Test often by piercing them with the point of a knife; they should be a bit resistant in the center, but not hard. Remove from the heat and drain. Slice, toss with the parsley and butter, and sprinkle with salt and pepper. Serve hot.

Creamed Jerusalem Artichokes. Just before serving, stir in *1 cup White Sauce* (p. 265) and sprinkle a little more *finely chopped parsley* on top. Serve hot.

ABOUT ASPARAGUS

Height of Season: April and May.
What to Look For: Round, firm, fresh-looking spears, very green with smooth, tight tips. Thickness does not affect tenderness.
Uses: Cooked, plain or with sauces, boiled, steamed, stir-fried, as an appetizer, in soups, in salads, in vegetable custards, or in quiches. *As a vegetable accompaniment,* particularly good with beef, veal, and salmon.
Amount: Six to eight per person.
Alternatives to Fresh: Frozen retain the taste of asparagus better than canned, but the texture suffers in both cases.

The asparagus is a perennial vegetable, well worth growing at home. Its fern makes a beautiful addition to any backyard, and asparagus cooked straight from the garden is a great spring feast. It may take a few years to get an asparagus patch established, but then it will provide succulent green spears for as long as thirty-five or forty years.

Basic Method for Cooking Asparagus

The shorter the cooking time, the fresher and greener the color.

(SERVES ABOUT FOUR)

24 large asparagus

Wash the asparagus and cut or break off the tough, colorless, woody bottom of each stalk. Peel with a vegetable peeler, lightly near the top and more deeply toward the bottom. Plunge the spears into a large pot of boiling water and boil gently until the bottoms are just tender when pierced with a knife. Begin testing after 5–8 minutes, depending on the thickness of the stalks. Drain well and serve with *melted butter, Hollandaise Sauce* (p. 272), or *Cheese Sauce* (p. 265).

Asparagus Vinaigrette. Spoon *½ cup French Dressing* (p. 450) over hot or cold asparagus, either ahead of time or just before serving.

Stir-fried Asparagus

Asparagus cooked in the Chinese way will be crisp and very green.

(SERVES TWO TO THREE)

1 pound (450 g) thin asparagus   Salt
2–3 tablespoons cooking oil   Freshly ground pepper

Wash the asparagus and trim the bottoms. Cut asparagus in ½-inch slices, slanted at the ends. Heat the oil in a wok or a skillet, add the asparagus, and sauté quickly, tossing frequently, until all the pieces are coated, about 2 minutes. Add 2 tablespoons water and cover. Cook over medium heat for about 3 minutes, until just tender. Season to taste, and serve immediately.

DRIED BEANS

See p. 322.

ABOUT GREEN BEANS

Availability: Year round, especially in spring and summer.
What to Look For: Crisp, firm beans, with good, fresh color; should snap when broken.
Uses: Hot or cold, boiled or steamed, as an appetizer, salad, or vegetable; add leftovers to soups or salads, or purée. *As a vegetable accompaniment,* good with just about everything.
Amount: One pound serves three or four.
Alternatives to Fresh: Frozen preferable to canned, but will be limp.

Green beans were once called string beans. Today they are stringless; just break off the ends as you wash them. Green beans, wax beans, and pole beans may all be cooked the same way, until just tender but crunchy. Try them fried whole in a beer batter for a change sometimes (see p. 358).

Basic Method for Cooking Green Beans

If you leave the beans whole, they will be less watery and more flavorful. If they are very thick, however, you may wish to slice them diagonally or "French" them.

(SERVES THREE TO FOUR)

1 pound (450 g) green beans   Salt
Butter   Freshly ground pepper

Wash the beans and remove the ends and strings, if there are any. Leave them whole or cut them in diagonal strips. Drop them into a large pot of boiling water and boil them gently until just done, allowing about 5–10 minutes, depending on the size and age of the beans. Taste one to see if it is done; it should still be very crunchy. Drain the beans and rinse them thoroughly in cold water to stop the cooking. Reheat them in lots of butter, salt, and pepper just before serving.

Green Beans with Herbs. As you reheat the beans in the butter, add *1 teaspoon fresh (or ½ teaspoon dried) thyme, rosemary,* or *savory,* and a *generous squeeze of lemon juice.*

Green Beans with Almonds. Cook *⅓ cup slivered, blanched almonds* in the butter until lightly browned, then reheat the beans with the nuts and the browned butter, adding salt and pepper to taste.

Green Beans Vinaigrette. Toss the beans with *½ cup French Dressing* (p. 450) and let them sit at room temperature for at least 1 hour before serving.

Green Beans au Gratin. Let the beans boil for only 2 or 3 minutes; they should be very crisp and underdone. Drain and combine them with *1½ cups Cheese Sauce* (p. 265). Arrange in buttered casserole, sprinkle with *buttered bread crumbs,* and bake, uncovered, in a preheated 400°F (205°C) oven just until bubbly and brown, about 20 minutes. Serve immediately. Frozen green beans, defrosted but uncooked, will work in this recipe.

Steamed Green Beans

Steaming is a perfectly acceptable alternative to cooking beans in lots of boiling water, although the color will not be as vivid. The method of cooking is less important than the timing: be sure that the beans are crunchy and not overcooked.

(SERVES THREE TO FOUR)

1 pound (450 g) green beans	Salt
Butter	Freshly ground pepper

Wash the beans and remove the ends and strings, if there are any. Leave them whole or cut them in diagonal strips. Steam them, covered, in a steamer basket over an inch or so of rapidly boiling water until just tender, but still crunchy, about 10–15 minutes. Drain, toss with butter, season to taste, and serve, or **see** variations in the preceding recipe.

ABOUT FRESH SHELL BEANS

Availability: Varies according to variety and region; check in farmers' markets or grow them yourself.
What to Look For: Fresh, firm beans with good color and pliable, velvety pods.
Uses: Cold, as a salad. *Hot,* in soups and casserole dishes. *As a vegetable accompaniment,* particularly good with ham.
Amount: One pound shelled (about 3 pounds unshelled) serves four or five.
Alternatives to Fresh: Frozen and canned are acceptable.

Competition from the frozen product has made fresh shell beans scarce in our markets. The best-known shell beans—lima beans, green soy beans, fava beans, and kidney beans—usually used in their dried form, are especially good when cooked fresh (for information about dried beans, see p. 322). If you can't get them, it's well worth the trouble of growing them yourself.

Most shell beans are shelled by breaking or cutting the pods open and squeezing the beans out. To shell green soy beans, drop them into boiling water, cover, and let stand for 5 minutes; then drain and press out the beans.

1. *artichokes with cross section showing choke and heart;* 2. *Jerusalem artichoke;*
3. *asparagus;* 4. *green beans;* 5. *shell beans;* 6. *lima beans;* 7. *beets;* 8. *broccoli;*
9. *Brussels sprouts;* 10. *broccoli rabe;* 11. *red cabbage;* 12. *Savoy cabbage;*
13. *Chinese cabbage.*

Fresh Lima Beans

2½ pounds (1¼ kg) unshelled   ½ cup (1 dL) heavy cream
   green lima beans   Salt
3 tablespoons butter   Freshly ground pepper

Prepare the limas by snapping open the pods or use a knife to cut them open; remove the beans. Put the beans and 2 quarts water in a large pan. Cover and cook for about 20 minutes or until tender; drain. Melt the butter in the pan, then add the beans, cream, and salt and pepper to taste. Shake the pan to keep the beans from sticking or burning and to coat them evenly. Serve when hot.

Fava Beans

Fava beans are large, shiny green beans, often called broad beans. They are found in the market in April, May, and June.

3 pounds (1⅓ kg) unshelled   1 teaspoon marjoram, crumbled
   fava beans   Salt
4 tablespoons butter   Freshly ground pepper
1 onion, chopped

Shell the beans. Melt the butter in a pan, add the onion, and stir until soft. Add the beans and just enough water to cover. Add the marjoram, cover, and cook for about 20 minutes or until the beans are tender. Drain, saving the liquid, and put the beans in a warm oven. Return the liquid to the pan, turn the heat on high, and reduce the liquid to about ½ cup. Season to taste. Pour over the beans and serve.

ABOUT BEETS

Availability: Year round, especially from June to October.

What to Look For: Smooth, firm, round beets—small or medium size—with deep red color and fresh-looking leaves.

Uses: Cold, pickled, as an hors d'oeuvre or salad. *Hot or cold,* in soups. *As a vegetable accompaniment,* especially good with pork and ground beef.

Amount: One pound serves three to four.

Alternatives to Fresh: Canned beets are acceptable in many recipes.

Beets are usually peeled after boiling, but very young ones may not need peeling at all. Young beets are tender and delicious; if you grow them in your garden, let them grow to the size of marbles before you thin the rows. Cook the beets you pull out with their delicate leaves still attached.

Basic Method for Cooking Beets

Young boiled beets need nothing for embellishment except, perhaps, a little butter. If your beets are old and not very flavorful, try sugaring them or pickling them (see opposite).

(SERVES THREE TO FOUR)

1 pound (450 g) beets
Butter
Salt

Freshly ground pepper
Chopped parsley

Cut off all but 1 inch of the beet tops; do not pare or remove the roots. Drop the beets into enough boiling water to cover them, and cook them, uncovered, until they are tender, allowing 30 minutes to 1 hour, depending on the age of the beets. Drain the beets, drop them in cold water for a minute or two to cool them slightly, then slip off the skins. Leave them whole or quarter them, or slice them with an egg slicer. Toss them with butter, salt and pepper to taste, and some chopped parsley, and reheat them, if necessary, before serving.

Sugared Beets. Toss each pound (about 2 cups) of sliced, cooked beets with *2 tablespoons butter, 1 teaspoon sugar, and ½ teaspoon salt.* Reheat, if necessary, before serving.

Pickled Beets. Mix *½ cup vinegar* with *¼ cup sugar* and boil for 5 minutes. Add *1 teaspoon caraway seeds* and *¼ teaspoon salt.* Pour over 1 pound (about 2 cups) of sliced, cooked beets and serve cold or at room temperature.

Baked Beets

Sweetly tender with such a nice taste. Leftovers done this way are particularly good in salad.

(SERVES FOUR)

1 pound (450 g) beets
Salt
2 tablespoons butter

Preheat the oven to 375°F (190°C). Butter a baking dish that will hold the beets in a single layer. Wash and trim the beets. Put them into the baking dish and sprinkle salt and bits of butter on top. Cover and bake for 1–1½ hours. If the skins are tough or unattractive, slip them off before serving.

Harvard Beets

(SERVES SIX)

½ cup (100 g) sugar
1½ teaspoons cornstarch
¼ cup (½ dL) cider vinegar

3 cups (¾ L) sliced or cubed
cooked beets
2 tablespoons butter

Mix the sugar, cornstarch, vinegar, and ¼ cup water in a pot and boil for 5 minutes. Add the beets, toss well, and let stand for 30 minutes or more. Just before serving, add the butter and reheat to the boiling point.

Beets and Greens

Use very young beets, the size of marbles, and cook them with their tender leaves. To cook mature beet greens, see About Collards and Other Greens (p. 376).

Beets and Greens (continued)

(SERVES TWO)

About 12–15 tiny beets and   Salt
    leaves   Freshly ground pepper
Butter

Wash the beets and leaves thoroughly and cut off the roots. Cut the leaves coarsely. Bring about ½ inch of water to a boil in a pot or skillet. Add the beets and greens, cover, and boil gently for 20–30 minutes, taking care that they do not burn. When the beets can be pierced easily with a fork, they are done. Drain. Toss with lots of butter, season to taste, and serve immediately.

Shredded Beets

(SERVES THREE TO FOUR)

1 pound (450 g) young beets   Salt
3 tablespoons butter   Freshly ground pepper
1 tablespoon lemon juice

Shred the beets by rubbing them against the large holes of a grater or in a food processor. Heat the butter in a skillet. Add the shredded beets, toss, then add the lemon juice and 1 tablespoon of water. Cover and cook over moderate heat, stirring frequently, for 5 minutes or until tender. Season to taste and serve hot.

ABOUT BROCCOLI

Availability: Year round, especially from October to May.
What to Look For: Tight, compact deep green or purple-green flowerets. Avoid
    wilted or yellowish flowerets and stems that are very thick.
Uses: Raw, with a dip, or as a first course or in salads. *Cooked,* boiled or steamed,
    in soups, purées, custards, and quiches; also, dipped in batter and fried. *As
    a vegetable accompaniment,* particularly good with grilled beef.
Amount: One pound serves two to three.
Alternatives to Fresh: Frozen best when puréed or combined with a sauce.

Broccoli belongs to the cabbage family. It is a very satisfactory vegetable to grow at home, for the more it is cut, the more it produces.

Basic Method for Cooking Broccoli

It's true for many vegetables, but especially true with broccoli: Don't overcook!

(SERVES TWO TO THREE)

1 pound (450 g) broccoli
Melted butter
Salt

Cut off and discard the tough end of the stems and coarse outer leaves of the broccoli. Cut the broccoli into flowerets with short stems and peel the stems lightly with a vegetable peeler. Peel more deeply the thick stems cut from the flowerets, and slice them diagonally, so that they will cook quickly. Drop the stems into a large pot of boiling, salted water and boil 3 or 4 minutes, then add the flowerets. Boil until the stems are just tender when pierced with a sharp knife, about 6–10 minutes in all. Drain. Toss with melted butter and salt or serve with *Hollandaise Sauce* (p. 272).

Puréed Broccoli. Put the cooked broccoli through a vegetable mill or purée it in a food processor. Reheat, seasoning to taste with lots of butter, salt, and pepper.

Steamed Broccoli

An alternative to the Basic Method, steamed broccoli will have a fine texture and taste, but the color fades. Take care that the broccoli is not overcooked.

(SERVES TWO TO THREE)

1 pound (450 g) broccoli
Melted butter

Clean and cut up the broccoli as directed in the preceding Basic Method for Cooking Broccoli. Steam it, covered, in a steamer basket over boiling water until the thickest stems are just tender when pierced with a sharp knife, about 10–15 minutes. Drain. Toss with melted butter or *Hollandaise Sauce* (p. 272).

Broccoli in Cheese Custard

This custard recipe may also be used with other cooked vegetables such as cauliflower, corn kernels, onions, spinach, and cabbage.

(SERVES SIX)

2 cups (½ L) chopped cooked broccoli
¾ cup (1¾ dL) grated Cheddar cheese
3 eggs

1½ cups (3½ dL) milk or light cream
¾ teaspoon salt
¼ teaspoon freshly ground pepper

Preheat the oven to 350°F (180°C). Butter a 1½-quart baking dish, put the chopped broccoli into it, and sprinkle with the cheese. Beat the eggs lightly in a bowl and stir in the milk or cream, salt, and pepper. Stir into the broccoli-cheese mixture. Put the baking dish in a shallow pan with hot water halfway up its sides. Bake for 45–60 minutes, or until the custard is set.

ABOUT BROCCOLI RABE

Availability: Late summer and fall, especially in Italian markets.
What to Look For: Thin, firm stems, and small, open, yellowish flowerets.
Uses: Cooked, cold in salads, or *hot,* boiled or blanched and then sautéed. *As a vegetable accompaniment,* especially suitable with meat and pasta dishes.
Amount: One pound serves two to three.

Broccoli rabe, a member of the broccoli family, has a strong, slightly bitter flavor. It profits from special treatment, like the addition of a little garlic and oil.

Sautéed Broccoli Rabe

(SERVES TWO TO THREE)

1 pound (450 g) broccoli rabe   Salt
2 cloves garlic, minced   Freshly ground pepper
3 tablespoons cooking oil

Wash the broccoli rabe and cut it into 2- or 3-inch pieces. Drop them into a large
pot of boiling water and boil for about 5 minutes, or until not quite tender; drain.
Sauté the garlic in the oil for a minute or two without browning, then add the
broccoli rabe and cook over medium heat, stirring frequently, until tender but
still firm. Season to taste and serve immediately.

ABOUT BRUSSELS SPROUTS

Height of Season: Late fall and winter.
What to Look For: Unblemished, tightly closed sprouts, bright green in color.
     Avoid soft, wilted, or yellowing sprouts.
Uses: Cooked, with chestnuts or in casserole dishes. *As a vegetable accompaniment,*
     good with pork and ham, not with delicate meats or fish.
Amount: One pound serves four.
Alternatives to Fresh: Frozen are good.

Brussels sprouts look like tiny cabbages. They grow close together on a long,
single stem which can reach as high as 3 feet. The plants are not much affected
by cold weather and you can often harvest them right through the winter.

Basic Method for Cooking Brussels Sprouts

Properly cooked Brussels sprouts should be bright green and never
overcooked.

(SERVES FOUR)

1 pound (450 g) Brussels sprouts
Melted butter
Salt

Wash the sprouts in cold water, removing any wilted leaves and cutting off the
stems. Drop them into a large pot of boiling, salted water for 8–10 minutes, or
until just tender. Taste one to see if it's done; it should still be slightly crunchy.
Drain. Toss with melted butter and salt to taste or *Hollandaise Sauce* (p. 272).

Brussels Sprouts with Chestnuts

Use the leftover broth to make a soup.

(SERVES SIX)

1 pound (450 g) Brussels   1 cup (¼ L) cooked (p. 375)
  sprouts, trimmed   or canned chestnuts
1½ cups (3½ dL) beef broth   Salt
3 tablespoons butter   Freshly ground pepper
1 teaspoon sugar

Put the Brussels sprouts in a pan with the beef broth. Simmer for about 10–15 minutes or until tender; drain. Melt the butter and sugar together in a pan, stirring until golden. Add the chestnuts and cook until they are slightly brown. Add the sprouts and cook over low heat, stirring occasionally, for 15 minutes more. Season lightly and serve.

ABOUT CABBAGE

Availability: Year round.

What to Look For: Crisp, firm, heavy heads with good color. Avoid those with blemishes or too many loose outer leaves.

Uses: Raw, for dipping or in salads, cole slaw. *Cooked,* boiled, steamed, braised, baked, sautéed, pickled, shredded, stuffed, in soups and stews. *As a vegetable accompaniment,* especially good with corned beef, game, pork, or smoked meats.

Amount: One pound serves three.

Cabbage has been cultivated as a vegetable since ancient times, when it was valued for its health-giving and healing properties. It comes in many varieties, the most common of which are smooth green cabbage, crinkly green Savoy cabbage, red cabbage, and Chinese cabbage.

A lot of people hate cabbage because it's usually cooked to lifelessness and served without texture or taste. It also has an unpleasant odor when it's been boiling for a long time. Except when it's being braised, cabbage should actually be cooked quickly until just tender and should retain its color and crispness.

Basic Method for Cooking Cabbage

(SERVES THREE)

1 pound (450 g) cabbage

Cut the cabbage in half; cut away and discard the hard, whitish core. Slice into wedges. Drop them into a large pot filled with boiling, salted water and boil until the cabbage is just tender, about 10–15 minutes. The cabbage should be crisp-tender and retain its color. Drain well.

Blanched, Buttered Cabbage

Beautiful color, mild taste, this is a marvelous method for those who are dubious about cabbage.

(SERVES SIX)

2 pounds (900 g) cabbage, cored
4 slices bacon
4 tablespoons butter, melted

Salt to taste
½ teaspoon coarsely ground pepper

Bring a big pot of water to boil. Tear the cabbage leaves into large pieces. Fry the bacon until crisp; drain, crumble, and set aside. Plunge the cabbage in and boil for just 1 minute; drain immediately. Return to the pot and toss with the melted butter, salt, pepper, and crumbled bacon. Serve hot.

Scalloped Cabbage

This dish has a pleasing texture: soft cabbage and cream sauce with crisp buttered crumbs on top.

(SERVES SIX)

2 pounds (900 g) cabbage, cut into 8 wedges
1½ cups (3½ dL) White Sauce (p. 265)

1 cup (¼ L) buttered crumbs

Preheat the oven to 400°F (205°C). Butter a 1½-quart casserole. Fill a large pot with salted water, and bring to a boil. Add the cabbage and boil for 6–8 minutes; drain and trim away the tough core. Coarsely chop the cabbage and put it into a casserole. Spoon the sauce over it and sprinkle the crumbs on top. Bake for 20 minutes.

Braised Red Cabbage and Apples

This is exceptionally good: moist, spicy, and faintly sweet. A roasted loin of pork would be a splendid companion.

(SERVES EIGHT)

4 tablespoons bacon fat
2 tablespoons sugar
1 onion, chopped
2 pounds (900 g) red cabbage, shredded
2 tart apples, peeled, cored, and sliced thin

2 tablespoons cider vinegar
½ teaspoon caraway seeds
¼ teaspoon nutmeg
⅛ teaspoon cayenne pepper
½ cup (1 dL) dry red wine
Salt

Melt the bacon fat in a skillet, add the sugar and cook, stirring, for 2 minutes. Add the onion and cook slowly until lightly colored. Stir in the cabbage, apples, vinegar, caraway seeds, nutmeg, cayenne, and red wine. Cook over low heat, covered, for 10 minutes, then add ½ cup water and cook, with cover askew, stirring occasionally, for 30–40 minutes more. Add salt to taste. Serve hot or cold.

Sauerkraut

Sauerkraut, German in origin, is shredded cabbage preserved in a salt-water brine. It is not necessary to wash the brine from the sauerkraut unless a milder taste is desired. Sauerkraut, with its assertive flavor, is very compatible with goose and with pork sausages.

(SERVES FOUR)

1 pound (450 g) sauerkraut
1 large tart apple, peeled, cored, and diced
1 cup (¼ L) beef bouillon

1 teaspoon caraway seeds
¼ teaspoon freshly ground pepper
Salt

Wash the sauerkraut in several changes of cold water if desired; drain thoroughly. Combine the sauerkraut, apple, bouillon, caraway seeds, and pepper. Cook over low heat, stirring occasionally, for about 30–35 minutes. Add salt to taste. Serve hot.

Braised Chinese Cabbage

(SERVES FOUR)

8 strips bacon
1 head Chinese cabbage,
   shredded

Salt
Freshly ground pepper
Soy sauce

Cook the bacon in a skillet until crisp; remove and drain. Pour off all but 2 tablespoons of bacon fat. Heat the remaining fat, then add the cabbage. Cover and cook slowly, stirring occasionally, until just tender, about 3 minutes. Crumble the bacon and stir it into the cabbage. Season to taste with salt and pepper and serve with soy sauce.

Hot Slaw

A tart, vinegary dressing that is a good foil for shredded cabbage. This would be nice with pork or ham.

(SERVES FOUR)

1 pound (450 g) cabbage
2 egg yolks
1 tablespoon butter

¼ cup (½ dL) cider vinegar
Salt

Shred the cabbage and have it ready in a bowl. Mix the egg yolks, ¼ cup of cold water, butter, and vinegar in a heavy-bottomed pan. Cook, stirring constantly, over low heat until thickened. Add the cabbage and stir briskly to coat. Add salt to taste. Heat through and serve.

ABOUT CARROTS

Availability: Year round.
What to Look For: Fairly small, firm, smooth carrots with good color and no cracks or green areas at the top.
Uses: Whole, diced, sliced, or grated. *Raw,* for dipping, in juice, salads. *Cooked,* boiled, braised, baked, as a seasoning, in stocks, soups, casserole dishes, cakes, breads, cookies. *As a vegetable accompaniment,* good with just about anything.
Amount: One pound serves three to four.
Alternatives to Fresh: Frozen preferable to canned, but texture is poor.

Carrots are rich in vitamin A. When small and new, they may not need peeling. If peeling is necessary, use a vegetable scraper and keep them in cold water until ready to use.

Cooked carrots, even old carrots, may be very sweet; use them with discretion or you may overpower the flavor of a soup, sauce, or stew.

If you plan to grow carrots yourself, choose one of the shorter varieties: it's hard to grow straight, long, tapered carrots unless you have specially prepared, rock-free soil.

Basic Method for Cooking Carrots

Cooking times vary greatly with carrots, depending on their size and age.

(SERVES THREE TO FOUR)

1 pound (450 g) carrots, trimmed and peeled	Salt
2 tablespoons butter	Freshly ground pepper

Slice or cube the carrots, or leave them whole if they are small. Cook them, covered, in about 2 inches of boiling water until they are tender, about 10–12 minutes if they are sliced, longer if they are whole. Drain. Coat with the butter, season to taste, and reheat, if necessary, before serving.

Candied Carrots. Melt *5 tablespoons butter* in a heavy skillet, stir in *¼ cup brown sugar*, and heat, stirring, until melted. Add the cooked, seasoned carrots and cook slowly until they are well glazed.

Carrots and Peas. Add *cooked green peas* to diced cooked carrots, dot with butter, season to taste with salt and freshly ground pepper, and reheat slowly.

Mashed or Puréed Carrots. Mash the cooked carrots, put them through a food mill, or purée them in a food processor. Season to taste with butter, salt, freshly ground pepper, and a whisper of *nutmeg*. Reheat slowly, preferably in the top of a double boiler.

Carrot Ring

A custard of puréed carrots baked in a ring mold—delicious with a mound of fresh cooked green peas in the center.

(1-QUART RING)

2½ cups, 6 dL (1 pound, 450 g) mashed cooked carrots	1 cup (¼ L) milk or light cream
1 teaspoon thyme, crumbled	½ teaspoon salt
3 tablespoons butter, melted	¼ teaspoon freshly ground pepper
2 eggs, well beaten	
1 tablespoon flour	

Preheat the oven to 350°F (180°C). Amply butter a 1-quart ring mold and lightly dust it with flour. Mix all ingredients in a bowl, stirring vigorously. Spoon into the mold. Set the mold in a shallow pan of hot water and bake until firm, about 45 minutes. Unmold, fill the center, if you like, with peas or another green vegetable, and serve.

Baked Carrots

(SERVES THREE TO FOUR)

1 pound (450 g) carrots	Pinch of nutmeg
3 tablespoons butter	Salt
1 small onion, chopped	Freshly ground pepper
1 teaspoon sugar	½ cup (1 dL) broth or stock

Preheat the oven to 350°F (180°C). Peel and grate the carrots and set them aside. Melt the butter in a small casserole, add the onion, and cook until soft and transparent. Stir in the carrots, season with the sugar and nutmeg, and add salt and pepper to taste. Add the broth or stock, cover, and bake until tender, about 30–40 minutes.

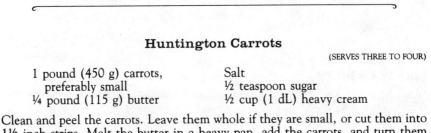

Huntington Carrots

(SERVES THREE TO FOUR)

1 pound (450 g) carrots,	Salt
preferably small	½ teaspoon sugar
¼ pound (115 g) butter	½ cup (1 dL) heavy cream

Clean and peel the carrots. Leave them whole if they are small, or cut them into 1½-inch strips. Melt the butter in a heavy pan, add the carrots, and turn them over and over in the butter until they are well coated. Season them with salt to taste and sugar, cover, and cook very slowly until thecarrots are tender, about 25–35 minutes. Turn them occasionally and be sure that they do not burn. Before serving, adjust the seasonings, add the cream, and reheat.

ABOUT CAULIFLOWER

Height of Season: Fall or winter.
What to Look For: Firm, white, compact flowerets without spots or bruises; crisp, green leaves.
Uses: Raw, in flowerets, for dipping or in salads. *Cooked,* whole or in flowerets, boiled, steamed, deep-fried in batter, and pickled. *As a vegetable accompaniment,* especially good with steak or chops.
Amount: One medium head, about two pounds, serves four to five.
Alternatives to Fresh: Frozen acceptable.

Cauliflower, like broccoli, is grown for its clusters of unopened flower buds, called curds. If you grow it yourself, the flowerets will most likely be tinged with purple (unless they are well shielded from the light) but will taste just fine.

Basic Method for Cooking Cauliflower

(SERVES FOUR TO FIVE)

1 medium cauliflower (about 2	Salt
pounds, 900 g)	Freshly ground pepper
Melted butter	

Remove the leaves from the cauliflower. Wash it well, leaving it whole or separating it into flowerets. Steam, covered, in a steamer basket over boiling water until tender, allowing about 10 minutes for flowerets, 20–30 minutes for the whole head. Drain. Pour melted butter over it and season to taste.

Cauliflower with Chopped Walnuts. Before serving, sprinkle with *½ cup coarsely chopped walnuts.*

Cauliflower au Gratin. Leave the cauliflower whole and put it on a shallow, ovenproof dish. Sprinkle with *¾ cup freshly grated Parmesan cheese* and *½ cup* *buttered bread crumbs.* Bake in a preheated 400°F (205°C) oven until brown on top, about 15 minutes.

Creamed Cauliflower au Gratin. Arrange cooked cauliflower flowerets in a baking dish, season with salt and freshly ground pepper, and cover with *1½ cups White Sauce* (p. 265). Sprinkle *½ cup grated Cheddar or Parmesan* over the top. Bake in a preheated 400°F (205°C) oven until hot and bubbly throughout and golden on top, 15 to 20 minutes.

ABOUT CELERY

Availability: Year round.
What to Look For: Fresh, firm, unwilted stalks, preferably with leaves.
Uses: Raw, with a dip or in salads. *Cooked,* steamed, sautéed, braised, as a
    seasoning, in stocks, soups, stews, and casserole dishes. Leaves also used
    for seasoning. *As a vegetable accompaniment,* it's good with everything.
Amount: One pound serves two to three.

The pale celery that we find in the markets is intentionally "blanched" while it is being grown. Many home gardeners do the same, planting celery in trenches which they gradually fill with soil as the celery grows. This keeps the light from the celery stalks, making them white and their flavor mild. Some people, however, prefer the strong flavor of unblanched green celery.

Braised Celery

Braising celery this way brings out its rich flavor.

(SERVES TWO TO THREE)

1 pound (450 g) celery	Salt
2 tablespoons butter	Freshly ground pepper
Chicken broth	

Wash the celery and cut off the leaves and any discolored parts. Cut the stalks in even lengths, about 3 inches long. Sauté in the butter for about 5 minutes, then add about ½ inch of broth, just enough to keep the celery from burning. Season with salt and pepper, unless the stock is already well seasoned. Cover and cook over low heat until the celery is just tender, about 12–15 minutes. Put the celery in a serving dish. Rapidly boil the liquid in the pan until it is reduced to just a few tablespoons. Pour over the celery and serve.

Braised Celery au Gratin. Arrange the braised celery in a shallow baking dish and add a little of the cooking liquid. Sprinkle with *½ cup freshly grated Parmesan cheese* and put under the broiler until the cheese has melted.

ABOUT CELERY ROOT OR CELERIAC

Height of Season: October through April; not all markets sell it.
What to Look For: Firm, unwilted root.
Uses: Raw, grated, as a first course or salad. *As a vegetable accompaniment,*
    especially good with veal and beef when braised.
Amount: One pound serves four.

Celery root or celeriac is also known as celeri-rave or celery knob. It is large, brown, and lumpy in appearance. It has a slightly mealy texture when cooked and an earthy, concentrated celery flavor with a slightly sweet overtone that is unusual and utterly delicious. Try it also in the Scalloped Potatoes with Celery Root or Celeriac, p. 401.

Braised Celery Root

(SERVES FOUR)

1 pound (450 g) celery root
2 tablespoons butter
About 2 cups (½ L) beef
  bouillon

2 tablespoons minced parsley

Peel the celery root and cut into ¼-inch slices. Arrange in a skillet—preferably not iron because it is apt to discolor the celery root—dot with butter, and cook over medium high heat with cover askew until tender, but not mushy, about 10 to 15 minutes. Then remove the celery root with a slotted spoon to a serving dish and keep warm while you boil down the remaining liquid until it is almost syrupy. Pour over the celery root and sprinkle with parsley.

Sautéed Celery Root or Celeriac

A combination of faintly sweet grapes and a fine, sharp celery flavor, this is a particularly nice dish to serve with fish.

(SERVES FOUR)

1 pound (450 g) celeriac
Juice of 1 lemon
3 tablespoons butter
2 teaspoons minced parsley

¾ cup (1¾ dL) green seedless
  grapes
Salt

Peel the celeriac and cut it into eighths. Put into a pot with 1 cup water, the lemon juice, and 1 tablespoon of the butter. Cover and simmer about 10–15 minutes or until tender. Drain off the liquid and add the remaining 2 tablespoons of butter, the parsley, the grapes, and salt to taste. Turn up the heat and shake the pan to coat the ingredients with the butter and to prevent sticking. Heat through and serve.

ABOUT CHESTNUTS

Height of Season: Winter, especially around Thanksgiving and Christmas.
What to Look For: It is hard to tell how fresh chestnuts are when they're in the shell. Feel them and be sure that the nut seems firm and has not drawn away from the shell.
Uses: Cooked, in stuffings or combined with other vegetables, such as Brussels sprouts or red cabbage. *As a vegetable accompaniment,* especially good with fowl or pork. Cooked in syrup and put through a ricer, chestnuts also make an elegant dessert, served with whipped cream.
Amount: One pound serves three or four.
Alternatives to Fresh: Canned (unsweetened).

Technically nuts, chestnuts are primarily used as a vegetable.

There's no substitute for their unique flavor. It's worth the bother of shelling them and removing the inner skin.

To shell, cut slits or crisscross gashes in the flat sides of the chestnuts and drop them into boiling water for a minute or two. While the chestnuts are still warm, remove the shells and inner skins, using a sharp knife. If any of the skins are especially difficult to peel, reboil the chestnuts for a few seconds.

Braised Chestnuts

(SERVES FOUR)

1 pound (450 g) chestnuts, shelled (above)
1 cup (¼ L) beef broth
¼ teaspoon salt

⅛ teaspoon freshly ground pepper
2 tablespoons butter

Put the chestnuts into a pan with the beef broth, salt, and pepper. Cover and simmer for about 15–20 minutes; drain. Add the butter, turn the heat up, and shake the pan so the chestnuts are well anointed with the butter. Serve hot.

Creamed Chestnuts. Add 4 *tablespoons heavy cream* with the butter.

Puréed Chestnuts. Put the buttered chestnuts through a food mill or purée them in a blender or food processor, beating in a little *hot heavy cream* if too thick.

ABOUT COLLARDS AND OTHER GREENS

Availability: Year round, especially summer and fall.
What to Look For: Crisp, green leaves without blemishes or discoloration.
Uses: As a vegetable accompaniment, especially good with ham or pork chops.
Amount: One pound serves two.

Beet greens, kale, turnip and mustard greens may all be cooked in the same fashion as collards. In fact, these greens often taste better in combination, cooked with a ham bone. If the stems are thick, remove them and cook them separately.

Braised Collards

It's fine to cook other greens by this method, although the cooking time may need adjusting.

(SERVES TWO)

1 pound (450 g) collards or other greens
⅛ pound (60 g) salt pork, diced

Salt
Freshly ground pepper

Wash the greens well, removing all sand, in several changes of cold water. Remove any tough ribs, then cut or tear into small pieces. Cook the salt pork over low heat until its fat is rendered and it turns golden. Meanwhile, drop the greens into a large pot of boiling water and blanch them for about 10 minutes; remove and drain well. Add the blanched, drained greens to the salt pork, cover, and cook over medium heat for 20–30 minutes. Season with a little salt and pepper, if necessary.

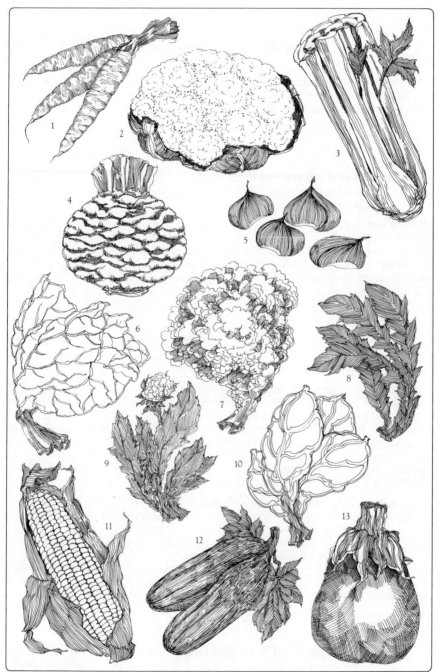

1. *carrots*; 2. *cauliflower*; 3. *celery*; 4. *celeriac*; 5. *chestnuts*; 6. *collards*; 7. *kale*;
8. *dandelion greens*; 9. *turnip greens*; 10. *beet greens*; 11. *corn*; 12. *cucumbers*;
13. *eggplant.*

Mixed Greens Southern-Style

Save a ham bone (with a little meat clinging to it) to make this. The greens can vary according to what is available, but there should be a good proportion of collards. Southerners would serve in soup plates with hot corn bread to mop up what they call the pot liquor.

(SERVES SIX)

1 ham bone
¼ pound (115 g) salt pork, cubed
3 pounds (1⅓ kg) collards, kale, turnip greens, and/or mustard greens

Salt
Freshly ground pepper

Boil the ham bone and salt pork in 6 cups water for 45 minutes. Wash the greens carefully, remove tough ends of the stalks, and chop up the rest along with the greens. Add to the pot and cook until tender, about 45 minutes. At that point the water should almost have disappeared and the salt pork will have melted away. Remove the ham bone and scrape any bits of meat back into the pot. Add salt and pepper to taste.

ABOUT CORN

Height of Season: Spring or summer, depending on region.
What to Look For: Moist, plump, juicy-looking yellow or white kernels, not too large; green, fresh-looking husks.
Uses: Cooked, boiled, roasted, pickled, on the cob or off, in succotash, soup, salads, puddings, and fritters. *As a vegetable accompaniment,* good with everything.
Amount: Two or more ears per person.
Alternatives to Fresh: Frozen better than canned.

The sugar in corn turns to starch very rapidly after it is picked. How lucky are those who can rush fresh ears from the field, husk them quickly, and plunge them into a pot of boiling water!

If you must hold corn for any length of time, keep it unhusked in the refrigerator until you are ready to cook it.

Cut the kernels from any leftover cooked, fresh corn and freeze them in a plastic container. Reheated quickly in a little boiling water, drained, and tossed with butter, home-frozen corn kernels make a delicious midwinter vegetable.

Basic Method for Cooking Corn on the Cob

There is nothing like fresh corn on the cob, quickly boiled, spread with lots of sweet butter, and sprinkled with salt. Two ears per person may seem like a proper serving, but appetites often run high when corn is in season and freshly picked.

12 ears of corn
Butter, softened
Salt

Just before cooking, husk the corn, pull off the silky threads, and cut out any blemishes with a pointed knife. Drop the corn into a large pot filled with boiling, unsalted water. Cover the pot and let the water return to a boil again, then turn off the heat and keep the pot covered. After about 5 minutes, remove enough ears for a first serving. You can keep the remaining corn warm in the water for another 10 minutes without its becoming tough. Serve with lots of butter and salt.

Buttered Corn Kernels. Cut the corn from the cob with a sharp knife. Heat the kernels in butter and season with salt and *freshly ground pepper.*

Foil-roasted Corn on the Cob

12 ears of corn
Butter
Salt

Preheat the oven to 400°F (205°C). Husk the corn and wrap each ear in foil, adding 2 teaspoons of butter to each packet. Bake for about 25 minutes. Or roast the foil-wrapped corn over hot coals, turning once during the cooking. Serve with more butter and salt.

Broiled Corn in the Husk

12 ears of corn
Butter
Salt

Soak the corn in cold water, for a few minutes. Broil on an outdoor grill over hot coals, turning frequently, for about 15–25 minutes, depending on the heat of the fire. Be careful not to scorch the corn. The husks and silk will pull off easily when cooked. Serve with lots of butter and salt.

Succotash

1 cup (¼ L) cooked corn kernels	Butter
	Cream
1 cup (¼ L) cooked lima beans or other shell beans	Salt
	Freshly ground pepper

Heat the corn and lima beans in butter and a little cream in a saucepan. Season to taste.

Southern Corn Pudding

Fresh corn kernels extracted from the cob give this a special quality.

(SERVES FOUR)

2 cups (½ L) fresh grated or
  chopped corn kernels
2 eggs, slightly beaten
2 tablespoons butter, melted

2 cups (½ L) hot milk
½ teaspoon salt
⅛ teaspoon freshly ground
  pepper

Preheat the oven to 350°F (180°C). Butter a 1½-quart casserole. Mix all ingredients together in a bowl. Pour into the casserole and place in a pan of hot water. Bake until firm, about 45 minutes.

Corn Soufflé

(SERVES SIX)

1 tablespoon butter
2 tablespoons flour
1 cup (¼ L) milk
2 eggs, separated
2 cups (½ L) cooked, canned,
  or frozen, thawed corn
  kernels

1 teaspoon salt
¼ teaspoon freshly ground
  pepper

Preheat the oven to 350°F (180°C). Generously butter a 1½-quart casserole. Melt the butter in a pan, slowly stir in the flour, and cook over moderate heat for 2 minutes, stirring constantly. Slowly add the milk and continue stirring constantly until thickened; continue to cook for 2 or 3 more minutes. Stir the egg yolks in a small bowl, then add a little of the hot milk mixture, stirring briskly. Add the yolk mixture to the milk mixture in the pan, stir for 1 minute, then remove from the heat and add the corn, salt, and pepper; set aside. Beat the egg whites until stiff but not dry. Fold a fourth of the whites into the corn mixture and blend, then gently fold in the remaining whites. Spoon into the baking dish and bake for about 30–35 minutes.

Scalloped Corn

(SERVES SIX)

3 tablespoons flour
1 teaspoon salt
¼ teaspoon paprika
¼ teaspoon dry mustard
Pinch of cayenne pepper
3 tablespoons butter
1 small green pepper, chopped
  fine

½ onion, chopped fine
1 cup (¼ L) milk
2 cups (½ L) fresh or canned,
  drained corn kernels
1 egg yolk, slightly beaten
⅔ cup (1½ dL) buttered bread
  crumbs

Preheat the oven to 400°F (205°C). Generously butter 1½-quart baking dish. Mix the flour, salt, paprika, mustard, and cayenne pepper together; set aside. Melt the butter in a skillet, add the green pepper and onion, and cook until soft. Stir in the flour mixture and cook, stirring and smoothing, for 2 or 3 minutes. Add the milk, stirring constantly, and bring it to the boiling point. Stir in the corn and egg yolk. Spoon into the baking dish and sprinkle with the crumbs. Bake for 25 minutes until the crumbs are brown.

Corn Oysters

Lightly browned, with a chewy texture, simple flavor, and fresh corn taste. Serve these with ham, perhaps with a few drops of maple syrup over them.

(TEN 2½-INCH OYSTERS; SERVES FOUR TO FIVE)

1 cup (¼ L) grated or chopped fresh corn kernels
1 egg, well beaten
¼ cup (35 g) flour

¼ teaspoon salt
⅛ teaspoon freshly ground pepper
4 tablespoons butter

Combine the corn with the egg, flour, salt, and pepper and mix well. Shape into patties (or "oysters") about 2½ inches in diameter. Heat the butter in a skillet until foaming, then add the corn oysters. Cook over medium heat for 3 or 4 minutes. Turn when golden brown, and brown the other side. Keep warm in a low oven until ready to serve.

ABOUT CUCUMBERS

Availability: Year round, especially good at farmers' markets in summer.
What to Look For: Firm, slender, well-shaped, dark-green cucumbers, preferably fresh, not waxed.
Uses: Raw, with dips or in soups, salads, or sandwiches. *Cooked,* in soups, stuffed, or pickled. *As a vegetable accompaniment,* good with fish or veal.
Amount: One large cucumber serves two.

Store cucumbers in the refrigerator and do not keep them too long. They contain a lot of water and are cooling and thirst-quenching. Salting draws the water out of cucumber slices, as does blanching. More often used raw, cucumbers are also delicious cooked, stewed as below, or stuffed (see p. 305).

Stewed Cucumbers

Pale, delicate green, and faintly piquant; good with fish or lamb.

(SERVES FOUR)

2 large cucumbers
6 tablespoons butter

½ teaspoon chervil, crumbled
Salt

Peel the cucumbers, slice lengthwise, scoop out the seeds, and cut into ½-inch slices. Put in a heavy-bottomed pan with a lid; add 1 cup water, 4 tablespoons of the butter, and the chervil. Cover and gently simmer for 8–10 minutes. Drain, then add salt to taste and the remaining 2 tablespoons of butter. Serve hot.

ABOUT EGGPLANT

Availability: Year round, especially in August and September.
What to Look For: Heavy, smooth, firm vegetables with shiny, unscarred skins.
Uses: Cooked, with or without skin, pan-fried, batter-fried, sautéed, baked,

chopped, stuffed, marinated. *Cold,* in salads. *Hot,* in stews and casserole dishes or as a main course. *As a vegetable accompaniment,* good with lamb and pork.

Amount: One medium eggplant, about 1½ pounds, serves four.

Eggplant is known as *aubergine* in France and England and *melanzana* in Italy. There are several varieties, including white eggplant and tiny purple eggplants only 3–4 inches long, but the large, tapered, purple vegetable is the one we usually see here.

Keep eggplants in the refrigerator and use them as soon as possible. Eggplant has a great capacity for absorbing oil, but if the slices are salted to drain them of excess water, then dried and fried in well-heated butter or oil, they will absorb less.

Baked Stuffed Eggplant

Bake this in a bowl so it holds its shape. The dark skin encasing a moist eggplant filling is most attractive.

(SERVES FOUR)

1 eggplant (about 1½ pounds, 675 g)	1 small onion, chopped fine
1 cup (¼ L) soft fresh bread crumbs	Salt
	Freshly ground pepper
4 tablespoons butter	1 egg, well beaten

Preheat the oven to 375°F (190°C). Put the eggplant in a large pot filled with boiling, salted water and cook for 12–15 minutes. Drain, then cut in half lengthwise. Remove the pulp carefully without breaking the skin. Chop the pulp, including the seeds, and stir in the bread crumbs; set aside. Melt the butter in a skillet. Add the onion and cook until soft; add to the eggplant mixture. Add salt and pepper to taste. Stir in the beaten egg and toss to mix well. Gently place the eggplant shells (skins) in an amply buttered round baking dish to cover the bottom and sides. Spoon the eggplant mixture into the dish and bake for 35–40 minutes. Unmold and serve hot or cold.

Scalloped Eggplant

(SERVES FOUR)

1 eggplant (about 1½ pounds, 675 g)	Salt
2 tablespoons butter	Freshly ground pepper
1 small onion, chopped fine	Buttered bread crumbs
1 tablespoon finely chopped parsley	Freshly grated Parmesan cheese

Preheat the oven to 375°F (190°C). Peel the eggplant and cut it into ½-inch cubes. Put the eggplant in a pot with an inch of boiling water, cover, and cook gently until tender, about 5–10 minutes. Drain. Melt the butter in a skillet, add the onion, and cook over low heat until soft but not brown. Stir in the eggplant and parsley, season with salt and pepper, and combine gently. Spoon into a buttered baking dish, cover with lots of bread crumbs and grated cheese, and bake until the eggplant is heated through and the crumbs are brown.

Golden Fried Eggplant

A simple preparation, good for eggplant lovers.

(SERVES FOUR)

1 medium eggplant (about 1½ pounds, 675 g)
Salt
Freshly ground pepper
¼ pound (115 g) butter

Cut the eggplant into slices ¼ to ½ inch thick. Sprinkle lightly with salt and pepper and let drain on paper towels for 30 minutes; pat dry. Melt the butter in a large skillet. Cook the eggplant slices over moderate heat, turning them once or twice, until they are golden. Serve hot.

ABOUT BELGIAN ENDIVE

Availability: Most of the year; usually quite expensive.
What to Look For: Fresh, crisp, tender stalks, without discoloration or signs of insect damage.
Uses: Raw, in salads. *Cooked,* braised, baked, sautéed. *As a hot vegetable accompaniment,* especially good with ham.
Amount: One to two stalks per serving.

Belgian endive, also known as witloof chicory, is a compact vegetable, budlike in form, which is grown in the dark to give it its creamy white color. It has a slightly bitter flavor, especially when cooked.

Braised Endive

Don't use an iron skillet, or the endive will turn black.

(SERVES FOUR)

8 small endive
3 tablespoons butter
Chicken broth
Salt

Wash the endive and cut off any discolored spots. Split them lengthwise if they are large; leave them whole if they are small. Sauté them in the butter for about 5 minutes, then add about ½ inch of broth. Cover and cook slowly until just tender when pierced with the tip of a sharp knife, about 20 minutes. Arrange the endive in a serving dish. Boil the cooking liquid rapidly until it is reduced to just a few tablespoons. Add salt to taste. Pour over the endive and serve.

ABOUT FLORENTINE FENNEL

Availability: Most of the year, especially in Italian markets.
What to Look For: Firm, fresh stalks and leaves.
Uses: Raw, like celery, or in salads. *Cooked,* in soups, stews, casserole dishes, stuffings. *As a vegetable accompaniment,* especially good with chicken, veal, or fish.
Amount: One pound serves three.

Florentine fennel, also called *finocchio*, has celerylike stalks that broaden to a bulb shape, with feather leaves at the stem end, and the licorice flavor of anise. It is not to be confused with common fennel, which is used as a seasoning but not as a vegetable.

Braised Fennel

(SERVES THREE)

1 pound (450 g) fennel	Salt
2 tablespoons butter	Freshly ground pepper
Chicken broth	

Wash the fennel and remove any tough or discolored outer parts. Slice—the bulb into ½-inch pieces, the tender part of the stems into smaller. Sauté in the butter in a skillet for about 5 minutes, then add about ½ inch of broth, enough so that the fennel does not burn. Cover and simmer over low heat until tender, about 15–20 minutes. Arrange the fennel in a serving dish. Boil the cooking liquid down to just a few tablespoons, and season to taste. Pour over the fennel and serve.

Braised Fennel au Gratin. Arrange the cooked fennel in a shallow baking dish and pour a little of the pan juices over it. Sprinkle generously with *freshly grated Parmesan cheese* and put under the broiler until the cheese has melted.

ABOUT FIDDLEHEADS

Availability: Found wild in the spring, or in specialty markets.
What to Look For: Young, curled, unopened fern shoots.
Uses: As an unusual vegetable accompaniment, good with ham.
Alternatives to Fresh: Frozen or canned, best with a sauce, like Hollandaise Sauce (p. 272).

Fiddleheads are feathery and a little crisp. If you pick them yourself, you must know what you are looking for—otherwise you may pick varieties that are quite bitter.

Basic Method for Cooking Fiddleheads

Fresh or frozen fiddleheads	Salt
Butter	Freshly ground pepper

Wash fresh fiddleheads, drain them, and rub off their woolly skins. If you are using frozen fiddleheads, let them defrost partially. Melt a tablespoon or two of butter in ½ inch of boiling water in a skillet, lay the fiddleheads flat in the pan, cover, and simmer for about 10 minutes. Season to taste with salt and pepper.

KALE

See About Collards and Other Greens, p. 376.

ABOUT KOHLRABI

Availability: June and July are height of season.
What to Look For: Small, young, tender globes.
Uses: Raw, with salt, as a snack or salad. *Cooked,* in soups or stews. *As a vegetable accompaniment,* especially good with pot roast.
Amount: Two or three small kohlrabi per person.

Kohlrabi is a strange-looking light-green and purple vegetable. It's in the cabbage family, as its leaves indicate. Its globe, however, resembles a turnip and tastes like one, too, though milder. The globe grows above ground, unlike a turnip, and is part of the stem, not the root.

Basic Method for Cooking Kohlrabi

If the kohlrabi tops are young and tender, cook them separately in boiling salted water, drain and chop them, and add them to the cooked kohlrabi globe.

(SERVES FOUR)

12 small kohlrabi   Salt
Melted butter   Freshly ground pepper

Cut off the tops of the kohlrabi and peel and slice the globes. Cook, uncovered, in boiling, salted water until tender, about 20–30 minutes. Drain. Toss with melted butter and season to taste.

Kohlrabi au Gratin. Put the cooked, seasoned kohlrabi in a shallow, buttered baking dish. Sprinkle with *½ cup freshly grated Parmesan cheese* and put under the broiler until the cheese has melted.

ABOUT LEEKS

Availability: Year round, especially in the fall.
What to Look For: Young, fresh-looking leeks, flexible not stiff; avoid discolored tops.
Uses: Cooked, braised, served hot or cold, as a first course, or in soups and stews.
     As a vegetable accompaniment, especially good with a roast of beef.
Amount: One pound serves three.

Although leeks are in the onion family, their sweet, delicate flavor is distinctively their own. Often quite expensive in stores, they are exceedingly easy to grow at home and an infinitely useful vegetable to have in a home garden. They are very hardy and may be dug until the ground has frozen.

Because the bottoms of leeks are grown underground, sand often gets inside the leaves and works it way down within them. Leeks thus require a good deal of washing. To clean them, cut off the soft tops, leaving 1–2 inches of green. Slice them lengthwise to within ½ inch of the bottom, spread the leaves, and wash well in cold water. Use the cut-off tops in soups and stocks.

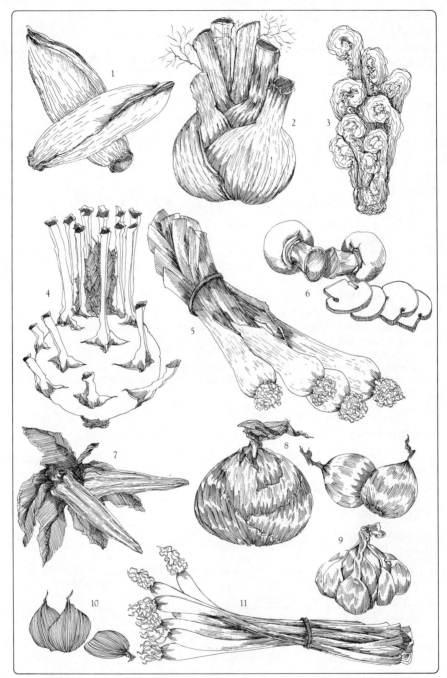

1. *endive;* 2. *fennel;* 3. *fiddleheads;* 4. *kohlrabi;* 5. *leeks;* 6. *mushrooms;* 7. *okra;* 8. *onions;* 9. *garlic;* 10. *shallots;* 11. *scallions.*

Braised Leeks

(SERVES THREE)

2 large bunches (about 1 pound, 450 g) leeks	Chicken broth
	Salt
2 tablespoons butter	Freshly ground pepper

Wash the leeks thoroughly (see preceding discussion) and trim them, leaving about 1½ inches of the green tops. Sauté them in butter in a skillet for about 5 minutes, then add about ½ inch of broth, enough so that the leeks will not burn. Cover, and simmer slowly until the leeks are tender, about 20–30 minutes. Arrange the leeks on a serving platter. Boil the cooking liquid down to a few tablespoons, season to taste, pour over the leeks, and serve.

Braised Leeks au Gratin. Arrange the cooked leeks in a shallow baking dish, spoon a little of the cooking liquid over them, and sprinkle with ½ cup *freshly grated Parmesan cheese.* Put under the broiler until the cheese melts.

ABOUT MUSHROOMS

Height of Season: Fall and winter.

What to Look For: Firm, white, fresh-looking mushrooms, caps closed around stems; avoid discoloration or soft spots.

Uses: Whole or sliced, cold or hot. *Raw or cooked,* as an hors d'oeuvre, with a dip, as a salad or first course. *Cooked,* sautéed, broiled, baked, coated in batter and fried, stuffed, in soups, stews, casserole dishes, quiches, duxelles. *As a vegetable accompaniment,* especially good with steak or chops.

Amount: One pound serves four.

Alternatives to Fresh: Canned or frozen will not have the flavor but may be used in a pinch. Dried varieties are delicious but have a different texture so cannot be used as substitutes in the recipes that follow. However, they are excellent to use in soups, sauces, and stews and can add a stronger mushroom accent, sometimes complementing blander fresh mushrooms. Dried mushrooms must be soaked for 30 minutes; save the soaking liquid to add to a soup or sauce.

Unless you're expert, don't eat wild mushrooms picked in the woods.

It's best not to wash mushrooms, since they will absorb too much water. Just wipe them clean, using a damp towel or cloth, and cut off ¼ inch from the bottoms of the stems.

Sautéed Mushrooms

(SERVES FOUR)

1 pound (450 g) mushrooms	2 teaspoons minced parsley
6 tablespoons butter	Salt
2 tablespoons minced shallots or scallions	Freshly ground pepper

Wipe the mushrooms clean and slice them. Melt the butter in a pan, add the shallots or scallions, and cook for 3 minutes, stirring often. Add the mushrooms and continue to cook over low heat for 10 minutes. Add the parsley, season to taste, and mix well.

Creamed Mushrooms

Cream and mushrooms complement each other—in a luscious way.

(SERVES FOUR)

1½ pounds (675 g) mushrooms	¾ cup (1¾ dL) heavy cream
¼ pound (115 g) butter	Salt
4 tablespoons Madeira wine	Freshly ground pepper

Wipe the mushrooms clean and cut caps in half with the stems attached. Melt the butter over medium heat until it foams, stir in the mushrooms, and turn the heat to low. Simmer for 5 minutes, then add the Madeira and cream. Continue to cook over low heat for 30 minutes, stirring once in a while. Season to taste. Serve hot.

Stuffed Mushrooms

(SERVES FOUR)

12 large mushroom caps	½ teaspoon salt
¼ pound (115 g) butter	½ teaspoon pepper
½ cup (1 dL) dry homemade bread crumbs	1 egg, lightly beaten
1 tablespoon finely chopped parsley	½ cup (1 dL) freshly grated Parmesan cheese
1 tablespoon finely chopped onion	

Preheat oven to 350°F (180°C). Generously butter a shallow baking dish. Wipe the mushroom caps clean. Melt 4 tablespoons of the butter in a small pan and let it cool a bit. Using the palms of your hands, thoroughly coat mushroom caps with butter and put them in the baking dish. Mix the bread crumbs, parsley, onion, salt, pepper, and egg together. Fill each mushroom cap with the mixture. Melt the remaining 4 tablespoons of butter. Sprinkle a little Parmesan cheese over each cap, drizzle a little melted butter on top, and bake for 15–20 minutes.

Mushrooms à l'Algonquin

Plump toothsome bites. Arrange five or six on a plate with toast and a mound of freshly cooked spinach.

(SERVES FOUR)

20 large mushroom caps	20 tiny oysters
¼ pound (115 g) butter	1 lemon
Salt	

Preheat the oven to 400°F (205°C). Butter a shallow baking dish. Wipe the mushroom caps clean. Melt the butter in a small pan. Dip the mushroom caps in the melted butter and coat thoroughly. Place the mushroom caps, saucer side up, in the baking dish, and sprinkle lightly with salt. Place an oyster in each one. Squeeze a few drops of lemon juice over each oyster and drizzle the remaining butter over each. Put in the oven for 8–10 minutes. Serve hot or cold.

Mushroom Duxelles

A French method of preserving mushrooms for use in fillings, soups, and sauces. Duxelles should be cooked until all moisture is absorbed.

(1½ CUPS)

4 tablespoons butter
½ onion, finely chopped
1 pound (450 g) mushrooms,
    finely chopped

Salt
Freshly ground pepper

Melt the butter in a very large skillet over medium heat, add the onion, and cook, stirring, for 2 minutes. Add the mushrooms and continue to cook over low heat, stirring occasionally, until all the moisture has evaporated—about 20 minutes. Season to taste. Cool, then put in a container and close tightly. Refrigerate or freeze until needed.

ABOUT OKRA

Availability: May to October height of season.
What to Look For: Small, green, tender, flexible pods, about 2–4 inches long.
Uses: Cooked, steamed, boiled, sautéed, in soups or stews, with other vegetables, in casserole dishes. *As a vegetable accompaniment,* especially good with chicken or fish.
Amount: One pound serves four.
Alternatives to Fresh: Frozen or canned acceptable.

Okra, actually the immature seed pod of the okra plant, is used a great deal in the southern United States. Its gummy texture provides a good thickening base for gumbos: indeed, okra is sometimes incorrectly called "gumbo," although "gumbo" really describes the dishes in which it appears.

Sautéed Okra

When okra is blanched and sautéed in butter, it has good flavor, a velvety outside, and a chewy texture.

(SERVES FOUR)

1 pound (450 g) okra
6 tablespoons butter

Salt
Freshly ground pepper

Start a large pot of water boiling. Wash the okra and snap or cut off the stems. Drop it in the boiling water for 1 minute; drain. Melt the butter over medium heat. Add the okra and cook for 3 minutes, shaking the pan often to coat the okra with butter. Season lightly with salt and pepper. Serve hot.

Sautéed Okra with Browned Crumbs. Drop the okra into boiling water and let cook 3 minutes. Drain. Sauté ¾ *cup freshly made bread crumbs* in the butter until browned. Add the okra, season, and toss together for a minute.

Okra, Tomatoes, and Corn

(SERVES SIX)

2 tablespoons butter
1 small onion, finely chopped
1 small green pepper, finely
  chopped
1 pound (450 g) okra, in ½-
  inch slices

2 large fresh tomatoes, peeled,
  seeded, and chopped
1 cup (¼ L) corn kernels
½ teaspoon oregano, crumbled
Salt
Freshly ground pepper

Melt the butter in a pan, add the onion and green pepper, and cook over medium heat for 3–4 minutes, stirring often. Add the okra slices and cook, stirring often, for 2 minutes. Add the tomatoes, corn, and oregano. Cover and simmer over low heat for 10 minutes. Season to taste. Serve hot.

ABOUT ONIONS

Availability: Year round.
What to Look For: Firm, well-shaped onions with dry skins and no sprouts.
Uses: Sliced, chopped, or whole. *Raw,* in salads, sandwiches, as a garnish.
  Cooked, boiled, baked, sautéed, fried, stuffed, pickled, braised, or roasted,
  in soups, stews, casserole dishes, sauces, and just about everything else.
Amount: One pound serves four.
Alternatives to Fresh: Canned or frozen in a pinch.

It's hard to imagine what food would be like without onions! Fortunately, they are readily available and in many varieties. Most familiar are the yellow cooking onions which have a strong flavor and often make your eyes water when you slice them. There are also sweet, mild Spanish or Italian onions; large, delicately flavored Bermudas; small white onions to glaze or cream or put in stews, and the scallions or green onions and shallots described below.

Keep onions in a cool, dry, dark place. Once you've peeled or sliced them, it's best to keep them in the refrigerator.

About Scallions or Green Onions

Availability: Year round.
What to Look For: Crisp, tender scallions with firm, white bottoms and fresh
  green tops.
Uses: Whole, sliced, or chopped. *Raw,* with a dip, in salads, sandwiches, as a
  garnish. *Cooked,* sautéed or braised, in sauces, soups, stews, as a flavoring.
  As a vegetable accompaniment, good with chopped beef or just about anything.

Green onions, or scallions, are onions that have been harvested while young. They have a milder flavor than mature onions. Keep them in the refrigerator.

About Shallots

Availability: Year round, mainly in specialty stores.
What to Look For: Clusters of crisp, tender, plump bulbs, with dry rust-colored
  skins and no sprouts.
Uses: *Raw* (used sparingly) or *cooked,* as a flavoring for sauces and an aromatic
  base for braising.

Shallots have a delicate, somewhat sweet flavor. They add a fine, subtle touch to sauces.

Baked Onions

A little sweet, opaque, mostly tender.

(SERVES FOUR)

4 medium onions, peeled	4 tablespoons butter
⅓ cup (¾ dL) seedless white raisins	Salt

Preheat the oven to 350°F (180°C). Put the onions in a small casserole, sprinkle the raisins around, and put bits of the butter evenly over and around them. Sprinkle with salt and cover with foil. Bake for 45–60 minutes. Serve hot.

Creamed Onions

(SERVES FOUR)

1 pound (450 g) baby white onions	Salt
¾ cup (1¾ dL) heavy cream	2 teaspoons minced parsley

To make peeling easier, bring a large pot of water to boil, drop the onions into the boiling water, and cook for 2 minutes; drain and peel. Put the onions into a pan, pour the cream over, and simmer, turning often, for 15–20 minutes. Add salt to taste. Sprinkle with parsley. Serve hot.

Creamed Onions in White Sauce. If you prefer a more traditional recipe with a thicker cream sauce, blanch and peel the onions as in the recipe for Creamed Onions. Then cook them in 1 cup lightly salted water until tender. Drain and combine them with *1 cup White Sauce* (p. 265) and reheat.

Glazed Onions

(SERVES FOUR)

1 pound (450 g) baby white onions	1½ tablespoons honey
5 tablespoons butter	Salt

Bring a pot of water to a boil. Add the onions and boil for 5 minutes; drain and peel. Melt the butter in a skillet and stir in the honey. Add the onions and cook over medium heat, stirring often, for about 10 minutes or until the onions are slightly browned. Sprinkle with salt and serve.

Braised White Baby Onions

Silky texture and a mildly sweet onion taste.

(SERVES FOUR)

1 pound (450 g) baby white onions	4 tablespoons butter
	Salt

Bring a large pot of water to boil. Drop the onions into the boiling water and cook for 3 minutes; drain and remove the outer skin. Melt the butter in a skillet with a lid. Add the onions, cover, and cook over low heat for 20 minutes. Shake the skillet often. Uncover and cook 5 minutes more. Add salt to taste.

Scalloped Onions. Boil the onions for 10 minutes before peeling. Drain and put the onions into a buttered baking dish. Add *1 cup White Sauce* (p. 265) and sprinkle *1 cup grated Cheddar cheese* on top. Bake in a 350°F (180°C) oven for 20 minutes.

Onions, Corn, and Green Peppers

A most agreeable mixture.

(SERVES SIX)

5 tablespoons butter
1 pound (450 g) onions, in ¼-inch slices
2 green peppers, in ¼-inch strips

1½ cups (3½ dL) cooked corn kernels
Salt

Melt the butter in a pan, add the onions, and cook, stirring, until they are limp. Add the peppers and continue to cook until they turn a little dull in color, about 5 minutes. Stir in the corn, add salt to taste, and heat through.

French-fried Onion Rings

Golden and good. Soaking the onions first in milk takes away some of their sharpness.

(SERVES EIGHT)

4 large Bermuda onions, in ¼-inch slices
2 cups (½ L) milk

½ cup (70 g) flour
Salt
Oil for deep frying

Separate the onion slices into rings. Put them in a shallow dish and pour the milk over them. Soak for 30 minutes, turning once or twice. Mix the flour with a sprinkle of salt, and dip the rings into this mixture, coating them all over. Heat oil to 370°F and deep-fry the rings several at a time until golden on both sides. Pat free of oil, keep warm while frying the rest, and sprinkle with more salt, if desired, before serving.

Braised Scallions or Green Onions

(SERVES FOUR)

4 bunches scallions, about 2 dozen
3 tablespoons butter

Trim the coarse or discolored green from the scallion tops, and trim off the bottom roots; rinse scallions. Melt the butter in a skillet with a lid. Add the scallions, sprinkle 2 tablespoons of water over them, cover, and turn the heat to low. Simmer for 4–6 minutes. Serve hot.

ABOUT PARSNIPS

Availability: Year round, especially late winter.
What to Look For: Small, well-shaped parsnips, smooth and firm.
Uses: Raw, with dips. *Cooked,* in soups, stews, fritters. *As a vegetable accompaniment,*
  good with beef or lamb.
Amount: One pound serves three or four.

Parsnips are a creamy pale color—a member of the carrot family, whose shape
they resemble. Their flavor becomes sweeter after they have been held for a while
at temperatures below 40°F. Use them in moderation, or their sweetness may
overpower other ingredients in a dish.

Basic Method for Cooking Parsnips

(SERVES FOUR)

1 pound (450 g) parsnips	Salt
2 tablespoons butter	Freshly ground pepper

Scrape the parsnips and cut them in ½-inch sticks, about 2 inches long. Cook
them, covered, in about 2 inches of boiling water until tender, about 10 minutes;
drain. Coat them with the butter, season to taste, and reheat them, if necessary,
before serving.

Candied Parsnips. Melt 4 *tablespoons butter* in a skillet, stir in 2 *teaspoons sugar,*
and cook, stirring, until the sugar dissolves. Add the parsnips, ½ *teaspoon salt,*
and ¼ *teaspoon freshly ground pepper,* and cook over medium-low heat, stirring
often, for 10–15 minutes or until the parsnips are golden. Serve hot.

Mashed or Puréed Parsnips. Mash the cooked, drained parsnips or purée them
through a food mill or in a food processor. Stir in *1 tablespoon butter, 1–2*
tablespoons heavy cream, and season to taste with salt and freshly ground pepper.
Reheat slowly, preferably in the top of a double boiler.

Parsnip Fritters

(SERVES FOUR)

1 pound (450 g) parsnips, cooked	½ teaspoon salt
4 tablespoons butter	½ teaspoon ginger

Mash the parsnips with 2 tablespoons of the butter and the salt and ginger,
beating until smooth. Flour your hands and shape into balls about 1¼ inches in
diameter, then flatten into patties. Melt the remaining 2 tablespoons of butter
in a skillet and fry the patties on each side until brown. Serve hot.

ABOUT GREEN PEAS

Availability: Most of the year, especially spring.
What to Look For: Fresh-looking, bright green pods. To test, crack open and
  taste; the peas should be sweet and tender.

Uses: Cooked, braised or boiled, in cold salads, or in soups, stews, casserole dishes, with other vegetables. *As a vegetable accompaniment,* good with everything.

Amount: One pound shelled peas serves four. Two pounds of unshelled peas yield about 1 pound of shelled peas.

Alternatives to Fresh: Frozen are good, better than canned.

About Snow Peas

Snow peas, also called sugar peas, Chinese peas, pea pods, or *mange tout,* are eaten crisp, barely cooked, in their flat, edible pods—and you eat the whole pod. They are available in Chinese food stores and also come frozen. They are also easy to grow and they yield enormously.

Basic Method for Cooking Green Peas

(SERVES FOUR)

| 2 pounds (900 g) fresh peas | 3 tablespoons butter |
| (1 pound shelled) | Salt |

Put the shelled peas, 1 cup water, and 1 tablespoon of the butter in a pan, cover, and cook over medium heat. After 6 minutes, check for doneness by pressing or tasting one or two; they should be tender but firm, which may take only a few minutes if young, or up to 20 minutes for older peas. Drain, coat with the remaining 2 tablespoons of butter, and lightly sprinkle salt over all.

Mint-flavored Peas. Add *1 tablespoon finely chopped mint* with the remaining 2 tablespoons of butter.

Purée of Green Peas. Add *1 slice onion* to the water. Add *½ cup heavy cream* with the remaining 2 tablespoons of butter. Put through a food mill or purée in a blender or food processor. Serve hot.

Braised Peas

(SERVES FOUR)

6 large lettuce leaves	4 tablespoons butter, melted
2 pounds (900 g) fresh peas	Salt
(1 pound shelled)	Freshly ground pepper

Rinse the lettuce leaves, leaving the drops of water on them. Use 3 of the leaves to line a heavy-bottomed pan with a lid. Put the shelled peas on the leaves and distribute the butter over them. Sprinkle with salt and pepper and cover with the remaining lettuce leaves. Cover the pan and simmer gently for 15–20 minutes or until the peas are tender. Usually one discards the lettuce leaves before serving the peas, but they taste good, so serve them if you wish.

Snow Peas

(SERVES FOUR)

1 pound (450 g) snow peas
3 tablespoons butter
Salt

Wash the snow peas and remove any strings. Bring a large pot of water to boil and drop the snow peas in; boil for 1 minute. Drain and quickly glisten with the butter, sprinkle with salt, and serve.

Stir-fried Snow Peas. Using a wok or a skillet, stir fry whole snow peas as you would sliced asparagus in Stir-fried Asparagus, p. 361, cooking only 2 minutes under cover.

ABOUT PEPPERS

Availability: Year round, especially in the summer.
What to Look For: Good color and sheen; smooth, firm sides.
Uses: Raw, with dips, in salads, stuffed. *Cooked,* in soups, sauces, stews, stuffed, with other vegetables, in casserole dishes. *As a vegetable accompaniment,* good with sausages and beef.
Amount: One per serving.

Peppers vary greatly in both appearance and taste. Sweet bell peppers, both red and green, are the most common. Red bell peppers are actually green peppers that have been allowed to mature fully; they are a bit sweeter than the green. Pimientos are roasted sweet red peppers packed in oil.

Tapered, light-green Italian peppers are found in stores more frequently these days. They have thinner skins and a sweeter, more delicate flavor than bell peppers.

Hot red and green chili peppers come in several varieties; they should be handled carefully—use gloves and don't touch your eyes—and should be used sparingly, as a seasoning in dishes that call for them. Chili powder and cayenne are made from hot peppers.

The membranes or ribs and seeds of sweet peppers are bitter and should be removed before the peppers are eaten or cooked.

Sautéed Sweet Red and Green Peppers

Red and green sweet bell peppers, slightly different in taste, are very compatible cooked together.

(SERVES FOUR)

4 tablespoons vegetable oil	Salt
2 sweet red peppers, in ¼-inch strips	Coarsely ground pepper
2 green peppers, in ¼-inch strips	

Heat the oil in a skillet. Put the peppers in the skillet and cook for 5–7 minutes, stirring to coat with the oil. Sprinkle with salt and pepper to taste.

Vegetarian Stuffed Green Peppers

This vegetarian stuffed pepper is good to look at and has lively flavor. For stuffed pepper using meat in the filling, see p. 305.

Vegetarian Stuffed Green Peppers (continued)

(SERVES SIX)

3 large green peppers, halved
and seeded
3 tablespoons olive oil
1 onion, finely chopped
2 cups (½ L) cooked corn
kernels
2 tomatoes, peeled and coarsely
chopped
2 tablespoons minced parsley

1 tablespoon chopped fresh
basil, or 1½ teaspoons dried,
crumbled
½ teaspoon salt
¼ teaspoon freshly ground
pepper
1 cup (¼ L) freshly made bread
crumbs

Preheat the oven to 350°F (180°C). Oil a shallow baking dish large enough to hold pepper halves in a single layer. Cook the peppers in boiling water for 2 minutes; drain and set aside. Heat the oil in a skillet and add the chopped onion. Cook, stirring, until soft. Put the onion in a bowl, add the corn, tomatoes, parsley, basil, salt, and pepper, and mix very well. Lightly fill each pepper half with some of the mixture. Sprinkle the tops with the bread crumbs. Bake for 30–40 minutes or until crumbs are lightly browned.

Rice-and-Cheese-stuffed Green Peppers. Substitute *1 cup cooked rice* and *1 cup grated Cheddar cheese* for the corn. Add *½ teaspoon savory, crumbled,* instead of the basil.

ABOUT POTATOES

Availability: Year round.

What to Look For: Firm, well-shaped potatoes without sprouts, cracks, or discolored spots.

Uses: Whole, sliced, cubed, grated, mashed, or puréed. *Cold,* in salads, soup. *Hot,* baked, boiled, fried, in soups, stews, casseroles, around a roast, with other vegetables, in pancakes. *As a vegetable accompaniment,* good with just about everything.

Amount: Allow one medium potato per person or a pound to serve about three.

Alternatives to Fresh: Canned potatoes are not very good, although sweet potatoes take to canning more successfully and their texture is better preserved. There are, of course, frozen French-fried potatoes, but once you've made your own—and it is a relatively simple task—you'll never settle for less. Instant mashed potatoes can be used in a pinch quite successfully, with lots of butter or a little cream but, again, aren't as good as the real thing.

The potato has fallen into disfavor in many American households, owing to the mistaken belief that it is fattening. Actually, a baked potato has 90 calories, 27 less than an apple. Nor is it always necessary to douse potatoes with lots of butter or cream. Prepare them simply and use them like any other vegetable accompaniment: they are wonderful for sopping up good juices and sauces.

There are many different kinds of potatoes. Most common are "all-purpose" potatoes which are used for boiling, baking, French frying, mashing, or just about any other kind of potato dish. Idaho and russet potatoes are very flaky and are best for baking. Red or white "new" potatoes are young potatoes which have not been kept in storage; they are ideal for salads, or you can boil or steam them in their skins until they are just tender, then toss them with a bit of butter, salt, and some chopped parsley.

Commercially frozen potatoes have been partially dehydrated so that they keep their texture after defrosting. Don't freeze potato dishes yourself, for they lose their consistency. Always store potatoes in a cool, dry, dark place and use them before they start to sprout. Do not refrigerate.

If they are not cooked immediately, peeled potatoes will discolor unless you cover them with cold water.

About Sweet Potatoes

There are two kinds of sweet potatoes: a light-colored, dry sweet potato and the sweeter, more common, deep-orange, moist type, generally referred to as a yam. Choose medium or small yams that are smooth and tapered at each end. Sweet potatoes or yams don't keep more than two weeks, store them in a very cool, dark place.

Baked Potatoes

(ALLOW ONE PER SERVING)

If you can, use Idaho or russet potatoes for baking; "all-purpose" will do but you won't get the same lovely, mealy texture. Incidentally, russets are very often packed in 5-pound bags in supermarkets, so read the labeling carefully when you are looking for them. Don't wrap potatoes for baking in foil—contrary to current fashion; foil steams them so that the jackets will be limp and the insides will taste steamed rather than having that good dry, baked taste and texture.

Scrub potatoes with a brush and water to remove all dirt. Place them slightly apart from each other on the oven rack and bake in a preheated 450°F (230°C) oven for 1 hour for large potatoes; 50 minutes for medium; 40–45 for small, childen-size potatoes. Test for doneness by piercing the potatoes with the point of a knife or by squeezing to see if the potato feels soft. Break baked potatoes apart with a fork while they are still very hot and add *butter* and *salt* to taste.

Crusty Baked Potatoes. If you want a marvelous, thick, crackly potato skin—for those who love to eat them—let them bake 1½ hours for medium, 2 hours for large.

Stuffed Baked Potatoes. Cut the baked potato in half lengthwise and scoop out the pulp, leaving the skins intact. Beat until fluffy, adding *2–4 tablespoons milk or cream* per potato, *1–2 tablespoons butter,* and *salt* and *freshly ground pepper* to taste. Refill the shells and sprinkle *2 tablespoons grated cheese* over the top, if desired. If the potatoes are at room temperature, reheat them in a 400°F (205°C) oven for 20 minutes before serving. If chilled, reheat them for 30–40 minutes.

Steamed New Potatoes

Steaming is a lovely way to treat very fresh potatoes, particularly very tiny ones. No butter is necessary, just a light sprinkling of salt.

(SERVES SIX)

2 pounds (900 g) tiny new
    unpeeled potatoes
Salt

Wash the potatoes well and place them in a steamer basket in a pot filled with a few inches of water. Cover, bring to a boil, and steam until the potatoes are just tender. Sprinkle lightly with salt and eat at once.

Parslied New Potatoes, Boiled

(SERVES SIX)

12 or more small new potatoes	6 tablespoons butter
2 tablespoons finely chopped parsley	Salt
	Freshly ground pepper

Scrub the potatoes—peeling is not necessary unless you prefer to for aesthetic reasons. Cover with cold water in a saucepan, bring to a boil, and boil gently for 15–20 minutes, or until tender when pierced with a knife; drain. Add the parsley and butter, season to taste, and shake the pan to coat the potatoes. Serve hot.

Pan-roasted Potatoes

Use either all-purpose or new potatoes. Peel them and cover them with cold water. Bring to a boil and boil 10–15 minutes or until barely tender. Drain well and place in a pan with roasting meat, at least 1 hour before the meat is done. Turn the potatoes all over in the meat drippings, then sprinkle with salt and freshly ground pepper. Baste with drippings and turn once or twice during roasting. They will be done in 1 hour, but more time won't hurt them.

Chantilly Potatoes

(SERVES FOUR TO FIVE)

3 cups (¾ L) mashed potatoes (following recipe)	Salt
½ cup (1 dL) heavy cream	Freshly ground pepper
½ cup (1 dL) grated Swiss or Gruyère cheese	

Preheat the oven to 350°F (180°C). Butter a shallow 1½-quart baking dish. Spread the mashed potatoes in the baking dish. Whip the cream until stiff, fold in the cheese, and add salt and pepper to taste. Spread over the potatoes. Bake for 25–30 minutes or until the top is delicately brown.

Mashed Potatoes

Don't try beating potatoes in a food processor: the fast spinning motion will develop the gluten in the potatoes and turn them into a gray, sticky mass. You can use an electric beater if your potatoes are mealy—russet or Idahoes.

(4 CUPS)

6 medium all-purpose potatoes	Salt
½–¾ cup (1–1¾ dL) hot milk	Freshly ground pepper
4 tablespoons butter	

Peel the potatoes and cut them into quarters. Put them in a pan and just cover them with cold water. Bring to a boil and boil gently for 15–20 minutes or until tender when pierced with a fork. Drain very well and return to very low heat.

Add ½ cup hot milk and the butter and start mashing with a potato masher or a fork (or put them through a potato ricer), smoothing out all the lumps. When you have worked the potatoes free of the lumps, transfer to a warm bowl and whip with a fork or whisk until light and fluffy, adding the remaining milk, if necessary, and salt and pepper to taste. Serve immediately, or keep hot, uncovered, in a double boiler.

Potato Cakes. Using leftover mashed potatoes, shape into small flat cakes. Dip lightly in *flour*, shake off any excess, and brown each side in hot *bacon fat* or *butter* over medium heat.

Potato Croquettes

(SERVES FOUR)

2 cups (½ L) mashed potatoes (opposite)
2 eggs
4 tablespoons flour

1 cup (¼ L) freshly made bread crumbs
½ cup (1 dL) vegetable oil

Put the potatoes into a bowl and lightly beat one of the eggs. Add the egg to the potatoes and mix well. Shape the potato mixture into 8 balls, cover, and chill. Beat the remaining egg lightly. Dip the potato balls into the flour, shake off any excess, dip into the egg, and then into the crumbs. Place on a piece of wax paper. Heat the oil in a skillet over medium-high heat. Add the balls and let them heat and brown for several minutes, turning the heat down if they brown too quickly. Turn the balls and brown on all sides. Keep the croquettes warm in a 300°F (150°C) oven until all are ready, then serve immediately.

Nut and Potato Croquettes

(SERVES FOUR)

2 cups (½ L) mashed potatoes (opposite)
½ cup (1 dL) heavy cream
1 teaspoon salt
¼ teaspoon freshly ground pepper
Pinch of cayenne pepper

1 tablespoon minced onion
2 egg yolks
1½ cups (3½ dL) freshly made bread crumbs
⅓ cup (¾ dL) finely chopped pecans
3 tablespoons shortening

Combine the potatoes, 3 tablespoons of the cream, ½ teaspoon of the salt, the pepper, cayenne pepper, onion, and 1 egg yolk. Beat until well blended; set aside. Cook ⅓ cup of the crumbs with the remaining 5 tablespoons of cream, stirring until a thick paste is formed; let cool. Put the cooled paste in a bowl and add the remaining egg yolk, the pecans, and the remaining ½ teaspoon salt. Mix well. Shape half the potato mixture into small nests, fill with the nut mixture, then cover with the remaining potato mixture. Pat to shape and make firm. Heat the shortening in a skillet. Dip the croquettes in the remaining crumbs, then fry until brown on both sides. Serve hot.

Potato and Spinach Croquettes. Add *1 egg yolk* and *¼ cup finely chopped cooked spinach* to the potato mixture. Proceed as directed.

French-fried Potatoes

It's water that makes hot fat sputter and spray, so be sure to dry the potatoes well and stand back when adding them to the hot fat. If you haven't had a lot of experience with deep-fat frying, you'll find a frying thermometer necessary. A frying basket that fits inside a pan is also very handy; if you don't have one, you can use a slotted spoon to extract the potatoes, but it takes longer and once your potatoes are fried to a turn, you want to get them out quickly. Be sure there's enough fat in the pan so that the potatoes will be completely submerged. You can fry just a few at a time, if necessary.

(ALLOW ONE POTATO PER SERVING)

Wash and peel firm, mature potatoes and cut them into long strips about ⅜ inch wide. Place in a bowl, cover with cold water, and let stand for at least 30 minutes. Drain and dry thoroughly with paper towels. Heat several inches of fat or oil in a pan until a frying thermometer reads 360°F. Add the potatoes without crowding and fry, moving them about with a fork or spoon until they are golden brown. Lift out and drain on paper towels. Keep hot in a warm oven until all are done.

Oven-fried Potatoes. Peel and slice potatoes as directed in the recipe for French-fried Potatoes. Dip the sliced potatoes in melted butter. Spread in a shallow pan and bake in a 400°F (205°C) oven for about 45 minutes or until brown and tender.

Potato Chips. Peel potatoes and slice them very thin. Soak them in cold water for about 1 hour, then pat them as dry as possible with paper towels. Fry as in the recipe for French-fried Potatoes, using oil that has been heated to 390°F. Salt before serving.

German Fried Potatoes

(SERVES FOUR)

6 tablespoons vegetable oil
4 cups (1 L) sliced cooked potatoes
Salt

Pour the oil into a large sauté pan and heat. Add the potatoes and turn the heat down to medium low. Cook, frequently turning, until well browned. Quickly remove to paper towels, lightly pat free of excess oil, and sprinkle with salt. Serve hot.

Cottage-fried or Hashed Brown Potatoes

(SERVES FOUR)

6 tablespoons bacon fat or oil
4 cups (1 L) finely diced
  potatoes, raw or cooked
1 tablespoon finely chopped
  onion

Salt to taste
1½ teaspoons coarsely ground
  pepper

Heat the fat or oil in a large skillet. Spread the potatoes evenly over the bottom and sprinkle the onion, salt, and pepper on top. Cook over low heat, pressing down on the potatoes firmly with a spatula several times. Cook until the bottom side is golden brown, allowing more time if the potatoes are raw; in fact, if you use raw potatoes, cover the pan and cook over a low heat to cook them through; then turn up the heat for a final browning. With the spatula cut down the middle of the potatoes and turn each side over. Cook until golden, again pressing down with a spatula several times. Serve hot.

Potato Pancakes

Crisp and brown, good with applesauce and roast pork. Peel and grate the potatoes immediately before cooking, or they will discolor: while this doesn't affect the taste of the pancakes, they will not look as appetizing. If you put grated potatoes in a bowl of cold water, they will not discolor, but you will then have to be especially careful to squeeze out the excess moisture before cooking.

(NINE 3½-INCH PANCAKES)

3 medium potatoes	1 egg, beaten
1 tablespoon flour	Salt to taste
1 tablespoon heavy or light cream	4 tablespoons bacon fat or oil

Peel and grate the potatoes. Place them on a double thickness of paper towels, fold the towels around them, and twist and squeeze until most of the moisture is extracted. Put the potatoes in a bowl, add the flour, cream, egg, and salt, and toss until well mixed. Heat the fat or oil in a large skillet. Put about 2 tablespoons of the potato mixture in the pan and press and shape with a spatula into a flat, 3½-inch pancake; repeat until the pan is full but not crowded. Cook each pancake about 5 minutes over medium-low heat until the bottom is crisp and brown; turn and cook the other side 5 minutes more. Keep warm in a 300°F (150°C) oven until all are ready, then serve immediately.

Scalloped Potatoes

Little rivers of buttery milk, lots of pepper, and creamy potatoes.

(SERVES FOUR)

4 medium potatoes, peeled and sliced ¼ inch thick	3 tablespoons flour
Salt	4 tablespoons butter
Freshly ground pepper	About 1½ cups (3½ dL) milk

Preheat the oven to 350°F (180°C). Butter a 1½-quart casserole. Cover the bottom of the casserole with a single layer of potatoes. Sprinkle generously with salt, pepper, flour, and a few dots of butter. Repeat until all the potato slices are used. Pour milk over the potato slices until the top is almost covered. Dot with the remaining butter. Bake for 1 hour or until the potatoes are soft.

Scalloped Potatoes with Celery Root or Celeriac. Alternate each layer of potatoes with a layer of *peeled, thinly sliced celery root.*

Creamed Potatoes

(SERVES FOUR)

8 or more new potatoes (about
  1½ pounds, 675 g)
1 celery stalk with leaves
1½ cups (3½ dL) heavy cream

½ cup (1 dL) freshly grated
  Parmesan cheese
Salt
Freshly ground pepper

Preheat the oven to 350°F (180°C). Peel and dice the potatoes, put them in a
pan, cover with cold water, and add the celery stalk, broken in half. Bring to a
boil and simmer for about 8 minutes or until barely tender; drain. Remove the
celery. Add the cream and cheese, season to taste, mix well, and place in a
shallow baking dish. Bake for 20–30 minutes or until bubbling. Serve hot.

Skillet Creamed Potatoes

(SERVES FOUR)

8 new potatoes (about 1½
  pounds, 675 g)
Salt

½ cup (1 dL) milk
2 tablespoons finely chopped
  parsley

Peel and dice the potatoes, put them in a pan, and cover with ½ cup boiling
water and a sprinkle of salt. Cook, covered, for 6–8 minutes. Uncover and
continue to cook until the water has evaporated. Add the milk and more salt,
if needed. Cook over low heat, stirring gently with a fork until well blended and
slightly thickened. Add the parsley. Serve hot.

Potatoes Hashed in Cream

(SERVES FOUR TO FIVE)

4 medium baking potatoes
2 tablespoons butter
1 tablespoon flour

1 cup (¼ L) heavy cream
Salt
Coarsely ground pepper

Preheat oven to 350°F (180°C). Butter a 2-quart baking dish. Scrub the potatoes
and bake them for about 1 hour or until barely tender; let cool, then peel and
dice. Melt the butter in a skillet and stir in the flour. Blend and stir for a couple
of minutes, then slowly add the cream. Cook, continuing to stir, until the sauce
bubbles and thickens. Add the potatoes, season to taste, mix well, and spoon
into the baking dish. Bake uncovered for about 30 minutes or until lightly
browned on top. Serve hot.

Lyonnaise Potatoes

(SERVES FOUR)

3 tablespoons butter
1 small onion, finely chopped
3 cups (¾ L) potatoes in small
  cubes (3–4 potatoes)

¼ cup (½ dL) beef stock or
  broth
Salt
Freshly ground pepper

Melt the butter in a skillet. Add the onion and cook until transparent. Add the
potatoes, and mix well. Stir in the stock or broth, lower the heat, and simmer,
covered, until the potatoes are tender and lightly browned on the bottom. Season
to taste. Serve hot.

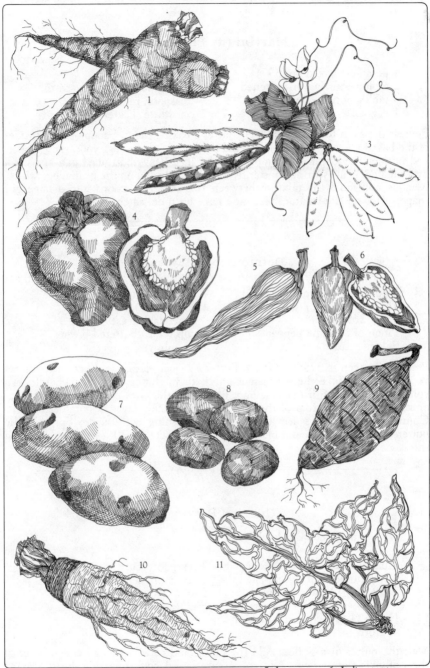

1. *parsnip*; 2. *peas*; 3. *snow peas*; 4. *green pepper*; 5. *hot pepper*; 6. *Italian pepper and cross section*; 7. *potato*; 8. *new potato*; 9. *sweet potato*; 10. *salsify*; 11. *spinach*.

Martinique Potatoes

(SERVES FOUR)

4 potatoes, baked (p. 397)   Salt to taste
2 tablespoons butter, softened   Freshly ground pepper to taste
3 tablespoons heavy cream   ¼ teaspoon nutmeg
1 egg yolk, slightly beaten   1 egg white, beaten stiff

Preheat the oven to 375°F (190°C). Butter a baking sheet. Scoop out the insides of the baked potatoes into a bowl. Add the butter, cream, egg yolk, salt, pepper, and nutmeg, and beat until smooth. Place in a heavy-bottomed pan and cook over medium heat, stirring constantly and gradually adding the beaten egg white. Remove and mold the mixture between two buttered spoons into a large egg shape, place on the baking sheet, and bake until delicately browned.

Delmonico Potatoes

(SERVES SIX)

6 potatoes, peeled and boiled   2 egg yolks, lightly beaten
1½ cups (3½ dL) White Sauce   ½ cup (1 dL) grated mild
  (p. 265)   Cheddar cheese
Pinch of cayenne pepper   1 cup (¼ L) buttered bread
Salt to taste   crumbs

Preheat the oven to 375°F (190°C). Butter a 2-quart casserole. Slice the potatoes ¼ inch thick. Make the white sauce and stir in the cayenne pepper, salt, egg yolks, and cheese. Stir over medium heat until the cheese melts. Spoon a film of sauce over the bottom of the casserole and place a layer of potatoes over it. Continue alternating sauce and potatoes, finishing with sauce. Sprinkle the buttered crumbs on top and place in the oven. Bake for 20–25 minutes or until the sauce is bubbling.

Curried Potatoes

Nice with chicken or lamb.

(SERVES FOUR)

4 tablespoons butter   2 teaspoons curry powder
1 small onion, finely chopped   2 teaspoons lemon juice
3 cups (¾ L) diced, cooked   Salt
  potatoes (about 4 potatoes)   Freshly ground pepper
½ cup (1 dL) chicken stock or
  broth

Melt the butter in a skillet. Add the onion and cook, stirring frequently, until the onion is transparent. Add the potatoes and cook over low heat, stirring occasionally, until the potatoes have absorbed the butter. Add the chicken stock or broth, curry powder, and lemon juice. Stir and blend all the ingredients and continue to cook over low heat until all the stock or broth has been absorbed. Season to taste.

Deerfoot Potatoes

(ALLOW ONE POTATO PER SERVING)

Preheat oven to 400°F (205°C). Wash and pare potatoes of uniform size. Cut out through the center of the potato a core the diameter of a sausage. Save two small slices from each core to fit the ends of each potato. Fill the cavity with a *country sausage* cut slightly less than the length, then insert a piece of potato core at each end. Rub the outside of the potatoes with *butter.* Put in a pan and bake for 1 hour or until soft enough to pierce with a fork.

Baked Sweet Potatoes or Yams

(ALLOW ONE MEDIUM POTATO PER SERVING)

Preheat the oven to 375°F (190°C). Scrub the potatoes and cut a small piece off one end so the potato won't burst during baking. Place the potatoes, slightly apart, on the oven rack. Bake for about 1 hour or until tender when pierced with a knife. Fork open and put a pat of butter inside to serve.

Boiled Sweet Potatoes or Yams

(ALLOW ONE MEDIUM POTATO PER SERVING)

Scrub the potatoes, put them into boiling water, cover, and boil gently for 20–30 minutes or until tender when pierced with a knife. Drain, peel, and add *butter, salt,* and *freshly ground pepper.*

Fried Sweet Potatoes or Yams

(ALLOW ONE MEDIUM POTATO PER SERVING)

Scrub the potatoes, put them into boiling water, and boil for 10 minutes. Drain, peel, and cut into ⅛-inch slices. Put enough oil in a pan to completely cover the slices. Heat to 375°F (190°C). Add the potatoes without crowding and fry until lightly browned. Remove and drain on paper towels. Keep hot in a warm oven until all the slices are fried. Add *salt* and serve.

Sweet Potato and Apple Scallop

(SERVES FOUR)

2 cups (½ L) thinly sliced
   boiled sweet potatoes or yams
   (about 2 medium potatoes)
1½ cups (3½ dL) peeled,
   thinly sliced tart apples

½ cup (1 dL) brown sugar
4 tablespoons butter
Salt

Preheat the oven to 350°F (180°C). Butter a 1½-quart baking dish. Put half the potatoes in the baking dish. Cover with half the apples, sprinkle with half the sugar, dot with half the butter, and sprinkle with salt. Repeat. Cover and bake for 30 minutes. Uncover and bake about 30 minutes more or until the apples are soft.

Candied Sweet Potatoes or Yams

(SERVES FOUR)

4 medium sweet potatoes or yams
4 tablespoons butter
⅓ cup (¾ dL) brown sugar

Boil the potatoes until tender; drain. Peel and cut in half lengthwise. Put the butter and sugar in a heavy skillet and heat, stirring occasionally, until melted. Add the potatoes and turn until lightly browned. Add ¼ cup water, cover, and simmer over low heat for about 10–15 minutes.

Baked Candied Sweet Potatoes or Yams. After the butter and sugar have melted, put the potatoes in a buttered baking dish, pour the butter-sugar mixture on top, cover, and bake in a preheated 350°F (180°C) oven for 45 minutes to 1 hour.

Mashed Sweet Potatoes or Yams

Add spices—nutmeg, allspice, cinnamon, or ginger—according to taste, but in small quantities, about ⅛ teaspoon per potato.

(SERVES FOUR)

4 medium sweet potatoes or yams
Butter
Salt
Spices (see above)
Orange juice or milk (optional)

Wash and peel the potatoes, put in a pot, and cover with cold water. Bring to a boil and cook gently until tender, about 30 minutes; drain. Mash with a potato masher, put through a ricer, or whip in an electric mixer, adding butter, salt, and spices to taste. Add a few tablespoons of orange juice or milk, if you wish, especially if you are using light, dry sweet potatoes. Beat until smooth.

Mashed Sweet Potatoes or Yams with Pineapple and Pecans. Add ¼ cup crushed, drained pineapple and ¼ cup chopped pecans to the finished mashed potatoes. (This may be done in advance.) Put the potato mixture into a 1-quart buttered baking dish. Bake in a 375°F (190°C) oven for 30–35 minutes or until hot.

Sweet Potatoes Georgian. Put the mashed potatoes in a 1-quart buttered baking dish. Combine 2 tablespoons molasses and 1 teaspoon butter in a small pan and boil for 1 minute. Pour over the potatoes and bake in a preheated 400°F (205°C) oven until slightly brown on top.

ABOUT PUMPKIN

Height of Season: Fall.
What to Look For: Hard rind, bright orange color, firm stem. The size does not seem to affect the taste and a good-sized pumpkin is always a good buy.
Uses: As a soup, a vegetable, in bread, and primarily as a filling for the all-American pie.
Amount: One pound serves two.
Alternatives to Fresh: Canned and frozen both good. In buying canned, be sure

not to purchase the kind that has been sweetened and spiced; it can only be used for pie and it is better to do your own flavoring.

Technically a member of the squash family, pumpkin can be prepared in the same ways as you would winter squash; it is particularly good cut into fair-sized pieces and baked with a little maple syrup and butter.

Puréed pumpkin: Steaming is more successful than boiling because the pulp is less watery and seems to retain both color and flavor better. Simply cut the pumpkin into large chunks and arrange on a steamer tray. Check after 30 minutes of vigorous steaming—it will take anywhere from 30 to 45 minutes. Remove when the interior is soft and scrape the pulp away from the skin. Either whip with a hand or electric beater or purée in a food processor. Use as is for soups, casseroles, and desserts; or, for an accompaniment to meats and poultry, beat in a little butter and cream, and add a sprinkling of nutmeg and salt and pepper to taste. Pumpkin purée keeps well, frozen.

Pumpkin seeds: Long popular in Mexican cooking, pumpkin seeds are relished today by the health-minded; they make a nourishing, chewy nibble and an interesting garnish for a pumpkin soup. When you are opening a pumpkin, scoop out the seeds, wash them under running water, then spread on paper towels to dry. Scatter them over an oiled cookie sheet and bake in a slow 250°F (120°C) oven to dry out completely for at least 1 hour, shaking them a few times and turning up the heat for about 5 minutes at the end of cooking to brown slightly. Remove, store in an airtight tin, salted or not, as you wish.

New England Vermont Pumpkin Casserole

Good with wedges of warm corn bread.

(SERVES FOUR)

4 cups (1 L) mashed or puréed pumpkin
1 cup (¼ L) Thick Cream Sauce (p. 265)
2 cups (3½ dL) diced ham
1⅓ cups (3¼ dL) coarsely grated sharp Cheddar cheese
2 hard-cooked eggs, sliced
½ cup (1 dL) broken soda crackers
2 tablespoons butter

Preheat the oven to 350°F (180°C). Mix together thoroughly the pumpkin, Cream Sauce, ham, and 1 cup of the cheese. Place half of this mixture in a 2-quart casserole, then cover with the sliced hard-cooked eggs, and top with the remaining pumpkin mixture. Sprinkle over the top the coarsely crumbled soda crackers, the remaining cheese, and dot with butter. Bake for 30 minutes.

ABOUT SALSIFY (OYSTER PLANT)

Height of Season: Fall or winter; look in specialty stores.
What to Look For: Firm roots with either black or white skin.
Uses: A good accent in stews or chicken and meat pies. As a vegetable accompaniment, especially good with roast beef, roast chicken, chops, and meat loaf.
Amount: One pound serves two to three.

Salsify is a root vegetable, long and tapering, of a grayish-white cast. It is sometimes called "oyster plant" because its delicate flavor is a little like oysters.

Basic Method for Cooking Salsify

(SERVES TWO TO THREE)

1 pound (450 g) salsify   Freshly ground pepper
Butter   Chopped parsley or chives
Salt

Have ready a bowl of cold water to which a little lemon juice or vinegar has been added. Cut off the tops of the salsify root, peel with a vegetable scraper, and drop immediately into the cold acidulated water to prevent discoloration. Cut into ½-inch-wide strips about 2 inches long. Drop them into a large pot filled with boiling water and cook, covered, until tender, about 20 minutes; taste to check doneness—the flesh should not become mushy. Drain. Add some butter, salt, pepper, and a sprinkling of parsley or chives and toss well before serving.

Mashed or Puréed Salsify. Mash the cooked, drained salsify or purée it through a food mill or in a food processor. Stir in some *butter, salt, freshly ground pepper,* and a little *cream.* Reheat, if necessary, preferably in the top of a double boiler. Or put in a shallow baking dish and sprinkle some bread crumbs dotted with butter on top and put under the broiler to brown.

Salsify Fritters

(SERVES THREE)

1 pound (450 g) salsify, cooked   1–2 tablespoons chopped
4 tablespoons butter   chives
Salt

Mash the cooked salsify with 2 tablespoons of the butter, adding salt and chives to taste. Beat until smooth. Shape into balls about 1¼ inches in diameter, then flatten into patties. Melt the remaining 2 tablespoons of butter in a skillet and fry the patties on each side until brown. Serve hot.

ABOUT SPINACH

Availability: Year round.
What to Look For: Fresh, dark-green leaves.
Uses: Raw, in salads. *Cooked,* as a bed for eggs, fish, or meat (dishes that are usually described as Florentine), in custards, quiches, soufflés, stuffings, soups. *As a vegetable accompaniment,* good with almost everything, especially with fish.
Amount: One pound serves two or three.
Alternatives to Fresh: Frozen perfectly acceptable but flavor not as good.

Loose, bulk spinach is far preferable to the spinach that comes prewashed in a package. If using the latter, be sure that it is fresh and not slimy.

Basic Method for Cooking Spinach

(SERVES TWO TO THREE)

1 pound (450 g) spinach   Salt
Melted butter   Freshly ground pepper

Wash the spinach leaves well in several changes of water and remove tougher stems. Bring a large pot of water to a fast boil, plunge the spinach into the boiling water, cook for 3–6 minutes, depending on how young it is, and drain it in a colander. Leave the cooked spinach whole or chop it, toss it with melted butter, season with salt and pepper, and serve at once.

Puréed Spinach. Purée the cooked spinach in a blender or food processor. Reheat it with some butter, season with salt and freshly ground pepper, and add a little *heavy cream*, if you wish.

Braised Baby Spinach

This method works well with tender, young spinach leaves.

(SERVES TWO TO THREE)

1 pound (450 g) young spinach	Salt
Melted butter	Freshly ground pepper

Wash spinach leaves well. Put them in a pot or skillet with the water still clinging to them. Cover and cook over low heat until the spinach is tender, about 2 minutes. Toss with melted butter, season with salt and pepper, and serve at once.

ABOUT SQUASH

Squash, a true American vegetable, is somewhat bland and very versatile, conducive to good seasonings and a natural partner to a number of vegetables and meats.

There are two main categories of squash: summer squash and winter squash. Summer squash have soft skins and a tender, more watery interior, while winter squash are hard-shelled and mealier inside.

About Summer Squash

Availability: Most of the year, especially summer.

What to Look For: Small, young, firm squash with good color and smooth, shiny green or yellow skins.

Uses: Raw, with a dip or in salad. *Cooked*, in soups, stews, stuffed (p. 304), baked, in casserole dishes, with other vegetables. *As a vegetable accompaniment*, good with fish, meat, and chicken.

Amount: One pound serves four.

Summer squash should be picked while still immature, about 6–9 inches long, and before the skins harden. If you grow squash yourself, you will soon learn how quickly the vegetables grow; picking them at the correct, early stage often involves split-second timing. Do not peel summer squash; the skins provide good taste and texture. Large summer squash are best scooped out and stuffed.

The larger summer squash are known outside the United States as vegetable marrows, the smaller as courgettes. There are many varieties available, among them smooth, yellow squash, both crooknecks and straightnecks; thin, dark-green zucchini, and scalloped, pale-green pattypan squash, also called cymlings. The various kinds of summer squash are interchangeable in recipes.

Unlike winter squash, summer squash is quite perishable: it should be kept refrigerated and used promptly.

About Winter Squash

Height of Season: Fall and winter.
What to Look For: Firm, hard squash without blemishes: often rough and bumpy.
Uses: Cooked, baked, puréed, in soups and in pie. *As a vegetable accompaniment,* excellent with all kinds of meats, particularly country ham.
Amount: One pound serves two.
Alternatives to Fresh: Frozen mashed winter squash is very good.

Winter squash are picked in the fall when they are mature and their skins have hardened. If you grow them yourself and plan to store them for future use, be sure to leave part of the stems attached or they will not keep very well.

Among the more common forms of winter squash are acorn squash, green hubbard squash, tan butternut squash, buttercup or turban squash, green and gold delicious squash, banana squash, and pumpkins. A recent variety is the spaghetti squash, about the size of a football, so called because when it has been cooked and the flesh is scraped out, it forms spaghettilike ribbons. Squash vary greatly in size, from the small, 1-pound acorn squash to the 5- or 6-pound, or more, hubbard.

Basic Method for Cooking Summer Squash

(SERVES FOUR)

1 pound (450 g) summer   Salt
    squash, in ½-inch slices   Freshly ground pepper
3 tablespoons butter

Bring 1½ cups water to a boil, add the squash, and simmer over medium heat, covered, for 3–5 minutes or until just tender; drain. Add the butter, season to taste, and toss to coat. Serve hot.

Summer Squash and Onion. Add *1 coarsely chopped onion* and cook with the squash.

Summer Squash and Tomatoes. Two minutes before the squash is done, add *2 tomatoes, peeled, seeded, and chopped with some of the liquid gently squeezed out.*

Summer Squash with Horseradish Cream. Mix *½ cup sour cream* with *1 tablespoon prepared horseradish,* add to the cooked squash, and reheat for a few minutes before serving.

Sautéed Summer Squash

This is another way to cook summer squash, equally basic and good with all sorts of variations. Any of the variations for the preceding recipe may be used with this sauté, too.

(SERVES FOUR)

3–4 tablespoons butter   Salt
1 pound (450 g) summer   Freshly ground pepper
    squash, in ½-inch slices

Melt the butter in a skillet, add the squash, and cook over low heat, stirring and tossing from time to time, until the squash is tender, about 8–10 minutes. Season to taste.

Variations:

Combine both *zucchini* and *yellow squash*.

Add 2 or more *thinly sliced scallions* as you sauté the squash.

Sprinkle with herbs—*parsley, chives, basil, summer savory*—before serving.

Toss in ¾ *cup buttered bread crumbs* during the last minute of cooking.

Sautéed Zucchini

(SERVES FOUR)

2 tablespoons olive or other oil   Salt
2 cloves garlic, minced   Freshly ground pepper
1 pound (450 g) zucchini, in
    ½-inch slices

Heat the oil in a skillet, add the minced garlic, and cook for a few minutes without letting the garlic brown. Add the zucchini and cook over low heat, stirring occasionally, until the squash is tender, about 10 minutes. Season to taste.

Zucchini Ring

Sweet marjoram tastes good in zucchini. Fill the center of the ring with braised carrots, cut into small matchstick shape.

(SERVES SIX)

3 cups (¾ L) cooked zucchini,   2 tablespoons finely grated
    drained and mashed   onion
1 teaspoon salt   3 eggs, well beaten
1 teaspoon chopped fresh   ½ cup (1 dL) buttered bread
    marjoram, or ½ teaspoon   crumbs
    dried

Preheat the oven to 350°F (180°C). Butter a 1½-quart ring mold generously. Put the zucchini, salt, marjoram, onion, and eggs together in a bowl and mix thoroughly. Sprinkle the bread crumbs evenly on the inside of the buttered mold. Spoon in the zucchini mixture. Set the mold in a shallow pan of hot water that comes up the side about 2 inches. Bake for 35–45 minutes or until firm. Turn the zucchini out of the mold onto a platter and fill if desired. Serve hot.

Baked Winter Squash

(SERVES FOUR)

2 small acorn or butternut   2 tablespoons butter
    squash   3 tablespoons maple syrup
Salt

Preheat the oven to 400°F (205°C). Split the squash and remove the seeds. Sprinkle the cut sides with salt. Place cut side down in a baking dish and bake for about 40–50 minutes or until the squash is easily pierced with a fork. Turn and make indentations with a fork across the cut side of the squash. Spread with the butter, drizzle with the maple syrup, and return to the oven for a minute or two. Serve hot.

Whipped Winter Squash

This can be prepared ahead and reheated in the oven.

(SERVES FOUR)

2 pounds (900 g) winter squash   ½ cup (1 dL) heavy cream
4 tablespoons butter   Salt
¼ teaspoon nutmeg

Preheat the oven to 350°F (180°C). Cut the squash in half and remove the fibers and seeds. Place cut side down in a baking pan. Bake for 40–50 minutes or until tender. Or, cut in large chunks and boil in salted water until tender, then drain well. Scoop out the pulp and put into a mixing bowl with the butter, nutmeg, and cream. Beat with an electric beater or by hand until smooth and well blended. Add salt to taste. Serve hot.

ABOUT SWISS CHARD

Availability: Summer and fall height of season.
What to Look For: Crisp, crinkly leaves, deep-green color.
Uses: Raw, in salads. *Cooked,* like spinach, in stuffings, quiches, and soups. *As a vegetable accompaniment,* especially good with meat, eggs, and fish.
Amount: One pound serves two.

Swiss chard looks like spinach, but has a coarser texture and a stronger taste with a sharp bite to it.

Older chard has thick stems which are good braised separately from the leaves. Rhubarb Swiss chard has thick, reddish stems that are also good cooked separately.

Basic Method for Cooking Swiss Chard

Swiss chard is most delicious when you cook the stems and the leaves separately following this method.

(SERVES SIX)

3 pounds (1⅓ kg) Swiss chard   2 tablespoons butter
3 tablespoons flour   Salt
2 tablespoons lemon juice

Separate the leaves from the stalks, pulling away the rib from the leaf along with the stem. Wash both thoroughly. Chop the stems into ½-inch pieces. Whisk the flour into 3 cups water, then bring to a boil, and drop the chopped stems in along with the lemon juice and ½ teaspoon of salt. Simmer gently for 20–30 minutes, depending on the tenderness of the stalks. Meanwhile bring a large pot of salted water to a boil and drop the leaves in. Boil rapidly for 10–15 minutes, depending on their tenderness. Drain and chop roughly; toss with butter and salt to taste. Place the cooked stems and their juice, which will have thickened to the consistency of cream sauce, in the center of a hot platter and surround with the greens.

Gratin of Swiss Chard. After preparing the Swiss chard as above (or use any leftover cooked Swiss chard), place both stems and greens in a shallow casserole, mix *2–3 tablespoons heavy cream* in with the chard sauce, correct seasoning, and top with *¼–½ cup bread crumbs and an equal amount of grated cheese.* Bake in a 425°F (220°C) oven for 15 minutes.

ABOUT TOMATOES

Availability: Almost year round but August and September height of season for fresh.

What to Look For: Firm, smooth, ripe but not overripe tomatoes, without bruises or soft spots.

Uses: Raw, like fruit, in salads, sandwiches, as a first course. *Cooked,* broiled, sautéed, stewed, and baked, in soups, stews, casserole dishes, and of course, as the foundation of an indispensable sauce (see p. 271). Also used for juice, tomato paste, catsup, chili sauce, and in relishes and pickles.

Amount: One per person.

Alternatives to Fresh: Canned plum tomatoes for sauces, stews, and casserole dishes.

The pale, hard-skinned hothouse tomatoes that most markets stock during the winter months lack flavor and have a mealy texture, having been grown mainly for their durability during shipping and handling. Tiny round cherry tomatoes or small pear-shaped or egg-shaped tomatoes, available most of the year, though also grown in hothouses, seem to have more flavor during the out-of-season months.

If tomatoes are not quite ripe, keep them at room temperature until they ripen. Do not refrigerate them: once they've been refrigerated, they will not ripen. Tomatoes actually taste best when they've not been refrigerated at all.

To peel a tomato, submerge it in boiling water for about a minute, then let it cool a bit. The skin can then be pulled off easily with a sharp knife. *To seed a tomato,* cut it in half and gently squeeze out the excess juice and seeds, scraping off those that adhere.

Green *tomatoes,* which are unripened tomatoes, are excellent fried, sautéed, or cooked in sauces or stews. Use small green tomatoes for pickling. Large, unblemished green tomatoes will ripen on a sunny window sill, or you can wrap them in newspaper and let them ripen slowly in a cool, dark place.

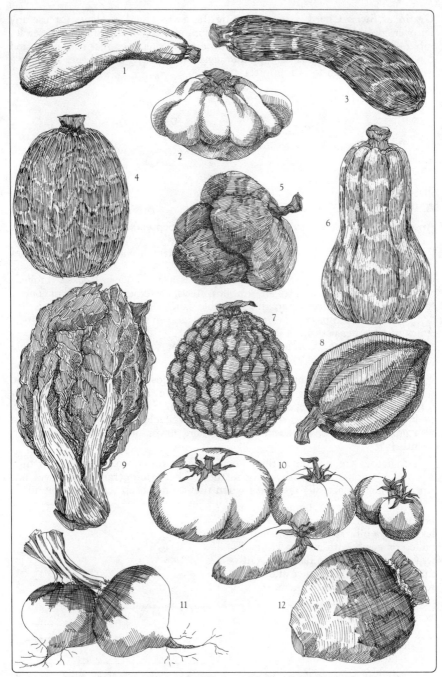

1. *yellow or crookneck squash;* 2. *patty pan squash;* 3. *zucchini;* 4. *spaghetti squash;* 5. *turban squash;* 6. *butternut squash;* 7. *hubbard squash;* 8. *acorn squash;* 9. *Swiss chard;* 10. *tomatoes;* 11. *turnip;* 12. *rutabaga.*

Sautéed Tomatoes

The secret of this recipe is to cook the tomatoes only slightly, browning them quickly in hot butter. They are firm and flavorful with the basil and cream.

(SERVES SIX)

6 large tomatoes
½ cup (70 g) flour
½ teaspoon freshly ground
  pepper
¼ pound (115 g) butter

2 tablespoons chopped fresh
  basil, or 1 tablespoon dried,
  crumbled
¾ cup (1¾ dL) heavy cream
Salt

Slice the tomatoes ½ inch thick. Mix the flour and pepper together. Heat the butter over medium high heat. Dip the tomato slices into the flour mixture and coat on each side; shake free of excess flour. Put the slices into the hot butter and cook just a minute on each side or until lightly golden. Remove and keep in warm oven. Pour off all but 1 tablespoon of the butter, then stir in the basil, cream, and salt to taste. Bring to a boil and boil rapidly about 3 or 4 minutes. Pour over the tomato slices and serve.

Braised Herb Tomatoes

(SERVES FOUR)

4 tablespoons butter
4 scallions, chopped
1 tablespoon finely chopped
  parsley
4 teaspoons chopped fresh basil,
  or 2 teaspoons dried,
  crumbled

2 teaspoons chopped fresh
  thyme, or 1 teaspoon dried,
  crumbled
8 medium tomatoes, peeled
Salt
Freshly ground pepper

Melt the butter in a skillet. Stir in the scallions, parsley, basil, and thyme. Cook over low heat, stirring often, for 5 minutes. Add the tomatoes, cover, and cook over low heat for 5 more minutes. Season to taste. Place the tomatoes on a platter and spoon the herb juices over them.

Stewed Tomatoes

This is the old-fashioned way of stewing tomatoes. If it seems too sweet for your taste, use less sugar.

(SERVES SIX)

6 large tomatoes, peeled
  (p. 413), or 2½ cups (6 dL)
  canned tomatoes
1 tablespoon butter
2 tablespoons finely chopped
  onion

2 teaspoons sugar
⅛ teaspoon cloves
Salt
Freshly ground pepper
1 slice fresh bread, torn in
  pieces (optional)

Cut the tomatoes into eighths. Melt the butter in a pan, add the onion and sugar, and cook for 3 or 4 minutes, stirring, over medium heat. Add the tomatoes and cloves. Cover and simmer for 15 minutes. Season to taste. If a thicker stew is desired, add the bread and cook another 10 minutes.

Broiled Tomatoes

Delicious with chops and roasts, particularly lamb.

(SERVES FOUR)

4 large tomatoes
2 teaspoons chopped fresh
  oregano or marjoram, or 1
  teaspoon dried, crumbled
1 teaspoon salt

1 cup (¼ L) buttered bread
  crumbs
¼ teaspoon freshly ground
  pepper

Cut the tomatoes in half and arrange them cut side up in a shallow, buttered baking dish. Mix the oregano or marjoram, salt, bread crumbs, and pepper together and sprinkle evenly over tomatoes. Place under the broiler, watching carefully, until the crumbs brown and the tomatoes heat slightly. Be careful not to overcook or you will ruin the texture and the shape. Serve hot or cold.

Broiled Tomatoes with Cheese. Add ½ cup *freshly grated Parmesan cheese* and ½ *clove garlic, minced,* to the seasoned crumbs.

Broiled Tomatoes with Mustard Cream. Omit the oregano or marjoram. Combine *1 cup heavy cream* and *1½ tablespoons prepared mustard* in a small pan and heat, stirring. Pour the mustard cream around the tomatoes just before serving.

Baked Stuffed Tomatoes

About 2 cups of stuffing will fill four large tomatoes nicely.

(SERVES FOUR)

4 firm large tomatoes
Salt
1¼ cups (3 dL) dried
  homemade bread crumbs
1 teaspoon chopped fresh
  basil, or ½ teaspoon dried,
  crumbled

2 tablespoons finely chopped
  onion
2 tablespoons finely chopped
  green pepper
1½ tablespoons olive oil
Coarsely ground pepper

Preheat the oven to 400°F (205°C). Film a shallow baking pan with oil, using a pan large enough so that 8 tomato halves will not be crowded. Carefully cut a slice from the top of each tomato and scoop out most of the pulp, leaving a thick shell so that the tomato will hold its shape. Sprinkle the insides of the tomatoes with salt, invert them on paper towels, and let them drain for about 15 minutes. Squeeze the juice out of the pulp and chop pulp fine. In a bowl, *lightly* toss the bread crumbs, basil, onion, green pepper, and tomato pulp, then add the olive oil and season to taste with salt and pepper. Lightly fill each tomato, without packing. Place on the baking pan and bake for 15–20 minutes.

Baked Tomatoes with Mushroom Stuffing. Omit the basil, green pepper, and olive oil and reduce the amount of bread crumbs to ½ cup. Clean and chop ½ *pound mushrooms* and sauté them with the onion in *4 tablespoons butter* over moderate heat for about 5 minutes; cool. Lightly toss the bread crumbs, tomato pulp, mushroom and onion mixture, salt, and pepper together and proceed as for Baked Stuffed Tomatoes.

Baked Tomatoes with Tuna Stuffing. Omit the basil and reduce the amount of bread crumbs to ½ cup and the onion and green pepper to 1 tablespoon each. Add *½ teaspoon chopped fresh tarragon or ¼ teaspoon dried tarragon, crumbled,* and *a 6½-ounce can tuna,* well drained and broken into small pieces. Lightly mix the bread crumbs, tomato pulp, tarragon, tuna, onion, and green pepper, then add the olive oil, salt, and pepper. Proceed as for Baked Stuffed Tomatoes.

Baked Tomatoes with Meat, Fish, or Chicken Stuffing. Omit the basil, green pepper, and olive oil and reduce the amount of bread crumbs to ½ cup. Add *1 teaspoon chopped fresh thyme or ½ teaspoon dried thyme, crumbled, 2 tablespoons melted butter,* and *1 cup minced cooked meat, fish, or chicken.* Proceed as for Baked Stuffed Tomatoes.

Baked Tomatoes with Spinach and Water Chestnut Stuffing. Omit the green pepper and reduce the amount of bread crumbs to ½ cup. Add *1 cup well-drained chopped cooked spinach* and *¼ cup sliced canned water chestnuts.* Proceed as for Baked Stuffed Tomatoes.

Creole Tomatoes

(SERVES SIX)

3 tablespoons butter
1 large green pepper, chopped
1 onion, chopped
6–7 medium tomatoes,
   quartered
⅛ teaspoon cayenne pepper

1 tablespoon chopped fresh
   thyme, or 1½ teaspoons
   dried, crumbled
Salt
2 tablespoons finely chopped
   parsley

Melt the butter in a large skillet, add the green pepper and onion, and cook slowly over medium-low heat, stirring occasionally, for about 10 minutes or until the onions are lightly colored. Add the tomatoes, cayenne pepper, and thyme. Cook for 5–6 minutes, stirring frequently. Add salt to taste, sprinkle with parsley, and serve.

Tomato Curry

(SERVES FOUR)

3 tablespoons butter
1 small onion, peeled and
   finely chopped
1 tart apple, peeled and
   chopped
2 cups (½ L) peeled and
   chopped fresh tomatoes, or
   canned tomatoes, partially
   drained and chopped

2 teaspoons curry powder
1 teaspoon vinegar
¼ teaspoon freshly ground
   pepper
1½ cups (3½ dL) cooked rice
Salt

Melt the butter in a large skillet, add the onion, and cook over medium heat, stirring often, until transparent. Add the apple and cook gently for 5 more minutes. Stir in the tomatoes, curry powder, vinegar, and pepper. Cook, stirring often, for 5 more minutes, then add the rice and salt to taste. Heat well before serving.

Curried Green Tomatoes

This is good hot or cold. The tomatoes should be barely cooked.

(SERVES FOUR)

2 tablespoons butter
½ onion, finely chopped
1½ teaspoons curry powder
Pinch of cayenne pepper

2 cups (½ L) coarsely chopped
  green tomatoes
Salt

Melt the butter in a skillet, add the onion, and cook slowly until onion is transparent. Add the curry powder and blend well. Stir in the cayenne pepper and green tomatoes. Cook, stirring, for 3 or 4 minutes. Add salt to taste.

ABOUT TURNIPS AND RUTABAGAS

Availability: White turnips, year round; rutabagas or yellow turnips, mainly fall and winter.
What to Look For: Firm, smooth, round, unblemished turnips.
Uses: Whole when small, or sliced or grated. *Raw,* julienned or sliced thin, salted, with dips. *Cooked,* in stews, casserole dishes, braised, puréed, creamed, around a roast, with other vegetables. *As a vegetable accompaniment,* especially good with pork and duck; yellow turnips or rutabagas puréed are excellent with beef, lamb, and a roast turkey.
Amount: One pound serves three.

White turnips, particularly the small ones, are somewhat milder than rutabagas and cook more quickly. Turnips are easy to grow and will thrive in about any kind of soil. The greens can be cooked like collards and other field greens (p. 376).

Basic Method for Cooking White Turnips

(SERVES FOUR)

1½ pounds (675 g) white
  turnips
3 tablespoons butter

Salt to taste
1 tablespoon finely chopped
  parsley

If the turnips are old, peel them; small young turnips need only be scrubbed. If large, cut them into quarters; if small, cut in half. Drop turnips into a large pot of boiling water and boil for 8–10 minutes or until tender when pierced with a knife or skewer; drain. Add the butter, sprinkle with salt and parsley, and toss until coated.

Whipped Turnips. After boiling, mash with a fork, then add *½ cup heavy cream, heated, 2 tablespoons softened butter, 1 teaspoon grated lemon rind,* and *½ teaspoon salt.* Beat by hand or with an electric mixer until smooth.

Creamed Turnips. After boiling, drain and dice. Melt *2 tablespoons butter* in a skillet, add the turnips, pour *1 cup heavy cream* over them, and stir in ¾ *teaspoon ginger* and *salt to taste.* Stir until well blended and hot. If a thicker sauce is desired, boil, drain, and dice the turnips, then toss them in *1 cup White Sauce* (p. 265).

Braised Turnips

Either white or yellow turnips can be done this way. Usually rutabagas are larger and will take longer to cook.

(SERVES FOUR)

3 tablespoons butter
1 cup (¼ L) beef broth
1 pound (450 g) small young
   turnips, peeled and halved

Salt
Freshly ground pepper

Melt the butter in a heavy-bottomed pan with a lid. Add the beef broth and bring it to a simmer. Add the turnips, cover, and simmer for 10–15 minutes or until tender. Remove from the heat, add salt and pepper to taste, and serve hot.

White Turnips Roasted with Meat or Fowl

Turnips taste wonderful roasted with a pork or beef roast or with turkey or duck: the rich pan drippings blend nicely with the sweet tangy character of the turnips.

(SERVES FOUR)

1½ pounds (675 g) medium
white turnips

Peel the turnips, drop them into boiling water, and let them boil for 10 or more minutes until they are barely tender. If they are quite large, halve or quarter them; otherwise place them whole around roast meat or fowl during the last hour of roasting. Turn them and baste them every 20–30 minutes with the pan juices.

Basic Method for Cooking Rutabagas

(SERVES FOUR)

1½ pounds (675 g) rutabagas
   or yellow turnips
Salt

Melted butter
Lemon juice

Peel the rutabagas and cut them up or dice them. Drop them into boiling water to cover and cook briskly until soft. Drain well, season with salt, toss with melted butter, and add a squeeze or so of lemon juice to taste.

Mashed or Puréed Rutabagas. Drain and mash the cooked rutabagas with a fork or potato masher or purée them in a food processor. Add a little *butter, salt, freshly ground pepper,* and *cream* to taste. A *dash of cinnamon or freshly grated nutmeg* is also a good accent.

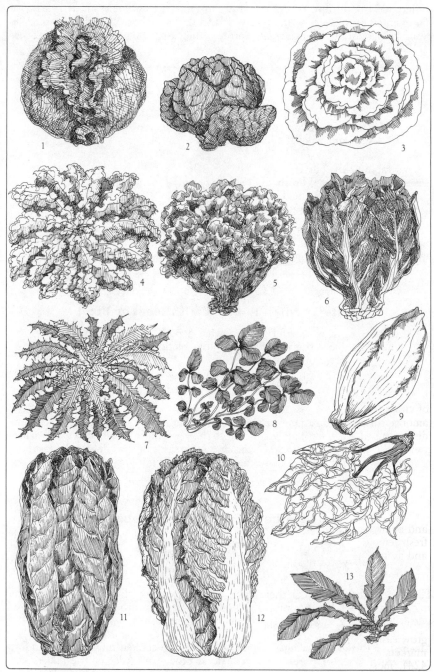

1. *iceberg lettuce;* 2. *Bibb lettuce;* 3. *Boston lettuce;* 4. *loose leaf lettuce;* 5. *red leaf lettuce;* 6. *escarole;* 7. *chicory;* 8. *watercress;* 9. *endive;* 10. *spinach;* 11. *romaine;* 12. *Chinese cabbage;* 13. *arugola.*

SALAD

ABOUT SALAD

The Role of Salad

Salads in all their various shapes and forms seem to play an increasingly large part in the American diet. A salad can be a whole meal, a starter, an accompaniment to the main course, a refresher after it, or even a dessert. With the abundance of fresh produce available year round and with the growing awareness of the role of vitamins and healthful raw foods, there is less concentration today, particularly among the young, on jellied salads made from synthetic flavors with overly sweet dressings and more concern for lightness, crispness, color, and balance of flavors.

Types of Salad

Green salad, in keeping with the tendency to serve simpler and fewer dishes at a meal, appears now as often as a first course as the pause between the main course and dessert. (Westerners have always preferred it first anyway.) So there are no rules about *when* it should appear, only *how*. A green salad should sparkle and be made of clean, chill, crisp greens, fresh oil, light tingling vinegar and/or fresh lemon juice, with salt, freshly ground pepper, sometimes mustard, herbs, and aromatics as accents.

The salad course need never be monotonous. There is such a variety of greens to choose from in our markets; in addition to the standby iceberg lettuce, there are leafy heads of Boston, romaine, and sometimes garden varieties, when in season, as well as greens with sharper flavor, such as spinach, chicory, watercress, escarole, and endive. Mustard greens, arugola, dandelion greens, and others that grow easily in home gardens are beginning to find their way into ethnic produce markets in urban areas. In addition, there are many salad "companions" (see p. 424), most of them available year round, to be used judiciously for a touch of contrast. And there are many ways to vary your dressings with herbs, the addition of mustard, garlic, or cheese.

Green salads should be dressed lightly just before serving or even at table. Most greens should be more or less bite size, torn by hand rather than chopped,

421

sometimes with smaller leaves or the heart just pulled apart, the shape left intact. Be subtle with sharp raw onion and garlic; red or sweet onions, scallions, and chives are milder and generally better to use in salads that require an accent. When you want a really garlicky salad, be sure the garlic is fresh and mince the clove very fine, then mash it into the dressing; always make it fresh—garlic, once it's crushed, does not keep well.

A molded salad should have good, intense—preferably natural—flavor. It should be attractive to look at, but not too gussied up, and while it must hold its shape, the jelly should never be overly firm and rubbery.

Vegetables used in salads can be raw or cooked. If raw, they should be young and tender. It is nice to use some of the skin for flavor and color, but avoid tough skins or ones that have been waxed. Cooked vegetables should have a crisp texture and bright color, which is best achieved by brief cooking in a lot of water. Leftover vegetables can be used, but the sooner the better, and if they have been tossed with butter, be sure to scald with boiling water to remove any congealed fat. The same goes for potatoes, macaroni, and rice, which form the basis of so many substantial salads; don't use refrigerator-weary leftovers.

A composed salad means one that has been arranged, the ingredients imaginatively combined and placed on a plate. You can create an attractive first course simply by making a circle of sliced garden tomatoes with chopped fresh parsley and maybe basil sprinkled on the top, or on a bed of watercress by placing a halved hard-boiled egg, dotted with coarse pepper, and a small stack of lightly cooked green beans with a few slivers of anchovy on top. There are further suggestions on p. 426 but use your ingenuity, too. Or you can choose from any of the American favorites like Crab Louis or Ravigote, Chicken or Lobster Salad, Hearts of Palm with Avocado, or shrimp and artichoke, arranged enticingly on separate plates, waiting at each place as you sit down to the meal.

Washing, Drying, and Storing Greens

Wash greens that are dirty as soon as you get them home, using very cold water, separating the leaves, and soaking in several changes of water if they are gritty. There are some you may not need to wash at all, like iceberg lettuce or endive, and in this case do not separate the leaves until you are ready to use them. The best way to dry greens is in a salad spinner—see p. 29. Lacking that, wrap loosely in a towel and shake. If your refrigerator has a salad crisper drawer, simply store the greens in that. Otherwise fold loosely in a towel. Avoid wrapping washed greens in plastic bags which create too much moisture so that the greens are apt to turn dank more quickly. There is no exact rule about how long they will keep; they're usable as long as they seem fresh and crisp—so much depends on how fresh they were when you bought them. It is a good idea to check and remove any leaves that have turned brown because they can infect the whole lot.

Salad Dressings

The amount of dressing on a salad is critical. Too much dressing drenches and wilts the greens and robs them of taste and texture. Not enough dressing leaves a salad unseasoned, unfinished. Here is a rough guide:

> For 2 quarts of mixed greens (2 quarts will serve four): use 5 tablespoons vinaigrette or 6 tablespoons mayonnaise-type dressing.
> 4 tablespoons mayonnaise will coat 2 cups moist, cooked chicken pieces. If the chicken is dry it will take 1 or 2 more tablespoons.
> ½ cup of mayonnaise will dress and moisten 2 cups well-drained tuna.

Salad Dressing Ingredients

Olive Oil. Price generally indicates the quality of the olive oil. It is better to buy a fine first-press olive oil and dilute it with a small amount of vegetable oil than to buy an inexpensive poor-quality olive oil.

Do not refrigerate olive oil. Again, a fine-quality olive oil won't turn rancid. Keep it in your coolest storage place and don't close airtight; let the can or bottle breathe a little by plugging it with a paper towel or cloth.

Buy in smaller quantity if your consumption is small.

Vinegar. There are many varieties of vinegars. Which you should use depends upon the salad ingredients. Soft, tender Bibb lettuce is nice with a mild wine vinegar and oil. Red wine vinegars are lusty and strong; white wine tarragon vinegar is light with an aromatic flavor. Japanese rice vinegars are wonderful on fruits. Many people who find vinegar too assertive prefer to use fresh *lemon juice*; or it may be used in combination with vinegar.

Yogurt. Now being used more and more in interesting ways as a base for salad dressing, yogurt is tart and delicious and you don't have to be a weight-watcher to enjoy it.

Mayonnaise. Homemade mayonnaise is delicious and easy to make—a simple sleight of hand. It is worth making if only to watch the liquids become transformed into a creamy, pale sauce. Such a lovely result for so little effort. And with the advent of the blender and the food processor, it can be even more simply made. There is no reason not to have some always on hand, particularly as you can freeze any excess amount. Mayonnaise is a basic sauce, and a variety of flavors can be added to make it more finished and to complement different ingredients—see the variations that follow the recipe, p. 453.

Avoid sweet dressings on most salads that go with a meal. They are fine with a fruit salad at the end and some people enjoy them with a main-course luncheon salad, but be careful not to overwhelm natural flavors with too much sweetness.

Types of Salad Greens

Iceberg. The all-purpose lettuce that is available year round. The head is large and tight, the leaves crisp, and it keeps well. Don't separate the leaves before storing. Iceberg has less taste than other lettuces, so for a salad it is best mixed with other greens and crunchy salad companions. It is particularly good in sandwiches, makes nice lettuce cups, and a bed of shredded iceberg will hold up well as a base for stuffed eggs, avocados, and other composed salads.

Boston or Butter Lettuce. Generally available, this looser head has large, deep-green, soft leaves and a lighter, tender heart. Its delicate flavor is best enhanced by a light vinaigrette.

Bibb or Limestone Lettuce. The heads are a little smaller and more pointy than Boston and the leaves are somewhat firmer. Some Bibb used to be grown in limestone, hence the alternate name for it. A prized lettuce for green salads, it too is best served by a light vinaigrette, though will hold up to something stronger.

Leaf Lettuce or Garden Lettuce. Fresh and tasty, the curly loose leaves of garden lettuce wilt quickly and should be kept very cold and used as soon as possible. Good by itself with a light vinaigrette, made perhaps with lemon and fresh herbs. The leaves are also an addition to any mixed salad.

Red-Leaf Lettuce. Another loose-leaf garden variety with leaves that are tinged in red—the color of oak in autumn. Red-leaf looks and tastes lovely in any kind of mixed green salad.

Escarole. A large spready head of longish leaves that splay out at the end with wide ribs at the base, escarole can be a bit tough on the outside, so some of the more mature leaves should be discarded; the heart is always tender. It makes a fine wintry salad that can stand up to a more robust dressing like a Roquefort or a cream dressing or vinaigrette spiked with garlic; walnuts and apples can also be good companions.

Chicory. Sometimes known as curly endive, the spiky, curly-edged leaves have a pleasing bitter taste and make a good foil for milder greens. Again, an assertive dressing holds up best.

Watercress. Deep green, the small flat leaves of watercress have a peppery taste that mixes well with other greens. For salads, trim off some of the stem. Watercress is good with astringent fruits like oranges and grapefruit, makes a handsome garnish for almost anything, and is good in sandwiches.

Belgian Endive. The slender, long blanched leaves from a head of endive offer contrast of color, texture, and a slightly bitter taste in a mixed salad. It's very expensive, but a little goes a long way and the crisp leaves, which can be left whole or broken in pieces, hold up well. A lovely salad can be made of just endive and beets, a perfect marriage, dressed in vinaigrette.

Spinach. For salad use young, tender, very fresh leaves and trim off the stems. Wash well—spinach can be gritty. A raw spinach salad of chopped hard-cooked eggs, sliced raw mushrooms, and bacon is good as a whole lunch or to balance out a meal, and a few crisp leaves are always welcome in a mixed salad. Young *dandelion leaves, beet greens, kale,* and *chard,* when very fresh, also add to a green salad.

Romaine. A long, sometimes quite fat head of crisp leaves that always give a wonderful crunch to a salad. When very young the tender heart is sometimes served whole, but more often leaves are torn into bite-size pieces; romaine takes well to an assertive dressing.

Chinese Cabbage. A long tight head of Chinese cabbage with its pale-green fringed leaves is a more familiar sight in our markets today. The leaves cut in pieces make a lovely-looking salad with a beautiful mild cabbagy flavor, particularly good with Lemon Soy Dressing.

Arugola or Rocket. More likely to be found in Italian neighborhoods, where it is much appreciated. A few arugola leaves add a surprising, pronounced flavor to a green salad. Aficionados will make a whole salad of it with a wine vinegar and olive oil dressing, but if you haven't had the arugola experience, you might be put off.

Fresh Herbs
Tossed on a green salad or blended in with the dressing, these fresh herbs are particularly pleasing: tarragon; basil (fresh far preferable); chives; Italian (flat-leafed) parsley; dill (particularly with cucumbers); summer savory (particularly with cooked vegetables); chervil.

Salad Companions
Use singly or in combination to give variety—a little contrast in texture, taste, and color—to a mixed green salad. It's up to you how much of anything to use, depending on the place of the salad in your meal; if the salad is simply a refresher after the main course, don't add any of the more substantial salad companions—and what you do include should be just a very light accent.

Raw Vegetables
Tomatoes. Peel only if tough-skinned, then slice or cut in wedges. Leave cherry tomatoes whole or halve them.

Cucumbers. Peel if skin is waxed. Leave unpeeled and scored, or semipeeled, if young and tender. Slice very thin or dice.

Radishes. Scrub and slice or grate.

Scallions or Spring Onions. Chop, using most of the green if tender.

Celery. Use tender stalks (leaves are a bit dominant for a mixed salad). Remove strings if necessary, then slice, dice, or julienne.

Fennel. Use bulb primarily, chopped or julienned, and a little of the feathery green, if liked. The flavor is assertive, so don't overpower with it.

Carrots. Scrape, then julienne or grate. Or make carrot curls for garnish.

Mushrooms. They should be very fresh to use raw. Wipe clean with a damp cloth, remove stems if at all woody, or just trim the ends. Don't peel. Slice or quarter.

Avocado. Peel at the last moment, then slice, dice, or chunk. If storing an unused portion, rub cut sides with lemon juice, keep the pit in the center, wrap tightly with plastic wrap, and refrigerate.

Baby Zucchini. Just scrub, don't peel, and cut in thin slivers.

Jicama. Peel, then dice, cut in slivers, or julienne.

Kohlrabi. Same as jicama.

Jerusalem Artichokes. Same as jicama.

Green or Sweet Red Pepper. Scrape out seeds and remove inner ribs, then dice or julienne.

Alfalfa Sprouts. Should be plump and fresh-looking. Rinse and remove any dank threads. Unused sprouts should be stored in water and refrigerated for up to a week.

Bean Sprouts. Same as alfalfa sprouts.

Raw Fruit

Grapefruit. Peel while whole and separate into segments.

Orange. Peel whole and separate into segments or cut across into slices.

Apple. Peel or not as you wish and dice or cut in thin slices.

Pear. Same as apple. A little pear is good in a winter salad with slightly bitter greens.

Preserved Things

Olives. Green, stuffed, ripe, or black Mediterranean. Pit and slice. Use sparingly in a green salad; more appropriate for a mixed concoction or a composed salad (in which case leave whole).

Pimiento. Again, more appropriate for a composed salad, sliced or chopped.

Anchovies. Use sparingly in tiny pieces or mash into the dressing—the flavor is very robust. More appropriate in special salads.

Capers. Drain and rinse if very briny. Same kind of use as anchovies.

Other Things

Hard-boiled Eggs. Chopped or quartered eggs are more suitable to a substantial salad, but grated they can give an attractive mimosa effect to a green salad.

Walnuts. Roughly chopped, walnuts can be particularly good as an accent in a winter salad of tart greens.

Beets. An exception to the raw vegetable practice, beets are usually added cooked to a green salad, either diced or julienned. Particularly good with endive and chicory.

Cottage Cheese. Better for a luncheon salad, placed on top in attractive mounds and sprinkled with chives, chopped scallions, or dusted with paprika.

Cream Cheese Balls. Same as cottage cheese.

Wheat Berries. Cooked until just tender, a scattering of wheat berries in a salad adds a nice chewy texture and a lot of nutrition.

Croutons. They give a pleasing contrast in texture. Be sure they taste fresh. Rubbing them with garlic is a good way of imparting that flavor to a salad.

Chickpeas or Garbanzo Beans. Cooked, just a few tablespoons scattered in a big salad are good.

Composed Salads

The exact amounts for a composed salad really depend upon the eye and appetite of the maker. For a rough guide, ⅓ cup of each of three basic ingredients per serving seems reasonable. This would be about 1 cup per serving. Too much is a greater error than too little.

Some Ideas for Composed Salads

Belgian endive, Red Delicious apple pieces, walnuts, soft cream cheese.

Raw snow peas, cooked chicken pieces, salted cashews, cilantro (Chinese parsley).

Cooked leeks, diced cooked potatoes, slices of sausage, hard-boiled eggs.

Cold cooked fish, sliced red onions, cucumber, cold cooked brown rice.

Grapefruit sections, asparagus, papaya slices, prosciutto, water chestnuts.

Artichoke hearts, mushrooms, black olives, marinated cold beef and capers.

TOSSED AND COMPOSED SALADS

Chef's Salad

This is a main dish for a summer evening or a lunch.

(SERVES FOUR)

1 head iceberg lettuce
12 radishes, trimmed, sliced
2 stalks celery, julienned
1½ cups (3½ dL) French Dressing (p. 450), Cream French Dressing (p. 451), or Russian Dressing (p. 453)
4 tomatoes, peeled, cut into 6 wedges each
¾ cup (1¾ dL) Swiss cheese strips, ⅛ inch wide, 1½ inches long

1 cup (¼ L) cooked ham or tongue (or both) strips, ⅛ inch wide, 1½ inches long
1 cup (¼ L) cooked chicken or turkey strips, ⅛ inch wide, 1½ inches long
4 hard-boiled eggs, quartered
Salt
Freshly ground pepper

Core the iceberg lettuce and save four outside leaves for the bed in which to put the salad. Place them around the edges of a large salad bowl. Cut or tear the remaining lettuce into bite-size pieces, place in the bowl, and toss with the radishes, celery, and half of the dressing. Arrange the tomato wedges around the inside edges of the lettuce. Combine the cheese, ham or tongue, and chicken or turkey, toss, and spread it over the lettuce and vegetables. Place the hard-boiled eggs between the tomato wedges. Salt and pepper lightly over the salad. Spoon the rest of the dressing over the salad.

Cucumber Salad

This is a sharp cucumber salad, maybe too much so for some tastes—
if so add a little sugar.

(SERVES SIX)

3 medium cucumbers
Salt
4 tablespoons sour cream or
  mayonnaise
3 tablespoons minced scallions

1 teaspoon lemon juice
2 tablespoons vinegar
½ teaspoon dry mustard
1 tablespoon minced dill or
  parsley

Peel the cucumbers and slice thin. Spread them over the bottom of a colander
and sprinkle salt on top. Let them drain for 30 minutes, press gently to remove
excess liquid, then chill. Blend the sour cream or mayonnaise, scallions, lemon
juice, vinegar, and dry mustard together. Add salt to taste. Toss the dressing with
the cucumbers. Sprinkle the dill or parsley on top and serve cold.

Wilted Cucumber Salad

(SERVES FOUR)

3 cucumbers, peeled, thinly
  sliced
1 clove garlic, peeled
Salt

4 tablespoons vinegar
2 tablespoons sugar
Watercress

Cover the cucumbers with water. Add the garlic and sprinkle well with salt,
stirring to dissolve the salt. Let stand 1 hour. Drain, pressing gently to rid of
excess liquid, and discard garlic. Stir the vinegar, sugar, and 2 tablespoons water
together until the sugar is dissolved. Pour over the cucumbers and stir. Add salt
to taste. Chill well and serve on a bed of watercress.

Raw Green Beans, Tomatoes, Olives,
Scallions, and Celery Salad

Pick vegetables with care: look for bright color and firm texture.

(7 CUPS)

4 cups (1 L) tiny tender green
  beans; if larger blanch 2
  minutes
1 cup (¼ L) small cherry
  tomatoes
¾ cup (1¾ dL) Greek olives
1 cup (¼ L) matchstick-size
  celery pieces

½ cup (1 dL) chopped scallions
½ cup (1 dL) French Dressing
  (p. 450)
Salt to taste
2 tablespoons chopped fresh
  dill, or 1 tablespoon dried,
  crumbled
2 tablespoons minced parsley

Wash and trim the green beans; cut them into 1½-inch lengths. Wash and dry
the tomatoes. Arrange the green beans, tomatoes, olives, scallions, and celery
in a shallow bowl, pour the dressing evenly over all, and sprinkle with salt, dill,
and parsley.

Caesar Salad

Caesar salad can be a tableside performance, made with gusto in front
of friends and family, or it can be privately assembled in the kitchen.
If you can find young romaine, use just the heart, left whole—one
per serving.

(SERVES FOUR)

2 medium or 4 small heads
   romaine lettuce
2-ounce (60-g) can anchovy
   fillets, drained
6 tablespoons olive oil
3 tablespoons lemon juice
2 teaspoons Dijon mustard
1 egg

Salt to taste
½ teaspoon freshly ground
   pepper
½ cup (1 dL) freshly grated
   Parmesan cheese
1½ cups (3½ dL) garlic
   croutons (p. 492)

Separate the leaves of romaine, discarding outer tough leaves, if any, wash, and
thoroughly dry. Tear into bite-size pieces. (Or trim small heads to the hearts and
leave whole, dipping in and out of cold water and then spinning dry.)

In a small bowl, mash the anchovies; stir in the olive oil and lemon juice,
whisking; add the mustard and blend. Put the romaine into the salad bowl, pour
the dressing over, add the egg, and toss the salad lightly (using your hands does
the best job) until the egg has disappeared. Add remaining ingredients, toss for
just a second, and serve.

Red Onion, Spinach, and Tomato
with Horseradish Dressing

(SERVES FOUR)

4 cups (1 L) fresh spinach
   leaves, washed, dried,
   trimmed of stems
4 tomatoes, trimmed and sliced
   ¼ inch thick
2 red onions, thinly sliced in
   rings

Salt to taste
4 tablespoons olive oil
1½ tablespoons vinegar
½ teaspoon freshly ground
   pepper
1 tablespoon prepared
   horseradish

Arrange a bed of spinach leaves on a platter. Place the slices of tomato over it,
and the onion rings over the tomatoes. Sprinkle salt evenly over all. Combine
the oil, vinegar, pepper, and horseradish in a small bowl and beat until blended.
Pour the dressing over the vegetables and serve.

Cole Slaw

(SERVES FOUR)

1 medium head cabbage
1 cup (¼ L) Boiled Dressing
   (p. 451)

1 teaspoon celery seed
Salt

Cut the head of cabbage in half, place in a bowl of cold water, and refrigerate
for 1 hour. Drain well. Shred finely, and add the dressing and celery seed. Toss
to mix well and add salt to taste.

Cole Slaw with Chinese Cabbage and Watercress

(SERVES FOUR)

2 cups (½ L) shredded cabbage
2 cups (½ L) shredded Chinese cabbage
1½ cups (3½ dL) thinly sliced celery
¾ cup (1¾ dL) mayonnaise
¼ cup (½ dL) heavy cream

1 tablespoon honey
3 tablespoons lemon juice
Salt to taste
½ teaspoon celery seed
½ teaspoon mustard seed
1 bunch watercress, washed, dried, chopped

Put both cabbages and the celery in a bowl of ice water and let stand 30 minutes in the refrigerator. Combine the mayonnaise, cream, honey, lemon juice, salt, celery seed, and mustard seed in a bowl and blend until well mixed. Drain the cabbages and celery, and thoroughly toss with the dressing. Just before serving sprinkle the watercress over the salad and around the edges.

Carrot Slaw

A great favorite with children.

(SERVES SIX)

6 medium carrots
¾ cup (1¾ dL) diced celery
¼ cup (½ dL) diced onion
⅓ cup (¾ dL) raisins

½ cup (1 dL) diced apple
½ cup (1 dL) mayonnaise
Salt
Freshly ground pepper

Grate the carrots by hand or in a food processor. Toss with the celery, onion, raisins, and apple. Mix in the mayonnaise, season well with salt and pepper, and chill thoroughly.

Spinach, Mushroom, and Bacon Salad

(SERVES FOUR)

1 pound (450 g) fresh young spinach
¼ pound (115 g) raw mushrooms, thinly sliced
2 hard-boiled eggs, coarsely chopped
½ cup (1 dL) vegetable oil
½ teaspoon sesame oil (optional)

1 teaspoon sugar
3 tablespoons lemon juice
½ teaspoon Dijon mustard
Freshly ground pepper
Salt to taste
5 strips bacon, fried crisp, crumbled

Wash and dry the spinach and discard the stems. If leaves are small, leave whole; if large, cut or tear into bite-size pieces. Toss the spinach, mushrooms, and eggs together in a salad bowl. Mix in a separate bowl the vegetable oil, sesame oil, if you want to use it, sugar, lemon juice, mustard, pepper, and salt. Beat well, then pour over the salad and toss until all leaves are coated. Serve on individual plates and sprinkle the bacon over each serving.

Bulgur Wheat Salad

Known as "tabbouli" in the Middle East, this cold salad is fresh and light with lemon juice, parsley, and mint. Serve it on crisp lettuce leaves.

(SERVES FOUR)

1 cup (¼ L) bulgur
5 tablespoons oil
½ cup (1 dL) lemon juice
About 1½ teaspoons salt
1 teaspoon freshly ground
  pepper

½ cup (1 dL) finely chopped
  parsley
3 tablespoons finely chopped
  mint
1 bunch scallions, chopped fine
2 tomatoes, diced

Put the bulgur in a bowl with 2 cups cold water and let stand for 1 hour; drain well and squeeze in a towel. Toss in the salad bowl with the remaining ingredients. Taste and correct the seasoning. Chill before serving.

Health Salad

(SERVES SIX)

1 cup (¼ L) grated carrots
½ cup (1 dL) grated young raw
  beets
1 cup (¼ L) grated zucchini
1 cup (¼ L) grated cucumber
4 tablespoons finely chopped
  red onion
Salt

2 bunches watercress, washed,
  dried
1½ cups (3½ dL) raw
  cauliflower flowerets
2 cups (½ L) cherry tomatoes
1 recipe Yogurt Dressing
  (p. 454)
1 cup (¼ L) alfalfa sprouts

Combine the carrots, beets, zucchini, cucumber, and onion in a bowl. Toss and gently mix. Salt to taste. Make a bed of the watercress. Pile the mixed grated vegetables in the center, and arrange the cauliflower flowerets and cherry tomatoes around them. Spoon some of the dressing over the top and pass the remainder. Sprinkle the alfalfa sprouts on top.

Watercress, Orange Slices, and Avocado Salad

(SERVES FOUR)

2 bunches watercress, washed,
  dried, stems trimmed
4 large oranges, peeled and
  sliced
1 large ripe avocado
4 tablespoons vegetable oil

4 tablespoons orange juice
1 tablespoon white vinegar
½ teaspoon celery seed
Salt
4 radishes, grated

Arrange the watercress on a large plate or individual salad plates. Distribute the orange slices over each plate. Peel and dice the avocado and scatter the pieces among the orange slices. Combine the oil, orange juice, vinegar, and celery seed in a jar or small bowl. Shake or whisk to blend the ingredients until smooth and well mixed. Add salt to taste. Pour the dressing over the salad and sprinkle the grated radishes over the top.

Dandelion Salad with Bacon

(SERVES FOUR)

4 tablespoons vinegar
1½ teaspoons sugar
1 clove garlic, minced
½ teaspoon freshly ground
   pepper
6 slices bacon

1 pound (450 g) dandelion greens,
   trimmed, washed, dried
2 large ripe tomatoes, sliced
   into 4 thick slices
½ cup (1 dL) finely sliced
   scallions

Mix the vinegar, sugar, garlic, and pepper in a small bowl. Let stand at least 30
minutes. Fry the bacon in a large skillet until crisp. Place on paper towels to free
of excess fat. Remove the skillet from the heat and add the greens to the hot
bacon fat in the skillet, gently stir for a minute or until the greens wilt a little.
Add the vinegar mixture and mix well.

Arrange the tomato slices on a large plate or individual salad plates, mound
a portion of dandelion greens on each slice, and sprinkle the scallions on top.

Belgian Endive with Beets

(SERVES FOUR)

4 Belgian endive
4 small beets, cooked tender
   but firm
4 hard-cooked eggs (optional)
1 recipe French Dressing
   (p. 450)

Salt to taste
¼ teaspoon freshly ground
   pepper
1 tablespoon chopped fresh
   dill, or 1½ teaspoons dried,
   crumbled

Remove five outer leaves from each endive and arrange on salad plates in the
form of a star, points outward. Slice the remaining endive into ⅛-inch rounds.
Peel the beets and coarsely chop. Coarsely chop the eggs if you wish to use them.
Combine remaining ingredients and mix well. Just before serving toss together
gently the endive slices, beets, eggs, and French dressing until thoroughly mixed.
Mound a portion in the center of each of the arranged endive leaves.

Wheat Berries, Bean Sprouts, Tomato,
and Avocado Salad

(SERVES FOUR)

1½ cups (3½ dL) cooked
   wheat berries
1½ cups (3½ dL) bean sprouts
2 tomatoes, chopped
1 large avocado, peeled and
   diced
8–12 spinach leaves, trimmed,
   washed, dried

½ teaspoon freshly ground
   pepper
6 tablespoons olive oil
½ teaspoon dried mustard
2 tablespoons lemon juice
2 teaspoons grated lemon rind
Salt to taste

Just before serving, combine the wheat berries, bean sprouts, tomatoes, and
avocado in a bowl. Arrange spinach leaves on a plate. Mix remaining ingredients
briskly until well blended, pour over the wheat berry mixture, and toss to mix.
Spoon onto the spinach leaves and serve.

Hearts of Palm Salad with Avocado

(SERVES FOUR)

4 tablespoons olive oil
1½ tablespoons vinegar
⅛ teaspoon freshly ground
    pepper
2 teaspoons minced parsley
1 teaspoon finely chopped
    scallions or chives (optional)

Salt
1 head Bibb or butter lettuce
2 ripe avocados
1 can hearts of palm, drained

Combine the oil, vinegar, pepper, and parsley. Add scallions or chives if you
wish, and salt to taste. Mix until well blended. Wash and dry the lettuce leaves
and arrange on four salad plates. Peel the avocados, cut in half, and remove seed.
Place one avocado half on each plate. Slice the hearts of palm in ¼-inch rounds,
and divide them evenly over each avocado half. Drizzle the vinaigrette over each
salad. Serve.

COOKED VEGETABLE SALADS

About Cooked Vegetable Salads

What makes a good mixed cooked vegetable salad? A combination of vegetables,
cooked until barely tender (sometimes less than a minute), well drained, and
chilled. You want to have contrast in color and in texture, so it is nice to have
one raw ingredient that will provide a crunchier foil. Use only enough dressing
to coat and flavor the vegetables. And don't select a vegetable that is so
overpowering that it smothers the flavor of its companions.

What makes a poor cooked vegetable salad? Too many vegetables, cooked
until limp, inadequately drained, and overdressed so that they are swimming in
oil or cream dressing. Don't use a heavy hand with onion or garlic, and don't
abuse herbs (too much dried tarragon, for instance, has ruined many a fine salad).
An all-too-common mixture is peas, diced carrots, and potatoes—a poor balance
because two of the vegetables tend to be sweetish in taste and there is too much
mealiness in texture.

In addition to the recipes that follow, some good combinations might be:

Whole green beans, sliced beets, and new potatoes.

Sliced yellow squash and zucchini, just blanched, diced cucumber, and
    strips of green pepper and celery.

Flowers of broccoli and of cauliflower, and strips of red pepper.

Eggplant and zucchini, sautéed in oil, and fresh tomato wedges.

Blanched Chinese cabbage and red pepper and cucumber strips (with
    Lemon Soy Dressing).

Single cooked vegetables, such as asparagus, green beans, beets, broccoli
flowerets, are also good by themselves, tossed with vinaigrette, French Dressing,
Boiled Dressing, Mayonnaise, or perhaps Avocado Dressing and a little chopped
scallions or chives and parsley, served on a bed of lettuce.

Zucchini, Potato, and Tomato Salad

Cook the vegetables only until tender: about 8 minutes for the zucchini, about 20 minutes for the potatoes (but check—potatoes vary). And remove the salad from the refrigerator half an hour before serving: it tastes better at room temperature.

(SERVES FOUR)

3 medium zucchini, cooked
  whole 8 minutes
4 new potatoes, cooked
2 ripe, fresh tomatoes, peeled,
  chopped
2 tablespoons finely chopped
  onion

1 recipe French Dressing
  (p. 450)
Salt to taste
¼ teaspoon freshly ground
  pepper

Trim away the ends of the zucchini and slice about ¼ inch thick. Peel and dice the potatoes. Combine the zucchini, potatoes, tomatoes, and onion in a bowl. Add the dressing and toss to coat well. Add salt and pepper. Mix well and chill.

Artichoke Hearts, Peas, and Jerusalem Artichoke Salad

(SERVES FOUR)

1 package frozen artichoke
  hearts, cooked, drained
1 cup (¼ L) small peas, cooked
¾ cup (1¾ dL) thinly sliced
  Jerusalem artichokes

½ cup (1 dL) mayonnaise
1½ tablespoons tarragon
  vinegar
Salt
1 bunch watercress, washed

Cut the artichoke hearts in half lengthwise and mix with the peas and sliced Jerusalem artichokes. Blend the mayonnaise and tarragon vinegar together, and salt to taste. Arrange the watercress on a platter and place the vegetables on top. Spoon the mayonnaise over. Serve chilled.

Cauliflower, Beets, and Green Bean Salad

(SERVES FOUR)

2 cups (½ L) cauliflower
  flowerets, cooked 5 minutes
2 cups (½ L) green beans,
  cooked 5 minutes, cut in
  1-inch pieces
2 beets, cooked and sliced

1 cup (¼ L) sliced mushrooms
1 recipe French Dressing
  (p. 450)
2 teaspoons Dijon mustard
Salt

Combine the cauliflower, green beans, beets, and mushrooms. Mix the dressing and mustard together until well blended, then stir into the combined vegetables and toss to mix well. Salt to taste. Serve chilled or at room temperature.

Variations. Omit the cauliflower and add *2 cups cooked corn kernels* or *2 cups cooked lima beans.*

SUBSTANTIAL SALADS

Macaroni Salad

One-half pound uncooked macaroni makes 4 cups cooked.

(SERVES SIX)

4 cups (1 L) cooked macaroni
1 cup (¼ L) sliced celery
½ cup (1 dL) sliced scallions
4 tablespoons coarsely chopped
   green pepper
2 tablespoons chopped
   pimiento
4 tablespoons pitted, chopped
   black olives

2 tablespoons finely chopped
   parsley
1 cup (¼ L) mayonnaise
2 tablespoons vinegar
½ teaspoon freshly ground
   black pepper
Salt

Combine macaroni, celery, scallions, green pepper, pimiento, olives, and parsley in a large bowl; toss to mix. In a small bowl mix the mayonnaise and vinegar together until smooth. Add to the macaroni mixture. Add pepper and salt to taste. Toss and mix well. Refrigerate several hours before serving.

Rice Salad

This is a salad that has so many possibilities for variations that a list of suggestions follows the basic recipe. So use your ingenuity.

(SERVES FOUR)

3 cups (¾ L) cooked rice
1 cup (¼ L) thin strips cooked
   ham
1 cup (¼ L) baby frozen peas,
   defrosted, or fresh young
   peas, blanched 1 minute
4-ounce (115-g) can whole
   pimientos, drained, chopped
2 tablespoons finely chopped
   chives or scallions

1 tablespoon finely chopped
   parsley
1 recipe French Dressing
   (p. 450)
1½ teaspoons Dijon mustard
Salt
Freshly ground pepper

Combine the rice, ham, peas, pimientos, chives or scallions, and parsley in a large bowl. In a small bowl mix the dressing and mustard until blended. Combine with the rice mixture, seasoning to taste.

Variations and Additions

   1 cup rare roast beef instead of the ham.

   1 cup vegetables cut in dice, such as tomatoes, green and red peppers,
      young raw zucchini, cucumbers in addition to, or in place of, the
      meat.

   ½ cup black olives, cut in half.

   1 cup cooked shrimp and/or other seafood such as crabmeat, mussels,
      lobster, baby clams.

Salade Niçoise

Full of the flavors of the Mediterranean.

(SERVES FOUR)

1 small head lettuce
1 cup (¼ L) lightly cooked
   green beans
1 can tuna fish
1 recipe French Dressing
   (p. 450), made with 1
   teaspoon minced garlic

4 anchovy fillets
8 black olives
½ green pepper, cut in thin
   strips
2 hard-boiled eggs, quartered

Tear up the lettuce and mix with the green beans. Drain and break up the tuna fish, and add it with all but a couple of tablespoons of the dressing. Toss in a salad bowl. Over the top arrange the anchovy fillets, olives, green pepper strips, and eggs decoratively, and drizzle the remaining dressing over.

Chickpea Salad

(SERVES FOUR)

2 cups (½ L) cooked or canned
   chickpeas
2 cloves garlic, minced
3 tablespoons oil
1 tablespoon vinegar
¼ teaspoon chili powder
Salt to taste

Freshly ground pepper to taste
4 large radishes, sliced
3 tablespoons chopped parsley
3–4 leaves fresh basil,
   chopped, or ½ teaspoon
   dried

Drain the chickpeas, reserving 1 tablespoon of their cooking or canning liquid. Add liquid to the garlic, oil, vinegar, chili powder, salt, and pepper, and stir to blend. Pour over the chickpeas, toss with the radishes, and sprinkle parsley and basil over the top.

Chickpea Salad with Sausage. Add ½ *cup sliced sausage* (salami, pepperoni, or cooked sausages), ½ *cup chopped pimiento*, and toss.

Chickpea Salad with Tuna. Add *1 can drained tuna fish, a dozen black olives, halved,* and toss. Lay *4 anchovy fillets* over the top.

Lentil Salad

(SERVES SIX)

1 cup (¼ L) lentils
Salt
3 tablespoons oil
1 tablespoon vinegar

1 medium onion, minced
Freshly ground pepper
¼ teaspoon dry mustard
2 tablespoons minced parsley

Simmer the lentils in 3 cups water with 1 teaspoon salt for 30–40 minutes, until tender. Drain. In a small bowl, mix the oil, vinegar, onion, pepper, and mustard. Toss with the lentils while they are hot. Refrigerate and, when cool, mix in the parsley and salt to taste.

Kidney and Green Bean Salad

A fine way of using up cooked green beans. Cut them up after rather than before cooking—they'll taste better.

(SERVES TWO)

1 cup (¼ L) red kidney beans
1 cup (¼ L) cooked green beans
3 finely sliced scallions, or ½
    small red onion, finely sliced

¼ cup (½ dL) French Dressing
    (p. 450), made with mustard

Drain the kidney beans and rinse them. Dry thoroughly. Cut the green beans about the same size as the kidney beans. Toss together with the scallions or red onion and the dressing. Refrigerate for several hours before serving.

Potato Salad

(SERVES SIX)

8 medium new potatoes
4 tablespoons lemon juice
4 tablespoons vegetable oil
Salt
½ teaspoon freshly ground
    pepper
2 celery ribs, finely chopped

4 hard-boiled eggs, coarsely
    chopped
1–1¼ cups (2¼–3 dL)
    mayonnaise
3 tablespoons cider vinegar
Six large lettuce leaves

Boil the potatoes just until tender when pierced with a fork. Drain, and as soon as you can handle them, peel and dice. Toss with the lemon juice, oil, and salt to taste (the flavor is better when they have this preliminary dressing while very warm, and the potatoes, thus coated, won't absorb as much mayonnaise later). Cool. Add the pepper, celery, and chopped eggs. Blend 1 cup mayonnaise with vinegar, then toss over the potato salad, gently folding until all pieces are coated. If the potatoes seem a little dry, add more mayonnaise. Line a bowl or a platter with lettuce leaves and pile the potato salad in the middle.

Variations and Additions

3 tablespoons finely chopped onion.

2 tablespoons dry mustard mixed into the mayonnaise.

3 tablespoons sweet pickle relish.

2 tablespoons minced parsley.

Hot or German Potato Salad

(SERVES SIX)

8 medium new potatoes
6 slices bacon
2½ tablespoons flour
6 tablespoons cider vinegar
1½ tablespoons sugar
1 teaspoon dry mustard

Salt to taste
½ teaspoon freshly ground
    pepper
10 romaine lettuce leaves
3 large ripe tomatoes

Boil the potatoes in their jackets until just tender. Meanwhile, fry the bacon until crisp. Reserving 4 tablespoons bacon fat, drain the bacon well and crumble;

set aside. Heat the bacon fat and stir in the flour. Cook slowly, continuing to stir for a minute. Off heat add 1½ cups hot water and the vinegar, mix well, return to low heat, and cook, stirring, until smooth and thickened. Add sugar, mustard, salt, and pepper, and cook 2 minutes. Drain the potatoes, peel and slice them warm. Toss with the dressing until well coated. Arrange lettuce leaves in a large bowl and mound the hot salad in the center. Cut the tomatoes in wedges and arrange around edge. Sprinkle the crumbled bacon on top and serve warm.

Avocado with Chicken Stuffing

(SERVES FOUR)

½ cup (1 dL) mayonnaise
2 tablespoons lemon juice
1½ cups (3½ dL) diced cooked
  chicken
¼ cup (½ dL) finely chopped
  celery

Salt
⅓ cup (¾ dL) coarsely
  chopped blanched almonds
2 ripe, firm avocados
8 leaves of Bibb lettuce

Blend the mayonnaise and lemon juice together. Mix with the diced chicken and celery. Salt to taste and stir in the almonds. Peel the avocados and cut in half lengthwise. On each salad plate, place two lettuce leaves with one avocado half on top. Spoon one-fourth of the chicken salad into the hollow of each avocado half, letting some spill over onto the lettuce.

Avocado with Seafood Stuffing: Substitute *1¾ cups cooked shellfish* or *fish*, or a combination thereof, for the chicken. Eliminate the almonds and sprinkle *½ dozen or so capers* on top of each serving.

Stuffed Tomato Salad

(SERVES FOUR)

4 firm ripe tomatoes
¾ cup (1¾ dL) cooked corn
  kernels
⅓ cup (¾ dL) chopped
  cucumber
½ cup (1 dL) finely diced ham
2 teaspoons minced chives

¼ cup (½ dL) cooked peas
¼ teaspoon freshly ground
  pepper
⅓ cup (¾ dL) mayonnaise
1½ teaspoons prepared
  horseradish
8 leaves of butter lettuce

Bring a large pot of water to a boil and drop in the tomatoes. Boil for about 20 seconds, remove, and slide the tomato skin off, trimming the little stubborn pieces away with a paring knife. Cut the core of the tomato out, and with a teaspoon, gently scoop out the inside of the tomato, leaving a good sturdy shell. Turn the tomatoes upside down on a rack to drain. Combine the corn, cucumber, ham, chives, peas, and pepper in a bowl. Mix the mayonnaise and horseradish together until well blended, then gently toss mixture with the vegetables to thoroughly coat. Spoon the vegetable filling into the hollowed tomatoes. Place the tomatoes on the lettuce leaves and serve cold.

Stuffed Tomato Salad with Bacon. Use *4 slices bacon* cooked until crisp, drained, and crumbled in place of the ham.

Stuffed Tomato Salad with Tuna Fish. Eliminate the corn, ham, and peas and use instead *1 can tuna fish, ¼ cup chopped green pepper,* and *⅓ cup chopped celery.* Instead of the horseradish, use *a few drops of lemon juice* for flavoring.

Egg Salad

Have all the ingredients chilled.

(SERVES FOUR)

⅔ cup (1½ dL) mayonnaise
2 tablespoons lemon juice
2 teaspoons vinegar
1 tablespoon finely chopped chives
1 tablespoon chopped fresh dill, or 1½ teaspoons dried, crumbled
⅛ teaspoon freshly ground pepper

Salt
⅓ cup (¾ dL) finely chopped green pepper
8 hard-boiled eggs, diced
4 crisp outer leaves of iceberg lettuce and 2 cups (½ L) shredded iceberg lettuce, or 1 head Boston or Bibb lettuce and several sprigs watercress

Combine the mayonnaise, lemon juice, vinegar, chives, dill, and pepper. Mix until well blended, and add salt to taste. Add the green pepper and eggs; gently toss to mix. Arrange one lettuce leaf on each salad plate and put ½ cup shredded lettuce on top. Or make a bed of lettuce leaves and watercress (reserving a few leaves for the top). Put a portion of egg salad on each lettuce bed. Serve.

Tuna Salad

Canned salmon or crab may be used instead of tuna, but omit the sweet pickle relish (some may not like it even with tuna). Add a teaspoon of capers to the salmon or crab. Chill all the ingredients.

(SERVES FOUR)

1½ cups (3½ dL) canned tuna, well drained, flaked
½ cup (1 dL) finely chopped celery
2 tablespoons sweet pickle relish (optional)
3 tablespoons lemon juice

½ cup (1 dL) mayonnaise
4 outer crisp leaves of iceberg lettuce and 2 cups (½ L) shredded iceberg lettuce, or 1 head Boston lettuce
1 tablespoon minced parsley

Combine the tuna, celery, pickle relish (if you wish), lemon juice, and mayonnaise. Toss until well mixed. Put the lettuce leaves on four salad plates with ½ cup shredded lettuce on top of each, or make a bed of loose lettuce leaves. Put a fourth of the tuna salad on each lettuce bed. Sprinkle with parsley and serve.

Chicken Salad

(SERVES FOUR)

4 cups (1 L) bite-size pieces cooked chicken
2 teaspoons grated onion or chopped scallions (optional)
1 cup (¼ L) sliced celery
⅔ cup (1½ dL) mayonnaise
4 tablespoons heavy cream

2 tablespoons vinegar
⅛ teaspoon freshly ground pepper
Salt to taste
1 head Bibb lettuce, washed, dried

Put chicken in a bowl and add the onion or scallions (if you like) and celery. Combine the mayonnaise, cream, and vinegar and blend well. Add pepper and salt, and toss with chicken, until well mixed. Make a bed of the lettuce leaves and spoon the chicken salad over.

Variations and Additions

Sprinkle *1 cup chopped almonds* over salad.

Instead of the celery add *1 cup seedless grapes* to chicken mixture.

Add *2 teaspoons curry powder* to the mayonnaise.

Omit the celery and add *½ cup peeled, seeded, diced cucumber* and *½ cup pineapple bits.*

Add *1 cup diced, unpeeled red apple* and *½ cup chopped walnuts.*

Shrimp and Artichoke Salad

(SERVES FOUR)

1½ pounds (675 g) medium-size raw shrimp	1 recipe Handmade Basic Mayonnaise (p. 452)
10-ounce (285-g) package frozen artichoke hearts	Salt
1 tablespoon minced parsley	1 head Bibb lettuce

Bring a pot with enough water to cover the shrimp to boil. Add the shrimp and cook only until pink (about 5 minutes). Drain, rinse with cold water, peel, shell, and remove any black vein, then chill in the refrigerator. Cook the artichoke hearts as directed. Drain and chill. Mix the parsley into the mayonnaise. Toss the shrimp and artichoke hearts in the mayonnaise until well coated. Add salt to taste. Arrange the shrimp mixture on lettuce leaves.

Crab Ravigote

(SERVES FOUR)

1 tablespoon olive oil	1 teaspoon minced parsley
3 tablespoons vinegar	2 cups (½ L) cooked crabmeat
⅛ teaspoon cayenne pepper	Salt to taste
1 teaspoon prepared mustard	1 cup (¼ L) Green
1 hard-boiled egg, chopped fine	Mayonnaise (p. 453)

Combine the oil, vinegar, cayenne pepper, mustard, egg, and parsley in a mixing bowl. Mix until well blended. Add the crab and salt. Spoon the crab mixture into scallop shells or small dishes, and cover with the mayonnaise.

Crab Louis

(SERVES FOUR)

½ large head iceberg lettuce, shredded	⅓ cup (¾ dL) whipped cream
3 cups (¾ L) cooked crabmeat	4 tablespoons chili sauce
1 cup (¼ L) mayonnaise	2 teaspoons grated onion
	Pinch of cayenne pepper

Arrange the lettuce on four salad plates. Divide crabmeat and place on top. Combine remaining ingredients and mix until well blended. Spoon over each serving of crabmeat.

Lobster Salad

Lobster salad is at its best when made very simply with lobster meat, a little crunchy celery, and adequately dressed with a creamy, mild homemade mayonnaise. Have all the ingredients chilled.

(SERVES FOUR)

3 cups (¾ L) cooked lobster meat
½ cup (1 dL) finely chopped celery

½ cup (1 dL) mayonnaise
1½ tablespoons heavy cream
Salt to taste
1 head Bibb lettuce

Cut the lobster meat into large bite-size pieces, place them in a bowl, and add the celery. Blend the mayonnaise and cream in a small bowl, then gently combine with the lobster, toss to mix, and add salt. Arrange a bed of lettuce leaves and put the lobster salad on top.

FRUIT SALADS

About Fruit Salads

What makes a good fruit salad? Luscious, ripe, fresh fruit that is sweet and firm with its own distinct flavor. Use fruits that mingle well. The pieces of fruit should be uniform in size and easy to eat. Each of the fruits should retain its own characteristic taste. Make and serve fruit salad fresh whenever possible and strive for good contrast in color and texture.

What makes a bad fruit salad? Unripe or overripe fruit with spoiled spots that go untrimmed. Don't mix fruits that aren't compatible—for instance, the acidity of grapefruit will overwhelm the delicate taste of melon. Fruit should be neatly cut and in not-too-large pieces. Don't prepare too far ahead or the fruits become limp and drained of their vitality. Avoid dullness in color and texture.

Fruit Salad Combinations

Use crisp lettuce or watercress as a bed for some of these salads or one or two sprigs of mint on top of the fruit. The following proportions are for one serving; multiply for the number to be served.

½ cup sliced peaches, ¼ cup diced pears, ¼ cup seedless grapes, dressed with 2 teaspoons mayonnaise thinned with 1 teaspoon cream, or Nut Pascagoula Dressing.

½ cup grapefruit sections, ½ cup banana slices, 1 tablespoon pomegranate seeds, if available, dressed with 1 tablespoon French Dressing, or if you prefer a sweeter dressing, Cleveland.

⅓ cup papaya cubes, ⅓ cup kiwi slices, ⅓ cup hearts of palm cut in rounds, dressed with 1 teaspoon vegetable oil, 1 teaspoon lime juice, and 1 teaspoon honey blended together, or Lime Dressing.

⅓ cup pineapple cubes, ⅓ cup cantaloupe balls, 5 strawberries, no dressing.

¾ cup orange sections, ¼ cup thin red onion rings, dressed with 1 tablespoon French Dressing.

⅓ cup pineapple cubes, ½ cup avocado slices, ⅓ cup mango slivers, 2 tablespoons grated coconut, dressed with 1 teaspoon lime juice blended with 2 teaspoons mayonnaise, or Pineapple Honey Dressing.

¾ cup honeydew melon balls, ¼ cup blueberries, dressed with 1 teaspoon lemon juice, 1 teaspoon vegetable oil, pinch of salt, ½ teaspoon sugar blended.

⅓ cup cantaloupe balls, ⅓ cup honeydew melon balls, ⅓ cup watermelon balls, served with mint sprig and lime wedge.

1 orange, sectioned, ½ banana, thinly sliced, dressed with 1 teaspoon lemon juice blended with 1 teaspoon honey.

⅓ cup chopped apples, ⅓ cup orange sections, ½ cup sliced bananas, dressed with 2 teaspoons Poppy-Seed Dressing.

Mixed Combinations

Prunes stuffed with cream cheese and walnut halves.

Pear halves, pitted cherries, watercress.

Cantaloupe rings with small mound of raspberries in the center.

Fruit Salad Additions

Sliced kumquats, raisins, nuts, cottage cheese, celery, cucumber, chopped dates.

Waldorf Salad

Sometimes it's pleasing to have two different kinds of apples in a Waldorf salad, if the season is right and you can get different varieties like a sweet Delicious and a tart Greening. In any case, be sure the apples you use are crisp.

(SERVES FOUR)

2 firm ripe green apples
1 firm ripe red apple
1 tablespoon lemon juice
1 cup (¼ L) sliced celery
½ cup (1 dL) coarsely chopped walnuts

½ cup (1 dL) mayonnaise
1½ teaspoons honey (optional)
Iceberg or Bibb lettuce leaves

Core and quarter the apples (leave the skin on unless it is tough) and slice thin. Put in a bowl and toss with the lemon juice to coat. Add the celery and walnuts. Cover and chill. Mix the mayonnaise and honey (if you like a little sweetness in the dressing) together until smooth, add to the apple mixture, and toss. Serve on a bed of lettuce.

Peaches with Cream Cheese Balls

Chill this salad well before serving.

(SERVES FOUR)

8 canned peach halves
8 ounces (225 g) cream cheese,
  softened
1½ teaspoons prepared
  horseradish

½ cup (1 dL) finely chopped
  pecans
Lettuce leaves

Drain the peaches, reserving 2 tablespoons of the syrup. Combine the cream cheese, peach syrup, and horseradish in a bowl or blender or food processor and cream until well blended. Chill until firm, shape into eight balls, then roll balls in the pecans. Arrange lettuce leaves on a cold platter and place peach halves on top. Put a cream cheese ball in each peach hollow.

MOLDED SALADS

About Aspics

Too many poorly conceived molded salads have, alas, graced (or disgraced) the American table. But a really fine-tasting fruit or vegetable jelly—not overly jellied—with combinations that are compatible, or a beautiful clear aspic studded with colorful morsels can be a credit to any good cook and looks so tempting on a buffet or a summer lunch table that it is worth mastering this very simple art.

An aspic is as good as the flavor and quality of the liquid that you set to jell. It follows that a good homemade broth—made of chicken or other poultry, beef, or fish, well seasoned—will provide the base for the most delicious aspics. There is no reason why you can't use a canned broth; however, it will taste better if you simmer it with aromatic vegetables. To 4 cups of canned broth add ½ cup minced carrots, onion, and some celery, plus 3 or 4 sprigs of parsley, ½ bay leaf, and a pinch of thyme. About ½ cup red wine plus a couple of teaspoons of tomato paste, if you like a strong flavor, is good with beef broth, and dry white wine enhances a chicken broth. Simmer the mixture gently for 30 minutes, then strain.

The best substitute for fish stock is bottled clam juice, but it must be cut in half with water, preferably mixed with a little dry white wine or vermouth, simmered for a few minutes with chopped onion and a few sprigs of parsley.

In using either a canned stock or your own homemade, you should determine first how much jelling power the broth has naturally. Test by refrigerating. If the broth is firmly jelled, to make the aspic you will need only 1 teaspoon gelatin to 2 cups liquid, but if it barely holds together, use the usual formula of 1 envelope (1 tablespoon) gelatin to 2 cups liquid. This will be firm enough to hold up to 2 cups of solids, unless you are including uncooked vegetables in your mold; they tend to give off some water, so 1 envelope gelatin to 2 cups liquid to 1 cup solids would be a safer rule. Never attempt to hold an aspic containing uncooked vegetables for more than a day or two, or they will release their water.

An aspic that is too firm is rubbery and unappealing. If you are serving an unmolded aspic that may have to sit around in warm weather, it is better to place your platter on a bed of ice than to try to increase its holding power by adding extra gelatin when you make it.

For a decorative transparent mold with attractively arranged shapes and colors, you want to be sure to have your aspic crystal clear, so it is necessary to clarify the stock. It's a fussy procedure, but if you follow the directions on p. 78 carefully, you should have no trouble, and other faster methods are just not as foolproof.

To ensure that the solids stay in place and don't all float to the top, you have to partially set a bottom layer of aspic in the mold by chilling, then arrange a decorative pattern on that, spoon in more aspic, which should be cool just to the point of being syrupy, about the consistency of lightly beaten egg white, and let that set before you proceed. Sometimes you may want to build several layers in this manner, but it is the bottom one that counts most, because when you unmold, you want the design to look attractive and orderly—the way you have arranged it. Jelling time varies; to be safe, for a large aspic with solids, allow 6 hours before unmolding.

If you're uneasy at first about making your own aspics, to get the feel of working with jelly try some of the simple jellied salads first, made with commercial flavored gelatins. And they're fine to fall back on if your family enjoys them. But they do tend to be sweet—more a dessert—and they haven't the pure essence of good flavor that your own delicious homemade aspics will have.

Simple Jellied Salads
Dissolve 1 package flavored gelatin in 1 cup of boiling water. Add 1 cup of cold liquid—this can be plain water or a fruit juice that is compatible with the flavor, or water or juice flavored with a little wine (sherry, dry white wine, or Port). Season to taste and chill.

When the jelly begins to thicken to about the consistency of lightly beaten egg white, fold in 1½ cups prepared fruits or vegetables; cooked meat or fish would not taste good in these sweetened jellies. Chill until firm—about 4 hours.

Some Ideas for Combinations

Lemon or lime gelatin with small diced cucumber and radishes plus 3 tablespoons chopped chives.

Apple gelatin with finely cut celery and ¼ cup chopped walnuts.

Lemon gelatin with 1 cup finely diced beets, 2 tablespoons minced red onion, 1 tablespoon prepared horseradish, and ¾ cup finely diced celery. Use ¾ cup beet juice and 3 tablespoons vinegar for the 1 cup cold liquid required.

Lemon, lime, or apple gelatin with 1 cup chopped nuts and ½ cup plumped raisins.

Raspberry gelatin with 1 cup canned black cherries poured into a mold lined with cream cheese balls (from a 4-ounce package). Use ¾ cup cherry juice and 3 tablespoons dry white wine, 1 tablespoon fresh lemon juice, and 2 tablespoons water for the 1 cup cold liquid required.

Cucumber Aspic

(SERVES FOUR)

½ cup (1 dL) freshly squeezed orange juice	3 scallions
1 envelope gelatin	4 sprigs parsley
2 medium cucumbers	1 teaspoon salt
	3 tablespoons lime juice

Put the orange juice in a small saucepan and sprinkle the gelatin over. Stir over low heat just until the gelatin dissolves. Peel and split the cucumbers lengthwise. Scoop out the seeds, then chop cucumber roughly and put in the blender or food processor. Roughly chop the scallions, using some of the green, and add them to cucumber along with the rest of the ingredients, including the gelatin dissolved in orange juice. Blend until puréed. Chill until the mixture begins to set, then stir well, and pour into a lightly oiled 4-cup mold. Chill until set.

Variation with Frozen Orange Juice. Use ½ *cup frozen orange juice diluted with* ½ *cup water* instead of freshly squeezed orange juice.

Bing Cherry Mold

Heightened by the fresh astringent flavor of cranberry juice, this tart mold is particularly good with cold chicken, or turkey, or duck. Serve garnished with watercress and cream cheese balls.

(SERVES SIX)

18-ounce (510-g) jar or can Bing cherries	1 cup (¼ L) cranberry juice 1 envelope gelatin

Drain cherries, add the juice to the cold cranberry juice and sprinkle the gelatin over. Heat until almost simmering. Remove from heat, and stir until gelatin is thoroughly dissolved. Pour into a 4-cup mold and cool. Pit the cherries, if necessary. When the liquid is about the consistency of egg whites, spoon in the cherries and chill until set.

Grapefruit Jelly Salad

Made with fresh juicy grapefruit at the peak of season, this tart and cleansing aspic needs no additional sugar and looks attractive un-molded with slices of grapefruit and avocado (or other fruit) inter-spersed. Decorate the serving platter with watercress and cream cheese balls.

(SERVES FOUR TO SIX)

1 envelope gelatin 1½ cups (3½ dL) freshly squeezed grapefruit juice, or canned or bottled, unsweetened 1 or more teaspoons sugar (optional)	1 small avocado Segments from 1 fresh grapefruit, or 1 cup (¼ L) canned

Sprinkle the gelatin over the cold grapefruit juice, add sugar, if desired, then heat it to a simmer and stir well to make sure the gelatin is dissolved. Pour enough of the hot liquid into a 3- or 4-cup mold to cover the bottom ½ inch. Chill until almost firm. Peel the avocado and cut into the same number of slices as you have grapefruit segments. Place alternating pieces of grapefruit and avocado on the slightly firm jelly, chill again, and then pour the last of the juice over. Refrigerate until firm. Unmold to serve.

Variations:

   Alternate *segments of orange* and grapefruit.

   Alternate *strips of peeled and seeded cucumber* and grapefruit.

Use *1½ cups cubed apples and seedless grapes* and distribute evenly through the gelatin-thickened grapefruit juice after chilling until it is about the consistency of egg whites.

Tomato Aspic

Tomato aspic is good with so many things—seafood, chicken, and other cold meats, or just by itself on a bed of lettuce with a dollop of good homemade mayonnaise on top.

(SERVES SIX)

2 envelopes gelatin
4 cups (1 L) tomato juice
1 onion, sliced thin
4 tablespoons chopped celery
    leaves
2½ teaspoons sugar

1 teaspoon salt
½ teaspoon freshly ground
    pepper
4 whole cloves
4 tablespoons lemon juice

Sprinkle the gelatin in a small bowl, add ⅓ cup water, stir, and let stand. Combine the tomato juice, onion, celery leaves, sugar, salt, pepper, and cloves in a pan. Bring to a boil, lower the heat to simmer, cook for 5 minutes, remove from the heat, strain, stir in the softened gelatin, and stir until the liquid clears. Add the lemon juice. Pour into a 1-quart mold and chill until set.

Tomato Aspic with Vegetables

(SERVES SIX)

1-pound-12-ounce (800-g) can
    tomatoes
½ teaspoon sugar
1 small onion, sliced
2 bay leaves
¼ teaspoon dried basil,
    crumbled, or 6 fresh leaves
½ teaspoon salt
¼ teaspoon freshly ground
    pepper

1 envelope gelatin
⅓ cup (¾ dL) beef bouillon
1½ cups (3½ dL) finely diced
    raw vegetables, such as
    celery, zucchini, cucumber,
    red and green peppers
Parsley sprigs
Black olives

Simmer the tomatoes, sugar, onion, bay leaves, basil, salt, and pepper 15 minutes. Soak the gelatin in the cold bouillon plus 2 tablespoons of water. Strain the tomatoes (saving the pulp for another use in a sauce or soup). Mix the gelatin into the hot liquid until thoroughly dissolved. Fill the bottom ½ inch of a 1-quart mold with the liquid; chill until just set. Distribute the vegetables over the surface and add remaining liquid. Chill until completely set. Unmold and decorate with parsley and black olives.

Tomato Aspic with Shrimp. After the ½ inch of aspic has chilled until barely set, distribute *small cooked shrimp* instead of the vegetables in a decorative pattern over the jelly, then spoon more liquid aspic over and around the shrimp and chill. When set, add the remaining liquid and refrigerate until ready to unmold and serve.

Fresh Tomato Aspic

If you are lucky to have a garden or have an abundance of vine-ripened tomatoes from a farmers' market, it is worth making a fresh tomato aspic. Be sure to taste the tomatoes, however, because even though they may look bursting with ripeness, they can have a lot of acidity and you may need to use a little sugar; lemon juice will help to bring up the flavor. The preceding Tomato Aspic with Vegetables and the variation with Shrimp will both taste delicious made this way.

(SERVES FOUR)

2 pounds (900 g) ripe tomatoes, about 5 cups (1¼ L), chopped
1 envelope gelatin
1 teaspoon grated onion
¼ cup (½ dL) minced celery and leaves

Salt
Up to 1 teaspoon sugar (optional)
1 tablespoon lemon juice (optional)

Boil the tomatoes with ¾ cup water over medium high heat, stirring often, for 15 minutes. Dissolve the gelatin in ¼ cup cold water. Put the tomatoes through a vegetable mill or strainer, then return the purée to the pan and add onion and celery. Add salt to taste—it will need quite a lot, up to 1 teaspoon—and sugar and lemon, if needed. Cook 5 minutes, stirring briskly. Remove from the fire and add the gelatin, stirring until thoroughly dissolved. Turn into a 1-quart ring mold and chill until firm.

Jellied Vegetable Ring

Vegetables should be varied according to what is in season. Young zucchini, yellow squash, and tender green beans, blanched for only 2 minutes and then chopped, are good, for instance, with pimientos for contrast. All ingredients should be cut in small cubes so that the mold can be cut neatly. Serve on a bed of lettuce or watercress with mayonnaise or Boiled Dressing (p. 451).

(SERVES SIX)

1 envelope gelatin
¼ cup (50 g) sugar
¼ cup (½ dL) cider vinegar
3 tablespoons lemon juice
1 teaspoon salt
½ cup (1 dL) chopped celery
⅓ cup (¾ dL) chopped cabbage

⅛ cup (¼ dL) peeled, seeded, and cubed cucumbers
¼ cup (½ dL) fresh peas, blanched 1 minute, or defrosted frozen baby peas
¼ cup (½ dL) cubed cooked beets

Mix 1 cup cold water, gelatin, and sugar in a saucepan; stir over low heat until dissolved. Add the vinegar, lemon juice, and salt, and chill until as thick as an unbeaten egg white. Stir in the vegetables, pour into a 4-cup ring mold, and chill.

Seafood Aspic

This may be varied with whatever combinations of seafood and fish are available, but it is interesting to have the crystal-clear aspic studded with contrasting shapes and colors.

(SERVES FOUR)

2 cups (½ L) clarified well-
   seasoned fish stock (p. 83)
1 envelope gelatin
2 tablespoons dry white wine
Salt

Freshly ground pepper
8 medium shrimp, cooked
8 mussels, cooked
8 scallops or chunks of white
   fish, cooked

Heat the fish stock. Soften the gelatin in the wine plus 2 tablespoons water. Add to the hot stock and mix until thoroughly dissolved. Taste, and season well with salt and pepper. Pour ½ inch of liquid into a 1-quart mold—a ring mold or a fish shape if you have one—and chill until just set. Distribute the seafood in a decorative contrasting pattern, then gently pour in the rest of the gelatin and chill until set.

Duck and Orange in Aspic

Next time you prepare a roast duck, cook an extra one so that you can make this elegant dish for a luncheon party or a buffet later in the week. Be sure to collect all the giblets from both ducks and save the carcass from the first one so that you'll have a good strong broth to make the aspic.

(SERVES FOUR)

Stock

Leftover bones and carcass
   from 1 cooked duck
Giblets from 2 ducks
1 onion, unpeeled

1 scraped carrot
1 stalk celery
1 parsley sprig
½ teaspoon salt

Combine all the above ingredients with 2 quarts water and simmer for 2½–3 hours. Strain into a bowl and chill. Then remove the congealed fat.

1 cooked duck
2 oranges, peeled, sliced, and
   pitted
2 envelopes gelatin
2 tablespoons Port wine

1 quart (1 L) duck stock,
   clarified (above)
Garnish: black olives and
   watercress sprigs

Carve the duck into 8 pieces: 2 thighs, 2 legs, the breast split, and each side cut in half. Trim off any obtruding pieces of bone and place duck in a shallow dish that will hold the pieces in one layer. Place a slice of orange over each piece of duck, using a few halved slices to tuck in around the edges. Soak the gelatin in the Port plus 2 tablespoons cold water, then add to the stock. Heat just to a simmer and stir to dissolve thoroughly. Chill the aspic until it has the thickness of slightly beaten egg white, then coat the pieces of duck. If you find the aspic slipping off, put both the dish and bowl of aspic back in the refrigerator and chill a little longer; then add another coat until all of the aspic is used up. Chill thoroughly before serving, garnished with olives and watercress.

Parslied Ham in Aspic

Serve this pretty aspic unmolded with a bowl of Mustard Mayonnaise
(p. 453) on the side.

(SERVES SIX)

2 envelopes gelatin
¼ cup (½ dL) Madeira wine
3½ cups (8 dL) hot chicken
   stock, clarified (p. 78)

3 cups (¾ L) ham, cut in
   ½-inch dice
¾ cup (1¾ dL) chopped
   parsley

Soak the gelatin in the Madeira plus 2 tablespoons cold water. Dissolve thoroughly
in the hot chicken stock. Pour ½ inch of the aspic into a 2-quart mold and chill
until just set. Also refrigerate the rest of the aspic. When it is the consistency
of lightly beaten egg whites, fold in the ham and the parsley. Fill the mold gently
with this mixture and chill until very firm.

Aspic of Cold Beef and Vegetables

No one would suspect that this handsome dish was made from leftover
beef; the pieces should be tender and free of fat. It requires some
patience to put together while layers of aspic set, but you can be
doing other kitchen tasks.

(SERVES EIGHT)

8 cups (2 L) clarified beef stock
   (p. 79)
4 envelopes gelatin
5 whole cooked carrots, halved
   lengthwise

16 tiny cooked onions
1 cooked beet
10 slices cold cooked beef

Pour 2 cups of the cold stock into a small bowl, sprinkle the gelatin over, and
let stand a few minutes. Heat the rest of the stock to simmering, add the gelatin
mixture, and stir until completely dissolved. Remove from the heat and refrigerate
until it has become syrupy. Line the bottom of a large bowl with about ¼ inch
of thickened aspic, chill until firm, then add another shallow layer of aspic. Place
carrots, as many as you need to fit, in rows 1½ inches apart on the bottom of
the bowl. Put tiny onions in between. Cut the beet in decorative slices and place
along the sides. Cover the vegetables with a thin layer of aspic and chill until
firm. Place the slices of beef upright through the center of the bowl, using
remaining carrot cut in small pieces to hold them evenly apart. Pour in the
remaining syrupy aspic to fill the bowl. Refrigerate until firm, at least 6 hours—
better overnight. Unmold and serve with a mustardy mayonnaise.

About Cream Molds and Mousses

Cream molds or mousses are made with the addition of mayonnaise and/or cream,
which adds richness and greater fullness to the dish. The molds should always
be lightly oiled before the mixture is poured in. They make enticing first courses,
done in small shapes and turned out on a bed of watercress or shredded lettuce
and garnished with something appropriate and colorful, such as black olives, a

few strips of pimiento, a shrimp, if it is a fish mousse. A large mold can be served as a main course at lunch or as an important feature of a buffet table, presented on a platter surrounded by watercress or other greens. If it is a ring mold, spoon dressing inside, or serve the dressing separately in a glass dish.

Remember in making any kind of aspic that cold tends to dull flavors, and thus you want to make the seasoning a little more intense than you would for a warm dish. Taste critically before you chill, and heighten the flavors if necessary.

Lemon Chicken and Asparagus Cream Mold

(SERVES FOUR TO SIX)

1 envelope gelatin
2 teaspoons lemon juice
¾ cup (1¾ dL) chicken broth
¼ pound (115 g) asparagus
½ cup (1 dL) sour cream
½ teaspoon salt
⅛ teaspoon freshly ground
   pepper

Grated rind of 1 small lemon
2 scallions, finely chopped,
   including green part
1¼ cups (3 dL) finely chopped
   cooked chicken
¾ cup (1¾ dL) heavy cream,
   whipped
Watercress sprigs

Soften the gelatin in 2 tablespoons cold water and the lemon juice. Heat the broth, then stir in gelatin until thoroughly dissolved. Cool. Meanwhile blanch the asparagus in boiling, salted water to cover for 5 minutes. Cut off an inch of the tips and reserve for garnish. Slice the stems in thin diagonals, then quarter the slices if the stems are thick. Add to the cooled broth along with the sour cream, salt, pepper, lemon rind, scallions, and chicken, mix well, and correct seasoning. Fold in the whipped cream and pour into a lightly oiled 4-cup ring mold. Chill until set. Unmold and garnish with asparagus tips and watercress. Serve with Yogurt Dressing (p. 454).

Chicken and Almond Mousse

(SERVES SIX)

1 envelope gelatin
1 cup (¼ L) cold chicken
   broth
3 egg yolks, lightly beaten
1 cup (¼ L) ground cooked
   white chicken
½ cup (1 dL) ground blanched
   almonds

Few drops of fresh lemon juice
Dash of cayenne pepper
1 teaspoon chopped fresh
   tarragon, or ½ teaspoon
   dried, crumbled
Salt
1 cup (¼ L) heavy cream,
   beaten stiff

Sprinkle the gelatin over the broth, then heat just until the gelatin has dissolved. Pour the hot liquid over the egg yolks in a steady stream, stirring vigorously, return the mixture to the saucepan, and heat gently, stirring constantly until it thickens slightly. Add the ground chicken and almonds (they may be ground very successfully in a food processor), lemon juice, cayenne pepper, and tarragon. Season liberally with salt, as chilled foods always become more bland. Chill until the mixture thickens to the consistency of an unbeaten egg white, then fold in the whipped cream. Pour into a 4-cup mold and chill.

Fish Mousse

If you have a fish-shaped mold, this delicate mousse will look very pretty when it is turned out on a platter garnished with black olives, sprigs of parsley, and lemon slices.

(SERVES SIX)

1 pound (450 g) lean fillets of turbot or flounder, fresh or frozen
2 cups (½ L) fish stock (p. 83), chilled
2 egg yolks, lightly beaten
2 envelopes gelatin
⅓ cup (¾ dL) dry white wine
¾ pound (340 g) cooked shrimp, or 1¼ cups small, canned
2 tablespoons chopped parsley
1 tablespoon chopped scallion greens or chives
1 tablespoon chopped fresh basil, or ½ teaspoon dried, crumbled
Few drops of fresh lemon juice
Salt
Freshly ground pepper
Several dashes of cayenne pepper
¾ cup (1¾ dL) heavy cream, whipped

Cover the fish fillets with cold fish stock and bring slowly to a boil. Simmer about 8 minutes, until fish is opaque through. Remove the fish and purée in a blender or in a food processor with a little of the stock. Temper the egg yolks by gradually adding the hot stock, then return to the pan and cook gently, stirring, until the liquid thickens enough to just coat the spoon. Remove from the heat. Soften the gelatin in the wine and mix into the hot stock until completely dissolved. Reserving 6 shrimp for garnish, cut the remaining into ½-inch pieces and toss with the chopped herbs and lemon juice. Combine the puréed fish, the shrimp mixture, and the stock, and season liberally with salt, pepper, and a little cayenne pepper. Refrigerate until the mixture is somewhat thickened—about the consistency of egg whites. Then fold in the whipped cream and pour into a lightly oiled 3-cup mold. Refrigerate until set. Turn out and decorate the platter with the remaining shrimp and other suggested garnishes.

SALAD DRESSINGS

French Dressing or Basic Vinaigrette

(SERVES FOUR)

2 tablespoons vinegar
½ teaspoon salt
¼ teaspoon freshly ground pepper
½ cup (1 dL) olive or salad oil

In a small bowl mix the vinegar and salt and let stand a few minutes. Add the pepper and slowly stir or whisk in the oil. Taste for acid and salt and add more if too bland. Stir to blend before using, or store in a jar with a tight lid and shake well before using.

Mustardy French Dressing. Add an additional *1–1½ tablespoons Dijon mustard.* Blend well. Include onion and garlic, if desired.

Onion or Garlic French Dressing. Add *1–2 tablespoons minced onion, scallions, or shallots* or *½–1 teaspoon minced garlic.*

French Dressing with Fresh Herbs. Add *2 teaspoons fresh chopped herbs,* such as basil, chervil, or tarragon.

Curried French Dressing. Add *1 teaspoon curry powder* and blend well.

Cream French Dressing. Add *3 tablespoons heavy cream* or *sour cream* and blend well.

Fruit Salad French Dressing. Use *lemon juice* instead of vinegar and add *⅓ cup honey.* Blend well.

Blue Cheese Dressing. Add *3 tablespoons crumbled blue cheese.* Blend well.

Cumberland Dressing. Add *1 tablespoon heavy cream, 1 tablespoon currant jelly,* and *¼ teaspoon grated lemon rind.* Mix until well blended.

Chiffonade Dressing. Add *1 tablespoon minced parsley, 2 tablespoons minced sweet red pepper, 1 tablespoon minced onion,* and *2 hard-boiled eggs, finely chopped.* Blend all ingredients well.

Boiled Dressing

(1¼ CUPS)

1½ tablespoons flour	1½ tablespoons butter, melted
1 teaspoon dry mustard	¾ cup (1¾ dL) milk
1 tablespoon sugar	¼ cup (½ dL) vinegar
2 egg yolks, slightly beaten	Salt
Pinch of cayenne pepper	

Combine the flour, mustard, and sugar in a heavy-bottomed pan. Slowly add the yolks, cayenne pepper, melted butter, milk, and vinegar. Heat, stirring constantly, over low heat until thickened and smooth. Add salt to taste. Remove and store covered in the refrigerator until needed.

Nut Pascagoula Dressing

For fruit salad.

(½ CUP)

5 pecan halves, blanched	¼ teaspoon sugar
10 almonds, blanched	1 tablespoon vinegar
¼ teaspoon dry mustard	5 tablespoons salad oil
¼ teaspoon paprika	Salt
½ teaspoon catsup	

Grind the nuts or whirl in blender to pulverize. Add the mustard, paprika, catsup, sugar, and vinegar. Blend. Slowly add the oil, then salt to taste.

Pineapple Honey Dressing

For fruit salads.

(¾ CUP)

½ cup (1 dL) honey
3 tablespoons crushed
    pineapple

¼ cup (½ dL) lemon juice
Salt

Combine honey, pineapple, and lemon juice in a jar, cover with a snug-fitting lid, and shake until well blended. Add salt to taste.

Lime Dressing

For fruit salads.

(⅓ CUP)

¼ cup (½ dL) salad oil
2 tablespoons lime juice
¼ teaspoon Tabasco
2 teaspoons sugar

¼ teaspoon freshly ground
    pepper
Salt to taste

Combine all ingredients in a jar with a snug-fitting lid. Shake until blended.

Thousand-Island Dressing

For green salads.

(½ CUP)

⅓ cup (¾ dL) salad oil
2 tablespoons orange juice
1 tablespoon lemon juice
½ teaspoon paprika
2 teaspoons minced onion

2 teaspoons Worcestershire
    sauce
½ teaspoon dry mustard
2 teaspoons minced parsley
Salt to taste

Combine all ingredients in a pint jar, place lid on securely, and shake until well blended.

Handmade Basic Mayonnaise

Have your eggs at room temperature. Always add the oil drop by drop when first incorporating it with the egg and seasonings. After emulsion has begun, the oil may be added in a slow thin stream. Be patient! If you follow these rules, you should have no trouble.

(1 CUP)

1 egg yolk
½ teaspoon Dijon mustard or
    dry mustard
½ teaspoon salt

Pinch of cayenne pepper
1 tablespoon vinegar
¾ cup (1¾ dL) olive oil or
    salad oil

Put the yolk, mustard, salt, cayenne pepper, and vinegar in a clean bowl, put the bowl on a towel so it will remain stationary, and whisk until blended. Beat in the oil, drop by drop. As the sauce thickens, increase the flow of oil, but be slow and patient. If it should separate, follow the suggestions on p. 264 for restoring "broken" mayonnaise. The sauce, when finished, should be very thick. Taste critically and adjust the seasoning, adding a little more vinegar or salt, if necessary.

Cream Mayonnaise. Fold into the finished mayonnaise *½ cup heavy cream, whipped.* Serve with fruit salads, cold fish.

Mustard Mayonnaise. Blend *2 additional tablespoons Dijon mustard* thoroughly into the finished mayonnaise.

Green Mayonnaise. Cover *10 sprigs watercress, 10 leaves spinach,* and *4 sprigs parsley* with boiling water. Let stand for 3 minutes. Drain, put in cold water, and drain again. Chop into a purée. Add to the finished mayonnaise and mix well.

Applesauce Mayonnaise. Add *1 cup unsweetened applesauce* and *1 tablespoon prepared horseradish* to the finished mayonnaise and mix well. Serve with cold ham or pork.

Russian Dressing. Add to the finished mayonnaise *1 cup chili sauce, 2 tablespoons minced celery, 2 tablespoons minced pimiento, 2 tablespoons minced green pepper,* and add more *salt to taste.* Blend well.

Blender Mayonnaise

A whole egg is needed when making mayonnaise in a blender. For a food processor 1 whole egg plus 1 yolk will give you the right consistency.

(1½ CUPS)

1 egg	1½ tablespoons vinegar or
¼ teaspoon salt	lemon juice
½ teaspoon dry mustard, or	Salt to taste
1 teaspoon Dijon mustard	
1 cup (¼ L) olive, peanut, or	
vegetable oil (or a combination)	

Place the egg, salt, mustard, and ¼ cup of the oil in the electric blender. Turn on the motor and add the remaining ¾ cup oil in a slow, thin stream. Add the vinegar or lemon juice, and 1 tablespoon boiling water. Taste, correct the seasoning, and refrigerate until needed.

Food Processor Mayonnaise. Use 1 egg *plus 1 egg yolk* and mix in the food processor. Add up to *½ cup more oil* and adjust the amount of vinegar or lemon juice. Omit the tablespoon of boiling water.

Green Mayonnaise (Machine-made)

This must be used within a few days; after that the greens tend to turn sour. If you plan to keep it longer, blanch the greens for a minute in boiling water, then squeeze dry before using.

Green Mayonnaise (continued)

(1¾ CUPS)

¾ cup (1¾ dL) fresh greens: parsley, watercress, young spinach leaves
¼ cup (½ dL) fresh herbs: basil, tarragon, chervil, or 2 tablespoons dill, or 1 tablespoon dried herbs (1 teaspoon if using dried dill)
1 egg

1 egg yolk
Freshly ground pepper to taste
1 cup (¼ L) olive, peanut, or vegetable oil (or a combination)
1½ tablespoons mild vinegar or lemon juice or a combination
Salt to taste

Place the greens and the herbs with the egg, egg yolk, and pepper in an electric blender or food processor and blend until the greens are puréed. Start adding the oil in a slow, thin stream until the mixture becomes too thick, then add the vinegar and/or lemon juice and continue until all the oil is used up. If too thick, add a small amount of boiling water. Taste, add salt, and refrigerate in a covered jar or bowl until needed.

Green Goddess Dressing

(1½ CUPS)

1 egg yolk
2 tablespoons tarragon vinegar
1 tablespoon anchovy paste
1 cup (¼ L) salad oil
4 tablespoons heavy cream
1 tablespoon lemon juice

2 tablespoons finely chopped chives
2 tablespoons finely chopped parsley
Salt to taste

Combine the egg yolk, vinegar, and anchovy paste in a bowl and stir until well mixed. Slowly beat in the oil, a drop at a time, increasing flow as the sauce emulsifies. The sauce should be smooth and thickened. Stir in remaining ingredients. Mix well. Serve on green salads.

Yogurt Dressing

(1¼ CUPS)

1 cup (¼ L) yogurt
2 tablespoons white vinegar
1½ tablespoons lemon juice
⅛ teaspoon freshly ground pepper

2 tablespoons finely chopped chives
2 tablespoons finely chopped parsley
Salt to taste

Combine all ingredients in a bowl and blend until well mixed. Refrigerate and use as needed.

Honey Yogurt Dressing. Add *2 tablespoons honey* and omit the chives and parsley.

Yogurt, Garlic, and Blue Cheese Dressing. Add *4 tablespoons crumbled blue cheese* and *2 cloves garlic, finely chopped.*

Yogurt and Mayonnaise Dressing. Add up to *1 cup mayonnaise* and mix well.

Avocado Mayonnaise

Serve on tomatoes with salad greens, or use as a dip for tacos.

(1 CUP)

1 ripe avocado	1 teaspoon Dijon mustard
2 tablespoons evaporated milk	⅛ teaspoon Tabasco
1 tablespoon lemon juice	Salt

Peel and remove pit from avocado. Put avocado in a bowl and mash it until smooth, slowly add the milk, lemon juice, mustard, and Tabasco. Beat until smooth and blended. Add salt to taste.

Cleveland Dressing

A very sweet dressing, for those who like them on fruit salads. The fruit should be tart and include some grapefruit segments.

(1¾ CUPS)

1 teaspoon dry mustard	¼ cup (½ dL) vinegar
½ cup (100 g) sugar	1 cup (¼ L) salad oil
1 teaspoon paprika	Salt

Combine the mustard, sugar, paprika, and vinegar in a bowl and chill in the refrigerator. With an electric or hand beater, slowly add the salad oil, beating constantly. Beat until thickened. Add salt to taste.

Poppy-Seed Dressing. Substitute *lemon juice* for the vinegar and add *1 tablespoon poppy seeds.* Mix well.

Sour-Cream Dressing

For fruit salads and vegetable salads.

(1¼ CUPS)

1 cup (¼ L) sour cream	1 teaspoon dry mustard
4 tablespoons vinegar	⅛ teaspoon cayenne pepper
2 teaspoons sugar (for fruit salad), or 1 teaspoon sugar (for vegetable salad)	Salt to taste

Combine all ingredients in a bowl and whisk until well blended.

Lemon Soy Dressing

(1 CUP)

2 tablespoons soy sauce
⅓ cup (¾ dL) fresh lemon juice
¼ cup (½ dL) salad oil

Mix together well or shake in a bottle all ingredients with ¼ cup water.

Bacon Dressing

Very good on bitter or robust greens, such as spinach.

(1¼ CUPS)

3 tablespoons bacon fat
2 tablespoons flour
2 teaspoons grated onion
½ teaspoon freshly ground
  pepper

¼ teaspoon sugar
2 teaspoons prepared mustard
1 tablespoon vinegar
Salt

Melt the bacon fat in a skillet, slowly stir in the flour and onion, and cook, stirring constantly, for 2 minutes. Add the pepper, sugar, mustard, and vinegar. Blend and stir, then slowly add 1 cup water. Continue to stir and cook over medium heat until thickened. Add salt to taste. Can be served hot or cold.

YEAST BREADS

ABOUT BREADMAKING

Baking bread at home is uniquely satisfying. It is an art involving patience, creativity, and an intuitive feeling for the constantly changing texture of the dough. It is a lovely feeling to sink your hands into the dough to mix and knead it; it's hard work but, like the best of physical exercise, thoroughly relaxing. There is a sense of mystery in watching basic ingredients like flour, water, sugar, and salt respond to the almost magical power of the yeast to lift and expand; that yeast matures according to its own timetable and cannot be hurried along to fit our crowded daily schedules commands our respect. When the yeasty smell of baking bread fills your home as it did the homes of earlier generations, when you cut thick slices of crusty, chewy, oven-warm bread baked expressly for your family and your friends, you cannot help but feel a special kind of pride and elation in your achievement.

Many families have begun to bake their own bread these days because they appreciate the wholesomeness and incomparable taste of their own product. They find that baking bread at home is no longer the time-consuming, uncertain process it once was. Modern calibrated ovens, stable, dependable yeasts, and the large variety of wholesome flours now easily available make bread baking infinitely easier today. Furthermore, there are machines that can aid you in the kneading (see illustration).

Many of the bread and roll recipes in this section can be traced back to the nineteenth century, but they have all been adapted for contemporary use. Each recipe is self-contained, but we urge you to look at the general notes about ingredients and breadmaking before proceeding to the recipes. They explain basic procedures to the novice and will also refresh the memories of those who do not bake bread regularly.

Ingredients

Yeast. Yeast is what releases the gases that make the dough rise, thus lightening the bread. It is really a tiny living fungus that thrives on sweetness, warmth, and moisture. Yeast should not be rushed in its activity: given sufficient

457

time, it will not only make dough rise but will work on the gluten in the flour to develop good flavor and texture.

Yeast comes in compressed cakes or in dry, granular form, both equally satisfactory. The compressed cakes must be stored in the refrigerator and will keep from one to two weeks; they may also be frozen but must be used immediately after defrosting. Dry yeast usually comes in ¼-ounce packages, each containing one tablespoon, but you can get it in larger amounts and measure out your own. Manufacturers tell us that one package of dry yeast is the equivalent of one ³/₅-ounce cake of compressed yeast, but many home breadmakers work out their own formulas, using somewhat less dry yeast to fresh proportionately. These recipes call for dry yeast, since it is available everywhere and keeps longer. It should be stored in a cool, dry place; note the expiration date on each package.

Yeast is usually stirred into a small amount of warm liquid and allowed to stand for about 5 minutes to dissolve. If you have any doubt about freshness, "proof" the yeast by dissolving it in ¼ cup of warm water and adding a teaspoon sugar and 2 tablespoons flour; if the yeast is active it will be spurred on by the sugar to feed on the flour, and within 10 minutes you will see it begin to expand and foam.

The temperature of the liquid in which yeast is dissolved is important. Yeast will not grow in a solution that is too cold, while one that is too hot will kill it. Compressed yeast should be dissolved in lukewarm water or milk at about 100–105°F; dry yeast will tolerate somewhat warmer temperatures—about 100–115°F. It's not necessary to use a thermometer: test the water with your fingers or on your wrist and you will soon have a good feel for it.

Flour. Yeast bread depends upon wheat flour, rich in a protein called "gluten," which makes dough strong and elastic. It is capable of expanding greatly, forming a network of hundreds of little pockets to trap the yeast-produced gases which would otherwise escape from the dough. True whole-wheat flour contains all of the wheat kernel including the bran and the germ. All-purpose white flour is made from the inner part of the wheat kernel, known as the endosperm.

Bread recipes that use yeast must contain at least some white or whole-wheat flour for the gluten they provide. Bread made with gluten-rich wheat flour is a perfect food except for a slight deficiency in fat, which is probably why the custom arose of spreading bread with butter.

The hard-wheat (winter wheat) flour used by professional bakers is richest in gluten and best for baking bread. Since it is not easy to come by, you can use all-purpose flour in these recipes whenever white flour is specified. All-purpose flour is readily available, is widely used, and produces a highly satisfactory loaf. The unbleached variety, less white than the bleached, has more food value.

Flours vary considerably and react in different ways, making it hard to specify an exact amount of flour in a bread recipe. That is one reason we suggest holding back the final cup, kneading it in only as necessary. With a little experience you will know when dough has reached the proper consistency.

There are special flours, such as rye, corn, barley, graham, soy bean, rice, and buckwheat, and meals, such as oat, corn, barley, and rye; they have good flavor and texture but *must* be used with white or whole-wheat flour in yeast-bread recipes, since they do not react to yeast. Bran, wheat germ, whole-wheat kernels, and wheat berries will add both texture and nutrients to your bread. Stoneground flours have a good, coarse texture and

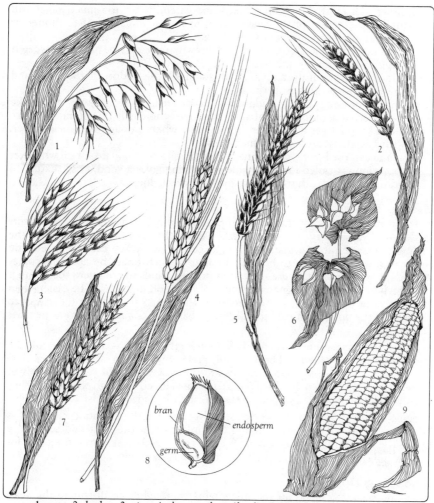

1. oats; 2. barley; 3. rice; 4. durum wheat (hard); 5. rye; 6. buckwheat; 7. soft wheat; 8. magnified cross section of wheat kernel; 9. corn.

are generally considered to be more nutritious as well. The list of special flours and grains is lengthy: as you become more experienced, you will want to seek them out and try them in these recipes.

Liquid. It is the liquid in the dough which, during baking, turns to steam and helps create the texture of the bread. As a general rule, about 2 cups of liquid are used for 1 package of yeast and 6 cups of flour, but this proportion will vary considerably from recipe to recipe, affecting the speed with which the dough will rise and the texture of the loaf itself.

Water, potato water, milk, or even beer can be used as the liquid. Milk produces a richer bread with a more tender crumb and a less grainy taste. Bread made with milk or potato water will keep longer than bread made with water.

Sweeteners. Sugar, used sparingly, makes the dough rise more quickly and helps brown the crust, but follow the recipe carefully, for too much sugar will inhibit the action of the yeast. Also, as an accompaniment to dinner, it is preferable not to serve a sweet bread.

Honey, molasses, corn syrup, or brown sugar can be used to sweeten bread, as can raisins and dates.

Salt. Salt is used primarily for flavor. It stabilizes the action of the yeast and strengthens the gluten in the flour.

Shortening. Shortening is often added to enrich bread, give it flavor, and make it tender. It is not essential to any recipe, though it does tend to make bread keep longer and better. Sometimes, when a dough is especially rich with fat, the yeast may act more slowly.

You can use butter, margarine, vegetable shortening, lard, or oil wherever shortening is called for. Vegetable shortening gives a good, crisp texture to nonsweet breads. Butter is best in rich, sweet doughs.

Mixing Dough

It is important to mix all the ingredients thoroughly and vigorously at the start so that the yeast is evenly distributed. Dough that is not well mixed at the beginning may result in a loaf with rough, coarse grain. You can use an electric beater or a wooden spoon to beat in the flour at first; once the dough becomes stiff, you'll find it easiest to use the spoon or your hands to complete the mixing. Hold back a cup of the designated amount of flour and mixing will be easier; then knead in later only what you need to keep the dough from being too sticky to handle. As the dough is mixed it will form a ball that comes away from the sides of the bowl.

Batter breads require no kneading. After the yeast is dissolved, all the ingredients are combined and beaten well, preferably with an electric beater. The dough is then set to rise. Batter breads are the easiest kind of yeasted breads to make. Since the gluten in the flour is not developed through kneading, they usually have a coarser, more porous texture than kneaded breads.

Some of the recipes in this book use a "sponge" method to start: the yeast is mixed with the full amount of liquid but only part of the flour and set to rise before the remaining flour is added. We use this speedy first rising in recipes for certain rolls and buns in which an airy texture is desirable.

Kneading Dough

Kneading serves to blend all the ingredients thoroughly, to distribute the yeast evenly, and to give the dough elasticity and a smooth, even texture.

After the dough is mixed, turn it out onto a lightly floured board for kneading. If you knead it for a minute or two and then let it rest for 10 minutes, it will be easier to work, although it still may be a bit sticky at first.

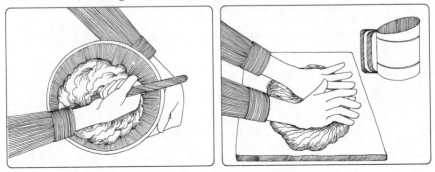

Sprinkle the dough with a little flour and flour your hands generously. Push the dough quickly away from you, using the heels of your hands. Pull the far end of the dough toward you with your fingertips, folding it over. Give the dough a quarter-turn and repeat these two motions, using not just your arms but your whole body and setting a vigorous rhythm as you work. Knead for about 10 minutes, until the dough holds together, becomes smooth and satiny, and is no longer sticky but elastic to the touch. Depress the dough with your fingers: if it springs back, it has been kneaded enough. Don't worry about kneading too much—it can never hurt. If dough is not well kneaded, the resulting loaf may have big holes in it.

If you must interrupt the kneading process for more than 10 or 15 minutes, turn a bowl over the dough so that it does not dry out.

Occasionally dough will become "bucky" and develop folds that remain while you are kneading. If that should happen, slam the dough down on a hard surface several times to make it pliable.

Bread dough can be kneaded in an electric mixer equipped with a dough hook. Machine kneading is quick and very efficient. It eliminates the unique pleasure of hand kneading, but you can always finish the kneading by hand. There are also less expensive kneading pails available, which you turn by hand. And a food processor works quite well, but will do only a single loaf at a time.

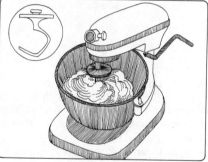

Raising Dough

Dough should not be disturbed during the rising period, when the yeast is producing the little gas bubbles that stretch the gluten in the flour and make the dough expand.

The time required for dough to rise will vary considerably, depending on a number of uncontrollable factors. Thus, these recipes describe how *much* the dough should rise, rather than how *long* it will take. As a general guideline, a first rising should take two or more hours in a warm place (longer if the dough contains no sugar and is in a cool kitchen under 70°F), a second rising (if there is one) about one and one-half hours, and the final phase, in the pans, about an hour or less.

If you "overproof" by letting the dough rise to more than the recipe suggests, the bread may be yeasty, lack good flavor and texture, or have a separation between the crumb and the crust. Or if it has overrisen in the final phase in the pans, it is apt to sink in the oven. If the dough is not given sufficient time to rise, it may be too moist and heavy. If you wish to extend the rising time for your own convenience, put the bowl in the refrigerator and cover it with a plate to retard the action of the yeast.

Prepare the dough for rising by greasing a large mixing bowl and placing the ball of kneaded dough in it. Turn the dough so that it is coated on all sides, then cover the bowl with a clean towel and set it in a warm place (75–85°F), away from any drafts. Let the dough rise to the desired bulk. Depress the raised dough with your fingers: if the indentations remain, the dough has fully risen.

Punch the dough down with your fist to let the trapped gases escape, and knead it if the recipe suggests; usually it isn't necessary. Some recipes call for a second rising, which produces a finer-textured bread and a more developed flavor. Others proceed directly to the final rising—after the dough has been shaped and put in a loaf pan or on a baking sheet. The loaves are covered with a towel and set in a warm place until the dough has risen the required amount. Remember to preheat the oven when the dough is almost ready to bake.

If the dough should rise too much in the pan, punch it down, knead it for a minute or two, reshape it, and let it rise again in the pan.

Forming Loaves

Once you have tried a few of the techniques we suggest for shaping loaves, you will find the way that seems most natural to you and will probably stick to it. Remember that part of the charm of homemade bread is in its appearance: seams and little imperfections keep it from being factory-perfect and make each loaf original.

Begin by cutting the dough with a knife into two or more parts, according to the number of loaves the recipe makes. Pat each piece into a ball and let it rest while you grease the bread pans.

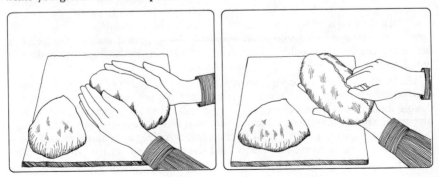

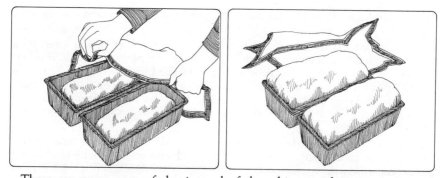

There are many ways of shaping a loaf, but this procedure is so easy and satisfactory that there really is no need to master more complicated techniques, unless you wish to play around with them. Simply pat the dough into an oval approximately the length of your bread pan. Then plump it up by drawing your hand down the sides, gently stretching the dough toward the bottom to make a smooth shape. If there is a fold on the bottom, pinch it together, but this is not absolutely necessary. Place the dough in the pan, with the seams or creases on the bottom. The ends should touch the sides of the pan; if they don't or if the shape seems uneven, just pat it to even out.

Two alternate methods are: *One*, patting the dough into a rectangle, making a dent in the center, then folding one side over, pinching the seams together, and placing in the pan seam side down with the ends tucked under. *Two*, patting the dough into an oval, then starting with the short end, rolling it up tightly, pinching the edges together, and placing it in the pan, seam side down.

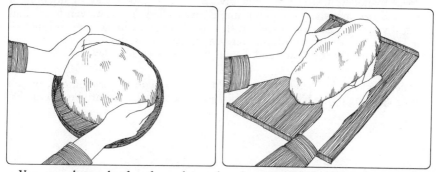

You can also make free-form shapes by plumping the dough into a round or oval loaf. To make the round shape, draw your hands down the sides, stretching the dough and turning it, until you have a perfect round; pinch the bottom where the dough comes together. An oval is shaped very much like the simple forming of the loaf for the bread pan above; simply taper the ends so that the loaf swells more in the center. Let these loaves rise on a greased cookie sheet, which will then go straight into the oven for baking.

Baking Bread

Baking kills the action of the yeast. When bread is baked properly, it will be well browned and will pull away from the sides of the pan and slip out easily.

Loaf pans should be filled one-half to two-thirds full. They come in two standard sizes: 9 × 5 × 3 inches and 8½ × 4½ × 2½ inches. Either size can be used in these recipes; the smaller size is preferable, as it produces a higher loaf. You can also get high, domed loaves by doubling a two-loaf recipe and baking three loaves in 9 × 5 × 3-inch pans.

The standard test to see if bread is done is to tap the bottom and listen for a hollow sound, but bread often sounds hollow when it is not yet done, so it is best to bake it for the full recommended time. A standard loaf needs 40–55 minutes in a 375°F oven, depending on the flours and meal used. If you have any question, you can put a bread back in the hot pan and bake it a little longer. Sometimes a loaf is removed from the pan when it's done and put back on the oven rack for a final crisping.

For a hard, crisp crust, brush the bread with cold water several times during baking. If you prefer a soft crust, brush the bread with milk or melted butter. Or mix an egg yolk with a tablespoon of milk for a glaze which will make the crust golden and shiny.

If you wish, you can make a few diagonal slashes, about ½ inch deep, across the top of the bread, using a sharp knife. The slashes are decorative and they will prevent cracking.

Cooling and Storing Bread

Bread should be cooled away from drafts to prevent shrinking. Remove the loaf from the pan immediately after taking it from the oven and let it cool on a rack. Cover it with a dishtowel while it is cooling if you want a soft crust.

Do not wrap bread until it is thoroughly cool. Store it in a plastic bag or wrapped in foil, in or out of the refrigerator. Most breads taste best the first or second day after baking, although some will keep longer, especially those that are very moist or are made from dough that is rich in butter and milk.

Bread freezes well. You can often save both time and money by doubling a recipe and freezing what you do not immediately need. You can even freeze half a loaf, if you wish. To defrost, reheat the bread, wrapped in foil and still frozen, in a 350°F oven for about 30 minutes. Or simply let the bread defrost at room temperature for about 3 hours and crisp it in a hot oven for a few minutes before serving.

Stale bread can be used for toast, stuffing, bread pudding, or croutons, or you can use a rolling pin, a blender, or a food processor to make it into bread crumbs.

LOAF BREADS (KNEADED)

White Bread

A pure, tender loaf, exactly what a basic white bread should be.

(2 LOAVES)

2 tablespoons shortening	1 cup (¼ L) hot milk
2½ teaspoons salt	1 package dry yeast
2 tablespoons sugar	6 cups (840 g) white flour

Mix the shortening, salt, and sugar in a large bowl, add the hot milk and 1 cup hot water, and let cool to lukewarm. In a small bowl or cup mix the yeast with ¼ cup warm water and let it stand for 5 minutes to dissolve. Add the dissolved yeast and 3 cups of the flour to the first mixture and beat until well blended. Add 2 more cups of flour, mix, and turn out onto a lightly floured board. Knead for a minute or two and then let rest for 10 minutes. Adding just enough of the remaining flour so that the dough is not sticky, resume kneading until the dough is smooth and elastic. Put the dough in a large, greased bowl, cover, and let rise in a warm spot until double in bulk. Punch down and shape into two loaves. Place in greased loaf pans, cover, and let double in bulk again. Preheat oven to 425°F (220°C). Bake bread for 15 minutes, reduce heat to 375°F (190°C), and bake for 30 minutes more. Remove from pans and cool on racks.

Cheese Bread. Mix *1 ½ cups grated Cheddar or other sharp cheese* with the last flour added.

Whole-Wheat Bread

You'll get fine-textured wheat slices with a whole-grain flavor from these loaves.

(2 LOAVES)

1 cup (¼ L) milk
¼ cup (50 g) sugar
2 teaspoons salt
1 package dry yeast

2 cups (280 g) whole-wheat flour
4 cups (560 g) white flour

Bring ½ cup water to a boil, mix it with the milk, sugar, and salt in a large bowl, and let cool to lukewarm. In a separate container, measure ½ cup warm water, stir in the yeast, and let it stand for 5 minutes to dissolve. Add the dissolved yeast, the whole-wheat flour, and 2 cups of the white flour to the first mixture. Beat thoroughly, then turn out onto a lightly floured board, adding enough flour so that the dough handles easily. Knead for a few minutes and let rest for 10 minutes. Add as much of the remaining flour as necessary to keep the dough from being sticky. Resume kneading for 10 minutes or until the dough is smooth and elastic. Place in a greased bowl, cover, and let rise in a warm spot until double in bulk. Punch down and shape into two loaves. Place in greased loaf pans, cover, and let rise again until almost double in bulk. Preheat oven to 375°F (190°C). Bake bread for about 45 minutes. Remove from pans and cool on racks.

Whole-Wheat Bread with Wheat Berries. Simmer *½–¾ cup dry wheat berries* in water to cover for several hours or until soft. Drain and knead them into the Whole-Wheat Bread dough after the first rising.

Whole-Wheat Bread with Wheat Germ. Mix *½ cup wheat germ* in with the flour.

Whole-Wheat Oatmeal Bread. Knead in *1 cup uncooked rolled oats* with the whole-wheat flour. You will need ½–1 cup less of the white flour if you add the oats.

Cracked-Wheat Bread

A good brown crust, nice tender crumb, and bits of cracked wheat make this a perfect loaf to balance a supper salad.

Cracked-Wheat Bread (continued)

(2 LOAVES)

1 cup (¼ L) milk	1 cup (¼ L) cracked wheat
¼ cup (½ dL) molasses	1 cup (140 g) whole-wheat
2 teaspoons salt	flour
1 package dry yeast	4 cups (560 g) white flour

Bring ½ cup water to a boil, mix it with the milk, molasses, and salt in a large bowl, and let cool to lukewarm. In a separate container, measure ½ cup warm water, stir in the yeast, and let it stand for 5 minutes to dissolve. Add the dissolved yeast, cracked wheat, whole-wheat flour, and 1 cup of the white flour to the first mixture and beat thoroughly. Add most of the remaining 3 cups of flour and beat well. Turn out onto a lightly floured board, knead for a minute or two, and let rest for 10 minutes. Resume kneading until the dough is smooth and elastic, adding the remaining flour only if necessary. Place in a greased bowl, cover, and let rise in a warm place until double in bulk. Punch down and form into two loaves. Place in greased loaf pans, cover and let rise until almost double in bulk. Preheat the oven to 375°F (190°C). Bake bread for 45–50 minutes. Remove from pans and cool on racks.

Water Bread and Rolls

Light and tender, good with delicate, subtle dishes.

(1 LOAF AND 8 ROLLS)

1 tablespoon butter	1½ teaspoons salt
1 tablespoon shortening	1 package dry yeast
1 tablespoon sugar	6 cups (840 g) white flour

Mix the butter, shortening, sugar, and salt in a large bowl. Bring 2 cups water to a boil, add it to mixture, and let cool to lukewarm. Measure ¼ cup warm water in a separate container, add the yeast, and let it stand for 5 minutes to dissolve. Add the dissolved yeast and 5 cups of the flour to the first mixture and mix thoroughly. Turn out onto a lightly floured board and let rest for about 10 minutes. Adding as much of the remaining flour as necessary, knead until smooth and elastic. Place the dough in a large, buttered bowl, cover, and let rise in a warm place until double in bulk. Punch the dough down and knead it once or twice. Half-fill a buttered loaf pan; break the remaining dough into pieces the size of small lemons and arrange them, sides touching, on a buttered 9-inch pie plate. Cover the pan and the pie plate and let the dough double in bulk once again. Preheat the oven to 375°F (190°C). Bake bread, allowing about 25 minutes for the rolls and about 45 minutes for the loaf. Remove from pans and cool on racks.

Oatmeal Bread

Honey-colored, chewy, and moist with a distinct molasses flavor.

(2 LOAVES)

1 cup (¼ L) instant oats	2 teaspoons salt
1 package dry yeast	1 tablespoon butter
½ cup (1 dL) molasses	5½ cups (770 g) white flour

Put the oats in a large bowl. Bring 2 cups water to a boil, pour it over oats, and let stand for at least 15 minutes. Stir the yeast into ¼ cup warm water and let it stand for 5 minutes to dissolve. Feel the oats at the bottom of the bowl to be sure they're lukewarm, then add the molasses, salt, butter, and dissolved yeast. Work in enough of the flour so that the dough is easy to handle. Turn out onto a lightly floured board, knead for a minute or two, and let rest for 10 minutes. Resume kneading until the dough is smooth and elastic, adding more flour as necessary. Place in a buttered bowl, cover, and let rise in a warm spot until double in bulk. Punch down and shape into two loaves. Place in buttered loaf pans, cover, and let rise again until double in bulk. Preheat oven to 375°F (190°C). Bake bread for 45 minutes. Remove from pans and cool on racks.

Oatmeal Bread with Honey. Use ⅓ *cup honey* instead of molasses.

Rye Bread

Rye flour will remain a bit sticky, even when it has been thoroughly kneaded. This recipe makes a light, moist loaf.

(2 LOAVES)

1 cup (¼ L) milk
2 tablespoons shortening
2 tablespoons dark-brown sugar
1 tablespoon salt

2 packages dry yeast
3 cups (420 g) rye flour
3 cups (420 g) white flour

Bring 1 cup water to a boil, mix it with the milk, shortening, sugar, and salt in a large bowl, and let cool to lukewarm. Measure ½ cup warm water in a separate container, stir in yeast, and let it stand for 5 minutes to dissolve. Add the dissolved yeast and the rye flour to the first mixture and combine thoroughly. Add enough of the white flour so that you can handle the dough. Turn out onto a lightly floured board, knead for a minute or two, then let rest for 10 minutes. Resume kneading for about 10 minutes, adding the remaining flour as necessary. Put the dough in a greased bowl, cover, and let rise in a warm place until almost double in bulk. Punch down and shape into two loaves. Place in greased loaf pans, cover, and let rise again until double in bulk. Preheat oven to 375°F (190°C). Bake bread for 45–50 minutes. Remove from pans and cool on racks.

German Caraway Bread

A dense, chewy loaf distinctly flavored with rye and caraway. Rye flour makes a sticky dough; if you flour your hands well, it will be easier to handle.

(2 LOAVES)

1 cup (¼ L) milk
2 tablespoons shortening
2 teaspoons salt
1 tablespoon sugar

1 tablespoon caraway seeds
2 packages dry yeast
2 cups (280 g) white flour
4 cups (560 g) rye flour

Bring 1 cup water to a boil, mix it with the milk, shortening, salt, sugar, and caraway seeds in a large bowl, and let cool to lukewarm. In a separate container, measure ¼ cup warm water, stir in the yeast, and let it stand for 5 minutes to dissolve. Add the dissolved yeast and the white flour to the first mixture and combine well. Beat in about 3 cups of the rye flour, or enough to make a moderately stiff dough. Turn out onto a lightly floured board, knead for a few minutes, and then let rest for 10 minutes. Resume kneading for about 10 minutes, adding the remaining rye flour as necessary; the dough will be a bit sticky even when thoroughly kneaded. Put the dough in a greased bowl, cover, and let rise in a warm spot until double in bulk. Punch down and form into two loaves. Place in greased loaf pans, cover, and let rise again until almost double in bulk. Or shape into two rounds or ovals and place on a greased cookie sheet, cover, and let rise. Preheat oven to 375°F (190°C). Bake bread for about 45 minutes. Remove from pans or cookie sheet and cool on racks.

French Bread

This is French bread, American style. Its soft, fine texture and light-brown crust make it a pleasing dinner bread.

(TWO 15-INCH LOAVES)

2 packages dry yeast	Salt
2 tablespoons sugar	6 cups (840 g) white flour
4 tablespoons melted	Cornmeal
shortening	1 egg white

Stir the yeast into 2 cups warm water in a large bowl and let it stand for 5 minutes to dissolve. Add the sugar, the shortening, and 1 tablespoon salt, and stir well. Add 2 cups of the flour and beat thoroughly. Add 3 more cups of the flour and mix well. Turn out onto a lightly floured board, knead for a few minutes, and let rest for 10 minutes. Resume kneading, adding some of the remaining flour until the dough is no longer sticky but very smooth and elastic. Place in a greased bowl, cover, and let rise in a warm spot until double in bulk. Punch down and knead for a few seconds. Shape by rolling and stretching into two long, cylindrical 15-inch loaves and place on a greased cookie sheet lightly sprinkled with cornmeal. Cover and let rise again until double in bulk. Preheat oven to 375°F (190°C).

Lightly beat egg white with 1 tablespoon water and 1 teaspoon salt. Brush tops of loaves with this glaze before baking. Bake for 35–45 minutes. Remove from pan and cool on racks.

Hot Buttered Bread. Soften *4 tablespoons unsalted butter.* After baking and cooling, cut French Bread in diagonal slices without cutting all the way through. Spread the butter between the slices, wrap the bread in foil, and heat in a 400°F (205°C) oven until very hot.

Garlic Bread. Mash *1 minced garlic clove* into *4 tablespoons softened butter* and proceed as for Hot Buttered Bread.

Herb Bread. Mix some *finely chopped chives, watercress, or mixed fresh herbs* and a few drops of *lemon juice* into the butter and proceed as for Hot Buttered Bread.

Cheesed Bread. Follow the directions for Hot Buttered Bread, spreading the slices with *soft cheese* or *butter mixed with grated Cheddar cheese.*

Brioche Bread and Rolls

Bread and rolls with a mildly sweet, pale yellow crumb and the gentle flavor of lemons and butter.

(1 LOAF AND 6 ROLLS)

2 packages dry yeast
1 cup (¼ L) warm milk
⅔ cup (1½ dL) butter
1 egg
4 egg yolks

½ cup (100 g) sugar
1½ teaspoons salt
Grated rind of 1 lemon
5½ cups (770 g) white flour

Stir the yeast into the milk in a large mixing bowl and let it stand for 5 minutes to dissolve. Add the butter, egg, egg yolks, sugar, salt, lemon rind, and about 2½ cups of the flour. Beat thoroughly, then add as much of the remaining flour as is necessary for a dough that handles easily. Turn out onto a lightly floured board. Knead for a minute or two and let rest for 10 minutes. Continue to knead until smooth and elastic. Put the dough in a large, buttered bowl, cover, and let rise in a warm spot until double in bulk. Punch down and let it rise again until slightly less than double in bulk, for at least 4 hours or in a covered bowl in the refrigerator overnight. Butter a loaf pan and a 6-cup muffin pan and fill them one-third full. Cover and let double once again. Preheat oven to 375°F (190°C). Bake bread, allowing about 20 minutes for the muffins and 45 minutes for the bread. Remove from pans and cool on racks.

Cornell Bread

This high-protein bread was developed for use in public institutions and has been acclaimed for providing excellent nutritional value at low cost. A creamy, light-textured loaf laced with tiny flecks of wheat germ, it is not only health-giving but appealing in looks and taste.

(2 LOAVES)

1 cup (¼ L) milk
2 tablespoons shortening
1 tablespoon salt
2 tablespoons brown sugar
1 package dry yeast

6 tablespoons soy flour
6 tablespoons nonfat dry milk
2 tablespoons wheat germ
5 cups (700 g) white flour

Bring 1 cup water to a boil, mix it with the milk, shortening, salt, and sugar in a large bowl, and let cool to lukewarm. In a separate container, measure ½ cup warm water, stir in the yeast, and let it stand for 5 minutes to dissolve. Add the dissolved yeast, soy flour, dry milk, wheat germ, and 2 cups of the white flour to the first mixture and beat until well blended. Add 2 more cups of the white flour, mix, and turn out onto a lightly floured board. Knead for a minute or two and then let rest for 10 minutes. Adding just enough of the remaining flour so that the dough is not sticky, resume kneading until smooth and elastic. Put the dough in a large greased bowl, cover, and let rise in a warm spot until double in bulk. Punch down and shape into two loaves. Place in greased loaf pans, cover, and let rise again until double in bulk. Preheat oven to 375°F (190°C). Bake bread for 45–50 minutes. Remove from pans and cool on racks.

Colonial Bread

A honey-colored bread, dotted with pieces of pecan and candied orange peel.

(2 LOAVES)

1 cup (¼ L) milk
¼ cup (½ dL) honey
2 teaspoons salt
1 package dry yeast
4 cups (560 g) white flour
2 cups (280 g) whole-wheat
  flour

½ cup (1 dL) finely chopped
  candied orange peel
1 cup (¼ L) pecans, in coarse
  pieces

Bring ½ cup water to a boil, mix it with the milk, honey, and salt in a large bowl, and let cool to lukewarm. In a separate container, stir the yeast into ½ cup warm water and let it stand for 5 minutes to dissolve. Add the dissolved yeast and 3 cups of the white flour to the first mixture and beat vigorously. Add the remaining cup of white flour and 1 cup of the whole-wheat flour and mix well. Turn it out onto a lightly floured board, knead for a minute or two, and let rest for 10 minutes. Using the remaining flour only if the dough is too sticky to handle, resume kneading until smooth and elastic. Place the dough in a greased bowl, cover, and let rise in a warm place until double in bulk. Punch down and knead in the candied orange peel and the pecans. Shape into two loaves, place in greased loaf pans, cover, and let rise until almost double in bulk. Preheat oven to 375°F (190°C). Bake bread for 45–55 minutes. Remove from pans and cool on racks.

Bran and Honey Bread

Sweet, light, and wholesome.

(2 LOAVES)

1 tablespoon butter
4 tablespoons honey
2½ teaspoons salt
1 cup (¼ L) milk

1 package dry yeast
1 cup (¼ L) bran
5 cups (700 g) white flour

Bring 1 cup water to a boil, mix it with the butter, honey, salt, and milk in a large bowl, and let cool to lukewarm. In a separate container, stir the yeast into ¼ cup warm water and let it stand for 5 minutes to dissolve. Add the dissolved yeast, the bran, and 2 cups of the white flour to the first mixture and stir vigorously. Add 2 more cups of white flour and mix well. Turn out onto a lightly floured board and let rest for 10 minutes. Adding as much of the remaining flour as necessary to keep the dough from sticking, knead until smooth and elastic— about 10 minutes. Put the dough in a greased bowl, cover, and let rise in a warm place until double in bulk. Punch down and shape into two loaves. Place in greased loaf pans, cover, and let rise again until double in bulk. Preheat oven to 425°F (220°C). Bake bread for 10 minutes, reduce heat to 375°F (190°C), and continue to bake for 30–35 minutes more. Remove from pans and cool on racks.

Raisin and Nut Bread

A soft-crumbed, tender loaf. It's good toasted, too—with honey.

(2 LOAVES)

1 cup (¼ L) milk	1 package dry yeast
4 tablespoons butter	6 cups (840 g) white flour
4 tablespoons sugar	¾ cup (1¾ dL) raisins
1 tablespoon salt	¾ cup (1¾ dL) chopped nuts

Bring 1 cup water to a boil, mix it with the milk, butter, sugar, and salt in a large bowl, and let cool to lukewarm. In a separate container, measure ½ cup warm water, stir in the yeast, and let it stand for 5 minutes to dissolve. Add the dissolved yeast and 3 cups of the flour to the first mixture and combine thoroughly. Add the raisins and nuts. Work in enough of the remaining flour so that the dough is easy to handle. Turn out onto a lightly floured board, knead for a few minutes, and let rest for 10 minutes. Resume kneading until the dough is smooth and elastic. Put the dough in a buttered bowl, cover, and let rise in a warm spot until double in bulk. Punch down and shape into two loaves. Place in buttered loaf pans, cover, and let rise again until almost double in bulk. Preheat oven to 375°F (190°C). Bake bread for 45–55 minutes. Remove from pans and cool on racks.

LOAF BREADS (BATTER)

Anadama Bread

Brown and crusty with a chewy, springy texture, this old-fashioned batter bread, quick and easy to make, is an American classic.

(2 LOAVES)

½ cup (1 dL) yellow cornmeal	2 teaspoons salt
1 package dry yeast	1 tablespoon butter
½ cup (1 dL) molasses	4½ cups (630 g) white flour

Put the cornmeal in a large mixing bowl. Bring 2 cups water to a boil and pour it over the cornmeal. Stir until smooth, making sure that the cornmeal does not lump. Let stand for 30 minutes. Stir the yeast into ½ cup warm water and let it stand for 5 minutes to dissolve. Add the molasses, salt, butter, and dissolved yeast to the cornmeal mixture. Stir in the flour and beat thoroughly. Spoon into 2 buttered loaf pans, cover, and let rise in a warm spot until double in bulk. Preheat oven to 350°F (180°C). Bake bread for 45–50 minutes. Remove from pans and cool on racks.

Entire Wheat Bread

The original recipe for this batter bread called for "entire wheat flour"—made from whole kernels of wheat with only the outer husk removed before grinding—which was probably not very different from the excellent, finely milled whole-wheat flours available in supermarkets today. Unusually tender and refined, it is a splendid wheat bread and requires no kneading.

(1 LOAF)

2 cups (½ L) hot milk	1 package dry yeast
⅓ cup (¾ dL) molasses	4⅓ cups (610 g) whole-wheat
1½ teaspoons salt	flour

Mix the milk, molasses, and salt in a large bowl and let cool to lukewarm. Stir the yeast into ¼ cup warm water and let it stand for 5 minutes to dissolve. Add the dissolved yeast and the flour to the first mixture. Beat well, cover, and let rise in a warm place until double in bulk. Beat briefly and turn into a greased loaf pan. Cover and let rise again to not quite double in bulk. Preheat oven to 375°F (190°C). Bake bread for about 45 minutes. Remove from pan and cool on a rack.

Third Bread

Called "third bread" because of the three types of flours—actually, two flours and one meal—that go into it, this is better balanced and lighter than most loaves made with several flours and requires no kneading.

(2 LOAVES)

1 package dry yeast	1 cup (140 g) rye flour
½ cup (1 dL) molasses	3 cups (420 g) white flour
1½ teaspoons salt	1 cup (¼ L) yellow cornmeal

In a large bowl stir the yeast into 2 cups warm water and let it stand for 5 minutes to dissolve. Add the molasses and salt and stir well. Beat in the rye flour, white flour, and cornmeal. Cover and put in a warm place until the dough doubles in bulk. Beat again briefly and form into two loaves. Place in greased loaf pans, cover, and let double in bulk once again. Preheat oven to 375°F (190°C). Bake bread for about 45 minutes. Remove from pans and cool on racks.

Graham Bread

Graham flour, a coarsely milled whole-wheat flour that includes the bran, was developed by the Reverend Sylvester Graham in the nineteenth century. A fat slice of this satisfying, richly flavored batter bread, some cheese, and a pear make a splendid lunch.

(2 LOAVES)

⅓ cup (¾ dL) molasses or	1 package dry yeast
honey	3 cups (420 g) white flour
1½ teaspoons salt	3 cups (420 g) graham flour

Mix the molasses or honey, salt, and 2½ cups warm water in a large bowl; let cool to lukewarm. Stir the yeast into ¼ cup warm water and let it stand for 5 minutes to dissolve. Add the dissolved yeast, the white flour, and 2½ cups of the graham flour to the lukewarm molasses mixture and beat well. Slowly add the remaining graham flour. Cover and let rise in a warm place until double in bulk. Beat again briefly and divide the dough evenly into two greased loaf pans. Cover and let rise to the tops of the pans. Preheat oven to 375°F (190°C). Bake bread for about 45 minutes. Remove from pans and cool on racks.

Cincinnati Coffee Bread

(1 LOAF)

1 cup (¼ L) hot milk	1 package dry yeast
⅓ cup (65 g) sugar	2 eggs, well beaten
5 tablespoons butter	4 cups (560 g) white flour
1 teaspoon salt	

Topping

½ cup (1 dL) bread crumbs	1 tablespoon cinnamon
2 tablespoons sugar	2 tablespoons melted butter

Mix the milk, sugar, butter, and salt in a large bowl and let cool to lukewarm. Stir the yeast into ¼ cup warm water and let stand for 5 minutes to dissolve. Add the dissolved yeast, eggs, and flour to the first mixture and beat very well. Cover and let rise until double in bulk. Stir down with a spoon and beat thoroughly. Spoon into a buttered loaf pan. Mix the topping ingredients together and sprinkle them on the batter, cover the pan, and let rise again until double in bulk. Preheat oven to 350°F (180°C). Bake loaf for about 40–50 minutes.

ROLLS, DOUGHNUTS, AND COFFEE CAKES

Standard Rolls

With this basic recipe you can make fine, light rolls and biscuits in a variety of shapes.

(2½–3 DOZEN ROLLS)

4 tablespoons butter	1 package dry yeast
2 tablespoons sugar	6 cups (840 g) white flour
2 teaspoons salt	Melted butter
2 cups (½ L) warm milk	

Mix the butter, sugar, salt, and milk in a large bowl and let cool to lukewarm. Stir the yeast into ¼ cup warm water and let it stand for 5 minutes to dissolve. Add 3 cups of the flour and the dissolved yeast to the first mixture and beat vigorously for 2 minutes. Cover and let rise in a warm place until double in bulk. Stir the dough vigorously and add as much of the remaining flour as necessary in order to knead the dough. Turn out onto a lightly floured board, knead for a minute or two, and let rest for 10 minutes. Resume kneading until smooth. Shape (see following suggestions). Arrange the shaped dough in buttered muffin tins or close together on buttered cookie sheets, brushing between them with melted butter so that they separate easily after baking. Cover and let rise again until double in bulk. Preheat oven to 425°F (220°C). Bake rolls for about 12–15 minutes.

Shaping Rolls

Biscuits. Using a rolling pin, roll out the dough for Standard Rolls on a lightly floured board until it is ⅓ inch thick; cut with a small, round biscuit cutter. Or shape the dough into a long, thin cylinder and with a floured knife cut off pieces about ⅓ inch thick.

Finger Rolls. Cut the dough for Standard Rolls as you would for Biscuits, then roll each piece with one hand on an unfloured board into a long, thin oval.

Clover Leaf Rolls. Shape the dough for Standard Rolls into 1-inch balls, brush with *melted butter,* and place three balls in each section of a buttered muffin tin.

Parker House Rolls. Using a rolling pin, roll out the dough for Standard Rolls until it is ⅓ inch thick and cut with a round biscuit cutter or with an oval Parker House roll cutter. Using the dull edge of a knife, make a crease through the center of each piece of dough, brush with *melted butter,* fold in half along the crease, and press edges lightly together. Place 1 inch apart on a buttered cookie sheet.

Bowknots or Twists. Using your hands, roll thin strips of the dough for Standard Rolls into sticks 8–10 inches long. Twist them or tie them loosely in knots.

Butter Rolls. Using a rolling pin, roll the dough for Standard Rolls into a rectangle about 12 × 16 inches. Spread with *softened butter.* Cut lengthwise into four strips and stack them evenly in a pile. Cut into 1-inch pieces and arrange them on their sides in a buttered muffin tin.

Pinwheel Biscuits. Using a rolling pin, roll out the dough for Standard Rolls until it is ¼ inch thick and spread it with *softened butter.* Roll from the long side like a jelly roll. Cut in ¾-inch pieces and place close together on a buttered cookie sheet, cut side down.

Feather Rolls

Feather rolls, as their name indicates, are high and very light.

(12 ROLLS)

1 package dry yeast	1 egg
4 tablespoons soft butter	¾ cup (1¾ dL) warm milk
1 tablespoon sugar	2 cups (280 g) white flour
¾ teaspoon salt	

Stir the yeast into ¼ cup warm water and let it stand for 5 minutes to dissolve. Mix the butter, sugar, salt, egg, milk, and dissolved yeast in a large bowl and beat until smooth. Add the flour and beat vigorously until well blended. Cover and let rise in a warm spot for about 1 hour. Stir down and fill buttered muffin tins half full. Cover and let rise for about 30 minutes. Preheat oven to 400°F (205°C). Bake rolls for 15–20 minutes.

1. *biscuits*; 2. *finger rolls*; 3. *clover leaf rolls*; 4. *Parker House rolls*; 5. *bowknots or twists*; 6. *butter rolls*; 7. & 8. *pinwheel biscuits.*

Hard Rolls

The secret to making hard rolls is to create steam in the oven so that
they will develop a good crust as they bake.

(1½ DOZEN ROLLS)

1 package dry yeast	3½ cups (490 g) white flour
1 tablespoon salt	Cornmeal

In a large bowl, mix the yeast in ¼ cup warm water and let stand a few minutes
until dissolved. Add another 1¼ cups warm water, stir in the salt, and then 3
cups of the flour. Turn out and knead for about 10 minutes, until smooth,
adding more flour as necessary. Place in an unbuttered bowl, cover, and let rise
in a warm place until double in bulk; it will take longer than other bread doughs
because it contains no sugar. Punch down and turn out onto a board. Pull off
pieces of dough slightly larger than a golf ball and turn them, cupping your hands
over and pulling the dough toward the bottom, until you have perfect rounds.
Pinch the seams at the bottoms and place on a cookie sheet, sprinkled with
cornmeal, 2 inches apart. Cover lightly with a towel and let rise again until
doubled. Preheat the oven to 450°F (230°C) about halfway through the final rising.
Brush the risen rolls with cold water, put in the oven, and immediately throw
several ice cubes on the floor of the oven, or put a pan of boiling water there,
or spray the oven quickly with a plant atomizer. If you use the latter system,
repeat twice during the first five minutes of baking. Check after 15 minutes;
when the rolls are browned, they should be done. Cool on racks.

Sesame or Poppy-Seed Rolls. Brush the rolls with an *egg white* beaten with 1
tablespoon cold water and sprinkle liberally with *sesame seeds* or *poppy seeds*.

Hard Whole-Wheat Rolls. Use ½ *cup whole-wheat flour* for white flour to give
these rolls a delicious light wheat flavor.

English Muffins

These are coarse, chewy muffins with fine character. Use two forks
to split them open and eat them toasted with lots of butter and jam.

(15 MUFFINS)

1 cup (¼ L) milk	1 tablespoon shortening
2 teaspoons salt	1 package dry yeast
1 tablespoon sugar	3 cups (420 g) white flour

Bring ½ cup water to a boil, mix it with the milk, salt, sugar, and shortening in
a large bowl, and let cool to lukewarm. Stir the yeast into ¼ cup warm water and
let it stand for 5 minutes to dissolve. Add the dissolved yeast and 2 cups of the
flour to the first mixture and beat vigorously. Cover and let rise in a warm place
until double in bulk. Stir, add the remaining flour, and beat well. Cover, and let
the dough double in bulk once again. Turn out onto a lightly floured board and
pat the dough until it is ½ inch thick. Cut into 3-inch rounds, cover, and let
rise until almost double. Cook on a well-greased, fairly hot griddle or in a skillet
for about 15 minutes on each side, turning muffins and adjusting the heat if they
are getting brown too fast. Cool a little, then split in half and toast.

Potato Biscuits

Old-fashioned potato biscuits are light, moist, and golden. And they do taste good!

(ABOUT 15 BISCUITS)

½ cup (1 dL) hot milk
2 tablespoons shortening
2 tablespoons sugar
½ cup (1 dL) warm mashed
   potatoes

1 teaspoon salt
3¼ cups (450 g) white flour
1 package dry yeast

Mix the hot milk, shortening, sugar, potatoes, salt, and ¼ cup of the flour in a large bowl and let cool to lukewarm. Stir the yeast into ¼ cup warm water and let it stand for 5 minutes to dissolve. Add the dissolved yeast to the first mixture and beat vigorously. Cover and let rise in a warm place until light. Stir, add the remaining 3 cups of flour, and mix well. Cover and let rise again to double in bulk. Turn out onto a lightly floured board. Pat the dough until it is ¼ inch thick and cut into 2-inch rounds. Place the rounds about 1 inch apart on a greased baking sheet, cover, and let rise until almost double. Preheat oven to 425°F (220°C). Bake biscuits for about 15 minutes.

Bread Sticks

Serve these crisp, brown bread sticks with an appetizer or with any kind of soup.

(ABOUT 3 DOZEN 6-INCH STICKS)

1 cup (¼ L) hot milk
4 tablespoons butter
1½ tablespoons sugar
2 teaspoons salt

1 package dry yeast
3 cups (420 g) white flour
1 egg white, lightly beaten
   with 1 tablespoon cold water

Mix the hot milk, butter, sugar, and salt in a large bowl and let cool to lukewarm. Stir the yeast into ¼ cup warm water and let it stand for 5 minutes to dissolve. Add the dissolved yeast and 2 cups of the flour to the first mixture, stir vigorously, and add enough of the remaining flour so that the dough pulls away from the sides of the bowl. Turn out onto a lightly floured board, knead for a minute or two, and let rest for 10 minutes. Resume kneading until smooth and elastic. Put in a buttered bowl, cover, and let rise in a warm place until double in bulk. Punch down and roll out with a rolling pin into a rectangle ½ inch thick. Cut into strips about ½ inch wide and of uniform length. Place 1 inch apart on buttered cookie sheets, cover, and let rise a little. Brush with the egg-white glaze before baking. Preheat oven to 300°F (150° C). Bake bread sticks for 30 minutes or until lightly browned.

Salt Sticks. Brush Bread Sticks with the glaze and sprinkle them with *coarse salt* before baking.

Sesame or Poppy-Seed Sticks. A few minutes before the Bread Sticks have finished baking, remove them from the oven, brush them with some more of the glaze, and roll them in *sesame or poppy seeds*. Return them to the oven and bake 5 minutes more.

Cheese Sticks. Remove the Bread Sticks from the oven a few minutes before they have finished baking, brush them with glaze, and roll them in *freshly grated Parmesan cheese,* seasoned with *salt* and *freshly ground pepper.* Return to the oven and bake 5 minutes more.

Cream Bread Fingers

Slender little golden breads, delicate in shape and flavor.

(12 FINGERS)

½ cup (1 dL) heavy cream,   1 package dry yeast
  heated   1¼ cups (175 g) white flour
1 tablespoon sugar   2 tablespoons milk
½ teaspoon salt

Mix the hot cream, sugar, and salt in a large bowl and let cool to lukewarm. Stir the yeast into ¼ cup warm water and let it stand for 5 minutes to dissolve. Add the dissolved yeast and the flour to the first mixture and beat well. Turn out onto a lightly floured board and, adding a little more flour only if necessary to handle the dough, knead until smooth. Put in a greased bowl, cover, and let rise in a warm place until double in bulk. Roll or pat into a rectangle ¼ inch thick. Cut into strips 1 inch wide and 4 inches long. Cover and let rise until almost double. Brush the tops with milk. Preheat oven to 375°F (190°C). Bake bread fingers for 6 minutes, turn, and bake for another 6 minutes or until tops are golden.

Sweet Rolls

These rolls are made from a dependable, basic sweet dough, good for buns and coffee cakes. The texture is fine, rather dense, and rich. Doughs like this, enriched with eggs, milk, butter, and more sugar than usual, do not rise as rapidly as plainer doughs.

(ABOUT 18 ROLLS)

¾ cup (1¾ dL) warm milk   2 eggs
¼ cup (50 g) sugar   1 package dry yeast
1 teaspoon salt   2½ cups (350 g) white flour
4 tablespoons soft butter

Mix the milk, sugar, salt, butter, and eggs in a large bowl and let cool to lukewarm. Stir the yeast into ¼ cup warm water and let it stand for 5 minutes to dissolve. Add the dissolved yeast to the firet mixture, beat thoroughly, and add 1½ cups of the flour, beating well. Cover and let rise in a warm place for about 1 hour. Add the remaining cup of flour and blend in well, adding more flour if necessary to make the dough firm enough to handle. Knead until smooth and elastic. Put the dough in a buttered bowl, cover, and let rise until almost double in bulk. Punch down, shape into rolls (see p. 474 for directions), and let rise for about 1 hour. Preheat oven to 400°F (205°C). Bake rolls for 15–20 minutes.

Cinnamon Buns. Add *1 tablespoon cinnamon* to the dough in the first step.

Orange Rolls. Use *¾ cup orange juice* instead of milk and add *1 tablespoon grated orange peel.* Shape like Parker House Rolls (p. 474). Dip *orange sections* in sugar and put one in the center of each roll before folding and baking.

Cinnamon Rolls

These rolls rise very high and are mildly sweet with a soft cinnamon flavor.

(ABOUT 16 ROLLS)

1 package dry yeast
4½ cups (630 g) white flour
1 cup (¼ L) lukewarm milk
¾ cup (145 g) granulated sugar
1 teaspoon salt
1 tablespoon cinnamon
2 eggs

2 tablespoons butter
½ cup (1 dL) raisins
Milk
¾ cup (1¾ dL) confectioners' sugar
1 teaspoon vanilla

Stir the yeast into ¼ cup warm water and let it stand for 5 minutes to dissolve. Add the dissolved yeast and 3 cups of the flour to the milk and blend well. Cover and let rise in a warm place until light. Add the granulated sugar, salt, cinnamon, eggs, butter, and ¾ cup of the flour and blend. Turn out onto a lightly floured board and knead gently, slowly adding the remaining ¾ cup of flour until the dough can be easily handled. Knead in the raisins. Pull off pieces of dough the size of medium lemons, roll each about 8 inches long, and wind it into a coil. Arrange on two buttered 9-inch cake pans, cover, and let rise until double in bulk, then brush tops with milk. Preheat oven to 375°F (190°C). Bake rolls for 25 minutes. Mix the confectioners' sugar and vanilla with 4 teaspoons warm water to make a glaze, and spread a thin layer on rolls immediately after removing from the oven.

Sally Lunn Tea Cakes

They say that Sally Lunn lived in Bath, England, and sold this kind of tender, semisweet tea cake—almost weightless with a light yellow crumb, they can also be made as one large cake.

(24 TEA CAKES OR ONE 10-INCH TUBE CAKE)

1 cup (¼ L) hot milk
¼ pound (115 g) butter
⅓ cup (65 g) sugar
1 teaspoon salt

1 package dry yeast
3 eggs
3½ cups (490 g) white flour

Mix the hot milk, butter, sugar, and salt in a large bowl and let cool to lukewarm. Stir the yeast into ¼ cup warm water and let it stand for 5 minutes to dissolve. Add the dissolved yeast and the eggs to the first mixture and beat vigorously. Gradually add the flour. Cover and let rise in a warm place until about double in bulk. Spoon the dough into buttered muffin tins, filling each section about half full, or put it all in a buttered 10-inch tube pan. Preheat oven to 425°F (220°C) for muffins, 350°F (180°C) for cake. Bake muffins for 20 minutes, tube cake for about 50 minutes.

Raised Doughnuts

The temperature of the cooking oil is very important when frying doughnuts: if it is too cool, the doughnuts will absorb it and be greasy; if it is too hot, the doughnuts will burn on the outside or remain uncooked inside. Unless you have had a great deal of experience with deep frying, a frying (candy) thermometer to establish and maintain the proper heat is essential. (See also Old-fashioned Doughnuts, p. 498.)

(ABOUT 24)

1 cup (¼ L) warm milk
1 package dry yeast
1 teaspoon salt
2 tablespoons granulated sugar
3½ cups (490 g) flour
¼ cup (½ dL) melted butter

1 cup (¼ L) light-brown sugar
2 eggs, well beaten
½ teaspoon nutmeg
Vegetable shortening or oil for
    frying
Confectioners' sugar

Put the milk, yeast, salt, granulated sugar, and 2 cups of the flour in a bowl and beat thoroughly. Cover and let rise until double in bulk. Stir down and add the butter, brown sugar, eggs, nutmeg, and an additional 1 cup flour. Beat well, cover, and let rise again until almost double in bulk. Stir down and turn out onto a lightly floured board, kneading in only enough flour so that the dough handles easily. Let rest for 10 minutes, then roll out about ½ inch thick. Cut with a doughnut cutter or a sharp knife into 3-inch rounds, cut out the centers and save these "holes," which can also be fried. Let rise, uncovered, for about 1 hour. Using a heavy pot and a thermometer, heat about 4 inches of shortening or oil to 360°F. Lower the doughnuts into the hot fat, cooking three or four at a time. Turn them when they are brown on one side, and brown the other side. Drain them on paper towels and sprinkle freely with confectioners' sugar.

Crullers (3 dozen). After the dough has risen for the second time, roll it out ⅓ inch thick. Cut in strips 8 inches long and ¾ inch wide. Let rise, uncovered, for about 1 hour. Twist each strip several times and pinch the ends. Fry, drain, and roll in *granulated sugar*.

Jelly Doughnuts (about 15). Cut the dough in 2½-inch rounds. Place heaping teaspoons of *strawberry or raspberry jelly or jam* on half of them, brush the edges with *slightly beaten egg white*, and cover with the other rounds, pressing the edges firmly together. Let rise, uncovered, for about 1 hour. Fry, drain, and dust with confectioners' sugar.

Christmas Stollen

Christmas Stollen are made from a sweet dough, rich in butter and eggs, with lemon rind, almonds, and candied fruit added for festive trimmings.

(TWO 14-INCH STOLLEN)

1 package dry yeast
¾ cup (1¾ dL) warm milk
¼ cup (50 g) granulated sugar

1 teaspoon salt
4 tablespoons soft butter
2 eggs

3 cups (420 g) white flour   ½ cup (1 dL) chopped almonds
1 tablespoon grated lemon rind   ¾ cup (1¾ dL) candied fruit

Glaze
1 cup (¼ L) confectioners' sugar
2 tablespoons lemon juice

Garnish
Candied fruit and nuts

Stir the yeast into ¼ cup warm water and let it stand for 5 minutes to dissolve. Mix the milk, granulated sugar, salt, butter, and eggs in a large mixing bowl. Add the dissolved yeast, beat thoroughly, and add 1½ cups of the flour, beating until well blended. Cover the bowl and let rise in a warm place for about 1 hour. Add enough of the remaining flour so that the dough is easy to handle. Cover and chill in the refrigerator for about 30 minutes. Turn out onto a lightly floured board and knead with the lemon rind, almonds, and candied fruit for a few

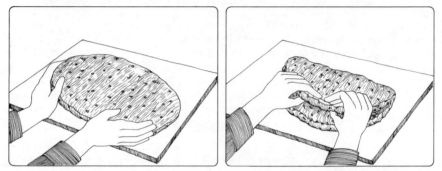

minutes. Pat dough into an oval ¼ inch thick. Fold the dough in half lengthwise bringing the upper half not quite to the edge of the lower half and press down along the edge to secure. Place on buttered cookie sheets, cover, and let double in bulk. Preheat oven to 375°F (190°C). Bake Stollen for 35 minutes. Mix the sugar, lemon juice, and 1–2 tablespoons water and glaze the cake while it is still warm. Decorate with garnish of candied fruit and nuts.

Ruth's Coffee Cake (one 10-inch tube cake). Prepare the dough for Christmas Stollen, omitting the lemon rind, almonds, and candied fruit. Roll it into a long cylinder about 1 inch in diameter. Cut off 1-inch pieces and form them into balls. Dip each ball into *melted butter* and then into a mixture of *cinnamon* and *sugar*, using 1 tablespoon cinnamon to ½ cup sugar. Arrange the balls in two layers in a buttered 10-inch tube pan, sprinkling each layer with *chopped nuts and/or raisins*. Bake in a preheated 350°F (180°C) oven for 50–60 minutes.

Swedish Bread

What could be better than warm Swedish bread with sweet butter to go with freshly ground coffee on a cold Sunday morning? Try shaping the dough into a lovely braid or tea ring to serve when you have guests for brunch.

(2 LOAVES)

½ cup (1 dL) melted butter	1 package dry yeast
⅔ cup (125 g) sugar	1 egg, well beaten
1 teaspoon salt	1 teaspoon almond extract
2¼ cups (5 dL) hot milk	7 cups (980 g) white flour

Mix the butter, sugar, salt, and hot milk in a large bowl and let cool to lukewarm. Stir the yeast into ¼ cup warm water and let it stand for 5 minutes to dissolve. Add the dissolved yeast, egg, almond extract, and 3 cups of the flour to the first mixture and mix vigorously. Add 3 more cups of the flour and mix well. Turn out onto a lightly floured board, knead for a minute or two, and let rest for 10 minutes. Adding the remaining flour only if the dough is too sticky, resume kneading until smooth and elastic. Put the dough in a large, buttered bowl, cover, and let rise in a warm place until double in bulk. Punch down, knead for a minute or two, and shape into two loaves. Place in buttered loaf pans, cover, and let rise until double in bulk once again. Preheat oven to 375°F (190°C). Bake bread for 40–50 minutes. Remove from pans and cool on racks.

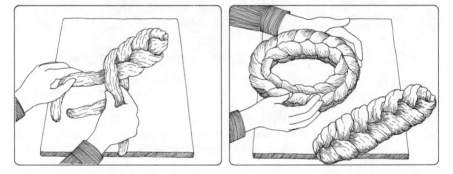

Swedish Braided Bread (two braids). After the dough has risen for the first time, punch it down, knead it for a minute or two and divide it into six equal pieces. Stretch and roll each piece with your hands until you have six long rolls of uniform size. Make two braids with them, pinching the three pieces of dough firmly together when you start the braiding and again when you finish. Leave as is or form each braid into a ring if you wish. Place them on buttered cookie sheets, cover, and let rise to about double in bulk. Brush with *1 egg yolk*, lightly beaten with 1 teaspoon cold water, and sprinkle with *blanched, chopped almonds*. Bake for only 25–30 minutes.

Swedish Tea Ring (one tea ring and one standard loaf). After the dough has risen for the first time, punch it down, knead it for a minute or two, and divide it in half. Roll and shape the first piece with your hands into a long, thin roll. Using a rolling pin and an unfloured board, roll it into a thin rectangle, about 7 × 16 inches; it will stick to the board but may easily be lifted with a knife.

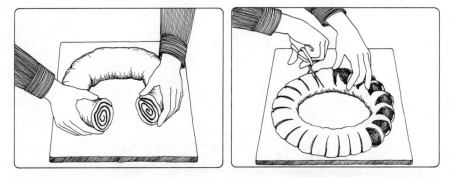

Spread with *melted butter* and sprinkle with *sugar, cinnamon, ¾ cup candied fruit or raisins,* and *½ cup chopped walnuts or almonds.* Starting with the long side, roll like a jelly roll. Trim, if necessary, and join the ends to form a ring. Place on a buttered cookie sheet, make perpendicular cuts, as illustrated, with a scissors, about 1 inch apart and then spread open, so that one side falls flat.Repeat with the other piece of dough, if you wish, or use the remaining dough to make one standard loaf of Swedish Bread. Cover and let rise to almost double in bulk. Bake for 25–30 minutes.

QUICK BREADS

ABOUT QUICK BREADS

Quick breads are made without yeast from batters which require no kneading and do not have to rise before going into the oven. These breads are valued for the ease and speed with which they can be turned out, as well as for their light, cakelike crumb, which is frequently embellished with fruits, nuts, and other seasonings. They rise quickly once they are in the oven, leavened by steam, air, and carbon dioxide gases created by baking powder, baking soda, beaten eggs and egg whites, and other combinations of leavening agents.

Quick breads are apt to crack in baking. There's no way to prevent this; the cracks are simply characteristic of this kind of bread.

Very fresh bread crumbles easily. If you make these quick loaves several hours ahead and let them cool thoroughly, you will find them easier to slice.

LOAF BREADS

Nut Bread

(1 LOAF)

2 cups (280 g) flour	1 egg
½ cup (1 dL) dark-brown sugar	1 cup (¼ L) milk
2 teaspoons baking powder	2 tablespoons melted butter
1 teaspoon salt	½ cup (1 dL) chopped nuts

Preheat the oven to 350°F (180°C). Butter a loaf pan. Mix the flour, brown sugar, baking powder, and salt in a large bowl, add the egg, milk, and butter, and stir until well blended. Add the nuts. Spoon into the pan and bake for 45 minutes. Remove from the pan and cool on a rack.

Quick Whole-Wheat Bread

Brown as a chestnut, moist, and honest in taste.

(1 LOAF)

½ cup (70 g) white flour
1 teaspoon baking powder
1 teaspoon baking soda
1 teaspoon salt
2 cups (280 g) whole-wheat
 flour

¼ cup (½ dL) melted
 shortening
1½ cups (3½ dL) sour milk
 (p. 11)
½ cup (1 dL) molasses

Preheat the oven to 375°F (190°C). Grease a loaf pan. Mix the white flour, baking powder, baking soda, salt, and whole-wheat flour in a large bowl, add the shortening, sour milk, and molasses, and stir until well blended. Spoon into the pan and bake for about 50 minutes. Remove from the pan and cool on a rack.

Winchester Nut Bread

A dark, sweet, moist, and nourishing whole-wheat bread.

(2 LOAVES)

½ cup (1 dL) dark-brown sugar
½ cup (1 dL) molasses
¾ cup (1¾ dL) milk
1 cup (140 g) white flour
2 cups (280 g) whole-wheat
 flour

1 teaspoon salt
2½ teaspoons baking powder
¾ teaspoon baking soda
1 cup (¼ L) coarsely chopped
 walnuts

Preheat the oven to 275°F (135°C). Grease two loaf pans. Put the brown sugar in a large bowl, add ¾ cup cold water, and stir until the sugar dissolves. Stir in the molasses and milk. Add the white flour, whole-wheat flour, salt, baking powder, and baking soda, and mix well. Stir in the walnuts. Spoon into the pans and bake for 2 hours. Remove from the pans and cool on racks.

Honey Bread

Honey bread has a fine, silky texture and the sweet, mild flavor of spice. Very long beating is the secret of its tender grain.

(1 LOAF)

2 cups (280 g) white flour
1 teaspoon baking powder
1 teaspoon baking soda
1 teaspoon salt
½ teaspoon cinnamon

1 teaspoon ginger
½ cup (1 dL) honey
1 egg, slightly beaten
1 cup (¼ L) milk

Preheat the oven to 350°F (180°C). Butter a loaf pan. Put the flour, baking powder, baking soda, salt, cinnamon, and ginger in a large bowl, add the honey, egg, and milk, and beat thoroughly with an electric beater for about 20 minutes. Spoon into the pan and bake for about 50 minutes. Remove from the pan and cool on a rack.

Date Nut Bread

Date nut bread is moist and sweet, and it keeps very well.

(1 LOAF)

1 cup (¼ L) chopped dates	1 teaspoon baking soda
½ cup (100 g) sugar	1¾ cups (245 g) flour
4 tablespoons butter	½ teaspoon salt
1 egg, well beaten	½ cup (1 dL) walnuts, chopped

Preheat the oven to 350°F (180°C). Butter a loaf pan. Bring ¾ cup water to a boil, mix it with the dates, sugar, and butter in a large bowl, and let cool to lukewarm. Stir in the egg, baking soda, flour, salt, and nuts, and blend well. Spoon into the pan and bake for about 50 minutes. Remove from the pan and cool on a rack.

Apricot Almond Bread

Brown and crusty on the outside, with bits of tart apricot and white almonds scattered throughout.

(1 LOAF)

1½ cups (3½ dL) coarsely chopped dried apricots	1 cup (140 g) whole-wheat flour
2 tablespoons butter	1 teaspoon baking soda
1 cup (200 g) sugar	1 cup (¼ L) almonds, chopped
1 teaspoon salt	1 egg, well beaten
1½ cups (210 g) white flour	1 teaspoon orange extract

Preheat the oven to 350°F (180°C). Butter a loaf pan. Put the apricots in a bowl and pour 1½ cups boiling water over them. Add the butter, sugar, and salt and let cool to lukewarm. Stir in remaining ingredients and mix very well. Spoon into the pan and bake for 1¼ hours. Remove from the pan and cool on a rack.

Orange Peel Bread

The flavor of orange is just right with the moist, slightly coarse texture of this outstanding bread.

(2 LOAVES)

5–6 oranges	2 cups (½ L) milk
1½ cups (300 g) sugar	4 cups (560 g) white flour
1 tablespoon butter	4 teaspoons baking powder
1 egg	½ teaspoon salt

Preheat the oven to 325°F (165°C). Butter two loaf pans. Peel outer skins of the oranges with a vegetable parer until you have enough to fill 1 cup loosely. Chop into small pieces and put in a small pan with just enough water to cover. Cook over medium-low heat, adding more water if necessary, for 15–20 minutes or until tender. Add 1 cup of the sugar and boil about 10 minutes, until thick and syrupy. Cream the butter with the remaining sugar, and add the egg and milk. Mix the flour, baking powder, and salt, and add to the batter, beating well. Add the cooked orange peel and syrup. Put in the pans and bake for 40–50 minutes. Remove from the pans and cool on racks.

Pumpkin Bread

(1 LOAF)

1½ cups (210 g) flour
½ teaspoon salt
1 cup (200 g) sugar
1 teaspoon baking soda
1 cup (¼ L) pumpkin purée
½ cup (1 dL) vegetable oil

2 eggs, beaten
¼ teaspoon nutmeg
¼ teaspoon cinnamon
¼ teaspoon allspice
½ cup (1 dL) chopped nuts

Preheat the oven to 350°F (180°C). Sift together the flour, salt, sugar, and baking soda. Mix the pumpkin, oil, eggs, ¼ cup water, and spices together, then combine with the dry ingredients, but do not mix too thoroughly. Stir in the nuts. Pour into a well-buttered 9 × 5 × 3-inch loaf pan. Bake 50–60 minutes until a straw comes out clean. Turn out of the pan and cool on a rack.

Cranberry Nut Bread

(1 LOAF)

1 orange
2 tablespoons butter
1 egg
1 cup (200 g) sugar
1 cup (¼ L) cranberries, chopped

½ cup (1 dL) chopped walnuts
2 cups (280 g) white flour
½ teaspoon salt
1½ teaspoons baking powder
½ teaspoon baking soda

Preheat the oven to 325°F (165°C). Butter a loaf pan. Grate the rind of the orange, and squeeze out all the juice into a measuring cup and add enough boiling water to make ¾ cup. Add the orange rind and the butter and stir to melt the butter. Beat the egg in another bowl and gradually add the sugar, beating well. Add remaining ingredients and orange mixture, and blend well. Spoon into the pan and bake for 1 hour. Remove from the pan and cool on a rack.

Peanut Butter Bread

Tan, moist, and close-textured, peanut butter bread is slightly sweet with a distinct peanut flavor. If you use "chunky" peanut butter, there will be bits of peanut in the bread.

(1 LOAF)

2 cups (280 g) white flour
⅓ cup (65 g) sugar
2 teaspoons baking powder
¼ teaspoon salt

¾ cup (1¾ dL) peanut butter
1 cup (¼ L) milk
1 egg, well beaten

Preheat the oven to 350°F (180°C). Grease a loaf pan. Put the flour, sugar, baking powder, and salt in a large bowl. Add the peanut butter, milk, and egg, and mix until well blended. Spoon into the pan and bake for about 50 minutes. Remove from the pan and cool on a rack.

Banana Nut Bread

This is pure and simple banana bread, heavy, moist, and dark.

(1 LOAF)

3 ripe bananas, well mashed
2 eggs, well beaten
2 cups (280 g) flour
¾ cup (145 g) sugar

1 teaspoon salt
1 teaspoon baking soda
½ cup (1 dL) coarsely chopped
    walnuts

Preheat the oven to 350°F (180°C). Grease a loaf pan. Mix the bananas and eggs together in a large bowl. Stir in the flour, sugar, salt, and baking soda. Add the walnuts and blend. Put the batter in the pan and bake for 1 hour. Remove from the pan to a rack. Serve still warm or cooled, as you like it.

Prune Bread

A dark and nourishing breakfast bread, good with spicy sausages and coffee.

(2 LOAVES)

1 cup (200 g) sugar
1 cup (140 g) whole-wheat
    flour
2 cups (280 g) white flour
1 teaspoon baking soda
¼ teaspoon baking powder
½ teaspoon salt

2 tablespoons melted butter
1 egg, well beaten
1 cup (¼ L) cooked, pitted
    prunes, in small pieces
½ cup (1 dL) prune juice
1 cup (¼ L) sour milk or
    buttermilk

Preheat the oven to 350°F (180°C). Butter two loaf pans. Put the sugar, whole-wheat flour, white flour, baking soda, baking powder, and salt in a large bowl. Stir in remaining ingredients and mix very well. Spoon into the pans and bake for 1 hour. Remove from the pans and cool on racks.

MUFFINS, TOAST, BREAKFAST BREADS, AND TEA BREADS

Basic Muffins

What could be nicer than warm muffins wrapped in a napkin on the morning breakfast table? And they are so quick and easy to make, particularly since the ingredients are only lightly mixed, not beaten smooth.

(12 MUFFINS)

2 cups (280 g) white flour
3 teaspoons baking powder
½ teaspoon salt
2 tablespoons sugar

1 egg, slightly beaten
1 cup (¼ L) milk
¼ cup (60 g) melted butter

Preheat the oven to 375°F (190°C). Butter muffin pans. Mix the flour, baking powder, salt, and sugar in a large bowl. Add the egg, milk, and butter, stirring only enough to dampen the flour; the batter should *not* be smooth. Spoon into the muffin pans, filling each cup about two-thirds full. Bake for about 20–25 minutes.

Blueberry Muffins. Use *½ cup sugar.* Reserve ¼ cup of the flour, sprinkle it over *1 cup blueberries,* and stir them into the batter last.

Pecan Muffins. Use *¼ cup sugar.* Add *½ cup chopped pecans* to the batter. After filling the cups, sprinkle with *sugar, cinnamon,* and more *chopped nuts.*

Whole-Wheat Muffins. Use *¾ cup whole-wheat flour* and *1 cup white flour.*

Date or Raisin Muffins. Add *½ cup chopped pitted dates* or *⅓ cup raisins* to the batter.

Bacon Muffins. Add *3 strips bacon, fried crisp and crumbled,* to the batter.

Oatmeal Muffins

(12 MUFFINS)

1½ cups (210 g) flour	½ cup (1 dL) milk
2 tablespoons sugar	1 egg, well beaten
4 teaspoons baking powder	2 tablespoons butter, melted
½ teaspoon salt	1 cup (¼ L) cooked oatmeal

Preheat the oven to 400°F (205°C). Butter the muffin pan. Combine flour, sugar, baking powder, and salt. In a separate bowl stir the milk, egg, and butter into the oatmeal. Stir until well blended. Combine the two mixtures and mix well. Spoon each muffin cup two-thirds full of batter. Bake for about 20 minutes, or until a broomstraw comes out dry when inserted in center.

Bran Muffins

Split, toasted, and lightly spread with butter, these are earthy and good.

(12 MUFFINS)

1 egg, slightly beaten	1 cup (140 g) white flour
1 cup (¼ L) milk	3 teaspoons baking powder
2 tablespoons melted butter	¼ cup (50 g) sugar
1 cup (¼ L) bran	½ teaspoon salt

Preheat the oven to 375°F (190°C). Butter muffin pans. Put the egg, milk, butter, and bran in a mixing bowl and let stand for 10 minutes. Add the flour, baking powder, sugar, and salt and stir just enough to dampen. Spoon into the muffin pans, filling each cup about two-thirds full. Bake for about 20 minutes.

Berkshire Muffins

A bit of leftover rice and some cornmeal give these muffins a rustic texture and taste.

Berkshire Muffins (continued)

(12 SMALL MUFFINS)

⅔ cup (1½ dL) milk	3 teaspoons baking powder
½ cup (1 dL) cornmeal	½ teaspoon salt
½ cup (1 dL) cooked rice	1 egg yolk, well beaten
½ cup (70 g) white flour	1 tablespoon melted butter
2 tablespoons sugar	1 egg white, beaten stiff

Preheat the oven to 375°F (190°C). Butter muffin pans. Scald the milk, slowly pour it on the cornmeal, and let stand 5 minutes. Stir in the rice, flour, sugar, baking powder, and salt. Add the egg yolk and butter, and blend well. Gently fold in the egg white and spoon into the muffin pans, filling each cup about one-half full. Bake for about 20 minutes.

Baking Powder Biscuits

Light-gold and crusty outside, moist and fine-textured inside.

(16 BISCUITS)

2 cups (280 g) flour	1 tablespoon sugar
½ teaspoon salt	½ cup (1 dL) vegetable
4 teaspoons baking powder	shortening
½ teaspoon cream of tartar	⅔ cup (1½ dL) milk

Preheat the oven to 425°F (220°C). Grease two 8-inch cake pans. Put the flour, salt, baking powder, cream of tartar, and sugar in a bowl. Cut the shortening into the flour with two knives or a pastry blender until the mixture resembles coarse meal. Add the milk all at once and stir just until the dough forms a ball around the fork. Turn the dough onto a lightly floured board and knead 14 times. Pat until ½ inch thick. Cut into rounds with a 2-inch cookie cutter. Place touching each other in the cake pans and bake for 15–20 minutes.

Crusty Baking Powder Biscuits. Roll biscuits to ¼ inch thick and place 1 inch apart. Bake in a 450°F (230°C) oven for 12 minutes. This will yield almost twice as many biscuits.

Buttermilk Biscuits. Use *⅔ cup buttermilk* instead of sweet milk and *½ teaspoon baking soda,* cutting the amount of baking powder in half—i.e., 2 teaspoons.

Cheese Biscuits. Add *½ cup grated sharp Cheddar cheese* to the dry ingredients.

Drop Biscuits. Add an additional *⅓ cup milk* and drop by teaspoonfuls onto a buttered baking sheet.

Hominy Gems

To make these old-fashioned gems, use the cereal hominy that comes in a box, also known as grits.

(12 MUFFINS)

¼ cup (½ dL) hominy	3 tablespoons sugar
½ teaspoon salt	3 tablespoons butter
1 cup (¼ L) scalded milk	3 teaspoons baking powder
1 cup (¼ L) cornmeal	2 eggs, separated

Preheat the oven to 400°F (205°C). Line a 12-cup muffin pan with cupcake papers or grease each cup. Put the hominy and salt in a bowl and pour ½ cup boiling water over. Let stand for a few minutes, until the hominy has absorbed the water. In a separate bowl, thoroughly mix the scalded milk, cornmeal, sugar, and butter. Combine the two mixtures, stir, and cool slightly. Add the baking powder. Beat the egg yolks and add to the mixture. Beat the egg whites until stiff but not dry. Stir a third of the whites into the batter and gently fold in the rest. Spoon the batter into the muffin cups. Bake 15–20 minutes, or until a broomstraw comes out dry when inserted in the center of a muffin.

French or German Toast

French toast is always better if your bread is a little dry—a day or two old, or leave the slices out overnight. Serve these crusty slices with bacon and warmed maple syrup, jam, or marmalade, or sprinkle them with a mixture of cinnamon and sugar.

(SIX SLICES)

3 eggs, slightly beaten
½ teaspoon salt
2 tablespoons sugar

1 cup (¼ L) milk
6 slices bread

Mix the eggs, salt, sugar, and milk in a shallow dish or pie pan. Soak the bread in the mixture until soft, turning once. Cook on a hot, well-greased skillet or frying pan, turning to brown each side.

Cinnamon Toast

Bread for toasting
Butter

Sugar
Cinnamon

Toast the bread. Butter one side generously and sprinkle it with a mixture of sugar and cinnamon, using 1 part cinnamon to 3 parts sugar. Toast under the broiler, sugared side up, or place in a hot oven until sugar melts.

Milk Toast

The image of Caspar Milquetoast—the "Timid Soul"—may have contributed to the fading reputation of this bland dish. Today it is mainly a curiosity, although sometimes comforting to the ill or convalescent.

(TWO SERVINGS)

Butter
4 slices white or wheat toast
2 cups (½ L) milk

¼ cup (½ dL) raisins
¼ teaspoon salt

Butter the toast generously and place it in two soupbowls. Heat the milk with the raisins and salt, and simmer for a minute or two so that the raisins plump up. Pour half the milk mixture over each serving.

Croutons

For soups and salads—a good way to use stale or slightly stale bread.

Sautéed Croutons. Cut slices of *bread* in even cubes, removing the crusts. Sauté in hot *butter*, turning to brown all sides. Drain on paper towels.

Baked Croutons. Lightly *butter* slices of *bread* on both sides, then cut in cubes, removing the crusts. Bake on a cookie sheet in a preheated 350°F (180°C) oven, turning a few times until evenly brown.

Garlic or Herb Croutons. Add a *minced clove garlic* or some *minced fresh herbs* to the butter when you sauté or butter the bread.

Popovers

Forget what you've read elsewhere. The secret in making good popovers is to start them in a cold oven.

(ABOUT 10 POPOVERS)

2 eggs
1 cup (¼ L) milk
1 tablespoon melted butter

1 cup (140 g) white flour
¼ teaspoon salt

Put all ingredients in a large bowl and mix thoroughly, without overbeating. Half-fill buttered muffin tins or custard cups. Put them in a cold oven and set the heat for 450°F (230°C). Bake for 15 minutes, then reduce heat to 350°F (180°C) and bake for another 15 to 20 minutes. Test one to be sure it's done by removing it from the pan: it should be crisp outside and moist and tender inside.

Whole-Wheat Popovers. Use ⅔ *cup whole-wheat flour* and ⅓ *cup white flour* instead of all white flour. (Whole-wheat popovers will not rise as high as regular popovers.)

Yorkshire Pudding

First cousin to the popover, this crisp, golden-brown puff is a glorious accompaniment to Roast Beef (p. 154). Remove the roast from the oven 25 minutes before it is to be served. It's essential that it be cooked in the roast beef fat and drippings, which flavor it so beautifully. The Yorkshire pudding will cook while the roast "rests" and can be brought to the table after you have carved the meat.

(SERVES SIX)

4 tablespoons roast beef pan
  drippings
2 eggs

1 cup (¼ L) milk
1 cup (140 g) flour
¾ teaspoon salt

Turn the oven up to 450°F (230°C) and pour the pan drippings into a 9 × 9-inch pan or an 11 × 7-inch pan. Put the pan in the oven to keep sizzling while you prepare the batter. Combine the eggs, milk, flour, and salt and beat until well blended. Pour batter into the prepared pan and bake 25–30 minutes. Serve piping hot from the baking pan, a generous square with each helping of roast beef.

Corn Bread

Sturdy, solid, slightly dry—a direct legacy from our American past.

(SIXTEEN 2-INCH SQUARES)

¾ cup (1¾ dL) yellow
  cornmeal
1 cup (140 g) flour
⅓ cup (65 g) sugar
3 teaspoons baking powder

½ teaspoon salt
1 cup (¼ L) milk
1 egg, well beaten
2 tablespoons melted
  shortening or bacon fat

Preheat the oven to 425°F (220°C). Grease an 8-inch square cake pan. Mix the cornmeal, flour, sugar, baking powder, and salt in a large bowl. Add the milk, egg, and shortening or bacon fat, and blend well. Spoon into the pan and bake for about 20 minutes. Cool and cut in squares.

Corn Muffins. Thoroughly grease a muffin pan and pour the batter into the cups about three-quarters full. You should have 12 muffins. For a richer version use the recipe for Rich Corn Cake that follows.

Rich Corn Cake

(SIXTEEN 2¼-INCH SQUARES)

1 cup (¼ L) yellow cornmeal
1 cup (140 g) flour
4 tablespoons sugar
1 teaspoon baking soda
2 teaspoons cream of tartar

¾ teaspoon salt
1 cup (¼ L) sour cream
¼ cup (½ dL) milk
2 eggs, well beaten
4 tablespoons butter, melted

Preheat the oven to 425°F (220°C). Butter a 9 × 9 × 2–inch pan. Combine the cornmeal, flour, sugar, baking soda, cream of tartar, and salt and mix well. Quickly add the sour cream, milk, eggs, and butter. Stir just to mix. Spoon into pan and bake for about 20 minutes. Cool and cut in squares.

Cornsticks. Heavily grease cornstick pans and place them in the oven empty to get them smoking hot. Then fill them two-thirds full of corn cake batter. Bake for about 15 minutes or until a broomstraw inserted comes out dry.

White Corn Cake

The soft, coarse crumb of this corn cake is fine with fried chicken and pan gravy.

(SIXTEEN 1-INCH SQUARES)

4 tablespoons butter
½ cup (100 g) sugar
1¼ cups (3 dL) white cornmeal
1¼ cups (175 g) flour

4 teaspoons baking powder
1 teaspoon salt
1⅓ cups (3¼ dL) milk
3 egg whites, beaten stiff

Preheat the oven to 425°F (220°C). Butter an 8-inch square cake pan. Cream the butter in a mixing bowl, slowly add the sugar, and beat until light. Mix together the cornmeal, flour, baking powder, and salt. Add the milk to the butter mixture, alternating it with the mixed dry ingredients, and beat thoroughly. Stir a third of the beaten egg whites into the batter, then fold in the remaining whites. Spoon into the pan and bake for about 30 minutes. Cool and cut in squares.

Littleton Spider Corn Cakes

This is a very old recipe from New Hampshire. The corn cakes have a more robust corn taste but are still moist and light. Originally the corn cake was undoubtedly cooked on a spider or skillet over the fire, but the oven gives more even baking.

(16 SQUARES)

1⅓ cups (3¼ dL) cornmeal
⅓ cup (50 g) flour
1 teaspoon baking soda
1 cup (¼ L) sour milk (p. 11)
2 eggs, well beaten

2 cups (½ L) regular milk
¼ cup (50 g) sugar
½ teaspoon salt
1½ tablespoons butter

Preheat the oven to 350°F (180°C). Mix the cornmeal, flour, and baking soda in a large bowl. Stir in the sour milk, eggs, 1 cup of the regular milk, sugar, and salt, and blend well. Melt the butter in a 9-inch square pan and film the sides. Add the mixture to the pan and pour the remaining cup of milk over the top. Bake for about 45 minutes. Cool and cut in squares.

Irish Bread

A large round biscuit with a brown, flaky crust and the flavor of raisins and caraway seeds. Serve with lots of butter.

(9-INCH ROUND LOAF)

2 cups (280 g) white flour
4 teaspoons baking powder
½ teaspoon salt
1 tablespoon sugar
3 tablespoons vegetable
    shortening

⅔ cup (1½ dL) milk
½ cup (1 dL) raisins
1 tablespoon caraway seeds

Preheat the oven to 375°F (190°C). Grease a 9-inch round cake pan. Put the flour, baking powder, salt, and sugar in a large bowl. Work in the shortening with a pastry blender, then quickly stir the milk into the dough. Add the raisins and caraway seeds, stirring just enough to distribute them evenly. Turn out onto a lightly floured board and knead about 20 times. Put the dough in the pan and bake for 20–30 minutes. Cut into wedges to serve.

Boston Brown Bread

This bread is traditionally served with baked beans. Use a 1-pound coffee tin if you do not have a pudding mold, and cover it with aluminum foil tied tight with string.

(10 OR MORE SLICES)

½ cup (70 g) rye flour
½ cup (1 dL) cornmeal
½ cup (70 g) whole-wheat
    flour

1 teaspoon baking soda
½ teaspoon salt
⅓ cup (¾ dL) molasses
1 cup (¼ L) sour milk (p. 11)

Mix the rye flour, cornmeal, whole-wheat flour, baking soda, and salt in a large bowl. Stir in the molasses and milk and blend well. Butter a 1-quart pudding mold or a 1-pound coffee tin and fill no more than two-thirds full. Cover tightly and place in a deep kettle. Add boiling water halfway up the mold. Cover the kettle and steam over moderate heat for 2 hours, replacing the water if necessary. Remove from mold. Cut slices with a string while hot by drawing the string around the bread, crossing, and pulling the ends. Or reheat, if necessary, in a 300°F (150°C) oven.

Raisin Brown Bread. Add *½ cup seedless raisins* to the batter.

Cream Scones

Wedge-shaped with lightly browned sides and tops, cream scones and English tea are traditional partners. Serve with a plump mound of butter and some marmalade or jam.

(12 WEDGES)

2 cups (280 g) flour	4 tablespoons butter
2 teaspoons baking powder	2 eggs, well beaten
1 tablespoon sugar	½ cup (1 dL) cream
½ teaspoon salt	

Preheat the oven to 425°F (220°C). Lightly butter a cookie sheet. Mix the flour, baking powder, sugar, and salt in a large bowl. Work in the butter with your fingers or a pastry blender until the mixture resembles coarse meal. Add the eggs and cream and stir until blended. Turn out onto a lightly floured board and knead for about a minute. Pat or roll the dough about ¾ inch thick and cut into wedges. Place on the cookie sheet and bake for about 15 minutes.

Quick Coffee Cake

Simple to make, good to eat.

(8-INCH SQUARE CAKE)

1 cup (200 g) sugar	1 egg, slightly beaten
1¾ cups (245 g) white flour	½ cup (1 dL) milk
2 teaspoons baking powder	1 tablespoon sugar mixed with
4 tablespoons butter	1½ teaspoons cinnamon

Preheat the oven to 375°F (190°C). Butter an 8-inch square cake pan. Mix the 1 cup sugar, the flour, and the baking powder in a large bowl. Work in the butter with your fingers or a pastry blender until the mixture resembles coarse meal. Add the egg and milk and blend. Spoon into the pan. Sprinkle the sugar-cinnamon mixture evenly over the top. Bake for 20 minutes.

GRIDDLECAKES, WAFFLES, AND DOUGHNUTS

Griddlecakes

The amount of milk you use will determine how thick these griddlecakes or pancakes are. Start with the smaller amount suggested and add more if the batter seems too thick. Try to have the milk at room temperature before mixing and take care not to overbeat: a few lumps in the batter will do no harm. You can make lighter, fluffier griddlecakes by separating the egg, beating the white, and folding it in last. Serve with maple syrup or honey.

(16 GRIDDLECAKES)

½–¾ cup (1–1¾ dL) milk
2 tablespoons melted butter
1 egg
1 cup (140 g) white flour

2 teaspoons baking powder
2 tablespoons sugar
½ teaspoon salt

Beat the milk, butter, and egg lightly in a mixing bowl. Mix the flour, baking powder, sugar, and salt and add them all at once to the first mixture, stirring just enough to dampen the flour. Lightly butter or grease a griddle or frying pan and set over moderate heat until a few drops of cold water sprinkled on the pan form rapidly moving globules. If you wish small pancakes, drop about 2 tablespoons of the batter onto the pan, or pour about ¼ cup from a measuring cup if larger pancakes are desired. Bake on the griddle until the cakes are full of bubbles on the top and the undersides are lightly browned. Turn with a spatula and brown the other sides. Place finished griddlecakes on a warm plate in a 200°F (95°C) oven until you have enough to begin serving.

Buttermilk Griddlecakes. Use *buttermilk, sour milk, or yogurt* instead of milk and substitute ½ *teaspoon baking soda* for the 2 teaspoons baking powder.

Whole-Wheat Griddlecakes. Use ⅓ *cup whole-wheat flour* and ⅔ *cup white flour*. If you wish, sweeten the batter with *2 tablespoons molasses or honey* instead of sugar.

Oatmeal Griddlecakes. Heat the ½ cup of milk, stir in ½ *cup quick-cooking oatmeal*, and let stand for 10 minutes. Add the remaining ingredients, reducing the flour to 2 tablespoons.

Buckwheat Cakes. Use ½ *cup buckwheat flour* and ½ *cup white flour*.

Apple Griddlecakes. Peel *1 tart, juicy apple*, cut it in thin slices, and stir it in.

Blueberry Griddlecakes. Add ½ *cup blueberries*. If you use canned blueberries, strain them before adding.

Rice Griddlecakes

This is a good way to use cooked rice. The yellow, rice-flecked griddlecakes can be made sweet with syrup or cinnamon-sugar, or spread with butter and served with meat or fish.

(ABOUT 18 GRIDDLECAKES)

1 cup (¼ L) milk
1 cup (¼ L) warm cooked rice
¼ teaspoon salt

2 eggs, separated
1 tablespoon melted butter
1 cup (140 g) white flour

Mix the milk, rice, and salt in a large bowl. Beat the egg yolks and add them, then stir in the butter and flour. Beat the egg whites until stiff, and gently fold them in. Drop by large spoonfuls onto a moderately hot, buttered griddle or frying pan. Turn with a spatula when the cakes are full of bubbles, and bake on the other side until lightly browned. Keep warm in a 200°F (95°C) oven until you have enough to serve.

Cottage Cheese Griddlecakes

Turn these tender pancakes gently, and let them cook a little longer than you would a traditional pancake.

(12 GRIDDLECAKES)

1 cup (¼ L) cottage cheese
3 eggs
2 tablespoons melted butter

¼ cup (35 g) white flour
¼ teaspoon salt

Dry the cottage cheese in a sieve, pressing it down firmly and letting it stand and drip for an hour or so. Beat the eggs well in a mixing bowl. Add the cottage cheese, butter, flour, and salt, and mix only enough to blend. Drop by large spoonfuls onto a buttered, moderately hot griddle or frying pan. Turn gently with a spatula when lightly browned on the underside and bake on the other side until light brown. Keep warm in a 200°F (95°C) oven until you have enough to serve.

Crêpes or French Pancakes

This crêpe recipe first appeared in the *Fannie Farmer Cook Book* in 1930, although the thin French pancakes that it produces seem always to have had a place in American cookery. Simple to make and extraordinarily versatile, they are good plain, stuffed and rolled, or sweetened. Like a velvet cape wrapped around a simple dress, they transform good leftovers (see p. 295 for recipes for savory fillings and p. 614 for sweet).

(ABOUT TWELVE 7-INCH PANCAKES OR SIXTEEN 5-INCH PANCAKES)

2 eggs
1 cup (¼ L) milk
½ teaspoon salt

1 cup (140 g) flour
2 tablespoons melted butter

Beat the eggs well, then beat in the milk, salt, flour, and butter. (Or mix all the ingredients in a blender until smooth.) Cover and let stand for at least 30 minutes. Heat a 7-inch or 5-inch skillet or crêpe pan until moderately hot, then film it with butter or shortening, using a brush or a folded paper towel. Using a ladle or small cup, pour in several tablespoons of batter, then quickly tilt the

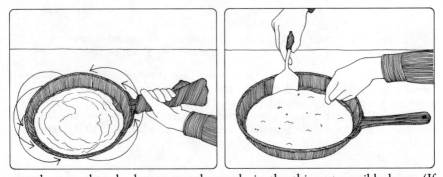

pan about so that the batter spreads evenly in the thinnest possible layer. (If
there is too much batter in the pan, pour it back into the bowl of batter and use
less for the next pancake.) Cook for a few more minutes, until the bottom is
lightly browned and the edges lift easily from the pan. The pancake should then
slide loosely about in the pan. Turn it with a spatula or by catching an edge with
your fingers and flipping it over. Cook the second side for a few minutes; it will
brown in spots, not as evenly as the first side, but it doesn't matter because this
side should be used inside when the crêpes are rolled. Remove to a plate and film
the pan again lightly with butter or shortening before cooking the next pancake.
If the batter seems to be getting too thick as you get toward the end of it, add
a little milk. Crêpes freeze very well simply stacked and wrapped in foil or plastic
with the edges tightly sealed. Defrost at room temperature before separating them.

Cheese Filling

(ENOUGH FOR TWELVE 7-INCH PANCAKES OR SIXTEEN 5-INCH PANCAKES)

Make 2 cups White Sauce (p. 265). Stir in 1½ cups grated Swiss or Cheddar cheese
and heat until melted. Spoon about 4 tablespoons of filling onto the bottom third
of each pancake; the mixture will be enough to fill the number of pancakes the
preceding recipe yields. Roll up the pancakes and arrange side by side in a shallow,
buttered baking dish. Sprinkle with ½ cup grated cheese. Heat in the upper part
of a preheated 350°F (180°C) oven until lightly browned. Or heat thoroughly
and then brown quickly under the broiler.

Old-fashioned Doughnuts

Easier to make and more cakelike than yeast-leavened doughnuts
(p. 480), these doughnuts have a fine, creamy crumb. The temperature
of the cooking oil is crucial, so use a frying (candy) thermometer.

(ABOUT 18 DOUGHNUTS)

½ cup (1 dL) milk
½ cup (100 g) sugar
2 teaspoons baking powder
¼ teaspoon nutmeg
½ teaspoon salt
1 egg, beaten
1 tablespoon melted butter

About 1¾ cups (245 g) white
   flour
Vegetable shortening or oil for
   frying
Confectioners' or granulated
   sugar for dusting

Mix the milk, sugar, baking powder, nutmeg, salt, egg, and butter in a large bowl. Add the flour gradually, using just enough so that the dough is firm enough to handle yet as soft as possible. Cover the dough and chill for about 1 hour. Turn out onto a lightly floured board and knead for a few minutes. Roll out about ½ inch thick. Cut with a doughnut cutter or sharp knife into 3-inch rounds, cutting out and saving the centers (which can also be fried). Place on a lightly floured piece of wax paper and let rest for about 5 minutes. Using a heavy pan and a thermometer, heat about 4 inches of shortening or oil to 360°F. Fry three or four doughnuts at a time, turning them with a fork or tongs when one side is browned and continuing to fry until brown all over. Drain on paper towels and dust with sugar.

Crullers (three dozen). Prepare the batter for Doughnuts. Roll it out ⅓ inch thick. Cut it in strips 8 inches long and ¾ inch wide. Let rest for 10 minutes, then twist each strip several times and pinch the ends. Fry, drain, and roll in sugar.

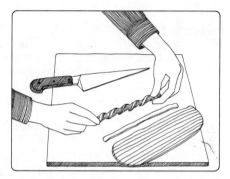

Chocolate Doughnuts. Mix ½ *cup unsweetened cocoa* with the flour. Dust the drained doughnuts with sugar or spread with *Creamy Chocolate Frosting* (p. 536).

Waffles

Many automatic waffle irons have thermostats that indicate when to add the batter. To test one that doesn't, put 1 teaspoon of water inside, close it, and turn it on; when the steaming stops, the iron is ready for the batter. Modern waffle irons do not need greasing. If the first waffle sticks, as it is often inclined to do, bake it a little longer and expect no problem with the others. Remember that a thin batter makes tender waffles. Serve them with melted butter and warmed maple syrup.

(8 WAFFLES)

2 eggs, well beaten
1 cup (¼ L) milk
3 tablespoons salad oil
1½ cups (215 g) flour

3 teaspoons baking powder
2 teaspoons sugar
½ teaspoon salt

Mix the eggs, milk, and oil in a large bowl or pitcher. Stir in the flour, baking powder, sugar, and salt and mix until blended. Heat the waffle iron, brush it with melted shortening or oil if necessary, pour in enough batter to just fill. Close and bake until the steaming stops and the waffles are crisp, tender, and brown.

Special Waffles

This method makes waffles extra-light.

(6 STANDARD-SIZE WAFFLES)

2 cups (280 g) flour
3 teaspoons baking powder
½ teaspoon salt
3 eggs, separated

1¾ cups (4 dL) milk
4 tablespoons butter, melted
3 tablespoons sugar

Combine the flour, baking powder, and salt in a bowl. In a separate bowl beat the egg yolks well, and add the milk and butter. Combine the flour and yolk mixture and beat until smooth. Beat the egg whites until stiff, but not dry. Slowly add the sugar, beating constantly. Mix a third of the beaten whites gently into the batter, then fold in the remaining whites very carefully. Spread ½ cup of waffle batter in the hot waffle iron. Bake until golden.

Cornmeal Waffles

(8 WAFFLES)

1¾ cups (245 g) white flour
1 cup (¼ L) yellow cornmeal
2½ teaspoons baking powder
½ teaspoon baking soda
1 teaspoon salt

3 eggs, separated
2½ cups (6 dL) buttermilk
4 tablespoons butter, melted
3 tablespoons sugar

Mix well together the flour, cornmeal, baking powder, baking soda, and salt. In a separate bowl, beat the egg yolks. Add the buttermilk and butter, and stir to blend. Combine with the flour mixture and mix well. Beat the egg whites until stiff but not dry, and slowly add the sugar, beating until it is absorbed. Stir a third of the whites into the flour mixture and gently fold the remaining whites in. Spoon ½ cup of waffle batter in a greased hot waffle iron. Bake until golden.

CAKES

ABOUT CAKEMAKING

Baking is not any more difficult than other kinds of cooking, but it *is* very different. That is why it sometimes seems a bit intimidating, even to those with lots of kitchen experience. When you're making a cake, you can't rely merely on good taste, instinct, and ingenuity, which mean so much in other kinds of cooking. Baking requires skill and accuracy: there are special techniques, like folding and whipping, to master, and there are basic rules of chemistry to obey. It is important to follow a recipe exactly, to measure accurately, and to use a well-regulated oven and properly prepared pans of the right size.

Once you accept these facts, however, you'll find that it does not take long to acquire a feeling for baking procedures and a respect for the wondrous process by which butter, sugar, eggs, flour, and a few other simple ingredients are transformed into the sweet, light, tempting array of confections that we call "cake." Using good, well-tested recipes like the ones in this chapter, you'll find that it's easy to make perfect cakes—cakes that are light, fine, and tender with an even-textured, slightly moist crumb. And your feeling of pride will be heightened by the pleasure that comes from knowing that your cakes are made with fresh, wholesome ingredients.

Kinds of Cakes

There are two basic kinds of cakes: those made with butter or some other kind of shortening and those made without any shortening.

Cakes Made with Shortening. Many of the cakes with which we are most familiar—standard white, gold, and chocolate cakes, spice cakes, pound cakes, fruit cakes, and gingerbreads—fall into this category and are frequently referred to as "butter" cakes. These cakes usually use baking powder or baking soda for leavening. More finely grained than those made without shortening, they are easy to fill and frost and make excellent layer cakes.

Sometimes the eggs in butter cakes are added whole; sometimes they are separated and the beaten egg whites are folded in just before baking. Butter cakes made with separately beaten egg whites are lighter and fluffier than cakes made with whole eggs.

Cakes Made Without Shortening. Sponge cakes and angel food cakes are made without butter or shortening. Sponge cakes use separately beaten egg yolks and whites; angel food cakes are made only with beaten egg whites.

Cakes in this category usually do not use chemical leavening but depend exclusively on the air beaten into eggs or egg whites instead. These cakes are delicate and need to be assembled with special care.

Tortes. Tortes are European in origin. They are usually light cakes made with separated eggs. Ground nuts or crumbs are often used instead of flour, although many tortes do contain some flour. Tortes are very rich and require no more finishing than a dusting of confectioners' sugar or a little whipped cream. They will stay fresh longer than other cakes.

Ingredients

Shortening. Butter, margarine, vegetable shortening, salad oil, or a combination of several of these may be used as shortening in cakes.

Vegetable shortening is cheaper than butter and somewhat easier to use because of its soft, spreadable consistency. It keeps indefinitely and requires no refrigeration. We use it in those cakes where the *flavor* of butter is not important, either because there is very little shortening in the cake or because the flavor of the spices and seasonings in the cake is stronger than the taste of butter. Because so many people are purists when it comes to using butter in baking, we've compared carefully the same cake made with butter and with shortening. The texture of the cake with vegetable shortening seemed a bit springier and the color was lighter, but we all found it hard to distinguish a noticeable difference in taste.

Butter, nevertheless, is generally favored by cooks and bakers. It should be fresh and, preferably, sweet (unsalted). Let it become slightly soft, not mushy, at room temperature before you use it.

Salad oil is used most often in chiffon cakes or in "quick" cakes that can be easily beaten without an electric beater.

Sugar. Sugar adds sweetness and tenderness to cakes. If your sugar is lumpy, be sure to sift it before using. Do not use lumpy brown sugar when baking; the hard lumps will *not* dissolve in baking. For storing brown sugar and keeping it soft, see p. 18.

Eggs. Eggs make a cake rich and give it good taste and texture. As elsewhere in this book use eggs that are officially graded "large." To substitute eggs of a different size in these recipes, follow the proportions outlined on p. 336.

Some cakes that call for separated eggs depend on beaten egg whites exclusively for leavening, so in these instances it is especially important that the whites be beaten properly. Always have the eggs at room temperature and follow the directions for beating and folding on p. 336.

Cutting corners in cakemaking doesn't pay. It would, of course, be easier to beat the egg whites when you first begin to mix a cake, while the beaters are clean and dry and have not yet been used to combine the other ingredients. Indeed, many cookbooks do recommend this method for that very reason. But we have found that egg whites have a tendency to deflate when they stand around for any length of time. And since their volume is so important to the success of a cake, we recommend that they be beaten last, just before they are folded into the batter.

Flour. All flour should be stored in airtight containers. The recipes in this chapter call either for all-purpose flour or for cake flour, a soft-wheat flour that contains more starch and less gluten than hard-wheat bread flour or all-purpose flour.

Cake flour makes a cake lighter and more crumbly. It can be used in any cake recipe, but since it is more expensive than all-purpose flour, we call for it only in recipes where we feel it will make a significant difference. It is even a bit difficult to find in some supermarkets today.

All-purpose flour produces fine cakes, and you can substitute it for cake flour whenever necessary. If you choose to use all-purpose flour in a recipe calling for cake flour, use 2 tablespoons less for each cup of cake flour specified; if you should wish to substitute cake flour for all-purpose flour, use 2 tablespoons more per cup.

Quick-mixing all-purpose flour, milled so fine it will pass right through a sifter, is not a substitute for cake flour. Since it will dissolve instantly in cold (but not hot) liquids, use it, if you wish, in sauces, fillings, and gravies, but not in cakes.

Do not use self-rising flour in these cake recipes; it is premixed with salt and leavening and requires adjustment of the recipe.

Sifting is a way of lightening flour and thoroughly mixing it with the other dry ingredients. In the past it was considered absolutely essential to sift flour in any cake recipe, and most cake recipes still call for sifted flour. Flour today, however, is sifted many times during milling before it is packaged and sent to the stores. We find that many cakes are just as good when made with unsifted flour, and this certainly makes them easier to prepare. At least one major flour company, after extensive research, has arrived at similar conclusions. Thus, you will find that we have eliminated the direction to sift in many of these recipes and suggest simply mixing the flour with the other dry ingredients, blending them well with a fork.

To measure flour without sifting, scoop it up in a dry-measure cup or spoon it lightly into the measuring cup. Level it off with a straight knife. Do not tap or bang the cup or the flour will settle. Better a little *less* flour in a cake than a little more.

We continue to recommend sifting in recipes for refined cakes like sponge or angel food cakes, where the lightness of sifted flour will make it easier to fold it into the beaten egg whites. When sifting, sift onto wax paper, from which the dry ingredients can then be added directly to the measuring cup or mixing bowl. It is better not to wash the sifter, since the flour residue may cake. Tap out as much of the remaining flour as possible and wrap the sifter in a plastic bag before putting it away.

Leavening. Use double-acting baking powder in these recipes. For information about baking powder, baking soda, and other leaveners, see p. 16.

Chocolate. Chocolate burns easily. It is best to melt it over simmering water, rather than over a direct flame. For information about kinds of chocolate, storing chocolate, melting chocolate, and substituting cocoa for chocolate, see p. 13.

Dried Fruit and Nuts. Dried fruit and nuts, when added to cake batters, are often floured first to keep them from settling to the bottom.

Dried fruit that is old and hard will not soften during baking. Soften it by boiling it in water for about 10 minutes, then drain it thoroughly and pat it dry before adding it to the batter. Fruit prepared specifically for use in fruit cakes is available in stores, especially at holiday time.

Nuts keep best when stored in the refrigerator or freezer. When grinding nuts for tortes, keep them light and fluffy and take care not to overgrind. If using a blender, do only ½ cup at a time and turn the motor on and off. Very finely ground or pulverized nuts will become oily and make a heavy, sodden cake.

Preparing Cake Pans

Make sure that you use the size pan that is called for in the recipe. For most cakes the pans should be greased and lightly floured so that the cakes do not stick. Pans and molds with designs in them need especially heavy greasing so that cakes will come out easily.

Prepare the pans for butter cakes before you begin to mix the ingredients so that the pans will be ready when you need them. First, grease them. Using your fingers, scoop up about a teaspoon of soft butter or vegetable shortening and smear it around the bottom and sides of the cake pan. Then sprinkle it liberally all over with flour, and shake out the excess.

Angel food cakes and sponge cakes do not call for greased pans: the beaten egg whites that leaven them will rise better and higher on an ungreased surface. Bake angel food cakes in clean, dry tube pans; sponge cakes in ungreased pans that have been fitted with a round of wax paper on the bottom. You can butter the bottom of the tube pan to keep the wax paper in place, if you wish. Some tube pans come with removable bottoms (in which case don't use a paper liner).

Jelly-roll pans are traditionally lined with wax paper: simply grease the bottom of the pan, then cover it with wax paper, leaving about 2 inches overlap at each of the short ends of the pan; the paper will peel off easily when the cake is turned out to cool.

Mixing Cake Batters

Have the ingredients at room temperature and measure them all out first before you begin to mix them. Try to get in the habit of turning on the oven to preheat while you assemble and mix the ingredients, so that it will be hot and ready when you need it.

It is almost impossible to give the exact amount of time that it will take to mix a cake batter—the time will vary, according to the recipe and the type of beater that you use. These recipes assume that you are using some form of electric beater which will combine the ingredients quickly and efficiently. Needless to say, if you are beating a cake by hand it will take more time and the ingredients should be added more gradually. In general, cake batters should be beaten just long enough to combine all the ingredients thoroughly.

The procedure for mixing the batter for a butter cake differs considerably from that used for sponge cakes. With butter cakes the shortening is usually softened, or "creamed," first, so that it blends more readily with the other ingredients. This can be done by beating it with a wooden spoon or at low speed with an electric beater. The sugar should then be added gradually and beaten in well. Shortening and sugar, when properly creamed together, will get light in color and creamy or fluffy in consistency. Eggs or egg yolks are usually added next, along with vanilla or other flavorings. Add them all at once if you're using an electric mixer; if you're beating by hand or with a less efficient beater, add the eggs one at a time, beating each one in well before adding the next. The mixed dry ingredients and the liquid are added next, again all at once if an electric mixer is used. When mixing by hand, it's best to add the dry and liquid ingredients alternately, beginning and ending with the dry ones, for this is the fastest way to incorporate them without overbeating the cake (that is why so many old recipes detail this method). If the butter cake recipe calls for separated eggs, the eggs whites should be beaten separately at the end and folded in just before baking.

Sponge cakes are very delicate, and their ingredients must be combined carefully. The egg yolks are generally beaten first, and then the sugar and other flavorings are added. The whites, which do the leavening, should be carefully beaten, but not overbeaten, just before they are to be folded in. We suggest beating a little sugar into the beaten egg whites to help them hold the air. Stir a little of the beaten whites into the egg yolk mixture to lighten it before folding in the remaining whites and the sifted flour very gently and with a light hand.

Filling Cake Pans
Most cake pans should be filled no more than two-thirds full to allow room for the cake to rise. Spread the batter up against the sides of the pan a bit and well into the corners.

You can substitute square, rectangular, or irregularly shaped pans for round layer pans. Measure the volume of the layer pan by filling it with water, then pour the water into the pan you wish to use to judge its volume. Adjust the amount of batter you prepare accordingly. Remember, when you substitute pans that are different from those called for in the recipe, the baking time may also vary.

Baking Cakes
Always bake cakes in a preheated oven unless the recipe says otherwise: many a cake has been ruined by a slow start in a cool oven. Make sure that your oven temperature is accurate. You can use an oven thermometer to check it out, but the best test is your own experience: if your cakes bake unevenly or consistently take more or less time than the recipe suggests, it's worth having the oven regulator checked by a reliable service company.

Glass or dark-colored pans will retain more heat than shiny ones. When using them, bake the same amount of time but reduce the oven temperature by 25 degrees.

Bake cakes on the center rack of the oven, or as near the center as possible to allow room for the heat to circulate. Do not overcrowd the oven or let pans touch each other. If using two racks, stagger the pans so that they are not right on top of each other. If the cake is baking unevenly, turn the pan several times during baking.

Begin to test a cake, 5–10 minutes before it is supposed to be done, by inserting a toothpick or a broomstraw near the center: if it comes out clean the cake is done. Use a long piece of straw or a long wooden skewer to test a high tube cake; do not use metal cake testers, for they do not work well. You can also test a cake by pressing it lightly with your fingertip: most cakes, unless they are very rich, will spring back, leaving no depression, when they are done. Remember also that a cake that is done will shrink a bit away from the sides of the pan.

High-Altitude Baking

At altitudes of 3,500 feet or higher, the amount of leavening in a cake must be reduced and the oven temperature raised, or the cake will be dry, coarse, and crumbly. Decrease the amount of baking powder or baking soda by one-third at 3,500 feet, by one-half at 5,000 feet, and by two-thirds above 5,000 feet. Raise the oven temperature by 25 degrees, and do not beat the eggs or egg whites quite as much as usual.

The agriculture departments in many states issue books of recipes especially adapted for baking at high altitudes.

Cooling Cakes

Let butter cakes cool and shrink in their pans for about 5 minutes, then turn them out on a wire rack to cool completely. If the cake should stick to the pan, use a spatula to loosen it gently.

Sponge cakes, angel food cakes, and chiffon cakes should be allowed to cool upside down by inverting the tube pans in which they were baked. If the pan does not have little "feet" to raise it above the surface on which it rests, set the pan over the neck of a bottle so that air can circulate around the cake while it is cooling. When completely cool, loosen with a spatula or a knife, if necessary, and unmold.

Frosting Cakes

For information about frosting and filling cakes, see p. 532.

Storing Cakes

Most cakes taste best when they are fresh, no more than a day or two old. If you plan to keep a cake for several days, wrap it well in foil or plastic wrap. Store it in a cake box, cover it with a deep bowl, or keep it in the refrigerator. Some cakes—those with perishable fillings or frostings—must be refrigerated. An iced cake will keep better than unfrosted layers.

All cakes freeze well. They should be wrapped tight before freezing to prevent the "freezer burn" that results when air gets into the wrappings.

Defrost cakes at room temperature for 1–2 hours. Let them thaw completely before you unwrap them.

Cakes can be frozen with or without frosting, though it's easier to freeze them without. To wrap and freeze a frosted cake, set it on a piece of foil on a plate in the freezer; *after* it is frozen, remove it from the plate, wrap it well, and return it to the freezer.

CAKES MADE WITH SHORTENING (BUTTER CAKES)

Chocolate Cake

A fine-grained, tender cake—ice water is its secret. If you wanted a chocolate cake for a birthday, this would be the one to pick.

(TWO 8-INCH ROUND LAYERS)

2 ounces (60 g) unsweetened chocolate
¼ pound (115 g) butter
1½ cups (300 g) sugar
2 eggs

2 teaspoons vanilla
2 cups (280 g) cake flour
1½ teaspoons baking soda
½ teaspoon salt

Preheat the oven to 350°F (180°C). Butter and lightly flour two 8-inch round cake pans. Melt the chocolate in a small pot or bowl over simmering water; set aside to cool. Cream the butter, slowly beat in the sugar, and beat until light. Add the eggs and the vanilla, mixing well. Add the chocolate and combine thoroughly. Mix the flour, baking soda, and salt together, add to the first mixture, and blend. Add 1 cup ice water and beat until smooth. Pour the batter into the pans and bake for 25–30 minutes, until a toothpick comes out clean. Cool in the pans for 5 minutes before turning out onto racks. Frost with *Portsmouth* (p. 535) or *Creamy Chocolate Frosting* (p. 536).

Huntington Chocolate Cake

This plain, satisfying chocolate cake can be made very quickly and easily. Double the recipe if you want a traditional layer cake.

(ONE 8-INCH ROUND LAYER)

2 ounces (60 g) unsweetened chocolate
½ cup (1 dL) shortening, or ¼ pound (115 g) butter
1 teaspoon vanilla
1 cup (140 g) cake flour

1 cup (200 g) sugar
1 teaspoon cream of tartar
½ teaspoon baking soda
½ teaspoon salt
½ cup (1 dL) milk
2 eggs

Preheat the oven to 350°F (180°C). Butter and lightly flour one 8-inch round cake pan. Melt the chocolate and shortening or butter together in a bowl or pot over simmering water; stir in the vanilla. Mix the flour, sugar, cream of tartar, baking soda, and salt together in a large bowl. Add the chocolate mixture, the milk, and the eggs and beat until smooth. Spread in the pan and bake for about 30 minutes. Cool in the pan for 5 minutes before turning out onto a rack. Frost with *Confectioners' Frosting I* (p. 535) or any other you wish.

Chocolate Buttermilk Cake

This eggless cake with its deep chocolate flavor can be made very quickly.

Chocolate Buttermilk Cake (continued)

(TWO 8-INCH ROUND LAYERS OR ONE 9 × 13-INCH CAKE)

1⅔ cups (235 g) flour
1 cup (200 g) sugar
½ cup (1 dL) cocoa
1 teaspoon baking soda
½ teaspoon salt

1 cup (¼ L) buttermilk or sour
 milk (see p. 11)
½ cup (1 dL) vegetable oil
2 teaspoons vanilla

Preheat the oven to 350°F (180°C). Butter and lightly flour two 8-inch round cake pans or one 9 × 13–inch pan. Mix the flour, sugar, cocoa, baking soda, and salt in a bowl. Add the buttermilk or sour milk, vegetable oil, and vanilla, beating until smooth. Spread in the pans or pan and bake, about 20–25 minutes for the small pans, 35–45 minutes for the large one. Test to see if a toothpick comes out clean. Cool for 5 minutes in the pan before turning out onto a rack. Frost with *Creamy Chocolate Frosting* (p. 536) or *Seven-Minute Coconut Frosting* (p. 540).

Rich Devil's Food Cake

(TWO 8-INCH ROUND LAYERS)

4 tablespoons cocoa
1 cup (200 g) plus 3
 tablespoons sugar
½ cup (1 dL) milk
¼ pound (115 g) butter, or ½
 cup (1 dL) shortening

1 teaspoon vanilla
2 eggs, separated
1 cup (140 g) flour
½ teaspoon cream of tartar
½ teaspoon salt
½ teaspoon baking soda

Preheat the oven to 350°F (180°C). Butter and lightly flour two 8-inch round cake pans. Put the cocoa, 3 tablespoons of the sugar, and 3 tablespoons water in a small pan and cook over low heat until smooth and blended. Remove from the heat and stir in the milk; set aside. Cream the butter or shortening, add the vanilla and ½ cup of the remaining sugar, and beat until light. Beat in the egg yolks, and then add the cocoa mixture, beating well. Mix the flour, cream of tartar, salt, and baking soda together, add to the first mixture, and blend until smooth. Beat the egg whites separately until they are foamy, slowly add the remaining ½ cup of sugar, and continue to beat until the whites are stiff but not dry. Fold the whites into the batter. Spread in the pans and bake for 30–35 minutes; test with a toothpick until it comes out clean. Cool in the pans for 5 minutes before turning out onto racks. Frost with *Confectioners' Frosting II* (p. 535) or *Fudge Frosting* (p. 537).

Fudge Layer Cake

A delicious, tender cake, black with chocolate.

(TWO 9-INCH LAYERS)

4 ounces (115 g) unsweetened
 chocolate
1½ cups (300 g) sugar
½ cup (1 dL) shortening
1 teaspoon vanilla

3 eggs
2 cups (280 g) cake flour
1 teaspoon baking soda
¼ teaspoon salt
⅔ cup (1½ dL) milk

Preheat the oven to 350°F (180°C). Butter and lightly flour two 9-inch cake pans. Put the chocolate, 6 tablespoons water, and ½ cup of the sugar in a heavy-bottomed small pan over low heat, stirring often. As the chocolate melts, stir vigorously to blend. Cook until the chocolate has completely melted and mixture is smooth. Set aside. Cream the shortening and remaining 1 cup sugar together until light. Add the vanilla and beat until well blended. Add the eggs, one at a time, beating thoroughly after each addition. Sift the flour, baking soda, and salt together on a piece of wax paper. Add the dry ingredients alternately with the milk in three parts. Add the chocolate mixture and beat until well blended. Pour the batter into the pans. Bake for 35–40 minutes, or until a straw comes out dry when inserted in center of cake. Cool in the pans for 10 minutes, then turn cakes out on racks. Frost with *Fudge Frosting* (p. 537).

Chocolate Fruit Cake

This combination of chocolate, cinnamon, and brandy is unusual and good. The raisins should be soaked in brandy for at least several hours before using, preferably overnight.

(TWO 8-INCH ROUND LAYERS)

⅓ cup (¾ dL) raisins	1 teaspoon vanilla
2 tablespoons brandy	1 cup (¼ L) milk
2 ounces (60 g) unsweetened chocolate	2 cups (280 g) cake flour
	2 teaspoons baking powder
¼ pound (115 g) butter, or ½ cup (1 dL) shortening	½ teaspoon salt
	2 teaspoons cinnamon
1¼ cups (250 g) sugar	⅓ cup (¾ dL) candied cherries
2 eggs	½ cup (1 dL) chopped walnuts

Preheat the oven to 350°F (180°C). Butter and lightly flour two 8-inch round cake pans. Soak the raisins in the brandy for at least 2 hours, or overnight if possible. Melt the chocolate in a pot or bowl over simmering water; set aside to cool. Cream the butter or shortening in a large mixing bowl, gradually add the sugar, and beat until light and fluffy. Add the eggs and beat well. Beat in the chocolate and the vanilla, then add the milk and beat well. Mix the flour, baking powder, salt, and cinnamon together and add to the batter, beating thoroughly. Stir in the raisins and brandy, cherries, and walnuts. Spread the batter in the pans and bake for about 35 minutes, testing until a toothpick comes out clean. Cool in the pans for 5 minutes before turning out onto a rack.

Walnut Mocha Cake

(TWO 8-INCH ROUND LAYERS OR ONE 8-INCH SQUARE CAKE)

¾ cup (1¾ dL) milk	3 eggs
3 tablespoons instant coffee	2¼ cups (315 g) cake flour
2 teaspoons vanilla	¾ teaspoon salt
¼ pound (115 g) butter	3 teaspoons baking powder
1½ cups (300 g) sugar	1 cup (¼ L) chopped walnuts

Preheat the oven to 350°F (180°C). Butter and lightly flour two 8-inch round cake pans or one 8-inch square pan. Heat the milk and stir in the instant coffee until it dissolves. Add the vanilla and let cool. Cream the butter and gradually add the sugar, beating until light. Add the eggs and beat well. Stir in the coffee mixture. Combine the flour, salt, and baking powder, and add them to the first mixture, mixing well. Stir in the walnuts. Spread batter in the pans and bake, about 30 minutes for the round layers, 40–50 minutes for the square cake. Test to see if a toothpick comes out clean. Cool in the pans for 5 minutes before turning out onto a rack. Frost with *Penuche Frosting* (p. 538).

Velvet Cake

This simple cake with its fine flavor and smooth, velvet texture is an old classic. It would be a good simple cake to fill and frost for a child's birthday.

(TWO 8-INCH ROUND LAYERS)

¼ pound (115 g) butter
1 cup (200 g) sugar
4 eggs, separated
1½ cups (210 g) cake flour

½ cup (1 dL) cornstarch
½ teaspoon salt
4 teaspoons baking powder

Preheat the oven to 350°F (180°C). Butter and lightly flour two 8-inch round cake pans. Cream the butter and slowly add the sugar, beating until light. Beat in the egg yolks and ½ cup cold water and combine well. Combine the flour, cornstarch, salt, and baking powder, add to the first mixture, and mix thoroughly. Beat the egg whites separately until stiff but not dry. Gently stir a third of the whites into the first mixture, then fold in the remaining whites. Spread the batter in the pans and bake for about 25 minutes, until a toothpick comes out clean. Cool in the pans for 5 minutes before turning out onto racks. Frost with *Chocolate Butter Frosting* (p. 539) or *Mocha Rum Butter Frosting* (p. 539).

Lord Baltimore Cake

This classic gold cake can be made with a variety of fillings and frostings. It becomes "Lord Baltimore Cake" when you use Lord Baltimore filling and frosting.

(TWO 8-INCH ROUND LAYERS)

¼ pound (115 g) butter
1 cup (200 g) sugar
5 egg yolks
1 whole egg
2 teaspoons vanilla

½ cup (1 dL) milk
2 cups (280 g) cake flour
2½ teaspoons baking powder
¼ teaspoon salt

Preheat the oven to 350°F (180°C). Butter and lightly flour two 8-inch round cake pans. Cream the butter and slowly add the sugar, beating until light. Add the egg yolks and beat well. Add the whole egg, vanilla, and milk and beat well. Combine the flour, baking powder, and salt, and add to the first mixture, beating until smooth. Spread in the pans and bake for about 25 minutes, until a toothpick comes out clean. Cool in the pans for 5 minutes before turning out onto racks. Fill with *Lord Baltimore Filling* (p. 543) and frost with *Seven-Minute Frosting* (p. 540).

Lady Baltimore Cake

A drift of pure white, Lady Baltimore Cake is fine, soft-textured, and lightly flavored. Fill the layers with its own special filling of nuts and dried fruit or use as a basic white cake with any frosting and filling you prefer.

¼ pound (115 g) butter	¼ teaspoon salt
1 cup (200 g) sugar	¾ cup (1¾ dL) milk
3 cups (420 g) cake flour	1 teaspoon vanilla
2 teaspoons baking powder	4 egg whites

Preheat the oven to 350°F (180°C). Butter and lightly flour two 8-inch round cake pans. Cream the butter until it is smooth, slowly add the sugar, and beat until light and fluffy. Combine the flour, baking powder, and salt, add to the first mixture, add the milk and vanilla, and beat until well blended. Beat the egg whites separately until stiff but not dry. Stir a quarter of the whites into the batter, then gently fold in the remaining whites. Spread in the pans and bake for 25–30 minutes or until a toothpick comes out clean. Cool in the pans for 5 minutes before turning out onto racks. Fill with *Lady Baltimore Filling* (p. 543) and frost with *Seven-Minute Frosting* (p. 540).

Fresh Coconut Cake

Light, tender, and moist—the fresh coconut adds a good texture.

1 coconut	2¼ cups (315 g) cake flour
¾ cup (1¾ dL) shortening	2 teaspoons baking powder
1½ cups (300 g) sugar	½ teaspoon salt
3 eggs, separated	1 cup (¼ L) milk
½ teaspoon coconut extract	

Preheat the oven to 350°F (180°C). Butter and lightly flour two 9-inch cake pans. Remove the meat from the coconut (see p. 13), and grate it in a hand grater or the food processor. You should have about 3 cups. Cream the shortening and slowly add the sugar. Beat until light and smooth. Add the egg yolks, one at a time, beating well after each addition. Stir in the coconut extract. Sift the flour, baking powder, and salt together on a piece of wax paper. Add the dry ingredients alternately in three parts with the milk, beating until well blended. Stir in 1 cup of grated coconut. Beat the egg whites until stiff but not dry, stir a third of the whites into the batter, and gently fold in the remainder. Spoon the batter into the cake pans. Bake for 25 minutes or until a straw inserted in the center of the cake comes out dry. Let the cakes cool for 10 minutes in the pans, then turn onto a cake rack. Cool. Frost with *Seven-Minute Coconut Frosting* (p. 540). Cover the top and sides of the cake with the remaining freshly grated coconut.

Pound Cake

½ pound (225 g) butter	½ teaspoon salt
1⅔ cups (325 g) sugar	1 teaspoon vanilla, or ½
5 eggs	teaspoon mace
2 cups (280 g) cake flour	

Preheat the oven to 325°F (165°C). Butter and lightly flour a 9 × 5–inch loaf pan. Cream the butter, slowly add the sugar, and beat until light. Add the eggs, one at a time, beating each in well. Stir in the flour, salt, and vanilla or mace and combine well. Spoon into the pan and bake for 1¼–1½ hours, or until a toothpick comes out clean. Cool in the pan for 5 minutes before turning out onto a rack. Serve very thin slices.

Birthday Cake

This is a charming, old-fashioned birthday cake, orange-flavored with pieces of candied orange peel, raisins, and walnuts.

(TWO 8-INCH ROUND LAYERS)

¼ pound (115 g) butter, or ½ cup (1 dL) shortening
1¼ cups (3 dL) dark-brown sugar, firmly packed
2 teaspoons orange extract
2 eggs
2 cups (280 g) flour

3 teaspoons baking powder
½ teaspoon salt
⅔ cup (1½ dL) milk
½ cup (1 dL) raisins
½ cup (1 dL) chopped walnuts
2 tablespoons minced candied orange peel

Preheat the oven to 325°F (165°C). Butter and lightly flour two 8-inch round cake pans. Cream the butter or shortening with the brown sugar until light. Add the orange extract and the eggs and beat well. Mix the flour, baking powder, and salt and stir into the first mixture. Add the milk and beat until smooth. Fold in the raisins, walnuts, and orange peel. Spoon into the pans and bake for 25–30 minutes or until a toothpick comes out clean. Cool in the pans for 5 minutes before turning out onto racks. Fill with *Lemon Coconut Cream Filling* (p. 543), frost with *Seven-Minute Frosting* (p. 540), and decorate with *Confectioners' Frosting II* (p. 535), tinted with a few drops of vegetable coloring.

Boston Favorite Cake

This is an excellent basic butter cake. It can also be made as cupcakes or one 7 × 11-inch rectangular.

(TWO 8-INCH LAYERS)

6 tablespoons butter
1 cup (200 g) sugar
2 eggs, separated
1½ teaspoons vanilla

1¾ cups (245 g) cake flour
2 teaspoons baking powder
½ teaspoon salt
⅔ cup (1 dL) milk

Preheat the oven to 350°F (180°C). Butter and lightly flour two 8-inch round cake pans. Cream the butter until softened and slowly add the sugar, beating until light. Add the egg yolks and vanilla and beat to blend well. Sift the flour, baking powder, and salt onto a piece of wax paper. Alternately blend the dry ingredients and the milk into the butter mixture in three stages. Beat until smooth. In a separate bowl, beat the egg whites until stiff but not dry. Stir a third of the whites into the cake batter and gently fold in the remaining. Spoon into the cake pans. Bake for 30–35 minutes, or until a straw inserted in the center of cake comes out dry. Cool in pans for 5 minutes before turning out onto racks. Fill and frost with *Creamy Chocolate Frosting* (p. 536) or *Maple Frosting* (p. 538).

Marble Cake. Divide the batter in half. Melt *1 ounce unsweetened chocolate* over simmering water and add it to half the batter. Fill the pans using large spoonfuls and alternating between the plain and the chocolate batters.

Priscilla Cake. For a richer cake use 1⅓ cups sugar and 3 eggs.

Boston Cream Pie

A simple cake filled with rich cream custard, its top dusted with powdered sugar, this variation of Boston Favorite Cake has become a great American favorite. If you are in a hurry, prepare the custard while the cake is in the oven, but do not fill the cake until it is completely cool.

(TWO-LAYER ROUND CAKE)

1 cup (¼ L) milk
½ cup (100 g) granulated sugar
3 tablespoons flour
⅛ teaspoon salt
2 egg yolks

1½ teaspoons vanilla
Two 8-inch layers Boston
    Favorite Cake (opposite)
Confectioners' sugar

Heat the milk in a pan until very hot, then briskly stir in the granulated sugar, flour, and salt. Cook over moderate heat, stirring constantly, until very thick. Add the egg yolks and cook, continuing to stir, for another 4–5 minutes. Remove from the heat, add the vanilla, and cool, stirring occasionally. Cover well and refrigerate until ready to use. Spread the custard between the cake layers and dust the top of the cake with confectioners' sugar. Keep refrigerated.

Gingerbread

Moist, spicy, and sweet.

(9-INCH SQUARE CAKE)

¼ pound (115 g) butter
1 cup (200 g) sugar
2 eggs
¾ cup (1¾ dL) molasses

2½ cups (350 g) flour
2 teaspoons baking soda
½ teaspoon salt
2 teaspoons powdered ginger

Preheat the oven to 350°F (180°C). Butter and lightly flour a 9-inch square cake pan. Cream the butter, add the sugar, and beat until light and fluffy. Add the eggs and beat well. Add ¾ cup boiling water and the molasses and blend. Mix together the flour, baking soda, salt, and ginger, add to the first mixture, and combine thoroughly. Pour into the pan and bake for 35–45 minutes, until a toothpick comes out clean. Cool in the pan for about 5 minutes before turning out onto a plate. Gingerbread is good served warm *with sweetened whipped cream.* You may serve it with *applesauce,* if you wish, or spread it with *Butter Frosting II* (p. 539).

Sour Cream Gingerbread

More cakelike than plain gingerbread, with a light texture and a creamy crumb.

(9-INCH SQUARE CAKE)

¼ pound (115 g) butter
1 cup (200 g) sugar
½ cup (1 dL) molasses
½ cup (1 dL) sour cream
2 eggs

1½ cups (210 g) flour
1 teaspoon baking powder
½ teaspoon baking soda
½ teaspoon salt
1½ teaspoons powdered ginger

Preheat the oven to 350°F (180°C). Butter and lightly flour a 9-inch square pan. Cream the butter and slowly add the sugar, beating until light and fluffy. Add the molasses and sour cream and blend well. Add the eggs, continuing to beat until well mixed. Mix together the flour, baking powder, baking soda, salt, and ginger, add to the first mixture, and beat until smooth. Pour into the pan and bake for 30–40 minutes, until a toothpick comes out clean. Cool in the pan for 5 minutes before turning out onto a rack.

Applesauce Cake

This cake keeps well and will stay fresh for picnics or trips. Add a teaspoon of powdered ginger if you want it very spicy.

(TWO 8-INCH ROUND LAYERS OR ONE 9 × 13-INCH CAKE)

¼ pound (115 g) butter, or	1½ teaspoons baking soda
½ cup (1 dL) shortening	½ teaspoon salt
1½ cups (300 g) sugar	2 teaspoons cinnamon
1 cup (¼ L) applesauce	½ teaspoon nutmeg
2 eggs	½ cup (1 dL) raisins
2 cups (280 g) flour	½ cup (1 dL) chopped walnuts

Preheat the oven to 350°F (180°C). Butter and lightly flour two 8-inch round cake pans or one 9 × 13–inch cake pan. Cream the butter or shortening, add the sugar gradually, and beat well. Add the applesauce and blend. Beat in the eggs and mix thoroughly. Mix together the flour, baking soda, salt, cinnamon, and nutmeg, add to the first mixture, and beat just until mixed. Stir in the raisins and nuts. Spread in the pans or pan and bake, 25–30 minutes for the layers, 35–40 minutes for the rectangle. Test to see if a toothpick comes out clean. Cool in the pans for 5 minutes before turning out onto racks. Spread with *Cream Cheese Frosting* (p. 538) before serving, if you wish.

Spice Cake

Cinnamon, cloves, nutmeg, and cayenne make this a lively cake.

(TWO 8-INCH ROUND LAYERS OR ONE 8-INCH SQUARE CAKE)

¼ pound (115 g) butter, or	2¼ cups (315 g) flour
½ cup (1 dL) shortening	1 teaspoon salt
1 cup (200 g) granulated sugar	½ teaspoon baking soda
½ cup (1 dL) dark-brown sugar	2 teaspoons cinnamon
4 eggs	¼ teaspoon cloves
½ cup (1 dL) milk	¼ teaspoon nutmeg
½ cup (1 dL) molasses	⅛ teaspoon cayenne pepper

Preheat the oven to 350°F (180°C). Butter and lightly flour two 8-inch round cake pans or one 8-inch square pan. Cream the butter or shortening and slowly add the two sugars, beating until light and fluffy. Beat in the eggs, then add the milk and molasses, beating thoroughly. Mix together the remaining ingredients and add to the first mixture, beating until well blended. Pour the batter into the pans or pan and bake, about 30 minutes for the round layers, 45–50 minutes for the square cake. Test to see if a toothpick comes out clean. Cool in the pans for 5 minutes before turning out onto racks. Frost with *Quick Caramel Frosting* (p. 537).

Jam Cake

¼ pound (115 g) butter, or
  ½ cup (1 dL) shortening
1½ cups (300 g) sugar
3 eggs
2¼ cups (315 g) flour
1 teaspoon allspice
1 teaspoon cinnamon
1 teaspoon nutmeg

½ teaspoon salt
1 teaspoon baking powder
½ teaspoon baking soda
1 cup (¼ L) blackberry,
  raspberry, or strawberry jam
¼ cup (½ dL) sour milk
  (p. 11)

Preheat the oven to 350°F (180°C). Butter and lightly flour two 8-inch round cake pans. Cream the butter or shortening, add the sugar, and beat until light and fluffy. Add the eggs and beat very well. Mix together the flour, allspice, cinnamon, nutmeg, salt, baking powder, and baking soda; add to the first mixture and beat until well mixed. Stir in the jam and sour milk and blend thoroughly. Spread in the pans and bake for 25 minutes, or until a toothpick comes out clean. Cool in the pans for 5 minutes before turning out on a rack. Frost with *Portsmouth Frosting* (p. 535).

Light Fruit Cake

This is exceptionally good. Any combination of candied fruits and nuts will do, but the stuffed dates, which you want to prepare before you start, are particularly good. Simply fill each date with a piece of nut and roll it in sugar. You'll need about 1 pound of dates and a dozen or so extra nuts for this.

½ pound (225 g) butter
2 cups (400 g) sugar
1 tablespoon vanilla
7 eggs, separated
2¾ cups (385 g) flour
1 teaspoon salt
2 teaspoons baking powder
1 cup (¼ L) milk
2 cups (½ L) seedless white
  raisins

2 cups (½ L) pecans in large
  pieces
1 cup (¼ L) candied cherries
1 cup (¼ L) candied pineapple
  in large pieces
2 cups (½ L) dates, stuffed
  with nuts and rolled in sugar

Preheat the oven to 325°F (165°C). Butter and lightly flour two 9 × 5-inch loaf pans. Cream the butter and slowly add the sugar, beating until light. Add the vanilla and the egg yolks and beat well. Mix the flour, salt, and baking powder, and stir them and ½ cup of the milk into the first mixture. Add the remaining ½ cup of milk and beat well. Stir in the raisins and the pecans. Beat the egg whites separately until they are stiff but not dry. Gently stir a third of the whites into the batter, then fold in the remaining whites carefully. Spoon a layer of batter into each loaf pan. Arrange several rows of candied cherries and pineapple and the dates on top of the batter, then cover with the remaining batter, filling each pan one-half to two-thirds full. Bake for about 1 hour or until a toothpick comes out clean. Cool in the pans for 5 minutes before turning out onto racks. When completely cool, wrap well and store in an airtight container up to two months.

Fresh Banana Cake

Moist and banana-sweet, with dark banana flecks throughout.

(9-INCH SQUARE CAKE)

¼ pound (115 g) butter, or
   ½ cup (1 dL) shortening
1½ cups (300 g) sugar
1 cup (¼ L) mashed banana
   (about 2 medium bananas)
2 eggs

1 teaspoon vanilla
2 cups (280 g) cake flour
1 teaspoon baking soda
½ teaspoon salt
½ cup (1 dL) sour milk
   (p. 11) or sour cream

Preheat the oven to 350°F (180°C). Butter and lightly flour a 9-inch square cake pan. Cream the butter or shortening, slowly add the sugar, and beat until light. Add the banana, eggs, and vanilla and beat well. Mix the flour, baking soda, and salt, add to the first mixture, and blend. Slowly add the sour milk or sour cream and beat until well blended. Spread in the pan and bake for about 45 minutes, or until a toothpick comes out clean. Cool in the pan for 5 minutes before turning out onto a rack. Split the cake and fill with *Banana Cream Filling* (p. 542) and frost with *Portsmouth Frosting* (p. 535).

Princeton Orange Cake

This orange-flavored velvet cake is fresh and bright with a delicate texture and keen orange taste.

(TWO 9-INCH ROUND LAYERS)

¼ pound (115 g) butter
1 cup (200 g) sugar
4 eggs, separated
½ cup (1 dL) orange juice
Grated rind of 1 large orange

1½ cups (210 g) cake flour
½ cup (1 dL) cornstarch
½ teaspoon salt
4 teaspoons baking powder

Preheat the oven to 350°F (180°C). Butter and lightly flour two 9-inch round cake pans. Cream the butter and slowly add the sugar, beating until light. Add the egg yolks, orange juice, and orange rind and beat well. Mix the flour, cornstarch, salt, and baking powder, stir into the first mixture, and blend until smooth. Beat the egg whites in a separate bowl until stiff but not dry. Gently stir a third of the egg whites into the first mixture, then fold in the remaining whites. Spread the batter in the pans and bake for 30–40 minutes, or until a toothpick comes out clean. Cool in the pans for 5 minutes before turning out onto racks. Frost with *White Mountain Cream* (p. 541) and sprinkle with ¾ *cup grated coconut,* if you wish.

Dark Fruit Cake

Every kitchen file should have a recipe for a distinguished dark fruit cake. This is as good as any to be found.

(TWO LOAVES)

¼ pound (115 g) butter, or
   ½ cup (1 dL) shortening

1 cup (¼ L) dark-brown sugar,
   firmly packed

1 teaspoon lemon extract
2 eggs
½ cup (1 dL) molasses
2 cups (280 g) flour
½ teaspoon baking soda
1 teaspoon cinnamon
½ teaspoon allspice
½ teaspoon mace
¼ teaspoon ground cloves

½ teaspoon salt
½ cup (1 dL) milk
2 cups (½ L) small pieces
  mixed candied fruit
½ cup (1 dL) small pieces
  candied citron
1 cup (¼ L) raisins
1 cup (¼ L) chopped pecans

Preheat the oven to 325°F (165°C). Butter two 9 × 5–inch loaf pans, line them with foil, then butter the foil. Cream the butter or shortening, add the brown sugar, and beat until light. Add the lemon extract and eggs and beat well. Stir in the molasses and blend. Mix together the flour, baking soda, cinnamon, allspice, mace, cloves, and salt; beat into the first mixture. Add the milk and beat until smooth. Stir in the candied fruit, citron, raisins, and pecans and mix well. Spoon into the pans and bake for 1–1¼ hours, until a toothpick comes out clean. Turn out onto racks to cool. When completely cool, wrap well and store in an airtight container.

Brandied Fruit Cake. Soak two large pieces of cheesecloth in *brandy*. Wrap each fruit cake in the cheesecloth, covering all sides, then wrap well in foil. Moisten the cheesecloth with additional brandy every few days for about a week. The brandy will flavor the cake and help preserve it too.

CAKES MADE WITHOUT SHORTENING (SPONGE CAKES)

True Sponge Cake

This is a classic sponge cake, made without any baking powder, leavened by air held within well-beaten eggs.

(9-INCH TUBE CAKE OR TWO 8-INCH ROUND LAYERS)

5 eggs, separated
1 tablespoon lemon juice
1 cup (200 g) sugar

¼ teaspoon salt
1 cup (140 g) cake flour

Preheat the oven to 325°F (165°C). Line the bottom of a 9-inch tube pan or of two 8-inch round cake pans with wax paper, cut to fit. Beat the egg yolks with the lemon juice until pale and thick. Gradually add ¾ cup of the sugar and beat thoroughly. Beat the egg whites until foamy, add the salt, and continue beating until the whites hold soft peaks, then slowly add the remaining ¼ cup of sugar and beat until stiff but not dry. Stir a fourth of the beaten whites into the egg yolk mixture. Spoon the remaining whites over the yolk mixture and sift the flour on top. Gently fold until blended. Spoon into the pan or pans. Bake for 45–55 minutes in the tube pan, 25–30 minutes in the layer pans, or until a toothpick or straw comes out clean. Invert the pan or pans on a rack and let the cake cool completely before removing from the pan. Dust with *confectioners' sugar*, sifted through a strainer, or frost with lemon-flavored *Confectioners' Frosting II* (p. 535) or any other light frosting you wish.

Hot-Water Sponge Cake

Hot-water sponge cake is made with baking powder, which ensures its lightness. It's an easy sponge cake for those new to baking.

(9-INCH SQUARE CAKE OR 12 CUPCAKES)

2 eggs, separated
1 teaspoon vanilla
¾ cup (145 g) sugar

⅛ teaspoon salt
1 cup (140 g) cake flour
1¼ teaspoons baking powder

Preheat the oven to 325°F (165°C). Line the bottom of a 9-inch square cake pan with wax paper or place 12 fluted paper liners in a muffin pan. Beat the egg yolks, ¼ cup hot water, and vanilla together until very thick and pale. Slowly beat in ½ cup of the sugar; set aside. Beat the egg whites until foamy, add the salt, and continue beating until they hold soft peaks. Gradually beat in the remaining ¼ cup sugar and beat until stiff but not dry. Stir a fourth of the whites into the yolk mixture and sift the flour and baking powder over them. Gently fold until blended. Spoon into the pan and bake, 25–30 minutes for the cake, 20 minutes for the cupcakes, or until a toothpick comes out clean. Invert the pan on a rack and let the cake or cupcakes cool completely before removing from the pan. Frost with *Quick Caramel Frosting* (p. 537).

Cream Sponge Cake

(8-INCH TUBE CAKE OR TWO 8-INCH ROUND LAYERS)

4 eggs, separated
1 tablespoon lemon juice
1 teaspoon vanilla
1 cup (200 g) sugar

¼ teaspoon salt
1 cup (140 g) cake flour
1¼ teaspoons baking powder

Preheat the oven to 325°F (165°C). Line the bottom of an 8-inch tube pan or of two 8-inch round cake pans with wax paper, cut to fit. Beat the egg yolks with the lemon juice, 1½ tablespoons cold water, and vanilla until thick and pale. Gradually add ¾ cup of the sugar and blend well; set aside. Beat the egg whites separately until foamy, add the salt, and continue beating until the whites form soft peaks. Gradually add the remaining ¼ cup of sugar and beat until stiff but not dry. Gently stir a fourth of the whites into the yolk mixture. Spoon the remaining whites onto the yolk mixture and sift the flour and baking powder on top. Carefully fold until blended. Spoon into the pan or pans and bake, allowing 40–50 minutes for the tube cake, about 25 minutes for the layers. Test to see if a straw or toothpick comes out clean. Invert each pan on a rack and let the cake cool completely before removing the pan. If you have used a tube pan, split the cake horizontally to make two even layers. Fill and frost with *Chocolate Whipped Cream Filling* (p. 545).

Chocolate Sponge Cake

This very delicate chocolate sponge cake is exceptionally good.

(9-INCH TUBE CAKE)

6 ounces (180 g) semisweet
  chocolate
4 eggs
¾ cup (145 g) sugar

1 teaspoon vanilla
⅛ teaspoon salt
½ cup (70 g) cake flour

Preheat the oven to 350°F (180°C). Line the bottom of a 9-inch tube pan with wax paper, cut to fit. Melt the chocolate in a small pan or bowl over simmering water; set aside to cool. Beat the eggs until light, then gradually add the sugar, vanilla, and salt. Stir in the melted chocolate. Sift the flour over the batter and fold in just until blended. Spoon into the pan and bake for 40–50 minutes, until a straw comes out clean. Invert the pan on a rack and let the cake cool completely before removing from the pan. Frost with *Portsmouth Frosting* (p. 535) or *Coffee Butter Frosting* (p. 539).

Daffodil Cake

Called daffodil because the bursts of yellow throughout the white cake look like flowers. As good to eat as it is to look at.

(10-INCH TUBE CAKE)

¼ teaspoon salt	1¼ cups (250 g) sugar
1½ teaspoons cream of tartar	1¼ cups (145 g) sifted flour
2 teaspoons vanilla	4 egg yolks
9 egg whites (1⅛ cups)	2 teaspoons grated orange rind

Preheat the oven to 375°F (190°C). In a large mixing bowl, sprinkle the salt, cream of tartar, and vanilla over the egg whites. Beat until the whites hold a soft peak, and slowly add 1 cup of the sugar. Beat just until the sugar is blended into the whites. Add the flour in four parts, folding in each time gently with a rubber spatula, until all the flour is incorporated. In another bowl, beat the egg yolks and orange rind until thick, slowly adding the remaining 4 tablespoons of sugar. Beat until thick and pale yellow. Fold a third of the egg white mixture into the yolk mixture, fold gently until blended. Fill an ungreased 10-inch tube pan, using large spoonfuls and alternating the yellow batter with the white batter until all is used. Bake about 35 minutes or until a straw comes out dry when inserted into the cake. Frost with *Fluffy Butter Frosting* (p. 539) to which *2 teaspoons grated orange rind* plus *½–1 teaspoon orange extract* are added (taste to determine how much is needed for a light orange flavor).

Sunshine Cake

An airy yellow cake, light in texture, sweet in taste.

(10-INCH TUBE CAKE)

7 egg yolks	10 egg whites
1 teaspoon lemon extract	1 teaspoon cream of tartar
1½ cups (3½ dL)	1 cup (140 g) cake flour
confectioners' sugar	¼ teaspoon salt

Preheat the oven to 325°F (165°C). Line the bottom of a 10-inch tube pan with wax paper, cut to fit. Beat the egg yolks, add the lemon extract and 1 cup of the confectioners' sugar, and beat until thick and pale; set aside. Beat the whites until foamy, add the cream of tartar, and beat until the whites form soft peaks. Gradually add the remaining ½ cup confectioners' sugar and beat until stiff. Stir a fourth of the whites into the yolk mixture. Spoon the remaining whites on top of the yolk mixture and sift the flour and salt over them. Carefully fold until blended. Spoon into the pan and bake for 50–60 minutes, until a straw comes out clean. Invert the pan on a rack and let the cake cool completely before removing from the pan. Frost with *Confectioners' Frosting I* (p. 535).

Angel Food Cake

Save your egg whites and freeze them until you have enough to make
this cake.

(10-INCH TUBE CAKE)

8 egg whites (1 cup, ¼ L)   1 teaspoon vanilla
¼ teaspoon salt   1¼ cups (250 g) sugar
1 teaspoon cream of tartar   1 cup (140 g) cake flour
1 teaspoon almond extract

Preheat the oven to 325°F (165°C). Beat the egg whites until foamy, add the salt
and cream of tartar, and beat until soft peaks form. Add the almond extract and
the vanilla, then gradually add the sugar, beating until stiff. Sift the flour over
the whites and gently fold it in. Bake in an ungreased 10-inch tube pan for
50–60 minutes, until a straw comes out clean. Invert the pan on a rack and let
the cake cool completely before removing from the pan. Frost with *Chocolate
Frosting* (p. 536).

TORTES, JELLY ROLLS, AND OTHER SPECIAL CAKES

Nut Torte

(TWO 8-INCH ROUND CAKES)

5 eggs, separated   1 teaspoon baking powder
1 cup (200 g) sugar   1 teaspoon vanilla
2 cups (½ L) ground walnuts   ⅛ teaspoon salt
1 cup (¼ L) bread crumbs

Preheat the oven to 325°F (165°C). Butter and lightly flour two 8-inch round
cake pans. Beat the egg yolks until pale and thick. Slowly add the sugar and
continue to beat until well blended. Stir in the walnuts, crumbs, baking powder,
and vanilla, and mix well. Beat the egg whites separately until foamy, add the
salt, and continue to beat until stiff but not dry. Gently stir a third of the whites
into the batter, then fold in the remaining whites. Spread in the pans and bake
for about 30 minutes, or until a toothpick comes out clean. Let cool in the pans
for 5 minutes before turning out onto racks. Serve spread with *sweetened whipped
cream* between the layers and dust the top with sifted *confectioners' sugar*.

Almond Torte ·

Moist, delicate, and mildly sweet, just right with sweetened whipped
cream.

(9-INCH ROUND CAKE)

4 eggs, separated   ½ cup (1 dL) chopped almonds
1½ cups (3½ dL)   2 ounces (60 g) unsweetened
  confectioners' sugar   chocolate, finely grated
½ cup (1 dL) fine cracker   1 teaspoon baking powder
  crumbs

Preheat the oven to 325°F (165°C). Butter and lightly flour a 9-inch springform pan. Beat the egg yolks until thick and pale. Slowly add 1 cup of the sugar and continue to beat until blended. Stir in the crumbs, almonds, chocolate, and baking powder, and mix well. Beat the egg whites separately until they hold soft peaks, then slowly beat in the remaining ½ cup of sugar, continuing to beat until stiff but not dry. Gently stir a third of the whites into the batter, then fold in the remaining whites. Spread lightly in the pan and bake for about 30 minutes, or until a toothpick comes out clean. Run a knife around the edge, remove the rim, and let cool. Serve with *sweetened whipped cream.*

Jelly Roll

This is the best sponge-cake jelly roll we've found. The cornstarch gives it a fine, springy texture. Fill it with jelly or jam, whipped cream, ice cream, or any other filling you wish.

(15-INCH JELLY ROLL)

5 eggs, separated	⅓ cup (¾ dL) cornstarch
1 teaspoon vanilla	⅓ cup (50 g) flour
½ teaspoon salt	Confectioners' sugar
⅓ cup (65 g) granulated sugar	Jelly or jam

Preheat the oven to 375°F (190°C). Grease a 10½ × 15½–inch jelly-roll pan and cover it with wax paper. Beat the egg yolks and add the vanilla; set aside.

Beat the egg whites until foamy, add the salt, and continue beating until the whites form soft peaks. Slowly add the granulated sugar and beat until stiff but not dry. Spoon the whites over the yolks and sprinkle the cornstarch and flour on top. Fold gently until blended. Spread in the pan and bake for about 12 minutes, until a toothpick comes out clean. Meanwhile, liberally dust a kitchen towel with confectioners' sugar. Turn the jelly roll out onto the towel, carefully remove the wax paper,

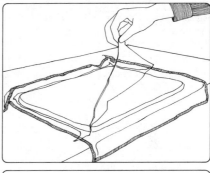

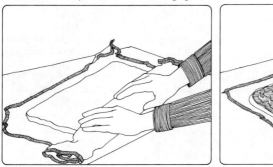

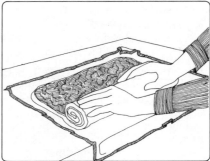

and trim off any crisp edges. Roll the cake up in the towel from the long side and let it rest for a minute, unroll it and let it rest for a few minutes, then roll it up in the towel again and let it cool completely. Unroll, spread all over with jelly or jam right to the edges, roll up—this time *without* the towel inside—and sprinkle with confectioners' sugar.

Jelly Roll Fillings

Whipped Cream Filling. Whip *1½ cups heavy cream,* flavoring it with *sugar to taste* and *2 teaspoons vanilla or 1 tablespoon instant coffee.* Spread on the jelly roll instead of the jelly or jam and roll up.

Ice Cream Filling. Omit the jelly or jam and spread the roll with *1 quart softened chocolate ice cream,* or another flavor, if you wish. Roll up and keep in the freezer until ready to serve.

Lemon Filling. Omit the jelly or jam and spread the roll with *1 recipe Lemon Filling* (p. 544).

Carrot Torte

(9- OR 10-INCH ROUND CAKE)

4 eggs, separated	1 tablespoon lemon juice
1 cup (200 g) sugar	½ cup (70 g) flour
1 cup (¼ L) grated raw carrots	1 teaspoon baking powder
Grated rind of 1 lemon	⅛ teaspoon salt

Preheat the oven to 325°F (165°C). Butter and lightly flour a 9- or 10-inch springform pan. Beat the egg yolks until they are pale and thick. Slowly add the sugar and continue to beat until smooth and blended. Stir in the carrots, lemon rind, lemon juice, flour, and baking powder and mix thoroughly. Beat the egg whites separately until foamy, add the salt, and continue to beat until stiff but not dry. Gently stir a third of the whites into the batter, then fold in the remaining whites. Spread in the pan and bake for 30–40 minutes, or until a toothpick comes out clean. Run a knife around the edge, remove the rim, and let cool. Sprinkle the top with *confectioners' sugar,* sifted through a strainer.

Nut Roll

This sophisticated version of the classic jelly roll is made with chopped nuts instead of flour.

(15-INCH ROLL)

6 eggs, separated	⅛ teaspoon salt
¾ cup (150 g) sugar	1½ cups (3½ dL) heavy cream
1½ cups (3½ dL) finely chopped walnuts	¼ cup (½ dL) confectioners' sugar
1 teaspoon baking powder	2 tablespoons rum

Preheat the oven to 350°F (180°C). Butter a 10½ × 15½–inch jelly-roll pan, line it with wax paper. Beat the egg yolks until they are pale and thick. Slowly add the granulated sugar and continue to beat until blended. Stir in the walnuts and baking powder; set aside. Beat the egg whites until foamy, then add the salt and continue to beat until stiff but not dry. Gently stir a third of the whites into the batter, then fold in the remaining whites. Spread lightly in the pan and bake for 12–15 minutes, until a toothpick comes out clean. Turn out onto a clean kitchen towel. Remove the wax paper and trim off any crisp edges. Roll the cake up in the towel, starting from the long side like a jelly roll, and let it rest for a minute. Unroll the cake, let it rest for a few minutes, then roll it up in the towel again and let it cool completely. Whip the cream, adding the confectioners' sugar and the rum. Spread it over the cake and roll up gently without the towel. Cover and refrigerate until ready to serve.

Chocolate Roll

(15-INCH ROLL)

5 eggs, separated
1¼ cups (3 dL) confectioners' sugar
¼ cup (½ dL) cocoa
¼ teaspoon salt

1½ cups (3½ dL) sweetened heavy cream, whipped, or 1 quart (1 L) vanilla ice cream, softened

Preheat the oven to 350°F (180°C). Butter a 10½ × 15½–inch jelly-roll pan and line it with wax paper. Beat the egg yolks until they are pale and thick; set aside. Sift the sugar and cocoa together onto a piece of wax paper. Beat the egg whites until they are foamy, add the salt, and continue to beat until they hold soft peaks. Fold the sugar and cocoa into the whites. Gently fold a third of the egg white mixture into the yolks, then lightly fold in the remaining whites. Spread evenly in the pan and bake for about 20 minutes, until a toothpick comes out clean. Turn the cake out onto a clean kitchen towel. Remove the wax paper and trim off any crisp edges. Roll the cake up with the towel from the long side, like a jelly roll (see p. 521), and let it rest for a minute. Unroll it and let it rest for a few minutes, then roll it up in the towel again and let it cool completely. Unroll and spread with sweetened whipped cream or softened ice cream. Roll up again without the towel. Dust the top of the roll with more confectioners' sugar sifted through a strainer. Refrigerate the whipped cream roll until ready to serve; keep the ice cream roll in the freezer.

Cottage Pudding Cake

This is a good basic recipe with the pleasing flavor of butter. A similar batter is used in the following recipes for apple cobbler, apple pandowdy, and pineapple and gingerbread upside-down cakes.

(8-INCH SQUARE CAKE)

1½ cups (210 g) flour
2 teaspoons baking powder
½ teaspoon salt
½ cup (100 g) sugar

¼ pound (115 g) butter
½ cup (1 dL) milk
1 egg

Preheat the oven to 400°F (205°C). Butter and lightly flour an 8-inch square cake pan. Mix the flour, baking powder, salt, and sugar together in a large bowl. Melt the butter in a small pan, remove from the heat, and stir in the milk and the egg, beating well. Add to the flour mixture and blend. Pour into the pan and bake for about 25 minutes, until a toothpick comes out clean. Cool in the pan for 5 minutes before turning out onto a rack. Serve warm with *Lemon Sauce* (p. 644). Or frost with *Creamy Chocolate Frosting* (p. 536) or *Sultana Nut Frosting* (p. 538).

Chocolate Chip Cake. Add *1 cup (6 ounces) chocolate chips* to the batter before pouring it into the pan.

Dutch Apple Cake. Spread the batter ¾ inch thick in a 10 × 6 × 2–inch baking dish. Pare and core *5 tart apples*, cut into wedges of eighths, and press them in uniform rows into the batter. Mix *½ cup sugar* with *½ teaspoon cinnamon* and *2 tablespoons raisins*. Sprinkle evenly over the top. Bake as directed. Serve with *heavy cream*.

Apple Cobbler

(8-INCH SQUARE CAKE)

12 tablespoons butter
2 cups (½ L) peeled and sliced
  tart apples
¾ teaspoon salt
¾ cup (150 g) sugar

½ cup (1 dL) milk
1 egg
1½ cups (215 g) flour
2 teaspoons baking powder

Preheat the oven to 375°F (190°C). Melt 4 tablespoons of the butter and pour it into an 8-inch square cake pan. Spread it evenly and arrange the apples over it. Mix ¼ teaspoon of the salt with ¼ cup of the sugar and sprinkle evenly over the apples; set aside. Melt the remaining 8 tablespoons of the butter in a small pan, remove from the heat, add the milk and egg, and beat well. Mix the flour, baking powder, the remaining ½ cup sugar, and the remaining ½ teaspoon salt in a bowl. Stir in the milk and egg mixture and beat until smooth. Pour over the apples and bake for about 30 minutes, or until a toothpick comes out clean. Serve from the pan in squares, fruit side up. Serve plain or with *whipped cream* or *vanilla ice cream,* if you wish.

Apple Pandowdy

A very tasty version of a time-honored New England dish.

(SERVES SIX)

3 cups (¾ L) peeled and sliced
  tart apples
½ teaspoon nutmeg
½ teaspoon cinnamon
¾ teaspoon salt
½ cup (1 dL) molasses

1½ cups (215 g) flour
2 teaspoons baking powder
½ cup (100 g) sugar
¼ pound (115 g) butter
½ cup (1 dL) milk
1 egg

Preheat the oven to 350°F (180°C). Butter a 1½-quart baking dish. Arrange the sliced apples in the dish. Sprinkle with the nutmeg, cinnamon, and ¼ teaspoon of the salt, and spoon the molasses evenly over them. Cover the baking dish with foil and bake for 30 minutes. While the apples are baking, combine the flour, baking powder, sugar, and the remaining ½ teaspoon salt in a large bowl. Melt the butter in a small pan, remove from the heat, and stir in the milk and the egg, beating well. Add to the flour mixture and blend. Pour the batter over the apples after they have baked for 30 minutes, and return them to the oven for 30 minutes more, or until a toothpick comes out clean. Serve from the dish or turn out onto a serving plate with the apples on top. Serve with *whipped cream,* if you wish.

Pineapple Upside-Down Cake

Sweet butter syrup over pineapple and fresh cake; make this in an old-fashioned black iron skillet or "spider," and decorate each pineapple ring with a pecan half or a fresh cherry, if you wish.

(8- OR 9-INCH ROUND CAKE)

12 tablespoons butter
1 cup (¼ L) dark-brown sugar

¼ cup (½ dL) pineapple juice
5 whole pineapple rings

½ cup (1 dL) milk
1 egg
1½ cups (215 g) flour

2 teaspoons baking powder
½ teaspoon salt
½ cup (100 g) granulated sugar

Preheat the oven to 400°F (205°C). Melt 4 tablespoons of the butter in an ovenproof skillet or an 8- or 9-inch cake pan. Stir in the brown sugar and continue to stir over low heat until it dissolves. Remove from the heat and add the pineapple juice. Arrange the pineapple rings in one layer in the pan; set aside. Melt the remaining 8 tablespoons butter in a small pan. Remove from the heat and stir in the milk and egg, beating well. Mix the flour, baking powder, salt, and granulated sugar in a bowl, then add the milk-egg mixture and beat until smooth. Pour over the pineapple slices and bake for about 35 minutes, until a toothpick comes out clean. Let cool in the pan for 10 minutes, then turn out onto a plate, fruit side up. Serve with *whipped cream,* if you wish.

Gingerbread Upside-Down Cake

(8-INCH SQUARE CAKE)

12 tablespoons butter
⅓ cup (¾ dL) dark-brown
 sugar
3 ripe pears, peeled, cored, and
 halved, or 6 canned pear
 halves
1½ cups (215 g) flour

2 teaspoons baking powder
2 teaspoons powdered ginger
½ teaspoon salt
½ cup (100 g) granulated sugar
½ cup (1 dL) milk
1 egg

Preheat the oven to 375°F (190°C). Melt 4 tablespoons of the butter in a small pan, add the brown sugar, and stir over low heat until blended. Pour into an 8-inch square cake pan and arrange the pear halves round side down in the pan; set aside. Mix the flour, baking powder, ginger, salt, and granulated sugar in a bowl. Melt the remaining 8 tablespoons of butter in a small pan. Remove from the heat, add the milk and the egg, and beat well. Add to the flour mixture and beat until smooth. Pour over the pears and bake for about 25 minutes, or until a toothpick comes out clean. Cool in the pan for about 10 minutes, then turn out onto a serving plate, fruit side up. Serve with *whipped cream,* if you wish.

Chiffon Cake

(10-INCH TUBE CAKE)

2¼ cups (315 g) cake flour
3 teaspoons baking powder
1½ cups (300 g) sugar
1 teaspoon salt
½ cup (1 dL) salad oil

5 egg yolks
2 teaspoons vanilla
8 egg whites
½ teaspoon cream of tartar

Preheat oven to 325°F (165°C). Line the bottom of a 10-inch tube pan with wax paper, cut to fit. Sift the flour, baking powder, sugar, and salt into a large bowl. Pour in the oil, egg yolks, ¾ cup cold water, and vanilla, and beat until smooth and shiny; set aside. Beat the egg whites separately until foamy, add the cream of tartar, and continue beating until stiff but not dry. Blend a fourth of the whites into the batter, then fold in the remaining whites. Spoon the batter into the tube pan and bake for 50–60 minutes, until a straw comes out clean. Invert the pan on a rack and let the cake cool completely before removing from the pan. Frost with *Seven-Minute Lemon or Orange Frosting* (p. 540).

Shortcake

Old-fashioned biscuit-dough shortcakes, warm from the oven, should be split, buttered, spread with sugared berries, and graced with lots of heavy cream.

(ONE 8-INCH ROUND CAKE OR EIGHT 2-INCH ROUND CAKES)

2 cups (280 g) flour
4 teaspoons baking powder
1 teaspoon salt
1½ tablespoons sugar
5 tablespoons butter

⅔ cup (1½ dL) milk
Berries or sliced fresh fruit,
   sweetened
Heavy cream

Preheat the oven to 425°F (220°C). Butter and lightly flour an 8-inch cake pan or a cookie sheet. Mix the flour, baking powder, salt, and sugar in a bowl. Cut the butter in bits and work it into the flour mixture with a pastry blender or your fingers until it resembles coarse meal. Slowly stir in the milk, using just enough to hold the dough together. Turn out onto a floured board and knead for a minute or two. Pat the dough into the cake pan or roll or pat it ¾ inch thick and cut it into eight 2-inch rounds, using a biscuit cutter. Arrange the rounds on a cookie sheet and bake them for 10–12 minutes or the larger cake for 12–15 minutes. Split with two forks while still warm, butter, fill with sugared fruit or berries, and serve warm with heavy cream.

Baba Cakes

(TWELVE 2½-INCH CUPCAKES)

1 package yeast
1¾ cups (245 g) flour
4 eggs, at room temperature

¼ cup (50 g) sugar
¼ teaspoon salt
¼ pound (115 g) soft butter

Stir the yeast into ½ cup warm water and let it stand for 5 minutes to dissolve. Add ½ cup of the flour and mix well with an electric beater. Beat in the eggs, one at a time, then add the sugar, salt, and remaining flour. Mix until the dough is smooth. Cover and let rise until double in bulk. Beat the softened butter into the dough, bit by bit, until smooth. Butter the muffin pans. Put 2 tablespoons of dough in each opening, cover, and let rest 45 minutes. Preheat oven to 400°F (205°C). Bake for about 20 minutes or until lightly golden on top. Remove from the pans and cool on a rack.

Rum Sauce
1 cup (200 g) sugar
½ cup (1 dL) rum

Mix the sugar with 1 cup water in a small pot and boil 10 minutes. Cool to lukewarm, then add the rum. Dip the Baba Cakes in this sauce and spoon some over the tops of each cake.

Savarin (two rings). Prepare 1 recipe of Baba Cake dough. Preheat the oven to 400°F (205°C). Butter two 8- or 9-inch ring molds and divide dough between them. Bake for 20 minutes or until golden brown. Turn each Savarin ring onto a rack placed over a shallow bowl. While still warm, spoon *Rum Sauce* (above) over the ring several times until the cake is moist and well flavored. Before serving, fill the center with *sugared strawberries, ice cream,* or *sweetened whipped cream.*

Lazy Daisy Cake

This small cake, made with hot milk, is high, light, delicate, and very easy to make. You can omit the broiled topping, if you wish, and frost the cake instead, once it has cooled. But the traditional Lazy Daisy topping is very, very good.

(8-INCH SQUARE CAKE)

2 eggs
1 teaspoon vanilla
1 cup (200 g) granulated sugar
1 cup (140 g) flour
1 teaspoon baking powder
¼ teaspoon salt

½ cup (1 dL) milk
4 tablespoons butter
3 tablespoons dark-brown sugar
2 tablespoons cream
½ cup (1 dL) grated coconut
    or chopped nuts

Preheat the oven to 350°F (180°C). Butter and lightly flour an 8-inch square cake pan. Beat the eggs with the vanilla until they have thickened slightly. Gradually add the granulated sugar and beat thoroughly. Mix the flour, baking powder, and salt together and add to the first mixture, blending until smooth. Heat the milk and 1 tablespoon of the butter together in a small pan. When the butter has melted, stir the milk and melted butter into the batter and mix well; the batter will be very liquid. Pour into the pan and bake for about 25 minutes, until a toothpick comes out clean. Remove the cake from the oven. Mix the 3 remaining tablespoons of butter, the brown sugar, the cream, and the coconut or nuts together in a small pan over low heat until melted and well blended. Spread over the hot cake and brown lightly under the broiler for a minute or two, taking care that it does not burn.

Cheese Cake

(9-INCH CAKE)

1 cup (¼ L) zwieback or
    graham cracker crumbs
4 tablespoons melted butter
¼ teaspoon cinnamon
¼ teaspoon nutmeg
1¼ cups (250 g) sugar
4 eggs, separated

1 cup (¼ L) sour cream
2 tablespoons flour
¼ teaspoon salt
1 teaspoon vanilla
1 pound (450 g) cream cheese,
    at room temperature

Combine the crumbs, melted butter, cinnamon, nutmeg, and ¼ cup of the sugar in a bowl and mix well. Butter a 9-inch springform pan and pat the crumb mixture over the bottom and 1 inch up the sides. Chill. Preheat the oven to 325°F (165°). Beat the egg yolks with an electric beater until they are thick and pale. Add the sour cream, flour, salt, ¾ cup of the sugar, and the vanilla and beat until well blended. Add the cream cheese and beat until smooth. Beat the egg whites until foamy, then gradually beat in the remaining ¼ cup of sugar, beating until the whites are stiff and shiny. Fold into the cream cheese mixture. Spoon into the crumb crust. Bake about 1 hour, or until the center does not tremble when the cake is gently shaken. Cool, then chill in the refrigerator.

Quick Chocolate Mocha Cake

Very black and very rich, you can make this excellent cake easily without an electric beater.

(8-INCH ROUND LAYER)

2 ounces (60 g) unsweetened chocolate
1 egg
1 cup (200 g) sugar
⅓ cup (¾ dL) vegetable oil

1 teaspoon vanilla
¾ cup (1¾ dL) strong coffee
1⅓ cups (190 g) flour
1 teaspoon baking powder
1 teaspoon baking soda

Preheat the oven to 350°F (180°C). Butter and lightly flour an 8-inch round cake pan. Melt the chocolate in a bowl or pot over simmering water; set aside. Beat the egg in a bowl and slowly add the sugar, continuing to beat until well blended. Add the oil, vanilla, melted chocolate, and coffee and beat well. Mix the flour, baking powder, and baking soda together and add, beating vigorously by hand for 3 or 4 minutes until smooth and blended, or for 2 minutes if using an electric beater. Spread in the pan and bake for 35–40 minutes, or until a toothpick comes out clean. Spread with *Broiled Frosting* (p. 534) while still in the pan and put under the broiler to brown. Or cool in the pan for 5 minutes, then turn out onto a rack and frost when cool with *Butter Frosting II* (p. 539).

Quick Gold Cake

(TWO 8- OR 9-INCH ROUND LAYERS)

2¼ cups (315 g) cake flour
3 teaspoons baking powder
1 teaspoon salt
1¼ cups (250 g) sugar

½ cup (1 dL) vegetable oil
1 cup (¼ L) milk
2 eggs
2 teaspoons vanilla

Preheat the oven to 350°F (180°C). Butter and lightly flour two 8- or 9-inch round cake pans. Mix the flour, baking powder, salt, and sugar in a bowl. Stir in the oil and milk, and beat for 2 minutes. Add the eggs and vanilla, and beat for another 2 minutes. Pour into the pans and bake for 25–30 minutes, or until a toothpick comes out clean. Cool in the pans for 5 minutes before turning out onto racks. Frost with *Fluffy Butter Frosting* (p. 539) or *Mocha Rum Butter Frosting* (p. 539).

Quick Date Cake

(9-INCH SQUARE CAKE)

5 tablespoons soft butter
1 cup (¼ L) dark-brown sugar
2 eggs
½ cup (1 dL) milk
1¾ cups (245 g) flour

2 teaspoons baking powder
½ teaspoon cinnamon
½ teaspoon nutmeg
½ pound (225 g) dates, cut in pieces

Preheat the oven to 350°F (180°C). Butter and lightly flour a 9-inch square cake pan. Combine all the ingredients in a mixing bowl and beat for 3 minutes with a wooden spoon. Pour into the pan and bake for 35–40 minutes, until a toothpick comes out clean. Cool in the pan for 5 minutes before turning out onto a rack. While still warm, dust with *confectioners' sugar* sifted through a strainer.

CUPCAKES

About Cupcakes

Just about any plain white, butter, or chocolate cake recipe can be used for cupcakes. Bake them in muffin pans, greased or lined with fluted paper cups. Fill each cup halfway. Cupcakes will bake in less time than layer cakes, usually about 15 minutes in a preheated 350°F oven, or until a straw inserted in the center comes out clean. Let cupcakes cool in the pan for about 5 minutes before turning them out onto a rack to cool thoroughly. The three recipes that follow make particularly nice cupcakes.

Boston Cupcakes

There's more than a little hint of mace to give these a true New England quality.

(12 MEDIUM CUPCAKES)

5 tablespoons butter	2 teaspoons baking powder
1 cup (200 g) sugar	¼ teaspoon mace
2 eggs	¼ teaspoon salt
1¼ cups (175 g) cake flour	½ cup (1 dL) milk

Preheat the oven to 350°F (180°C). Butter muffin tins for 12 cupcakes or line them with fluted paper cups. Cream the butter, gradually add the sugar, and beat until light and fluffy. Stir in the eggs and beat well. Mix the flour, baking powder, mace, and salt together. Add to the first mixture, then stir in the milk and beat until well combined. Spoon into the pans, filling each cup about two-thirds full. Bake for 15 minutes, until a straw or toothpick comes out clean. Cool in the pan for 5 minutes before turning out onto a rack. Frost with *Creamy Chocolate Frosting* (p. 536) or *Coffee Butter Frosting* (p. 539).

Almond Cakes

These are moistly delicate, lovely for afternoon tea or with a dish of vanilla ice cream with caramel sauce.

(8 CAKES)

¼ pound (115 g) butter	¼ teaspoon salt
¾ cup (150 g) sugar	⅓ cup (¾ dL) milk
2 eggs, well beaten	1 cup (¼ L) blanched
1⅓ cups (190 g) cake flour	almonds, cut into pieces
2 teaspoons baking powder	

Preheat the oven to 375°F (190°C). Line a muffin tin with cupcake papers or grease well. Cream together the butter and sugar until light and fluffy. Add the eggs, beating thoroughly. Stir in the flour, baking powder, and salt; beat, and add the milk. Mix well and stir in the almonds. Spoon the batter into the muffin tins two-thirds full. Bake for 15–20 minutes or until center is dry when a straw is inserted.

Date Nut Cakes

These make a delicious dessert crowned with a generous amount of whipped cream.

(12 CAKES)

1 teaspoon baking soda
1 cup (¼ L) pitted chopped
  dates
1 tablespoon butter, softened
1 cup (200 g) sugar

½ teaspoon salt
2 eggs, well beaten
1 cup (140 g) flour
1 cup (¼ L) coarsely chopped
  walnuts

Preheat the oven to 325°F (165°C). Line a 12-cup muffin pan with cupcake liners or grease well. Mix 1 cup boiling water with the soda, then add the dates. Set aside to cool. Combine the butter, sugar, salt, eggs, and flour. Mix well. Add the date mixture and walnuts. Beat until well blended. Spoon into each cup until almost full. Bake 40–50 minutes, or until a toothpick comes out clean when inserted. Serve with *softly whipped cream.*

YESTERDAY'S CAKES

Yesterday's cake can return, in a different disguise, sometimes reaching new heights with such simple, good additions as Chocolate Cream Filling (p. 542), Lemon Filling (p. 544), or just softly whipped sweetened cream flavored with rum. When cake loses its appeal or becomes dry, take what is left and cut into bite-size cubes, place in a bowl, add a flavored cream or custard, and gently mix with the cake pieces. Cover and refrigerate at least 4 hours. A lovely change takes place: textures and taste are fresh and new. The remains of a spice cake or a light cake can be cut into strips, spread with a little jam or jelly, rolled up, enclosed in plastic wrap, refrigerated for several hours, and served with coffee or as dessert. Some other suggested additions for recreating cake are: Flavored whipped creams, custards, fresh sliced fruit, berries, ice cream, nuts, liqueurs.

Rum Cake

Use the equivalent of one layer of plain (not chocolate or spice) cake. Cut into serving pieces, or smaller, then sprinkle ⅓–½ cup rum over the pieces. Place them in a 1½-quart serving dish—glass, if possible. Whip 1½ cups heavy cream, sweeten with 3–4 tablespoons sugar and flavor with ½ cup (or more) apricot preserves or raspberry jam. Spread over and around the cake. Press gently, so the cake settles down. Cover and chill for at least 4 hours. Serve from its dish.

Icebox Cake

Line a mold or large bowl with strips of leftover sponge cake, angel food cake, pound cake, or other plain cake. If there is enough cake, have the pieces overlap at the edges. Fill with one of the following fillings:

Butter Filling

¼ pound (115 g) sweet butter,   4 eggs, separated
  softened   2 teaspoons vanilla, or 3
1 cup (¼ L) confectioners'   tablespoons rum
  sugar

Beat the butter, slowly adding the sugar. Continue to beat until light and fluffy. Add the egg yolks, one at a time, beating well after each addition. Add vanilla or rum. In a separate bowl beat the egg whites until stiff but not dry. Gently fold the whites into the butter mixture, then spoon into the cake-lined mold. Cover and chill overnight. Unmold and serve with *whipped cream*.

Chocolate Filling. Melt *1 ounce unsweetened chocolate* with 2 tablespoons water. Cool and add to the butter mixture before folding in the egg whites. Continue as directed.

Lemon Filling. Add the *grated rind and juice of 1 lemon* to the butter mixture before folding in the egg whites.

Coffee Filling. Add *3 tablespoons instant coffee* to the butter mixture before folding in the egg whites.

Tipsy Pudding

½ cup (1 dL) sherry   1 cup (¼ L) heavy cream,
3 cups (¾ L) unfrosted cake   whipped
  cut in 1-inch cubes   1 cup (¼ L) macaroon crumbs
1 recipe Soft Custard (p. 608)   (optional)

Put the sherry in a bowl, add the cake cubes, and lightly toss to get some sherry on each piece. Cover with Soft Custard, spoon whipped cream on top, and sprinkle with crumbs, if you wish. Cover and refrigerate at least 2 hours.

English Trifle. Add *a cup or so of fresh diced fruit*—peaches, bananas, plums, berries—or *canned fruit* to the cake cubes when you toss them.

Tipsy Pudding with Ladyfingers. Instead of using cake, line the bowl with *1 dozen or so ladyfingers*, then pour Soft Custard (p. 608), flavored with sherry, over.

FROSTINGS &
FILLINGS

ABOUT FROSTINGS AND FILLINGS

You can add a complex blend of flavors and textures to a plain cake by using a special filling between the layers and a contrasting frosting on the sides and top of the cake. Most frequently, however, layer cakes are filled and frosted with the same frosting. In general, 1½–2 cups of frosting will fill and cover two 8- or 9-inch layers. Since this varies, depending on the thickness of the frosting, we indicate with the recipe how much cake each frosting will cover. Again as a general rule, ½–¾ cup of filling will fill a two-layer cake.

Whenever possible, spread *uncooked* frostings on cakes that are still slightly warm. *Cooked* frostings, on the other hand, should be used after the cake has cooled completely.

Frostings that are too thin can be thickened: stir in some confectioners' sugar to thicken an *uncooked* frosting; put *cooked* frostings in the top of a double boiler and beat them over hot water until they thicken. To thin any frosting that is too thick, very gradually beat in a few drops of hot water.

Frostings made with eggs or butter should be refrigerated if you are not serving the cake until the next day. Frostings will keep a long time refrigerated; there's no need to freeze them.

If a cake is lopsided or uneven, do not hesitate to reshape it before you frost it. Use a sharp knife and slice off whatever is necessary to make a cake regular or cake layers uniform. If you are making a three-layer cake and the middle layer has a rounded top, slice off the raised portion so that the layers fit together evenly. You can also slice through cake layers horizontally to make a cake with lots of filling and four or more thin layers. Before you slice through horizontally, as illustrated, first make a shallow vertical cut to mark the place where you'll need to fit the layers together later.

Frosting Cakes

Place the bottom layer upside down on a serving plate. Tuck strips of wax paper or foil around to catch any icing that may drip down.

Spread filling on the bottom layer and then set the top layer over it, right side up, so that the two level surfaces are face to face. (If you are doing several layers, align the vertical cuts you made before slicing the layers in half.) Using a wide knife or a spatula, cover the sides first, then pile the remaining frosting on the top and swirl it to the edges. (If you dip the knife or spatula in warm water from time to time, the frosting will be shiny and spread more easily.) If you are not going to decorate, you can make a simple cross hatching with the tines of a fork on the top.

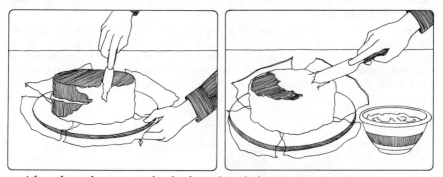

After the cake is completely frosted and the frosting has had time to set, remove the strips of paper or foil protecting the serving plate.

Decorating Cakes

You can decorate a cake very simply, using chopped or whole nuts, coconut, tiny candies, colored sugar, or candied fruit or flowers. Arrange them in patterns or sprinkle them at random over the cake. Candles are, of course, essential for birthday cakes; they should be in holders, which you can buy—or even make yourself, if you are inventive.

If you wish to do something elaborate, decorate your cake with icing pushed through a pastry bag. A pastry bag is a worthwhile investment, and far easier and more satisfactory to use than metal cake decorators. Pastry bags come with a set of tips; each is cut in a special way to make specific patterns.

If you don't have a pastry bag, or if you are using a number of different colors and need a different bag for each, try making your own pastry bags out of sheets of heavy typing paper or baking parchment. Fold each sheet into a tight cornucopia with a sharp point, and fasten it firmly with Scotch tape. Pinch the point flat and cut it according to the design you want: straight across to make a ribbon design, in two points to make leaves, or in three points to make stars. Or drop metal decorating tips into the bags.

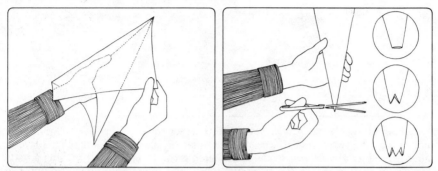

Confectioners' Frosting II (opposite), *Royal Frosting* (p. 536), or any butter frosting will work well in a pastry bag. Before filling the bag, fold one-third of the top back. Also, push the fabric down into the large end of the metal tube to block the opening. Fill the bag half full—about to the level where you have folded the top down; then unfold and twist the top of the pastry bag firmly around the filling.

Spread out a piece of wax paper near the cake. Push a little frosting out onto the paper to make sure there are no air bubbles in the cone and practice a little before you tackle the cake. Then decorate the cake itself; one hand should be near the nozzle guiding the tip and squeezing the bag slightly while the other hand holds the twisted end and exerts a little downward pressure.

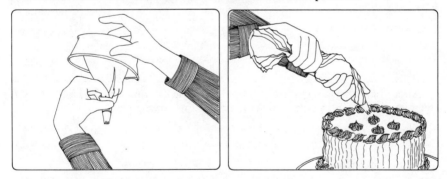

FROSTINGS

Broiled Frosting

This simple frosting, also used as lazy daisy topping, is to be spread on a warm, freshly baked one-layer cake which is then set under the broiler to brown. Watch carefully to be sure that the topping browns lightly and evenly.

(FROSTS 8-INCH SQUARE CAKE)

3 tablespoons melted butter
3 tablespoons dark-brown sugar
2 tablespoons cream

½ cup (1 dL) shredded coconut
or chopped nuts

Mix all the ingredients together and spread over a warm cake while it is still in the pan. Set the pan under the broiler until the frosting bubbles and turns golden.

Confectioners' Frosting I

You can give this sweet frosting different flavors by substituting the same amount of hot coffee, lemon juice, or orange juice for the hot water. Or substitute 1 teaspoon of vanilla for the hot water. For a fine creamy consistency, be sure to beat the frosting very well.

(MAKES 1 CUP)

About 2½ cups (6 dL)
confectioners' sugar

Put 3 tablespoons hot water in a small bowl and beat in the confectioners' sugar until the frosting is thick enough to spread. Continue to beat for several minutes until very creamy. This will be enough frosting for an 8-inch two-layer cake.

Confectioners' Frosting II

This pure-white, creamy frosting is excellent for decorating cakes; the shortening will keep it from becoming dry and it can be tinted with vegetable coloring, if you wish.

(MAKES ABOUT 1 CUP)

⅓ cup (¾ dL) vegetable
shortening
⅛ teaspoon salt
About 2 cups (½ L)
confectioners' sugar

About 2 tablespoons cream or
milk

Cream the shortening and the salt together, then beat in the sugar. Stir in the cream or milk and beat well, adding more sugar or more milk if necessary to get the proper consistency. This is enough to frost an 8-inch two-layer cake.

Portsmouth Frosting

This tastes of butter and cream, and what could be nicer?

(MAKES ABOUT 1¾ CUPS)

4 tablespoons melted butter
¼ cup (½ dL) cream
1 teaspoon vanilla or rum

About 3 cups (¾ L)
confectioners' sugar

Mix the butter, cream, and vanilla or rum together in a bowl. Slowly beat in the sugar until thick and creamy. This is enough to fill and frost an 8- or 9-inch two-layer cake.

Royal Frosting

This is a fine basic frosting, light and airy rather than creamy. If you wish, flavor it with 1 teaspoon of any kind of extract.

(MAKES ABOUT 2 CUPS)

1 cup (¼ L) confectioners' sugar
¼ teaspoon cream of tartar
1 egg white

Mix all the ingredients in a bowl. Add ⅓ cup boiling water. Beat at high speed for 6–10 minutes, until the frosting is thick enough to stand in peaks. This will be enough to fill and frost an 8- or 9-inch two-layer cake.

Chocolate Frosting

Smooth, shiny, and thick.

(MAKES ABOUT 1 CUP)

2 ounces (60 g) unsweetened chocolate
1 tablespoon butter
⅓ cup (¾ dL) milk (more if necessary)

2 cups (½ L) confectioners' sugar
1 teaspoon vanilla

Melt the chocolate, butter, and milk together in a small bowl or pot over simmering water. Cool to lukewarm, then stir in the sugar and vanilla. Beat until thick enough to spread. This will be enough to frost an 8- or 9-inch two-layer cake.

Creamy Chocolate Frosting

(MAKES ABOUT 2 CUPS)

2 ounces (60 g) unsweetened chocolate, grated
1 cup (200 g) sugar
3 tablespoons cornstarch

1 tablespoon butter
1 teaspoon vanilla
⅛ teaspoon salt

Combine the chocolate, sugar, and cornstarch in a heavy-bottomed pan. Stir in 1 cup boiling water, and cook, stirring constantly, until thick and smooth. Remove from the heat and add the butter, vanilla, and salt. Beat well. You will have enough to fill and frost an 8- or 9-inch two-layer cake.

Chocolate Frosting for Cream Puffs and Éclairs

For Cream Puffs and Éclairs, see p. 596.

3 ounces (85 g) semisweet chocolate
2 tablespoons butter

Melt the chocolate and the butter in a small pan over moderate heat, stirring constantly until smooth. Spoon over filled cream puffs or éclairs and let drip down the sides.

Fudge Frosting

(MAKES ABOUT 2 CUPS)

2 ounces (60 g) unsweetened
   chocolate, cut in bits
1½ cups (300 g) sugar
½ cup (1 dL) milk

4 tablespoons butter
1 tablespoon corn syrup
¼ teaspoon salt
1 teaspoon vanilla

Stir together all the ingredients except the vanilla in a heavy-bottomed pan.
Bring to a rolling boil and cook, stirring vigorously, for just 1 minute; cool. Add
the vanilla and beat until thick. This will fill and frost an 8- or 9-inch two-layer
cake.

Quick Fudge Frosting

(MAKES ABOUT 2 CUPS)

2 ounces (60 g) unsweetened
   chocolate
1 can sweetened condensed
   milk

1 teaspoon vanilla
⅛ teaspoon salt

Melt the chocolate with the milk in a heavy-bottomed pan, stirring constantly.
Remove from the heat and beat in the vanilla and salt. Add about 1 tablespoon
hot water, a few drops at a time, until the frosting is thin enough to spread. You
will have enough to fill and frost an 8- or 9-inch two-layer cake.

Vanilla Fudge Frosting

(MAKES ABOUT 1½ CUPS)

1 tablespoon butter
1½ cups (300 g) sugar
½ cup (1 dL) milk

⅛ teaspoon salt
1 teaspoon vanilla

Mix the butter, sugar, milk, and salt in a heavy-bottomed pan. Bring to the
boiling point over moderate heat, then boil without stirring until the mixture
reaches 234°F, or the "soft-ball stage" (see p. 677). Let cool, then beat until thick
enough to spread. Add the vanilla. You will have enough to fill and frost an 8-
or 9-inch two-layer cake.

Quick Caramel Frosting

(MAKES ABOUT 1½ CUPS)

¼ pound (115 g) butter
½ cup (1 dL) dark-brown sugar
¼ cup (½ dL) milk

2 cups (½ L) confectioners'
   sugar

Melt the butter and brown sugar in a heavy-bottomed pan, stirring over moderate
heat until the sugar is dissolved. Add the milk and blend. Cool, then beat in the
confectioners' sugar until thick enough to spread. You will have enough to fill
and frost an 8- or 9-inch two-layer cake.

Penuche Frosting

Excellent caramel flavor.

(MAKES 1½–2 CUPS)

1½ cups (3½ dL) dark-brown
  sugar
¾ cup (150 g) granulated sugar
⅛ teaspoon salt

½ cup (1 dL) milk
3 tablespoons butter
1½ tablespoons corn syrup
1½ teaspoons vanilla

Mix all the ingredients except the vanilla in a heavy-bottomed pan. Bring slowly to the boiling point, stirring constantly, and boil for just 1 minute. Cool to lukewarm, add the vanilla, and beat until thick enough to spread. You will have enough to fill and frost an 8- or 9-inch two-layer cake.

Maple Frosting

(MAKES ABOUT 2½ CUPS)

1½ cups (3½ dL) maple syrup
⅛ teaspoon salt
¼ teaspoon cream of tartar

¼ cup (50 g) sugar
2 egg whites

Combine all the ingredients in the top of a double boiler or in a bowl. Beat the mixture over simmering water until it stands in stiff peaks, about 5–7 minutes, no longer. You will have enough to fill and frost an 8- or 9-inch two-layer cake.

Sultana Nut Frosting

Creamy and good, with a praline taste.

(MAKES ABOUT 2¼ CUPS)

2 cups (½ L) dark-brown sugar
¾ cup (1¾ dL) heavy cream
¼ cup (½ dL) seedless raisins

¼ cup (½ dL) finely chopped
  walnuts

Mix the brown sugar and cream in a heavy-bottomed pan and boil without stirring until the mixture reaches 234°F, or the "soft-ball stage" (see p. 677). Pour onto a large platter and let cool. Work with a spatula until creamy, then stir in the raisins and walnuts. You will have enough to fill and frost an 8- or 9-inch two-layer cake.

Cream Cheese Frosting

(MAKES ABOUT 1¼ CUPS)

4 tablespoons cream cheese,
  softened
1½ cups (3½ dL)
  confectioners' sugar

1 egg white, slightly beaten
½ teaspoon vanilla
⅛ teaspoon salt

Beat all the ingredients together until light and of spreading consistency. You will have enough to fill and frost an 8-inch two-layer cake.

Butter Frosting I

If you want more frosting, double the butter and the sugar, but use only the one yolk.

(MAKES ABOUT ¾ CUP)

4 tablespoons butter
1 egg yolk
1 cup (¼ L) confectioners' sugar

Beat the butter until light and creamy. Stir in the egg yolk and continue to beat, adding the sugar, 2 tablespoons at a time. Beat until all the sugar is added and the frosting is fluffy. You will have enough to frost an 8-inch two-layer cake.

Butter Frosting II

(MAKES ABOUT 1 CUP)

½ cup (100 g) sugar
1 egg yolk
¼ pound (115 g) chilled butter

Boil the sugar and ¼ cup water without stirring in a heavy-bottomed pan until the mixture reaches 240°F, or the "medium soft-ball stage" (see p. 677). While the sugar syrup is cooking, beat the egg yolk well. Slowly pour the 240° syrup over the beaten yolk, beating constantly. Beat in bits of the cold butter until it is all incorporated. Continue to beat until the frosting is of spreading consistency. You will have enough to frost a 9-inch two-layer cake.

Chocolate Butter Frosting. Melt *4 ounces semisweet chocolate* and add to the frosting after the butter has been incorporated.

Coffee Butter Frosting. Add *2 teaspoons instant coffee* to the frosting after the butter has been incorporated.

Mocha Rum Butter Frosting. Add *1½ tablespoons rum* and *2 teaspoons instant coffee* after the butter has been incorporated.

Fluffy Butter Frosting

Light and airy.

(MAKES ABOUT 1½ CUPS)

4 tablespoons butter
1½ cups (3½ dL) confectioners' sugar
2 egg whites

Cream the butter until light. Gradually add ½ cup of the sugar; set aside. Beat the egg whites until foamy, slowly add the remaining cup of sugar and continue to beat until stiff. Combine the two mixtures and blend. Add more sugar if necessary to make the frosting thick enough to spread. You will have enough to fill and frost an 8- or 9-inch two-layer cake.

Seven-Minute Frosting

A light, billowy frosting with a sheen, very much like a "boiled" frosting. Seven-minute frosting dries out quickly, so keep it refrigerated if you're not using it within a few hours.

(MAKES ABOUT 2 CUPS)

1½ cups (300 g) sugar
¼ teaspoon cream of tartar
⅛ teaspoon salt

2 egg whites
2 teaspoons vanilla

Mix sugar, cream of tartar, salt, egg whites, and ¼ cup water in a pot or bowl over simmering water. Beat steadily over low heat with a rotary or electric hand beater until the frosting stands in peaks, about 5–7 minutes, no more. Remove from the heat and continue to beat until thick enough to spread. Add the vanilla before spreading. You will have enough to fill and frost an 8- or 9-inch two-layer cake.

Caramel Frosting. Omit the vanilla and substitute *1 cup dark-brown sugar* for 1 cup of the white sugar.

Coconut Frosting. Omit the vanilla and stir in *½ cup shredded coconut* (p. 13) before spreading.

Coffee Frosting. Omit the vanilla and add *1 tablespoon instant coffee* before spreading.

Lemon or Orange Frosting. Omit the vanilla and substitute *¼ cup lemon or orange juice* for the water. Add *1 teaspoon grated lemon or orange rind* before spreading.

Peppermint Frosting. Omit the vanilla. Add *½ teaspoon oil of peppermint* and a few drops of *green food coloring* before spreading.

Italian Meringue

This light, fluffy frosting should be applied very generously to the cake. Cooking procedures are important here to prevent the syrup from crystallizing or becoming grainy.

(MAKES ABOUT 5 CUPS)

3 egg whites
Pinch of salt

1 cup (200 g) sugar
1½ teaspoons vanilla

Combine the egg whites and salt in a bowl and beat until the whites are stiff but not dry; set aside. Combine the sugar and ½ cup water in a small, heavy-bottomed pan. Heat, without stirring, until the mixture begins to boil. Cover for 3 minutes to dissolve any sugar crystals on the sides of the pan. Remove the lid and let the syrup boil without stirring for about 10–15 minutes until it "spins a thread" (see p. 677) or reaches 230–232°F on a candy thermometer. Very slowly pour the syrup over the beaten whites, beating constantly all the while; continue to beat until the meringue has cooled to room temperature. Beat in the vanilla. You will have frosting enough to fill and frost an 8- or 9-inch two- or even three-layer cake.

White Mountain Cream

This is the classic "boiled" frosting, fluffy with a marshmallowlike consistency. A hot sugar syrup cooks the egg whites as it thickens them.

(MAKES ABOUT 1½ CUPS)

1 cup (200 g) sugar
⅛ teaspoon cream of tartar
⅛ teaspoon salt

2 egg whites
1 teaspoon vanilla

Mix the sugar, ⅓ cup water, cream of tartar, and salt in a heavy-bottomed pan. Boil without stirring until the mixture reaches 240°F, or the "medium soft-ball stage" (see p. 677). Beat the egg whites until stiff, then pour the 240° sugar syrup over them in a slow, thin stream, beating constantly until thick enough to spread. Stir in the vanilla. You will have enough to fill and frost an 8- or 9-inch two-layer cake.

Petits Fours Frosting

Use this on any cake or to cover Petits Fours (p. 568).

(FROSTING FOR 80 PETITS FOURS)

2 cups (400 g) granulated sugar
⅛ teaspoon cream of tartar

1½ cups (3½ dL) or more
confectioners' sugar

Combine the granulated sugar, cream of tartar, and 1 cup water in a saucepan. Bring to a boil and boil without stirring until the mixture becomes a thin syrup, 226°F on a candy thermometer. Cool until slightly above lukewarm (100°F). Gradually stir in confectioners' sugar until the syrup is just thick enough to coat a spoon. Test it by pouring a little over a cake to see if it's the proper consistency. Use while warm or reheat over simmering water.

Colored Petits Fours Frosting. Divide Petits Fours Frosting into separate bowls and tint each with a different shade of vegetable coloring. Or tint the frosting delicately, frost one row of petits fours, then add more coloring, making each row of cakes a bit deeper in color. White, pink, rose, and red make a good series, as do white, yellow, pale orange, and deep orange.

Chocolate Petits Fours Frosting. Melt 3 *ounces unsweetened chocolate* over simmering water and stir it into warm Petits Fours Frosting. Use less chocolate if you are flavoring only part of the frosting.

Basic Glaze

Use hot orange juice, lemon juice, strong coffee, or another liquid of your choice instead of the hot water, if you wish to change the flavor of this basic glaze.

Confectioners' sugar

Add hot water *very gradually* to the confectioners' sugar, a few drops at a time, and beat constantly until the glaze is thin enough to pour. Pour it over cake and let it dribble down the sides.

Chocolate Glaze

Unsweetened chocolate
Butter

Melt the chocolate with the butter over simmering water, using 1 table-spoon of butter for each ounce of chocolate. Let the glaze cool slightly, then dribble it over white frosting after it has set. Use the tines of a fork to create a lined or crisscrossed effect in the chocolate.

Apricot Glaze

1 small jar apricot preserves

Melt the apricot preserves over low heat until liquid. Strain and spread on the cake.

FILLINGS

Basic Cream Filling

Also known as *crème patissière*, this basic custard is good by itself or used in cream puffs, pies, and other pastries.

(MAKES ABOUT 1¾ CUPS)

1 cup (¼ L) milk
½ cup (100 g) sugar
3 tablespoons flour

⅛ teaspoon salt
2 egg yolks, slightly beaten
2 teaspoons vanilla

Heat the milk in a heavy-bottomed pan until very hot but not boiling. Mix the sugar, flour, and salt together in a bowl, stir in the hot milk, and beat until well blended. Pour back into the pan and continue to stir vigorously over low heat for 4–5 minutes, until very thick and smooth. Add the egg yolks and cook for a few more minutes. Cool, stirring from time to time, then add the vanilla. You will have about enough filling for an 8- or 9-inch three-layer cake.

Banana Cream Filling. Omit the vanilla. Mash *1 large banana* and beat it until smooth, add *2 tablespoons lemon juice,* and stir the mixture into the cooled filling.

Chocolate Cream Filling. Melt *2 ounces unsweetened chocolate* in the milk and use *1 cup sugar* instead of ½ cup.

Butter Cream Filling

Use dollops of butter cream filling as a topping for poached fruit.

(MAKES ABOUT 3½ CUPS)

⅓ cup (65 g) sugar
⅓ cup (50 g) flour
2 cups (½ L) milk

½ pound (225 g) butter
2 teaspoons vanilla

Mix the sugar and flour in a small, heavy-bottomed pan. Place over moderate heat and slowly stir in the milk. Cook, stirring constantly, until thick and smooth. Add the butter, bit by bit, stirring over moderate heat until all the butter has been incorporated. Cool, then stir in the vanilla. You will have enough filling for an 8- or 9-inch four-layer cake.

Lord Baltimore Filling and Frosting

Use this with Lord Baltimore Cake (p. 510).

(MAKES ABOUT 3½ CUPS)

One recipe Seven-Minute
  Frosting (p. 540)
½ cup (1 dL) dry macaroon
  crumbs
¼ cup (½ dL) chopped pecans

¼ cup (½ dL) chopped
  blanched almonds
12 candied cherries, in quarters
2 teaspoons lemon juice
½ teaspoon orange extract

Divide the frosting in half. Fold all of the remaining ingredients into half the frosting and use as a filling between two yellow 8-inch cake layers. Use the remaining plain frosting to cover the sides and the top of the cake.

Lady Baltimore Filling and Frosting

Use this with Lady Baltimore Cake (p. 510).

(MAKES ABOUT 3 CUPS)

One recipe Seven-Minute
  Frosting (p. 540)
⅓ cup (¾ dL) chopped pecans

3 dried figs, cut in bits
½ cup (1 dL) raisins
½ teaspoon almond extract

Divide the frosting in half. Fold the pecans, figs, raisins, and almond extract into half the frosting and use it as a filling between two white 8-inch cake layers. Use the remaining plain frosting to cover the sides and the top of the cake.

Lemon Coconut Cream Filling

(MAKES ABOUT 2 CUPS)

Juice and grated rind of 1
  lemon
1 cup (200 g) sugar

2 egg yolks, slightly beaten
1 cup (¼ L) shredded coconut

Mix the lemon juice and rind, sugar, and egg yolks in a heavy-bottomed pan and cook over moderate heat, stirring constantly, until smooth and thickened. Remove from the heat, stir in the coconut, and cool. You will have enough filling for an 8- or 9-inch three-layer cake.

Lemon Filling

Lemon filling also makes a delightful dessert topped with chilled, sliced strawberries, oranges, or bananas.

(MAKES ABOUT ½ CUP)

1 cup (200 g) sugar	Grated rind of 2 lemons
2½ tablespoons flour	1 egg
¼ cup (½ dL) lemon juice	1 tablespoon butter

Mix all the ingredients together in a heavy-bottomed pan. Cook over moderate heat, stirring constantly, until thick and smooth. Cool before spreading between layers. You will have enough filling for an 8- or 9-inch three-layer cake.

Orange Filling

Orange filling can also make a pretty and unusual dessert with cooked prunes or pears spooned over it.

(MAKES ABOUT 1¼ CUPS)

¾ cup (150 g) sugar	1 tablespoon lemon juice
¼ cup (35 g) flour	2 egg yolks, slightly beaten
Grated rind of 1 orange	⅛ teaspoon salt

Mix all the ingredients in a heavy-bottomed pan and cook over moderate heat, stirring constantly, until thickened and smooth. Cool. You will have enough filling for an 8- or 9-inch three-layer cake.

Butterscotch Filling

Good, also, with sliced bananas or some softened vanilla ice cream.

(MAKES ABOUT 1¾ CUPS)

½ cup (1 dL) dark-brown sugar	½ teaspoon salt
2 tablespoons butter	2 eggs, slightly beaten
1 cup (¼ L) milk	½ teaspoon vanilla
3 tablespoons flour	

Mix the sugar and butter in a heavy-bottomed pot. Cook over low heat, stirring constantly, until the sugar has melted and blended with the butter. Add ½ cup of the milk and continue cooking until well blended. Mix the flour and salt with the remaining ½ cup of milk, add to the first mixture, and cook, stirring constantly, until thickened. Add the eggs and cook for another 2 minutes. Cool, then stir in the vanilla. You will have enough filling for an 8- or 9-inch three-layer cake.

French Cream Filling

(MAKES ABOUT 3 CUPS)

1 egg white	¼ cup (½ dL) confectioners'
⅛ teaspoon salt	sugar
1 cup (¼ L) heavy cream	1 teaspoon vanilla

Beat the egg white until foamy, then add the salt and continue beating until stiff but not dry. Beat the cream separately until it forms soft peaks, then slowly beat in the sugar and the vanilla. Fold the two mixtures together. You will have enough filling for an 8- or 9-inch three-layer cake.

French Coffee Filling. Add *2 teaspoons instant coffee* instead of the vanilla.

French Strawberry Filling. Use *⅓ cup confectioners' sugar* instead of ¼ cup and fold in *½ cup mashed strawberries* at the end.

Chocolate Whipped Cream Filling

Try this as a filling for Chocolate Roll (p. 523).

(MAKES ABOUT 2½ CUPS)

4 ounces (115 g) unsweetened chocolate
2 tablespoons butter
1 cup (¼ L) heavy cream

2 cups (½ L) confectioners' sugar
⅛ teaspoon salt

Melt the chocolate and butter together in a small pan or bowl over simmering water. Combine the cream, 1 cup of the confectioners' sugar, and the salt in a bowl; add the melted chocolate and butter mixture. Beat, slowly adding the remaining cup of sugar, for about 10 minutes, until the filling is light and fluffy. You will have enough filling for an 8- or 9-inch three-layer cake.

COOKIES &
CAKE SQUARES

ABOUT MAKING COOKIES AND CAKE SQUARES

See About Cakemaking, p. 501.

Cookies and cake squares, so good to eat and so easy to make, are often the enticements that first lure youngsters into the mysterious ways of the kitchen. Many accomplished adult cooks recall childhood "apprenticeships" in the family kitchen, mixing doughs and batters, buttering pans, and shaping cookies.

Ingredients

As with cakes, it's best to have all the ingredients for cookies and cake squares at room temperature before you mix them.

Use all-purpose white flour, unless otherwise indicated. It is not necessary to sift flour when making cookies or cake squares.

As elsewhere, use "large" eggs in these recipes, or make the correct adjustment (see p. 336).

Preparing Pans for Cookies and Cake Squares

Use sturdy cookie sheets that are the right size for your oven, allowing room for the heat to circulate freely around them. Do not use pans with high sides for cookie baking: they will deflect the heat and the cookies will not bake properly.

Greasing cookie sheets is unnecessary when the cookie dough contains a lot of shortening, but you can always put a light film of butter or shortening on the pans if you have any question. Use your fingers or a piece of crumpled paper towel to grease the pans, dipping it into soft butter or vegetable shortening and running it lightly over the pans. Cookie sheets don't need washing or regreasing between batches; just wipe off any crumbs.

Cake squares are usually baked in greased and lightly floured pans, 1½–2 inches deep. Be sure to use the pan size called for in the recipe if you want the cake to turn out right.

Mixing Cookie Doughs and Cake-Square Batters

Preheat the oven, prepare the pans, and measure out the ingredients before you begin to combine them.

Many cookie doughs and cake-square batters can easily be blended together with a wooden spoon, or you can use an electric beater if you find it more convenient.

Filling Cookie and Cake-Square Pans

Dropped Cookies. To make dropped cookies, take a spoonful or less of the dough and drop or push it off onto a cookie sheet. Leave 1–2 inches of space between the cookies, for they will spread, thin doughs more than thick ones.

Thicker doughs can be placed on the cookie sheets and then pressed flat with the back of a floured spoon or the bottom of a glass. Or spread them flat with a knife that has been dipped in cold water.

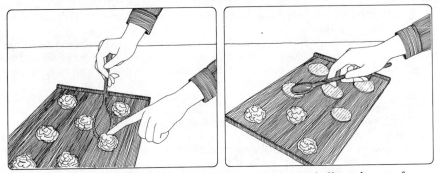

Or shape dropped cookies by forming them into balls with your fingers and arranging them on a cookie sheet, flattening them if you wish.

If cookies are flattened before baking, they will be more uniform in shape than if they are allowed to spread naturally.

Rolled Cookies. Chill the dough for rolled cookies so that it will not stick when you roll it out on a board. If the dough still seems sticky, sprinkle the rolling pin and the board lightly with flour or confectioners' sugar.

Roll the dough until it is ⅛–¼ inch thick and then cut it into shapes, using cookie cutters or the rim of a glass. Or cut the rolled dough into squares or diamonds, using a sharp knife.

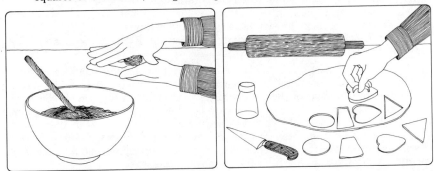

After the shaped cookies have been cut out, gather up all the scraps of dough, put them together, and roll or pat them out again to make more cookies.

Refrigerator Cookies. Shape the dough for refrigerator cookies by hand into rolls about 2 inches in diameter, then wrap the rolls with foil or plastic wrap. Or use a cookie mold designed for this purpose. Well-wrapped cookie dough will keep in the refrigerator for at least a week and can also be frozen.

Use a sharp knife to slice off each cookie, making the slices as thin or as thick as you wish. Bake them on ungreased pans. Refrigerator cookies are practical, especially for small families, because you can bake only as many as you need at a particular time.

Any cookie recipe that uses at least ¼ cup of butter or shortening for each cup of flour may be used for refrigerator cookies; doughs that use less shortening, however, may dry out or crumble.

Pressed Cookies. If you use a cookie press, you can make cookies in a variety of professional-looking shapes to suit a number of occasions. The doughs for Norwegian Butter Cookies (p. 562) and Refrigerator Cookies (p. 562) work particularly well in a cookie press. Select disks with the shapes you want, pack the dough into the press, and push the cookies out onto cookie sheets. Electric cookie presses are also available; follow the manufacturer's directions when using them.

Holiday and Christmas Cookies. Christmas cookies and cookies shaped for other occasions can be made with a cookie press or with molds or be shaped by hand—stars, Santas, bells, Christmas trees, or whatever you like. It's fun to assemble an assortment of different sizes, shapes, and flavors.

For holiday giving select cookies that keep well so you can make them a week or two ahead. Store them in airtight containers. You can also make gift cookies ahead of time and freeze them. Cookies tend to take on each other's flavors if stored together for even a few days: pack different kinds of cookies separately until you are ready to combine them in gift boxes, or wrap them in separate boxes if they are very strongly flavored.

Cookies can also be ornaments to hang on the Christmas tree. To create a loop for hanging them, cut string in 3-inch pieces, fold each piece in half, and press the cut ends into the underside of unbaked cookies. The finished cookies will have loops baked right into them.

Cookie Bars and Cake Squares. Bars and squares are the easiest small confections to make. The dough or batter is mixed, spooned into a greased pan of the right size, spread evenly with a spatula, baked, and cut into bars or squares.

Baking Cookies and Cake Squares

Always bake cookies in a preheated oven unless the recipe says not to and do only one sheet at a time, unless your oven is wide enough to accommodate two sheets on the same rack. The cookie sheet should be on the center rack, allowing room for heat to circulate around it, and turn it if the cookies are baking unevenly.

Watch cookies carefully while they are baking: many thin cookies require 5 minutes or less to brown, and the baking time may vary a bit each time you bake, depending on the heat of the oven and the placement of the pan. If some bake more quickly, remove them with a spatula when they are done and continue baking the rest. If you like cookies chewy and slightly soft, keep them in the oven for a shorter time than called for; leave them in longer if you want them to be very crisp. Let the pans cool off a bit before putting new cookies on them, or the next batch may not hold their shapes.

Cake squares should also be baked in the center of the oven. Check them to see if they're done about 5 minutes before the suggested baking time is over. If you like them very chewy, shorten the baking time a little.

Cooling Cookies and Cake Squares

Remove cookies from the hot pans as soon as they are firm enough to handle, or they will continue to bake. Use a spatula and be careful that they do not crumble. Let very delicate cookies cool slightly before trying to remove them. If the cookies should harden and stick to the pan, put them back in the hot oven for a few minutes to soften them again.

Let warm cookies cool on a plate without touching one another. Do not stack or store them until they have cooled completely or they will not be crisp.

Cake squares are usually left to cool in the pan for about 10–15 minutes before they are cut and removed. If they seem very crumbly, cut them but let them cool thoroughly in the pan before removing them.

Storing Cookies and Cake Squares

Store cookies and cake squares in a tightly covered jar or airtight box to keep them crisp. If they should become soggy, you can freshen them by heating them for a few minutes in a 300°F oven.

If you are storing soft cookies, and you wish them to remain that way, a small slice of apple in the cookie jar will keep them from drying out. Put sheets of wax paper between layers if the cookies or cake squares are very delicate.

All cookies and cake squares freeze well, wrapped in foil or freezer paper or packed in plastic containers or clean coffee tins. Frozen cookies will defrost quickly; indeed, many taste just fine while they are still partially frozen.

Decorating Cookies and Cake Squares

You can decorate cookies and cake squares before they are baked by sprinkling them with plain or colored sugar, or by pressing into them lightly a few nuts, raisins, or bits of citron, coconut, angelica, dates, figs, or candied fruit or fruit peel. Or make a depression in the center of each cookie and fill it with chocolate chips, jam or jelly, candied ginger, or candied orange or lemon peel.

Cookies or cake squares can be dipped in confectioners' sugar while they are still warm, or frosted with tinted frostings, such as Confectioners' Frosting II (p. 535) or Portsmouth Frosting (p. 535). See also Decorating Cakes, p. 533.

COOKIES

Sugar Cookies

Old-fashioned sugar cookies are sweet, rich, and delectable, the essence of what a "plain" cookie should be.

(ABOUT 40 COOKIES)

¼ pound (115 g) butter
¾ cup (150 g) sugar
1 egg
½ teaspoon vanilla

1 tablespoon cream or milk
1¼ cups (175 g) flour
⅛ teaspoon salt
¼ teaspoon baking powder

Preheat the oven to 350°F (180°C). Cream the butter, then gradually add the sugar, beating until light. Add the egg, vanilla, and cream or milk, and beat thoroughly. Mix the flour, salt, and baking powder together, add to the first mixture, and blend well. Arrange by teaspoonfuls on cookie sheets, 1 inch apart. Bake for 8–10 minutes or until lightly browned.

Almond Spice Cookies. Fold ⅓ *cup finely chopped, blanched almonds, ½ teaspoon cinnamon, ½ teaspoon ground cloves, ½ teaspoon nutmeg,* and the *grated rind of ½ lemon* into the cookie dough.

Coconut Cookies. Add ½ *cup finely chopped coconut* to the dough.

Lemon Sugar Cookies. Omit the vanilla and add ½ *teaspoon lemon extract* and *2 teaspoons grated lemon rind* to the dough.

Nut Cookies. Add ½ *cup chopped nuts* to the dough.

Raisin Cookies. Add ½ *cup chopped raisins* to the dough.

Filled Sugar Cookies. Add *about ¼ cup flour* to the dough, just enough so that it can be rolled out. Roll ¼ inch thick and cut into 3-inch circles. Spread half the circles with *jam, jelly, mincemeat,* or the *Fruit and Nut Filling* that follows. Cover with the remaining circles and press the edges together with a fork. Prick well. Bake on buttered cookie sheets in a preheated 325°F (165°C) oven until lightly browned, about 12 minutes.

Fruit and Nut Filling for Filled Sugar Cookies. In a saucepan mix ½ *cup chopped raisins, ½ cup finely cut dates, ¼ cup chopped walnuts, ½ cup water, ½ cup sugar,* and *1 teaspoon flour.* Cook slowly until thick. Use as recommended above.

Rich Butter Cookies

(ABOUT 60 COOKIES)

½ pound (225 g) butter	2 eggs
1 teaspoon vanilla	1½ cups (215 g) flour
⅔ cup (130 g) sugar	½ teaspoon salt

Preheat the oven to 375°F (190°C). Cream the butter and the vanilla. Gradually add the sugar and the eggs and beat well. Mix the flour and salt together, add to the first mixture, and blend thoroughly. Arrange by half-teaspoonfuls on cookie sheets, leaving 2 inches between the cookies—they will spread during baking. Flatten them with a knife dipped in cold water. Bake for about 8 minutes or until lightly browned.

Sour Cream Cookies

(ABOUT 60 COOKIES)

2 eggs	½ teaspoon vanilla
1 cup (200 g) sugar, white or light brown	2 cups (280 g) flour
½ cup (1 dL) sour cream	½ teaspoon baking soda
5 tablespoons melted butter	¼ teaspoon nutmeg

Preheat the oven to 375°F (190°C) and butter some cookie sheets. Beat the eggs well, then add the sugar, sour cream, butter, and vanilla, beating until well incorporated. Mix the flour, baking soda, and nutmeg together and add to the first mixture, beating well. Arrange by teaspoonfuls, 1 inch apart, on the cookie sheets and bake for about 10 minutes or until lightly browned.

Butter Stars

(ABOUT 40 COOKIES)

½ pound (225 g) butter
1 egg yolk
6 tablespoons confectioners' sugar
3 cups (420 g) flour

1 tablespoon sherry or brandy
1 egg white
½ cup (100 g) granulated sugar
⅓ cup (¾ dL) finely chopped almonds

Preheat the oven to 325°F (165°C). Cream the butter, then add the egg yolk, confectioners' sugar, flour, and sherry or brandy and mix thoroughly. Chill for at least 20 minutes. Roll out ⅜ inch thick. Cut with a star cutter, or any other shape you desire, and arrange on ungreased cookie sheets. Beat the egg white until stiff, then gradually beat in the granulated sugar. Put a spoonful of beaten egg white on each cookie and sprinkle with the chopped nuts. Bake for 25 minutes or until lightly browned.

Boston Cookies

Chewy, wholesome, full of good tastes and textures.

(ABOUT 30 COOKIES)

4 tablespoons butter
½ cup (100 g) sugar
1 egg, well beaten
1 cup (140 g) flour
¼ teaspoon baking soda

Few grains of salt
½ teaspoon cinnamon
½ cup (1 dL) chopped nuts
½ cup (1 dL) raisins

Preheat the oven to 350°F (180°C) and butter some cookie sheets. Cream the butter, then gradually add the sugar, mixing well. Beat in the egg. Mix together the flour, baking soda, salt, and cinnamon and add to the first mixture, blending thoroughly. Add the nuts and raisins and mix well. Arrange by spoonfuls, 1 inch apart, on the cookie sheets and bake about 10–12 minutes or until delicately brown.

Molasses Cookies

Some like these plain—some spicy.

(ABOUT 40 COOKIES)

¼ cup (½ dL) molasses
½ cup (1 dL) shortening
¾ cup (1¾ dL) dark-brown sugar

1 egg
1 cup (140 g) flour
½ teaspoon salt
½ teaspoon baking soda

Preheat theoven to 375°F (190°C). Mix the molasses, shortening, brown sugar, and egg in a bowl, combining well. Mix the flour, salt, and baking soda together, add to the first mixture, and blend thoroughly. Arrange by teaspoonfuls on ungreased cookie sheets, about 1 inch apart, and bake for 7–10 minutes or until crisp and lightly browned.

Spiced Molasses Cookies. Add *¼ teaspoon powdered ginger, ¼ teaspoon ground cloves, ¼ teaspoon cinnamon, and ¼ teaspoon nutmeg to the flour mixture.*

Cape Cod Oatmeal Cookies

A fine, chewy oatmeal cookie, wholesome and nourishing.

(ABOUT 70 COOKIES)

1½ cups (210 g) flour
½ teaspoon baking soda
1 teaspoon cinnamon
½ teaspoon salt
1 egg, lightly beaten
1 cup (200 g) sugar
½ cup (1 dL) melted
   shortening

½ cup (115 g) melted butter
1 tablespoon molasses
¼ cup (½ dL) milk
1¾ cups (4 dL) uncooked
   oatmeal
½ cup (1 dL) raisins
½ cup (1 dL) chopped nuts

Preheat the oven to 350°F (180°C). Mix the flour, baking soda, cinnamon, and salt together in a large bowl. Stir in the remaining ingredients. Arrange by teaspoonfuls on unbuttered cookie sheets and bake until the edges are brown, about 12 minutes.

Applesauce Cookies

(ABOUT 40 COOKIES)

¼ pound (115 g) butter
½ cup (1 dL) brown sugar
½ cup (100 g) granulated sugar
1 egg
1 cup (¼ L) applesauce
2 cups (280 g) flour
1 teaspoon baking soda

½ teaspoon salt
1 teaspoon cinnamon
1 teaspoon nutmeg
½ teaspoon ground cloves
1 cup (¼ L) raisins
½ cup (1 dL) chopped nuts

Preheat the oven to 375°F (190°C) and grease some cookie sheets. Cream the butter and add the two sugars, beating until light. Stir in the egg and the applesauce. Mix together the flour, baking soda, salt, cinnamon, nutmeg, and cloves, and add to the first mixture, beating until smooth. Add the raisins and nuts. Arrange by spoonfuls on the cookie sheets and bake for 5–7 minutes or until lightly browned.

Chocolate Coconut Cookies

Almost a candy, these are chewy, not too sweet but very chocolaty.

(ABOUT 40 COOKIES)

14-ounce (400-g) can
   sweetened condensed milk
3 ounces (85 g) unsweetened
   chocolate

2 cups (½ L) shredded coconut
1 cup (¼ L) pecan pieces
1 teaspoon vanilla
Dash of salt

Preheat the oven to 300°F (150°C). Grease some cookie sheets very well. Heat the sweetened condensed milk and the chocolate together in a small pot over simmering water until the chocolate has melted. Remove from the heat and stir in the remaining ingredients. Arrange by teaspoonfuls on the cookie sheets and bake for about 15 minutes, taking care that the bottoms do not burn.

Chocolate Chip Cookies

Is there anyone in America who does not know and love these cookies? They were, incidentally, created by a Massachusetts housewife in 1929.

(ABOUT 50 COOKIES)

¼ pound (115 g) butter
½ cup (1 dL) dark-brown sugar
½ cup (100 g) granulated sugar
1 egg
¾ teaspoon vanilla
1⅛ cups (155 g) flour

½ teaspoon salt
½ teaspoon baking soda
½ cup (1 dL) chopped nuts
1 cup (¼ L, 6 ounces)
semisweet chocolate chips

Preheat the oven to 375°F (190°C) and grease some cookie sheets. Cream the butter, then gradually add the two sugars, beating until light and smooth. Beat in the egg and the vanilla. Mix the flour, salt, and baking soda together and add it to the first mixture, blending well. Stir in the nuts and the chocolate chips. Drop by teaspoonfuls onto the cookie sheets about 1 inch apart and bake for 8–10 minutes or until lightly browned.

Chocolate Chip Oatmeal Cookies. Use ½ *cup uncooked oatmeal* instead of the chopped nuts.

Nut Cookies

(ABOUT 50 COOKIES)

2 eggs, separated
1 cup (¼ L) brown sugar
1 cup (¼ L) chopped nuts

Dash of salt
6 tablespoons flour

Preheat the oven to 350°F (180°C). Beat the egg yolks until they are pale and thick. Gradually beat in the sugar, then add the nuts and salt. Beat the egg whites separately until stiff but not dry. Fold them into the first mixture, then stir in the flour. Drop by teaspoonfuls onto ungreased cookie sheets, leaving about 2 inches between cookies for them to spread. Flatten with a knife. Bake for 5–8 minutes or until firm.

Peanut Butter Cookies

(ABOUT 50 COOKIES)

¼ pound (115 g) butter
½ cup (1 dL) chunk-style
  peanut butter
½ cup (100 g) granulated sugar
½ cup (1 dL) dark-brown sugar

1 egg
½ teaspoon vanilla
½ teaspoon salt
½ teaspoon baking soda
1 cup (140 g) flour

Preheat the oven to 350°F (180°C) and grease some cookie sheets. Cream the butter and peanut butter together. Beat in the two sugars, then add the egg and the vanilla and mix well. Mix together the salt, baking soda, and flour and add to the first mixture, combining thoroughly. Arrange by teaspoonfuls on the cookie sheets, about 1½ inches apart. Press each one flat with the back of a floured spoon. Bake about 7 minutes or until firm.

Chocolate Walnut Wafers

Take care not to overbake this chewy, brownielike cookie.

(ABOUT 50 COOKIES)

2 ounces (60 g) unsweetened
   chocolate
¼ pound (115 g) butter
1 cup (200 g) sugar
2 eggs

1 cup (¼ L) chopped walnuts
⅔ cup (100 g) flour
¼ teaspoon salt
¼ teaspoon vanilla

Preheat the oven to 350°F (180°C) and grease some cookie sheets well. Melt the chocolate in a bowl or pot over simmering water; set aside to cool. Cream the butter and gradually beat in the sugar and the eggs, blending well. Add the chocolate and the walnuts and combine thoroughly. Mix the flour and salt together and add to the first mixture, along with the vanilla. Mix well. Arrange by teaspoonfuls on the cookie sheets and bake for 10–12 minutes or until firm but chewy.

Swedish Nut Wafers

Thin, crisp, and nut-flavored, these are exceptionally good—and thrifty as well: a little bit of batter goes a long way.

(ABOUT 75 COOKIES)

4 tablespoons butter
¾ cup (150 g) sugar
1 egg, well beaten
2 tablespoons milk
1 teaspoon vanilla

1⅓ cups (190 g) flour
1 teaspoon baking powder
½ teaspoon salt
⅓ cup (¾ dL) chopped nut
   meats

Preheat the oven to 325°F (165°C). Lightly butter a cookie sheet or jelly-roll pan. Cream the butter, then gradually beat in the sugar, until well blended. Add the egg, milk, and vanilla and beat well. Mix together the flour, baking powder, and salt and beat into the first mixture. Spread the dough on the cookie sheet as thin as possible, just enough to cover the bottom. Sprinkle with the chopped nuts and press them gently into the dough. Mark with a sharp knife into cookie-sized rectangles and bake about 12 minutes or until delicately browned. Cut while still warm.

Swedish Almond Wafers

These buttery, lacelike cookies are so delicate they must be handled with extreme care. They are exceptionally easy to prepare, but they really spread in baking, so use scant teaspoonfuls of batter and space them far apart on the cookie sheet.

(ABOUT 50 COOKIES)

¾ cup (1¾ dL) finely ground,
   unblanched almonds
¼ pound (115 g) butter

½ cup (100 g) sugar
1 tablespoon flour
2 tablespoons light cream

Preheat the oven to 350°F (180°C). Mix all the ingredients in a heavy saucepan and cook, stirring, over moderate heat until the butter has melted. Arrange by scant teaspoonfuls, 3 inches apart, on a lightly buttered cookie sheet and bake for 3–5 minutes, watching carefully, until delicately brown at the edges but still bubbling slightly in the center. As soon as the edge is firm enough to lift the cookies with a spatula, remove them to a plate and let them cool. Do not stack the cookies until cool, and handle them with care.

Lace Cookies

Thin, crisp, and almost transparent, these splendid cookies are exceedingly simple to make. The little lumps of dough that you put on the baking sheet will spread, melt, and bubble as the cookies bake.

(ABOUT 60 COOKIES)

1½ cups (3½ dL) uncooked oatmeal
1½ cups (3½ dL) light-brown sugar
2 tablespoons flour

½ teaspoon salt
⅔ cup (150 g) melted butter
1 egg, slightly beaten
½ teaspoon vanilla

Preheat the oven to 350°F (180°C). Mix the oatmeal, brown sugar, flour, and salt in a bowl. Stir in the melted butter, then add the egg and vanilla and combine well. Arrange the batter by half-teaspoonfuls, about 2 inches apart, on ungreased cookie sheets. Bake until lightly browned, about 5 minutes. Cool slightly, removing the cookies from the cookie sheet with a spatula as soon as they are firm.

Sand Tarts

(60 COOKIES)

¼ pound (115 g) butter
1½ cups (300 g) sugar
1 egg
2 cups (280 g) flour

¼ teaspoon salt
1 egg white, slightly beaten
1 teaspoon cinnamon

Preheat the oven to 400°F (205°C). Beat the butter until softened, then slowly add 1¼ cups of the sugar, continuing to beat until creamy and smooth. Add the egg and mix well. Add the flour and salt and beat until well blended. Chill the dough for 30 minutes. Sprinkle a surface lightly with flour and roll out the dough *very* thin, then brush it with beaten egg white. Mix the remaining ¼ cup of sugar with the cinnamon and sprinkle over the dough. Cut into desired cookie shapes and place on ungreased cookie sheets. Bake for about 6 minutes or until the edges of the cookies turn slightly golden. Remove from oven; let cool a minute or two before removing to racks to cool. Store in airtight container.

Macaroons

True macaroons are made of egg whites, sugar, and almond paste.

(30 COOKIES)

½ pound (225 g) almond paste
1 cup (200 g) granulated sugar
3 egg whites
⅓ cup (¾ dL) confectioners'
sugar

2 tablespoons cake flour
⅛ teaspoon salt

Preheat the oven to 300°F (150°C). Cover cookie sheets with parchment paper or brown paper. Using your hands or the food processor, soften the almond paste. Gradually blend in the granulated sugar and egg whites; then mix in the confectioners' sugar, flour, and salt. Force through a cookie press or drop by teaspoonfuls onto the paper-covered cookie sheets. Cover and let stand 30 minutes. Bake 25 minutes; lay the paper linings on a damp cloth, let cool, and peel off the macaroons.

Cherry Macaroons. Add 2 *tablespoons chopped candied cherries* to the dough.

Almond Macaroons. Sprinkle before baking with 2 *tablespoons chopped blanched almonds.*

Cornflake "Macaroons"

(18 MACAROONS)

1 egg white
½ cup (100 g) sugar
½ cup (1 dL) shredded coconut
1 cup (¼ L) cornflakes

¼ teaspoon almond extract
¼ teaspoon vanilla
Dash of salt

Preheat the oven to 350°F (180°C) and grease some cookie sheets. Beat the egg white until stiff, then stir in the remaining ingredients. Place by teaspoonfuls on the cookie sheets and bake for about 10 minutes or until lightly browned.

Peanut "Macaroons"

(16 MACAROONS)

1 egg white
¼ cup (50 g) sugar

½ cup (1 dL) chopped peanuts
1 teaspoon vanilla

Preheat the oven to 300°F (150°C) and grease some cookie sheets. Beat the egg white until stiff, then gradually add the sugar, beating constantly. Stir in the peanuts and the vanilla. Place by teaspoonfuls on the cookie sheets, about 1½ inches apart. Bake until dry, about 12–15 minutes.

English Rolled Wafers

These ginger-molasses cookies that are shaped around a wooden spoon are also known as "brandy snaps" because sometimes they are served in England as an elegant dessert filled with whipped cream that has been flavored with a touch of brandy. More often they appear just plain at tea time.

(ABOUT 40 COOKIES)

½ cup (1 dL) molasses
¼ pound (115 g) butter
1 cup (140 g) flour

⅔ cup (130 g) sugar
1 teaspoon powdered ginger

Preheat the oven to 300°F (150°C). Heat the molasses in a pot until it reaches the boiling point, then add the butter and stir until melted. Remove from the

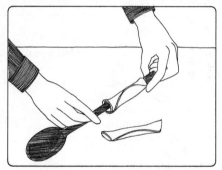

heat. Mix the flour, sugar, and ginger together and stir into the hot molasses mixture. Arrange by teaspoonfuls on ungreased cookie sheets, allowing 2 inches between cookies for them to spread. Bake for about 15 minutes; the cookies will be bubbly and lightly browned. Remove one from the cookie sheet with a spatula as soon as it is firm enough to handle. Shape it into a tube while it is still warm by rolling it around the handle of a wooden spoon. Remove and roll only one cookie at a time so that the others remain warm on the pan and pliable enough to shape. You can also serve them unrolled, of course.

Jubilees

Use jams of various colors to fill the centers of these crisp, chewy cookies.

(ABOUT 40 COOKIES)

¼ pound (115 g) butter
1 cup (200 g) sugar
2 eggs
1 teaspoon vanilla
1½ cups (215 g) flour

1 teaspoon baking powder
¼ teaspoon baking soda
½ teaspoon salt
Cornflakes, slightly crumbled
Jam or jelly

Preheat the oven to 350°F (180°C) and grease some cookie sheets. Cream the butter, then add the sugar gradually, combining well. Add the eggs and vanilla and mix well. Mix together the flour, baking powder, baking soda, and salt. Add to the first mixture and combine thoroughly. Chill until firm enough to handle, then shape with your fingers into 1-inch balls. Roll in cornflakes and place on the cookie sheets, about 2 inches apart. Indent each in the center with your finger and fill with a little jam or jelly. Bake for 15–20 minutes or until firm.

Charleston Benne Wafers

Crisp and sweet with good sesame flavor.

(ABOUT 36 COOKIES)

½ cup (1 dL) sesame seeds
1 tablespoon butter
1 cup (¼ L) light-brown sugar
3 tablespoons flour

1 egg, beaten
1 teaspoon vanilla
¼ teaspoon salt

Preheat the oven to 350°F (180°C). Butter some cookies sheets *very well*. Put the sesame seeds in a small pan and stir or shake them over moderate heat until they are slightly brown. Remove from the heat, stir in the remaining ingredients, and mix well. Drop by teaspoonfuls onto the cookie sheets, leaving 2 inches between them for the cookies to spread. Bake until just slightly brown, 3–5 minutes. Remove from the cookie sheets very carefully while still warm.

Mincemeat Cookies

(ABOUT 85 COOKIES)

1 cup (¼ L) shortening
½ teaspoon vanilla
1 cup (¼ L) honey, or 1½ cups
   (300 g) sugar
3 eggs
3¼ cups (455 g) flour

1 teaspoon salt
1 teaspoon baking soda
1 cup (¼ L) chopped nuts
1½ cups (3½ dL) mincemeat,
   drained if necessary

Preheat the oven to 350°F (180°C). Lightly grease some cookie sheets. Cream the shortening, then beat in the vanilla, honey or sugar, and eggs. Mix the flour, salt, and baking soda together and add to the first mixture, blending well. Stir in the nuts and the mincemeat. Arrange by teaspoonfuls on the cookie sheets. Bake until light brown, about 8–10 minutes.

Wasps' Nests

A traditional Christmas cookie, wonderful all year round.

(40 COOKIES)

½ pound (225 g) almonds,
   blanched and slivered
½ cup (100 g) granulated sugar
6 ounces (180 g) semisweet
   chocolate

3 egg whites
1¼ cups (3 dL) confectioners'
   sugar

Preheat the oven to 300°F (150°C). Butter and flour cookie sheets. In a heavy-bottomed pan, cook the granulated sugar in ¼ cup water until the syrup spins a thread or a thermometer registers 240°F. Stir in the almonds and remove from the heat. Grate the chocolate or use the food processor. Beat the egg whites until they are very stiff, adding spoonfuls of confectioners' sugar during the last few minutes of beating. Fold in the almond mixture and the grated chocolate and drop by teaspoonfuls on the cookie sheets. Bake until the cookies are dry, about 20 minutes. Let stand 5 minutes, and remove from the pan.

Old-fashioned Gingersnaps

(ABOUT 50 GINGERSNAPS)

½ cup (1 dL) molasses
4 tablespoons shortening
1½ cups (215 g) flour

¼ teaspoon baking soda
1½ teaspoons powdered ginger
¾ teaspoon salt

Preheat the oven to 350°F (180°C). Heat the molasses to the boiling point, pour it over the shortening, and stir to combine well. Mix together the flour, baking soda, ginger, and salt and add to the molasses mixture, blending well. Using a rolling pin, roll the dough out on an unfloured board as thin as possible. Cut into 1½-inch rounds with a small cutter or the edge of a small drinking glass. Bake on ungreased cookie sheets for about 5 minutes or until crisp and dry.

Meringues

Make these sweet confections, sometimes known as "kisses," anytime you have a few extra egg whites. Be sure the whites are at room temperature before you begin to beat them, and add the sugar very gradually so that the beaten whites do not lose any volume. Meringues are baked in a very slow oven and then left in the turned-off oven for a long time to crisp.

(ABOUT 12 SMALL MERINGUES)

2 egg whites
8 tablespoons sugar, preferably
    superfine

1 teaspoon vanilla

Preheat the oven to 250°F (120°C). Cover a cookie sheet with brown paper or parchment. Beat the egg whites until stiff but not dry, and add 6 tablespoons of the sugar, a spoonful at a time, beating well between each addition. Add the

vanilla, and fold in the remaining 2 tablespoons of sugar. Shape the meringues on the cookie sheet with a pastry bag and tube or a spoon. Bake for 1 hour. Turn off the oven and let the meringues remain in the oven for 6 more hours. Don't open the oven door—they must dry out to be nice and crisp.

Meringue Shells. Using a spoon or a pastry bag, shape the egg-white mixture into 3-inch rings. Bake at 250°F (120°C) until completely dry but not colored. Fill with *whipped cream* or *ice cream* and top with *crushed strawberries, blueberries,* or *chocolate sauce.*

Nut Meringues. Add about ½ *cup chopped nuts.*

Chocolate Meringues. Add 4 *tablespoons unsweetened cocoa* to the egg whites after you have beaten in the sugar.

Ladyfingers

These light and airy finger-shaped confections are good by themselves with afternoon tea. For dessert serve them with fruits, berries, or applesauce. Or line a mold with ladyfingers and fill it with Bavarian cream or soft custard spiked with sherry to make what was known in many a childhood as Tipsy Pudding (see p. 531). The store-bought kind can't touch the ones you make yourself.

(ABOUT 20 LADYFINGERS)

2 egg yolks
½ teaspoon vanilla
⅛ teaspoon salt
3 egg whites

⅓ cup (65 g) sugar
⅓ cup (50 g) sifted flour
Sugar

Preheat the oven to 350°F (180°C). Butter ladyfinger tins or muffin tins or line a cookie sheet with parchment paper. Beat the egg yolks, vanilla, and salt together until thick and pale yellow. Using clean beaters, beat the egg whites until they hold soft peaks, then slowly beat in the sugar. Fold the egg whites into the egg yolks until just blended, then gradually fold in the flour. Spoon the mixture into the tins or pipe it through a pastry bag onto the lined cookie sheets, making "fingers" 4–5 inches long. Sprinkle with a little sugar. Bake for 10–12 minutes until lightly colored.

Crescents

(24 COOKIES)

½ pound (225 g) almond paste
½ cup (1 dL) confectioners'
  sugar
1 egg white
½ cup (1 dL) chopped
  blanched almonds

1 recipe Confectioners' Frosting
  I made with lemon juice
  (p. 535)
2–4 tablespoons lemon juice

Preheat the oven to 300°F (150°C). Cover cookie sheets with aluminum foil, parchment paper, or brown paper. Using your hands or a food processor, soften the almond paste. Add the sugar and egg white and blend thoroughly. Shape the mixture into a long roll. Cut in ¾-inch pieces, roll each piece in chopped almonds, and shape into crescents. Put on the cookie sheet, cover, and let stand 20 minutes. Bake for 20 minutes; lay the paper linings on a damp cloth, let cool, and peel off the cookies. When they are cool, paint them with frosting.

Viennese Crescents

The meltingly light taste of these rich, buttery confections makes them disappear almost as quickly as you can make them.

(ABOUT 50 SMALL COOKIES)

½ pound (225 g) butter
¼ cup (50 g) granulated sugar
2 cups (280 g) flour

1 cup (¼ L) ground nuts
1 teaspoon vanilla
Confectioners' sugar

Preheat the oven to 300°F (150°C). Cream the butter, then add the granulated sugar, flour, nuts, and vanilla and mix thoroughly. Shape with your fingers into delicate crescents, about 2 inches long and ½ inch wide and thick. Roll in confectioners' sugar and bake on ungreased cookie sheets for about 30 minutes, until just faintly browned. Cool, then roll in more confectioners' sugar before serving.

Scotch Shortbreads

Sandy and crumbly, as the perfect shortbread should be.

(ABOUT TWENTY-FOUR 1 × 2-INCH BARS)

½ pound (225 g) butter
½ cup (1 dL) confectioners'
sugar

2 cups (280 g) flour
¼ teaspoon salt
¼ teaspoon baking powder

Preheat the oven to 350°F (180°C). Cream the butter, then gradually add the sugar, beating well. Mix the flour, salt, and baking powder together and add to the first mixture, combining thoroughly. Roll out the dough with a rolling pin until it is ¼ inch thick, then cut into rectangles or any other shape desired. Put them on ungreased cookie sheets, prick each cookie with a fork, and bake for 20–25 minutes or until they turn lightly brown around the edges.

Gingerbread Men

(ABOUT EIGHT 5 × 3½-INCH MEN OR TWENTY-FOUR 2 × 1½-INCH MEN)

½ cup (1 dL) molasses
¼ cup (50 g) sugar
3 tablespoons butter or
shortening
1 tablespoon milk
2 cups (280 g) flour

½ teaspoon baking soda
½ teaspoon salt
½ teaspoon nutmeg
½ teaspoon cinnamon
½ teaspoon ground cloves
½ teaspoon powdered ginger

Preheat the oven to 350°F (180°C) and butter some cookie sheets. Heat the molasses to the boiling point, then add the sugar, butter or shortening, and milk. Mix the flour with the baking soda, salt, nutmeg, cinnamon, cloves, and ginger. Add to the first mixture and blend well. Add a few tablespoons of water, enough so that the dough holds together and handles easily. Roll or pat out the dough about ¼ inch thick. Cut into large or small gingerbread men, using special cookie cutters or a very sharp knife. Bake for 5–7 minutes. When cool, frost with *Confectioners' Frosting I* (p. 535) and decorate with *candies, raisins, or bits of citron.*

Refrigerator Cookies

A basic refrigerator cookie—sweet, crisp, and chewy.

(ABOUT 60 COOKIES)

¼ pound (115 g) butter	1 egg
1 teaspoon vanilla	1½ cups (210 g) flour
⅔ cup (1½ dL) brown sugar	¼ teaspoon cream of tartar
⅓ cup (65 g) granulated sugar	¼ teaspoon salt

Cream the butter and vanilla together, then beat in both sugars and the egg. Mix the flour, cream of tartar, and salt together, add to the first mixture, and combine well. Shape in a roll or rolls about 2 inches in diameter. Wrap in foil and store in the refrigerator until ready to bake; the dough will keep well for at least a week and may also be frozen. Before baking, preheat the oven to 400°F (205°C). Using a sharp knife, slice in rounds ⅛ to ¼ inch thick. Bake on ungreased cookie sheets for about 8 minutes, until crisp and lightly browned.

Cinnamon or Nutmeg Refrigerator Cookies. Add ⅓ *teaspoon cinnamon* or *nutmeg* to the flour mixture.

Chocolate Refrigerator Cookies. Add *2 ounces melted, unsweetened chocolate* with the egg.

Raisin, Nut, or Coconut Refrigerator Cookies. Add ½ *cup chopped nuts, raisins,* or *shredded coconut* to the cookie dough before shaping it into a roll.

Norwegian Butter Cookies

These are excellent cookie-press cookies.

(ABOUT 30 COOKIES)

¼ pound (115 g) butter	1 cup (140 g) flour
2 hard-cooked egg yolks	½ teaspoon lemon or vanilla
¼ cup (50 g) sugar	extract

Preheat the oven to 375°F (190°C). Cream the butter, then add the egg yolks, and beat well. Beat in the sugar. Add the flour and the lemon or vanilla extract and combine thoroughly. Put through a cookie press or arrange by teaspoonfuls on ungreased cookie sheets. Bake for 10–12 minutes or until lightly browned.

Date-filled Oatmeal Cookies

(ABOUT 24 COOKIES)

1 cup (¼ L) pitted dates, chopped	1½ cups (210 g) flour
½ cup (100 g) granulated sugar	¼ teaspoon baking soda
¼ pound (115 g) butter	½ teaspoon salt
½ cup (1 dL) brown sugar	1¼ cups (3 dL) oatmeal

Preheat the oven to 350°F (180°C). Put the dates, granulated sugar, and ½ cup water in a small pot and cook slowly until thick and smooth, about 15 minutes; set aside. Cream the butter, then add the brown sugar, and mix well. Mix together the flour, baking soda, and salt and add to the dates and sugar, beating well. Combine with the oatmeal, mixing thoroughly. Add about 2–4 tablespoons water, enough to form the dough into a ball so that it can be rolled. Refrigerate for about 15 minutes to facilitate rolling. Roll ⅛ inch thick. Cut into 2-inch rounds. Put them together in pairs with the date mixture as a filling and press the edges firmly together. Bake about 15 minutes, until browned.

Chocolate Cookies

These work well in a cookie press.

(ABOUT 50 COOKIES)

2 ounces (60 g) unsweetened
  chocolate
¾ cup (1¾ dL) shortening
1 cup (200 g) sugar
1 egg

½ teaspoon vanilla
¼ teaspoon salt
2 tablespoons milk
2 cups (280 g) flour

Preheat the oven to 375°F (190°C). Melt the chocolate in a small pot or bowl over simmering water; set aside. Cream the shortening, then gradually add the sugar, creaming well. Add the egg, vanilla, salt, chocolate, and milk and beat well. Gently stir in the flour and combine thoroughly. Put through a cookie press or arrange by teaspoonfuls on ungreased cookie sheets. Bake for 8–10 minutes or until crisp.

CAKE SQUARES AND BARS

Brownies

Don't overbake: brownies should be moist and chewy.

(16 BROWNIES)

3 ounces (85 g) unsweetened
  chocolate
6 tablespoons butter
1½ cups (300 g) sugar
3 eggs

¼ teaspoon salt
¾ cup (105 g) flour
¾ cup (1¾ dL) chopped
  walnuts
1½ teaspoons vanilla

Preheat the oven to 350°F (180°C). Butter a 9-inch square cake pan. Melt the chocolate and the butter in a bowl or pot over simmering water, stirring until smooth. Remove from heat, and stir in the sugar, eggs, salt, flour, walnuts, and vanilla. Combine well. Spread in the pan and bake for about 40 minutes, until dry on top and almost firm to the touch. Set the pan on a rack to cool for about 15 minutes, then cut the brownies into squares approximately 2¼ inches.

Butterscotch Brownies

(16 BROWNIES)

½ cup (115 g) melted butter
2 cups (½ L) dark-brown sugar
2 eggs
½ teaspoon salt

1½ cups (210 g) flour
2 teaspoons baking powder
1 teaspoon vanilla
1 cup (¼ L) chopped nuts

Preheat the oven to 350°F (180°C). Butter a 9-inch square cake pan. Mix all the ingredients together, combining them well. Spread in the pan and bake for 35–40 minutes or until dry on top and almost firm to the touch. Let cool for 10–15 minutes, then cut in squares approximately 2¼ inches.

Peanut Butter Brownies

Very sweet with a distinct peanut flavor, especially appealing to young children. They dry out quickly, if not kept in an airtight container.

(16 BROWNIES)

2 eggs
1 cup (200 g) granulated sugar
½ cup (1 dL) light-brown sugar
¼ cup (½ dL) chunk-style
   peanut butter
1 teaspoon vanilla

2 tablespoons soft butter
1⅓ cups (190 g) flour
2 teaspoons baking powder
½ teaspoon salt
¼ cup (½ dL) chopped salted
   peanuts

Preheat the oven to 350°F (180°C). Butter a 9-inch square cake pan. Put the eggs, both sugars, peanut butter, vanilla, and butter in a bowl and beat well with an electric or rotary beater. Mix the flour, baking powder, and salt together and stir into the first mixture. Spread in the pan. Sprinkle with the chopped peanuts and press them in lightly. Bake for about 30 minutes. Cool in the pan for 10–15 minutes, then cut in squares.

Coconut Squares

Coconut and nuts give these good texture. They are chewy, moist, and sweet.

(16 SQUARES)

2 eggs
2 cups (½ L) light-brown sugar
⅛ teaspoon salt
½ teaspoon vanilla

2 cups (½ L) shredded coconut
   (p. 13)
¼ cup (½ dL) chopped walnuts
6 tablespoons flour

Preheat the oven to 350°F (180°C). Butter a 9-inch square cake pan. Using a whisk or an electric beater, beat the eggs until they are foamy, then beat in the brown sugar, salt, and vanilla. Stir in the coconut and walnuts, then sprinkle the flour over the batter and stir in lightly. Spread in the pan and bake for about 30 minutes. Cool in the pan for 10–15 minutes, then cut in squares.

Hermits

(36 SQUARES OR ABOUT 60 COOKIES)

¼ cup (½ dL) raisins or
   currants
¼ cup (½ dL) chopped nuts
2 cups (280 g) flour
4 tablespoons butter
½ cup (100 g) sugar
½ teaspoon salt
2 eggs

½ cup (1 dL) molasses
1 teaspoon baking soda
½ teaspoon cream of tartar
1 teaspoon cinnamon
½ teaspoon ground cloves
¼ teaspoon mace
¼ teaspoon nutmeg

Preheat the oven to 350°F (180°C). Grease a 9 × 13–inch cake pan or some cookie sheets. Toss the raisins or currants and the chopped nuts in ¼ cup of the flour; set aside. Cream the butter, then add the sugar and blend well. Add the salt, eggs, and molasses and beat well. Mix together the remaining 1¾ cups flour, the baking soda, cream of tartar, cinnamon, cloves, mace, and nutmeg, add to the butter-sugar-egg mixture, and beat thoroughly. Stir in the raisins and nuts. Spread in the pan or drop by teaspoonfuls onto the cookie sheets. Bake only until the top is firm and the center chewy, about 15–20 minutes for the squares, 8–10 minutes for the cookies.

Concord Hermits. Substitute *1 cup dark-brown sugar* for the white sugar and molasses and add *½ cup sour cream.* You may also add *3 tablespoons chopped citron or candied orange peel,* if you wish.

Coconut Bars

Rich and sweet as candy, this delicious confection has a pastry base with a chewy coconut topping.

(16 BARS)

¼ pound (115 g) butter
2 tablespoons confectioners'
   sugar
1 cup (140 g) plus 2
   tablespoons flour
2 eggs
1¼ cups (3 dL) light-brown
   sugar

1 teaspoon vanilla
¼ teaspoon salt
1 teaspoon baking powder
1 cup (¼ L) coarsely chopped
   nut meats
1–1½ cups (2 dL–3½ dL)
   moist shredded coconut
   (p. 13)

Preheat the oven to 350°F (180°C). Line an 8 × 8–inch square pan with wax paper. Cream the butter, then add the confectioners' sugar, and the cup of flour and blend. Pat evenly into the pan and bake for 15 minutes. While the pastry is baking, beat the eggs, then add the brown sugar and vanilla, beating until thick. Mix the remaining 2 tablespoons of flour, salt, and baking powder together and add to the egg mixture, incorporating well. Beat in the nuts and coconut. Spread evenly over the pastry and bake for 25–30 minutes. Cool in the pan, then cut into 1 × 4–inch bars.

Pecan Squares

These have a good butter and pecan taste, and a nice short texture.

(36 SQUARES)

½ pound (225 g) butter
1 cup (200 g) sugar
1 egg, separated

1 teaspoon vanilla
2 cups (280 g) flour
1 cup (¼ L) chopped pecans

Preheat the oven to 375°F (190°C). Grease a jelly-roll pan about 9 × 15 inches. Cream the butter and sugar together until smooth and light. Beat in the egg yolk, vanilla, and flour until well mixed. Pat evenly into pan. Beat the egg white slightly and brush over the dough. Sprinkle the pecans evenly on top and press them in the dough slightly. Bake 16–18 minutes or until golden brown. Cool in the pan and cut into small squares.

Date Lebkuchen

Dense, moist, with a fine flavor, this makes a good picnic sweet.

(6½ DOZEN SQUARES)

Grated rind and juice of 1
    lemon
Grated rind and juice of 1
    orange
1 pound (450 g) dates, pitted,
    cut small
4 eggs
1 pound (450 g) dark-brown
    sugar
2 cups (280 g) flour

¼ teaspoon salt
1 teaspoon instant coffee
2 teaspoons baking powder
2 teaspoons cinnamon
1 cup (¼ L) chopped walnuts
3 tablespoons orange juice
1 teaspoon butter, melted
1 cup (¼ L) or more
    confectioners' sugar

Preheat oven to 375°F (190°C). Butter a 12 × 15–inch pan. Combine the rind and juice of the lemon and orange in a bowl, add the dates, and let marinate for 1 hour, turning them in the juices often. Beat the eggs until light. Gradually add the brown sugar, flour, salt, coffee, baking powder, and cinnamon. Beat until well blended. Stir in the dates and walnuts. Spread in the pan and bake for 30 minutes. Cool in pan. In a small bowl combine the 3 tablespoons orange juice and the melted butter, and add confectioners' sugar until you have the consistency of softened butter. Spread over the lebkuchen and cut into 1½-inch squares.

Linzer Schnitten

A very good, rather heavy, spicy cookie.

(40 COOKIES)

3 eggs
2¼ cups (450 g) sugar
¾ cup (180 g) butter, melted
3½ cups (490 g) flour
1 teaspoon baking powder
2 teaspoons cinnamon

1 teaspoon powdered cloves
¼ teaspoon salt
Grated rind and juice of 1
    lemon
1 cup (¼ L) apricot preserves

Preheat oven to 375°F (190°C). Beat 2 of the eggs until light. Gradually add 1½ cups of the sugar and the butter, blending well. Sift the flour, baking powder, cinnamon, cloves, and salt together, then stir into the egg mixture and mix well. Add the lemon rind and juice. Mix well. Turn dough onto a floured board and knead until smooth. Cover with a bowl and let stand 1 hour. Roll out to ½ inch thick. Cut in strips 1½ × 10 inches. Mark a groove down the center of each strip with the handle of a wooden spoon. Fill the grooves with apricot preserves. Place on ungreased cookie sheet and bake 20 minutes or until lightly browned. Beat the remaining 1 egg and ¾ cup sugar together, brush over the baked strips while they are still hot, and cut immediately into diagonal pieces.

Noels

Very rich and very chewy.

(16 SQUARES)

2 eggs
1 teaspoon vanilla
1 cup (¼ L) dark-brown sugar
5 tablespoons flour
⅛ teaspoon baking soda

¼ teaspoon salt
1 cup (¼ L) coarsely chopped nuts
2 tablespoons butter
Confectioners' sugar

Preheat the oven to 350°F (180°C). Beat the eggs and vanilla together lightly. Mix together the brown sugar, flour, baking soda, salt, and nuts. Add to the eggs and mix well. Melt the butter in a 9-inch square pan. Pour the batter into the pan and bake for about 20–25 minutes, until firm to the touch. Turn out onto wax paper, buttered side up. Dust lightly with confectioners' sugar while still warm, then cut into squares.

Honey Date and Nut Bars

(16 BARS)

2 tablespoons melted butter
½ cup (1 dL) honey
2 eggs, well beaten
¾ cup (105 g) flour
½ teaspoon baking powder

Dash of salt
½ cup (1 dL) dates, cut fine
½ cup (1 dL) chopped nuts
Confectioners' sugar

Preheat the oven to 350°F (180°C). Butter an 8-inch square cake pan. Mix all the ingredients except confectioners' sugar together in the order given. Spread in the pan and bake for about 25 minutes or until firm and delicately brown. Cool for 5–10 minutes, then cut in bars 1 × 4 inches and roll in confectioners' sugar while still warm.

Walnut Meringue Bars

(24 BARS)

¼ pound (115 g) butter
2 cups (½ L) light-brown sugar
½ teaspoon salt
2 teaspoons vanilla

2 eggs, separated
1¼ cups (175 g) flour
1½ teaspoons baking powder
1 cup (¼ L) chopped walnuts

Preheat the oven to 300°F (150°C). Butter a pan about 8 × 12 inches. Cream the butter and 1 cup of the sugar together until light and smooth. Beat in the salt, 1 teaspoon vanilla, and egg yolks. Add the flour and baking powder. Beat well. Spread evenly in the pan. Beat the egg whites until soft peaks are reached, then slowly beat in the remaining 1 cup brown sugar until all is incorporated. Gently stir in the walnuts and remaining teaspoon of vanilla. Spread over the cookie dough. Bake 35 minutes. Cool. Cut in bars 4 × 1 inches.

Jam or Marmalade Bars

(16 BARS)

½ cup (1 dL) shortening
½ cup (100 g) sugar
½ teaspoon vanilla
½ teaspoon almond extract
1 egg
1½ cups (215 g) flour

1 teaspoon baking powder
½ teaspoon cinnamon
¼ teaspoon ground cloves
½ teaspoon salt
Raspberry jam or marmalade

Preheat the oven to 400°F (205°C). Grease an 8-inch square pan. Cream the shortening with the sugar, vanilla, and almond extract. Stir in the egg and blend well. Mix together the flour, baking powder, cinnamon, cloves, and salt, add to the first mixture, and combine thoroughly. Spread half the dough in the pan. Cover with a layer of jam or marmalade. Pat the remaining dough on top and bake for about 25 minutes. Cool, then cut into bars 4 × 1 inches.

Rum Balls

(50 BALLS)

2 cups (½ L) vanilla wafer
   crumbs
1 cup (¼ L) sweetened
   shredded coconut

2½ cups (6 dL) confectioners'
   sugar
2 tablespoons light corn syrup
⅓ cup (¾ dL) rum

Prepare the vanilla wafer crumbs in the blender or food processor. Combine the crumbs, coconut, 1 cup of the confectioners' sugar, corn syrup, and rum in a bowl. Mix well and shape into small firm balls ¾ inch in diameter. Sift the remaining 1½ cups confectioners' sugar on a piece of wax paper. Roll the balls in the sugar. Store until needed.

Petits Fours

These pretty, small cakes are lovely for parties and buffets.

(ABOUT 80 SMALL CAKES)

2 eggs
2 egg yolks
1 cup (200 g) sugar
2 cups (280 g) flour

2 teaspoons baking powder
½ cup (1 dL) milk
5 tablespoons melted butter

Preheat the oven to 350°F (180°C). Butter and lightly flour a 10½ × 15½–inch jelly-roll pan. Beat the eggs and egg yolks until they are blended, gradually add the sugar, and beat until very pale and fluffy, about 10 minutes with an electric beater. Sift the flour and baking powder over the egg mixture, add the milk, and fold together lightly until the batter is well mixed. Add the melted butter and combine thoroughly. Spread the batter in the pan and bake for 12–15 minutes, until a toothpick comes out clean. Turn the cake out onto a sheet of wax paper and cool completely. Cut into small squares, rectangles, or triangles and arrange them in rows on a fine-mesh cake rack with plenty of space between the rows.

Set the cake rack over a shallow pan or raised over a piece of wax paper. Heat *Petits Fours Frosting* (p. 541) in a pan over simmering water until it is thin enough to pour; you can thin it with water or thicken it with confectioners' sugar if the consistency is not right when the icing is heated. Pour the frosting over the cakes, moving slowly down each row and back again and letting the icing spread over the cakes and drip down through the cake rack. Lift the cake rack and move it gently back and forth to loosen any icing that is clinging to the underside. Scrape up the drippings and reuse them, heating them again over simmering water. When the cakes are dry, lift them from the rack with a spatula and trim the bottom edges with a sharp knife. Decorate each little cake with *a whole nut, some candied fruit, tiny candies, sprinkles,* or *coconut.*

PIES & PASTRIES

ABOUT MAKING PIES

A light-brown flaky crust holding fresh fruit, custard, or cream—pie, the traditional American dessert, is such a welcome sight on the table.

Learn to make your own piecrusts; it's not hard, and the results are so much better than commercial products. Each of the piecrusts we offer here differs from the others in taste, texture, and structure. Try them all; you will soon develop your own favorites.

Kinds of Pie Pastry

Basic Pastry is flaky and tender and at its best when freshly baked. It should be made with vegetable shortening for the lightest, flakiest results.

Tart Pastry is buttery, crisp, and strong, with a crumbly, rather than a flaky, consistency. It includes an egg, which gives it extra firmness, enough to hold a filling without a pan to support the sides. The butter in tart pastry adds strength as well as good taste.

Hot-Water Pastry and *Stirred Pastry* are interchangeable with basic pastry and somewhat easier to make. Hot-water pastry calls for melted shortening and stirred pastry uses vegetable oil, both of which are *stirred*, rather than *cut*, into the flour. The ease of blending these doughs makes them less intimidating to beginners. Once you've got the knack of it, however, you'll find that basic pastry is also easy to assemble and, we believe, the lightest and flakiest of the three.

Catherine's Pastry is a sturdy pastry using both lard and butter and is especially good with meat and other savory fillings. It will be particularly delicious if you live on or near a farm and have access to pure, unadulterated lard.

Crumb Crusts, made with cracker crumbs, are not true pastry. They are the simplest pie shells to make and are especially good with chiffon and other cold fillings.

Special pastry flour may be used in these piecrusts, but all-purpose white flour is just fine for any crust.

Rolling and Shaping Pie Doughs

Do not chill *basic pastry* before you roll it out; line the pie pan with it first and then refrigerate it. Pastry made with butter, such as *tart pastry*, will, however, be easier to handle if you chill it for 30 minutes or so *before* you roll it out (see p. 576).

No matter what piecrust you use, let the bottom crust chill in the pie pan in the refrigerator while you prepare the filling and the top crust. Chilling the bottom crust and assembling the pie just before you bake it will help keep the baked bottom crust from being soggy.

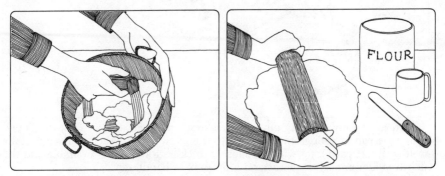

Bottom Crust. Divide the dough in half, if you have made enough for a two-crust pie, and pat each piece into a ball. Flatten one of the balls with the heel of your hand, keeping it round. Place it on a lightly floured board or on a pastry cloth and sprinkle the top with a little flour. Using a rolling pin, start in the center and roll lightly in all directions, lifting and turning the dough frequently to make sure it is not sticking to the board. Do not roll quite to the edge of the dough until the last few turns.

If the dough seems to be sticking, dust the board with more flour. Roll the dough until you have a round piece about ⅛ inch thick and 2 inches greater in diameter than the pie pan you plan to use. Fold the dough in half and lift it gently into the pan with the fold in the center. Unfold it and fit it to the pan, easing it in loosely without stretching it. Pat it into all the edges, then trim the extra dough hanging over the edge so that it is ¾ inch larger than the pan.

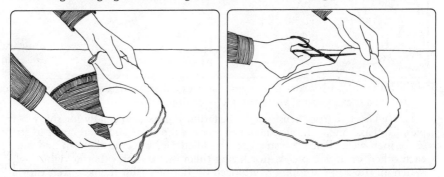

Refrigerate the bottom crust until you are ready to fill and bake it.

Pie Shell. If you are making a pie shell for a single-crust, open-face pie, fold the extra ¾ inch under along the rim of the pan so that it is double in thickness, then crimp using one of the following methods: 1) press the tines of a fork all around the rim (below left). 2) Using your thumb and forefinger, press and pinch the dough together at even intervals around the rim (as has been done on the crust, p. 574). 3) Build the dough up around the rim about ¾ inch; then using your two forefingers press and pleat at intervals to make a stand-up, scalloped edge (below right).

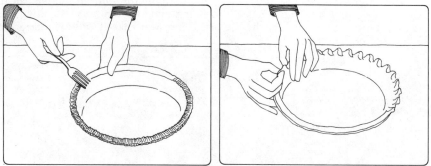

Instead of using a rolling pin when making a pie shell, you can pat the dough into a pie pan or springform pan with your fingers. This method works especially well with tart pastry, for which a slightly thick bottom crust is desirable and the dough is firm enough to withstand a little extra handling.

Top Crust. For a two-crust pie, roll out the second piece of dough just like the first. Fill the bottom crust generously with the pie filling, then fold the dough for the top crust in half and gently lift it onto the filling with the fold in the center. Unfold it and trim it so that the dough for both crusts extends over the rim of the pan by about ¾ inch. Press the edges of the top and bottom crusts together, tucking the top one over the bottom one to make a thick edge. Crimp the edges with the tines of a fork or flute them with your fingers.

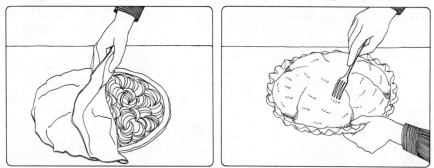

Prick the top with a fork in several places or cut vents or a small design or two so that steam can escape while the pie is baking.

Lattice Crust. Lattice crusts make beautiful finishes, especially for shiny berry pies. To make one, roll out the dough as for a top crust and then cut it in strips ½–¾ inch wide. Place the strips on the filled pie, weaving them in and out of each other, or, if you prefer, just laying them across each other at right angles. When all the strips are loosely arranged on the pie, trim them so that they are even with the overhanging bottom crust. Fold the edge of the bottom crust up over the ends of the strips and press together. Crimp or flute the edge all around.

Lattice strips may also be twisted to give a spiral effect.

Using a Food Processor to Make Pastry

The food processor does not prepare good *basic pastry:* it blends the flour and shortening into a paste, instead of keeping bits of shortening separate from the flour to create a flaky texture when baked. ·

The food processor will, however, blend *tart pastry* most satisfactorily. Be sure to have the butter very chilled. Use the metal blade and follow the directions on p. 576. Process just until a ball of dough forms on the blade; do *not* overblend.

The food processor will make perfect crumbs for crumb crusts. You can also use the slicing blade to prepare many fruits for pie fillings.

Glazing Pies

We sometimes like to sprinkle granulated sugar over lattice tops or top crusts before we bake a pie.

Melted currant jelly makes a nice glaze for an open fruit tart (p. 579). You can also put a sugar glaze on a two-crust pie right after it comes out of the oven (p. 579).

Baking Pies and Pie Shells

For a crisp bottom crust, be sure to bake pies on the lowest rack of a thoroughly preheated oven.

Use heavy-gauge steel or aluminum pans for the best results. Glass and ceramic pans also work well, and glass has the added advantage of letting you see how brown the bottom crust is getting. However, pies baked in glass or ceramic pans should be baked at about 25 degrees less oven heat than the recipe calls for.

Foil pans are often not strong enough to hold certain fillings firmly in place. They also overheat because they are so thin. But they are very welcome in emergencies.

Beware of some of the newer finishes in bakeware: predarkened tin-oxide pans brown pies and breads too quickly and you have to compensate by shortening the baking time. White Teflon-finished pans, on the other hand, often produce pastries and breads that are pale and colorless.

Unfilled Pie Shells. Unfilled pie shells should be baked at 425°F for 12 minutes for a tart shell, 18–20 minutes for the Basic Pastry—or until lightly browned. Let them cool before filling them.

If the dough has been fitted to the pan loosely without stretching, the

pie shell is less likely to buckle up during baking. Many books recommend
that unfilled pie shells be covered with foil and then weighted down with
beans or rice to prevent the pastry from puffing up in spots while it is
baking. We have found, however, that this method often creates an
undesirable moist bottom. We prefer to prick the bottom all over with a
fork before baking and then, after the pie shell has been in the oven for
about 5 minutes, to open the door to see if any spots have begun to swell;
if so, push them down gently. Repeat this again, if necessary, after 5 minutes
and you will have a dry, flaky pie shell.

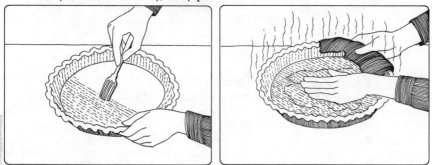

Filled Pies and Filled Pie Shells. Filled pies are generally baked at 425°F for the first
10 minutes and then at 350°F for the remainder of the baking time. The
higher baking temperature at the beginning helps produce a crisp crust.
Baking temperatures vary, of course, with specific pies, so follow the
instructions given with the recipe.

   If the tops or edges of a piecrust begin to brown too quickly, cover the
pie lightly with a piece of foil and continue baking.

Storing and Freezing Pie Dough and Pies

Unbaked Pie Dough. Unbaked pie dough will keep in the refrigerator, tightly
wrapped, for about 4 days. Pat the dough into a ball and wrap it well with
foil or plastic wrap. Let it soften a bit at room temperature before you roll
it out. Unbaked pie dough can also be frozen for at least 3 months. Save
bits and scraps each time you make pastry and you will soon have enough
for a complete pie. Or line small tart shells with unbaked pastry scraps and
keep them in the freezer; filled with savories or sweets, they make delightful
appetizers or desserts.

   When you are preparing a pie ahead of time, roll the dough out, line the
pan with it, wrap well with foil or plastic, and put it in the refrigerator. If
you are making a two-crust pie, roll the top out, too, and place it on a
piece of wax paper over the lined pan. Cover it all securely and keep
refrigerated until you are ready to fill and bake the pie. Wrapped this way,
unbaked piecrusts will keep in the refrigerator for about 4 days or in the
freezer for at least 3 months. You can make several pies at the same time,
following this procedure; stack the rolled-out crusts carefully, one on top
of another, with wax paper separating the layers.

Unfilled Pie Shells. Unfilled pie shells may be frozen either baked or unbaked, but
unbaked is preferable by far. Wrapped well in foil or freezer paper, an
unbaked pie shell will keep in the freezer for at least 3 months. Unbaked
shells should be unwrapped and baked while still frozen in a 450°F oven
for 15–20 minutes (less for a tart shell, longer for a basic piecrust) or until
browned. Allow approximately 3 minutes more than usual baking time for
frozen dough.

Baked pie shells should not be held in the freezer for more than 6 weeks. Their texture may lose some crispness in the freezing-defrosting process; try crisping in a preheated 450°F oven for 10 minutes. They are great to have in an emergency, since they will defrost in less than 2 hours and may be filled with a variety of cold fillings for a quick, delicious dessert.

Filled Pies and Filled Pie Shells. Although you should not freeze pies with custard or cream fillings, pies and pie shells filled with fruit and other mixtures will keep well in the freezer for at least 3 months. We find that unbaked pies remain crisper and more tender and pleasing after freezing than baked pies. Do not defrost them before baking them: bake them unwrapped, directly from the freezer, in a preheated 425°F oven for 15–20 minutes and then in a 350°F oven for the remainder of the baking time. The total baking time for a frozen pie will be about 20 minutes longer than for an unfrozen one.

Baked pies should be frozen only when necessary: if you are left with an uneaten pie on your hands, for example, or are preparing large quantities of pies in advance for the town fair. Let baked frozen pies defrost unwrapped at room temperature for about 3 hours, then crisp them in a preheated 450°F oven for about 20 minutes.

PIE PASTRY

Basic Pastry

Don't handle this pastry dough any more than necessary or it will be tough: treat it firmly, not timidly, but don't fuss with it. The flour and shortening should not be blended too well: it is the bits of shortening left in the dough that puff and expand during baking and give the pastry its flaky identity. For that reason, the dough cannot be mixed as successfully in a food processor. Follow illustrated details pp. 571–574.

(8-INCH PIE SHELL)

1 cup (140 g) plus 2 tablespoons flour	⅓ cup (¾ dL) shortening
¼ teaspoon salt	2–3 tablespoons cold water

(8-INCH TWO-CRUST PIE)

2 cups (280 g) flour	⅔ cup (1½ dL) shortening
½ teaspoon salt	⅓ cup (¾ dL) cold water

(9-INCH PIE SHELL)

1½ cups (215 g) flour	½ cup (1 dL) shortening
¼ teaspoon salt	3–4 tablespoons cold water

(9-INCH TWO-CRUST PIE)

2½ cups (350 g) flour	¾ cup (1¾ dL) shortening
½ teaspoon salt	6–7 tablespoons cold water

Mix the flour and salt. Cut in the shortening with a pastry blender or two knives (see illustration p. 571). Combine lightly only until the mixture resembles coarse meal or very tiny peas: its texture will not be uniform but will contain crumbs and small bits and pieces. Sprinkle water over the flour mixture, a tablespoon at a time, and mix lightly with a fork, using only enough water so that the pastry will hold together when pressed gently into a ball.

Pie Shell

Roll the dough out 2 inches larger than the pie pan, then fit it loosely but firmly into the pan. Crimp or flute the edges. For a *baked pie shell* (sometimes known, incidentally, as baking blind) prick the bottom dough all over with a fork and bake the shell for 16–18 minutes in a preheated 425°F (220°C) oven (for a partially baked shell, bake 10 minutes). Open the oven door once or twice during the baking and see if the shell again has begun to swell up in spots; if it has, push it down gently. Or fill the *unbaked pie shell* with pie filling and then bake the pie as directed in the filling recipe.

Two-Crust Pie

Divide the dough into two balls. Roll the bottom crust out 2 inches larger than the pie pan. Ease it into the pan, fitting it loosely but firmly. Roll out the top crust. Fill the pie generously, then put on the top crust and prick in several places with a fork or cut vents in it. Or cover the pie with lattice strips. Crimp or flute the edges. Bake as indicated in the filling recipe.

Tart Pastry

This well-balanced, basic recipe produces a firm, crisp crust with the taste of butter. You can sweeten it slightly, if you wish, by adding 1½ tablespoons of sugar to the flour. Unlike the preceding basic pastry, tart pastry will not get tough if you handle it a lot and you can mix it in a food processor.

(ONE 9-INCH TART)

1 cup (140 g) flour   1 egg yolk
¼ teaspoon salt
6 tablespoons cold butter, in
   small pieces

Mix the flour and salt in a bowl. Cut in the butter with your fingers or a pastry blender until the mixture resembles coarse meal or tiny peas. Whisk the egg yolk and 2 tablespoons water together in another bowl, add to the flour mixture, and blend until the pastry is smooth and holds together in a ball. It can be mixed in a food processor; process first the flour, salt, and butter quickly together, then add the egg yolk and water through the funnel and process until the dough balls up around the blade. Wrap in foil or plastic and refrigerate it for at least 20 minutes. You can roll this dough out with a rolling pin, but you would have to chill it, wrapped in plastic, for at least 20 minutes. We find it easier to pat it into a pie pan or springform with our hands. Pull pieces of dough from the ball and press them over the bottom and sides of the pan, using the heel of your hand. The dough should be thick enough to hold the filling, but be careful that it is not too thick around the bottom edge or the finished tart will seem coarse. If there's time, cover the lined pan snugly with foil and refrigerate it before filling and baking it. Bake as directed in the filling recipe. Or prick the bottom with a fork and bake it unfilled for 12 minutes in a preheated 425°F (220°C) oven. If you use a springform pan, do not remove the sides until you are ready to serve the tart.

Hot-Water Pastry

This is a good recipe for beginners. Somewhat less flaky and tender than the preceding Basic Pastry, it is still very acceptable.

(8- OR 9-INCH PIE SHELL)

½ cup (1 dL) shortening
1½ cups (210 g) flour

½ teaspoon salt
¼ teaspoon baking powder

Put the shortening in a bowl, add ⅓ cup boiling water, and stir until the shortening melts. Add the flour, salt, and baking powder, and mix with a fork until blended. Form the dough into a ball. Roll it out 2 inches larger than the pie pan. Ease the dough into the pan and fit it loosely, but firmly. Cover the pan and let the dough chill in the refrigerator for at least 4 hours before baking. Bake for 15 minutes in a preheated 425°F (220°C) oven. Or fill first and bake as directed in the filling recipe.

Stirred Pastry

(8-INCH TWO-CRUST PIE OR 9-INCH LATTICE-TOP PIE)

2 cups (280 g) flour
1½ teaspoons salt
1½ teaspoons sugar

½ cup (1 dL) vegetable oil
¼ cup (½ dL) milk

Mix the flour, salt, and sugar in a bowl. Pour in the oil and milk, and stir lightly with a fork until no dry flour shows. Pat the dough into two balls. Roll the bottom crust out 2 inches larger than the pie pan. Ease the dough into the pie pan and fit it loosely but firmly. Roll out the top crust. Fill the pie, then put on the top crust and cut vents in it. Or cover the pie with lattice strips. Crimp or flute the edges. Bake as indicated in the filling recipe.

Catherine's Pastry

This flaky crust is very durable. Try it if you can get some good fresh lard. It is fine for meat or other main-dish pies.

(8-INCH TWO-CRUST PIE OR 9-INCH LATTICE-TOP PIE)

2 cups (280 g) flour
1 teaspoon salt
½ teaspoon baking powder

⅓ cup (¾ dL) lard
⅓ cup (75 g) butter

Mix the flour, salt, and baking powder in a bowl. Work in the lard until it resembles coarse meal or very small peas. Sprinkle in up to ⅓ cup ice water, drop by drop, stirring lightly with a fork and using only enough water to hold the dough together. Roll out the dough into a rectangle. Dot with a third of the butter, then roll up the dough like a jelly roll. Roll out again until ¼ inch thick and dot with a third of the butter. Roll up the dough and repeat once more. Chill 30 minutes. Roll the bottom crust out 2 inches larger than the pie pan. Fit the dough in the pan. Roll out the top crust. Fill the pie, then put on the top crust and cut vents in it. Or cover the top with lattice strips. Crimp or flute the edges. Bake as indicated in the filling recipe.

Chocolate Coconut Crust

Fill this with ice cream for a quick, delectable dessert.

2 ounces (60 g) unsweetened
   chocolate
2 tablespoons butter
1 cup (¼ L) confectioners'
   sugar

1½ cups (3½ dL) flaked
   coconut

Melt the chocolate and butter in a small pan over low heat. Mix the sugar and 3 tablespoons hot water together in a small bowl. Add the chocolate and butter to the sugar, then stir in the coconut. Press the mixture firmly into a pie pan and chill.

Crumb Crust

1½ cups (3½ dL) fine crumbs
   (graham cracker, gingersnap,
   rusk, zwieback, or vanilla or
   chocolate wafers)

⅓ cup (65 g) sugar
⅓ cup (75 g) butter, melted

Mix the crumbs, sugar, and butter together in a bowl. Press and pat the crumb mixture into the pie pan. Bake 8–10 minutes in a preheated 350°F (180°C) oven or fill unbaked as directed in the filling recipe.

PIE TOPPINGS

Meringue Topping

Meringue toppings for pies often "weep," shrink, or turn rubbery. Follow this somewhat unconventional method and yours will hold up well and stay light for several days. Be sure to refrigerate a meringue pie if it isn't served within a few hours of making it.

3 egg whites, at room
   temperature
⅓ cup (65 g) sugar

⅛ teaspoon salt
½ teaspoon vanilla

4 egg whites, at room
   temperature
6 tablespoons sugar

¼ teaspoon salt
½ teaspoon vanilla

Put the egg whites and sugar in a mixing bowl and place the bowl in a pan of hot water. Stir constantly until the whites feel warm, then add the salt and vanilla. Remove the bowl from the hot water and beat with an electric beater until the meringue is stiff and shiny. Spread the meringue over a filled and baked pie shell. Be sure that the meringue touches the inner edges of the crust; this will keep it from shrinking. Put the pie under the broiler and let the meringue peaks brown a little. Watch carefully, as this will take only a minute or two.

Glaze for Fruit Tarts

(FOR 10-INCH TART)

1 cup (¼ L) red currant jelly or 1½ cups (3½ dL) apricot or strawberry preserves

Melt the jelly or preserve over low heat, stirring. If you are using preserves, strain. Let cool a bit, then spread over the fruit-filled tart.

Sugar Glaze for Piecrusts

(FOR 9-INCH PIE)

½ cup (1 dL) confectioners' sugar
1 tablespoon water

Mix the sugar with the water and brush it on a hot baked pie immediately after it is removed from the oven.

PIES

Apple Pie

Apple pie is a symbol of the many good things in the American home. You will not be disappointed with this one. It is especially good served warm with a wedge of sharp Cheddar cheese or a spoonful of whipped cream.

(9-INCH PIE)

Basic Pastry dough for 9-inch
  two-crust pie (p. 575)
¾–1 cup (150–200 g) sugar
½ teaspoon salt
1 teaspoon cinnamon

½ teaspoon nutmeg
1½ tablespoons flour
6 large, firm, tart apples
2 tablespoons butter

Preheat the oven to 425°F (220°C). Line a 9-inch pie pan with half the pastry dough. Mix the sugar, salt, cinnamon, nutmeg, and flour in a large bowl. Peel, core, and slice the apples and toss them in the sugar mixture, coating them well. Pile them into the lined pan and dot with the butter. Roll out the top crust and drape it over the pie. Crimp the edges and cut several vents in the top. Bake 10 minutes, then lower the heat to 350°F (180°C) and bake 30–40 minutes more or until the apples are tender when pierced with a skewer and the crust is browned.

Fresh Peach Pie

If you submerge peaches in boiling water for a minute or two, then plunge them into cold water, their skins will be easier to peel.

(9-INCH PIE)

Basic Pastry dough for 9-inch   4 cups (1 L) peeled and sliced
  two-crust pie (p. 575)   fresh peaches
1 cup (200 g) sugar   1 tablespoon lemon juice
4 tablespoons flour

Preheat the oven to 425°F (220°C). Line a 9-inch pie pan with half the pastry dough. Mix the sugar and flour in a large bowl. Add the peaches and lemon juice and toss well. Pile the fruit into the lined pie pan. Roll out the top crust and drape it over the pie. Crimp or flute the edges and cut several vents in the top. Bake for 10 minutes, then lower the heat to 350°F (180°C) and bake 30–40 minutes more, until the top is browned.

Apricot Pie

(9-INCH PIE)

Basic Pastry dough for 9-inch   1 cup (200 g) sugar
  two-crust pie (p. 575)   2 tablespoons tapioca
4 cups (1 L) pitted, halved   1½ tablespoons lemon juice
  apricots   2 tablespoons butter

Preheat the oven to 425°F (220°C). Line a 9-inch pie pan with half the pastry dough. Spread half the apricots in the lined pan and sprinkle half the sugar over them. Spread the remaining apricots on top and sprinkle with the remaining sugar and the tapioca and lemon juice. Dot with the butter. Roll out the top crust and drape it over the pie. Crimp or flute the edges and cut several vents in the top. Bake for 10 minutes, then lower the heat to 350°F (180°C) and bake 30–40 minutes, until the top is browned.

Blueberry Pie

(9-INCH PIE)

Basic Pastry dough for 9-inch   1 cup (200 g) sugar
  two-crust pie (p. 575)   ⅛ teaspoon salt
4 cups (1 L) fresh or frozen   1 tablespoon lemon juice
  blueberries   1 tablespoon butter
3 tablespoons flour

Preheat the oven to 425°F (220°C). Line the pie pan with half the pastry dough. Wash and pick over the blueberries if you are using fresh ones; if you are using frozen berries, it is not necessary to defrost them completely. Mix the flour, sugar, and salt in a large bowl. Add the blueberries and lemon juice and toss well. Pile the mixture into the lined pie pan and dot with the butter. Roll out the top crust and drape it over the pie. Crimp or flute the edges and cut several vents in the top. Bake for 10 minutes, then lower the heat to 350°F (180°C) and bake for 30–40 minutes or until the top is browned.

Open Blueberry Pie

Blueberries and cream in a crisp, prebaked pie shell.

(9-INCH OPEN PIE)

Tart Pastry dough for 9-inch
  tart (p. 576)
1 cup (200 g) sugar
3 tablespoons cornstarch
⅛ teaspoon salt

1 tablespoon butter
4 cups (1 L) fresh or frozen
  blueberries
1 cup (¼ L) heavy cream
Sugar

Preheat the oven to 425°F (220°C). Line a 9-inch pie pan with the pastry dough, prick the dough all over, and bake for 10–15 minutes, until lightly browned. Mix the sugar, cornstarch, salt, and 1 cup water in a pan. Cook over low heat, stirring constantly, until thickened. Add the butter, stir until melted, and let cool. Fold in the blueberries and pile into the baked pie shell. Before serving, whip the cream, adding sugar to taste, and spread it over the blueberry filling.

Sour Cherry Pie

There's nothing like the flavor of sour cherries wrapped in flaky pastry. Serve slightly warm for the best flavor.

(8-INCH LATTICE PIE)

Basic Pastry dough for 8-inch
  two-crust pie (p. 575)
1 cup (200 g) sugar
1½ tablespoons flour

⅛ teaspoon salt
4 cups (1 L) fresh or canned
  sour cherries, pitted

Preheat the oven to 425°F (220°C). Line an 8-inch pie pan with half the pastry dough. Mix the sugar, flour, and salt in a large bowl, add the cherries (if canned, drain them; use only ¼ cup sugar and add ½ cup of the juice to the sugar mixture), and toss until well coated. Pile into the lined pie pan. Use the remaining dough to make a lattice top. Crimp the edges. Bake for 10 minutes, then reduce the heat to 350°F (180°C) and bake for 30–40 minutes more or until the crust is browned.

Sweet Cherry Pie

(8-INCH PIE)

Basic Pastry dough for 8-inch
  two-crust pie (p. 575)
3 cups (¾ L) fresh or canned
  sweet cherries, pitted

¼ cup (50 g) sugar
2½ tablespoons quick-cooking
  tapioca
2 teaspoons butter

Preheat the oven to 425°F (220°C). Line an 8-inch pie pan with half the pastry dough. Drain the cherries, saving ½ cup of the juice. (If you are using fresh cherries, the natural juices which bubble up during baking are sufficient.) Mix the juice, sugar, and tapioca in a bowl, add the cherries, and toss well. Pile into the lined pan and dot with the butter. Roll out the top crust and drape it over the pie. Crimp the edges and cut several vents in the top. Bake for 10 minutes, reduce the heat to 350°F (180°C), continue to bake for 30–40 minutes more, until the crust is lightly browned.

Glazed Fresh Strawberry Tart

Wait until the spring when strawberries are plump and juicy, then fill a buttery prebaked tart shell with glazed berries topped with clouds of lightly sweetened whipped cream. Other fresh berry tarts can be made the same way—substituting blueberries, raspberries, blackberries for the quart of strawberries.

(9-INCH TART)

Tart Pastry dough for 9-inch
  tart (p. 576)
1 cup (200 g) granulated sugar
3 tablespoons cornstarch
¼ teaspoon salt
¾ cup (1¾ dL) orange juice

1 tablespoon lemon juice
1 quart (1 L) strawberries,
  hulled and sliced
1 cup (¼ L) heavy cream
Confectioners' sugar

Preheat the oven to 425°F (220°C). Line a 9-inch pie pan or springform with the tart dough, prick the dough all over, and bake for 12 minutes or until lightly browned. Combine the granulated sugar, cornstarch, salt, orange juice, and lemon juice in a saucepan. Cook over low heat, stirring constantly, until thickened, then continue to cook for about 10 minutes. Spoon into a bowl to cool. Fill the baked tart shell with the strawberries and cover them with the cornstarch mixture. Before serving, whip the cream, sweetening it to taste with confectioners' sugar. Spread over the strawberry filling.

Deep-Dish Peach Pie

(SERVES EIGHT)

1½ recipes Basic Pastry dough
  for 8-inch pie shell (p. 575)
2 tablespoons lemon juice
6 cups (1½ L) peeled, pitted,
  sliced peaches
1¼ cups (250 g) plus 2
  tablespoons sugar

⅛ teaspoon salt
¼ teaspoon nutmeg
¼ teaspoon cinnamon
3 tablespoons flour
4 tablespoons butter
1 cup (¼ L) heavy cream,
  whipped

Preheat the oven to 450°F (230°C). Prepare the pastry dough and set it aside. Sprinkle the lemon juice over the peaches in a large bowl. Mix 1¼ cups of the sugar with the salt, nutmeg, cinnamon, and flour, then add to the peaches and toss until they are evenly coated. Spread the peaches in a 1½- to 2-quart baking dish and dot all over with the butter. Roll out the pastry dough to cover the top of the dish with a 1½-inch overhang. Press the pastry to the edge of the dish and flute it. Cut two or three vents on top for steam to escape. Sprinkle the top with the remaining 2 tablespoons of sugar. Bake for 10 minutes, then reduce heat to 350°F (180°C) and continue to bake for 30 minutes more. Serve with whipped cream.

Deep-Dish Apple Pie. Substitute 6 *cups peeled, cored, sliced apples* for the peaches and use *2 teaspoons cinnamon.*

Deep-Dish Blueberry Pie. Substitute 6 *cups blueberries* for the peaches and use ½ *teaspoon cinnamon.*

Rhubarb Pie

Rhubarb is sometimes called "pie plant." Use only the stalks: the leaves are poisonous. Flatter this pie, if you wish, by adding a cup of crushed, drained strawberries or pineapple to the rhubarb filling.

(9-INCH LATTICE PIE)

Basic Pastry dough for 9-inch
   two-crust pie (p. 575)
1¼ cups (250 g) sugar
4 tablespoons flour

⅛ teaspoon salt
4 cups (1 L) ¼-inch pieces
   rhubarb stalks
2 tablespoons butter

1 Eggs
¼ c. Orange Juice
1½ c. Strawberries

Preheat the oven to 425°F (220°C). Line a 9-inch pie pan with half the pastry dough. Combine the sugar, flour, and salt in a bowl. Add the rhubarb and toss well. Pile the rhubarb filling into the lined pie pan and dot with the butter. Roll out the remaining dough and make a lattice top. Crimp the edges. Bake for 10 minutes, then reduce the heat to 350°F (180°C) and bake for 30–40 minutes more, until the filling is tender when pierced with a skewer and the crust is browned.

Pecan Pie

When you serve this pie, pass around a bowl filled with billows of unsweetened whipped cream.

(9-INCH OPEN PIE)

Tart Pastry dough for 9-inch
   tart (p. 576)
3 eggs, slightly beaten
¾ cup (150 g) sugar
⅛ teaspoon salt
1 cup (¼ L) dark corn syrup

1 teaspoon vanilla
1 cup (¼ L) pecans, broken in
   pieces
1 cup (¼ L) heavy cream,
   whipped

Preheat the oven to 425°F (220°C). Line a 9-inch pie pan with the pastry dough. Combine the eggs, sugar, salt, corn syrup, and vanilla in a bowl and blend well. Stir in the pecans. Pour into the lined pan. Bake for 10 minutes, then reduce the heat to 350°F (180°C) and bake for another 35 minutes. Serve with unsweetened whipped cream.

Cornish Treacle Tart

Treacle tart, an English sweet, is a great national favorite. To the English, treacle usually means molasses, but in the case of this tart golden syrup is used; we recommend using dark corn syrup. This isn't a traditional American kind of pie; the treacle is just a sweet thick coating that lies between the crisp bottom crust and the lattice crust.

(8-INCH LATTICE PIE)

Basic Pastry dough for 8-inch
   two-crust pie (p. 575)
4 tablespoons fresh white bread
   crumbs

¾ cup (1¾ dL) dark corn syrup
Grated rind of 1 lemon
1 teaspoon lemon juice

Preheat the oven to 425°F (220°C). Line an 8-inch pie pan with half the pastry dough. Mix the syrup, lemon rind, crumbs, and lemon juice together and pour into the lined pan. Roll out the remaining dough and make a lattice top. Crimp or flute the edges. Bake for 10 minutes, then lower the heat to 350°F (180°C) and bake for about 25 minutes more or until lightly browned.

Prune Pie

(9-INCH LATTICE PIE)

1 pound (450 g) dried prunes	1 tablespoon flour
Basic Pastry dough for 9-inch	Grated rind of 1 lemon
two-crust pie (p. 575)	2 tablespoons lemon juice
½ cup (100 g) sugar	2 tablespoons butter

Cook the prunes slowly in water to cover until they are tender, about 30 minutes. Drain them, reserving ½ cup of the juice. Preheat the oven to 425°F (220°C). Line a 9-inch pie pan with half the pastry dough. Pit the prunes and cut them in quarters. Mix the reserved prune juice, sugar, flour, lemon rind, and lemon juice in a small bowl. Spoon the prunes into the lined pie pan and pour the juice evenly on top. Dot with the butter. Roll out the remaining dough and make a lattice top. Crimp or flute the edges. Bake for 10 minutes, then lower the heat to 350°F (180°C) and continue baking for about 35 minutes or until the crust is browned.

Raisin Pie

Fill a child's hands with raisins or, better still, put the raisins in a pie faintly flavored with lemon and orange. This old-fashioned recipe will please grownups, too.

(9-INCH LATTICE PIE)

1 cup (¼ L) orange juice	1½ cups (300 g) sugar
2 cups (½ L) raisins	4 tablespoons flour
Basic Pastry dough for 9-inch	3 tablespoons lemon juice
two-crust pie (p. 575)	⅛ teaspoon salt

Put the orange juice and 1 cup water in a pan and bring to a boil. Remove from the heat and stir in the raisins. Let stand for 2 hours. Preheat the oven to 425°F (220°C). Line a 9-inch pie pan with half the pastry dough. Add the sugar, flour, lemon juice, and salt to the raisin mixture. Cook over low heat, stirring frequently, for about 10 minutes or until well thickened. Pile the filling into the lined pie pan. Roll out the remaining dough and make a lattice top. Crimp the edges. Bake for 10 minutes, then lower the heat to 350°F (180°C) and bake about 35 minutes longer, until the top is browned.

Apple-Cranberry-Raisin Pie

(9-INCH PIE)

Basic Pastry dough for 9-inch	1 cup (¼ L) cranberries
two-crust pie (p. 575)	½ cup (1 dL) raisins
1 cup (200 g) sugar	Grated rind of 1 lemon
½ teaspoon salt	5 large tart apples
3 tablespoons flour	2 tablespoons butter

Preheat the oven to 425°F (220°C). Line a 9-inch pie pan with half the pastry dough. Stir the sugar, salt, and flour together in a large bowl. Add the cranberries, raisins, and lemon rind. Peel, core, and slice the apples and toss them in the sugar mixture. Pile the filling into the lined pie pan and dot with the butter. Roll out the top crust and drape it over the pie. Crimp the edges together and cut several small vents in the top. Bake for 10 minutes, then lower the heat to 350°F (180°C) and continue baking for 30–40 minutes or until the apples are tender when pierced with a skewer and the crust is browned.

Mince Pie

In the first edition Fannie Farmer recommended puff paste for special Thanksgiving or Christmas mincemeat pies. Try using puff pastry, if you wish, but basic pastry dough makes a splendid mince pie.

(9-INCH PIE)

Basic Pastry dough for 9-inch
two-crust pie (p. 575)

1 pint (½ L) Mincemeat
(following recipes)

Preheat the oven to 425°F (220°C). Line a 9-inch pie pan with half the pastry dough. Fill the lined pan with the prepared mincemeat. Roll out the remaining dough and make a top crust or lattice crust. Crimp the edges. Cut vents if a top crust is used. Bake 10 minutes, then lower the heat to 350°F (180°C) and bake about 40 minutes more, until the top is lightly browned. Serve with softly *whipped cream* or *Hard Sauce* (p. 641), if you wish.

Mincemeat I

Mincemeat developed as a way of preserving meat without salting or smoking it. Traditionally, the minced beef and suet are combined with fruits, spices, and spirits, packed in jars, and sealed with wax. Make it well ahead of time: it keeps indefinitely, mellows with age, and is grand to have on hand as the holiday season approaches.

This is enough mincemeat for ten pies. You can make it in smaller quantities, if you wish, but before you reduce the recipe, consider the fine, old-fashioned holiday gifts that jars of homemade mincemeat make!

(20 PINTS)

4 pounds (1¾ kg) chopped
lean beef
2 pounds (900 g) chopped beef
suet
3 pounds (1½ kg) dark-brown
sugar
2 cups (½ L) molasses
2 quarts (2 L) cider
3 pounds (1½ kg) dried
currants
4 pounds (1¾ kg) seeded
raisins

½ pound (225 g) citron,
chopped
3 pounds (1½ kg) apples,
peeled, cored, and sliced
1 quart (1 L) brandy
1 tablespoon cinnamon
1 tablespoon mace
1 tablespoon ground cloves
1 teaspoon nutmeg
1 teaspoon allspice
2 teaspoons salt

Put the beef, suet, brown sugar, molasses, cider, currants, raisins, and citron in a large pot. Cook slowly, stirring occasionally, until the sugar and citron melt. Add the apples and cook until tender. Add the remaining ingredients and cook 15 minutes more, stirring frequently. Spoon into clean, hot jars, leaving 1-inch headspace. Close the jars and process at 10 pounds pressure for 20 minutes. You can then store the mincemeat indefinitely. If you do not want to process it, it is safer to refrigerate.

Mincemeat II

This recipe for meatless mincemeat will provide enough filling for two 8- or 9-inch pies.

(4 PINTS)

1 pound (450 g) suet, ground
1½ pounds (675 g) apples, peeled, cored, and chopped
1½ cups (3½ dL) dark-brown sugar
1 pound (450 g) dried currants
1 pound (450 g) golden raisins
1 pound (450 g) seedless raisins
4 ounces (115 g) candied lemon peel, diced

4 ounces (115 g) candied orange peel, diced
4 ounces (115 g) citron, diced
Grated rind of 2 lemons
Juice of 3 lemons
1 teaspoon cinnamon
½ teaspoon nutmeg
½ teaspoon mace
1 teaspoon allspice
1 cup (¼ L) brandy

Put all the ingredients in a large bowl and mix with your hands until well blended. Pack into sterilized jars and seal. Store in a cool place. It is not necessary to process this mincemeat because it doesn't contain fresh meat, but if you feel more comfortable about it, follow the directions for processing in the preceding recipe.

Mincemeat Tart

Fill a prebaked tart shell with this simple, meatless "mincemeat" mixture for a quick, easy, delicious version of mincemeat pie.

(9-INCH TART)

Tart Pastry dough for 9-inch tart (p. 576)
1½ cups (3½ dL) seedless raisins
4 tart apples, peeled and cored
½ orange, including rind
½ lemon, including rind
½ cup (1 dL) cider vinegar
1½ cups (3½ dL) dark-brown sugar

½ teaspoon salt
½ teaspoon cinnamon
½ teaspoon nutmeg
½ teaspoon ground cloves
Topping: 1½ cups (3½ dL) heavy cream; 3 tablespoons confectioners' sugar

Preheat the oven to 425°F (220°C). Line a 9-inch pie pan or springform pan with the pastry dough. Prick the dough all over and bake for 10–15 minutes, until lightly browned. Chop the raisins, apples, orange, and lemon coarsely. Add the vinegar and heat to the boiling point, then reduce the heat and simmer for 10 minutes. Add the sugar, salt, cinnamon, nutmeg, and cloves and simmer 15 minutes more. Let cool. Before serving, fill the tart with the cooled mincemeat. Whip the cream, sweetening it with the sugar, and spread over the mincemeat filling.

Pumpkin Pie

A really good pumpkin pie that deservedly goes with Thanksgiving.

(9-INCH OPEN PIE)

Basic Pastry dough for 9-inch
  pie shell (p. 575)
1 cup (200 g) sugar
½ teaspoon salt
1½ teaspoons cinnamon
½ teaspoon powdered ginger
½ teaspoon ground cloves

1½ cups (3½ dL) cooked or
  canned (unseasoned)
  pumpkin, mashed or puréed
1½ cups (3½ dL) evaporated
  milk
½ cup (1 dL) milk
2 eggs, slightly beaten

Preheat the oven to 425°F (220°C). Line a 9-inch pie pan with the pastry dough. Combine the remaining ingredients in a large bowl and beat until smooth. Pour into the lined pie pan. Bake for 10 minutes, then lower the heat to 300°F (150°C) and bake for about 45 minutes or until the filling is firm.

Sweet Potato Pie

Long ago the sweet potato was called a "long potato" or "Virginia potato." Southern states take pride in this very American pie.

(9-INCH OPEN PIE)

Tart Pastry dough for 9-inch
  tart (p. 576)
2 cups (½ L) mashed cooked
  sweet potatoes
2 eggs, well beaten
1¼ cups (3 dL) milk

¾ cup (150 g) sugar
½ teaspoon salt
½ teaspoon cinnamon
½ teaspoon nutmeg
2 tablespoons rum
4 tablespoons melted butter

Preheat the oven to 425°F (220°C). Line a 9-inch pie pan with the pastry dough. Combine the remaining ingredients in a large bowl and beat until smooth and well blended. Pour into the lined pan. Bake for 10 minutes, then reduce the heat to 300°F (150°C) and bake for about 50 minutes more or until the filling is firm.

Rich Squash Pie

(9-INCH OPEN PIE)

Basic Pastry dough for 9-inch
  pie shell (p. 575)
1 cup (¼ L) puréed cooked
  winter squash
1 cup (¼ L) heavy cream
1 cup (200 g) sugar
3 eggs, slightly beaten

3 tablespoons brandy
1 teaspoon cinnamon
1 teaspoon nutmeg
½ teaspoon powdered ginger
½ teaspoon salt
¼ teaspoon mace

Preheat the oven to 425°F (220°C). Line a 9-inch pie pan with the pastry dough. Combine the remaining ingredients in a large bowl and beat until smooth and well blended. Pour into the lined pie pan. Bake for 10 minutes, then reduce the heat to 300°F (150°C) and bake for 45–60 minutes more or until the filling is firm.

Parsnip Pie

Even if you've been prejudiced about parsnips since childhood, you should try this surprisingly delicious pie with a tantalizing flavor that most people are hard put to identify. Proportions are large because it is worth serving at a dinner party or a holiday feast.

(10-INCH OPEN PIE)

1 recipe Basic Pastry using 2
   cups flour (p. 575)
3 cups (¾ L) puréed plain
   parsnips, unseasoned
   (p. 393)
2 tablespoons soft butter
½ cup (1 dL) plus 2
   tablespoons honey

2 tablespoons orange rind
2 eggs, lightly beaten
½ teaspoon cinnamon
½ teaspoon mace
¼ teaspoon allspice
¼ teaspoon powdered cloves
1 teaspoon fresh lemon juice

Preheat the oven to 425°F (220°C). Line a 10-inch pie pan with the pastry dough. Beat all the other ingredients together until smooth, reserving the 2 additional tablespoons of honey. Prick the bottom of the pastry dough all over and bake for 5 minutes. Pour the parsnip filling into the partially baked shell and drizzle the remaining honey over the top. Lower the heat to 375°F (190°C). Bake 50–60 minutes or until the filling is firm in the center. Serve with a pitcher of *heavy cream* or a bowl of *lightly whipped cream* after the pie has cooled to room temperature.

Cottage Cheese Pie

This uses a graham-cracker crumb crust.

(8-INCH OPEN PIE)

Crumb Crust for 9-inch pie
   shell (p. 578), using graham
   crackers
2 cups (½ L) cottage cheese
¼ teaspoon salt
½ cup (100 g) sugar

½ cup (1 dL) light cream
3 eggs, well beaten
2 tablespoons butter, melted
Grated rind of 1 lemon
Juice of 1 lemon

Preheat the oven to 350°F (180°C). Set aside ½ cup of the crumb mixture to sprinkle on top of the pie. Pat the remaining crumbs into an 8-inch pie pan and refrigerate. Using a blender or a food processor or beating by hand, combine all the remaining ingredients until they are smooth and well mixed. Pour into the lined pie pan and sprinkle the reserved crumbs on top. Bake for 40–50 minutes, until a knife comes out clean.

Lemon Crumb Pie

(9-INCH OPEN PIE)

Crumb Crust for 9-inch pie
   shell (p. 578), using vanilla
   wafers
3 eggs, separated
Grated rind and juice of 2
   lemons

14-ounce (400-g) can
   sweetened condensed milk
⅛ teaspoon salt

Preheat the oven to 325°F (165°C). Line a 9-inch pie pan with the crumb crust mixture, reserving ¼ cup of the crumbs for the top. Refrigerate. Beat the egg yolks until they are thick and pale. Stir in the grated lemon rind, juice, milk, and salt. Beat the egg whites until stiff but not dry and fold them into the yolk mixture. Pour into the lined pie pan. Sprinkle the reserved crumbs on top and bake for 40 minutes.

Lemon Meringue Pie

A classic filling for a prebaked pie shell.

(9-INCH OPEN PIE)

Basic Pastry dough for 9-inch pie shell (p. 575)	4 eggs yolks, slightly beaten
4 tablespoons cornstarch	Grated rind of 1 lemon
4 tablespoons flour	½ cup (1 dL) lemon juice
¼ teaspoon salt	2 tablespoons butter
1¼ cups (250 g) sugar	Meringue Topping for 9-inch pie (p. 578)

Preheat the oven to 425°F (220°C). Line a 9-inch pie pan with the pastry dough, prick the dough all over, and bake for 16–18 minutes, until lightly browned. Mix the cornstarch, flour, salt, sugar, and 1½ cups water in a saucepan. Cook over low heat, stirring constantly, until thickened, then cook 10 minutes more, stirring frequently, until clear. Remove from the heat. Stir ½ cup of the hot mixture into the egg yolks, then stir the yolks into the remaining hot mixture and cook, stirring, for another 3 minutes. Remove from the heat and stir in the lemon rind, lemon juice, and butter. Let cool a bit. Spread the lemon mixture in the baked pie shell and cover with the meringue. Run under the broiler until the meringue peaks are delicately browned, taking care not to burn them. This particular meringue will hold up as long as two days without weeping and shrinking. Refrigerate for storage, but serve at room temperature.

Butterscotch Pie

A butterscotch custard, covered with soft whipped cream—most children love this pie.

(8-INCH OPEN PIE)

Tart Pastry for 8-inch tart (p. 576)	5 tablespoons flour
4 tablespoons butter	¼ teaspoon salt
¾ cup (1¾ dL) dark-brown sugar	2 eggs, slightly beaten
2 cups (½ L) milk	¼ teaspoon vanilla
	Topping: 1 cup (¼ L) heavy cream; sugar

Preheat the oven to 425°F (220°C). Line an 8-inch pie pan with the pastry dough, prick the dough all over, and bake for 12 minutes, until lightly browned. Put the butter and brown sugar in a sturdy pan and cook over medium heat for 2 minutes or until the mixture is brown and syrupy. Add 1⅔ cups of the milk, stir, and cook until very hot. Blend the flour, salt, and the remaining ⅓ cup of milk together in a small bowl until smooth. Add to the hot mixture and cook, stirring frequently, for 15 minutes. Stir some of the hot mixture into the beaten eggs, then return egg mixture to the pan. Cook, stirring, for 2 minutes. Cool. Add the vanilla, spread in the baked pie shell, and chill. Before serving, whip the cream, sweetening slightly, and spread it over the pie filling.

Orange Meringue Pie

(8-INCH OPEN PIE)

Basic Pastry dough for 8-inch
  pie shell (p. 575)
4 eggs, separated
½ cup (100 g) sugar
3 tablespoons flour

1 cup (¼ L) orange juice
Juice of 1 lemon
Meringue Topping for 8-inch
  pie (p. 578)

Preheat the oven to 425°F (220°C). Line an 8-inch pie pan with the pastry dough, prick the dough all over, and bake for 16–18 minutes, until lightly browned. Beat the egg yolks until they are thick and pale. Mix the sugar, flour, orange juice, and lemon juice together in a small pot. Add the egg yolks and cook over moderate heat, stirring constantly, until thick, about 10 minutes. Let cool. Spread the cooled mixture in the baked pie shell. Cover with meringue topping and run under the broiler until the meringue peaks are delicately browned, taking care not to burn them. Try not to do the meringue too far ahead.

Pineapple Meringue Pie

(8-INCH OPEN PIE)

Basic Pastry dough for 8-inch
  pie shell (p. 575)
2 cups (½ L) canned crushed
  pineapple
2 tablespoons cornstarch
¼ teaspoon salt

1 tablespoon butter, softened
1 tablespoon grated lemon rind
1 tablespoon lemon juice
Meringue Topping for 8-inch
  pie (p. 578)

Preheat the oven to 425°F (220°C). Line an 8-inch pie pan with the pastry dough, prick the dough all over, and bake for 16–18 minutes, until lightly browned. Mix the pineapple, cornstarch, and salt together in a saucepan and cook over low heat until clear and thickened. Cool, then blend in the butter, lemon rind, and lemon juice. Spread in the baked pie shell and cover with the meringue. Run under the broiler until the meringue peaks are delicately browned, taking care not to burn them. Try not to do the meringue too far ahead and serve at room temperature.

Banana Custard Pie

Nourishing, wholesome, and very pleasant to eat. The crisp, prebaked tart shell may be prepared in advance.

(9-INCH OPEN PIE)

Tart Pastry dough for 9-inch
  tart (p. 576)
⅔ cup (130 g) sugar
3 tablespoons flour
¼ teaspoon salt
4 eggs, separated

2 cups (½ L) milk
2 teaspoons vanilla
1½ tablespoons butter, melted
2 bananas, sliced
Meringue Topping for 9-inch
  pie (p. 578)

Preheat the oven to 425°F (220°C). Line a 9-inch pie pan with the pastry dough, prick the dough all over, and bake for 16–18 minutes, until lightly browned. Combine the sugar, flour, salt, and lightly beaten egg yolks in a bowl. (Reserve the whites for the Meringue Topping.) Scald the milk in a pan and slowly add it to the egg mixture, stirring constantly. Pour back into the pan and cook over moderate heat, stirring constantly, until thickened. Remove from the heat and pour into a bowl. Stir in the vanilla. Spread melted butter with a knife over the top of the custard to prevent a skin from forming. Cover and chill. Shortly before serving, cover the bottom of the baked pie shell with the sliced bananas. Add the chilled custard, spreading it evenly with a spatula. Cover with the meringue and run under the broiler until the meringue peaks are delicately browned, taking care not to burn them.

Slipped Custard Pie

This pie is a dandy, sitting smugly on its crisp prebaked crust. An easy, old-fashioned method keeps the piecrust flaky and the custard silken: they meet just before they are served.

(9-INCH OPEN PIE)

Basic Pastry dough for 9-inch pie shell (p. 575)
½ cup (100 g) sugar
¼ teaspoon salt

2½ cups (6 dL) milk, scalded
1½ teaspoons vanilla
4 eggs, slightly beaten

Preheat the oven to 425°F (220°C). Line a 9-inch pie pan with the pastry dough, prick the dough all over, and bake for 16–18 minutes, until lightly browned. Set aside. Reduce the oven heat to 350°F (180°C). Combine the sugar, salt, milk, and vanilla, add the eggs, and mix well. Pour into a buttered 9-inch pie pan the *same size and shape* as the baked pie shell. Set the pan in a larger pan filled with ½ inch hot water. Bake about 35 minutes or until the custard is barely set; overbaking will make it watery. Remove from the oven and cool; refrigerate if the custard is not to be served within a couple of hours. Assemble the pie as close to serving time as possible: loosen the edge of thecustard with a sharp knife, shaking gently to free the bottom; hold over the pie shell and ease the filling gently into the shell, shaking it a bit if necessary to make it settle into place.

Coconut Custard Pie. Add 1 *cup grated coconut* to the custard before baking.

Cream Pie

Fill prebaked pie shells with cream filling as close to serving time as possible so that they do not get soggy.

(9-INCH OPEN PIE)

Tart Pastry dough for 9-inch tart (p. 576)
¾ cup (150 g) sugar
½ cup (70 g) flour
¼ teaspoon salt

3 cups (¾ L) milk
3 egg yolks, slightly beaten
2 tablespoons butter
1 teaspoon vanilla

Preheat the oven to 425°F (220°C). Line a 9-inch pie pan with the pastry dough, prick the dough all over, and bake for 12 minutes until lightly browned. Set aside. Combine the sugar, flour, and salt in a saucepan. Stir in the milk and cook over low heat, stirring constantly, until thick. Add the egg yolks and continue to cook, stirring, for about 3 minutes. Remove from the heat and blend in the butter and vanilla. Let the custard cool for about 15 minutes, then pour it into the pie shell and refrigerate until ready to serve.

Chocolate Cream Pie. Before adding the milk, heat it with *2 ounces unsweetened chocolate,* stirring until the milk and chocolate are smoothly blended.

Coconut Cream Pie. Add *½ cup shredded coconut* together with the butter and vanilla. Sprinkle the top of the pie with *5 tablespoons shredded coconut.*

Banana Cream Pie. Peel and slice *2 ripe bananas* and arrange over the top of the finished pie shortly before serving.

Chocolate Chiffon Pie

(9-INCH OPEN PIE)

Crumb Crust (p. 578) or
   Chocolate Coconut Crust
   (p. 578)
1½ cups (3½ dL) cold milk
1 envelope gelatin

½ cup (100 g) sugar
⅛ teaspoon salt
4 eggs, separated
6 tablespoons cocoa

Preheat the oven to 350°F (180°C). Pat the crumb mixture into a 9-inch pie pan and bake for 8–10 minutes; set aside. Put the milk in a saucepan, sprinkle the gelatin over it, and let it soften for about 3 minutes. Stir in the sugar, salt, and egg yolks and beat thoroughly. Cook, stirring, over moderate heat until thickened; do not boil. Add the cocoa and stir until dissolved. Chill just until the mixture mounds when dropped from a spoon. Beat the egg whites until they are stiff but not dry. Fold them into the gelatin mixture. Spoon into the pie shell and chill until ready to serve.

Coffee Chiffon Pie. Substitute *2 tablespoons instant coffee* for the cocoa.

Eggnog Chiffon Pie. Substitute *3 tablespoons rum* for the cocoa. Top the finished pie with a thin layer of *whipped cream* and sprinkle with *nutmeg.*

Strawberry Chiffon Pie

(9-INCH OPEN PIE)

Crumb Crust for 9-inch pie
   shell (p. 578)
1 pint (½ L) strawberries
¾ cup (150 g) sugar

1 envelope gelatin
1 tablespoon lemon juice
⅛ teaspoon salt
2 egg whites

Preheat the oven to 350°F (180°C). Pat the crumb mixture into a 9-inch pie pan and bake for 8–10 minutes; set aside. Reserve 6 whole strawberries for a garnish, then slice the rest and toss them in ½ cup of the sugar. Sprinkle the gelatin over ¾ cup cold water and let it soften for about 3 minutes. Add the lemon juice, salt, and remaining ¼ cup sugar. Cook over moderate heat, stirring, until the gelatin dissolves; do not let the mixture boil. Cool a little, then stir in the sliced strawberries. Chill until the mixture mounds when dropped from a spoon. Beat the egg whites until stiff but not dry and fold them into the strawberry mixture. Spoon into the baked pie shell, garnish with the whole strawberries, and chill until ready to serve.

Lemon Chiffon Pie

(9-INCH OPEN PIE)

Crumb Crust for 9-inch pie
   shell (p. 578), using graham
   crackers
1 envelope gelatin
1 cup (200 g) sugar

⅛ teaspoon salt
1 teaspoon grated lemon rind
½ cup (1 dL) lemon juice
4 eggs, separated

Preheat the oven to 350°F (180°C). Pat the crumb mixture into a 9-inch pie pan and bake for 8–10 minutes; set aside. Put ¼ cup cold water in a saucepan, sprinkle the gelatin on top, and let it soften for about 3 minutes. Stir in ½ cup of the sugar and the salt, lemon rind, and lemon juice. Add the egg yolks and stir vigorously until well blended. Cook, stirring, over moderate heat until the gelatin has dissolved; do not allow to boil. Chill until the mixture mounds when dropped from a spoon. Beat the egg whites until they are foamy, then gradually add the remaining ½ cup of sugar, continuing to beat until smooth and shiny. Fold the whites into the lemon mixture, spread in the pie shell, and chill until ready to serve.

Lime Chiffon Pie. Using gingersnap crumbs in the crust substitute *1 teaspoon grated lime rind* and *½ cup lime juice* for the lemon rind and juice.

Orange Chiffon Pie. Using vanilla wafers in the crust substitute *1 teaspoon grated orange rind* and *½ cup orange juice plus 2 tablespoons lemon juice* for the lemon rind and juice.

Black-Bottom Pie

(9-INCH OPEN PIE)

Crumb Crust for 9-inch pie
   shell (p. 578), using
   chocolate wafers
1½ cups (3½ dL) cold milk
1 envelope gelatin
½ cup (100 g) sugar
⅛ teaspoon salt

4 eggs, separated
1½ ounces (45 g) unsweetened
   chocolate, melted
1 teaspoon vanilla
1 tablespoon rum
½ cup (1 dL) heavy cream

Preheat the oven to 350°F (180°C). Pat the crumb mixture into a 9-inch pie pan and bake for 8–10 minutes; set aside. Put the milk in a saucepan, sprinkle in the gelatin, and let it soften for about 3 minutes. Stir in the sugar, salt, and egg yolks and beat to blend thoroughly. Cook over moderate heat, stirring, until thickened; do not let the mixture boil. Remove from the heat and divide in half. Add the melted chocolate and the vanilla to one half and the rum to the other. Chill until the mixtures mound when dropped from a spoon. Beat the egg whites until stiff but not dry. Divide the beaten whites in half. Fold half into the chocolate mixture and the other half into the rum mixture. Spread the chocolate mixture over the crumb crust, then spread the rum mixture over the chocolate mixture. Whip the cream and spread that over all. Refrigerate until ready to serve.

Angel Pie

This angel pie has a crunchy, light-golden meringue crust filled with lemon custard, covered with clouds of sweetened whipped cream, and garnished with fresh strawberries. Meringues are temperamental: it's better to make them on a cool, dry day than a warm, humid one. Don't be alarmed when the crust collapses a bit and cracks as it cools. This is as it should be—the cracks won't show once it's filled.

(9-INCH OPEN PIE)

4 eggs, separated and at room temperature
⅛ teaspoon salt
¼ teaspoon cream of tartar
1½ cups (300 g) granulated sugar

¼ cup (½ dL) lemon juice
1½ cups (3½ dL) heavy cream
⅓ cup (¾ dL) confectioners' sugar
8 whole strawberries

Preheat the oven to 275°F (135°C). Butter a 9-inch pie pan. Combine the egg whites, salt, and cream of tartar in a large mixing bowl. Beat with an electric beater until soft peaks form. Slowly add 1 cup of the granulated sugar and beat until shiny peaks form. Spread the mixture over the bottom of the pie pan and build it up around the rim about 1 inch higher than the edge of the pan. Bake for about 1 hour or until lightly brown and firm to the touch. Turn off the heat and let cool in the oven with the door open. While the crust is cooling, beat the egg yolks until they are thick and pale. Slowly beat in the remaining ½ cup of the granulated sugar. Add the lemon juice. Cook over moderate heat, stirring constantly, until the mixture thickens. Cool. Spread in the meringue shell. Shortly before serving, whip the cream, slowly adding the confectioners' sugar until it holds soft peaks. Spoon the cream over the top and decorate with the strawberries. Refrigerate until ready to serve.

SMALL TARTS

Tarts are open pies—filled pastry shells without a top crust. Made with strong, buttery tart pastry, both small and large tarts are often freestanding, needing no pans to support their crisp, golden sides after they are baked. Small tarts are easy to serve and tidy to eat, conveniences you'll appreciate when you have a large group of guests. And they look so enchanting, filled with a variety of different sweets and set out on a large platter.

Making small tarts is a fine way to use up leftover pie dough or tart pastry. Even if you have only a little bit of leftover dough, it's often nice to have a few tarts on hand. Or wrap and freeze bits and scraps of leftover dough until you have enough for a big batch of tarts. If you have tart tins, line them with the dough and then freeze them; it's very handy to have some small tarts in the freezer, ready to bake at a moment's notice.

The most common small tart tin is 4 inches in diameter and 1 inch deep, holding ½ cup of filling. If you don't have small tart tins, invert a muffin tin and pat the pastry dough over the

bottoms of the inverted cups and about an inch up the sides. Bake, then let the pastry cool a bit before easing the baked tarts from the tins.

Fruit or Berry Tarts

(6 SMALL TARTS)

Tart Pastry dough for 9-inch
tart (p. 576)
3 cups (¾ L) drained cooked
fruit or fresh berries, sugared

1½ cups (3½ dL) currant jelly,
or 1 cup (¼ L) heavy cream,
whipped with some sugar

Preheat the oven to 375°F (190°C). Line six 4-inch tart tins with the pastry dough, prick the bottoms, and bake for about 10 minutes, or until the pastry is golden. Cool and remove from the tins. Just before serving, fill each baked tart shell with ½ cup fruit or berries. Melt the currant jelly in a pan over low heat and pour it over the fruit to glaze. Or top each tart with sweetened whipped cream.

Lemon Tarts

(6 SMALL TARTS)

Tart Pastry dough for 9-inch
tart (p. 576)
¼ pound (115 g) butter
1½ cups (300 g) sugar
Grated rind of 2 lemons

Juice of 3 lemons
6 eggs, slightly beaten
Topping: 1 cup (¼ L) heavy
cream, whipped

Preheat the oven to 375°F (190°C). Line six 4-inch tart tins with the pastry dough, prick the bottoms, and bake for about 10 minutes or until the pastry is golden. Cool and remove from the tins. Mix the butter, sugar, lemon rind, lemon juice, and eggs together in a heavy-bottomed pan or double boiler. Cook over moderate heat, stirring constantly, until thick. Cool in the refrigerator. Before serving, fill the tart shells with lemon filling and top with whipped cream.

Pecan Tarts

(6 SMALL TARTS)

Tart Pastry dough for 9-inch
tart (p. 576)
3 eggs
¾ cup (1¾ dL) dark-brown
sugar
¼ teaspoon salt
1 cup (¼ L) dark corn syrup

½ teaspoon vanilla
2 tablespoons melted butter
1 cup (¼ L) pecan pieces
Topping: 1 cup (¼ L) heavy
cream, whipped; sugar

Preheat the oven to 375°F (190°C). Line six 4-inch tart tins with the pastry dough; set aside. Beat the eggs in a bowl for a minute or less, then add the brown sugar, salt, corn syrup, vanilla, and melted butter. Stir vigorously, then add the pecans. Pour filling into tarts. Bake for 25 minutes or until the filling is set. Before serving, top with lightly sweetened whipped cream.

Raisin Tarts

(24 SMALL TARTS)

Basic Pastry dough for 8-inch
  two-crust pie (p. 575)
¾ cup (1¾ dL) raisins
2 tablespoons chopped citron
3 tablespoons honey

2 tablespoons melted butter
1 tablespoon grated orange peel
¼ cup (½ dL) dark-brown
  sugar
Milk

Preheat the oven to 450°F (230°C). Roll the pastry dough very thin. Cut 2½-inch rounds, 48 in all. Mix the raisins, citron, honey, butter, orange peel, and brown sugar in a bowl. Place a rounded teaspoonful in the center of half the pastry rounds. Moisten the edges with milk and place an unfilled round on top of each filled one. Seal the edges with the tines of a fork and prick the top. Bake 10–15 minutes or until golden.

Banbury Tarts

Banbury tarts come from Banbury, England, where street vendors sold them steaming hot from flannel-lined baskets.

(12 SMALL TARTS)

Basic Pastry dough for 8-inch
  two-crust pie (p. 575)
1 cup (¼ L) raisins
1 cup (200 g) sugar

1 egg, slightly beaten
1 tablespoon cracker crumbs
Grated rind and juice of 1
  lemon

Preheat the oven to 350°F (180°C). Roll the dough out ⅛ inch thick and cut it in 3 × 3½–inch squares. Mix the raisins, sugar, egg, cracker crumbs, lemon rind and juice together in a bowl and toss until well mixed. Put about 2 teaspoonfuls on one half of each piece of pastry. Moisten the edges with cold water, fold in half into little triangles, and press the edges together with a fork dipped in flour. Prick the tops. Bake on an ungreased cookie sheet for about 20 minutes.

Cream Puffs

Cream puffs are versatile. In addition to the charming sweet described below, the puffs may be filled with cold mixed seafood, flavored cream cheese, or chicken salad. You can make tiny puffs, fill them with a variety of fillings, and use them as appetizers.

It is best to assemble cream puffs as close to serving time as possible, since the pastry will remain crisper if it is not refrigerated. Make the filling ahead and keep it refrigerated until you are ready to assemble the puffs.

(FOURTEEN 2-INCH PUFFS)

4 tablespoons butter
½ cup (70 g) flour
2 eggs, at room temperature

Preheat the oven to 375°F (190°C). Combine ½ cup water and the butter in a saucepan and bring to a boil. Remove from the heat and add the flour all at once, stirring vigorously with a wooden spoon. Return to moderate heat and stir constantly until the dough leaves the sides of the pan and forms a ball. Remove from the heat and let cool for about 5 minutes. Add the eggs, one at a time, beating hard until the dough is smooth. Place large, rounded tablespoons of dough on an ungreased cookie sheet, 2 inches apart. Bake for 30 minutes or until the puffs are golden. Carefully slice the tops off the puffs and scoop out the centers. Cool on a rack. Fill with *Basic Cream Filling* (p. 542). Replace the tops and cover them with *Chocolate Frosting for Cream Puffs and Éclairs* (p. 536).

Éclairs (8 éclairs). Prepare 1 recipe Cream Puff dough. Put the dough in a pastry bag and pipe onto an ungreased cookie sheet in strips about 4½ inches long and 1 inch wide. Bake as above. Carefully split the éclairs lengthwise and cool them on a rack. Scoop out the insides and fill with *Basic Cream Filling* (p. 542) or with *whipped cream*. Replace the top halves and ice with *Chocolate Frosting for Cream Puffs and Éclairs* (p. 536).

PUFF PASTRY

Puff pastry, basic to French cuisine, has been popular in this country for a long time. The first edition of this book gave instructions for making it, cautioning the novice baker to "work rapidly and with a light touch"—there were no refrigerators then to chill the dough and let it rest between rollings-out.

Sometimes referred to as the "pastry of a thousand leaves," its many buttery, crisp layers, light enough to be all but airborne, are a flaky miracle of levitation. It is often used to make small patty shells which can lift meat, fish, or cheese mixtures to glorious heights or present delectable frames for custards, creams, and fruits. It is well worth learning to make puff pastry, if only for the confidence it inspires.

Puff pastry, like many marriages, unites separate identities in a compatible relationship, in this case between the butter and the dough. Both should have approximately the same consistency and temperature: adding a small amount of butter to the dough and a small amount of flour to the butter helps to achieve this.

The process of rolling, folding, and turning creates hundreds of alternating sheets of butter and dough. The heat of the oven melts the butter and creates steam which puffs the dough into light, flaky layers. Keeping this in mind will encourage you to roll it out lightly: you do not want to smear the butter into the flour.

Don't try to make puff pastry when the temperature in your kitchen is over 75°F. The dough must be somewhat chilled before you begin rolling it out—but don't let it get too cold. By the same token the butter shouldn't get too cold or you won't be able to pat it into the dough.

While rolling the dough, lift and move it constantly so it doesn't stick to the surface. Dust the working surface lightly with flour as needed. Brush off any excess flour before folding the dough. If it sticks or some butter shows through, lightly dust the spot with flour.

It is important to let the dough relax and cool in the refrigerator between each rolling-out, so that it will lose some of its elasticity and firm up. Moreover, while you are rolling it out, if it ever becomes too warm and smeary, stop right away and just fold it up in thirds, envelope-fashion, wrap it in foil or plastic, and return it to the refrigerator. If it is ever too cold when you take it out, leave it at room temperature a few minutes and, if necessary, give it a few whacks with the rolling pin in different places to loosen up the chilled butter inside.

All this sounds very complicated but as soon as you actually make the puff pastry, adhering carefully to the directions in the recipe that follows, you will find it surprisingly easy.

Basic Puff Pastry

2 cups (280 g) all-purpose   ½ pound (225 g) unsalted butter
    white flour   ½ teaspoon salt

Put 1¾ cups of the flour, 4 tablespoons of the butter, the salt, and ½ cup water into a bowl—the bowl of your electric mixer, if you have one. Beat with an electric hand-held beater or your mixer for 4 minutes at medium speed. Shape the dough into a ball, wrap in foil or wax paper, and refrigerate for 15 minutes. Put the remaining butter in the mixer bowl with the remaining ¼ cup of flour and beat until the butter and flour are blended and smooth. If the butter feels too soft and smeary, refrigerate it for about 5 minutes: the dough and the butter must be at about the same temperature. Roll the dough into a 12-inch circle. Pat

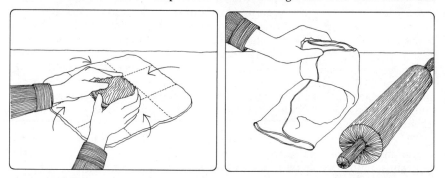

the butter into a 4-inch square in the center of the dough. Fold the dough over the butter making a plump, square package. Place, folded sides down, on a lightly floured board. Roll out into a rectangle about 6–8 inches wide and 14–18 inches long, then fold the dough into thirds like an envelope. This rolling out and folding is known as the first "turn." With the narrow end of the "envelope"

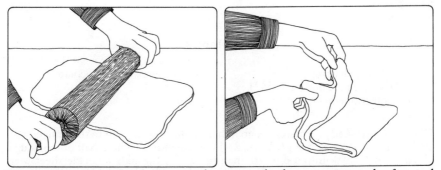

facing you, roll the dough into another rectangle the same size as the first and then fold that rectangle into thirds once again—the second "turn." Make two indentations in the dough with your fingers to remind you it has had two "turns." Let the dough chill in the refrigerator for about 45 minutes. Take it out of the refrigerator and give it two more "turns," then refrigerate again for 45 minutes. Altogether the dough should have six "turns." After the sixth, fold it again in an envelope form, wrap it in foil or plastic, and refrigerate for at least 1 hour before preparing it for baking. If you want to freeze puff pastry dough for use at another time, wrap it well and freeze it after the fourth "turn." Let it defrost in the refrigerator, then give it the final two "turns" before preparing it for baking.

Patty Shells

Fill these crisp, airy shells with creamed seafood or poultry for a main course, or with glazed fruit, custard, or whipped cream for dessert.

(6–8 PATTY SHELLS)

Basic Puff Pastry (preceding recipe)

Preheat the oven to 425°F (220°C). Roll the puff pastry dough into a rectangle ¼ inch thick or a little less. Cut it into circles 3 inches in diameter; you will need two circles to make each patty shell. Remove the centers from half the

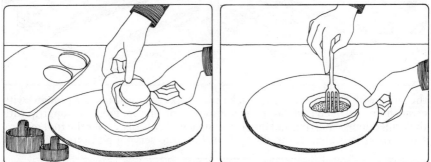

rounds with a small round cutter 2 inches in diameter. Sprinkle a cookie sheet with water and shake off the excess. Place the whole rounds on the cookie sheet and brush the edges of the rounds with water. Place a cut-out ring on top of each round and press gently to seal evenly. Prick the bottom of each unbaked shell in several places with a fork. Bake for 20–25 minutes. Remove from the oven and cool on a rack. Carefully remove uncooked pastry from the center, using a knife or a teaspoon.

Napoleons

(8–10 NAPOLEONS)

Basic Puff Pastry (p. 598)
Basic Cream Filling (p. 542)
Confectioners' Frosting I
(p. 535)

1 square semisweet chocolate
(optional)

Divide the prepared puff pastry dough in half, returning one half to the refrigerator. Preheat the oven to 425°F (220°C). Roll out the unrefrigerated half of the dough about ⅛ inch thick into a 6 × 16–inch rectangle. Sprinkle a cookie sheet with water and shake off the excess. Place the dough on the sheet and prick it all over with a fork. Bake for 20–25 minutes. Cool on a rack. Roll and bake the other half of the dough in the same fashion. Carefully cut each pastry rectangle into three long strips, 2 inches wide, and slice each strip in half lengthwise. Spread three of

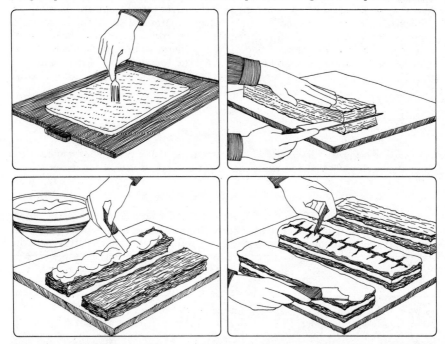

the strips with the cream filling. Make two stacks of strips, two strips high, with cream filling between each layer and unfrosted strip on top. Frost the top strip with the confectioners' frosting and drizzle warm melted chocolate over the top, making a pattern as indicated in the illustration. Cut into serving portions.

Cream Horns

(12 HORNS)

Basic Puff Pastry (page 598)
1 egg white

Preheat the oven to 450°F (230°C). Roll puff paste into a rectangle about 8 × 10 inches. Cut into twelve 10-inch strips. Roll each strip over a special cone-shaped form, having the edges overlap. Chill 20 minutes. Beat the egg white with 1 teaspoon water and brush the mixture over the horns. Place horns on cookie sheet and bake for 8 minutes, then reduce heat to 350°F (180°C) and bake until lightly golden. Remove from oven, and slip the forms out of the pastry. When cool, fill with *sweetened whipped cream flavored with rum* or *Basic Cream Filling* (p. 542).

Palm Cookies

A full recipe of Basic Puff Pastry (p. 598) will make 60 cookies, but chances are you'll be making these with leftover pieces of dough, instead. It's a great way to use up the sometimes considerable amounts of puff pastry dough that are left after special shapes are cut.

Puff pastry dough
Sugar

Fit leftover pieces of dough together as best you can, overlapping the edges slightly and then roll out with a rolling pin on a lightly floured board into a rectangle about ⅛ inch thick. Sprinkle the dough heavily with sugar. Fold the long edges of the dough lengthwise to the center. Fold the folded edges lengthwise to meet in the center. Flatten slightly with a rolling pin, then close the halves together as if shutting a book; you will have a long roll. Slice the roll into cookies ⅛ inch thick. Arrange each cookie on a heavily sugared baking sheet. Chill for 30 minutes. Preheat the oven to 450°F (230°C). Bake for about 6 minutes,

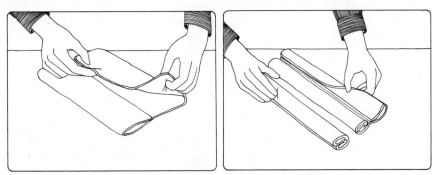

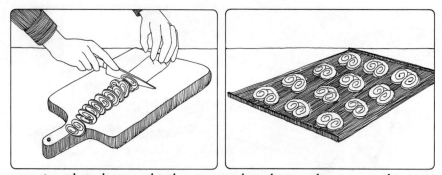

removing when the sugar has begun to melt and caramelize; turn cookies over and bake another few minutes, taking care that they do not burn. Remove and cool. Palm cookies will keep in an airtight container for about 3 days. They also freeze well.

DESSERTS &
DESSERT SAUCES

ABOUT DESSERTS

Imagine a world without creamy custards, sweet soufflés, rich creams, icy sherbets, simple puddings—what joy we would lose. Desserts are mostly just to please. It's not an accident that sweet dishes end a meal; we leave the table with such a benign view of the world.

It is like unearthing a collection of old treasures to discover the goodness of the simple desserts that families loved in the last century. An egg or two, milk, bread, rice or somesuch, a bit of sugar, flavor—simple combinations of these good things become splendid, wholesome dishes, easy to prepare and more economical and delicious than commercially packaged desserts.

If you are young and new to cooking, some of these lovely old dessert names may sound only vaguely familiar to you. Try them anyway, starting with Baked Rice Pudding or Chocolate Bread Pudding—you will be impressed.

Custards and Puddings
Custards. A custard is a cooked, egg-thickened dessert with eggs, milk, and sugar as its basic ingredients. Baked Custard in simple brown custard cups is one of the most familiar, homy American desserts. Soft Custard, also called "boiled custard," is a thinner, almost runny, custard, often used like a sauce with fruits or other desserts. It is made with whole eggs and usually cooked over very low heat or in the top of a double boiler. English Custard, or Crème Anglaise, is a richer, creamier soft custard, made with egg yolks, rather than whole eggs. It is also used as a sauce and as the base for other desserts, such as Bavarian Cream.
Blancmange. Blancmange is a starch-thickened dessert. Its name comes from the French and means "white food."
Puddings. "Pudding" used to be the general name for most desserts. It now usually refers to a cooked or steamed dessert that has been thickened.

Steamed Puddings
Steamed puddings are cooked by steam slowly. They are sometimes served cold, but we like them best served warm, and usually with a sauce. They make fine winter desserts.

Some steamed puddings are made with ground suet (beef fat), which gives them a rich, distinctive flavor. The suet dissolves during the steaming and moistens the pudding. You can have your own suet on hand if you collect and freeze the fat from various cuts of beef as you use them. When you have enough fat for a pudding, defrost it and grind it, leaving it at room temperature so that it can be creamed and blended with the other ingredients.

Steamed puddings should be made in a well-buttered mold or container. Fill the container no more than two-thirds full to allow room for expansion.

The pudding mold or container must be tightly covered. Use a standard pudding mold with a lid that clamps snugly, or cover a can with a double thickness of foil and tie the foil down securely with string.

Choose a large pot with a cover in which the pudding mold or container will fit when the pot is tightly covered. Set a canning rack or other rack in the pot to raise the mold so that water can circulate all around it. Or put a Mason jar ring or a hollowed-out ring from a small tuna fish can under the mold to raise it. Add enough water to the pot so that the mold will be covered halfway up its sides. Bring the water to a boil, then place the covered mold on the rack and cover the pot. Lower the heat so that the water boils gently, and cook as directed in the recipe, adding more water if necessary.

Dessert Soufflés

If you want to do a little spellbinding during a meal, include a soufflé in the menu. Simple as they are to prepare, soufflés demand attention. When a soufflé is served, everyone feels that you have done something special.

A true dessert soufflé has a cream-sauce base to which sugar, flavoring, and egg yolks are usually added. This flavored base can be prepared well in advance of serving, even several days ahead if necessary. All that remains to be done before baking is to fold beaten egg whites into the base. A soufflé made with a cream-sauce base will bake in just about the time it takes to eat the main course. Put it in the oven right before you sit down to dinner.

"Fruit soufflés," made with fruit purée, sugar, and egg whites, are really "whips" (see p. 619). The ingredients are folded together and baked into a fluffy froth. More fragile than soufflés with a cream-sauce base, they take only about 20 minutes to bake. To have them ready for dessert, you may have to be absent from the table for a few minutes during the meal.

Follow the same rules about beating and folding egg whites (p. 336) carefully as you would for a savory soufflé.

Butter the soufflé dish amply and sprinkle sugar all over the bottom and the sides. Fill the dish almost to the top.

You can help a soufflé to rise well above the .top of the dish by forming a collar as follows: cut a piece of wax paper or foil long enough to encircle the soufflé dish. Fold it in half lengthwise to give it extra strength. Butter the inside of the paper, then wrap it around the dish extending above the top rim, and tie a string around, fastening the top part with Scotch tape or a paper clip.

Put the soufflé dish in the oven on a cookie sheet so that the heat is

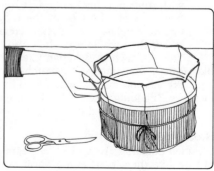

evenly distributed. For our basic two-quart soufflés, bake in a preheated 375°F oven, allowing 25–30 minutes if you wish a moist center, 35–45 minutes if you prefer it somewhat drier.

It is often nice to dust the top of a dessert soufflé with confectioners' sugar before presenting it.

Gelatin Desserts

For instructions on using unflavored gelatin, see Gelatin, p. 16.

Jellies. Lightest of all desserts are the jellies. Unfortunately, they have been replaced in many recipe files by the artificially flavored and colored commercial gelatins that have abounded in the past fifty years or so. Try wine jelly or orange jelly made with freshly squeezed fruit at your next Sunday dinner and you'll see why it's time to bring such old-fashioned jellies back.

Creams. Bavarian cream is English custard with gelatin and whipped cream added. Charlotte Russe is Bavarian cream made in a plain, cylindrical mold which has been lined with sponge cake or ladyfingers.

Using Molds for Chilled or Frozen Desserts. A chilled and frozen dessert often looks nicer when turned out from a nicely shaped mold, rather than being served from a simple bowl. But for many the struggle to remove the dessert from its molded prison is so irritating and the results so likely to be a mess that they avoid it. Unmolding a dessert is really not difficult, however, if you have patience and do not allow yourself to get flustered. Begin by using a sharp knife to loosen the edges of the chilled dessert. Select a pot or pan into which the mold can easily be set, and figure out how much water must be added to cover the mold right up to its rim. Heat the water until it is very hot. Dip the mold in the water for a few seconds, then cover it with a serving platter and turn it over until the dessert loosens. If it doesn't loosen immediately, let it sit for a while. If necessary, you can help it along by covering the mold for a few seconds with a hot, damp towel.

There is a pure-vegetable spray-on coating available now in most supermarkets which is guaranteed to make unmolding easy. Spray the inside of the mold with it generously before you put in the dessert. After the dessert has chilled, turn the mold over onto a serving platter; it should slide out easily and unscarred.

The exception to the unmolding rule comes when you make a chilled "soufflé." Fortified by gelatin and well-beaten egg whites and whipped cream, the soufflé mixture, usually with a puréed fruit or berry base, is poured into a slightly too-small soufflé mold with a collar around it so that when the collar is removed, it stands proudly a couple of inches above the mold just like a beautifully risen soufflé.

Frozen Desserts

Mousses. The word "mousse" is used to describe a variety of desserts, both chilled and frozen, made with any one of a number of combinations of egg yolks, egg whites, cream, gelatin, sugar, and flavorings. Their one consistent feature is a light, airy texture. Early in this century mousses in most cookbooks were all frozen. We give them here, together with an unfrozen, egg-white-lightened French chocolate mousse which appears with the custards and puddings.

Parfaits. A parfait is a whipped, frozen dessert, made with Italian meringue, a flavoring, and whipped cream. The flavoring may be vanilla, coffee, maple, a liqueur, or a purée of berries or fruit. Actually, anything served in a

parfait glass can be called a "parfait," and in this country we often find a
frozen ice cream parfait in tall glasses, made with several flavors of ice
cream, sauces, crushed fruit, and other embellishments.

Frozen Soufflés. A frozen soufflé is made of the same mixture of ingredients as a
parfait except that it is poured into a soufflé mold with a collar around it,
just like the previously mentioned chilled soufflé. It makes a handsome
presentation when it comes to the table "risen" above the rim of the mold,
particularly if you decorate the top with rosettes of whipped cream, fresh
fruit, and maybe even candied violets.

Ice Creams, Sherbets, and Ices

Although ice cream was much in favor among the European nobility of the
eighteenth century and was known in this country before President Madison's
time, it was Dolley Madison who first made it popular in the United States when
she served it to her guests at the White House. Today America produces and
consumes more ice cream than any other country in the world; half of it is
vanilla.

Making ice cream at home can be an event—an exciting one if everyone
participates. You can choose your own flavorings and fresh, wholesome ingredients
and the results will be so much better than anything you can buy. Although ice
cream will taste the same whether it's made in an electric ice cream maker or a
hand-cranked machine, the hand-cranked machine is certainly more fun to use.
Even the youngest member of the family can take a turn at cranking, and, of
course, in getting that first taste when the dripping dasher is passed around for
everyone to lick.

Ice cream is made with cream, sugar, and flavoring; ices with water, sugar, and
flavoring, and sherbet with milk or water, sugar, and flavoring. Gelatin is
sometimes used as a stabilizer in ice creams and sherbets.

Making Ice Creams, Sherbets, and Ices. The familiar old-fashioned two-quart ice
cream freezer that is hand-cranked and sits inside a wooden pail of ice and
rock salt has long been a fixture in many American households, and it is
still a splendid way to produce the very best ice cream, particularly if you
have those young hands available to help crack the ice and turn the crank.
In addition to the electric models in different sizes that work on the same
principle as the hand-cranked kind, there are electric ice cream makers
that go into the freezer and do the churning there so that you don't need
to pack them in ice and salt; their yield is usually only one quart and the
ice cream is apt to be a little more grainy, but, if that equipment appeals
to you and if you have sufficient freezer space, the end result is satisfactory
enough. Try anything that will encourage making your own good ice cream!
You may have to reduce the proportions in some of the recipes in this
chapter, if you have a model that yields only a small amount, but that is
a matter of simple arithmetic.

For the old-fashioned ice-packed method, you will need lots of ice—
about 20 pounds for the 2-quart model; get it already crushed, if you can.
Rock salt is usually recommended at the ratio of 1 part salt to 8 parts ice.
But at least one of the new machines we have tried calls for much less ice
and recommends that you use cubes straight from the refrigerator, as well
as ordinary table salt—and it works beautifully. So be sure to read the
manufacturer's instructions. The more salt you use, the faster the ice cream
will freeze, but it is *slow* freezing that gives ice cream its velvety texture.

Have the ice cream mixture cold (prepare it a day ahead, if you wish) before pouring it into the freezer can. Fill the container two-thirds to three-quarters full to allow for expansion during freezing. Place the container in the tub or pail. Fit the dasher in place with the crank secure on top.

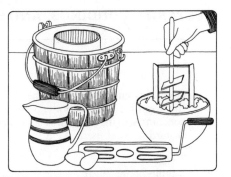

Fill the tub or pail one-third of the way up with crushed ice, then add the remaining ice and salt in layers until it is slightly above the level of the mixture in the can. Pack the ice down firmly and let it stand for 5 minutes. Or some manufacturers will recommend pouring a glass of ice water over the ice. If you are hand-cranking, slowly begin turning the crank, gradually increasing the speed and replenishing the ice and salt as it melts. When the ice cream is frozen the crank will turn with difficulty; an electric ice cream maker will shut off automatically.

Finished ice cream should be allowed to mellow or ripen for a few hours, if possible, either in the ice cream maker or in the refrigerator freezer. Drain off the water, wipe the lid of the can, remove it, and lift out the dasher. Pack the ice cream down with a spoon, cover the container with a double layer of foil, plug the hole, and replace the lid. Repack the tub or pail with ice and salt, cover with newspapers, and let stand for a few hours. Or simply store the ice cream in a home freezer, if convenient.

Freezing in Refrigerator Trays. Some ice cream, sherbets, and ices can be made and frozen in ice cube trays in the home freezer. A standard ice cube tray will hold one pint of ice cream. You can also freeze ice cream in metal bowls or other metal containers.

If you plan to freeze ice cream in a refrigerator tray, it is better to use only recipes that have been specially adapted to this method, but if you want to modify recipes for refrigerator freezing, keep the proportion of sugar low—not more than one to four—or substitute corn syrup for one-third of the sugar. Beaten egg whites help lighten the mixture.

Dessert Sauces

Dessert sauces, known as "pudding sauces" at the turn of the century, do good things to simple puddings, cooked fruits, and ice creams. It's like a prince marrying a peasant—the peasant becomes royal.

Use a heavy-bottomed pan to cook sauces: it will hold and diffuse the heat evenly and help prevent the scorching and burning that sugar is so inclined to do.

CUSTARDS, PUDDINGS, AND SWEET OMELETS

Soft Custard or Boiled Custard

Cook this custard over low heat in a heavy-bottomed saucepan or in the top of a double boiler over hot water. Either method requires constant stirring. As thick as whipped cream but heavier, this plain custard is good used like a sauce with fruits and other desserts.

(2½ CUPS)

3 eggs
6 tablespoons sugar
⅛ teaspoon salt

2 cups (½ L) scalded milk
1 teaspoon vanilla

Put the eggs in a heavy-bottomed pan and whisk just enough to blend. Add the sugar and salt and slowly pour in the hot milk, stirring constantly. Cook over medium heat until the custard coats the spoon, in 7–10 minutes. As soon as you see small bubbles forming around the edge of the pan, remove from the heat quickly; if it boils, the eggs will curdle. Stir in the vanilla, and strain into a bowl or pitcher. Cover and chill. The custard will thicken as it cools.

Floating Island

An ingenious mind conceived this simple, wonderful dessert. All the pieces fit together perfectly, like a puzzle.

(SERVES SIX)

2¼ cups (5½ dL) milk
3 egg whites
1 cup (200 g) sugar

5 egg yolks
2 teaspoons vanilla

Put the milk in a skillet and bring to a simmer over moderately low heat. While the milk is heating, beat the egg whites in a large bowl, slowly adding ⅓ cup of the sugar and beating until shiny and stiff. Using two soupspoons, shape the "islands" by scooping the meringue onto one spoon and placing the other spoon gently on top to shape. Slide the meringues into the barely simmering milk, only three or four at a time. Poach them 1 or 2 minutes on each side, just until they

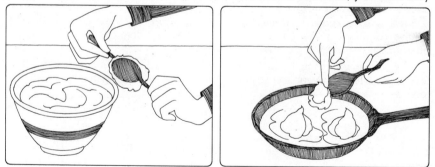

feel firm to the touch, then remove them to paper towels to drain. Continue to poach the remaining "islands" until all the meringue is used. You will have about 12 meringues, measuring 1½ × 2½ inches. Put the egg yolks in a bowl and beat them until they are thick and pale, slowly adding the remaining ⅔ cup of sugar.

Gradually add the simmering milk in which the meringues were poached, stirring well. Transfer to a heavy-bottomed pan and cook over low heat, stirring constantly, until the mixture thickens; do *not* boil. Pour into a bowl, stir in the vanilla, and let cool. Put the custard in a shallow bowl and arrange the "islands" on top. Chill well before serving.

Baked Custard

This kindly old dessert still nourishes and comforts. Traditionally served in familiar brown custard cups, it can also be made in one large baking dish.

(SERVES EIGHT)

2 egg yolks	3 cups (¾ L) very hot milk
3 eggs	1½ teaspoons vanilla
½ cup (100 g) sugar	Nutmeg
⅛ teaspoon salt	

Preheat the oven to 325°F (165°C). Butter a 1-quart baking dish or 8 ramekins. Set a shallow pan large enough to hold the baking dish or ramekins in the oven, and fill it with 1 inch of hot water. Beat the yolks and eggs together just enough to blend. Stir in the sugar and salt and slowly add the hot milk, stirring constantly. Add the vanilla. Strain into the baking dish or dishes and sprinkle with some nutmeg. Put in the pan and bake for about 45 minutes; the custard is set when a knife inserted in the center comes out clean.

Coconut Custard. Add ½ cup *flaked coconut* to the custard mixture before putting it into the baking dishes.

Chocolate Custard. Melt *1½ ounces unsweetened chocolate* in the milk while it is being heated to make the custard.

Caramel Custard. Melt *½ cup sugar* in a heavy-bottomed skillet and cook without stirring, swirling the pan so that the sugar moves about as it melts. When the sugar becomes caramel-colored, pour about 1 tablespoon of the caramelized sugar into each custard cup and swirl around to coat the bottom and sides. (Or if you are using a large baking dish, pour all the caramelized sugar into it and swirl quickly to coat the bottom and sides.) The caramel will harden at first, but don't worry, the next step takes care of that. Pour the custard on top of the caramel-lined cups (or dish) and bake as above.

Coffee Custard. Add *2 tablespoons instant coffee* to the milk before it is heated to make the custard.

Crème Brûlée

Crème brûlée, or "burnt cream," is a simple and sublime custard dessert. Its brown-sugar topping is melted under the broiler, forming a very thin candied sheet.

(SERVES SIX TO EIGHT)

2 egg yolks, slightly beaten	2 cups (½ L) very hot heavy cream
2 eggs, slightly beaten	
⅓ cup (65 g) granulated sugar	1½ cups (3½ dL) dark-brown sugar, sifted or sieved
⅛ teaspoon salt	

Crème Brulée (continued)

Mix the egg yolks, eggs, granulated sugar, and salt together in the top of a double boiler. Add the hot cream slowly, beating constantly; cook, stirring constantly, until slightly thickened. Pour into a 10 × 6–inch baking dish about 2 inches deep. Cover and refrigerate. Just before serving, preheat the broiler. Sprinkle the brown sugar *evenly* all over the top of the cream, no more than ¼ inch thick. Run the dish under the broiler and, watching carefully, heat just until the brown sugar melts and turns shiny. Remove and serve immediately.

Blancmange

Blancmange, a cornstarch pudding, once seemed so romantic: it is the dessert that Jo of *Little Women* often carried to Laurie, her frail neighbor, to help restore his health. When you want a basic vanilla or chocolate pudding, this is the recipe to use.

(SERVES FIVE)

3 tablespoons cornstarch	2 cups (½ L) milk
4 tablespoons sugar	1 teaspoon vanilla
⅛ teaspoon salt	

Mix the cornstarch, sugar, and salt with ¼ cup of the milk. Heat the remaining milk, then slowly add it to the cornstarch mixture, stirring constantly. Cook until thickened, stirring constantly, in a heavy-bottomed pan over moderately low heat or in a double boiler over simmering water. Continue to cook for about 15 minutes so that the raw taste of the cornstarch disappears. Let cool, then add the vanilla. Cover and chill.

Chocolate Blancmange. When you heat the milk, add *2 ounces unsweetened chocolate* and stir until smooth.

French Chocolate Mousse

Lighter than many mousses, this has no cream. Serve small portions and you will leave the table feeling almost guiltless.

(SERVES SIX TO EIGHT)

6-ounce (180-g) package semi-sweet chocolate bits	1 teaspoon vanilla, or 1 tablespoon rum
4 eggs, separated	

Melt the chocolate bits in a heavy-bottomed pan over very low heat, stirring often to prevent burning; set aside. Beat the egg yolks until pale and lemon-colored. Slowly stir in the chocolate and blend well. Beat the egg whites until stiff but not dry. Add a third of the whites to the yolks and chocolate, add the vanilla or rum, mix well, then carefully fold in the remaining whites. Spoon into individual serving dishes or a serving bowl. Cover and chill at least 8 hours before serving.

Rice Cream

Snowy white, creamy, and faintly sweet, good with a little maple syrup on top.

1 envelope gelatin
3 cups (¾ L) milk
3 tablespoons rice
1½ tablespoons sugar

⅛ teaspoon salt
1 cup (¼ L) heavy cream
1 teaspoon vanilla

Soak the gelatin in 3 tablespoons cold water. Put 2 cups of the milk in a heavy-bottomed saucepan, add the rice, and cook, stirring often to prevent scorching, until the rice is tender, about 20 minutes. Add the gelatin and stir to dissolve, then add the remaining cup of milk, sugar, and salt. Let cool. Whip the cream until soft peaks form, add the vanilla, and fold into the rice mixture. Cover and chill.

Baked Rice Pudding

This bears no resemblance to the standard cafeteria version. Long, slow baking gives the rice a golden color and a thick creamy texture. Some purists don't even like the addition of nutmeg, but it does give the pudding a lovely flavor. Serve warm or cold, with heavy cream.

(SERVES SIX TO EIGHT)

4 cups (1 L) milk
½ teaspoon salt
⅔ cup (125 g) sugar

½ teaspoon nutmeg (optional)
3 tablespoons rice

Preheat the oven to 300°F (150°C). Put all the ingredients in a buttered baking dish and stir to blend. Bake for 3½ hours, stirring three times during the first hour of baking so the rice doesn't settle.

Raisin Rice Pudding. Add ½ cup raisins to the ingredients.

Chocolate Rice Pudding. Add 2 ounces melted unsweetened chocolate to the ingredients.

Tapioca Cream

Don't be deterred by the children who used to call pearl tapioca "fish eyes." It is time that this almost-forgotten dessert be revived—it tastes wonderful.

(SERVES FOUR TO SIX)

3 tablespoons quick-cooking
    tapioca
⅛ teaspoon salt
5 tablespoons sugar

2 cups (½ L) milk
2 eggs, separated
1 teaspoon vanilla

Mix the tapioca, salt, 3 tablespoons of the sugar, milk, and slightly beaten egg yolks in a heavy-bottomed pot. Let stand for 5 minutes. Cook over medium heat, stirring constantly, for about 6 minutes until the mixture comes to a full boil; remove from the heat. Beat the egg whites until foamy, then slowly add the remaining 2 tablespoons of sugar and continue beating until stiff but not dry. Slowly stir the whites into the hot tapioca mixture, then add the vanilla and blend. Serve warm or cold.

Butterscotch Tapioca

(SERVES FOUR TO SIX)

3 tablespoons quick-cooking
  tapioca
⅛ teaspoon salt
2 cups (½ L) milk

1 tablespoon butter
½ cup (1 dL) dark-brown sugar
¼ cup (½ dL) finely chopped
  pecans

Mix the tapioca, salt, and milk in a heavy-bottomed pan and let stand for 5 minutes. Cook over moderate heat, stirring constantly, for about 6 minutes, until the mixture comes to a full boil; remove from the heat. Melt the butter in a small skillet and stir in the brown sugar. Cook over moderate heat, stirring, until the sugar melts and bubbles for 1 minute. Stir into the tapioca mixture and add the pecans. Serve warm or cold.

Chocolate Bread Pudding

Soft as a pillow with a full, light, chocolate-pudding taste.

(SERVES EIGHT)

2 ounces (60 g) unsweetened
  chocolate
1 quart (1 L) scalded milk
2 cups (½ L) homemade bread
  crumbs

⅓ cup (65 g) sugar
¼ cup (60 g) butter, melted
2 eggs, slightly beaten
¼ teaspoon salt
1 teaspoon vanilla

Preheat the oven to 325°F (165°C). Butter a 1½- or 2-quart baking dish. Break the chocolate into bits and melt in the milk, stirring until smooth. Add the bread crumbs and set aside to cool. When lukewarm, add remaining ingredients. Mix well, pour into the buttered dish, and bake for about 50 minutes or until set. Serve with *whipped cream.*

Lemon Pudding

An old favorite, a delicious dessert with its soft lemony custard on the bottom and sponge cake texture on top. Don't let it get too brown.

(SERVES SIX)

2 tablespoons butter
⅞ cup (170 g) sugar
3 eggs
1 cup (¼ L) milk

1½ tablespoons flour
⅓ cup (¾ dL) lemon juice
Grated rind of 1 lemon

Preheat oven to 350°F (180°C). Beat the butter until soft, then gradually add the sugar, beating until it is all incorporated. Separate the eggs and beat in the egg yolks one by one. Add the milk, flour, lemon juice, and rind, and beat to mix well, although the mixture will have a curdled look. Beat the egg whites until they form soft peaks, then fold into the batter. Turn into a 1½-quart baking dish and set it in a pan of hot water that comes halfway up the sides of the dish. Bake for 50–60 minutes. Let cool and serve either tepid or chilled, with a pitcher of *heavy cream*.

Indian Pudding

Spicy, coarse, and dark brown, an old-fashioned dessert that celebrates the Indians' gift of corn.

(SERVES EIGHT TO TEN)

4 cups (1 L) milk
½ cup (1 dL) yellow cornmeal
⅓ cup (¾ dL) dark-brown
  sugar
⅓ cup (65 g) granulated sugar

⅓ cup (¾ dL) molasses
1 teaspoon salt
4 tablespoons butter
½ teaspoon powdered ginger
½ teaspoon cinnamon

Preheat the oven to 275°F (135°C). Heat 2 cups of the milk until very hot and pour it slowly over the cornmeal, stirring constantly. Cook in a double boiler over simmering water for 10–15 minutes, until the cornmeal mixture is creamy. Add the remaining ingredients and mix well. Spoon into a buttered 1½-quart baking dish, pour the remaining 2 cups of milk on top, set into a pan of hot water, and bake for 2½–3 hours or until set. The pudding will become firmer as it cools. Serve with *heavy cream* or *vanilla ice cream*.

Bread-and-Butter Pudding

A delectable old-fashioned dessert that emerges puffy from the oven, then falls slowly; golden and slightly crusty on top, it's soft and spoonable inside. Some purists don't even care to flavor this pudding with vanilla and cinnamon, preferring just the good buttery flavor. The important thing is to use a good textured white bread, preferably homemade, which can be a few days old; an equivalent amount of Italian or French bread will do, too, and it's a good way to use up pieces that turn stale so quickly.

(SERVES SIX)

Soft butter
7 slices good quality white
  bread
1 quart (1 L) milk
3 eggs, slightly beaten
½ cup (100 g) sugar

¼ teaspoon salt
½ cup (1 dL) raisins
1 teaspoon vanilla (optional)
½ teaspoon cinnamon
  (optional)

Preheat the oven to 325°F (165°C). Butter a 2-quart baking dish. Spread a generous amount of butter on one side of each slice of bread and line the bottom and sides of the baking dish. Mix together the milk, eggs, sugar, salt, raisins, and vanilla and cinnamon, if you are using them, and pour over the bread. Place any extra pieces of bread on top and press down so they are submerged. Let stand about 10 minutes, a little longer if the bread is particularly dry. Bake covered for 30 minutes, then uncover and bake for 30 minutes more. If you like a crustier brown top, slip the dish under a hot broiler a few minutes until deep golden. Serve warm with a pitcher of *heavy cream*.

Sweet Omelet

A sweet omelet is a satisfying way to end a meal.

(SERVES ONE)

2 eggs	½ teaspoon vanilla
⅛ teaspoon salt	1 tablespoon butter
1½ tablespoons granulated sugar	2 tablespoons confectioners' sugar

Combine the eggs, salt, granulated sugar, and vanilla and beat only long enough to blend. Put a 7-inch nonstick skillet over the heat. When the pan is hot, add the butter and as soon as it foams, tilt the pan so the butter coats the bottom. Pour in the eggs. Shake the pan forward and backward, pulling the eggs with a fork and letting the uncooked part run out to the edges, until the whole is creamy (see illustration p. 341). Fold it in half and roll it out onto a warm plate. Sprinkle with confectioners' sugar.

Sweet Omelet with Rum. Add *2 tablespoons rum* to the eggs when mixing.

Sweet Omelet with Jam. Spread *¼ cup jam or preserves* across the omelet before folding it.

Sweet Omelet with Berries and Cream. Garnish the finished omelet with *2 tablespoons sour cream* and *¼ cup sweetened strawberries,* or *other berries.*

Dessert Crêpes or French Pancakes

(SIXTEEN 5-INCH PANCAKES)

Follow the recipe for Crêpes (p. 497), adding *2 tablespoons sugar* to the batter.

Jelly Crêpes. Spread warm crêpes with *jelly, jam,* or *fruit preserves (apricot* is particularly good). Roll them and dust them with *confectioners' sugar.*

Whipped-Cream Crêpes. Whip *1 cup heavy cream,* sweetening it with *2 tablespoons confectioners' sugar.* Fold in *1 cup chopped toasted almonds.* Spread on the pancakes and roll them up. Dust with confectioners' sugar and a sprinkling of additional *chopped almonds.*

Crêpes Suzette. Cream *1 cup butter* and add *1 cup confectioners' sugar,* mixing together until light. Add the *grated rind of 3 oranges,* the *juice of 1½ oranges,* and *5 tablespoons Grand Marnier* or *other brandy.* Melt over low heat in a skillet or chafing dish until hot. Fold the pancakes in quarters and add a few at a time to the pan. Heat very slowly, spooning the sauce over them until well saturated. Remove to a heatproof platter and keep warm until all are ready to serve. Pour the sauce in the pan over them and serve. If you wish to flambé, warm ¼ cup brandy, ignite, and pour flaming over the crêpes.

Strawberry (or Other Fresh Berry) Crêpes. Fill each crêpe with about *2 tablespoons crushed strawberries* (or other berries) that have been tossed first with a little sugar and left to stand a short while. Frozen berries, drained of some of the juice, are also good. Roll the crêpe up, top with *confectioners' sugar* and a dollop of *sour cream* or *whipped cream.*

Coeur à la Crème

A dense, faintly sweet dessert cheese, traditionally made in a heart-shaped mold. When it is served, a little cream is poured over the cheese, and strawberries or raspberries are spooned around it.

(SERVES FOUR)

1 cup (¼ L) cream cheese; or 1 cup (¼ L) cottage cheese that has been rubbed through a sieve or puréed in a food processor

1½ cups (3½ dL) heavy cream
2 tablespoons sugar
2 egg whites, stiffly beaten
2 cups (½ L) berries

Blend the cheese with 1 cup of the heavy cream until smooth. Fold in the sugar and egg whites. Line a heart-shaped basket or mold with holes in it, using several layers of cheesecloth. Spoon the mixture into the mold, place it in a shallow bowl, and allow to drain overnight in the refrigerator. Unmold, pour on the remaining ½ cup cream, and garnish with the fruit.

STEAMED PUDDINGS

Steamed Chocolate Pudding

Dark, moist, and chocolate, not quite as sweet as chocolate cake, just right served with Foamy Sauce.

(SERVES EIGHT)

3 ounces (85 g) unsweetened chocolate
6 tablespoons butter
1 cup (200 g) sugar
2 eggs

⅔ cup (1½ dL) milk
2 teaspoons vanilla
2 cups (280 g) flour
3 teaspoons baking powder
½ teaspoon salt

Butter a 2-quart mold; if it doesn't have a tight lid, see p. 604. Heat water in a pot large enough to hold the mold. Melt the chocolate and butter in a small, heavy-bottomed pan. Remove from the heat and pour into a mixing bowl. Stir in the sugar and eggs, beat until smooth, then add the milk and vanilla. Stir in the flour, baking powder, and salt, and beat until smooth and creamy. Spoon into the mold and cover. Put in the large pot and steam (see p. 604) for 1½ hours. Remove and let cool for 10 minutes before unmolding. Serve warm with *Foamy Sauce* (p. 640).

Ohio Pudding

Mixing this steamed carrot pudding takes a little patience—the moisture from the carrots and potatoes makes blending a slow process, unless you have an electric mixer.

Ohio Pudding (continued)

1 cup (200 g) sugar
1 cup (140 g) flour
2 teaspoons baking powder
1 teaspoon salt
1 teaspoon baking soda
1 cup (¼ L) currants

1 cup (¼ L) raisins
1 cup (¼ L) finely grated raw
  potato
1 cup (¼ L) finely grated raw
  carrot

Butter a 2-quart mold; if it doesn't have a tight lid, see p. 604. Heat water in a pot large enough to hold the mold. Mix the sugar, flour, baking powder, salt, and baking soda together in a large bowl. Add the currants, raisins, potato, and carrot and mix very thoroughly with your hands. Spoon into the mold and cover. Put in the large pot and steam (see p. 604) for about 3 hours. Remove and cool for 10 minutes before unmolding. Serve warm.

Steamed Fig Pudding

3 tablespoons butter, melted
¾ cup (1¾ dL) dark-brown
  sugar
½ cup (1 dL) milk
2 cups (280 g) flour
½ teaspoon baking soda

½ teaspoon salt
¼ teaspoon allspice
1 cup (¼ L) dried figs,
  chopped fine
1 tart apple, peeled, cored, and
  chopped fine

Butter a 2-quart mold; if it doesn't have a tight lid, see p. 604. Heat water in a pot large enough to hold the mold. Put the melted butter in a large bowl and stir in the sugar and milk. Add the flour, baking soda, salt, and allspice and beat until smooth. Stir in the figs and apple. Spoon into the mold and cover. Put in the large pot and steam (see p. 604) for 2½ hours. Remove and cool for 10 minutes before unmolding. Serve warm with *Foamy Sauce* (p. 640).

Sterling Pudding

½ cup (1 dL) finely chopped
  beef suet
2⅔ cups (5¾ dL) dry bread
  crumbs
1 cup (¼ L) grated carrots
4 eggs, separated
1⅓ cups (3¼ dL) dark-brown
  sugar
Grated rind of 1 lemon

1 tablespoon vinegar
2 tablespoons flour
1 teaspoon salt
1 teaspoon cinnamon
½ teaspoon nutmeg
¼ teaspoon ground cloves
1 cup (¼ L) raisins
¾ cup (1¾ dL) currants

Butter a 2-quart mold; if it doesn't have a tight lid, see p. 604. Heat water in a pot large enough to hold the mold. Using an electric mixer or a spoon, beat the suet in a bowl until it is creamy. Add the bread crumbs and carrots and mix well. Beat the egg yolks in a separate bowl until light, add the brown sugar, continue to beat until smooth, and add to the suet mixture. Stir in the lemon rind and vinegar. Add the flour, salt, cinnamon, nutmeg, cloves, raisins, and currants and stir briskly until well blended. Beat the egg whites until they are stiff but not dry. Stir a third of the whites into the pudding mixture, then fold the remaining whites in gently, until no white shows. Spoon pudding batter into the mold and cover. Put in the large pot and steam (see p. 604) for 3½ hours. Remove and cool for 10 minutes before unmolding. Serve warm with *Hard Sauce* (p. 641).

Thanksgiving Pudding

(SERVES EIGHT)

2½ cups (6 dL) homemade dry bread crumbs
¾ cup (1¾ dL) milk
4 eggs, well beaten
1 cup (¼ L) dark-brown sugar
¾ teaspoon salt
2 teaspoons baking powder
½ teaspoon cinnamon
¼ teaspoon nutmeg

⅓ cup (¾ dL) ground suet
1 cup (¼ L) finely chopped dried figs
½ cup (1 dL) coarsely chopped walnuts
½ cup (1 dL) raisins
¾ cup (1¾ dL) currants
2 tablespoons flour

Butter a 2-quart mold, if it doesn't have a tight lid, see p. 604. Heat water in a pot large enough to hold the mold. Soak the bread crumbs in the milk, then add the eggs, sugar, salt, baking powder, cinnamon, and nutmeg and combine thoroughly. Work the suet in another bowl until it is creamy, then add the figs. Combine with the bread and milk mixture. Dredge the walnuts, raisins, and currants with the flour. Add to the mixture and beat very well to blend thoroughly. Spoon into the mold and cover. Put in the large pot and steam (see p. 604) for 3 hours. Remove and let cool for 10 minutes before unmolding. Serve warm with *Brandy Hard Sauce* (p. 641).

English Plum Pudding

English plum pudding makes a lovely Christmas gift. Wrapped well in a brandy-dampened towel, it will keep in the refrigerator for several months. Reheat in the top of a double boiler before serving.

(SERVES SIX)

10 slices white bread
1 cup (¼ L) scalded milk
½ cup (100 g) sugar
4 eggs, separated
1⅓ cups (3¼ dL) raisins, lightly floured
½ cup (1 dL) finely chopped dried figs
3 tablespoons finely chopped citron

¾ cup (1¾ dL) finely chopped suet
3 tablespoons brandy
1 teaspoon nutmeg
½ teaspoon cinnamon
¼ teaspoon ground cloves
¼ teaspoon mace
1 teaspoon salt

Butter a 2-quart mold, if it doesn't have a tight lid, see p. 604. Heat water in a pot large enough to hold the mold. Crumb the bread, and soak it in the hot milk. Cool and add the sugar, the well-beaten egg yolks, raisins, figs, and citron. Break the suet up with a fork and mash until it is creamy or use a food processor. Add to the crumb mixture, then stir in the brandy, nutmeg, cinnamon, cloves, mace, and salt. Beat until well blended. Beat the egg whites until they are stiff but not dry. Stir a third of the whites into the pudding mixture, then gently fold in the remaining whites. Spoon the mixture into the mold and cover. Put in the large pot and steam (see p. 604) for 6 hours. Remove and let cool for 10 minutes before unmolding. Serve warm with *Hard Sauce* (p. 641).

Steamed Cranberry Pudding

(SERVES EIGHT)

⅓ cup (80 g) butter, softened
1 cup (200 g) sugar
2 eggs, well beaten
2⅓ cups (330 g) flour
¼ teaspoon salt

2½ teaspoons baking powder
⅓ cup (¾ dL) milk
1½ cups (3½ dL) cranberries
½ cup (1 dL) chopped walnuts
1 tablespoon grated orange rind

Butter a 2-quart mold, if it doesn't have a tight lid, see p. 604. Heat water in a pot large enough to hold the mold. Cream the butter in a bowl and slowly add the sugar. Stir in the eggs. Mix the flour, salt, and baking powder together and add with the milk to the butter mixture, beating until well blended. Add the cranberries, walnuts, and grated orange rind and mix well. Pour into the buttered mold and cover. Put in the large pot and steam (see p. 604) for 2½ hours. Remove and let cool for 10 minutes before unmolding. Serve warm with *sweetened whipped cream.*

DESSERT SOUFFLÉS

Basic Dessert Soufflé

Serve a soufflé the moment it leaves the oven. A dessert soufflé must be delicate, so it cannot stand without falling.

(SERVES SIX TO EIGHT)

4 egg yolks
½ cup (100 g) sugar
3 tablespoons butter
3 tablespoons flour

⅛ teaspoon salt
1 cup (¼ L) milk
5 egg whites
2 teaspoons vanilla

Preheat the oven to 375°F (190°C). Butter a 2-quart soufflé dish or baking dish and sprinkle it with sugar. Beat the yolks and slowly add ¼ cup of the sugar, beating until thick and blended; set aside. Melt the butter in a skillet and stir in the flour and salt. Cook for several minutes over low heat, stirring, then slowly stir in the milk. Cook over medium heat, stirring, until the sauce reaches the boiling point and becomes smooth and thick. Remove from the heat, pour a little of the hot sauce into the yolk-sugar mixture, and stir well. Add the remaining yolk mixture to the sauce, stirring constantly, then return to the heat and cook for another minute; remove and let cool. Put the 5 egg whites in a large bowl and beat until foamy. Slowly add the remaining ¼ cup of sugar and beat until the whites are stiff but not dry. Whisk a fourth of the whites into the sauce to lighten it, then fold in the remaining whites. Stir in the vanilla. Pour into the soufflé dish. Bake for 35 minutes if a slightly runny center is desired and 45–50 minutes for a dry soufflé.

Coffee Soufflé. Add 2 *tablespoons instant coffee* to the milk and heat until the coffee is dissolved.

Soufflé Grand Marnier. Use *2 tablespoons Grand Marnier* instead of the vanilla. Sprinkle *ladyfingers or dry sponge-cake slices* with *Grand Marnier* until dampened and line the soufflé dish with them before adding the soufflé mixture.

Chocolate Soufflé

This is a first-rate chocolate soufflé, light and yet very chocolaty. Most chocolate soufflés are so dense with flavor that their essential lightness is lost.

(SERVES SIX)

1½ ounces (45 g) unsweetened chocolate	⅛ teaspoon salt
5 tablespoons sugar	¾ cup (1¾ dL) milk
2 tablespoons butter	3 eggs, separated
2 tablespoons flour	1 teaspoon vanilla

Preheat the oven to 325°F (165°C). Butter a 1½-quart soufflé dish and sprinkle it with sugar. Put the chocolate, 2 tablespoons of the sugar, and 2 tablespoons hot water in a small pan and heat slowly, stirring occasionally, until the chocolate is melted and smooth; remove from the heat andset aside. Melt the butter in a skillet, then add the flour and salt. Cook over low heat, stirring, for several minutes, then gradually stir in the milk. Cook to the boiling point, stirring; the sauce will become smooth and thick. Blend in the chocolate mixture. Beat the egg yolks well. Stir a little of the hot sauce into the yolks, then add the yolks to the remaining sauce. Stir well, then set aside to cool. Beat the egg whites until foamy, slowly add the remaining 3 tablespoons of sugar, and continue beating until stiff but not dry. Stir a fourth of the whites into the chocolate mixture, then fold in the remaining whites. Stir in the vanilla. Spoon into the soufflé dish and bake for 35–40 minutes. Serve with *whipped cream.*

Fruit Soufflé

This fruit soufflé, made without a cream-sauce base, is as light as a cloud, a delicate reminder of summer during the long, cold winter months. Use canned applesauce, apricots, sour cherries, or pineapple or fresh berries, apricots, pears, or peaches. None of these fruits need cooking, but they should be well drained. The hot fruit purée will set and stabilize the egg whites.

(SERVES FOUR TO FIVE)

¾ cup (1¾ dL) fresh or canned fruit purée	Pinch of salt
1 tablespoon freshly squeezed lemon juice	Sugar to taste
	3 egg whites

Preheat the oven to 375°F (190°C). Butter a 1-quart soufflé dish and sprinkle it with sugar. Heat the fruit purée in a small pan. Add the lemon juice, salt, and sugar, and stir to blend; remove from the heat. Beat the egg whites until stiff but not dry and stir them into the hot purée until evenly blended. Spoon into the soufflé dish and bake for 20–25 minutes.

Lemon Soufflé

(SERVES FOUR)

4 eggs, separated   2 tablespoons lemon juice
⅔ cup (130 g) sugar   Grated rind of 1 lemon

Preheat the oven to 325°F (165°C). Butter a 1½-quart soufflé dish and sprinkle it with sugar. Beat the yolks, slowly adding ⅓ cup of the sugar and continuing to beat until thick and lemon-colored. In a large bowl beat the egg whites until they are foamy, then slowly add the remaining ⅓ cup of sugar and beat until stiff but not dry. Gently stir in the lemon juice and grated rind. Stir a fourth of the whites into the yolk mixture, then fold in the remaining whites. Spoon into the soufflé dish and bake for 35–40 minutes.

Marmalade Soufflé

This dish graced many tables during the servantless days of the late 1930s and 40s and was considered a "ritzy" addition to any dinner. A splendid solution for the cook who is also the host, it will hold for much longer than the hour of cooking time and will not collapse if a draft nips it.

(SERVES FOUR TO SIX)

3 egg whites   3 tablespoons orange marmalade
3 tablespoons sugar   Grated rind of 1 orange

Start some water simmering in the bottom of a double boiler; butter the top part of the double boiler. Beat the egg whites in a large bowl until foamy, then slowly add the sugar and continue beating until the whites are stiff but not dry. Gently fold in the marmalade and orange rind. Spoon into the buttered pot. Cover and cook over barely simmering water for 1 hour. Serve with *whipped cream* flavored with a touch of sherry.

GELATIN DESSERTS (JELLIES AND CREAMS)

Lemon Jelly

Fruit jellies, made with unflavored gelatin and fresh fruit juices, have true, unadulterated flavor. They bear no resemblance to commercially packaged, flavored gelatin mixes.

(SERVES EIGHT)

2 envelopes gelatin   1 cup (¼ L) freshly squeezed
1 cup (200 g) sugar   lemon juice

Sprinkle the gelatin over ½ cup cold water and let it soften for 5 minutes. Bring 2 cups water to a boil, add the sugar, lemon juice, and gelatin, and cook over low heat, stirring constantly, for about 3 minutes, until the gelatin dissolves and the liquid is clear. Remove from the heat and pour into individual glasses or a bowl. Chill until firm. Serve with *Old-fashioned Gingersnaps* (p. 559).

Apricot and Wine Jelly

(SERVES EIGHT)

2 envelopes gelatin
1 cup (200 g) sugar
1 cup (¼ L) apricot juice

1 tablespoon freshly squeezed
  lemon juice
1 cup (¼ L) sherry

Mix the gelatin and sugar in a small pan. Add 1½ cups water, stir, and let stand for 5 minutes to soften. Cook over low heat, stirring constantly, until the gelatin dissolves and the liquid is clear. Remove from the heat and add the apricot juice, lemon juice, and sherry. Pour into individual dishes or a bowl and chill until firm.

Orange Jelly

(SERVES SIX)

2 envelopes gelatin
1½ cups (3½ dL) freshly
  squeezed orange juice

¾ cup (150 g) sugar
Juice of 1 lemon

Sprinkle the gelatin over ½ cup cold water and let it soften, then pour on 1¾ cups boiling water. Mix well to dissolve. Add the orange juice, sugar, and lemon juice. Pour into a 1-quart mold and chill until firm. Serve with *lightly whipped cream*.

Orange Jelly with Grapes. Spread *1½ cups peeled seedless grapes* around the mold before adding the liquid and chilling.

Coffee Jelly

(SERVES SIX)

1 envelope gelatin
6 tablespoons sugar
2 cups (½ L) *very* strong coffee

Mix the gelatin, sugar, and ½ cup cold water together in a small pan and let soften for 5 minutes. Add the coffee and cook over low heat, stirring constantly, until the gelatin dissolves and the liquid is clear. Pour into individual dishes or a bowl and chill until firm. Serve with *heavy cream*.

Wine Jelly

(SERVES SIX TO EIGHT)

2 envelopes gelatin
1 cup (200 g) sugar
⅓ cup (¾ dL) freshly squeezed
  orange juice

3 tablespoons freshly squeezed
  lemon juice
1 cup (¼ L) sherry or Madeira
  wine

Mix the gelatin and sugar together in a small bowl, stir in ½ cup cold water and let soften for 5 minutes. Pour 1½ cups boiling water over and mix well to dissolve. Add the orange juice, lemon juice, and wine. Pour into individual dishes or a bowl and chill until firm.

Snow Pudding

(SERVES SIX)

1 envelope gelatin
1 cup (200 g) sugar

¼ cup (½ dL) lemon juice
3 egg whites

Sprinkle the gelatin over ¼ cup cold water and let it stand for 5 minutes. Pour in 1 cup boiling water and stir to dissolve, then add the sugar and lemon juice and heat gently until everything has dissolved; remove and let cool. When the gelatin mixture is thick and syrupy, whip until frothy. Beat the egg whites until stiff but not dry and fold them into the gelatin mixture. Pile by spoonfuls into a dish and chill. Serve around some *Soft Custard* (p. 608). You will have about 4 cups.

Coffee Sponge

Make the coffee very strong or the flavor will be lost when the sponge is chilled.

(SERVES SIX)

1 envelope gelatin
⅔ cup (130 g) sugar

2 cups (½ L) strong hot coffee
2 egg whites

Sprinkle the gelatin over ¼ cup cold water and let it soften for 5 minutes. Put the sugar and coffee in a small pan with the gelatin and heat, stirring, until the gelatin dissolves. Remove from the heat and chill until the mixture is as thick as unbeaten egg white. Add the egg whites and beat until the mixture is thick enough to hold its shape. Spoon into a dish or individual dessert dishes and chill. Serve with *whipped cream*. You will have about 4 cups.

Bavarian Cream

Bavarian cream is basically English custard made with beaten egg whites, gelatin, and freshly whipped cream. It should be chilled until firm.

(SERVES SIX)

1 envelope gelatin
2 eggs, separated
1¼ cups (3 dL) milk
½ cup (100 g) sugar

Pinch of salt
1½ teaspoons vanilla
1 cup (¼ L) heavy cream

Sprinkle the gelatin over ¼ cup cold water and let it soften for 5 minutes. Beat the egg yolks slightly. Heat the milk in a heavy-bottomed pan until very hot, then stir a little into the beaten yolks. Return the yolks to the remaining milk in the pan and add the sugar, salt, and gelatin. Stir constantly over medium heat until slightly thickened; do not overcook or boil or the egg yolks will curdle. Remove from the heat and refrigerate for about 15 minutes or until cool. Add the vanilla. Beat the egg whites until they are stiff but not dry and fold them into the custard. Beat thecream until it barely holds soft peaks and fold it into the custard. Spoon into a 2-quart mold, cover, and chill until firm. Unmold before serving.

Spanish Cream

1 envelope gelatin
3 cups (¾ L) milk
½ cup (100 g) sugar

3 eggs, separated
¼ teaspoon salt
4 tablespoons sherry

Sprinkle the gelatin over ½ cup cold water and let it soften for 5 minutes. Heat the milk, sugar, and gelatin in a heavy-bottomed pan until the milk is barely scalded, stirring often; do not boil. Beat the egg yolks slightly and pour some of the hot milk mixture over them, stirring constantly. Pour back into the pan and cook over medium heat, stirring, until the custard begins to thicken; be careful not to overcook or boil or the yolks will curdle. Remove from the heat and add the salt and sherry. Beat the egg whites until stiff but not dry and fold them in. Spoon into a 2-quart mold or individual dessert dishes and chill until firm. You will have about 6½ cups.

Macaroon Cream

Crunchy, creamy, and very good.

1 envelope gelatin
2 cups (½ L) milk
3 eggs, separated
⅓ cup (65 g) sugar

⅛ teaspoon salt
1 cup (¼ L) coarsely crushed
  macaroons
2 teaspoons vanilla

Sprinkle the gelatin over ¼ cup cold water and let it soften for 5 minutes. Heat the milk to almost boiling and stir a little into the slightly beaten egg yolks. Stir the remainder of the yolks and the sugar into the milk, add the gelatin and salt, and cook over medium heat, stirring constantly, just until the custard begins to thicken; do not overcook or boil or the yolks will curdle. Remove from the heat and add the macaroons and vanilla. Beat the egg whites until they are stiff but not dry and fold them into the custard. Spoon into a 1½-quart mold or individual dessert dishes and chill until firm. You will have about 6 cups.

Charlotte Russe

This fine dish, considered the invention of the great French chef Antonin Carême, became very popular in this country during the nineteenth century. It is made in a cylindrical mold lined with a thin layer of sponge cake and filled with Bavarian cream.

1 envelope gelatin
⅓ cup (65 g) sugar
½ cup (1 dL) milk

1½ teaspoons vanilla
1 cup (¼ L) heavy cream
Sponge cake

Sprinkle the gelatin over ¼ cup cold water and let it soften for 5 minutes. Mix the sugar and milk in a pan, add the gelatin, and cook over medium heat, stirring constantly, until the sugar and gelatin dissolve. Remove from the heat and add the vanilla. Chill until thick and syrupy, then beat until fluffy. Whip the cream to soft peaks and fold in the gelatin mixture. Line individual molds or a 1½-quart mold with ½-inch-thick slices of sponge cake. Spoon in the filling and chill until firm. Unmold before serving.

Caramel Charlotte. After softening the gelatin, melt the sugar slowly in a small skillet until it turns golden, then add it to the milk, stirring, and heat until blended. Add the gelatin and cook a minute or two more until the gelatin is dissolved. Remove from the heat, add the vanilla, and proceed as directed.

Burnt Almond Charlotte. Fold in *½ cup finely chopped, blanched, toasted almonds* with the cream.

Chocolate Charlotte. Melt *1 ounce unsweetened chocolate* with *3 tablespoons hot water* and *⅓ cup confectioners' sugar* and add these with the vanilla to the hot gelatin mixture.

Orange Charlotte

Sections of orange, placed around the mold before the charlotte is spooned in, offer good contrast in taste and texture.

(SERVES EIGHT TO TEN)

1 envelope gelatin	3 egg whites
1 cup (200 g) sugar	1 cup (¼ L) heavy cream
4 tablespoons lemon juice	Orange sections
1 cup (¼ L) orange juice	

Sprinkle the gelatin over ¼ cup cold water and let it soften for 5 minutes. Mix the sugar, ¾ cup water, lemon juice, and orange juice together in a pan, add the gelatin, and heat, stirring, until the gelatin dissolves. Chill until as thick as unbeaten egg white, then beat until frothy. Beat the egg whites stiff but not dry and fold them in. Whip the cream to soft peaks and fold it in. Line a 2-quart mold with orange sections, spoon in the charlotte, and chill. Unmold before serving.

Cold Rhubarb Soufflé

(SERVES SIX)

4 cups (1 L) chopped rhubarb	4 egg whites
2¼ cups (450 g) sugar	1 teaspoon vanilla
1 envelope gelatin	12 fresh strawberries
1 cup (¼ L) heavy cream	Additional whipped cream

Cook the rhubarb with ¼ cup water and 1¾ cups of the sugar in a heavy-bottomed saucepan for about 10 minutes until soft. Strain and cook down the juice to ½ cup. Purée the rhubarb in a food mill or a blender, or put through a vegetable mill. Soften the gelatin in 2 tablespoons cold water, then add to the hot rhubarb juice and stir until completely dissolved. Add the purée. Beat the cream until stiff. Beat the egg whites until they begin to stiffen, then add the remaining ½ cup sugar and the vanilla, continuing to beat until stiff peaks form. Fold first the egg-white mixture into the rhubarb, then the whipped cream. Make a collar of wax paper (see illustration p. 604) and fit it around a 1½-quart soufflé mold. Chill for at least six hours. Remove the collar and decorate the top with fresh strawberries and rosettes of whipped cream piped from a pastry tube.

Cold Apricot Soufflé. Use *3 cups sweetened puréed apricots* instead of the rhubarb-

and-sugar purée and use ½ *cup warm apricot juice* to dissolve the softened gelatin. Decorate the top with *fresh apricots,* if available, or *walnuts* and whipped-cream rosettes.

Cold Strawberry or Raspberry Soufflé. Use *3 cups sweetened purée of strawberries or raspberries* and save about ½ cup strawberry or raspberry juice to heat and dissolve the softened gelatin. Decorate the top with *whole strawberries or raspberries* and whipped cream.

FROZEN DESSERTS (MOUSSES AND PARFAITS)

Frozen Vanilla Mousse

Light and icy cold, plumped up with rich cream, frozen vanilla mousse provides a gentle end to a hot and spicy meal.

(SERVES SIX)

2 egg whites
½ cup (1 dL) confectioners' sugar

2 cups (½ L) heavy cream
2 teaspoons vanilla

Beat the egg whites until foamy, slowly add ¼ cup of the sugar, and continue beating until the whites hold stiff peaks. Whip the cream, slowly adding the remaining ¼ cup sugar, until the cream barely holds soft peaks. Stir in the vanilla, then fold in the egg whites. Spoon into a mold and freeze. Unmold before serving.

Frozen Apricot Mousse. Gently add *1 cup apricot purée* after the egg whites and cream have been folded together.

Frozen Coffee Mousse. Dissolve *3 tablespoons instant coffee* in ¼ *cup hot water.* Follow the recipe for Frozen Vanilla Mousse, gently stirring in the coffee after the egg whites and cream have been folded together.

Frozen Chocolate Mousse

(SERVES SIX)

1 cup (¼ L) cold milk
1 envelope gelatin
2 ounces (60 g) unsweetened chocolate

¾ cup (150 g) sugar
2 teaspoons vanilla
2 cups (½ L) heavy cream

Put the milk in a heavy-bottomed pan, sprinkle the gelatin over it, and let soften for 5 minutes. Add the chocolate and sugar and cook over moderate heat, stirring constantly, until the chocolate melts and is well blended. Chill until lukewarm. Add the vanilla. Whip the cream until it holds soft peaks, then fold it into the chocolate mixture. Spoon into a mold and freeze. Unmold and serve with *unsweetened whipped cream.*

Frozen Pineapple Mousse

(SERVES SIX)

1¼ cups (3 dL) syrup from
   canned pineapple
1 envelope gelatin
½ cup (100 g) sugar

Pinch of salt
2 tablespoons freshly squeezed
   lemon juice
2 cups (½ L) heavy cream

Put the pineapple syrup in a heavy-bottomed pan; sprinkle the gelatin over it and
let it soften for 5 minutes. Add the sugar and salt and cook over low heat,
stirring, until the sugar and gelatin dissolve. Remove from the heat and add the
lemon juice. Chill until thick but not set, then beat until light. Whip the heavy
cream and fold it into the pineapple mixture. Spoon into a mold or into ice cube
trays and freeze.

Angel Parfait

This whipped cream dessert has a sugar-syrup foundation. The syrup
is poured over stiffly beaten egg whites, and whipped cream and
vanilla are folded in. When you taste it you will understand its name:
it is truly angelic.

(SERVES SIX TO EIGHT)

3 egg whites
Pinch of salt
1 cup (200 g) sugar

2 teaspoons vanilla
2 cups (½ L) heavy cream

Combine the egg whites and salt in a bowl and beat until stiff but not dry; set
aside. Combine the sugar and ½ cup water in a small, heavy-bottomed pan. Heat
without stirring until the syrup boils. Cover with a lid to steam the sugar crystals
down the sides and continue to boil for 3 minutes. Remove the lid and boil
without stirring for 10–15 minutes more until the syrup registers 230°–232°F on
a candy thermometer or "spins a thread" (see p. 49). Slowly pour the syrup over
the beaten egg whites and beat constantly until the meringue is almost at room
temperature. Add the vanilla and blend. Whip the cream to soft peaks and fold
it in. Spoon into a mold, bowl, or parfait glasses, cover, and freeze until ready
to serve. You will have about 5 cups.

Strawberry Parfait

Try this during the summer when strawberries are abundant. It is
wonderful.

(SERVES EIGHT TO TEN)

1 quart (1 L) strawberries,
   washed and hulled
1¾ cups (250 g) sugar

3 egg whites
Pinch of salt
2 cups (½ L) heavy cream

Combine the strawberries and ¾ cup of the sugar. Purée in a blender or food
processor and refrigerate. Combine the egg whites and salt in a bowl and beat
until stiff but not dry; set aside. Put the remaining cup of sugar and ½ cup water
in a heavy-bottomed pan and bring to a boil *without stirring*. Cover with a lid to
steam the sugar crystals down the sides and boil for 3 minutes. Remove the lid

and continue boiling without stirring until the syrup registers 230°–232°F on a candy thermometer or "spins a thread" (see p. 49). Slowly pour the syrup over the beaten egg whites, beating constantly until the meringue is at room temperature. Whip the cream to soft peaks and gently fold it in. Fold in the cold strawberry mixture. Spoon into a mold, a dish, or parfait glasses, cover, and freeze until ready to serve. You will have about 7 cups.

Frozen Raspberry Soufflé

By freezing this in a straight-sided dish with a collar around it, the final presentation will look like a soufflé rising above the dish. Pipe extra whipped cream on top and decorate with a few extra raspberries, if you want it to look particularly elegant.

(SERVES EIGHT)

5 egg whites
¾ cup (150 g) sugar
3 cups (¾ L) raspberries

2 cups (½ L) heavy cream, whipped

Combine the egg whites and sugar in a metal bowl and place over hot water until the mixture is tepid (warm to the touch). Remove from the heat and beat with an electric beater until stiff. Set aside. Purée the raspberries and remove the seeds by forcing the purée through a strainer. Fold the raspberry purée into the egg-white mixture and fold in the whipped cream. Make a collar around a 1½-quart soufflé dish. Spoon the raspberry mousse into the dish and freeze at least six hours. Remove the collar to serve.

Frozen Strawberry Soufflé. Use *3 cups strawberries* instead of the raspberries.

Frozen Apricot Soufflé. Use *3 cups mashed apricots* (dried apricots that have been stewed in a little water until soft are fine) instead of the raspberries.

Frozen Lemon Yogurt Soufflé

(SERVES SIX)

1 cup (200 g) sugar
2 pints (1 L) unflavored yogurt
1 teaspoon vanilla
Juice and grated rind of 2
  lemons

2 egg whites
½ cup (1 dL) heavy cream

Beat ⅔ cup of the sugar into the yogurt, then add the vanilla and lemon juice and rind, mixing well. Beat the egg whites until they begin to thicken, then add the remaining ⅓ cup sugar, and continue to beat until stiff peaks are formed. In a separate chilled bowl whip the cream until stiff. Fold first the egg whites, then the whipped cream into the yogurt mixture. Turn into a 1½-quart soufflé dish with a collar around it and freeze at least 8 hours. Remove the collar and serve, decorated, if you like, with additional whipped cream.

Maple Mousse

Although this rich and pure maply-tasting mousse should be put in the freezer for 4 hours or more, it will have a more pleasing texture if you remove it to the refrigerator an hour before serving.

Maple Mousse (continued)

1 egg white
¾ cup (1¾ dL) hot maple
  syrup

1 cup (¼ L) heavy cream
1 dozen or so pecans or walnuts
  (optional)

Beat the egg white until it begins to thicken. Slowly add the hot maple syrup and continue beating until it is all absorbed and you have a thick meringuelike mixture. Beat the cream in a chilled bowl until stiff, incorporating as much air as possible into the whipped cream. Fold into the maple mixture. Pour into a 1-quart mold and freeze. Decorate the top, if you like, with pecans or walnuts.

English Toffee Bisque

2 cups (½ L) milk
3 egg yolks
⅓ cup (65 g) sugar
¾ tablespoon vanilla

¼ pound (115 g) English toffee
1 cup (¼ L) heavy cream
Pinch of salt

Heat the milk in a heavy-bottomed saucepan to the boiling point. Beat the egg yolks and sugar together, then add the hot milk in a slow, steady stream. Return the mixture to the saucepan and cook over medium heat, stirring constantly, until slightly thickened, or until the custard coats the spoon. Cool. Stir in the vanilla. Chop the toffee up into small bits, or put through a food processor. Add to the custard and stir in the cream and the salt. Pour into a 1-quart mold and freeze.

Nut Brittle Bisque. Instead of the toffee, add *1 cup nut brittle, preferably walnut,* broken into small pieces.

Biscuit Tortoni

1½ cups (3½ dL) dry
  macaroon crumbs
2 cups (½ L) light cream

½ cup (1 dL) sugar
⅓ cup (¾ dL) sherry
2 cups (½ L) heavy cream

Put 1 cup of the macaroon crumbs in a bowl, pour the light cream over them, and let soak for 1 hour. Stir in the sugar and sherry. Pour into a metal bowl or 2 ice cube trays and freeze until "mushy." Whip the heavy cream until stiff, fold the crumb mixture in, and blend gently. Spoon into individual cups, small fluted paper cups, or cupcake papers. Sprinkle the remaining ½ cup macaroon crumbs over the tops. Freeze until firm.

Baked Alaska

The wonder of a baked Alaska: its cold, frozen filling comes right from the hot oven where its topping has just been browned. In this true American dessert, invented by a physicist around 1800, ice cream rests on sponge cake and is covered by meringue which is browned in the oven so quickly that the ice cream doesn't have time to melt. Any kind of ice cream that appeals to you can be used.

(SERVES EIGHT TO TEN)

Hot-Water Sponge Cake
  (p. 518)
4 egg whites
⅛ teaspoon cream of tartar

½ cup (100 g) sugar
1 quart (1 L) ice cream, frozen
hard

Preheat the oven to 450°F (230°C). Chose a board that will fit into your oven, wet it on both sides, then shake off the excess water. Put a piece of brown paper on top of the board. Place the cake on it. Put the egg whites and cream of tartar in a bowl and beat until foamy. Slowly add the sugar and continue to beat until stiff but not dry. Cut the ice cream in slices to cover the cake, leaving a ½-inch rim all around. Cover completely with the meringue. Lightly brown in the oven for about 5 minutes. Serve at once.

ICE CREAMS, SHERBETS, AND ICES

French Vanilla Ice Cream

Excellent, creamy, and smooth, this French ice cream takes a little more trouble to make than the recipe that follows. Use vanilla bean for real French vanilla flavor; vanilla extract is best in the variations. Either this or the Philadelphia Ice Cream that follows lends itself to the many variations in flavor on p. 630.

(3 PINTS)

½ cup (100 g) sugar
⅛ teaspoon salt
4 egg yolks, slightly beaten
2 cups (½ L) very hot milk

1 teaspoon finely grated vanilla
bean, or 1 tablespoon vanilla
extract
1 pint (½ L) heavy cream

Mix the sugar, salt, and egg yolks together in a heavy-bottomed pan. Slowly stir in the hot milk and the grated vanilla bean if used. Cook, continuing to stir, until slightly thickened; remove and cool. Strain, then add the cream. Add the vanilla extract, if you are not using vanilla bean. Chill. Freeze in a hand-cranked or electric ice cream freezer (see p. 606).

Philadelphia Ice Cream

Deep in flavor, light in texture, easy to make—Philadelphia ice cream is richer and creamier than French vanilla ice cream. If it is too rich for your taste, use one part light cream to one part heavy—a better proportion for some of the rich variations that follow.

(3 PINTS)

1 quart (1 L) heavy cream, or
  2 cups (½ L) heavy cream
  and 2 cups (½ L) light
  cream
¾ cup (150 g) sugar

Pinch of salt
1 teaspoon finely grated vanilla
  bean, or 2 teaspoons vanilla
  extract

Mix everything together and stir until the sugar is dissolved. Freeze in a hand-cranked or electric ice cream freezer (see p. 606).

Flavored Ice Creams

Using either one of the preceding recipes for French Vanilla Ice Cream or Philadelphia Ice Cream, vary the flavorings as follows:

Butterscotch Ice Cream. First cook the sugar with *2 tablespoons butter* until melted and well browned. Then heat the milk or cream and dissolve the sugar-butter in it. Add the rest of the ingredients and cool before freezing.

Caramel Ice Cream. First caramelize half the sugar (see p. 609). Then heat the milk or cream and dissolve the caramelized sugar in it. Proceed with the rest of the recipe and be sure to cool the mixture before freezing.

Burnt Almond Ice Cream. Add, along with the vanilla, *1 cup finely chopped almonds* that have been *blanched and toasted* until golden.

Coffee Ice Cream. Add *2 tablespoons instant coffee* at the same time as you add the vanilla.

Ginger Ice Cream. Add *½ cup finely chopped preserved ginger* and *3 tablespoons ginger syrup* when adding the vanilla.

Maple and Maple Walnut Ice Cream. Use *½ cup maple syrup* instead of the sugar. Add *1 cup chopped walnuts,* if desired.

Mint Ice Cream. Use *1 teaspoon oil of peppermint* instead of vanilla. Color lightly with *green vegetable coloring.*

Pistachio Ice Cream. Omit the vanilla and add *1 teaspoon almond extract* and *½ cup pistachio nuts, chopped fine.* Color lightly with *green vegetable coloring.*

Chocolate Chip Ice Cream. Use only ½ teaspoon vanilla and add *1 cup chocolate chips* to the mixture before freezing.

Chestnut Ice Cream. Add *1 cup chopped preserved chestnuts and their syrup* and use only half the amount of sugar called for.

Peanut Brittle Ice Cream. Omit the sugar. Crush *½ pound peanut brittle* or pulverize in the blender, then sift into the ice cream mixture. Taste and add additional sugar if necessary.

Peppermint Candy Ice Cream. Omit the sugar. Crush *½ pound peppermint-stick candy* and add to heated milk or cream. Cool before freezing.

Praline Ice Cream. Add *1 cup finely chopped almonds* that have been *blanched and toasted* until golden. Caramelize half the sugar, heat the milk or cream, and then add the caramelized sugar slowly. Cool before freezing.

Old-fashioned Custard Ice Cream

Good and substantial, with a dense, full texture.

(3 PINTS)

2 cups (½ L) milk
1 tablespoon flour
¾ cup (150 g) sugar
2 egg yolks, slightly beaten

1 pint (½ L) heavy cream
1 tablespoon vanilla
¼ teaspoon salt

Heat 1½ cups of the milk until very hot. Mix the flour, sugar, and remaining ½ cup milk in a bowl, add the hot milk slowly, and stir until smooth. Return to the pan and cook, stirring constantly, for about 8 minutes. Pour a little of the milk mixture over the yolks, then stir the yolks into the pan. Cook for another minute, then strain and cool. Add the cream, vanilla, and salt. Chill. Freeze in a hand-cranked or electric ice cream freezer (see p. 606).

Fresh Fruit Ice Cream

Using light cream or milk makes this a fresh fruit sherbet; heavy cream makes a rich ice cream.

(ABOUT 1½ QUARTS)

2 cups (½ L) milk
2 cups (½ L) heavy cream
1¼ cups (250 g) sugar
  (depending on how sweet
  the fruit)

1½ cups (3½ dL) fresh puréed
  peeled peaches, apricots,
  strawberries, or raspberries
Pinch of salt

Put the milk and cream in a pan and heat to the boiling point. Remove from the heat and add half the sugar; stir to dissolve. Cool. Sprinkle the remaining half of sugar over the puréed fruit, taste for sweetness and add more sugar, if needed, after adding the sweetened milk and cream. Stir in the salt and blend well. Freeze in a hand-cranked or electric ice cream freezer (see p. 606).

Chocolate Ice Cream

A rich, chocolate ice cream that is very smooth in texture—and easy to make.

(3 PINTS)

½ pound (225 g) semisweet
  chocolate, in pieces
2 cups (½ L) milk
3 eggs

1 cup (200 g) sugar
1 pint (½ L) light cream
1 tablespoon vanilla
⅛ teaspoon salt

Put the chocolate and milk in a pan and cook over low heat, stirring frequently, until melted, about 20 minutes. Beat the eggs in a bowl, slowly adding the sugar. Add the cream, vanilla, and salt and mix well. Stir in the chocolate mixture and chill. Freeze in a hand-cranked or electric ice cream freezer (see p. 606).

Old-fashioned Chocolate Ice Cream

There is even more richness and depth to this lovely ice cream—a must for chocolate ice cream lovers.

Old-fashioned Chocolate Ice Cream (continued)

1¼ cups (250 g) sugar   2 cups (½ L) milk
1 tablespoon flour   2 squares bitter chocolate
Dash of salt   2 cups (½ L) cream
2 eggs, slightly beaten   1 tablespoon vanilla

Mix the sugar, flour, and salt together, and add the eggs. Heat the milk and melt the chocolate in it. Combine the mixtures and cook over medium heat in a heavy-bottomed saucepan, stirring constantly, until lightly thickened. Cool, then add the cream and the vanilla. Strain and freeze in a hand-cranked or electric ice cream freezer (see p. 606).

Fresh Fruit or Berry Ice Cream

A basic, creamy ice cream that lets the flavor of the fresh fruit dominate. Taste the fruit pulp for flavor and to determine how much sugar is needed; if the fruit is too bland, adjust with lemon juice to bring up its flavor. This ice cream can be made with peaches, pears, apricots, mangoes, or berries.

4 cups (1 L) fresh fruit or   Up to ¼ cup (½ dL) fresh
  berries, crushed   lemon juice
Pinch of salt   1 cup (¼ L) heavy cream
¾ cup (150 g) sugar or more,   1 cup (¼ L) light cream
  as needed

Sprinkle the crushed fruit or berries with salt and half the sugar. Taste and add more sugar and lemon juice, if needed. Put the cream and remaining sugar into the freezer container of a hand-cranked or electric freezer and chill until slightly firm (see p. 606). Then add the sweetened fruit or berries and finish freezing.

Frozen Yogurt

So very simple and good—and so much less caloric than the usual ice cream—no wonder frozen yogurt has become so popular in America. And, particularly if you make your own yogurt (see p. 17), this can be a very inexpensive treat to have available in the family freezer.

3 pints (1½ L) unflavored yogurt
1½ teaspoons vanilla (optional)
Sugar (optional)

Mix the yogurt and vanilla and, if you wish, as much sugar as desired. Freeze in a hand-cranked or electric ice cream freezer (see p. 606).

Frozen Fruit Yogurt. Use 2½ pints yogurt and add *1 cup sugar* and *1 cup mashed fruit* or *berries*, fresh, frozen, or canned. If using fresh, let stand with a tablespoon or so of sugar, depending on the sweetness of the fruit or berries, for about 20 minutes to develop flavor before adding to the yogurt and freezing.

Rich Coffee Ice Cream

(1½ QUARTS)

1 cup (¼ L) milk
¼ cup (½ dL) finely ground
  coffee, preferably mocha
1 cup (200 g) sugar

3 eggs
Pinch of salt
3 cups (¾ L) light cream
1 tablespoon vanilla

Heat the milk to the boiling point, add the coffee and ½ cup of the sugar. Beat the eggs, then add the milk-coffee mixture in a steady stream, beating constantly. Add the remaining sugar and the salt and heat this mixture in a heavy-bottomed saucepan, stirring constantly, until thickened. Add 1 cup of the cream and the vanilla, and let stand 30 minutes. Cool, strain through cheesecloth or a textured synthetic towel. Add the remaining cream and freeze in a hand-cranked or electric ice cream freezer (see p. 606).

Brown Bread Ice Cream

There is a delicious contrast between the pure, rich vanilla cream and the tiny, crisp bits of brown wheat.

(2 QUARTS)

1½ cups (3½ dL) homemade
  dried whole-wheat bread
  crumbs
3 pints (1½ L) heavy cream

1¼ cups (250 g) sugar
¼ teaspoon salt
4 teaspoons vanilla

Soak the crumbs in 4 cups of the heavy cream for 15 minutes. Add the sugar, salt, vanilla, and remaining 2 cups of cream. Chill. Freeze in a hand-cranked or electric ice cream freezer (see p. 606).

Orange Ice Cream

Light ice-milk texture and a fine, sharp orange flavor.

(2 QUARTS)

1½ cups (300 g) sugar
2 cups (½ L) freshly squeezed
  orange juice
2 cups (½ L) very hot light
  cream

2 egg yolks, slightly beaten
2 cups (½ L) heavy cream

Combine the sugar and 1 cup water in a pan and boil for 5 minutes. Stir in the orange juice and the hot light cream. Whisk in the egg yolks and cook over low heat, stirring constantly, until thick. Cool. Whip the cream and fold it in. Freeze in a hand-cranked or electric ice cream freezer (see p. 606).

Grape Ice Cream

A simple and surprisingly delicious ice cream, the color of lilacs.

(1 QUART)

1 pint (½ L) heavy cream
1¼ cups (3 dL) unsweetened
   grape juice

⅓ cup (65 g) sugar
Few drops of fresh lemon or
   lime juice

Mix the cream, grape juice, and sugar together and stir until the sugar is dissolved.
Add fresh lemon or lime juice to taste. Freeze in a hand-cranked or electric ice
cream freezer (see p. 606).

Refrigerator Ice Cream

Refrigerator ice cream is light and creamy, although it never achieves
the thick, dense creaminess of cranked ice cream.

(1 QUART)

1 teaspoon gelatin
1 cup (¼ L) hot milk
¼ cup (50 g) sugar
3 tablespoons corn syrup
1 teaspoon flour

Pinch of salt
1 egg, separated
2 cups (½ L) heavy cream
2 teaspoons vanilla

Put the gelatin and ¼ cup cold water in the top of a double boiler and let the
gelatin soften for 5 minutes. Stir in the milk, sugar, corn syrup, flour, and salt,
and cook, stirring frequently, until thickened. Cover and cook over hot water
for 10 minutes. Beat the egg yolk slightly, stir it in slowly, and cook 1 minute
more. Strain into two ice cube trays or a metal bowl and chill. When cool, pour
into a large bowl and beat until very light. Beat the egg white in another bowl
until stiff but not dry, then fold it into the ice cream mixture. Whip the cream
separately and fold it in. Stir in the vanilla. Pour back into the trays or bowl and
freeze in the refrigerator freezer.

Lemon Milk Sherbet

Pleasingly acid, light, and creamy. The unchilled mixture may look
curdled, but it will be smooth after freezing.

(3 PINTS)

1 cup (¼ L) freshly squeezed
   lemon juice
1½ cups (300 g) sugar

Pinch of salt
1 quart (1 L) milk

Mix all the ingredients together in a bowl. Freeze in metal bowls or three ice
cube trays in the refrigerator freezer.

Orange Cream Sherbet

Keen flavor and light texture.

(3 PINTS)

1 cup (200 g) sugar
2 cups (½ L) freshly squeezed
   orange juice

Pinch of salt
2 cups (½ L) milk
1 cup (¼ L) heavy cream

Mix all the ingredients in a bowl and stir until blended. Freeze in a hand-cranked or electric ice cream freezer (see p. 606).

Cranberry Sherbet

Icy crisp, light, and fresh—a touch tart, a touch sweet.

(1 QUART)

1½ cups (3½ dL) cranberry
   jelly
Grated rind and juice of 1
   lemon

Juice of 1 orange
2 egg whites

Beat the cranberry jelly, lemon rind and juice, and orange juice together until well blended. Freeze to a mush in two ice cube trays. Beat the egg whites until stiff but not dry and whisk them in. Freeze in the ice cube trays or in a metal bowl in the refrigerator freezer.

Fruit Sherbet

A clean, light taste, refreshing and nice.

(1 QUART)

1 envelope gelatin
¼ cup (50 g) sugar
2 cups (½ L) puréed fresh (see
   p. 648), cooked, or canned
   fruit

Pinch of salt
Sugar
2 tablespoons freshly squeezed
   lemon juice

Sprinkle the gelatin over ¼ cup water and let it soften for 5 minutes. Put the sugar and ¾ cup water in a pan, stir in the gelatin, and cook over low heat until it dissolves. Add the fruit purée, salt, and sugar to taste and cook, stirring, until the sugar has dissolved. Remove and add the lemon juice. Freeze in two ice cube trays or a metal bowl in the refrigerator freezer.

Ginger Sherbet

Such a clean, tingling taste at the end of a good meal.

(1½ QUARTS)

1 cup (200 g) sugar
¼ pound (115 g) preserved
   Canton ginger
½ cup (1 dL) freshly squeezed
   orange juice

⅓ cup (¾ dL) freshly squeezed
   lemon juice

Bring the sugar and 4 cups water to a boil. Cut the ginger into small pieces and drop into the boiling syrup. Boil 5 minutes. Add the fruit juices and cool. Strain, mashing the ginger to extract all its flavor. Freeze in a hand-cranked or electric ice cream freezer (see p. 606).

Pineapple Ice

Simple and very good.

(3 PINTS)

¾ cup (150 g) sugar
2 cups (½ L) fresh or canned
    crushed unsweetened
    pineapple

½ cup (1 dL) lemon juice
Pinch of salt

Boil 2 cups water with the sugar in a pan for 5 minutes. Remove from the heat and stir in the pineapple, lemon juice, and salt. Cool. Pour into three ice cube trays and freeze in the refrigerator freezer.

Lemon Ice

Lovely, fresh, and sharp.

(3 PINTS)

1¾ cups (350 g) sugar
1 tablespoon grated lemon rind
¾ cup (1¾ dL) lemon juice

Bring 3 cups water to a boil, and stir in the sugar until dissolved. Cool, then add the lemon rind and juice. Freeze in a hand-cranked or electric ice cream freezer (see p. 606) or in the refrigerator freezer, using three ice cube trays or a metal bowl.

Orange Ice. Omit the lemon rind and juice and substitute *3 cups orange juice, ½ cup lemon juice,* and the *grated rind of 2 oranges.*

Grape Ice. Omit the lemon rind and juice and substitute *2 cups grape juice, ⅔ cup orange juice,* and *¼ cup lemon juice.*

Raspberry Ice. Omit the lemon rind and juice and substitute *2 cups raspberry juice.*

Bombes and Molds

Chill a melon mold or another decoratively shaped mold. Spoon in whatever ice cream or ice you are using for the outside coating; it will help if this ice cream is slightly soft. Spread it all around to make a lining about ¾ inch thick, using the back of a spoon to smooth it in. Fill to overflowing with the contrasting ice cream, ice, or other filling that you have chosen. Put on the cover and press down; the object is to have the mold so well filled that when you press down, the mixture is forced into all the corners and crevices. If you do not have a cover for the mold, use heavy foil and a plate. Freeze either by packing in salt and ice, using 4 parts ice to 1 part salt, or, if you have space, put in the freezer for 4 hours. To serve: invert the mold on a serving dish. Wipe with a cloth that has been soaked in very hot water and then wrung out; repeat if the mold does not lift easily from the ice cream. Decorate with a border of whipped cream, fresh-cut fruit or berries, nuts, flowers—whatever seems attractive.

Suggested combinations for the bombes or molds are:

Coating	Center
Ice cream of any flavor	Ice cream of contrasting flavor that is compatible
Raspberry Ice	Vanilla Ice Cream or Vanilla Mousse
Chocolate Ice Cream	Chocolate Chip, Mint, Pistachio Ice Cream, Orange Ice, or Apricot Mousse
Coffee Ice Cream	Italian Meringue, English Toffee or Burnt Walnut Bisque, or Pistachio Ice Cream
Vanilla Ice Cream	Maple Walnut or Burnt Almond Ice Cream, Peanut or Walnut Brittle folded into Italian Meringue

☼ Other Suggestions for Using Ice Cream

The cool creaminess of ice cream makes a delicious filling, providing just the right contrast for certain baked textures. Try spreading a Chocolate Roll with softened vanilla ice cream instead of whipped cream; or fill Éclairs or Cream Puffs with vanilla ice cream and drizzle some Chocolate or Butterscotch Sauce over the top. The crunchy, slightly chewy texture of meringues is marvelously enhanced by a scoop of ice cream, any flavor you like, topped by whipped cream, crushed fruit or berries, or perhaps Chocolate Sauce. All of these concoctions should be served immediately, before the ice cream melts. A rum cake can be made with layers of leftover sponge cake, sprinkled generously with rum, interspersed with layers of vanilla, coffee, or chocolate ice cream, then firmed in the refrigerator; serve this with Rum Sauce (p. 526). And fruits and ice cream, of course, invariably make for a fine marriage. Peach or Pear Melba is simply made by filling poached peach or pear halves, hollow sides up, with scoops of vanilla ice cream and topping with Melba (raspberry) Sauce (p. 641); a dessert of black cherries flamed over ice cream becomes Cherries Jubilee (p. 656); and for Strawberries Romanoff (p. 674) the berries are folded into softened vanilla ice cream and whipped cream. Experiment with your own combinations, but use the best of ingredients and aim for a delicate balance of textures and flavors that seem really compatible.

DESSERT SAUCES

Butterscotch Sauce

A thick, translucent sauce, perfect over ice cream or frozen desserts.

(1 CUP)

½ cup (1 dL) dark-brown sugar   2 tablespoons butter
½ cup (1 dL) light corn syrup   1 teaspoon vanilla
¼ teaspoon salt

Stir the brown sugar and corn syrup together in a small, heavy-bottomed pan. Cook over low heat, stirring occasionally, for about 6 minutes. Remove from heat, stir in the salt, butter, and vanilla, and blend well.

Rich Butterscotch Sauce

Creamy and not very thick, this is good over mousses, custards, and the like.

(2 CUPS)

¼ pound (115 g) butter
2⅔ cups (6½ dL) light-brown
  sugar (1 pound, 450 g)

½ teaspoon vinegar
½ cup (1 dL) heavy cream
Pinch of salt

Mix all the ingredients together in a heavy-bottomed pan. Cook over low heat, stirring occasionally, for 30 minutes.

Caramel Sauce

A thin caramel syrup, clear and deep gold, this is just right over egg custards or vanilla pudding. It will keep indefinitely.

(1 CUP)

1 cup (200 g) sugar

Put the sugar in a small, heavy-bottomed pan and swirl it over very low heat *without stirring;* it will slowly melt and turn golden. When completely melted, stir in 1 cup boiling water. Cook for 3–4 minutes.

Chocolate Sauce

A good, shiny, all-purpose sauce, not very thick and not overly rich.

(1 CUP)

2 tablespoons butter
2 ounces (60 g) unsweetened
  chocolate

1 cup (200 g) sugar
Pinch of salt
1½ teaspoons vanilla

Put the butter and chocolate in a heavy-bottomed saucepan and stir over low heat until the chocolate is melted. Remove from the heat and stir in the sugar, salt, and ½ cup water. Blend well, return to moderate heat, and cook, stirring often, for about 5 minutes. Remove and cool a little, then add the vanilla.

Fudge Sauce

A medium-thick, silky sauce with deep chocolate taste. It is just right over vanilla ice cream.

(2 CUPS)

2 ounces (60 g) unsweetened
  chocolate
¾ cup (150 g) sugar
¼ teaspoon salt

½ cup (1 dL) light corn syrup
½ cup (1 dL) milk
2 tablespoons butter
1 tablespoon vanilla

Mix the chocolate, sugar, salt, corn syrup, and milk together in a heavy-bottomed pan. Cook over low heat, stirring often, for 20–25 minutes or until thickened. Add the butter. Cool a little, then add the vanilla.

Creamy Chocolate Sauce

A thick chocolate sauce, milder than the preceding chocolate and fudge sauces and very good over cakes and puddings.

(1½ CUPS)

1½ cups (3½ dL) milk	1 tablespoon flour
2 ounces (60 g) unsweetened chocolate	Pinch of salt
½ cup (100 g) sugar	2 tablespoons butter
	1 teaspoon vanilla

Heat the milk and chocolate in a heavy-bottomed pan until the chocolate melts; beat until smooth. Mix the sugar, flour, and salt together and stir slowly into the chocolate mixture. Cook, stirring constantly, for 5 minutes. Remove from the heat and blend in the butter and vanilla.

English Custard (Crème Anglaise)

A pale-yellow softly flavored vanilla sauce, one of the best of all the dessert sauces and basic to many Bavarian creams and mousses.

(SERVES FIVE)

2 cups (½ L) milk	½ cup (100 g) sugar
4 egg yolks	1½ teaspoons vanilla

Heat the milk in a heavy-bottomed pan until it is very hot. Beat the egg yolks for about 3 minutes while slowly adding the sugar until mixture is a pale lemon color and thick. Very slowly pour in the hot milk, stirring constantly, until blended. Return the mixture to the pan and cook over medium-low heat to just below the boiling point, stirring constantly, until slightly thickened and the froth has disappeared. Do not boil or the sauce will "curdle." Remove from the heat, quickly pour into a bowl, and stir for a minute or two to cool. When completely cool add the vanilla and blend. Cover and chill until needed. You will have about 2½ cups of custard.

Sea-Foam Sauce

Creamy, but not heavy; beaten egg white is added just before serving. Try this over Steamed Chocolate Pudding (p. 615) or Chocolate Bread Pudding (p. 612).

(1½ CUPS)

2 tablespoons butter	1 egg, separated
2 tablespoons flour	1 teaspoon vanilla
½ cup (100 g) sugar	

Cream the butter, flour, and sugar together in a small saucepan. Beat the egg yolk with ½ cup water, then add to the creamed mixture. Cook over low heat, stirring constantly, until thickened. Cool. Just before serving, add the vanilla. Beat the egg white until stiff but not dry and fold it in.

Foamy Sauce

This sauce holds well and is wonderful with Steamed Chocolate Pudding (p. 615). Flavored with sherry, it is also very good with Christmas cakes.

(1½ CUPS)

1 cup (¼ L) confectioners' sugar	1 egg, well beaten
¼ pound (115 g) butter, softened	Pinch of salt
	1 teaspoon vanilla, or 2 tablespoons sherry

Beat the sugar into the softened butter in the top of a double boiler. Blend in the egg and salt. Beat over simmering water until light, about 5 minutes. Stir in the vanilla or sherry.

Orange Sauce

This sauce has a sweet, sharp citrus taste that is grand over Rice Cream (p. 610), Blancmange (p. 610), or Marmalade Soufflé (p. 620). Make it just before using—it thins out after an hour.

(1½ CUPS)

3 egg whites	Grated rind and juice of 2 oranges
1 cup (¼ L) confectioners' sugar	Juice of 1 lemon

Beat the egg whites until they are stiff but not dry. Gradually beat in the sugar. Stir in the orange rind and juice and lemon juice and blend well.

Coffee Custard Sauce

Splendid over Caramel Custard (p. 609), cake, or vanilla pudding.

(2 CUPS)

3 egg yolks, slightly beaten	1 cup (¼ L) hot strong coffee
¼ cup (50 g) sugar	⅓ cup (¾ dL) heavy cream
⅛ teaspoon salt	

Put the yolks, sugar, and salt in a heavy-bottomed pan and cook over moderate heat, stirring and slowly adding the hot coffee. Cook, stirring constantly, until thickened. Remove from the heat and cool. Whip the cream to soft peaks and fold it in. Refrigerate until needed.

Honey Cream Sauce

This honey-colored sauce is good over spice cake or puddings. Taste it by itself; you'll find it sweet, with a bit of tang.

(1 CUP)

½ cup (1 dL) heavy cream
½ cup (1 dL) honey
1 teaspoon lemon juice

Whip the cream until it holds soft peaks. Stir in the honey and lemon juice and whip well. Refrigerate until needed; it will keep for 5–7 days if made with regular cream and for at least a month if sterilized cream is used.

Sabayon Sauce

This sauce is especially good over fruit. It is also sometimes served by itself in small glasses as a very light whipped-custard dessert. It must be served at once or it will slowly fall.

(1½ CUPS)

Grated rind of ½ lemon
Juice of ½ lemon
¼ cup (½ dL) sherry or
   Madeira wine

⅓ cup (65 g) sugar
2 eggs, separated

Put the lemon rind, lemon juice, wine, sugar, and egg yolks into the top of a double boiler. Beat with a whisk over simmering water until thick; remove from the heat. Beat the egg whites until stiff but not dry and fold them in. Serve at once.

Hard Sauce

Traditionally served with English Plum Pudding (p. 617), hard sauce is very sweet and good with many other steamed puddings. Serve it cool, but not chilled.

(1 CUP)

5 tablespoons butter
1 cup (¼ L) confectioners' sugar
½ teaspoon vanilla

Cream the butter, then slowly add the sugar, beating well with an electric beater or by hand until creamy and pale yellow. Add the vanilla and blend. Cover and refrigerate until needed.

Brandy or Wine Hard Sauce. Use *2 tablespoons brandy* or *3 tablespoons sherry* or *Madeira wine* instead of the vanilla.

Lemon Hard Sauce. Use *1 tablespoon freshly squeezed lemon juice* and *1 tablespoon grated lemon rind* in place of the vanilla.

Mocha Hard Sauce. Omit the vanilla and add *2 teaspoons instant coffee* and *2 teaspoons powdered cocoa.*

Raspberry Hard Sauce. Omit the vanilla and add *3 tablespoons raspberry juice* or *4 tablespoons raspberry jam.*

Melba Sauce I

Nothing more than sweetened raspberry juice, but very good over peaches, ice cream, or vanilla mousse.

(1 CUP)

1 cup (¼ L) fresh or frozen raspberries
¼ cup (50 g) sugar

Melba Sauce I (continued)

Purée the raspberries in a blender or food processor. Strain the purée to remove the seeds, put it in a small pan, and stir in the sugar. Cook over medium heat, stirring frequently, until the sugar dissolves; remove and cool. Cover and refrigerate.

Melba Sauce II

This is thicker and finer than the preceding Melba Sauce I. The currant jelly adds a nice tartness, so don't sweeten the raspberries too much.

(1½ CUPS)

2 cups (½ L) fresh or frozen
  raspberries
½ cup (1 dL) currant jelly

Sugar
1 teaspoon cornstarch

Crush the raspberries, then strain them to remove the seeds. Put them into a small pan, add the currant jelly, and bring to the boiling point. Stir in sugar to taste and simmer for 2 minutes. Mix the cornstarch with 1 tablespoon cold water in a small bowl until smooth. Slowly stir the cornstarch mixture into the raspberry sauce, then cook, stirring, until thick and clear. Cool and store in a covered container until needed.

Strawberry Sauce I

This sauce has the consistency of a creamy frosting. Use it on a plain white or yellow cake or over pancakes or waffles.

(1 CUP)

5 tablespoons butter, softened
1 cup (¼ L) confectioners' sugar
⅔ cup (1½ dL) strawberries

Cream the butter, then add the sugar gradually, beating well. Crush the strawberries and add them a little at a time, beating after each addition until the sauce is smooth. Cover and refrigerate until needed.

Strawberry Sauce II

The addition of an egg white makes this lighter than Strawberry Sauce I. It is very nice over delicate desserts such as poached pears, vanilla mousse, or fresh, sliced strawberries.

(1½ CUPS)

5 tablespoons butter, softened
1 cup (¼ L) confectioners'
  sugar

⅔ cup (1½ dL) strawberries
1 egg white

Cream the butter, then slowly add the sugar, blending well. Crush the strawberries and add them a little at a time, beating until smooth. Add the egg white and beat until the sauce is light and barely holds soft peaks. Cover and refrigerate.

Sterling Sauce

The brown-sugar version of Hard Sauce (p.641).

(1 CUP)

5 tablespoons butter, softened
¾ cup (1¾ dL) light-brown
   sugar

2 tablespoons heavy cream
2 tablespoons sherry
1 tablespoon brandy

Cream the butter in a mixing bowl and slowly add the sugar, beating well with an electric beater or by hand until smooth and creamy. Slowly add the cream and blend well, then add the sherry and brandy and mix thoroughly. Cover and refrigerate until needed.

Cambridge Sauce

A rather thin sauce with a smooth texture and a light butter-vanilla flavor. Very good over a rich, robust pudding.

(1 CUP)

2 teaspoons flour
5 tablespoons butter
1 cup (¼ L) confectioners'
   sugar

2 teaspoons vanilla

Put ½ cup water in a small saucepan and bring to a boil. Stir 2 tablespoons cold water into the flour and mix until smooth. Gradually stir the flour mixture into the boiling water, lower the heat, and simmer, stirring, for 5 minutes; remove from the heat and cool. Cream the butter, then add the confectioners' sugar and beat until smooth. Add the flour mixture and the vanilla and blend well. Cover and refrigerate until needed.

Whipped Cream

Heavy cream and whipping cream are the same. There are two kinds of heavy cream available today: "old-fashioned" pasteurized heavy cream which will remain fresh for five to seven days, and the new "sterilized" or "ultrapasteurized" cream that keeps for five to six weeks, having been heated to a high temperature to protect it from bacteria. Use whipped cream as a cake frosting or as a topping for desserts. Sweeten it or not, flavor it or not, depending on how sweet the dessert is and whether you want an additional flavor. Incidentally, sweetened whipped cream with a little vanilla is also known as Chantilly Cream.

(1½-2 CUPS)

1 cup (¼ L) heavy cream
1–2 tablespoons confectioners'
   sugar (optional)

½ teaspoon or 1½-2
   tablespoons sweet liqueur
   (optional)

Using a whisk or an electric beater, whip the cream until soft peaks form. With an electric beater the cream can turn buttery very suddenly after it has thickened, so watch it carefully. The more air you can incorporate, the greater the volume of the whipped cream will be; ideally you should double the volume. This is easier to accomplish with a balloon whisk, and if you beat the cream over another bowl of ice, the whipping will go very quickly. Add the sugar and vanilla or liqueur any time after you have started to beat. If you are using a sweet liqueur, you will need very little sugar. Whipped cream will keep in the refrigerator for several hours, but it is better to store it in a strainer set over a bowl so that the liquid that accumulates will drain off.

Whipped Evaporated Milk. *Canned evaporated milk* will whip nicely if it is chilled well.

Whipped Light Cream, Half-and-Half, or Coffee Cream. Sprinkle *1 teaspoon gelatin* over *1 tablespoon cold water* in a small metal bowl and let it soften for 5 minutes. Dissolve it by putting the bowl into a pan of simmering water and stirring until clear. Add the gelatin and *1 egg white* to *1 cup light cream*. Beat until soft peaks form.

Mock Devonshire Cream. Beat *3 ounces softened cream cheese*, then slowly add *½ cup heavy cream* and beat until smooth.

Lemon Sauce

A good old-fashioned sauce for Cottage Pudding Cake (p. 523) and for steamed puddings.

(ABOUT 1 CUP)

½ cup (100 g) sugar	3 tablespoons lemon juice
1 tablespoon cornstarch	Grated rind of 1 lemon
1 cup (¼ L) boiling water	Few gratings nutmeg (optional)
2 tablespoons butter	Pinch of salt

Mix the sugar and cornstarch together in a small saucepan. Add the boiling water, stirring constantly. Boil 5 minutes. Remove from the heat and swirl in the butter, lemon juice and rind, optional nutmeg, and pinch of salt. Serve warm.

FRUITS &
FRUIT DESSERTS

ABOUT FRUIT

Whether it is served squeezed for breakfast or cut up over cereal, tucked into a lunch box or munched as an afternoon snack, arranged on a salad plate or in tall sherbet glasses to begin dinner, fruit is one food we can eat with unabashed pleasure, never feeling guilty. As children we learn how good it is for us, and most of us never get over the joy of anticipating the first strawberries and the tart freshness of an apple just shaken from the tree. Today with modern transportation more fruits are available year round and less familiar kinds like papaya and kumquats and mangoes are seen more in our markets. But both these exotic varieties and out-of-season fruits are expensive, and for daily use the sensible cook will try to concentrate on seasonal fruits, which offer not only better value but also much better flavor.

In addition to enjoying fruits whole and raw and cut up in fresh compotes, we have a rich heritage of delectable fruit desserts—pies, shortcakes, whips, soufflés, fritters, and puddings (some with charming names like Brown Betty and Rolypoly and Grunt) that have come down to us from our forebears, who clearly enjoyed making the most of each harvest and of adding variety to their diets during the lean, cold months. If you grew up on these delicious, old-fashioned desserts, you will want to share such treasures with your family; if they weren't part of your past, you'll soon discover why they are held in such affection.

Buying and Storing Fruit

The chances are that when you buy fruit, it will not be fully ripened; see individual listings that follow as to what to look for. Leave fruits out at room temperature or, to hasten the ripening process, put them in a paper bag, twist the top so the air is locked in, and leave until they are ready to eat. If fruits are fully ripe, store them in the refrigerator. If there are any bruised or soft spots, cut them out and don't store the fruits too close together.

645

Frozen Fruits and Juices

Try not to let frozen fruits and juices defrost on their journey home from market, and store them quickly in the freezer. Depending on how well they have been handled by purveyors, frozen fruits and juices can have better flavor than their out-of-season counterparts. Berries are apt to have a softer texture when defrosted but are fine for sauces and purées and, of course, cooked.

For freezing your own fruits, see p. 731.

Canned Fruits

See the individual listings for recommendations. While sliced or cut-up fruits may be a better value than whole, they are also more permeated with syrup so tend to taste less of their own natural flavors; for compotes and baked fruit dishes whole canned fruits are therefore preferable.

For canning your own fruits, see p. 717.

A Bowl of Fresh Fruit

Placing a beautiful and bountiful bowl of fruit in the middle of the table, providing each diner with a handy fruit knife, and encouraging all to help themselves is one of the pleasantest ways to end a dinner, particularly a substantial one when the cleansing lightness of fruit is so welcome. The fruits should look inviting and not disappoint when they are bitten into; market well enough ahead so that unripened fruits will have plenty of time to develop. Select different varieties depending on what's in season and look for nice shapes and contrasting colors that will make up an attractive composition. Polish apples and pears until they shine, freshen anything that looks a little weary in ice water, add leaves or sprigs of holly to the bowl, and include a surprising touch like a sprinkling of bright berries or wedges of pineapple with a few spiky leaves left on. The contrast of dried fruits and nuts is nice, too, particularly in winter.

Here are some suggestions for seasonal fruit bowls:

Fall Fruit Bowls. You might have a mixture of local apples of different kinds, some red-brown small Seckel pears as well as large, yellow Bartletts, small clusters of green seedless grapes and of blue Concords, some tangerines, dried figs, and raisins and mixed nuts.

Winter Fruit Bowls. Include some longer-keeping apples like Red and Golden Delicious and McIntosh, Anjou and russet pears, kumquats, bananas, red winter grapes and purple Malagas, a pineapple cut into wedges (the pieces loosened and speared with toothpicks for easy handling), dates, dried apricots, and nuts.

Spring Fruit Bowls. These could welcome some of the tropical fruits that ripen early—papayas and mangoes cut in slim wedges—along with navel oranges, greening apples, early nectarines, and a sprinkling of the first strawberries, unhulled.

Summer Fruit Bowls. Early summer could include apricots and the first peaches and plums, and cherries. Later, there will be more plums—from tiny sweet sugarplums to luscious greengage—fresh figs, and cantaloupes, honeydews and watermelons, which can be cut in thin manageable slices to distribute around the fruit bowl. Decorate with berries as they come into season.

Fruit Cups

See also Fruit Salads, p. 440.

Ideally a festive and truly delicious fruit cup should be made up of fresh fruits, pitted, peeled (unless you want to leave a little tender skin for color and flavor), and cut into not-too-small pieces. Follow the same principles of selection you would for a fruit bowl—let the seasons guide you. Use small berries as they appear and cut some fruits into balls with a melon-ball cutter. Sometimes a teaspoon or so of fresh lemon juice will help to heighten flavors of fruits not quite at their peak (and it's a good idea whenever you include peaches, since they discolor after peeling); toss your mixture with sugar and let it chill.

To serve as a first course, cut-up fruits look lovely in sherbet glasses or goblets with a sprig of mint on top, or arrange them attractively in a large glass bowl. For dessert, a small scoop of a fruit ice is nice, too. Sometimes you may want to macerate the fruits in some sweet sauterne or kirsch or a very small amount of brandy, but go easy—you want to taste the fruit, and strong liquors like brandy and rum tend to overwhelm it. Sour cream, crème fraîche, or whipped cream lightly flavored with a liqueur and sprinkled with brown sugar can make good toppings. Serve with Lace Cookies (p. 555), or Chocolate Walnut Wafers (p. 554), or other delicate cookies.

Fruit Desserts

Whips. A whip is made with stiffly beaten egg whites, lightly sugared, with chopped or puréed fruit folded in. It may be baked or unbaked. Prune whip, which adorned many tables at the turn of the century, was a great American favorite. Cold puréed fruit or berry soufflés (see p. 625) are a variation on the whip with a little gelatin and whipped cream added to make the airy dessert stand up in a soufflé dish.

Snows. Snows are always unbaked. They are made with stiffly beaten egg whites, sugared, sometimes stabilized with gelatin and flavored with fruit purée or fruit juice.

Brown Betty. Brown Betty, an all-time treasure, is a baked fruit dish with spicy buttered crumbs on top. Occasionally the crumbs are strewn throughout as well. A close cousin is the *Crisp,* another baked fruit dessert with a topping of sugar, flour, and butter.

Summer Pudding. Sometimes known as Blueberry Bread Pudding, Summer Puddings are made by lining a bowl with lightly buttered bread, then pouring over hot, sweetened, lightly stewed berries—whatever kind of fresh berry is in season at that point in the summer. The dessert is then weighted and chilled and emerges tasting like the essence of summer.

Fritters. Certain fruits, like apples, bananas, and pineapple, make especially good fritters. Coated in a batter that becomes crisp when deep-fried, the interior bursts with warm, sweet juices. Morning is a grand time to eat fritters, straight from the pan, just dusted with confectioners' sugar. The fritter batter made with beer (p. 358) gives a pleasant tangy taste that goes well with fruit, but here is a slightly sweeter batter if you prefer that.

Fruit Fritters

Use peeled apples, bananas, or pineapple, cut in pieces no more than ½ inch thick.

(SERVES EIGHT TO TEN)

2 eggs	1 teaspoon baking powder
2 teaspoons granulated sugar	¼ teaspoon salt
⅔ cup (1½ dL) milk	Vegetable oil for frying
1 teaspoon salad oil	5 cups (1¼ L) fruit, in large,
1 teaspoon lemon juice	bite-size pieces
1 cup (140 g) flour	Confectioners' sugar

Beat the eggs until light. Add the granulated sugar, milk, salad oil, and lemon juice and mix until blended. Add the flour, baking powder, and salt and stir until smooth. If possible, refrigerate for an hour or so before using. Pour about 2 inches of vegetable oil into a heavy skillet and heat to 370°F. Turn the oven on to 250°F (120°C). Pat the pieces of fruit as dry as possible. Spear each piece with a fork and dip it into the batter, letting only excess batter drain back into the bowl, then lower it carefully into the hot oil. Don't overcrowd the pan: fry about 6 pieces at a time. Allow about 2 minutes until the first side is golden brown, turn with a slotted spoon, and brown the other side. Drain on paper towels, patting to absorb the excess fat. Keep finished fritters warm in the oven until all are fried. Dust with confectioners' sugar and serve.

Fruit Purées

Fruit purées, particularly made with fresh fruits, are lovely tasting and are also used as a base in soufflés and other dishes.

Fresh Fruit Purée

(¾ CUP)

½ pound (225 g) fresh fruit,
     peeled and cut in pieces
Sugar

If the fruit is hard, cook it in a little water until soft. Purée it by forcing it through a food mill or whirling it in a blender or food processor. Taste and add sugar, if necessary.

Dried Fruit Purée. Cook the dried fruit according to the directions on the package. Or measure the fruit, combine it in a pot with an equal amount of water, cover, and simmer for 10–15 minutes, until soft. Add sugar to taste, stirring to dissolve. Proceed as for Fruit Purée.

Canned Fruit Purée. Drain canned fruit and proceed as for Fruit Purée.

Cooked Fruits

See individual listings for recipes for each kind of fruit. But here are two fine recipes for canned fruits used in attractive combinations.

Hot Fruit Compote

(SERVES EIGHT)

1 can pears	1 tablespoon slivered orange peel
1 can Bing cherries	1 tablespoon brandy or rum, or
1 can whole apricots, pitted	1 teaspoon vanilla

Drain the juice from the cans. Add to the juice the slivered orange peel, and simmer gently for 30 minutes. Add the fruit and the brandy, rum, or vanilla, and heat through. Serve with *whipped cream* flavored with the same flavoring you have used in the fruit.

Other combinations:

> Peaches, plums, raisins (added to the juice for the last 10 minutes of simmering), and slivered toasted almonds scattered over the cream.
>
> Peaches, pears, apricots, and chestnuts.
>
> Plums, apricots, and cherries.
>
> Pineapple, mandarin orange sections, and black cherries.
>
> Prunes, apricots, and greengage plums.
>
> Cooked apple slices, raisins (simmered as above), and walnut halves on top of the cream.

Baked Fruit Compote

(SERVES FOUR)

2 cups (½ L) canned fruit: peaches, apricots, pears, greengage plums, cherries	Grated rind and juice of ½ lemon
2 tablespoons brown sugar	½ cup (1 dL) macaroon or other cookie crumbs

Preheat the oven to 350°F (180°C). Arrange layers of fruit in a deep baking dish, sprinkling each layer with brown sugar, lemon rind, and lemon juice. Then pour the reserved juice from the can(s) on top, sprinkle on the crumbs, and bake 35 minutes. Serve warm or cold with *cream*.

ABOUT APPLES

Availability: Height of season is late summer and fall, but many varieties available through winter and spring, even summer.

What to Look For: Firm, unblemished, bright fruit. Green does not necessarily mean sour; varieties like greenings and Granny Smiths are tart, keep well, and are good for both eating and cooking. Crabapples are small, very hard and sour, best for preserves.

Uses: Raw, for eating whole, particularly good with both soft and firm cheeses; also in fresh cut-up fruit bowls and salads. *Cooked,* baked, sautéed, stewed, frittered, and fried, especially as an accompaniment to pork, duck, and goose; baked in fruit desserts, pies, pudding, cakes. Also good in stuffings and preserves.

Amount: One per person raw; two when cooked in a compote or applesauce.

Alternatives to Fresh: Dried fruit can be tastier than canned, but some brands of canned applesauce are good. Bottled or canned juice very good if not too full of preservatives; frozen juice is fine; and, of course, freshly pressed cider excellent.

At the height of the season there is such a variety of apples available that we have an embarrassment of riches in this country. Take advantage of your local varieties and eat them raw—hard, juicy, and tart. Many regional types—like Jonathans, Northern Spys, winesaps, and Newtons—don't seem to keep well through the winter, and the ubiquitous McIntosh, Red and Yellow Delicious apples, and later greenings are what you'll find in the supermarkets most of the winter. For cooking, you need tart apples, but for a baked apple you want one that will keep its shape, so Delicious, Rome Beauty, or Cortland if you can find it, are your best bet.

Applesauce

Use a food mill for this, if you have one: you won't have to peel or core the apples if you do, and cooking them with their skins adds taste and color. Late summer and fall apples are so flavorful that they don't need spices, but apples that are kept long into winter will need some tarting up and the added smoothness of butter.

(SERVES FOUR)

8 tart apples
Sugar
½-inch cinnamon stick
  (optional)

2 cloves (optional)
2 tablespoons butter (optional)
Few gratings of nutmeg
  (optional)

Cut the apples in large chunks; pare and core them if you do not have a food mill. Put them in a pan, add a very small amount of water, about 2 tablespoons sugar, and the cinnamon and cloves, if you wish. Cover and cook slowly until tender, about 15–20 minutes. Put the apples through a food mill to remove the skins, seeds, and spices, or simply remove the spices if you have peeled and cored the apples before cooking them. Stir in the butter, if you like, and add more sugar to taste and nutmeg if desired.

Cape Cod Apple Pudding

(SERVES SIX)

4 cups (1 L) peeled and sliced
  apples
¾ cup (150 g) sugar
¼ teaspoon salt

½ teaspoon cinnamon
Baking Powder Biscuits
  (p. 490)

Put the apples, sugar, salt, cinnamon, and ¼ cup water in a 2-quart saucepan. Stir occasionally and cook until the apples are tender. Meanwhile, prepare the dough for the biscuits. Roll out and spread over the cooked apples in the pan. Cover tight and cook over moderate heat for 15 minutes. Turn into a shallow bowl and serve with *heavy cream.*

Apple Crisp

Sweet soft apples, mildly spiced, with cinnamony crisp brown crumbs on top.

(SERVES SIX)

5 cups (1¼ L) peeled and
  sliced apples
¾ cup (105 g) flour
1 cup (200 g) sugar

½ teaspoon cinnamon
¼ teaspoon salt
¼ pound (115 g) butter, in
  small pieces

Preheat the oven to 350°F (180°C). Butter a 1½-quart baking dish, spread the apples in it, and sprinkle ⅓ cup water on top. Combine the flour, sugar, cinnamon, and salt in a bowl, and rub in the butter with your fingers until it resembles coarse crumbs. Spread evenly over the apples. Bake for about 30 minutes or until the crust is browned. Serve with *heavy cream.*

Apple Brown Betty

If your apples are full of flavor, you won't need the lemon.

(SERVES SIX)

5 tablespoons melted butter
2 cups (½ L) homemade dry
   bread crumbs
5 cups (1¼ L) (about 1½
   pounds, 675 g) peeled, sliced
   tart apples

½ cup (1 dL) brown sugar
½ teaspoon cinnamon
Grated rind and juice of ½
   lemon (optional)

Preheat the oven to 350°F (180°C). Butter a 1½-quart casserole or baking dish, preferably one with a lid. Toss the melted butter and crumbs together lightly in a bowl. Spread about a third of the crumbs in the baking dish. Toss the apples, sugar, cinnamon, lemon rind, and lemon juice together in a bowl. Spread half the apple mixture over the crumbs, add another layer of crumbs, a layer of the remaining apples, and a final layer of crumbs on top. Add ⅓ cup hot water. Cover with a lid or with foil and bake for 25 minutes. Uncover and bake 20 minutes more. Serve with *heavy cream.*

Peach Brown Betty. Omit the cinnamon, and optional lemon juice and rind, and substitute *5 cups sliced peaches* for the apples.

Apricot Brown Betty. Substitute *3 cups fresh apricots* or *stewed and drained dried apricots* for the apples and use *⅓ cup stewing liquid* instead of the water.

Apple Compote

(SERVES FOUR)

1 cup (200 g) sugar
Grated rind of 1 lemon

8 tart apples, pared, cored,
   and quartered

Combine the sugar, grated lemon rind, and 1 cup water in a saucepan and simmer for 5 minutes. Add the apple pieces, a few at a time, and cook until tender enough to pierce with a toothpick. Continue to cook until all the apples are done. Strain the syrup over the apples. Serve cold.

Apple Snow

(SERVES FOUR)

4 tart apples, pared, cored, and
   sliced
3 egg whites

½–¾ cup (100–150 g) sugar
1 tablespoon lemon juice

Put the apples and ¼ cup water in a saucepan, cover, and cook over low heat for 7–10 minutes or until mushy, stirring occasionally. Mash or beat until smooth. There should be 1 cup or a bit more of thick applesauce. Beat the egg whites until foamy, then gradually add the sugar and lemon juice, beating until stiff but not dry. Fold into the applesauce and chill. Or serve warm by turning the apple snow into a buttered double-boiler top, covering, and cooking over simmering water for 30 minutes. Serve with *Soft Custard* (p. 608) or *English Custard* (p. 639).

Glazed Baked Apples

Use firm apples that will hold their shape, such as Delicious, Rome Beauty, Cortland, greening, or other hard fall apples.

(4 APPLES)

4 firm apples
½ cup (100 g) sugar

Preheat the oven to 375°F (190°C). Core the apples and pare them one-third of the way down from the stem end. Put them close together in a baking dish, peeled side up. Add ½ inch of water and bake, basting every 10 minutes or so with the pan juices, until the apples can be pierced easily with a fork but still hold their shape. Turn up the oven heat to 425°F (220°C). Sprinkle the apples with the sugar and bake until the sugar dissolves and the tops are crisp and lightly browned, about 5–10 minutes. Serve with some of the juices.

Cinnamon Apples

Cinnamon apples are a fine dessert. Try them also as a relish with roast pork.

(6 APPLES)

1 cup (200 g) sugar
2 tablespoons tiny red
    cinnamon candies

12 cloves
6 apples, pared and cored

Combine the sugar, cinnamon candies, and 1½ cups water in a saucepan and simmer for 5 minutes. Stick two cloves in each apple. Put the apples in the saucepan, cover, and cook over low heat, basting every 10 minutes until tender when pierced with a toothpick. Remove the apples from the pan and put in a dish to cool. Remove the cloves. Strain the syrup over the apples and serve warm or chilled.

ABOUT APRICOTS

Availability: June and July.
What to Look For: Small, plump, juicy, orangy-yellow fruit which should yield to slight pressure when pressed.
Uses: Raw, whole for hand-eating; in fresh fruit compotes, salads, jelly, ice cream, sherbet, and mousses. *Cooked,* in compotes, soufflés, baked, puréed, whipped. Excellent preserved in jam and as a glaze.
Amount: Three or four per person.
Alternatives to Fresh: Canned very good. Dried excellent both for cooking and just for munching.

Fresh apricots are more scarce today unless you live in the heart of rich apricot country, like Oregon and Washington, and the ones that have traveled far are apt to soften quite quickly. But when you can find plump fresh ones, take advantage and eat them raw. *To peel:* dip in boiling water, then plunge in cold, and slip off the skins with your fingers. Dried apricots today seldom need presoaking. Simply cook them gently in water to cover for about 15 minutes until just soft; they are delicious served with a dollop of sour cream or crème fraîche.

Baked Apricots. See Baked Fruit Compote (p. 649).

Apricot Brown Betty. See variation of Apple Brown Betty (p. 651).

Apricot Soufflé, hot or cold. See Cold Apricot Soufflé (p. 624) or Frozen Apricot Soufflé (p. 627).

Apricot Whip

(SERVES FOUR)

1 cup (¼ L) fresh or dried apricots	2 teaspoons lemon juice
¼ cup (50 g) sugar	⅛ teaspoon salt
	3 egg whites

To make a purée of apricots, slice the fresh apricots (you do not need to peel them) or, if using dried apricots, cook them in water to cover for about 10 minutes, then drain. Put the apricots through a food mill or purée in a blender or food processor.

Preheat the oven to 300°F (150°C). Combine the apricot purée and the sugar in a heavy-bottomed saucepan and cook over moderately low heat until thickened, stirring often to prevent sticking or burning. Remove from the heat and add the lemon juice and salt. Taste and add more sugar, if necessary. Let cool to lukewarm. Beat the whites until they are stiff but not dry. Whisk a third of the whites into the purée, then fold the mixture gently into the remaining whites. Spoon into a 1-quart soufflé dish. Set the dish in a pan of hot water and bake for about 45 minutes, or until firm to the touch. Serve warm.

Apricot Bavarian Cream

(6 CUPS)

1 envelope unflavored gelatin	1 cup (¼ L) milk
4 egg yolks	1 cup (¼ L) apricot purée
½ cup (100 g) sugar	1 cup (¼ L) heavy cream,
1 teaspoon vanilla	whipped

Dissolve gelatin in ¼ cup cold water. Beat the yolks and slowly add the sugar, until the mixture is thick and creamy; add the vanilla. Heat the milk to the boiling point, then, stirring constantly, pour it slowly over the egg mixture. Blend well, return to the saucepan, and cook over medium heat, stirring constantly, until slightly thickened. Remove from the heat and stir in the gelatin until completely dissolved. Cool and add the apricot purée. Fold in the whipped cream. Spoon into a mold. Chill at least six hours.

ABOUT BANANAS

Availability: Year round.

What to Look For: Ripe fruit should be yellow flecked with brown, firm but not
    hard. Unripe fruit will be hard and slightly green at the ends; use for
    cooking, if not too hard. Red bananas are a uniform brown-red and a little
    softer.

Uses: Raw, eaten whole or cut up with cream, on cereal, in fresh fruit compote.
    Used as a side dish with curry; also mashed in milk shakes. *Cooked,* sautéed,
    baked, or frittered.

Amount: One per person.

Alternatives to Fresh: Dried, good for munching.

Highly nutritious, bananas seem to be one of our favorite foods from babyhood
on, good for breakfast, lunch, or supper. Cut them up only just before serving
because they blacken quickly. They also ripen quickly, so don't worry if you find
only unripened ones in the market. Just leave out in a cool spot in the kitchen;
refrigerate bananas only when fully ripe, and—be forewarned—the skins will
turn black but that won't affect their taste.

Baked Bananas

(4 BANANAS)

4 tablespoons butter	4 firm ripe bananas
1 teaspoon grated lemon rind	4 tablespoons dark-brown sugar
1 tablespoon lemon juice	

Preheat the oven to 350°F (180°C). Put the butter, lemon rind, and lemon juice
in a baking dish and place it in the oven for 2–3 minutes, just long enough to
melt the butter; remove and stir. Peel the bananas and put them in the baking
dish, turning so they are coated with the butter mixture. Sprinkle the brown
sugar over them and bake for 15 minutes. Serve hot with *heavy cream.*

Baked Bananas Flambéed with Rum. Pour ¼ *cup warm rum* over the bananas
when baked and set aflame, spooning the burning liquor over the bananas.

Sautéed Bananas

This lovely dessert is also a fine accompaniment to curry or chicken
dishes.

(4 BANANAS)

4 tablespoons butter
4 firm ripe bananas
4 tablespoons confectioners' sugar

Melt the butter in a skillet. Peel the bananas and cut them in half lengthwise.
Cook over moderate heat for 5 minutes, turning once. Remove to a dish and
spoon the butter from the pan over them. Sift the confectioners' sugar on top.

ABOUT BLACKBERRIES

Height of Season: Midsummer.
What to Look For: Plump, juicy, dark berries.
Uses: Raw, as is with sugar and heavy cream, and in a fresh fruit compote.
  Cooked, in puddings, compotes, pies, and tarts. *Preserved,* in jams, jellies,
  and syrup.
Amount: Raw, ½ cup per person; cooked, ¾ cup.
Alternatives to Fresh: Frozen have good flavor. Canned acceptable in pies and
  purées.

The last of the berries of summer, blackberries can be used in all the recipes that
call for raspberries when they have vanished.

For use in a lovely bread-and-butter dessert, see Summer Pudding, (p. 656).

Blackberry Rolypoly

You may substitute any other berry for the blackberries.

(SERVES SIX)

6 cups (1½ L) blackberries
1 cup (200 g) sugar
½ teaspoon salt
1 recipe Shortcake dough
  (p. 526)

2 tablespoons butter, melted
1½ cups (3½ dL) heavy cream,
  whipped

Preheat the oven to 425°F (220°C). Butter an 8 × 10–inch pan. Combine the
berries, sugar, and salt in a bowl. Toss very gently to mix. Set aside. Roll the
shortcake dough into a rectangle ½ inch thick. Brush with the melted butter.
Spread half the berries over the dough. Roll up like a jelly roll and put into the
pan, fold side down. Put the rest of the berries around the roll. Bake for 30
minutes. Slice and serve warm or cold with whipped cream.

ABOUT BLUEBERRIES AND HUCKLEBERRIES

Availability: Midsummer for wild; from spring through fall for cultivated.
What to Look For: Blueberries are bright blue with a slightly frosted look; they
  should be firm, dry, well rounded. The cultivated berries are fatter and
  fleshier and have not the same intensity of flavor that you get in wild
  berries. Huckleberries are larger and darker and have bigger seeds.
Uses: Raw, as is or with cream and sugar, in fresh fruit compote, particularly nice
  with melon balls and/or strawberries; good in tarts. *Cooked,* in pies, muffins,
  and other baked goods, pancakes, puddings, stewed as a dessert sauce.
  Preserved, in jams.
Amount: Raw, ½ cup per person; cooked, ¾ cup.
Alternatives to Fresh: Canned and frozen acceptable for cooking; frozen better for
  use fresh but the berries will have softened somewhat.

If you are in a part of the country where blueberries grow wild, by all means get
a bucket and go out picking. It may spoil your taste for the cultivated variety,
but the treat is worth it.

Summer Pudding or Blueberry Bread Pudding

Summer puddings are made with raspberries or blackberries, too. Just use the same proportions.

(SERVES SIX)

7 thin slices white bread	3 cups (¾ L) blueberries
Soft butter	½–⅔ cup (100–125 g) sugar

Butter each slice of bread lightly and line a round 3- to 4-cup bowl with the slices, butter side out. Fill in the interstices with bread trimmed to fit so the bowl is completely covered, saving one slice for the top. Cook the blueberries with the sugar (adjusting according to how sweet the berries are) and ⅓ cup water for 10 minutes, then pour into the bread-lined bowl. Place a slice on top and fold the edges over to meet. Place a saucer on top and press down. Pour off excess liquid and serve with the pudding or reserve for a sauce or ice cream. Chill at least 6 hours before serving. Serve with *heavy cream*.

ABOUT CHERRIES

Availability: June, July, and into August.

What to Look For: Bing cherries should be deep red, large, and plump almost to bursting. Equally good and sweet but not as common are the bright reddish brown Lambert cherries. Sour cherries are smaller, paler red (and only for cooking).

Uses: Raw, whole with stems left on, or stemmed and pitted in fresh fruit compotes and in tarts. *Cooked*, in pies, in compotes, and as a sauce. Sour and wild cherries make good jellies and syrups.

Amount: ¼ pound per person.

Alternatives to Fresh: Canned and frozen both acceptable.

Cherries Jubilee

(SERVES SIX)

2 cups (½ L) fresh Bing cherries, or 1 large can black cherries	1 tablespoon cornstarch
	¼ cup (½ dL) brandy
	1 quart (1 L) vanilla ice cream
Sugar	

If using fresh cherries, stem and pit them, then cook them about 5 minutes in 1 cup water and 3 tablespoons sugar. If using canned cherries, add only 1 tablespoon sugar. Dissolve the cornstarch in 1 tablespoon water, then add 1 cup of the cherry cooking juice or of the canned juice, bring to a boil, and simmer with the cherries for 2 minutes. Heat the brandy, add to the cherries, then light and pour them flaming over the ice cream.

ABOUT COCONUTS

Availability: Year round in some areas, but primarily September through December.

What to Look For: The outside should be hard, with a brown, fibrous husk. Shake it and listen for the liquid sloshing inside; if you can't hear it, the meat,

1. *apples;* 2. *apricots;* 3. *bananas;* 4. *blackberries;* 5. *blueberries;* 6. *cherries;*
7. *cranberries;* 8. *currants;* 9. *dates;* 10. *figs;* 11. *gooseberries.*

when you open it, will be dried up. Watch out also for mold around the
eyes.

Uses: What is called the "milk" doesn't have much flavor and is at best used with
other fruits or alcohol in cool drinks. To make the "milk" that is often used
in South American cooking, grated coconut must be steeped in this interior
liquid. We use the coconut meat, grated, shredded, or flaked for cakes,
cookies, desserts, and with other fruits, particularly oranges.

Alternatives to Fresh: Vacuum-packed in cans or plastic pouches, keeps well and
tastes fine, although sweeter than fresh.

Amount: The meat of a coconut varies but an average-size coconut of about 1
pound usually yields about 2½ cups of grated coconut.

It is best to refrigerate a fresh coconut.

To extract the meat from a coconut, crack it open by putting it on the middle
rack of a preheated 425°F (220°C) oven for 15–20 minutes, until the shell has
split and cracked in several places.

Using an ice pick and hammer, deeply puncture the three eyes, turn upside
down over a bowl, and let the coconut milk drain out. (This liquid can be
strained to drink or used in cooking.) Tap the shell with the hammer until it
splits open. Or, if it is convenient, just go outside and drop it on the hard ground
or on a stone. Dislodge the white meat from the shell with a thin screwdriver
or knife, and pare off the brown covering with a vegetable peeler. Grate on a
hand grater, or in a blender or food processor. Store in an airtight container in
the refrigerator or freezer.

ABOUT CRANBERRIES

Availability: September through January.

What to Look For: The test of a good cranberry is its bounce. Good firm ones will
bounce like rubber balls.

Uses: Raw in a relish. *Cooked* in cranberry sauce, jelly, pudding, bread, pie,
punch.

Alternatives to Fresh: Frozen. Bottled juice is good and healthful.

ABOUT CURRANTS

Availability: Midsummer.

What to Look For: Small, bright red, almost translucent berries.

Uses: Raw, stemmed and generously sugared; delicious with raspberries. *Cooked*,
principally used cooked, in jellies and jams.

Alternatives to Fresh: Preserved. Dried currants are not really currants but Corinth
grapes; they look like small raisins and are used the same way.

ABOUT DATES

Availability: Year round packaged.

What to Look For: Plump, not-too-hard, sticky fruit, preferably pitted.

Uses: Plain as a snack or with cream cheese; stuffed with nuts (and sometimes
rolled in confectioners' sugar). An addition, chopped, to baked goods,
desserts, cakes, cookies. See Date Nut Cakes (p. 530) for a favorite dessert
cake.

ABOUT FIGS

Availability: Midsummer for fresh figs. Dried available year round.

What to Look For: Fresh figs can be purple or pale green. They should be a little soft and look well filled out and, when cut, pink and juicy inside. There are many varieties of dried figs—those from the Mediterranean and Middle East are particularly plump and good; sometimes they are sold packaged, sometimes in bulk in stores featuring imported foods and spices.

Uses: Raw, for eating whole or sliced with a little crème fraîche; delicious served sliced with thin pieces of country ham or prosciutto, as an appetizer. Dried stewed figs, baked goods, puddings (a lovely Steamed Fig Pudding is on p. 616).

Alternatives to Fresh: Dried as noted above, and canned.

Stewed Figs

(SERVES SIX)

1 pound (450 g) dried figs
1 cup (¼ L) sour cream or
  Soft Custard (p. 608)

Cover the figs with cold water and simmer until they are tender, about 15 minutes. Chill. Spoon into goblets with a few tablespoons of their juice and top with sour cream or Soft Custard.

ABOUT GOOSEBERRIES

Availability: Midsummer.

What to Look For: Round—the size of marbles—green, almost translucent fruit.

Uses: Cooked, in puddings and tarts, and as a sauce. *Preserved,* as a relish and in jam.

Once abundant in this country, gooseberry shrubs are now subject to stringent laws in many states because of a fungus they harbor which is destructive to pines. We almost never see fully ripened gooseberries in our markets, and the appearance of green ones is fleeting, so grab them while you can if you love their flavor. They can be stewed into a simple sauce to eat with cream or custard on top or, following British tradition, as an accompaniment to fish, particularly mackerel.

ABOUT GRAPEFRUIT

Availability: Year round, but inferior in quality and more expensive during the summer months.

What to Look For: Firm, heavy, well-filled-out fruits. A coarse, thick-skinned grapefruit, or one that narrows at the stem end, is apt to yield less juice and taste pithy. A few exterior scars don't hurt, but soft skins and dents are not good signs.

Uses: Raw, halved and scooped out, peeled and segmented as a breakfast fruit, in fresh fruit salads and compotes, jellies, ices. *Cooked,* baked, or broiled as a first course or dessert. The juice makes an excellent drink.

Amount: Half a grapefruit per person eaten whole. The juice of one grapefruit make about ⅔ cup, but yield varies considerably.

Alternatives to Fresh: Frozen concentrated juice very good; also canned—unsweetened preferred.

The juicy, almost seedless grapefruit we find today is very much a product of American enterprise of this century. Happily, we have taken to the grapefruit with enthusiasm: since the thirties, grapefruit has become almost as popular as oranges in this country, particularly among dieters.

To *prepare a grapefruit half,* use a special curved grapefruit knife to cut around each segment and loosen it from the surrounding membrane and skin. Actually a small sharp paring knife works just as well: run it around the whole circumference, then slice between the pulp and membrane on both sides of each segment. If you want to decorate the center with a strawberry or cherry or sprig of mint, cut out the core; otherwise it is not necessary.

To *extract whole grapefruit segments,* put the fruit on a cutting board. Hold it firmly with your left hand and pare off the skin with a long, very sharp knife. Cut away the white layer beneath the skin as you pare. Remove the pulp by sections, cutting it away from the membrane, first on one side of a section, then the other, see illustration for sectioning an orange, p. 665. Cut off any white bits that remain, so that you have perfect whole sections of fruit.

Grapefruit Coupe

(SERVES FOUR)

Mint sprigs
3–4 teaspoons sugar

2–3 grapefruit cut in segments,
enough to make 2 cups

Crush about 6–8 leaves of mint with the sugar and sprinkle it over the grapefruit segments. Macerate in the refrigerator for several hours. Serve in chilled sherbet glasses or goblets with a sprig of mint on top.

Grapefruit Baskets. Cut the fruit in half. Remove the pulp and scrape out the white membrane and the core. Scallop the edge with scissors, if you like. Fill with fresh fruit compote, grapefruit segments, and avocado slices or sherbet.

Baked Grapefruit

(SERVES FOUR)

2 grapefruit
2 tablespoons melted butter

2 tablespoons white or brown
sugar or honey

Preheat the oven to 450°F (230°C). Cut each grapefruit in half crosswise. With a sharp knife, cut each section to loosen the flesh from the membrane and remove any seeds. Spread the melted butter on each half. Sprinkle the sugar or honey over the tops. Bake for 15 minutes.

Broiled Grapefruit. Broil for about 5 minutes, until hot and bubbly.

ABOUT GRAPES

Availability: Summer and fall for green grapes and local varieties; late summer, fall, and winter for red dark grapes.

What to Look For: Plump, unblemished fruit of good color, firmly attached to the stems. Check around the stem area for signs of off-color and deterioration. Unripened grapes will not develop much flavor after they've been cut.

Uses: Raw, for hand-eating; stemmed, pitted, and sometimes even peeled, in fresh fruit salads and compotes; with fish; in fruit jellies and other desserts. Bottled grape juice excellent as a refreshing drink; good, too, as a flavoring in homemade ice cream. Raisins eaten raw or cooked, in baked goods, desserts, preserves.

Amount: A pound should serve three.

Alternatives to Fresh: Frozen concentrated juice, as well as the bottled, good. Raisins are dried grapes, available black and yellow; small seedless sultanas are not to be confused with currants. Both domestic and imported varieties excellent.

Cool grapes are good just by themselves. Fortunately, they have an extended season—the bright red Tokay and Cardinal grapes, then the deep red Emperors and almost black Malagas, replace the early pale green seedless Thompsons on the market. For a quite different flavor, don't miss the native Northeastern Concords when they mature in the fall—deep blue with tougher skins that slip easily off the exceptionally juicy, almost slippery flesh.

For a fancier presentation, pile seedless grapes in sherbet glasses or goblets and top with whipped cream flavored with a little kirsch, or crème fraîche with slivered toasted almonds on top.

Frosted grapes are fun at Christmastime. Simply beat an egg white until frothy, then pour over a perfect bunch of Malagas, coating each grape. Dust with granulated sugar and let dry before adding to the fruit bowl.

ABOUT KUMQUATS

Availability: Late fall and winter.

What to Look For: Small, firm fruit with a bright color (kumquats look like tiny oranges, only more oblong in shape).

Uses: Raw, for eating whole (the rind is sweet and flavorful). *Cooked,* in marmalades, jellies, candied as a condiment.

Amount: Three or four per person as dessert.

ABOUT LEMONS

Availability: Year round.

What to Look For: Heavy, firm (but not hard) fruit, bright yellow color, fairly thin skins; avoid coarse, thick-skinned lemons, which will yield little juice.

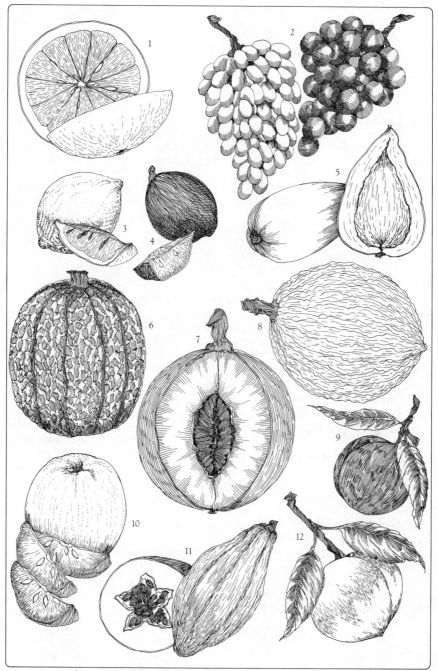

1. grapefruit; 2. grapes; 3. lemon; 4. lime; 5. mangoes; 6. cantaloupe; 7. honeydew melon; 8. cranshaw melon; 9. nectarine; 10. orange; 11. papaya; 12. peach.

Uses: Fresh slices and wedges are a much-used garnish. Lemon juice, used discreetly, is greatly valued as a seasoning to bring out natural flavors; it is useful as an aid in blanching and to prevent discoloration of certain fruits and vegetables; the juice—and often the yellow part of the skin, known as the zest—is an essential flavoring in many savory as well as sweet sauces, in marinades, desserts, baked goods, sherbets, ices, toddies, and cool refreshing drinks.

Alternatives to Fresh: Frozen concentrated juice is acceptable in baking and in drinks, but only fresh will do as a zestful flavoring. Bottled lemon juice should be avoided, as well as the kind that comes in plastic lemon-shaped containers; the taste is disagreeable and would not add real lemon flavor.

Amount: The juice of 1 lemon makes about ¼ cup, but yield varies considerably.

No good kitchen should be without a fresh lemon or two, and since they're always available and keep well, there's no reason not to have them on hand. Just a few drops can make such a difference in giving character to a bit of sauce, heightening the flavor of fruits and vegetables, bringing out the essence of fish and shellfish. The more you use lemons, the more they will reveal their secret powers. But they are perverse, too; while their high vitamin C count inhibits cut peaches, pears, bananas, avocados, and apples from turning black and blanches artichoke bottoms, Swiss chard stems, and sweetbreads, at the same time lemon juice can turn certain green vegetables, like beans and broccoli, brownish and red cabbage blue! So get to know your lemons.

One of the most amazing properties of the lemon is its effect on raw flesh, so that when fish is marinated in a lemon bath, the raw fish turns opaque after several hours and is in essence "cooked" (see recipe for Seviche, p. 123). In the same way the acidity breaks down tough fibers so that lemons are invaluable in marinades to tenderize meat.

ABOUT LIMES

Availability: Year round.

What to Look For: Full, heavy fruit with deep, bright green color and glossy skin that isn't too thick.

Uses: Fresh slices and wedges for garnish. The juice, and occasionally the grated rind, is sometimes used with fish and is particularly desirable for chilled desserts and ices, and cool drinks.

Amount: The juice of 1 lime makes less than ¼ cup but can vary.

Alternatives to Fresh: Frozen concentrated juice is fine for drinks and desserts. Bottled lime juice, used discreetly, has its own special flavor in drinks.

You can use limes in many of the ways you use lemons to blanch and to penetrate fibers because the citric acid content has the same properties (see recipe for Seviche, p. 123). But as a flavoring lime juice does impart a different taste.

ABOUT MANGOES

Availability: Midsummer. Increasingly available in our markets.

What to Look For: The skin is sometimes orange, sometimes a deep red with just a little green, and the fruit should be soft to the touch.

Uses: Raw, eaten whole; good in ice cream and ices. *Preserved,* in chutneys.

Amount: One mango per person.

A ripe, sweet mango has an indescribably delicious and refreshing taste of ginger and lemon; it should not be puckery—that means it isn't ripe. There is an art to eating a mango. Don't try to remove the seed to which the flesh clings so tenaciously. Simply cut a circle all around the fruit, then peel back the skin, and eat the flesh with a spoon, scraping it away from the pit.

ABOUT MELONS

Availability: Cantaloupes or muskmelons from May through September; casaba, July to November; Crenshaws, August and September; honeydews, July through October; watermelons, June through August. Expensive, imported varieties in winter months.

What to Look For: Ripe cantaloupes, casabas, Crenshaws, and honeydews should have lost any greenish cast and the flower end should yield slightly to pressure and should give off a pleasant melon smell (except for casabas, which have no aroma). Only a farmer with his trick of plugging a melon can judge accurately the ripeness of a watermelon before it is opened, but most markets will display a cut piece; look for firm, juicy, red-colored flesh and dark seeds.

Uses: Raw, halved, quartered, or cut in smaller slices, cut in chunks or balls in salads and fruit bowls; also for sherbets and ices. The rind of watermelon makes a fine pickle.

Individual tastes assert themselves when it comes to eating melons. Some people like to sprinkle sugar on top, some a dash of salt, and sometimes a squirt of lemon or lime will bring out sluggish natural flavor. But a really good melon requires no artful additions. A slice of juicy melon is always a welcome sight at breakfast or lunch, or as a first or last course at dinner.

Melon and ham as an appetizer is simple and delicious. Arrange peeled slices of almost any kind of ripe melon (except watermelon) with two or three very thin slices of country ham or Italian prosciutto.

For dessert a scoop of vanilla ice cream or a few tablespoons of raspberries can be nice filling the cavity of a melon. A small half cantaloupe is sometimes very pleasing filled with Port. Combinations of different kinds of melons make lovely dishes, particularly when the fruit is scooped out with a melon baller. Balls of melon are also good with blueberries and a sprinkling of kirsch and sugar.

ABOUT NECTARINES

Availability: June through September.

What to Look For: Plump fruit of a good color—orangy yellow, deepening to red in areas. When fully ripe, along the seam there will be a little softening.

Uses: Raw, whole for hand-eating; cut up in fresh fruit salads, compotes, tarts. *Cooked,* may be used in any of the desserts and preserves that call for peaches.

ABOUT ORANGES

Availability: Year round, but (except for Valencias) the quality is poor and the fruit expensive during summer months.

What to Look For: Fresh, heavy fruit with bright-looking color and skin that is not too thick and coarse, particularly if you are interested in good juicing oranges. Navel oranges (good for peeling and segmenting) and Valencias should be rich orange, but with other varieties the color is not a guide; for instance, greening is apt to occur late in the season and is not indicative of immaturity. A few scars don't matter, either. Check for discoloration around the stem end—a sign that the fruit is starting to deteriorate, which can affect the taste of the juice.

Uses: Raw, peeled and segmented for hand-eating; sliced or segmented in green salads, mixed fruit salads, and compotes, or alone as a dessert; as a flavoring in baked goods; grated peel used in both savory and sweet sauces, frostings, fillings, and dessert; juice in jellies and in sherbets and ices. *Baked*, as a quick relish.

Alternatives to Fresh: Frozen concentrated juice, good; canned not desirable. Freshly squeezed bottled juice acceptable if not kept too long.

The healthy aspect of the average American is often attributed to the amount of orange juice he drinks. Today with the easy availability of frozen concentrated juice, we are drinking even more, but there is nothing like the taste of your own freshly squeezed juice, particularly when oranges are at their peak of flavor. Treat your family to it for breakfast at least sometimes, or add some fresh juice and pulp to the pitcher of frozen to give it a lift. Eating an orange cut in half and sectioned like a grapefruit (see p. 660) is a very nice way, too, to start the morning. Try desserts like fresh orange jelly—you will revel in their goodness. Or make a coupe out of segments or slices.

To extract segments from an orange, first peel it, by starting at the top with a sharp knife and peeling around and down in a spiral, cutting close to the flesh and removing the white pith at the same time as the peel. Trim away any white bits that you missed. Then remove each section, cutting it away from the membrane, first on one side and then on the other.

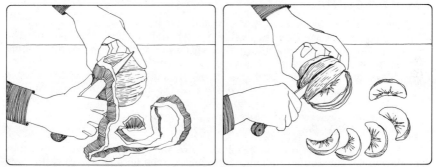

To make orange slices: Remove the peel in a spiral pattern with a sharp paring knife. Cut away any remaining bits of white. Cut ¼-inch slices, discarding the end pieces. Remove any pits.

Oranges Amandine

(SERVES FOUR)

2 cups (½ L) orange sections or slices
4 teaspoons grated maple sugar
4 tablespoons toasted slivered almonds

Sprinkle the orange sections or slices with the sugar and almonds and chill thoroughly.

Ambrosia

(SERVES SIX)

3 cups (¾ L) sliced oranges
¾ cup (1¾ dL) shredded
coconut, fresh if possible

Sprinkle the orange slices with the coconut and chill well. (Sliced bananas may be added at the last, but it is not strictly ambrosia then.)

ABOUT PAPAYAS

Availability: Usually May and June.
What to Look For: Pear-shaped fruit with smooth skin; firm but soft enough to dent slightly with a little pressure of your thumb; not too large, with good orange or yellow color.
Uses: Raw, halved and chilled, or cut up in fruit salads and fresh fruit compotes; as papaya juice.

Papaya is a tropical fruit, also known as "pawpaw." In the United States, it is grown mainly in Florida. The ripe, raw fruit has moist, juicy orange flesh and many edible black seeds. Serve it in wedges with most of the seeds removed, accompanied by a slice of lemon or lime. It is cooling on a hot summer day.

ABOUT PEACHES

Availability: Spring through fall, but especially in the summer months.
What to Look For: Green peaches will *not* ripen well at home: be sure that the peaches you buy are ripe and golden with a well-rounded shape; they should be slightly soft but without any tan or brownish spots.
Uses: Uncooked and whole for hand-eating, or sliced, with or without heavy cream, or in fruit salads. *Broiled or baked.* As a relish, pickled, brandied, spiced. In desserts, such as mousses, pies, cakes, betties, crisps, cobblers, ice cream. *Preserved*, in jellies, jams, and preserves.
Alternatives to Fresh: Frozen taste more like fresh peaches than canned.

Of the thousands of varieties of peaches, there are two general types: freestone and clingstone. Freestones are more desirable, for the flesh separates easily from the pit. Clingstones are used mainly for canning, since they hold their shape well.

To peel peaches, dip them briefly in boiling water before removing the skin with a sharp knife.

To prevent darkening in sliced peaches, sprinkle them with a little lemon juice.

To serve sliced peaches, arrange in shallow bowls, accompanied by heavy cream or whipped cream, or sprinkle them with blueberries. Or pour a sauce over them, made with sweetened, puréed strawberries and/or raspberries flavored with a few drops of lemon juice.

To bake or broil peaches, slice them in half and remove the stones. Fill the cavities with any one or a combination of the following: butter, sugar, lemon juice, a sprinkle of nutmeg, chopped nuts, raisins, a little brandy. Bake about

15–20 minutes in a 350°F (180°C) oven, or place at least 6 inches below the broiler and watch carefully.

Peach Brown Betty. See variation of recipe for Apple Brown Betty (p. 651).

ABOUT PEARS

Availability: Some varieties like Bartlett available in August and fall; others like Anjou, Bosc, and Comice are around through the winter.

What to Look For: Firm fruit with no bad spots; color will vary according to the variety. Most pears you buy will need several days' ripening.

Uses: Raw, whole for hand-eating, cut into tart green salads and mixed with other fruits in salads and compotes. *Cooked,* stewed, baked, in tarts. *Preserved,* spiced.

Alternatives to Fresh: Canned pears are not as good as fresh, but they are all right in a pinch.

There are literally thousands of varieties of pears that come in a great range of colors: yellow, gold, green, brown. Bartlett, Anjou, Bosc, and Seckel are among the most familiar.

Pears are particularly good with cheese—a firm cheese like aged Cheddar, a soft cheese like Brie or Camembert, or a good Roquefort; serve them with one kind or a selection for dessert. They are also good as a salad peeled, halved, and cored with a ball of cream cheese inside and on a bed of lettuce.

Pears with Chocolate Sauce

Peel pears, cut them in quarters lengthwise, and remove the cores. Sauté them in butter until tender and golden brown. Serve warm with Creamy Chocolate Sauce (p. 639).

Stewed or Baked Pears

(SERVES FOUR)

4 firm pears	Heavy cream or Soft Custard
½ cup (100 g) sugar	(p. 608)
Lemon rind or cinnamon stick	

Peel the pears, cut them in quarters lengthwise, and remove the cores. Combine the sugar with ½ cup water and some lemon rind or cinnamon stick; cook rapidly for 5 minutes. Add the pears, cover, and cook slowly until tender but still firm; or bake in a 300°F (150°C) oven. Serve warm or cold with cream or custard.

Pears with Cointreau. When pears are cooked, remove them from the syrup and cook the syrup until it is as thick as honey. Add *1 tablespoon Cointreau,* pour over the pears, and chill. Serve with cream.

Pears in Port Wine. Pour *Port wine* over the cooked pears, cover, and let sit for at least 1 hour.

Pears Helene. When pears are cooked, add *vanilla or brandy* to taste and let cool in the syrup. Serve with *vanilla ice cream* and top with *Creamy Chocolate Sauce* (p. 639).

ABOUT PERSIMMONS

Availability: October through December.
What to Look For: Deep orange or red color with green cap intact and no signs of damage. Persimmons will ripen at room temperature. When ripe, they should be quite soft, with some slight resistance.
Uses: Raw, in fruit salads. *Cooked* and puréed, in cakes.

Persimmons are very bitter when not ripe, sweet and delicious when fully ripened. Serve them chilled and cut in half.

ABOUT PINEAPPLES

Availability: Year round, especially in the spring.
What to Look For: Large, heavy, sweet-smelling fruit with no soft spots and healthy-looking leaves (leaves pulling out easily is *not* a sign of ripeness). Moreover, pineapples will *not* ripen further after they've been picked.
Uses: Raw, in wedges, chunks, in salad. *Cooked*, in desserts, cakes, cookies, pies, breads; as juice; in sauces; pickled, spiced; as a garnish for ham and other pork dishes.
Amount: A 2-pound pineapple yields 2½ to 3 cups diced fruit.
Alternatives to Fresh: Canned pineapple comes packed in sweet syrup or unsweetened and packed in water.

An interesting fact about pineapple is that if it is used fresh with gelatin, the gelatin will not jell because pineapple contains an enzyme that destroys its jelling power. However, canned pineapple works perfectly well.

For large slices of pineapple, hold the fruit upright and pare with a sharp knife, then dig out the "eyes." Cut in long slices.

To dice a pineapple, cut off the crown. Then cut crosswise in 1- to 2-inch slices. Cut off the rind and the "eyes" and remove the core. Then cut into cubes. Or use the same method, as for Quartered Pineapples, opposite, simply scooping the fruit out instead of leaving it on the shell; this is by far the easiest method, although you may not get quite as much fruit.

To shred a pineapple, hold upright, pare, and remove the "eyes." Shred the pulp with the tines of a fork.

Pineapple in the Shell. Without paring or removing the top leaves, cut the pineapple lengthwise into halves. Cut the flesh from the rind either in one piece or in chunks. Then remove the core, scraping out any flesh under the core. Slice or chop all the pieces and arrange on the shell. Sprinkle with *sugar, kirsch,* or *white wine* and garnish with *fresh cherries, strawberries, raspberries,* or *sprigs of mint.*

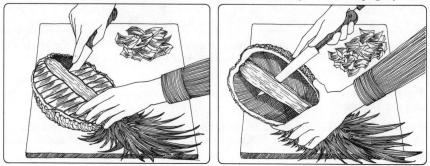

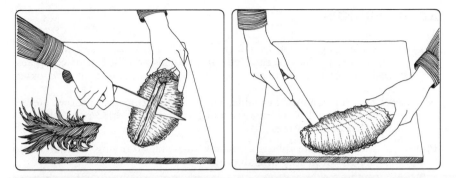

Quartered Pineapple on the Shell. Remove the top leaves, unless you want to keep them on for display. Cut the pineapple lengthwise into quarters. Cut out the core, then slice lengthwise down the center, going through just to the skin. Run the knife under the flesh along the skin to loosen it on both sides. Then cut the loosened strip on each side into bite-size pieces. Serve one quarter per person, or put the quartered shells in a fruit bowl with other fresh fruits, spearing each loosened chunk with a toothpick.

ABOUT PLUMS

Height of Season: July and August.

What to Look For: Plump fruit with good color, slightly soft but with smooth, unshriveled skins. Don't necessarily fall for very large fat plums—their flavor can be bland and watery.

Uses: Raw and whole for hand-eating, sliced in salads and fresh fruit compotes, and over ice cream. *Cooked*, in breads, cakes, pies, puddings, jellies, jams, and preserves.

Alternatives to Fresh: Canned, cooked plums are satisfactory in most cooked dishes.

Plums come in many color combinations—purple, red, blue, yellow, green—and may be round or oval in shape. Familiar varieties are red-skinned Santa Rosas, large purply-blue Presidents, tiny blue Damsons, and sweet small yellowy-red sugarplums, later greengages and Kelseys. See also About Prunes (p. 670).

To stew plums, cover them with just enough water to keep them from burning and cook gently until soft, about 10 minutes. Add *sugar* to taste and serve with the juices poured over them. If desired, sprinkle with a little *brandy* and serve over *vanilla ice cream.*

ABOUT POMEGRANATES

Height of Season: Fall.

What to Look For: Fruit about the size of an apple, with good color, not too dry looking.

Uses: Cut and eat raw; use seeds as a garnish for salads.

An exotic, refreshing, wonderful-looking fruit. Suck the seed coverings, chew or spit out the seeds, drink the juice, eat the crimson flesh—and wear old clothes: it's a delightfully messy experience.

ABOUT PRUNES

Availability: Summer and fall.

What to Look For: Slightly soft fruit with deep blue-black color, smooth skin.

Uses: Raw, whole, for hand-eating, cut up in salads and fresh fruit compotes, stewed, in compotes; as juice. *Dried and cooked*, in cakes, muffins, cookies, pies, and whips.

Alternatives to Fresh: Canned available, but it is easy to make your own stewed prunes, which will be more tasty and less limp, and dried prunes have so many other delicious uses.

Prunes are a form of plum that is especially adaptable to drying. In the United States they are grown mainly in California.

To *stew dried prunes*, put them in a pot with just enough water to cover and simmer gently until they are plump and tender. Serve in their own juices, with *heavy cream*, if desired.

To *purée dried prunes*, stew them, remove the pits and put the prunes through a food mill, or purée them in a blender or food processor.

Prune Whip

Prune whip was a frequent visitor to nineteenth- and early-twentieth-century tables.

(SERVES FOUR)

1 cup (¼ L) puréed fresh or dried prunes (see above)
¼ cup (50 g) sugar

1 tablespoon lemon juice
⅛ teaspoon salt
3 egg whites

Preheat the oven to 300°F (150°C). Combine the prune purée and the sugar in a heavy-bottomed saucepan and cook over moderate heat until thickened, stirring frequently. Remove from the heat and add the lemon juice and the salt. Taste and add more sugar, if necessary. Let cool to lukewarm. Beat the whites until they are stiff but not dry. Whisk a third of the whites into the purée mixture and then fold the mixture gently into the remaining whites. Spoon into a 1-quart soufflé dish. Set the dish in a pan of hot water and bake for about 45 minutes, or until firm to the touch. Serve warm.

ABOUT QUINCES

Availability: Occasionally in specialty stores (unless you know someone with a quince tree).

What to Look For: Firm fruit with a deep yellow color. Don't worry if they are a bit gnarled.

Uses: Mainly in jellies and preserves—quinces have lots of natural pectin.

Baked Quinces

Quinces
Sugar
Sliced oranges

Preheat the oven to 300°F (150°C). Peel the quinces, cut them in quarters, and remove the cores. Arrange them in a casserole and sprinkle them with sugar, allowing 2 tablespoons for each quince. Cover with water by ½ inch. Add some sliced oranges, 1 orange for every 4 quinces. Bake about 2 hours, until tender. Serve cold.

ABOUT RASPBERRIES

Height of Season: June and July.
What to Look For: Fresh, clean berries with good color, no green spots or signs of mold or wetness. Stains on the container may indicate spoilage.
Uses: Raw with heavy cream, with sugar, in fresh fruit salads, and compotes, in ice cream, mousses, sherbets. *Cooked,* in pies, tarts, puddings, soufflés, cakes, pancakes; as juice; puréed, in syrups and sauces; preserved, in jams and jellies.
Amount: One pint serves three.
Alternatives to Fresh: Frozen in dry-pack form is better than frozen in syrup.

ABOUT RHUBARB

Availability: January through June.
What to Look For: Firm, thick, bright reddish stalks, fairly thick and not fibrous.
Uses: Cooked, in pies, often with strawberries; as a stewed fruit, sometimes with apples; makes a good cold soufflé, see p. 624.
Amount: One pound produces about 2 cups of cooked rhubarb.

Do not eat the leaves of rhubarb: they are poisonous. Though used as a fruit, rhubarb is really a vegetable, belonging to the sorrel family.

Baked Rhubarb

(SERVES FOUR)

1 pound (450 g) rhubarb stalks
½ cup (100 g) sugar

Preheat the oven to 350°F (180°C). Wash the rhubarb and cut off the leaves and the stem ends. Don't peel it unless it is very tough. Cut in 1-inch pieces. Put the rhubarb in a casserole and sprinkle the sugar over it. Cover and bake for about 25 minutes, adding more sugar if the rhubarb is too tart.

Stewed Rhubarb

(SERVES FOUR)

1 pound (450 g) rhubarb stalks
½ cup (100 g) sugar
1 teaspoon grated lemon rind

Wash and trim the rhubarb, peeling it if it is tough. Cut into 1-inch pieces and put in a heavy-bottomed saucepan. Add the sugar, lemon rind, and ¼ cup water, cover, and cook gently for 5–7 minutes.

Rhubarb Betty

2 pounds (900 g) trimmed
　rhubarb stalks, in 2-inch
　pieces
1½ cups (300 g) sugar

2½ cups (6 dL) homemade dry
　bread crumbs
6 tablespoons butter, melted

Preheat the oven to 350°F (180°C). Place the rhubarb in a saucepan with the sugar and ¼ cup water, cover, and cook until tender, about 7 minutes. Set aside ⅓ cup of the rhubarb syrup. Put the bread crumbs in a bowl with the melted butter and toss. Place half the crumbs in the bottom of a baking dish. Arrange the rhubarb on top of the crumbs and pour the syrup over it. Top with the remaining crumbs. Bake about 40 minutes, covering with foil if the crumbs begin to get too brown. Serve with *whipped cream,* if you wish.

ABOUT STRAWBERRIES

Availability: Hothouse variety most of the year, but peak of the season in May and
　June.
What to Look For: Bright, red, shiny, well-formed berries, with no signs of mold
　or wetness. Stains on the container may indicate spoilage.
Uses: Raw, dipped in or sprinkled with sugar, or served with heavy cream,
　whipped cream, sour cream, or yogurt: in fresh fruit salads and compotes;
　with cereals. *Cooked,* in pies, tarts, shortcakes; puréed, in syrups and sauces,
　mousses, ice cream; as juice; preserved, in jellies, jams, and preserves.
Amount: One quart serves four to five.
Alternatives to Fresh: Frozen in dry-pack form is better than frozen in syrups, but
　only for cooking purposes.

Wash strawberries, if necessary, in cold water; hull them after washing so they don't get soggy unless you want to serve them unhulled in a fruit bowl or to dip in sugar. Wash and sugar berries shortly before eating, so they do not soften.

Strawberries in Sherry Cream

Sherry cream has a caramel flavor and a slightly golden color. It is exceptionally good with strawberries.

5 egg yolks
1 cup (200 g) sugar
1 cup (¼ L) sherry

1 cup (¼ L) heavy cream
6 cups (1½ L) strawberries,
　washed and hulled

Put the egg yolks in a heavy-bottomed pan over low heat or in a double boiler over hot water. Beat with a whisk or electric mixer until thick and pale. Beat in the sugar and sherry. Cook over low heat, stirring constantly, until thickened, about 7–8 minutes. Remove from the heat and let cool. Just before serving, whip the cream and fold it and the strawberries into the cooled egg yolks.

1. *pears*; 2. *persimmon*; 3. *pineapple*; 4. *pomegranate*; 5. *plums*; 6. *prunes*;
7. *pumpkin*; 8. *quince*; 9. *raspberry*; 10. *rhubarb*; 11. *strawberries*; 12. *tangerine*;
13. *watermelon*.

Strawberries Romanoff

(SERVES EIGHT)

1 pint (½ L) vanilla ice cream
1 cup (¼ L) heavy cream
Juice of 1 lemon

4 tablespoons Cointreau
2 quarts (2 L) strawberries,
   washed and hulled

Put the ice cream in a 2-quart bowl and beat lightly to soften. Whip the cream until soft peaks form. Fold the cream, lemon juice, and Cointreau into the ice cream. Add the strawberries and stir gently. Serve immediately.

ABOUT TANGERINES

Height of Season: Winter months.
What to Look For: Heavy-feeling fruit with a deep orange color and a nice sheen. The skin, which should be unblemished, peels very easily, which is why it seems less firm than an orange skin.
Uses: Peeled and sectioned, with ice cream and other simple desserts; cut up into fruit salads.

ABOUT WATERMELONS

Availability: May through September, but especially in the summer.
What to Look For: A firm, well-shaped melon; one side will be light-colored from resting on the soil. A cut watermelon is easier to judge for quality: it should have juicy, deep-pink flesh with no white streaks, and the seeds should be dark and shiny.
Uses: Raw, in wedges or in fresh fruit salads and compotes. The white rind is often pickled and used as a relish.
Amount: Watermelons vary greatly in size and can be bought in sections by the pound. Be generous in serving: watermelon is 92 percent water, to say nothing of all the seeds.

For watermelon cocktail, cut the pink part of the melon into cubes or balls and remove the seeds. Sprinkle with a little lemon juice and chill. Serve alone or combined with other kinds of melon balls.

CANDIES &
CONFECTIONS

ABOUT MAKING CANDY

There is no reason except pure pleasure to make candy. A gift of homemade candy, made from real cream, butter, fresh nuts, and rich chocolate, is a rare and wonderful surprise. A lively family can finish off a batch in a day. Everyone enjoys being offered a small rich sweet; it's a lovely indulgence at the end of a good meal.

Making candy is as exacting as it is fun, as much chemistry as it is cooking. The basic requirements are strict attention and a few good tools. Don't be discouraged by tales of failure. Too many novice candymakers have been disappointed by inadequate directions.

Kinds of Candy

Candy is simply sugar, liquid, and flavoring that are melted together and heated to a high enough temperature to solidify. The degree to which the syrup is heated dictates the final consistency of the candy; the higher the heat, the harder the candy.

Between certain stages (234° to 240°F) the sugar syrup solidifies but the candy remains creamy. The best example of this category is fudge. (Not necessarily chocolate!—it's a generic term, meaning a soft, creamy candy.) A bit higher up the scale (242° to 268°F), candy becomes firm and chewy; caramels and taffy belong in this group. And at very high heats (270° to 310°F), a great deal of moisture is evaporated with a resulting hard and brittle candy, like crunchy toffee or nut brittles.

Then, of course, there are confections, uncooked as well as cooked little delicacies, usually made of fruit or nuts. These have the added appeal of often being quick to prepare—a bonus for the sweet tooth in a hurry.

Conditions for Candymaking

Since humidity sometimes causes candy to sugar and soften, it's better to make it on a cold clear day. If humidity is a factor, let some of the moisture evaporate by cooking the candy syrup to two degrees higher than specified.

Candy cooks faster at high altitudes; for each 500 feet above sea level cook the syrup one degree less than the recipe specifies.

Equipment

For cooking, a heavy, deep, straight-sided pot helps keep the candy from burning and the cook from being burned. Pots made of copper or enameled cast iron are particularly good. Use a pot that is about fourtimes greater in volume than the dissolved ingredients, because the candy will boil up dramatically as it cooks. A 4-quart saucepan with a cover is a good all-purpose size.

For stirring, use a sturdy wooden spoon with a long handle; a metal-handled spoon can get too hot. A spoon with a flattened tip will pick up all the syrup from the bottom of the pot.

For spading, turning, and spreading, procedures used for fondant, nougat, and brittles respectively, a heavy-duty metal spatula—a pancake turner—is an all-purpose tool.

For testing, an accurate candy thermometer is almost indispensable. At certain stages each degree is crucial, and a thermometer will let you know the exact state of the syrup.

For cooling to the pouring stage, a marble surface will absorb the heat of the cooking pan quickly and evenly, but it is not essential—the pan can be elevated on a cake rack or set on a thick mat.

To become firm, candy should be poured out of the cooking pan onto a cooling surface. This can be any heat-absorbent surface: a cookie sheet, a platter, or a pastry marble. You can use a baking pan, which will give you neat edges and contain the candy, thus making it thicker, if you want it that way. But there is no need to be rigid about sizes, and any flat surface will do. Most candy solidifies quickly when it is poured out to cool, and there is little danger of its spreading too thin. However, if you are uncertain, and fear that the hot candy mixture might spread, play safe and use a pan with sides; that is why we are recommending a jelly-roll pan.

Ingredients

Use only butter for candymaking. It imparts its own good taste. Use mineral oil or flavorless cooking oils for greasing the pan. They won't become rancid if the candy is stored for a long time.

Setting Up

Because everything happens so quickly in candymaking, it is essential to have all equipment immediately at hand. Put a large platter right by the stove to hold the candy spoon, thermometer or testing spoon, cup of cold water, pastry brush, and a small plate for catching drips. Oil the cooling pan in advance. Have a rack or cooling surface nearby and all ingredients prepared and waiting.

Cooking Candy Syrups

Testing. The concentration of the sugar syrup—the degree to which the syrup is heated—can be measured with a thermometer or by eye and hand, using the cold-water test.

Because the temperature may change rapidly, it is important to gauge constantly, watching the candy syrup vigilantly as it cooks. There is some tolerance within each stage, but if the syrup should go a few degrees above the highest point, add 3–4 tablespoons of cold water or more, if needed, to coax the temperature back down again, then let it cook to the proper degree.

Thermometer Test. Buy a heavy-gauge thermometer that registers to 320°F and test its accuracy by immersing it in a pan of water, bringing the water to the boiling point and letting it boil for 10 minutes. It should read 212°F at sea level, one degree less for every 500 feet above sea level.

When using a thermometer for candy testing, warm it up gradually so it doesn't crack: hold it under increasingly hot water, or put it in the candy pan at the very beginning, making sure that the bulb is completely immersed without touching the bottom or sides of the pan. Attach the thermometer by its clip, or prop it at a slight angle on the side of the pan. Stir around it, but don't move it in and out, as this might cause sugaring (see below). Remove it quickly from the finished syrup, holding it over a small plate so any lingering sugar crystals don't fall back into the pan.

Cold-Water Test. The concentration of the candy syrup can be tested in cold water, although the reading will not be as exact. Remove the pan of cooking syrup from the heat for each test. Spoon out ½ teaspoon of the syrup, drop it into a cup of cold fresh water, and work it with your fingers for a few seconds to determine the stage.

Stages for Candy Syrup

Stage	On a Thermometer	In Cold Water	Examples
Soft Ball	234°–240°F	Makes a soft ball which does not hold its shape; flattens when held in the fingers.	Fudge Fondant Pralines
Firm Ball	242°–248°F	Makes a firm ball which holds its shape.	Caramels
Hard Ball	250°–268°F	Makes a hard but pliable ball.	Taffy
Soft Crack	270°–288°F	Makes hard separate threads that bend when removed from water.	Butterscotch
Hard Crack	290°–310°F	Makes brittle threads that remain brittle out of water.	Nut Brittles Candy Apples Lollipops

Sugaring. Sugar crystals, the bane of every candy cook, are bits of undissolved sugar which cause candy to "sugar" and become grainy. Even one recalcitrant crystal can turn a velvety mixture into a granular mass. Some recipes call for corn syrup and cream of tartar as partial insurance against sugaring, but careful cooking is the best precaution.

Preventing Sugar Crystals. Before heating, stir all the ingredients together so they dissolve as much as possible.

When the syrup boils, cover the pan and let it boil for 2–3 minutes; the rising steam will wash down the sides of the pan. Uncover and proceed.

Have ready a cup of cold water and a clean pastry brush, preferably one kept specifically for this purpose. As the syrup boils, dip the brush liberally

in the water and thoroughly wash down the sides of the pot so that any remaining undissolved crystals go back into the syrup. The extra water will simply boil away.

After the boiling point has been reached, it is ideal not to interrupt the heating syrup by stirring, but this is not always possible. Candies made with milk, butter, and chocolate are sometimes stirred slowly to prevent scorching, and brittles and other highly heated candies must be stirred, albeit briefly, if they start to burn. Always stir slowly and in one continuous direction, and, to avoid picking up sugar crystals, don't touch the sides of the pot with the spoon.

Cooling Candy

If the candy is to be beaten or stirred after it has cooled, let it rest, undisturbed, until it is lukewarm (about 110°F); the bottom of the pot will be cool enough to touch. Be patient! This may take half an hour or longer.

Set the pot on a cooling rack or heat-absorbent surface or, for faster results, immediately set it in a pan of ice water. Don't stir. When the syrup has cooled, beat or stir without stopping until it has thickened and lost its gloss.

When pouring hot syrup from the pot, use only what pours easily, leaving the thick residue in the bottom of the pot. This thick mass may have cooked more than the free-flowing candy and could turn the whole batch granular.

Some candies are better in flavor and texture if they age overnight. Often candies that aren't creamy at first will become so after setting for eight hours or so. Professionals call this the "relaxing" of the sugar syrup.

Cleaning Up

Most pots and implements will wash clean after a preliminary soaking, but any hard brittle can easily be removed by filling the pan with water, putting in the utensils, putting it back on the stove, and letting the water simmer until the residue has dissolved.

Storing Candies

All candy should be stored airtight. For creamy candy this keeps the moisture in; for brittle candy it keeps the moisture out. For special occasions or gifts, pieces of candy can be individually wrapped in foil or plastic wrap, but for everyday storage, candy keeps very well between layers of wax paper in metal, plastic, or glass containers. It's best to use tins for brittle candies; plastic can absorb too much moisture.

In general, the harder the candy the longer it will stay fresh at room temperature. Brittles can be stored for two weeks or longer. Caramels, wrapped individually and stored in a tin, will stay fresh for a week or more. Even creamy candies should not be refrigerated unless the weather is very hot. Humid weather can affect both hard and soft candies, causing them to "melt" or become sticky, and in very hot weather all kinds of candy should be kept in the refrigerator.

Wrapped airtight, candy can be frozen. Although creamy candy, particularly chocolate, will sometimes lose its "bloom," the taste will not be affected. To keep the moisture in, defrost creamy candy still sealed in its package, either in the refrigerator or at room temperature.

BASIC CANDIES

Chocolate Fudge

Old-fashioned basic fudge, smooth and chocolaty.

(1½ POUNDS)

2 ounces (60 g) unsweetened chocolate, in small pieces, or 4 tablespoons unsweetened cocoa
2 cups (400 g) sugar

¾ cup (1¾ dL) milk
2 tablespoons light corn syrup
2 tablespoons butter, in small pieces
2 teaspoons vanilla

Oil a jelly-roll pan or an 8 × 8–inch pan. Combine the chocolate or cocoa, sugar, milk, and corn syrup in a 3-quart heavy pot, stirring to blend all the ingredients. Set over low heat and, stirring slowly, bring to a boil. Cover the pot and let boil for 2–3 minutes. Uncover and wash down the sides of the pot with a pastry brush dipped in cold water, then continue to boil slowly, without stirring, until the syrup reaches the soft-ball stage (234°F). Remove from the heat, add the butter without stirring, and set the pot on a cooling surface or rack. Do not stir until the syrup is lukewarm (110°F), then add the vanilla and stir without stopping until the mixture loses its gloss and thickens. Pour it into the oiled pan and mark into squares. When firm, cut into pieces and store airtight.

Chocolate Sour-Cream Fudge. Substitute ¾ *cup plus 2 tablespoons sour cream* for the milk and butter.

Chocolate Nut Fudge. Stir in *1 cup chopped nuts* before turning the candy out of the pot.

Chocolate Marshmallow Fudge. Add *1½ cups small marshmallows* before turning the candy out of the pot.

Twenty-Minute Fudge

An uncooked fudge with a deep chocolate taste.

(1½ POUNDS)

1 egg, well beaten
3 tablespoons heavy cream
2 teaspoons vanilla
1 pound (450 g) confectioners' sugar, sifted

¼ teaspoon salt
4 ounces (115 g) unsweetened chocolate
1 tablespoon butter
1 cup (¼ L) chopped walnuts

Oil a jelly-roll pan or an 8 × 8–inch pan. In a large bowl, combine the egg, cream, vanilla, confectioners' sugar, and salt and mix until well blended. Melt the chocolate and butter together over low heat in a small heavy-bottomed pan. Cool a little, then add to the sugar mixture, stirring vigorously to blend. Stir in the walnuts and spread in the oiled pan. Cut into squares when firm and store airtight.

Million-Dollar Fudge

A very fast, very easy method, resulting in a fine, creamy fudge.

(2 POUNDS)

12 ounces (340 g) semisweet
  chocolate bits, or squares, in
  small pieces
1 cup (¼ L) marshmallow
  cream
2 cups (400 g) sugar

2 tablespoons butter
¾ cup (1¾ dL) evaporated
  milk
⅛ teaspoon salt
1 teaspoon vanilla
1 cup (¼ L) chopped nuts

Oil a jelly-roll pan or a 9 × 9–inch pan. Combine the chocolate and the marshmallow cream in a large bowl and set aside. Mix the sugar, butter, and milk in a 3-quart heavy pot, stirring to combine well. Gradually bring to a boil over low heat, stirring until the sugar dissolves. Dip a pastry brush in cold water and wash down the sides of the pot. Continue to boil, stirring constantly without touching the sides of the pot, for 5 minutes, then pour the mixture over the chocolate mixture and add the salt and vanilla. Stir until the chocolate melts and the mixture is smooth, then stir in the nuts. Spread on the cookie sheet or pan and let stand until firm. Cut into squares and store airtight.

Opera Fudge

A cream-colored, vanilla-flavored fudge. For the best flavor, let it mellow overnight.

(1 POUND)

2 cups (400 g) sugar
1 cup (¼ L) heavy cream

⅛ teaspoon salt
1 teaspoon vanilla

Oil a jelly-roll pan or 8 × 8–inch pan. Combine the sugar, cream, and salt in a 3-quart heavy pot, stirring to blend well. Place over medium heat and, stirring, bring to a boil. Cover and let boil for 2–3 minutes. Uncover and wash down the sides of the pot with a pastry brush dipped in cold water. Continue to boil over medium heat, without stirring, until the syrup reaches the soft-ball stage (234°F). Remove the pot to a cooling surface or rack and, without stirring, let cool to lukewarm (110°F). Add the vanilla, stir until creamy, then spread in the oiled pan. To keep it creamy, cover the top of the candy with a damp cloth or paper towels for 30 minutes. Uncover, let it set until firm, then cut into squares and store airtight.

Peanut Butter Fudge

A firm fudge, rich in peanut butter flavor.

(1 POUND)

2 cups (400 g) sugar
⅛ teaspoon salt
¾ cup (1¾ dL) milk or cream

2 tablespoons light corn syrup
¼ cup (½ dL) peanut butter
1 teaspoon vanilla

Oil a jelly-roll pan or 8 × 8–inch pan. Combine the sugar, salt, milk or cream, and corn syrup in a heavy 3-quart pot, stirring to mix well. Stir over medium heat until it boils, then cover and let boil for 2–3 minutes. Uncover and wash down the sides of the pot with a pastry brush dipped in cold water. Continue to boil over medium heat, without stirring, to the soft-ball stage (234°F). Put the pot on a cooling surface or rack and, without stirring, let the syrup cool to lukewarm (110°F). Mix in the peanut butter and vanilla, stirring until thickened. Spread in the oiled pan. Cut into squares when firm, and store airtight.

Marshmallow Peanut Butter Fudge

The marshmallow cream lightens both the texture and the taste.

(2 POUNDS)

2 cups (400 g) sugar
⅔ cup (1½ dL) milk
1 cup (¼ L) marshmallow
  cream

1 cup (¼ L) peanut butter
2 teaspoons vanilla

Oil a jelly-roll pan or a 9 × 9–inch pan. Combine the sugar and milk in a 3-quart heavy pot. Stir to mix well and place over moderate heat. Bring to a boil, stirring until the sugar dissolves, then cover and let boil for 2–3 minutes. Uncover and wash down the sides of the pot with a pastry brush dipped in cold water. Continue to boil over medium heat, without stirring, to the soft-ball stage (234°F). Remove from the heat and stir in the marshmallow cream, peanut butter, and vanilla. Mix well and spread in the oiled pan. Cool and cut into squares. Store airtight.

Pecan Penuche

Penuche is firmer than classic fudge, but because of its deep sweet flavor, it's often called "brown sugar fudge."

(1½ POUNDS)

2 cups (½ L) firmly packed
  dark-brown sugar
¾ cup (1¾ dL) milk
⅛ teaspoon salt
2½ tablespoons butter, in small
  pieces

1 teaspoon vanilla
¾ cup (1¾ dL) chopped
  pecans

Oil a jelly-roll pan or an 8 × 8–inch pan. Combine the sugar, milk, and salt in a 3-quart heavy pot, stirring to mix well. Place over medium heat and bring to a boil, stirring constantly until the sugar dissolves. Cover and let boil for 2–3 minutes. Uncover, and wash down the sides of the pot with a pastry brush dipped in cold water. Continue to boil over medium heat to the firm-ball stage (244°F), stirring only if it starts to burn. Remove from the heat and immediately place the pot into a larger pan filled with cold water; this will stop the cooking process and bring the temperature down. Drop in the butter and let cool slightly, without stirring. Beat until it starts to thicken, add the vanilla and the pecans, and continue to beat until the candy loses some of its gloss. Spread evenly in the pan and mark into squares. When firm, cut into pieces and store airtight.

Chantilly Cream Squares

A creamy candy, soft and delicate.

(2 POUNDS)

2 cups (400 g) sugar
¾ cup (1¾ dL) heavy cream
1 cup (¼ L) milk
2 tablespoons light corn syrup

⅛ teaspoon salt
1 teaspoon vanilla
1 cup (¼ L) chopped nuts

Oil a jelly-roll pan or an 8 × 8–inch pan. Combine the sugar, cream, milk, corn syrup, and salt in a 4-quart heavy pot, stirring to mix well. Bring to a boil over moderately low heat, stirring slowly. Cover and let boil for 2–3 minutes. Uncover and wash down the sides of the pot with a pastry brush dipped in cold water. Continue to boil slowly, without stirring, to the soft-ball stage (234°F). Remove from the heat, cool slightly, and stir in the vanilla. Beat until it starts to thicken, then stir in the nuts and spread in the oiled pan. When firm, cut into squares and store airtight.

Maple Pralines

Pecans are especially good in this candy.

(1½ POUNDS)

2 cups (½ L) confectioners'
   sugar
1 cup (¼ L) maple sugar or
   maple syrup

½ cup (1 dL) heavy cream
2 cups (½ L) large pieces of
   nuts

Combine the confectioners' sugar, maple sugar or syrup, and cream in a 3-quart heavy pot, stirring to blend well. Bring to a boil over medium heat, stirring constantly until the sugar dissolves. Cover and let boil for 2–3 minutes, then uncover and wash down the sides of the pot with a pastry brush dipped in cold water. Without stirring, boil to the soft-ball stage (234°F). Remove from the heat to a cooling surface and let stand, without stirring, until lukewarm (110°F). Beat with a wooden spoon until it starts to thicken and becomes cloudy, then beat in the nuts. Using two metal tablespoons, scoop up the mixture and drop small patties onto a sheet of wax paper. Let stand until firm, then store airtight.

Caramels

Lovely, classic, chewy caramels. Take care that the easily scorched syrup doesn't burn or become granular: stir it continuously over medium-low heat, without touching the sides of the pan. Light cream is called for but you can as easily use half-and-half or ¾ cup milk mixed with ¾ cup heavy cream.

(1 POUND)

1 cup (200 g) sugar
⅔ cup (1½ dL) corn syrup

1½ cups (3½ dL) light cream
1 teaspoon vanilla

Oil a jelly-roll pan or an 8 × 8–inch pan. Put the sugar, corn syrup, and ½ cup of light cream or milk-and-cream combination in a 3-quart heavy pot. Stir until well mixed, then bring to a boil, stirring over medium-low heat until the sugar dissolves. Cover and let boil for 2–3 minutes. Uncover and wash down the sides of the pot with a pastry brush dipped in cold water. Continue to boil over medium-low heat, stirring gently without touching the sides of the pot with the spoon. When the syrup reaches the soft-ball stage (234°F), slowly, without breaking the boil, stir in another ½ cup of light cream. Continue to boil, stirring constantly until the soft-ball stage (234°F) is again reached, then slowly add, without breaking the boil, the remaining ½ cup light cream. Keep it boiling gently, stirring constantly, to the firm-ball stage (244°F). Remove from the heat and stir in the vanilla. Turn into the oiled pan, spreading a layer about ¾ inch deep. Mark into squares and let stand until cool. When firm, cut with a sharp knife into pieces and wrap each piece in plastic wrap or wax paper. Store airtight in a cool place.

Mr. B's Caramels

Mr. B's secret is the honey.

(2½ POUNDS)

1¼ cups (3 dL) light corn syrup	1 tablespoon butter
½ cup (1 dL) honey	½ teaspoon salt
2 cups (400 g) sugar	2 cups (½ L) heavy cream
	1 teaspoon vanilla

Oil a jelly-roll pan or a 9 × 9–inch pan. Combine the syrup, honey, sugar, butter, salt, and 1 cup of the cream in a 4-quart heavy pot. Stir to mix well. Place over medium-low heat and bring to a boil, stirring until the sugar dissolves. Cover and let boil for 2–3 minutes, then uncover and, when the foam subsides, wash down the sides of the pot with a pastry brush dipped in cold water. Continue to boil, stirring without touching the sides of the pot, to the firm-ball stage (244°F). Very slowly, without breaking the boil, add the remaining 1 cup cream. Then, still stirring, bring back to the firm-ball stage (244°F). Remove from the heat, stir in the vanilla, and pour into the prepared pan. When cool and firm, cut into squares and wrap in pieces of wax paper or plastic wrap. Store in a cool place.

Divinity

Divinity is meant to be eaten up in short order: it dries out quickly.

(1 POUND)

1½ cups (3½ dL) firmly packed light-brown sugar	Pinch of salt
1 teaspoon vinegar	1 teaspoon vanilla
1 egg white, at room temperature	½ cup (1 dL) chopped nuts

Combine the sugar, ½ cup water, and the vinegar in a 3-quart heavy pot, stirring to mix well. Bring to a boil over medium heat, stirring until the sugar is dissolved. Cover and boil for 2–3 minutes, then uncover and wash down the sides of the pot with a pastry brush dipped in cold water. Continue to boil without stirring until the syrup reaches the firm-ball stage (244°F). While it is cooking, beat the egg white and salt in the large bowl of an electric mixer until stiff but not dry. As soon as the syrup is ready, remove it from the heat, turn on the mixer, and pour it slowly onto the beaten egg white, beating until creamy. Stir in the vanilla and nuts and drop by teaspoonfuls onto a sheet of wax paper. Store airtight.

Toffee

A smooth dark brittle with a deep butterscotch taste.

(1 POUND)

2 cups (½ L) firmly packed
   dark-brown sugar
¼ cup (60 g) butter

1 tablespoon vinegar
Pinch of salt

Oil a jelly-roll pan or an 8 × 8–inch pan. Combine all the ingredients with 2 tablespoons boiling water in a 3-quart heavy pot, stirring to blend well. Place over moderate heat, stirring as the sugar dissolves and the mixture comes to a boil. Cover and let boil for 2–3 minutes, then uncover and wash down the sides of the pot with a pastry brush dipped in cold water. Boil slowly over moderate heat until it reaches the hard-crack stage (290°F), stirring gently, without touching the sides of the pot, only if it starts to scorch. Pour it out into the oiled pan and let cool partially, then cut into squares. When completely cool and hard, cut or break into pieces and transfer to an airtight tin.

Peanut Brittle

A light, clear, crisp brittle.

(1 POUND)

1 cup (¼ L) skinned salted
   peanuts
1 cup (200 g) sugar

½ cup (1 dL) light corn syrup
1½ tablespoons butter, cut in
   pieces

Oil a jelly-roll pan and spread the nuts close together in one layer on the bottom. Grease a sturdy wooden spoon or metal spatula and set aside. Combine the sugar, syrup, and ½ cup water in a 3-quart heavy pot and bring to a boil over moderate heat, stirring until the sugar dissolves. Cover and let boil for 2–3 minutes, then uncover and wash down the sides of the pot with a pastry brush dipped in cold water. Continue to boil over moderate heat, stirring only if it starts to scorch, until the syrup becomes golden and reaches the hard-crack stage (295°F). Remove from the heat, stir in the butter, and pour the syrup evenly over the nuts. Use the greased spoon or spatula to spread it out slightly. When cool, blot with paper towels, break into irregular pieces, and store in an airtight tin.

Walnut Brittle. Use *1 cup coarsely chopped walnuts* in place of peanuts.

Old-fashioned Peanut Brittle

A thick, opaque, golden brittle.

(1½ POUNDS)

1½ cups (3½ dL) skinned
   salted peanuts
2 cups (400 g) sugar
1 cup (¼ L) light corn syrup

2 tablespoons butter, cut in
   pieces
2 teaspoons baking soda

Oil two jelly-roll pans and divide the nuts evenly between them, spreading them close together in one layer. Combine the sugar, corn syrup, and ¼ cup water in a heavy 3- or 4-quart pot, stirring to blend well. Stir over moderate heat until the sugar dissolves and comes to a boil. Cover and let boil for 2–3 minutes, then uncover and wash down the sides of the pot with a pastry brush dipped in cold water. Without stirring, continue to boil over moderate heat to the soft-crack stage (280°F). Remove from the heat and drop the butter in, swirling the pan gently so the butter melts; the syrup will turn golden. Return to the heat and cook to the hard-crack stage (295°F). Remove from the heat, thoroughly stir in the baking soda (the syrup will foam up), and pour it evenly over the nuts. When the brittle is cool enough to handle, in just a few minutes, pick it up and pull and stretch it as thin as possible. When cold, blot it with paper towels and break into irregular pieces. Store in an airtight tin.

Molasses Taffy

Taffy can be made alone, but it's more fun with two; its unique texture and cylindrical shape are the result of vigorous pulling.

(1 POUND)

½ cup (1 dL) unsulfured
   molasses
1½ cups (300 g) sugar
1½ cups (3½ dL) cider vinegar

¼ teaspoon cream of tartar
¼ cup (60 g) butter, melted
⅛ teaspoon baking soda

Oil a marble slab or large cookie sheet. Combine the molasses, sugar, ½ cup water, and the vinegar in a 3-quart heavy pot, stirring to blend well. Stirring constantly, bring to a boil over moderately low heat. Stir in the cream of tartar. Cover and let boil for 2–3 minutes. Uncover, and wash down the sides of the pot with a pastry brush dipped in cold water. Without stirring, continue to boil over moderate heat to the hard-ball stage (256°F), adding the melted butter and baking soda right before it is done. Pour it out onto the slab or cookie sheet. As the candy cools around the edges, oil your fingertips and fold it toward the center to form a mass. When it is cool enough to handle, the best method is to find a partner to help pull; both of you should oil or butter your hands and, using your fingertips and thumbs, pull the taffy out about 12 inches. Otherwise, just use your own two hands, well greased. Fold it back on itself, twist, pull again, and repeat until it is porous, light-colored, and almost too hard to pull. Shape into a long rope and cut with a greased knife or scissors into small pieces. Put on wax paper to harden, then store between sheets of wax paper in an airtight tin. Keep it in a cool place so it doesn't get sticky.

Butterscotch Nut Brittle

A dark-brown glossy brittle with a distinct toffee taste.

(1 POUND)

1 cup (¼ L) chopped salted
   mixed nuts
¼ cup (½ dL) unsulfured
   molasses

1 cup (200 g) sugar
¼ pound (115 g) butter
1 tablespoon cider vinegar

Oil a jelly-roll pan and sprinkle the nuts close together in one layer over the bottom. Grease a sturdy wooden spoon or metal spatula and set aside. Combine the molasses, sugar, butter, vinegar, and 2 tablespoons water in a 3-quart heavy pot, stirring to mix well. Stir over moderate heat until the sugar dissolves and it comes to a boil. Cover and boil for 2–3 minutes, then uncover and wash down the sides of the pot with a pastry brush dipped in cold water. Continue to cook at a slow boil over moderate heat; stir, without touching the sides of the pan, only if the syrup starts to scorch. Cook to the hard-crack stage (290°F), then pour out over the nuts, using the greased spoon or spatula to spread it evenly. Cool, blot with paper towels, and break into irregular pieces. Store in an airtight tin.

French Nougat

A light, dry brittle—delicious over ice cream.

(1 POUND)

1 cup (¼ L) confectioners' sugar
1 cup (¼ L) finely chopped
toasted almonds

Oil a marble slab or large cookie sheet. Oil a heavy wooden spoon or metal spatula and set aside. Put the sugar in a 3-quart heavy pot, set over low heat, and stir now and then as it becomes very hot. Stir continuously as it starts to melt. It may take 10 minutes to begin to melt; as it does it will almost immediately turn to caramel. When completely melted and caramelized, stir in the almonds and turn out onto the slab or cookie sheet. For flat pieces, use the greased spatula or spoon to spread it out until it stops moving, then let it cool and break into pieces. For small rounds, keep it moving at this point; fold it over onto itself with the spatula, keeping it constantly in motion. As soon as it is cool enough to handle, divide into four parts and shape into long rolls about ⅓ inch thick. Keep the rolls moving until they are almost cold. With a sharp knife cut each roll into five sections. Store in an airtight container.

FONDANT

About Fondant

Fondant is a grand thing to learn to make; its uses are so varied it truly could be called the heart of the candy world. Variously flavored, it becomes the center of bonbons and chocolate creams. As a coating it can be used for nuts and dried fruits. Melted with liquid it becomes a smooth shiny glaze for cakes and pastries.

Making fondant is an almost magical process; a simple sugar syrup becomes a creamy white mass literally under the heat of your hands. Once made and stored airtight in the refrigerator, it keeps almost indefinitely, always ready for a spectrum of sophisticated ends.

Basic Fondant

(1 POUND)

2 cups (400 g) sugar
⅛ teaspoon cream of tartar

Wipe a marble slab or large heavy cookie sheet with a damp cloth. Have ready a heavy metal spatula (a pancake turner). Put the sugar, cream of tartar, and 1 cup water in a 3-quart heavy pot, stirring to blend thoroughly. Place over medium heat and let it come to a boil, stirring until the sugar is completely dissolved. Cover the pot and let boil for 2–3 minutes. Uncover, dip a pastry brush in cold water, and wash down the sides of the pot. Boil without stirring until the syrup reaches the soft-ball stage (238°F). Remove from the heat and, without scraping the pot, pour out the syrup onto the slab or cookie sheet. Let it cool for about 10 minutes, until it is just lukewarm. Start to work it with the spatula, spreading it out and turning it over and over on itself. Professionals call this procedure "spading," and this exactly describes the motion. As it starts to thicken and whiten, it is easier to knead with your hands. Continue to knead until it is white, creamy, and too stiff to knead any more. If it crumbles too much, sprinkle on a little water and continue to knead; fondant cannot be overkneaded. Cover with a damp cloth and let it stand for 30 minutes. Knead again for a minute, then wrap in damp cheesecloth and store in an airtight container in the refrigerator. Let it mellow for 3–4 days before using.

Fondant Glaze. Put the fondant in the top of a double boiler over hot water. Stir in about a tablespoon of liquid for each cup of fondant and stir gently until it melts into a thick cream. Use immediately, as a glaze for pastries, cakes, or petits fours. Pour it out evenly, working carefully but quickly; it hardens fast.

Butter Fondant. Let the fondant come to room temperature. For each cup of fondant, mix in *2 tablespoons soft butter* and *½ teaspoon vanilla,* kneading thoroughly until mixed.

Flavored Fondant. Any flavoring, liqueur, fruit juice, or powdered ingredient can be kneaded into fondant. Try *cocoa, instant coffee, rum, peppermint extract,* or *vanilla,* adding a bit or a few drops at a time until you reach the desired flavor. A drop or two of vegetable coloring can be kneaded in to visually emphasize a particular taste.

Fondant Confections

Bonbons. Let the fondant come to room temperature, kneading in flavoring if desired. Roll bits into 1-inch balls and set them on a cake rack to dry, then roll them in *finely chopped nuts, shredded coconut,* or *cocoa.* Let dry again before storing.

Chocolate Bonbons. Follow the procedure for Bonbons, dipping the 1-inch balls into *chocolate* that has been melted and cooled to about 85°F. Dip one at a time. Use a fork or improvise a dipper by bending a piece of wire into a circle at one end and bending up the straight piece so it is like a ladle. Let them dry thoroughly on wax paper or a rack.

Cream Mints. Melt 1 cup of fondant over hot water, flavoring with 1–2 drops of *oil of peppermint.* Color pale green if desired. Drop from the tip of a spoon onto wax paper and dry thoroughly before using.

Fondant-covered Nuts. Use *whole almonds* or *walnut* or *pecan halves.* Melt the fondant over hot water. Spear the nuts with a fork, or use tweezers to dip. Dry thoroughly on a rack before storing.

ALMOND PASTE AND MARZIPAN

Almond Paste

Homemade almond paste will stay fresh for months in the refrigerator. To keep it moist, cover with a piece of dampened cheesecloth and store it in an airtight container.

(2 POUNDS)

¼ cup (½ dL) confectioners' sugar
2 cups (400 g) granulated sugar

1 pound (450 g) blanched almonds, finely ground
½ cup (1 dL) orange juice

Dust a marble slab or board with the confectioners' sugar. Put the granulated sugar and 1 cup water in a 3-quart heavy pot and stir to blend. Bring to a boil over moderate heat, stirring until the sugar is dissolved, cover, and let boil for 2–3 minutes. Uncover and wash down the sides of the pot with a pastry brush dipped in cold water. Cook without stirring to the soft-ball stage (240°F). Remove from the heat and stir in the almonds and orange juice, stirring until creamy. Turn out onto the slab or board and let stand until cool, then knead together. Wrap in a piece of damp cheesecloth and store in an airtight container in the refrigerator. Let it mellow for a week before using, then let it come to room temperature and knead it briefly to soften.

Blender Almond Paste

An almost instant version.

(1½ POUNDS)

½ cup (1 dL) orange juice
2 cups (½ L) blanched almonds
1 cup (200 g) sugar

Put the orange juice, 1 cup of the almonds, and the sugar into a blender or food processor and whirl until the nuts are very fine. Add the remaining cup of almonds and whirl again until very fine. Knead together, cover with dampened cheesecloth, and store in an airtight container in the refrigerator.

Marzipan

Malleable marzipan can be used as a cake filling as well as for a range of beguiling and decorative miniature shapes.

(1¾ CUPS)

1 cup (¼ L) or ½ pound (225 g) almond paste (preceding recipes), at room temperature

1 cup (¼ L) confectioners' sugar
1½ teaspoons rosewater

Combine the almond paste, sugar, and rosewater, mixing well with your hands. Put it on a marble slab or board and knead for 10–20 minutes, until it is very pliable. Wrap in damp cheesecloth and store in an airtight container. It will keep for months in the refrigerator.

Marzipan Miniatures. Although tiny fruits and vegetables are traditional, any number, letter, or shape that strikes your fancy can be molded from marzipan; think of it as edible modeling clay. Paint the molded shapes with food coloring, using a small brush, or dip them into a small bowl of coloring. Or roll the shapes in confectioners' sugar or spices. (For example, a little potato shape can be covered with a mixture of cocoa and confectioners' sugar.) Use tweezers to apply finishing touches like leaves and stems. They can be made of marzipan too, or use candied fruit or spices; whole cloves as stems, bits of angelica for leaves. The range of possibilities is almost endless. Let the molded shapes dry on a cake rack, then store them in an airtight container in the refrigerator. They can be eaten, of course, or used over and over again to decorate gingerbread houses, desserts, pastries, and birthday cakes.

NUTS AND POPCORN

Roasted Chestnuts

With a sharp paring knife, cut a ½-inch crisscross gash on the flat side of each nut, cutting down to the meat.

To roast in the oven, preheat the oven to 450°F (230°C). Spread the nuts out on a cookie sheet and bake, stirring once or twice, for 10–20 minutes, until the shells open and the nuts can easily be dislodged. Peel them while they are still warm.

To roast over a fire, use a perforated-bottom chestnut roasting pan or a popcorn popper, shaking the nuts gently over the fire until the shells open and the nuts become toasty and brown.

Sherry Walnuts

Sugared nutmeats with a real sherry flavor. Served with a strong cup of coffee, they're a perfect way to end dinner.

(ABOUT 4 CUPS)

1½ cups (300 g) sugar	½ teaspoon cinnamon
½ cup (1 dL) sherry	3 cups (¾ L) walnut halves
Pinch of salt	

Lightly oil a cookie sheet. Mix the sugar, sherry, and salt together in a 3-quart heavy pot. Stir over low heat until the sugar has dissolved, bring to a boil, cover, and let boil for 2–3 minutes. Uncover and wash down the sides of the pot with a pastry brush dipped in cold water. Cook without stirring to the soft-ball stage (236°F). Remove from the heat, stir in the cinnamon and walnuts, and stir vigorously until the mixture looks cloudy. Turn out onto the cookie sheet and separate the nuts with two forks. Let cool. Then store in a tin at room temperature.

Brazil Nut Chips

Very worthwhile to make!

Brazil nuts, shelled
1 tablespoon butter for each cup of nuts
Salt

Preheat oven to 350°F (180°C). Put the nuts in a saucepan, cover with cold water, bring slowly to a boil, lower the heat, and simmer for 3 minutes. Drain and cool. With a sharp paring knife, cut the nuts into thin lengthwise strips and spread in one layer in a shallow baking pan. Dot with butter and sprinkle with salt. Bake for 15 minutes, stirring once or twice. Blot dry on paper towels and store in a sealed jar.

Spiced Nuts

Sweet, spicy, and delicious.

(ABOUT 4 CUPS)

1 cup (200 g) sugar
1 teaspoon cinnamon
Pinch of salt

6 tablespoons milk
1 teaspoon vanilla
3 cups (¾ L) walnut halves

Lightly oil a cookie sheet. Mix the sugar, cinnamon, salt, and milk together in a 3-quart heavy pot and stir over low heat until the sugar dissolves. Bring to a boil, cover, and let boil for 2–3 minutes. Uncover, wash down the sides of the pot with a pastry brush dipped in cold water, and continue to cook, without stirring, to the soft-ball stage (236°F). Remove from the heat, stir in the vanilla and walnuts, and stir vigorously until creamy. Spread out on the cookie sheet and separate the nuts with two forks. Let cool. Keep them in a tin at room temperature.

Popcorn Balls

An authentic old-fashioned version.

(FIFTEEN 3-INCH BALLS)

3 quarts (3 L) popped corn
  (p. 73), unsalted, unbuttered
2 cups (½ L) light corn syrup

1 tablespoon cider vinegar
½ teaspoon salt
2 teaspoons vanilla

Put the popped corn into a large greased bowl and keep warm in a 250°F (120°C) oven. Oil a large fork and set aside. Combine the corn syrup, vinegar, and salt in a 3-quart heavy pot. Cook over medium heat, stirring occasionally, until the syrup reaches the hard-ball stage (250°F). Remove from the heat and add the vanilla. Slowly pour the syrup over the popcorn, tossing with the fork until it is well distributed. As soon as the mixture is cool enough to handle, quickly and gently shape it into 3-inch balls. Let them stand on wax paper until they are cool and no longer sticky, then wrap each in plastic wrap, a tied plastic bag, or tissue paper, and store at room temperature.

COCONUT

Coconut Cakes

These are chewy, toasted, and just sweet enough. A fine complement to fresh fruit desserts.

(20 SMALL BALLS)

2 cups (½ L) coarsely grated
    fresh coconut (see p. 13)
2 tablespoons light corn syrup
½ cup (100 g) sugar

Pinch of salt
1 egg white
¼ teaspoon coconut or almond
    extract

Mix the coconut, corn syrup, sugar, and salt together in a 3-quart heavy pot. Stir over medium heat until the mixture thickens a little, about 5–6 minutes. Stir in the egg white and cook, stirring, for another 5–6 minutes, until the mixture feels sticky; cool a little and feel it with your fingers. Stir in the coconut or almond extract. Remove from the heat. Rinse a shallow pan with cold water, shake out the excess, and spread the mixture over the bottom. Rinse paper towels in cold water, wring them out, and place them over the mixture. Refrigerate until chilled. Preheat oven to 300°F (150°C). Lightly grease a cookie sheet. Dip your hands in cold water, then shape the coconut mixture into small balls. Heat the cookie sheet slightly and place the balls on it. Bake for 20 minutes or until golden on top. Store in an airtight container at room temperature.

CANDIED PEEL AND CRYSTALLIZED LEAVES

Candied Citrus Peel

Refreshing, addictive, and absolutely satisfying at the end of a meal. Candied citrus peel keeps so well that it's a good idea to double the recipe.

(2 CUPS)

2 grapefruit or 3 oranges or
    6 lemons

2 cups (400 g) sugar
3 tablespoons light corn syrup

Peel the fruit in large strips, using only the zest and white peel. If the white is very thick, trim it down a little. Put the peel in a pan, cover with cold water, and simmer for 30 minutes. Drain, cover with cold water, and simmer until tender. Drain and cut the peel into small strips, about ¼ inch wide and 2 inches long. Mix 1 cup of the sugar with the corn syrup and ¾ cup water in a heavy saucepan and stir over low heat until dissolved. Dip a pastry brush in cold water and wash down the sides of the pan, then add the peel and cook very gently over low heat until most of the syrup has been absorbed. Cover and let stand overnight. Reheat and bring to the simmer again, then cool a little and drain. Spread several thicknesses of paper towels with the remaining cup of sugar and roll the peel in it, turning so that all the pieces are well coated. Let them stand until they are dry enough to handle. Stored airtight, they will stay fresh for several months. If they become too dry, put a lemon in the container for a day or two and the peel will soften.

Crystallized Mint Leaves

Frosted leaves with the pure essence of mint. As enlivening to the palate as they are to the plate. You can treat violets and lemon balm the same way, if you are lucky enough to have them in your garden.

(36 LEAVES)

36 fresh mint leaves, without stems
1 egg white, beaten stiff

¼ teaspoon peppermint extract
¾ cup (150 g) superfine sugar

Preheat the oven to 250°F (120°C). Wash the mint leaves, pat dry, and spread on paper towels until thoroughly dry. Brush both sides of each leaf with the beaten egg white. Mix the peppermint extract into the sugar and mix and toss with a fork or your hands until the peppermint is well distributed. Dip each leaf into the flavored sugar. Cover a cake rack or two with wax paper, place the leaves close together on it, and let stand in the oven until dry, about 10–15 minutes. Turn them once so they will dry completely on both sides. Use as both a confection and a decoration. They are very fragile and won't keep long.

UNCOOKED CONFECTIONS

Stuffed Dates or Prunes

Very nice to have on hand or give as a present.

(36 PIECES)

36 large dates or prunes, pitted
36 walnut halves or large pieces
½–¾ cup (100–150 g) sugar

If the dates or prunes are very dry, put them in a strainer, cover loosely, and soften them over boiling water for 10–15 minutes. Cool, then fill each one with a walnut piece: use halves for prunes and large pieces for dates. Sprinkle a piece of wax paper with sugar, and roll the dates or prunes in it until coated. Store airtight in the refrigerator; they will keep for several months.

Fruit Leather

A notable specialty of Charleston, South Carolina—wonderful to take on hikes. Apricots and peaches are traditional, but other dried fruit combinations can be substituted.

(1½ POUNDS)

1 pound (450 g) dried apricots
½ pound (225 g) dried peaches
¼–½ cup (50–100 g) sugar

Put the apricots and peaches through a meat grinder twice or finely chop them together in a food processor. Liberally sprinkle a board with sugar. Pat and roll out the fruit mixture to ⅛ inch thick and cut into 1¼ × 2-inch strips. Roll each strip lengthwise into a tight roll. Stored in an airtight container, these keep well at room temperature for several months.

Walnut Balls

Nut bonbons, with a dusting of confectioners' sugar.

(½ POUND)

¼ cup (½ dL) light corn syrup
1 teaspoon vanilla
⅛ teaspoon salt
½ cup (1 dL) instant nonfat
  dry milk

¼ cup (½ dL) finely chopped
  walnuts, or other nuts
¼ cup (½ dL) confectioners'
  sugar

Mix the syrup, vanilla, salt, dry milk, and walnuts together in a bowl, using your hands to blend well. Sprinkle a board with a little of the confectioners' sugar and knead the candy on the board until it becomes creamy. Shape into 1-inch balls and dust with the remaining confectioners' sugar. These keep best in the refrigerator.

Peanut Butter Chewies

A bonanza for peanut lovers: nut-covered nuggets of peanut butter.

(½ POUND)

½ cup (1 dL) crunchy peanut
  butter
3 tablespoons honey
1 teaspoon vanilla
¾ cup (1¾ dL) instant nonfat
  dry milk

Pinch of salt
3 tablespoons confectioners'
  sugar
½ cup (1 dL) finely chopped
  unsalted peanuts

Mix the peanut butter, honey, vanilla, dry milk, salt, and sugar together in a bowl. Using your hands, blend until very well mixed, then shape the mixture into 1-inch balls and roll them in the peanuts. For longer than a day, store in the refrigerator.

PRESERVES, PICKLES, & CANNED FRUITS & VEGETABLES

ABOUT PRESERVES, PICKLES, AND CANNED FRUITS AND VEGETABLES

Back in the days when our country was more rural and people really lived off their land, the practice of "putting by" summertime produce for winter use was a necessity, not a luxury. Now, of course, with good, commercially canned and frozen products available just about everywhere, it isn't really essential for most of us to do our own preserving, pickling, and canning. Yet many people still do—not just those who are following thrifty, long-established family habits but health-minded young cooks who are wary of chemical preservatives in commercial products.

There's great satisfaction in filling tidy shelves with colorful, glistening jars of home-canned fruits, vegetables, pickles, jams, jellies, and preserves. Set a few aside for giving—they make precious gifts for special friends—and use the others throughout the winter, a source of happy summer memories and of pride in your own well-ordered home.

Whether the foods you process are the extra fruits and vegetables from your own family garden or are purchased at a rural farm stand or a city market, canning is an economical way to use fruits and vegetables when they are abundant. For city dwellers, canning is an especially gratifying way to feel a relationship with the changing seasons.

For Detailed Information

The U.S. Department of Agriculture publishes excellent, up-to-date information about preserving, pickling, and canning. You can get these materials from the U.S. Government Printing Office, Washington, D.C., as well as other information put out by the makers of canning equipment; they provide detailed information, especially useful if you plan to can on a large-scale basis.

Canning versus Freezing

With the advent of the large, freestanding home freezer, those who have the space usually prefer to freeze meats and vegetables rather than to can them. Vegetables, in particular, will have better texture when frozen rather than canned, especially low-acid vegetables which must be processed for a long time and then reboiled before eating.

Pickles, jellies, and preserves, on the other hand, are most appealing in clear jars that let their colors gleam through. They may also be frozen very satisfactorily. If you freeze them, processing will not, of course, be necessary.

A Few Words of Warning

Canned foods must be properly processed to prevent the growth of a toxin that causes botulism poisoning and to prevent other forms of spoilage caused by yeasts, molds, and bacteria. Always use reliable recipes, follow them carefully, and do not take shortcuts.

Botulism. Many people are dissuaded from canning altogether because of an irrational fear of botulism. While botulism *can* be deadly (one tiny bite of contaminated food may be fatal), it is also very rare. Most important, there's no mystery about botulism: if you understand its causes, you can prevent it with self-assurance.

Botulism spores grow naturally in an air-free environment, usually in low-acid foods. They are destroyed by processing at the right temperature and for the designated amount of time.

Since botulism is not readily detectable through sight, smell, or taste, your only safeguard is to be particularly careful when you can your own low-acid foods. Follow the directions in each recipe. If you are in doubt about a home-canned product you have not prepared yourself, empty the contents into a pot and boil for 15 minutes before tasting: high heat and air will destroy the botulism toxin.

Molds, Yeasts, and Bacteria. Molds, yeasts, and bacteria can spoil canned foods if proper processing procedures have not been followed. Molds and yeasts are more likely to be found in acid foods and are easily destroyed by a temperature of 212°F, the maximum reached in a water-bath canner.

Bacteria, on the other hand, thrive in low-acid foods, where they may cause an unpleasant flavor called "flat-sour." They are harder to destroy than molds and yeasts, requiring processing at 240°F in a steam-pressure canner. Signs of possible spoilage include a broken seal, leaky jars, fermented contents, or a heavy layer of mold. Do not use canned foods if any of these signs are present.

Differentiating Between High-Acid and Low-Acid Foods

High-Acid Foods. High-acid foods include fruits, tomatoes, rhubarb, sauerkraut, jellies, jams, preserves, and pickles. Jellies, jams, preserves, and pickles may be prepared by the open-kettle method; some prefer a simmering-water bath at 185°C, but only because it assures a good seal. In the case of pickles, again, processing assures a reliable seal and thus you risk less chance of spoilage, but it *does* destroy some of the crunchiness, so you should weigh the pros and cons and make your own choice. All other high-acid foods require a boiling-water bath at 212°F in a water-bath canner.

Low-Acid Foods. Low-acid foods—most vegetables and all meats, poultry, and seafood—require processing at 240°F in a steam-pressure canner.

Equipment for Preserving, Pickling, and Canning

Canning requires special equipment, some of it used exclusively for that purpose. Check before you get started to be sure you have everything you need.

Jars. Do not use ordinary kitchen jars for canning. Use special canning jars that can be vacuum-sealed so that air does not get in. The best and most commonly used are those with screwbands and flat metal lids edged with a sealing compound.

    Canning jars are sealed by vacuum which creates the pressure that holds the lid down: the red rubber seal at the edge of the metal lid keeps air from getting into the jars. Inspect the jars you plan to use: be sure they have no nicks or cracks and that the lids are not rusty. Make sure you have enough lids and screwbands. You can reuse the screwbands, but you must use a *new* metal lid for each jar that you process.

    Jars should be spotlessly clean. Run them through the dishwasher so that they will be clean and hot, or wash or rinse them thoroughly and let them sit in hot water until you are ready to use them. It is not necessary to sterilize jars if they are going to be processed in a water-bath canner or a steam-pressure canner, but you may prefer to boil them anyway. To sterilize jars, boil them gently for 10 minutes and leave them in the hot water until ready to use.

Canners and Pots. Depending on the acidity of the food you intend to can, you will need one or both of the following: a water-bath canner with a rack and a cover or a steam-pressure canner with a well-functioning pressure gauge. You will also need pots of different sizes for cooking the foods you plan to can.

Other Equipment. Jar tongs, a ladle, a long-handled spoon, a slotted spoon, a wide-mouthed funnel, and labels are all useful. You may wish to use paraffin and a candy-jelly thermometer for jellies and jams.

Filling Jars

Fill jars tightly or loosely, according to the recipe instructions. There should be enough juices, water, or syrup to cover the food entirely so that it does not darken. Be sure to leave the specified amount of headspace between the top of the food and the cover of the jar, usually ½–1 inch. Avoid sudden changes of temperature when filling the jars so that they don't crack. To remove air bubbles, run a table knife between the jar and the food.

Open-Kettle Method. In the open-kettle method, food is cooked uncovered, then poured while boiling hot into hot, sterilized jars and quickly sealed. No processing is necessary.

Raw-Pack Method. In the raw-pack or cold-pack method, clean jars are filled with raw food and then processed.

Hot-Pack Method. The hot-pack method involves filling clean jars with hot or cooked food before they are processed.

Processing Jars

After the jars are filled, wipe the rims clean with a hot, damp cloth. If you are using jars with metal lids and screwbands, place the flat lid on the jar with the sealing compound next to the glass rim. Screw the metal band on tight; there will still be space for air to escape during processing. Do not tighten the screwband after the jar has been processed.

Water-Bath Method. The water-bath method is required for acid foods: fruits, tomatoes, rhubarb, sauerkraut, and, if you wish, pickles. The maximum temperature reached in a boiling-water bath is 212°F, enough to destroy any harmful organisms in acid foods; a simmering-water bath at 185°F is enough for jellies, jams, and preserves, if you chose to process them.

The water-bath method requires a water-bath canner—a large pot with a cover, fitted with a rack or basket to keep the jars from touching the bottom of the pot. The pot should be deep enough so that the water will cover the tops of the jars by at least 1 inch. Canners are sold complete with racks, or you can buy the racks separately and fit them into a very large pot. In many households, the canner doubles as the pot in which corn on the cob is cooked in.

To use a water-bath canner, fill it with 4–5 inches of water: use boiling water if the food is "hot-packed" or hot water if the food is "raw-packed." Jars should be put in the pot slightly apart as soon as they are filled and closed. They should not touch the bottom or sides of the pot. When all the jars have been added, cover them with boiling water by at least 1 inch. Cover the pot and begin timing when the water reaches a boil. Boil gently and steadily (or simmer for jams and preserves), adding more time if you are canning in a high-altitude area (see p. 698).

Steam-Pressure Method. The steam-pressure method is recommended for all low-acid foods—most vegetables and all meats, poultry, and seafood—because food can be processed under 10 pounds of pressure at 240°F, enough to destroy botulism spores and the bacteria that grow in low-acid foods.

A special steam-pressure canner is required, a heavy pot with a cover that can be clamped down tight, equipped with a rack, a safety valve, a pressure gauge, and a petcock (vent). A steam-pressure canner can also be used as a water-bath canner if the cover is left unfastened and the vent wide open.

Before canning, make sure that the canner is clean and functioning properly. Run a heavy string through the petcock and safety valve openings to be sure they are clear.

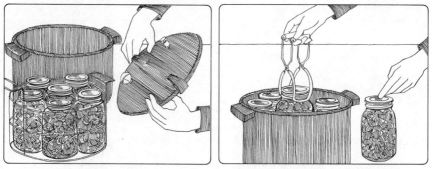

Add about 3 inches of water to the canner, then put in the filled, covered jars. The jars should not touch each other or the bottom or sides of the pot. Clamp down the pot cover, leaving the petcock open until steam has escaped for 10 minutes. Close the petcock and bring the pressure to 10 pounds, following the manufacturer's directions carefully. Start to time after the pressure has reached 10 pounds. Adjust the pressure if processing at a high altitude (see below).

Follow the manufacturer's instructions when opening the canner, being sure to let the pressure return to zero and waiting for a few minutes before slowly opening the petcock.

A pressure cooker may be used to process small jars, but add 20 minutes to the cooking time because the pan heats and cools quickly.

Processing at High Altitudes. When using a water-bath canner at high altitudes, increase the processing time 1 minute for every 1,000 feet above sea level if the total processing time is 20 minutes or less. Increase by 2 minutes for every 1,000 feet above sea level if the total processing time is more than 20 minutes.

When steam-pressure canning at high altitudes, increase the pressure to 11½ pounds at altitudes between 2,000 and 3,000 feet above sea level. Add ½ pound of pressure for every 1,000 feet thereafter.

Cooling and Storing Jars

Use jar tongs to remove jars from boiling water after the processing time is up. Let the jars cool on a towel, set somewhat apart from each other, in a draft-free place; avoid sudden changes in temperature.

When the jars are cool, check the seal. Press the metal lid to see if it's down tight. You may remove the screwbands after 24 hours and reuse them. If a jar has failed to seal properly, process all over again, using a new lid, or refrigerate and use as you would any cooked food.

Label the jars. Store them in a cool, dry place, out of direct sunlight. Do not, of course, open them until you are ready to use the contents.

Using Home-Canned Foods

Save the liquid left over from home-canned foods: it's a good addition to soups or stocks. Extra pickle juices may be used to make another batch of similar pickles.

Pickles and preserves should stand for a few weeks after canning to develop their full flavor. If jellies are kept *too* long, their bright colors may fade.

PRESERVES

About Preserves

For general information, see About Preserves, Pickles, and Canned Fruits and Vegetables (p. 694).

There is nothing more delicious with breakfast or afternoon tea than a homemade preserve served with freshly baked bread, muffins, or rolls. Homemade jellies and jams are also often used as a condiment with roasts, and homemade preserves, added to ice cream, trifles, cookies, or cakes, will transform them into exceptional desserts. With their concentrated goodness and rich, jewellike colors, homemade preserves make wonderful gifts.

Kinds of Preserves

Jellies. Jellies are made from fruit juices and sugar. They have a firm but spreadable consistency and may be clear or translucent, depending on how the fruit juices are extracted. Jellies differ from other types of jams and preserves because they require two separate cooking processes, one to extract the juice and the other to make the jelly.

Jams. Jams are made with sugar and crushed or chopped fruit. They have a softer consistency than jellies.

Preserves. Preserves are fruits cooked with sugar so that they keep their shape within a jellylike syrup.

Conserves. Conserves are jamlike mixtures of two or more fruits to which nuts or raisins are usually added.

Marmalades. Marmalades are like soft jellies with pieces of fruit or fruit peel in them.

Butters. Butters are thick and smooth for easy spreading. They are made from fruit pulp and sugar which are cooked together, sometimes with spices, and usually strained.

Equipment for Preserving

(For general canning equipment, see p. 696.)

Whether you are making jellies, jams, or preserves, you will need a large, heavy-bottomed pot, big enough to hold four times the volume of the ingredients you are using. A jelly or candy thermometer is extremely useful when making jellies, jams, or preserves, especially those without commercial pectin.

When making jelly, a jellmeter is helpful for measuring the natural pectin in fruit juices. You will need a jelly bag and stand for extracting the juices, or some cheesecloth and a colander to improvise one.

You may use either screwtops or paraffin or both to seal jars of preserves made by the open-kettle method. Since paraffin smokes and flames easily, melt it in the top of a double boiler over warm, not boiling, water. Use a single, very thin layer of paraffin, about ⅛ inch thick, and make sure that it touches the glass all around. Prick any air bubbles that form, or they may become holes as the wax hardens. After the paraffin is hard, you may cover the jelly jars with metal lids, if desired, but it's not necessary.

Ingredients

Fruit. Fruit, which gives jellies and jams their flavor and color, also provides at least some of the pectin and acid required for jelling. Fruit that is firm and just barely ripe will be richest in pectin and acid.

   The following fruits are rich in pectin: tart apples, crabapples, green barberries, tart blackberries, boysenberries, cranberries, loganberries, red currants, green gooseberries, Concord grapes, sour guavas, fresh prunes, plums, and quinces. Low-pectin fruits, such as strawberries, blueberries, peaches, apricots, cherries, figs, pears, raspberries, and pineapples, should be combined with pectin-rich fruits like apples and quinces, unless you wish to use commercial pectins.

Pectin. Jellies, which must be firm enough to hold their shape, require more pectin than jams or preserves.

The pectin content of fruit juices will determine the amount of sugar needed for a jelly to jell. It can be tested with a jellmeter, a glass tube through which the extracted juice is passed. The rate of flow determines the pectin content of the juice and thus the amount of sugar to be used. Follow the manufacturer's instructions when using a jellmeter.

Another test for pectin content requires mixing 1 teaspoon of grain or ethyl alcohol with 1 teaspoon of extracted fruit juice. If the mixture comes together in one transparent, firm mass when poured into another glass, equal quantities of sugar and juice should be used. If the mixture is soft, use half as much sugar as juice, and if it forms two or three separate masses, use two-thirds as much sugar as juice. Do not taste this mixture.

Commercial pectins, made from apples or citrus fruits, come in liquid or powdered form. They reduce the cooking times of jellies and jams and eliminate any uncertainty about jelling. They also require a higher proportion of sugar to fruit, and thus many cooks prefer not to use them. None of the recipes in this chapter requires commercial pectins. If you wish to use them, follow the manufacturer's directions carefully.

Acid. Acid is necessary in jellied products, both for flavor and for jelling. Lemon juice is often called for in recipes for jellies and jams using low-acid fruits.

Sugar. Sugar adds sweetness, aids in preserving, and helps make a jelly or jam jell. Either beet or cane sugar may be used. Honey may be substituted for up to one-half the sugar in a recipe.

Testing for the Jellying Point

Since jellies and jams thicken as they cool, it is often difficult to determine when the hot jelly or jam has reached the proper consistency. There are three ways to test the jellying point:

Thermometer Test. A jelly or candy thermometer is probably the most accurate way to test for the jellying point. First it is necessary to know the boiling point of water in your locality, which can be determined by taking the temperature of water with your jelly thermometer. Jelly should register 8 degrees higher than the boiling point of water to assure the proper amount of jell.

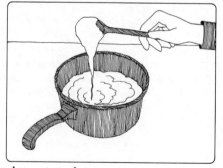

Sheet Test. Using a cool metal spoon, scoop up a bit of the boiling jelly mixture. Tip the spoon and let the jelly run off the side. When the jelly separates from the spoon in a sheet, rather than in separate drops, it is done.

Freezer Test. Remove the jelly from the heat while making this test. Put a few drops on a plate and cool it quickly in the freezer to see if it will jell when cool.

Processing Preserves

See Water-Bath Method, p. 697.

Jellies, jams, preserves, conserves, marmalades, and butters may be made safely by the open-kettle method. The only reason for processing in a simmering-water bath at 185°F for 10–15 minutes is that it does no harm and will assure a better seal.

PRESERVES

Basic Method for Preparing Fruit Jelly

The standard proportion in fruit jellies is about ¾ cup sugar for each cup of fruit juice, but this will vary according to the fruit. You may test the pectin content of the juice (see p. 700) to adjust the amount of sugar, or follow the general guidelines given in this recipe and its variations, adjusting according to your own experience. Do not peel any fruit except pineapple; fruit skin is rich in pectin. Do not core fruits, except for quinces, which have bitter cores. Old cookbooks will tell you that if you warm the sugar in a moderate oven before adding it to the fruit, it will keep the jelly from clouding, but this is an old wives' tale. In all probability sugar was heated in the old days to get the dampness and consequent lumps out of it, but this is not necessary today with our refined sugar and would simply be a waste of energy. Don't squeeze or press the jelly bag; you will get more jelly but it will not be crystal clear.

(ABOUT FOUR 6-OUNCE JARS)

3 pounds (1⅓ kg) fruit (to yield about 4 cups, 1 L, juice)

Sugar (about ¾ cup, 150 g, for each cup of juice)

Wash the fruit thoroughly and cut it into pieces. To extract the juice, put the fruit in a large, heavy-bottomed pot. If the fruit is soft, crush it a little and add just enough water to keep it from burning. If the fruit is hard, add water to just below the top layer. Cover and cook over low heat until the juice flows freely, from 3–15 minutes depending on the fruit. Strain through a colander. Pour the juice into a damp jelly bag or through several layers of damp cheesecloth draped over a colander and set over a bowl so the juice will drip freely. Be patient, allowing an hour or more for the juice to drip through. You should have about 4 cups of juice.

To make the extracted juice into jelly, measure no more than 4 cups of juice at a time into a large pot. Boil for 5 minutes, then add the sugar, allowing ¾ cup sugar for each cup of juice. Boil until the mixture jells, from 10–30 minutes depending on the kind of fruit. Test for the jellying point, using a thermometer, the sheet test, or the freezer test (see p. 700). Skim off the foam and pour the jelly into hot, sterilized jars (see p. 696). Seal immediately with metal lids or paraffin and cool, label, and store (see p. 698).

Apple Jelly. Use *3 pounds apples* and 3 cups water to produce 4 cups of extracted juice.

Blueberry Apple Jelly. Use *2 cups blueberry juice* and *2 cups apple juice* and add *2 tablespoons lemon juice.*

Crabapple Jelly. Use *3 pounds crabapples* and 3 cups water to produce 4 cups of extracted juice. Use *1 cup sugar* for each cup of juice.

Mint Jelly. Use light-colored apples or crabapples or peel the apples if they have very bright skins. After the juice and sugar are combined, add *1 cup chopped mint leaves and stems* for every 4 cups of juice. While the jelly is boiling, color lightly with *green vegetable coloring.*

Spiced Apple Jelly. Use *3 pounds apples, ½ cup mild vinegar, 2½ cups water,* and a spice bag containing *1 teaspoon whole cinnamon, 1 teaspoon whole allspice,* and *½ teaspoon whole cloves.* Extract the juice and proceed as the basic recipe directs.

Currant Jelly. Use *2½ quarts currants* (with leaves, but not stems, removed) and 1 cup water to produce 4 cups of extracted juice. Use *up to 1 cup sugar* for each cup of juice.

Currant Raspberry Jelly. Use *2 cups currant juice* and *2 cups raspberry juice.*

Gooseberry Jelly. Remove the stems and blossom ends from the gooseberries and extract the juice in the same way as for Currant Jelly. Use *4 cups gooseberry juice* instead of currant juice.

Grape Jelly. Use Concord or wild grapes, including lots of green, unripened grapes and removing about half the stems. Crush the grapes in the pot, using *3½ pounds grapes* and ½ cup water to produce 4 cups of extracted juice. Store the juice in the refrigerator overnight so that crystals and sediment will settle. Discard the sediment and proceed according to the basic recipe.

Spiced Grape (Venison) Jelly. Follow the recipe for Grape Jelly, using *½ cup vinegar, 1 tablespoon whole cloves,* a *1-inch stick of cinnamon,* and *4 cups grapes.* Cook slowly for about 15 minutes. Strain and allow the sediment to settle. To make into jelly, boil the juice for 20 minutes before adding sugar, and use *up to 1 cup sugar* for each cup of juice.

Guava Jelly. Follow the Basic Method for Preparing Fruit Jelly, cooking the fruit for 45 minutes or more to extract the juice and adding the *juice of 1 lime* to each 4 cups of guava juice.

Quince Jelly. Wash the quinces and rub off the fuzz. Remove the stems, cores, and seeds and slice. Follow the Basic Method for Preparing Fruit Jelly, using *3½ pounds quinces* and 7 cups water to produce 4 cups of juice and cooking 45 minutes or more to extract the juice. Use *1 cup sugar* for each cup of juice.

Quince Apple Jelly. Follow the recipe for Quince Jelly, using *2 cups quince juice* and *2 cups apple juice*.

Raspberry or Blackberry Jelly. Use *4 cups raspberry* or *blackberry juice*.

Basic Method for Preparing Fruit Jam

The basic proportions for jam are ¾ cup sugar for each cup of prepared fruit.

(2–3 PINTS)

4 cups (1 L) prepared fruit
3 cups (600 g) sugar

Wash the fruit thoroughly. Peel and remove cores, pits, stems, and seeds. Berries and small fruits may be crushed in the pan. Other fruits should be cut into small pieces. Measure the fruit before putting it into the pan. Cook until tender, adding just enough water to prevent burning. Add the sugar to the fruit, stirring until it dissolves. Boil rapidly until the jam is thick, stirring to prevent sticking. Test for the jellying point, using a thermometer, the sheet test, or the freezer test (p. 700). Pour into hot, sterilized jars and seal.

Raspberry Jam

Since it's easy to overcook this jam, it's best to use a jelly thermometer when you make it.

(ABOUT 2 PINTS)

4 cups (1 L) raspberries
3 cups (600 g) warm sugar

Clean the raspberries, put them in a large pot, and crush them with a potato masher. Cook for 15 minutes to reduce the juices. Add the sugar and bring to a boil. Cook stirring, until the mixture registers 214°F degrees on a jelly thermometer. Skim off the foam and let stand until cool. Pour into hot, *sterilized* jars and seal.

Blackberry Jam. Substitute *4 cups blackberries* for the raspberries. If you prefer to remove the seeds, put the cooked berries through a food mill or coarse sieve.

Raspberry Currant Jam. Use *3 cups raspberries* and *1 cup currants*.

Apricot Pineapple Jam

(ABOUT 4 PINTS)

1 pound (450 g) dried apricots   Sugar
8-ounce (225-g) can crushed
  pineapple and juice

Put the apricots in a pot, barely cover with cold water, and cook until soft. Drain, reserving the juice. Chop the fruit and return to the juice. Add the canned pineapple with its juices and measure. Put in a large pot and bring to a boil. Measure the sugar, using about two-thirds as much sugar as fruit and stir in. Boil rapidly, stirring to prevent sticking, until thick. Test for the jellying point, using a thermometer, the sheet test, or the freezer test (p. 700). Pour into hot, *sterilized* jars and seal.

Gooseberry Jam

Use currant juice that has been extracted as for jelly; it is not necessary to drip it through a jelly bag; just put it through a mesh strainer. This jam must be processed because it is cooled before it is packed.

(ABOUT 6 PINTS)

4 pounds (1¾ kg) gooseberries
3 pounds (1⅓ kg) sugar
2 cups (½ L) red currant juice

Wash and clean the gooseberries and set them aside. Bring the currant juice to a boil in a large pot, then add the sugar and boil together for 5 minutes. Add the gooseberries and boil for 40 minutes, skimming occasionally. Cool and set aside for 24 hours. Drain off the syrup. Pack the gooseberries in clean jars. Boil the syrup until it is as thick as honey, pour it over the berries, and close the jars. Process in a simmering-water bath at 185°F for 10–15 minutes.

Black Currant Jam

If you are lucky enough to find some wild black currants, wash them well and pick off the stems. Chop them, then put them through a coarse sieve, or purée them briefly in a food processor. Measure, then add an equal amount of sugar. Bring quickly to a boil and cook gently for 20 minutes, stirring. Pour into hot, *sterilized* jars and seal.

Strawberry Preserves

(ABOUT 2 PINTS)

3 cups (600 g) sugar
1 quart (1 L) strawberries

Cook the sugar and 1 cup water together until the mixture reaches 238°F on a jelly thermometer (soft-ball stage, p. 677). Wash and hull the berries, add to the syrup, cover, and remove from heat. Let stand for 10 minutes. Skim off any foam. Remove the berries and set aside. Cook the syrup to 238°F again, add the berries, and let stand over very low heat for 15 minutes. Skim, remove the berries, and reheat again to 238°F. Add the berries once more and cook slowly until the syrup is thick. Let stand for 24 hours before putting into *sterilized* jars and closing them. Refrigerate, freeze, or process in a simmering-water bath at 185°F for 10–15 minutes.

Peach Preserves

(ABOUT 7 HALF-PINT JARS)

10 large peaches, peeled,
pitted, and sliced
6 cups (1200 g) sugar

Combine the peaches and the sugar and let stand in a cool place overnight. Boil gently, stirring frequently, until the fruit is clear and the syrup thick, about 45 minutes. Pour into hot, *sterilized* jars and seal.

Raspberry Currant Preserves

(ABOUT SIX 8-OUNCE JARS)

2 quarts (2 L) raspberries
Juice from 1½ pounds (675 g)
   currants (see p. 701)

1½ pounds (675 g) sugar

Wash the raspberries and set aside. Put the currant juice in a large pot and add the sugar. Heat to the boiling point, then cook slowly for 20 minutes. Add a third of the raspberries. Bring the syrup to the boiling point, then spoon the raspberries into clean, *sterilized* jars. Repeat until all the berries are used. Fill each jar with the boiling syrup and seal.

Kumquat Preserves

(SIX 6-OUNCE JARS)

2 cups (400 g) sugar
1 quart (1 L) fresh kumquats

Combine the sugar with 1 cup water in a pot and boil for 5 minutes. Add the kumquats and cook gently until tender, about 45 minutes. Pour into hot, *sterilized* jars and seal.

Grape Conserve

(ABOUT TEN 6-OUNCE JARS)

5 pounds (2¼ kg) Concord
   grapes
½ orange, in thin slivers

Sugar
½ cup (1 dL) walnut pieces

Wash the grapes, remove the stems, and separate the pulp from the skins; reserve the skins. Heat the pulp gently to free the seeds, stirring to prevent sticking. Put through a sieve or food mill and discard the seeds. Add the orange to the grape pulp and skins and measure. Add an equal amount of sugar to the grape mixture. Cook slowly in a large, flat skillet, in two batches, if necessary. Use the freezer test (p. 700) to see if the conserve is thick, then add the walnuts. Spoon into hot, *sterilized* jars and seal.

Rhubarb Conserve

(SIX 6-OUNCE JARS)

2 pounds (900 g) rhubarb
2½ pounds (1¼ kg) sugar
½ pound (225 g) raisins

Grated rind and juice of 1 orange
Grated rind and juice of ½ lemon

Wash the rhubarb and cut it into 1-inch pieces. Put in a pot with the remaining ingredients, mix well, cover, and let stand for 30 minutes. Bring to a boil, then simmer for 45 minutes, stirring frequently. Pour into hot, *sterilized* jars and seal.

Cranberry Conserve

For Cranberry Jelly and other quick relishes, see p. 282.

(ABOUT THREE 6-OUNCE JARS)

4 cups (1 L) cranberries
⅔ cup (1½ dL) boiling apple
  or pineapple juice
¼ pound (115 g) seedless
  raisins

1 orange, sliced, seeded, and
  cut small
1½ pounds (675 g) sugar
½ pound (225 g) walnut or
  filbert meats, cut in pieces

Wash the cranberries and put them in a large pot. Add ⅔ cup cold water and cook until the skins break. Force through a strainer or food mill. Add the apple or pineapple juice, raisins, orange, and sugar. Bring to a boil, then simmer for 20 minutes. Add the nuts and let cool. Spoon into clean jars, close the jars, and process in a simmering-water bath at 185°F for 10–15 minutes.

Cranberry Ginger Conserve. Add ½ *cup preserved ginger, cut small,* along with the raisins and orange.

Rhubarb Fig Marmalade

(ABOUT SIX 6-OUNCE JARS)

1 pound (450 g) rhubarb, cut
  fine
1 pound (450 g) sugar

¼ pound (115 g) dried figs, cut
  small
Juice of ½ lemon

Combine the ingredients in a large pot, cover, and let stand 24 hours. Cook rapidly, stirring frequently, until the jellying point is reached (p. 700). Pour into hot, *sterilized* jars and seal.

Tomato Marmalade

(ABOUT SIX 6-OUNCE JARS)

3 pounds (1⅓ kg) red or green
  tomatoes, peeled and cut in
  pieces

1 orange, seeded and sliced thin
½ lemon, seeded and sliced thin
1½ pounds (675 g) sugar

Combine all the ingredients in a large pot and cook slowly, stirring frequently, until thick, about 3 hours. Pour into hot, *sterilized* jars and seal.

Orange Marmalade

(ABOUT 3 PINTS)

6 large oranges
2 lemons
Sugar

Peel the oranges and cut the peel into very thin slices. Cut up the orange pulp.

Slice the lemons very thin. Combine the fruit in a large pot and add 1½ quarts water. Bring to a boil and simmer for about 10 minutes; then let stand overnight in a cool place. Bring to a boil again and cook rapidly until the peel is tender. Measure the fruit and liquid. For each cup of undrained fruit measure ¾ cup sugar and add it to the fruit. Heat, stirring, until the sugar is dissolved, then cook rapidly until the jellying point is reached (p. 700), about 30 minutes. Pour into hot, *sterilized* jars and seal.

Ginger Marmalade. Add *2½ cups chopped preserved ginger* to each quart of fruit before boiling to the jellying point.

Three-Fruit Marmalade

(ABOUT TWELVE 6-OUNCE JARS)

1 grapefruit	Sugar
2 oranges	Salt
2 lemons	

Scrub the fruit and slice very thin, saving the juice. Discard the seeds and the grapefruit core. Measure the fruit and juice. Put the fruit and juice in a large pot and add three times as much water. Simmer, covered, for 2 hours, then let stand overnight. Measure the fruit and liquid, then add an equal amount of sugar and a sprinkle of salt. Cook rapidly, in two or three batches, until the jellying point is reached (p. 700), stirring frequently. Pour into hot, *sterilized* jars and seal.

Spiced Orange Slices

Fine with roast duckling.

(ABOUT EIGHT 6-OUNCE JARS)

6 large oranges	1 stick cinnamon
3½ cups (700 g) sugar	2 teaspoons cloves
1 cup (¼ L) cider vinegar	

Cut the oranges in ¼-inch slices and remove the seeds. Put in a pot, cover with water, simmer for 30 minutes, and drain. In another saucepan, combine the remaining ingredients and boil for 5 minutes. Cook the orange slices in the syrup in batches, so that each batch of slices is completely covered by the syrup. Remove the slices when they are clear, after about 30 minutes. Cover the cooked slices with the syrup and let stand overnight. Drain the slices and cook the syrup separately until it is thick. Add the orange slices and heat to the boiling point. Pour into hot, *sterilized* jars and seal.

Apple Butter

This recipe works for other fruit butters as well: use fresh apricots, peaches, plums, or the pulp in the jelly bag after the juice has been extracted. When using fruits that are juicier than apples, crush them and add just enough water, not cider or vinegar, to keep the fruit from sticking.

Apple Butter (continued)

(ABOUT TEN 6-OUNCE JARS)

4 pounds (1¾ kg) tart apples
2 cups (½ L) cider, cider
   vinegar, or water
Sugar
Salt
About 2 teaspoons cinnamon

About 1 teaspoon ground
   cloves
About ½ teaspoon allspice
Grated rind and juice of 1
   lemon

Cut the apples into pieces without peeling or coring them. Put them in a pot, cover with the cider, vinegar, or water, and cook until soft. Put through a sieve or food mill. Measure. Add ½ cup sugar for each cup of apple pulp. To the whole mixture, add a dash of salt and the cinnamon, cloves, allspice, and lemon rind and juice. Cook, covered, over low heat until the sugar dissolves, taste, and adjust the seasonings. Uncover and cook quickly, stirring constantly to prevent burning, until thick and smooth when a bit is spooned onto a cold plate. Pour into hot, *sterilized* jars and seal.

Brandied Peaches

Use perfect peaches for this. If the skins are thin, it is not necessary to peel them: simply rub off the fuzz with a clean cloth and prick each peach twice with a fork. Store these for a month before using.

(2 OR 3 PINT JARS)

6 peaches
2 cups (400 g) sugar
Brandy

Peel the peaches, if you wish, dipping them quickly in hot water before removing the skins. Combine the sugar with 3 cups water and boil for 10 minutes. Cook the peaches, a few at a time, in the sugar syrup until tender when pricked with a toothpick, about 5 minutes. Pack into clean, hot jars, adding 2 tablespoons of brandy to each pint jar. Fill the jars with syrup, close the jars, and process in a simmering-water bath at 185°F for 10–15 minutes.

Brandied Cherries. Substitute *2 pounds firm cherries* for the peaches.

Tutti-Frutti

A large stone crock is the traditional container, but a large glass jar or casserole will do. Tutti-frutti and ice cream are a splendid combination.

(ABOUT 6 QUARTS)

5–6 quarts (5–6 L) assorted
   fruits: berries, cherries,
   currants, apricots, peaches,
   pineapple

1 quart (1 L) brandy
Sugar

Put the brandy in a crock that will hold at least 2 gallons. Add the fruits, hulling strawberries and raspberries; pitting cherries; pitting, peeling, and cutting up apricots and peaches; and cutting pineapple into chunks. Add 2 cups sugar for each 2 cups fruit. Cover tight, or seal in *sterilized* jars, and store for 3 months before using.

PICKLES

About Pickles

For general information, see About Preserves, Pickles, and Canned Fruits and Vegetables (p. 694).

Pickles and relishes, so much a part of our heritage, have given a lift to many a homely meal. Serve them with snacks and sandwiches, as an hors d'oeuvre on a relish tray, or as an accompaniment to meats and poultry. Used in small quantities, they add nice flavor to certain salads, salad dressings, and sauces, and, like preserves, they make very special gifts.

Kinds of Pickles

Brined Pickles. Old-fashioned brined pickles are cured in a water and salt solution over a period of weeks. Dill pickles, sauerkraut, and green tomatoes are frequently cured that way. Although it is possible to brine pickles at home, the method requires controlled temperatures and conditions as well as patience. Most home cooks these days use the fresh-pack, or short-brine, method.

Fresh-Pack Pickles. Fresh-pack, or short-brine, pickles are soaked in a salt solution for several hours or more to extract moisture, then drained and preserved in vinegar.

Relishes. Relishes usually combine several fruits or vegetables that are chopped or sliced, cooked and seasoned, then packed in jars and processed. Some relishes are mild and subtly flavored; others are spicy and hot. Chutneys, as we know them in this country, are sweet-spicy fruit relishes, often dotted with raisins.

Fruit Pickles. Fruit pickles are made from whole or sliced fruits that are simmered in a spicy sweet-sour syrup.

Equipment for Pickling

For general canning equipment, see p. 696.

Pickles preserved in vinegar are high in acid, which prevents toxic growth. Read the advantage and disadvantage of processing on p. 695 before you decide which way is for you. If processed do so at 212°F in a boiling-water bath. For this you will need a water-bath canner, equipped with a rack so that the jars do not touch the bottom of the pot (p. 696).

Do not use copper, brass, or iron utensils, which may react unfavorably to the acid in the pickles.

Ingredients

Vegetables and Fruits. Use fresh, young, tender vegetables and fruits, as free as possible from bruises and blemishes. Wash them very carefully and cut away any bad spots. Slightly underripe vegetables will produce crisper pickles. Do not use waxed cucumbers if you are pickling them whole; the waxed skins will not absorb liquid.

Vinegar. Cider vinegar or any vinegar with a mild flavor is good for pickling. Be sure the label indicates that the vinegar has at least 4 to 6 percent acidity, or your pickled vegetables may spoil. Don't dilute vinegar; if the mixture seems too sour, add sugar to achieve the proper balance. Although cider vinegar may darken pickles slightly, it is desirable for its pleasantly mild flavor. White vinegar has a sharper taste, but should be used when pickling light-colored vegetables like onions.

Water. The water used when pickling should be soft or artificially softened.

Salt. Use pure, granulated salt, if you can get some, or uniodized table salt. Iodized table salt will darken pickles.

Spices. Spices should be fresh, of course. They are usually used whole, and often put in a cloth bag for easy removal. If spices stay in the pickled product too long, they will darken it. You can vary the amount of spices in these recipes to suit your own tastes.

Alum and Lime. Neither alum nor lime is necessary to produce crisp pickles if you use the right ingredients and procedures.

Processing Pickles

See Water-Bath Method, p. 697.

If you do decide to process pickles, be sure not to overprocess them; you want to retain as much crispness as possible. Begin counting the processing time when the jars are first inserted into the boiling water; do not wait for the water to return to a boil again, as you do with other home-canned products.

Bread-and-Butter Pickles

Use Kirby cucumbers or other small, unwaxed cucumbers, and tiny white onions, if possible.

(ABOUT 4 PINTS)

6 cups (1½ L) thin-sliced
    cucumbers
1 pound (450 g) onions
1 green pepper, shredded
¼ cup (½ dL) salt
2 cups (½ L) brown sugar

½ teaspoon turmeric
¼ teaspoon ground cloves
1 tablespoon mustard seed
1 teaspoon celery seed
2 cups (½ L) cider vinegar

Mix the cucumbers, onions (sliced if large), green pepper, and salt. Cover and let stand for 3 hours. Mix the remaining ingredients in a large pot, bring slowly to the boiling point, and boil for 5 minutes. Drain the vegetables in a colander and rinse them well with cold water. Add them to the hot syrup and heat to just below the boiling point. Spoon into hot *sterilized* jars, fill with the cooking syrup, leaving ⅛-inch headspace, and seal. Or, if you prefer, process in a boiling-water bath for 10 minutes.

Dill Pickles

(6–8 QUARTS)

About 50 unwaxed 3–4-inch
    cucumbers
1 quart (1 L) cider vinegar

¾ cup (1¾ dL) salt
Fresh dill sprigs
Garlic cloves, peeled

Put the cucumbers in the sink, cover with cold water and let stand overnight. Drain and pack them into hot, *sterilized* jars. Combine the vinegar and salt with 2 quarts water in a pot and bring to the boiling point. Pour over the cucumbers, leaving ¼-inch headspace. Add a sprig or two of dill and a clove of peeled garlic to each jar and seal. Or close the jars and process in a boiling-water bath for 15 minutes.

Icicle Pickles

(ABOUT 6 PINTS)

Twenty 6-inch cucumbers,
  quartered lengthwise
6 cups (1½ L) vinegar

6 cups (1200 g) sugar
½ cup (1 dL) salt

Cover the cucumbers with ice water and let stand overnight. Drain and pack upright in clean jars. Combine the vinegar and sugar with 2 cups water in a pot, boil for 3 minutes, then add the salt. Pour over the cucumbers, leaving ¼-inch headspace. Close the jars and process in a boiling-water bath for 10 minutes.

Mustard Pickles

Be careful not to overcook so these pickles remain crisp.

(8 PINTS)

3 pounds (1½ kg) small
  cucumbers, sliced
3 large cucumbers, cubed
2 pounds (900 g) green
  tomatoes, diced
1½ pounds (675 g) small white
  onions, peeled
4 green peppers, diced

1 large cauliflower, in small
  pieces
½ cup (1 dL) salt
1 cup (140 g) flour
6 tablespoons dry mustard
1 tablespoon turmeric
2 quarts (2 L) cider vinegar
2 cups (400 g) sugar

Put the cucumbers, tomatoes, onions, peppers, and cauliflower in a large bowl. Mix the salt with 4 quarts cold water, pour over the vegetables, cover, and let stand for 8 hours or overnight. Drain and rinse under cold water. Put the vegetables in a pot, cover them with fresh cold water, bring to the boiling point, and drain in a colander once again. Put the flour, mustard, and turmeric in the pot. Stir in enough vinegar to make a smooth paste, then gradually add the remaining vinegar and the sugar, stirring well. Bring to a boil, stirring constantly, and cook until thick and smooth. Add the vegetables and cook, stirring, until heated through. Spoon into hot, *sterilized* jars, leaving ¼-inch headspace, and seal. Or close the jars and process in a boiling-water bath for 10 minutes.

Pickled Onions

(ABOUT 8 PINTS)

4 quarts (4 L) small white
  pickling onions, peeled
  (p. 391)
1 cup (¼ L) salt
2 quarts (2 L) white vinegar
2 cups (400 g) sugar

¼ cup (½ dL) mustard seed
2 tablespoons prepared
  horseradish
White peppercorns
Bay leaves
Pimiento slices

Sprinkle the onions with the salt. Cover with cold water and let stand 6–8 hours or overnight. Rinse thoroughly with cold water, and drain well. Combine the vinegar, sugar, mustard seed, and horseradish in a pot and simmer for 10 minutes. Spoon the onions into hot, *sterilized* jars, adding a few peppercorns, a bay leaf, and some pimiento slices to each jar. Pour the boiling hot vinegar mixture over the onions, leaving ¼-inch headspace, and seal. Or close the jars and process in a boiling-water bath for 10 minutes.

Pickled Beets

(4 PINTS)

4 pounds (1¾ kg) small beets   ½ teaspoon whole allspice
1 quart (1 L) vinegar   1 stick cinnamon
1½ cups (300 g) sugar   1 teaspoon cloves

Cook the beets in boiling water until tender when pierced with a fork. Hold them under cold water and slip off the skins. Slice them only if they are large. Mix the remaining ingredients in a large saucepan, add the beets, and bring to a boil. Reduce the heat and simmer for 15 minutes. Spoon into clean, hot, *sterilized* jars, fill with the cooking liquid, leaving ½-inch headspace, and seal. If you wish, process in a boiling-water bath for 30 minutes.

Corn Relish

Use sweet pimiento for a mild relish, hot red pepper for a spicy one. A food processor will be handy here.

(ABOUT 6 PINTS)

18 ears of corn   6 green peppers, chopped fine
1 head green cabbage, chopped   2 quarts (2 L) vinegar
   fine   2 cups (400 g) sugar
8 white onions, chopped fine   ¼ cup (½ dL) salt
½ cup (1 dL) chopped   2 teaspoons celery seed
   pimiento, or 4 small hot red 2 teaspoons mustard seed
   peppers

Cut the kernels from the corn ears. Combine them with the remaining ingredients in a large pot, bring to the boiling point, and simmer for 40 minutes. Spoon into hot, *sterilized* jars, leaving ⅛-inch headspace, and seal. If you wish, process in a boiling-water bath for 15 minutes.

Red or Green Pepper Relish

You can chop the vegetables for this and other relishes coarse or fine, according to your preference. Use a food processor, if you have one, to save time and effort.

(6–7 PINTS)

24 sweet red or green peppers   2 cups (400 g) sugar
   or a combination   3 tablespoons salt
12 onions, peeled   1 tablespoon mustard or celery
6 stalks celery   seed
1 quart (1 L) cider vinegar

Chop the peppers, onions, and celery, cover with boiling water, then drain. Put them in a pot, cover with cold water, bring to the boiling point, then drain again. Mix the vinegar, sugar, salt, and mustard or celery seed in a pot, heat to the boiling point, add the vegetables, and simmer for about 10 minutes, adjusting the seasonings if necessary. Spoon into clean, hot jars, fill with the cooking liquid, leaving ⅛-inch headspace, and seal. If you wish, process in a boiling-water bath for 10 minutes.

Celery Relish

Sweet and crunchy.

(3 PINTS)

½ cup (100 g) sugar
2 teaspoons salt
¼ teaspoon dry mustard
¼ teaspoon ground cloves
¼ teaspoon allspice
¼ teaspoon cinnamon

¼ teaspoon celery seed
1–1½ cups (2¼–3½ dL) cider vinegar
2 bunches celery, chopped
6 large tomatoes, chopped
1 sweet red pepper, chopped

Mix all the ingredients well in a large pot. Bring to the boiling point, reduce the heat, and simmer until thick, about 1 hour. Spoon into hot, *sterilized* jars, fill with the cooking liquid, leaving ⅛-inch headspace, and seal. If you wish, process in a boiling-water bath for 10 minutes.

Chow-Chow

A beautiful, golden relish with a mustardy tang.

(8 PINTS)

2½ pounds (1¼ kg) green tomatoes
6 small cucumbers
2 sweet red or green peppers
1 small cauliflower
1 bunch celery
2 pounds (900 g) small white onions, peeled
1 pound (450 g) green beans, in 1-inch lengths

¾ cup (1¾ dL) salt
2 quarts (1 L) cider vinegar
2½ cups (500 g) sugar
2 tablespoons celery seed
3 tablespoons dry mustard
4 tablespoons turmeric
1 tablespoon whole allspice
1 tablespoon freshly ground pepper
1 tablespoon ground cloves

Cut the tomatoes, cucumbers, red or green peppers, cauliflower, and celery in small pieces. Combine with the onions and green beans. Cover with 3 quarts boiling water and the salt and let stand for 1 hour. Drain. Rinse well in cold water and drain again. Mix the remaining ingredients in a large pot and heat to the boiling point. Add the vegetables and cook until tender, stirring frequently. Spoon into hot, *sterilized* jars, fill with the cooking liquid, leaving ⅛-inch headspace, and seal. If you wish, process in a boiling-water bath for 10 minutes.

Piccalilli

Sweet and spicy.

(6 PINTS)

12 green tomatoes
4 green peppers
2 sweet red peppers
6 onions, peeled
1 small cabbage
¼ cup (½ dL) salt
3 cups (¾ L) light-brown sugar

1½ teaspoons celery seed
1 tablespoon mustard seed
1 tablespoon cloves
2-inch stick cinnamon
1 tablespoon whole allspice
2 cups (½ L) cider vinegar

Chop the tomatoes, peppers, onions, and cabbage coarsely. Sprinkle them with the salt, cover, and let stand overnight. Cover with cold water and then drain. Mix the remaining ingredients in a large pot. Add the vegetables and bring to the boiling point. Reduce the heat and simmer for about 15 minutes. Spoon into hot, *sterilized* jars, fill with the cooking liquid, leaving ⅛-inch headspace, and seal. If you wish, process in a boiling-water bath for 10 minutes.

Green Tomato Relish

(4 PINTS)

4 pounds (1¾ kg) green
  tomatoes, chopped (about 8
  cups, 2 L)
¼ cup (½ dL) salt
1 teaspoon freshly ground
  pepper
1½ teaspoons dry mustard
1½ teaspoons cinnamon

½ teaspoon allspice
1½ teaspoons ground cloves
¼ cup (½ dL) mustard seed
1 quart (1 L) cider vinegar
1 cup (¼ L) light-brown sugar
2 sweet red or green peppers,
  chopped
1 onion, chopped

Mix the tomatoes with the salt, cover, and let stand overnight or for 24 hours. Wash in cold water and drain. Mix the remaining ingredients in a pot, add the tomatoes, and bring to a boil. Cook gently for about 15 minutes. Spoon into hot, *sterilized* jars, leaving ⅛-inch headspace, and seal. If you wish, process in a boiling-water bath for 10 minutes.

Tomato Relish

This is a tart, red tomato relish. Add more sugar if you want it to be sweet.

(2 PINTS)

1 bunch celery
2 large green peppers
1 onion
6 large tomatoes, peeled and
  cut in pieces

1 tablespoon salt
1 tablespoon sugar
1¼ cups (3 dL) cider vinegar

Chop the celery, peppers, and onion and mix in a large pot. Add the tomatoes, salt, sugar, and vinegar and simmer, stirring occasionally, until thick, about 1½ hours. Spoon into hot, *sterilized* jars, leaving ⅛-inch headspace, and seal. If you wish, process in a boiling-water bath for 10 minutes.

Sweet Chili Sauce

Good with hamburgers and steak.

(3–4 PINTS)

3 pounds (1⅓ kg) (about 4
  cups, 1 L) ripe tomatoes,
  peeled and cut up
2 green peppers, chopped fine

2 onions, chopped fine
2 apples, cored and chopped
  fine
½–1 cup (100–200 g) sugar

1 tablespoon salt
½ teaspoon freshly ground
   pepper
1 teaspoon cinnamon

1 teaspoon ground cloves
½ teaspoon allspice
1 teaspoon nutmeg
1 cup (¼ L) cider vinegar

Cook the tomatoes slowly for about 30 minutes, until they are soft. Stir in the peppers, onions, and apples and cook 30 minutes more. Add the remaining ingredients, adjusting the amount of sugar to taste. Boil until thick, about 10 minutes, stirring frequently and taking care not to let the mixture burn. Spoon into hot, *sterilized* jars, leaving ⅛-inch headspace, and seal. If you wish, process in a boiling-water bath for 15 minutes.

Tomato Catsup

A clean, spicy flavor, very different from the commercial product.

(1 PINT)

10 pounds (4½ kg) ripe
   tomatoes, peeled and cut up
3 onions, chopped fine
2 sweet red or green peppers,
   seeded and chopped
1 small clove garlic, minced
2-inch stick cinnamon
1 teaspoon peppercorns
1 teaspoon cloves

1 teaspoon whole allspice
1 teaspoon celery seed
¾ cup (1¾ dL) dark-brown
   sugar
1 cup (¼ L) cider vinegar
1 tablespoon salt
2 teaspoons paprika
¼ teaspoon cayenne pepper

Combine the tomatoes, onions, red or green peppers, and garlic in a pot and cook slowly until soft, at least 30 minutes. Strain through a food mill or a fine sieve. Return to the pot and simmer until the mixture is reduced by one-half, about 30–40 minutes, stirring frequently to be sure that it does not stick or burn. Tie the cinnamon, peppercorns, cloves, allspice, and celery seed in a cheesecloth bag and add them and the remaining ingredients to the tomato mixture. Cook slowly until the catsup is very thick, stirring frequently to prevent burning. Remove the bag of spices. Spoon into small clean, hot jars, leaving ⅛-inch headspace. Close the jars and process in a boiling-water bath for 10 minutes.

Peach Chutney

(THREE OR FOUR 6-OUNCE JARS)

2 cups (½ L) cider vinegar
3 cups (600 g) sugar
4 cups (1 L) (about 2 pounds,
   900 g) peaches, peeled,
   pitted, and cut up

½ pound (225 g) currants or
   raisins
2 cloves garlic, minced
2 tablespoons candied ginger,
   cut fine

Combine the vinegar and sugar in a pot and bring to a boil. Add the remaining ingredients, and cook slowly for about 2 hours, stirring occasionally to prevent sticking. Spoon into hot, *sterilized* jars, leaving ¼-inch headspace, and seal. If you wish, process in a boiling-water bath for 10 minutes.

Apple Chutney

A splendid sweet-and-spicy partner to ham and other pork dishes. Use ripe, red tomatoes, if you wish. You may add ½ cup of finely cut mint leaves, if you have them.

(7 PINTS)

1½ pounds (675 g) green tomatoes, chopped (about 3 cups, ¾ L)
4 tablespoons salt
1 quart (1 L) cider vinegar
1 pound (450 g) dark-brown sugar

12 large, tart apples, cored and chopped
2 Spanish onions, peeled and chopped
1 pound (450 g) raisins
2 tablespoons ground ginger

Put the tomatoes in a bowl, toss them with 2 tablespoons of the salt, cover, and let stand for about 12 hours. Drain and soak them in cold water for a few minutes, then drain again. Heat the vinegar, the remaining 2 tablespoons of salt, and the sugar in a large pot. Add the drained tomatoes, the apples, onions, raisins, and ginger, and cook over low heat for about 30 minutes, until the apples and onions are tender. Spoon into hot, *sterilized* jars, leaving ¼-inch headspace, and seal. If you wish, process in a boiling-water bath for 10 minutes.

Ginger Apple Chutney. Omit the ground ginger and substitute 6 *ounces preserved ginger, cut small.*

Watermelon Pickle

Sweet and spicy, this will appeal to thrifty souls because it uses the watermelon rind that would otherwise go uneaten.

(2 QUARTS)

Rind from 1 large watermelon
½ cup (1 dL) salt
2½ cups (6 dL) cider vinegar
2 cups (400 g) sugar

2 teaspoons cloves
1 small stick cinnamon, in pieces
2 tablespoons whole allspice

Remove the pink pulp from the watermelon and cut the rind into manageable pieces. Cover with boiling water and boil for 5 minutes; drain and cool. Cut off the green outer skin of the watermelon rind and remove any remaining bits of pink pulp. Cut the rind into 1-inch strips or squares or any shape you prefer. You should have about 8 cups of cut-up rind. Mix the salt with 1½ quarts cold water and pour over the rind. Let stand at room temperature for about 6 hours. Drain, soak in several changes of fresh, cold water, and drain again. Cover with fresh, cold water, bring to a boil, and simmer until just tender when pierced with a fork; drain. Mix the vinegar, 1 cup water, and the sugar in a pot, then add the cloves, cinnamon, and allspice tied in a cheesecloth bag. Simmer until the sugar dissolves. Add the watermelon rind and simmer until it is clear, adding more water only if necessary. Remove the spice bag. Pack in hot, *sterilized* jars and cover with the boiling liquid, leaving ¼-inch headspace, and seal. If you wish, process in a boiling-water bath for 10 minutes.

Ginger Watermelon Pickle. Add *1–2 tablespoons chopped preserved ginger* to the vinegar mixture.

Pickled Crabapples

(ABOUT 3 PINTS)

30 crabapples
1 cup (¼ L) cider vinegar
1 cup (¼ L) brown sugar

1 cup (200 g) granulated sugar
1 tablespoon cloves
1 stick cinnamon, in pieces

Cut off the blossom end of the crabapples but do not peel. Prick them several times with a fork. Combine the remaining ingredients with 1 cup water in a pot and boil for 5 minutes. Add the fruit, in batches if necessary, and simmer until tender. Spoon the crabapples into clean, hot jars. Fill with the hot cooking syrup, leaving ¼-inch headspace. Prepare more syrup, if necessary. Seal and process, if you wish, in a boiling-water bath for 15 minutes.

Pickled Pears. Use *Seckel pears*. Peel them, if you wish, or leave the skin on, pricking it well. Use *white vinegar* instead of cider vinegar.

Horseradish

Horseradish roots
Salt
White vinegar

Scrape the outside of the horseradish roots until clean and drop them into cold water to prevent discoloration. Drain and chop in a food processor or in a blender with a little vinegar. Spoon into clean pint jars, filling them about two-thirds full. Add 1 teaspoon of salt to each jar, then fill with white vinegar. Close the jars and refrigerate.

CANNED FRUITS AND HIGH-ACID VEGETABLES

About Canned Fruits and High-Acid Vegetables

For general information, see About Preserves, Pickles, and Canned Fruits and Vegetables, p. 694. For freezing fruits, see p. 731.

Equipment for Canning Fruits and High-Acid Vegetables

All fruits and a few vegetables, such as tomatoes and rhubarb, are high in natural acid. Do not use tomatoes when they are overripe; they are less acid. Fruits and acid vegetables do not require high-heat processing under pressure but should be processed in a boiling-water bath at 212°F. For this you will need a water-bath canner, equipped with a rack so that the jars do not touch the bottom of the pot (p. 696).

Preparing Fruits and High-Acid Vegetables for Canning

Use firm, fresh produce. Wash fruits and vegetables thoroughly before hulling or removing the skins, pits, cores, or seeds.

To prevent prepared fruit from darkening, drop it into a salt-vinegar-water mixture (2 tablespoons each of salt and vinegar to 1 gallon of water) for no more than 20 minutes. Rinse the fruit before cooking it or packing it into jars. Leave the designated headspace.

Fruits and vegetables may be raw-packed or hot-packed (p. 697), according to the recipe, in sweetened or unsweetened liquid. Sugar syrup is often used to help preserve the shape, color, and flavor of fruit, but it is not necessary for preserving: fruit juices or plain water will preserve just as well.

Sugar Syrup. Each quart of fruit requires from 1 to 1½ cups of sugar syrup. Sugar syrup is made by cooking sugar in water or fruit juice until it dissolves. Use the following proportions:

Light Syrup: 2 cups sugar to 4 cups water = 5 cups syrup

Medium Syrup: 3 cups sugar to 4 cups water = 5½ cups syrup

Heavy Syrup: 4¾ cups sugar to 4 cups water = 6½ cups syrup

If you wish, you can replace up to half the sugar with honey or corn syrup. This sugar syrup is also used in freezing fruits (see p. 731).

Processing Fruits and High-Acid Vegetables
See Water-Bath Method, p. 697.

Canned Apples
(ALLOW 2½–3 POUNDS FOR EACH QUART JAR)

Peel, core, and slice the *apples* or cut them into quarters. Boil in *light syrup* (above) for 5 minutes. Pack into clean, hot jars and cover with boiling syrup, leaving ½-inch headspace. Close the jars and process in a boiling-water bath for 20 minutes.

Applesauce

Follow instructions for making *Applesauce* (p. 650). Heat the applesauce until it boils, then spoon it into clean, hot jars, leaving ½-inch headspace. Close the jars and process in a boiling-water bath for 20 minutes.

Canned Apricots
(ALLOW 2–3 POUNDS FOR EACH QUART JAR)

Cut the *apricots* in half and remove the pits. Cook gently in *medium* or *heavy syrup* (above) until heated through. Pack into clean, hot jars and cover with boiling syrup, leaving ½-inch headspace. Close the jars and process in a boiling-water bath, allowing 20 minutes for pint jars and 25 minutes for quarts.

Canned Blackberries and Raspberries
(ALLOW 1½ QUARTS FOR EACH QUART JAR)

Wash the *berries* and remove the caps and stems. Spoon them into clean, hot jars. Cover them with boiling *light* or *medium syrup* (above), leaving ½-inch headspace. Close the jars and process in a boiling-water bath, allowing 15 minutes for pint jars and 20 minutes for quarts.

Canned Blueberries

(ALLOW 2 QUARTS FOR 3 PINT JARS)

Wash the *blueberries* and remove the stems. Put them in a square of cheesecloth and gather up the ends to form a bag. Dip the berries into boiling water for about 30 seconds or until spots appear on the bag. Dip into cold water. Pack the berries tightly into jars, leaving ½-inch headspace. Do *not* add sugar or liquid. Close the jars and process in a boiling-water bath, allowing 15 minutes for pint jars and 20 minutes for quarts.

Canned Cherries

(ALLOW 2–2½ POUNDS FOR EACH QUART JAR)

Stem and pit the *cherries,* or leave the pits in, if desired. Wash them and pack them into jars. Fill with boiling *light syrup* (opposite), leaving ½-inch headspace. Close the jars and process in a boiling-water bath, allowing 20 minutes for pint jars and 25 minutes for quarts.

Sour Cherries. Use *medium* or *heavy syrup* (opposite).

Canned Peaches

(ALLOW 2–3 POUNDS FOR EACH QUART JAR)

Wash *freestone peaches* and dip them into boiling water, then cold water. Peel them, then cut in half and remove the stones. Slice, if desired. Cook gently in *medium or heavy syrup* (opposite) until heated through. Spoon into clean, hot jars, and cover with boiling syrup, leaving ½-inch headspace. Close the jars and process in a boiling-water bath, allowing 20 minutes for pint jars and 25 minutes for quarts.

Canned Pears

(ALLOW 2–3 POUNDS FOR EACH QUART JAR)

Wash the *pears* and peel them. Leave them whole or cut them in half and core them. Cook gently in *light syrup* (opposite) for 5–6 minutes, about 10 minutes if whole. Pack into clean, hot jars and cover with boiling syrup, leaving ½-inch headspace. Close the jars and process in a boiling-water bath, allowing 20 minutes for pint jars and 25 minutes for quarts.

Canned Pineapple

(ALLOW 2 POUNDS FOR EACH QUART JAR)

Cut the *pineapple* crosswise in ½-inch slices. Pare the outer shell and cut out the cores. Dice, if desired. Simmer in *light syrup* (opposite) until tender. Pack into clean, hot jars and cover with boiling syrup, leaving ½-inch headspace. Close the jars and process in a boiling-water bath, allowing 15 minutes for pint jars and 20 minutes for quarts.

Canned Plums

(ALLOW 1½–2½ POUNDS FOR EACH QUART JAR)

Wash the *plums*, cut them in half, and remove the pits, or prick the skins and use them whole. Heat to the boiling point in *medium* or *heavy syrup* (p. 718). Pack in clean, hot jars and cover with boiling syrup, leaving ½-inch headspace. Close the jars and process in a boiling-water bath, allowing 20 minutes for pint jars and 25 minutes for quarts.

Canned Rhubarb

(ALLOW 1 POUND FOR EACH PINT JAR)

Clean the *rhubarb* and cut the stalks into ½-inch pieces. Measure and add ¼ *cup sugar* for each pint. Mix well and let stand for at least 1 hour, then bring slowly to the boiling point and boil for about 1 minute. Pack into clean, hot jars, leaving ½-inch headspace. Close the jars and process in a boiling-water bath for 10 minutes.

Canned Strawberries

Strawberries do not can well. It's best to use them in jams and preserves (p. 704) or to freeze them (p. 731).

Canned Tomatoes

(ALLOW 3 POUNDS FOR EACH QUART JAR)

Dip barely ripe *tomatoes* in boiling water for a minute or two and then in cold water. Peel them and cut out the stems and any white cores. Slice them or leave them whole. Pack into clean, hot jars and press down until the jars fill up with liquid, leaving ½-inch headspace. Add 1 teaspoon *salt* for each quart. Close the jars and process in a boiling-water bath, allowing 35 minutes for pint jars and 45 minutes for quarts.

Canned Tomato Purée

Dip barely ripe *tomatoes* in boiling water for a minute or two and then in cold water. Peel them and cut out the stems and any white cores. Slice them and cook over low heat until soft. Press through a food mill or strainer, then return to the pot and continue to cook until thick, stirring constantly to prevent sticking. Season with *salt*, if you wish. Pack in clean, hot jars, leaving ¼-inch headspace. Close the jars and process in a boiling-water bath, allowing 30 minutes for pint jars.

Spicy Tomato Purée. Add to the peeled tomatoes any one or all of the following: *chopped onion, chopped fresh herbs, chopped celery, chopped carrot, chopped green pepper.* Process pint jars for 45 minutes.

Canned Tomato Juice

Wash barely ripe *tomatoes* and cut away the stem ends and any bad spots. Cut in small pieces and simmer over low heat until very soft. Strain through a sieve or a food mill. Reheat the juice to the boiling point, adding salt, a touch of sugar and spices to taste, if you wish. Pour into clean, hot jars, leaving ¼-inch headspace. Close the jars and process in a boiling-water bath, allowing 10 minutes for pint jars and 15 minutes for quarts.

Canned Fruit Juice

Extract the *juice* from fruit as for jelly (p. 701). Sweeten with *sugar*, if desired. Pour into clean, hot jars, leaving ¼-inch headspace. Close the jars and process in a simmering-water bath at 185°F for 15 minutes.

CANNED LOW-ACID VEGETABLES

About Canned Low-Acid Vegetables

For general information, see About Preserves, Pickles, and Canned Fruits and Vegetables (p. 694). For freezing vegetables, see p. 733.

Note: All home-canned low-acid foods should be boiled in an uncovered pot for 15 minutes before tasting or serving.

Equipment for Canning Low-Acid Vegetables

Most vegetables are low in acid and must be processed under 10 pounds of pressure at a temperature of 240°F. (To adjust temperature when processing at high altitudes, see p. 698.) A steam-pressure canner is necessary for processing low-acid vegetables; it should be equipped with a cover that can be clamped down tight, a safety valve, a pressure gauge, and a petcock (vent).

Preparing Low-Acid Vegetables for Canning

Vegetables should be washed thoroughly to remove all traces of soil. Pack them whole or cut up, loosely enough for water to circulate, leaving the designated amount of headspace.

Salt is not necessary for preserving purposes, but is usually used for flavoring. Although low-acid vegetables may be raw-packed or hot-packed, we generally prefer the hot-pack method.

Broccoli, Brussels sprouts, cabbage, cauliflower, celery, cucumbers, eggplant, kohlrabi, onions, parsnips, and turnips are not recommended for canning.

Processing Low-Acid Vegetables

See Steam-Pressure Method, p. 697.

Using Canned Low-Acid Vegetables

There's no way to keep canned, low-acid vegetables crisp, given the long processing times required and the need to boil them for 15 minutes before they are tasted. It's best to use home-canned vegetables in soups or stews or to freeze them rather than can them.

Asparagus

(ALLOW 1½ POUNDS FOR EACH QUART JAR)

Wash *asparagus* thoroughly and trim off the scales and tough ends. Leave whole or cut into 1-inch pieces. Drop into boiling water and boil for 3 minutes. Pack into clean, hot jars, add ½ teaspoon *salt* for each pint, and cover with the boiling water, leaving ½-inch headspace. Close the jars and process at 10 pounds pressure in a steam-pressure canner, allowing 25 minutes for pint jars and 30 minutes for quarts.

Green or Wax Beans

Use young, tender beans, if possible. Older beans require 15 minutes more processing time. Beans are particularly susceptible to spoilage, so be sure jars are sterilized and check that caps have not bulged before opening.

(ALLOW ¾ POUND FOR EACH PINT JAR)

Wash *beans* thoroughly and trim the ends. Leave whole or cut into 1–2-inch lengths. Drop into boiling water and boil for 3 minutes. Pack into hot, clean jars, add ½ teaspoon *salt* for each pint, and cover with the boiling water, leaving 1-inch headspace. Close the jars and process at 10 pounds pressure in a steam-pressure canner, allowing 20 minutes for pint jars and 25 minutes for quarts.

Lima Beans

(ALLOW 2 POUNDS UNSHELLED BEANS FOR EACH PINT JAR)

Shell tender young *beans*, then wash and drain them. Drop into boiling water and boil for 3 minutes. Pack into hot, clean jars, add ½ teaspoon *salt* for each pint, and cover with the boiling water, leaving 1-inch headspace. Close the jars and process at 10 pounds pressure in a steam-pressure canner, allowing 40 minutes for pint jars and 50 minutes for quarts. (If beans are very large, add 10 minutes more processing time.)

Beets

(ALLOW 1–1½ POUNDS FOR EACH PINT JAR)

Wash *beets* thoroughly and trim, leaving 1 inch of stems. Boil about 15 minutes, until the skins slip off easily. Remove skins and trim; leave whole or slice. Pack beets into clean, hot jars, add ½ teaspoon *salt* for each pint, and cover with boiling water, leaving 1-inch headspace. Close the jars and process at 10 pounds pressure in a steam-pressure canner, allowing 30 minutes for pint jars and 35 minutes for quarts.

Carrots

(ALLOW 2–3 POUNDS FOR EACH QUART JAR)

Scrape *carrots* and wash them very well. Leave whole, slice, or dice. Drop into boiling water and boil for 3 minutes. Pack into clean, hot jars, add *1 teaspoon salt* for each quart, and cover with boiling water, leaving 1-inch headspace. Close the jars and process at 10 pounds pressure in a steam-pressure canner, allowing 25 minutes for pint jars and 30 minutes for quarts.

Corn—Whole Kernel

(ALLOW 4–6 CORN EARS FOR EACH PINT JAR)

Husk *corn*, remove the silk, and cut the kernels off without scraping the cob. Measure, then add ½ *teaspoon salt* and 1 cup boiling water for each pint. Bring to a boil, then pour at once into clean, hot jars, leaving 1-inch headspace. Close the jars and process at 10 pounds pressure in a steam-pressure canner, allowing 55 minutes for pint jars and 1 hour and 25 minutes for quarts.

Corn—Cream Style

(ALLOW 4–6 EARS FOR EACH PINT JAR)

Husk *corn*, remove the silks, and cut off the tips of the kernels. Scrape out the pulp. Measure, then add ½ *teaspoon salt* and 1¼ cups boiling water for each pint. Boil for 3 minutes, then pour into clean, hot jars, leaving 1-inch headspace. Close the jars and process at 10 pounds pressure in a steam-pressure canner, allowing 1 hour and 25 minutes for pint jars.

Peas

(ALLOW 2 POUNDS UNSHELLED PEAS FOR EACH PINT JAR)

Shell *peas*, wash them, then drop into boiling water and boil for 3–5 minutes. Pack into clean, hot jars, add ½ *teaspoon salt* for each pint, and cover with the boiling water, leaving 1-inch headspace. Close the jars and process at 10 pounds pressure in a steam-pressure canner for 40 minutes.

Potatoes

Wash tender *new potatoes* thoroughly; peel. Cook in boiling water for 10 minutes; drain. Pack into clean, hot jars, add ½ *teaspoon salt* for each pint, and cover with boiling water, leaving 1-inch headspace. Close the jars and process at 10 pounds pressure in a steam-pressure canner, allowing 30 minutes for pint jars and 40 minutes for quarts.

Pumpkin and Winter Squash

Because of the density of mashed pumpkin and winter squash, which makes it difficult for heat to reach the center, experts recommend that you can them cubed rather than mashed.

(ALLOW 1½ TO 2 POUNDS FOR EACH QUART JAR)

Wash and peel *pumpkin or winter squash* and cut it into cubes. Cook in a little water until tender. Pack into clean, hot jars and cover with boiling water, leaving 1-inch headspace. Close the jars and process at 10 pounds pressure in a steam-pressure canner, allowing 40 minutes for quart jars.

Summer Squash

(ALLOW 2–4 POUNDS FOR EACH QUART JAR)

Wash *squash* thoroughly, but do not peel it. Cut into ¼-inch slices and boil for 3 minutes. Pack into clean, hot jars, add ½ *teaspoon salt* for each pint, and cover with the boiling water, leaving 1-inch headspace. Close the jars and process at 10 pounds pressure in a steam-pressure canner, allowing 30 minutes for pint jars and 40 minutes for quarts.

Succotash

Husk fresh *corn*, remove the silk, and boil for 5 minutes. Cut the kernels from the cobs. Cook an equal amount of fresh *lima beans* in boiling water for 3 minutes. Mix the corn and lima beans and pack in clean, hot jars. Add ½ *teaspoon salt* for each pint and cover with boiling water, leaving 1-inch headspace. Close the jars and process at 10 pounds pressure in a steam-pressure canner, allowing 1 hour for pint jars and 1 hour and 25 minutes for quarts.

CANNED MEAT, POULTRY, AND SEAFOOD

Meat, poultry, and seafood contain very little natural acid and must be processed at 240°F in a steam-pressure canner under 10 pounds of pressure.

The home freezer offers a simpler and more efficient method for keeping meat, poultry, and seafood; it has virtually replaced the canning of these products in most households these days.

FROZEN FOODS

ABOUT FREEZING

Freezing is the best way to preserve the fresh, natural colors, textures, flavors, and food values of most foods. It is also easier than canning, requiring less equipment and processing time. No wonder home freezing has replaced or supplemented canning in many parts of our country, even in rural areas where preserving is done on a large scale.

Most homeowners today would find it hard to imagine living without some kind of freezer space. But as freezers become increasingly indispensable to our way of life, they are also being taken for granted, with all the resulting abuses that come with careless handling, packaging, and storing of frozen food. It's important to develop good freezer habits so that you can use your freezer comfortably, productively, and creatively.

While freezing arrests the growth of harmful bacteria, molds, and yeasts, it does not destroy them. Use high-quality, fresh foods when freezing, for no matter how carefully foods are packaged and stored, freezing will not transform food into something better than it was when it was first purchased and prepared.

Owning and Maintaining a Freezer

Although freezer-lockers are available in many towns on a rental basis, it pays to invest in a freezer of your own. You'll save money and reduce shopping time, for you can buy large quantities of foods that are in season or on sale and freeze them for future use. You can also save cooking time by cooking in quantity.

Freezers help you to plan and organize your life. You can prepare weeks ahead for special occasions, and you can always have something on hand for emergencies.

Types of Freezers. A separate, freestanding storage freezer that is opened infrequently provides the most satisfactory storage. Such freezers come in upright and chest styles and in a variety of sizes.

Refrigerator-freezer combinations, with a separate freezer door that is located at the top, bottom, or side, are also very efficient. However, since they hold ice cubes and other everyday items, they will be opened more frequently than a storage freezer and thus will not preserve flavor or quality for quite as long a time.

Old-style freezer–ice cube compartments that are within the refrigerator itself should be used only for the very short-term storage of commercially frozen products and leftovers.

Temperature. Food should be frozen quickly at 0°F or below. Quick freezing will prevent the formation of large ice crystals between the food fibers which break down the structure of foods and affect their quality.

The best way to check the temperature of your freezer is to use a freezer thermometer. It's good to keep the freezer at −10°F so that when you add unfrozen food the temperature will not rise above 0°F. It is especially important to control the temperature when you are adding a large quantity of unfrozen food at one time.

In Case of Power Failure. During a power failure, a fully loaded freezer will stay cold for one to two days; a partially loaded freezer will hold for a much shorter time. Don't open the freezer door when the power is off.

If the failure threatens to last for more than a day or two, you can buy some dry ice and put it in the freezer. Be sure to handle dry ice carefully, wearing gloves, and place it in the freezer on a piece of cardboard, not directly on the food. A 50-pound cake of dry ice, if added soon after a power failure, will prevent thawing for two or three days.

Defrosting a Freezer. Unless your freezer is the self-defrosting kind, it will need defrosting whenever the ice on the sides is about ¾ inch thick. Transfer frozen foods to the refrigerator during defrosting, or wrap them in layers of newspapers or blankets to keep them insulated. To speed defrosting, set pans of hot water inside the freezer.

Self-defrosting freezers, although they use more electricity than others, are very convenient.

All freezers, including frostless ones, should be thoroughly cleaned while empty once a year. Use a solution of warm water and baking soda, about ¼ cup baking soda to each quart of water.

Unwanted Odors. If you are troubled by off-odors in your freezer, put a few lumps of charcoal in the freezer to absorb them.

Packaging Food for Freezing

Foods should be packed for freezing in quantities geared to your family's needs and your entertaining patterns. If your family is small, for example, use several small containers to pack a stew; you can always defrost an extra package if you have unexpected guests, but a large amount of stew, once defrosted, may leave you with unwanted leftovers that will not benefit from refreezing.

Before you package food for freezing, decide how you will be defrosting it and proceed with that in mind. If you put soup or other liquid cooked foods in a rigid, heavy plastic or metal container, you'll be able to speed up defrosting by heating the container in a pot of barely simmering water until the contents are soft enough to pour into a pot for slow heating. Casserole dishes should be frozen in the kind of heavy-duty casseroles or foil or glass containers that can go straight from the freezer into a preheated oven. If you are going to need a particular casserole dish and therefore do not want to leave it in the freezer, line it with foil and, once the contents are frozen solid, remove them and wrap and store them; when they are ready to serve, the frozen food will fit neatly into the same casserole for reheating.

Herbed butters and jams can also be frozen the same way by foil-lining crocks in which the butter is packed, then freezing it and removing it, so that it can later be served in the same crocks.

Cakes with frostings should first be frozen and then wrapped in foil, plastic, or other freezer paper; in that way the frosting will not stick to the paper as it freezes. Cooked meat will keep better if frozen unsliced, but if it's more convenient to freeze it in serving portions, slice it and pack it with a little gravy which will help preserve it and make it easy to heat.

Small amounts of stock and concentrated sauces or gravies may be frozen first in ice cube trays and then turned into plastic bags for storage. This will reduce thawing time and make it possible to extract just a small amount.

Containers and Wrappings. All freezer wrappings should be moisture-proof and vapor-proof. Air is the great enemy of frozen food: exposure to air during freezing may cause an off flavor, the loss of moisture and color, or the development of a tough, dry surface known as "freezer burn."

But although exposure to air is to be avoided, it is important to leave some headspace when packaging soft and liquid food, for many foods expand as they freeze. Leave ½-inch headspace for soft or liquid foods in pint containers and 1-inch headspace for soft or liquid foods in quart containers. Dry-packed fruits and vegetables should have about ½-inch headspace. Headspace is especially important when using glass freezer jars, which might break without room for expansion.

Plastic containers or glass jars with wide mouths are commonly used for freezing foods that have a soft or liquid consistency. An initial investment in good heavy-duty containers is worthwhile, for they can be reused indefinitely. Square or rectangular containers stack well and use space more economically than round ones. There's no reason not to reuse round coffee or nut tins with plastic lids or the extra-heavy plastic containers that come with certain ice cream and dairy products—after all, they're free and work perfectly satisfactorily.

Liquid foods can also be packed in special plastic bags that seal with heat. These freeze-and-cook bags, which come with directions for use, can be submerged in boiling water, an excellent way to reheat frozen cooked food.

Foods that are not liquid, especially those with bulky shapes, should be wrapped in plastic bags or in flexible wrapping paper suitable for freezing. When using plastic bags, press out all the air, then twist the tops and seal them with the ties that come with the bags.

It's easiest to wrap meat, cakes, pies, and other dry or bulky products in flexible wrappings like foil, plastic wrap, or special freezer wrap. Freezer wrap is fine when used by a butcher, but unless you have a special knack for wrapping, you may find it awkward to use at home. We find that heavy-duty foil, while expensive, provides splendid protection and is very easy to use, for it can be pressed to fit the shape of the food and does not need to be sealed with tape. Single-weight foil, used in several layers, is also very satisfactory, as is flexible, transparent plastic wrap. Contrary to popular belief, meats and other supermarket products, if they are not to be held more than a few months, may be frozen in the plastic-wrap packages in which they are sold.

Do not use cellophane tape to seal covers or packages: it will not hold. We recommend ordinary masking tape, which is a lot cheaper and just as effective as special freezer tape.

Labeling. Be sure to label foods before you freeze them, indicating the contents, the quantity, and the date. Include other pertinent information when relevant: "needs seasoning," "thin before using," etc. Use a pencil, a crayon, or a special marking pen for labeling; many ordinary pens and felt-tipped pens will fade or smudge in the freezer and become illegible. Don't write directly on containers you plan to reuse. Make labels with masking tape instead and be sure to put the tape on the package before you freeze it; it will not adhere to a frozen surface.

Loading a Freezer
Don't overtax your freezer by putting in a lot of fresh food at the same time. Add only as much food as will freeze within 24 hours, about 3 pounds for each cubic foot of interior space.

Whenever possible, let newly added food packages touch the freezer walls or shelves for quick freezing. Set them apart from each other so that cold air can circulate around them. After they are frozen, stack them neatly.

Store foods in groups, keeping meats in one place, soups in another, and so on. Keep foods that have been in the freezer longest near the front so that they will be used in chronological order.

As you fill your freezer, keep an inventory of its contents. Make up a list of all the foods inside, including the dates they were frozen and the quantities in which they were packed. Keep the list taped to the door, crossing off items as you use them and penciling in others as new foods are added. An inventory list will show at a glance just what you have in the right quantity for a particular meal. The dates will enable you to use foods within the proper amount of time. Moreover, if you know what you're looking for before you open the freezer, you won't keep the door open unnecessarily while you rummage around.

Storing Foods
Frozen foods will not turn bad if they are stored too long, but they will gradually lose quality. Cooked foods, cakes, cookies, breads, unbaked pastries, chopped meat, pork products, fish, and liver should be used within a three- to six-month period. Most other fruits, vegetables, and meats, frozen under proper conditions, may be kept for about a year.

Defrosting Foods and Refreezing Them
Defrosted food will spoil more rapidly than fresh and should therefore be used promptly.

Whenever possible, it's best to cook frozen foods directly from a frozen state without defrosting them. When foods require complete defrosting, try to use them while they are still chilled.

It really doesn't matter with most foods how they are defrosted, as long as they are used soon after. However, with some meats and poultry, and with fish especially, the texture is preserved better when they defrost slowly in the refrigerator, provided you have the time to do so. Room-temperature defrosting is, of course, much quicker, and in an emergency, you can even put most foods in front of a fan to speed defrosting, or run the package under cool, or even warm, water. You can also use a microwave oven to defrost foods, following the manufacturer's instructions.

Any defrosted food that is safe to eat may also be safely refrozen. Although the quality, and especially the texture, of food may suffer after refreezing, the only *danger* in refreezing food is that spoilage may have set in before the food was refrozen. Things like bread, butter, and nuts may be defrosted and refrozen several times without noticeable change.

Sometimes, when uncooked foods like meat and poultry have accidentally defrosted, you may find it convenient to cook them and then freeze them in their cooked form. It's a good way to guard against spoilage and to avoid the loss of texture and quality that often comes with refrozen food.

It's good to know when a package has been thawed and refrozen, so that you don't repeat the process over and over again. Be sure to make an appropriate note on the label.

Do not eat thawed foods if you have any question about their taste, smell, or appearance.

WHAT TO FREEZE

Freezing information for specific foods appears throughout this book in the introductions to the individual chapters. This section contains general information about freezing cooked foods and specific information about freezing uncooked meat, fruits, and vegetables.

There are no hard-and-fast rules for what the perfectly planned freezer should contain. The contents of a well-stocked freezer will vary from home to home, depending on individual tastes and eating habits, styles of cooking and enter-taining, and, of course, the nature of the household itself. But regardless of whether the food in the freezer is commercially prepared or homemade, whether it's geared toward everyday basics or special indulgences, it is possible for every freezer owner to have good things on hand for all occasions.

Storing Staples in the Freezer
Almost everything freezes well: just look through the frozen food section of any large supermarket. Meat, poultry, fish, hard cheeses, breads, cakes, desserts, pastries, cookies, candies, nuts, dried fruits, and coffee are among the uncooked or commercially prepared unfrozen staples that you can store in your freezer. Some things, like nuts and coffee, are better stored in the freezer than at room temperature. Parsley and fresh herbs, wrapped in foil, will keep their flavor for many months. Milk and cream keep well in the freezer, and it's good to have some on hand for emergencies. If you allow heavy cream to defrost completely, then shake it well, it will whip up just fine. Fruits and vegetables, purchased in season, may be frozen uncooked or partially cooked (see pp. 731, 733).

Foods That Don't Freeze Well
Potatoes, unless mashed, become mushy in the freezer: it's best to freeze soups and stews without them and to add potatoes later. Cream cheese, soft cheeses, chopped liver, cream fillings, custards, egg-thickened sauces, meringue, and many cake frostings (especially those made with brown sugar or egg whites) will not freeze well. Hard-boiled egg whites get rubbery in the freezer, most fried or breaded foods become soggy, and foods made with gelatin do not keep their consistency. Salad greens, radishes, cucumbers, celery, uncooked tomatoes, scallions, and bananas should not be frozen.

Freezing Home-Cooked Foods
The best way to have a very special supply of frozen food at hand is to cook specifically for your freezer. This is doubly useful during harvest times, when low prices tempt you to buy in quantity or when you have a lot of extra produce from your own garden. Cook seasonal vegetables and fruits like tomatoes, squash, and berries; use them in sauces, pies, soups, and casserole dishes and then freeze them for future use.

Stews, casseroles, meat pies, gravies, soups, stocks, and cooked meat and poultry all freeze well. Home-baked breads, pies, cakes, cookies, preserves, pickles, and candies may also be kept in the freezer. Many foods that are to be frozen should be slightly undercooked, since they will cook further when they are reheated. This is especially true for vegetable soups, stews, and pasta dishes.

You may have to readjust the seasonings of frozen cooked foods before you use them. Some seasonings—pepper, garlic, vanilla—increase in flavor in the freezer, while others—like salt—seem to diminish. Cool cooked foods thoroughly before freezing them, but do not let them sit around once they have cooled.

It's good to get in the habit of cooking double or even triple amounts of favorite dishes that freeze well, and then putting the extras away for another meal. The additional work is minimal—you're making the dish anyway—and the pleasure of having a meal or two prepared and waiting in the freezer cannot be overestimated.

If your freezer contains a crusty, home-baked bread, some nourishing soup made from last summer's vegetables, a few hard cheeses, and some cookies, ice cream, or sherbet, you'll always be able to put together a quick, impromptu meal.

You can prepare an elegant crêpe dinner if you have some easy-to-defrost crêpes in the freezer, some frozen cooked chicken, and some frozen duxelles. Bind the filling with a velouté sauce, perhaps a very special one made with your own defrosted chicken stock.

Frozen pot roast and gravy are always good to have on hand, as are home-baked cakes and cookies, which defrost readily when you have unexpected guests. Indeed, some cookies are even better when still partially frozen.

If you use your free time every once in a while to make and freeze a supply of special cooking ingredients that take time to prepare—beef stock or puff pastry, for example—you'll find that the creation of "elaborate" dishes at a later date will be a snap.

Freezing Leftovers
The freezer is like a savings bank: use it to collect good things for the future— leftover meat and poultry that can later be used in pies, casseroles, and fillings; leftover vegetables juices, gravies, meat juices, bits, or sauces—no matter how small the amount, it will come in handy to add flavor to soups and sauces. Save bones and giblets for making stock, adding bits of other leftovers as they accumulate. Leftover cooked beans, even rice and noodles, may be frozen and combined with meats and sauces in the future. Save the livers from each chicken you cook until you have enough for a meal. Freeze leftover egg whites, unbeaten, until you have enough for angel cake or meringue. Leftover egg yolks or whole eggs out of the shell will freeze well if you add sugar (1 teaspoon per 6 yolks) or salt (½ teaspoon per 6 yolks). Use the sugared eggs in dessert recipes and the salted ones in sauce and egg dishes.

Freezing Meat and Poultry
Freeze meat in the quantities in which you plan to use it—for example, enough individual hamburger patties or boned chicken breasts for your family or a 2-pound package of chopped meat for a meat loaf. Beef, lamb, veal, and chicken will keep in the freezer for about a year, pork for three to six months, and variety meats for several months. Leftover cooked meat, carefully wrapped, may be frozen for three to six months, but cured meat tends to turn rancid in the freezer because of its high concentration of salt.

If you should forget to defrost a piece of meat and find yourself with, say, a hard-frozen leg of lamb at three in the afternoon, don't despair. You can cook meat that is still frozen if you allow the amount of time you would if the meat had been at room temperature and then add half as much time again. This is true for all meat except pork which, for safety's sake, should never be cooked frozen.

Freezing Fruits

Uncooked fruit may be packed for freezing in a variety of ways, depending on the fruit and the way in which it will be used. Always select fruit that is ripe and wash it well with cold water, handling it gently to avoid bruising. Most fruits will have good flavor after freezing, but their texture will become softer. Puréed fruit and fruit juices retain their character best after defrosting.

Pack fruits in sugar syrup if you intend to use them as desserts. If you plan to cook the fruit after defrosting it, or to use it in pies, jams, or sauces, pack it dry, with or without sugar. When cooking defrosted fruit, be sure to make allowances for any sugar that was added before freezing.

To Prevent Darkening. An ascorbic acid (vitamin C) solution is recommended to prevent the darkening of certain fruits, especially apricots, cherries, peaches, nectarines, and plums. To make the solution, dissolve ½ teaspoon ascorbic acid crystals in ¼ cup cold water for each quart of sugar syrup or of prepared fruit. There are also commercially prepared ascorbic acid mixtures. When using them, follow the printed directions.

Lemon juice is sometimes substituted for ascorbic acid, but it may change the flavor of the finished product. Steaming is recommended to prevent the darkening of apple and pear slices.

Dry Pack Without Sugar. (See chart, p. 732.) To pack fruit dry without sugar is very simple: wash the fruit, dry it, sprinkle it with ascorbic acid (if recommended), pack in containers, and freeze.

You can make a loose pack by spreading the fruit out on a tray and freezing it, then packing it in containers and sealing. When fruit is loose-packed, it is easy to use in small quantities.

Dry Pack with Sugar. (See chart, p. 732.) Wash and dry the fruit, add ascorbic acid (if recommended), then sprinkle with sugar, using ½–¾ cup sugar for each quart of prepared fruit. Toss the fruit gently, then let it stand for about 10 minutes until the sugar dissolves and the juices are drawn out.

Syrup Pack. (See chart at the end of this section.) The sugar syrup used for freezing fruit is the same as that used for canning fruit (p. 718). Make the syrup, using the strength recommended on the chart on the next page. Cool the syrup thoroughly before adding the fruit. If ascorbic acid is recommended, add it to the syrup just before combining the syrup with the fruit.

You will need ½–¾ cup sugar syrup for each pint package of fruit. Pack the fruit so that it is completely covered with the syrup, leaving the recommended headspace. Cover the top of the fruit with a piece of crumpled foil to hold it under the syrup.

Wet Pack Without Sugar. You can also crush unsweetened fruit and pack it in its own juices, or leave it whole and add water to which ascorbic acid (if recommended) has been added. Leave the proper amount of headspace (p. 727).

Puréed Fruit. Puréed fruit, of which applesauce is the most familiar example, freezes beautifully. Sugar may be added or not, according to taste. For fruits that work well as purées, see the chart on the next page.

Fruit Juice. To extract fruit juices, see p. 701. All fruit juices freeze well.

For Freezing Fruits

Fruit	Preparation	Dry pack without sugar	Dry pack with sugar (amount of sugar per 1-quart package)	Syrup pack (see p. 718)	Wet pack without sugar	Purée	Use ascorbic acid
Apples	Peel, slice, steam 2–3 minutes over boiling water.	Yes	½ cup	Medium		Yes	Yes
Apricots	Halve and pit; peel and slice, if desired.		½ cup	Medium	Pack in water	Yes	Yes
Berries (except strawberries)	Remove leaves and stems.	Yes	¾ cup	Medium	Pack in berry juice		
Cherries— Sweet and Sour	Pit, if desired.		¾ cup	Heavy			Yes
Cranberries	Remove stems.	Yes		Heavy			
Currants	Remove stems.	Yes	¾ cup	Heavy			
Gooseberries	Remove stems and ends.	Yes	¾ cup	Heavy			
Grapes	Stem; leave whole if seedless; halve and remove seeds if not.	Yes		Medium			
Melons	Peel, remove seeds, cut in cubes or balls.			Light		Yes	
Nectarines	Halve and pit; peel and slice, if desired.		⅔ cup	Medium	Pack in water	Yes	Yes
Oranges and Grapefruit	Peel, section, remove seeds.			Medium			
Peaches	Halve and pit; peel and slice, if desired.		⅔ cup	Medium	Pack in water	Yes	Yes
Pears	Peel, core, slice; heat in boiling, medium syrup 1–2 minutes.			Medium			Yes
Pineapple	Pare; cube or crush.	Yes		Light	Pack in water		
Plums and Prunes	Halve and pit or leave whole.	Yes	¾ cup	Medium or heavy		Yes	Yes
Rhubarb	Trim, cut in 1-inch pieces; heat 1 minute in boiling water.	Yes	1 cup	Medium			
Strawberries	Hull; leave whole or slice.	Yes	¾ cup	Heavy	Pack in berry juice	Yes	

Freezing Vegetables

Blanching. Most vegetables should be prepared for freezing by a process known as blanching, during which they are scalded in boiling water for a short, designated period of time (see chart, below). In addition to helping preserve fresh vegetable flavor, bright color, and vitamin content, blanching will destroy harmful enzymes that might otherwise cause deterioration. Blanching also makes vegetables less bulky and thus easier to pack.

You'll need a large pot. Allow a gallon of water for each pound or quart of vegetables to be blanched. Bring the water to a boil while you are preparing the vegetables.

For best results, use vegetables that are very fresh. Wash them in cold water and prepare them as you would for cooking. When necessary, cut the vegetables into pieces small enough for packaging. Place them in a wire basket or a cheesecloth bag.

Submerge the basket or bag into the boiling water, using a small enough amount of vegetables at one time so that the water will return to a boil within a minute. Cover the pot and begin timing; follow the recommended amount of time in the chart.

When the time is up, plunge the vegetables into a large bowl full of ice water to stop them from cooking further. Leave them there for about as much time as they spent in the boiling water.

Drain the vegetables and pat them dry. Pack them without any liquid in freezer bags or containers and freeze.

You can use the same pot of boiling water for scalding other batches of the same vegetable.

Exceptions to Blanching. To freeze *beets*, cook them until they are tender, then peel them, slice them if you wish, and pack and freeze them.

Potatoes, sweet potatoes, winter squash, and *pumpkin* should be cooked until soft, then mashed, packed, and frozen. Reheat them in the top of a double boiler, adding butter and seasonings to taste.

To freeze *mushrooms*, sauté them, whole or sliced, in a little butter, then freeze immediately. Or make duxelles (p. 389), which freezes splendidly.

Green pepper should be cleaned, sliced or chopped, wrapped, and frozen without any blanching.

Onions may be parboiled and then frozen, or left raw, chopped and frozen without any blanching.

Cooking Frozen Vegetables. Cook frozen vegetables for a shorter time than you would fresh.

Many frozen vegetables should be cooked directly from a frozen state. Others, like broccoli and greens, are better when they are partially thawed and broken up, then cooked very quickly. Corn on the cob should be thoroughly defrosted, then buttered, wrapped in foil, and reheated in a moderate oven.

For Blanching Vegetables

*(Add 1 minute to blanching time if you live
5,000 feet or more above sea level.)*

Vegetable	Preparation	Blanching Time in Minutes
Asparagus	Cut or break off woody bottom of each stalk. Peel stalks with vegetable peeler.	Thin: 2 Thick: 3
Beans, Green, Wax	Wash and trim off ends.	3

For Blanching Vegetables

*(Add 1 minute to blanching time if you live
5,000 feet or more above sea level.)*

Vegetable	Preparation	Blanching Time in Minutes
Beans, Lima and Other Shell Beans	Remove shells and sort by size.	Small: 1 Medium: 2 Large: 3
Beans, Green Soy	Preserve only the newly formed beans in the green stage. Blanch whole pods, cool, then squeeze beans out.	5
Broccoli	Use only the firm young stalks with bright flowerets. Separate the flowerets from the stems, peel stems and slice diagonally, cut into 1½" lengths.	3
Brussels Sprouts	Wash and remove wilted outer leaves. Trim the stems.	3
Carrots	Scrub young carrots but scrape skin off older carrots. Cut the medium size and larger lengthwise and in 2" lengths; younger small carrots in 2" lengths.	2
Cauliflower	Use only firm heads. Trim and break into flowerets, about 1" in diameter, and wash.	2
Corn on the Cob	Remove husks, and silk threads; wash.	6
Corn, Whole-kernel	Remove husks and silk threads. Scrape kernels from cob after blanching.	6
Kohlrabi	Use mature but tender stems. Trim top and bottom, peel away the tough fibers. Cut crosswise ¼" thick—unless very young, then leave whole.	2
Okra	Use young pods. Remove the stem at end.	Small: 3 Large: 4
Parsnips	Use firm roots. Remove top, wash, and peel. Slice into ½" pieces.	3
Peas, Black-eyed	Use only young, tender black-eyed peas. Shell.	Small: 1 Large: 2
Peas, Green	Use only the young. Shell.	1
Succotash	Blanch whole-kernel corn and lima beans separately as above. Mix equal parts.	2
Turnips and Rutabagas	Remove tops, peel. Slice into ½" pieces.	1

APPENDIXES &
INDEX

BEVERAGES

ABOUT COFFEE

Making Good Coffee

A good cup of coffee should have a pleasing, never bitter taste, and it should be full bodied with a rich aroma. Too often the coffee we make misses the mark because the coffee isn't sufficiently fresh and/or we have been careless making it. To brew a good cup of coffee is really a simple procedure, if you bear in mind the following rules:

• Start with fresh coffee. A vacuum-packed can of coffee is fine when just opened, but because the beans are ground, they lose their aroma quickly; aroma is the key to freshness. Keep the tin well sealed and store in a cool place, preferably the refrigerator. If you can buy freshly roasted beans and grind your own each time you make it, you will have much more delicious coffee. Store beans in a tightly sealed jar in the refrigerator or freezer; in the latter case, simply remove what you need and grind the beans still frozen.

• Use 2 level tablespoons of coffee to 1 cup of water. If you want stronger coffee, increase the amount of coffee; don't try to compensate by brewing longer: that only leads to overextraction and consequent bitterness. To make weaker coffee, use the recommended proportions, which preserve the proper balance, and then add boiling water after, rather than reduce the amount of coffee.

• For methods requiring boiling water, ideally the water should be at 205°F (96°C)—just under boiling. But rather than hover over the kettle to catch the water before it comes to the boil, let the kettle rest a moment after boiling before pouring over the grounds.

• Be sure to use the right grind for the particular kind of coffee you are making: Drip for drip method; Regular for percolator, steeped, and boiled coffee; Fine or Vacuum for espresso.

• Glass and porcelain coffee makers are the best. Metal pots tend to make coffee taste bitter; stainless steel has the least ill effect.

• Always be sure that your coffee-making equipment is scrupulously clean, particularly if you are using any kind of metal. Wash after each use with a mild detergent or baking soda; soak any filters.

- Don't leave coffee sitting on the grounds too long.
- Don't repour coffee through the grounds.
- Try to avoid reheating coffee; it is better to make just what you need.
- To make *iced coffee*, double the amount of coffee, prepare by one of the methods outlined below, and leave to cool. If you add ice cubes while the coffee is still hot, you may want to make an even stronger brew.

TYPES OF COFFEE

The kind of coffee you like best is a matter of individual taste. Sample different brands until you are satisfied. If you have the opportunity to experiment with freshly roasted beans, try mixing your own blends. The results are more satisfying than using just one individual type, and with a good blend one flavor will enhance another. Many people like to combine one part light-roasted coffee such as Mocha with one part of a full-bodied Brazilian Santos, or Colombian, or Java, and one part of dark-roasted French. Ask questions about the nature of different beans and work out blends that please you.

Usually an after-dinner coffee is stronger than a morning cup, particularly if it is served in demitasses. You can simply double the strength of your usual brew or use French or Italian coffee or combinations thereof.

Steeped Coffee. You can use a clean saucepan or a special glass coffee maker with a plunger (see illustration opposite, the third pot in at top). Measure 2 level tablespoons of regular grind coffee for each cup, then pour barely boiling water over and let steep 5 minutes. If using a saucepan, pour off the coffee through a fine-meshed strainer; for the special glass model, simply push down the plunger, so the grounds remain at the bottom.

"Boiled" Coffee. This is somewhat of a misnomer because to make coffee successfully using this old-style camping method, you shouldn't boil the coffee; rather let it come just to the boil. Measure 2 level tablespoons of regular grind coffee for each cup desired into the bottom of a clean saucepan or an old-fashioned coffee pot and pour the required number of cups of cold water on top. Add a pinch of salt and cover. Bring the coffee slowly to the boil and just as soon as the bubbles break through the surface crust, stir it and remove from the fire. Sprinkle a little cold water on top and let settle a few minutes before pouring. Some outdoorsmen crack an egg and mix it, crumpled-up shell and all, into the coffee grounds before pouring on the water. It helps the grounds to settle. In either case one is apt to have a slightly muddy but good strong brew. Coffee purists may frown on this method but it can produce a delicious cup.

Percolator Coffee. Be sure that all parts of the percolator are absolutely clean. Fill the basket with the correct amount of regular grind coffee—that is, 2 tablespoons per cup—and pour the measured amount of cold water for the particular percolator into the bottom. Insert the basket and percolate over low heat 6–8 minutes. Electric percolators have the disadvantage of not enabling you to control the timing or the heat so that sometimes overextraction of the beans occurs, causing bitterness.

Drip Coffee. Use 2 level tablespoons drip grind per cup. It's better not to make more than you need, and preheating the pot with boiling water will help to hold

the warmth while the coffee is dripping so you needn't reheat. After pouring the first splashes of barely boiling water on the grounds, stir to be sure they are all moistened, then continue. We recommend drip coffee makers of glass or porcelain that use paper filters. Automatic electric drip coffee makers are excellent, provided you don't allow the finished coffee to sit on the warmer too long. Follow the manufacturer's instructions for use, but ignore any suggestions for using less than 2 tablespoons of coffee per cup of water.

Espresso Coffee. One needs a special espresso maker to produce this kind of strong coffee. Use the fine or vacuum grind of French or Italian coffee, 2 tablespoons to 3–4 ounces of water—and follow the manufacturer's instructions. The type of machine that pushes under pressure both steam and hot water through the coffee will give you the true espresso experience, but the two-cylinder pot (above, top right) is more familiar for home use and it simulates a fine espresso.

Here are two coffee recipes for special occasions.

Irish Coffee

(SERVES ONE)

1 jigger Irish whiskey
1 teaspoon sugar
1 cup (¼ L) very hot after-
  dinner coffee

2 tablespoons whipped cream

Put the Irish whiskey in the bottom of a glass or mug. Stir in the sugar and add piping hot strong coffee. Top with the whipped cream and serve immediately.

Café Brûlot

Café Brûlot, which has long been a specialty of New Orleans, can provide a dramatic climax to a fine meal. In New Orleans, it is usually prepared in and served from a special silver brûlot bowl that is warmed over an alcohol flame. A chafing dish will do the job effectively.

(SERVES SIX)

1½-inch stick cinnamon	2 lumps sugar
5 cloves	⅓ cup (¾ dL) brandy
3 tablespoons slivered orange peel	2 tablespoons curaçao
3 tablespoons slivered lemon peel	3 cups (¾ L) hot after-dinner coffee

Put the cinnamon, cloves, orange and lemon peels, and sugar in a chafing dish or brûlot bowl with a flame under and mash together with the back of a spoon or a pestle. Add the brandy and curaçao, and when hot, ignite. Stir to dissolve the sugar, then gradually add the coffee. Serve in demitasses.

ABOUT TEA

Making Good Tea

To make good tea. the leaves must be steeped in boiling water. Loose tea is the best kind to use, but tea bags are perfectly serviceable as long as they are put in a warm pot, cup, or mug and *boiling* water is used. The way tea is served in most public places—a cup of hot water with a tea bag alongside it—is an insult to anyone who cares about tea and should be protested because it is impossible to produce a decent cup that way.

The important points to remember in making tea are:

• The water you use should always be cold and freshly drawn—not water that has been boiled before or has sat around in a kettle. Bring it to a rolling boil and use immediately.

• Earthenware or china pots are best. Metal is apt to alter the flavor ever so slightly.

• Warm the teapot (mug, or cup) by pouring boiling water in and swirling it around, then discard.

• Put 1 teaspoon of tea into the steaming pot (or a tea bag into the warm cup or mug) for every cup of water, then gently pour over the leaves water that has just come to a rolling boil. Give a good stir, cover, and let steep 5 minutes. (For the single cup or mug, use a saucer to cover; 3–4 minutes of quiet steeping should be enough; don't dunk the bag.)

• Give a final stir to the pot, let the tea settle, and pour—through a tea strainer or not, depending on whether you mind a few leaves in your cup.

• If the tea is too strong when you pour it out, add boiling water. You may find that for your own taste the proportion of 1 teaspoon per cup for certain strong blends like Irish Breakfast is too strong and that you want to use slightly less tea. But remember that it is easier to weaken tea with boiling water after it is made than to try to add more leaves after it has been brewed.

• Serve with cream or milk, slices of lemon, and sugar on the side for those who want them. Always have available a pot of hot water.

• To make *iced tea,* double the amount of tea per cup, make in the usual way, and then pour off into a pitcher. Add ice when cool; if you are in a hurry and want to add the ice while still hot, triple the amount of tea used because the ice will weaken it. Refrigerating iced tea will make it cloudy. Add, if you wish, a sprig of mint and a slice of lemon and/or orange, to each glass and let each person sweeten according to his taste. Instant iced tea makes a beverage that tastes little like real tea.

• A tea cozy provides a nice way of keeping the pot warm. But don't let tea sit around too long. It is better to make a fresh pot for latecomers. Or you may pour the tea off into another preheated pot and keep warm over a candle.

• Store loose tea and tea bags in airtight tins and keep away from strong light. Tea that is fresh when bought should keep as long as six months this way. Tea bags lose their flavor much more quickly.

Types of Tea
Most of the tea that we buy in tea bags is advertised as Pekoe and Orange Pekoe, which actually refers to the cut and size of the leaf and tells us nothing about the type or origin. If you become interested in tea, as so many Americans have in the past decade or so, you should start sampling some of the various types and blends of imported tea packed in tins and perhaps seek out sources where you can buy your own loose tea. The basic types of tea are the black, fermented teas, which include Ceylon, Darjeeling, Keemun, and Assam, all rich and full-tasting; the green, unfermented teas, which we associate primarily with Japan and China; and the semifermented Oolong teas. Certain teas, like black Lapsang Souchong, have a smoky flavor that comes from the curing process, and others have a perfume because they have been fired with jasmine or other kinds of blossoms.

The most familiar blends are English Breakfast Tea, made up primarily of Keemun; Irish Breakfast, a strong blend of Assam and Ceylon, more often drunk with milk in it; Earl Grey, a delicately scented tea; and Russian, usually a blend of black teas and China green.

Spiced Teas and Herbal Teas. Spiced teas are made from real tea with the addition of such spices as cloves, dried orange or lemon peel, and sometimes with cinnamon, anise, or cardamom. Mint tea can be made of pure mint leaves— usually peppermint or spearmint—or blended with a strong black tea; mint teas are particularly good cold on a hot day.

ABOUT PUNCH
Punches and eggnogs are for celebrations and holidays. They should be served from a large punch bowl, ladled out into small cups or glasses. Here are several to choose from—both with spirits and without. Count on about ¾ cup for each serving.

Rum Punch

(ABOUT 5 QUARTS)

1 cup (¼ L) sugar
1½ cups (3½ dL) lemon juice
1½ cups (3½ dL) grapefruit
  juice
5 cups (1¼ L) orange juice

6 cups (1½ L) unsweetened
  pineapple juice
1 fifth (¾ L) dark Jamaica rum
2 fifths (1½ L) light West
  Indian punch

Make a sugar syrup by boiling the sugar with 1 cup of water for 5 minutes. Let cool. Mix together with all the other ingredients and let mellow for at least 1 hour. Pour over a large block of ice in a punch bowl and serve when thoroughly chilled.

Regent Punch

(5½ QUARTS)

1 quart (1 L) rye whiskey
1 quart (1 L) rum
1 quart (1 L) strong tea
¾ cup (1¾ dL) lemon juice

1½ cups (3½ dL) orange juice
1 fifth (¾ L) champagne
1 quart (1 L) soda water

Mix together the rye, rum, tea, and the fruit juices and pour over a large block of ice in a punch bowl. Just before serving add the champagne and soda water.

Champagne Punch

(6 QUARTS)

2 cups (½ L) sugar
1¼ cups (3 dL) lemon juice
2 cups (½ L) apricot nectar
One 6-ounce (1¾ dL) can
  frozen orange juice
  concentrate

3 cups (¾ L) unsweetened
  apple juice
2 cups (½ L) unsweetened
  pineapple juice
2 quarts (2 L) ginger ale
2 fifths (1½ L) champagne

Make a sugar syrup by boiling the sugar with 2 cups of water for 1 minute. Cool. Add the lemon juice, apricot nectar, orange, apple, and pineapple juices to the sugar syrup. Chill. Pour over a large block of ice in a punch bowl and just before serving add the ginger ale and champagne.

Creole Champagne Punch

(8½ QUARTS)

2 cups (½ L) sugar
2 fifths (1½ L) dry white wine
1 pint (½ L) curaçao
1 pineapple

4 quarts (3¾ L) soda water
2 fifths (1½ L) champagne
1 quart (1 L) strawberries

Stir the sugar into the wine and curaçao until completely dissolved. Shred half the pineapple by cutting it into quarters, removing the core, and either putting peeled pieces in a food processor or scraping unpeeled quarters against the large holes of a grater. Peel the other half and cut into slices. Add the grated pineapple to the wine mixture and pour over a large block of ice in a punch bowl. Just before serving, add the soda water and champagne and float the pieces of pineapple and the strawberries, halved if they are large, on top.

Cider Punch

(6½ QUARTS)

1 gallon (3¾ L) sweet cider	1 cup (¼ L) brandy
2 quarts (2 L) soda water	3 tablespoons lemon juice
1¼ cups (3 dL) sherry	Peel of 1 lemon, cut into strips

Mix all the ingredients together and pour over a block of ice in a punch bowl.

Fish House Punch

Fish House is the informal name of The State in Schuylkill, the oldest men's club in America, and this is the authentic recipe for its much-esteemed and highly potent punch. For a milder version, more suitable for a wedding reception or holiday bowl, try the variation, but if you want the real thing, this is it.

(4 QUARTS)

2 cups (½ L) sugar	2 fifths (1½ L) dark rum
1 quart (1 L) lemon or lime juice, or a combination	1 fifth (¾ L) cognac
	2–3 ounces peach brandy

Dissolve the sugar in the citrus juice and 2 cups water. Mix in the rest of the ingredients and "brew" by letting it sit 2 hours to exchange flavors. Pour over a block of ice in a punch bowl and serve.

Milder Fish House Punch. Dissolve the sugar in 2 cups water and 2 cups citrus juice. Use only 1 fifth rum and add 3½ *cups tea* and 3 *quarts ginger ale* to the mixture.

Basic Fruit Punch (nonalcoholic)

(3½ QUARTS)

1½ cups (3½ dL) sugar	1 cup (¼ L) lemon juice
1 quart (1 L) strong hot tea	1 quart (1 L) ginger ale
1 quart (1 L) orange juice	Fresh mint leaves

Dissolve the sugar in the hot tea. Mix together with the citrus juices. Pour over a large block of ice and just before serving add the ginger ale and scatter fresh mint leaves on top.

Variations. Use ½ *cup fruit syrup* such as raspberry or strawberry instead of the sugar. You may need some additional sugar; taste and add what is needed. Add *fresh fruits,* such as shredded pineapple, strawberries, sliced peaches or mangoes, to the bowl.

Sangria

(ABOUT 4½ QUARTS)

1 quart (1 L) orange juice
3 quarts (2¾ L) dry red wine
2 oranges, washed and sliced
4 fresh peaches, peeled and
    sliced

1 lemon, washed and sliced
Up to ¾ cup (1¾ dL)
    confectioners' sugar
    (optional)
Soda water (optional)

Mix together all except the optional ingredients in several large pitchers and let stand for 4–6 hours. Add ice and taste. If you wish it sweeter, stir in confectioners' sugar to taste. If you like it a little lighter, splash in some soda water. Pour into large wine or old-fashioned glasses, letting a little of the fruit fall into each glass.

Eggnog

(ABOUT 8 QUARTS)

1 dozen eggs, separated
½ teaspoon salt
2¼ or more cups (450 g) sugar
2 or more cups (½ L) bourbon
½ cup (1 dL) rum

1 quart (1 L) milk
2 tablespoons vanilla extract
3 pints (1½ L) heavy cream
Nutmeg

Beat together the egg yolks and salt in a large mixing bowl, slowing adding 1½ cups of the sugar. Continue beating until thick and pale. Stir in the bourbon, rum, milk, and vanilla until well mixed. Beat the egg whites until foamy and slowly add the remaining ¾ cup sugar, continuing to beat until stiff and all the sugar has been incorporated. Whip the cream until stiff. Now fold the egg whites into the yolk mixture and then fold in the whipped cream. Taste and add more bourbon and/or sugar if necessary. Pour into a punch bowl and sprinkle the top with nutmeg.

COCOA AND MILK DRINKS

Hot Cocoa

(6 CUPS)

4 tablespoons unsweetened
    cocoa
2 tablespoons sugar
Pinch of salt

4 cups milk
Few drops of vanilla extract
    (optional)
Whipped cream (optional)

Mix the cocoa, sugar, and salt with ½ cup water in a medium-sized saucepan and boil gently for 2 minutes. Add the milk and heat slowly just to the boiling point. Beat well with a beater or whisk and, if you wish, flavor with a few drops of vanilla. Pour into cups and top with a dollop of whipped cream, if desired.

Basic Milk Shake

Vary this shake according to what flavor you want—strawberry ice cream with strawberry syrup, coffee with coffee, maple walnut with maple syrup, etc.

(SERVES ONE)

¾ cup (1¾ dL) milk
2 teaspoons vanilla extract or 2
    tablespoons syrup of your
    choice

1–2 scoops ice cream

Beat together all the ingredients or spin quickly in a blender.

Basic Ice Cream Soda

Again, the combination of syrup and ice cream is up to you.

(SERVES ONE)

3 tablespoons chocolate,
    strawberry, or other fruit,
    caramel, or coffee syrup

1 cup (¼ L) soda water
1–2 scoops ice cream

Mix everything in a tall glass, stir a bit, and serve with a straw.

Jack's Health Drink

A colorful and delicious drink that is good for you.

(SERVES ONE)

1 cup (¼ L) skim milk
1 tablespoon wheat germ
½ ripe banana

½ papaya, peach, or pear,
    peeled and seeded

Put all the ingredients into a blender and blend until smooth. Pour into a tall glass. If the drink is thicker than desired, add a couple of ice cubes.

MENUS &
TABLE SETTINGS

For thoughts about what constitutes a good menu, consult Menu Planning for Family and Friends, p. 5. The suggestions that follow should serve simply as guidelines. The more you cook, the more you'll want to vary meals your own way and create menus that reflect your particular mood, the occasion, the season, or express some motif that may have meaning for you.

No matter how simple the meal, it's nice to have the table properly set. Knives, then spoons should be on the right side of each place setting, forks on the left. The easiest rule is to place the utensils in the order of their use during the particular meal, starting at the outside. The setting below, at right, would be for a dinner that begins with soup, followed by a main course (large knife and fork), salad (small fork), and dessert; the butter and/or cheese knife goes to the right of the big knife. If you were having salad as a first course, the two forks would be reversed and no soup spoon would be needed, as in left illustration.

All these rules assume that you have plenty of silver. If you haven't, don't worry, and certainly don't hesitate to serve more than just one course because of lack of tableware. You can always slip out between courses and wash up whatever is needed or simply ask guests to keep a knife or a fork. The French use special knife-and-fork rests for just this purpose.

Napkins should go to the left of the forks or under them. Or you can do something fancy, if you're good at that sort of thing, like making the napkin into a fan shape and putting it in the middle of each place setting or stuffing it into a large goblet. Glasses for wine and water are always to the right of the setting. If you are serving both red and white wine, put the smaller glass for white wine on the outside. Butter plates, when used, are to the left.

Most important, whether for guests or when you're just family, remember always to have your plates and serving bowls and platters warm whenever you are serving hot food. It is so unpleasant to have nice hot food congealing on a cold plate after it is served. Warm everything in a low oven or on the back of the stove, if you have room; if not, a radiator, a hot plate, and even the drying cycle of a dishwasher make excellent plate warmers.

FAMILY DINNERS

Here are some suggestions for traditional family dinners. The dishes are relatively simple to make and not too expensive, with many of the main course ingredients providing leftovers that could be used to create another dish for another meal—see Other Suggestions at the end of the Chicken, Beef, Lamb, and Ham recipe sections.

Pan-fried Chicken
Corn Fritters
Cranberry Jelly
Swiss Chard OR *Spinach*
~
Lemon Pudding

Meat Loaf
Hashed Brown Potatoes
Green Beans
~
Baked Bananas

Irish Stew
Garlic OR *Herb Bread*
Green Salad
~
Chocolate Bread Pudding

Pot Roast
Potato Pancakes
Brussels Sprouts
~
Baked Custard

Picnic Ham
Sweet Potato & Apple Scallop
OR *Spoon Bread*
Scalloped Cabbage
~
Gingerbread & Whipped Cream

Salmon Loaf
Rice
Peas
~
Baked Pears OR *Apples*

New England Boiled Dinner
Corn Sticks
Cole Slaw OR *Sliced Tomatoes*
~
Apple Crisp

Meatballs in Onions & Sour Cream
Buttered Noodles
Sautéed Zucchini
~
Indian Pudding

FAMILY SUPPERS

There are so many good supper dishes to choose from that use little or no meat—an important consideration these days when meat is so expensive and world food supplies so limited. A good pasta, rice, or bean dish, eggs in various guises, stuffed vegetables, a hearty soup with your own homemade bread all make delicious and satisfying main courses for family dinners.

Spaghetti & Meatballs OR *Macaroni and Cheese*
Mixed Green Salad
Hard Rolls
~
Marmalade Soufflé

Filled Omelets OR *Baked Eggs*
Cottage Fried Potatoes
Buttered Peas
~
Pineapple Upside Down Cake

Spanish Rice OR *Rice & Pecan Loaf*
Baked Carrots
Watercress, Orange, & Avocado Salad
~
Cottage Pudding Cake

Waffles
Creamed Chipped Beef
Braised Spinach
~
Fruit Salad
Crackers & Cheese

Baked Beans OR *Beans Bretonne*
Boston Brown Bread
Wilted Cucumber Salad
~
Floating Island

Stuffed Eggplant OR *Green Peppers*
Scalloped Corn
~
Boston Cream Pie

Mixed Greens, Southern-style OR *Chicken Gumbo Soup*
Corn Bread
~
Brown Betty

Old-fashioned Fish Chowder, Black Bean, Oxtail, OR *Split Pea Soup*
Entire Wheat OR *Graham Bread*
~
Fruit Compote
Applesauce Cake

LATE SUPPERS

Soups are also good for a late supper after a basketball game or the theater, or at the end of an evening of talk or cards. Here are two attractive possibilities:

Cioppino OR *Mulligatawny Soup*
Potato Biscuits
~
Ginger Ice Cream
Charleston Benne Wafers

Pumpkin OR *Onion Soup*
Small Biscuits & Ham
~
Meringue Shells with Ice Cream OR *Strawberries*

SMALL DINNER PARTIES

Nothing in these menus requires too much last-minute attention, so that the dishes can be prepared ahead as time allows and the host-cook can relax with the guests. Even vegetables can be blanched ahead and heated up in butter between the first and second courses. With everything made at home, the dishes should not be too expensive. Meats are costly, particularly the roast beef and the crown roast of lamb, but these would be for special occasions, or could be replaced with less expensive cuts.

Clear Tomato Soup

~

Mushroom-stuffed Chicken Breasts
Buttered Broccoli
Feather Rolls

~

Deep-Dish Peach OR *Apple Pie*

Cold Artichokes OR
Green Beans Vinaigrette

~

Roast Pork
Scalloped Potatoes
Braised Red Cabbage & Apples
Corn Sticks

~

Pears with Chocolate Sauce &
Lace Cookies

Platter of mixed hors d'oeuvre, such
as slices of pâté, olives, celery,
tomatoes, stuffed eggs

~

Sole Baked in Herbed Cream
Parslied New Potatoes, Boiled
Braised Baby Spinach
Bread Sticks

~

Carrot Torte

Watercress, Orange Slices, &
Avocado Salad

~

Crown Roast of Lamb
Scalloped Eggplant

~

Date & Nut Cakes with Whipped
Cream

Stuffed Clams OR *Oysters*

~

Standing Rib Roast of Beef
Yorkshire Pudding
Sautéed Mushrooms
OR *Puréed Parsnips*

~

Mixed Green Salad
Platter of Cheeses
French Bread

~

Lemon OR *Raspberry Ice*

Cream of Jerusalem Artichoke Soup

~

Roast Ducks
Wild Rice OR *a combination of*
long-grain & wild rice
Puréed Rutabagas

~

Romaine & Chicory Salad

~

Strawberry Tart

LUNCH PARTIES

Unless you are a family who sits down together and has dinner in the middle of the day, lunch is apt to be a very informal meal, improvised from what is on hand (and the chapter Filled Things offers some tempting ideas). The lunch menus that follow are primarily suggestions for small luncheon parties.

<table>
<tr><td>

Beef Bouillon

~

Eggplant Quiche with
Tomatoes & Olives

~

Cold Rhubarb OR
Apricot Soufflé

</td><td>

Asparagus OR *Artichokes Vinaigrette*

~

Cheese OR *Spinach & Ham Soufflé*

~

Rhubarb Pie with Lattice Crust

</td></tr>
</table>

<table>
<tr><td>

Avocados Stuffed with
Chicken OR *Seafood*
Popovers

~

Lemon, Lime, OR *Orange*
Chiffon Pie

</td><td>

Corn Chowder

~

Spinach, Mushroom, & Bacon Salad
Hominy Gems OR *Nut Bread*

~

Dessert Crêpes with Berries OR *Jam*

</td></tr>
</table>

<table>
<tr><td>

Crêpes Stuffed with Chicken
& Mushrooms
Green Salad

~

Orange Jelly with Grapes &
Whipped Cream

</td><td>

Baked Eggs in Mornay Sauce
Sautéed Sweet Red & Green Peppers
Baking Powder Biscuits

~

Fresh Cut-up Fruit
Macaroons, Crescents, OR *Other*
Cookies

</td></tr>
</table>

TWO MENUS FOR SUMMER:

<table>
<tr><td>

Cold Cucumber Soup

~

Chicken OR *Lobster Salad*
Cream Bread Fingers

~

Summer Berry Pudding

</td><td>

A Slice of Melon with Country Ham
Sliced Paper Thin

~

Lemon Chicken & Asparagus Mold
with Watercress
Whole-Wheat Muffins

~

Bowl of Fresh Fruit
Brownies

</td></tr>
</table>

BUFFETS

Here are several ideas for a buffet table—some more elaborate than others.

Cold Fish Mousse
Swedish Meatballs
Buttered Slices of Rye Bread
Chickpea OR Lentil Salad
Green Beans OR Blanched Broccoli
Vinaigrette
~
Strawberry Shortcake OR
Nut Roll with Whipped Cream

Moussaka
Assortment of Aromatic Vegetables
Chicken & Pork Pâté
Buttered Slices of German
Caraway Bread
Hot Stuffed Risolettes OR
Hot Savory Tarts
~
Almond Torte
Fruit Sherbets

Country Terrine
Seafood Aspic
Chicken Divan
French Bread
Rice Salad
Green Salad
~
Bowl of Fresh Fruits
Walnut Mocha Cake

Baked Clams
Cannelloni OR Stuffed Manicotti
Health Salad OR Mixed Green Salad
~
Watermelon Filled with
Melon Chunks
Fresh Banana Cake OR
Chocolate Cake

Quiche
Cold Bass OR Salmon with
Green Mayonnaise
Baked Ham OR
Parslied Ham in Aspic
Water Bread OR
Parker House Rolls
Red Onion, Spinach, & Tomato
Salad OR Other Mixed Vegetable
Salad
~
Frozen Raspberry Soufflé OR
Ice Cream Bombe
Daffodil Cake

Chicken & Oysters in a Chafing
Dish
Stuffed Zucchini
Southern Corn Pudding OR
Scalloped Corn
Brioche Rolls OR
Corn Bread
Watercress, Orange Slices, &
Avocado Salad
~
Pecan AND/OR Squash Pie

BRUNCHES

Brunch is a good way to combine breakfast and lunch for your family on a lazy weekend morning or to get together with friends for a relaxed midday meal. It's a fine time to enjoy a lot of the old favorites that used to grace our breakfast tables and to savor some of the wonderful sweet breads that taste so good with a steaming pot of coffee or tea. If you have a large crowd, combine several of the dishes suggested in the different menus.

Grapefruit
Goldenrod Eggs
Apple Griddlecakes
Sausages OR *Scrapple*
Cinnamon Rolls

Watermelon
Codfish Cakes
Creole Tomatoes
Corn Muffins

Fruit Cup
Sautéed Kidneys
Omelets
Orange Peel Bread

Cut-up Pineapple
Sautéed Chicken Livers
Scrambled Eggs
Apricot Almond Bread

Melon
Finnan Haddie Baked in Milk
Frittata with Cheese & Vegetables
Swedish Braided Bread

Strawberries
Eggs Benedict
Broiled Tomatoes
Quick Coffee Cake

PRESSURE COOKING CHARTS

PRESSURE COOKING CHART FOR FRESH VEGETABLES

This chart provides a general guide to pressure cooking vegetables. It is geared to average-sized vegetables bought in the market. If your vegetables have been picked very young and are garden fresh, you'll want to cook them a shorter time. You may also find that you like your vegetables slightly less or more done than recommended here. In any case, make notes of your results and keep a record for future use.

It is possible to cook more than one vegetable at once provided both vegetables require the same amount of cooking time. It is better to season vegetables after cooking because you can judge better what is needed; pressure-cooked vegetables retain more of their own natural mineral salts and their flavor is apt to be more intense, so you may need less seasoning. Always make sure that the vent of your pressure cooker is open. Put it up to the light to see if the hole is clear; if not, clean it out with a pipe cleaner. Place vegetables on the rack and do not have the pressure cooker more than two-thirds full.

Vegetable	Preparation	Amount of Water	Time
Artichokes	Wash and trim (p. 358). Leave whole.	1 cup	10 minutes
Asparagus	Break off stems, wash, and peel. Leave whole.	½ cup	2 minutes
Beans (green, wax, and pole)	Wash. Remove ends and strings, if any. Leave whole, unless very thick—then French or cut into 1-inch pieces.	½ cup	2 minutes
Beans (lima, shell, and fava)	Shell.	½ cup	2 minutes
Beets	Wash. Cut off all but 1 inch of the top; leave roots on. After cooking, cool and slip off skins.	1½ cups	15 minutes

Vegetable	Preparation	Amount of Water	Time
Broccoli	Wash and prepare (p. 366). After cooking, cut flowerets diagonally, peeled stems together.	½ cup	2 minutes
Broccoli Rabe	Wash and cut into 2-inch pieces.	½ cup	2 minutes
Brussels Sprouts	Wash. Remove wilted outer leaves and cut a cross in the root ends.	½ cup	3 minutes
Cabbage (green and red)	Remove wilted outside leaves, cut away inner core, and cut into 2-inch wedges.	½ cup	3 minutes
Carrots	Wash and peel. Leave small carrots whole or slice ¼ inch thick.	1 cup ½ cup	5 minutes 2 minutes
Cauliflower	Remove outer leaves and stalk. Break into flowerets and wash.	½ cup	2 minutes
Celery	Separate stalks. Remove strings and wash. Leave whole or cut into pieces.	½ cup	2 minutes
Celery Root or Celeriac	Peel, wash, and cut into ½-inch slices.	½ cup	3 minutes
Corn (on the cob)	Remove husk and silk.	½ cup	3 minutes
Fennel	Wash, trim away tough outer part, slice ½ inch thick.	½ cup	2 minutes
Greens (collards, beet greens, Swiss chard, and turnip greens)	Remove wilted leaves and tough root ends. Wash thoroughly in several changes of water.	½ cup	3 minutes
Jerusalem Artichokes	Scrub and peel. Leave whole.	1 cup	3 minutes
Kohlrabi	Wash, peel, and cut into ½-inch cubes.	1 cup	2 minutes
Onions	Wash and peel. Leave whole—up to 2-inch diameter; larger than that, cut in halves or quarters.	1 cup	5 minutes
Parsnips	Wash and peel or scrape. Trim root ends and leave whole.	1 cup	8 minutes
Peas (green)	Shell.	½ cup	2 minutes
Potatoes	Wash and scrub. Don't peel new potatoes. Leave whole unless very large; if so, cut into pieces 1½ inches thick.	1 cup	10 minutes
Spinach	Wash thoroughly in several changes of water. Remove tough stems.	½ cup	1 minute
Squash (winter) and Pumpkin	Wash and cut into 1½–2-inch chunks. Scrape out meat when cooked.	1½ cups	12 minutes
Sweet Potatoes	Wash and scrub. Leave whole.	1 cup	10 minutes
White Turnips and Rutabagas	Wash, peel, and cut into 1-inch cubes or slices.	½ cup	3 minutes

PRESSURE COOKING CHART FOR DRIED VEGETABLES

Dried vegetables can be cooked very successfully in the pressure cooker, and it will save you a good deal of time and energy. Vegetables should be presoaked, even lentils and those labeled "no soaking necessary," because of their tendency to foam and clog the vent. Cover with cold water in the pressure-cooker pot, add 2 tablespoons of cooking oil for every cup of dried vegetables, and soak overnight; or bring to a boil, cook 2 minutes, and let soak 1 hour (lentils and others marked "no soaking" need only be brought just to the boil and then soaked 20 minutes). When you are ready to proceed with the pressure cooking, add 1 teaspoon salt to every cup of dried beans, use the same water they have soaked in, and follow the recommended cooking times. Make sure the vent pipe is open and don't fill the pressure cooker more than half full (no rack is needed). After cooking, let the pressure drop of its own accord before removing the cover.

Vegetable	Time
Black Beans	35 minutes
Black-eyed Peas	20 minutes
Chickpeas or Garbanzo Beans	45 minutes
Great Northern Beans	30 minutes
Kidney Beans	25 minutes
Lentils	15 minutes
Lima Beans	25 minutes
Navy Beans or Small White Beans	25 minutes
Pink Beans	30 minutes
Pinto Beans	25 minutes
Red Beans	35 minutes
Split Peas (green or yellow)	5 minutes

TABLE OF CALORIES

The number of calories that appears in the left-hand column is approximate. For more detailed information consult government bulletins.

Beverages

0 Coffee, tea, any amount

90 Buttermilk, 8-ounce glass
185 Chocolate milk, 8-ounce glass
270 Eggnog, 8-ounce glass
165 Milk, Grade A whole, 8-ounce glass
85 Milk, skim, 8-ounce glass

123 Apple juice, 8-ounce glass
115 Cider, 8-ounce glass
163 Cranberry juice cocktail, 8-ounce glass
87 Grapefruit juice, 8-ounce glass
168 Grape juice, 8-ounce glass
108 Orange juice, 8-ounce glass
95 Pineapple juice, 8-ounce glass
197 Prune juice, 8-ounce glass

50 Tomato juice, 8-ounce glass

96 Cola, 8-ounce glass
85 Ginger ale, 8-ounce glass
320 Ice cream soda, chocolate, 1 fountain serving
100 Root beer, 8-ounce glass
5 Seltzer (carbonated water), 8-ounce glass
97 Seven-Up, 8-ounce glass
3 Tab, 8-ounce glass

125 Beer, lager, 8-ounce glass
75 Distilled spirits, 1 ounce
110 Sherry, 3-ounce glass
105 Vermouth, 4-ounce glass
96 Wine, dry red, 4-ounce glass
90 Wine, dry white, 4-ounce glass

Breads, Cereals, Grains, Pasta, and Rice

170 Bread crumbs, dry and grated, ½ cup
55 Bread sticks, salted, 1 large
105 Corn bread, 2" × 2½" × 1½" piece
80 Cracked-wheat bread, 3" × 4" × ½" slice
60 French bread, 1½" × 2" oval × 1"
104 Italian bread, 3" × 3½" oval × 1"
25 Pumpernickel bread, 3½" × 3½" × ⅛" slice
80 Raisin bread, 3" × 4" × ½" slice
55 Rye bread, 3½" × 4½" oval × ⅜"
16 Rye Krisp, 3½" × 2" wafer
65 White enriched bread, 4" × 4½" × ½" slice
55 Whole-wheat bread, 4" × 4½" × ½" slice

125 Bagel, 1 medium
130 Baking powder muffin, 2½" diameter
100 Blueberry muffin, 2½" diameter
80 Bran muffin, 3½" diameter
140 Cinnamon roll, 2½" diameter
150 Coffee cake, 3" × 2" × ¾" piece
105 Corn muffin, 2" × 2½" × 1½" piece
230 Doughnut, jelly, 1 medium
136 Doughnut, plain, 1 medium with hole
125 English muffin, toasted, standard
155 Hamburger roll, standard
160 Hot dog roll, standard
47 Pancake, buckwheat, 4" diameter
60 Pancake, wheat, enriched flour, 4" diameter

125 Parker House roll, 2¾" diameter
60 Popover, 3" diameter
135 Sweet roll, 3½" diameter
215 Waffle, 4½" × 5⅝" × ½" piece

98 Cheerios, 8-ounce cup
95 Cornflakes, 8-ounce cup
149 Raisin bran cereal, 8-ounce cup
125 Rice Krispies, 8-ounce cup
100 Shredded wheat, 1 biscuit
70 Special K, 8-ounce cup
125 Wheaties, 8-ounce cup

110 Cream of Wheat, cooked, 8-ounce
    cup
148 Oatmeal, cooked, 8-ounce cup
200 Ralston health cereal, cooked,
    8-ounce cup
120 Wheatena, cooked, 8-ounce cup

98 Barley, pearled, light, dry,
   2 tablespoons
115 Bran flakes, 8-ounce cup
250 Granola, 4-ounce cup
246 Wheat germ, stirred, 8-ounce cup

209 Macaroni, cooked, 8-ounce cup
107 Noodles, cooked, 8-ounce cup
245 Pizza, ⅙ of 14" diameter
218 Spaghetti, cooked, 8-ounce cup
396 Spaghetti, cooked, with tomato
    sauce, 8-ounce cup

200 Rice, brown, cooked, 8-ounce cup
184 Rice, converted, cooked, 8-ounce
    cup
155 Rice, wild, cooked, 8-ounce cup
184 Rice, white, boiled, 8-ounce cup

Dairy Products

100 Butter, 1 tablespoon
100 American cheese, 1 slice
    (1 ounce)
52 Blue cheese, 1 tablespoon
85 Camembert cheese, 1 triangle
   (1 ounce)
113 Cheddar cheese, 1 ounce
30 Cheddar cheese, grated,
   1 tablespoon
230 Cottage cheese, creamed, 8-ounce
    cup
106 Cream cheese, 1 ounce
35 Parmesan cheese, dry, grated,
   1 tablespoon
101 Swiss cheese, processed, 1 ounce
50 Cream, heavy, 1 tablespoon

30 Cream, light, 1 tablespoon
58 Cream, sour, 1 tablespoon
81 Eggs, raw, whole, 1 large
   (white—18; yolk—63)
81 Egg, boiled, 1 large
110 Egg, fried, with 1 teaspoon butter,
    1 large
81 Egg, poached, 1 large
114 Egg, scrambled, with 1 teaspoon
    butter, 1 large
    Milk, see under Beverage
123 Yogurt, plain, skim, 1 cup
153 Yogurt, plain, whole, 1 cup
260 Yogurt, fruit, 1 cup
200 Yogurt, vanilla, 1 cup

Fats and Oils

100 Bacon fat, 1 tablespoon
    Butter, see under Dairy Products
100 Corn oil, 1 tablespoon
110 Crisco, 1 tablespoon

126 Lard, 1 tablespoon
125 Olive oil, 1 tablespoon
118 Peanut oil, 1 tablespoon
110 Vegetable fat, 1 tablespoon

Soups

191 Bean, Navy, 8-ounce cup
9 Bouillon, clear, 8-ounce cup
2 Bouillon, 1 cube
100 Broth, beef, 8-ounce cup
50 Broth, chicken, 8-ounce cup
86 Clam chowder, 8-ounce cup
198 Corn chowder, creamed, 8-ounce
    cup
200 Creamed soups (most), 8-ounce
    cup

150 Mulligatawny, 8-ounce cup
150 Oxtail, 8-ounce cup
200 Oyster stew, half cream and half
    milk, 8-ounce cup
141 Split pea, 8-ounce cup
90 Tomato, 8-ounce cup
82 Vegetable, 8-ounce cup

Meats

159 Beef, corned, 3 ounces (lean)
120 Beef, corned and hashed, 3 ounces
336 Beef, dried, 8-ounce cup
235 Beef, flank steak, 3½ ounces
    without bone
326 Beef, hamburger, broiled, 4 ounces
262 Beef, rib roast, 4 ounces with bone
247 Beef, T-bone steak, 3½ ounces
 90 Beef heart, 3 ounces
350 Beef stew, 8-ounce cup
235 Beef tongue, 4 ounces
100 Beef tripe, ½ cup (4 ounces)
467 Bologna, 1″ thick × 1½″ diameter
    piece
106 Brains, all animals, 3 ounces
120 Calves' liver, 3 ounces
124 Frankfurter, 1 average
265 Ham, baked, 4¼″ × 4″ × ½″ slice
172 Ham, boiled, 2-ounce slice
180 Lamb, roast leg, 4 ounces with
    bone

223 Lamb chop, loin, broiled,
    3½ ounces without bone
252 Lamb stew, 8-ounce cup
150 Liverwurst, 2-ounce slice
316 Meatball, 1 medium (3 ounces)
316 Meat loaf, 3-ounce slice
170 Pastrami, 2 medium slices
    (2 ounces)
287 Pork, loin, roasted, 4 ounces with
    bone
287 Pork chop, 4 ounces with bone
467 Salami, 1″ thick × 1½″ diameter
    piece
 63 Sausage, 1 pork link
100 Sweetbreads, broiled, ½ cup
    (¼ pound)
198 Veal, roast rump, 4 ounces without
    bone
207 Veal chop, 3½-ounce portion
250 Veal stew, 8-ounce cup
225 Venison, 4-ounce slice

Poultry

210 Chicken, broiled, ½ medium,
    boned, 8 ounces
216 Chicken, creamed, ½ cup
    (4 ounces)
204 Chicken, fried, 5 ounces, boned

155 Chicken liver, sautéed, 3 ounces
325 Duck, roast, 4 ounces, boned
180   Stuffing, ¼ cup
327 Turkey, dark, 4 ounces
280 Turkey, light, 4 ounces

Fish and Shellfish

360 Bass, baked or broiled, 8 ounces
352 Bluefish, baked or broiled,
    8 ounces
 35 Caviar, 1 tablespoon
180 Clams, canned, cherrystone,
    8 ounces
196 Cod, 7 ounces
125 Codfish cakes, 1″ thick ×
    2½″ diameter
 90 Crabmeat, 3 ounces
376 Halibut, broiled, 8 ounces
 88 Lobster, fresh, 12 ounces
318 Mackerel, 7 ounces
 75 Mussels, 6 medium
200 Oysters, raw, Blue Point, 8 ounces
170 Perch, sea, 8 ounces

220 Porgy, 8 ounces
190 Red snapper, 8 ounces
204 Salmon, baked or broiled, 4″ × 3″
    × ½″ piece
285 Salmon, smoked, 3 ounces
180 Sardines, with oil drained,
    3 ounces
350 Scallops, broiled, 8 ounces
382 Shad, 8 ounces
200 Shad roe, 4 ounces
 75 Shrimps, 6 medium (3 ounces)
200 Sole, filet, 8 ounces
223 Swordfish, 3″ × 3″ × ½″ piece
100 Trout, brook, 7 ounces
240 Tuna, canned, drained, 6 ounces

Sauces, Gravies, and Salad Dressings

 17 Chili sauce, 1 tablespoon
 34 Cranberry sauce, 1 tablespoon
 35 Cream sauce, 1 tablespoon
100 Garlic sauce with butter,
    1 tablespoon

 45 Hard sauce, 1 tablespoon

100 Hollandaise sauce, 1 tablespoon
 25 Lemon sauce, 1 tablespoon
 68 Tartar sauce, 1 tablespoon
  5 Tomato sauce, 1 tablespoon
 27 White sauce, 1 tablespoon

 50 Gravy, thick, 1 tablespoon

35 Gravy, thin, 1 tablespoon

95 Blue cheese dressing, 1 tablespoon
80 French or vinaigrette dressing,
    1 tablespoon
124 Oil, salad or cooking, 1 tablespoon

100 Roquefort dressing, 1 tablespoon
106 Russian dressing, 1 tablespoon
100 Thousand Island dressing,
    1 tablespoon
2 Vinegar, 1 tablespoon

Vegetables and Salad Greens

20 Artichokes, 4 bottoms
53 Artichokes, boiled and drained,
    1 average size
36 Asparagus spears, 1 cup
279 Avocado, half of average size
325 Beans, baked (with pork and
    molasses), 8-ounce cup
35 Beans, green, 3½ ounces
152 Beans, lima, 8-ounce cup
68 Beets, diced, 8-ounce cup
44 Broccoli flowerets and cut-up
    stems, 8-ounce cup
44 Brussels sprouts, 8-ounce cup
40 Cabbage, cooked, 8-ounce cup
24 Cabbage, raw, shredded, 8-ounce
    cup
21 Carrot, raw, 5½" × 1" diameter
44 Carrots, cooked, diced, 8-ounce
    cup
30 Cauliflower, 8-ounce cup
24 Celery, cooked, diced, 8-ounce cup
7 Celery, raw, 1 large outer stalk
84 Corn, 1 average ear
140 Corn, kernels, 8-ounce cup
6 Cucumber, 6 slices
24 Eggplant, 3½ ounces

5 Garlic, 1 clove
7 Lettuce, 2 large or 4 small leaves
20 Mushrooms, raw, sliced, 8-ounce
    cup
4 Onion, raw, chopped, 1 tablespoon
79 Onions, cooked, 8-ounce cup
72 Olives, 10
94 Parsnips, cooked, 8-ounce cup
111 Peas, green, 8-ounce cup
17 Pepper, cooked, 1 medium
185 Pepper, stuffed, 1 medium
102 Potato, baked, unpeeled,
    1 medium
105 Potato, boiled, peeled, 1 medium
183 Potato, sweet, baked, peeled,
    1 medium
157 Potatoes, French fried, 8 pieces
4 Radishes, 4 small
46 Spinach, cooked, 8-ounce cup
22 Spinach, raw, 4 ounces
34 Squash, summer, 8-ounce cup
97 Squash, winter, baked and
    mashed, 8-ounce cup
30 Tomato, raw, 1 medium
46 Tomatoes, stewed, 8-ounce cup
42 Turnips, cooked, 8-ounce cup

Fruits

76 Apple, 1 medium
54 Apricots, 3 medium
88 Banana, 1 medium
85 Blueberries, 8-ounce cup
37 Cantaloupe, half of 5" diameter
40 Date, pitted, 1-ounce piece
52 Fig, dried, 1 large
90 Figs, fresh, 3 small
75 Grapefruit, half of medium
102 Grapes, 8 ounces
49 Honeydew melon, 2" × 7" wedge
19 Lemon, 1 medium
87 Mango, fresh, 1 medium

70 Orange, 1 medium
71 Papaya, cubed, 8-ounce cup
46 Peach, 1 medium
95 Pear, 1 medium
74 Pineapples, fresh, diced, 8-ounce
    cup
29 Plum, 2" diameter
75 Pomegranate, 1 medium
26 Raisins, dried, 1 tablespoon
70 Raspberries, red, 8-ounce cup
19 Rhubarb, diced, 8-ounce cup
54 Strawberries, 8-ounce cup
120 Watermelon, 4" × 8" wedge

Desserts, Pastries, and Ice Cream

110 Angel food cake, 1/12 of
    8" diameter
300 Cheese cake, 3" × 2" × 1½" piece
161 Cup cake with icing, 1¾" diameter
105 Fruit cake, 2" × 2" × ½" piece
180 Gingerbread, 2" × 2" × 2" piece

155 Layer cake, chocolate, with icing,
    1" × 1½" × 1" piece
100 Layer cake, white, with icing,
    1" × 1½" × 1" piece
130 Pound cake, 2¾" × 3" × ⅝" piece
117 Sponge cake, 1/12 of 8" diameter

Desserts, Pastries and Ice Cream (*continued*)

320 Strawberry shortcake, 3″ × 3″
     × 2″ piece
135 Brownie, 2″ × 2″ × ¾″ piece
40 Chocolate chip cookie,
     2″ diameter
109 Cookies, plain or assorted,
     3″ diameter
25 Graham cracker, 3½″ square
40 Oatmeal cookie, 3″ diameter
40 Shortbread, 1¾″ square
38 Vanilla wafer, 3½″ diameter

50 Applesauce, unsweetened, ½ cup
142 Custard, ½ cup (4 ounces)
155 Gelatin, plain, 8-ounce cup
172 Jell-O, all fruit flavors, 8-ounce
     cup
150 Tapioca, ½ cup
138 Vanilla pudding, ½ cup

1,165 Banana split, fountain size
298 Chocolate chip ice cream, 1 scoop
     (½ cup)
298 Chocolate ice cream, 1 scoop
     (½ cup)
150 Vanilla ice cream, 1 scoop (½ cup)

300 Chocolate éclair, 1 medium
250 Danish pastry, 1 medium
225 French pastry, 1 medium
200 Tart with fruit filling

331 Apple pie, ⅐ section
260 Cream pie, ⅐ section
302 Lemon meringue pie, ⅐ section
341 Mince pie, ⅐ section
263 Pumpkin pie, ⅐ section
328 Rhubarb pie, ⅐ section

Candies, Nuts, Jams, and Condiments (including sugars)

250 Candy bar, average, 2 ounces
120 Caramel, 1″ square (1 ounce)
110 Chocolate cream, 1-ounce piece
10 Cough drop, 1 piece
100 Fruit drops, 3 medium pieces
115 Fudge, 1-ounce square
9 Gum, chewing, 1 stick
35 Gumdrop, 1 large
50 Jelly beans, 6 pieces
5 Life Savers, 1 piece
108 Lollipop, 1-ounce size
105 Maple sugar, 1¾″ × 1¼″ ×
     ½″ piece
90 Marshmallow, 1-ounce piece
90 Mint, after-dinner, chocolate,
     1½″ diameter
125 Peanut brittle, 1-ounce piece
65 Popcorn, 1 cup
50 Saltwater taffy, 1 average kiss
20 Sour ball, 1 average piece

424 Almonds, shelled, ½ cup
452 Brazil nuts, shelled, ½ cup
     (16 kernels)
164 Cashews, roasted, 1 ounce
191 Chestnuts, 3½ ounces
349 Coconut, shredded, 1 cup

100 Hazelnuts, 8–10 nuts
100 Hickory nuts, 12–15 nuts
805 Peanuts, shelled, 1 cup
752 Pecans, halved, 1 cup
100 Pistachios, 12 medium
568 Sesame seeds, whole, 3½ ounces
654 Walnuts, halved, 1 cup

27 Sugar, 1 cube
51 Sugar, brown, 1 tablespoon
54 Sugar, granulated, 1 tablespoon
870 Sugar, granulated, 1 cup

62 Honey, 1 tablespoon
55 Jams and preserves (most flavors),
     1 tablespoon
50 Jellies (most flavors), 1 tablespoon

42 Syrup, chocolate, 1 tablespoon
70 Syrup, maple, 1 tablespoon

17 Catsup, 1 tablespoon
92 Mayonnaise, 1 tablespoon
21 Mustard, 1 ounce
92 Peanut butter, 1 tablespoon
24 Worcestershire sauce, 1 tablespoon

METRICS

The metric measurements given throughout the book represent the nearest, most convenient equivalents in every case. We feel that it is important at this stage for American cooks to get familiar with easy conversions rather than be frightened off by long numbers and decimals which represent a kind of precision that not only doesn't count when it comes to cooking but does not reflect at all the measures that the average European uses in the kitchen or at the market. For that reason we have stuck to liters and deciliters ($\frac{1}{10}$ of a liter) in our liquid measures rather than going in for centiliters ($\frac{1}{100}$ of a liter) or milliliters ($\frac{1}{1000}$th). *To convert a quart to a liter, the accepted rule is to multiply by 0.95**. This means that our quart is just a negligible 5 centiliters larger than the European liter—an amount that makes virtually no difference in cooking. Only when you are dealing with large quantities does the differential become great enough to be of consequence. The abbreviation for the liter is L and for the deciliter dL. For the record, *to convert one ounce to milliliters multiply by 29.57†*. Our cup would therefore be precisely 237 mL (instead of $\frac{1}{4}$ L) and our quart 946 mL (instead of 1 L)—not very easy figures to cook by. Incidentally, there is no need for Americans to give up measuring with familiar cups and spoons in order to work with metrics. The following tables (and those on the endpapers of this book) should give you all the guidelines you need and, as you will see, tablespoons and cups are part of the calculations.

* To convert a liter to a quart, multiply the liter by 1.057.

† To convert a milliliter to an ounce multiply the milliliter by 0.034.

Conversion of Liquid Measures

Spoons, cups, pints, and quarts	Ounces	Deciliters and liters (nearest convenient equivalents)
1 Tb	1 oz	¼ dL or 1 Tb
¼ c or 4 Tbs	2 oz	½ dL or 4 Tbs
⅓ c	2⅔ oz	¾ dL
½ c	4 oz	1 dL
⅔ c	5⅓ oz	1½ dL
¾ c	6 oz	1¾ dL
1 c	8 oz	¼ L
1¼ c	10 oz	3 dL
1⅓ c	10⅔ oz	3¼ dL
1½ c	12 oz	3½ dL
1⅔ c	13⅓ oz	3¾ dL
1¾ c	14 oz	4 dL
2 c; 1 pt	16 oz	½ L
2½ c	20 oz	6 dL
3 c	24 oz	¾ L
3½ c	28 oz	⅘ L; 8 dL
4 c; 1 qt	32 oz	1 L
5 c	40 oz	1¼ L
6 c; 1½ qt	48 oz	1½ L
8 c; 2 qt	64 oz	2 L
10 c; 2½ qt	80 oz	2½ L
12 c; 3 qt	96 oz	2¾ L
4 qt	128 oz	3¾ L
5 qt		4¾ L
6 qt		5¾ L
8 qt		7½ L

Conversion of Solid Measures

To convert ounces to grams multiply ounces by 28.35. If you want to translate grams to ounces, multiply by .035. As you can see from the chart opposite, you are soon dealing in large numbers of grams when you get up over 2 pounds. Therefore, whenever possible in our lists of ingredients we have converted to a fraction of the kilogram rather than the precise number of grams. It's not only less cumbersome but also more in keeping with European style—in common parlance one would always speak of a kilo and a half, for instance, rather than 1500 grams.

Ounces	Pounds	Grams (nearest convenient equivalents)	Kilograms
1 oz		30 g	
2 oz		60 g	
3 oz		85 g	
4 oz	¼ lb	115 g	
5 oz		140 g	
6 oz		180 g	
8 oz	½ lb	225 g	
9 oz		250 g	¼ kg
10 oz		285 g	
12 oz	¾ lb	340 g	
14 oz		400 g	
16 oz	1 lb	450 g	
18 oz	1⅛ lb	500 g	½ kg
20 oz	1¼ lb	560 g	
24 oz	1½ lb	675 g	
28 oz	1¾ lb	800 g	
32 oz	2 lb	900 g	
	2¼ lb	1000 g	1 kg
	2½ lb	1125 g	1¼ kg
	3 lb	1350 g	1⅓ kg
	3½ lb	1500 g	1½ kg
	4 lb	1800 g	1¾ kg
	4½ lb		2 kg
	5 lb		2¼ kg
	5½ lb		2½ kg
	6 lb		2¾ kg
	7 lb		3¼ kg
	8 lb		3½ kg
	9 lb		4 kg
	10 lb		4½ kg
	12 lb		5½ kg
	14 lb		6¼ kg
	15 lb		6¾ kg
	16 lb		7¼ kg
	18 lb		8 kg
	20 lb		9 kg
	25 lb		11¼ kg
	50 lb		22½ kg

Conversion of Linear Measures

To convert inches to centimeters, multiply the inch by 2.54. To translate centimeters to inches, multiply the centimeter by .39. In the recipes we have not given the equivalent of every pan and dish size in metrics, feeling that it would be too distracting in the recipe text, but in the opening chapter About the Kitchen metric conversions are offered in the equipment section.

Inches	Centimeters (nearest convenient equivalent)	Inches	Centimeters (nearest convenient equivalent)
1/16 in	1/4 cm	5 in	13 cm
1/8 in	1/2 cm	6 in	15 cm
1/4 in	3/4 cm	7 in	18 cm
3/8 in	1 cm	8 in	20 cm
1/2 in	1 1/2 cm	9 in	23 cm
3/4 in	2 cm	10 in	25 cm
1 in	2 1/2 cm	12 in, 1 ft.	30 cm
1 1/2 in	4 cm	14 in	35 cm
2 in	5 cm	15 in	38 1/2 cm
2 1/2 in	6 1/2 cm	16 in	40 cm
3 in	8 cm	18 in	45 cm
3 1/2 in	9 cm	20 in	50 cm
4 in	10 cm	24 in, 2 ft.	60 cm

Conversion of Temperatures

To convert Fahrenheit degrees to Celsius, subtract 32, multiply by 5, and divide by 9—and we hope you have a pocket calculator. *To translate Celsius to Fahrenheit, multiply by 9, divide by 5, and add 32.* Below are the nearest equivalent conversions you are most likely to need in cooking. Incidentally, Celsius and Centigrade are the same. Celsius is the term that has been agreed on internationally so it is replacing Centigrade in Europe.

Fahrenheit°	Celsius°	Fahrenheit°	Celsius°
85°F	29°C	212°F	100°C
100°F	38°C	225°F	110°C
110°F	43°C	250°F	120°C
115°F	46°C	275°F	135°C
135°F	57°C	300°F	150°C
140°F	60°C	325°F	165°C
150°F	66°C	350°F	180°C
160°F	71°C	375°F	190°C
165°F	74°C	400°F	205°C
170°F	77°C	425°F	220°C
180°F	82°C	450°F	230°C
190°F	88°C	475°F	245°C
200°F	95°C	500°F	260°C
205°F	96°C		

INDEX

G

A Note on the Type

The text of this book has been set in a VIP version of Goudy Old Style, one of the more than one hundred typefaces designed by Frederic William Goudy, 1865–1947. Although Goudy began his career as a bookkeeper, he was so inspired by the appearance of several newly published books from the Kelmscott Press that he devoted the remainder of his life to typography and to an attempt to bring a better understanding of the movement led by William Morris to the printers of the United States.

Produced in 1914, Goudy Old Style reflects the absorption of a generation of designers with things "ancient." Its smooth, even color combined with its generous curves and ample cut, mark it as one of Goudy's finest achievements.

Composed by Monotype Composition Company, Inc., Baltimore, Maryland.

Designed by Anthea Lingeman.

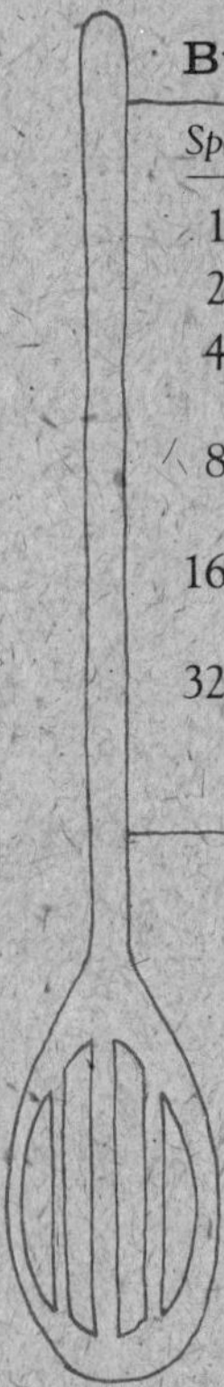

Butter, Shortening, Cheese, and Other Solid Fats

Spoons and cups		Ounces	Grams
1 tablespoon	⅛ stick	½ ounce	15 grams
2 tablespoons	¼ stick	1 ounce	30 grams
4 tablespoons (¼ cup)	½ stick	2 ounces	60 grams
8 tablespoons (½ cup)	1 stick	4 ounces (¼ pound)	115 grams
16 tablespoons (1 cup)	2 sticks	8 ounces (½ pound)	225 grams
32 tablespoons (2 cups)	4 sticks	16 ounces (1 pound)	450 grams (500 grams = ½ kilogram)

To beat egg whites successfully, always have them at room temperature and use a clean, dry bowl and beaters. A single egg white increases its volume to ½ cup, but 3 egg whites will mount to 2⅔ cups, or 9 times their volume.

To measure flour, scoop the amount required into a metal measuring cup exactly that size and level off excess by sweeping a knife or spatula across the top.

Flour (unsifted)

Spoons and cups	Ounces
1 tablespoon	¼ ounce
¼ cup (4 tablespoons)	1¼ ounces
⅓ cup (5 tablespoons)	1½ ounces
½ cup	2½ ounces
⅔ cup	3¼ ounces
¾ cup	3½ ounces
1 cup	5 ounces
1½ cups	7½ ounces
2 cups	10 ounces
3½ cups	16 ounces (1 pound

Note: 1 cup sifted flour = 1 cup unsifted flour

Granulated Sugar

Spoons and cups	Ounces	Grams
1 teaspoon	⅛ ounce	5 grams
1 tablespoon	½ ounce	15 grams
¼ cup (4 tablespoons)	1¾ ounces	60 grams
⅓ cup (5 tablespoons)	2¼ ounces	75 grams
½ cup	3½ ounces	100 grams
⅔ cup	4½ ounces	130 grams
¾ cup	5 ounces	150 grams
1 cup	7 ounces (6¾ ounces)	200 grams
1½ cups	9½ ounces	300 grams
2 cups	13½ ounces	400 grams

Egg yolks should always be "tempered" by mixing them with a little hot liquid before incorporating them into a hot sauce. Unless the sauce is bound by flour, don't let it boil again after the egg yolks have been added or they will curdle.